Mafatih al-Jinan

A Treasury of Islamic Piety

(Translation with the Arabic Texts)

VOLUME TWO

The Book of Ziyarah

Shaykh Abbas Qummi

Translated & Annotated by

Ali Quli Qarai

First Edition 2019
ISBN: 978-1-955725-35-4

Contents

Book Three: Ziyārāt

The following table shows the system followed in transliterating the Arabic texts.

ا	*alif*	a		ع	*ᶜayn*	ᶜ	
		ā	*(long vowel)*	غ	*ghayn*	gh	
		â	*(with madd)*	ف	*fā*	f	
ب	*bā*	b		ق	*qāf*	q	
ت	*tā*	t		ك	*kāf*	k	
ث	*thā*	th		ل	*lām*	l	
ج	*j¢m*	j		م	*mīm*	m	
ح	*ḥā*	ḥ		ن	*nūn*	n	
خ	*khā*	kh				ⁿ	*(for nazal nūn)*
د	*dāl*	d		ه	*hā*	h	
ذ	*dhāl*	dh		و	*wāw*	w	*(consonantal)*
ر	*rā*	r				ū	*(long vowel)*
ز	*zāy*	z				û	*(with madd)*
س	*sīn*	s		ى	*yā*	y	*(consonantal)*
ش	*sh¢n*	sh				ī	*(long vowel)*
ص	*ṣād*	ṣ				î	*(with madd)*
ض	*ḍād*	ḍ		ء	*hamzah*	’ ’a, ’i, ’u	*depending on the vowel*
ط	*ṭā*	ṭ					
ظ	*ẓā*	ẓ					

Short vowels َ____ *(fatḥah)* = a

____ ِ *(kasrah)* = i ُ____ *(ḍammah)* = u

(ṣ) stands for *Ṣallallāhu ‘alayhi wa ālihī wa sallam*, an invocation of blessings for the Prophet, meaning ‘May God bless him and his Family.’

(‘*a*) stands for *‘alayhis/‘alayhas salām*, meaning ‘May peace be upon him/her.’

(*r*) stands for *riḍwānullāh ‘alayhi/‘alayhā*, meaning ‘May God be pleased with him/her.’

Book Three

This book pertains to the *ziyārahs* and it consists of an introduction, several chapters and a conclusion.

Introduction

The Etiquette of Journey

When intending to undertake a journey, it is advisable to fast for three days—Wednesday, Thursday and Friday—and to choose Saturday, Tuesday or Thursday for setting out.[1] One should avoid setting out on Mondays and Wednesdays, as well as before noon on Friday.[2] The days of the [lunar] month that are to be avoided by the prospective traveller are mentioned in the following lines of verse:

هفت روزی نحس باشد در مهی　　زان حذر کن تا نیابی هیچ رنج

سه و پنج وسیزده با شانزده　　بیست‌ویك‌با بیست‌وچار وبیست‌وپنج

Seven days are inauspicious in the month,
Avoid them to avert trouble:
The third day, the fifth, the thirteenth, and the sixteenth,
The twenty-first,[3] the twenty-fourth and the twenty-fifth.

One should avoid travelling during moonless nights of the month or when the moon is in the House of Scorpio.[4] However, when travel is a necessity during these times, one may set out at any time one wishes after reciting the supplication of journey and offering charity (*ṣadaqah*).[5]

It is reported[6] that one of the companions of Imam Muḥammad

[1] *Tahdhīb*, vi, 76, b 22, h 19, whence *Wasā'il*, xiv, 539, b 77, h 19777 *Biḥār*, xcviii, 147, b 17, h 38.

[2] For traditions concerning journey on the days of the week see *Wasā'il*, xi, 348-367, b 3-11, h 14985-15035. *Faqīh*, ii, 266-267, h 2389-2403.

[3] According to some reports, the twenty-first of a month is a good day for starting on a journey, but the eighth and the twenty-third are bad. (Compiler)

[4] *Faqīh*, ii, 267, h 2401, thence and from *Kafī* in *Wasā'il*, xi, 267. b 11, h 15035. See also the traditions in *Wasā'il*, xi, 370-374, b 15, h 15041-15050 concerning warnings about reliance on astrology.

[5] For traditions pertaining to giving charity before journey, see *Wasā'il*, xi, 375-377, b 15, h 15051-15057; *Faqīh*, ii, 269-270, bāb iftitāḥ al-safar bi al-ṣadaqah, h 2404-2408.

[6] *Daᶜā'im* al-Islām, i, 346, whence *Mustadrak*, viii, 125, b 12, h 9223/2. For a report describing this practice of Imam ᶜAli b. al-Ḥusayn (ᶜ*a*), see *Maḥāsin*, ii,

al-Bāqir (ʿ*a*), who was intending to make a journey, came to bid him farewell. The Imam told him, "Whenever my father, ʿAlī ibn al-Ḥusayn (ʿ*a*), wanted to go out on visits to some of his estates, he would buy his safety from God Almighty by offering whatever charity was feasible for him. He would do so when putting his foot in the stirrup. Again, on returning safely from a journey he would thank God and give whatever charity that was feasible for him." The man departed taking the Imam's leave, but did not carry out the Imam's advice. He perished on the way. When Imam Muḥammad al-Bāqir (ʿ*a*) heard about it, he said, "He was given advice, had he been one to take it!"

It is apt to take a bath before setting out.[1] Before leaving, one should gather one's family members, offer a two-*rakʿah* prayer and petition God Almighty for welfare and safety. After reciting the Throne Verse (2:255), praising God and invoking blessings on the Apostle of Allah and his Family (ṣ), one should say,[2]

[1]O Allah, today I entrust to Your care myself, my family, my property, my children and all those who belong to me in some way, including those who are present and those who are absent.

اَللّٰهُمَّ إِنِّي أَسْـــتَوْدِعُكَ الْيَوْمَ نَفْسِى وَ أَهْــلِي وَ مَالِي وَ وُلْدِى وَ مَنْ كَانَ مِنِّي بِسَبِيلٍ، اَلشَّاهِدَ مِنْهُمْ وَ الْغَائِبَ.

[2]O Allah, protect us with the safety of faith and take care of what belongs to us!

اَللّٰهُمَّ احْفَظْنَا بِحِفْظِ الْإِيمَانِ وَ احْفَظْ عَلَيْنَا.

[3]O Allah, draw us into Your mercy and do not deprive us of Your grace! Indeed we implore You!

اَللّٰهُمَّ اجْعَلْنَــا [اجْمَعْنَا] فِي رَحْمَتِكَ وَ لَا تَسْلُبْنَا فَضْلَكَ، إِنَّا إِلَيْكَ رَاغِبُونَ.

[4]O Allah, we seek refuge with You from the hardships of the journey, distress at destination, and from coming up against misfortune in family, property, and children,

اَللّٰهُمَّ إِنَّا نَعُوذُ بِكَ مِنْ وَعْثَاءِ السَّفَرِ، وَ كَآبَةِ الْمُنْقَلَبِ، وَ سُـــوءِ الْمَنْظَرِ فِي الْأَهْــلِ وَ الْمَالِ وَ الْــوَلَدِ فِي الدُّنْيَا وَ

348, b 8, h 25, whence *Biḥār*, lxxiii, 231, b 48, h 9; *Faqīh*, ii, 270, 2408, whence *Wasā'il*, xi, 376, b 15, h 15055; *Makārim*, 243, whence *Biḥār*, lxxiii, 233, b 48, h 14.

1 *Amān*, 33, whence *Wasā'il*, 369-370, b 13, h 15038-15040, and *Biḥār*, lxxiii, 235, b 48, h 19.

2 Ṭūsī's *Miṣbāḥ*, 717, whence *Biḥār*, xcviii, 257, b 18, h 41. *Amān*, 41, whence *Biḥār*, lxxiii, 236, b 48, h 20. *Biḥār*, xcvii, 105, b 1, h 11.

either in the world or the Hereafter! الْآخِرَةِ.

[5]O Allah, I turn to You, seeking Your pleasure and nearness.

اَللّٰهُمَّ إِنِّي أَتَوَجَّهُ إِلَيْكَ هٰذَا التَّوَجُّهَ طَلَبًا لِمَرْضَاتِكَ وَ تَقَرُّبًا إِلَيْكَ.

[6]O Allah, enable me to attain whatever I do hope and expect from You and Your *awliyā*, O Most Merciful of the merciful!

(اَللّٰهُمَّ) فَبَلِّغْنِي مَا أُؤَمِّلُهُ وَ أَرْجُوهُ فِيكَ وَ فِي أَوْلِيَائِكَ يَا أَرْحَمَ الرَّاحِمِينَ.

Then, after bidding farewell to one's family, while standing at the door, one should recite the *tasbīḥ* of Ḥaḍrat Fatimah (*ᶜa*), followed by al-Fātiḥah, first facing in the direction one is to proceed, and then to one's right and left. Likewise, one should recite the Throne Verse (2:255) in the three directions, and then say,[1]

[1]O Allah, I turn my face to You and place in Your hands my family, my property, and whatever You have given me to possess, putting my reliance in You. So do not disappoint me, O You who do not disappoint those who look up to You, and those whom You protect do not perish. [2]O Allah, bless Muḥammad and his Family and take care of what I am leaving behind and do not abandon me to my own devices, O Most Merciful of the merciful!

اَللّٰهُمَّ إِلَيْكَ وَجَّهْتُ وَجْهِي، وَ عَلَيْكَ خَلَّفْتُ أَهْلِي وَ مَالِي وَ مَا خَوَّلْتَنِي، وَ قَدْ وَثِقْتُ بِكَ، فَلَا تُخَيِّبْنِي يَا مَنْ لَا يُخَيِّبُ مَنْ أَرَادَهُ، وَ لَا يُضَيِّعُ مَنْ حَفِظَهُ اَللّٰهُمَّ صَلِّ عَلَىٰ مُحَمَّدٍ وَ آلِهِ، وَ احْفَظْنِي فِيمَا غِبْتُ عَنْهُ، وَ لَا تَكِلْنِي إِلَىٰ نَفْسِي يَا أَرْحَمَ الرَّاحِمِينَ.

Then one should recite Sūrat al-Tawḥīd 11 times, followed by Surat al-Qadr, the Throne Verse, Surat al-Nās, and Surat al-Falaq, and draw one's hand over one's body and luggage. Then offer any charity that is feasible, and say,[2]

[1]O Allah, with this charity I buy my

اَللّٰهُمَّ إِنِّي اشْتَرَيْتُ بِهٰذِهِ الصَّدَقَةِ

[1] *Amān*, 106, whence *Biḥār*, lxxiii, 241, b 48, h 21, xcvii, 106, b 1, h 12; and *Mustadrak*, viii, 130, b 16, h 9233/2.

[2] *Biḥār*, xcvii, 107, b 1, h 13, from *Miṣbāḥ al-Zā'ir*. *Amān* 38, whence *Biḥār*, lxxiii, 236, b 48, h 20.

safety and that of my journey and whatever is with me.	سَلاٰمَتِي وَ سَلاٰمَةَ سَفَرِى وَ مَا مَعِي.
[2]O Allah, keep me safe and protect me and whatever is with me from harm, and enable me and whatever is with me to reach the destination with Your good and gracious conveyance.	اَللّٰهُمَّ احْفَظْنِي وَ احْفَظْ مَا مَعِيَ، وَ سَلِّمْنِي وَ سَلِّمْ مَا مَعِيَ، وَ بَلِّغْنِي وَ بَلِّغْ مَا مَعِيَ بِبَلاٰغِكَ الْحَسَنِ الْجَمِيلِ.

It is also recommended to carry along a staff made of the wood of the bitter almond tree, as it is mentioned in a report that one setting out on journey should carry along a staff made of the wood of bitter almond and recite the following verses of the Qur'ān (28:22-28) so that God Almighty may grant him safety from predatory beasts, bandits and any kind of poisonous creature till he returns home, and that seventy-seven angels may plead for forgiveness of his sins until he returns home and lays down his staff.[1]

[22]And when he turned his face toward Midian, he said, 'Maybe my Lord will show me the right way.' [23]When he arrived at the well of Midian, he found there a throng of people watering [their flocks], and he found, besides them, two women holding back [their flock]. He said, 'What is your business?' They said, 'We do not water [our flock] until the shepherds have driven out [their flocks], and our father is an aged man.'	وَ لَمَّا تَوَجَّهَ تِلْقَاءَ مَدْيَنَ قَالَ عَسىٰ رَبِّي أَنْ يَهْدِيَنِى سَوَاءَ السَّبِيلِ. وَ لَمَّا وَرَدَ مَاءَ مَدْيَنَ وَجَدَ عَلَيْهِ أُمَّةً مِنَ النَّاسِ يَسْقُونَ، وَ وَجَدَ مِنْ دُونِهِمُ امْرَأَتَيْنِ تَذُودَانِ، قالَ مَا خَطْبُكُمَا، قَالَتَا لَا نَسْقِي حَتَّىٰ يُصْدِرَ الرِّعَاءُ وَ أَبُونَا شَيْخٌ كَبِيرٌ.
[24]So he watered their flock for them. Then he withdrew toward the shade and said, 'My Lord! I am indeed in need of any good You may send down to me!' [25]Then one of the two women approached him, walking bashfully. She said, 'Indeed my fa-	فَسَقَىٰ لَهُمَا، ثُمَّ تَوَلَّىٰ إِلَى الظِّلِّ فَقَالَ: رَبِّ إِنِّي لِمَا أَنْزَلْتَ إِلَيَّ مِنْ خَيْرٍ فَقِيرٌ. فَجَاءَتْهُ إِحْدَاهُمَا تَمْشِي عَلَى اسْتِحْيَاءٍ. قَالَتْ إِنَّ أَبِي يَدْعُوكَ

1 *Amān*, 49. *Biḥār*, xcvii, 108, b 1, h 14, from *Miṣbāḥ al-Zā'ir*. *Jāmi*ᶜ *al-Akhbār*, 120.

لِيَجْزِيَكَ أَجْرَ مٰا سَقَيْتَ لَنٰا.
فَلَمّٰا جاءَهُ وَ قَصَّ عَلَيْهِ الْقَصَصَ قالَ
لاٰ تَخَـفْ، نَجَوْتَ مِنَ الْقَوْمِ الظّٰالِمِينَ.
قالَتْ إِحْدٰاهُمٰا: يٰا أَبَتِ اسْتَأْجِرْهُ، إِنَّ
خَيْرَ مَنِ اسْتَأْجَرْتَ الْقَوِيُّ الْأَمِينُ.
قالَ إِنِّي أُرِيـدُ أَنْ أُنْكِحَكَ إِحْدَى
ابْنَـتَيَّ هاتَـيْنِ عَلىٰ أَنْ تَأْجُرَنِي ثَمٰانِيَ
حِجَجٍ، فَإِنْ أَتْمَمْتَ عَشْراً فَمِنْ عِنْدِكَ،
وَ مٰا أُرِيدُ أَنْ أَشُـقَّ عَلَيْكَ، سَتَجِدُنِي
إِنْ شاءَ اللّٰهُ مِنَ الصّٰالِحِينَ. قالَ: ذٰلِكَ
بَيْنِي وَ بَيْنَكَ أَيَّمَا الْأَجَلَيْنِ قَضَيْتُ فَلاٰ
عُدْوانَ عَلَيَّ، وَ اللّٰهُ عَلىٰ مٰا نَقُولُ وَكِيلٌ.

ther invites you to pay you the wages for watering (our flock) for us.' So when he came to him and recounted the story to him, he said, 'Do not be afraid. You have been delivered from the wrongdoing lot.' [26]One of the two women said, 'Father, hire him. Indeed, the best you can hire is a powerful and trustworthy man.'

[27]He said, 'Indeed, I desire to marry you to one of these two daughters of mine, on condition that you hire yourself to me for eight years. And if you complete ten, that will be up to you, and I do not want to be hard on you. God willing, you will find me to be one of the righteous.' [28]He said, 'This will be [by consent] between you and me. Whichever of the two terms I complete, there shall be no reprisal against me, and Allah is witness over what we say.'

It is *sunnah* to go out wearing a turban (*ᶜammāmah*) with its loose end drawn under the chain. It is said to gguard against thieves and the risk of drowning and burning.[1] It is also recommended that one should take along a little of the soil (*turbah*) taken from the shrine of Imam al-Ḥusayn (*ᶜa*), and say while holding it,[2]

اَللّٰهُمَّ هٰذِهِ طِينَةُ قَبْرِ الْحُسَـيْنِ عَلَيْهِ
السَّـلاٰمُ وَلِيِّكَ وَ ابْنِ وَلِيِّكَ، اِتَّخَذْتُهٰا
حِرْزاً لِمٰا أَخٰافُ وَ مٰا لاٰ أَخٰافُ.

O Allah, this soil is from the tomb of Ḥusayn, Your *walī* and son of Your *walī*, may peace be upon him. I carry it as an amulet to protect myself from what I fear and what I do not.

1 *Maḥāsin*, ii, 373, b 35, h 137, whence *Biḥār*, lxxiii, 238, b 48, h 12. *Thawāb*, 187, whence *Biḥār*, lxxiii, 230, b 48, h 4. *Faqīh*, ii, 301, h 2519, whence *Wasā'il*, xi, 452, b 59, h 15238. *Makārim* 120. *Amān* 102. *Biḥār*, xcvii, 109, b 1, h 18 from *Miṣbāḥ al-Zā'ir*. *Aᶜlām al-Dīn*, 396.

2 *Tahdhīb*, vi, 74, b 22, h 15. *Amān*, 47, whence *Biḥār*, xcvii, 109, b 1, h 18, 19. *Kāmil al-Ziyārāt*, 283, b 93, h 10.

It is also recommended that one be wearing a ring of agate or turquoise, especially one studded with a yellow agate with the words مَا شَاءَ اللهُ لَا قُوَّةَ إِلَّا بِاللهِ أَسْتَغْفِرُ اللهَ inscribed on one side and the words "*Muḥammad wa ʿAlī*" on the other.[1]

Sayyid Ibn Ṭāwūs, in *Amān al-Akhṭār*, cites a report[2] of Ṣāfī, a servant of Imam ʿAlī al-Naqī (ʿ*a*), narrated from him by Abū Muḥammad al-Qāsim b. ʿAlā. Ṣāfī says, 'When I was taking the Imam's leave for pilgrimage to the shrine of his grandfather, Imam ʿAlī al-Riḍā (ʿ*a*), he said to me, 'Carry along a ring studded with a yellow agate with the words "*Mā shâ' Allāhu lā quwwata illā billāh. Astaghfirullāh*" inscribed on one side and "*Mūḥammad wa ʿAlī*" on the other. When you carry this ring with you, you will be secure from the evil of bandits and thieves and it will be useful for the safety of your person and faith.' "

Ṣāfī says, "Having obtained a ring like the one Imam had mentioned, I went back to bid him farewell. After departing, when I had gone some distance, he sent for me. When I came back, he said to me, 'O Ṣāfī, you should carry a ring of turquoise too, for between Ṭūs and Nayshābūr your caravan will come up against a lion that will block your way. You should approach him and show him this ring and say, "My master tells you to get out of our way." Have the words اللهُ المَلِكُ inscribed on one side of it and المُلْكُ لِلهِ الوَاحِدِ القَهَّارِ on the other, as اللهُ المَلِكُ was the inscription on the ring of the Commander of the Faithful (ʿ*a*). After the caliphate was restored to him, he had the words المُلْكُ لِلهِ الوَاحِدِ القَهَّارِ inscribed on his ring, which was studded with turquoise. Such a ring is protection against the danger of wild beasts and brings victory in battle.' "

Ṣāfī says, "I proceeded on the journey and, by God, at the very place that the Imam had mentioned a lion appeared in our way. I did as the Imam had commanded and it went away. On returning from the pilgrimage, I recounted to him what had happened. He said, 'There is one thing which you have not mentioned. I will describe it if you wish.' I said, 'Master, perhaps I have forgotten something.' He said, 'One night at Ṭūs when you were resting near the holy tomb, a group of jinn who had come for pilgrimage to the Imam's tomb saw the ring in your hand. On noting its inscription, they took it out of your hand and carried it for one of their sick. They washed the ring in water and gave it to the sick person to drink and he was cured. Then they restored the ring to you. You had been wearing it in your right hand, but they put it in your left. This caused you much amazement, but you

1 *Amān*, 48, whence *Wasā'il*, xi, 428, b 45, h 15175.

2 *Amān*, 48.

did not know how it had happened. You found a ruby lying near your head and it is now in your possession. Take it to the market. You will be able to sell it for 80 gold coins. It is a gift brought to you by those jinn.' " Ṣāfī says, "I took the ruby to the market and sold it for eighty gold coins, as the master had said."

Imam Jaᶜfar al-Ṣādiq (ᶜa) is reported[1] to have said that those who recite the Throne Verse every night during journey, they and those who are with them will remain safe from harm. Also, it is recommended[2] that the traveller should say,

O Allah, let my journey be a lesson, and let my silence be informed with contemplation, and my speech with Your remembrance!	اَللّٰهُمَّ اجْعَلْ مَسِيرِى عَبَراً، وَ صَمْتِي تَفَكُّراً، وَ كَلَامِى ذِكْرًا.

Imam Zayn al-ᶜĀbidīn (ᶜa) is reported[3] to have said concerning the following supplication, "When I say these words, I do not care even if all humans and jinn rally to inflict harm upon me,"

In the Name of Allah, by Allah, from Allah, toward Allah, and in the way of Allah. O Allah, I surrender my self to You, turn my face toward You, and resign my affairs to You. So protect me with the shield of faith, from my front and rear, from my right and left, and from above and below, and shield me with Your power and strength. For indeed there is no power or forceexcept what derives from Allah, the All-exalted, the All-great!	بِسْمِ اللّٰهِ وَ بِاللّٰهِ وَ مِنَ اللّٰهِ وَ إِلَى اللّٰهِ وَ فِي سَبِيلِ اللّٰهِ. اَللّٰهُمَّ إِلَيْكَ أَسْلَمْتُ نَفْسِى، وَ إِلَيْكَ وَجَّهْتُ وَجْهِى، وَ إِلَيْكَ فَوَّضْتُ أَمْرِى، فَاحْفَظْنِي بِحِفْظِ الْإِيمَانِ مِنْ بَيْنِ يَدَىَّ وَ مِنْ خَلْفِي وَ عَنْ يَمِينِي وَ عَنْ شِمَالِي وَ مِنْ فَوْقِي وَ مِنْ تَحْتِي، وَ ادْفَعْ عَنِّي بِحَوْلِكَ وَ قُوَّتِكَ، فَإِنَّهُ لَا حَوْلَ وَ لَا قُوَّةَ إِلَّا بِاللّٰهِ الْعَلِيِّ الْعَظِيمِ.

1 *Makārim*, 254, whence *Biḥār*, lxxiii, 252, b 48, h 47.

2 *Faqīh*, ii, 273, whence *Wasā'il*, xi, 392, b 21, h 15089. *Makārim*, 254, whence *Biḥār*, lxxiii, 252, b 48, h 47. *Amān*, 112. *Biḥār*, xcvii, 110, b 1, h 20, from *Miṣbāḥ al-Zā'ir*.

3 Ṭusī's *Amālī*, 208, whence *Biḥār*, xcii, 215, b 107, h 7. *Amān*, 125, whence *Biḥār*, lxxiii, 258, b 48, h 52. Kafᶜamī's *Miṣbāḥ*, 247. *Biḥār*, xcvii, 110, b 1, h 20, from *Miṣbāḥ al-Zā'ir*.

Some Points of Etiquette

The supplications recommended for journey and the points of etiquette relating to it are many. Here we will briefly mention some points pertaining to the subject.

(1) While riding (a mount or vehicle), not to forget saying *"Bismillāh."*[1]

(2) To be careful of one's provisions and baggage and to place them in a safe place. It is mentioned in a tradition that taking good care of one's means is part of the traveller's wisdom.[2]

(3) To offer help and assistance to one's companions during the journey and not to spare any assistance and service they may need, so that God Almighty may spare one of 73 troubles and save one from the world's sorrows and worries and the great anguish of the Day of Resurrection.[3]

It has been reported that Imam Zayn al-ᶜĀbidīn (ᶜ*a*) did not travel except in the company of people who did not know him so that he might be able to serve them on the way. That was because if they knew him, they would not allow him to do anything for them.[4]

We get a similar picture of the the noble characteristics of the

[1] *Maḥāsin*, ii, 628, b 12, h 101 & *Kāfī*, vi, 539, 540, h 13, whence *Wasā'il*, xi, 388, b 20, h 15081, .& *Biḥār*, lx, 204, b 3, h 31. *Thawāb*, 191, whence *Biḥār*, lxxvii, 296, b 55, h 25. *Tahdhīb*, vi, 165, b 77, h 8, 10. *Makārim*, 248, 264, whence *Biḥār*, lxi, 209, b 8, h 14. *Daᶜawāt*, 294, h 51, whence *Biḥār*, lxxiii, 242, b 48, h 22. *Aᶜlām, al-Dīn*, 396.

Ṣiffīn, 132, whence *Mustadrak*, viii, 135, b 17, h 9238/1. Ṭūsī's *Amālī*, 515, majlis 18, h 1126/33, , whence *Wasā'il*, xi, 390, b 20, h 15085 & *Biḥār*, lxxiii, 295,299, b 55, h 23, 38. *Makārim*, 108. *Manāqib*, 297, whence *Biḥār*, lx, 324, b 98, h 6 & *Mustadrak*, iii, 326, b 48, h 3699/28.

[2] *Biḥār*, lxxiii, 270, b 49, h 25 citing *Maḥāsin*, gives the wording as مِن فِقهِ الْمُسَافِرِ حِفظُ نَفَقَتِهِ. However, in *Maḥāsin*, ii, 358, b 19, h 74, whence *Biḥār*, xcvi, 122, b 20, h 3, and *Faqīh*, ii, 280, h 2448, whence *Wasā'il*, xi, 419, b 38, h 15152, the text cited is مِن قُوَّةِ الْمُسَافِرِ حِفظُ نَفَقَتِهِ, which means that taking proper care of one's belongings and means during journey is part of the traveller's strengths.

[3] *Maḥāsin*, ii, 362, b 25, h 95, 96, whence *Biḥār*, lxxiii, 247, 287, b 49, h 28, b 54, h 1, 2. *Kāfī*, ii, 199, h 2, whence *Wasā'il*, xvi, 372, b 29, h 21793, & *Biḥār*, vii, 197, b 8, h 71, lxxi, 320, b 20, h 86. *Faqīh*, ii, 292, h 2497, whence *Wasā'il*, xi, 429, b 46, h 15176,. *Jaᶜfariyāt*, 198, whence *Mustadrak*, viii, 219, b 35, h 9297/1. *Makārim*, 266. Rāwandī's *Nawādir*, 8, whence *Biḥār*, vii, 183, b 8, h 31, lxxiii, 288, b 54, h 4.

[4] *ᶜUyūn Akhbār, al-Riḍā*, ii, 145, b 40, h 13, whence *Wasā'il*, xi, 430, b 46, h 15177 & *Biḥār*, xlvi, 69, b 5, h 41.

Apostle of Allah (ṣ) from the following story. Once when he was travelling with some companions, they needed to prepare food. One of them said, "I will slaughter the sheep." Another said, "I will do the skinning." Another one said, "I will do the cooking." The Prophet said, "I will gather firewood." They said, "O Apostle of Allah, we will do that ourselves. Do not trouble yourself." He said, "I know that you will do it. But I do not like to have any advantage over you. God Almighty hates to see any of His servants preferring himself to his companions."[1]

One should know that the most difficult of companions during journey is one who does nothing despite having no physical disability and expects others to do things for him.

(4) To travel in the company of someone who is like oneself in spending.[2]

(5) Not to drink water at any halt during the journey without mixing it with water remaining from the previous halt. It is also recommended that the traveller should carry along some of the soil of his hometown and put a little of it in the water container, which should be stirred somewhat and then allowed to settle. After the water has become clear it may be used for drinking.[3]

(6) To observe good manners and to be patient and forbearing. We will mention that which is appropriate in this regard while describing the etiquette pertaining to the *ziyārah* of Imam al-Ḥusayn (ᶜ*a*).

(7) To carry along one's provisions for the journey. The dignified thing for a person to do is to carry good provisions, especially during the journey to Makkah.[4] However, it is not desirable during the journey of *ziyārah* to the shrine of Imam al-Ḥusayn (ᶜ*a*) to carry delicious preparations such as pilau, sweetmeats etc., as will be mentioned in the section pertaining to the *ziyārah* of that Imam.

Ibn Aᶜsam has authored the following verses on the topic.

مِنْ شَرَفِ الإِنْسَانِ فِي الأَسْفَارِ   تَطْيِيبُهُ الزَّادَ مَعَ الإِكْثَارِ

1 *Makārim* 251, whence *Biḥār*, lxxiii, 273, b 49, h 31.

2 *Maḥāsin*, ii, 357, b 15, h 64, 65, whence *Biḥār*, lxxiii, 267, 268, b 49, h 10, 11. *Kāfī*, iv, 286, 287, h 6, 7 & *Faqīh*, ii, 278, 279, h 2441, 2442, whence *Wasā'il*, xi, 413, 414, b 33, h 15137, 15139. *Makārim*, 251. ᶜ*Awālī*, iv, 31, h 104.

3 *Ṭibb al-Riḍā* (ᶜ*a*), 44-45, whence *Biḥār*, lix, 325.

4 *Maḥāsin*, ii, 360, b 21, h 81, whence *Biḥār*, lxxiii, 269, b 49, h 21. *Kāfī*, viii, 303, h 467. *Faqīh*, ii, 281, whence *Wasā'il*, xi, 423,, b 42, h 15160, 2454. *Mustadrak*, viii, 216, b 30, h 9290/1, from Abū al-Qāsim al-Kūfī's *Kitāb al-Akhlāq*. *Makārim*, 253. Amān, 56. Kafᶜamī's *Miṣbāḥ*, 185.

وَ لْيُحْسِنِ الْإِنْسَانُ فِي حَالِ السَّفَرِ أَخْلَاقَهُ زِيَادَةً عَلَى الْحَضَرِ

وَ لْيَدْعُ عِنْدَ الْوَضْعِ لِلْخِوَانِ مَنْ كَانَ حَاضِرًا مِنَ الْإِخْوَانِ

وَ لْيُكْثِرِ الْمَزْحَ مَعَ الصَّحْبِ إِذَا لَمْ يُسْخِطِ اللهَ وَ لَمْ يَجْلِبْ أَذَى

مَنْ جَاءَ بَلْدَةً فَذَا ضَيْفٌ عَلَى إِخْوَانِهِ فِيهَا إِلَى أَنْ يَرْحَلَا

يُبَرُّ لَيْلَتَيْنِ ثُمَّ لَيَأْكُلِ مِنْ أَكْلِ أَهْلِ الْبَيْتِ فِي الْمُسْتَقْبِلِ

It is decent during journeys to carry provisions good and ample,
To observe superior manners when travelling, better than we do at home.
When the table has been laid out, invite the folks present.
Let there be some humour, not causing Heaven displeasure or the companions annoyance.
When someone arrives in town, he is guest of the brethren until he leaves,
Receiving the guest's especial attention for two nights,
Dining thereafter with the host's family, eating their usual bread.

(8) What is very important during journeys is to be careful of one's obligatory prayers and to perform them with punctuality and due observance of their prerequisites. It is often observed that pilgrims on journeys of ḥajj or *ziyārah* neglect their prayers during travel and either do not perform their obligatory prayers on time or make them while riding, or with *tayammum*, or in a state of ritual impurity of the body or clothes. Such conduct is indicative of negligence and indifference to their prayers, although, as pointed out by Imam Jaᶜfar al-Ṣādiq (*ᶜa*) in a report, the obligatory prayer is better than 20 ḥajj pilgrimages and a single ḥajj is better than a house full of gold given away in charity.[1]

Also, one should not forget to say 30 times "*Suḥānallāhi, wal hamdulillāhi, wa lā ilāha illallāhu, wallāhu akbar,*" after the shortened (*qaṣr*) prayers made during journey, a practice that has been urged in the traditions.[2]

[1] *Kāfī*, iii, 265, h 7, whence *Wasā'il*, iv, 39, b 10, h 4456; *Faqīh*. i, 209, h 630, ii, 221, h 2237; *Tahdhīb*, ii, 236, b 12, h 4, v, 21, b 3, h 7; whence *Biḥār*, lxxix, 227, b 1, h 55. *Rawḍat al-Wāᶜiẓīn*, ii, 318. *ᶜAawālī*, i, 415, h 85, i, 319, h 47.

[2] *Faqīh*, i, 452, h 1312. *ᶜUyūn Akhbār al-Riḍā*, ii, 182, b 44, whence *Wasā'il*, viii, 523, b 24, h 11342 & *Biḥār*, lxxxii, 32, b 23, h 23. *Mustadrak*, vi, 544, b 17, h 7471/1, from Ṣadūq's *al-Muqniᶜ*. *Tahdhīb*, iii, 230, b 23, h 103, whence *Wasā'il*, viii, 523, b 24, h 11341, 11342. *Biḥār*, lxxxvi, 60.

Chapter One

The Etiquette of Ziyarah

The points of etiquette pertaining to *ziyārah* are many and here we shall confine ourselves to noting a few.

(1) To take a bath before going out on the journey for *ziyārah*.[1]

(2) To refrain from useless and vain talk, quarrels and disputes on the way.[2]

(3) To take a bath for the *ziyārah* of each of the Imams[3] and to recite the prescribed supplication, which will be mentioned at the beginning of *Ziyārah al-Wārith* (p. 276).

(4) Being in a state of ritual purity (*ṭahārah*) from major and minor impurity (*ḥadath*).[4]

(5) To wear clean and new clothes,[5] preferably white.[6]

(6) To walk calmly and with dignity, walking with humility, taking short steps, while proceeding towards the holy shrine, with the head lowered and without looking up and around.[7]

(7) To apply perfume to oneself, except when making *ziyārah* of the shrine of Imam al-Ḥusayn (ᶜ*a*).[8]

(8) While on the way to the shrine, to engage in *dhikr*, *takbīr*, *tasbīḥ* and *tahlīl* and invoking blessings (*ṣalawāt*) on the Prophet Muḥammad and his Family (ᶜ*a*).[9]

(9) To stop at the shrine gate and ask for leave of admittance, while trying to bring about in one's heart a feeling of reverence, hu-

1 *Faqīh*, ii, 602, h 3210. *Amān*, 33 whence *Wasā'il*, xi, 369, b 13, h 15038 & *Biḥār*, lxxiii, 235, b 48, h 19, xcvii, 104.

2 *Wasā'il*, xii, 182-187, b 117, h 16023-16043; xii, 236-238, b 135, h 16180-16188. *Biḥār*, ii, 124-140, b 17, h 1-60. *Mustadrak*, ix, 26-35, b 103, h 10109/1-10133/25, ix, 73-77, b 117, h 10240/1-10255/16.

3 *Wasā'il*, xiv, 390-393, b 29, h 19443-19449. *Durūs*, ii, 22.

4 *Durūs*, ii, 22, dars 128.

5 *Durūs*, ii, 22-23.

6 *Kāfī*, vi, 445, h 1-3. *Wasā'il*, v, 26-, b 14, h 5796-5798, 5800-5801. *Mustadrak*, iii, 247, b 10, h 3499/1-3500/2.

7 *Faqīh*, ii, 609, h 3213. *Tahdhīb*, i, 95, b 46, h 1. *Wasā'il*, xiv, 390-393, b 29, h 19443-19449.

8 *Al-Mazār al-Kabīr*, 205. *Iqbāl*, 608. Thence in *Wasā'il*, xiv, 392, b 29, h 19448 & *Biḥār*, xcvii, 236, 373, b 2, h 3, b 5, h 9. *Farḥat al-Gharī*, 93.

9 *Wasā'il*, xiv, 392-393, b 29, h 19445, 19448, 19449 .

mility and tenderness by contemplating the greatness and majesty of the personage whose shrine is being visited, remembering that he/she sees one standing at the shrine door, hears one's speech and responds to one's greeting. One testifies to the truth of all these matters while reciting the leave of admittance.[1]

Also, one should call to one's mind the love and kindness they have for their followers and visitors, and reflect over one's shortcomings and the affronts one might have committed in relation to those personages, either by disregarding their multifarious advices and injunctions, or by offending them, or their friends and favourites, which also amount to offending them. Indeed, if one were to do some introspection, one's feet would tremble and fail to move forward, and one's heart would be filled with anxiety and eyes with tears, and such a state is the soul of the etiquette.

Here it would be appropriate to mention certain verses of Sakhāwī as well as the report cited by ᶜAllāmah Majlisī (r) in the *Biḥār* from *ᶜUyūn al-Muᶜjizāt*. As for Sakhāwī's verses, which are worthy of being mused upon in this state, they are as follows:

قَالُوا غَـداً نَأْتِي دِيَارَ الْحِمَىٰ   وَ يَنْزِلُ الرَّكْبُ بِمَغْنَاهُـمُ

فَـكُلُّ مَـنْ كَانَ مُطِيعًا لَهُمْ   أَصْبَحَ مَسْـرُورًا بِلُقْـيَاهُمُ

قُلْتُ فَلِي ذَنْبٌ فَـمَا حِيلَتِي   بِـأَيِّ وَجْـهٍ أَتَلَقَّاهُـمُ

قَالُوا أَلَيْسَ الْعَفْـوُ مِنْ شَأْنِهِمْ   لا سِـيَّمَا عَمَّـنْ تَرَجَّاهُمُ

فَجِئْتُهُمْ أَسْـعَى إِلَـىٰ بَابِهِمْ   أَرْجُوهُمُ طَـوْرًا وَأَخْشَاهُمُ

I was told, Tomorrow we shall be within the sanctuary,
And the caravan will alight in the courtyard of safety and peace,
Whereat all who had kept their faith with them rejoiced at the prospect of the union..
And I said to myself, I carry guilt, what shall I do, what face have I to face them!
I was told, Is it not their custom to pardon, above all those who expect that of them?
And so I came hurrying at their door, hopeful and with a heart tremulous with awe.[2]

1 *Durūs*, ii, 23.

2 It will be appropriate to summon up as well the following verses.

As for the report cited by ᶜAllāmah Majlisī,[1] it is as follows.

Ibrāhīm Jammāl, a Shīᶜī, wanted to meet ᶜAlī b. Yaqṭīn, the vizier of Hārūn al-Ras͟hīd. Apparently, his status was not such as to permit him to enter ᶜAlī's presence, and accordingly he was denied admittance by the vizier. By chance, during the same year ᶜAlī b. Yaqṭīn came for hajj pilgrimage and wanted to meet Imam Mūsā ibn Jaᶜfar (*ᶜa*). The Imam refused to meet him. The second day ᶜAlī chanced to meet the Imam outside his house and said to him, "Master, what was my fault that you refused to see me?" The Imam replied, "You refused admittance to your brother Ibrāhīm Jammāl and God Almighty will not accept your efforts unless Ibrāhīm pardons you."

ᶜAlī said, "My master and lord, how can I find Ibrāhīm at this time? I am in Madīnah and he is in Kūfah." The Imam said to him, "At nightfall go to the cemetery at Baqīᶜ without any of your subordinates and servants knowing about it. There you will find a saddled camel. Ride that camel and depart for Kūfah.

At night ᶜAlī b Yaqṭīn went to Baqīᶜ and mounted the camel. In a short time he was at the door of Ibrāhīm's house. Having seated the camel, he knocked at the door. "Who is that?" inquired Ibrāhīm,. "It is ᶜAlī b. Yaqṭīn," he answered. "What is ᶜAlī b. Yaqṭīn doing at my door," asked Ibrāhīm. "Come out, I am in a dire situation!" cried ᶜAlī, and entreated him to allow him to enter.

When he entered, he said to Ibrāhīm, "O Ibrāhīm, my master and lord has refused to accept my acts of worship unless you pardon me." "May God forgive you," Ibrāhīm answered. Then ᶜAlī fell on his knees and placing his face on the ground entreated Ibrāhīm to place his foot on his face and to trample it. Ibrāhīm refused to do so, but when ᶜAlī adjured him, he put his foot on ᶜAlī b. Yaqṭīn's face and rubbed it underneath, while ᶜAlī was saying, "O God, be witness!"

هَـا عَبْــــدُكَ وَاقِفٌ ذَلِيلٌ   بِالْبَابِ يَمُــــدُّ كَفَّ سَائِلٍ
قَدْ عَــــزَّ عَلَيَّ سُــوءُ حَالِي   مَا يَفْــعَلُ مَا فَعَلْتُ عَاقِلٌ
يَا أَكْــــرَمَ مَنْ رَجَاهُ رَاجٍ   عَنْ بَـــــابِكَ لا يُرَدُّ سَائِلٌ

Here stands your humble servant, his hand stretched like the beggar's
Restrained by his own wretchedness, does any sane person do what I have done?
O most magnanimous of those in whom are placed hopes,
The needy are not turned away from your door! (The Compiler's note)

[1] *Biḥār*, xlviii, 85, b 4, h 105.

Then coming out, he mounted the camel and returned the same night to Madīnah where he got the camel seated at the door of Imam Mūsā ibn Jaᶜfar (ᶜ*a*). Thereupon, the Imam granted him admittance and accepted his apology.

This report shows how important are the rights of one's brethren-in-faith.

(10) To embrace the threshold of the blessed shrine, and the Shahīd Awwal (r) has said that it will be better for the visitor to prostrate with the intent of prostrating to God in gratitude for enabling him to reach that place.[1]

(11) To enter with the right foot and to put the left foot forward while leaving, as in the case of a mosque.[2]

(12) To approach the blessed tomb so closely as to be able to embrace it. It is a delusion to imagine that standing at a distance is a mark of reverence, as the reports enjoin one to embrace it and to lean upon it.[3]

(13) To stand facing the luminous tomb, with one's back towards the *qiblah*. Apparently, this etiquette is restricted to the tombs of the Infallibles (ᶜ*a*). After performing the *ziyārah*, to supplicate while placing the right cheek on the tomb and then the left, and to humbly petition God with insistent entreaties to grant one the benefit of the intercession of the owner of the tomb by the rights of that personage. Then one should move towards the head of the tomb and supplicate facing the *qiblah*.[4]

(14) To stand while reciting the *ziyārah*, unless one has an excuse, such as weakness, backache, leg pain and the like.

(15) To say *takbīr* on sighting the blessed tomb and before reciting the *ziyārah*. It is mentioned in a report[5] that those who say *takbīr* while coming face to face with the Imam (ᶜ*a*) and say *Lā ilāha illallāh, waḥdahū lā sharīka lah* are written down as those who obtain 'God's greatest approval' (*riḍwān Allāh al-akbar*).

(16) To recite the texts of *ziyārah* narrated from those teachers of humankind (ᶜ*a*)[6] and to refrain from reading faked *ziyārahs*, which are compositions of ignorant laymen mingled with part of the authentic texts for the use of the unwary.

1 *Durūs*, ii, 24-25.
2 *Durūs*, ii, 23.
3 *Durūs*, ii, 23.
4 *Ibid*.
5 Source not found.
6 *Durūs*, ii, 23.

Shaykh Kulaynī (*r*) reports[1] that ʿAbd al-Raḥīm al-Qaṣīir, one of the companions of Imam Jaʿfar al-Ṣādiq (*ʿa*) said to the Imam, "May I be made your ransom, I have composed a supplication." The imam (*ʿa*) said to him, "Spare me of your compositions. When you have some need, take resort with the Apostle of Allah (ṣ), offer two *rakʿahs* of prayer and make a gift of them to him (ṣ)..."

(17) To offer the prayer of *ziyārah*, which is at least two *rakʿahs.* Shahīd Awwal says that when performing the *ziyārah* of the Apostle of Allah (ṣ) the prayer should be offered within his holy shrine, and when it is in the shrine of one of the Imams (*ʿa*) to offer it at the head of the tomb, and that it is permissible to offer the two *rakʿahs* within the mosque adjoining the shrine.[2] ʿAllāmah Majlisī (*r*) says that in his opinion it is better to pray at the head of the tomb or behind the head. ʿAllāmah Baḥr al-ʿUlūm too has said in the *Durrah*,

وَمِنْ حَدِيثِ كَرْبَلا وَالْكَعْبَةِ لِكَرْبَلا بَانَ عُلُوُّ الرُّتْبَةِ

وَ غَيْرُهَا مِنْ سَائِرِ الْمَشَاهِدِ أَمْثَالُهَا بِالنَّقْلِ ذِي الشَّوَاهِدِ

وَ رَاعِ فِيهِنَّ اقْتِرَابَ الرَّمْسِ وَ آثِرِ الصَّلاةَ عِنْدَ الرَّأْسِ

وَ صَلِّ خَلْفَ الْقَبْرِ فَالصَّحِيحُ كَغَيْرِهِ فِي نَدْبِهَا صَرِيحُ

وَ الْفَرْقُ بَيْنَ هٰذِهِ الْقُبُورِ وَ غَيْرِهَا كَالنُّورِ فَوْقَ الطُّورِ

فَالسَّعْيُ لِلصَّلاةِ عِنْدَهَا نُدِبَ وَقُرْبُهَا بَلِ اللُّصُوقُ قَدْ طُلِبَ

The lofty rank of Karbalā is evident from reports about it and the Ka'bah,
And other similar shrines as well, as borne out by the evidence of traditions.
Observe therein nearness to the tomb, and prefer prayer at the head.
Pray behind the tomb, as reliable reports recommend it, like other desirable acts.
Their distinction over other tombs is like that of the Light over the Mount.
Pray diligently in their neighbourhood,
And keep close to them, or rather cling to them.

1 *Kāfī*, iii, 476, whence *Wasāʾil*, iii, 333, b 20, h 2799, viii, 130, b 28, h 10234 & *Biḥār*, xcix, 229, h 3. *Faqīh*, i, 559. *Tahdhīb*, i, 116, b 5, h 37.

2 *Durūs*, ii, 23.

(18) To recite Sūrat Yā Sīn in the first *rakʿah* and Sūrat al-Raḥmān in the second of the prayer of *ziyārah* if no specifics are mentioned for the prayer to be performed.[1] To supplicate after the prayer, by reciting a text narrated in the sources, or anything that may occur to one's mind for one's well-being in mundane and religious matters. Supplicating for the general good is recommended, for it is more likely to be answered.

(19) Shahīd Awwal (r) says[2] that when on entering the shrine one observes that con)gregational prayers are being held, one should first attend the prayer before making the *ziyārah*. Also, if the time for obligatory prayers sets in, one should postpone the *ziyārah* and start the prayer. Otherwise, it is preferable to perform the *ziyārah* first, because that is the main objective of entering the shrine. If the prayers commence while one is in the middle of a *ziyārah*, it is preferable for the pilgrims to discontinue the *ziyārah* and join the prayers, it being undesirable to put off the prayer. It is the duty of those who administer the shrine to ask the people to join the prayers.

(20) Shahīd Awwal considers[3] it a part of the etiquette of *ziyārah* to read the Qur'ān by the blessed tomb and to make a gift of its reward to the spirit of the visited saint. The visitor is also the beneficiary of this act which is a gesture of reverence for the visited one.[4]

(21) One should refrain from unworthy and idle talk and gossip and engaging in mundane conversation. They are reprehensible and ugly in all places and a cause of denial of Divine blessings and provision. They sicken the heart, and are especially harmful in these sacred spots and sublime shrines, whose greatness and glory is mentioned by God Almighty in the verses of Sūrat al-Nūr,

فِى بُيُوتٍ أَذِنَ اللهُ أَنْ تُرْفَعَ وَ يُذْكَرَ فِيهَا اسْمُهُ يُسَبِّحُ لَهُ فِيهَا بِالْغُدُوِّ وَ الْآصالِ رِجالٌ لا تُلْهِيهِمْ تِجارَةٌ وَ لا بَيْعٌ عَنْ ذِكْرِ اللهِ وَ إِقامِ الصَّلاةِ وَ إِيتاءِ الزَّكاةِ يَخافُونَ يَوْماً تَتَقَلَّبُ فِيهِ الْقُلُوبُ وَ الْأَبْصارُ

[1] *Kāmil al-Ziyārāt*, 213, 239, 311 *Faqīh*, ii, 604. *ʿUyūn Akhbār al-Riḍā*, ii, 270, b 68, h 1. Mufid's *Mazār*, 83, b 44, 114, b 44. Ṭūsī's *Miṣbāḥ*, 744. *Tahdhīb*, vi, 63, b 18, 88, b 35. Kafʿamī's *Miṣbāḥ*, 378. *Balad*, 294. Thence in *Biḥār*, xcvii, 134, b 3, h 24, xcvii, 179, b 2, xcvii, 320, b 4, h 25. xcviii, 166, 186, 21, b 18, h 17, 30, 33, xcix, 16, 46, b 2, h 9, b 5, h 1.

[2] *Durūs*, ii, 25.

[3] *Durūs*, ii, 23.

[4] *Durūs*, ii, 23.

In houses Allah has allowed to be raised and wherein His Name is celebrated, He is glorified therein, morning and evening, by men whom neither trading nor bargaining distracts from the remembrance of Allah, and the maintenance of prayer and the giving of zakāt. They are fearful of a day wherein the hearts and the sights will be transformed . . . (24:36-37).

(22) To refrain from raising one's voice when reciting the *ziyārah*, as mentioned by us in *Hadīyyat al-Zā'irīn.*

(23) To bid the Imam farewell when leaving the town, either by reciting a text narrated in the sources or something else.

(24) To perform repentance and plead for forgiveness of one's sins and to improve one's character and speech to be better than what they had been before the *ziyārah.*[1]

(25) To provide financial assistance to the staff serving at the blessed shrine. It is behooving that the serving staff should be good and honourable persons possessing piety, generosity and patience. They should restrain their anger when faced with improper conduct on behalf of the visitors and refrain from rude and harsh manners. They should try to assist those who stand in need of their help and guide foreigners who have lost their way.[2] In brief, it is the duty of the service staff to be sincere in their work and provide the essential services for the cleanliness, safety and maintenance of the shrine and care of its visitors.

(26) To offer financial help to the local needy and poor belonging to the Imam's town, especially the sayyids and the religious scholars and students facing poverty and penury, each of whose efforts in upholding the sanctity of the Divine sacraments and other aspects is sufficient to underscore the necessity of assistance.

(27) Shahīd Awwal has said[3] that one of the points of etiquette is to make haste in leaving when one has obtained one's share of the *ziyārah* in order to enhance one's reverence and eagerness to return. He also says that the women should perform the *ziyārah* separately from men and it is better for them to perform it during nighttime. They should also modify their dress to suit the occasion, by putting on simple and plain clothes divested of fineries, in order to be indistinguishable from others. They should come out incognito taking care not to be seen and identified by strangers. It is however per-

[1] *Durūs*, ii, 24.
[2] *Durūs*, ii, 24.
[3] *Durūs*, ii, 24.

missible for them to perform the *ziyārah* alongside men, though it is undesirable (*makrūh*).

The compiler says: These statements indicate the outrageousness of what has become a common practice. These days women adorn themselves in the name of going out for *ziyārah* and emerge from their homes in their finery. Within the holy shrines they either jostle through the crowd of strange men, or stand clinging to the holy tomb, or engage in reading the *ziyārah* while sitting at the *qiblah* of the menfolk, causing distraction for the people and diverting the attention of the worshippers and those engaged in prayers, petitions, entreaties and lamentation. Thus, they inadvertently join the ranks of those who bar the way of God. In fact, this kind of *ziyārah* should be considered an act of impiety, not worship, and classed with mortal sins, not with devotions that bring one close to God.

It is mentioned in a report of Imam Jaᶜfar al-Ṣādiq (ᶜ*a*) that the Commander of the Faithful (ᶜ*a*) once remarked in an address to the people of Iraq,

يَا أَهْلَ الْعِرَاقِ نُبِّئْتُ أَنَّ نِسَاءَكُمْ يُدَافِعْنَ الرِّجَالَ فِي الطَّرِيقِ أَ مَا تَسْتَحُونَ

"O people of Iraq! It has been reported to me that your womenfolk jostle men on the streets. Have you no shame?"[1]

He also said,

لَعَنَ اللهُ مَنْ لَا يَغَارُ

"Allah distances from His mercy those who have no sense of manly honour (*ghayrah*).[2]

In *Faqīh* is cited a report of Aṣbagh b. Nubātah that he heard the Commander of the Faithful (ᶜ*a*) say,

يَظْهَرُ فِي آخِرِ الزَّمَانِ وَ اقْتِرَابِ السَّاعَةِ وَ هُوَ شَرُّ الْأَزْمِنَةِ نِسْوَةٌ كَاشِفَاتٌ عَارِيَاتٌ، مُتَبَرِّجَاتٌ مِنَ الدِّينِ، دَاخِلَاتٌ فِي الْفِتَنِ مَائِلَاتٌ إِلَى الشَّهَوَاتِ، مُسْرِعَاتٌ إِلَى اللَّذَّاتِ، مُسْتَحِلَّاتٌ لِلْمُحَرَّمَاتِ، فِي جَهَنَّمَ خَالِدَاتٌ

1 *Maḥāsin*, i, 115, b 54, h 116. *Kāfī*, v, 536, h 6, whence *Biḥār*, lxxvi, 115, b 84, h 7 and *Wasā'il*, xx, 235, b 132, h 25520. *Mishkāt al-Anwār*, 235.

2 *Maḥāsin*, i, 115, b 54, h 116, whence *Biḥār*, lxxvi, 115, b 84, h 7 and *Wasā'il*, xx, 235, b 132, h 25520.

> There will appear in the ultimate era—which is the worst of eras and near the Hour of Resurrection—women who will display their adornments and charms, being bereft of the veil of modesty and devoid of faith, fallen to temptations, inclined toward lust and avid for pleasures. They will regard what God has forbidden as lawful and permissible and so will be destined to languish in hell.[1]

(28) It is advisable that when there is a large throng of pilgrims, those who have succeeded in approaching the *ḍarīḥ* should shorten the time of *ziyārah* and leave so that others may have the opportunity to approach the *ḍarīḥ* like them.

In the chapter on the *ziyārah* of Imam al-Ḥusayn (ʿ*a*), we will mention the etiquette to be observed for the *ziyārah* of that Imam.

1 *Faqīh*, iii, 390, h 4374, whence *Wasāʾil*, xx, 35, b 7, h 24961. *Makārim*, 201.

Chapter Two

Appeal for the Leave of Entry

In this chapter, we will mention texts for making the appeal seeking admittance into any of the holy shrines.

First Appeal for Admittance

<u>Sh</u>ay<u>kh</u> Kafʿamī says,[1] when one wants to enter the Mosque of the Apostle of Allah (ṣ) or the shrine one of the Imams (ʿa), one should say,

اَللّٰهُمَّ إِنِّي وَقَفْتُ عَلىٰ بَابٍ مِنْ أَبْوَابِ
بُيُوتِ نَبِيِّكَ صَلَوَاتُكَ عَلَيْهِ وَآلِهِ، وَ
قَدْ مَنَعْتَ النَّاسَ أَنْ يَدْخُلُوا إِلَّا بِإِذْنِهِ،
فَقُلْتَ: يَا أَيُّهَا الَّذِينَ آمَنُوا لَا تَدْخُلُوا
بُيُوتَ النَّبِيِّ إِلَّا أَنْ يُؤْذَنَ لَكُمْ.

O Allah, I stand at a door from among the doors of the houses of Your Prophet, may Your blessings be upon him and his Family, and You have forbidden people from entering them without his leave and You have said, "*O you who have faith! Do not enter the Prophet's houses unless you are granted permission.*"(33:53)

اَللّٰهُمَّ إِنِّي أَعْتَقِدُ حُرْمَةَ صَاحِبِ هٰذَا
الْمَشْهَدِ الشَّرِيفِ فِي غَيْبَتِهِ، كَمَا
أَعْتَقِدُهَا فِي حَضْرَتِهِ، وَ أَعْلَمُ أَنَّ
رَسُولَكَ وَ خُلَفَاءَكَ عَلَيْهِمُ السَّلَامُ
أَحْيَاءٌ عِنْدَكَ يُرْزَقُونَ، يَرَوْنَ مَقَامِي وَ
يَسْمَعُونَ كَلَامِي، وَ يَرُدُّونَ سَلَامِي، وَ
أَنَّكَ حَجَبْتَ عَنْ سَمْعِي كَلَامَهُمْ، وَ
فَتَحْتَ بَابَ فَهْمِي بِلَذِيذِ مُنَاجَاتِهِمْ،

O Allah, I believe in the inviolability of the owner of this holy shrine in his absence as much as I believe in it during his presence, and I know that Your Apostle and Your vicegerents, may peace be upon them, are alive with You, provided by You, and that they observe my standing in this place and hear my speech and return my greetings and that You have drawn a veil between my hearing and their speech, while opening the door to my understanding with the charm of intimate discourse with them.

[1] Kafʿamī's *Miṣbāḥ*, 472. *Balad*, 275.

وَإِنِّي أَسْتَأْذِنُكَ يَا رَبِّ أَوَّلًا، وَأَسْتَأْذِنُ
رَسُولَكَ صَلَّى اللهُ عَلَيْهِ وَآلِهِ ثَانِيًا، وَ
أَسْتَأْذِنُ خَلِيفَتَكَ الْإِمَامَ الْمَفْرُوضَ
عَلَيَّ طَاعَتُهُ فُلَانَ بْنَ فُلَان

My Lord, first I seek Your permission, secondly the permission of Your Apostle, may Allah bless him and his Family, and thirdly the permission of Your vicegerent, the Imam obedience to whom is obligatory on me, so-and-so, son of so-and-so,

Mention the name of the Imam whose shrine one is visiting and that of his father. For instance, if it is Imam al-Ḥusayn (ᶜa) say *"al-Ḥusayn ibna ᶜAlīyin, ᶜalayhis salām,"* and if it is Imam ᶜAlī al-Riḍā (ᶜa) say *ᶜAlī-y-abna Mūsar Riḍā, alayhis salām*, and so on. Then say,

وَالْمَلَائِكَةَ الْمُوَكَّلِينَ بِهٰذِهِ الْبُقْعَةِ
الْمُبَارَكَةِ ثَالِثًا،

and that of the angels entrusted with this blessed shrine.

أَأَدْخُلُ يَا رَسُولَ اللهِ؟ أَأَدْخُلُ يَا
حُجَّةَ اللهِ؟ أَأَدْخُلُ يَا مَلَائِكَةَ اللهِ
الْمُقَرَّبِينَ الْمُقِيمِينَ فِي هٰذَا الْمَشْهَدِ؟

Shall I enter O Apostle of Allah? Shall I enter O Testament of Allah? Shall I enter O Angels brought near to Allah, who reside in this shrine?

فَأْذَنْ لِي يَا مَوْلَايَ فِي الدُّخُولِ أَفْضَلَ
مَا أَذِنْتَ لِأَحَدٍ مِنْ أَوْلِيَائِكَ، فَإِنْ لَمْ
أَكُنْ أَهْلًا لِذٰلِكَ، فَأَنْتَ أَهْلٌ لِذٰلِكَ.

Permit me to enter, O my master, with the most gracious of permissions that You have granted to any of your friends! For even if I should not be worthy of it, you are indeed worthy of it!

Then embrace the blessed threshold and enter. Then say,

بِسْمِ اللهِ وَبِاللهِ وَفِي سَبِيلِ اللهِ وَ
عَلَىٰ مِلَّةِ رَسُولِ اللهِ صَلَّى اللهُ عَلَيْهِ
وَآلِهِ. اَللّٰهُمَّ اغْفِرْ لِي وَارْحَمْنِي وَتُبْ
عَلَيَّ، إِنَّكَ أَنْتَ التَّوَّابُ الرَّحِيمُ.

In the name of Allah, by Allah, in the way of Allah, and following the creed of the Apostle of Allah, may Allah bless him and his Family! O Allah, forgive me, have mercy on me and accept my repentance! Indeed, You are the All-clement and the All-merciful!

Second Appeal for Admittance

ʿAllāmah Majlisī has cited the following text[1] for leave of admittance while entering the holy basement at Sāmarrā and the luminous shrines of the Imams (ʿ*a*), which he quotes from an old manuscript of a Shīʿī work.

اَللّٰهُمَّ إِنَّ هٰذِهِ بُقْعَةٌ طَهَّرْتَهَا، وَ عَقْوَةٌ شَرَّفْتَهَا، وَ مَعَالِمُ زَكَّيْتَهَا، حَيْثُ أَظْهَرْتَ فِيهَا أَدِلَّةَ التَّوْحِيدِ وَ أَشْبَاحَ الْعَرْشِ الْمَجِيدِ، اَلَّذِينَ اصْطَفَيْتَهُمْ مُلُوكًا لِحِفْظِ النِّظَامِ، وَ اخْتَرْتَهُمْ رُؤَسَاءَ لِجَمِيعِ الْأَنَامِ، وَ بَعَثْتَهُمْ لِقِيَامِ الْقِسْطِ فِي ابْتِدَاءِ الْوُجُودِ إِلَىٰ يَوْمِ الْقِيَامَةِ،

O Allah, this is a shrine which You have made pure, precincts that You have honoured, a place You have made chaste by manifesting in it the proofs of Your unity and the theophanies of Your glorious Throne—those whom You chose as sovereigns for preservation of the world's order and elected them as heads of all the people and sent them for the establishment of justice at the beginning of existence until the Day of Resurrection.

ثُمَّ مَنَنْتَ عَلَيْهِمْ بِاسْتِنَابَةِ أَنْبِيَائِكَ لِحِفْظِ شَرَايِعِكَ وَ أَحْكَامِكَ، فَأَكْمَلْتَ بِاسْتِخْلَافِهِمْ رِسَالَةَ الْمُنْذِرِينَ، كَمَا أَوْجَبْتَ رِيَاسَتَهُمْ فِي فِطَرِ الْمُكَلَّفِينَ.

Then You favoured them with the successorship of Your prophets for the preservation of Your precepts and laws. Through their vicegerency You completed the mission of the warners and implanted their leadership in the disposition of those obligated to observe the precepts of religion.

فَسُبْحَانَكَ مِنْ إِلٰهٍ مَا أَرْأَفَكَ! وَ لَا إِلٰهَ إِلَّا أَنْتَ مِنْ مَلِكٍ مَا أَعْدَلَكَ! حَيْثُ طَابَقَ صُنْعُكَ مَا فَطَرْتَ عَلَيْهِ الْعُقُولَ، وَ وَافَقَ حُكْمُكَ مَا قَرَّرْتَهُ فِي الْمَعْقُولِ وَ الْمَنْقُولِ، فَلَكَ الْحَمْدُ عَلَىٰ

Glory be to You, how kind a god You are! There is no god except You, how just a sovereign You are! Your handiwork is in accordance with the nature of the intellects and Your ordinances accord with what You have established in the realms of reason and revelation. So, to You belongs all praise for Your good and beautiful design

[1] *Biḥār*, xcix, 115, b 7.

and to You are due thanks for Your ordainments, justified by the most perfect justification.	تَقْدِيرِكَ الْحَسَنِ الْجَمِيلِ، وَ لَكَ الشُّكْرُ عَلٰى قَضَائِكَ الْمُعَلَّلِ بِأَكْمَلِ التَّعْلِيلِ.
So, glory be to You who are not questioned concerning Your acts and not contested in Your commands! Glory be to You who made mercy incumbent upon Yourself before the beginning of Your creation!	فَسُبْحَانَ مَنْ لَا يُسْأَلُ عَنْ فِعْلِهِ وَ لَا يُنَازَعُ فِي أَمْرِهِ، وَ سُبْحَانَ مَنْ كَتَبَ عَلٰى نَفْسِهِ الرَّحْمَةَ قَبْلَ ابْتِدَاءِ خَلْقِهِ،
All praise belongs to Allah who favoured us with rulers who act as His surrogates, were He present in this place.	وَ الْحَمْدُ لِلّٰهِ الَّذِى مَنَّ عَلَيْنَا بِحُكَّامٍ يَقُومُونَ مَقَامَهُ لَوْ كَانَ حَاضِرًا فِي الْمَكَانِ،
There is no god except Allah, who has honoured us with the legatees who safeguard the laws during all ages. May Allah be magnified, who manifested them for us by the means of miracles which are beyond the power of humans and jinn.	لَا إِلٰهَ إِلَّا اللّٰهُ الَّذِى شَرَّفَنَا بِأَوْصِيَاءَ يَحْفَظُونَ الشَّرَايِعَ فِي كُلِّ الْأَزْمَانِ، وَ اللّٰهُ أَكْبَرُ الَّذِى أَظْهَرَهُمْ لَنَا بِمُعْجِزَاتٍ يَعْجِزُ عَنْهَا الثَّقَلَانِ،
There is no power for force except what derives from Allah, the All-exalted, and the All-supreme, who bestowed upon us His gifts among the past nations!	لَا حَوْلَ وَ لَا قُوَّةَ إِلَّا بِاللّٰهِ الْعَلِيِّ الْعَظِيمِ الَّذِى أَجْرَانَا عَلٰى عَوَائِدِهِ الْجَمِيلَةِ فِي الْأُمَمِ السَّالِفِينَ.
O Allah, to You belongs all praise and extolment, even as eternity belongs exclusively to Your Face, and for Your making the best of the prophets our prophet and the best of creatures our sovereigns, and for electing them over all the world's beings with Your knowledge!	اَللّٰهُمَّ فَلَكَ الْحَمْدُ وَ الثَّنَاءُ الْعَلِيُّ، كَمَا وَجَبَ لِوَجْهِكَ الْبَقَاءُ السَّرْمَدِيُّ، وَ كَمَا جَعَلْتَ نَبِيَّنَا خَيْرَ النَّبِيِّينَ، وَ مُلُوكَنَا أَفْضَلَ الْمَخْلُوقِينَ، وَ اخْتَرْتَهُمْ عَلٰى عِلْمٍ عَلَى الْعَالَمِينَ،
Enable us to hasten to their doors, busy until the Day of Retribution,	وَفِّقْنَا لِلسَّعْيِ إِلٰى أَبْوَابِهِمُ الْعَامِرَةِ إِلٰى

يَوْمِ الدِّينِ، وَ اجْعَلْ أَرْوَاحَنَا تَحِنُّ إِلَىٰ مَوْطِئِ أَقْدَامِهِمْ، وَ نُفُوسَنَا تَهْوِى النَّظَرَ إِلَىٰ مَجَالِسِهِمْ وَ عَرَصَاتِهِمْ، حَتَّىٰ كَأَنَّنَا نُخَاطِبُهُمْ فِي حُضُورِ أَشْخَاصِهِمْ.

and make our spirits hanker for the marks of their footsteps, and our souls yearn for the view of their gatherings and their courtyards, so that we may converse with them as if in the presence of their persons.

فَصَلَّى اللهُ عَلَيْهِمْ مِنْ سَادَةٍ غَائِبِينَ، وَ مِنْ سُلَالَةٍ طَاهِرِينَ، وَ مِنْ أَئِمَّةٍ مَعْصُومِينَ.

May the blessings of Allah be upon them, the invisible chiefs, the seed of the pure ones, and the infallible Imams!

اَللّٰهُمَّ فَأْذَنْ لَنَا بِدُخُولِ هٰذِهِ الْعَرَصَاتِ الَّتِي اسْتَعْبَدْتَ بِزِيَارَتِهَا أَهْلَ الْأَرَضِينَ وَ السَّمَاوَاتِ، وَ أَرْسِلْ دُمُوعَنَا بِخُشُوعِ الْمَهَابَةِ، وَ ذَلِّلْ جَوَارِحَنَا بِذُلِّ الْعُبُودِيَّةِ وَ فَرْضِ الطَّاعَةِ، حَتَّىٰ نُقِرَّ بِمَا يَجِبُ لَهُمْ مِنَ الْأَوْصَافِ، وَ نَعْتَرِفَ بِأَنَّهُمْ شُفَعَاءُ الْخَلَائِقِ إِذَا نُصِبَتِ الْمَوَازِينُ فِي يَوْمِ الْأَعْرَافِ، وَ الْحَمْدُ لِلّٰهِ، وَ سَلَامٌ عَلَىٰ عِبَادِهِ الَّذِينَ اصْطَفَىٰ مُحَمَّدٍ وَ آلِهِ الطَّاهِرِينَ.

O Allah, permit us to enter these precincts, visiting which You have made a duty for the denizens of the heavens and the earths, and let our tears flow in humility and awe. Give meekness to our bodily members, the meekness of servants bound with the duty of obedience, so that we may acknowledge the attributes that are due to them and admit that they are the intercessors of all the creatures when the Scales are setup on the Day of the Elevations. All praise belongs to Allah and may peace be upon His chosen servants, Muḥammad and his pure Family!

Then embrace the threshold and enter in a state of humility and with flowing tears, for indeed that is your permission of entry from them, may the blessings of Allah be upon them all.

Chapter Three

The Ziyārah of Madīnah Munawwarah

Ziyārah of the Apostle of Allah (ṣ), Fatimah Zahrā' (ᶜa) and the Imams at Baqīᶜ (ᶜa)

It is a strongly urged *mustaḥab* for the generality of people, especially those on ḥajj pilgrimage, to perform the *ziyārah* of the blessed tomb and radiant shrine of the Chief of the Apostles, Muḥammad ibn ᶜAbd Allāh, may Allah's blessings be upon him and his Family. Neglecting his *ziyārah* would be counted a slight and act of discourtesy towards him on the Day of Resurrection.

The Shahīd Awwal is of the opinion that if the people neglect the *ziyārah* of the Prophet, it is the duty of the ruler (*imam*) to force them to perform it, because the neglect of his *ziyārah* amounts to an impermissible breach of his rights (*al-jafā al-muḥarram*).[1]

Shaykh Ṣadūq reports Imam Jaᶜfar al-Ṣādiq (ᶜ*a*) as having said, "Whenever any of you performs ḥajj, he should conclude his pilgrimage with our *ziyārah*, for that completes his ḥajj.[2]

He also reports the Commander of the Faithful (ᶜ*a*) as having said, "Complete your ḥajj with the *ziyārah* of the Apostle of Allah (ṣ), for to neglect his *ziyārah* after ḥajj is an injustice and breach of etiquette, as you have been commanded to carry it out. Complete the pilgrimage to God's House with visit to the tombs whose *ziyārah* and observance of whose rights has been made incumbent upon you by God Almighty, and seek your provision from God Almighty at the side of their tombs."[3]

He has also cited a report on the authority of Abū al-Ṣalṭ al-Harawī that he said to Imam ᶜAlī al-Riḍā (ᶜ*a*), "O son of the Apostle of Allah, what do you say concerning the tradition narrated by some that the faithful will visit their Lord in paradise." His question was about the meaning of the tradition. For if considered authentic, it implied something which was not consistent with the correct doc-

1 *Durūs*, ii, 5.

2 *ᶜUyūn Akhbār al-Riḍā*, ii, 262, b 66, 28, whence *Wasā'il*, xiv, 324, b 2, h 19316. *ᶜIlal*, ii, 459, b 221, h 1, whence *Biḥār*, xcvi, 374, b 66, h 1, xcvii, 139, b 1, h 1..

3 *Khiṣāl*, ii, 616, whence *Biḥār*, xcvii, 139, b 1, h 3.

trine. The Imam replied to him, "O Abū al-Ṣalt! God Almighty has given Muḥammad (ṣ) a merit above all His creation including the prophets and the angels, by considering obedience to him as obedience to Himself and allegiance to him as allegiance to Himself, and a visit paid to him as a visit paid to Himself. Hence He has said, '*Whoever obeys the Apostle certainly obeys Allah,*'[1] and He has said, '*Indeed, those who swear allegiance to you, swear allegiance only to Allah: the hand of Allah is above their hands...*'[2] And the Apostle of Allah has himself said, 'Whoever visits me during my life, or after death, is like someone who visits God Almighty.' "[3]

Ḥimyarī reports in *Qurb al-Isnād* from Imam Jaᶜfar al-Ṣādiq (ᶜ*a*) that the Prophet (ṣ) said, "Whoever visits me in life or after death, I will intercede for him on the Day of Resurrection."[4]

It is reported that once on a day of ᶜ*īd* in Madīnah, Imam Jaᶜfar al-Ṣādiq (ᶜ*a*) entered the Prophet's shrine and greeted him. Then turning to those who were present, he said, "We have an advantage over people of all other towns, including Makkah and other places, for being able to greet the Apostle of Allah (ṣ)."[5]

Shaykh Ṭūsī reports in *Tahdhīb* from Yazīd b. ᶜAbd al-Malik from his grandfather that he said, "I visited Fāṭimah, and she was the first to greet. When she asked me the purpose of my visit, I told her that it was for the sake of its blessing (*barakah*). She said, 'My father has told me, and he is present here, that someone who greets him and me for three days will be admitted by Allah into paradise.' I asked her if that was true during her life and his. She said, 'Yes, and after our death as well.'"[6]

ᶜAllāmah Majlisī says that it is mentioned in a reliable report of ᶜAbd Allāh b. ᶜAbbās that the Apostle of Allah (ṣ) said, those who

1 The Qur'ān, 4:80

2 The Qur'ān, 48:10.

3 Ṣadūq's *Amālī*, 460, malis 70, h 7; *Tawḥīd*, 117, b 8, h 21, whence *Wasā'il*, xiv, 325, b 2, h 19320; ᶜ*Uyūn Akhbār al-Riḍā*, i, 115, b 11, 3, whence *Biḥār*, iv, 3, b 1, h 4, iv, 31, b 5, h 6, xcvii, 139, b 1, h 4. Muḥammad b. ᶜAlī b. Ibrāhīm's *al-ᶜIlal*, whence *Biḥār*, lxxvii, 192, b 2 h 53, whence *Mustadrak*, i, 262, b 12, h 547/4. *Iḥtijāj*, ii, 408.

4 *Qurb al-Isnād*, 31, whence *Biḥār*, xcvii, 139, b 1, h 2 & *Wasā'il*, xiv, 336, b 3, h 19343.

5 *Kāmil al-Ziyārāt*, 331, b 108, h 9, whence *Biḥār*, xcvii, 144, b 1, h 33 & *Wasā'il*, xiv, 249, b 10, h 19367.

6 *Tahdhīb*, iv, 9, b 3, h 11 whence *Biḥār*, xcvii, 194, b 5, h 9 & *Wasā'il*, xiv, 367, b 18, h 19404. *Manāqib*, iii, 365, whence *Biḥār*, xliii, 185, b 7, h 17. Mufīd's *Mazār*, 177, b 6, h 1. *Kashf al-Yaqīn*, 354.

visit the tomb of Imam al-Ḥasan (ᶜa) at Baqīᶜ, their feet will remain steady on the day when most feet shall tremble while passing over the Bridge over hell (*ṣirāṭ*).[1]

In the *Muqniᶜah* Imam Jaᶜfar al-Ṣādiq (ᶜa) is reported to have said, "Those who visit me shall be forgiven their sins and they will not be destitute at death."[2]

Shaykh Ṭūsī reports in *Tahdhīb* from Imam al-Ḥasan al-ᶜAskarī (ᶜa) that he said that those who visit the tombs of Imam Jaᶜfar al-Ṣādiq (ᶜa) and his father will not suffer from eye pain or disease, nor will they die in a state of misery.[3]

Ibn Qūlawayh has cited an elaborate report of Hishām b. Sālim from Imam Jaᶜfar al-Ṣādiq (ᶜa) in his *Kāmil al-Ziyārāt* in which among other things it is mentioned that a man asked the Imam if one should visit his father's tomb. He answered, "Yes." Asked as to what benefit it had for the visitor, the Imam replied, "It will earn him admittance into paradise, if he had followed him in life." Asked as to what would happen if one were not to do so out of indifference or disregard, he replied, "It will cause him regret on the Day of Regret."[4]

There are many traditions on this topic and those cited suffice our purpose.

Ziyarah of the Apostle of Allah (ṣ)

The manner of performing the *ziyārah* of the Apostle of Allah (ṣ) is as follows. When, God willing, you enter the city of the Prophet (ṣ), perform the bath for *ziyārah*. When entering the Prophet's Mosque, stand at the door and recite the first appeal for admittance and then enter with the right foot from the Door of Gabriel. Then say a hundred times *Allāhu akbar* and offer two *rakᶜahs* of the prayer of *taḥiyyah* of the mosque. Then approach the blessed tomb chamber and embrace it and draw your hand on it and say,[5]

1 *Faḍā'il*, 10.

2 *Muqniᶜah*, 474, b 20, *Tahdhīb*, vi, 78, b 26, h 1, whence *Wasā'il*, xiv, 543, b 79, h 19784 & *Biḥār*, xcvii, 145, b 1, h 34. *Rawḍat al-Wāᶜiẓīn*, i, 212. *Manāqib*, iv, 281. *Jāmiᶜ al-Akhbār*, 27, faṣl 12.

3 *Muqniᶜah*, 474, b 20, *Tahdhīb*, vi, 78, b 26, h 2, whence *Wasā'il*, xiv, 543, b 79, h 19785 & *Biḥār*, xcvii, 145, b 1, h 35. *Rawḍat al-Wāᶜiẓīn*, i, 212.

4 *Kāmil al-Ziyārāt*, 123, b 44, h 2, 128, b 46, h 3, 198, b 78, h 7, whence *Wasā'il*, xiv, 533, b 38, h 19638, xiv, 442, b 42, h 19559 & *Biḥār*, xcvii, 145, b 1, h 36, xcviii, 5, b 1, h 19, xcviii, 78, b 10, h 39 & *Mustadrak*, x, 258, b 27, h 11964/4, x, 350, b 61, h 12158/2.

5 *Biḥār*, xcvii, 160, b 2, h 41 from Shaykh Mufīd.

اَلسَّلَامُ عَلَيْكَ يَا رَسُولَ اللهِ، اَلسَّلَامُ عَلَيْكَ يَا نَبِيَّ اللهِ، اَلسَّلَامُ عَلَيْكَ يَا مُحَمَّدَ بْنَ عَبْدِ اللهِ، اَلسَّلَامُ عَلَيْكَ يَا خَاتَمَ النَّبِيِّينَ،

Peace be to you O Apostle of Allah! Peace be to you O Prophet of Allah! Peace be to you O Muḥammad ibne ᶜAbdillāh! Peace be to you O Seal of the Prophets!

أَشْهَدُ أَنَّكَ قَدْ بَلَّغْتَ الرِّسَالَةَ، وَ أَقَمْتَ الصَّلَاةَ وَ آتَيْتَ الزَّكَاةَ، وَ أَمَرْتَ بِالْمَعْرُوفِ وَ نَهَيْتَ عَنِ الْمُنْكَرِ، وَ عَبَدْتَ اللهَ مُخْلِصًا حَتَّىٰ أَتَاكَ الْيَقِينُ، فَصَلَوَاتُ اللهِ عَلَيْكَ وَ رَحْمَتُهُ وَ عَلَىٰ أَهْلِ بَيْتِكَ الطَّاهِرِينَ.

I testify that you fulfilled your mission, maintained the prayer, gave *zakāt*, bade what is right and forbade what is wrong, and worshipped Allah dedicatedly until your demise! May the blessings of Allah be upon you and your immaculate Family!

(Shaykh Ṭūsī, citing a report from Imam Jaᶜfar al-Ṣādiq (ᶜ*a*) cited in *Kāfī*, says),[1] "Then stand facing in the direction of the *qiblah* at the pillar to the right side at the head of the grave, with the grave to one's left and the *minbar* to one's right, a position which is at the head of the Prophet's tomb, and say,

أَشْهَدُ أَنْ لَا إِلٰهَ إِلَّا اللهُ وَحْدَهُ لَا شَرِيكَ لَهُ، وَ أَشْهَدُ أَنَّ مُحَمَّدًا عَبْدُهُ وَ رَسُولُهُ،

I testify that there is no god except Allah, He is one and has no partner, and I testify that Muḥammad is His servant and apostle.

وَ أَشْهَدُ أَنَّكَ رَسُولُ اللهِ، وَ أَنَّكَ مُحَمَّدُ بْنُ عَبْدِ اللهِ، وَ أَشْهَدُ أَنَّكَ قَدْ بَلَّغْتَ رِسَالَاتِ رَبِّكَ، وَ نَصَحْتَ لِأُمَّتِكَ، وَ جَاهَدْتَ فِي سَبِيلِ اللهِ، وَ عَبَدْتَ اللهَ حَتَّىٰ أَتَاكَ الْيَقِينُ، بِالْحِكْمَةِ وَ الْمَوْعِظَةِ الْحَسَنَةِ، وَ أَدَّيْتَ

I testify that you are the apostle of Allah and that you are Muḥammad, son of ᶜAbd Allāh, and I testify that you delivered the messages of your lord and were a well-wisher for your *ummah* and you struggled in the way of Allah and worshipped Allah until your demise with wisdom and good advice and

[1] *Kāfī*, iv, 550, h 1, whence *Wasā'il*, xiv, 341, b 6, h 19353. *Faqīh*, ii, 565-567. *Kāmil al-Ziyārāt*, 15, h 1, whence *Biḥār*, xcvii, 150, b 2, h 17. *Tahdhīb*, vi, 5, b 3, h 1. Ṭūsī's *Miṣbāḥ*, 709-710. Kafᶜamī's *Miṣbāḥ*, 472. *Balad*, 276. A longer version cited in *Biḥār*, xcvii, 169, b 2, h 42.

الَّذِى عَلَيْكَ مِنَ الْحَقِّ، وَ أَنَّكَ قَدْ رَؤُفْتَ
بِالْمُؤْمِنِينَ، وَ غَلُظْتَ عَلَى الْكَافِرِينَ،

you fulfil led your obligations and that you were kind to the faithful and harsh towards the faithless.

فَبَلَّغَ اللهُ بِكَ أَفْضَلَ شَرَفِ مَحَلِّ
الْمُكَرَّمِينَ. اَلْحَمْدُ لِلّٰهِ الَّذِى اسْتَنْقَذَنَا بِكَ
مِنَ الشِّرْكِ وَ الضَّلَالَةِ.

May Allah make you attain the station of highest honour among the honoured ones. All praise belongs to Allah, who delivered us by your means from idolatry and misguidance.

اَللّٰهُمَّ فَاجْعَلْ صَلَوَاتِكَ وَ صَلَوَاتِ
مَلَائِكَتِكَ الْمُقَرَّبِينَ، وَ أَنْبِيَائِكَ
الْمُرْسَلِينَ، وَ عِبَادِكَ الصَّالِحِينَ، وَ أَهْلِ
السَّمَاوَاتِ وَ الْأَرَضِينَ، وَ مَنْ سَبَّحَ لَكَ يَا
رَبَّ الْعَالَمِينَ مِنَ الْأَوَّلِينَ وَ الْآخِرِينَ، عَلَى
مُحَمَّدٍ عَبْدِكَ وَ رَسُولِكَ وَ نَبِيِّكَ وَ أَمِينِكَ
وَ نَجِيِّكَ وَ حَبِيبِكَ وَ صَفِيِّكَ وَ خَاصَّتِكَ
وَ صَفْوَتِكَ وَ خِيَرَتِكَ مِنْ خَلْقِكَ.

O Allah, let Your blessings, the blessings of Your angels brought near to You, and those of Your prophets, apostles, Your righteous servants and the denizens of the heavens and the earths and those who glorify You from the earliest of the generations to the last of them, O Lord of all the worlds, be upon Muḥammad, Your servant, apostle, prophet, trustee, confidant, beloved, elect, intimate, best friend and the chosen of Your creatures!

اَللّٰهُمَّ أَعْطِهِ الدَّرَجَةَ الرَّفِيعَةَ، وَ آتِهِ
الْوَسِيلَةَ مِنَ الْجَنَّةِ، وَ ابْعَثْهُ مَقَامًا مَحْمُودًا
يَغْبِطُهُ بِهِ الْأَوَّلُونَ وَ الْآخِرُونَ.

O Allah, grant him the highest rank, grant him the station of mediation with regard to paradise, and raise him to a praiseworthy station envied by the former and latter generations!

اَللّٰهُمَّ إِنَّكَ قُلْتَ: وَ لَوْ أَنَّهُمْ إِذْ ظَلَمُوا
أَنْفُسَهُمْ جَاءُوكَ فَاسْتَغْفَرُوا اللهَ وَ
اسْتَغْفَرَ لَهُمُ الرَّسُولُ لَوَجَدُوا اللهَ تَوَّابًا
رَحِيمًا، وَ إِنِّي أَتَيْتُكَ مُسْتَغْفِرًا تَائِبًا مِنْ

O Allah, You have said, "*Had they, when they wronged themselves, come to you and pleaded to Allah for forgiveness, and the Apostle had pleaded for forgiveness for them, they would have surely found Allah all-clement, all-merciful.*"(4:64) Indeed, I have come to you pleading forgiveness and repenting for my sins, and I turn to Allah, my Lord and yours, by your means, so that He may forgive my sins!

ذُنُوبِي، وَ إِنِّي أَتَوَجَّـــهُ بِكَ إِلَى اللهِ رَبِّي وَ رَبِّكَ لِيَغْفِرَ لِي ذُنُوبِي.

"Should you have any petition to make to God, lift up your hands while facing in the direction of *qiblah* and with the grave of the Apostle of Allah (ṣ) at the back of your shoulder, make your petition, which will be granted, God willing."

Ibn Qūlawayh reports[1] with a reliable *isnād* from Muḥammad ibn Masᶜūd that he once saw Imam Jaᶜfar al-Ṣādiq (ᶜ*a*) approach the grave of the Prophet (ṣ). The Imam put his blessed hand on the grave and said,

I beseech Allah, who chose you and elected and guided you, and guided (mankind) by your means, to bless you!

أَسْـــأَلُ اللهَ الَّذِى اجْتَبَـــاكَ وَ اخْتَارَكَ وَ هَدَاكَ وَ هَدَىٰ بِكَ أَنْ يُصَلِّيَ عَلَيْكَ.

Then he said,

Indeed Allah and His angels bless the Prophet: O you who have faith, invoke blessings on him and Peace in a worthy manner. (33:56)

إِنَّ اللهَ وَ مَلٰائِكَتَهُ يُصَلُّونَ عَلَى النَّبِيِّ، يٰا أَيُّهَا الَّذِينَ آمَنُوا صَلُّوا عَلَيْهِ وَسَلِّمُوا تَسْلِيمًا

Shaykh Ṭūsī says in the *Miṣbāḥ*, "After having supplicated Allah near the holy tomb, move on towards the *minbar*, caress it with your hand and take hold of the two knobs below shaped like pomegranates and rub your face and eyes on it, for therein is a cure for the eyes. Then stand near the *minbar* and praise and extol Allah and make your petition. The Apostle of Allah (ṣ) has said, 'There is a garden from among the gardens of paradise between my grave and *minbar*, and my *minbar* stands at one of the doors of paradise.' Then proceeds towards the Station of the Prophet (ṣ) and stand there for prayer for as much as you would. Pray a lot in the Mosque of the Prophet, for each prayer performed therein is equal to a thousand prayers."

[1] *Kāfī*, iv, 552, h 4, whence *Wasā'il*, xiv, 344, b 6, h 19357. *Kāmil al-Ziyārāṭ*, 17, h 4, whence *Biḥār*, xcvii, 154, b 2, h 23 & *Mustadrak*, x, 192, b 6, h 11826/4. Kafᶜamī's *Miṣbāḥ*, 474. *Balad*, 277.

"Invoke blessings upon the Prophet (ṣ) whenever you enter or leave the Mosque, and offer prayer in the house of Fāṭimah, may Allah's blessings be upon her. Then go to the station of Gabriel (*ʿa*), which is situated under the waterspout and that is the place where Gabriel (*ʿa*) used to stand while seeking the Apostle's leave for entering, and say,[1]

أَسْــأَلُكَ أَىْ جَوَادُ أَىْ كَرِيمُ أَىْ قَرِيبُ
أَىْ بَعِيدُ أَنْ تَرُدَّ عَلَيَّ نِعْمَتَكَ .

I beseech You, O Generous One, O Munificent One, O Nearmost and Farmost, to restore Your blessings to me!

ZIYARAH OF FATIMAH ZAHRA (ʿA)

Then perform the *ziyārah* of Ḥaḍrat Fatimah (*ʿa*) near the holy tomb. There is a difference of opinion concerning the location of the Lady's grave. Some say that she is buried in the 'garden' between the Prophet's grave and his *minbar*. Some believe that she was buried in her own house, and some others are of the opinion that she was buried in the graveyard at Baqīʿ. The majority of our scholars hold that her *ziyārah* should be performed near the Prophet's tomb and it is preferable to perform her *ziyārah* at all the three locations. When standing in any of these locations for her *ziyārah*, say,[2]

يَا مُمْتَحَنَةُ امْتَحَنَكِ اللّٰهُ الَّذِى خَلَقَكِ
قَبْلَ أَنْ يَخْلُقَكِ، فَوَجَدَكِ لِمَا امْتَحَنَكِ
صَابِــرَةً، وَ زَعَمْنَــا أَنَّا لَــكِ أَوْلِيَاءُ وَ
مُصَدِّقُونَ وَ صَابِــرُونَ لِكُلِّ مَا أَتَانَا بِهِ
أَبُوكِ صَلَّى اللّٰهُ عَلَيْهِ وَآلِهِ وَأَتَى بِهِ وَصِيُّهُ،

O you who were tested before your creation by Allah, who created you, and, in His test found you to be patient and constant! We declare that we are your friends, who affirm while being constant in following what was brought by your father, may Allah bless him and his Family, and by his legatee!

1 This more complete version, which includes the *ṣalawāt*, is from: *Kāfī*, iv, 557, h 1, whence *Biḥār*, xcvii, 147, b 2, h 8 and *Wasā'il*, xiv, 346, b 8, h 19361. *Tahdhīb*, vi, 8, b 3, h 10. Cited without it in: *Faqīh*, ii, 568, whence *Mustadrak*, ix, 426, b 62, h 11256/1. *Miṣbāḥ*, 710.

2 The text is cited here from *Tahdhīb*, vi, 9, b 3, h 12, thence (with a slight loss) in *Biḥār*, xcvii, 194, b 5, h 11 and *Wasā'il*, xiv, 367, b 18, h 19405. Variants appear in: *Miṣbāḥ*, 711. *Kitāb al-Mazār*, 178, b 7. *Jamāl*, 32, whence *Biḥār*, xcix, 213.

فَإِنَّا نَسْأَلُكِ إِنْ كُنَّا صَدَّقْنَاكِ إِلَّا
أَلْحَقْتِنَا بِتَصْدِيقِنَا لَهُمَا، لِنُبَشِّرَ أَنْفُسَنَا
بِأَنَّا قَدْ طَهُرْنَا بِوِلَايَتِكِ.

So, we adjure you, should we be telling you the truth, to unite us with our affirmation of them (after death), so that we may rejoice in the hope that we have been purged (of sins) by virtue of your friendship!

It is also *mustaḥabb* to say,[1]

اَلسَّلَامُ عَلَيْكِ يَا بِنْتَ رَسُولِ اللهِ،
اَلسَّلَامُ عَلَيْكِ يَا بِنْتَ نَبِيِّ اللهِ،
اَلسَّلَامُ عَلَيْكِ يَا بِنْتَ حَبِيبِ اللهِ،
اَلسَّلَامُ عَلَيْكِ يَا بِنْتَ خَلِيلِ اللهِ،
اَلسَّلَامُ عَلَيْكِ يَا بِنْتَ صَفِيِّ اللهِ،
اَلسَّلَامُ عَلَيْكِ يَا بِنْتَ أَمِينِ اللهِ،

Peace be to you O daughter of the Apostle of Allah! Peace be to you, O daughter of the Prophet of Allah! Peace be to you, O daughter of the beloved of Allah! Peace be to you, O daughter of Allah's dedicated friend! Peace be to you, O daughter of the elect of Allah! Peace be to you, O daughter of the trustee of Allah!

اَلسَّلَامُ عَلَيْكِ يَا بِنْتَ خَيْرِ خَلْقِ اللهِ،
اَلسَّلَامُ عَلَيْكِ يَا بِنْتَ أَفْضَلِ أَنْبِيَاءِ
اللهِ وَ رُسُلِهِ وَ مَلَائِكَتِهِ، اَلسَّلَامُ
عَلَيْكِ يَا بِنْتَ خَيْرِ الْبَرِيَّةِ،

Peace be to you, O daughter of the best of Allah's creation! Peace be to you, O daughter of the best of Allah's prophets, apostles and angels! Peace be to you, O daughter of the best of creatures!

اَلسَّلَامُ عَلَيْكِ يَا سَيِّدَةَ نِسَاءِ الْعَالَمِينَ
مِنَ الْأَوَّلِينَ وَ الْآخِرِينَ، اَلسَّلَامُ عَلَيْكِ
يَا زَوْجَةَ وَلِيِّ اللهِ وَ خَيْرِ الْخَلْقِ بَعْدَ
رَسُولِ اللهِ، اَلسَّلَامُ عَلَيْكِ يَا أُمَّ الْحَسَنِ
وَ الْحُسَيْنِ سَيِّدَيْ شَبَابِ أَهْلِ الْجَنَّةِ،

Peace be to you, O mistress of the world's womankind, of the former generations and the latter! Peace be to you, O spouse of Allah's *walī* and the best of His creation after the Apostle of Allah! Peace be to you, O mother of al-Ḥasan and al-Ḥusayn, the doyens of the youth of paradise!

[1] *Faqīh*, ii, 572. *Tahdhīb*, vi, 10, b 3, h 12, whence *Biḥār*, xcvii, 195, b 5, h 12 and *Wasā'il*, xiv, 367, b 18, h 19405. Ṭūsī's *Miṣbāḥ*, 711. Kafʿamī's *Miṣbāḥ*, 475. *Balad*, 278.

اَلسَّلَامُ عَلَيْكِ أَيَّتُهَا الصِّدِّيقَةُ الشَّهِيدَةُ،
اَلسَّـــلَامُ عَلَيْكِ أَيَّتُهَا الرَّضِيَّةُ الْمَرْضِيَّةُ،
اَلسَّـــلَامُ عَلَيْكِ أَيَّتُهَا الْفَاضِلَةُ الزَّكِيَّةُ،
اَلسَّـــلَامُ عَلَيْكِ أَيَّتُهَا الْحَوْرَاءُ الْإِنْسِيَّةُ،
اَلسَّـــلَامُ عَلَيْكِ أَيَّتُهَا التَّقِيَّـــةُ النَّقِيَّةُ،
اَلسَّلَامُ عَلَيْكِ أَيَّتُهَا الْمُحَدَّثَةُ الْعَلِيمَةُ،
اَلسَّلَامُ عَلَيْكِ أَيَّتُهَا الْمَظْلُومَةُ الْمَغْصُوبَةُ،
اَلسَّـــلَامُ عَلَيْـــكِ أَيَّتُهَـــا الْمُضْطَهَدَةُ
الْمَقْهُورَةُ، اَلسَّلَامُ عَلَيْكِ يَا فَاطِمَةُ بِنْتَ
رَسُـــولِ اللهِ وَ رَحْمَةُ اللهِ وَ بَرَكَاتُهُ، صَلَّى
اللهُ عَلَيْـــكِ وَ عَلَىٰ رُوحِـــكِ وَ بَدَنِكِ،

Peace be to you, O truthful one, O martyr! Peace be to you, who are pleasing to Allah and pleased with Him! Peace be to you, O excellent and immaculate one! Peace be to you, O human houri! Peace be to you, O Godwary and pure one! Peace be to you, O receiver of inspiration and possessor of sacred knowledge! Peace be to you, who were made victim of tyranny and usurped of your rights! Peace be to you, who were made victim of injustice and oppression! Peace be to you, O Fāṭimah, daughter of the Apostle of Allah and may Allah's mercy and His benisons be upon you! May Allah's blessings be upon you, your spirit and your body!

أَشْهَدُ أَنَّكِ مَضَيْتِ عَلَىٰ بَيِّنَةٍ مِنْ رَبِّكِ،
وَ أَنَّ مَـــنْ سَرَّكِ فَقَدْ سَرَّ رَسُـــولَ اللهِ
صَـــلَّى اللهُ عَلَيْهِ وَ آلِهِ، وَ مَـــنْ جَفَاكِ
فَقَدْ جَفَا رَسُـــولَ اللهِ صَـــلَّى اللهُ عَلَيْهِ
وَ آلِهِ، وَ مَنْ آذَاكِ فَقَدْ آذَىٰ رَسُـــولَ اللهِ
صَـــلَّى اللهُ عَلَيْـــهِ وَ آلِهِ، وَ مَنْ وَصَلَكِ
فَقَدْ وَصَلَ رَسُـــولَ اللهِ صَلَّى اللهُ عَلَيْهِ
وَ آلِهِ، وَ مَنْ قَطَعَكِ فَقَدْ قَطَعَ رَسُـــولَ
اللهِ صَلَّى اللهُ عَلَيْهِ وَ آلِهِ، لِأَنَّكِ بَضْعَةٌ

I testify that you departed from the world with a manifest proof from your Lord and that those who make you glad bring gladness to the Apostle of Allah, may Allah bless him and his Family, that those who offend you cause offence to the Apostle of Allah, may Allah bless him and his Family, that those who hurt you hurt the Apostle of Allah, may Allah bless him and his Family, that those who befriend you befriend the Apostle of Allah, may Allah bless him and his Family, and that those who break with you break with the Apostle of Allah, may Allah bless him and his

Family, for you are indeed a part of him and his soul, (as declared by him, may Allah bless him and his Family!)

مِنْهُ وَ رُوحُهُ الَّذِي بَيْنَ جَنْبَيْهِ،
(كَمَا قَالَ صَلَّى اللّٰهُ عَلَيْهِ وَ آلِهِ،)

I call to witness Allah, His apostles and angels that I approve those whom you approve of and resent those whom you resent, I repudiate those whom you repudiate and befriend those whom you befriend, I treat as enemy those whom you treat as enemy, and hate those whom you hate, and I love those whom you love and Allah suffices as witness and reckoner, retributor and rewarder.

أُشْهِدُ اللّٰهَ وَ رُسُلَهُ وَ مَلٰائِكَتَهُ أَنِّي
رَاضٍ عَمَّنْ رَضِيتِ عَنْهُ، سَاخِطٌ
عَلٰى مَنْ سَخِطْتِ عَلَيْهِ، مُتَبَرِّئٌ مِمَّنْ
تَبَرَّأْتِ مِنْهُ، مُوَالٍ لِمَنْ وَالَيْتِ، مُعَادٍ
لِمَنْ عَادَيْتِ، مُبْغِضٌ لِمَنْ أَبْغَضْتِ،
مُحِبٌّ لِمَنْ أَحْبَبْتِ، وَ كَفَى بِاللّٰهِ
شَهِيدًا وَ حَسِيبًا وَ جَازِيًا وَ مُثِيبًا.

Then invoke blessings on the Apostle (ṣ) and the immaculate Imams (ᶜa).[1]

We have cited another *ziyārah* for Haḍrat Fāṭimah (ᶜa) in the observances of the 3rd day of Jumādā II (vol. 1, p. 783).

The scholars have cited an elaborate *ziyārah* for that lady, which is similar to the one we have cited from Shaykh Ṭūsī's work, from its opening, "*Assalāmu alayki yā binta Rasūlillāh,*" until before the words "*Ushhidullāha wa rasūlahū wa malâ'ikatahū...*" [2] Thereafter, its continuation is as follows:

I call to witness Allah and His angels that I befriend those who befriend you and treat as enemy those who treat you as enemy and I am at war with those who are at war with you.

أُشْهِدُ اللّٰهَ وَ مَلٰائِكَتَهُ أَنِّي وَلِيٌّ لِمَنْ
وَالَاكِ، وَ عَدُوٌّ لِمَنْ عَادَاكِ، وَ حَرْبٌ
لِمَنْ حَارَبَكِ،

My Lady, I have convinced faith in you, your father, your husband and the Imams of your progeny, and I have faith in their *wilāyah* and am

أَنَا يَا مَوْلَاتِي بِكِ وَ بِأَبِيكِ وَ بَعْلِكِ وَ
الْأَئِمَّةِ مِنْ وُلْدِكِ مُوقِنٌ، وَ بِوِلَايَتِهِمْ

[1] A *ṣalawāt* for this occasion is cited in *Faqīh*, ii, 572, whence *Biḥār*, xcvii, 196, b 5, h 13.

[2] *Iqbāl*, 624, whence *Biḥār*, xcvii, 199, b 5, h 20.

مُؤْمِنٌ، وَ لِطَاعَتِهِمْ مُلْتَزِمٌ، أَشْهَدُ أَنَّ
الدِّينَ دِينُهُمْ، وَ الْحُكْمَ حُكْمُهُمْ، وَ هُمْ
قَدْ بَلَّغُوا عَنِ اللهِ عَزَّ وَ جَلَّ، وَ دَعَوْا
إِلىٰ سَبِيلِ اللهِ بِالْحِكْمَةِ وَ الْمَوْعِظَةِ
الْحَسَنَةِ، لَا تَأْخُذُهُمْ فِي اللهِ لَوْمَةُ لَائِمٍ،

committed to their obedience. I testify that their religion is the [true] religion and their judgement is the right judgement, and that they communicated Allah's messages and summoned to the way of Allah with wisdom and good counsel undeterred by the blame of any blamer.

وَ صَلَوَاتُ اللهِ عَلَيْكِ وَ عَلىٰ أَبِيكِ وَ
بَعْلِكِ وَ ذُرِّيَّتِكِ الْأَئِمَّةِ الطَّاهِرِينَ.

May Allah's blessings be upon you, your father, your husband and your descendants, the Immaculate Imams!

اَللّٰهُمَّ صَلِّ عَلىٰ مُحَمَّدٍ وَ أَهْلِ بَيْتِهِ، وَ
صَلِّ عَلَى الْبَتُولِ الطَّاهِرَةِ الصِّدِّيقَةِ
الْمَعْصُومَةِ، التَّقِيَّةِ النَّقِيَّةِ، اَلرَّضِيَّةِ
الْمَرْضِيَّةِ، اَلزَّكِيَّةِ الرَّشِيدَةِ، اَلْمَظْلُومَةِ
الْمَقْهُورَةِ، اَلْمَغْصُوبَةِ حَقُّهَا، اَلْمَمْنُوعَةِ
إِرْثُهَا، اَلْمَكْسُورَةِ ضِلْعُهَا، اَلْمَظْلُومِ
بَعْلُهَا، اَلْمَقْتُولِ وَلَدُهَا، فَاطِمَةَ بِنْتِ
رَسُولِكَ، وَ بَضْعَةِ لَحْمِهِ وَ صَمِيمِ قَلْبِهِ
وَ فِلْذَةِ كَبِدِهِ، وَ النُّخْبَةِ مِنْكَ لَهُ، وَ
التُّحْفَةِ خَصَصْتَ بِهَا وَصِيَّهُ، وَ حَبِيبَةِ
الْمُصْطَفَىٰ، وَ قَرِينَةِ الْمُرْتَضَىٰ، وَ سَيِّدَةِ
النِّسَاءِ، وَ مُبَشِّرَةِ الْأَوْلِيَاءِ، حَلِيفَةِ
الْوَرَعِ وَ الزُّهْدِ، وَ تُفَّاحَةِ الْفِرْدَوْسِ

O Allah, bless Muḥammad and his Family and bless the Virgin, the immaculate one, the truthful one, the infallible one, the God-wary one, the pure one, the one who is pleased with You and is pleasing to You, the blameless, the rightly guided, the victim of injustice and oppression, whose rights were usurped, who was denied her inheritance, whose ribs were broken, whose husband was oppressed and whose children were slain, Fāṭimah, daughter of Your Apostle, the flesh of his flesh, the pith of his heart and his own blood, Your choicest prize to him and Your gift to his legatee, the beloved of al-Muṣṭafā and the consort of al-Murtaḍā, the princess of womankind, the herald of good news to the *awliyā'*, the ally of piety and renunciation, the apple of the eternal paradise, whose birth You had honoured with presence of the women of

وَ الْخُلْدِ، اَلَّتِي شَرَّفْتَ مَوْلِدَهَا بِنِسَاءِ
الْجَنَّةِ، وَ سَلَلْتَ مِنْهَا أَنْوَارَ الْأَئِمَّةِ، وَ
أَرْخَيْتَ دُونَهَا حِجَابَ النُّبُوَّةِ.

paradise and from whose descent You brought forth the lights of the Imams and let fall before her the curtain of prophethood!

اَللَّهُمَّ صَلِّ عَلَيْهَا صَلاَةً تَزِيدُ فِي مَحَلِّهَا
عِنْدَكَ، وَ شَرَفِهَا لَدَيْكَ، وَ مَنْزِلَتِهَا مِنْ
رِضَاكَ، وَبَلِّغْهَا مِنَّا تَحِيَّةً وَسَلاَمًا، وَآتِنَا
مِنْ لَدُنْكَ فِي حُبِّهَا فَضْلاً وَ إِحْسَانًا، وَ
رَحْمَةً وَ غُفْرَانًا، إِنَّكَ ذُو الْعَفْوِ الْكَرِيمِ.

O Allah, bless her with a blessing that may enhance her station before You, her dignity with You and the degree of Your approval, and covey to her our greetings and *salām*, and grant us from Yourself, by virtue of our love for her, grace and goodness, mercy and forgiveness. Indeed, you are the All-pardoning, All-magnanimous!

Shyakh Ṭūsī remarks[1] in the *Tahdhīb* that the reports that have been narrated concerning the excellence of the *ziyārah* of that august lady are more than can be counted and ᶜAllāmah Majlisī cites a report[2] from *Miṣbāḥ al-anwār* that Ḥadrat Fāṭimah (ṣ) said, "The Apostle of Allah (ṣ) told me, 'God Almighty will forgive those who invoke blessings on you and join them with me in whatever place I happen to be in paradise.' "

Ziyarah of the Prophet (ṣ) from Distance

Allāmah Majlisī, while describing the observances of the 17th day of Rabīᶜ al-Awwal,[3] the day on which the Prophet's birthday is celebrated, says: "Shaykh Mufīd, Shahīd al-Awwal and Sayyid Ibn Ṭāwus have said that when one wants to perform the *ziyārah* of the Apostle of Allah (ṣ) in a place other than the holy city of Madīnah, one should perform a bath and, picturing the Prophet's tomb in front of oneself and with the heart's attention turned towards him, say,

أَشْهَدُ أَنْ لاَ إِلٰهَ إِلاَّ اللهُ وَحْدَهُ لاَ شَرِيكَ
لَهُ، وَ أَشْهَدُ أَنَّ مُحَمَّدًا عَبْدُهُ وَ رَسُولُهُ،

I testify that there is no god except Allah, He is One and has no partner, and I testify that Muḥammad

1 *Tahdhīb*, vi, 9, b 3.
2 *Biḥār*, xcvii, 194, b 5, h 10, whence *Mustadrak*, x, 211, b 14, h 11877/2.
3 *Iqbāl*, 604, whence *Biḥār*, xcvii, 183, b 3, h 11.

وَ أَنَّهُ سَـيِّدُ الْأَوَّلِينَ وَ الْآخِرِينَ، وَ أَنَّهُ سَـيِّدُ الْأَنْبِيَاءِ وَ الْمُرْسَلِينَ. اَللّٰهُمَّ صَلِّ عَلَيْهِ وَ عَلىٰ أَهْلِ بَيْتِهِ الْأَئِمَّةِ الطَّيِّبِينَ.	is his servant and apostle, and that he is the master of the former and the latter generations and that he is the chief of the prophets and apostles. O Allah, bless him and the personages of his Family, the immaculate Imams.

Then say,

اَلسَّـلَامُ عَلَيْكَ يَا رَسُـولَ اللهِ، اَلسَّلَامُ عَلَيْكَ يَا خَلِيلَ اللهِ، اَلسَّـلَامُ عَلَيْكَ يَا نَبِيَّ اللهِ، اَلسَّـلَامُ عَلَيْكَ يَا صَفِيَّ اللهِ، اَلسَّـلَامُ عَلَيْكَ يَا رَحْمَةَ اللهِ، اَلسَّـلَامُ عَلَيْكَ يَا خِيَرَةَ اللهِ، اَلسَّـلَامُ عَلَيْكَ يَا حَبِيبَ اللهِ، اَلسَّلَامُ عَلَيْكَ يَا نَجِيبَ اللهِ،	Peace be to you, O Apostle of Allah! Peace be to you, O Allah's dedicated friend! Peace be to you, O prophet of Allah! Peace be to you, O elect of Allah! Peace be to you, O mercy of Allah! Peace be to you, O chosen of Allah! Peace be to you, O beloved of Allah! Peace be to you, O distinguished with Allah!
اَلسَّلَامُ عَلَيْكَ يَا خَاتَمَ النَّبِيِّينَ، اَلسَّلَامُ عَلَيْكَ يَا سَيِّدَ الْمُرْسَلِينَ اَلسَّلَامُ عَلَيْكَ يَا قَائِمًا بِالْقِسْطِ، اَلسَّلَامُ عَلَيْكَ يَا فَاتِحَ الْخَيْرِ، اَلسَّـلَامُ عَلَيْكَ يَا مَعْدِنَ الْوَحْيِ وَ التَّنْزِيلِ، اَلسَّـلَامُ عَلَيْكَ يَا مُبَلِّغًا عَنِ اللهِ، اَلسَّلَامُ عَلَيْكَ أَيُّهَا السِّرَاجُ الْمُنِيرُ،	Peace be to you, O Seal of the Prophets! Peace be to you, O prince of the Apostles! Peace be to you, O maintainer of justice! Peace be to you, O initiator of all good! Peace be to you, O repository of revelation! Peace be to you, O communicator of Allah's messages! Peace be to you, O radiant lamp!
اَلسَّلَامُ عَلَيْكَ يَا مُبَشِّرُ، اَلسَّلَامُ عَلَيْكَ يَا نَذِيرُ، اَلسَّلَامُ عَلَيْكَ يَا مُنْذِرُ، اَلسَّلَامُ عَلَيْكَ يَا نُورَ اللهِ الَّذِي يُسْتَضَاءُ بِهِ،	Peace be to you, O bearer of good news! Peace be to you, O warner! Peace be to you, O bringer of warnings! Peace be to you, O light of Allah which is sought for illumination!

Peace be to you and the people of your Family, the good ones, the immaculate, rightly-guided and true guides! Peace be to you and your grandfather, ʿAbd al-Muṭṭalib, and your father ʿAbd Allāh! Peace be to your mother, Āminah, daughter of Wahb! Peace be to your uncle, Ḥamzah, the chief of the martyrs! Peace be to your uncle ʿAbbās, son of ʿAbd al-Muṭṭalib, and your uncle and guardian Abū Ṭālib! Peace be to your cousin Jaʿfar, who flies in the eternal paradise!

اَلسَّلَامُ عَلَيْكَ وَ عَلَىٰ أَهْلِ بَيْتِكَ الطَّيِّبِينَ الطَّاهِرِينَ الْهَادِينَ الْمَهْدِيِّينَ، اَلسَّلَامُ عَلَيْكَ وَ عَلَىٰ جَدِّكَ عَبْدِ الْمُطَّلِبِ، وَ عَلَىٰ أَبِيكَ عَبْدِ اللهِ، اَلسَّلَامُ عَلَىٰ أُمِّكَ آمِنَةَ بِنْتِ وَهْبٍ، اَلسَّلَامُ عَلَىٰ عَمِّكَ حَمْزَةَ سَيِّدِ الشُّهَدَاءِ، اَلسَّلَامُ عَلَىٰ عَمِّكَ الْعَبَّاسِ بْنِ عَبْدِ الْمُطَّلِبِ، اَلسَّلَامُ عَلَىٰ عَمِّكَ وَ كَفِيلِكَ أَبِي طَالِبٍ، اَلسَّلَامُ عَلَى ابْنِ عَمِّكَ جَعْفَرٍ الطَّيَّارِ فِي جِنَانِ الْخُلْدِ،

Peace be to you O Muḥammad! Peace be to you, O Aḥmad! Peace be to you, O Allah's testament to the former and the latter generations, the foremost in obeying the Lord of all the worlds, the guardian over His apostles and the Seal of His prophets, the witness over His creation, the intercessor with Him, the eminent with Him, obeyed in His dominions, the most praiseworthy with respect to attributes, the praised one for all the honours, the honoured one with the Lord, the one who was spoken to from behind the veil, the foremost and unapproachable! This *salām* is from someone who is cognizant of your rights, admits his shortcoming in observing what is your due, does not deny

اَلسَّلَامُ عَلَيْكَ يَا مُحَمَّدُ، اَلسَّلَامُ عَلَيْكَ يَا أَحْمَدُ، اَلسَّلَامُ عَلَيْكَ يَا حُجَّةَ اللهِ عَلَى الْأَوَّلِينَ وَ الْآخِرِينَ، وَ السَّابِقَ إِلَىٰ طَاعَةِ رَبِّ الْعَالَمِينَ، وَ الْمُهَيْمِنَ عَلَىٰ رُسُلِهِ، وَ الْخَاتِمَ لِأَنْبِيَائِهِ، وَ الشَّاهِدَ عَلَىٰ خَلْقِهِ، وَ الشَّفِيعَ إِلَيْهِ، وَ الْمَكِينَ لَدَيْهِ، وَ الْمُطَاعَ فِي مَلَكُوتِهِ، اَلْأَحْمَدَ مِنَ الْأَوْصَافِ، اَلْمُحَمَّدَ لِسَائِرِ الْأَشْرَافِ، اَلْكَرِيمَ عِنْدَ الرَّبِّ، وَ الْمُكَلَّمَ مِنْ وَرَاءِ الْحُجُبِ، اَلْفَائِزَ بِالسِّبَاقِ، وَ الْفَائِتَ عَنِ اللِّحَاقِ، تَسْلِيمَ عَارِفٍ بِحَقِّكَ، مُعْتَرِفٍ بِالتَّقْصِيرِ فِي

قِيامِهِ بِوَاجِبِكَ، غَيْرَ مُنْكِرٍ مَا انْتَهَى
إِلَيْهِ مِنْ فَضْلِكَ، مُوقِنٍ بِالْمَزِيدَاتِ
مِنْ رَبِّكَ، مُؤْمِنٍ بِالْكِتَابِ الْمُنْزَلِ
عَلَيْكَ، مُحَلِّلٍ حَلَالَكَ، مُحَرِّمٍ حَرَامَكَ.
أَشْهَدُ يَا رَسُولَ اللهِ مَعَ كُلِّ شَاهِدٍ، وَ
أَتَحَمَّلُهَا عَنْ كُلِّ جَاحِدٍ، أَنَّكَ قَدْ بَلَّغْتَ
رِسَالَاتِ رَبِّكَ، وَ نَصَحْتَ لِأُمَّتِكَ، وَ
جَاهَدْتَ فِي سَبِيلِ رَبِّكَ، وَ صَدَعْتَ
بِأَمْرِهِ، وَ احْتَمَلْتَ الْأَذَى فِي جَنْبِهِ، وَ
دَعَوْتَ إِلَى سَبِيلِهِ بِالْحِكْمَةِ وَ الْمَوْعِظَةِ
الْحَسَنَةِ الْجَمِيلَةِ، وَ أَدَّيْتَ الْحَقَّ الَّذِي
كَانَ عَلَيْكَ، وَ أَنَّكَ قَدْ رَؤُفْتَ بِالْمُؤْمِنِينَ،
وَ غَلُظْتَ عَلَى الْكَافِرِينَ، وَ عَبَدْتَ اللهَ
مُخْلِصًا حَتَّى أَتَاكَ الْيَقِينُ،

any of your excellences that have reached him, is convinced of the abundant bounties of your Lord, has faith in the Scripture that was revealed to you, regards what you have permitted as lawful and whatever your have forbidden as unlawful.

O Apostle of Allah, I testify with every witnesses and stand by it in face of every denier, that you communicated the messages of your Lord, admonished your *ummah*, and struggled in the way of your Lord, complied with His ordinances, and suffered torments for His sake, and summoned to His path with wisdom and good and graceful counsel, and fulfilled the duties that lay upon you, and that you were kind to the faithful and severe with the faithless, and you worshiped Allah with exclusive faith until your demise

.

فَبَلَغَ اللهُ بِكَ أَشْرَفَ مَحَلِّ الْمُكَرَّمِينَ، وَ
أَعْلَى مَنَازِلِ الْمُقَرَّبِينَ، وَ أَرْفَعَ دَرَجَاتِ
الْمُرْسَلِينَ، حَيْثُ لَا يَلْحَقُكَ لَاحِقٌ، وَ لَا
يَفُوقُكَ فَائِقٌ، وَ لَا يَسْبِقُكَ سَابِقٌ، وَ لَا
يَطْمَعُ فِي إِدْرَاكِكَ طَامِعٌ.

Thereat Allah made you attain the noblest of the stations of the honoured ones and the most exalted of the stations of those near to Him, and the highest of the degrees of the apostles, unequalled, unapproached and unsurpassed by anyone, which no aspirer can hope to attain!

اَلْحَمْدُ لِلّٰهِ الَّذِي اسْتَنْقَذَنَا بِكَ مِنَ

All praise belongs to Allah who rescued us from destruction by your means, guided us out of error, and gave us the light to emerge from darkness O Apostle of Allah, may Allah reward you with the best of what He has rewarded any prophet on behalf of his *ummah* or any apostle on behalf of those to whom he had been sent!

May my father and mother be sacrificed for your sake, O Apostle of Allah! I have paid you this visit knowing your rights, admitting your excellence, perceiving the error of those who opposed you and your Family, and recognizing the rightness of your guidance!

May my father and mother, my soul, my family, children and property be sacrificed for your sake, I bless you in the manner that Allah has blessed you and as His angels, prophets and apostles have blessed you, a blessing that is continuous, abundant, perpetual, uninterrupted, timeless and everlasting. May Allah bless you and your good and immaculate Family as is worthy of you!

الْهَلَكَةِ، وَ هَدَانَا بِكَ مِنَ الضَّلَالَةِ، وَ
نَوَّرَنَا بِكَ مِنَ الظُّلْمَةِ، فَجَزَاكَ اللهُ يَا
رَسُولَ اللهِ مِنْ مَبْعُوثٍ أَفْضَلَ مَا جَازَىٰ
نَبِيًّا عَنْ أُمَّتِهِ، وَ رَسُولًا عَمَّنْ أُرْسِلَ إِلَيْهِ.
بِأَبِي أَنْتَ وَ أُمِّي يَا رَسُولَ اللهِ، زُرْتُكَ
عَارِفًا بِحَقِّكَ، مُقِرًّا بِفَضْلِكَ، مُسْتَبْصِرًا
بِضَلَالَةِ مَنْ خَالَفَكَ وَ خَالَفَ أَهْلَ
بَيْتِكَ، عَارِفًا بِالْهُدَىٰ الَّذِي أَنْتَ عَلَيْهِ،
بِأَبِي أَنْتَ وَ أُمِّي وَ نَفْسِي وَ أَهْلِي وَ مَالِي
وَ وَلَدِي، أَنَا أُصَلِّي عَلَيْكَ كَمَا صَلَّىٰ
اللهُ عَلَيْكَ، وَ صَلَّىٰ عَلَيْكَ مَلَائِكَتُهُ
وَ أَنْبِيَاؤُهُ وَ رُسُلُهُ، صَلَاةً مُتَتَابِعَةً وَافِرَةً
مُتَوَاصِلَةً لَا انْقِطَاعَ لَهَا وَ لَا أَمَدَ وَ لَا
أَجَلَ، صَلَّى اللهُ عَلَيْكَ وَ عَلَىٰ أَهْلِ بَيْتِكَ
الطَّيِّبِينَ الطَّاهِرِينَ كَمَا أَنْتُمْ أَهْلُهُ.

Then stretching out your hands say,

O Allah, grant the totality of Your blessings, Your exuberant bounties, Your choicest benisons, the noblest of Your greetings, honours and mercies, and let the blessings of Your archangels, Your prophets and emissaries, Your chosen leaders, Your right-

اَللّٰهُمَّ اجْعَلْ جَوَامِعَ صَلَوَاتِكَ وَ نَوَامِيَ
بَرَكَاتِكَ وَ فَوَاضِلَ خَيْرَاتِكَ وَ شَرَائِفَ
تَحِيَّاتِكَ وَ تَسْلِيمَاتِكَ وَ كَرَامَاتِكَ
وَ رَحَمَاتِكَ، وَ صَلَوَاتِ مَلَائِكَتِكَ

الْمُقَرَّبِينَ، وَ أَنْبِيَائِكَ الْمُرْسَلِينَ، وَ أَئِمَّتِكَ الْمُنْتَجَبِينَ، وَ عِبَادِكَ الصَّالِحِينَ، وَ أَهْلِ السَّمَاوَاتِ وَ الْأَرَضِينَ، وَ مَنْ سَبَّحَ لَكَ يَا رَبَّ الْعَالَمِينَ مِنَ الْأَوَّلِينَ وَ الْآخِرِينَ، عَلَىٰ مُحَمَّدٍ عَبْدِكَ وَ رَسُولِكَ وَ شَاهِدِكَ وَ نَبِيِّكَ وَ نَذِيرِكَ وَ أَمِينِكَ وَ مَكِينِكَ وَ نَجِيِّكَ وَ نَجِيبِكَ وَ حَبِيبِكَ وَ خَلِيلِكَ وَ صَفِيِّكَ وَ صَفْوَتِكَ وَ خَاصَّتِكَ وَ خَالِصَتِكَ وَ رَحْمَتِكَ وَ خَيْرِ خِيَرَتِكَ مِنْ خَلْقِكَ، نَبِيِّ الرَّحْمَةِ، وَ خَازِنِ الْمَغْفِرَةِ، وَ قَائِدِ الْخَيْرِ وَ الْبَرَكَةِ، وَ مُنْقِذِ الْعِبَادِ مِنَ الْهَلَكَةِ بِإِذْنِكَ، وَ دَاعِيهِمْ إِلَىٰ دِينِكَ، الْقَيِّمِ بِأَمْرِكَ، أَوَّلِ النَّبِيِّينَ مِيثَاقًا، وَ آخِرِهِمْ مَبْعَثًا، الَّذِي غَمَسْتَهُ فِي بَحْرِ الْفَضِيلَةِ وَ الْمَنْزِلَةِ الْجَلِيلَةِ وَ الدَّرَجَةِ الرَّفِيعَةِ وَ الْمَرْتَبَةِ الْخَطِيرَةِ ،

eous servants, the denizens of the heavens and the earths and those who celebrate Your glory from the former and the latter generations, O Lord of all the worlds, be upon Muḥammad, Your servant and apostle, Your witness and prophet, Your warner and trustee, eminent with You and Your confidant, distinguished with You and Your beloved, Your dedicated friend and elect, Your bosom friend and favourite, Your devoted one, Your mercy, the best of the elect of Your creation, the Prophet of Mercy, the dispenser of forgiveness, the director of all good and bounties, the saviour of the servants from destruction with Your will, the summoner to Your religion, the custodian of Your ordinances, the first of the prophets with respect to the covenant and the last of them to be sent forth, whom You submerged in the ocean of excellence, majesty of station, exalted degrees and distinguished rank.

وَ أَوْدَعْتَهُ الْأَصْلَابَ الطَّاهِرَةَ، وَ نَقَلْتَهُ مِنْهَا إِلَى الْأَرْحَامِ الْمُطَهَّرَةِ، لُطْفًا مِنْكَ لَهُ وَ تَحَنُّنًا مِنْكَ عَلَيْهِ، إِذْ وَكَّلْتَ لِصَوْنِهِ وَ حِرَاسَتِهِ، وَ حِفْظِهِ وَ حِيَاطَتِهِ، مِنْ قُدْرَتِكَ عَيْنًا عَاصِمَةً حَجَبْتَ بِهَا عَنْهُ مَدَانِسَ الْعَهْرِ، وَ

You lodged him in chaste loins and moved him from them to chaste wombs, with Your kindness and compassion for him, assigning for his preservation, protection, safety and custody a sentinel with Your power, by means of which You shielded him from the defilements of fornication and the blemishes of unchastity, until by his means You exalted the visions of Your servants and revived the lifeless communities, and with the light of his birth You dispelled the covers of darkness and, by his means, draped Your sanctuary in light!

مَعَايِبَ السِّفَاحِ، حَتَّىٰ رَفَعْتَ بِهِ نَوَاظِرَ
الْعِبَادِ، وَ أَحْيَيْتَ بِهِ مَيْتَ الْبِلَادِ، بِأَنْ
كَشَفْتَ عَنْ نُورِ وِلَادَتِهِ ظُلَمَ الْأَسْتَارِ،
وَ أَلْبَسْتَ حَرَمَكَ بِهِ حُلَلَ الْأَنْوَارِ.

O Allah, even as You have singled him out for the dignity of this noble rank and reserved for him this supreme virtue, bless him for having fulfilled Your covenant, communicated Your messages, fought the opponents of Your unity, dissociating himself from faithless kinsmen for the exaltation of Your religion, and putting up with adversities in struggle against Your enemies, and You granted him for every injury that he suffered and for every plot that he came up against of the group that tried to kill him an excellence surpassing all merits, whereby he came into possession of Your abundant gifts, concealing his sorrow, repressing his sighs, suppressing his rage and never overstepping or disregarding what he had received of Your revelations.

اَللّٰهُمَّ فَكَمَا خَصَصْتَهُ بِشَرَفِ هٰذِهِ
الْمَرْتَبَةِ الْكَرِيمَةِ، وَ ذُخْرِ هٰذِهِ الْمَنْقَبَةِ
الْعَظِيمَةِ، صَلِّ عَلَيْهِ كَمَا وَفَىٰ بِعَهْدِكَ، وَ
بَلَّغَ رِسَالَاتِكَ، وَ قَاتَلَ أَهْلَ الْجُحُودِ عَلَىٰ
تَوْحِيدِكَ، وَ قَطَعَ رَحِمَ الْكُفْرِ فِي إِعْزَازِ
دِينِكَ، وَ لَبِسَ ثَوْبَ الْبَلْوَىٰ فِي مُجَاهَدَةِ
أَعْدَائِكَ، وَ أَوْجَبْتَ لَهُ بِكُلِّ أَذًى
مَسَّهُ، أَوْ كَيْدٍ أَحَسَّ بِهِ مِنَ الْفِئَةِ الَّتِي
حَاوَلَتْ قَتْلَهُ، فَضِيلَةً تَفُوقُ الْفَضَائِلَ،
وَ يَمْلِكُ بِهَا الْجَزِيلَ مِنْ نَوَالِكَ، وَ قَدْ
أَسَرَّ الْحَسْرَةَ، وَ أَخْفَى الزَّفْرَةَ، وَ تَجَرَّعَ
الْغُصَّةَ، وَ لَمْ يَتَخَطَّ مَا مَثَّلَ لَهُ وَحْيُكَ .

O Allah, bless him and his Family with a blessing that You approve for them and convey to them on our behalf many greetings and *salāms*, and grant us from Yourself grace, beneficence, mercy and forgiveness by virtue of our attachment to them. Indeed, You

اَللّٰهُمَّ صَلِّ عَلَيْهِ وَ عَلَىٰ أَهْلِ بَيْتِهِ صَلَاةً
تَرْضَاهَا لَهُمْ، وَ بَلِّغْهُمْ مِنَّا تَحِيَّةً كَثِيرَةً
وَ سَلَامًا، وَ آتِنَا مِنْ لَدُنْكَ فِي مُوَالَاتِهِمْ
فَضْلًا وَ إِحْسَانًا، وَ رَحْمَةً وَ غُفْرَانًا،

are dispenser of a mighty grace!

إِنَّكَ ذُو الْفَضْلِ الْعَظِيمِ.

Then offer a four-*rakʿah* prayer of *ziyārah* with two *salāms*, reciting any sūrahs of your choice. Thereafter, perform the *tasbīḥ* of Ḥaḍrat Fāṭimah (ʿ*a*) and say,[1]

O Allah, You have said to Your Prophet, Muḥammad, may Allah bless him and his Family, “*Had they, when they wronged themselves, come to You and pleaded to Allah for forgiveness, and the Apostle had pleaded for forgiveness for them, they would have surely found Allah all-clement, all-merciful.*”(4:64) But I was not present during the times of Your Apostle, peace be to him and his Family.

اَللّٰهُمَّ إِنَّكَ قُلْتَ لِنَبِيِّكَ مُحَمَّدٍ صَلَّى اللّٰهُ عَلَيْهِ وَ آلِهِ: وَ لَوْ أَنَّهُمْ إِذْ ظَلَمُوا أَنْفُسَهُمْ جَاءُوكَ فَاسْتَغْفَرُوا اللّٰهَ وَ اسْتَغْفَرَ لَهُمُ الرَّسُولُ لَوَجَدُوا اللّٰهَ تَوَّابًا رَحِيمًا، وَ لَمْ أَحْضُرْ زَمَانَ رَسُولِكَ عَلَيْهِ وَ آلِهِ السَّلَامُ.

O Allah, I have visited him eagerly, repenting my evil conduct and pleading to You for forgiveness of my sins, confessing them before You, though You know them better than I do, turning to You through the mediation of Your Prophet, the Prophet of Mercy, may Your blessings be upon him and his Family. Make me, O Allah, through Muḥammad, distinguished with Yourself in the world and the Hereafter and of those near to You!

اَللّٰهُمَّ وَ قَدْ زُرْتُهُ رَاغِبًا تَائِبًا مِنْ سَيِّئِ عَمَلِي، وَ مُسْتَغْفِرًا لَكَ مِنْ ذُنُوبِي، وَ مُقِرًّا لَكَ بِهَا وَ أَنْتَ أَعْلَمُ بِهَا مِنِّي، وَ مُتَوَجِّهًا إِلَيْكَ بِنَبِيِّكَ نَبِيِّ الرَّحْمَةِ صَلَوَاتُكَ عَلَيْهِ وَ آلِهِ، فَاجْعَلْنِي اللّٰهُمَّ بِمُحَمَّدٍ وَ أَهْلِ بَيْتِهِ عِنْدَكَ وَجِيهًا فِي الدُّنْيَا وَ الْآخِرَةِ وَ مِنَ الْمُقَرَّبِينَ.

O Muḥammad, O Apostle of Allah! O Prophet of Allah, you are dear to me than my father and mother! O master of Allah’s creation, I turn through your mediation to Allah, your Lord and mine, that He may forgive my sins, accept my

يَا مُحَمَّدُ يَا رَسُولَ اللّٰهِ، بِأَبِي أَنْتَ وَ أُمِّي يَا نَبِيَّ اللّٰهِ، يَا سَيِّدَ خَلْقِ اللّٰهِ، إِنِّي أَتَوَجَّهُ بِكَ إِلَى اللّٰهِ رَبِّكَ وَ رَبِّي، لِيَغْفِرَ لِي ذُنُوبِي، وَ يَتَقَبَّلَ مِنِّي عَمَلِي،

[1] *Iqbāl*, 606, whence *Biḥār*, xcvii, 186, b 3, h 11.

works, and fulfil my needs. So by my intercessor with your Lord and mine, for how excellent a Master my Lord is who is besought and how excellent an intercessor you are, O Muḥammad, may peace be to you and your Family!

وَ يَقْضِيَ لِي حَوَائِجِي، فَكُنْ لِي شَفِيعًا عِنْدَ رَبِّكَ وَ رَبِّي، فَنِعْمَ الْمَسْئُولُ الْمَوْلَىٰ رَبِّي، وَ نِعْمَ الشَّفِيعُ أَنْتَ يَا مُحَمَّدُ، عَلَيْكَ وَ عَلَىٰ أَهْلِ بَيْتِكَ السَّلَامُ.

O Allah, grant me forgiveness, mercy and an expansive, good and beneficial provision, such as You would grant those who came to Your Prophet, Muḥammad, may Your blessings be upon him and his Family, during his life and confessed before him to their sins and Your Apostle, may peace be to him and his Family, would plead forgiveness for them, whereupon You would forgive them with Your mercy, O Most Merciful of the merciful!

اَللّٰهُمَّ وَ أَوْجِبْ لِي مِنْكَ الْمَغْفِرَةَ وَ الرَّحْمَةَ، وَ الرِّزْقَ الْوَاسِعَ الطَّيِّبَ النَّافِعَ، كَمَا أَوْجَبْتَ لِمَنْ أَتَى نَبِيَّكَ مُحَمَّدًا صَلَوَاتُكَ عَلَيْهِ وَ آلِهِ وَ هُوَ حَيٌّ فَأَقَرَّ لَهُ بِذُنُوبِهِ، وَ اسْتَغْفَرَ لَهُ رَسُولُكَ عَلَيْهِ وَ آلِهِ السَّلَامُ، فَغَفَرْتَ لَهُ بِرَحْمَتِكَ يَا أَرْحَمَ الرَّاحِمِينَ.

O Allah, I put my hope in You and stand before You in expectation, imploring You, to the exclusion of all others, and I hope for Your generous reward, while I confess, without denying, and repent to You from whatever I have perpetrated, and seek refuge with You right here where I stand from the deeds that I have sent ahead and concerning which You had forewarned me and from which You had forbidden me and threatened me with retribution!

اَللّٰهُمَّ وَ قَدْ أَمَّلْتُكَ وَ رَجَوْتُكَ، وَ قُمْتُ بَيْنَ يَدَيْكَ، وَ رَغِبْتُ إِلَيْكَ عَمَّنْ سِوَاكَ، وَ قَدْ أَمَّلْتُ جَزِيلَ ثَوَابِكَ، وَ إِنِّي لَمُقِرٌّ غَيْرُ مُنْكِرٍ، وَ تَائِبٌ إِلَيْكَ مِمَّا اقْتَرَفْتُ، وَ عَائِذٌ بِكَ فِي هٰذَا الْمَقَامِ مِمَّا قَدَّمْتُ مِنَ الْأَعْمَالِ الَّتِي تَقَدَّمْتَ إِلَيَّ فِيهَا، وَ نَهَيْتَنِي عَنْهَا وَ أَوْعَدْتَ عَلَيْهَا الْعِقَابَ،

I seek refuge with Your magnanimous Face, lest You should make me stand in the position of disgrace and humiliation on a day

وَ أَعُوذُ بِكَرَمِ وَجْهِكَ أَنْ تُقِيمَنِي مَقَامَ الْخِزْيِ وَ الذُّلِّ يَوْمَ تُهْتَكُ فِيهِ الْأَسْتَارُ،

وَ تَبْدُو فِيهِ الْأَسْرَارُ وَ الْفَضَائِحُ، وَ تَرْعَدُ فِيهِ الْفَرَائِصُ، يَوْمَ الْحَسْرَةِ وَ النَّدَامَةِ، يَوْمَ الْآفِكَةِ، يَوْمَ الْآزِفَةِ، يَوْمَ التَّغَابُنِ، يَوْمَ الْفَصْلِ، يَوْمَ الْجَزَاءِ، يَوْمًا كَانَ مِقْدَارُهُ خَمْسِينَ أَلْفَ سَنَةٍ، يَوْمَ النَّفْخَةِ، يَوْمَ تَرْجُفُ الرَّاجِفَةُ تَتْبَعُهَا الرَّادِفَةُ، يَوْمَ النَّشْرِ، يَوْمَ الْعَرْضِ، يَوْمَ يَقُومُ النَّاسُ لِرَبِّ الْعَالَمِينَ، يَوْمَ يَفِرُّ الْمَرْءُ مِنْ أَخِيهِ، وَ أُمِّهِ وَ أَبِيهِ، وَ صَاحِبَتِهِ وَ بَنِيهِ، يَوْمَ تَشَقَّقُ الْأَرْضُ وَ أَكْنَافُ السَّمَاءِ،

when all the hidden matters will be exposed, all secrets and scandals will be divulged, and feet shall tremble, the day of regret and remorse, the day of overturning, the approaching day, the day of dispossession, the day of judgement, the day of retribution, the day whose span will be fifty-thousand years, the day of the blowing (of the Trumpet), *the day when the Quaker quakes and is followed by the Successor*, the Day of Resurrection, the day of presentation, *the day when mankind will stand before the Lord of all the worlds, the day when a man will evade his brother, his mother and his father, his spouse and his sons, the day when the earth and the sides of the sky will be split open,*

يَوْمَ تَأْتِي كُلُّ نَفْسٍ تُجَادِلُ عَنْ نَفْسِهَا، يَوْمَ يُرَدُّونَ إِلَى اللهِ فَيُنَبِّئُهُمْ بِمَا عَمِلُوا، يَوْمَ لَا يُغْنِي مَوْلًى عَنْ مَوْلًى شَيْئًا وَ لَا هُمْ يُنْصَرُونَ، إِلَّا مَنْ رَحِمَ اللهُ إِنَّهُ هُوَ الْعَزِيزُ الرَّحِيمُ، يَوْمَ يُرَدُّونَ إِلَى عَالِمِ الْغَيْبِ وَ الشَّهَادَةِ، يَوْمَ يُرَدُّونَ إِلَى اللهِ مَوْلَاهُمُ الْحَقِّ، يَوْمَ يَخْرُجُونَ مِنَ الْأَجْدَاثِ سِرَاعًا كَأَنَّهُمْ إِلَى نُصُبٍ يُوفِضُونَ، وَ كَأَنَّهُمْ جَرَادٌ

The day when every soul will come pleading for itself, the day they will be returned to Allah whereat He will inform them about what they have done, the day when a friend will not avail a friend in any way, nor will they be helped, except for him on whom Allah has mercy. Indeed, He is the All-mighty, the All-merciful,[44:41-42] *the day they will be returned to the Knower of the visible and the Unseen, the day they will be returned to Allah, their true Master, the day when they will emerge from the graves, hastening, as if racing toward a target,*[70:43] *as if they were scattered locusts, scrambling toward the summoner,*[54:7] towards Allah, on the day of the Imminent, *the day when the earth is shaken violently,*[56:4] the day when *the sky will be like molten copper, and the mountains like* [tufts of] *dyed wool,* [10] and *no friend will inquire about* [the welfare of his] *friend,*[70:8-10] the day of *the witness and the witnessed,* and the day when the angels will stand in arrays!

مُنْتَشِرٌ، مُهْطِعِينَ إِلَى الدَّاعِ إِلَى اللهِ،
يَوْمَ الْوَاقِعَةِ، يَوْمَ تُرَجُّ الْأَرْضُ رَجًّا،
يَوْمَ تَكُونُ السَّمَاءُ كَالْمُهْلِ، وَ تَكُونُ
الْجِبَالُ كَالْعِهْنِ، وَ لَا يُسْأَلُ حَمِيمٌ
حَمِيمًا، يَوْمَ الشَّاهِدِ وَ الْمَشْهُودِ، يَوْمَ
تَكُونُ الْمَلَائِكَةُ صَفًّا صَفًّا.

O Allah, on that day have mercy on my situation for the sake of this situation of mine today and do not humiliate me in that stage on account of the harms I have inflicted upon my own soul. O my Lord, let me walk that day with Your chosen friends, gather me in the fold of Muḥammad and his Family, may peace be to them, let my entrance be at his Pool and my emergence with the noble and the honoured ones. Give my book of deeds in my right hand, so that I succeed on account of my good works, with my face brightened thereby, my reckoning having been made easy, and the weight of my good deeds in the Scales made preponderant, and dispatch me in the company of the triumphant of Your righteous servants towards Your pleasure and paradise, O God of all the worlds!

اَللّٰهُمَّ ارْحَمْ مَوْقِفِي فِي ذٰلِكَ الْيَوْمِ بِمَوْقِفِي
فِي هٰذَا الْيَوْمِ، وَ لَا تُخْزِنِي فِي ذٰلِكَ الْمَوْقِفِ
بِمَا جَنَيْتُ عَلٰى نَفْسِي، وَ اجْعَلْ يَا رَبِّ
فِي ذٰلِكَ الْيَوْمِ مَعَ أَوْلِيَائِكَ مُنْطَلَقِي، وَ فِي
زُمْرَةِ مُحَمَّدٍ وَ أَهْلِ بَيْتِهِ عَلَيْهِمُ السَّلَامُ
مَحْشَرِي، وَ اجْعَلْ حَوْضَهُ مَوْرِدِي، وَ
فِي الْغُرِّ الْكِرَامِ مَصْدَرِي، وَ أَعْطِنِي
كِتَابِي بِيَمِينِي، حَتّٰى أَفُوزَ بِحَسَنَاتِي، وَ
تُبَيِّضَ بِهِ وَجْهِي، وَ تُيَسِّرَ بِهِ حِسَابِي، وَ
تُرَجِّحَ بِهِ مِيزَانِي، وَ أَمْضِيَ مَعَ الْفَائِزِينَ
مِنْ عِبَادِكَ الصَّالِحِينَ إِلٰى رِضْوَانِكَ وَ
جِنَانِكَ، إِلٰهَ الْعَالَمِينَ.

O Allah, I seek refuge with You, lest You should humiliate me on that day in front of the creatures because of my insolence, or lest I

اَللّٰهُمَّ إِنِّي أَعُوذُ بِكَ مِنْ أَنْ تَفْضَحَنِي فِي
ذٰلِكَ الْيَوْمِ بَيْنَ يَدَيِ الْخَلَائِقِ بِجَرِيرَتِي،

أَوْ أَنْ أَلْقَى الْخِزْيَ وَ النَّدَامَةَ بِخَطِيئَتِي،
أَوْ أَنْ تُظْهِرَ فِيهِ سَيِّئَاتِي عَلَىٰ حَسَنَاتِي،
أَوْ أَنْ تُنَوِّهَ بَيْنَ الْخَلَائِقِ بِاسْمِي، يَا كَرِيمُ
يَا كَرِيمُ، اَلْعَفْوَ الْعَفْوَ، اَلسَّتْرَ اَلسَّتْرَ.

encounter disgrace and remorse for my misconduct, or lest You make my vices preponderant over my virtues, or lest You announce my name for the creatures! O Magnanimous One, O Magnanimous One, pardon me! Pardon me! Cover my sins! Cover my sins!

اَللّٰهُمَّ وَ أَعُوذُ بِكَ مِنْ أَنْ يَكُونَ فِي
ذٰلِكَ الْيَوْمِ فِي مَوَاقِفِ الْأَشْرَارِ مَوْقِفِي،
أَوْ فِي مَقَامِ الْأَشْقِيَاءِ مَقَامِي، وَ إِذَا مَيَّزْتَ
بَيْنَ خَلْقِكَ فَسُقْتَ كُلًّا بِأَعْمَالِهِمْ زُمَرًا
إِلَىٰ مَنَازِلِهِمْ، فَسُقْنِي بِرَحْمَتِكَ فِي عِبَادِكَ
الصَّالِحِينَ، وَ فِي زُمْرَةِ أَوْلِيَائِكَ الْمُتَّقِينَ
إِلَىٰ جَنَّاتِكَ، يَا رَبَّ الْعَالَمِينَ!

O Allah, I take refuge with You, lest on that day my place should be among the evil ones and I stand along with the wretched. When You set apart the creatures into different groups and drive forth each of them on the basis of their deeds towards their destinations, direct me with You mercy in the company of Your righteous servants and in the fold of Your *awliyā'*, the Godwary, towards Your paradise, O Lord of all the worlds!

When bidding the Prophet (ṣ) farewell, say,[1]

اَلسَّلَامُ عَلَيْكَ يَا رَسُولَ اللّٰهِ، اَلسَّلَامُ
عَلَيْكَ أَيُّهَا الْبَشِيرُ النَّذِيرُ، اَلسَّلَامُ
عَلَيْكَ أَيُّهَا السِّرَاجُ الْمُنِيرُ، اَلسَّلَامُ
عَلَيْكَ أَيُّهَا السَّفِيرُ بَيْنَ اللّٰهِ وَ بَيْنَ خَلْقِهِ،

Peace be to you, O Apostle of Allah! Peace be to you, O bearer of good news and warner! Peace be to you, O radiant lamp! Peace be to you, O Allah's envoy to His creatures.

أَشْهَدُ يَا رَسُولَ اللّٰهِ أَنَّكَ كُنْتَ نُورًا فِي
الْأَصْلَابِ الشَّامِخَةِ، وَ الْأَرْحَامِ الْمُطَهَّرَةِ،
لَمْ تُنَجِّسْكَ الْجَاهِلِيَّةُ بِأَنْجَاسِهَا، وَ لَمْ
تُلْبِسْكَ مِنْ مُدْلَهِمَّاتِ ثِيَابِهَا،

O Apostle of Allah, I testify that you have been a light that resided in exalted loins and immaculate wombs, undefiled by any of the filth of paganism, and never overcast by any of its glooms!

[1] *Iqbāl*, 607, whence *Biḥār*, xcvii, 187, b 3, h 11.

I testify, O Apostle of Allah, that I have faith in you and in the Imams of your Family, and have convinced faith in all that you have brought, approving it and believing in it. I testify that the Imams of your Family are the banners of guidance and the firmest handle and testament to the people of the world!

وَ أَشْهَدُ يَا رَسُولَ اللهِ أَنِّي مُؤْمِنٌ بِكَ وَ
بِالْأَئِمَّةِ مِنْ أَهْلِ بَيْتِكَ، مُوقِنٌ بِجَمِيعِ
مَا أَتَيْتَ، بِهِ رَاضٍ مُؤْمِنٌ، وَ أَشْهَدُ أَنَّ
الْأَئِمَّةَ مِنْ أَهْلِ بَيْتِكَ أَعْلَامُ الْهُدَىٰ وَ
الْعُرْوَةُ الْوُثْقَىٰ وَ الْحُجَّةُ عَلَىٰ أَهْلِ الدُّنْيَا.

O Allah, let this not be my last time to perform the *ziyārah* of Your Prophet, may peace be to him and his Family, and should You make me die, I will testify after death to what I have testified in my life, that You are Allah, there is no god besides You, You are One and You have no partner, and that Muḥammad is Your servant and apostle and that the imams of his Family are Your *awliyā*, Your helpers and Your testaments to Your creatures, and Your vicegerents amongst Your servants, Your standards in Your lands, the custodians of Your knowledge, the keepers of Your secrets, and the interpreters of Your revelations!

اَللّٰهُمَّ لَا تَجْعَلْهُ آخِرَ الْعَهْدِ مِنْ زِيَارَةِ
نَبِيِّكَ عَلَيْهِ وَ آلِهِ السَّلَامُ، وَ إِنْ تَوَفَّيْتَنِي
فَإِنِّي أَشْهَدُ فِي مَمَاتِي عَلَىٰ مَا أَشْهَدُ عَلَيْهِ
فِي حَيَاتِي أَنَّكَ أَنْتَ اللهُ لَا إِلٰهَ إِلَّا أَنْتَ،
وَحْدَكَ لَا شَرِيكَ لَكَ، وَ أَنَّ مُحَمَّدًا
عَبْدُكَ وَ رَسُولُكَ، وَ أَنَّ الْأَئِمَّةَ مِنْ أَهْلِ
بَيْتِهِ أَوْلِيَاؤُكَ وَ أَنْصَارُكَ، وَ حُجَجُكَ
عَلَىٰ خَلْقِكَ، وَ خُلَفَاؤُكَ فِي عِبَادِكَ، وَ
أَعْلَامُكَ فِي بِلَادِكَ، وَ خُزَّانُ عِلْمِكَ وَ
حَفَظَةُ سِرِّكَ وَ تَرَاجِمَةُ وَحْيِكَ.

O Allah, bless Muḥammad and the Family of Muḥammad and convey my greetings and *salāms* to the spirit of Muḥammad, Your Prophet, and his Family, at this hour and at all hours.

اَللّٰهُمَّ صَلِّ عَلَىٰ مُحَمَّدٍ وَ آلِ مُحَمَّدٍ، وَ بَلِّغْ
رُوحَ نَبِيِّكَ مُحَمَّدٍ وَ آلِهِ فِي سَاعَتِي هٰذِهِ
وَ فِي كُلِّ سَاعَةٍ تَحِيَّةً مِنِّي وَ سَلَامًا،

Peace be to you, O Apostle of Allah, and may Allah's mercy and His blessings be upon You. May Allah not make this my last *salām* to you!

وَ السَّلَامُ عَلَيْكَ يَا رَسُولَ اللهِ وَ رَحْمَةُ اللهِ وَ
بَرَكَاتُهُ، لَا جَعَلَهُ اللهُ آخِرَ تَسْلِيمِي عَلَيْكَ.

Shaykh Ṭūsī in *Miṣbāḥ* and Sayyid Ibn Ṭāwūs in *Jamāl,* while describing the observances pertaining to Friday, say that it is *mustaḥab* to perform the *ziyārah* of the Apostle of Allah (ṣ) and the Imams (ᶜ*a*) on the day of Friday.[1]

Imam Jaᶜfar al-Ṣādiq (ᶜ*a*) is reported[2] to have said, "Someone who wants to perform the *ziyārah* of the tomb of the Apostle of Allah (ṣ) or that of the Commander of the Faithful (ᶜ*a*) or Fāṭimah, al-Ḥasan, al-Ḥusayn or any of the Immaculate Imams (ᶜ*a*) in his own town, should perform a bath on Friday and putting on clean clothes go out into the wilderness (or ascend to the roof of his house, according to another report) and offer four *rak*ᶜ*ahs* of prayer, reciting any *sūrahs* that are feasible. After *tashahhud* and *salām*, he should stand up facing the *qiblah*, and say,

اَلسَّلاَمُ عَلَيْكَ أَيُّهَا النَّبِيُّ وَ رَحْمَةُ اللهِ وَ بَرَكَاتُهُ، اَلسَّلاَمُ عَلَيْكَ أَيُّهَا النَّبِيُّ الْمُرْسَلُ، وَ الْوَصِيُّ الْمُرْتَضَىٰ، وَ السَّيِّدَةُ الْكُبْرَىٰ، وَ السَّيِّدَةُ الزَّهْرَاءُ، وَ السِّبْطَانِ الْمُنْتَجَبَانِ، وَ الْأَوْلَادُ الْأَعْلَامُ، وَ الْأُمَنَاءُ الْمُنْتَجَبُونَ،

Peace be to you O Prophet and may Allah's mercy and blessings be upon you! Peace be to you, O prophetic emissary, and peace be to your legatee, al-Murtaḍā, to the great lady, Sayyidah Zahrā, and to the two grandsons, the chosen ones, and their distinguished descendants, the elect trustees!

جِئْتُ انْقِطَاعًا إِلَيْكُمْ وَ إِلَىٰ آبَائِكُمْ وَ وَلَدِكُمُ الْخَلَفِ عَلَىٰ بَرَكَةِ الْحَقِّ، فَقَلْبِي لَكُمْ مُسَلِّمٌ، وَ نُصْرَتِي لَكُمْ مُعَدَّةٌ، حَتَّىٰ يَحْكُمَ اللهُ بِدِينِهِ، فَمَعَكُمْ مَعَكُمْ لَا مَعَ عَدُوِّكُمْ، إِنِّي لَمِنَ الْقَائِلِينَ بِفَضْلِكُمْ، مُقِرٌّ بِرَجْعَتِكُمْ، لَا أُنْكِرُ لِلّٰهِ قُدْرَةً، وَ لَا أَزْعُمُ إِلَّا مَا شَاءَ اللهُ.

I come wholeheartedly to you, to your ancestors and descendant, with the blessing of God, my heart compliant to you and my help held ready for you until Allah issues His verdict! Indeed, I stand by your side, not with your enemies! I hold with those believe in your excellence, acknowledge your return, not denying Allah's power, nor maintaining except what He wills!

1 Ṭūsī's *Miṣbāḥ*, 288 . *Jamāl*, 231.

2 Ṭūsī's *Miṣbāḥ*, 288, and *Jamāl*, 231; whence *Biḥār*, lxxxvi, 330, b 4, h 3, xcvii, 189, b 3, h 12, and *Wasā'il*, xiv, 579, b 96, h 19857.

سُبْحَانَ اللهِ ذِى الْمُلْكِ وَ الْمَلَكُوتِ،
يُسَبِّحُ اللهَ بِأَسْمَائِهِ جَمِيعُ خَلْقِهِ، وَ
السَّلَامُ عَلَىٰ أَرْوَاحِكُمْ وَ أَجْسَادِكُمْ،
وَ السَّلَامُ عَلَيْكُمْ وَ رَحْمَةُ اللهِ وَ بَرَكَاتُهُ.

Glory be to Allah, the Lord of the natural and supra natural realms. The glory of Allah is celebrated with His Names by all His creation. Peace be to your spirits and bodies! Peace be to you and may Allah's mercy and blessings be upon you!"

There are many reports that mention that wherever one may be, the *salāms* and greetings addressed to the Apostle of Allah (ṣ) do reach him. There is a tradition that there is an angel who has been appointed to say to every believer who says "*Ṣallallāhu ᶜalā Muḥammadin wa ālihī wa sallam,*" (May Allah's blessings and *salām* be upon Muḥammad and his Family), "*wa ᶜalayk*" Then he says to the Prophet (ṣ), "O Apostle of Allah, so-and-so has sent you *salāms,*" whereupon the Prophet (ṣ) says, "*Wa ᶜalayhis salām!*"[1]

It is mentioned in a reliable report that the Prophet (ṣ) said, "Whoever visits my tomb after my death is like someone who has migrated to join me during my life. If you do not have the capacity to visit my tomb, send me your *salām* and it shall reach me."[2]

There are many similar reports and in Book One (vol. 1, pp. 171-175), while mentioning the *ziyārah*s of the Infallible Ones during the days of the week, we have cited two *ziyārah*s of the Apostle of Allah (ṣ) to be recited on Saturdays. Those desirous should refer to that section and earn the reward of reciting them.[3]

It is fitting to invoke blessings on the Prophet (ṣ) with the *ṣalawāt* that was pronounced by the Commander of the Faithful (*ᶜa*) in one of his Friday sermons, as mentioned in *Kāfī,* "kitāb al-rawḍah."[4]

[1] Ṭūsī's *Amālī*, 678, majlis 37, h 1437/16, whence *Wasā'il*, xii, 71, b 43, h 15670, *Biḥār*, xci, 70, b 29, h 61, xcvii, 181, b 3, h 2 & *Mustadrak*, v, 332, b 31, h 6018/9, x, 187, b 4, h 11816/5. *Majmūᶜah Warrām*, ii, 83.

[2] *Kāmil al-Ziyārāt*, xiv, b 2, h 17, whence *Biḥār*, xcvii, 143, b 1, h 29. Mufī's *Mazār*, 168, b 1, h 1. *Daᶜā'im*, i, 296 , whence *Biḥār*, xcvi, 279, b 1, h 16, thence and *Ja ᶜfarīyāt*, 76 in *Mustadrak*, x, 185, 189, b 3, h 11808/2, b 4, h 11820/9. *Tahdhīb*, vi, 3, b 2, h 1, whence *Wasā'il*, xiv, 337, b 4, h 19344. *Iqbāl*, 604.

[3] A short *ziyārah* of the Prophet (ṣ) has to be recited along with the appeal of admittance at the entrance of the tomb chamber of the Commander of the Faithful (*ᶜa*). (The Compiler)

[4] *Kāfī*, viii, 175, whence *Biḥār*, lxxiv, 352, b 14, h 31.

إِنَّ اللهَ وَ مَلاَئِكَتَهُ يُصَلُّونَ عَلَى النَّبِيِّ، يَا أَيُّهَا الَّذِينَ آمَنُوا صَلُّوا عَلَيْهِ، وَ سَلِّمُوا تَسْلِيمًا.

Indeed, Allah and His angels bless the Prophet; O you who have faith! Invoke blessings on him and invoke Peace upon him in a worthy manner.

اَللّٰهُمَّ صَلِّ عَلٰى مُحَمَّدٍ وَ آلِ مُحَمَّدٍ، وَ بَارِكْ عَلٰى مُحَمَّدٍ وَ آلِ مُحَمَّدٍ، وَ تَحَنَّنْ عَلٰى مُحَمَّدٍ وَ آلِ مُحَمَّدٍ، وَ سَلِّمْ عَلٰى مُحَمَّدٍ وَ آلِ مُحَمَّدٍ، كَأَفْضَلِ مَا صَلَّيْتَ وَ بَارَكْتَ وَ تَرَحَّمْتَ وَ تَحَنَّنْتَ وَ سَلَّمْتَ عَلٰى إِبْرَاهِيمَ وَ آلِ إِبْرَاهِيمَ، إِنَّكَ حَمِيدٌ مَجِيدٌ.

O Allah, bless Muḥammad and the Family of Muḥammad, give benison to Muḥammad and the Family of Muḥammad, be compassionate to Muḥammad and the Family of Muḥammad! Greet Muḥmmad and the Family of Muḥammad with the best of blessings, benisons, mercy, compassion and peace that You have granted to Abraham and the progeny of Abraham! Indeed, You are all-laudable and all-glorious!

اَللّٰهُمَّ أَعْطِ مُحَمَّدًا الْوَسِيلَةَ، وَ الشَّرَفَ وَ الْفَضِيلَةَ، وَ الْمَنْزِلَةَ الْكَرِيمَةَ. اَللّٰهُمَّ اجْعَلْ مُحَمَّدًا وَ آلَ مُحَمَّدٍ أَعْظَمَ الْخَلاَئِقِ كُلِّهِمْ شَرَفًا يَوْمَ الْقِيَامَةِ، وَ أَقْرَبَهُمْ مِنْكَ مَقْعَدًا، وَ أَوْجَهَهُمْ عِنْدَكَ يَوْمَ الْقِيَامَةِ جَاهًا، وَ أَفْضَلَهُمْ عِنْدَكَ مَنْزِلَةً وَ نَصِيبًا.

O Allah, grant Muḥammad the mediation, the dignity, the excellence and the honoured station! O Allah, make Muḥammad and the Family of Muḥammad the supreme of Your creation with regard to dignity on the Day of Resurrection and place them nearmost to You in station and make them the most eminent with You on the Day of Resurrection and the best of them with respect to station and rank.

اَللّٰهُمَّ أَعْطِ مُحَمَّدًا أَشْرَفَ الْمَقَامِ وَ حِبَاءَ السَّلاَمِ وَ شَفَاعَةَ الْإِسْلاَمِ.

O Allah, grant Muḥammad the most honoured station, the award of Peace, and the intercession of Islam!

اَللّٰهُمَّ وَ أَلْحِقْنَا بِهِ غَيْرَ خَزَايَا وَ لاَ نَاكِثِينَ وَ لاَ نَادِمِينَ وَ لاَ مُبَدِّلِينَ، إِلٰهَ الْحَقِّ آمِينَ.

O Allah, join us to him, without deserving disgrace for breaking his covenant, and being regretful for having changed his religion, O God of Truth! Amen!

A series of *ṣalawāts* for the Prophet (ṣ) and his Family will also be mentioned at the end of the Book of *Ziyārah* (p. 546).

Ziyarah of the Imams of al-Baqi‘

The Imāms al-Ḥasan al-Mujtabā, ᶜAlī Zayn al-ᶜĀbidīn, Muḥammad al-Bāqir and Jaᶜfar al-Ṣādiq (ᶜa)

When intending to perform the *ziyārah* of these Imams, one should observe the points mentioned in the section on the etiquette of *ziyārah*, such as taking bath, observing ritual purity, wearing clean and good garments, applying perfume, and seeking leave of admittance, and the like. Then one should say,[1]

O my masters, O sons of the Apostle of Allah! Your servant and son of your maidservant stands in front of you, lowly and inadequate before the loftiness of your station. He acknowledges your rights and comes to you seeking refuge with you, betakes to your shrine, seeking nearness to your station and your mediation with Allah, the Exalted!	يَا مَوَالِيَّ يَا أَبْنَاءَ رَسُولِ اللّٰهِ، عَبْدُكُمْ وَ ابْنُ أَمَتِكُمْ، اَلذَّلِيلُ بَيْنَ أَيْدِيكُمْ، وَ الْمُضْعَفُ فِي عُلُوِّ قَدْرِكُمْ، وَ الْمُعْتَرِفُ بِحَقِّكُمْ، جَاءَكُمْ مُسْتَجِيرًا بِكُمْ، قَاصِدًا إِلَىٰ حَرَمِكُمْ، مُتَقَرِّبًا إِلَىٰ مَقَامِكُمْ، مُتَوَسِّلًا إِلَى اللّٰهِ تَعَالَىٰ بِكُمْ،
May I enter, O my masters? May I enter O *awliyā* of Allah? May I enter O Allah's angels who surround this shrine and reside in this sanctuary?	أَ أَدْخُلُ يَا مَوَالِيَّ؟ أَ أَدْخُلُ يَا أَوْلِيَاءَ اللّٰهِ؟ أَ أَدْخُلُ يَا مَلَائِكَةَ اللّٰهِ الْمُحْدِقِينَ بِهٰذَا الْحَرَمِ، اَلْمُقِيمِينَ بِهٰذَا الْمَشْهَدِ؟

Then advance humbly and tearfully, and enter with the right foot, and say,

May Allah be magnified worthily; may He be praised greatly; and may He be glorified morning and evening! All praise belongs to Allah, the Singular, the All-embracing, the All-praiseworthy, the	اَللّٰهُ أَكْبَرُ كَبِيرًا، وَ الْحَمْدُ لِلّٰهِ كَثِيرًا، وَ سُبْحَانَ اللّٰهِ بُكْرَةً وَ أَصِيلًا، وَ الْحَمْدُ لِلّٰهِ الْفَرْدِ الصَّمَدِ الْمَاجِدِ الْأَحَدِ،

1 *Biḥār*, xcvii, 211, b 6, h 10 from *al-Mazār al-Kabīr*, 88.

One, the Gracious, the Favourer, the All-bountiful and the All-compassionate, who grants out of His bounty. He facilitated my pilgrimage to my masters with His kindness. He did not keep me from their pilgrimage, but blessed me with His bounty and favour!

اَلْمُتَفَضِّلِ الْمَنَّانِ، اَلْمُتَطَوِّلِ الْحَنَّانِ، اَلَّذِى مَنَّ بِطَوْلِهِ، وَ سَهَّلَ زِيَارَةَ سَادَاتِى بِإِحْسَانِهِ، وَ لَمْ يَجْعَلْنِى عَنْ زِيَارَتِهِمْ مَمْنُوعًا، بَلْ تَطَوَّلَ وَ مَنَحَ.

Then approach their graves and stand facing them with the back turned towards the *qiblah*, and say,[1]

Peace be to you O Imams of guidance! Peace be to you O prime models of Godwarniness! Peace be to you O (God's) testaments to the people of the world! Peace be to you O maintainers of justice amongst creatures!

اَلسَّلَامُ عَلَيْكُمْ أَئِمَّةَ الْهُدَىٰ، اَلسَّلَامُ عَلَيْكُمْ أَهْلَ التَّقْوَىٰ، اَلسَّلَامُ عَلَيْكُمْ أَيُّهَا الْحُجَجُ عَلَى أَهْلِ الدُّنْيَا، اَلسَّلَامُ عَلَيْكُمْ أَيُّهَا الْقُوَّامُ فِى الْبَرِيَّةِ بِالْقِسْطِ،

Peace be to you O prime possessors of excellence! Peace be to you O progeny of the Apostle of Allah! Peace be to you O lovers of intimate communion (with Allah)!

اَلسَّلَامُ عَلَيْكُمْ أَهْلَ الصَّفْوَةِ، اَلسَّلَامُ عَلَيْكُمْ آلَ رَسُولِ اللهِ، اَلسَّلَامُ عَلَيْكُمْ أَهْلَ النَّجْوَىٰ،

I testify that you communicated (Allah's messages), exhorted (the *ummah*), and patiently bore (hardships) for the sake of Allah. You were impugned and mistreated, but you forgave that. I testify that you are the rightly-guided Imams and guides, that obedience to you is obligatory, and whatever you said is the truth. You summoned (to Allah), but your summons went unanswered. You commanded, but you were not

أَشْهَدُ أَنَّكُمْ قَدْ بَلَّغْتُمْ وَ نَصَحْتُمْ وَ صَبَرْتُمْ فِى ذَاتِ اللهِ، وَ كُذِّبْتُمْ وَ أُسِىءَ إِلَيْكُمْ فَغَفَرْتُمْ، وَ أَشْهَدُ أَنَّكُمُ الْأَئِمَّةُ الرَّاشِدُونَ الْمُهْتَدُونَ، وَ أَنَّ طَاعَتَكُمْ مَفْرُوضَةٌ، وَ أَنَّ قَوْلَكُمُ الصِّدْقُ، وَ أَنَّكُمْ دَعَوْتُمْ فَلَمْ تُجَابُوا، وَ أَمَرْتُمْ فَلَمْ تُطَاعُوا، وَ أَنَّكُمْ دَعَائِمُ الدِّينِ،

---

[1] *Kāfī*, iv, 559, h 1. *Kāmil al-Ziyārāt*, 53-54, b 15, h 2. Ṭūsī's *Miṣbāḥ*, 713. *Tahdhīb*. vi, 79, b 27. *Kitāb al-Mazār*, 187, h 13. *Balad*, 279.

وَ أَرْكَانُ الْأَرْضِ، لَمْ تَزَالُوا بِعَيْنِ اللهِ،
يَنْسَخُكُمْ مِنْ أَصْلَابِ كُلِّ مُطَهَّرٍ،
وَ يَنْقُلُكُمْ مِنْ أَرْحَامِ الْمُطَهَّرَاتِ، لَمْ
تُدَنِّسْكُمُ الْجَاهِلِيَّةُ الْجَهْلَاءُ، وَ لَمْ
تَشْرَكْ فِيكُمْ فِتَنُ الْأَهْوَاءِ،

obeyed. (It testify) that you are the supports of the faith and the pillars of the world. You have never ceased to enjoy Allah's special care, and He would make you pass from one chaste loin to another and from one chaste womb to another, without ever being defiled by the filth of paganism and without ever being associated with the seductions of heretical beliefs.

طِبْتُمْ وَ طَابَ مَنْبِتُكُمْ، مَنَّ بِكُمْ
عَلَيْنَا دَيَّانُ الدِّينِ، فَجَعَلَكُمْ فِي
بُيُوتٍ أَذِنَ اللهُ أَنْ تُرْفَعَ وَ يُذْكَرَ فِيهَا
اسْمُهُ، وَ جَعَلَ صَلَاتَنَا عَلَيْكُمْ
رَحْمَةً لَنَا، وَ كَفَّارَةً لِذُنُوبِنَا، إِذِ
اخْتَارَكُمُ اللهُ لَنَا، وَ طَيَّبَ خَلْقَنَا
بِمَا مَنَّ عَلَيْنَا مِنْ وِلَايَتِكُمْ، وَ كُنَّا
عِنْدَهُ مُسَمِّينَ بِعِلْمِكُمْ، مُعْتَرِفِينَ
بِتَصْدِيقِنَا إِيَّاكُمْ،

You are good and pure, and good and pure is the source of your birth and origin. The Judge of the Day of Retribution favoured us by your means and He set you *in houses Allah has allowed to be raised and wherein His Name is celebrated,*[24:36] and He has appointed our invocation of blessing on you as a mercy for us and as atonement for our sins, as He has chosen you for us and made our creation chaste by favouring us with your *wilāyah* and we are well-known with Him as those who know you and acknowledge and affirm you!

وَ هٰذَا مَقَامُ مَنْ أَسْرَفَ وَ أَخْطَأَ،
وَ اسْتَكَانَ وَ أَقَرَّ بِمَا جَنَىٰ، وَ رَجَا
بِمَقَامِهِ الْخَلَاصَ، وَ أَنْ يَسْتَنْقِذَهُ
بِكُمْ مُسْتَنْقِذُ الْهَلْكَىٰ مِنَ الرَّدَىٰ،
فَكُونُوا لِي شُفَعَاءَ، فَقَدْ وَفَدْتُ
إِلَيْكُمْ إِذْ رَغِبَ عَنْكُمْ أَهْلُ الدُّنْيَا،

Here stand I—someone who is guilty of excesses and errors and who, having surrendered humbly, admits his offenses and, as he stands in this place, hopes for deliverance, and that He who rescues the perishing may rescue me by your means from destruction. So be my intercessors!! I have come to you, when the people of the world have disregarded you, taking the signs of Allah in derision and being disdainful of them!

وَ اتَّخَذُوا آيَاتِ اللهِ هُزُوًا، وَ اسْتَكْبَرُوا عَنْهَا،

At this point raise your head and say,

O You, who are the Sustainer (of the world) and who do not err. O Everlasting One who do not forget and who comprehend all things! You have favoured me by granting me this success and giving me the knowledge of the *wilāyah* on which You have made me stand, while Your servants bar the way to it and disregard its knowledge, making light of its rights and turning their backs on it.

يَا مَنْ هُوَ قَائِمٌ لَا يَسْهُو، وَ دَائِمٌ لَا يَلْهُو، وَ مُحِيطٌ بِكُلِّ شَيْءٍ، لَكَ الْمَنُّ بِمَا وَفَّقْتَنِي وَ عَرَّفْتَنِي بِمَا أَقَمْتَنِي عَلَيْهِ، إِذْ صَدَّ عَنْهُ عِبَادُكَ، وَ جَهِلُوا مَعْرِفَتَهُ، وَ اسْتَخَفُّوا بِحَقِّهِ، وَ مَالُوا إِلَىٰ سِوَاهُ،

It is due to Your favour that I have been singled out by You along with some communities. All praise belongs to You! Even as You have taken note of my standing here and placed that on record, do not deprive me of what I expect and do not disappoint my supplication by the sanctity of Muḥammad and his immaculate Family! May Allah bless Muḥammad and the Family of Muḥammad!

فَكَانَتِ الْمِنَّةُ مِنْكَ عَلَيَّ مَعَ أَقْوَامٍ خَصَصْتَهُمْ بِمَا خَصَصْتَنِي بِهِ، فَلَكَ الْحَمْدُ إِذْ كُنْتُ عِنْدَكَ فِي مَقَامِي هٰذَا مَذْكُورًا مَكْتُوبًا، فَلَا تَحْرِمْنِي مَا رَجَوْتُ، وَ لَا تُخَيِّبْنِي فِيمَا دَعَوْتُ، بِحُرْمَةِ مُحَمَّدٍ وَ آلِهِ الطَّاهِرِينَ، وَ صَلَّى اللهُ عَلَىٰ مُحَمَّدٍ وَ آلِ مُحَمَّدٍ.

Then supplicate and make whatever requests you may have.

Shaykh Ṭūsī says that after this, one should offer eight *rakʿahs* as prayer of *ziyārah*, two *rakʿahs* for each of the Imams.

According to Shaykh Ṭūsī and Sayyid Ibn Ṭāwūs,[1] while bidding farewell to the Imams of Baqīʿ, one should say,

1 *Muqniʿah*, 476, b 22. *Tahdhīb*. vi, 80, b 28. Ṭūsī's *Miṣbāḥ*, 714. *Kitāb al-Mazār*, 189. *Biḥār*, xcvii, 206, b 6, h 6 from *Miṣbāḥ al-Zā'ir*. Kafʿamī's *Miṣbāḥ*, 476, whence *Biḥār*, xcvii, 207, b 6, h 7. *Balad*, 279.

Peace be to you, O Imams of guidance, and may Allah's mercy and His blessings be upon you. I commend you to the care of Allah and give you my *salām*. We have faith in Allah and the Apostle and whatever you have brought and pointed out. O Allah, write us among the witnesses!	اَلسَّلَامُ عَلَيْكُمْ أَئِمَّةَ الْهُدَىٰ وَ رَحْمَةُ اللهِ وَ بَرَكَاتُهُ، أَسْتَوْدِعُكُمُ اللهَ وَ أَقْرَأُ عَلَيْكُمُ السَّلَامُ، آمَنَّا بِاللهِ وَ بِالرَّسُولِ وَ بِمَا جِئْتُمْ بِهِ وَ دَلَلْتُمْ عَلَيْهِ، اَللّٰهُمَّ فَاكْتُبْنَا مَعَ الشَّاهِدِينَ.

Then supplicate earnestly and pray to Allah to bring you back again for their *ziyārah* and not to make this your last opportunity.

ᶜAllāmah Majlisī (*r*) has cited an elaborate *ziyārah* in the *Biḥār* from an old manuscript. However, as he and other scholars have pointed out, the best of *ziyārahs* are the so-called *ziyārāt jāmiᶜah*, which will be cited later on in this book (pp. 519-542, 578). Therefore, we have confined ourselves to the ones already cited.

In the chapter on observances of the days of the week in Book One, we have cited a *ziyārah* for Imam al-Ḥasan (*ᶜa*) (p. 177) and another for the three other Imams (p. 179), and these are not to be neglected.

With the exception of the Imams of Baqīᶜ, we have mentioned a *ṣalawāt* for each of the Imams in the chapters dealing with their *ziyārah*. The reader will find the *ṣalawāt* for the Imams of Baqīᶜs at the end of the Book of *Ziyārah* (p. 549-552). Hence the pilgrim should recite this *ṣalawāt* addressed to them and thus add to his collection of virtues and good deeds.

My desire and ardour for those noble shrines brings to my mind the panegyric (*qaṣīdah*) of Shaykh Uzrī (*r*) sung in the praise of the Prophet's Family, and it would be appropriate to cite it here. Muḥammad Ḥasan, the author of *Jawāhir al-Kalām*, the doyen of the leading jurists and the seal of the august *mujtahids*, so much admired it that he is reported to have said that he would consent to an exchange with Uzrī and have the *Jawāhir* written in Uzrī's account if the *qaṣīdah* could be written among his own deeds. Uzrī's poem is as follows.

إِنَّ تِلْكَ الْقُلُوبَ أَقْلَقَهَا الْوَجْدُ ... وَ أَدْمَىٰ تِلْكَ الْعُيُونَ بُكَاهَا
كَانَ أَنْكَى الْخُطُوبِ لَمْ يُبْكِ مِنِّي ... مُقْلَةً لٰكِنِ الْهَوَىٰ أَبْكَاهَا
كُلَّ يَوْمٍ لِلْحَادِثَاتِ عَوَادٍ ... لَيْسَ يَقْوَىٰ رَضْوَىٰ عَلَىٰ مُلْتَقَاهَا

كَيْفَ يُرْجَى الْخَلاصُ مِنْهُنَّ إِلَّا   بِذِمَامٍ مِنْ سَيِّدِ الرُّسْلِ طٰهٰ
مَعْقِلُ الْخَائِفِينَ مِنْ كُلِّ خَوْفٍ   أَوْفَرُ الْعُرْبِ ذِمَّةً أَوْفَاهَا
مَصْدَرُ الْعِلْمِ لَيْسَ إِلَّا لَدَيْهِ   خَبَرُ الْكَائِنَاتِ مِنْ مُبْتَدَاهَا
فَاضَ لِلْخَلْقِ مِنْهُ عِلْمٌ وَ حِلْمٌ   أَخَذَتْ مِنْهُمَا الْعُقُولُ نُهَاهَا
نَوَّهَتْ بِاسْمِهِ السَّمَاوَاتُ وَ الْأَرْ   ضُ كَمَا نَوَّهَتْ بِصُبْحٍ ذُكَاهَا
وَ غَدَتْ تَنْشُرُ الْفَضَائِلَ عَنْهُ   كُلُّ قَوْمٍ عَلَى اخْتِلافِ لُغَاهَا
طَرِبَتْ لِاسْمِهِ الثَّرَىٰ فَاسْتَطَالَتْ   فَوْقَ عُلْوِيَّةِ السَّمٰا سُفْلاهَا
جَازَ مِنْ جَوْهَرِ التَّقَدُّسِ ذَاتًا   تَاهَتِ الْأَنْبِيَاءُ فِي مَعْنَاهَا
لا تُجِلْ فِي صِفَاتِ أَحْمَدَ فِكْرًا   فَهِيَ الصُّورَةُ الَّتِي لَنْ تَرَاهَا
أَيُّ خَلْقٍ لِلّٰهِ أَعْظَمُ مِنْهُ   وَ هُوَ الْغَايَةُ الَّتِي اسْتَقْصَاهَا
قَلَّبَ الْخَافِقَيْنِ ظَهْرًا لِبَطْنٍ   فَرَأَىٰ ذَاتَ أَحْمَدَ فَاجْتَبَاهَا
لَسْتُ أَنْسَىٰ لَهُ مَنَازِلَ قُدْسٍ   قَدْ بَنَاهَا التُّقَىٰ فَأَعْلَىٰ بِنَاهَا
وَ رِجَالًا أَعِزَّةً فِي بُيُوتٍ   أَذِنَ اللّٰهُ أَنْ يُعَزَّ حِمَاهَا
سَادَةٌ لا تُرِيدُ إِلا رِضَى اللّٰهِ   كَمَا لا يُرِيدُ إِلَّا رِضَاهَا
خَصَّهَا مِنْ كَمَالِهِ بِالْمَعَانِي   وَ بِأَعْلَىٰ أَسْمَائِهِ سَمَّاهَا
لَمْ يَكُونُوا لِلْعَرْشِ إِلَّا كُنُوزًا   خَافِيَاتٍ سُبْحَانَ مَنْ أَبْدَاهَا
كَمْ لَهُمْ أَلْسُنٌ عَنِ اللّٰهِ تُنْبِي   هِيَ أَقْلامُ حِكْمَةٍ قَدْ بَرَاهَا

وَ هُمُ الْأَعْيُنُ الصَّحِيحَاتُ تَهْدِي   كُلَّ عَيْنٍ مَكْفُوفَةٍ عَيْنَاهَا
عُلَمَاءُ أَئِمَّةٌ حُكَمَاءُ   يَهْتَدِي النَّجْمُ بِاتِّبَاعِ هُدَاهَا
قَادَةٌ عِلْمُهُمْ وَ رَأْيُ حِجَاهُمْ   مَسْمَعَا كُلِّ حِكْمَةٍ مَنْظَرَاهَا
مَا أُبَالِي وَلَوْ أُهِيلَتْ عَلَى الْأَرْ   ضِ السَّمَاوَاتُ بَعْدَ نَيْلِ وِلاهَا

These hearts are disconsolate with grief and the eyes red with weeping blood
My worst hardships could not bring out a single tear, but it was love that made me cry
And every day brings such calamities as even Mount Raḍwā would not bear

How can one expect relief from them save with the aegis of Ṭā Hā, the Prince of the Apostles?
The fugitive's refuge from every danger, the most faithful of Arabs to his pledges
The springs of knowledge are to be found nowhere except with him, and the tidings of the universe since its beginnings
Founts of knowledge and forbearance have flown from him to the creatures, and from them the intellects receive their acumen
The heavens and the earth proclaim his fame, as the dawn blazoned by its glow
To the point that all nations celebrate his virtues in their various tongues
The earth has been enraptured by his name, and its lowest reaches mock the heaven's heights
His being has surpassed the essence of holiness and its reality bewilders the prophets
Let not your thoughts wander in pursuit of Ahmad's attributes, for it is a form that you will never see
What creature of God is greater than him? He is the furthest limit probed by the Divine Explorer
He ransacked the east and the west thoroughly, and seeing Ahmad's being, took him for His chosen
I will not forget the mansions of sanctity built by Godfearing and raised high
Mighty men in houses, their bulwarks made inviolable by God's leave
Masters seeking nothing but God's pleasure, and He desiring nothing except to make them pleased
He singled them out for His perfections and styled them with His most exalted Names
They weren't but the Throne's hidden treasures, glory be to Him who manifested them!
They're the many tongues that speak of God, and they're the pens of wisdom He has carved
They're the healthy eyes that restore the light of guidance to every eye that has lost its vision
Learned and wise leaders, the stars find their way with their guidance
Leaders, whose knowledge and thoughts are wisdom's light and vision
What do I care if the heaven should fall on earth, blessed as I am

with their *wilāyah*!

OTHER ZIYĀRAHS OF MADĪNAH
(Cited from Miṣbāḥ al-Zā'ir and other sources)

ZIYARAH OF IBRAHIM ('A), THE PROPHET'S SON

Standing by the graveside of Ibrāhīm, son of the Apostle of Allah (ṣ), say,[1]

Peace be to the Apostle of Allah! Peace be to the Prophet of Allah! Peace be to the beloved of Allah! Peace be to the sincere friend of Allah! Peace be to Allah's elect! Peace be to Muḥammad, son of ᶜAbd Allāh and the chief of the prophets and Seal of the Apostles, Allah's chosen one from His creatures in His heaven and earth!

اَلسَّلَامُ عَلَىٰ رَسُولِ اللهِ، اَلسَّلَامُ عَلَىٰ نَبِيِّ
اللهِ، اَلسَّلَامُ عَلَىٰ حَبِيبِ اللهِ، اَلسَّلَامُ عَلَىٰ
صَفِيِّ اللهِ، اَلسَّلَامُ عَلَىٰ نَجِيِّ اللهِ، اَلسَّلَامُ
عَلَىٰ مُحَمَّدِ بْنِ عَبْدِ اللهِ سَيِّدِ الْأَنْبِيَاءِ وَ
خَاتَمِ الْمُرْسَلِينَ، وَ خِيَرَةِ اللهِ مِنْ خَلْقِهِ فِي
أَرْضِهِ وَ سَمَائِهِ،

Peace be to all His prophets and apostles! Peace be to all the martyrs, the felicitous and the righteous! Peace be to us and Allah's righteous servants!

اَلسَّلَامُ عَلَىٰ جَمِيعِ أَنْبِيَائِهِ وَ رُسُلِهِ، اَلسَّلَامُ
عَلَى الشُّهَدَاءِ وَ السُّعَدَاءِ وَ الصَّالِحِينَ.
اَلسَّلَامُ عَلَيْنَا وَ عَلَىٰ عِبَادِ اللهِ الصَّالِحِينَ.

Peace be to you O immaculate spirit! Peace be to you, O noble soul! Peace be to you O pure offspring! Peace be to you, O immaculate soul!

اَلسَّلَامُ عَلَيْكِ أَيَّتُهَا الرُّوحُ الزَّاكِيَةُ،
اَلسَّلَامُ عَلَيْكِ أَيَّتُهَا النَّفْسُ الشَّرِيفَةُ،
اَلسَّلَامُ عَلَيْكِ أَيَّتُهَا السُّلَالَةُ الطَّاهِرَةُ،
اَلسَّلَامُ عَلَيْكِ أَيَّتُهَا النَّسَمَةُ الزَّاكِيَةُ،

Peace be to you O son of the best of creatures! Peace be to you O son of the chosen Proph-

اَلسَّلَامُ عَلَيْكَ يَا ابْنَ خَيْرِ الْوَرَىٰ، اَلسَّلَامُ
عَلَيْكَ يَا ابْنَ النَّبِيِّ الْمُجْتَبَىٰ، اَلسَّلَامُ

[1] *Biḥār*, xcvii, 217, b 7, h 16 from Mufīd, Ibn Ṭāwūs and Shahīd Awwal.

عَلَيْكَ يَا ابْنَ الْمَبْعُوثِ إِلَىٰ كَافَّةِ الْوَرَىٰ،

et! Peace be to you O son of God's envoy to the entire people of the world!

اَلسَّلَامُ عَلَيْكَ يَا ابْنَ الْبَشِيرِ النَّذِيرِ، اَلسَّلَامُ عَلَيْكَ يَا ابْنَ السِّرَاجِ الْمُنِيرِ، اَلسَّلَامُ عَلَيْكَ يَا ابْنَ الْمُؤَيَّدِ بِالْقُرْآنِ، اَلسَّلَامُ عَلَيْكَ يَا ابْنَ الْمُرْسَلِ إِلَى الْإِنْسِ وَ الْجَانِّ،

Peace be to you O son of the bearer of good news and warner! Peace be to you O son of the Radiant Lamp! Peace be to you O son of him who was strengthened with the Qur'ān! Peace be to God's envoy to humans and the Jinn!

اَلسَّلَامُ عَلَيْكَ يَا ابْنَ صَاحِبِ الرَّايَةِ وَ الْعَلَامَةِ، اَلسَّلَامُ عَلَيْكَ يَا ابْنَ الشَّفِيعِ يَوْمَ الْقِيَامَةِ، اَلسَّلَامُ عَلَيْكَ يَا ابْنَ مَنْ حَبَاهُ اللهُ بِالْكَرَامَةِ، اَلسَّلَامُ عَلَيْكَ وَرَحْمَةُ اللهِ وَبَرَكَاتُهُ

Peace be to you O son of the bearer of the banner and the standard (of *ḥamd*)! Peace be to you O son of the Intercessor on Resurrection's Day! Peace be to you O son of him who was dignified by Allah! Peace be to you, and may Allah's mercy and blessings be upon you!

أَشْهَدُ أَنَّكَ قَدِ اخْتَارَ اللهُ لَكَ دَارَ إِنْعَامِهِ، قَبْلَ أَنْ يَكْتُبَ عَلَيْكَ أَحْكَامَهُ، أَوْ يُكَلِّفَكَ حَلَالَهُ وَ حَرَامَهُ، فَنَقَلَكَ إِلَيْهِ طَيِّبًا زَاكِيًا مَرْضِيًّا طَاهِرًا مِنْ كُلِّ نَجَسٍ، مُقَدَّسًا مِنْ كُلِّ دَنَسٍ، وَ بَوَّأَكَ جَنَّةَ الْمَأْوَىٰ، وَ رَفَعَكَ إِلَى الدَّرَجَاتِ الْعُلَىٰ، وَ صَلَّى اللهُ عَلَيْكَ صَلَاةً تَقَرُّ بِهَا عَيْنُ رَسُولِهِ، وَ تُبَلِّغُهُ أَكْبَرَ مَأْمُولِهِ.

I testify that Allah chose for you the abode of His blessings before making you liable to follow His laws or obligating you to observe what He has made lawful and unlawful, taking you while you were immaculate, good, pleasing and pure from every defilement, from every uncleanliness, and settled you in the abode of His paradise and raised you to the highest degrees! May Allah bless you with a blessing that would delight His Apostle and meet his highest hopes!

اَللّٰهُمَّ اجْعَلْ أَفْضَلَ صَلَوَاتِكَ وَ أَزْكَاهَا، وَ أَنْمَىٰ بَرَكَاتِكَ وَ أَوْفَاهَا، عَلَىٰ رَسُولِكَ وَ

O Allah, grant the best of Your blessings and the purest, most complete and proliferating of Your benisons to Your Apostle,

نَبِيِّكَ وَ خِيَرَتِكَ مِنْ خَلْقِكَ مُحَمَّدٍ خَاتَمِ
النَّبِيِّينَ، وَ عَلٰى مَنْ نَسَلَ مِنْ أَوْلَادِهِ
الطَّيِّبِينَ، وَ عَلٰى مَنْ خَلَّفَ مِنْ عِتْرَتِهِ
الطَّاهِرِينَ، بِرَحْمَتِكَ يَا أَرْحَمَ الرَّاحِمِينَ.

Prophet and the chosen of Your creatures, Muḥammad, the Seal of the Prophets, and those of his immaculate descent and the posterity of his immaculate progeny, with Your mercy, O Most Merciful of the merciful!

اَللّٰهُمَّ إِنِّي أَسْأَلُكَ بِحَقِّ مُحَمَّدٍ صَفِيِّكَ، وَ
إِبْرَاهِيمَ نَجْلِ نَبِيِّكَ، أَنْ تَجْعَلَ سَعْيِي بِهِمْ
مَشْكُورًا، وَ ذَنْبِي بِهِمْ مَغْفُورًا، وَ حَيَاتِي
بِهِمْ سَعِيدَةً، وَ عَاقِبَتِي بِهِمْ حَمِيدَةً، وَ
حَوَائِجِي بِهِمْ مَقْضِيَّةً، وَ أَفْعَالِي بِهِمْ
مَرْضِيَّةً، وَ أُمُورِي بِهِمْ مَسْعُودَةً، وَ
شُؤُونِي بِهِمْ مَحْمُودَةً.

O Allah, I beseech You by the right of Muḥammad, Your best friend, and Ibrāhīm, the offspring of Your Prophet, to bless by their means my efforts and forgive my sins, and for their sake and by their means, make my life felicitous and its conclusion commendable, fulfil my needs, approve my works, bless my concerns and make my character worthy.

اَللّٰهُمَّ وَ أَحْسِنْ لِيَ التَّوْفِيقَ، وَ نَفِّسْ
عَنِّي كُلَّ هَمٍّ وَ ضِيقٍ.

O Allah, enable me to succeed in the best manner and dispel all my worries and anxieties.

اَللّٰهُمَّ جَنِّبْنِي عِقَابَكَ، وَ امْنَحْنِي ثَوَابَكَ،
وَ أَسْكِنِّي جِنَانَكَ، وَ ارْزُقْنِي رِضْوَانَكَ وَ
أَمَانَكَ، وَ أَشْرِكْ لِي فِي صَالِحِ دُعَائِي وَالِدَيَّ
وَ وُلْدِي وَ جَمِيعَ الْمُؤْمِنِينَ وَ الْمُؤْمِنَاتِ،
اَلْأَحْيَاءِ مِنْهُمْ وَ الْأَمْوَاتِ، إِنَّكَ وَلِيُّ
الْبَاقِيَاتِ الصَّالِحَاتِ، آمِينَ رَبَّ الْعَالَمِينَ.

O Allah, spare me from Your punishments and grant me Your rewards, settle me in Your paradise and grant me Your approval and security, and include in my rightful supplications my parents, children and all the faithful, men and women, the living and the dead. Indeed, You are the patron of lasting righteous deeds. Amen, O Lord of all the worlds!

Then make any petition that you wish and offer two *rakʿahs* as prayer of *ziyārah*.

Ziyarah of Fatimah Bint Asad

Stand by the graveside of the honoured mother of the Commander of the Faithful (ʿa) and say,[1]

Peace be to the Prophet of Allah! Peace be to the Apostle of Allah! Peace be to Muḥammad, the master of the apostles! Peace be to Muḥammad, the master of the former generations! Peace be to Muḥammad, the master of the latter generations! Peace be to him who was sent by Allah as a mercy to all the worlds! Peace be to you O Prophet, and my Allah's mercy and blessings be upon you!

Peace be to Fāṭimah, daughter of Asad, of the Hashimite clan! Peace be to you O truthful and admirable one! Peace be to you, O Godwary and blameless one! Peace be to you, O honoured and approved one! Peace be to you, O guardian of Muḥammad, the Seal of the Prophets! Peace be to you, O mother of the head of legatees!

Peace be to you, who showed loving care for the Apostle of Allah, the Seal of the Prophets! Peace be to you who were entrusted with the up bringing of the *walī* of Allah! Peace be to you, to your spirit and your immaculate body! Peace be to you and your offspring and may Allah's mercy and His blessings be upon you!

اَلسَّلَامُ عَلىٰ نَبِيِّ اللهِ، اَلسَّلَامُ عَلىٰ رَسُولِ
اللهِ، اَلسَّلَامُ عَلىٰ مُحَمَّدٍ سَيِّدِ الْمُرْسَلِينَ،
اَلسَّلَامُ عَلىٰ مُحَمَّدٍ سَيِّدِ الْأَوَّلِينَ، اَلسَّلَامُ
عَلىٰ مُحَمَّدٍ سَيِّدِ الْآخِرِينَ، اَلسَّلَامُ عَلىٰ
مَنْ بَعَثَهُ اللهُ رَحْمَةً لِلْعَالَمِينَ، اَلسَّلَامُ
عَلَيْكَ أَيُّهَا النَّبِيُّ وَ رَحْمَةُ اللهِ وَ بَرَكَاتُهُ.
اَلسَّلَامُ عَلىٰ فَاطِمَةَ بِنْتِ أَسَدٍ الْهَاشِمِيَّةِ،
اَلسَّلَامُ عَلَيْكِ أَيَّتُهَا الصِّدِّيقَةُ الْمَرْضِيَّةُ،
اَلسَّلَامُ عَلَيْكِ أَيَّتُهَا التَّقِيَّةُ النَّقِيَّةُ، اَلسَّلَامُ
عَلَيْكِ أَيَّتُهَا الْكَرِيمَةُ الرَّضِيَّةُ، اَلسَّلَامُ
عَلَيْكِ يَا كَافِلَةَ مُحَمَّدٍ خَاتَمِ النَّبِيِّينَ،
اَلسَّلَامُ عَلَيْكِ يَا وَالِدَةَ سَيِّدِ الْوَصِيِّينَ،
اَلسَّلَامُ عَلَيْكِ يَا مَنْ ظَهَرَتْ شَفَقَتُهَا عَلىٰ
رَسُولِ اللهِ خَاتَمِ النَّبِيِّينَ، اَلسَّلَامُ عَلَيْكِ يَا
مَنْ تَرْبِيَتُهَا لِوَلِيِّ اللهِ الْأَمِينِ، اَلسَّلَامُ عَلَيْكِ
وَ عَلىٰ رُوحِكِ وَ بَدَنِكِ الطَّاهِرِ، اَلسَّلَامُ
عَلَيْكِ وَ عَلىٰ وَلَدِكِ وَ رَحْمَةُ اللهِ وَ بَرَكَاتُهُ.

[1] *Biḥār*, xcvii, 218, b 7, h 17 from Mufīd, Ibn Ṭāwūs and Shahīd Awwal.

أَشْهَدُ أَنَّكِ أَحْسَنْتِ الْكَفَالَةَ، وَ أَدَّيْتِ الْأَمَانَةَ، وَ اجْتَهَدْتِ فِي مَرْضَاةِ اللهِ، وَ بَالَغْتِ فِي حِفْظِ رَسُولِ اللهِ، عَارِفَةً بِحَقِّهِ، مُؤْمِنَةً بِصِدْقِهِ، مُعْتَرِفَةً بِنُبُوَّتِهِ، مُسْتَبْصِرَةً بِنِعْمَتِهِ، كَافِلَةً بِتَرْبِيَتِهِ، مُشْفِقَةً عَلَىٰ نَفْسِهِ، وَاقِفَةً عَلَىٰ خِدْمَتِهِ، مُخْتَارَةً رِضَاهُ،

I testify that you did a superb job as guardian, fulfilled your trust and endeavoured for the sake of Allah's pleasure, doing your utmost in taking care of the Apostle of Allah, knowing well his rights, having faith in his truthfulness, acknowledging his prophethood, aware of his blessedness, taking charge of his up bringing, giving him loving care, with devotion to his service and giving precedence to his will and wish over your own!

وَ أَشْهَدُ أَنَّكِ مَضَيْتِ عَلَى الْإِيمَانِ، وَ التَّمَسُّكِ بِأَشْرَفِ الْأَدْيَانِ، رَاضِيَةً مَرْضِيَّةً، طَاهِرَةً زَكِيَّةً، تَقِيَّةً نَقِيَّةً، فَرَضِيَ اللهُ عَنْكِ وَ أَرْضَاكِ، وَ جَعَلَ الْجَنَّةَ مَنْزِلَكِ وَ مَأْوَاكِ.

I testify that you departed from the world with faith, holding on to the best of religions, and you were pleasing to Allah and well pleased with Him, immaculate, pure, pious and blameless! May Allah be pleased with you, make you pleased with Him, and may He make paradise your home and abode!

اَللّٰهُمَّ صَلِّ عَلَىٰ مُحَمَّدٍ وَ آلِ مُحَمَّدٍ، وَ انْفَعْنِي بِزِيَارَتِهَا، وَ ثَبِّتْنِي عَلَىٰ مَحَبَّتِهَا، وَ لَا تَحْرِمْنِي شَفَاعَتَهَا وَ شَفَاعَةَ الْأَئِمَّةِ مِنْ ذُرِّيَّتِهَا، وَ ارْزُقْنِي مُرَافَقَتَهَا، وَ احْشُرْنِي مَعَهَا وَ مَعَ أَوْلَادِهَا الطَّاهِرِينَ.

O Allah, bless Muḥammad and the Family of Muḥammad and grant me the benefit of her *ziyārah*, make me steady on her love, do not deprive me of her intercession and the intercession of the Imams of her progeny. Grant me her companionship and resurrect me with her and her immaculate descendants!

اَللّٰهُمَّ لَا تَجْعَلْهُ آخِرَ الْعَهْدِ مِنْ زِيَارَتِي إِيَّاهَا، وَ ارْزُقْنِي الْعَوْدَ إِلَيْهَا أَبَدًا مَا أَبْقَيْتَنِي، وَ إِذَا تَوَفَّيْتَنِي فَاحْشُرْنِي فِي

O Allah, do not make this my last opportunity of her *ziyārah* and grant me to keep on returning to her as long as You keep me alive, and when You make me die gather me in her fold and admit me into her intercession, with Your mercy, O Most Merciful of the merciful!

زُمْرَتِهَا، وَ أَدْخِلْنِي فِي شَفَاعَتِهَا بِرَحْمَتِكَ
يَا أَرْحَمَ الرَّاحِمِينَ.

O Allah, for the sake of her rights with You and her station in Your eyes, forgive me, my parents and all the faithful, men and women, and give us good in this world and good in the Hereafter, and save us with Your mercy from the punishment of the Fire.(2:201)

اَللّٰهُمَّ بِحَقِّهَا عِنْدَكَ وَ مَنْزِلَتِهَا لَدَيْكَ،
اِغْفِرْ لِي وَ لِوَالِدَيَّ وَ لِجَمِيعِ الْمُؤْمِنِينَ وَ
الْمُؤْمِنَاتِ، وَ آتِنَا فِي الدُّنْيَا حَسَنَةً، وَ فِي
الْآخِرَةِ حَسَنَةً، وَ قِنَا بِرَحْمَتِكَ عَذَابَ النَّارِ.

Then offer a two-*rakʿah* prayer of *ziyārah,* supplicate for your need, and leave.

Ziyarah of Ḥadrat Ḥamzah (r) at Uhud

When visiting the cemetery at Uḥud, stand by his graveside and say,[1]

Peace be to you O uncle of Allah's Apostle, may Allah bless him and his Family! Peace be to you O best of the martyrs! Peace be to you O lion of Allah and His Apostle!

I testify that you struggled for the sake of Allah, Almighty and Glorious, strove earnestly and acted in good faith towards the Apostle of Allah, desiring that which is with Allah, may He be glorified!

اَلسَّلَامُ عَلَيْكَ يَا عَمَّ رَسُولِ اللهِ صَلَّى اللهُ
عَلَيْهِ وَآلِهِ، اَلسَّلَامُ عَلَيْكَ يَا خَيْرَ الشُّهَدَاءِ،
اَلسَّلَامُ عَلَيْكَ يَا أَسَدَ اللهِ وَ أَسَدَ رَسُولِهِ،
أَشْهَدُ أَنَّكَ قَدْ جَاهَدْتَ فِي اللهِ عَزَّ وَ
جَلَّ، وَ جُدْتَ بِنَفْسِكَ، وَ نَصَحْتَ رَسُولَ
اللهِ صَلَّى اللهُ عَلَيْهِ وَ آلِهِ، وَ كُنْتَ فِيمَا
عِنْدَ اللهِ سُبْحَانَهُ رَاغِبًا.

May my father and mother be sacrificed for you, I have come to you [seeking nearness to Allah, the Almighty and Glorious, through your *ziyārah*] seeking

بِأَبِي أَنْتَ وَ أُمِّي، أَتَيْتُكَ مُتَقَرِّبًا إِلَى
رَسُولِ اللهِ صَلَّى اللهُ عَلَيْهِ وَ آلِهِ بِذٰلِكَ،
رَاغِبًا إِلَيْكَ فِي الشَّفَاعَةِ، أَبْتَغِي بِزِيَارَتِكَ

1 *Biḥār*, xcvii, 220, b 7, h 18 from Mufīd, Ibn Ṭāwūs and Shahīd Awwal.

thereby nearness to the Apostle of Allah, may Allah bless him and his Family, asking for your intercession and desiring through your *ziyārah* my own salvation and your protection from the Fire, which the likes of me deserve on account of the offenses that I have committed against my own soul. Fleeing the sins that have piled up on my back, I seek shelter with you, hoping for the mercy of my Lord. I come to you from a distant place seeking to free my neck from the Fire, with a heavy burden of sins on my back! I have perpetrated what is displeasing to my Lord and do not find anyone with whom I may find shelter better than you, the Family of mercy! So intercede for me on the day of my privation and need!

خَلَاصَ نَفْسِي، مُتَعَوِّذًا بِكَ مِنْ نَارٍ اسْتَحَقَّهَا مِثْلِي بِمَا جَنَيْتُ عَلَىٰ نَفْسِي، هَارِبًا مِنْ ذُنُوبِيَ الَّتِي احْتَطَبْتُهَا عَلَىٰ ظَهْرِي، فَزِعًا إِلَيْكَ رَجَاءَ رَحْمَةِ رَبِّي، أَتَيْتُكَ مِنْ شُقَّةٍ بَعِيدَةٍ طَالِبًا فَكَاكَ رَقَبَتِي مِنَ النَّارِ، وَ قَدْ أَوْقَرَتْ ظَهْرِي ذُنُوبِي وَ أَتَيْتُ مَا أَسْخَطَ رَبِّي، وَ لَمْ أَجِدْ أَحَدًا أَفْزَعُ إِلَيْهِ خَيْرًا لِي مِنْكُمْ أَهْلَ بَيْتِ الرَّحْمَةِ، فَكُنْ لِي شَفِيعًا يَوْمَ فَقْرِي وَ حَاجَتِي،

I have come to you with my sorrow and distress, shedding tears by your graveside, having come all alone! You are one of those attachment to whom has been urged by Allah, who has urged me to be good to them, shown me their excellence, guided me to their love, encouraged me to visit them and inspired me to seek the fulfilment of my needs by their side. You are a Family whose friends are never wretched, and those who come to them are never disappointed, and those who seek them do not lose, and those who hate them never attain felicity!

فَقَدْ سِرْتُ إِلَيْكَ مَحْزُونًا، وَ أَتَيْتُكَ مَكْرُوبًا، وَ سَكَبْتُ عَبْرَتِي عِنْدَكَ بَاكِيًا، وَ صِرْتُ إِلَيْكَ مُفْرَدًا، وَ أَنْتَ مِمَّنْ أَمَرَنِيَ اللهُ بِصِلَتِهِ، وَ حَثَّنِي عَلَىٰ بِرِّهِ، وَ دَلَّنِي عَلَىٰ فَضْلِهِ، وَ هَدَانِي لِحُبِّهِ، وَ رَغَّبَنِي فِي الْوِفَادَةِ إِلَيْهِ، وَ أَلْهَمَنِي طَلَبَ الْحَوَائِجِ عِنْدَهُ، أَنْتُمْ أَهْلُ بَيْتٍ لَا يَشْقَىٰ مَنْ تَوَلَّاكُمْ، وَلَا يَخِيبُ مَنْ أَتَاكُمْ، وَ لَا يَخْسَرُ مَنْ يَهْوَاكُمْ، وَ لَا يَسْعَدُ مَنْ عَادَاكُمْ.

Then offer two *rakʿahs* as prayer of *ziyārah* facing the *qiblah*. After the prayer, clinging to the grave, say,

O Allah, bless Muḥammad and the Family of Muḥammad. O Allah, I place myself before Your mercy by clinging to the grave of the uncle of Your Prophet, may Allah bless him and his Family, that You may shelter me from Your vengeance [Your displeasure and Your disgust] on the day of confusion of voices, wherein every soul will be preoccupied with what it has sent ahead and will be pleading for itself! So if You have mercy on me that day, I will have no fear or grief, and if You punish me, the Master has total power over His servant. Do not disappoint me after today and do not turn me away without granting my request, for I cling to the grave of Your Prophet's uncle and by his means seek nearness to You, seeking Your approval and expecting Your mercy!

اَللّٰهُـمَّ صَلِّ عَلىٰ مُحَمَّـدٍ وَ آلِ مُحَمَّدٍ،
اَللّٰهُـمَّ إِنِّي تَعَرَّضْتُ لِرَحْمَتِكَ بِلُزُومِي
لِقَبْرِ عَمِّ نَبِيِّكَ صَلَّى اللّٰهُ عَلَيْهِ وَ آلِهِ،
لِيُجِيرَنِي مِـنْ نِقْمَتِكَ فِي يَوْمٍ تَكْثُرُ
فِيـهِ الْأَصْوَاتُ، وَ تَشْـغَلُ كُلَّ نَفْسٍ
بِمَا قَدَّمَـتْ وَ تُجَادِلُ عَنْ نَفْسِـهَا،
فَإِنْ تَرْحَمْنِي الْيَوْمَ فَلَا خَوْفٌ عَلَيَّ وَ لَا
حُزْنٌ، وَ إِنْ تُعَاقِبْ فَمَوْلًى لَهُ الْقُدْرَةُ
عَلىٰ عَبْدِهِ، وَ لَا تُخَيِّبْنِي بَعْدَ الْيَوْمِ، وَ
لَا تَصْرِفْنِي بِغَيْرِ حَاجَتِي، فَقَدْ لَصِقْتُ
بِقَبْرِ عَمِّ نَبِيِّـكَ، وَ تَقَرَّبْتُ بِهِ إِلَيْكَ
ابْتِغَاءَ مَرْضَاتِكَ وَ رَجَاءَ رَحْمَتِكَ،

So accept from me and return my ignorance with Your forbearance and my offenses against my soul with Your compassion, for my offense has indeed been great. I am not afraid that You will do me injustice, but I fear the ills ensuing from the reckoning of my deeds. Yet observe today my writhing at the grave of Your Prophet's uncle and release me on its account from the Fire.

فَتَقَبَّلْ مِنِّي وَ عُدْ بِحِلْمِكَ عَلىٰ جَهْلِي،
وَ بِرَأْفَتِكَ عَلىٰ جِنَايَـةِ نَفْسِي، فَقَدْ
عَظُمَ جُرْمِي، وَ مَا أَخَافُ أَنْ تَظْلِمَنِي
وَ لٰكِنْ أَخَافُ سُوءَ الْحِسَابِ، فَانْظُرِ
الْيَوْمَ تَقَلُّبِي عَلىٰ قَبْرِ عَمِّ نَبِيِّكَ، فَبِهِمَا
فُكَّنِي مِنَ النَّارِ،

Do not fail my effort; do not dis-

وَ لَا تُخَيِّبْ سَعْيِي، وَ لَا يَهُونَنَّ عَلَيْكَ

ابْتِهَالِي، وَ لَا تَحْجُبَنَّ عَنْكَ صَوْتِي، وَ لَا تَقْلِبْنِي بِغَيْرِ حَوَائِجِي، يَا غِيَاثَ كُلِّ مَكْرُوبٍ وَ مَحْزُونٍ، وَ يَا مُفَرِّجًا عَنِ الْمَلْهُوفِ الْحَيْرَانِ الْغَرِيقِ الْمُشْرِفِ عَلَى الْهَلَكَةِ، فَصَلِّ عَلَىٰ مُحَمَّدٍ وَ آلِ مُحَمَّدٍ، وَ انْظُرْ إِلَيَّ نَظْرَةً لَا أَشْقَىٰ بَعْدَهَا أَبَدًا، وَ ارْحَمْ تَضَرُّعِي وَ عَبْرَتِي وَ انْفِرَادِي، فَقَدْ رَجَوْتُ رِضَاكَ، وَ تَحَرَّيْتُ الْخَيْرَ الَّذِي لَا يُعْطِيهِ أَحَدٌ سِوَاكَ، فَلَا تَرُدَّ أَمَلِي.

regard my entreaties; do not shut away my cries, and do not turn me away without granting my requests, O Succour of all those who are distressed and grieved, O Reliever of all those who are troubled, baffled and drowning, who stand at the edge of destruction! Bless Muḥammad and the Family of Muḥammad and cast at me a look after which I will never be wretched and have mercy on my entreaties, my tears and my lonesomeness, for I indeed expect Your approval and aspire for the good which none can bestow upon me except You, so do not turn away my hope!

اَللّٰهُمَّ إِنْ تُعَاقِبْ فَمَوْلًى لَهُ الْقُدْرَةُ عَلَىٰ عَبْدِهِ وَ جَزَائِهِ بِسُوءِ فِعْلِهِ، فَلَا أَخِيبَنَّ الْيَوْمَ، وَ لَا تَصْرِفْنِي بِغَيْرِ حَاجَتِي، وَ لَا تُخَيِّبَنَّ شُخُوصِي وَ وِفَادَتِي، فَقَدْ أَنْفَدْتُ نَفَقَتِي، وَ أَتْعَبْتُ بَدَنِي، وَ قَطَعْتُ الْمَفَازَاتِ، وَ خَلَّفْتُ الْأَهْلَ وَ الْمَالَ وَ مَا خَوَّلْتَنِي، وَ آثَرْتُ مَا عِنْدَكَ عَلَىٰ نَفْسِي، وَ لُذْتُ بِقَبْرِ عَمِّ نَبِيِّكَ صَلَّى اللّٰهُ عَلَيْهِ وَ آلِهِ، وَ تَقَرَّبْتُ بِهِ ابْتِغَاءَ مَرْضَاتِكَ، فَعُدْ بِحِلْمِكَ عَلَىٰ جَهْلِي، وَ بِرَأْفَتِكَ عَلَىٰ ذَنْبِي، فَقَدْ عَظُمَ جُرْمِي،

O Allah, should you punish me, the master has authority over his slave to repay him for his evil conduct! Yet do not disappoint me today and do not turn me away without granting my petition, and do not disappoint my journey and my arrival, for I have spent my means, put my body to hardship, traversed through deserts, leaving behind my family, property and whatever You have given into my possession, preferring for myself that which is with You, and I have taken refuge with the grave of the uncle of Your Prophet, may Allah's blessings be upon him and his Family, and I seek nearness to him desiring Your pleasure! So return my ignorance with Your forbearance and my sin with Your compassion, for my guilt has indeed been great, O Magnanimous One, O Magnanimous One!

بِرَحْمَتِكَ يَا كَرِيمُ يَا كَرِيمُ.

The excellences of Ḥaḍrat Ḥamzah, may Allah's peace be upon him, and the virtues of his *ziyārah* are more than can be mentioned here. Fakhr al-Muḥaqqiqīn (r), in his *Risālah Fakhriyyah*, says that it is *mustaḥab* to perform the *ziyārah* of Ḥamzah and other martyrs at Uḥud as the Apostle of Allah (ṣ) is reported to have said, "Whoever pays me a visit without visiting my uncle Ḥamzah's tomb has been unfair to me."[1]

I have described in *Bayt al-Aḥzān fī Maṣā'ib Sayyadat al-Niswān* that after the death of her great father, Ḥaḍrat Fāṭimah, may Allah's blessings be upon her, used to make regular visits every week, on Mondays and Thursdays, to Uḥud for the *ziyārah* of Ḥamzah and other martyrs.[2] There she would offer prayers and make supplications, a practice that she continued until her demise.

Maḥmūd b. Labīd reports[3] that that august lady would arrive at Ḥamzah's graveside and do mourning. On one of these days I visited Ḥamzah's grave for *ziyārah* and saw her engaged in mourning. I waited until she stopped crying. Then I approached and greeted her. I said to her, 'O princess of the womenfolk, by God, you have wrenched my heart with this mourning of yours.' She replied, 'O Abu ᶜAmr, it behooves me to weep, for I have been bereft of the best of fathers, the Apostle of Allah!' She added, 'How much I pine for the Apostle of Allah!' Then she recited this verse:

إِذَا مَـاتَ يَوْمًـا مَيِّتٌ قَـلَّ ذِكْرُهُ وَ ذِكْـرُ أَبِي مُذْ مَـاتَ وَ اللهِ أَكْثَرُ

The memories of the departed fade with every passing day,
But my father's memories, by God, have grown since he passed away.

Shaykh Mufīd writes,

During his lifetime, the Apostle of Allah, may Allah bless him and his Family, used to urge people to visit the grave of Ḥamzah, may peace be to him, and he himself used to call on him and the other

1 *Risālah Fakhriyyah*, 79. According to the author of *Sadād al-ᶜIbād*, 402, the tradition has been narrated in Shīᶜī as well as Sunnī sources.

2 *Kāfī*, iii, 228, h3, iv, 561, h 3, whence *Wasā'il*, iii, 223, b 55, h 3467, xiv, 356, b 13, h 19380 & *Biḥār*, xliii, 195, b 7, h 24, xcvi, 216, b 7, h 12.

3 *Kifāyat al-Athar*, 197, whence *Biḥār*, xxxvi, 352, b 41, h 224.

martyrs. After his demise, may Allah bless him and his Family, Fāṭimah, peace be to her, continued to make frequent visits to his tomb, and Muslims frequented it for *ziyārah* and stayed by his graveside.[1]

ZIYARAH OF THE MARTYRS OF UHUD (R)

When intending to perform their *ziyārah*, say,[2]

Peace be to the Apostle of Allah! Peace be to the Prophet of Allah! Peace be to Muḥammad ibn ᶜAbd Allāh! Peace be to his immaculate Family!	اَلسَّلَامُ عَلَىٰ رَسُولِ اللهِ، اَلسَّلَامُ عَلَىٰ نَبِيِّ اللهِ، اَلسَّلَامُ عَلَىٰ مُحَمَّدِ بْنِ عَبْدِ اللهِ، اَلسَّلَامُ عَلَىٰ أَهْلِ بَيْتِهِ الطَّاهِرِينَ،
Peace be to you, O faithful martyrs! Peace be to you, O members of the house of faith and monotheism! Peace be to you, O helpers of Allah's religion and helpers of His Apostle, may peace be to him and his Family! *Peace be to you for your patience.' How excellent is the reward of the [ultimate] abode!*(13:24)	اَلسَّلَامُ عَلَيْكُمْ أَيُّهَا الشُّهَدَاءُ الْمُؤْمِنُونَ، اَلسَّلَامُ عَلَيْكُمْ يَا أَهْلَ بَيْتِ الْإِيمَانِ وَ التَّوْحِيدِ، اَلسَّلَامُ عَلَيْكُمْ يَا أَنْصَارَ دِينِ اللهِ وَ أَنْصَارَ رَسُولِهِ عَلَيْهِ وَ آلِهِ السَّلَامُ، سَلَامٌ عَلَيْكُمْ بِمَا صَبَرْتُمْ فَنِعْمَ عُقْبَى الدَّارِ،
I testify that Allah chose you for His faith and elected you for His Apostle, and I testify that you wage *jihād* for the sake of Allah, a *jihād* which is worthy of Him, and you defended the religion of Allah and His Prophet and sacrificed yourselves for him.	أَشْهَدُ أَنَّ اللهَ اخْتَارَكُمْ لِدِينِهِ، وَ اصْطَفَاكُمْ لِرَسُولِهِ، وَ أَشْهَدُ أَنَّكُمْ قَدْ جَاهَدْتُمْ فِي اللهِ حَقَّ جِهَادِهِ، وَ ذَبَبْتُمْ عَنْ دِينِ اللهِ وَ عَنْ نَبِيِّهِ، وَ جُدْتُمْ بِأَنْفُسِكُمْ دُونَهُ،
I testify that you were slain while following the path of the Apostle of Allah! So may Allah grant you the best reward on behalf of His Prophet and of Islam	وَ أَشْهَدُ أَنَّكُمْ قُتِلْتُمْ عَلَىٰ مِنْهَاجِ رَسُولِ اللهِ، فَجَزَاكُمُ اللهُ عَنْ نَبِيِّهِ وَ عَنِ الْإِسْلَامِ وَ أَهْلِهِ أَفْضَلَ الْجَزَاءِ، وَ عَرَّفَنَا

1 *Al-Fuṣūl al-Mukhtārah*, 131, whence *Biḥār*, x, 442.

2 *Biḥār*, xcvii, 221, b 7, h 19 from Mufīd, Ibn Ṭāwūs and Shahīd Awwal.

and its people, and may He introduce you to us in the abode of His pleasure and the place of His hospitality in the company of the prophets, the truthful, the martyrs and the righteous, and excellent companions are they![(4:69)]

وُجُوهَكُمْ فِي مَحَلِّ رِضْوَانِهِ وَ مَوْضِعِ إِكْرَامِهِ، مَعَ النَّبِيِّينَ وَ الصِّدِّيقِينَ وَ الشُّهَدَاءِ وَ الصَّالِحِينَ، وَ حَسُنَ أُولٰئِكَ رَفِيقًا.

I testify that you are the party of Allah and that those who waged war against you waged war against Allah, and that you were indeed among those brought near to Allah and the triumphant ones, *who are living and provided near their Lord!* So, may Allah's curse be on those who slew you and that of all the angels and humans!

أَشْهَدُ أَنَّكُمْ حِزْبُ اللهِ، وَ أَنَّ مَنْ حَارَبَكُمْ فَقَدْ حَارَبَ اللهَ، وَ أَنَّكُمْ لَمِنَ الْمُقَرَّبِينَ الْفَائِزِينَ الَّذِينَ هُمْ أَحْيَاءٌ عِنْدَ رَبِّهِمْ يُرْزَقُونَ، فَعَلىٰ مَنْ قَتَلَكُمْ لَعْنَةُ اللهِ وَ الْمَلَائِكَةِ وَ النَّاسِ أَجْمَعِينَ.

O people of *tawḥīd*, I have come to you as a pilgrim, aware of your rights, seeking nearness to Allah through your *ziyārah*, and knowing part of your noble deeds and admirable works! So, may Allah's peace, His mercy and blessings be upon you, and may Allah's curse and His wrath and displeasure be on those who slew you!

أَتَيْتُكُمْ يَا أَهْلَ التَّوْحِيدِ زَائِرًا، وَ بِحَقِّكُمْ عَارِفًا، وَ بِزِيَارَتِكُمْ إِلَى اللهِ مُتَقَرِّبًا، وَ بِمَا سَبَقَ مِنْ شَرِيفِ الْأَعْمَالِ وَ مَرْضِيِّ الْأَفْعَالِ عَالِمًا، فَعَلَيْكُمْ سَلَامُ اللهِ وَ رَحْمَتُهُ وَ بَرَكَاتُهُ، وَ عَلىٰ مَنْ قَتَلَكُمْ لَعْنَةُ اللهِ وَ غَضَبُهُ وَ سَخَطُهُ.

O Allah, grant me the benefit of their *ziyārah* and make me steadfast in pursuing their goals, and make me die with the faith that You made them die with, and unite me with them in the abode of Your mercy! I testify that you have preceded us and we are about to join you!

اَللّٰهُمَّ انْفَعْنِي بِزِيَارَتِهِمْ، وَ ثَبِّتْنِي عَلىٰ قَصْدِهِمْ، وَ تَوَفَّنِي عَلىٰ مَا تَوَفَّيْتَهُمْ عَلَيْهِ، وَ اجْمَعْ بَيْنِي وَ بَيْنَهُمْ فِي مُسْتَقَرِّ دَارِ رَحْمَتِكَ، أَشْهَدُ أَنَّكُمْ لَنَا فَرَطٌ وَ نَحْنُ بِكُمْ لَاحِقُونَ.

Also recite the Sūrat al-Qadr as much as is feasible. Some scholars recommend offering a two-*rakʿah* prayer at the graveside of each martyr visited.

Some Notable Mosques of Madinah

Important among the mosques of Madīnah is Masjid Qubā, *a mosque founded on Godwariness from the very first day,* in the words of the Qur'ān. It is mentioned in a report that those who visit that mosque and offer two *rakʿahs* of prayer in it return with the reward of performing an *ʿumrah.* Hence one should visit that holy mosque and offer two *rakʿahs* of prayer of *taḥiyyah.* Then perform the *tasbīḥ* of Ḥazrat Fāṭimah (*ʿa*) and recite the *ziyārah jāmiʿah* that begins with the words, *"Assalāmu ʿalā awliyā'illāh..."* (p. 519), which is the first *ziyārah* cited by us in the section on *ziyārat jāmiʿah* at the end of this Book. Then supplicate Allah and recite the supplication which begins with the words, "*Yā kā'inan qabla kulli shay.*" This is an elaborate supplication, not cited here for reasons of space. Those who are interested should refer to the chapters of the *Biḥar* on the topic of *mazār.*[1]

(ʿAllāmah Majlisī writes:)[2] "One should also visit and offer prayer in the *mashrabah* of Umm Ibrāhīm, mother of Ibrāhīm, the Prophet's son, where the Apostle of Allah (ṣ) used to stay and pray, as well as Masjid Faḍīkh, which is near the Qubā Mosque, also known as the Masjid Radd al-Shams. Also visit and offer prayer in Masjid al-Fatḥ, also known as Masjid al-Aḥzāb. After prayer in Masjid al-Fatḥ, say,

يَا صَرِيخَ الْمَكْرُوبِينَ، وَ يَا مُجِيبَ دَعْوَةِ
الْمُضْطَرِّينَ، وَ يَا مُغِيثَ الْمَهْمُومِينَ،
اِكْشِفْ عَنِّي ضُرِّي وَ هَمِّي وَ كَرْبِي وَ
غَمِّي كَمَا كَشَفْتَ عَنْ نَبِيِّكَ صَلَّى اللهُ
عَلَيْهِ وَ آلِهِ هَمَّهُ، وَ كَفَيْتَهُ هَوْلَ عَدُوِّهِ،
وَ اكْفِنِي مَا أَهَمَّنِي مِنْ أَمْرِ الدُّنْيَا وَ
الْآخِرَةِ يَا أَرْحَمَ الرَّاحِمِينَ.

O Rescuer of the troubled, O Responder to the calls of the distressed, O Succour of the worried! Relieve my distress, worries, troubles and grief, even as You removed the worries of Your Prophet, may Allah bless him and his Family, and sufficed him against the fear of his enemy. Suffice me with regard to what worries me in relation to the concerns of the world and the Hereafter, O Most Merciful of the merciful!

1 *Biḥār*, xcvii, 223-224.

2 *Biḥār*, xcvii, 224-225.

"One should also visit the house of Imam Zayn al-ʿAbidīn (ʿa), the house of Imam Jaʿfar al-Ṣādiq (ʿa), Masjid Salmān, Masjid Amīr al-Mu'minīn, which is in the vicinity of Ḥamzah's tomb, and the Masjid al-Mubāhalah and offer prayers there and supplicate as much as one can and make whatever petitions one may want to make..."

The Farewell Ziyarah

When intending to leave Madīnah, take a bath and after performing the Prophet's *ziyārah* as described earlier, bid him farewell and say,[1]

Peace be to you, O Apostle of Allah! I commend you to Allah's care and His protection, and give you my *salām*! I have faith in Allah and believe what you have brought and what you have preached.

O Allah, let this not be my last opportunity to visit Your Prophet's tomb, and if You take me away before that, I will testify after my death to what I have testified in my life, that there is no god except You and that Muḥammad is Your servant and Apostle, may Allah bless him and his Family!

اَلسَّلَامُ عَلَيْكَ يَا رَسُولَ اللهِ، أَسْتَوْدِعُكَ
اللهَ وَ أَسْتَرْعِيكَ وَ أَقْرَأُ عَلَيْكَ السَّلَامَ،
آمَنْتُ بِاللهِ وَ بِمَا جِئْتَ بِهِ وَ دَلَلْتَ عَلَيْهِ
اَللّٰهُمَّ لَا تَجْعَلْهُ آخِرَ الْعَهْدِ مِنِّي لِزِيَارَةِ
قَبْرِ نَبِيِّكَ، فَإِنْ تَوَفَّيْتَنِي قَبْلَ ذٰلِكَ فَإِنِّي
أَشْهَدُ فِي مَمَاتِي عَلَىٰ مَا شَهِدْتُ عَلَيْهِ فِي
حَيَاتِي أَنْ لَا إِلٰهَ إِلَّا أَنْتَ، وَ أَنَّ مُحَمَّدًا
عَبْدُكَ وَ رَسُولُكَ صَلَّى اللهُ عَلَيْهِ وَ آلِهِ.

Imam al-Ṣādiq (ʿa) told Yūnus b. Yaʿqūb to say the following while bidding farewell to the Apostle of Allah(ṣ),[2]

Allah bless you! Peace be to you! May Allah not make this my last opportunity to greet you!

صَلَّى اللهُ عَلَيْكَ، اَلسَّلَامُ عَلَيْكَ،
لَا جَعَلَهُ اللهُ آخِرَ تَسْلِيمِي عَلَيْكَ.

As I have pointed out in my book *Hadiyyat al-Zā'irīn*, among things which are important for the pilgrims when they are in the holy city of Madīnah is to make the best use of the opportunity to offer prayers in the Mosque of the Apostle of Allah (ṣ), wherein every prayer per-

1 *Al-Mazār al-Kabīr*, 108, whence *Biḥār*, xcvii, 180, b 2, h 45.

2 *Kāfī*, iv, 563, h 2, whence *Wasā'il*, xiv, 359, b 15, h 19384. *Kāmil al-Ziyārāt*, 26, b 7, h 2, whence *Biḥār*, xcvi, 381, b 2, h 8, xcvii, 182, b 3, h 5.

formed equals ten thousand prayers performed elsewhere,[1] the best place for prayer within the mosque being the "Garden" (*rawḍah*) between the Prophet's tomb and his *minbar*.[2]

As mentioned by our teacher in his work *Taḥiyyah*, for being the burial ground for the blessed bodies of our Prophet and the Imams, may Allah's blessings be upon them, these precincts are holier than the holy Kaᶜbah, a matter on which there is a consensus of all jurists, as expressly mentioned by Shahīd Awwal (*r*) in his work, *al-Qawā'id*.[3]

In a credible (*ḥasan*) report transmitted by Ḥaḍramī from Imam Jaᶜfar al-Ṣādiq (*ᶜa*), he says that the Imam enjoined him to pray as much as he could in the Prophet's Mosque, adding that he will not always have the opportunity to be present in that blessed place whenever he liked.[4]

Shaykh Ṭūsī (*r*) reports in *Tahdhīb* with reliable *isnād* from Murāzim that Imam Jaᶜfar al-Ṣādiq (*ᶜa*) said to him, "It is not obligatory to do fasting in Madīnah and to pray by the pillars of the Mosque, but it is good for someone who wishes to do so. All that is obligatory is the fivefold daily prayers and fasting during the month of Ramaḍān. So, perform as much prayer in this mosque as you can, as it is good for you. When someone is clever in worldly matters, the people praise him and say, 'How clever is he!' So how will it be if someone were to be clever in matters pertaining to the Hereafter?!"[5]

Perform the *ziyārah* of the Apostle of Allah (*ṣ*) every day, repeatedly, and so also that of the Imams at Baqīᶜ, as much as is feasible.

1 *Kāfī*, iv, 556, h 11, 12. *Tahdhīb*, iii, 250, 254 b 25, h 21, 6. *Wasā'il*, v 279-282, b 57, h 6543-55 from many sources..

2 *Kāfī*, iv, 554, 556, h 3, 5, 8, 10. *Wasā'il*, xiv, 344-346, b 7, h 19358-60.

3 *Al-Qawāᶜid wal-Fawā'id*, ii, 124. However, Shahīd Awwal in "qāᶜidah 189" (ii, 117), titled *Madhhab al-aṣḥāb anna Makkah ashraf al-biqāᶜ wa afḍaluhā*," states that the opinion of the majority of Shīᶜī scholars (*akthar al-jumhūr*) is that Makkah is superior in station to all other places, but some scholars believe Madīnah to be such. After citing the reasons offered by the two sides, he argues in favour of the superiority of Makkah. At the end of the "qāᶜidah," he mentions that one Sunnī scholar of the west has claimed consensus concerning the superiority of the place where the Prophet (ṣ) is buried over all other places (there is no mention of the Kaᶜbah in the Shahīd's remarks) and that his claim concerning both the superiority and the consensus has been disputed by another scholar. In the editor's footnote, it is pointed out that the claim of consensus has been made by Qāḍī ᶜIyāḍ (d. 544/1149), a Mālikī, and that it has been disputed by a Shāfiᶜī scholar. (Tr.)

4 *Kāmil al-Ziyārāt*, 12, b 2, h 5, whence *Wasā'il*, xiv, 338, b 4, h 19349 & *Biḥār*, xcvii, 157, b 2, h 33.

5 *Tahdhīb*, i, 19, b 5, h 23, whence *Wasā'il*, xiv, 351, b 11, h 19369.

Whenever your eyes fall on the Prophet's shrine, salute him. As long as you are in Madīnah, be careful of your conduct and guard yourself against sin and wrongful acts. Contemplate the sublimity of that place, especially about its blessed mosque whose grounds have been trodden by the blessed feet of the Apostle of Allah (ṣ), who walked through the allies and bazaars of that town and prayed in its mosque. It is the place of descent of God's revelations and that of Gabriel and the archangels. And well has someone said,

أَرْضٌ مَشَىٰ جِبْرِيلُ فِي عَرَصَاتِهَا وَ اللهُ شَرَّفَ أَرْضَهَا وَ سَمَاءَهَا

It is the land whose stretches have been trodden by Gabriel,
And God has honoured its ground and skies.

Give as much charity as you can while you are in Madīnah, especially in the Mosque and particularly to the sayyids and descendants of the Apostle (ṣ), which have a great reward. ʿAllāmah Majlisī says that a dirham given there in charity equals ten thousand spent elsewhere. If possible one should take up residence in that blessed city as it is *mustaḥab* to take residence in the Prophet's vicinage and a considerable number of reports have been transmitted concerning its virtues.

سَقَى اللهُ قَبْرًا بِالْمَدِينَةِ غَيْثَهُ فَقَدْ حَلَّ فِيهِ الْأَمْنُ بِالْبَرَكَاتِ

نَبِيُّ الْهُدَىٰ صَلَّى عَلَيْهِ مَلِيكُهُ وَبَلَّغَ عَنَّا رُوحَهُ التُّحَفَاتِ

وَ صَلَّى عَلَيْهِ اللهُ مَا ذَرَّ شَارِقٌ وَ لاحَتْ نُجُومُ اللَّيْلِ مُبْتَدِرَاتِ

God has drenched the shrine in Madīnah with the downpours of
His blessings
Hence peace and blessing have settled in its environs
His angels invoke blessings upon the Prophet of true guidance,
May our offerings and gifts be delivered to his spirit.
May God bless him as long as the sun shines
And the stars glitter at the fall of night.

Chapter Four

The Ziyārah of Najaf A<u>sh</u>raf

This chapter deals with the virtues of the *ziyārah* of our Master, the Commander of the Faithful (ᶜ*a*), and the manner of its performance. It consists of several sections.

The Virtues of Imam 'Ali's Ziyarah

<u>Sh</u>ay<u>kh</u> Ṭusī cites a *ṣaḥīḥ* report[1] of Muḥammad b. Muslim from Imam Jaᶜfar al-Ṣādiq (ᶜ*a*) that he said, "God has not created any creatures more numerous than the angels. Indeed, every day seventy thousand of them descend and arrive at the Bayt al-Maᶜmūr and circuit it, after which they proceed to circuit the Kaᶜbah. After going around the Kaᶜbah, they arrive at the tomb of the Apostle of Allah (*ṣ*) and salute him. Then they come to the tomb of the Commander of the Faithful (ᶜ*a*) and salute him. Thereafter they arrive at the tomb of Imam al-Ḥusayn (ᶜ*a*) and salute him, after which they ascend back to the heaven. A similar group of them continues to descend every day, and this will go on until the Day of Resurrection."

Then he added, "For those who perform the *ziyārah* of the Commander of the Faithful (ᶜ*a*), without pride and arrogance and with an awareness of his merits—that is, knowing that he is the Prophet's direct successor and an Imam obeying whom is obligatory—God Almighty writes for them the reward of a hundred thousand martyrs and forgives their past and future sins. He will raise them on the Day of Resurrection among those who are spared from that day's horrors and He will take a lenient reckoning of their deeds. As they arrive for the *ziyārah*, they are welcomed by the angels, who escort them to their homes when they return. When they fall sick, the angels come to visit them, and when they die, they accompany their funeral procession to the grave and plead to Allah for their forgiveness."

Sayyid ᶜAbd al-Karīm ibn Ṭāwūs, in *Farḥat al-<u>Gh</u>arī*, reports[2] that

1 Ṭūsī's *Amālī*, 214, majlis 8, h 374/22, whence *Wasā'il*, xiv, 375, b 23, h 19419 and *Biḥār*, xcvii, 257, b 3, 1. Ibn al-<u>Sh</u>ay<u>kh</u>'s *Amālī*, whence *Biḥār*, lvi, 176, b 23, h 8. *Bi<u>sh</u>ārat al-Muṣṭafā*, 108, whence *Biḥār*, xcvii, 122, b 2, h 27 and *Mustadrak*, x, 213, b 16, h 11884/5.

2 *Tah<u>dh</u>īb*, vi, 20, b 7, h 3, whence *Wasā'il*, xiv, 380, b 24, h 19430. *Farḥat al-<u>Gh</u>arī*,

Imam Jaᶜfar al-Ṣādiq (ᶜ*a*) said, "Those who go for the *ziyārah* of the Commander of the Faithful (ᶜ*a*) on foot, God Almighty writes for them the reward of a *ḥajj* and an ᶜ*umrah* for each and every step, and the reward of two *ḥajj* and two ᶜ*umrah* pilgrimages for every step of those who return on foot."

He also reports[1] the Imam to have said to Ibn Mārid, "O son of Mārid, whoever performs the *ziyārah* of my grandfather, the Commander of the Faithful (ᶜ*a*), with awareness of his merits, God Almighty writes for him the reward of a well-received ḥajj and an approved ᶜ*umrah* for every one of his steps. O son of Mārid, by God, the fire of hell will not touch the feet that were covered with dust during pilgrimage to the tomb of the Commander of the Faithful (ᶜ*a*), regardless of whether he makes the journey on foot or mounted. O son of Mārid, write this ḥadīth with gold-water."

He further reports[2] Imam Jaᶜfar al-Ṣādiq (ᶜ*a*) to have said, "We say that behind the city of Kūfah there is a grave where no person suffering from any affliction takes shelter without being healed by God Almighty."

The compiler says: That which is disclosed by reliable traditions is that God Almighty has made the grave of the Commander of the Faithful (ᶜ*a*) and those of his infallible descendants, a sanctuary for the afraid and the distressed and a place of security for the earth's denizens. By his graveside the sorrows of those who suffer from grief are removed and those suffering from maladies are cured when they embrace his grave, and those who take shelter in his shrine remain secure.

Sayyid ᶜAbd al-Karīm ibn Ṭāwūs cites[3] a tradition of Muḥammad b. ᶜAlī Shaybānī who reports saying,

> "One night, in the company of my father and uncle, Ḥusayn, we went on a secret journey for the *ziyārah* of the grave of the Commander of the Faithful (ᶜ*a*). I was a child and the year was 260 H. and odd. On approaching the grave, we saw a ring of black (or reclining) stones placed around the grave and there was nothing

75, whence *Biḥār*, xcvii, 260, b 3, h 9.

1 *Farḥat al-Gharī*, whence *Biḥār*, ii, 147, b 19, h 17 and xcvii, 260, b 3, h 10. *Wasā'il*, xiv, 377, b b 23, h 19421, from Mufīd.

2 Mufīd's *Kitāb al-Mazār*, 224, b 29, h 6. *Tahdhīb*, vi, 34, b 10, h 14, whence *Wasā'il*, xiv, 377, b 23, h 19423. *Makārim* , 387, whence *Biḥār*, xcii, 15, b 55, h 16. *Farḥat al-Gharī*, 91, whence *Biḥār*, xcvii, 261, b 3, h 13.

3 *Farḥat al-Gharī*, 140, b 15, whence *Biḥār*, xlii, 315, b 129, h 2.

built over it. Arriving at the graveside, some of us started reciting the Qur'ān, some stood up for prayer, and some others began reciting his *ziyārah*. While we were thus engaged, there appeared a lion and it approached us. When it came nearer, approaching within the distance of a spear's length, we said to ourselves, let us withdraw from the grave and see what it is up to. So we drew back and the lion approached the grave and began to rub its arm against it. One of us went forward to observe closely and he came back to inform us. Our fear abated and all of us came forward to watch it rubbing its arm on the grave. There was a wound in the arm and it kept on rubbing it for some time, after which it withdrew from the grave and left. We resumed our engagements of prayer, *ziyārah* and recitation of the Qur'ān."

Shaykh Mufīd writes,

> One day Hārūn al-Rashīd went out of Kūfah for hunting. Turning towards Gharīyayn and Thuwayyah, he spotted there some gazelles. He had the hunting dogs and falcons released in pursuit of the gazelles and they went forth after them. The gazelles took refuge on a hillside, where they rested. The falcons came down in one area and the dogs came back. Hārūn was surprised at what he saw. Again, when the gazelles descended from the hill, they were pursued by the dogs and the falcons, and once again they took refuge on the hill. The falcons came down and the dogs returned once again. When this happened three times, Hārūn ordered his men to gallop forth and bring him anyone they found. They brought to him an old man belonging to Banū Asad. Hārūn asked him about the hill. The man said to him, "I will tell you, if you will spare my life." Hārūn swore by God that he intended no harm. The man said, "I was told by my father, who heard it from his father that they believed that the grave of ʿAlī ibn Abī Ṭālib was situated on the hill. God has made it a sanctuary, and anyone who takes refuge there remains secure from danger." Hārūn asked for water to be brought and performing ablutions offered prayer on the hill.[1]

The compiler says: There is an Arabian proverb which says, أَحْمَى مِنْ مُجِيرِ الجَرَادِ, which means, 'a bigger defender than the man who gave

[1] *Irshād*, i, 25. *Manāqib*, ii, 349. *Farḥat al-Gharī*, whence *Biḥār*, xlii, 329, h 16.

refuge to the locust.' The story behind it is that there was a Bedouin named Mudlij b. Suwayd belonging to the tribe of Ṭayy. One day, while he was sitting in his tent, he saw a group of his tribesmen approach with sacks and pots. When asked, they told him that a large number of locusts had come down in the vicinity of his camp, which they had come to gather. On hearing this, Mudlij caught hold of his spear and mounted his horse, declaring to them, "By God, I will kill anyone who puts his hand on them. Is it possible that the locusts should be in my neighbourhood and you should want to catch them? That shall not be!" He continued to stand in their defence until the sun rose high and the locust flew away. Thereat he said to them, "The locust have left my neighbourhood. Now you are free to do whatever you wish."

The author of the *Qāmūs* writes that "Dhū al-Aʿwād" was the nickname of a man who was held in great respect. Some say that he was the ancestor of Ak<u>th</u>am b. Ṣayfī, and the tribe of Muḍar used to pay him a yearly tribute. When he became very old, they seated him on a wooden cot and took him around the Arab tribes and oases to collect the tribute. He was held in such respect that anyone taking shelter by his cot was considered safe from harm. Any wretched person who came to him was honoured, and anyone suffering from hunger who approached him found relief.

Therefore, if an Arab man can attain such honour and exalted station, there should be no wonder if God Almighty makes the tomb of His *walī*, whose coffin was carried by the Imams al-Ḥasan and al-Ḥusayn (*ʿa*) and the archangels Gabriel and Michael, a refuge for the frightened, a sanctuary for the fugitive, a bastion for the weak and healing for the afflicted. Hence go to him wherever you may be, cling to him and entreat him so that he may respond to your call and save you from the perils of this world and the Hereafter.

لُذْ إِلَى جُـــودِهِ تَجِـــدْهُ زَعِيمًا   بِنَجَـــاةِ الْعُصَاةِ يَـــوْمَ لِقَاهَا

عَائِـــدٌ لِلْمُؤَمِّلِـــينَ مُجِيـــبٌ   سَـــامِعٌ مَا تُسِرُّ مِـــنْ نَجْوَاهَا

Take refuge in his generosity, you will find him the saviour of the sinners on Judgement's Day.

He fulfils the hopes of the petitioners, and hears the pleadings made in secret.

In *Dār al-Salām*, it is related, citing <u>Sh</u>ay<u>kh</u> Daylamī, from a group of the pious of Najaf A<u>sh</u>raf that someone saw in a dream that every grave in that holy shrine and those outside it were connected with a rope to the blessed tomb of the Commander of the Faithful (ṣ), who is the firmest cord of Allah. Thereupon, he composed the following verses.

إِذَا مُتُّ فَادْفِنِّي إِلىٰ جَنْبِ حَيْدَرٍ　　أَبِي شَبَّرٍ أَكْرِمْ بِهِ وَ شَبِيْرِ

فَلَسْتُ أَخَافُ النَّارَ عِنْدَ جِوَارِهِ　　وَ لا أَتَّقِي مِنْ مُنْكَرٍ وَ نَكِيرٍ

فَعَارٌ عَلىٰ حَامِي الْحِمىٰ　　إِذَا ضَلَّ فِي الْبَيْدَاءِ عِقَالُ بَعِيرٍ

Bury me by Ḥaydar's side, the venerable father of <u>Sh</u>abbar and <u>Sh</u>abīr.
I will not be afraid of the Fire in his vicinage, nor have any fright of Munkar and Nakīr.
For it goes against the repute of the sanctuary's patron that while his ward is under his protection,
His camel's reins should be lost in the desert.

The Ziyārah of Imām ᶜAlī (ᶜa)

The texts recited for *ziyārah* of the Commander of the Faithful (ᶜ*a*) as narrated from the Imams are of two kinds. First, those which are of a general kind, not meant for any special occasion. Others are meant for particular occasions. These two groups of *ziyārah* will be mentioned in two different sections.

1. The General Ziyārahs

The general *ziyārah*s are many and here we will confine ourselves to citing a few.

The First Ziyarah

(ᶜAllāmah Majlisī writes in *Biḥār*,)[1] This *ziyārah* has been cited by <u>Sh</u>ay<u>kh</u> Mufīd, <u>Sh</u>ahīd al-Awwal, Sayyid Ibn Ṭāwūs and others. The manner of its performance is as follows. When intending to proceed for the *ziyārah*, one should take a bath and put on clean clothes and

[1] The entire texts of this *ziyārah*, up to the supplication *Allāhumma lā budda min amrik...* (p. 100), is cited from *Biḥār*, xcvii, 282-287, b 4, h 18.

apply some perfume to oneself, if available. On coming out of your house, say,

O Allah, I leave my home seeking Your grace and to visit the Legatee of Your Prophet, may Your blessings be upon them. So make it, O Allah, easy for me and provide me with the means for undertaking the *ziyārah*, and take care of my family in my absence, making good for it in the best manner, O Most Merciful of the merciful!

اَللّٰهُمَّ إِنِّي خَرَجْتُ مِنْ مَنْزِلِي أَبْغِي
فَضْلَكَ، وَ أَزُورُ وَصِيَّ نَبِيِّكَ صَلَوَاتُكَ
عَلَيْهِمَا، اَللّٰهُمَّ فَيَسِّرْ ذٰلِكَ لِي، وَ سَبِّبِ
الْمَزَارَ لَهُ، وَاخْلُفْنِي فِي عَاقِبَتِي وَ حُزَانَتِي
بِأَحْسَنِ الْخِلَافَةِ، يَا أَرْحَمَ الرَّاحِمِينَ.

Then set out with the following dhikr on your lips.

All praise belongs to Allah! Glory be to Allah! There is no god except Allah!

الْحَمْدُ لِلّٰهِ وَ سُبْحَانَ اللّٰهِ وَ لَا إِلٰهَ إِلَّا
اللّٰهُ

On reaching the periphery of Kūfah, say,

Allah is greater! Allah is greater, the possessor of supremacy, majesty and greatness! Allah is greater, worthy of magnification and celebration of His sanctity and glory, and bestower of bounties! Allah is greater than what I may fear and beware of!

Allah is greater, He is my support and in Him do I put my trust! Allah, the greater, is my hope and to Him do I turn penitently!

O Allah, You are the dispenser of my blessings and have the power to grant my requests. You know my need and what passes in the breasts and what crosses the minds.

اَللّٰهُ أَكْبَرُ، اَللّٰهُ أَكْبَرُ أَهْلَ الْكِبْرِيَاءِ
وَ الْمَجْدِ وَ الْعَظَمَةِ، اَللّٰهُ أَكْبَرُ أَهْلُ
التَّكْبِيرِ وَ التَّقْدِيسِ وَ التَّسْبِيحِ وَ
الْآلَاءِ، اَللّٰهُ أَكْبَرُ مِمَّا أَخَافُ وَ أَحْذَرُ،
اَللّٰهُ أَكْبَرُ عِمَادِي وَ عَلَيْهِ أَتَوَكَّلُ، اَللّٰهُ
أَكْبَرُ رَجَائِي وَ إِلَيْهِ أُنِيبُ.
اَللّٰهُمَّ أَنْتَ وَلِيُّ نِعْمَتِي، وَ الْقَادِرُ عَلَى
طَلِبَتِي، تَعْلَمُ حَاجَتِي وَ مَا تُضْمِرُهُ
هَوَاجِسُ الصُّدُورِ وَ خَوَاطِرُ النُّفُوسِ،

I beseech You, by Muḥammad, Your chosen one by whose means You have refuted the arguments of the contenders and pretexts of those who advance excuses, and made him a mercy for all the worlds, not to deprive me of the reward of the *ziyārah* of Your *walī*, the brother of Your Prophet and the Commander of the Faithful, and from setting out towards him. Grant me to be among his worthy visitors and his pious followers, with Your mercy, O Most Merciful of the merciful!

فَأَسْأَلُكَ بِمُحَمَّدٍ الْمُصْطَفَى، اَلَّذِى قَطَعْتَ بِهِ حُجَجَ الْمُحْتَجِّينَ وَ عُذْرَ الْمُعْتَذِرِينَ، وَ جَعَلْتَهُ رَحْمَةً لِلْعَالَمِينَ، أَنْ لَا تَحْرِمَنِي ثَوَابَ زِيَارَةِ وَلِيِّكَ وَ أَخِي نَبِيِّكَ أَمِيرِ الْمُؤْمِنِينَ وَ قَصْدَهُ، وَ تَجْعَلَنِي مِنْ وَفْدِهِ الصَّالِحِينَ وَ شِيعَتِهِ الْمُتَّقِينَ، بِرَحْمَتِكَ يَا أَرْحَمَ الرَّاحِمِينَ.

On sighting the dome of his holy shrine, say,

All praise belongs to Allah, who favoured me with a good birth and chose me for the honour of the friendship of the pious ones, the immaculate emissaries, and the elect of the signs (of Your guidance)!

اَلْحَمْدُ لِلّٰهِ عَلَى مَا اخْتَصَّنِي بِهِ مِنْ طِيبِ الْمَوْلِدِ، وَ اسْتَخْلَصَنِي إِكْرَامًا بِهِ مِنْ مُوَالَاةِ الْأَبْرَارِ، اَلسَّفَرَةِ الْأَطْهَارِ، وَ الْخِيَرَةِ الْأَعْلَامِ،

O Allah, accept my endeavour toward You, my entreaties before You, and forgive my sins which are not hidden from You. Indeed, You are the All-forgiving Sovereign!

اَللّٰهُمَّ فَتَقَبَّلْ سَعْيِي إِلَيْكَ، وَ تَضَرُّعِي بَيْنَ يَدَيْكَ، وَ اغْفِرْ لِيَ الذُّنُوبَ الَّتِي لَا تَخْفَى عَلَيْكَ، إِنَّكَ أَنْتَ اللّٰهُ الْمَلِكُ الْغَفَّارُ.

The compiler says: On sighting the shining dome of the tomb, the pilgrim is animated with a feeling of reverent eagerness wherein he wishes to turn all his attention to that personage and to address him expressing his ardour and admiration in some manner. Particularly, if the pilgrim is a person of scholarly merit he may want to express his feelings by murmuring lines of eloquent poetry.

Accordingly, it occurred to me to cite some verse of Uzrī's *Hā'iyyah*, a panegyric suitable for this place, with a strong hope that the readers will convey the greetings of the author of these pages to the occupant of that luminous shrine and not forget to remember him in their prayers. These are his verses:

أَيُّهَا الرَّاكِبُ الْمُجِدُّ رُوَيْدًا   بِقُلُوبٍ تَقَلَّبَتْ فِي جَوَاهَا

إِنْ تَرَاءَتْ أَرْضُ الْغَرِيَّيْنِ فَاخْضَعْ   وَ اخْلَعِ النَّعْلَ دُونَ وَادِي طُوَاهَا

وَ إِذَا شِمْتَ قُبَّةَ الْعَالَمِ   الْأَعْلَىٰ وَ أَنْوَارُ رَبِّهَا تَغْشَاهَا

فَتَوَاضَعْ فَثَمَّ دَارَةُ قُدْسٍ   تَتَمَنَّى الْأَفْلَاكُ لَثْمَ ثَرَاهَا

قُلْ لَهُ وَ الدُّمُوعُ سَفْحُ عَقِيقٍ   وَ الْحَشَا تَصْطَلِي بِنَارِ غَضَاهَا

يَا ابْنَ عَمِّ النَّبِيِّ أَنْتَ يَدُ اللهِ   الَّتِي عَمَّ كُلَّ شَيْءٍ نَدَاهَا

أَنْتَ قُرْآنُهُ الْقَدِيمُ وَ أَوْصَا   فُكَ آيَاتُهُ الَّتِي أَوْحَاهَا

خَصَّكَ اللهُ فِي مَآثِرَ شَتَّىٰ   هِيَ مِثْلُ الْأَعْدَادِ لَا تَتَنَاهَىٰ

لَيْتَ عَيْنًا بِغَيْرِ رَوْضِكَ تَرْعَىٰ   قَذِيَتْ وَ اسْتَمَرَّ فِيهَا قَذَاهَا

أَنْتَ بَعْدَ النَّبِيِّ خَيْرُ الْبَرَايَا   وَ السَّمَا خَيْرُ مَا بِهَا قَمَرَاهَا

لَكَ ذَاتٌ كَذَاتِهِ حَيْثُ لَوْ لَا   أَنَّهَا مِثْلُهَا لَمَا آخَاهَا

قَدْ تَرَاضَعْتُمَا بِثَدْيِ وِصَالٍ   كَانَ مِنْ جَوْهَرِ التَّجَلِّي غِذَاهَا

يَا أَخَا الْمُصْطَفَىٰ لَدَيَّ ذُنُوبٌ   هِيَ عَيْنُ الْقَذَا وَ أَنْتَ جَلَاهَا

لَكَ فِي مُرْتَقَى الْعُلَىٰ وَ الْمَعَالِي   دَرَجَاتٌ لَا يُرْتَقَىٰ أَدْنَاهَا

لَكَ نَفْسٌ مِنْ مَعْدِنِ اللُّطْفِ صِيغَتْ   جَعَلَ اللهُ كُلَّ نَفْسٍ فِدَاهَا

O rider, hurry not with the hearts that are in a flutter in these environs,

Approach with humility on sighting the land of Gharī and remove your shoes on reaching this valley of Ṭuwā.

On sighting the sublime dome enveloped in the lights of its Lord,

Be humble, for here is the abode of sanctity, to embrace whose dust the heavens aspire.

Tell him, with tears falling like ruby beads, and a heart burning in its embers,

O Cousin of the Prophet, you are the hand of God, whose generosity embraces all things.

You are His eternal scripture, your attributes His revealed signs,

God has given you eminence through many glorious deeds, limitless like numbers.

May thorns never cease to trouble the eye that looks away from the garden of your merits

Best of creation after the Prophet, the heaven's best adornments are its sun and moon.

Your being like his being, for if you were not like him, he would not have made you his brother.

The two of you were nursed with the milk of Divine union, and your nourishment was from the quintessence of Divine manifestation

O brother of Muṣṭafā, I am laden with sins, these are thorns in my eye, and you are its healer

Your stations are in exalted peaks of sublimity and merit, whose lowest ranks cannot be scaled

Yours is a soul fashioned in the mine of Divine grace and beneficence, may all souls be sacrificed for your sake!

On reaching the city gates, say,

اَلْحَمْدُ لِلّٰهِ الَّذِي هَدَانَا لِهٰذَا وَ مَا كُنَّا لِنَهْتَدِيَ لَوْ لَا أَنْ هَدَانَا اللّٰهُ.

All praise belongs to Allah, who guided us to this. We would have never been guided had not Allah guided us.(7:43)

اَلْحَمْدُ لِلّٰهِ الَّذِي سَيَّرَنِي فِي بِلَادِهِ، وَ حَمَلَنِي عَلَىٰ دَوَابِّهِ، وَ طَوَىٰ لِيَ الْبَعِيدَ، وَ صَرَفَ عَنِّي الْمَحْذُورَ، وَ دَفَعَ عَنِّي الْمَكْرُوهَ، حَتَّىٰ أَقْدَمَنِي حَرَمَ أَخِي رَسُولِهِ صَلَّى اللّٰهُ عَلَيْهِ وَ آلِهِ.

All praise belongs to Allah, who has taken me through His towns, carried me on His beasts, taken me over far distances, removing all obstacles from my way, sparing me of unpleasant evens, until He brought me at the shrine of the brother of His Apostle, may Allah bless Him and his Family!

While entering the city, say,

All praise belongs to Allah, who has brought me into this holy place, which He has blessed and chosen for the Legatee of His Prophet.	اَلْحَمْــدُ لِلّٰهِ الَّذِى أَدْخَلَنِي هٰــذِهِ الْبُقْعَةَ الْمُبَارَكَةَ الَّتِي بَارَكَ اللهُ فِيهَا، وَ اخْتَارَهَا لِوَصِيِّ نَبِيِّهِ،
O Allah, let it be a testimony in my favour!	اَللّٰهُمَّ فَاجْعَلْهَا شَاهِدَةً لِي.

On arriving at the precincts of the shrine, say,

O Allah, I stand at Your door, having alighted in Your courtyard. I cling to Your cord, expose myself to Your mercy, seek the mediation of Your *walī*, may Your blessings be upon him! Let it be a visit that is well-received and a supplication that is well-answered!	اَللّٰهُمَّ لِبَابِكَ وَقَفْتُ، وَ بِفِنَائِكَ نَزَلْتُ، وَ بِحَبْلِــكَ اعْتَصَمْــتُ، وَ لِرَحْمَتِــكَ تَعَرَّضْــتُ، وَ بِوَلِيِّــكَ صَلَوَاتُكَ عَلَيْهِ تَوَسَّــلْتُ، فَاجْعَلْهَا زِيَــارَةً مَقْبُولَةً وَ دُعَاءً مُسْتَجَابًا.

On reaching the gate of the shrine's courtyard, say,

O Allah, this shrine is Your sanctuary, and this place belongs to You. I enter it to commune with You privately concerning what You know better than me, knowing as well my secret thoughts and discourses!	اَللّٰهُمَّ إِنَّ هٰذَا الْحَــرَمَ حَرَمُكَ، وَ الْمَقَامَ مَقَامُكَ، وَ أَنَا أَدْخُــلُ إِلَيْهِ أُنَاجِيكَ بِمَا أَنْتَ أَعْلَمُ بِهِ مِنِّي وَ مِنْ سِرِّى وَ نَجْوَاى.
All praise belongs to Allah, the All-compassionate, the Favourer, the All-bountiful, with whose bounty and kindness was facilitated this visit of mine to my master. He did not deprive me of his *ziyārah* nor kept me away from his *wilāyah*, but rather grant-	اَلْحَمْــدُ لِلّٰهِ الْحَنَّــانِ الْمَنَّــانِ الْمُتَطَوِّلِ الَّذِى مِنْ تَطَوُّلِهِ سَــهَّلَ لِي زِيَارَةَ مَوْلَاىَ بِإِحْسَــانِهِ، وَ لَمْ يَجْعَلْنِي عَــنْ زِيَارَتِهِ مَمْنُوعًا، وَ لَا عَنْ وِلَايَتِــهِ مَدْفُوعًا، بَلْ

ed me His kindness and bounty!

تَطَوَّلَ وَ مَنَحَ.

O Allah, even as You have favoured me by enabling me to know him, make me one of his followers and admit me into paradise with his intercession, O Most Merciful of the merciful!

اَللّٰهُمَّ كَمَا مَنَنْتَ عَلَيَّ بِمَعْرِفَتِهِ، فَاجْعَلْنِي مِنْ شِيعَتِهِ، وَ أَدْخِلْنِي الْجَنَّةَ بِشَفَاعَتِهِ، يَا أَرْحَمَ الرَّاحِمِينَ.

Then enter the shrine's courtyard and say,

All praise belongs to Allah who has honoured me with the knowledge of Him and His Apostle and of those whom He has made it my duty to obey, out of His mercy and grace to me, and favoured me with faith!

اَلْحَمْدُ لِلّٰهِ الَّذِي أَكْرَمَنِي بِمَعْرِفَتِهِ وَ مَعْرِفَةِ رَسُولِهِ وَ مَنْ فَرَضَ عَلَيَّ طَاعَتَهُ، رَحْمَةً مِنْهُ لِي وَ تَطَوُّلًا مِنْهُ عَلَيَّ، وَ مَنَّ عَلَيَّ بِالْإِيمَانِ.

All praise belongs to Allah, who admitted me into the shrine of the brother of His Apostle and enabled me to view it in the state of well being! All praise belongs to Allah who has made me one of the pilgrims to the tomb of the Legatee of His Apostle.

اَلْحَمْدُ لِلّٰهِ الَّذِي أَدْخَلَنِي حَرَمَ أَخِي رَسُولِهِ وَ أَرَانِيهِ فِي عَافِيَةٍ. اَلْحَمْدُ لِلّٰهِ الَّذِي جَعَلَنِي مِنْ زُوَّارِ قَبْرِ وَصِيِّ رَسُولِهِ.

I testify that there is no god other than Allah, He is One and has no partner, and I testify that Muḥammad is His servant and Apostle, who brought the truth from Allah. I testify that ʿAlī is the servant of Allah and brother of the Apostle of Allah!

أَشْهَدُ أَنْ لَا إِلٰهَ إِلَّا اللّٰهُ وَحْدَهُ لَا شَرِيكَ لَهُ، وَ أَشْهَدُ أَنَّ مُحَمَّدًا عَبْدُهُ وَ رَسُولُهُ، جَاءَ بِالْحَقِّ مِنْ عِنْدِ اللّٰهِ، وَ أَشْهَدُ أَنَّ عَلِيًّا عَبْدُ اللّٰهِ وَ أَخُو رَسُولِ اللّٰهِ.

Allah is greater, Allah is greater, Allah is greater! There is no god other than Allah, and Allah is greater! All praise belongs to Allah for His guidance and for en-

اَللّٰهُ أَكْبَرُ، اَللّٰهُ أَكْبَرُ، اَللّٰهُ أَكْبَرُ، لَا إِلٰهَ إِلَّا اللّٰهُ وَ اللّٰهُ أَكْبَرُ، وَ الْحَمْدُ لِلّٰهِ عَلَىٰ هِدَايَتِهِ وَ تَوْفِيقِهِ لِمَا دَعَا إِلَيْهِ مِنْ

abling us to answer His summons to His way!

سَبِيلِهِ.

O Allah, You are the best of those who are sought and the noblest of those who are visited, and I come to You seeking nearness to You by the mediation of Your Prophet, the prophet of mercy, and that of his brother, the Commander of the Faithful, ᶜAlī ibn Abī Ṭālib, may peace be to them!

اَللّٰهُمَّ إِنَّكَ أَفْضَلُ مَقْصُودٍ وَ أَكْرَمُ مَأْتِيٍّ، وَ قَدْ أَتَيْتُكَ مُتَقَرِّبًا إِلَيْكَ بِنَبِيِّكَ نَبِيِّ الرَّحْمَةِ، وَ بِأَخِيهِ أَمِيرِ الْمُؤْمِنِينَ عَلِيِّ بْنِ أَبِي طَالِبٍ عَلَيْهِمَا السَّلَامُ،

So bless Muḥammad and the Family of Muḥammad, and do not cause my efforts to fail and cast at me a merciful glance whereby You will revive me and make me distinguished with You in the world and the Hereafter and one of those brought near to You!

فَصَلِّ عَلَىٰ مُحَمَّدٍ وَ آلِ مُحَمَّدٍ، وَ لَا تُخَيِّبْ سَعْيِي، وَ انْظُرْ إِلَيَّ نَظْرَةً رَحِيمَةً تَنْعَشُنِي بِهَا، وَ اجْعَلْنِي عِنْدَكَ وَجِيهًا فِي الدُّنْيَا وَ الْآخِرَةِ وَ مِنَ الْمُقَرَّبِينَ.

When you reach the door of the entrance hall, stop and say,

Peace be to the Apostle of Allah, who was entrusted by Allah with His revelations and His prime commandments, the seal of the previous prophesies and inaugurator of what is to come, and custodian of all that. May Allah's mercy and His blessings be upon him!

اَلسَّلَامُ عَلَىٰ رَسُولِ اللّٰهِ أَمِينِ اللّٰهِ عَلَىٰ وَحْيِهِ وَ عَزَائِمِ أَمْرِهِ، اَلْخَاتِمِ لِمَا سَبَقَ، وَ الْفَاتِحِ لِمَا اسْتُقْبِلَ، وَ الْمُهَيْمِنِ عَلَىٰ ذٰلِكَ كُلِّهِ، وَ رَحْمَةُ اللّٰهِ وَ بَرَكَاتُهُ.

Peace be to the recipient of tranquillity. Peace to him who is buried at Madīnah! Peace be to him who has been helped and strengthened by Allah. Peace be to Abū al-Qāsim Muḥammad, son of ᶜAbd Allāh, and may Allah's mercy and blessings be upon him!

اَلسَّلَامُ عَلَىٰ صَاحِبِ السَّكِينَةِ، اَلسَّلَامُ عَلَى الْمَدْفُونِ بِالْمَدِينَةِ، اَلسَّلَامُ عَلَى الْمَنْصُورِ الْمُؤَيَّدِ، اَلسَّلَامُ عَلَىٰ أَبِي الْقَاسِمِ مُحَمَّدِ بْنِ عَبْدِ اللّٰهِ، وَ رَحْمَةُ اللّٰهِ وَ بَرَكَاتُهُ.

Appeal for Admittance at the Door of the Tomb Chamber

Then enter the entrance hall with the right foot and standing at the door (of the shrine chamber) say,

I testify that there is no god other than Allah, He is one and has no partner, and I testify that Muḥammad is His servant and Apostle, who brought the truth from Him and confirmed the apostles.

أَشْهَدُ أَنْ لَا إِلٰهَ إِلَّا اللهُ وَحْدَهُ لَا شَرِيكَ لَهُ، وَ أَشْهَدُ أَنَّ مُحَمَّدًا عَبْدُهُ وَ رَسُولُهُ، جَاءَ بِالْحَقِّ مِنْ عِنْدِهِ وَ صَدَّقَ الْمُرْسَلِينَ.

Peace be to you O Apostle of Allah! Peace be to you, O beloved of Allah and His chosen one from His creation! Peace be to the Commander of the Faithful, the servant of Allah and brother of the Apostle of Allah!

اَلسَّلَامُ عَلَيْكَ يَا رَسُولَ اللهِ، اَلسَّلَامُ عَلَيْكَ يَا حَبِيبَ اللهِ وَ خِيَرَتَهُ مِنْ خَلْقِهِ، اَلسَّلَامُ عَلَىٰ أَمِيرِ الْمُؤْمِنِينَ عَبْدِ اللهِ وَ أَخِي رَسُولِ اللهِ.

My master, O Commander of the Faithful! This servant, son of your servant and maidservant, has come to you seeking shelter in your sanctuary! He has set out for your shrine, turned toward your station, seeking your mediation with Allah the Most High!

يَا مَوْلَایَ يَا أَمِيرَ الْمُؤْمِنِينَ، عَبْدُكَ وَ ابْنُ عَبْدِكَ وَ ابْنُ أَمَتِكَ، جَاءَكَ مُسْتَجِيرًا بِذِمَّتِكَ، قَاصِدًا إِلَىٰ حَرَمِكَ، مُتَوَجِّهًا إِلَىٰ مَقَامِكَ، مُتَوَسِّلًا إِلَى اللهِ تَعَالَىٰ بِكَ،

May I enter, O my master? May I enter, O Commander of the Faithful? May I enter, O testament of Allah? May I enter, O trustee of Allah? May I enter, O angels residing in this shrine?

أَ أَدْخُلُ يَا مَوْلَایَ؟ أَ أَدْخُلُ يَا أَمِيرَ الْمُؤْمِنِينَ؟ أَ أَدْخُلُ يَا حُجَّةَ اللهِ؟ أَ أَدْخُلُ يَا أَمِينَ اللهِ؟ أَ أَدْخُلُ يَا مَلَائِكَةَ اللهِ الْمُقِيمِينَ فِي هٰذَا الْمَشْهَدِ؟

O master, do you allow me to enter with the best of leaves that you have given to any of your friends? For though I may not be worthy of that, it is indeed worthy of you!

يَا مَوْلَایَ أَ تَأْذَنُ لِي بِالدُّخُولِ أَفْضَلَ مَا أَذِنْتَ لِأَحَدٍ مِنْ أَوْلِيَائِكَ؟ فَإِنْ لَمْ أَكُنْ لَهُ أَهْلًا فَأَنْتَ أَهْلٌ لِذٰلِكَ.

Then embrace the threshold and enter, advancing with the right foot, and while entering say,

بِسْمِ اللّٰهِ وَ بِاللّٰهِ وَ فِي سَبِيلِ اللّٰهِ وَ عَلٰى مِلَّةِ رَسُولِ اللّٰهِ صَلَّى اللّٰهُ عَلَيْهِ وَ آلِهِ،

In the Name of Allah, by Allah, in the way of Allah, and upholding the creed of the Apostle of Allah, may Allah bless him and his Family!

اَللّٰهُمَّ اغْفِرْ لِي وَ ارْحَمْنِي وَ تُبْ عَلَيَّ، إِنَّكَ أَنْتَ التَّوَّابُ الرَّحِيمُ.

O Allah, forgive me, have mercy on me, and accept my repentance! Indeed, You are the All-clement and the All-merciful!

Then move on and stand facing the noble tomb, yet stop before reaching it, and facing it say,

اَلسَّلَامُ مِنَ اللّٰهِ عَلٰى مُحَمَّدٍ رَسُولِ اللّٰهِ، أَمِينِ اللّٰهِ عَلٰى وَحْيِهِ وَ رِسَالَاتِهِ وَ عَزَائِمِ أَمْرِهِ، وَ مَعْدِنِ الْوَحْيِ وَ التَّنْزِيلِ، اَلْخَاتِمِ لِمَا سَبَقَ، وَ الْفَاتِحِ لِمَا اسْتُقْبِلَ، وَ الْمُهَيْمِنِ عَلٰى ذٰلِكَ كُلِّهِ، اَلشَّاهِدِ عَلَى الْخَلْقِ، اَلسِّرَاجِ الْمُنِيرِ، وَ السَّلَامُ عَلَيْهِ وَ رَحْمَةُ اللّٰهِ وَ بَرَكَاتُهُ.

May Allah's salutations of 'Peace' be to Muḥammad, the Apostle of Allah, entrusted by Allah with His revelations, messages and His prime commandments, the repository of revelations and revealed texts, the seal of the previous prophesies and inaugurator of what is to come and custodian of all that, witness to the entire creation and the radiant lamp! May peace be to him and may Allah's blessings and mercy be upon him!

اَللّٰهُمَّ صَلِّ عَلٰى مُحَمَّدٍ وَ أَهْلِ بَيْتِهِ الْمَظْلُومِينَ أَفْضَلَ وَ أَكْمَلَ وَ أَرْفَعَ وَ أَشْرَفَ مَا صَلَّيْتَ عَلٰى أَحَدٍ مِنْ أَنْبِيَائِكَ وَ رُسُلِكَ وَ أَصْفِيَائِكَ.

O Allah, bless Muḥammad and his Family, sufferers of wrong and injustice, with the best, most perfect, sublimest and noblest of blessings with which You have blessed any of Your prophets, apostles and elect!

اَللّٰهُمَّ صَلِّ عَلٰى أَمِيرِ الْمُؤْمِنِينَ عَبْدِكَ وَ خَيْرِ خَلْقِكَ بَعْدَ نَبِيِّكَ، وَ أَخِي رَسُولِكَ،

O Allah, bless the Commander of the Faithful, Your servant and the best of Your creatures after Your

Prophet, Your Prophet's brother and the Legatee of Your beloved one, whom You chose from among Your creation, who is the guide to him whom You sent with Your messages, who judges in accordance with Your justice, and decides amongst Your creatures in accordance with Your decrees! May peace be to him and may Allah's mercy and His blessings be upon him!

وَ وَصِيِّ حَبِيبِكَ، اَلَّذِي انْتَجَبْتَهُ مِنْ خَلْقِكَ، وَ الدَّلِيلِ عَلَىٰ مَنْ بَعَثْتَهُ بِرِسَالَاتِكَ، وَ دَيَّانِ الدِّينِ بِعَدْلِكَ، وَ فَصْلِ قَضَائِكَ بَيْنَ خَلْقِكَ، وَ السَّلَامُ عَلَيْهِ وَ رَحْمَةُ اللهِ وَ بَرَكَاتُهُ.

O Allah, bless the Imams of his progeny, who are after him the maintainers of Your religion, the immaculate ones whom You have approved as helpers of Your religion, as keepers of Your secrets, as witnesses to Your creation, and as beacons of guidance for Your servants, may Your blessings be upon them all!

اَللّٰهُمَّ صَلِّ عَلَى الْأَئِمَّةِ مِنْ وُلْدِهِ، اَلْقَوَّامِينَ بِأَمْرِكَ مِنْ بَعْدِهِ، اَلْمُطَهَّرِينَ الَّذِينَ ارْتَضَيْتَهُمْ أَنْصَارًا لِدِينِكَ، وَ حَفَظَةً لِسِرِّكَ، وَ شُهَدَاءَ عَلَىٰ خَلْقِكَ، وَ أَعْلَامًا لِعِبَادِكَ، صَلَوَاتُكَ عَلَيْهِمْ أَجْمَعِينَ.

Peace be to the Commander of the Faithful, ʿAlī ibn Abī Ṭālib, the Legatee of the Apostle of Allah, his successor and the maintainer of His religion after him, the chief of the legatees, and may Allah's mercy and His blessings be upon him.

اَلسَّلَامُ عَلَىٰ أَمِيرِ الْمُؤْمِنِينَ عَلِيِّ بْنِ أَبِي طَالِبٍ، وَصِيِّ رَسُولِ اللهِ وَ خَلِيفَتِهِ، وَ الْقَائِمِ بِأَمْرِهِ مِنْ بَعْدِهِ، سَيِّدِ الْوَصِيِّينَ وَ رَحْمَةُ اللهِ وَ بَرَكَاتُهُ.

Peace be to Fāṭimah, daughter of the Apostle of Allah, may Allah bless him and his Family, the Lady of the world's womankind!

اَلسَّلَامُ عَلَىٰ فَاطِمَةَ بِنْتِ رَسُولِ اللهِ صَلَّى اللهُ عَلَيْهِ وَ آلِهِ، سَيِّدَةِ نِسَاءِ الْعَالَمِينَ.

Peace be to al-Ḥasan and al-Ḥusayn, the doyens of the youth of paradise from among the entire creation!

اَلسَّلَامُ عَلَى الْحَسَنِ وَ الْحُسَيْنِ سَيِّدَيْ شَبَابِ أَهْلِ الْجَنَّةِ مِنَ الْخَلْقِ أَجْمَعِينَ.

Peace be to the rightly-guided Imams! Peace be to all the prophets and apostles! Peace be to the

اَلسَّلَامُ عَلَى الْأَئِمَّةِ الرَّاشِدِينَ. اَلسَّلَامُ عَلَى الْأَنْبِيَاءِ وَ الْمُرْسَلِينَ. اَلسَّلَامُ عَلَى

Imams, the custodians! Peace be to the elect of Allah out of His creation! Peace be to the Seers! Peace be to the faithful who maintain His ordinances, provide support to the *awliyā'* of Allah and are fearful (of God) like them! Peace be to the angels brought near to Allah! Peace be to Allah's righteous servants!

الْأَئِمَّةِ الْمُسْتَوْدَعِينَ. اَلسَّلَامُ عَلَىٰ خَاصَّةِ
اللهِ مِنْ خَلْقِهِ. اَلسَّلَامُ عَلَى الْمُتَوَسِّمِينَ.
اَلسَّلَامُ عَلَى الْمُؤْمِنِينَ الَّذِينَ قَامُوا بِأَمْرِهِ،
وَ وَازَرُوا أَوْلِيَاءَ اللهِ؛ وَ خَافُوا بِخَوْفِهِمْ.
اَلسَّلَامُ عَلَى الْمَلَائِكَةِ الْمُقَرَّبِينَ. اَلسَّلَامُ
عَلَيْنَا وَ عَلَىٰ عِبَادِ اللهِ الصَّالِحِينَ.

Then drawing near the tomb, facing it with the *qiblah* at your back say,

Peace be to you, O Commander of the Faithful! Peace be to you, O beloved of Allah! Peace be to you, O elect of Allah! Peace be to you, O testament of Allah! Peace be to you, O Imam of guidance! Peace be to you, O standard of guidance! Peace be to you, O good, pious, blameless and loyal legatee! Peace be to you, O father of al-Ḥasan and al-Ḥusayn!

اَلسَّلَامُ عَلَيْكَ يَا أَمِيرَ الْمُؤْمِنِينَ، اَلسَّلَامُ
عَلَيْكَ يَا حَبِيبَ اللهِ، اَلسَّلَامُ عَلَيْكَ يَا
صَفْوَةَ اللهِ، اَلسَّلَامُ عَلَيْكَ يَا وَلِيَّ اللهِ،
اَلسَّلَامُ عَلَيْكَ يَا حُجَّةَ اللهِ، اَلسَّلَامُ
عَلَيْكَ يَا إِمَامَ الْهُدَىٰ، اَلسَّلَامُ عَلَيْكَ يَا
عَلَمَ التُّقَىٰ، اَلسَّلَامُ عَلَيْكَ أَيُّهَا الْوَصِيُّ
الْبَرُّ التَّقِيُّ النَّقِيُّ الْوَفِيُّ، اَلسَّلَامُ عَلَيْكَ يَا
أَبَا الْحَسَنِ وَ الْحُسَيْنِ،

Peace be to you, O pillar of the faith! Peace be to you, O chief of the legatees and trustee of the Lord of all the worlds, judge on the Day of Retribution, the best of the faithful, the doyen of the truthful, and elect of the offspring of the prophets, the door of the wisdom of the Lord of all

اَلسَّلَامُ عَلَيْكَ يَا عَمُودَ الدِّينِ، اَلسَّلَامُ
عَلَيْكَ يَا سَيِّدَ الْوَصِيِّينَ، وَ أَمِينَ رَبِّ
الْعَالَمِينَ، وَ دَيَّانَ يَوْمِ الدِّينِ، وَ خَيْرَ
الْمُؤْمِنِينَ، وَ سَيِّدَ الصِّدِّيقِينَ، وَ الصَّفْوَةَ
مِنْ سُلَالَةِ النَّبِيِّينَ، وَ بَابَ حِكْمَةِ رَبِّ

the worlds, custodian of His revelations, repository of His knowledge, well-wisher of the *ummah* of His Prophet, successor of His Apostle and his self-sacrificing supporter, the declarer of His proofs, the summoner to His Law, and follower of his *sunnah*!

الْعَالَمِينَ، وَ خَازِنَ وَحْيِهِ، وَ عَيْبَةَ
عِلْمِهِ، وَ النَّاصِحَ لِأُمَّةِ نَبِيِّهِ، وَ التَّالِىَ
لِرَسُولِهِ، وَ الْمُوَاسِىَ لَهُ بِنَفْسِهِ، وَ
النَّاطِقَ بِحُجَّتِهِ، وَ الدَّاعِىَ إِلَىٰ شَرِيعَتِهِ،
وَ الْمَاضِىَ عَلَىٰ سُنَّتِهِ.

O Allah, I testify that he delivered what he had received from Your Apostle, guarded what he had been given to preserve, preserved what he had been entrusted with, permitted what You have made lawful and forbade what You made unlawful, implemented Your laws and waged *jihād* in Your way against those who broke their oaths of allegiance, those who violated Your ordinances, and those who defected from Your command, with patience and in anticipation of Your reward, without fearing the blame of any blamer.

اَللّٰهُمَّ إِنِّى أَشْهَدُ أَنَّهُ قَدْ بَلَّغَ عَنْ
رَسُولِكَ مَا حُمِّلَ، وَ رَعَىٰ مَا اسْتُحْفِظَ،
وَ حَفِظَ مَا اسْتُوْدِعَ، وَ حَلَّلَ حَلَالَكَ،
وَ حَرَّمَ حَرَامَكَ، وَ أَقَامَ أَحْكَامَكَ،
وَ جَاهَدَ النَّاكِثِينَ فِى سَبِيلِكَ، وَ
الْقَاسِطِينَ فِى حُكْمِكَ، وَ الْمَارِقِينَ
عَنْ أَمْرِكَ، صَابِرًا مُحْتَسِبًا، لَا تَأْخُذُهُ
فِيكَ لَوْمَةُ لَائِمٍ.

O Allah, bless him with the best of what You have blessed any of Your *awliyā'*, Your elect and the legatees of Your prophets!

اَللّٰهُمَّ صَلِّ عَلَيْهِ أَفْضَلَ مَا صَلَّيْتَ
عَلَىٰ أَحَدٍ مِنْ أَوْلِيَائِكَ وَ أَصْفِيَائِكَ وَ
أَوْصِيَاءِ أَنْبِيَائِكَ.

O Allah, this is the grave of Your *walī*, obedience to whom You have enjoined and allegiance to whom You have made incumbent upon Your servants. [It is the grave] of Your vicegerent for whose sake You give and take, reward and punish. I have set out to visit him,

اَللّٰهُمَّ هٰذَا قَبْرُ وَلِيِّكَ الَّذِى فَرَضْتَ
طَاعَتَهُ، وَ جَعَلْتَ فِى أَعْنَاقِ عِبَادِكَ
مُبَايَعَتَهُ، وَ خَلِيفَتِكَ الَّذِى بِهِ تَأْخُذُ
وَ تُعْطِى، وَ بِهِ تُثِيبُ وَ تُعَاقِبُ، وَ قَدْ

aspiring for what You have prepared for Your *awliyā'*. So, for the sake of the greatness of his merit with You, the honour he has with You, and the nearness of his station to You, bless Muḥammad and the Family of Muḥammad and treat me as is worthy of You, for indeed You are magnanimous and munificent.

قَصَدْتُهُ طَمَعًا لِمَـا أَعْدَدْتَهُ لِأَوْلِيَائِكَ، فَبِعَظِيمِ قَـدْرِهِ عِنْدَكَ، وَ جَلِيلِ خَطَرِهِ لَدَيْـكَ، وَ قُرْبِ مَنْزِلَتِهِ مِنْكَ، صَلِّ عَلَىٰ مُحَمَّدٍ وَ آلِ مُحَمَّـدٍ، وَ افْعَلْ بِي مَا أَنْتَ أَهْلُهُ، فَإِنَّكَ أَهْلُ الْكَرَمِ وَ الْجُودِ.

Peace be to you, my master, and to Adam and Noah, who lie buried at your graveside, and may Allah's mercy and His blessings be on you!

وَ السَّـلَامُ عَلَيْـكَ يَا مَـوْلَايَ وَ عَلَىٰ ضَجِيعَيْكَ آدَمَ وَنُوحٍ وَرَحْمَةُ اللهِ وَبَرَكَاتُهُ

Then kiss the *ḍarīḥ* and standing at the head of the grave say,

My master, I have come to you, seeking your mediation with my Lord in achieving my goal! I testify that those who seek your mediation are not disappointed and those who seek you with understanding are not sent away except with satisfaction of their needs. So be my intercessor with Allah, your Lord and mine, with regard to fulfilment of my needs, facilitation of my affairs and removal of my distress, forgiveness of my sins, expansion of my provision, prolongation of my life-span, granting of my requests with regard to my fate in the Hereafter and my life in this world!

يَا مَوْلَايَ إِلَيْكَ وُفُودِي، وَ بِكَ أَتَوَسَّـلُ إِلَىٰ رَبِّي فِي بُلُوغِ مَقْصُودِي، وَ أَشْهَدُ أَنَّ الْمُتَوَسِّـلَ بِكَ غَيْرُ خَائِبٍ، وَ الطَّالِبَ بِكَ عَنْ مَعْرِفَةٍ غَيْرُ مَرْدُودٍ إِلَّا بِقَضَاءِ حَوَائِجِهِ، فَكُنْ لِي شَفِيعا إِلَى اللهِ رَبِّكَ وَ رَبِّي فِي قَضَـاءِ حَوَائِجِي، وَ تَيْسِـيرِ أُمُورِي، وَ كَشْـفِ شِـدَّتِي، وَ غُفْرَانِ ذَنْبِي، وَ سَعَةِ رِزْقِي، وَ تَطْوِيلِ عُمْرِي، وَ إِعْطَاءِ سُؤْلِي فِي آخِرَتِي وَ دُنْيَايَ.

O Allah, damn those who killed the Commander of the Faithful! O Allah, damn those who killed al-Ḥasan and al-Ḥusayn! O Allah, damn those who killed the Imams.

اَللّٰهُمَّ الْعَنْ قَتَلَةَ أَمِيرِ الْمُؤْمِنِينَ، اَللّٰهُمَّ الْعَنْ قَتَلَةَ الْحَسَـنِ وَ الْحُسَيْنِ، اَللّٰهُمَّ الْعَنْ قَتَلَةَ الْأَئِمَّةِ وَ عَذِّبْهُمْ عَذَابًا أَلِيمًا

لَا تُعَذِّبُهُ أَحَدًا مِنَ الْعَالَمِينَ، عَذَابًا كَثِيرًا لَا انْقِطَاعَ لَهُ وَ لَا أَجَلَ وَ لَا أَمَدَ، بِمَا شَاقُّوا وُلَاةَ أَمْرِكَ، وَ أَعِدَّ لَهُمْ عَذَابًا لَمْ تُحِلَّهُ بِأَحَدٍ مِنْ خَلْقِكَ.

Punish them with such painful punishment as You do not mete out to any of the world's creatures, a punishment that is manifold, unceasing, and unlimited by term and duration, for their defiance of Your vicegerents. Prepare for them such punishment as You would not inflict on any other of Your creatures!

اَللّٰهُمَّ وَ أَدْخِلْ عَلىٰ قَتَلَةِ أَنْصَارِ رَسُولِكَ، وَ عَلىٰ قَتَلَةِ أَمِيرِ الْمُؤْمِنِينَ، وَ عَلىٰ قَتَلَةِ الْحَسَنِ وَ الْحُسَيْنِ، وَ عَلىٰ قَتَلَةِ أَنْصَارِ الْحَسَنِ وَ الْحُسَيْنِ، وَ قَتَلَةِ مَنْ قُتِلَ فِي وِلَايَةِ آلِ مُحَمَّدٍ أَجْمَعِينَ، عَذَابًا أَلِيمًا مُضَاعَفًا فِي أَسْفَلِ دَرْكٍ مِنَ الْجَحِيمِ، لَا يُخَفَّفُ عَنْهُمُ الْعَذَابُ وَ هُمْ فِيهِ مُبْلِسُونَ مَلْعُونُونَ، نَاكِسُوا رُؤُوسِهِمْ عِنْدَ رَبِّهِمْ، قَدْ عَايَنُوا النَّدَامَةَ وَ الْخِزْيَ الطَّوِيلَ لِقَتْلِهِمْ عِتْرَةَ أَنْبِيَائِكَ وَ رُسُلِكَ وَ أَتْبَاعَهُمْ مِنْ عِبَادِكَ الصَّالِحِينَ.

O Allah, mete out to the guilty who killed helpers of Your Apostle, killed the Commander of the Faithful, killed al-Ḥasan and al-Ḥusayn, killed the supporters of al-Ḥasan and al-Ḥusayn, and killed those who were slain for the sake of friendship with the Family of Muḥammad, a painful and manifold punishment in the lowest reach of hell, a punishment that is ever undiminished, wherein they remain despondent and cursed, their heads downcast before their Lord, having experienced regret and abiding disgrace for having murdered the progeny of Your prophets and apostles and Your righteous servants from amongst their followers!

اَللّٰهُمَّ الْعَنْهُمْ فِي مُسْتَسِرِّ السِّرِّ وَ ظَاهِرِ الْعَلَانِيَةِ فِي أَرْضِكَ وَ سَمَائِكَ.

O Allah, damn them in the hidden and secret, and in the open and manifest quarters of Your earth and heaven!

اَللّٰهُمَّ اجْعَلْ لِي قَدَمَ صِدْقٍ فِي أَوْلِيَائِكَ، وَ حَبِّبْ إِلَيَّ مَشَاهِدَهُمْ وَ مُسْتَقَرَّهُمْ حَتّىٰ تُلْحِقَنِي بِهِمْ، وَ تَجْعَلَنِي لَهُمْ تَبَعًا

O Allah, assign me a worthy standing with Your *awliyā* and endear their shrines and abodes to me until You join me with them and make me follow them in the world and

the Hereafter, O most merciful of the merciful!	فِي الدُّنْيَا وَ الْآخِرَةِ يَا أَرْحَمَ الرَّاحِمِينَ.

Ziyarah of Imam al-Ḥusayn (ʿa)

Then kiss the *ḍarīḥ* and facing in the direction of the shrine of Imam al-Ḥusayn (ʿ*a*), with the back towards the *qiblah*, say,

Peace be to you, O Abū ʿAbdillāh! Peace be to you, O son of the Apostle of Allah! Peace be to you, O son of the Commander of the Faithful! Peace be to you, O son of Fāṭimah Zahrā, the mistress of the world's womankind Peace be to you, O father of the Imams, the guides and the rightly-guided ones! Peace be to you, O martyr fallen on the battlefield, for whom the tears flow! Peace be to you, O subject of the persistent and unfading tragedy!	اَلسَّـــلَامُ عَلَيْكَ يَا أَبَا عَبْدِ اللهِ، اَلسَّلَامُ عَلَيْكَ يَا ابْنَ رَسُولِ اللهِ، اَلسَّلَامُ عَلَيْكَ يَا ابْنَ أَمِيرِ الْمُؤْمِنِينَ، اَلسَّـــلَامُ عَلَيْكَ يَا ابْنَ فَاطِمَةَ الزَّهْرَاءِ سَيِّدَةِ نِسَاءِ الْعَالَمِينَ، اَلسَّـــلَامُ عَلَيْكَ يَا أَبَا الْأَئِمَّـــةِ الْهَادِينَ الْمَهْدِيِّـــينَ، اَلسَّـــلَامُ عَلَيْـــكَ يَا صَرِيعَ الدَّمْعَـــةِ السَّـــاكِبَةِ، اَلسَّـــلَامُ عَلَيْكَ يَا صَاحِبَ الْمُصِيبَةِ الرَّاتِبَةِ،
Peace be to you and to your grandfather and your father! Peace be to you, your mother and your brother! Peace be to you and to the Imams of your descent and your sons!	اَلسَّلَامُ عَلَيْكَ وَعَلَىٰ جَدِّكَ وَأَبِيكَ، اَلسَّلَامُ عَلَيْـــكَ وَ عَلَىٰ أُمِّكَ وَ أَخِيكَ، اَلسَّـــلَامُ عَلَيْكَ وَ عَلَى الْأَئِمَّةِ مِنْ ذُرِّيَّتِكَ وَ بَنِيكَ،
I testify that Allah imbued the earth with fragrance by virtue of your blood. He made the Scripture explicit through you, and made you, your father, grandfather, brother and sons an object lesson for those who possess intellect.	أَشْـــهَدُ لَقَدْ طَيَّبَ اللهُ بِـــكَ التُّرَابَ، وَ أَوْضَحَ بِكَ الْكِتَـــابَ، وَ جَعَلَكَ وَ أَبَاكَ وَ جَـــدَّكَ وَ أَخَاكَ وَ بَنِيـــكَ عِبْرَةً لِأُولِي الْأَلْبَابِ،
O son of the blessed and immaculate ones, who stand next to	يَا ابْنَ الْمَيَامِينِ الْأَطْيَابِ التَّالِينَ الْكِتَابَ،

the Scripture! I address my greeting of "Peace" to you. May Allah's blessings and peace be on you, and may He make the hearts of a part of the people fond of you! Not disappointed are those who cling to you and take refuge in you.	وَجَّهْتُ سَــلَامِي إِلَيْــكَ، صَلَوَاتُ اللهِ وَ سَــلَامُهُ عَلَيْكَ، وَ جَعَــلَ أَفْئِدَةً مِنَ النَّــاسِ تَهْــوِي إِلَيْكَ، مَا خَــابَ مَنْ تَمَسَّكَ بِكَ وَ لَجَأَ إِلَيْكَ.

Then moving towards the feet of the grave, stand there and say,

Peace be to the progenitor of all the Imams, the dedicated friend of the Prophet and his exclusive brother! Peace be to the leader of religion and faith, the Word of the All-beneficent! Peace be to the Scales of deeds, the changer of states, the sword of the Majestic Lord, the server-host of the clear and cold fount of Salsabīl!	اَلسَّــلَامُ عَلَىٰ أَبِي الْأَئِمَّــةِ، وَ خَلِيــلِ النُّبُوَّةِ، وَ الْمَخْصُوصِ بِالْأُخُوَّةِ. اَلسَّلَامُ عَلَىٰ يَعْسُــوبِ الدِّينِ وَ الْإِيمَانِ وَ كَلِمَةِ الرَّحْمَنِ. اَلسَّلَامُ عَلَىٰ مِيزَانِ الْأَعْمَالِ، وَ مُقَلِّبِ الْأَحْوَالِ، وَ سَيْفِ ذِي الْجَلَالِ، وَ سَاقِي السَّلْسَبِيلِ الزُّلَالِ.
Peace be to 'the righteous one among the faithful,' heir to the knowledge of the prophets, and judge on the Day of Retribution! Peace be to the tree of Godfearing and hearer of [the Prophet's] secret and intimate discourses!	اَلسَّــلَامُ عَلَىٰ صَالِحِ الْمُؤْمِنِينَ، وَ وَارِثِ عِلْــمِ النَّبِيِّينَ، وَ الْحَاكِــمِ يَوْمَ الدِّينِ. اَلسَّلَامُ عَلَىٰ شَــجَرَةِ التَّقْوَىٰ، وَ سَامِعِ السِّرِّ وَ النَّجْوَىٰ.
Peace be to Allah's conclusive testament, His abundant blessing, and His crushing vengeance! Peace be to the clear path, the bright star, the benign Imam, and the kindler of the torch (of guidance in the hearts), and may the mercy of Allah and His blessings be upon you!	اَلسَّلَامُ عَلَىٰ حُجَّةِ اللهِ الْبَالِغَةِ، وَ نِعْمَتِهِ السَّابِغَةِ، وَ نِقْمَتِهِ الدَّامِغَةِ. اَلسَّلَامُ عَلَى الصِّرَاطِ الْوَاضِــحِ، وَ النَّجْمِ اللَّائِحِ، وَ الْإِمَــامِ النَّاصِحِ، وَ الزِّنَــادِ الْقَادِحِ، وَ رَحْمَةُ اللهِ وَ بَرَكَاتُهُ.

Then say,

O Allah, bless the Commander of the Faithful, ᶜAlī ibn Abī Ṭālib, brother of Your Prophet, his friend, helper, legatee, minister, custodian of his knowledge and repository of his secrets, the door of his wisdom and declarer of his proofs, the summoner to his *sharīᶜah* and his successor in his *ummah*, who often relieved the Prophet of his anguish, crushed the faithless, humiliated the wicked, and whom You assigned a station in relation to Your Prophet as Aaron held in relation to Moses!

اَللّٰهُمَّ صَلِّ عَلٰى أَمِيرِ الْمُؤْمِنِينَ عَلِيِّ بْنِ
أَبِي طَالِبٍ، أَخِي نَبِيِّكَ وَ وَلِيِّهِ، وَ نَاصِرِهِ
وَ وَصِيِّهِ، وَ وَزِيرِهِ وَ مُسْتَوْدَعِ عِلْمِهِ، وَ
مَوْضِعِ سِرِّهِ، وَ بَابِ حِكْمَتِهِ، وَ النَّاطِقِ
بِحُجَّتِهِ، وَ الدَّاعِي إِلٰى شَرِيعَتِهِ، وَ خَلِيفَتِهِ
فِي أُمَّتِهِ، وَ مُفَرِّجِ الْكَرْبِ عَنْ وَجْهِهِ، وَ
قَاصِمِ الْكَفَرَةِ، وَ مُرْغِمِ الْفَجَرَةِ، اَلَّذِي
جَعَلْتَهُ مِنْ نَبِيِّكَ بِمَنْزِلَةِ هَارُونَ مِنْ
مُوسٰى،

O Allah, befriend those who befriend him and hate those who hate him, help those who help him and forsake those who forsake him. Damn those of the former and latter generations who regard him with enmity, and bless him with the best blessings that You have given to any of the legatees of Your prophets, O Lord of all the worlds!

اَللّٰهُمَّ وَالِ مَنْ وَالَاهُ، وَ عَادِ مَنْ عَادَاهُ،
وَ انْصُرْ مَنْ نَصَرَهُ، وَ اخْذُلْ مَنْ خَذَلَهُ،
وَ الْعَنْ مَنْ نَصَبَ لَهُ مِنَ الْأَوَّلِينَ وَ
الْآخِرِينَ، وَ صَلِّ عَلَيْهِ أَفْضَلَ مَا صَلَّيْتَ
عَلٰى أَحَدٍ مِنْ أَوْصِيَاءِ أَنْبِيَائِكَ، يَا رَبَّ
الْعَالَمِينَ!

Ziyarah of Adam and Noah (ʿa)

Then return to the head of the grave for *ziyārah* of Adam (ᶜ*a*) and Noah (ᶜ*a*). Then address Adam (ᶜ*a*) and say,

Peace be to you, O elect of Allah! Peace be to you, O beloved of Allah! Peace be to you, O prophet of Allah! Peace be to you, O trustee of Allah! Peace be

اَلسَّلَامُ عَلَيْكَ يَا صَفِيَّ اللّٰهِ، اَلسَّلَامُ
عَلَيْكَ يَا حَبِيبَ اللّٰهِ، اَلسَّلَامُ عَلَيْكَ
يَا نَبِيَّ اللّٰهِ، اَلسَّلَامُ عَلَيْكَ يَا أَمِينَ اللّٰهِ،

اَلسَّلاَمُ عَلَيْكَ يَا خَلِيفَةَ اللهِ فِي أَرْضِهِ، اَلسَّلاَمُ عَلَيْكَ يَا أَبَا الْبَشَرِ، اَلسَّلاَمُ عَلَيْكَ وَ عَلَىٰ رُوحِكَ وَ بَدَنِكَ، وَ عَلَى الطَّاهِرِينَ مِنْ وُلْدِكَ وَ ذُرِّيَّتِكَ، وَ صَلَّى اللهُ عَلَيْكَ صَلاَةً لاَ يُحْصِيهَا إِلاَّ هُوَ، وَ رَحْمَةُ اللهِ وَ بَرَكَاتُهُ.

to you, O vicegerent of Allah on His earth!

Peace be to you, O father of humankind! Peace be to you, to your spirit and body, and to the immaculate ones of your progeny and descent. May Allah bless you with a blessing that cannot be compassed by anyone except Him, and may His mercy and bounties be upon you!

Then addressing Noah (ʿ*a*) say,

اَلسَّلاَمُ عَلَيْكَ يَا نَبِيَّ اللهِ، اَلسَّلاَمُ عَلَيْكَ يَا صَفِيَّ اللهِ، اَلسَّلاَمُ عَلَيْكَ يَا وَلِيَّ اللهِ، اَلسَّلاَمُ عَلَيْكَ يَا حَبِيبَ اللهِ، اَلسَّلاَمُ عَلَيْكَ يَا شَيْخَ الْمُرْسَلِينَ،

Peace be to you, O prophet of Allah! Peace be to you, O elect of Allah! Peace be to you, O *walī* of Allah! Peace be to you, O beloved of Allah! Peace be to you, O patriarch of the apostles!

اَلسَّلاَمُ عَلَيْكَ يَا أَمِينَ اللهِ فِي أَرْضِهِ، صَلَوَاتُ اللهِ وَ سَلاَمُهُ عَلَيْكَ وَ عَلَىٰ رُوحِكَ وَ بَدَنِكَ، وَ عَلَى الطَّاهِرِينَ مِنْ وُلْدِكَ، وَ رَحْمَةُ اللهِ وَ بَرَكَاتُهُ.

Peace be to you, O trustee of Allah on His earth! May Allah's blessings and His peace be upon you, your spirit, your body and the immaculate ones of your progeny. May Allah's mercy and His bounties be upon you!

Then offer six *rakʿahs* of prayer, two for the Commander of the Faithful (ʿ*a*) with Sūrat al-Raḥmān after al-Fātiḥah in the first and Sūrat Yā Sīn after al-Fātiḥah in the second *rakʿah*. After the prayer, perform the *tasbīḥ* of Ḥaḍrat Fāṭimah Zahrā (ʿ*a*) and plead to Allah for forgiveness and supplicate for your needs, then say,

اَللّٰهُمَّ إِنِّي صَلَّيْتُ هَاتَيْنِ الرَّكْعَتَيْنِ هَدِيَّةً مِنِّي إِلَىٰ سَيِّدِي وَ مَوْلاَيَ، وَلِيِّكَ

O Allah, I have offered these two *rakʿahs* as a gift from me to my master and guardian, Your *walī* and brother of Your Apostle, the

Commander of the Faithful and Chief of the Legatees ʿAlī ibn Abī Ṭālib, may Allah's blessings be upon him and his progeny!

وَ أَخِي رَسُولِكَ، أَمِيرِ الْمُؤْمِنِينَ وَ سَيِّدِ الْوَصِيِّينَ عَلِيِّ بْنِ أَبِي طَالِبٍ صَلَوَاتُ اللهِ عَلَيْهِ وَ عَلَى آلِهِ.

O Allah, bless Muḥammad and the Family of Muḥammad and accept it from me, and grant me for it a reward that is granted to the virtuous!

اَللّٰهُمَّ فَصَلِّ عَلَى مُحَمَّدٍ وَ آلِ مُحَمَّدٍ، وَ تَقَبَّلْهَا مِنِّي وَ اجْزِنِي عَلَى ذٰلِكَ جَزَاءَ الْمُحْسِنِينَ.

O Allah, I have prayed to You, bowed and prostrated—You are one and have no partner—for prayer, bowing and prostrating is not permissible for anyone except before You, for You are Allah and there is no god besides You!

اَللّٰهُمَّ لَكَ صَلَّيْتُ وَ لَكَ رَكَعْتُ وَ لَكَ سَجَدْتُ، وَحْدَكَ لَا شَرِيكَ لَكَ، لِأَنَّهُ لَا تَكُونُ الصَّلَاةُ وَ الرُّكُوعُ وَ السُّجُودُ إِلَّا لَكَ، لِأَنَّكَ أَنْتَ اللهُ لَا إِلٰهَ إِلَّا أَنْتَ.

O Allah, bless Muḥammad and the Family of Muḥammad and accept my *ziyārah* and grant my request for the sake of Muḥammad and his immaculate Family!

اَللّٰهُمَّ صَلِّ عَلَى مُحَمَّدٍ وَ آلِ مُحَمَّدٍ، وَ تَقَبَّلْ مِنِّي زِيَارَتِي، وَ أَعْطِنِي سُؤْلِي بِمُحَمَّدٍ وَ آلِهِ الطَّاهِرِينَ.

Then offer the remaining four *rakʿahs* as gift to Adam (*ʿa*) and Noah (*ʿa*) and make a prostration of thanksgiving and while prostrating say,

O Allah, I turn to You and take recourse in You and in You do I trust! O Allah, You are my trust and my hope, so suffice me with regard to that which concerns me and that which does not cause me concern and You know it better than me! Mighty are those who take refuge in You. Exalted is Your praise, and there is no god besides

اَللّٰهُمَّ إِلَيْكَ تَوَجَّهْتُ وَ بِكَ اعْتَصَمْتُ وَ عَلَيْكَ تَوَكَّلْتُ، اَللّٰهُمَّ أَنْتَ ثِقَتِي وَ رَجَائِي، فَاكْفِنِي مَا أَهَمَّنِي وَ مَا لَا يُهِمُّنِي وَ مَا أَنْتَ أَعْلَمُ بِهِ مِنِّي، عَزَّ جَارُكَ وَ جَلَّ ثَنَاؤُكَ وَ لَا إِلٰهَ غَيْرُكَ،

صَلِّ عَلٰى مُحَمَّدٍ وَ آلِ مُحَمَّدٍ وَ قَرِّبْ
فَرَجَهُمْ.

You! Bless Muḥammad and the Family of Muḥammad and hasten their relief!

Then laying your right cheek on the ground say,

اِرْحَمْ ذُلِّي بَيْنَ يَدَيْكَ، وَ تَضَرُّعِي إِلَيْكَ،
وَ وَحْشَتِي مِنَ النَّاسِ، وَ أُنْسِي بِكَ يَا
كَرِيمُ يَا كَرِيمُ يَا كَرِيمُ.

Have mercy on my weakness in front of You, my entreaties before You, my estrangement from people and my intimacy with You! O Magnanimous One! O Magnanimous One! O Magnanimous One!

Then laying the left cheek on the ground, say,

لَا إِلٰهَ إِلَّا اللهُ أَنْتَ رَبِّي حَقًّا حَقًّا،
سَجَدْتُ لَكَ يَا رَبِّ تَعَبُّدًا وَ رِقًّا، اَللّٰهُمَّ
إِنَّ عَمَلِي ضَعِيفٌ فَضَاعِفْهُ لِي يَا كَرِيمُ
يَا كَرِيمُ يَا كَرِيمُ.

There is no god besides You, my Lord, in all truth! I prostrate to You as a servant and slave! O Allah, my works are trivial, so enhance them for me, O Magnanimous One! O Magnanimous One! O Magnanimous One!

Then prostrate again and say 100 times "*Shukran!*" Exert yourself in making supplication, for this is the place for making petitions. Plead for forgiveness, as this is also the place where sins are forgiven. Ask God Almighty to fulfil your needs, as this is the place where supplications are answered and requests are granted.

Supplication to be Said After the Prayers

Sayyid Ibn Ṭāwūs and other scholars remind that as long as one is in Najaf, one should recite the following supplication after prayers, obligatory and supererogatory.[1]

اَللّٰهُمَّ لَا بُدَّ مِنْ أَمْرِكَ، وَ لَا بُدَّ مِنْ
قَدَرِكَ، وَ لَا بُدَّ مِنْ قَضَائِكَ، وَ لَا حَوْلَ

O Allah, Your edicts are inescapable, Your ordainments are inevitable, Your decrees are unavoida-

[1] *Tahdhīb*, iii, 93, h 25. Ṭūsī's *Miṣbāḥ*, 567. *Iqbāl*, 178, whence *Biḥār*, xcv, 135, b 7, h 3. *Farḥat al-Gharī*, 66, whence *Biḥār*, xcvii, 269, b 4, h 12. Kafʿamī's *Miṣbāḥ*, 575.

ble, and there is no power or force except what derives from You!

وَ لَا قُوَّةَ إِلَّا بِكَ.

O Allah, whatever You may ordain and decide concerning us, give us the patience to surmount it and triumph over it, and make it the cause of our rising in Your estimation, enhancing in our virtues, merit, seniority, nobility, dignity, blessings, and honour, in this world and the Hereafter, and do no diminish our good works!

اَللّٰهُمَّ فَمَـــا قَضَيْتَ عَلَيْنَا مِنْ قَضَاءٍ، أَوْ
قَـــدَّرْتَ عَلَيْنَا مِنْ قَـــدَرٍ، فَأَعْطِنَا مَعَهُ
صَبْرًا يَقْهَـــرُهُ وَ يَدْمَغُـــهُ، وَ اجْعَلْهُ لَنَا
صَاعِدًا فِي رِضْوَانِكَ، يُنْمَىٰ فِي حَسَنَاتِنَا
وَ تَفْضِيلِنَا وَ سُؤْدَدِنَا وَ شَرَفِنَا وَ مَجْدِنَا وَ
نَعْمَائِنَا وَ كَرَامَتِنَا فِي الدُّنْيَا وَ الْآخِرَةِ، وَ
لَا تَنْقُصْ مِنْ حَسَنَاتِنَا.

O Allah, whatever gifts You have granted us, whatever advantage You bestowed on us, whatever honour You give us, also give us, with it, a gratitude that prevails over it and make it the cause of our rising in Your approval, enhancing in our virtues and in our merit, seniority, blessings and honour in this world and the Hereafter, and do no make it a cause of hubris and pride, temptation and abominable conduct, punishment and disgrace in the world and the Hereafter! O Allah, protect us from the pitfalls of speech, from ending up in an evil station with our works weighing light in the scales (of Your justice)!

اَللّٰهُـــمَّ وَ مَـــا أَعْطَيْتَنَا مِـــنْ عَطَاءٍ، أَوْ
فَضَّلْتَنَا بِهِ مِنْ فَضِيلَةٍ، أَوْ أَكْرَمْتَنَا بِهِ
مِنْ كَرَامَةٍ، فَأَعْطِنَا مَعَهُ شُكْرًا يَقْهَرُهُ وَ
يَدْمَغُهُ، وَ اجْعَلْهُ لَنَا صَاعِدًا فِي رِضْوَانِكَ
وَ فِي حَسَـــنَاتِنَا وَ سُـــؤْدَدِنَا وَ شَرَفِنَا وَ
نَعْمَائِكَ وَ كَرَامَتِكَ فِي الدُّنْيَا وَ الْآخِرَةِ،
وَ لَا تَجْعَلْهُ لَنَا أَشَرًا وَ لَا بَطَرًا وَ لَا فِتْنَةً
وَ لَا مَقْتًا وَ لَا عَذَابًا وَ لَا خِزْيًا فِي الدُّنْيَا
وَ الْآخِرَةِ. اَللّٰهُـــمَّ إِنَّا نَعُوذُ بِكَ مِنْ عَثْرَةِ
اللِّسَانِ وَ سُوءِ الْمَقَامِ وَ خِفَّةِ الْمِيزَانِ.

O Allah, bless Muḥammad and the Family of Muḥammad, and join us to our good works after death, do not show us our deeds

اَللّٰهُمَّ صَلِّ عَلَىٰ مُحَمَّدٍ وَ آلِ مُحَمَّدٍ، وَ لَقِّنَا
حَسَـــنَاتِنَا فِي الْمَمَاتِ، وَ لَا تُرِنَا أَعْمَالَنَا

as a cause of regret, do not humiliate us at Your judgement and do not put us to shame due to our misdeeds on the day of our encounter with You, and make our hearts remember You—not forgetting You—fearing You as if they see You, until the day we meet You!

حَسَرَاتٍ، وَ لَا تُخْزِنَا عِنْدَ قَضَائِكَ، وَ
لَا تَفْضَحْنَا بِسَيِّئَاتِنَا يَوْمَ نَلْقَاكَ، وَ
اجْعَلْ قُلُوبَنَا تَذْكُرُكَ وَ لَا تَنْسَاكَ، وَ
تَخْشَاكَ كَأَنَّهَا تَرَاكَ حَتَّىٰ نَلْقَاكَ،

Bless Muḥammad and the Family of Muḥammad and change our vices into virtues, and make our virtuous deeds into degrees, our degrees into lofty abodes, and our lofty abodes into the loftiest of stations! O Allah, expand the provision of the needy among us, with the bountifulness that You have prescribed for Your own self.

وَ صَلِّ عَلَىٰ مُحَمَّدٍ وَ آلِ مُحَمَّدٍ، وَ بَدِّلْ
سَيِّئَاتِنَا حَسَنَاتٍ، وَ اجْعَلْ حَسَنَاتِنَا
دَرَجَاتٍ، وَ اجْعَلْ دَرَجَاتِنَا غُرُفَاتٍ، وَ
اجْعَلْ غُرُفَاتِنَا عَالِيَاتٍ. اَللّٰهُمَّ وَ أَوْسِعْ
لِفَقِيرِنَا مِنْ سَعَةِ مَا قَضَيْتَ عَلَىٰ نَفْسِكَ.

O Allah, bless Muḥammad and the Family of Muḥammad and favour us with guidance as long as You make us survive, and with honour as long as You keep us alive, with pardon (and honour) when You make us die, with protection in what remains of our lives, and with blessing in what You provide us, and with help in carrying out the obligations You have laid on us, with steadfastness in bearing what You have laid on us, and do not punish us for the wrongs we have done, do not judge us by our ignorance, and do not lead us in gradual steps towards perdition through our mistakes, and establish the best of what we declare in our hearts.

اَللّٰهُمَّ صَلِّ عَلَىٰ مُحَمَّدٍ وَ آلِ مُحَمَّدٍ، وَ مُنَّ
عَلَيْنَا بِالْهُدَىٰ مَا أَبْقَيْتَنَا، وَ الْكَرَامَةِ
مَا أَحْيَيْتَنَا، وَ الْمَغْفِرَةِ [وَ الْكَرَامَةِ] إِذَا
تَوَفَّيْتَنَا، وَ الْحِفْظِ فِيمَا بَقِيَ مِنْ عُمْرِنَا،
وَ الْبَرَكَةِ فِيمَا رَزَقْتَنَا، وَ الْعَوْنِ عَلَىٰ مَا
حَمَّلْتَنَا، وَ الثَّبَاتِ عَلَىٰ مَا طَوَّقْتَنَا، وَ لَا
تُؤَاخِذْنَا بِظُلْمِنَا، وَ لَا تُقَايِسْنَا بِجَهْلِنَا،
وَ لَا تَسْتَدْرِجْنَا بِخَطَايَانَا، وَ اجْعَلْ
أَحْسَنَ مَا نَقُولُ ثَابِتًا فِي قُلُوبِنَا ،

Make us eminent with You and lowly in our own eyes, grant us the benefit of what You have taught

وَ اجْعَلْنَا عُظَمَاءَ عِنْدَكَ وَ أَذِلَّةً فِي
أَنْفُسِنَا، وَ انْفَعْنَا بِمَا عَلَّمْتَنَا، وَ زِدْنَا

عِلْمًا نَافِعًا، وَ أَعُــوذُ بِكَ مِنْ قَلْبٍ لَا يَخْشَــعُ، وَ مِنْ عَيْنٍ لَا تَدْمَــعُ، وَ مِنْ صَلَاةٍ لَا تُقْبَلُ، أَجِرْنَا مِنْ سُــوءِ الْفِتَنِ يَا وَلِيَّ الدُّنْيَا وَ الْآخِرَةِ.	us and increase us in beneficial knowledge! I take refuge in You from a heart that is not humble, from an eye that does not shed tears, from a prayer that is not received, and save us from evil temptations, O my Guardian in the world and the Hereafter!

Sayyid ibn Ṭāwūs in *Miṣbāḥ al-Zā'ir* cites another supplication, beginning with the words "*Yâ Allāhu, yâ Allāhu yâ Allāh! Yā mujība da*c*watil muḍṭarrīn,*" which it is *mustaḥab* to recite after the *ziyārah* of the Commander of the Faithful (c*a*).[1] This, however, is the same as the supplication of Ṣafwān, known as *Du*c*ā* c*Alqamah,* and, God willing, will be cited after the *ziyārah* of cĀshūrā' (p. 349).

Ziyarah of Imam Ḥusayn's Head

It is *mustḥab* to perform the *ziyārah* of Imam al-Ḥusayn's blessed head by the tomb of the Commander of the Faithful (c*a*), and a section has been assigned to this topic in the *Wasā'il* and *Mustadrak.*[2] The *Mustadrak*, citing Muḥammad ibn al-Mashhadī's *Mazār*, reports[3] that Imam Jacfar al-Ṣādiq (c*a*) performed the *ziyārah* of Imam al-Ḥusayn's head by the grave of the Commander of the Faithful (c*a*), where he offered also four *rak*c*ahs* of prayer. That *ziyārah* is as follows.

اَلسَّلَامُ عَلَيْكَ يَا ابْنَ رَسُولِ اللهِ، اَلسَّلَامُ عَلَيْكَ يَا ابْنَ أَمِيرِ الْمُؤْمِنِينَ، اَلسَّـــلَامُ عَلَيْكَ يَا ابْنَ الصِّدِّيقَةِ الطَّاهِرَةِ سَيِّدَةِ نِسَاءِ الْعَالَمِينَ، اَلسَّلَامُ عَلَيْكَ يَا مَوْلَايَ يَا أَبَا عَبْدِ اللهِ وَ رَحْمَـــةُ اللهِ وَ بَرَكَاتُهُ.	Peace be to you, O son of the Apostle of Allah! Peace be to you, O son of the Commander of the Faithful! Peace be to you, O son of the truthful and the immaculate Lady, the mistress of the world's womankind! Peace be to you, O my master, O Abū cAbdillāh, and may Allah's mercy and His bless-

1 Ṭūsī's *Miṣbāḥ*, 777, whence *Biḥār*, xcviii, 296, b 24, h 3. *Biḥār*, xcvii, 308, 352, b 4, h 23 from Ibn Ṭāwūs. Kafcamī's *Miṣbāḥ*, 485. *Balad*, 271.

2 *Wasā'il*, xiv, 298-403, b 32, h 19452-19462. *Mustadrak*, x, 225-227, b 23, h. 11903/1-11905/3.

3 *Muqni*c*ah*, 469, b 15. *Biḥār*, xcvii, 293, b 4, h. 19; xcviii, 256, b 18, h 40. *Mustadrak*, x, 226-227, b 23, h 11905/3.

ings be upon you!

I testify that You maintained the prayer, gave *zakāt*, bade what is right and forbade what is wrong, and followed the Scripture as is due, and waged *jihād* for the sake of Allah, a *jihād* that is worthy of Him, and You patiently bore all torments for His sake, expecting His reward, until your demise!

أَشْــهَدُ أَنَّكَ قَدْ أَقَمْتَ الصَّــلَاةَ، وَ آتَيْتَ الزَّكَاةَ، وَ أَمَــرْتَ بِالْمَعْرُوفِ، وَ نَهَيْتَ عَنِ الْمُنْكَرِ، وَ تَلَــوْتَ الْكِتَابَ حَقَّ تِلَاوَتِهِ، وَ جَاهَدْتَ فِي اللهِ حَقَّ جِهَادِهِ، وَ صَبَرْتَ عَلَى الْأَذَىٰ فِي جَنْبِهِ مُحْتَسِبًا حَتَّىٰ أَتَاكَ الْيَقِينُ،

I bear witness that those who opposed you and fought against you, and those who forsook you and slew you were the accursed ones, cursed by the tongue of the untaught Prophet, and those who made false accusations were losers. May Allah damn all those who wronged you from the former and the latter generations and may He mete out to them a twofold painful punishment!

وَ أَشْــهَدُ أَنَّ الَّذِينَ خَالَفُوكَ وَ حَارَبُوكَ وَ أَنَّ الَّذِينَ خَذَلُوكَ وَ الَّذِينَ قَتَلُوكَ مَلْعُونُونَ عَلَىٰ لِسَــانِ النَّبِيِّ الْأُمِّيِّ، وَ قَدْ خَابَ مَنِ افْــتَرَىٰ. لَعَنَ اللهُ الظَّالِمِــينَ لَكُمْ مِنَ الْأَوَّلِينَ وَ الْآخِرِيــنَ، وَ ضَاعَفَ عَلَيْهِمُ الْعَذَابَ الْأَلِيمَ.

O my master, O son of the Apostle of Allah! I have come to you as a pilgrim, knowing your rights, befriending your friends, hating your enemies, possessing insight of the guidance you hold with and of the error of those who opposed you! So intercede for me with your Lord!

أَتَيْتُكَ يَا مَوْلَايَ يَا ابْنَ رَسُولِ اللهِ زَائِرًا عَارِفًا بِحَقِّكَ، مُوَالِيًــا لِأَوْلِيَائِكَ، مُعَادِيًا لِأَعْدَائِكَ، مُسْتَبْصِرًا بِالْهُدَى الَّذِي أَنْتَ عَلَيْهِ، عَارِفًا بِضَلَالَةِ مَنْ خَالَفَكَ، فَاشْفَعْ لِي عِنْدَ رَبِّكَ.

It is appropriate to recite the same *ziyārah* at the Masjid Ḥannānah, as Shaykh Muḥammad b. al-Mas͟hhadī reports that Imam Jaᶜfar al-Ṣādiq (ᶜ*a*) performed this *ziyārah* at this mosque and offered four *rakᶜahs* in prayer.[1] Masjid Ḥannānah is one of the holy mosques of Najaf As͟hraf and there is a tradition that Imam al-Ḥusayn's head

1 *Biḥār*, xcvii, 283, 455, b 4, h 18, b 7, h 29; xcviii, 257, b 18, h 40.

is there.[1] Imam Ja^cfar al-Ṣādiq (*ᶜa*) is reported to have offered two *rakᶜahs* there, and when asked about the prayer he had performed, he replied, "This is the place where they had placed the head of my forefather al-Ḥusayn ibn ᶜAli (*ᶜa*) on returning from Karbalā, after which they carried it for ᶜUbayd Allah b. Ziyād."[2] The tradition reports that the Imam recommended that the following supplication be recited there:

O Allah, You see my place and hear my speech and nothing of my affairs is hidden from You. And how can what You have created and brought into existence be hidden from You? I have come to You seeking the intercession of Your Prophet, the Prophet of Mercy, and seeking the mediation of the Legatee of Your Apostle. I beseech You by them to make my feet steady and grant me guidance and forgiveness in the world and the Hereafter!

اَللّٰهُمَّ إِنَّكَ تَرَىٰ مَكَانِي، وَ تَسْمَعُ كَلاٰمِي،
وَ لاٰ يَخْفَىٰ عَلَيْـــكَ شَيْءٌ مِنْ أَمْرِى، وَ
كَيْفَ يَخْفَىٰ عَلَيْـــكَ مَا أَنْتَ مُكَوِّنُهُ وَ
بَارِئُهُ؟ وَ قَدْ جِئْتُكَ مُسْتَشْفِعًا بِنَبِيِّكَ
نَبِيِّ الرَّحْمَةِ، وَ مُتَوَسِّـــلًا بِوَصِيِّ رَسُولِكَ،
فَأَسْـــأَلُكَ بِهِمَا ثَبَاتَ الْقَدَمِ وَ الْهُدَىٰ وَ
الْمَغْفِرَةَ فِي الدُّنْيَا وَ الْآخِرَةِ.

The Second Ziyarah: Ziyarah Amin Allah

This famous *ziyārah* is known as "*Ziyārah Amīn Allāh.*" It possesses utmost reliability, and has been cited in all works on the subject of *mazār* and is cited as well by the *Miṣbaḥs*. ᶜAllamah Majlisī remarks that it is the best of *ziyārahs* from the viewpoint of content and *isnād*, and he recommends its regular recital in shrines of all the Imams.[3]

1 *Biḥār*, xcviii, 256, b 18, h 40.

2 *Biḥār*, xcvii, 281, b 4, h 18. *Mustadrak*, x, 403, b 86, h 12260/3.

3 In *Biḥār*, where ᶜAllāmah Majlisī cites this *ziyārah* from *Kāmil al-Ziyārāt* and *Farḥat al-Gharī*, he says that he has cited it repeatedly because of variant wordings and because it is one of the *ziyārahs* with the most reliable *isnād* (*min aṣaḥ al-ziyārāt sanadan wa aᶜammihā mawridan*), but makes no remark about its contents. However, in *Zād al-Maᶜād*, 265, he cites the *ziyārah* for the Prophet's birthday with the remark that it is the best of *ziyārahs* with respect to wording and meaning, and that it has been reported with very reliable *isnād*. Also in the same work, p. 301, he remarks about the longer *Ziyārah Jāmiᶜah* that it is the most complete of them. (Tr.)

This *ziyārah* has been reported[1] with reliable chains of transmission from Imam Muḥammad al-Bāqir (*ᶜa*) by Jābir b. ᶜAbd Allāh, who said that Imam Zayn al-ᶜĀbidīn (*ᶜa*) once visited the tomb of the Commander of the Faithful (*ᶜa*). There, he wept as he stood by the graveside and said,

اَلسَّلَامُ عَلَيْكَ يَا أَمِينَ اللهِ فِي أَرْضِهِ، وَ حُجَّتَهُ عَلَىٰ عِبَادِهِ، اَلسَّلَامُ عَلَيْكَ يَا أَمِيرَ الْمُؤْمِنِينَ،

Peace be to you, O Allah's trustee on His earth and His testament to His servants! Peace be to you, O Commander of the Faithful!

أَشْهَدُ أَنَّكَ جَاهَدْتَ فِي اللهِ حَقَّ جِهَادِهِ، وَ عَمِلْتَ بِكِتَابِهِ، وَ اتَّبَعْتَ سُنَنَ نَبِيِّهِ صَلَّى اللهُ عَلَيْهِ وَ آلِهِ حَتَّىٰ دَعَاكَ اللهُ إِلَىٰ جِوَارِهِ، فَقَبَضَكَ إِلَيْهِ بِاخْتِيَارِهِ، وَ أَلْزَمَ أَعْدَاءَكَ الْحُجَّةَ مَعَ مَا لَكَ مِنَ الْحُجَجِ الْبَالِغَةِ عَلَىٰ جَمِيعِ خَلْقِهِ. اَللّٰهُمَّ فَاجْعَلْ نَفْسِي مُطْمَئِنَّةً بِقَدَرِكَ، رَاضِيَةً بِقَضَائِكَ، مُولَعَةً بِذِكْرِكَ وَ دُعَائِكَ، مُحِبَّةً لِصَفْوَةِ أَوْلِيَائِكَ، مَحْبُوبَةً فِي أَرْضِكَ وَ سَمَائِكَ، صَابِرَةً عَلَىٰ نُزُولِ بَلَائِكَ، شَاكِرَةً لِفَوَاضِلِ نَعْمَائِكَ، ذَاكِرَةً لِسَوَابِغِ آلَائِكَ، مُشْتَاقَةً إِلَىٰ فَرْحَةِ لِقَائِكَ، مُتَزَوِّدَةً

I testify that you waged *jihād* for the sake of Allah, a *jihād* that is worthy of Him, and that you acted according to His Scripture and followed the *sunnah* of His Prophet, may Allah bless him and his Family, until Allah summoned you to His vicinage, taking your soul by His own will and choice, binding your enemies with an evidence along with the conclusive testimonies that you hold against all His creatures! O Allah, let my soul be at rest in Your ordainments; may I be pleased with Your decrees, cherishing Your remembrance and eager to supplicate You. Make me affectionate towards the elect of Your *awliyā*, grant me to be well-loved on Your earth and in Your heaven, patient in undergoing Your tests, grateful for Your abundant blessings, mindful of Your plentiful bounties, eager for the joy of meeting You, while cultivating piety as a provision for the day of Your retribution, walking

[1] *Kāmil al-Ziyārāṭ*, 39, whence *Biḥār*, xcvii, 264, b 4, h 2. Ṭūsī's *Miṣbāḥ*, 738, whence *Wasā'il*, xiv, 395, b 30, h 19451. *Iqbāl*, 470. *Farḥat al-Gharī*, 40, 43, whence *Biḥār*, xcvii, 266, b 4, h 9. Kafᶜamī's *Miṣbāḥ*, 480. *Balad*, 295.

in the ways of Your *awliyā*, avoiding the traits of Your enemies, and disengaging myself from mundane occupations to praise and extol You!

التَّقْوَىٰ لِيَوْمِ جَزَائِكَ، مُسْتَنَّةً بِسُنَنِ أَوْلِيَائِكَ، مُفَارِقَةً لِأَخْلَاقِ أَعْدَائِكَ، مَشْغُولَةً عَنِ الدُّنْيَا بِحَمْدِكَ وَ ثَنَائِكَ.

Then laying his blessed cheek on the grave, he said,

O Allah, the hearts of the humble long for You. The pathways of the eager lead them to You. The banners of Your seekers are manifest; the hearts of Your gnostics are full of awe; the voices of the supplicants rise to You; the doors of acceptance lie open for them; the calls of those who implore You secretly are heard; the repentance of those who turn to You is accepted; the tears of those who weep for the fear of You are beheld with mercy; Your succour is ready for those who seek Your succour; Your promises to Your servants are fulfilled; the stumbles of those who seek Your pardon are forgiven; the works of those who strive for You are safe with You; Your provisions to the creatures are coming down from You and Your further gifts keep on reaching them; the sins of those who plead to You for forgiveness are forgiven; the needs of Your creatures stand fulfilled with You; the awards of those who ask of You are plentiful and further

اَللّٰهُمَّ إِنَّ قُلُوبَ الْمُخْبِتِينَ إِلَيْكَ وَالِهَةٌ، وَ سُبُلَ الرَّاغِبِينَ إِلَيْكَ شَارِعَةٌ، وَ أَعْلَامَ الْقَاصِدِينَ إِلَيْكَ وَاضِحَةٌ، وَ أَفْئِدَةَ الْعَارِفِينَ مِنْكَ فَازِعَةٌ، وَ أَصْوَاتَ الدَّاعِينَ إِلَيْكَ صَاعِدَةٌ، وَ أَبْوَابَ الْإِجَابَةِ لَهُمْ مُفَتَّحَةٌ، وَ دَعْوَةَ مَنْ نَاجَاكَ مُسْتَجَابَةٌ، وَ تَوْبَةَ مَنْ أَنَابَ إِلَيْكَ مَقْبُولَةٌ، وَ عَبْرَةَ مَنْ بَكَىٰ مِنْ خَوْفِكَ مَرْحُومَةٌ، وَ الْإِغَاثَةَ لِمَنِ اسْتَغَاثَ بِكَ مَوْجُودَةٌ، وَ الْإِعَانَةَ لِمَنِ اسْتَعَانَ بِكَ مَبْذُولَةٌ، وَ عِدَاتِكَ لِعِبَادِكَ مُنْجَزَةٌ، وَ زَلَلَ مَنِ اسْتَقَالَكَ مُقَالَةٌ، وَ أَعْمَالَ الْعَامِلِينَ لَدَيْكَ مَحْفُوظَةٌ، وَ أَرْزَاقَكَ إِلَى الْخَلَائِقِ مِنْ لَدُنْكَ نَازِلَةٌ، وَ عَوَائِدَ الْمَزِيدِ إِلَيْهِمْ وَاصِلَةٌ، وَ ذُنُوبَ الْمُسْتَغْفِرِينَ مَغْفُورَةٌ، وَ حَوَائِجَ خَلْقِكَ عِنْدَكَ مَقْضِيَّةٌ، وَ جَوَائِزَ السَّائِلِينَ عِنْدَكَ مُوَفَّرَةٌ، وَ عَوَائِدَ الْمَزِيدِ مُتَوَاتِرَةٌ، وَ

gifts are perpetual; the tables are ready for those who desire to be fed and the springs are brimful for the thirsty!

مَوَائِدَ الْمُسْتَطْعِمِينَ مُعَدَّةٌ، وَ مَنَاهِلَ الظِّمَاءِ مُتْرَعَةٌ.

O Allah, answer my supplication, receive my eulogy and join me with my *awliyā*, by the right of Muḥammad, ʿAlī, Fāṭimah, al-Ḥasan and al-Ḥusayn. You are indeed the patron of my blessings, the goal of my hopes, and the aim of my expectations in this temporary abode and the permanent one!

اَللّٰهُمَّ فَاسْتَجِبْ دُعَائِى، وَ اقْبَلْ ثَنَائِى، وَ اجْمَعْ بَيْنِى وَ بَيْنَ أَوْلِيَائِى، بِحَقِّ مُحَمَّدٍ وَ عَلِيٍّ وَ فَاطِمَةَ وَ الْحَسَنِ وَ الْحُسَيْنِ، إِنَّكَ وَلِيُّ نَعْمَائِى، وَ مُنْتَهَىٰ مُنَاىَ، وَ غَايَةُ رَجَائِى فِى مُنْقَلَبِى وَ مَثْوَاىَ.

The following passage occurs in the *Kāmil al-Ziyārāt* following the text above.[1]

You are my God, my Master and Guardian! Forgive our friends, hold back our enemies, and distract them from tormenting us! Cause the word of truth to prevail, and make it uppermost. Nullify the word of falsehood and make it the lowermost! Indeed, You have power over all things!

أَنْتَ إِلٰهِى وَ سَيِّدِى وَ مَوْلَاىَ، اِغْفِرْ لِأَوْلِيَائِنَا، وَ كُفَّ عَنَّا أَعْدَاءَنَا، وَ اشْغَلْهُمْ عَنْ أَذَانَا، وَ أَظْهِرْ كَلِمَةَ الْحَقِّ وَ اجْعَلْهَا الْعُلْيَا، وَ أَدْحِضْ كَلِمَةَ الْبَاطِلِ وَ اجْعَلْهَا السُّفْلَىٰ، إِنَّكَ عَلَىٰ كُلِّ شَىْءٍ قَدِيرٌ.

Then Imam Muḥammad al-Bāqir (ʿa) said, "Should any of our followers recite this *ziyārah* and supplication by the tomb of the Commander of the Faithful (ʿa) or by the grave of any of the Imams (ʿa), God Almighty will cause that *ziyārah* and supplication to be taken up in an epistle of light and set the seal of the Prophet Muḥammad (ṣ) upon it, preserving it until it is delivered to the Qāʾim of the Family of Muḥammad (ʿa), who will welcome its author with honour, greetings and good news, God Almighty willing."

This sublime *ziyārah* is considered a general one, that is, for all occasions. It is also one of special *ziyārahs* for the Festival day of Ghadīr,[2] as well as a 'common' *ziyārah*, that is, one which can be re-

---

[1]   *Kāmil al-Ziyārāt*, 41.

[2]   In Ṭūsī's *Miṣbāḥ*, 738, it is cited as a *ziyārah* for the Day of Ghadīr.

cited in the shrine of any Imam.

The Third Ziyarah

Sayyid ᶜAbd al-Karīm ibn Ṭāwūs[1] cites a report of Ṣafwān b. Mihrān al-Jammāl, who states, "When we reached Kūfah in the company of Imam Jaᶜfar al-Ṣādiq (ᶜ*a*), who was on his way to meet Abū Jaᶜfar al-Manṣūr, he said to me, 'Ṣafwān, make the camel kneel down, for this is the place of the grave of my ancestor, the Commander of the Faithful (ᶜ*a*).' Then he dismounted, took a bath, changed his clothes and bared his feet. Then he said to me, 'Do as I am doing.' Then, as he set out towards the hillocks of Najaf, he said to me, 'Take short steps and lower your head, for indeed for every step that you take there will be written for you a hundred thousand good deeds and a hundred thousand of your sins will be forgiven. Your station with God will be exalted by a hundred thousand degrees, and a hundred thousand of your needs will be fulfilled. A reward will be written for you equal to that of every saint and every martyr who is slain.'

"He walked ahead and I followed him. We went on peacefully, in a dignified manner, glorifying God and declaring His holiness and oneness, until we reached the hillocks. There, he stopped and looked to the right and left and drew a line on the ground with his staff. Then he said to me, 'Look around.' I made a search and found the traces of the grave. Then, as tears streamed down his blessed cheeks, he said, *'Innā lillāhi wa innā ilayhi rājiᶜūn!'* Then he said,

Peace be to you, O pious and Godwary legatee [of the Apostle of Allah]! Peace be to you, O Great Tiding! Peace be to you, O truthful and rightly-guided one! Peace be to you, O pious and immaculate one! Peace be to you, O legatee of the Apostle of the Lord of all the worlds! Peace be to you, O chosen one of Allah over all the creation!	اَلسَّـــلَامُ عَلَيْكَ أَيُّهَا الْوَصِيُّ الْبَرُّ التَّقِيُّ، اَلسَّلَامُ عَلَيْكَ أَيُّهَا النَّبَأُ الْعَظِيمُ، اَلسَّلَامُ عَلَيْكَ أَيُّهَا الصِّدِّيقُ الرَّشِـيدُ، اَلسَّـلَامُ عَلَيْكَ أَيُّهَا الْبَرُّ الزَّكِيُّ، اَلسَّلَامُ عَلَيْكَ يَا وَصِيَّ رَسُولِ رَبِّ الْعَالَمِينَ، اَلسَّلَامُ عَلَيْكَ يَا خِيَرَةَ اللهِ عَلَى الْخَلْقِ أَجْمَعِينَ،

1 *Farḥat al-Gharī*, 94, whence *Biḥār*, vol. 97, 279, b 4, h 15. *Al-Mazār al-Kabīr*, 240-241. *Irshād al-Qulūb*, ii, 441.

أَشْهَدُ أَنَّكَ حَبِيبُ اللهِ وَ خَاصَّةُ اللهِ
وَ خَالِصَتُهُ، اَلسَّلَامُ عَلَيْكَ يَا وَلِيَّ اللهِ
وَ مَوْضِعَ سِرِّهِ وَ عَيْبَةَ عِلْمِهِ وَ خَازِنَ
وَحْيِهِ.

I testify that you are the beloved of Allah and His exclusive and dedicated friend. Peace be to you, O *walī* of Allah, custodian of His secrets, bearer of His knowledge and preserver of His revelations!

Then clasping the grave, he said,

بِأَبِي أَنْتَ وَ أُمِّي يَا أَمِيرَ الْمُؤْمِنِينَ، بِأَبِي
أَنْتَ وَ أُمِّي يَا حُجَّةَ الْخِصَامِ، بِأَبِي أَنْتَ
وَ أُمِّي يَا بَابَ الْمَقَامِ، بِأَبِي أَنْتَ وَ أُمِّي يَا
نُورَ اللهِ التَّامَّ،

O Commander of the Faithful, you are dearer to me than my parents! O proof against the adversaries, you are dearer to me than my parents! O door to Divine vicinage, you are dearer to me than my parents! O Allah's perfect light, you are dearer to me than my parents!

أَشْهَدُ أَنَّكَ قَدْ بَلَّغْتَ عَنِ اللهِ وَ عَنْ
رَسُولِ اللهِ صَلَّى اللهُ عَلَيْهِ وَ آلِهِ مَا
حُمِّلْتَ، وَ رَعَيْتَ مَا اسْتُحْفِظْتَ، وَ
حَفِظْتَ مَا اسْتُودِعْتَ، وَ حَلَّلْتَ حَلَالَ
اللهِ، وَ حَرَّمْتَ حَرَامَ اللهِ، وَ أَقَمْتَ
أَحْكَامَ اللهِ، وَ لَمْ تَتَعَدَّ حُدُودَ اللهِ، وَ
عَبَدْتَ اللهَ مُخْلِصًا حَتَّى أَتَاكَ الْيَقِينُ،
صَلَّى اللهُ عَلَيْكَ وَ عَلَى الْأَئِمَّةِ مِنْ بَعْدِكَ.

I testify that you communicated what you received from Allah and the Apostle of Allah, may Allah bless him and his Family, and you took good care of what you were given to preserve, and preserved what you were entrusted with, and allowed what God has made lawful and forbade what He has made unlawful, implemented Allah's laws and never violated His bounds, and that you worshipped Allah dedicatedly until demise. May Allah bless you and the Imams after you!

"Then he rose and offered several *rakʿahs* of prayer. Then he said, 'Ṣafwān, whoever performs this *ziyārah* of the Commander of the Faithful and offers this prayer will return to his family in such a state that his sins will have been forgiven and his works will have been well-received, and there will be written for him a reward of all the angels that arrive for his *ziyārah*.' Ṣafwān, amazed at the Imam's words, asked him, 'The reward of every angel that does his *ziyārah*?'

The Imam said, 'Yes. Every night 70 hosts of angels perform his *ziyārah*.' Ṣafwān asked him, 'How many is a single host?' 'It consists of a hundred thousand angels,' replied the Imam. Then, walking backwards, the Imam withdrew from the graveside, and as he returned, he was saying,

يَا جَدَّاهْ، يَا سَيِّدَاهْ، يَا طَيِّبَاهْ، يَا طَاهِرَاهْ، لَا جَعَلَهُ اللهُ آخِرَ الْعَهْدِ مِنْكَ، وَ رَزَقَنِي الْعَوْدَ إِلَيْكَ وَ الْمَقَامَ فِي حَرَمِكَ وَ الْكَوْنَ مَعَكَ وَ مَعَ الْأَبْرَارِ مِنْ وُلْدِكَ، صَلَّى اللهُ عَلَيْكَ وَ عَلَى الْمَلَائِكَةِ الْمُحْدِقِينَ بِكَ.

O grandfather! O Master! O good and pure one! May Allah not make this my last visit to you, and may He grant me to come back to you again to stand in your shrine and to be with you and your pious descendants! May Allah bless you and the angels who surround you!

Ṣafwān says, "I said to him, 'Do you permit me to inform my friends from Kūfah and show them the location of this grave?' 'Yes,' he replied. Then he gave me some money with which I had the tomb repaired."

The Fourth Ziyarah

The *Mustadrak* cites a report[1] of Imam Muḥammad al-Bāqir (ʿa) from an ancient work on *mazār*. In it, the Imam is reported to have said, "In the company of my father, we went for the *ziyārah* of the tomb of my ancestor, the Commander of the Faithful (ʿa) in Najaf. Standing by the holy graveside, he wept and said,

اَلسَّلَامُ عَلَى أَبِي الْأَئِمَّةِ، وَ خَلِيلِ النُّبُوَّةِ، وَ الْمَخْصُوصِ بِالْأُخُوَّةِ. اَلسَّلَامُ عَلَى يَعْسُوبِ الْإِيمَانِ، وَ مِيزَانِ الْأَعْمَالِ، وَ سَيْفِ ذِي الْجَلَالِ. اَلسَّلَامُ عَلَى صَالِحِ الْمُؤْمِنِينَ، وَ وَارِثِ عِلْمِ النَّبِيِّينَ، اَلْحَاكِمِ فِي يَوْمِ الدِّينِ.

Peace be to the patriarch of the Imams, the dedicated friend of the Prophet and his exclusive brother. Peace be to the leader of the faith, the Scales of Works and the sword of the Lord of majesty. Peace be to 'the righteous one among the faithful,' heir to the knowledge of the prophets and judge on the Day of Retribution!

اَلسَّلَامُ عَلَى شَجَرَةِ التَّقْوَى، اَلسَّلَامُ عَلَى

Peace be to the tree of Godfear-

[1] *Mustadrak*, x, 222, b 21, h 11900/1.

حُجَّةِ اللهِ الْبَالِغَةِ، وَ نِعْمَتِهِ السَّابِغَةِ، وَ نِقْمَتِهِ الدَّامِغَةِ. اَلسَّلَامُ عَلَى الصِّرَاطِ الْوَاضِحِ، وَ النَّجْمِ اللَّائِحِ، وَ الْإِمَامِ النَّاصِحِ، وَ رَحْمَةُ اللهِ وَ بَرَكَاتُهُ.

ing! Peace be to Allah's conclusive testament, His bounteous blessing, and His crushing vengeance! Peace be to the manifest path, the bright star, and the benign guide, and may Allah's mercy and His blessings be upon him!

Then he said,

أَنْتَ وَسِيلَتِي إِلَى اللهِ وَ ذَرِيعَتِي، وَ لِي حَقُّ مُوَالاتِي وَ تَأْمِيلِي، فَكُنْ لِي شَفِيعِي إِلَى اللهِ عَزَّ وَ جَلَّ فِي الْوُقُوفِ عَلَى قَضَاءِ حَاجَتِي وَ هِيَ فَكَاكُ رَقَبَتِي مِنَ النَّارِ، وَ اصْرِفْنِي فِي مَوْقِفِي هٰذَا بِالنُّجْحِ وَ بِمَا سَأَلْتُهُ كُلِّهِ بِرَحْمَتِهِ وَ قُدْرَتِهِ.

You are my recourse and means to Allah, and I have a right by virtue of my friendship and hope. So be my intercessor with Allah, Almighty and Glorious, at the halt in fulfilling my need, which is my release from the Fire. Let my return from this place where I stand be one marked with success in obtaining all I have asked for, by His mercy and power!

اَللّٰهُمَّ ارْزُقْنِي عَقْلًا كَامِلًا، وَ لُبًّا رَاجِحًا، وَ قَلْبًا زَكِيًّا، وَ عَمَلًا كَثِيرًا، وَ أَدَبًا بَارِعًا، وَ اجْعَلْ ذٰلِكَ كُلَّهُ لِي وَ لَا تَجْعَلْهُ عَلَيَّ، بِرَحْمَتِكَ يَا أَرْحَمَ الرَّاحِمِينَ.

O Allah, grant me a perfect intellect, a serene mind, a pure heart, diligence in works, and excellent manners. Let all that be for my good, not to my detriment, by Your mercy, O Most Merciful of the merciful!

The Fifth Ziyarah

Shaykh Kulaynī cites a report[1] wherein Imam ʿAlī al-Naqī (ʿa) has recommended
the following text for *ziyārah* at the tomb of the Commander of the Faithful (ʿa).

اَلسَّلَامُ عَلَيْكَ يَا وَلِيَّ اللهِ، أَنْتَ أَوَّلُ

Peace be to you, O *walī* of Allah! You are the first one to have been

1 *Kāfī*, iv, 569, h 1, whence *Tahdhīb*, vi, 28, h 2, and *Wasā'il*, xiv, 394, b 30, h 19450. *Kāmil al-Ziyārāt*, 45, h 3. *Faqīh*, ii, 586, h 3196. *Farḥat al-Gharī*, 111.

wronged and the first one whose rights were usurped. You bore it with patience and expecting Allah's reward until demise.

مَظْلُومٍ وَ أَوَّلُ مَنْ غُصِبَ حَقُّهُ، صَبَرْتَ
وَ احْتَسَبْتَ حَتَّىٰ أَتَاكَ الْيَقِينُ،

I testify that You met Allah as a martyr. May Allah punish your assassin with all kinds of punishments and perpetually renew his torments. I come to you as one knowing your rights, appreciating your station, hating your enemies and those who were unjust to you, and I shall meet my Lord with this belief, God willing!

فَأَشْهَدُ أَنَّكَ لَقِيتَ اللهَ وَ أَنْتَ شَهِيدٌ،
عَذَّبَ اللهُ قَاتِلَكَ بِأَنْوَاعِ الْعَذَابِ، وَ
جَدَّدَ عَلَيْهِ الْعَذَابَ، جِئْتُكَ عَارِفًا بِحَقِّكَ،
مُسْتَبْصِرًا بِشَأْنِكَ، مُعَادِيًا لِأَعْدَائِكَ وَ مَنْ
ظَلَمَكَ، أَلْقَىٰ عَلَىٰ ذٰلِكَ رَبِّي إِنْ شَاءَ اللهُ.

O *walī* of Allah, I am guilty of many sins, so intercede in my favour with your Lord, as You have an illustrious station with Allah and eminence and right of mediation, and Allah, the Most High, has said (concerning the intercession of the intercessors), *"They do not intercede except for someone He approves of."*(21:28)

يَا وَلِيَّ اللهِ، إِنَّ لِي ذُنُوبًا كَثِيرَةً، فَاشْفَعْ
لِي إِلَىٰ رَبِّكَ، فَإِنَّ لَكَ عِنْدَ اللهِ مَقَامًا
مَعْلُومًا، وَ إِنَّ لَكَ عِنْدَ اللهِ جَاهًا وَ
شَفَاعَةً، وَ قَدْ قَالَ اللهُ تَعَالَىٰ: وَ لَا
يَشْفَعُونَ إِلَّا لِمَنِ ارْتَضَىٰ.

The Sixth Ziyarah

This *ziyārah* has been cited by a group of scholars, among them is Shaykh Muḥammad ibn al-Mashhadī,[1] who states that Muḥammad b. Khālid Ṭayalisī reports from Sayf b. ᶜAmīrah, who said: "We went out towards Najaf in the company of Ṣafwān al-Jammāl and a group of companions and performed the *ziyārah* of the Commander of the Faithful (*ᶜa*). When we had finished, he turned in the direction of the tomb of Imam al-Ḥusayn, saying, 'I am performing the *ziyārah* of Imam al-Ḥusayn from this place, at the head of the tomb of the Commander of the Faithful (*ᶜa*).'

"He further said, 'I came here once with Imam Jaᶜfar al-Ṣādiq (*ᶜa*) and he performed such a *ziyārah* as this, followed by a prayer and supplication as I am going to perform. The Imam said to me, "Ṣaf-

1 *Al-Mazār al-Kabīr*, 214-222. *Biḥār*, xcvii, 305-310, from *Miṣbāḥ al-Zā'ir*.

wān, record this *ziyārah* and recite this supplication and perform the *ziyārah* of the Commander of the Faithful (ᶜ*a*) and Imam al-Ḥusayn in this manner. I guarantee, by Allah, that those who perform this *ziyārah* and make this supplication, whether from far or near, their *ziyārah* will be well-received and their efforts rewarded and their greetings will be acknowledged and their petitions, no matter how great and many, will be granted by Allah." ' "

God willing, the rest of this report pertaining to the excellence of this observance will be mentioned at the end of Ṣafwān's supplication in the section on *ziyārah* for the day of ᶜĀshūrā (p. 348-357). The *ziyārah* of the Commander of the Faithful (ᶜ*a*) to be recited facing his tomb [as mentioned in this report] is as follows.

Peace be to you, O Apostle of Allah! Peace be to you, O elect of Allah! Peace be to you, O trustee of Allah! Peace be to you, whom Allah chose, singled out and preferred from among His creatures! Peace be to you, O dedicated friend of Allah as long as nights fall and grow dark and days rise and brighten! Peace be to you as long as there is silence of the silent and speech of speakers and the resplendent sun rises over the horizon, and may Allah's mercy and His blessings be upon you!

اَلسَّـــلَامُ عَلَيْكَ يَا رَسُولَ اللهِ، اَلسَّلَامُ
عَلَيْكَ يَا صِفْوَةَ اللهِ، اَلسَّلَامُ عَلَيْكَ يَا
أَمِينَ اللهِ، اَلسَّلَامُ عَلَىٰ مَنِ اصْطَفَاهُ اللهُ
وَ اخْتَصَّهُ وَ اخْتَارَهُ مِنْ بَرِيَّتِهِ، اَلسَّلَامُ
عَلَيْكَ يَا خَلِيلَ اللهِ مَـــا دَجَا اللَّيْلُ وَ
غَسَقَ، وَ أَضَاءَ النَّهَارُ وَ أَشْرَقَ، اَلسَّلَامُ
عَلَيْكَ مَا صَمَتَ صَامِتٌ وَ نَطَقَ نَاطِقٌ
وَ ذَرَّ شَارِقٌ، وَ رَحْمَةُ اللهِ وَ بَرَكَاتُهُ.

Peace be to our master, ᶜAlī ibn Abī Ṭālib, the Commander of the Faithful, unmatched in his record of era of Islam, his virtues and heroism, destroyer of the hosts (of the infidels), great in strength, supreme in might, of unshakeable foundations, who will satiate the faithful with cups of drink from the Pond of the distinguished and trusted Apostle! Peace be to you,

اَلسَّلَامُ عَلَىٰ مَوْلَانَا أَمِيرِ الْمُؤْمِنِينَ عَلِيِّ بْنِ
أَبِي طَالِبٍ، صَاحِبِ السَّوَابِقِ وَ الْمَنَاقِبِ
وَ النَّجْدَةِ، وَ مُبِيدِ الْكَتَائِبِ، اَلشَّـــدِيدِ
الْبَـــأْسِ، اَلْعَظِيـــمِ الْمِـــرَاسِ، اَلْمَكِينِ
الْأَسَاسِ، سَاقِي الْمُؤْمِنِينَ بِالْكَأْسِ مِنْ
حَوْضِ الرَّسُولِ الْمَكِينِ الْأَمِينِ. اَلسَّلَامُ

blessed with a perfect intellect, virtues, bounties, noble deeds, and divine gifts! Peace be to you, hero of the faithful, lion of the monotheists, slayer of the polytheists and legatee of the Apostle of the Lord of the worlds, and may Allah's mercy and His blessings be upon you!

عَلٰى صَاحِبِ النُّهٰى وَ الْفَضْلِ وَ الطَّوَائِلِ، وَ
الْمَكْرُمَاتِ وَ النَّوَائِلِ. اَلسَّلَامُ عَلٰى فَارِسِ
الْمُؤْمِنِينَ، وَ لَيْثِ الْمُوَحِّدِينَ، وَ قَاتِلِ
الْمُشْرِكِينَ، وَ وَصِيِّ رَسُولِ رَبِّ الْعَالَمِينَ، وَ
رَحْمَةُ اللهِ وَ بَرَكَاتُهُ.

Peace be to you whom Allah strengthened by Gabriel, assisted by the means of Michael, brought near to Himself in both the worlds and granted all that is a cause of comfort and delight. May Allah bless you and your immaculate progeny and the elect of your descendants and the rightly guided Imams, who bade what is right and forbade what is wrong and enjoined us to perform the prayer and to give *zakāt* and familiarized us with the fasts of the month of Ramaḍān and recitation the Qur'ān!

اَلسَّلَامُ عَلٰى مَنْ أَيَّدَهُ اللهُ بِجَبْرَئِيلَ، وَ أَعَانَهُ
بِمِيكَائِيلَ، وَ أَزْلَفَهُ فِي الدَّارَيْنِ، وَ حَبَاهُ
بِكُلِّ مَا تَقِرُّ بِهِ الْعَيْنُ، وَ صَلَّى اللهُ عَلَيْهِ وَ
عَلٰى آلِهِ الطَّاهِرِينَ، وَ عَلٰى أَوْلَادِهِ الْمُنْتَجَبِينَ،
وَ عَلَى الْأَئِمَّةِ الرَّاشِدِينَ، اَلَّذِينَ أَمَرُوا
بِالْمَعْرُوفِ، وَ نَهَوْا عَنِ الْمُنْكَرِ، وَ فَرَضُوا
عَلَيْنَا الصَّلَوَاتِ، وَ أَمَرُوا بِإِيتَاءِ الزَّكَاةِ، وَ
عَرَّفُونَا صِيَامَ شَهْرِ رَمَضَانَ وَ قِرَاءَةَ الْقُرْآنِ.

Peace be to you, O Commander of the Faithful, the preceptor of the faith and the leader of the devout! Peace be to you, O door of Allah! Peace be to you, O watchful eye of Allah, His outstretched hand, His listening ear, His far-reaching wisdom, His plenteous blessing, and His crushing vengeance!

اَلسَّلَامُ عَلَيْكَ يَا أَمِيرَ الْمُؤْمِنِينَ، وَ
يَعْسُوبَ الدِّينِ، وَ قَائِدَ الْغُرِّ الْمُحَجَّلِينَ.
اَلسَّلَامُ عَلَيْكَ يَا بَابَ اللهِ، اَلسَّلَامُ عَلَيْكَ
يَا عَيْنَ اللهِ النَّاظِرَةَ، وَ يَدَهُ الْبَاسِطَةَ، وَ
أُذُنَهُ الْوَاعِيَةَ، وَ حِكْمَتَهُ الْبَالِغَةَ، وَ نِعْمَتَهُ
السَّابِغَةَ، وَ نِقْمَتَهُ الدَّامِغَةَ،

Peace be to you, O dispenser

اَلسَّلَامُ عَلٰى قَسِيمِ الْجَنَّةِ وَ النَّارِ. اَلسَّلَامُ

عَلَىٰ نِعْمَــةِ اللهِ عَلَى الْأَبْــرَارِ، وَ نِقْمَتِــهِ عَلَى الْفُجَّارِ. اَلسَّــلَامُ عَلَىٰ سَيِّدِ الْمُتَّقِينَ الْأَخْيَارِ،

of paradise and hell! Peace be to you, O Allah's blessing for the pious and His vengeance for the wicked! Peace be to you, O prince of the elect of the Godwary!

اَلسَّــلَامُ عَلَىٰ أَخِي رَسُولِ اللهِ وَ ابْنِ عَمِّهِ وَ زَوْجِ ابْنَتِــهِ وَ الْمَخْلُوقِ مِــنْ طِينَتِهِ. اَلسَّــلَامُ عَلَى الْأَصْلِ الْقَدِيــمِ، وَ الْفَرْعِ الْكَرِيمِ. اَلسَّلَامُ عَلَى الثَّمَرِ الْجَنِيِّ. اَلسَّلَامُ عَلَىٰ أَبِي الْحَسَــنِ عَلِيٍّ. اَلسَّلَامُ عَلَىٰ شَجَرَةِ طُوبَىٰ وَ سِدْرَةِ الْمُنْتَهَىٰ.

Peace be to you, O brother of the Apostle of Allah, his cousin and son-in-law, who were created of the same substance as he! Peace be to you, O eternal root and the noble branch! Peace be to you, O ripe fruit! Peace be to you, O Abul Ḥasan Alī! Peace be to the Tree of Ṭūbā and the Lote Tree of Ultimate Boundary!

اَلسَّــلَامُ عَلَىٰ آدَمَ صَفْوَةِ اللهِ، وَ نُوحٍ نَبِيِّ اللهِ، وَ إِبْرَاهِيمَ خَلِيلِ اللهِ، وَ مُوسَىٰ كَلِيمِ اللهِ، وَ عِيسَىٰ رُوحِ اللهِ، وَ مُحَمَّدٍ حَبِيبِ اللهِ، وَ مَنْ بَيْنَهُمْ مِنَ النَّبِيِّينَ وَ الصِّدِّيقِينَ وَ الشُّهَدَاءِ وَ الصَّالِحِينَ، وَ حَسُنَ أُولٰئِكَ رَفِيقًا.

Peace be to Adam, the elect of Allah, to Noah, the prophet of Allah, to Abraham, the dedicated friend of Allah, to Moses, the interlocutor of Allah, to Jesus the spirit of Allah, to Muḥammad, the beloved of Allah, and to all the prophets who lived in the eras between them, and to all the truthful, the martyrs and the righteous, and excellent companions are they!

اَلسَّلَامُ عَلَىٰ نُورِ الْأَنْوَارِ، وَ سَلِيلِ الْأَطْهَارِ، وَ عَنَاصِرِ الْأَخْيَارِ. اَلسَّلَامُ عَلَىٰ وَالِدِ الْأَئِمَّةِ الْأَبْرَارِ. اَلسَّــلَامُ عَلَىٰ حَبْلِ اللهِ الْمَتِينِ، وَ جَنْبِهِ الْمَكِينِ، وَ رَحْمَةُ اللهِ وَ بَرَكَاتُهُ.

Peace be to the light of lights, the descendant of the immaculate ones, and of the breed of the chosen ones! Peace be to the progenitor of the pious Imams! Peace be to the firm cord of Allah and His preeminent vicinage, and may Allah's mercy and His blessings be upon you!

اَلسَّــلَامُ عَلَىٰ أَمِيــنِ اللهِ فِي أَرْضِــهِ وَ

Peace be to the trustee of Allah on His earth, His vicegerent, who judged according to His laws, maintained His religion, spoke with His wisdom and acted in accordance with His scripture, the brother of the Apostle, the spouse of the Virgin, and the drawn-out sword of Allah! Peace be to the master of manifest proofs and signs and possessor of overpowering [glaring] miracles, the saviour from mortal dangers whom Allah has mentioned in His definitive verses, saying, "He is with Us, in the Mother Book, sublime (ʿAlī) and wise.

خَلِيفَتِهِ، وَ الْحَاكِمِ بِأَمْرِهِ، وَ الْقَيِّمِ بِدِينِهِ، وَ النَّاطِقِ بِحِكْمَتِهِ، وَ الْعَامِلِ بِكِتَابِهِ، أَخِ الرَّسُولِ وَ زَوْجِ الْبَتُولِ وَ سَيْفِ اللهِ الْمَسْلُولِ. اَلسَّلَامُ عَلَىٰ صَاحِبِ الدَّلَالَاتِ وَ الْآيَاتِ الْبَاهِرَاتِ وَ الْمُعْجِزَاتِ الْقَاهِرَاتِ، وَ الْمُنْجِي مِنَ الْهَلَكَاتِ، اَلَّذِي ذَكَرَهُ اللهُ فِي مُحْكَمِ الْآيَاتِ، فَقَالَ تَعَالَىٰ: وَ إِنَّهُ فِي أُمِّ الْكِتَابِ لَدَيْنَا لَعَلِيٌّ حَكِيمٌ.

Peace be to the admirable name of Allah, His radiant face and His exalted vicinage, and may Allah's mercy and blessings be upon him!

اَلسَّلَامُ عَلَى اسْمِ اللهِ الرَّضِيِّ، وَ وَجْهِهِ الْمُضِيءِ، وَجَنْبِهِ الْعَلِيِّ، وَرَحْمَةُ اللهِ وَبَرَكَاتُهُ

Peace be to the testaments of Allah, the legatees of His (Apostle), His exclusive, chosen and dedicated friends and trustees, and may Allah's mercy and blessings be upon them!

اَلسَّلَامُ عَلَىٰ حُجَجِ اللهِ وَ أَوْصِيَائِهِ، وَ خَاصَّةِ اللهِ وَ أَصْفِيَائِهِ، وَ خَالِصَتِهِ وَ أُمَنَائِهِ، وَ رَحْمَةُ اللهِ وَ بَرَكَاتُهُ.

My master, O trustee and testament of Allah, I have come to you as a pilgrim, knowing your rights, befriending your friends and hating your enemies, and seeking nearness to Allah by the means of your *ziyārah*, so be my intercessor with Allah, your Lord and mine, in delivering me from the Fire and fulfilment of my needs pertaining to this world and the Hereafter!

قَصَدْتُكَ يَا مَوْلَايَ يَا أَمِينَ اللهِ وَ حُجَّتَهُ، زَائِرًا عَارِفًا بِحَقِّكَ، مُوَالِيًا لِأَوْلِيَائِكَ، مُعَادِيًا لِأَعْدَائِكَ، مُتَقَرِّبًا إِلَى اللهِ بِزِيَارَتِكَ، فَاشْفَعْ لِي عِنْدَ اللهِ رَبِّي وَ رَبِّكَ فِي خَلَاصِ رَقَبَتِي مِنَ النَّارِ، وَ قَضَاءِ حَوَائِجِي حَوَائِجِ الدُّنْيَا وَ الْآخِرَةِ.

Then clasping the tomb, embrace it and say,

سَلَامُ اللهِ وَ سَلَامُ مَلَائِكَتِهِ الْمُقَرَّبِينَ وَ الْمُسَلِّمِينَ لَكَ بِقُلُوبِهِمْ يَا أَمِيرَ الْمُؤْمِنِينَ، وَ النَّاطِقِينَ بِفَضْلِكَ، وَ الشَّاهِدِينَ عَلَىٰ أَنَّكَ صَادِقٌ أَمِينٌ صِدِّيقٌ عَلَيْكَ، وَ رَحْمَةُ اللهِ وَ بَرَكَاتُهُ.

O Commander of the Faithful, may Allah's greeting of peace be to you, those of His archangels, and of those who accept you with their hearts, declare your excellence, and testify to your sincerity, trustworthiness and truthfulness, and may Allah's mercy and blessings be upon you!

أَشْهَدُ أَنَّكَ طُهْرٌ طَاهِرٌ مُطَهَّرٌ، مِنْ طُهْرٍ طَاهِرٍ مُطَهَّرٍ، أَشْهَدُ لَكَ يَا وَلِيَّ اللهِ وَ وَلِيَّ رَسُولِهِ بِالْبَلَاغِ وَ الْأَدَاءِ، وَ أَشْهَدُ أَنَّكَ جَنْبُ اللهِ وَ بَابُهُ، وَ أَنَّكَ حَبِيبُ اللهِ وَ وَجْهُهُ الَّذِى يُؤْتَىٰ مِنْهُ، وَ أَنَّكَ سَبِيلُ اللهِ، وَ أَنَّكَ عَبْدُ اللهِ وَ أَخُو رَسُولِهِ صَلَّى اللهُ عَلَيْهِ وَ آلِهِ،

I testify that You are pure, immaculate and blameless, descended from pure, immaculate and blameless ancestors! I testify, O *walī* of Allah and His Apostle that You communicated and fulfilled (what you were charged with) and I testify that you are Allah's vicinage and His door, Allah's beloved and His Face by which He is approached, and that you are the way of Allah, that you are Allah's servant and brother of His Apostle, may Allah bless him and his Family!

أَتَيْتُكَ مُتَقَرِّبًا إِلَى اللهِ عَزَّ وَ جَلَّ بِزِيَارَتِكَ، رَاغِبًا إِلَيْكَ فِي الشَّفَاعَةِ، أَبْتَغِي بِشَفَاعَتِكَ خَلَاصَ رَقَبَتِي مِنَ النَّارِ، مُتَعَوِّذًا بِكَ مِنَ النَّارِ، هَارِبًا مِنْ ذُنُوبِيَ الَّتِي احْتَطَبْتُهَا عَلَىٰ ظَهْرِى، فَزِعًا إِلَيْكَ رَجَاءَ رَحْمَةِ رَبِّي،

I come to you seeking nearness to Allah, Almighty and Glorious, by your *ziyārah*, asking for your intercession and seeking it for my deliverance from the Fire, taking refuge with you from the Fire, seeking shelter with you and fleeing from my sins that are like firewood that I have piled up on my back, expecting the mercy of my Lord!

أَتَيْتُكَ أَسْتَشْفِعُ بِكَ يَا مَوْلَاى، وَ

My master, I come to you seeking your intercession and seeking

أَتَقَرَّبُ بِكَ إِلَى اللهِ لِيَقْضِيَ بِكَ حَوَائِجِي، فَاشْفَعْ لِي يَا أَمِيرَ الْمُؤْمِنِينَ إِلَى اللهِ، فَإِنِّي عَبْدُ اللهِ وَ مَوْلَاكَ وَ زَائِرُكَ، وَ لَكَ عِنْدَ اللهِ الْمَقَامُ الْمَحْمُودُ، وَ الْجَاهُ الْعَظِيمُ، وَ الشَّأْنُ الْكَبِيرُ، وَ الشَّفَاعَةُ الْمَقْبُولَةُ.

nearness to Allah by your means, that He may fulfil my needs! O Commander of the Faithful, intercede for me with Allah, for I am a servant of Allah, your friend and pilgrim, and you have an admirable station with Allah, a great standing, a supreme eminence and an intercession that is heard!

اَللّٰهُمَّ صَلِّ عَلٰى مُحَمَّدٍ وَ آلِ مُحَمَّدٍ، وَ صَلِّ عَلٰى أَمِيرِ الْمُؤْمِنِينَ عَبْدِكَ الْمُرْتَضٰى، وَ أَمِينِكَ الْأَوْفٰى، وَ عُرْوَتِكَ الْوُثْقٰى، وَ يَدِكَ الْعُلْيَا، وَ جَنْبِكَ الْأَعْلٰى، وَ كَلِمَتِكَ الْحُسْنٰى، وَ حُجَّتِكَ عَلَى الْوَرٰى، وَ صِدِّيقِكَ الْأَكْبَرِ، وَ سَيِّدِ الْأَوْصِيَاءِ، وَ رُكْنِ الْأَوْلِيَاءِ، وَ عِمَادِ الْأَصْفِيَاءِ، أَمِيرِ الْمُؤْمِنِينَ، وَ يَعْسُوبِ الدِّينِ، وَ قُدْوَةِ الصَّالِحِينَ، وَ إِمَامِ الْمُخْلِصِينَ، اَلْمَعْصُومِ مِنَ الْخَلَلِ، اَلْمُهَذَّبِ مِنَ الزَّلَلِ، اَلْمُطَهَّرِ مِنَ الْعَيْبِ، اَلْمُنَزَّهِ مِنَ الرَّيْبِ، أَخِي نَبِيِّكَ وَ وَصِيِّ رَسُولِكَ، اَلْبَائِتِ عَلٰى فِرَاشِهِ، وَ الْمُوَاسِي لَهُ بِنَفْسِهِ، وَ كَاشِفِ الْكَرْبِ عَنْ وَجْهِهِ، اَلَّذِي جَعَلْتَهُ سَيْفًا لِنُبُوَّتِهِ، وَ آيَةً لِرِسَالَتِهِ، وَ شَاهِدًا عَلٰى أُمَّتِهِ، وَ دِلَالَةً عَلٰى حُجَّتِهِ، وَ

O Allah, bless Muḥammad and the Family of Muḥammad and bless the Commander of the Faithful, Your most approved servant and most loyal trustee, Your firmest handle, Your exalted hand, your most elevated vicinage, Your best word, Your testament to the entire creation, Your supreme truthful one, the prince of the legatees, the pillar of the *awliyā* and the elect, the Commander of the Faithful, the leader of the faith, the exemplar of the righteous, the Imam of Your dedicated servants, preserved from fallibility, refined from lapses, purified from defects, free from all doubt, brother of Your Prophet, legatee of Your Apostle, who slept in his bed (to save his life), supported him in a self-sacrificing manner, removed the anguish from his face, whom You made a sword in the service of his prophethood, a sign of his apostleship, a witness to his *ummah*, a proof in support of his testament, the bearer of his banner, the shield of his life, the guide of his *ummah*, the arm of his strength, the crown of his head, the door of his secrets and the key of his triumphs, so that he defeated the armies of idolatry with Your will and decimated the troops of infidelity with Your command, sacrificing his self for the pleasure of Your Apostle and dedicating himself to obeying him! O Allah, so bless him with a blessing that is perpetual and everlasting!

حَامِلًا لِرَايَتِهِ، وَ وِقَايَةً لِمُهْجَتِهِ، وَ هَادِيًا لِأُمَّتِهِ، وَ يَدًا لِبَأْسِهِ، وَ تَاجًا لِرَأْسِهِ، وَ بَابًا لِسِرِّهِ، وَ مِفْتَاحًا لِظَفَرِهِ، حَتّٰى هَزَمَ جُيُوشَ الشِّرْكِ بِإِذْنِكَ، وَ أَبَادَ عَسَاكِرَ الْكُفْرِ بِأَمْرِكَ، وَ بَذَلَ نَفْسَهُ فِي مَرْضَاةِ رَسُولِكَ، وَ جَعَلَهَا وَقْفًا عَلٰى طَاعَتِهِ، فَصَلِّ اللّٰهُمَّ عَلَيْهِ صَلَاةً دَائِمَةً بَاقِيَةً.

Then say,

Peace be to you, O *walī* of Allah, the piercing flame, the eternal light, and the scion of the pure ancestors! O secret of Allah! Between me and Allah there are many sins that weigh heavily on my back and nothing can take them away except His pleasure. So, by the right of Him who has entrusted you with His secrets and made you guardian of the affairs of His creatures, to be my intercessor with Allah, my refuge from the Fire, and my supporter in the hardships of the times, for indeed I am Allah's servant, your friend and pilgrim, may Allah bless you!

اَلسَّلَامُ عَلَيْكَ يَا وَلِيَّ اللهِ وَ الشِّهَابَ الثَّاقِبَ، وَ النُّورَ الْعَاقِبَ، يَا سَلِيلَ الْأَطَائِبِ، يَا سِرَّ اللهِ، إِنَّ بَيْنِي وَ بَيْنَ اللهِ تَعَالٰى ذُنُوبًا قَدْ أَثْقَلَتْ ظَهْرِي، وَ لَا يَأْتِي عَلَيْهَا إِلَّا رِضَاهُ، فَبِحَقِّ مَنِ ائْتَمَنَكَ عَلٰى سِرِّهِ، وَ اسْتَرْعَاكَ أَمْرَ خَلْقِهِ، كُنْ لِي إِلَى اللهِ شَفِيعًا، وَ مِنَ النَّارِ مُجِيرًا، وَ عَلَى الدَّهْرِ ظَهِيرًا، فَإِنِّي عَبْدُ اللهِ وَ وَلِيُّكَ وَ زَائِرُكَ، صَلَّى اللهُ عَلَيْكَ.

Then offer 6 *rakʿahs* as prayer of *ziyārah* and make any petition you wish. Then say,

Peace be to you, O Commander of

اَلسَّلَامُ عَلَيْكَ يَا أَمِيرَ الْمُؤْمِنِينَ،

the Faithful! May Allah's peace be to you so long as I live and as long as day and night endure!

عَلَيْكَ مِنِّي سَلَامُ اللهِ أَبَدًا مَا بَقِيتُ وَ بَقِيَ اللَّيْلُ وَ النَّهَارُ.

Then turn towards the tomb of Imam al-Ḥusayn (ʿa) and say,[1]

Peace be to you, O Abū ʿAbdillāh! Peace be to you, O son of the Apostle of Allah! I have come to the two of you as a pilgrim, seeking your mediation with Allah, your Lord and mine, turning to Him with your mediation, seeking your intercession with Allah in regard to this need of mine. So intercede for me, for indeed you have an admirable station with Allah and a preeminent eminence, an exalted station and mediation.

اَلسَّلَامُ عَلَيْكَ يَا أَبَا عَبْدِ اللهِ، اَلسَّلَامُ عَلَيْكَ يَا ابْنَ رَسُولِ اللهِ، أَتَيْتُكُمَا زَائِرًا وَ مُتَوَسِّلًا إِلَى اللهِ تَعَالَى رَبِّي وَ رَبِّكُمَا، وَ مُتَوَجِّهاً إِلَى اللهِ بِكُمَا، مُسْتَشْفِعاً بِكُمَا إِلَى اللهِ فِي حَاجَتِي هٰذِهِ، فَاشْفَعَا لِي، فَإِنَّ لَكُمَا عِنْدَ اللهِ الْمَقَامَ الْمَحْمُودَ، وَ الْجَاهَ الْوَجِيهَ، وَ الْمَنْزِلَ الرَّفِيعَ وَ الْوَسِيلَةَ.

I am returning from my visit to you, awaiting the fulfilment of this need and its satisfaction and completion by Allah and with your intercession with Him in my favour in this regard. So let me not be disappointed, nor let my return be one of failure. Rather, let my return be regarded with favour and let it be one of success and satisfaction, accompanied with fulfilment of all my needs. So intercede in my favour with Allah.

إِنِّي أَنْقَلِبُ عَنْكُمَا مُنْتَظِرًا لِتَنَجُّزِ الْحَاجَةِ وَ قَضَائِهَا وَ نَجَاحِهَا مِنَ اللهِ بِشَفَاعَتِكُمَا لِي إِلَى اللهِ فِي ذٰلِكَ، فَلَا أَخِيبُ وَ لَا يَكُونُ مُنْقَلَبِي عَنْكُمَا مُنْقَلَبًا خَاسِرًا، بَلْ يَكُونُ مُنْقَلَبِي مُنْقَلَبًا رَاجِحًا مُفْلِحًا مُنْجِحًا مُسْتَجَابًا لِي بِقَضَاءِ جَمِيعِ الْحَوَائِجِ فَاشْفَعَا لِي.

I return as Allah wishes—there being no power or force except what proceeds from Allah—

أَنْقَلِبُ عَلَى مَا شَاءَ اللهُ، لَا حَوْلَ وَ لَا قُوَّةَ إِلَّا بِاللهِ، مُفَوِّضًا أَمْرِي إِلَى اللهِ،

[1] The following passage is cited in the *Mafātīḥ* until the words: *fī ḥājatī hādhihī*. The complete text has been cited here (until the words *innahū qarībun mujīb*) from *Biḥār*. (Tr.)

مُلْجِئاً ظَهْــرِى إِلَى اللهِ، مُتَوَكِّلًا عَلَى
اللهِ، وَ أَقُــولُ حَسْــبِيَ اللهُ وَ كَــفَىٰ،
سَــمِعَ اللهُ لِمَنْ دَعَا، لَيْسَ وَرَاءَ اللهِ وَ
وَرَاءَكُمْ يَا سَادَتِي مُنْتَهىٰ، مَا شَاءَ اللهُ
رَبِّي كَانَ، وَ مَا لَمْ يَشَأْ لَمْ يَكُنْ.

entrusting my matters to Allah, falling back on Allah, putting trust in Allah, and believing that Allah is sufficient for me and that He hears those who call Him, and I do not have any resort beyond Allah and beyond you, my masters! Whatever my Lord wishes occurs and what He does not wish does not come about.

يَا سَيِّدِى يَا أَمِيرَ الْمُؤْمِنِينَ وَ مَوْلَاىَ وَ
أَنْتَ يَا أَبَا عَبْدِ اللهِ، سَلَامِى عَلَيْكُمَا
مُتَّصِلٌ مَا اتَّصَلَ اللَّيْلُ وَ النَّهَارُ، وَاصِلٌ
إِلَيْكُمَا غَيْرُ مَحْجُوبٍ عَنْكُمَا سَلَامِى
إِنْ شَاءَ اللهُ، وَ أَسْأَلُهُ بِحَقِّكُمَا أَنْ يَشَاءَ
ذٰلِكَ وَ يَفْعَلَ، فَإِنَّهُ حَمِيدٌ مَجِيدٌ

I am departing, O my master and guardian, the Commander of the Faithful, and you, my master, Abū ʿAbdillāh! Peace be to you on my behalf, forever as long as day and night continue and may my greeting reach you, without being kept out from your presence, God willing. I beseech Him by your right to do so with His will, indeed He is praiseworthy and glorious.

أَنْقَلِــبُ يَا سَــيِّدِى عَنْكُمَــا تَائِبًا
حَامِدًا لِلّٰهِ شَــاكِرًا رَاضِيًا مُسْتَيْقِنًا
لِلْإِجَابَةِ غَيْرَ آيِسٍ وَ لَا قَانِطٍ، عَائِدًا
رَاجِعًــا إِلَىٰ زِيَارَتِكُمَا، غَيْرَ رَاغِبٍ
عَنْكُمَا، بَلْ رَاجِعٌ إِنْ شَاءَ اللهُ تَعَالَىٰ
إِلَيْكُمَا، يَا سَــادَاتِي رَغِبْــتُ إِلَيْكُمَا
بَعْدَ أَنْ زَهِدَ فِيكُمَا وَ فِي زِيَارَتِكُمَا
أَهْــلُ الدُّنْيَا، فَلَا يُخَيِّبُــنِى اللهُ فِيمَا
رَجَوْتُ وَ مَا أَمَّلْــتُ فِي زِيَارَتِكُمَا،

O my masters, I depart from you as someone who is penitent, praising and thanking Allah, pleased with Him, being certain that my prayers will be heard, not being despondent and lacking in hope, being ever keen to return and come back again and again to visit the two of you, never being indifferent to you and your *ziyārah*, but keen to come back again and again, God willing. My masters, I have been keen to visit the two of you, while the world's people remain indifferent to you and your *ziyārah*, so may not Allah disappoint me with regard to my hopes and expecta-

إِنَّهُ قَرِيبٌ مُجِيبٌ.

tions from your *ziyārah*. Indeed, He is nearmost and responsive!

Then facing in the direction of *qiblah*, recite the following supplication.[1]

يَـا اَللّٰهُ يَا اَللّٰهُ يَـا اَللّٰهُ، يَا مُجِيبَ دَعْوَةِ الْمُضْطَرِّينَ، وَ يَا كَاشِفَ كَرْبِ الْمَكْرُوبِينَ، وَ يَا غِيَاثَ الْمُسْتَغِيثِينَ، وَ يَا صَرِيخَ الْمُسْتَصْرِخِينَ، وَ يَا مَنْ هُوَ أَقْرَبُ إِلَيَّ مِنْ حَبْلِ الْوَرِيدِ، يَا مَنْ يَحُولُ بَيْنَ الْمَرْءِ وَ قَلْبِهِ، وَ يَا مَنْ هُوَ بِالْمَنْظَرِ الْأَعْلَىٰ وَ بِالْأُفُقِ الْمُبِينِ، وَ يَا مَنْ هُوَ الرَّحْمٰنُ الرَّحِيمُ،

O Allah, O Allah, O Allah! O Answerer of the calls of the distressed! O Reliever of the anxieties of the troubled! O Succour of those who appeal for help! O Rescuer of those who cry out in distress! O You who are nearer to me than my jugular vein! O You who intervene between a person and his heart! O You who are on the highest viewpoint and on the manifest horizon! O You who are the All-beneficent and the All-merciful.

يَا مَنْ عَلَى الْعَرْشِ اسْتَوىٰ، يَا مَنْ يَعْلَمُ خَائِنَةَ الْأَعْيُنِ وَ مَا تُخْفِي الصُّدُورُ، وَ يَا مَنْ لَا تَخْفَىٰ عَلَيْهِ خَافِيَةٌ، يَا مَنْ لَا تَشْتَبِهُ عَلَيْهِ الْأَصْوَاتُ، يَا مَنْ لَا تُغَلِّطُهُ الْحَاجَاتُ، يَا مَنْ لَا يُبْرِمُهُ إِلْحَاحُ الْمُلِحِّينَ، يَا مُدْرِكَ كُلِّ فَوْتٍ، يَا جَامِعَ كُلِّ شَمْلٍ، يَا بَارِئَ النُّفُوسِ بَعْدَ الْمَوْتِ، يَا مَنْ هُوَ كُلَّ يَوْمٍ فِي شَأْنٍ،

O You who are settled on the Throne! O You *who know the treachery of the eyes and what the breasts hide!* O You from whom no hidden thing is concealed! O You who are not led into error by the great number of petitions! O You who are not wearied by the entreaties of the importunate! O Restorer of everything that is missing! O Bringer about of all unions! O Reviver of the souls after death! O You who are engaged in some work every day!

يَا قَاضِيَ الْحَاجَاتِ، يَا مُنَفِّسَ الْكُرُبَاتِ، يَا مُعْطِيَ السُّؤْلَاتِ، يَا وَلِيَّ الرَّغَبَاتِ، يَا كَافِيَ

O Fulfiller of all needs! O Dispeller of agonies O Granter of requests! O Patron of all peti-

[1] The *Mafātīḥ* does not cite the complete text to be recited here. The full text is given here for the reader's convenience. *Biḥār*, xcviii, 296-298, b 24, h 3, from Ṭūsī's Miṣbāḥ, 778. (Tr.)

الْمُهِمَّاتِ، يَا مَنْ يَكْفِي مِنْ كُلِّ شَيْءٍ وَ لَا يَكْفِي مِنْهُ شَيْءٌ فِي السَّمَاوَاتِ وَ الْأَرْضِ،

tions! O Sufficer in all concerns! O You who suffice against all things, and against whom nothing in the heavens and the earth can suffice!

أَسْأَلُكَ بِحَقِّ مُحَمَّدٍ خَاتَمِ النَّبِيِّينَ، وَ عَلِيٍّ أَمِيرِ الْمُؤْمِنِينَ، وَ بِحَقِّ فَاطِمَةَ بِنْتِ نَبِيِّكَ، وَ بِحَقِّ الْحَسَنِ وَ الْحُسَيْنِ، فَإِنِّي بِهِمْ أَتَوَجَّهُ إِلَيْكَ فِي مَقَامِى هٰذَا، وَ بِهِمْ أَتَوَسَّلُ وَ بِهِمْ أَسْتَشْفِعُ إِلَيْكَ،

I beseech You by the right of Muḥammad, the Seal of the Prophets, and ʿAlī, the Commander of the Faithful, and by the right of Fāṭimah, daughter of Your Prophet, and by the rights of al-Ḥasan and al-Ḥusayn, for I turn to You through their intermediacy in this place where I stand and take recourse in their mediation and their intercession.

وَ بِحَقِّهِمْ أَسْأَلُكَ وَ أُقْسِمُ وَ أَعْزِمُ عَلَيْكَ، وَ بِالشَّأْنِ الَّذِى لَهُمْ عِنْدَكَ، وَ بِالَّذِى فَضَّلْتَهُمْ عَلَى الْعَالَمِينَ، وَ بِاسْمِكَ الَّذِى جَعَلْتَهُ عِنْدَهُمْ، وَ بِهِ خَصَصْتَهُمْ دُونَ الْعَالَمِينَ، وَ بِهِ أَبَنْتَهُمْ وَ أَبَنْتَ فَضْلَهُمْ مِنْ كُلِّ فَضْلٍ، حَتَّىٰ فَاقَ فَضْلُهُمْ فَضْلَ الْعَالَمِينَ جَمِيعًا،

I beseech You by their right and adjure and implore You by the standing and worth they have with You and by the preference You have granted them over all the world's denizens, and by Your Name that You have conferred on them to exclusion other denizens of the world, thus distinguishing them and exalting their excellence over that of all the world's denizens, so that their merit surpasses the merits of all the world's denizens.

وَ أَسْأَلُكَ أَنْ تُصَلِّيَ عَلَىٰ مُحَمَّدٍ وَ آلِ مُحَمَّدٍ، وَ أَنْ تَكْشِفَ عَنِّي غَمِّي وَ هَمِّي وَ كَرْبِي، وَ أَنْ تَكْفِيَنِي الْمُهِمَّ مِنْ أُمُورِى، وَ تَقْضِيَ عَنِّي دَيْنِي، وَ تُجِيرَنِي مِنَ الْفَقْرِ، وَ تُجِيرَنِي مِنَ الْفَاقَةِ،

I beseech You to bless Muḥammad and the Family of Muḥammad and to remove my grief, worries and anguish, to take care of my concerns of consequence, to pay my debts, and shelter me from poverty and need, to spare me from asking the creatures, to protect me from those I fear would cause me worry, those I fear would cause me hardship, those I fear would cause me grief, and from the evil of those whose evil I fear, the cunning of those whose cunning I fear, from the envy of those whose envy I fear, from injustice of those whose injustice I fear, from tyranny of those whose tyranny I fear, from authority of those whose authority I fear, and from the guile of those whose guile I fear, and turn away from their guile and cunning and the power over me of those whose power I fear, and to repel from me the stratagems of the cunning and the ruses of the guileful.

وَ تُغْنِيَنِي عَنِ الْمَسْأَلَةِ إِلَى الْمَخْلُوقِينَ، وَ تَكْفِيَنِي هَمَّ مَنْ أَخَافُ هَمَّهُ، وَ عُسْرَ مَنْ أَخَافُ عُسْرَهُ، وَ حُزُونَةَ مَنْ أَخَافُ حُزُونَتَهُ، وَ شَرَّ مَنْ أَخَافُ شَرَّهُ، وَ مَكْرَ مَنْ أَخَافُ مَكْرَهُ، وَ بَغْيَ مَنْ أَخَافُ بَغْيَهُ، وَ جَوْرَ مَنْ أَخَافُ جَوْرَهُ، وَ سُلْطَانَ مَنْ أَخَافُ سُلْطَانَهُ، وَ كَيْدَ مَنْ أَخَافُ كَيْدَهُ، وَ اصْرِفْ عَنِّي كَيْدَهُ وَ مَكْرَهُ وَ مَقْدُرَةَ مَنْ أَخَافُ مَقْدُرَتَهُ عَلَيَّ، وَ تَرُدَّ عَنِّي كَيْدَ الْكَيَدَةِ وَ مَكْرَ الْمَكَرَةِ.

O Allah, whoever aims to harm me, direct it at him! Whoever plots against me, scheme against him, and turn away from me his guile and schemes, his violence and designs and keep him off from me in whatever manner You wish!

اَللّٰهُمَّ مَنْ أَرَادَنِي بِسُوءٍ فَأَرِدْهُ، وَ مَنْ كَادَنِي فَكِدْهُ، وَ اصْرِفْ عَنِّي كَيْدَهُ وَ بَأْسَهُ وَ أَمَانِيَّهُ، وَ امْنَعْهُ عَنِّي كَيْفَ شِئْتَ وَ أَنَّى شِئْتَ.

O Allah, distract him from troubling me with a poverty which You will not redress, an affliction You will not shield him from, a want You will not remove, a malady from which You will not cure, a disgrace You will not turn to honour, and a privation You will not relieve!

اَللّٰهُمَّ اشْغَلْهُ عَنِّي بِفَقْرٍ لَا تَجْبُرُهُ، وَ بَلَاءٍ لَا تَسْتُرُهُ، وَ بِفَاقَةٍ لَا تَسُدُّهَا، وَ بِسُقْمٍ لَا تُعَافِيهِ، وَ بِذُلٍّ لَا تُعِزُّهُ، وَ مَسْكَنَةٍ لَا تَجْبُرُهَا.

O Allah, make degradation his prospect, send poverty into his home and let disease and sick-

اَللّٰهُمَّ اضْرِبْ بِالذُّلِّ نَصْبَ عَيْنَيْهِ، وَ أَدْخِلِ الْفَقْرَ فِي مَنْزِلِهِ، وَ الْعِلَّةَ وَ السُّقْمَ

فِي بَدَنِهِ، حَتَّىٰ تَشْغَلَهُ عَنِّي بِشُغْلٍ شَاغِلٍ
لَا فَرَاغَ لَهُ، وَ أَنْسِهِ ذِكْرِي كَمَا أَنْسَيْتَهُ
ذِكْرَكَ، وَ خُذْ عَنِّي بِسَمْعِهِ وَ بَصَرِهِ وَ
لِسَانِهِ وَ يَدِهِ وَ رِجْلِهِ وَ قَلْبِهِ، وَ جَمِيعِ
جَوَارِحِهِ، وَ أَدْخِلْ عَلَيْهِ فِي جَمِيعِ ذَلِكَ
السُّقْمَ، وَ لَا تَشْفِهِ حَتَّىٰ تَجْعَلَ ذٰلِكَ
شُغْلًا شَاغِلًا بِهِ عَنِّي وَ عَنْ ذِكْرِي،
وَ اكْفِنِي يَا كَافِيَ مَا لَا يَكْفِي سِوَاكَ،
فَإِنَّكَ الْكَافِي لَا كَافِيَ سِوَاكَ، وَ مُفَرِّجٌ لَا
مُفَرِّجَ سِوَاكَ، وَ مُغِيثٌ لَا مُغِيثَ سِوَاكَ،
وَ جَارٌ لَا جَارَ سِوَاكَ، خَابَ مَنْ كَانَ
جَارُهُ سِوَاكَ، وَ مُغِيثُهُ سِوَاكَ، وَ مَفْزَعُهُ
إِلَىٰ سِوَاكَ، وَ مَهْرَبُهُ إِلَىٰ سِوَاكَ، وَ مَلْجَأُهُ
إِلَىٰ غَيْرِكَ، وَ مَنْجَاهُ مِنْ مَخْلُوقٍ غَيْرِكَ،
فَأَنْتَ ثِقَتِي وَ رَجَائِي وَ مَفْزَعِي وَ مَهْرَبِي
وَ مَلْجَئِي وَ مَنْجَايَ، فَبِكَ أَسْتَفْتِحُ وَ
بِكَ أَسْتَنْجِحُ، وَ بِمُحَمَّدٍ وَ آلِ مُحَمَّدٍ
أَتَوَجَّهُ إِلَيْكَ وَ أَتَوَسَّلُ وَ أَتَشَفَّعُ،
فَأَسْأَلُكَ يَا اَللّٰهُ يَا اَللّٰهُ يَا اَللّٰهُ، فَلَكَ
الْحَمْدُ وَ لَكَ الشُّكْرُ، وَ إِلَيْكَ الْمُشْتَكَىٰ

ness into his body, thus distracting him from troubling me with a preoccupation from which he finds no release. Make him forget me as You have made him forget You, and turn aside from me his hearing, sight, tongue, hands, feet, heart and all his bodily members and afflict him in all these with an illness which You will not heal, so that You make it the cause of his preoccupation which will distract him from troubling me and remembering me. Suffice me, O Sufficer, nothing besides whom can suffice, for You are the All-sufficing and there is no sufficer besides You. You are the Reliever and there is no reliever besides You. You are the Succourer and there is no succourer besides You. You are the Granter of refuge and there is no refuge besides You! Disappointment is the lot of those who take refuge in anyone other than You, and look for succour, sanctuary, shelter, haven with anyone other than You, and seek safety with a creature and not You.

So, You are my reliance and my hope, my sanctuary and my shelter, my haven and my safety, and You do I implore for victory and success, and to You do I turn with the intermediacy of Muḥammad and the Family of Muḥammad and seek their mediation and intercession! I beseech You, O Allah, O Allah, O Allah, for to You belongs all praise and to You are due all thanks; to You are addressed all complaints and You are the one who is sought for help!

I beseech You, O Allah, O Allah, O Allah, by the right of Muḥammad and the Family of Muḥammad to bless Muḥammad and the Family of Muḥammad, and to remove my grief, my worries and my anguish in this place that I stand even as You removed the grief, worries and anguish of Your Prophet and sufficed him against (protected him from) the fear of his enemies! Remove my afflictions as You removed his, give me relief as You gave him relief, suffice me as You sufficed him, repel from me the dangers, troubles and worries that I fear, without my having to bear any trouble on that account, and let my return be accompanied with fulfilment of my need and Your having taken care of all that is of concern to me of affairs pertaining to my Hereafter and my life in this world, O most merciful of the merciful!

وَ أَنْتَ الْمُسْتَعَانُ،
فَأَسْأَلُكَ يَا اَللّٰهُ يَا اَللّٰهُ يَا اَللّٰهُ، بِحَقِّ مُحَمَّدٍ
وَ آلِ مُحَمَّدٍ، أَنْ تُصَلِّيَ عَلٰى مُحَمَّدٍ وَ آلِ
مُحَمَّدٍ، وَ أَنْ تَكْشِفَ عَنِّي غَمِّي وَ هَمِّي
وَ كَرْبِي فِي مَقَامِي هٰذَا، كَمَا كَشَفْتَ عَنْ
نَبِيِّكَ هَمَّهُ وَ غَمَّهُ وَ كَرْبَهُ، وَ كَفَيْتَهُ هَوْلَ
عَدُوِّهِ، فَاكْشِفْ عَنِّي كَمَا كَشَفْتَ عَنْهُ،
وَ فَرِّجْ عَنِّي كَمَا فَرَّجْتَ عَنْهُ، وَ اكْفِنِي
كَمَا كَفَيْتَهُ، وَ اصْرِفْ عَنِّي هَوْلَ مَا أَخَافُ
هَوْلَهُ، وَ مَؤُونَةَ مَنْ أَخَافُ مَؤُونَتَهُ، وَ هَمَّ
مَنْ أَخَافُ هَمَّهُ، بِلَا مَؤُونَةٍ عَلٰى نَفْسِي
مِنْ ذٰلِكَ، وَ اصْرِفْنِي بِقَضَاءِ حَوَائِجِي وَ
كِفَايَةِ مَا أَهَمَّنِي هَمُّهُ مِنْ أَمْرِ دُنْيَايَ وَ
آخِرَتِي وَ دُنْيَايَ، يَا أَرْحَمَ الرَّاحِمِينَ.

Then turn towards the tomb of the Commander of the Faithful (*ʿa*) and say,

Peace be to you, O Commander of the Faithful, and peace be to Abū'Abd Allāh al-Ḥusayn so long as I live and so long as day and night endure! May Allah not make this my last opportunity to perform your ziyārah and may He never separate me from

اَلسَّلَامُ عَلَيْكَ يَا أَمِيرَ الْمُؤْمِنِينَ، وَ
السَّلَامُ عَلٰى أَبِي عَبْدِ اللّٰهِ الْحُسَيْنِ مَا
بَقِيتُ وَ بَقِيَ اللَّيْلُ وَ النَّهَارُ، لَا جَعَلَهُ اللّٰهُ
آخِرَ الْعَهْدِ مِنِّي لِزِيَارَتِكُمَا، وَ لَا فَرَّقَ

اللهُ بَيْنِي وَ بَيْنَكُمَا.

you!

As mentioned earlier, the supplication of Ṣafwān is the same as the famous *Du^cā Alqamah* and, God willing, will be cited (fully) in the section pertaining to *ziyārah* of Ā<u>sh</u>ūrā (p. 340).

THE SEVENTH ZIYARAH

This *ziyārah* has been cited by Sayyid Ibn Ṭāwūs in the *Miṣbāḥ al-Zā'ir*.[1] Its manner of performance is as follows: One should approach the shrine from "Bāb al-Salām," the door from which the blessed *ḍarīḥ* can be seen. On reaching it, say 34 times "*Allāhu akbar.*" Then say,

سَلَامُ اللهِ وَ سَلَامُ مَلَائِكَتِهِ الْمُقَرَّبِينَ وَ أَنْبِيَائِهِ الْمُرْسَلِينَ وَ عِبَادِهِ الصَّالِحِينَ وَ جَمِيعِ الشُّهَدَاءِ وَالصِّدِّيقِينَ عَلَيْكَ يَا أَمِيرَ الْمُؤْمِنِينَ

Allah's greetings of 'Peace' be to you as well as those of His archangels, prophets and emissaries, His righteous servants and all the martyrs and the truthful, O Commander of the Faithful!

اَلسَّلَامُ عَلَىٰ آدَمَ صِفْوَةِ اللهِ، اَلسَّلَامُ عَلَىٰ نُوحٍ نَبِيِّ اللهِ، اَلسَّلَامُ عَلَىٰ إِبْرَاهِيمَ خَلِيلِ اللهِ، اَلسَّلَامُ عَلَىٰ مُوسَىٰ كَلِيمِ اللهِ، اَلسَّلَامُ عَلَىٰ عِيسَىٰ رُوحِ اللهِ،

Peace be to Adam, the elect of Allah! Peace be to Noah, the prophet of Allah! Peace be to Abraham, the dedicated friend of Allah! Peace be to Moses, the interlocutor of Allah! Peace be to Jesus, the spirit of Allah!

اَلسَّلَامُ عَلَىٰ مُحَمَّدٍ حَبِيبِ اللهِ، وَ رَحْمَةُ اللهِ وَ بَرَكَاتُهُ. اَلسَّلَامُ عَلَى اسْمِ اللهِ الرَّضِيِّ، وَ وَجْهِهِ الْعَلِيِّ، وَ صِرَاطِهِ السَّوِيِّ. اَلسَّلَامُ عَلَى الْمُهَذَّبِ الصَّفِيِّ، اَلسَّلَامُ عَلَىٰ أَبِي الْحَسَنِ عَلِيِّ بْنِ أَبِي طَالِبٍ، وَ رَحْمَةُ اللهِ وَ بَرَكَاتُهُ.

Peace be to Muḥammad, the beloved of Allah, and may Allah's mercy and His bounties be upon them! Peace be to the admirable Name of Allah, His exalted Face and His straight path! Peace be to the purified, cultivated and refined personage. Peace be to Abū al-Ḥasan ^cAlī ibn Abī Ṭālib and may Allah's mercy and His bounties be upon him!

اَلسَّلَامُ عَلَىٰ خَالِصِ الْأَخِلَّاءِ، اَلسَّلَامُ عَلَىٰ

Peace be to the most dedicated

[1] *Biḥār*, xcvii, 302, b 4, h 22, from Ibn Ṭāwūs.

of God's friends. Peace be to the chosen spouse of the Mistress of the world's womankind! Peace be to him who was born in the Kaᶜbah and was wed in the heaven! Peace be to to the Lion of God in the thick of battle. Peace be to him through whom Makkah and Minā rose in honour!

الْمَخْصُوصِ بِسَيِّدَةِ النِّسَاءِ، اَلسَّلَامُ عَلَى الْمَوْلُودِ فِي الْكَعْبَةِ، اَلْمُزَوَّجِ فِي السَّمَاءِ، اَلسَّلَامُ عَلَىٰ أَسَدِ اللهِ فِي الْوَغَىٰ، اَلسَّلَامُ عَلَىٰ مَنْ شُرِّفَتْ بِهِ مَكَّةُ وَ مِنًى،

Peace be to master of the Pool and the bearer of the Banner. Peace be to him who was one of the five People of the Cloak! Peace be to him who slept on the Prophet's bed to save him from the enemies at the cost of his own life!

اَلسَّلَامُ عَلَىٰ صَاحِبِ الْحَوْضِ وَ حَامِلِ اللِّوَاءِ، اَلسَّلَامُ عَلَىٰ خَامِسِ أَهْلِ الْعَبَاءِ، اَلسَّلَامُ عَلَى الْبَائِتِ عَلَىٰ فِرَاشِ النَّبِيِّ وَ مُفْدِيهِ بِنَفْسِهِ مِنَ الْأَعْدَاءِ،

Peace be to him who pulled out the gate of the stronghold of Khaybar and held it level in the air! Peace be to him who spoke with the youth in their Cave in the tongue of the prophets! Peace be to him who made the dry well spring water in the waterless desert! Peace be to him who plucked the rock which a group of stalwarts were unable to move! Peace be to him who addressed the serpent from the *minbar* at Kūfah in the tongue of the eloquent! Peace be to him who addressed the wolf and conversed with the skull at Nahrawān after its bones had decayed!

اَلسَّلَامُ عَلَىٰ قَالِعِ بَابِ خَيْبَرَ وَ الدَّاحِي بِهِ فِي الْفَضَاءِ، اَلسَّلَامُ عَلَىٰ مُكَلِّمِ الْفِتْيَةِ فِي كَهْفِهِمْ بِلِسَانِ الْأَنْبِيَاءِ، اَلسَّلَامُ عَلَىٰ مُنْبِعِ الْقَلِيبِ فِي الْفَلَا، اَلسَّلَامُ عَلَىٰ قَالِعِ الصَّخْرَةِ وَ قَدْ عَجَزَ عَنْهَا الرِّجَالُ الْأَشِدَّاءُ، اَلسَّلَامُ عَلَىٰ مُخَاطِبِ الثُّعْبَانِ عَلَىٰ مِنْبَرِ الْكُوفَةِ بِلِسَانِ الْفُصَحَاءِ، اَلسَّلَامُ عَلَىٰ مُخَاطِبِ الذِّئْبِ وَ مُكَلِّمِ الْجُمْجُمَةِ بِالنَّهْرَوَانِ وَ قَدْ نَخِرَتِ الْعِظَامُ بِالْبِلَىٰ،

Peace be to the possessor of the station of intercession for the creatures on the Day of Resurrection, and may Allah's mercy and bounties be upon you! Peace be

اَلسَّلَامُ عَلَىٰ صَاحِبِ الشَّفَاعَةِ فِي يَوْمِ الْوَرَىٰ، وَ رَحْمَةُ اللهِ وَ بَرَكَاتُهُ. اَلسَّلَامُ عَلَى الْإِمَامِ الزَّكِيِّ حَلِيفِ الْمِحْرَابِ،

اَلسَّلَامُ عَلَىٰ صَاحِبِ الْمُعْجِزِ الْبَاهِرِ وَ النَّاطِقِ بِالْحِكْمَةِ وَ الصَّوَابِ، اَلسَّلَامُ عَلَىٰ مَنْ عِنْدَهُ تَأْوِيلُ الْمُحْكَمِ وَ الْمُتَشَابِهِ وَ عِنْدَهُ أُمُّ الْكِتَابِ،

to the immaculate Imam and the indweller of the prayer niche! Peace be to the performer of manifest miracles and the voice of wisdom and righteousness! Peace be to him who knows the interpretation of the definitive and metaphorical verses and with whom is the Mother Book!

اَلسَّلَامُ عَلَىٰ مَنْ رُدَّتْ عَلَيْهِ الشَّمْسُ حِينَ تَوَارَتْ بِالْحِجَابِ، اَلسَّلَامُ عَلَىٰ مُحْيِي اللَّيْلِ الْبَهِيمِ بِالتَّهَجُّدِ وَ الْإِكْتِيَابِ، اَلسَّلَامُ عَلَىٰ مَنْ خَاطَبَهُ جَبْرَئِيلُ بِإِمْرَةِ الْمُؤْمِنِينَ بِغَيْرِ ارْتِيَابٍ، وَ رَحْمَةُ اللهِ وَ بَرَكَاتُهُ.

Peace be to him for whom the sun was brought back after it had disappeared behind the veil of the horizon! Peace be to him who would spend nights in prayer and sorrow! Peace be to him who was undoubtedly addressed by Gabriel as 'the Commander of the Faithful', and may Allah's mercy and His bounties be upon him!

اَلسَّلَامُ عَلَىٰ سَيِّدِ السَّادَاتِ، اَلسَّلَامُ عَلَىٰ صَاحِبِ الْمُعْجِزَاتِ، اَلسَّلَامُ عَلَىٰ مَنْ عَجِبَ مِنْ حَمَلَاتِهِ فِي الْحُرُوبِ مَلَائِكَةُ سَبْعِ سَمَاوَاتٍ، اَلسَّلَامُ عَلَىٰ مَنْ نَاجَى الرَّسُولَ فَقَدَّمَ بَيْنَ يَدَيْ نَجْوَاهُ صَدَقَاتٍ،

Peace be to the chief of the *sayyids!* Peace be to the author of miracles! Peace be to him whose assaults during battles filled the angels of the seven heavens with wonder! Peace be to him who held secret conferences with the Apostle and offered charity before his confidential talks!

اَلسَّلَامُ عَلَىٰ أَمِيرِ الْجُيُوشِ وَ صَاحِبِ الْغَزَوَاتِ، اَلسَّلَامُ عَلَىٰ مُخَاطِبِ ذِئْبِ الْفَلَوَاتِ، اَلسَّلَامُ عَلَىٰ نُورِ اللهِ فِي الظُّلُمَاتِ، اَلسَّلَامُ عَلَىٰ مَنْ رُدَّتْ لَهُ الشَّمْسُ فَقَضَىٰ مَا فَاتَهُ مِنَ الصَّلَاةِ، وَ

Peace be to the commander of the armies of Islam and the director of its campaigns! Peace be to him who spoke to the wolves in the wilderness! Peace be to the light of Allah in the darkness! Peace be to him for whom the sun was brought back whereat he offered the prayer he had missed, and may Allah's mercy

رَحْمَةُ اللهِ وَ بَرَكَاتُهُ.

and bounties be upon him!

اَلسَّلَامُ عَلَىٰ أَمِيرِ الْمُؤْمِنِينَ، اَلسَّلَامُ عَلَىٰ سَيِّدِ الْوَصِيِّينَ، اَلسَّلَامُ عَلَىٰ إِمَامِ الْمُتَّقِينَ، اَلسَّلَامُ عَلَىٰ وَارِثِ عِلْمِ النَّبِيِّينَ، اَلسَّلَامُ عَلَىٰ يَعْسُوبِ الدِّينِ، اَلسَّلَامُ عَلَىٰ عِصْمَةِ الْمُؤْمِنِينَ، اَلسَّلَامُ عَلَىٰ قُدْوَةِ الصَّادِقِينَ، وَ رَحْمَةُ اللهِ وَ بَرَكَاتُهُ.

Peace be to the Commander of the Faithful! Peace be to the chief of the Legatees! Peace be to the Imam of the Godwary! Peace be to the heir to the knowledge of the prophets! Peace be to the leader of the faith! Peace be to the protector of the faithful! Peace be to the exemplar of the truthful, and may Allah's mercy and His bounties be upon him!

اَلسَّلَامُ عَلَىٰ حُجَّةِ الْأَبْرَارِ، اَلسَّلَامُ عَلَىٰ أَبِي الْأَئِمَّةِ الْأَطْهَارِ، اَلسَّلَامُ عَلَى الْمَخْصُوصِ بِذِي الْفَقَارِ، اَلسَّلَامُ عَلَىٰ سَاقِي أَوْلِيَائِهِ مِنْ حَوْضِ النَّبِيِّ الْمُخْتَارِ صَلَّى اللهُ عَلَيْهِ وَ آلِهِ مَا اطَّرَدَ اللَّيْلُ وَ النَّهَارُ،

Peace be to the Proof of the pious! Peace be to the father of the Infallible Imams! Peace be to him who was single out for the <u>Dh</u>ul Fiqār! Peace be to him who hands out the drink to his friends from the Pool of the Chosen Prophet, may Allah bless him and his Family as long as the night and day follow one another in succession

اَلسَّلَامُ عَلَى النَّبَإِ الْعَظِيمِ، اَلسَّلَامُ عَلَىٰ مَنْ أَنْزَلَ اللهُ فِيهِ: وَإِنَّهُ فِي أُمِّ الْكِتَابِ لَدَيْنَا لَعَلِيٌّ حَكِيمٌ، اَلسَّلَامُ عَلَىٰ صِرَاطِ اللهِ الْمُسْتَقِيمِ، اَلسَّلَامُ عَلَى الْمَنْعُوتِ فِي التَّوْرَاةِ وَ الْإِنْجِيلِ وَ الْقُرْآنِ الْحَكِيمِ، وَ رَحْمَةُ اللهِ وَ بَرَكَاتُهُ.

Peace be to the Great Tiding! Peace be to him concerning whom Allah revealed that *"He is with Us, in the Mother Book, sublime (ᶜAlī) and wise"!* Peace be to Allah's straight path. Peace be to him who has been praised in the Torah, the Evangel, and the Wise Qur'ān, and may Allah's mercy and bounties be upon him!

Then leaning on the *ḍarīḥ*, embrace it and say,

يَا أَمِينَ اللهِ، يَا حُجَّةَ اللهِ، يَا وَلِيَّ اللهِ، يَا

O trustee of Allah, O testament of Allah, O *walī* of Allah, O path of

صِرَاطَ اللهِ، زَارَكَ عَبْدُكَ وَ وَلِيُّكَ اللَّائِذُ بِقَبْرِكَ، وَ الْمُنِيخُ رَحْلَهُ بِفِنَائِكَ، اَلْمُتَقَرِّبُ إِلَى اللهِ عَزَّ وَ جَلَّ، وَ الْمُسْتَشْفِعُ بِكَ إِلَى اللهِ، زِيَارَةَ مَنْ هَجَرَ فِيكَ صَحْبَهُ، وَ جَعَلَكَ بَعْدَ اللهِ حَسْبَهُ،

Allah! Your servant and friend has come to visit you, taking refuge in your tomb and having landed in your courtyard, seeking nearness to Allah, Glorious and Exalted, and seeking your intercession with Him, a visit by someone who has left all his companions for your sake, considering you sufficient for himself after Allah!

أَشْهَدُ أَنَّكَ الطُّورُ وَ الْكِتَابُ الْمَسْطُورُ، وَ الرَّقُّ الْمَنْشُورُ، وَ بَحْرُ الْعِلْمِ الْمَسْجُورُ.

I testify that you are the *'the Mount and the Book inscribed on an unrolled parchment,'* and *'the surging sea'* of knowledge.

يَا وَلِيَّ اللهِ إِنَّ لِكُلِّ مَزُورٍ عِنَايَةً فِيمَنْ زَارَهُ وَ قَصَدَهُ وَ أَتَاهُ، وَ أَنَا وَلِيُّكَ وَ قَدْ حَطَطْتُ رَحْلِي بِفِنَائِكَ، وَ لَجَأْتُ إِلَى حَرَمِكَ، وَ لُذْتُ بِضَرِيحِكَ لِعِلْمِي بِعَظِيمِ مَنْزِلَتِكَ وَ شَرَفِ حَضْرَتِكَ، وَ قَدْ أَثْقَلَتِ الذُّنُوبُ ظَهْرِي وَ مَنَعَتْنِي رُقَادِي، فَمَا أَجِدُ حِرْزًا وَ لَا مَعْقِلًا وَ لَا مَلْجَأً أَلْجَأُ إِلَيْهِ إِلَّا اللهَ تَعَالَى وَ تَوَسُّلِي بِكَ إِلَيْهِ، وَ اسْتِشْفَاعِي بِكَ لَدَيْهِ، فَهَا أَنَا نَازِلٌ بِفِنَائِكَ، وَ لَكَ عِنْدَ اللهِ جَاهٌ عَظِيمٌ وَ مَقَامٌ كَرِيمٌ، فَاشْفَعْ لِي عِنْدَ اللهِ رَبِّكَ يَا مَوْلَايَ.

O *walī* of Allah, every visitor is treated with favour by those whom he comes to see and visit, and I am your friend who has arrived in your courtyard, taking refuge in your shrine and seeking shelter by your tomb because of my knowledge of your great station and the dignity of your presence! Sins weigh heavily on my back and they keep me from sleep and rest, and I do not know any protection, sanctuary or shelter where I may take refuge except Allah, the Most High, and your mediation with Him and my petition to intercede for me with Him. And here am I, having arrived in your courtyard, and you have a great eminence and an honoured station with Allah, so intercede for me with Allah, your Lord, O my master!

Then kiss the *ḍarīḥ* and facing towards the *qiblah* say,[1]

[1] In the following text, the epithets *al-anzaʿ* and *al-baṭīn*, by which Imam ʿAlī (*ʿa*) was often referred to by the Umayyāds, are attributed to him. Literally *al-anzaʿ* means someone with a receding forehead and *al-baṭīn* is one who is

O Allah, I seek nearness to You, O keenest of hearers, O keenest of observers, O swiftest of reckoners, O most generous of the generous, for the sake of Muḥammad, the Seal of the Prophets and Your Apostle to the world's denizens, and for the sake of his brother, son of his uncle, far removed from polytheism and great in knowledge, the manifest possessor of knowledge, ᶜAlī, the Commander of the Faithful, and for the sake of al-Ḥasan and al-Ḥusayn, the martyred Imams, and for the sake of ᶜAlī ibn al-Ḥusayn Zayn al-ᶜĀbidīn, and Muḥammad ibn ᶜAlī exponent of the sciences of the ancients, and for the sake of Jaᶜfar ibn Muḥammad, the most blameless of the truthful, and for the sake of Mūsā ibn Jaᶜfar who manifestly suppressed his rage and remained in the prisons of oppressors, and for the sake of ᶜAlī ibn Mūṣa, the admirable trustee, and for the sake of Muḥmmad ibn ᶜAlī, the generous one and the standard of the

اَللّهُـــمَّ إِنِّي أَتَقَـــرَّبُ إِلَيْكَ يا أَسْـــمَعَ السَّـــامِعِينَ، وَ يا أَبْـــصَرَ النَّاظِرِينَ، وَ يَـــا أَسْرَعَ الْحَاسِـــبِينَ، وَ يا أَجْوَدَ الْأَجْوَدِيـــنَ، بِمُحَمَّدٍ خَاتَـــمِ النَّبِيِّينَ رَسُولِكَ إِلَى الْعَالَمِينَ، وَ بِأَخِيهِ وَ ابْنِ عَمِّهِ الْأَنْزَعِ الْبَطِـــينِ الْعَالِمِ الْمُبِينِ، عَلِيٍّ أَمِـــيرِ الْمُؤْمِنِـــينَ، وَ الْحَسَـــنِ وَ الْحُسَيْنِ الْإِمَامَيْنِ الشَّهِيدَيْنِ، وَ بِعَلِيِّ بْنِ الْحُسَيْنِ زَيْنِ الْعَابِدِينَ، وَ بِمُحَمَّدِ بْنِ عَلِيٍّ بَاقِـــرِ عِلْمِ الْأَوَّلِينَ، وَ بِجَعْفَرِ بْنِ مُحَمَّـــدٍ زَكِيِّ الصِّدِّيقِينَ، وَ بِمُوسَى بْنِ جَعْفَرٍ الْكَاظِـــمِ الْمُبِينِ وَ حَبِيسِ الظَّالِمِينَ، وَ بِعَلِيِّ بْـــنِ مُوسَى الرِّضَا الْأَمِـــينِ، وَ بِمُحَمَّدِ بْـــنِ عَلِيٍّ الْجَوَادِ

portly and and potbellied. The translation given here is in accordance with the following tradition of the Prophet (ṣ) reported from Imam ᶜAlī al-Naqī (ᶜ*a*), from his father (ᶜ*a*), from Imam Jaᶜfar al-Ṣādiq (ᶜ*a*), Imam ᶜAlī al-Riḍā (ᶜ*a*), and Zayd b. ᶜAlī from the Prophet (ṣ).

قَالَ رَسُولُ الله: يا عَلِيُّ إِنَّ اللهَ عَزَّ وَ جَلَّ قَدْ غَفَرَ لَكَ وَ لِشِيعَتِكَ وَ لِمُحِبِّي شِيعَتِكَ وَ مُحِبِّي مُحِبِّي شِيعَتِكَ، فَأَبْشِرْ فَإِنَّكَ الْأَنْزَعُ الْبَطِينُ مَنْزُوعٌ مِنَ الشِّرْكِ بَطِينٌ مِنَ الْعِلْمِ

See *Ṣaḥīfat al-Riḍā*, 63, h 105. ᶜ*Uyūn Akhbār al-Riḍā*, ii, 47, b 31, h 182, whence *Biḥār*, xxvii, 79, b 4, h 13, xxxv, 52, b 2, h 6. Ṭūsī's *Amālī*, 293, majlis 11, h 570/17, whence *Biḥār*, lxv, 101, b 18, h 19. *Bishārat al-Muṣṭafā*, 184. *Musnad Zayd ibn ᶜAlī*, 456. *Irshād al-Qulūb*, ii, 258. *Kashf al-Ghummah*, i, 13, whence *Biḥār*, xl, 203, b 94, h 8. *Biḥār*, xl, 78, b 91, h 113 from *Firdaws al-Akhbār*. (Tr.)

عَلَمِ الْمُهْتَدِينَ، وَ بِعَلِيِّ بْنِ مُحَمَّدٍ الْبَرِّ
الصَّادِقِ سَــيِّدِ الْعَابِدِينَ، وَ بِالْحَسَنِ
بْــنِ عَلِيٍّ الْعَسْــكَرِيِّ وَلِيِّ الْمُؤْمِنِينَ،
وَ بِالْخَلَــفِ الْحُجَّةِ صَاحِــبِ الْأَمْرِ
مُظْهِرِ الْبَرَاهِينِ، أَنْ تَكْشِــفَ مَا بِي
مِنَ الْهُمُــومِ، وَ تَكْفِيَنِي شَرَّ الْبَلَاءِ
الْمَحْتُــومِ، وَ تُجِيرَنِي مِــنَ النَّارِ ذَاتِ
السَّمُومِ، بِرَحْمَتِكَ يَا أَرْحَمَ الرَّاحِمِينَ.

rightly-guided, and for the sake of ᶜAlī ibn Muḥammad, the pious and truthful one and the prince of the devout, and for the sake of al-Ḥasan ibn ᶜAlī al-ᶜAskarī, the guardian of the faithful, and for the sake of their scion, the Testament, the dispenser of Divine authority, the proclaimer of the proofs, to remove my worries and to protect me from the evil of the affliction certain to occur and to shelter me from the Fire and its infernal miasma, with Your mercy, O Most Merciful of the merciful!

Then make any petition that you may have, and depart taking leave of the Imam.

Sayyid ᶜAbd al-Karīm ibn Tāwūs reports[1] in his book *Farḥat al-Gharī* that once Imam Zayn al-Abidīn (*ᶜa*) arrived in Kufah and entered its mosque. Abu Ḥamzah al-Thumālī, one of the city's religious leaders and known for his piety and asceticism was present there. There the Imam offered two *rakᶜahs* of prayer. Abū Ḥamzah says, "Never have I heard anyone speak in a more refined accent. I went nearer to know what he was saying. I heard him utter these words,

إِلَهِي إِنْ كَانَ [كُنْتُ] قَدْ عَصَيْتُكَ فَإِنِّي قَدْ أَطَعْتُكَ فِي أَحَبِّ الْأَشْيَاءِ إِلَيْك

"My God, though I may have been disobedient to you, I have indeed obeyed you in things which are most cherished by you."

This is a well-known supplication, which will be cited in observances pertaining to the city of Kufah and its Mosque [where its full text appears on the basis of another version of this report].

In that report[2] Abū Ḥamzah describes how the Imam approached the seventh pillar, and, after taking off his shoes, said a *takbīr* while standing and raising his hands to the ears, which filled Abū Ḥamzah

1 *Farḥat al-Gharī*, 46, whence *Biḥār*, xcvii, 245, b .2, h 31 & *Mustadrak*, iii, 405, b 35, h 3886/12.

2 *Biḥār*, xcvii, 388, b 6, h 12, xcvii, 443, b 7, 22, from the works of Shahīd Awwal's *Mazār*, 258 and Muḥammad b. al-Mashhadī's *Mazār al-Kabīr*, 140, b 6..

with a feeling of awe. Then he offered four *rakᶜahs* of prayer, performing the kneelings and prostrations in a worthy manner. Then he recited the above-mentioned supplication.

To continue with the present report, Abū Ḥamzah says that when the Imam rose and left the mosque, he followed him until they reached the travellers' halt in Kufah. At a place where the camels were lodged, he saw a black slave with a camel of good breed and a she-camel. Abū Ḥamzah says, "I asked the salve as to who the man was. He replied, 'Can't you tell from his features? He is ᶜAlī ibn al-Ḥusayn!' Thereupon I fell at the Imam's feet to kiss them. But he lifted me up with his hands and said to me, 'No, Abū Ḥamzah! Prostration is exclusively for Allah, the Almighty and Glorious.' I said to him, 'O son of the Apostle of Allah, what has brought you here?' He replied, 'That which you have already seen.' (By which he meant prayer in the Mosque of Kufah.) 'Had the people known the merit of it, they would come here even if they had to crawl on their knees.' Then he said to me, 'Would you like to visit with me the tomb of my grandfather, ᶜAlī ibn Abī Ṭālib, may peace be to him?' 'Sure!' I said. As I walked in the shade of his camel, he kept talking to me, until we reached the two hills where there was a white spot radiant with light. He alighted from his mount and rubbed his cheeks on the ground. Then turning to me, he said, O Abū Ḥamzah, this is the grave of my grandfather, ᶜAlī ibn Abī Ṭālib, may peace be upon him!' Then he greeted him with a *ziyārah* that began with the words,

اَلسَّلَامُ عَلَى اسْمِ اللهِ الرَّضِيِّ وَ نُورِ وَجْهِهِ الْمُضِيءِ

> 'Peace be to the admirable Name of Allah, and the light of His radiant Face...'

Then he bade farewell to his grandfather and left for Madīnah and I returned to Kufah."

I was disappointed that the Sayyid had not cited this *ziyārah* in *Farḥat al-Gharī* and was on the lookout for it until I found one such *ziyārah* for the Commander of the Faithful (*ᶜa*). However, I did not find any that began with these two phrases, for in the one that I found, the first sentence is the same but the second is slightly different. It is probable that it is the same *ziyārah*, and the small difference of wording is not of much consequence. If there were an objection that this *ziyārah* opens with the words "*Salāmullāhi wa salāmu malā'ikatihī...*" whereas the one mentioned above begins with the words "*Assalāmu ᶜalā ismillāhir raḍī ...,*" I will say that this *ziyārah* is the same and begins with the words "*Assalāmu ᶜalā ismillāhir raḍī ...*" and the *salāms* that occur in the preceding passages are meant as a kind of prelude and request for leave of admittance. Such a claim is supported by the close correspondence between this *ziyārah* and the *ziyārah* meant for the day of the Prophet's birthday anniversary. The reader may refer to it in order to be convinced of this matter. Also, it should be noted that in the Sixth Ziyārah and the *ziyārah* for the day of the Prophet's birthday (p. 169), these two phrases occur without the word *nūr*, and Allah knows best.

In any case, the seven general *ziyārahs* cited here are sufficient for our purpose, and those desiring something more elaborate may recite one of the Ziyārāt Jāmiᶜah or the elaborate *ziyārah* that will be cited hereafter for the Day of Ghadīr (p. 140), for recitation of the latter *ziyārah* has been recommended as something desirable and profitable irrespective of time and place.

Performance of the *ziyārah* of the Commander of the Faithful (*ᶜa*) and the offering of prayer in his shrine are to be held in great regard, for a prayer by his tomb equals two hundred thousand prayers said elsewhere.[1]

Imam Jaᶜfar al-Ṣādiq is reported[2] to have said that a reward equal to that of a *ḥajj* and *ᶜumrah* is written for those who visit the shrine of an Imam obedience to whom is obligatory and offer four *rakᶜahs* of prayer by his graveside.

In our book *Hadīyat al-Zā'irīn*,[3] I have mentioned the virtues of staying in the neighbourhood of the shrine of the Commander of the Faithful (*ᶜa*), but that is true on condition that those who stay there observe the obligations entailed by his vicinage. Such a thing is very difficult and is not possible for everyone. This is not the place for further details in this regard, and those who are desirous should refer to the book *Kalimah Ṭayyibah*.[4]

1 Based, apparently, on a report said to have been cited in Ṣadūq's lost work *Madīnat al-ᶜIlm*. The text, though, is cited in many works of the jurists. *Kashf al-Ghiṭā'*, iii, 67, for instance, without citing any source, states it as folows: روى: أنّ الصلاة عند قبر علي عليه السلام بمائتي ألف صلاة.

Similar reports cited in *Faqīh*, i, 228, h 680 and *Tahdhīb*, vi, 31, b 10, h 2 state that a prayer offerred in Kūfah, a *ḥaram* of Allah, His Apostle and ᶜAlī, equals a thousand prayers offered elsewhere. (Tr.)

2 *Tahdhīb*, vi, 79, b 26, h 4, whence *Wasā'il*, xiv, 330, b 2, h 19329. Mufīd's *Mazār*, 134, b 59, h 3, 185, b 11, h 3, thence Wasā'il, xiv, 332, b 2, h 19333.

3 *Hadīyat al-Zā'irīn*, 198-201.

4 *Kalimah Ṭayyibah*, bāb 5, on the rights and duties arising from neighbourhood.

The Leave of Departure

When intending to bid farewell to the Imam (ᶜa), one may recite the following request for the leave of departure, which is cited after the Fifth Ziyārah in the works of the scholars.[1]

Peace be to you and may Allah's mercy and blessings be upon you! I commend You to Allah's care, committing you to His protection, and give you my *salām!* We have faith in Allah and the apostles and whatever they have brought, summoned us to and guided to, so write our names among the witnesses.

اَلسَّلَامُ عَلَيْكَ وَ رَحْمَةُ اللهِ وَ بَرَكَاتُهُ.
أَسْتَوْدِعُكَ اللهَ وَ أَسْتَرْعِيكَ وَ أَقْرَأُ
عَلَيْكَ السَّلَامَ، آمَنَّا بِاللهِ وَ بِالرُّسُلِ وَ بِمَا
جَاءَتْ بِهِ وَ دَعَتْ إِلَيْهِ وَ دَلَّتْ عَلَيْهِ،
فَاكْتُبْنَا مَعَ الشَّاهِدِينَ.

O Allah, do not let this be my last opportunity of his *ziyārah*, and if You take me away before that I will testify after my death to what I have testified in my life, that ᶜAlī, the Commander of the Faithful, and al-Ḥasan and al-Ḥusayn, ᶜAlī ibn al-Ḥusayn, Muḥammad ibn ᶜAlī, Jaᶜfar ibn Muḥammad, Mūsā ibn Jaᶜfar, ᶜAlī ibn Mūsā, Muḥammad ibn ᶜAlī, ᶜAlī ibn Muḥammad, al-Ḥasan ibn ᶜAlī, and the Ḥujjah, son of al-Ḥasan, may Your blessings be on them all, are my Imams.

اَللّٰهُمَّ لَا تَجْعَلْهُ آخِرَ الْعَهْدِ مِنْ زِيَارَتِي
إِيَّاهُ، فَإِنْ تَوَفَّيْتَنِي قَبْلَ ذٰلِكَ، فَإِنِّي أَشْهَدُ
فِي مَمَاتِي عَلَىٰ مَا شَهِدْتُ عَلَيْهِ فِي حَيَاتِي،
أَشْهَدُ أَنَّ أَمِيرَ الْمُؤْمِنِينَ عَلِيًّا وَ الْحَسَنَ
وَ الْحُسَيْنَ وَ عَلِيَّ بْنَ الْحُسَيْنِ وَ مُحَمَّدَ بْنَ
عَلِيٍّ وَ جَعْفَرَ بْنَ مُحَمَّدٍ وَ مُوسَىٰ بْنَ جَعْفَرٍ
وَ عَلِيَّ بْنَ مُوسَىٰ وَ مُحَمَّدَ بْنَ عَلِيٍّ وَ عَلِيَّ
بْنَ مُحَمَّدٍ وَ الْحَسَنَ بْنَ عَلِيٍّ وَ الْحُجَّةَ بْنَ
الْحَسَنِ صَلَوَاتُكَ عَلَيْهِمْ أَجْمَعِينَ أَئِمَّتِي،

I testify that those who slew them and waged war against them were idolaters and those who rejected them will be in lowest reaches of

وَ أَشْهَدُ أَنَّ مَنْ قَتَلَهُمْ وَ حَارَبَهُمْ
مُشْرِكُونَ، وَ مَنْ رَدَّ عَلَيْهِمْ فِي أَسْفَلِ

[1] *Faqīh*, ii, 591, h 3198. *Kitāb al-Mazār*, 86-87, b 45. *Kāmil al-Ziyārāt*, 46, h 1, whence *Biḥār*, xcvii, 266, b 4, h 8. *Tahdhīb*, vi, 30, b 9. Ṭūsī's *Miṣbāḥ*, 746. *Farḥat al-Gharī*, 85-86. Kafᶜamī's *Miṣbāḥ*, 480. *Balad*, 295.

دَرَكٍ مِنَ الْجَحِيمِ،

hell.

وَ أَشْهَدُ أَنَّ مَنْ حَارَبَهُمْ لَنَا أَعْدَاءُ وَ نَحْنُ مِنْهُمْ بُرَآءُ، وَ أَنَّهُمْ حِزْبُ الشَّيْطَانِ، وَ عَلَىٰ مَنْ قَتَلَهُمْ لَعْنَةُ اللهِ وَ الْمَلَائِكَةِ وَ النَّاسِ أَجْمَعِينَ، وَ مَنْ شَرِكَ فِيهِمْ وَ مَنْ سَرَّهُ قَتْلُهُمْ.

And I testify that those who waged war against them are our enemies, we repudiate them, and they are the confederates of Satan, and may Allah's curse be upon them and that of the angels and all humankind, as well as on as those who shared their guilt and felt glad on account of their murder!

اَللّٰهُمَّ إِنِّي أَسْأَلُكَ بَعْدَ الصَّلَاةِ وَ التَّسْلِيمِ أَنْ تُصَلِّيَ عَلَىٰ مُحَمَّدٍ وَ عَلِيٍّ وَ فَاطِمَةَ وَ الْحَسَنِ وَ الْحُسَيْنِ وَ عَلِيٍّ وَ مُحَمَّدٍ وَ جَعْفَرٍ وَ مُوسَىٰ وَ عَلِيٍّ وَ مُحَمَّدٍ وَ عَلِيٍّ وَ الْحَسَنِ وَ الْحُجَّةِ، وَ لَا تَجْعَلْهُ آخِرَ الْعَهْدِ مِنْ زِيَارَتِهِ، فَإِنْ جَعَلْتَهُ فَاحْشُرْنِي مَعَ هٰؤُلَاءِ الْمُسَمَّيْنَ الْأَئِمَّةِ.

O Allah, I beseech You, after my blessing and greeting, to bless Muḥammad, ᶜAlī, Fāṭimah, al-Ḥasan, al-Ḥusayn, ᶜAlī, Muḥammad, Jaᶜfar, Mūsa, ᶜAlī, Muḥammad, Alī, al-Ḥasan and the Ḥujjah, and do not let it be my last opportunity of his *ziyārah*, and if You ordain it to be such, raise me at resurrection with the Imams that I have named!

اَللّٰهُمَّ وَ ذَلِّلْ قُلُوبَنَا لَهُمْ بِالطَّاعَةِ وَ الْمُنَاصَحَةِ وَ الْمَحَبَّةِ وَ حُسْنِ الْمُوَازَرَةِ وَ التَّسْلِيمِ.

O Allah, make our hearts submissive to them with obedience, sincerity and loyalty, love, gracious support and compliance.

2. Ziyārahs for Special Days

There are several *ziyārah*s of the Commander of the Faithful (ᶜ*a*) meant for specific days. The first of them is the *ziyārah* for the day of G͟hadīr.

Ziyarah for ʿĪd al-Ghadir

Imam ᶜAlī al-Riḍā (ᶜa) is reported[1] to have told Ibn Abī Naṣr, "O son of Abū Naṣr, at whatever place you may be at the time, try to be present at the shrine of the Commander of the Faithful (ᶜa) on the day of Ghadīr. For indeed, on this day, God, the Most High, forgives 60 years of sins of the faithful, men and women, and rescues from hellfire twice the number of sinners that He rescues during the month of Ramaḍān and on the nights of Qadr and ᶜĪd al-Fiṭr."

It is to be noted that several *ziyārahs* have been prescribed for this noble day. The first of them is Ziyārah Amīn Allāh, the second of the *ziyārahs* cited above (p. 105).

Another *ziyārah* is the one reported with reliable *isnād* from Imam Muḥammad al-Taqī (ᶜa),[2] who is reported to have performed this *ziyārah* on a visit to the tomb of the Commander of the Faithful (ᶜa) during the year he was summoned by al-Muᶜtaṣim, the Abbasid caliph. Its manner of performance is as follows:

When intending to perform the *ziyārah*, one should request admittance while standing at the gate of the holy shrine. Shahīd Awwal suggests that at this time one should be wearing on one's cleanest clothes after having performed a bath. While seeking leave of admittance, one should recite the text cited at the beginning of this Book (p. 17), beginning with the words "*Allāhumma innī waqaftu ᶜalā bābin...*" Then entering with the right foot, one should approach the sacred *ḍarīḥ* and, with the back towards the *qiblah*, say,

Peace be to Muḥammad, the Apostle of Allah, the Seal of the Prophets, the Chief of the Envoys, the elect of the Lord of all the worlds, who was entrusted by Allah with His revelations and His prime commandments, and who is the seal of the previous prophesies and inaugurator of what is yet to come, and is the custodian of all that! May

اَلسَّلاَمُ عَلَىٰ مُحَمَّدٍ رَسُولِ اللهِ خَاتَمِ
النَّبِيِّينَ وَ سَيِّدِ الْمُرْسَلِينَ وَ صَفْوَةِ
رَبِّ الْعَالَمِينَ، أَمِينِ اللهِ عَلَىٰ وَحْيِهِ
وَ عَزَائِمِ أَمْرِهِ، وَ الْخَاتِمِ لِمَا سَبَقَ، وَ
الْفَاتِحِ لِمَا اسْتُقْبِلَ، وَ الْمُهَيْمِنِ عَلَىٰ

1 Ṭūsī's *Miṣbāḥ*, 727. *Tahdhīb*, vi, 24, b 7, h 9, whence *Wasā'il*, xiv, 388, b 28, h 19442. *Iqbāl*, 468. *Farḥat al-Gharī*, 106, whence *Biḥār*, xciv, 118, b 60, h 9. *Biḥār*, xcvii, 358, b 5, h2 from *Miṣbāḥ al-Zā'ir*..

2 *Al-Mazār al-Kabīr*, 263. *Biḥār*, xcvii, 359, b 5, h 6, from Mufīd. Referred in *Farḥat al-Gharī*, 112.

Allah's mercy and His blessings, bounties and greetings be upon him!

ذٰلِكَ كُلِّهِ، وَ رَحْمَةُ اللهِ وَ بَرَكَاتُهُ وَ صَلَوَاتُهُ
وَ تَحِيَّاتُهُ.

Peace be to the prophets of Allah, His apostles, archangels and His righteous servants!

اَلسَّلَامُ عَلىٰ أَنْبِيَاءِ اللهِ وَ رُسُلِهِ وَ
مَلَائِكَتِهِ الْمُقَرَّبِينَ وَ عِبَادِهِ الصَّالِحِينَ.

Peace be to you, O Commander of the Faithful, head of the Legatees, heir to the knowledge of the prophets, friend of the Lord of all the worlds, and my guardian and guardian of all the faithful! May Allah's mercy and His blessings be upon you!

اَلسَّلَامُ عَلَيْكَ يَا أَمِيرَ الْمُؤْمِنِينَ، وَ
سَيِّدَ الْوَصِيِّينَ، وَ وَارِثَ عِلْمِ النَّبِيِّينَ،
وَ وَلِيَّ رَبِّ الْعَالَمِينَ، وَ مَوْلَايَ وَ مَوْلَى
الْمُؤْمِنِينَ، وَ رَحْمَةُ اللهِ وَ بَرَكَاتُهُ.

Peace be to you, O my guardian, O Commander of the Faithful, O Allah's trustee on His earth, His envoy among His creatures and His conclusive testament to His servants!

اَلسَّلَامُ عَلَيْكَ يَا مَوْلَايَ يَا أَمِيرَ
الْمُؤْمِنِينَ، يَا أَمِينَ اللهِ فِي أَرْضِهِ، وَ سَفِيرَهُ
فِي خَلْقِهِ، وَ حُجَّتَهُ الْبَالِغَةَ عَلىٰ عِبَادِهِ.

Peace be to you, O Allah's true religion and His straight path! Peace be to you, O *great tiding, the one about which they differ,*[78:1-3] and concerning which they will be questioned.

اَلسَّلَامُ عَلَيْكَ يَا دِينَ اللهِ الْقَوِيمَ، وَ صِرَاطَهُ
الْمُسْتَقِيمَ اَلسَّلَامُ عَلَيْكَ أَيُّهَا النَّبَأُ الْعَظِيمُ
الَّذِي هُمْ فِيهِ مُخْتَلِفُونَ، وَ عَنْهُ يُسْأَلُونَ.

Peace be to you, O Commander of the Faithful! You had faith in Allah while others worshipped other gods; you affirmed the truth while they gainsaid it; you waged *jihād* for the sake of Allah, while they shrank away from it; and you worshipped Allah putting your exclusive faith in him, bearing hardships patiently for the sake of God until your last breath. Indeed may Allah's curse

اَلسَّلَامُ عَلَيْكَ يَا أَمِيرَ الْمُؤْمِنِينَ،
آمَنْتَ بِاللهِ وَ هُمْ مُشْرِكُونَ، وَ صَدَّقْتَ
بِالْحَقِّ وَ هُمْ مُكَذِّبُونَ، وَ جَاهَدْتَ
(فِي اللهِ) وَ هُمْ مُحْجِمُونَ، وَ عَبَدْتَ
اللهَ مُخْلِصًا لَهُ الدِّينَ صَابِرًا مُحْتَسِبًا
حَتّىٰ أَتَاكَ الْيَقِينُ، أَلَا لَعْنَةُ اللهِ عَلَى

be upon the wrongdoers!

الظَّالِمِينَ .

Peace be to you, O master of Muslims, leader of the faithful, Imam of the Godwary, and leader of the devout, and may Allah's mercy and blessings be upon you!

اَلسَّلَامُ عَلَيْكَ يَا سَيِّدَ الْمُسْلِمِينَ، وَ يَعْسُوبَ الْمُؤْمِنِينَ، وَ إِمَامَ الْمُتَّقِينَ، وَ قَائِدَ الْغُرِّ الْمُحَجَّلِينَ، وَ رَحْمَةُ اللهِ وَ بَرَكَاتُهُ

I testify that you are the brother of the Apostle of Allah, his legatee, heir to his knowledge, trustee of his *sharīʿah*, his successor within his *ummah*, the first to have faith in Allah and to affirm what was revealed to His Prophet!

أَشْهَدُ أَنَّكَ أَخُو رَسُولِ اللهِ وَ وَصِيُّهُ وَ وَارِثُ عِلْمِهِ، وَ أَمِينُهُ عَلَىٰ شَرْعِهِ، وَ خَلِيفَتُهُ فِي أُمَّتِهِ، وَ أَوَّلُ مَنْ آمَنَ بِاللهِ وَ صَدَّقَ بِمَا أُنْزِلَ عَلَىٰ نَبِيِّهِ،

I testify that he communicated whatever Allah had revealed concerning you, that he complied with His orders and made your *wilāyah* and obedience to you mandatory for his *ummah*, by taking from them the pledge of allegiance to you and giving you a preeminent authority over the faithful, such as Allah had given him. Thereafter, he invoked Allah to be witness over them, and he said, "Have I not communicated this matter to you?" and they replied, "By Allah, yes." Whereat he said, "O Allah, be witness, and You suffice as witness, and judge between Your servants." So may Allah's curse be upon those who disputed your authority after having acknowledged it, and broke their covenant after they had pledging it solemnly.

وَ أَشْهَدُ أَنَّهُ قَدْ بَلَّغَ عَنِ اللهِ مَا أَنْزَلَهُ فِيكَ، فَصَدَعَ بِأَمْرِهِ، وَ أَوْجَبَ عَلَىٰ أُمَّتِهِ فَرْضَ طَاعَتِكَ وَ وِلَايَتِكَ، وَ عَقَدَ عَلَيْهِمُ الْبَيْعَةَ لَكَ، وَ جَعَلَكَ أَوْلَىٰ بِالْمُؤْمِنِينَ مِنْ أَنْفُسِهِمْ كَمَا جَعَلَهُ اللهُ كَذٰلِكَ، ثُمَّ أَشْهَدَ اللهَ تَعَالَىٰ عَلَيْهِمْ فَقَالَ: أَ لَسْتُ قَدْ بَلَّغْتُ؟ فَقَالُوا اللّٰهُمَّ بَلَىٰ، فَقَالَ: اَللّٰهُمَّ اشْهَدْ وَ كَفَىٰ بِكَ شَهِيدًا وَ حَاكِمًا بَيْنَ الْعِبَادِ. فَلَعَنَ اللهُ جَاحِدَ وِلَايَتِكَ بَعْدَ الْإِقْرَارِ، وَ نَاكِثَ عَهْدِكَ بَعْدَ الْمِيثَاقِ،

I testify that you fulfilled the

وَ أَشْهَدُ أَنَّكَ وَفَيْتَ بِعَهْدِ اللهِ تَعَالَىٰ،

وَ أَنَّ اللهَ تَعَالَىٰ مُوفٍ لَكَ بِعَهْدِهِ، وَ مَنْ أَوْفَىٰ بِمَا عَاهَدَ عَلَيْهِ اللهَ فَسَيُؤْتِيهِ أَجْرًا عَظِيمًا.

covenant of Allah, the Most High, and that Allah will fulfil His covenant with you *and whoever fulfils the covenant he has made with Allah, He will give him a great reward.*(48:10)

وَ أَشْهَدُ أَنَّكَ أَمِيرُ الْمُؤْمِنِينَ الْحَقُّ الَّذِى نَطَقَ بِوِلَايَتِكَ التَّنْزِيلُ، وَ أَخَذَ لَكَ الْعَهْدَ عَلَى الْأُمَّةِ بِذٰلِكَ الرَّسُولُ.

And I testify that you are the true Commander of the Faithful whose authority has been proclaimed by God's revelations and the Apostle made the *ummah* pledge itself to that.

وَ أَشْهَدُ أَنَّكَ وَ عَمَّكَ وَ أَخَاكَ الَّذِينَ تَاجَرْتُمُ اللهَ بِنُفُوسِكُمْ، فَأَنْزَلَ اللهُ فِيكُمْ: إِنَّ اللهَ اشْتَرَىٰ مِنَ الْمُؤْمِنِينَ أَنْفُسَهُمْ وَ أَمْوَالَهُمْ بِأَنَّ لَهُمُ الْجَنَّةَ، يُقَاتِلُونَ فِي سَبِيلِ اللهِ فَيَقْتُلُونَ وَ يُقْتَلُونَ، وَعْدًا عَلَيْهِ حَقًّا فِي التَّوْرٰيةِ وَ الْإِنْجِيلِ وَ الْقُرْآنِ، وَ مَنْ أَوْفَىٰ بِعَهْدِهِ مِنَ اللهِ؟ فَاسْتَبْشِرُوا بِبَيْعِكُمُ الَّذِى بَايَعْتُمْ بِهِ، وَ ذٰلِكَ هُوَ الْفَوْزُ الْعَظِيمُ. اَلتَّائِبُونَ الْعَابِدُونَ الْحَامِدُونَ السَّائِحُونَ الرَّاكِعُونَ السَّاجِدُونَ الْآمِرُونَ بِالْمَعْرُوفِ وَ النَّاهُونَ عَنِ الْمُنْكَرِ وَ الْحَافِظُونَ لِحُدُودِ اللهِ، وَ بَشِّرِ الْمُؤْمِنِينَ؛

I testify that you, your uncle and your brother made a deal with Allah in exchange for your souls, whereat He revealed this verse concerning you, stating, "Indeed Allah has bought from the faithful their souls and their possessions for paradise to be theirs: they fight in the way of Allah, kill, and are killed. A promise binding upon Him in the Torah and the Evangel and the Qur'ān. And who is truer to his promise than Allah? So rejoice in the bargain you have made with Him, and that is the great success. [The faithful are] penitent, devout, celebrators of Allah's praise, wayfarers, who bow [and] prostrate [in prayer], bid what is right and forbid what is wrong, and keep Allah's bounds —and give good news to the faithful."(9:111-112)

أَشْهَدُ يَا أَمِيرَ الْمُؤْمِنِينَ أَنَّ الشَّاكَّ فِيكَ مَا آمَنَ بِالرَّسُولِ الْأَمِينِ، وَ أَنَّ الْعَادِلَ بِكَ

O Commander of the Faithful, I testify that those who have doubts about you[r Imamate] do not have faith in the trust-

غَيْرَكَ عَانِدٌ عَنِ الدِّيـنِ الْقَوِيمِ الَّذِى ارْتَضَاهُ لَنَـا رَبُّ الْعَالَمِينَ، وَ أَكْمَلَهُ بِوِلَايَتِكَ يَوْمَ الْغَدِيرِ.

ed Apostle and that those who put others on a par with you deviate from the upright religion which has been approved for us by the Lord of all the worlds, who perfected it with your *wilāyah* on the Day of Ghadīr.[5:3]

وَ أَشْهَدُ أَنَّكَ الْمَعْنِيُّ بِقَوْلِ الْعَزِيزِ الرَّحِيمِ: وَ أَنَّ هٰذَا صِرَاطِى مُسْتَقِيمًا فَاتَّبِعُوهُ وَ لَا تَتَّبِعُوا السُّبُلَ فَتَفَرَّقَ بِكُمْ عَنْ سَبِيلِهِ. ضَلَّ وَ اللهِ وَ أَضَلَّ مَنِ اتَّبَعَ سِوَاكَ، وَ عَنَدَ عَنِ الْحَقِّ مَنْ عَادَاكَ.

I testify that you are the one who is meant by the words of the Almighty and the All-merciful, "*This indeed is my straight path, so follow it, and do not follow the (other) ways, for they will separate you from His way.*"[6:153] By God, those who follow others besides you go astray and mislead others and those who are hostile to you deviate from the truth.

اَللّٰهُمَّ سَمِعْنَا لِأَمْرِكَ وَ أَطَعْنَا، وَ اتَّبَعْنَا صِرَاطَكَ الْمُسْتَقِيمَ، فَاهْدِنَا رَبَّنَا وَ لَا تُزِغْ قُلُوبَنَا بَعْدَ إِذْ هَدَيْتَنَا إِلَىٰ طَاعَتِكَ، وَ اجْعَلْنَا مِنَ الشَّاكِرِينَ لِأَنْعُمِكَ.

O Allah, we have heard Your command and we obey and follow Your straight path, so guide us, Our Lord! Do not make our hearts swerve after You have guided us, and enable us to be of those who are grateful for Your blessings!

وَ أَشْهَدُ أَنَّكَ لَمْ تَزَلْ لِلْهَوَىٰ مُخَالِفًا، وَ لِلتُّقَىٰ مُحَالِفًا، وَ عَلَىٰ كَظْمِ الْغَيْظِ قَادِرًا، وَ عَنِ النَّاسِ عَافِيًا غَافِرًا، وَ إِذَا عُصِيَ اللهُ سَاخِطًا، وَ إِذَا أُطِيعَ اللهُ رَاضِيًا، وَ بِمَا عَهِدَ إِلَيْكَ عَامِلًا، رَاعِيًا لِمَا اسْتُحْفِظْتَ، حَافِظًا لِمَا اسْتُودِعْتَ، مُبَلِّغًا مَا حُمِّلْتَ، مُنْتَظِرًا مَا وُعِدْتَ.

I testify that you always opposed self-seeking impulses and were committed to Godfearing, that you were well able to suppress your rage and pardon and forgive the people, that you were displeased when God was disobeyed and were pleased when God was obeyed, that you did what you were enjoined with, observed what was committed to your care, preserved what you were entrusted with, delivered what you were charged with, and await what you were promised.

وَ أَشْهَدُ أَنَّكَ مَا اتَّقَيْتَ ضَارِعًا، وَ لَا أَمْسَكْتَ عَنْ حَقِّكَ جَازِعًا، وَ لَا أَحْجَمْتَ عَنْ مُجَاهَدَةِ غَاصِبِيكَ نَاكِلًا، وَ لَا أَظْهَرْتَ الرِّضَىٰ بِخِلَافِ مَا يُرْضِي اللّٰهَ مُدَاهِنًا، وَ لَا وَهَنْتَ لِمَا أَصَابَكَ فِي سَبِيلِ اللّٰهِ، وَ لَا ضَعُفْتَ وَ لَا اسْتَكَنْتَ عَنْ طَلَبِ حَقِّكَ مُرَاقِبًا، مَعَاذَ اللّٰهِ أَنْ تَكُونَ كَذٰلِكَ، بَلْ إِذْ ظُلِمْتَ احْتَسَبْتَ رَبَّكَ، وَ فَوَّضْتَ إِلَيْهِ أَمْرَكَ، وَ ذَكَّرْتَهُمْ فَمَا ادَّكَرُوا، وَ وَعَظْتَهُمْ فَمَا اتَّعَظُوا، وَ خَوَّفْتَهُمُ اللّٰهَ فَمَا تَخَوَّفُوا.

I testify that you did not conciliate with your opponents out of humiliation and weakness, nor your restraint in obtaining your right was due to fear, nor your desisting from fighting the usurpers of your right was due to evasion, nor did you express approval of what was contrary to what God approves on account of laxity, nor did you falter for what befell you in the way of Allah, neither did you weaken nor abased yourself by failing to restore your right out of caution (to avoid danger or harm). God forbid, that you should be such! Rather, when treated unjustly you resigned yourself to your Lord's will, leaving your matter to Him, and you admonished them but they would not be admonished, you advised them and they would not take advice, and you called on them to fear Allah, but they would not fear Him.

وَ أَشْهَدُ أَنَّكَ يَا أَمِيرَ الْمُؤْمِنِينَ جَاهَدْتَ فِي اللّٰهِ حَقَّ جِهَادِهِ، حَتَّىٰ دَعَاكَ اللّٰهُ إِلَىٰ جِوَارِهِ، وَ قَبَضَكَ إِلَيْهِ بِاخْتِيَارِهِ، وَ أَلْزَمَ أَعْدَاءَكَ الْحُجَّةَ بِقَتْلِهِمْ إِيَّاكَ، لِتَكُونَ الْحُجَّةُ لَكَ عَلَيْهِمْ مَعَ مَا لَكَ مِنَ الْحُجَجِ الْبَالِغَةِ عَلَىٰ جَمِيعِ خَلْقِهِ.

O Commander of the Faithful, I testify that you waged *jihād* for the sake of Allah, a *jihād* that is worthy of Him, until Allah summoned you to His vicinage and took you away by His will, and He took a testimony against your enemies for assassinating you, so that it may be a proof in your favour and against them, along with the conclusive proof that you have against all His creation!

اَلسَّلَامُ عَلَيْكَ يَا أَمِيرَ الْمُؤْمِنِينَ، عَبَدْتَ اللّٰهَ مُخْلِصًا، وَ جَاهَدْتَ فِي اللّٰهِ صَابِرًا،

Peace be to you, O Commander of the Faithful! You worshipped Allah with total dedication and struggled

وَ جُدْتَ بِنَفْسِكَ مُحْتَسِبًا، وَ عَمِلْتَ بِكِتَابِهِ، وَ اتَّبَعْتَ سُنَّةَ نَبِيِّهِ، وَ أَقَمْتَ الصَّلَاةَ، وَ آتَيْتَ الزَّكَاةَ، وَ أَمَرْتَ بِالْمَعْرُوفِ، وَ نَهَيْتَ عَنِ الْمُنْكَرِ مَا اسْتَطَعْتَ، مُبْتَغِيًا مَا عِنْدَ اللهِ، رَاغِبًا فِيمَا وَعَدَ اللهُ، لَا تَحْفِلُ بِالنَّوَائِبِ؛ وَ لَا تَهِنُ عِنْدَ الشَّدَائِدِ، وَ لَا تَحْجِمُ عَنْ مُحَارِبٍ،

patiently for His sake. You sacrificed yourself while putting your trust in Him. You acted in accordance with His Scripture, followed the *sunnah* of His Prophet, maintained the prayer, paid *zakāt*, bade what is right and forbade what is wrong to the utmost extent of your capacity, seeking that which is with Allah, desiring that which He has promised, being indifferent to adversities, without showing weakness in hardships, and being unflinching in the face of any opponent.

أَفِكَ مَنْ نَسَبَ غَيْرَ ذٰلِكَ إِلَيْكَ، وَ افْتَرَىٰ بَاطِلًا عَلَيْكَ، وَ أَوْلَىٰ لِمَنْ عَنَدَ عَنْكَ.

Those who attribute to you any quality other than that lie and fabricate falsehoods against you, and woe to those who have swerved from you!

لَقَدْ جَاهَدْتَ فِي اللهِ حَقَّ الْجِهَادِ، وَ صَبَرْتَ عَلَى الْأَذَىٰ صَبْرَ احْتِسَابٍ، وَ أَنْتَ أَوَّلُ مَنْ آمَنَ بِاللهِ، وَ صَلَّىٰ لَهُ، وَ جَاهَدَ وَ أَبْدَىٰ صَفْحَتَهُ فِي دَارِ الشِّرْكِ، وَ الْأَرْضُ مَشْحُونَةٌ ضَلَالَةً، وَ الشَّيْطَانُ يُعْبَدُ جَهْرَةً، وَ أَنْتَ الْقَائِلُ لَا تَزِيدُنِي كَثْرَةُ النَّاسِ حَوْلِي عِزَّةً، وَ لَا تَفَرُّقُهُمْ عَنِّي وَحْشَةً، وَ لَوْ أَسْلَمَنِي النَّاسُ جَمِيعًا لَمْ أَكُنْ مُتَضَرِّعًا.

Certainly you waged *jihād* for the sake of Allah a worthy *jihād*, suffered patiently all the torments with a patience sprung from trust in Allah, and you were the first of those who believed in Allah, prayed to Him, struggled, and were the first of those who openly proclaimed their faith in Him in the abode of idolatry and in a land filled with error, where Satan was worshipped openly! You are the one who said, "The large number of people surrounding me does not increase my might and honour, nor their forsaking me makes me feel lonely and desolate, and if all mankind were to forsake and betray me I will not feel humiliated."

You held fast to Allah and enjoyed honour and might, and you chose the Hereafter over this world and led an ascetic life. Allah strengthened you and guided you; He made you dedicated in your faith and chose you. Hence there was neither any contradiction in your actions, nor any inconsistency in your statements, nor any dissonance in your states. You did not make any false claims and fabrications against Allah, nor you had any greed for worldly vanities, nor were you defiled by sins. You have never ceased to be on a manifest proof from your Lord and conviction in all your affairs, and you guided others to the truth and to the straight path.

اِعْتَصَمْتَ بِاللهِ فَعَزَزْتَ، وَ آثَرْتَ الْآخِرَةَ عَلَى الْأُولٰى فَزَهِدْتَ، وَ أَيَّدَكَ اللهُ وَ هَدَاكَ، وَ أَخْلَصَكَ وَ اجْتَبَاكَ، فَمَا تَنَاقَضَتْ أَفْعَالُكَ، وَ لَا اخْتَلَفَتْ أَقْوَالُكَ، وَ لَا تَقَلَّبَتْ أَحْوَالُكَ، وَ لَا ادَّعَيْتَ وَ لَا افْتَرَيْتَ عَلَى اللهِ كَذِبًا، وَ لَا شَرِهْتَ إِلَى الْحُطَامِ، وَ لَا دَنَّسَكَ الْآثَامُ، وَ لَمْ تَزَلْ عَلٰى بَيِّنَةٍ مِنْ رَبِّكَ، وَ يَقِينٍ مِنْ أَمْرِكَ، تَهْدِي إِلَى الْحَقِّ وَ إِلٰى صِرَاطٍ مُسْتَقِيمٍ.

I testify, with a testimony that is honest, and swear by Allah, with an oath that is genuine, that Muḥammad and his Family, may Allah bless them, are the leaders of the creation, and that you are my master and the guardian of the faithful, and that you are a servant of Allah and His *walī* and brother of the Apostle and his heir and legatee. I testify what the Apostle said to you: "By Him who has sent me with the truth, those who deny you do not believe in me, and those who repudiate you do not acknowledge faith in Allah. Those who turn their back on you go astray, and those who are not guided by you will not be guided to Allah or to me. And that is the meaning of the words of my

أَشْهَدُ شَهَادَةَ حَقٍّ، وَ أُقْسِمُ بِاللهِ قَسَمَ صِدْقٍ، أَنَّ مُحَمَّدًا وَ آلَهُ صَلَوَاتُ اللهِ عَلَيْهِمْ سَادَاتُ الْخَلْقِ، وَ أَنَّكَ مَوْلَايَ وَ مَوْلَى الْمُؤْمِنِينَ، وَ أَنَّكَ عَبْدُ اللهِ وَ وَلِيُّهُ، وَ أَخُو الرَّسُولِ وَ وَصِيُّهُ وَ وَارِثُهُ، وَ أَنَّهُ الْقَائِلُ لَكَ: وَ الَّذِي بَعَثَنِي بِالْحَقِّ مَا آمَنَ بِي مَنْ كَفَرَ بِكَ، وَ لَا أَقَرَّ بِاللهِ مَنْ جَحَدَكَ، وَ قَدْ ضَلَّ مَنْ صَدَّ عَنْكَ، وَ لَمْ يَهْتَدِ إِلَى اللهِ وَ لَا إِلَيَّ مَنْ لَا يَهْتَدِي بِكَ، وَ

Lord, Almighty and Glorious, '*Indeed I am an all-forgiving Lord toward those who repent, become faithful and act righteously, and then walk on the right path*' of your *wilāyah*."(20:82)

هُوَ قَوْلُ رَبِّي عَزَّ وَ جَلَّ: وَ إِنِّي لَغَفَّارٌ لِمَنْ
تَابَ وَ آمَنَ وَ عَمِلَ صَالِحًا ثُمَّ اهْتَدَىٰ
إِلَىٰ وِلَايَتِكَ.

My master, your excellence cannot be hidden and your light cannot be extinguished, and those who repudiate you are the most unjust and wretched [of creatures]. My master, you are Allah's testament to His servants and His guide to rectitude, and the provision for the Day of Resurrection.

مَوْلَايَ فَضْلُكَ لَا يَخْفَىٰ، وَ نُورُكَ
لَا يُطْفَأُ، وَ أَنَّ مَنْ جَحَدَكَ الظَّلُومُ
الْأَشْقَىٰ، مَوْلَايَ أَنْتَ الْحُجَّةُ عَلَى الْعِبَادِ،
وَ الْهَادِي إِلَى الرَّشَادِ، وَ الْعُدَّةُ لِلْمَعَادِ.

My master, Allah has certainly exalted your station in this world and elevated your rank in the Hereafter, and He enabled you to perceive that to which your opponents were blind and who became an obstacle between you and Allah's gifts to you. May Allah's curse be on those who violated your sanctity and usurped your right, and I testify that they were the greatest losers, "the Fire will scorch their faces, and they will be morose in it."(23:104.)

مَوْلَايَ لَقَدْ رَفَعَ اللهُ فِي الْأُولَىٰ مَنْزِلَتَكَ،
وَ أَعْلَىٰ فِي الْآخِرَةِ دَرَجَتَكَ، وَ بَصَّرَكَ مَا
عَمِيَ عَلَىٰ مَنْ خَالَفَكَ، وَ حَالَ بَيْنَكَ
وَ بَيْنَ مَوَاهِبِ اللهِ لَكَ، فَلَعَنَ اللهُ
مُسْتَحِلِّي الْحُرْمَةِ مِنْكَ، وَ ذَائِدِي الْحَقِّ
عَنْكَ، وَ أَشْهَدُ أَنَّهُمُ الْأَخْسَرُونَ الَّذِينَ
تَلْفَحُ وُجُوهَهُمُ النَّارُ وَ هُمْ فِيهَا كَالِحُونَ.

I testify that you never advanced, nor stepped back, nor spoke, nor were silent except by the command of Allah and His Apostle, and you said, "By Him in whose hand is my soul, the Apostle of Allah, may Allah bless him and his Family, saw me striking with the sword on the battlefront, whereupon he said to me,

وَ أَشْهَدُ أَنَّكَ مَا أَقْدَمْتَ وَ لَا أَحْجَمْتَ
وَ لَا نَطَقْتَ وَ لَا أَمْسَكْتَ إِلَّا بِأَمْرٍ مِنَ
اللهِ وَ رَسُولِهِ، قُلْتَ: وَ الَّذِي نَفْسِي بِيَدِهِ،
لَقَدْ نَظَرَ إِلَيَّ رَسُولُ اللهِ صَلَّى اللهُ عَلَيْهِ وَ
آلِهِ أَضْرِبُ بِالسَّيْفِ قُدُمًا، فَقَالَ: يَا عَلِيُّ

أَنْتَ مِنِّي بِمَنْزِلَةِ هَارُونَ مِنْ مُوسَىٰ إِلَّا أَنَّهُ لَا نَبِيَّ بَعْدِي، وَ أُعْلِمُكَ أَنَّ مَوْتَكَ وَ حَيَاتَكَ مَعِي وَ عَلَىٰ سُنَّتِي، فَوَ اللهِ مَا كَذِبْتُ وَ لَا كُذِبْتُ، وَ لَا ضَلَلْتُ وَ لَا ضُلَّ بِي، وَ لَا نَسِيتُ مَا عَهِدَ إِلَيَّ رَبِّي، وَ إِنِّي لَعَلَىٰ بَيِّنَةٍ مِنْ رَبِّي، بَيَّنَهَا لِنَبِيِّهِ وَ بَيَّنَهَا النَّبِيُّ لِي، وَ إِنِّي لَعَلَى الطَّرِيقِ الْوَاضِحِ أَلْفِظُهُ لَفْظًا.

ʻO ʻAlī, your position in relation to me is that of Aaron in relation to Moses, except that there shall be no prophet after me. I am informing you that your life and death is with me and in accordance with my *sunnah*.' By Allah, I do not lie, nor what I have been told is a lie. Neither have I gone astray nor have I been misled, nor have I forgotten what my Lord has enjoined upon me. Indeed I am on a manifest proof from my Lord, which He clarified for His Prophet and the Prophet clarified it for me, and I am on a clear path, which I know word by word."

صَدَقْتَ وَ اللهِ وَ قُلْتَ الْحَقَّ، فَلَعَنَ اللهُ مَنْ سَاوَاكَ بِمَنْ نَاوَاكَ، وَ اللهُ جَلَّ اسْمُهُ يَقُولُ: هَلْ يَسْتَوِي الَّذِينَ يَعْلَمُونَ وَ الَّذِينَ لَا يَعْلَمُونَ؟

By Allah, what you have said is true, and, by Allah, what you have stated is the truth, so may Allah's curse be upon those who equate you with those who dissociated themselves from you. Allah, may glory be to His Name, says, "Are those who know equal to those who do not know?"'(39:9)

فَلَعَنَ اللهُ مَنْ عَدَلَ بِكَ مَنْ فَرَضَ اللهُ عَلَيْهِ وِلَايَتَكَ، وَ أَنْتَ وَلِيُّ اللهِ، وَ أَخُو رَسُولِهِ، وَ الذَّابُّ عَنْ دِينِهِ، وَ الَّذِي نَطَقَ الْقُرْآنُ بِتَفْضِيلِهِ، قَالَ اللهُ تَعَالَىٰ: وَ فَضَّلَ اللهُ الْمُجَاهِدِينَ عَلَى الْقَاعِدِينَ أَجْرًا عَظِيمًا، دَرَجَاتٍ مِنْهُ وَ مَغْفِرَةً وَ رَحْمَةً وَ كَانَ اللهُ غَفُورًا رَحِيمًا،

May Allah's curse be upon those who equate you with those who were obligated by Allah to submit to your *wilāyah*. You are Allah's *walī*, brother of His Apostle and defender of His religion, and you are the one whose merit has been declared by the Qur'ān. Allah, the Most High, has said, "Allah has graced those who wage *jihād* over those who sit back with a great reward: ranks from Him, forgiveness, and mercy, and Allah is all-forgiving, all-merciful."(4:95-96)

وَ قَالَ اللّٰهُ تَعَالَىٰ: أَ جَعَلْتُمْ سِقَايَةَ الْحَاجِّ وَ عِمَارَةَ الْمَسْجِدِ الْحَرَامِ كَمَنْ آمَنَ بِاللّٰهِ وَ الْيَوْمِ الْآخِرِ، وَ جَاهَدَ فِي سَبِيلِ اللّٰهِ، لَا يَسْتَوُونَ عِنْدَ اللّٰهِ، وَ اللّٰهُ لَا يَهْدِي الْقَوْمَ الظَّالِمِينَ. اَلَّذِينَ آمَنُوا وَ هَاجَرُوا وَ جَاهَدُوا فِي سَبِيلِ اللّٰهِ بِأَمْوَالِهِمْ وَ أَنْفُسِهِمْ أَعْظَمُ دَرَجَةً عِنْدَ اللّٰهِ، وَ أُولٰئِكَ هُمُ الْفَائِزُونَ، يُبَشِّرُهُمْ رَبُّهُمْ بِرَحْمَةٍ مِنْهُ وَ رِضْوَانٍ وَ جَنَّاتٍ لَهُمْ فِيهَا نَعِيمٌ مُقِيمٌ، خَالِدِينَ فِيهَا أَبَدًا، إِنَّ اللّٰهَ عِنْدَهُ أَجْرٌ عَظِيمٌ.

And Allah, the Most High, has said, "Do you regard the providing of water to ḥajj pilgrims and the maintenance of the Holy Mosque as similar [in worth] to someone who has faith in Allah and [believes in] the Last Day and wages *jihād* in the way of Allah? They are not equal with Allah, and Allah does not guide the wrongdoing lot. Those who have believed and migrated, and waged *jihād* in the way of Allah with their possessions and persons have a greater rank near Allah, and it is they who are the triumphant. Their Lord gives them the good news of His mercy and [His] pleasure, and for them there will be gardens with lasting bliss, to remain in them forever. With Allah indeed is a great reward."(9:19-23)

أَشْهَدُ أَنَّكَ الْمَخْصُوصُ بِمِدْحَةِ اللّٰهِ، اَلْمُخْلِصُ لِطَاعَةِ اللّٰهِ، لَمْ تَبْغِ بِالْهُدَىٰ بَدَلًا، وَ لَمْ تُشْرِكْ بِعِبَادَةِ رَبِّكَ أَحَدًا، وَ أَنَّ اللّٰهَ تَعَالَىٰ اسْتَجَابَ لِنَبِيِّهِ صَلَّى اللّٰهُ عَلَيْهِ وَ آلِهِ فِيكَ دَعْوَتَهُ، ثُمَّ أَمَرَهُ بِإِظْهَارِ مَا أَوْلَاكَ لِأُمَّتِهِ، إِعْلَاءً لِشَأْنِكَ، وَ إِعْلَانًا لِبُرْهَانِكَ، وَ دَحْضًا لِلْأَبَاطِيلِ، وَ قَطْعًا لِلْمَعَاذِيرِ، فَلَمَّا أَشْفَقَ مِنْ فِتْنَةِ الْفَاسِقِينَ، وَ اتَّقَىٰ فِيكَ

I testify that you were singled out by Allah for acclaim, you were exclusively dedicated to obeying Allah, never seeking any substitute for guidance and never associating anyone in the worship of your Lord, and that Allah, the Most High, answered the prayer of His Prophet, may Allah bless him and his family, regarding you, and then commanded him to proclaim what He had bestowed upon you for the sake of his *ummah*, in order to exalt your station, to promulgate your testament, to refute falsehoods and to preclude all excuses. So when he was apprehensive of the seditions of the evildoers and was wary of the hypocrites on your account, the Lord of the worlds revealed to him, "*O Apostle! Communicate that which has been sent down to you from your Lord, and if you do not, you will not have communicated His message, and Allah shall protect you from the people.*"(5:67)

الْمُنَافِقِينَ، أَوْحَىٰ إِلَيْهِ رَبُّ الْعَالَمِينَ:
يَا أَيُّهَا الرَّسُولُ بَلِّغْ مَا أُنْزِلَ إِلَيْكَ
مِنْ رَبِّكَ، وَ إِنْ لَمْ تَفْعَلْ فَمَا بَلَّغْتَ
رِسَالَتَهُ، وَ اللهُ يَعْصِمُكَ مِنَ النَّاسِ؛

Thereupon he made the caravan halt and bring down its burdens in mid journey, and rose in the intense heat (of the day of Ghadīr) to deliver a sermon, calling upon them to listen, and crying out to them to communicate (Allah's edicts). Then he asked their assembly, "Have I delivered?" They said, "Yes, indeed!" Whereat he said, "O Allah, be witness!" Then he said, "Am I not more entitled to (direct the affairs of) the faithful than themselves?" "Yes, indeed," they answered. Then he took your hand and declared, "Of whomever I am master and guardian, 'Ali is his master and guardian. O Allah, befriend those who befriend him and be the enemy of those who are his enemies! Help those who help him and forsake those who forsake him!"

فَوَضَعَ عَلَىٰ نَفْسِهِ أَوْزَارَ الْمَسِيرِ، وَ
نَهَضَ فِي رَمْضَاءِ الْهَجِيرِ، فَخَطَبَ
وَ أَسْمَعَ، وَ نَادَىٰ فَأَبْلَغَ، ثُمَّ سَأَلَهُمْ
أَجْمَعَ، فَقَالَ: هَلْ بَلَّغْتُ؟ فَقَالُوا
اللّٰهُمَّ بَلَىٰ، فَقَالَ اللّٰهُمَّ اشْهَدْ، ثُمَّ
قَالَ: أَ لَسْتُ أَوْلَىٰ بِالْمُؤْمِنِينَ مِنْ
أَنْفُسِهِمْ؟ فَقَالُوا: بَلَىٰ، فَأَخَذَ بِيَدِكَ
وَ قَالَ: مَنْ كُنْتُ مَوْلَاهُ فَهٰذَا عَلِيٌّ
مَوْلَاهُ، اَللّٰهُمَّ وَالِ مَنْ وَالَاهُ، وَ عَادِ
مَنْ عَادَاهُ، وَ انْصُرْ مَنْ نَصَرَهُ، وَ
اخْذُلْ مَنْ خَذَلَهُ؛

Yet none except a few believed in what Allah had revealed concerning you, and it did not increase the majority of them except in loss. Indeed Allah had formerly revealed concerning you, something which they regarded with aversion, "O you who have faith! Should any of you desert his religion, Allah will soon bring a people whom He loves

فَمَا آمَنَ بِمَا أَنْزَلَ اللهُ فِيكَ عَلَىٰ
نَبِيِّهِ إِلَّا قَلِيلٌ، وَ لَا زَادَ أَكْثَرَهُمْ
غَيْرَ تَخْسِيرٍ، وَ لَقَدْ أَنْزَلَ اللهُ تَعَالَىٰ
فِيكَ مِنْ قَبْلُ وَ هُمْ كَارِهُونَ: يَا
أَيُّهَا الَّذِينَ آمَنُوا مَنْ يَرْتَدَّ مِنْكُمْ

عَنْ دِينِهِ فَسَوْفَ يَأْتِي اللّٰهُ بِقَوْمٍ يُحِبُّهُمْ وَ يُحِبُّونَهُ، أَذِلَّةٍ عَلَى الْمُؤْمِنِينَ، أَعِزَّةٍ عَلَى الْكَافِرِينَ، يُجَاهِدُونَ فِي سَبِيلِ اللّٰهِ وَ لَا يَخَافُونَ لَوْمَةَ لَائِمٍ، ذٰلِكَ فَضْلُ اللّٰهِ يُؤْتِيهِ مَنْ يَشَاءُ، وَ اللّٰهُ وَاسِعٌ عَلِيمٌ؛ إِنَّمَا وَلِيُّكُمُ اللّٰهُ وَ رَسُولُهُ وَ الَّذِينَ آمَنُوا الَّذِينَ يُقِيمُونَ الصَّلَاةَ وَ يُؤْتُونَ الزَّكَاةَ وَ هُمْ رَاكِعُونَ، وَ مَنْ يَتَوَلَّ اللّٰهَ وَ رَسُولَهُ وَ الَّذِينَ آمَنُوا فَإِنَّ حِزْبَ اللّٰهِ هُمُ الْغَالِبُونَ.

and who love Him, (who will be) humble towards the faithful, stern towards the faithless, waging *jihād* in the way of Allah, not fearing the blame of any blamer. That is Allah's grace which He grants to whomever He wishes, and Allah is all-bounteous, all-knowing. Your guardian is only Allah, His Apostle, and the faithful who maintain the prayer and give the *zakāt* while bowing down. Whoever takes for his guardians Allah, His Apostle and the faithful (should know that) the confederates of Allah are indeed the victorious."[5:54-56]

رَبَّنَا آمَنَّا بِمَا أَنْزَلْتَ وَ اتَّبَعْنَا الرَّسُولَ، فَاكْتُبْنَا مَعَ الشَّاهِدِينَ؛ رَبَّنَا لَا تُزِغْ قُلُوبَنَا بَعْدَ إِذْ هَدَيْتَنَا، وَ هَبْ لَنَا مِنْ لَدُنْكَ رَحْمَةً، إِنَّكَ أَنْتَ الْوَهَّابُ.

"Our Lord, we believe in what You have sent down, and we follow the Apostle, so write us among the witnesses."[3:53] "Our Lord! Do not make our hearts swerve after You have guided us, and bestow Your mercy on us. Indeed You are the All-munificent."[3:8]

اَللّٰهُمَّ إِنَّا نَعْلَمُ أَنَّ هٰذَا هُوَ الْحَقُّ مِنْ عِنْدِكَ، فَالْعَنْ مَنْ عَارَضَهُ وَ اسْتَكْبَرَ، وَ كَذَّبَ بِهِ وَ كَفَرَ، وَ سَيَعْلَمُ الَّذِينَ ظَلَمُوا أَيَّ مُنْقَلَبٍ يَنْقَلِبُونَ.

O Allah, we know that this is the truth from You, so let Your curse be on those who oppose it, deny it and gainsay it out of arrogance, "and the wrongdoers will soon know at what goal they will end up."[26:227]

اَلسَّلَامُ عَلَيْكَ يَا أَمِيرَ الْمُؤْمِنِينَ، وَ سَيِّدَ الْوَصِيِّينَ، وَ أَوَّلَ الْعَابِدِينَ، وَ أَزْهَدَ الزَّاهِدِينَ، وَ رَحْمَةُ اللّٰهِ وَ بَرَكَاتُهُ وَ صَلَوَاتُهُ

Peace be to you, O Commander of the Faithful, chief of the Legatees, the foremost of the devout, and the most self-denying of the ascetics, and may Allah's mercy

وَ تَحِيَّاتُهُ،

and His bounties, blessings and greetings be to you!

أَنْتَ مُطْعِمُ الطَّعَامِ عَلٰى حُبِّهِ مِسْكِينًا وَ يَتِيمًا وَ أَسِيرًا لِوَجْهِ اللهِ، لَا تُرِيدُ مِنْهُمْ جَزَاءً وَ لَا شُكُورًا،

You are the one who gave food, "for the love of Him, to the needy, the orphan and the prisoner, (saying,) 'We feed you only for the sake of Allah,'[76:8-9] not desiring from them any reward or thanks.

وَ فِيكَ أَنْزَلَ اللهُ تَعَالٰى: وَ يُؤْثِرُونَ عَلٰى أَنْفُسِهِمْ وَ لَوْ كَانَ بِهِمْ خَصَاصَةٌ، وَ مَنْ يُوقَ شُحَّ نَفْسِهِ فَأُولٰئِكَ هُمُ الْمُفْلِحُونَ؛ وَ أَنْتَ الْكَاظِمُ لِلْغَيْظِ وَ الْعَافِي عَنِ النَّاسِ وَ اللهُ يُحِبُّ الْمُحْسِنِينَ؛

And it was concerning you that Allah revealed, "They prefer [others] to themselves, though poverty be their own lot. And those who are saved from their own greed —it is they who are the felicitous.[59:9] You were the one *who suppressed your anger, and excused [the faults of] the people, and Allah loves the virtuous.*[3:134]

وَ أَنْتَ الصَّابِرُ فِي الْبَأْسَاءِ وَ الضَّرَّاءِ وَ حِينَ الْبَأْسِ، وَ أَنْتَ الْقَاسِمُ بِالسَّوِيَّةِ، وَ الْعَادِلُ فِي الرَّعِيَّةِ، وَ الْعَالِمُ بِحُدُودِ اللهِ مِنْ جَمِيعِ الْبَرِيَّةِ،

You are the one who were *patient in stress and distress, and in the heat of battle.*[2:177] You distributed the public funds equitably and carried out justice amongst the subjects. You knew Allah's laws better than the entire creation.

وَ اللهُ تَعَالٰى أَخْبَرَ عَمَّا أَوْلَاكَ مِنْ فَضْلِهِ بِقَوْلِهِ: أَ فَمَنْ كَانَ مُؤْمِنًا كَمَنْ كَانَ فَاسِقًا لَا يَسْتَوُونَ؛ أَمَّا الَّذِينَ آمَنُوا وَ عَمِلُوا الصَّالِحَاتِ فَلَهُمْ جَنَّاتُ الْمَأْوٰى نُزُلًا بِمَا كَانُوا يَعْمَلُونَ؛

Allah, the Most High, has informed us concerning the grace that He bestowed upon you when He said, "Is someone who is faithful like someone who is a transgressor? They are not equal. As for those who have faith and do righteous deeds, for them are gardens of the Abode—a hospitality for what they used to do." [32:18-19]

وَ أَنْتَ الْمَخْصُوصُ بِعِلْمِ التَّنْزِيلِ، وَ حُكْمِ التَّأْوِيلِ، وَ نَصِّ الرَّسُولِ، وَ

You are the one endowed with the knowledge of (the Qur'ānic) revelation, the rules of interpretation, the Apostle's texts, and to

لَكَ الْمَوَاقِفُ الْمَشْهُودَةُ، وَ الْمَقَامَاتُ الْمَشْهُورَةُ، وَ الْأَيَّامُ الْمَذْكُورَةُ، يَوْمَ بَدْرٍ وَ يَوْمَ الْأَحْزَابِ، إِذْ زَاغَتِ الْأَبْصَارُ وَ بَلَغَتِ الْقُلُوبُ الْحَنَاجِرَ، وَ تَظُنُّونَ بِاللهِ الظُّنُونَا، هُنَالِكَ ابْتُلِيَ الْمُؤْمِنُونَ وَ زُلْزِلُوا زِلْزَالًا شَدِيدًا، وَ إِذْ يَقُولُ الْمُنَافِقُونَ وَ الَّذِينَ فِي قُلُوبِهِمْ مَرَضٌ مَا وَعَدَنَا اللهُ وَ رَسُولُهُ إِلَّا غُرُورًا، وَ إِذْ قَالَتْ طَائِفَةٌ مِنْهُمْ يَا أَهْلَ يَثْرِبَ لَا مُقَامَ لَكُمْ فَارْجِعُوا، وَ يَسْتَأْذِنُ فَرِيقٌ مِنْهُمُ النَّبِيَّ، يَقُولُونَ إِنَّ بُيُوتَنَا عَوْرَةٌ، وَ مَا هِيَ بِعَوْرَةٍ، إِنْ يُرِيدُونَ إِلَّا فِرَارًا،

you belong the prominent and noteworthy occasions and illustrious stations, the historic days such as the Day of Badr and the Day of the Confederates "when the eyes rolled [with fear] and the hearts leapt to the throats, and you entertained misgivings about Allah, it was there that the faithful were tested and jolted with a severe agitation. And when the hypocrites were saying, as well as those in whose hearts is a sickness, 'Allah and His Apostle did not promise us [anything] except delusion.' And when a group of them said, 'O people of Yathrib! [This is] not a place for you,[1] so go back!' And a group of them sought the Prophet's permission, saying, 'Our homes lie exposed [to the enemy],' although they were not exposed. They only sought to flee." (33:10-13)

وَ قَالَ اللهُ تَعَالَىٰ: وَ لَمَّا رَأَى الْمُؤْمِنُونَ الْأَحْزَابَ قَالُوا هٰذَا مَا وَعَدَنَا اللهُ وَ رَسُولُهُ، وَ صَدَقَ اللهُ وَ رَسُولُهُ، وَ مَا زَادَهُمْ إِلَّا إِيمَانًا وَ تَسْلِيمًا.

And Allah, the Most High, has said, "But when the faithful saw the confederates, they said, 'This is what Allah and His Apostle had promised us, and Allah and His Apostle spoke the truth.' And it only increased them in faith and submission." (33:22)

فَقَتَلْتَ عَمْرَهُمْ، وَ هَزَمْتَ جَمْعَهُمْ، وَ رَدَّ اللهُ الَّذِينَ كَفَرُوا بِغَيْظِهِمْ لَمْ يَنَالُوا خَيْرًا، وَ كَفَى اللهُ الْمُؤْمِنِينَ الْقِتَالَ وَ كَانَ اللهُ قَوِيًّا عَزِيزًا.

There, you slew 'Amr, their warrior, and routed their hosts and "Allah sent back the faithless in their rage, without their attaining any advantage, and Allah spared the faithful of fighting, and Allah is all-strong, all-mighty." (33:25)

وَيَوْمَ أُحُدٍ إِذْ يُصْعِدُونَ وَلَا يَلْوُونَ عَلَىٰ أَحَدٍ، وَ الرَّسُولُ يَدْعُوهُمْ فِي أُخْرَاهُمْ، وَ أَنْتَ تَذُودُ بُهَمَ الْمُشْرِكِينَ عَنِ النَّبِيِّ ذَاتَ الْيَمِينِ وَ ذَاتَ الشِّمَالِ، حَتَّىٰ رَدَّهُمُ اللهُ تَعَالَىٰ عَنْكُمَا خَائِفِينَ، وَ نَصَرَ بِكَ الْخَاذِلِينَ.

And on the day of Uḥud, "when they were fleeing without paying any attention to anyone, while the Apostle was calling them from their rear,"[3:153] and you were chasing away the warriors of the idolaters from the Prophet to the right and to the left until Allah made them withdraw from the two of you in fear, and through you gave victory to those who had forsaken the battlefield.

وَ يَوْمَ حُنَيْنٍ عَلَىٰ مَا نَطَقَ بِهِ التَّنْزِيلُ: إِذْ أَعْجَبَتْكُمْ كَثْرَتُكُمْ، فَلَمْ تُغْنِ عَنْكُمْ شَيْئًا، وَ ضَاقَتْ عَلَيْكُمُ الْأَرْضُ بِمَا رَحُبَتْ، ثُمَّ وَلَّيْتُمْ مُدْبِرِينَ، ثُمَّ أَنْزَلَ اللهُ سَكِينَتَهُ عَلَىٰ رَسُولِهِ وَ عَلَى الْمُؤْمِنِينَ، وَ الْمُؤْمِنُونَ أَنْتَ وَ مَنْ يَلِيكَ وَ عَمُّكَ الْعَبَّاسُ يُنَادِي الْمُنْهَزِمِينَ يَا أَصْحَابَ سُورَةِ الْبَقَرَةِ، يَا أَهْلَ بَيْعَةِ الشَّجَرَةِ، حَتَّىٰ اسْتَجَابَ لَهُ قَوْمٌ قَدْ كَفَيْتَهُمُ الْمُؤْنَةَ، وَ تَكَفَّلْتَ دُونَهُمُ الْمَعُونَةَ، فَعَادُوا آيِسِينَ مِنَ الْمَثُوبَةِ، رَاجِينَ وَعْدَ اللهِ تَعَالَىٰ بِالتَّوْبَةِ، وَ ذٰلِكَ قَوْلُ اللهِ جَلَّ ذِكْرُهُ: ثُمَّ يَتُوبُ اللهُ مِنْ بَعْدِ ذٰلِكَ

And on the day of Ḥunayn, as declared in the revelation, "when your great number impressed you, but it did not avail you in any way, and the earth became narrow for you in spite of its expanse, whereupon you turned your backs (to flee). Then Allah sent down His composure upon His Apostle and upon the faithful."[9:25-26] 'The faithful' were you and your comrades and ʿAbbās, your uncle, who was shouting to the fleeing Muslim warriors, "O disciples of the Sūrat al-Baqarah! O performers of the Allegiance of the Tree!" Whereupon they responded to him after you had spared them the hardships of warfare and took upon yourself the defence of Islam without them. Thereat they returned having lost hope of the Divine reward and yet hopeful of the fulfilment of the promise of Allah through repentance, and that is referred to in the words of Allah, glorified be His name, "Then Allah shall turn clemently after that to whomever

عَلٰى مَنْ يَشَـاءُ، وَ أَنْتَ حَائِـزٌ دَرَجَةَ الصَّبْرِ، فَائِزٌ بِعَظِيمِ الْأَجْرِ،

He wishes,"(9:27.) while you enjoyed the high station of fortitude and attained a great reward.

وَ يَوْمَ خَيْبَرَ إِذْ أَظْهَرَ اللّٰهُ خَوَرَ الْمُنَافِقِينَ، وَ قَطَعَ دَابِرَ الْكَافِرِينَ، وَ الْحَمْدُ لِلّٰهِ رَبِّ الْعَالَمِينَ ،وَ لَقَدْ كَانُوا عَاهَدُوا اللّٰهَ مِنْ قَبْلُ لَا يُوَلُّونَ الْأَدْبَارَ، وَ كَانَ عَهْدُ اللّٰهِ مَسْؤُولًا؛

And again on the day of <u>Kh</u>aybar, when Allah divulged the weakness of the hypocrites and decimated the infidels, and all praise belongs to Allah, the Lord of all the worlds, "though they had certainly pledged to Allah before that they would not turn their backs (to flee), and pledges given to Allah are accountable."(33:15)

مَوْلَایَ أَنْتَ الْحُجَّةُ الْبَالِغَةُ، وَ الْمَحَجَّةُ الْوَاضِحَةُ، وَ النِّعْمَةُ السَّابِغَةُ، وَ الْبُرْهَانُ الْمُنِيرُ، فَهَنِيئًا لَكَ بِمَـا آتَاكَ اللّٰهُ مِنْ فَضْلٍ، وَ تَبًّا لِشَانِئِكَ ذِی الْجَهْلِ.

My master, you are (Allah's) conclusive testament, the clear path, the bountiful blessing, and the shining proof. Hence congratulations to you for the grace bestowed on you by Allah, and woe to your ignorant enemies!

شَهِدْتَ مَعَ النَّبِيِّ صَلَّى اللّٰهُ عَلَيْهِ وَ آلِهِ جَمِيعَ حُرُوبِهِ وَ مَغَازِيـهِ، تَحْمِلُ الرَّايَةَ أَمَامَهُ، وَ تَـضْرِبُ بِالسَّـيْفِ قُدَّامَهُ، ثُمَّ لِحَزْمِكَ الْمَشْـهُورِ، وَ بَصِيرَتِكَ فِی الْأُمُورِ، أَمَّرَكَ فِی الْمَوَاطِنِ، وَ لَمْ يَكُنْ عَلَيْكَ أَمِيرٌ،

You participated with the Prophet, may Allah bless him and his Family, in all his battles and campaigns, carrying the banner before him and fighting at his fore with the sword. On account of your well-known judiciousness and your insight in all matters, the Prophet made you commander on many occasions and never was anyone appointed a commander over you.

وَ كَمْ مِـنْ أَمْرٍ صَدَّكَ عَـنْ إِمْضَاءِ عَزْمِـكَ فِيهِ التُّقَىٰ، وَ اتَّبَـعَ غَيْرُكَ فِی مِثْلِهِ الْهَـوَىٰ، فَظَـنَّ الْجَاهِلُونَ أَنَّكَ

Many were the cases when your Godfearing withheld you from carrying out your resolve, whereas others followed their desires in similar cases, leading the ignorant to imagine that you lacked the

عَجَزْتَ عَمَّا إِلَيْهِ انْتَهَى، ضَلَّ وَ اللهِ الظَّانُّ لِذٰلِكَ وَ مَا اهْتَدَىٰ، وَ لَقَدْ أَوْضَحْتَ مَا أَشْكَلَ مِنْ ذٰلِكَ لِمَنْ تَوَهَّمَ وَ امْتَرَىٰ، بِقَوْلِكَ صَلَّى اللهُ عَلَيْكَ: قَدْ يَرَى الْحُوَّلُ الْقُلَّبُ وَجْهَ الْحِيلَةِ، وَ دُونَهَا حَاجِزٌ مِنْ تَقْوَى اللهِ، فَيَدَعُهَا رَأْيَ الْعَيْنِ، وَ يَنْتَهِزُ فُرْصَتَهَا مَنْ لَا حَرِيجَةَ لَهُ فِي الدِّينِ.

ability to carry out a task. By God, those who imagined such a thing went astray and were not rightly guided. You have certainly clarified the misconceptions of those who have entertained them and disputed (your abilities) with your statement, may Allah's blessings be upon you, "The experienced and ingenious person sights the course of artifice and, short of it, sees the barrier posed by Godfearing, whereat he disregards it right away at the first sight, but those who have no scruples in religion seize the opportunity provided by it."

صَدَقْتَ (وَ اللهِ) وَ خَسِرَ الْمُبْطِلُونَ، وَ إِذْ مَاكَرَكَ النَّاكِثَانِ فَقَالَا نُرِيدُ الْعُمْرَةَ، فَقُلْتَ لَهُمَا لَعَمْرُكُمَا مَا تُرِيدَانِ الْعُمْرَةَ، لَكِنْ تُرِيدَانِ الْغَدْرَةَ، فَأَخَذْتَ الْبَيْعَةَ عَلَيْهِمَا، وَ جَدَّدْتَ الْمِيثَاقَ، فَجَدَّا فِي النِّفَاقِ، فَلَمَّا نَبَّهْتَهُمَا عَلَىٰ فِعْلِهِمَا أَغْفَلَا، وَ عَادَا وَ مَا انْتَفَعَا، وَ كَانَ عَاقِبَةُ أَمْرِهِمَا خُسْرًا.

(By God,) you have stated the truth and those who pursued false notions were losers. When the two who broke their oath of allegiance tried to deceive you, saying that they intended to perform *'umrah* pilgrimage, you told them, "By your lives, your intention is not to perform *'umrah*, but to carry out treason!" Then you took their oath of allegiance and had them renew their pledge, but they rallied to sedition. So when you apprised them of their conduct, they disregarded it and went back without drawing any benefit, "and the outcome of their conduct was ruin."

ثُمَّ تَلَاهُمَا أَهْلُ الشَّامِ، فَسِرْتَ إِلَيْهِمْ بَعْدَ الْإِعْذَارِ، وَ هُمْ لَا يَدِينُونَ دِينَ الْحَقِّ، وَ لَا يَتَدَبَّرُونَ الْقُرْآنَ، هَمَجٌ رَعَاعٌ ضَالُّونَ، وَ بِالَّذِي أُنْزِلَ عَلَىٰ

Then they were followed by the Syrians and you marched towards them after having vindicated your stand, whereas they neither followed the true religion nor reflected upon the Qur'ān. They were the misguided rabble, who disbelieved

مُحَمَّدٍ فِيكَ كَافِرُونَ، وَ لِأَهْلِ الْخِلَافِ عَلَيْكَ نَاصِرُونَ، وَ قَدْ أَمَرَ اللهُ تَعَالَىٰ بِاتِّبَاعِكَ، وَ نَدَبَ الْمُؤْمِنِينَ إِلَىٰ نَصْرِكَ، وَ قَالَ عَزَّ وَ جَلَّ: يَا أَيُّهَا الَّذِينَ آمَنُوا اتَّقُوا اللهَ وَ كُونُوا مَعَ الصَّادِقِينَ.

what had been revealed to Muḥammad and supported the antagonists against you, whereas Allah, the Most High, had commanded them to follow you and urged the faithful to support you, and He, the Almighty and Glorious, had declared, "O you who have faith! Be wary of Allah, and be with the Truthful."(9:119)

مَوْلَاىَ بِكَ ظَهَرَ الْحَقُّ، وَ قَدْ نَبَذَهُ الْخَلْقُ، وَ أَوْضَحْتَ السُّنَنَ بَعْدَ الدُّرُوسِ وَ الطَّمْسِ، فَلَكَ سَابِقَةُ الْجِهَادِ عَلَىٰ تَصْدِيقِ التَّنْزِيلِ، وَ لَكَ فَضِيلَةُ الْجِهَادِ عَلَىٰ تَحْقِيقِ التَّأْوِيلِ، وَ عَدُوُّكَ عَدُوُّ اللهِ، جَاحِدٌ لِرَسُولِ اللهِ، يَدْعُو بَاطِلًا، وَ يَحْكُمُ جَائِرًا، وَ يَتَأَمَّرُ غَاصِبًا، وَ يَدْعُو حِزْبَهُ إِلَى النَّارِ.

My master, it was through you that the truth was disclosed, while the people disregarded it, and you expounded the precepts of Islam after they had become obliterated and effaced. Thus you enjoyed precedence in waging *jihād* for affirming the Revelation and yours was the merit of waging *jihād* for giving concrete form to its meanings. Your enemies are the enemies of Allah and deniers of the Apostle of Allah, who summon to untruth, judge unjustly, usurp power and invite their confederates to hellfire.

وَ عَمَّارٌ يُجَاهِدُ وَ يُنَادِي بَيْنَ الصَّفَّيْنِ: اَلرَّوَاحَ الرَّوَاحَ إِلَى الْجَنَّةِ، وَ لَمَّا اسْتَسْقَىٰ فَسُقِيَ اللَّبَنَ كَبَّرَ وَ قَالَ: قَالَ لِي رَسُولُ اللهِ صَلَّى اللهُ عَلَيْهِ وَ آلِهِ آخِرُ شَرَابِكَ مِنَ الدُّنْيَا ضَيَاحٌ مِنْ لَبَنٍ، وَ تَقْتُلُكَ الْفِئَةُ الْبَاغِيَةُ، فَاعْتَرَضَهُ أَبُو الْعَادِيَةِ الْفَزَارِيُّ فَقَتَلَهُ، فَعَلَىٰ أَبِي الْعَادِيَةِ

And there was 'Ammār, (your helper) who, as he fought, cried out between the ranks of the confronting armies, "Come on! Let's set out for paradise!" When he asked for water, he was given milk to drink, whereat he magnified God and said, "The Apostle of Allah, may Allah bless him and his Family, had told me, 'Your last drink in the world will be curdled milk, and you will be slain by the rebellious party.'" Thereupon Abul 'Ādiyah al-Fazārī engaged him and slew him. May Al-

لَعْنَةُ اللهِ وَ لَعْنَةُ مَلائِكَتِهِ وَ رُسُلِهِ أَجْمَعِينَ، وَ عَلىٰ مَنْ سَلَّ سَيْفَهُ عَلَيْكَ وَ سَلَلْتَ سَيْفَكَ عَلَيْهِ يا أَمِيرَ الْمُؤْمِنِينَ مِنَ الْمُشْرِكِينَ وَ الْمُنافِقِينَ إِلىٰ يَوْمِ الدِّينِ، وَ عَلىٰ مَنْ رَضِيَ بِما ساءَكَ وَ لَمْ يَكْرَهْهُ، وَ أَغْمَضَ عَيْنَهُ وَ لَمْ يُنْكِرْ، أَوْ أَعانَ عَلَيْكَ بِيَدٍ أَوْ لِسانٍ، أَوْ قَعَدَ عَنْ نَصْرِكَ، أَوْ خَذَلَ عَنِ الْجِهادِ مَعَكَ، أَوْ غَمَطَ فَضْلَكَ، وَ جَحَدَ حَقَّكَ، أَوْ عَدَلَ بِكَ مَنْ جَعَلَكَ اللهُ أَوْلىٰ بِهِ مِنْ نَفْسِهِ، وَ صَلَواتُ اللهِ عَلَيْكَ وَ رَحْمَةُ اللهِ وَ بَرَكاتُهُ وَ سَلامُهُ وَ تَحِيّاتُهُ، وَ عَلَى الْأَئِمَّةِ مِنْ آلِكَ الطّاهِرِينَ، إِنَّهُ حَمِيدٌ مَجِيدٌ.

lah's curse and that of His angels and all His apostles be until the Day of Retribution upon Abul ʿĀdiyah and on those who drew their swords against you and on those against whom you, O Commander of the Faithful, drew your sword, from among the polytheists and the hypocrites, as well as on those who view what offended you with approval and did not decry it, or looked the other way without disapproving, or provided their support against you by word or deed, or denied you their help or deserted their duty of waging *jihād* alongside you, or those who belittled your merits, contested your right, or regarded as your equals such persons over whom Allah had given you a greater right than they had over themselves, may Allah's blessings, His mercy, His bounties and His greetings and salutations be upon you and the immaculate Imams of your descent! Indeed He is all-praiseworthy and all-glorious!

وَ الْأَمْرُ الْأَعْجَبُ، وَ الْخَطْبُ الْأَفْظَعُ، بَعْدَ جَحْدِكَ حَقَّكَ غَصْبُ الصِّدِّيقَةِ الطّاهِرَةِ الزَّهْراءِ سَيِّدَةِ النِّساءِ فَدَكًا، وَ رَدُّ شَهادَتِكَ وَ شَهادَةِ السَّيِّدَيْنِ سُلالَتِكَ وَ عِتْرَةِ الْمُصْطَفىٰ صَلَّى اللهُ عَلَيْكُمْ، وَ قَدْ أَعْلَى اللهُ تَعالىٰ عَلَى

But what is more amazing, and outrageous after the denial of your right, is the wrongful usurpation of Fadak from Zahrā, the truthful and pure one, the mistress of the world's womankind, and the rejection of your testimony and that of your illustrious sons and the progeny of al-Muṣṭafā, may Allah's blessings be upon you, while Allah, the Most High, had elevated your rank over the entire *ummah* and exalted your station, and He had made manifest your excellence and honoured you above all the world's denizens, keeping all impurity from you and purifying you with utmost purification.

الْأُمَّةِ دَرَجَتَكُمْ، وَ رَفَعَ مَنْزِلَتَكُمْ،
وَ أَبَانَ فَضْلَكُمْ، وَ شَرَّفَكُمْ عَلَى
الْعَالَمِينَ، فَأَذْهَبَ عَنْكُمُ الرِّجْسَ وَ
طَهَّرَكُمْ تَطْهِيرًا،

Allah, the Almighty and Glorious, has said, "*Indeed man has been created covetous: he is anxious when an ill befalls him and grudging when good comes his way—[all are such] except the prayerful, (who are persevering in their prayers).*"(17:19-23) Thus Allah, the Most High, made His Prophet and you, O chief of the Legatees, an exception in relation to all the creatures.

قَالَ اللهُ عَزَّ وَ جَلَّ: إِنَّ الْإِنْسَانَ خُلِقَ
هَلُوعًا، إِذَا مَسَّهُ الشَّرُّ جَزُوعًا، وَ إِذَا
مَسَّهُ الْخَيْرُ مَنُوعًا، إِلَّا الْمُصَلِّينَ،
فَاسْتَثْنَى اللهُ تَعَالَىٰ نَبِيَّهُ الْمُصْطَفَىٰ وَ
أَنْتَ يَا سَيِّدَ الْأَوْصِيَاءِ مِنْ جَمِيعِ الْخَلْقِ.

So how misguided were those who wronged you with respect to your right, and then, for the sake of deception, assigned you the share of the kinsmen, while denying it unfairly to its rightful claimants!

فَمَا أَعْمَهَ مَنْ ظَلَمَكَ عَنِ الْحَقِّ، ثُمَّ
أَفْرَضُوكَ سَهْمَ ذَوِي الْقُرْبَىٰ مَكْرًا، وَ
أَحَادُوهُ عَنْ أَهْلِهِ جَوْرًا،

So when temporal power came into your hands, you let the situation remain as it was before in regard to your rights, disregarding them for the sake of your reward with Allah. So your ordeal in relation to the two was like the ordeal of the prophets, peace be to them, in their loneliness and absence of helpers.

فَلَمَّا آلَ الْأَمْرُ إِلَيْكَ أَجْرَيْتَهُمْ عَلَىٰ مَا
أَجْرَيَا رَغْبَةً عَنْهُمَا بِمَا عِنْدَ اللهِ لَكَ،
فَأَشْبَهَتْ مِحْنَتُكَ بِهِمَا مِحَنَ الْأَنْبِيَاءِ
عَلَيْهِمُ السَّلَامُ عِنْدَ الْوَحْدَةِ وَ عَدَمِ
الْأَنْصَارِ،

Your conduct in sleeping in the Prophet's bed (on the night of the flight from Makkah) was like that of Ishmael, may peace be to him, when you assented and obeyed,

وَ أَشْبَهْتَ فِي الْبَيَاتِ عَلَى الْفِرَاشِ
الذَّبِيحَ عَلَيْهِ السَّلَامُ، إِذْ أَجَبْتَ كَمَا
أَجَابَ، وَ أَطَعْتَ كَمَا أَطَاعَ إِسْمَاعِيلُ

as he did, patiently and seeking God's pleasure, when Abraham said to him, 'My son! I see in a dream that I am sacrificing you. See what you think.' He said, 'Father! Do whatever you have been commanded. If Allah wishes, you will find me to be patient.'[37:102]

صَابِرًا مُحْتَسِبًا، إِذْ قَالَ لَهُ: يَا بُنَيَّ إِنِّي أَرَىٰ فِي الْمَنَامِ أَنِّي أَذْبَحُكَ، فَانْظُرْ مَا ذَا تَرَىٰ. قَالَ: يَا أَبَتِ افْعَلْ مَا تُؤْمَرُ، سَتَجِدُنِي إِنْ شَاءَ اللهُ مِنَ الصَّابِرِينَ.

And so were you when the Prophet, may Allah bless him and his Family, bade you to sleep in his bed, and in this manner you shielded him from harm by risking your own life. You were prompt to comply, having obediently prepared yourself mentally to be killed, whereupon Allah, the Most High, appreciated your obedience and expressed the gracefulness of your action in His words, may His Name be glorified, "And among the people is he who sells his soul seeking the pleasure of Allah."[2:207]

وَ كَذٰلِكَ أَنْتَ لَمَّا أَبَاتَكَ النَّبِيُّ صَلَّى اللهُ عَلَيْهِ وَ آلِهِ، وَ أَمَرَكَ أَنْ تَضْجَعَ فِي مَرْقَدِهِ وَاقِيًا لَهُ بِنَفْسِكَ، أَسْرَعْتَ إِلَىٰ إِجَابَتِهِ مُطِيعًا، وَ لِنَفْسِكَ عَلَى الْقَتْلِ مُوَطِّنًا، فَشَكَرَ اللهُ تَعَالَىٰ طَاعَتَكَ، وَ أَبَانَ عَنْ جَمِيلِ فِعْلِكَ بِقَوْلِهِ جَلَّ ذِكْرُهُ: وَ مِنَ النَّاسِ مَنْ يَشْرِي نَفْسَهُ ابْتِغَاءَ مَرْضَاتِ اللهِ.

Yet again there was your ordeal during the Battle of Siffīn, when the tomes were raised on the spears as a deceptive stratagem, whereupon doubts arose in minds and the truth was set aside and conjecture was followed. It was similar to the ordeal of Aaron when he was appointed by Moses to lead his people, whereupon they forsook him while he kept calling them, saying, "O my people! You are only being tested by it. Indeed your Lord is the All-beneficent. So follow me and obey my command!" But they had said,

ثُمَّ مِحْنَتُكَ يَوْمَ صِفِّينَ وَ قَدْ رُفِعَتِ الْمَصَاحِفُ حِيلَةً وَ مَكْرًا فَأَعْرَضَ الشَّكُّ وَ عُزِفَ الْحَقُّ وَ اتُّبِعَ الظَّنُّ، أَشْبَهَتْ مِحْنَةَ هَارُونَ إِذْ أَمَّرَهُ مُوسَىٰ عَلَىٰ قَوْمِهِ، فَتَفَرَّقُوا عَنْهُ، وَ هَارُونُ يُنَادِي بِهِمْ وَ يَقُولُ: يَا قَوْمِ إِنَّمَا فُتِنْتُمْ بِهِ، وَ إِنَّ رَبَّكُمُ الرَّحْمٰنُ، فَاتَّبِعُونِي وَ أَطِيعُوا أَمْرِي، قَالُوا: لَنْ نَبْرَحَ عَلَيْهِ عَاكِفِينَ

"We will keep on attending to it until Moses returns to us." (20:90-91)

حَتَّىٰ يَرْجِعَ إِلَيْنَا مُوسَىٰ.

Such was your case, when the tomes were raised and you were saying, 'O my people, you are being misled and deceived by this means.' But they disobeyed you and demanded the appointment of arbiters, whereat you declined their demand and, deploring their conduct before Allah, left them to their devices.

وَ كَذٰلِكَ أَنْتَ لَمَّا رُفِعَتِ الْمَصَاحِفُ قُلْتَ: يَا قَوْمِ إِنَّمَا فُتِنْتُمْ بِهَا وَ خُدِعْتُمْ، فَعَصَوْكَ وَ خَالَفُوا عَلَيْكَ، وَ اسْتَدْعَوْا نَصْبَ الْحَكَمَيْنِ، فَأَبَيْتَ عَلَيْهِمْ، وَ تَبَرَّأْتَ إِلَى اللهِ مِنْ فِعْلِهِمْ، وَ فَوَّضْتَهُ إِلَيْهِمْ،

So when the truth was revealed and their wrong stand was discredited, and they admitted their mistake and oversight of the goal. But then they fell into disagreement and blamed on you the folly of arbitration, which you had opposed and they had desired and which you had warned them against while they considered it legitimate, and they held you responsible for the sin that they had themselves committed, although you were on the path of insight and guidance and they were in error and blindness.

فَلَمَّا أَسْفَرَ الْحَقُّ، وَ سَفِهَ الْمُنْكَرُ، وَ اعْتَرَفُوا بِالزَّلَلِ وَ الْجَوْرِ عَنِ الْقَصْدِ، اِخْتَلَفُوا مِنْ بَعْدِهِ، وَ أَلْزَمُوكَ عَلَىٰ سَفَهِ التَّحْكِيمِ الَّذِي أَبَيْتَهُ، وَ أَحَبُّوهُ وَ حَظَرْتَهُ، وَ أَبَاحُوا ذَنْبَهُمُ الَّذِي اقْتَرَفُوهُ، وَ أَنْتَ عَلَىٰ نَهْجِ بَصِيرَةٍ وَ هُدًى، وَ هُمْ عَلَىٰ سُنَنِ ضَلَالَةٍ وَ عَمًى،

Yet they persisted in their hypocrisy and perversity until Allah made them taste the evil consequences of their conduct. Those who opposed you, became wretched and perished, and He slew them with your sword. He revived through those who were felicitous your proofs and they were rightly guided.

فَمَا زَالُوا عَلَى النِّفَاقِ مُصِرِّينَ، وَ فِي الْغَيِّ مُتَرَدِّدِينَ، حَتَّىٰ أَذَاقَهُمُ اللهُ وَبَالَ أَمْرِهِمْ، فَأَمَاتَ بِسَيْفِكَ مَنْ عَانَدَكَ فَشَقِيَ وَ هَوَىٰ، وَ أَحْيَا بِحُجَّتِكَ مَنْ سَعِدَ فَهُدِيَ،

May Allah's blessings be upon you at every beginning and end of

صَلَوَاتُ اللهِ عَلَيْكَ غَادِيَةً وَ رَائِحَةً، وَ

عَاكِفَةً وَ ذَاهِبَةً، فَمَا يُحِيطُ الْمَادِحُ وَصْفَكَ، وَ لَا يُحْبِطُ الطَّاعِنُ فَضْلَكَ، أَنْتَ أَحْسَنُ الْخَلْقِ عِبَادَةً، وَ أَخْلَصُهُمْ زَهَادَةً، وَ أَذَبُّهُمْ عَنِ الدِّينِ،

your days and during all your movements and pauses. No admirer can encompass your merits and no detractor can obscure your excellences. You are the best of the creatures with regard to worship, the most dedicated in piety, and the most zealous in defending the faith.

أَقَمْتَ حُدُودَ اللهِ بِجُهْدِكَ، وَ فَلَلْتَ عَسَاكِرَ الْمَارِقِينَ بِسَيْفِكَ، تُخْمِدُ لَهَبَ الْحُرُوبِ بِبَنَانِكَ، وَ تَهْتِكُ سُتُورَ الشُّبَهِ بِبَيَانِكَ، وَ تَكْشِفُ لَبْسَ الْبَاطِلِ عَنْ صَرِيحِ الْحَقِّ، لَا تَأْخُذُكَ فِي اللهِ لَوْمَةُ لَائِمٍ،

With your efforts you maintained the laws of Allah and with your sword subdued the armies of the renegades. With your hands you extinguished the flames of war and with your discourses removed the veils of doubt, separated the adulterating falsehoods from the pure truth without being deterred by the blame of any blamer in any matter pertaining to Allah.

وَ فِي مَدْحِ اللهِ تَعَالَىٰ لَكَ غِنًى عَنْ مَدْحِ الْمَادِحِينَ، وَ تَقْرِيظِ الْوَاصِفِينَ، قَالَ اللهُ تَعَالَىٰ: مِنَ الْمُؤْمِنِينَ رِجَالٌ صَدَقُوا مَا عَاهَدُوا اللهَ عَلَيْهِ، فَمِنْهُمْ مَنْ قَضَىٰ نَحْبَهُ، وَ مِنْهُمْ مَنْ يَنْتَظِرُ، وَ مَا بَدَّلُوا تَبْدِيلًا.

The compliments of Allah, the Most High, regarding you suffice you to do without the praise of any admirer and compliments of any praiser. And Allah, the Most High, has said, “Among the faithful are men who fulfil what they have pledged to Allah. Of them are some who have fulfilled their pledge, and of them are some who still wait, and they have not changed in the least.” (33:23)

وَ لَمَّا رَأَيْتَ أَنْ قَتَلْتَ النَّاكِثِينَ وَ الْقَاسِطِينَ وَ الْمَارِقِينَ، وَ صَدَقَكَ رَسُولُ اللهِ صَلَّى اللهُ عَلَيْهِ وَ آلِهِ وَعْدَهُ، فَأَوْفَيْتَ بِعَهْدِهِ، قُلْتَ: أَمَا

Having seen that you had to fight the perfidious, the perverse and the renegades, and that the prophecy of the Apostle of Allah, may Allah bless him and his Family, had come true in what he had told you, and being content that you had fulfilled your pledge to him, you would say,

آنَ أَنْ تُخْضَبَ هٰذِهِ مِنْ هٰذِهِ؟ أَمْ مَتَىٰ يُبْعَثُ أَشْقَاهَا؟ وَاثِقًا بِأَنَّكَ عَلَىٰ بَيِّنَةٍ مِنْ رَبِّكَ، وَ بَصِيرَةٍ مِنْ أَمْرِكَ، قَادِمٌ عَلَى اللهِ، مُسْتَبْشِرٌ بِبَيْعِكَ الَّذِي بَايَعْتَهُ بِهِ، وَ ذٰلِكَ هُوَ الْفَوْزُ الْعَظِيمُ.

'Is it not the time yet for this (beard of mine) to be dyed in (the blood of) this (head of mine)?' or 'When will the most wretched man from among this people rise up?' You were convinced that you possessed a manifest proof from your Lord and full insight of your own affair, and that you will meet Allah rejoicing in the bargain you had made with Him, and that is the great success.

اَللّٰهُمَّ الْعَنْ قَتَلَةَ أَنْبِيَائِكَ وَ أَوْصِيَاءِ أَنْبِيَائِكَ بِجَمِيعِ لَعَنَاتِكَ، وَ أَصْلِهِمْ حَرَّ نَارِكَ، وَ الْعَنْ مَنْ غَصَبَ وَلِيَّكَ حَقَّهُ، وَ أَنْكَرَ عَهْدَهُ، وَ جَحَدَهُ بَعْدَ الْيَقِينِ وَ الْإِقْرَارِ بِالْوِلَايَةِ لَهُ يَوْمَ أَكْمَلْتَ لَهُ الدِّينَ.

O Allah, let Your anathema, accompanied with all Your curses, be on those who slew Your prophets and the legatees of Your prophets, and make them enter Your Fire. Let Your curse be on those who usurped the rights of Your *walī*, refused to acknowledge his covenant, and opposed him, after acknowledging and being certain of his authority on the day when You perfected the religion for them.

اَللّٰهُمَّ الْعَنْ قَتَلَةَ أَمِيرِ الْمُؤْمِنِينَ وَ مَنْ ظَلَمَهُ وَ أَشْيَاعَهُمْ وَ أَنْصَارَهُمْ.

O Allah, let Your curse be on those who killed the Commander of the Faithful and those who wronged him, and their followers and supporters.

اَللّٰهُمَّ الْعَنْ ظَالِمِي الْحُسَيْنِ وَ قَاتِلِيهِ، وَ الْمُتَابِعِينَ عَدُوَّهُ وَ نَاصِرِيهِ، وَ الرَّاضِينَ بِقَتْلِهِ وَ خَاذِلِيهِ لَعْنًا وَبِيلًا.

O Allah, bring down Your terrible curse on those who wronged al-Ḥusayn and those who slew him, as well as those who followed and helped his enemies, those who approved of his murder, and those who forsook him.

اَللّٰهُمَّ الْعَنْ أَوَّلَ ظَالِمٍ ظَلَمَ آلَ مُحَمَّدٍ وَ مَانِعِيهِمْ حُقُوقَهُمْ.

O Allah, let Your curse be on the one was first to wrong the Family of Muḥammad and those who denied them their rights.

اَللّٰهُمَّ خُصَّ أَوَّلَ ظَالِمٍ وَ غَاصِبٍ لِآلِ

O Allah, single out for Your curse until the Day of Resurrection the

مُحَمَّدٍ بِاللَّعْنِ، وَ كُلَّ مُسْتَنٍّ بِمَا سَنَّ إِلَىٰ يَوْمِ الْقِيٰامَةِ.

one who was first to have wronged the Family of Muḥammad and usurp their rights, as well as those who pursued his policies.

اَللّٰهُمَّ صَلِّ عَلىٰ مُحَمَّدٍ خَاتَمِ النَّبِيِّينَ، وَ عَلىٰ عَلِيٍّ سَيِّدِ الْوَصِيِّينَ وَ آلِهِ الطَّاهِرِينَ، وَ اجْعَلْنَا بِهِمْ مُتَمَسِّكِينَ، وَ بِوِلاٰيَتِهِمْ مِنَ الْفَائِزِينَ الْآمِنِينَ، اَلَّذِينَ لاٰ خَوْفٌ عَلَيْهِمْ وَ لاٰ هُمْ يَحْزَنُونَ.

Allah, bless Muḥammad, Seal of the Prophets, and 'Alī, chief of the Legatees, and his immaculate progeny, and appoint us to be amongst their adherents and those who obtain victory and security through their *wilāyah* and who will neither have any fear nor will ever grieve.

In our book *Hadīyat al-Zā'irīn* we have mentioned the *isnād* of this *ziyārah*[1] and noted that this *ziyārah* may be recited everyday from far and near, and this is an immensely useful point that will be appreciated by the lovers of worship and ardent performers of the *ziyārah* of the Prince of *Wilāyah*.

SUPPLICATION AFTER ZIYARAH

This supplication is reported in *Iqbāl*[2] from Imam Jaᶜfar al-Ṣādiq (*ᶜa*). The Imam is reported to have said that when someone is in the vicinity of the shrine of the Commander of the Faithful (*ᶜa*) on the day of Ghadir, he should approach the tomb and recite the following supplication after prayer. When in a distant town or place on that occasion, one should, after prayer, recite this supplication while pointing toward his shrine.

اَللّٰهُمَّ صَلِّ عَلىٰ وَلِيِّكَ، وَ أَخِي نَبِيِّكَ، وَ وَزِيرِهِ وَ حَبِيبِهِ وَ خَلِيلِهِ، وَ مَوْضِعِ سِرِّهِ، وَ خِيَرَتِهِ مِنْ أُسْرَتِهِ، وَ وَصِيِّهِ وَ صَفْوَتِهِ

Oh Allah, bless Your *wali* and the brother of Your Prophet and his minister, his beloved, dedicated friend, repository of his secrets, elect of his family, his legatee, sincere friend, trustee,

1 *Hadīyat al-Zā'irīn*, 241 from Muḥammad b. al-Mashhadī's *al-Mazār al-Kabīr*, 263.

2 *Iqbāl*, 493, whence *Biḥār*, xcvii, 372, b 5, h 8 and *Mustadrak*, x, 220, b 19, h 11896/1. Kafᶜamī's *Miṣbāḥ*, 685, whence *Biḥār*, xcv, 292, b 3, h 1.

وَ خَالِصَتِهِ، وَ أَمِينِهِ وَ وَلِيِّهِ وَ أَشْرَفِ
عِتْرَتِهِ الَّذِينَ آمَنُوا بِهِ، وَ أَبِي ذُرِّيَّتِهِ،
وَ بَابِ حِكْمَتِهِ، وَ النَّاطِقِ بِحُجَّتِهِ، وَ
الدَّاعِي إِلَىٰ شَرِيعَتِهِ، وَ الْمَاضِي عَلَىٰ سُنَّتِهِ،
وَ خَلِيفَتِهِ عَلَىٰ أُمَّتِهِ، سَيِّدِ الْمُسْلِمِينَ، وَ
أَمِيرِ الْمُؤْمِنِينَ، وَ قَائِدِ الْغُرِّ الْمُحَجَّلِينَ،
أَفْضَلَ مَا صَلَّيْتَ عَلَىٰ أَحَدٍ مِنْ خَلْقِكَ
وَ أَصْفِيَائِكَ وَ أَوْصِيَاءِ أَنْبِيَائِكَ.

walī, and the most distinguished of his kindred who had faith in him, and the father of his descendants, the gateway of his wisdom, the declarer of his proofs, the summoner to his *sharīʿah*, the adherent to his *sunnah*, his successor within his community, the chief of the Muslims, the Commander of the Faithful, and the leader of the devout, with the best of blessings that You have showered on any of Your creatures, Your elect servants, and the legatees of Your prophets!

اَللّٰهُمَّ إِنِّي أَشْهَدُ أَنَّهُ قَدْ بَلَّغَ عَنْ نَبِيِّكَ
صَلَّى اللّٰهُ عَلَيْهِ وَ آلِهِ مَا حُمِّلَ، وَ رَعَىٰ
مَا اسْتُحْفِظَ، وَ حَفِظَ مَا اسْتُودِعَ،
وَ حَلَّلَ حَلَالَكَ، وَ حَرَّمَ حَرَامَكَ، وَ
أَقَامَ أَحْكَامَكَ، وَ دَعَا إِلَىٰ سَبِيلِكَ،
وَ وَالَىٰ أَوْلِيَاءَكَ، وَ عَادَىٰ أَعْدَاءَكَ،
وَ جَاهَدَ النَّاكِثِينَ عَنْ سَبِيلِكَ، وَ
الْقَاسِطِينَ وَ الْمَارِقِينَ عَنْ أَمْرِكَ،
صَابِرًا مُحْتَسِبًا مُقْبِلًا غَيْرَ مُدْبِرٍ، لَا
تَأْخُذُهُ فِي اللّٰهِ لَوْمَةُ لَائِمٍ، حَتَّىٰ بَلَغَ
فِي ذٰلِكَ الرِّضَا، وَ سَلَّمَ إِلَيْكَ الْقَضَاءَ،
وَ عَبَدَكَ مُخْلِصًا، وَ نَصَحَ لَكَ مُجْتَهِدًا

O Allah, I testify that he communicated whatever he was charged with by Your Prophet, may Allah bless him and his Family, and safeguarded whatever he was given to guard, preserved whatever he had been entrusted with, allowed whatever You had made lawful, forbade whatever You had made unlawful, enforced Your laws, summoned to Your path, befriended Your friends and despised Your enemies, fought, patiently and seeking Your pleasure, the perfidious who broke from Your way, the perverse, and the renegades who had reneged from Your commands, without ever flinching and without being kept back by the blame of any blamer in the way of Allah, until he attained to the station of Your approval, surrendered to Your decrees,

حَتَّىٰ أَتَاهُ الْيَقِينُ، فَقَبَضْتَهُ إِلَيْكَ شَهِيدًا سَعِيدًا، وَلِيًّا تَقِيًّا، رَضِيًّا زَكِيًّا، هَادِيًا مَهْدِيًّا.

worshipped You dedicatedly, was a diligent well-wisher for Your sake, until your demise, whereat You received him as a martyr, felicitous, intimate friend, Godwary, pleasing, pure, guiding and well-guided.

اَللّٰهُمَّ صَلِّ عَلىٰ مُحَمَّدٍ وَ عَلَيْهِ أَفْضَلَ مَا صَلَّيْتَ عَلىٰ أَحَدٍ مِنْ أَنْبِيائِكَ وَ أَصْفِيائِكَ يا رَبَّ الْعَالَمِينَ!

O Allah bless Muḥammad and him with the best of blessings that You have bestowed upon any of Your prophets and Your elect servants, O Lord of all the worlds!

Sayyid Ibn Ṭāwūs has cited another *ziyārah* for this auspicious day in his book *Miṣbāḥ al-Zā'ir* and there is no indication that it is meant specifically for this day. It is composed of two *ziyārahs* and ᶜAllamah Majlisī, in his book *Tuḥfah*, has cited them as second and third *ziyārahs*.

ZIYARAH FOR THE PROPHET'S BIRTHDAY

Shaykh Mufid, Shahīd Awwal, and Sayyid Ibn Ṭāwūs report in their books[1] that Imam Jaᶜfar al-Ṣādiq (ᶜ*a*) performed the *ziyārah* of the Commander of the Faithful (ᶜ*a*) with this text on 17th of Rabīᶜ al-Awwal and taught this *ziyārah* to Muḥammad b. Muslim al-Thaqafī, an eminent disciple of the Imam and a trustworthy traditionist. He says, "When you arrive at the shrine of the Commander of the Faithful (ᶜ*a*), perform a bath for *ziyārah*, put on the neatest of your clothes, apply perfume to yourself, and proceed toward the shrine walking in a relaxed and dignified manner. On reaching the Bāb al-Salām, turn towards the *qiblah* and say 30 times *Allāhu akbar*. Then say,

اَلسَّلَامُ عَلىٰ رَسُولِ اللّٰهِ، اَلسَّلَامُ عَلىٰ خِيَرَةِ اللّٰهِ، اَلسَّلَامُ عَلَى الْبَشِيرِ النَّذِيرِ السِّرَاجِ الْمُنِيرِ، وَ رَحْمَةُ اللّٰهِ وَ بَرَكَاتُهُ.

Peace be to the Apostle of Allah! Peace be to the chosen of Allah! Peace be to the bearer of good news and warnings and the radiant lamp, and may Allah's mercy and His bounties be upon him!

1 *Iqbāl*, 608. *Biḥār*, xcvii, 373-376, b 5, h 9, from Shaykh Mufīd, Ibn Ṭāwūs and Shahīd Awwal's *Mazār*, 89-98. The report is cited without the text of the *ziyārah* in *Farḥat al-Gharī*, 93, and *Biḥār*, xcvii, 236, b 2, h 3, from Muḥammad b. al-Mashhadī's *al-Mazār al-Kabīr*.

اَلسَّلاٰمُ عَلَى الطُّهْرِ الطَّاهِرِ، اَلسَّلاٰمُ عَلَى الْعَلَمِ الزَّاهِرِ، اَلسَّلاٰمُ عَلَى الْمَنْصُورِ الْمُؤَيَّدِ، اَلسَّلاٰمُ عَلىٰ أَبِي الْقَاسِمِ مُحَمَّدٍ، وَ رَحْمَةُ اللهِ وَ بَرَكَاتُهُ.

Peace be to the pure and immaculate one! Peace be to the shining standard! Peace be to him who was blessed with divine help and approval! Peace be to Abū al-Qāsim Muḥammad and may Allah's mercy and His bounties be upon him!

اَلسَّلاٰمُ عَلىٰ أَنْبِيٰاءِ اللهِ الْمُرْسَلِينَ، وَ عِبَادِ اللهِ الصَّالِحِينَ، اَلسَّلاٰمُ عَلىٰ مَلاٰئِكَةِ اللهِ الْحَافِّينَ بِهٰذَا الْحَرَمِ وَ بِهٰذَا الضَّرِيحِ، اَللاّٰئِذِينَ بِهِ.

Peace be to the prophetic emissaries of Allah and His righteous servants! Peace be to Allah's angels who surround this sanctuary and shrine, having made it their refuge!

"Then approach the tomb and say,

اَلسَّلاٰمُ عَلَيْكَ يَا وَصِيَّ الْأَوْصِيٰاءِ، اَلسَّلاٰمُ عَلَيْكَ يَا عِمَادَ الْأَتْقِيٰاءِ، اَلسَّلاٰمُ عَلَيْكَ يَا وَلِيَّ الْأَوْلِيٰاءِ، اَلسَّلاٰمُ عَلَيْكَ يَا سَيِّدَ الشُّهَدَاءِ،

Peace be to you, O successor to all the legatees! Peace be to you, O pillar of the pious! Peace be to you, O guardian of Allah's friends! Peace be to you, O doyen of the martyrs!

اَلسَّلاٰمُ عَلَيْكَ يَا آيَةَ اللهِ الْعُظْمَىٰ، اَلسَّلاٰمُ عَلَيْكَ يَا خَامِسَ أَهْلِ الْعَبَاءِ، اَلسَّلاٰمُ عَلَيْكَ يَا قَائِدَ الْغُرِّ الْمُحَجَّلِينَ الْأَتْقِيٰاءِ، اَلسَّلاٰمُ عَلَيْكَ يَا عِصْمَةَ الْأَوْلِيٰاءِ،

Peace be to you, O greatest of Allah's signs! Peace be to you, O one of the five personages of the Cloak! Peace be to you, O leader of the singularly devout! Peace be to you, O preserver of the friends of Allah!

اَلسَّلاٰمُ عَلَيْكَ يَا زَيْنَ الْمُوَحِّدِينَ النُّجَبَاءِ، اَلسَّلاٰمُ عَلَيْكَ يَا خَالِصَ الْأَخِلاّٰءِ، اَلسَّلاٰمُ عَلَيْكَ يَا وَالِدَ الْأَئِمَّةِ الْأُمَنَاءِ،

Peace be to you, O gem of the elect of the monotheists! Peace be to you, O sinceremost of the Prophet's dedicated friends! Peace be to you, O progenitor of the trusted Imams!

اَلسَّلاٰمُ عَلَيْكَ يٰا صٰاحِبَ الْحَوْضِ وَ حٰامِلَ اللِّوٰاءِ، اَلسَّلاٰمُ عَلَيْكَ يٰا قَسِيمَ الْجَنَّةِ وَ لَظىٰ، اَلسَّلاٰمُ عَلَيْكَ يٰا مَنْ شُرِّفَتْ بِهِ مَكَّةُ وَ مِنىٰ،

Peace be to you, O master of the Pool and the bearer of the Banner (of Allah praise)! Peace be to you, O dispenser of paradise and hell! Peace be to you through whom were exalted Makkah and Minā!

اَلسَّلاٰمُ عَلَيْكَ يٰا بَحْرَ الْعُلُومِ وَ كَنَفَ الْفُقَرٰاءِ، اَلسَّلاٰمُ عَلَيْكَ يٰا مَنْ وُلِدَ فِي الْكَعْبَةِ وَ زُوِّجَ فِي السَّمٰاءِ بِسَيِّدَةِ النِّسٰاءِ، وَ كٰانَ شُهُودُهَا الْمَلاٰئِكَةَ الْأَصْفِيٰاءَ،

Peace be to you, O ocean of knowledge and refuge of the needy! Peace be to you, who were born in the Ka'bah and were wed to the princess of world's womankind in the heaven as witnessed by God's chosen angels!

اَلسَّلاٰمُ عَلَيْكَ يٰا مِصْبٰاحَ الضِّيٰاءِ، اَلسَّلاٰمُ عَلَيْكَ يٰا مَنْ خَصَّهُ النَّبِيُّ بِجَزِيلِ الْحِبٰاءِ، اَلسَّلاٰمُ عَلَيْكَ يٰا مَنْ بٰاتَ عَلىٰ فِرٰاشِ خٰاتَمِ الْأَنْبِيٰاءِ، وَ وَقٰاهُ بِنَفْسِهِ شَرَّ الْأَعْدٰاءِ،

Peace be to you, O lamp of light! Peace be to you who were singled out by the Prophet for the most abundant gifts! Peace be to you who slept on the bed of the Seal of the Prophets and saved him from the evil of the enemies at the risk of your own life!

اَلسَّلاٰمُ عَلَيْكَ يٰا مَنْ رُدَّتْ لَهُ الشَّمْسُ فَسٰامىٰ شَمْعُونَ الصَّفٰا، اَلسَّلاٰمُ عَلَيْكَ يٰا مَنْ أَنْجَى اللّٰهُ سَفِينَةَ نُوحٍ بِاسْمِهِ وَ اسْمِ أَخِيهِ حَيْثُ الْتَطَمَ الْمٰاءُ حَوْلَهٰا وَ طَمىٰ،

Peace be to you, for whom the sun was turned back, thus surpassing Peter Simon! Peace be to you, for the sake of whose name and that of his brother Allah delivered the Ark of Noah when jolted by the heaving waters surrounding it!

اَلسَّلاٰمُ عَلَيْكَ يٰا مَنْ تٰابَ اللّٰهُ بِهِ وَ بِأَخِيهِ عَلىٰ آدَمَ إِذْ غَوىٰ، اَلسَّلاٰمُ عَلَيْكَ يٰا فُلْكَ النَّجٰاةِ الَّذِي مَنْ رَكِبَهُ نَجٰا، وَ مَنْ تَأَخَّرَ عَنْهُ هَوىٰ،

Peace be to you, for whose sake and that of his brother Allah accepted the repentance of Adam at the time of his fall! Peace be to you, O ship of deliverance: those who board it are saved and those who lag behind perish!

اَلسَّلَامُ عَلَيْكَ يَا مَنْ خَاطَبَ الثُّعْبَانَ
وَ ذِئْبَ الْفَلَا، اَلسَّلَامُ عَلَيْكَ يَا أَمِيرَ
الْمُؤْمِنِينَ وَ رَحْمَةُ اللهِ وَ بَرَكَاتُهُ،

Peace be to you, who spoke to the python and to the wolf of the wild! Peace be to you, O Commander of the Faithful and may Allah's mercy and His bounties be upon you!

اَلسَّلَامُ عَلَيْكَ يَا حُجَّةَ اللهِ عَلَىٰ مَنْ
كَفَرَ وَ أَنَابَ، اَلسَّلَامُ عَلَيْكَ يَا إِمَامَ
ذَوِي الْأَلْبَابِ، اَلسَّلَامُ عَلَيْكَ يَا مَعْدِنَ
الْحِكْمَةِ وَ فَصْلَ الْخِطَابِ، اَلسَّلَامُ
عَلَيْكَ يَا مَنْ عِنْدَهُ عِلْمُ الْكِتَابِ،
اَلسَّلَامُ عَلَيْكَ يَا مِيزَانَ يَوْمِ الْحِسَابِ،

Peace be to you, O Allah's testament against those who reneged their faith as well as those who returned penitently! Peace be to you, O leader of those who possess intellects! Peace be to you, O fount of wisdom and decisive speech! Peace be to you, who have the knowledge of the Scripture! Peace be to you, O scale of justice on the Day of Reckoning!

اَلسَّلَامُ عَلَيْكَ يَا فَاصِلَ الْحُكْمِ النَّاطِقَ
بِالصَّوَابِ، اَلسَّلَامُ عَلَيْكَ أَيُّهَا الْمُتَصَدِّقُ
بِالْخَاتَمِ فِي الْمِحْرَابِ، اَلسَّلَامُ عَلَيْكَ
يَا مَنْ كَفَى اللهُ الْمُؤْمِنِينَ الْقِتَالَ بِهِ يَوْمَ
الْأَحْزَابِ،

Peace be to you, O giver of definitive judgment and author of right statements! Peace be to you, through whom Allah spared the faithful of fighting on the day of the Battle with the confederate tribes!

اَلسَّلَامُ عَلَيْكَ يَا مَنْ أَخْلَصَ لِلّٰهِ
الْوَحْدَانِيَّةَ وَ أَنَابَ، اَلسَّلَامُ عَلَيْكَ يَا
قَاتِلَ خَيْبَرَ وَ قَالِعَ الْبَابِ،

Peace be to you, whose dedication to the One God was unmingled, and to Allah did you ever turn! Peace be to you, O subduer of Khaybar, who tore away its gate!

اَلسَّلَامُ عَلَيْكَ يَا مَنْ دَعَاهُ خَيْرُ الْأَنَامِ
لِلْمَبِيتِ عَلَىٰ فِرَاشِهِ، فَأَسْلَمَ نَفْسَهُ
لِلْمَنِيَّةِ وَ أَجَابَ، اَلسَّلَامُ عَلَيْكَ يَا مَنْ

Peace be to you, who were called upon by the Best of the Creation to sleep on his bed, whereupon you surrendered yourself to destiny and complied! Peace be to you, blessed with happiness and

لَهُ طُوبىٰ وَ حُسْــنُ مَــآبٍ، وَ رَحْمَةُ اللهِ وَ بَرَكَاتُهُ.

excellent destination, and may Allah's mercy and His bounties be upon you!

اَلسَّــلَامُ عَلَيْكَ يَا وَلِيَّ عِصْمَةِ الدِّينِ وَ يَا سَيِّدَ السَّادَاتِ، اَلسَّلَامُ عَلَيْكَ يَا صَاحِبَ الْمُعْجِزَاتِ، اَلسَّلَامُ عَلَيْكَ يَا مَنْ نَزَلَتْ فِي فَضْلِهِ سُورَةُ الْعَادِيَاتِ، اَلسَّلَامُ عَلَيْكَ يَا مَنْ كُتِبَ اسْمُهُ فِي السَّمَاءِ عَلَى السُّرَادِقَاتِ،

Peace be to you, O protecting guardian of the faith and chief of the *sayyids!* Peace be to you, O author of miracles! Peace be to you, concerning whose virtues Sūrat al-ᶜĀdiyāt was revealed! Peace be to you, whose name is written on the curtains (of the Throne) in the heaven!

اَلسَّــلَامُ عَلَيْكَ يَا مُظْهِــرَ الْعَجَائِبِ وَ الْآيَاتِ، اَلسَّلَامُ عَلَيْكَ يَا أَمِيرَ الْغَزَوَاتِ، اَلسَّلَامُ عَلَيْكَ يَا مُخْبِرًا بِمَا غَبَرَ وَ بِمَا هُوَ آتٍ،

Peace be to you, O manifestor of wonders and miraculous signs! Peace be to you, O commander of the troops of Islam during the Prophet's campaigns! Peace be to you, who gave accounts of what is past and that which is yet to come!

اَلسَّلَامُ عَلَيْكَ يَا مُخَاطِبَ ذِئْبِ الْفَلَوَاتِ، اَلسَّــلَامُ عَلَيْكَ يَا خَاتِمَ الْحَصَىٰ وَ مُبَيِّنَ الْمُشْكِلَاتِ، اَلسَّلَامُ عَلَيْكَ يَا مَنْ عَجِبَتْ مِنْ حَمَلَاتِهِ فِي الْوَغَىٰ مَلَائِكَةُ السَّمَاوَاتِ،

Peace be to you, who addressed the wolf in the desert! Peace be to you, who set your seal on the pebbles and expounded all difficult problems! Peace be to you, whose forays on the battlefield led the angels in the heavens to wonder!

اَلسَّلَامُ عَلَيْكَ يَا مَنْ نَاجَى الرَّسُولَ فَقَدَّمَ بَيْنَ يَدَيْ نَجْوَاهُ الصَّدَقَاتِ، اَلسَّلَامُ عَلَيْكَ يَا وَالِدَ الْأَئِمَّةِ الْبَرَرَةِ السَّادَاتِ، وَ رَحْمَةُ اللهِ وَ بَرَكَاتُهُ.

Peace be to you, who held secret talks with the Apostle of Allah and offered charity before such sessions! Peace be to you, O progenitor of the Imams, the righteous masters, and may Allah's mercy and His bounties be upon you!

اَلسَّــلَامُ عَلَيْكَ يَا تَالِيَ الْمَبْعُوثِ، اَلسَّلَامُ

Peace be to you, who are next in station to the Messenger!

Peace be to you, O inheritor of the knowledge of the best of precursors, and may Allah's mercy and His bounties be upon you!

عَلَيْكَ يا وَارِثَ عِلْـمِ خَيْرِ مَوْرُوثٍ، وَ رَحْمَةُ اللهِ وَ بَرَكَاتُهُ.

Peace be to you, O chief of the Legatees! Peace be to you, O leader of the Godwary! Peace be to you, O succour of the suffering! Peace be to you, O protector of the faithful! Peace be to you, O proclaimer of the proofs!

اَلسَّـلامُ عَلَيْكَ يـا سَـيِّدَ الْوَصِيِّينَ،
اَلسَّـلامُ عَلَيْـكَ يـا إِمَـامَ الْمُتَّقِينَ،
اَلسَّـلامُ عَلَيْكَ يا غِيَاثَ الْمَكْرُوبِينَ،
اَلسَّـلامُ عَلَيْكَ يا عِصْمَـةَ الْمُؤْمِنِينَ،
اَلسَّـلامُ عَلَيْكَ يـا مُظْهِـرَ الْبَرَاهِينِ،

Peace be to you, O Ṭā Hā and Yā Sīn! Peace be to you, O firm cord of Allah! Peace be to you, who gave away his ring to the poor man during your prayer! Peace be to you, who removed the rock from the mouth of the well of Qalīb and made clear water to gush forth!

اَلسَّـلامُ عَلَيْكَ يا طٰهٰ وَ يٰسٓ، اَلسَّـلامُ عَلَيْكَ يا حَبْلَ اللهِ الْمَتِينَ، اَلسَّلامُ عَلَيْكَ يا مَـنْ تَصَدَّقَ فِي صَلاتِـهِ بِخَاتَمِهِ عَلَى الْمِسْكِينِ، اَلسَّلامُ عَلَيْكَ يا قَالِعَ الصَّخْرَةِ عَنْ فَمِ الْقَلِيـبِ وَ مُظْهِرَ الْمَاءِ الْمَعِينِ،

Peace be to you, O watchful eye of Allah, His open hand, His tongue which is His spokesman for all the creatures! Peace be to you, O heir to the knowledge of the prophets, the repository of the knowledge of all the seers of former and latter generations, the standard bearer of divine praise, the server of drink to his friends from the Pool of the Seal of the Prophets!

اَلسَّـلامُ عَلَيْكَ يا عَيْنَ اللهِ النَّاظِرَةَ، وَ يَدَهُ الْبَاسِطَةَ، وَ لِسَـانَهُ الْمُعَبِّرَ عَنْهُ فِي بَرِيَّتِهِ أَجْمَعِينَ، اَلسَّـلامُ عَلَيْكَ يا وَارِثَ عِلْمِ النَّبِيِّينَ، وَ مُسْتَوْدَعَ عِلْمِ الْأَوَّلِينَ وَ الْآخِرِينَ، وَ صَاحِبَ لِوَاءِ الْحَمْدِ، وَ سَاقِيَ أَوْلِيَائِهِ مِنْ حَوْضِ خَاتَمِ النَّبِيِّينَ،

Peace be to you, O preceptor of the faith, forerunner of the matchless devout, and father of all the admirable Imams, and

اَلسَّـلامُ عَلَيْكَ يا يَعْسُـوبَ الدِّينِ، وَ قَائِـدَ الْغُرِّ الْمُحَجَّلِـينَ، وَ وَالِدَ الْأَئِمَّةِ

الْمَرْضِيِّينَ، وَ رَحْمَةُ اللهِ وَ بَرَكَاتُهُ.

may Allah's mercy and His bounties be upon you!

اَلسَّلَامُ عَلَى اسْمِ اللهِ الرَّضِيِّ، وَ وَجْهِهِ الْمُضِيءِ، وَ جَنْبِهِ الْقَوِيِّ، وَ صِرَاطِهِ السَّوِيِّ، اَلسَّلَامُ عَلَى الْإِمَامِ التَّقِيِّ، اَلْمُخْلِصِ الصَّفِيِّ، اَلسَّلَامُ عَلَى الْكَوْكَبِ الدُّرِّيِّ، اَلسَّلَامُ عَلَى الْإِمَامِ أَبِي الْحَسَنِ عَلِيٍّ، وَ رَحْمَةُ اللهِ وَ بَرَكَاتُهُ.

Peace be to the admirable Name of Allah, His radiant Face, His strong arm, and His straight path! Peace be to the Godwary Imam, dedicated and sincere! Peace be to the shining star! Peace be to the Imam Abū al-Ḥasan ʿAlī, and may Allah's mercy and his bounties be upon him!

اَلسَّلَامُ عَلَى أَئِمَّةِ الْهُدَى، وَ مَصَابِيحِ الدُّجَى، وَ أَعْلَامِ التُّقَى، وَ مَنَارِ الْهُدَى، وَ ذَوِي النُّهَى، وَ كَهْفِ الْوَرَى، وَ الْعُرْوَةِ الْوُثْقَى، وَ الْحُجَّةِ عَلَى أَهْلِ الدُّنْيَا، وَ رَحْمَةُ اللهِ وَ بَرَكَاتُهُ.

Peace be to the Imams of guidance, the lamps in the darkness, the banners of piety, the minarets of guidance, the possessors of wisdom, the refuge of the creatures, the firm handle, and testaments to the world's people, and may Allah's mercy and His bounties be upon them!

اَلسَّلَامُ عَلَى نُورِ الْأَنْوَارِ، وَ حُجَّةِ الْجَبَّارِ، وَ وَالِدِ الْأَئِمَّةِ الْأَطْهَارِ، وَ قَسِيمِ الْجَنَّةِ وَ النَّارِ، اَلْمُخْبِرِ عَنِ الْآثَارِ، اَلْمُدَمِّرِ عَلَى الْكُفَّارِ، مُسْتَنْقِذِ الشِّيعَةِ الْمُخْلِصِينَ مِنْ عَظِيمِ الْأَوْزَارِ،

Peace be to the light of lights, the testament of the All-compeller, the progenitor of the immaculate Imams, the dispenser of paradise and hell, the informer concerning the legacies of the past seers, the destroyer of the faithless, the saviour of his dedicated followers from the great burden of sins!

اَلسَّلَامُ عَلَى الْمَخْصُوصِ بِالطَّاهِرَةِ التَّقِيَّةِ ابْنَةِ الْمُخْتَارِ، اَلْمَوْلُودِ فِي الْبَيْتِ ذِي الْأَسْتَارِ، اَلْمُزَوَّجِ فِي السَّمَاءِ بِالْبَرَّةِ

Peace be to you, who were singled out to wed the pure and pious daughter of the chosen Prophet, who were born in the House of God, draped in curtains, who were wed in the heaven to the good and pure mother of the immaculate Imams, she who was pleased with Allah and pleasing to Him, and may Allah's mercy and His bounties be upon you!

الطَّاهِرَةِ الرَّضِيَّةِ الْمَرْضِيَّـةِ وَالِدَةِ الْأَئِمَّةِ الْأَطْهَارِ، وَ رَحْمَةُ اللهِ وَ بَرَكَاتُهُ.

Peace be to the Great Tiding about whom the people are in disagreement, before whom they shall be presented and concerning whom they shall be questioned! Peace be to you, the brightest light of Allah and His most resplendent radiance, and may Allah's mercy and His bounties be upon you!

اَلسَّـلَامُ عَلَى النَّبَإِ الْعَظِيـمِ الَّذِى هُمْ فِيـهِ مُخْتَلِفُونَ، وَ عَلَيْـهِ يُعْرَضُونَ وَ عَنْهُ يُسْـأَلُونَ، اَلسَّـلَامُ عَلَىٰ نُورِ اللهِ الْأَنْوَرِ، وَ ضِيَائِهِ الْأَزْهَرِ، وَ رَحْمَةُ اللهِ وَ بَرَكَاتُهُ.

Peace be to you, O *walī* and testament of Allah, and His chosen friend and favourite.

اَلسَّـلَامُ عَلَيْكَ يَا وَلِيَّ اللهِ وَ حُجَّتَهُ، وَ خَالِصَةَ اللهِ وَ خَاصَّتَهُ،

I testify that you, Allah's *walī*, struggled in the way of Allah with a struggle worthy of Him, followed the path of the Apostle of Allah, may Allah bless him and his Family. You allowed what Allah had made lawful and forbade what Allah has made unlawful, implemented His laws, maintained the prayer, paid the *zakāt*, bade what is right and forbade what is wrong, and waged *jihād* in the way of Allah, patiently, sincerely, diligently and expecting a great reward from Allah, until your demise!

أَشْـهَدُ أَنَّكَ يَا وَلِيَّ اللهِ لَقَدْ جَاهَدْتَ فِي سَبِيلِ اللهِ حَقَّ جِهَادِهِ، وَ اتَّبَعْتَ مِنْهَاجَ رَسُـولِ اللهِ صَـلَّى اللهُ عَلَيْـهِ وَ آلِهِ، وَ حَلَّلْتَ حَلَالَ اللهِ، وَ حَرَّمْتَ حَرَامَ اللهِ، وَ شَرَعْتَ أَحْكَامَـهُ، وَ أَقَمْتَ الصَّلَاةَ، وَ آتَيْتَ الـزَّكَاةَ، وَ أَمَـرْتَ بِالْمَعْرُوفِ، وَ نَهَيْتَ عَنِ الْمُنْكَرِ، وَ جَاهَدْتَ فِي سَبِيلِ اللهِ صَابِرًا نَاصِحًا مُجْتَهِدًا مُحْتَسِـبًا عِنْدَ اللهِ عَظِيمَ الْأَجْرِ حَتَّىٰ أَتَاكَ الْيَقِينُ،

May Allah's curse be upon those who usurped your rights and dispossessed you of your

فَلَعَنَ اللهُ مَـنْ دَفَعَكَ عَـنْ حَقِّكَ، وَ أَزَالَكَ عَنْ مَقَامِكَ، وَ لَعَنَ اللهُ مَنْ بَلَغَهُ

ذٰلِكَ فَرَضِيَ بِهِ.

station, and may Allah's curse be on those who came to know about it and approved of it!

أُشْهِدُ اللّٰهَ وَ مَلَائِكَتَهُ وَ أَنْبِيَاءَهُ وَ رُسُلَهُ أَنِّي وَلِيٌّ لِمَنْ وَالَاكَ، وَ عَدُوٌّ لِمَنْ عَادَاكَ، اَلسَّلَامُ عَلَيْكَ وَ رَحْمَةُ اللّٰهِ وَ بَرَكَاتُهُ.

I call upon Allah, His angels and His apostles and prophets to be witness that I befriend those who befriend you and despise those who regard you with enmity! Peace be to you, and may Allah's mercy and His bounties be upon you!

"Then leaning against the tomb, embrace it and say,

أَشْهَدُ أَنَّكَ تَسْمَعُ كَلَامِي، وَ تَشْهَدُ مَقَامِي، وَ أَشْهَدُ لَكَ يَا وَلِيَّ اللّٰهِ بِالْبَلَاغِ وَ الْأَدَاءِ. يَا مَوْلَايَ يَا حُجَّةَ اللّٰهِ يَا أَمِينَ اللّٰهِ يَا وَلِيَّ اللّٰهِ، إِنَّ بَيْنِي وَ بَيْنَ اللّٰهِ عَزَّ وَ جَلَّ ذُنُوبًا قَدْ أَثْقَلَتْ ظَهْرِي، وَ مَنَعَتْنِي مِنَ الرُّقَادِ، وَ ذِكْرُهَا يُقَلْقِلُ أَحْشَائِي، وَ قَدْ هَرَبْتُ إِلَى اللّٰهِ عَزَّ وَ جَلَّ وَ إِلَيْكَ، فَبِحَقِّ مَنِ ائْتَمَنَكَ عَلَىٰ سِرِّهِ، وَ اسْتَرْعَاكَ أَمْرَ خَلْقِهِ، وَ قَرَنَ طَاعَتَكَ بِطَاعَتِهِ، وَ مُوَالَاتَكَ بِمُوَالَاتِهِ، كُنْ لِي إِلَى اللّٰهِ شَفِيعًا وَ مِنَ النَّارِ مُجِيرًا وَ عَلَى الدَّهْرِ ظَهِيرًا.

I testify that you hear my speech and observe my presence in this place. I testify, O *walī* of Allah, that you communicated and delivered all that you were charged with! My master, O testament of Allah, O trustee of Allah, O *walī* of Allah! There are certain sins that intervene between me and Allah; they weigh heavily on my back and deprive me of sleep and their mention makes me tremble. I have fled to seek refuge with Allah, Almighty and Glorious, and with you. So, for the sake of Him who has entrusted you with His secrets and made you guardian of the affairs of His creatures, equating obedience to you with obedience to Himself and love of you with love for Him, be my intercessor with Allah, my refuge from hellfire, and my supporter in hard times!

"Then leaning again against the tomb, kiss it and say,

يَا وَلِيَّ اللهِ يَا حُجَّــةَ اللهِ يَا بَابَ حِطَّةِ
اللهِ، وَلِيُّــكَ وَ زَائِرُكَ، وَ اللَّائِذُ بِقَبْرِكَ،
وَ النَّازِلُ بِفِنَائِــكَ، وَ الْمُنِيخُ رَحْلَهُ فِي
جِوَارِكَ، يَسْأَلُكَ أَنْ تَشْفَعَ لَهُ إِلَى اللهِ فِي
قَضَاءِ حَاجَتِهِ، وَ نُجْحِ طَلِبَتِهِ فِي الدُّنْيَا وَ
الْآخِرَةِ، فَإِنَّ لَكَ عِنْدَ اللهِ الْجَاهَ الْعَظِيمَ،
وَ الشَّــفَاعَةَ الْمَقْبُولَــةَ، فَاجْعَلْــنِي يَا
مَوْلَايَ مِنْ هَمِّكَ، وَ أَدْخِلْنِي فِي حِزْبِكَ،

O *walī* of Allah, O testament of Allah, O Allah's door for remission of sins! Your friend and pilgrim clings to your grave having, landed in your courtyard, your neighbourhood being the end of his journey. He asks you to intercede for him with Allah with regard to the fulfilment of his needs and success in attaining what he seeks in the life of the world and in the Hereafter. For indeed you have a great station with Allah and an intercession blessed with approval! So, my master, bless me with your attention and interest and admit me into your party!

وَ السَّلَامُ عَلَيْكَ وَ عَلَىٰ ضَجِيعَيْكَ آدَمَ
وَ نُوحٍ، وَ السَّلَامُ عَلَيْكَ وَ عَلَىٰ وَلَدَيْكَ
الْحَسَنِ وَالْحُسَيْنِ، وَعَلَى الْأَئِمَّةِ الطَّاهِرِينَ
مِــنْ ذُرِّيَّتِــكَ، وَ رَحْمَــةُ اللهِ وَ بَرَكَاتُهُ.

Peace be to you and to Adam and Noah, who are buried at your graveside. Peace be to you and to your sons, al-Ḥasan and al-Ḥusayn, and to the immaculate Imams of your descent, and may Allah's mercy and His bounties be upon you!

"After this, offer six *rakʿahs* of prayer: two for the Commander of the Faithful (ʿ*a*), two for Ḥaḍrat Adam (ʿ*a*) and two for Ḥaḍrat Noah (ʿ*a*), and entreat God greatly. God willing, your appeals will be granted."

The author of *al-Mazār al-Kabīr* says that this *ziyārah* should be recited at sunrise on the 17th of Rabīʿ al-Awwal.[1] But ʿAllāmah Majlisī (*r*) says, "This is one of the best *ziyārah*s and has been cited in reliable works with trustworthy chains of transmission. From what can be gathered from certain reports, it appears that this *ziyārah* is not specifically meant for the Prophet's birthday anniversary and may be performed on other days as well."[2]

Here the question may arise as to why the *ziyārah* of the Commander of the Faithful (ʿ*a*) has been prescribed as an observance for

1 *Al-Mazār al-Kabīr*, 205.
2 *Biḥār*, xcvii, 377, b 5, h 9.

the day of the Prophet's birth, or for the first day of his ministry (*mabᶜath*), whereas the appropriate thing would have been to prescribe specific *ziyārahs* on these days for the Prophet (ṣ). The answer is that this is on account of the intensity of the close relationship between these two personages, which arises from the unity of those two immaculate lights, so much so that anyone who performs the *ziyārah* of the Commander of the Faithful (*ᶜa*) is like one who has performed the *ziyārah* of the Apostle of Allah (ṣ) himself. The evidence for this is the phrase "our souls" in the Qur'ānic verse (3:61),[1]

وَ هُــوَ فِى آيَــةِ التَّبَاهُــلِ نَفْسُ الْمُصْطَفىٰ لَيْــسَ غَــيرُهُ إِيَّاهَا

He is the Prophet's 'soul' in accordance with the *āyah* of *Mubāhalah,* and no one except him has that station.

As for traditions, there are many reports, including the one reported by Shaykh Muḥammad ibn al-Mashhadi from Imam Jaᶜfar al-Ṣādiq (*ᶜa*).[2]

A Bedouin came to visit the the Apostle of Allah (*ᶜa*) and said to him, "O Apostle of Allah, the place where I live is far away from you and I come whenever I want to see you but do not always succeed in meeting you. When I do not find you, I go and visit ᶜAli ibn Abī Ṭālib, and he acquaints me with his teaching and advice. However, I return feeling sad and regretful for not having been able to meet you."

The Prophet said to him, "Whoever meets ᶜAlī is like someone who has met me. And whoever befriends him is like someone who befriends me, and whoever regards him with enmity is like someone who is my enemy. Convey this message to your people on my behalf and tell them that whoever visits and meets ᶜAlī has indeed met me and I, Gabriel and the righteous among the faithful will reward him on the day of resurrection."

1 This verse is as follows.

فَمَــنْ حَاجَّــكَ فِيهِ مِنْ بَعْدِ مَا جاءَكَ مِنَ الْعِلْــمِ فَقُلْ تَعالَوْا نَدْعُ أَبْناءَنَا وَ أَبْنَاءَكُمْ وَ نِسَــاءَنَا وَ نِسَاءَكُمْ وَ أَنْفُسَنَا وَ أَنْفُسَكُمْ ثُمَّ نَبْتَهِلْ فَنَجْعَلْ لَعْنَتَ اللهِ عَلَى الْكَاذِبِينَ

Should anyone argue with you (O Muḥammad) concerning him (.e. Jesus), after the knowledge that has come to you, say, 'Come! Let us call our sons and your sons, our women and your women, our souls and your souls, then let us pray earnestly and call down Allah's curse upon the liars.'

2 *Al-Mazār, al-Kabīr,* 38, whence *Biḥār*, xcvii, 262, b 3, h 17 & *Mustadrak*, x, 214, b 16, h 11885/6.

In a reliable report[1] from Imam Jaᶜfar al-Ṣādiq (ᶜ*a*), he is reported to have said that someone who visits the remains of Adam (ᶜ*a*) and Noah (ᶜ*a*) and the body of ᶜAlī ibn Abī Ṭālib (ᶜ*a*) at Najaf, is like someone who has paid a visit to these patriarchs, Muḥammad, the Seal of the Prophets, and ᶜAlī, the best of the Legatees.

In the sixth *ziyārah* cited above, the Imam was mentioned as having said, "Stand facing the grave of the Commander of the Faithful (ᶜ*a*) and say, *Assalāmu ᶜalayka yā rasūlallāh. Assalāmu ᶜalayka yā ṣafwatallāh*... (Peace be to you O Apostle of Allah! Peace be to you O elect of Allah!...)" and well has Shaykh Jābir said in his *tasmīṭ* of the *Qaṣīdah Uzriyyah* while referring to the shrine of Imam ᶜAlī (ᶜ*a*),

فَاعْتَمِــدْ لِلنَّبِيِّ أَعْظَــمَ رَمْسٍ　　فِيــهِ لِلطُّهْــرِ أَحْمَــدٍ أَيِّ نَفْسٍ
اَوْ تَرَي الْعَرْشَ فِيهِ اَنْوَرَ شَــمْسٍ　　فَتَوَاضَــعْ فَثَــمَّ دَارَةُ قُــدْسٍ
تَتَمَنَّى الْأَفْــلَاكُ لَثْــمَ ثَرَاهَا

Rest assured that here is the Prophet's greatest shrine
Where rests the great soul of Aḥmad, the immaculate one.
Or you will see the throne with the most resplendent sun on it,
Be reverent, for here is the abode of sanctity,
Whose dust the heavens aspire to embrace!

And Hakīm Senā'ī has said:

مرتضـايي که کـرد يزدانــش　　همره جــان مصطــفى جانش
هر دويك قبلــه و خردشان دو　　هر دو يك روح و كالبدشان دو
دو رونده چو اختر گــــردون　　دو برادر چــو موسى و هارون
هر دويك دُر زيك صدف بودند　　هر دو پيرايه شــــرف بودند
تا نـــه بگشاد علم حيدر در　　ندهــد ســنت پيمــبر بــر

Murtaḍā, the soul that Allah united with Mustafa's,
Spirits with a single presence, bodies of a single soul,
Two voyagers like the heaven's stars,
Two brothers, as Moses and Aaron
Pearls, two, gathered from a single shell
Embodiments, both, of honour and majesty
Until Ḥaydar opens the gate of knowledge

1 *Kāmil al-Ziyārāt*, 38, b 10, h 2, whence *Biḥār*, xcvii, 258, b 3, h 4. *Tahdhīb*, vi, 22, b 7, h 8, whence *Wasā'il*, xxxiv, 384, b 27, h 19435. *Farḥat al-Gharī*, 72. *Jāmi ᶜ al-Akhbār*, 20.

The Apostle's *sunnah* will bear no fruit!

Ziyarah for the Eve and Day of Mab'ath

There are three *ziyārahs* meant for the 27th day of Rajab. The first of them is the Ziyārah Rajabīyah which begins with the words *Alḥamdu lillāhil ladhî ashhadanā mashhada awliyâ'ih...* and was cited in the section pertaining to the observances of the month of Rajab (vol. 1, p. 375). It is a *ziyārah* that can be recited in any of the holy shrines during the month of Rajab. However, Shaykh Muḥammad ibn al-Mashhadī and the author of *al-Mazār al-Qadīm* have considered it to be among *ziyārahs* meant specifically for the eve of *Mabᶜath*.[1] They also mention that after reciting the *ziyārah* one should offer a two-*rakᶜah* prayer, followed by any petition one may like to make.

The second *ziyārah* is the one which begins with the words *As-salāmu ᶜalā abil a'immati wa maᶜdinin nubūwwah...*[2] ᶜAllāmah Majlisī cites it as the seventh among *ziyārahs* meant particularly for this day in his book *Tuḥfat al-Zā'r*,[3] and the author of *al-Mazār al-Qadīm* says that it is specific for the eve of 27th of Rajab. We have cited it similarly in our book *Hadīyat al-Zā'irīn*.[4]

The third *ziyārah* is the one cited by Shaykh Mufid, Sayyid Ibn Ṭāwūs and Shahīd Awwal.[5] The manner of its performance is that when intending the *ziyārah* of the Commander of the Faithful (*ᶜa*) on the eve of *mabᶜath*, or during its day, one should stand at the shrine's door facing the tomb and say,

أَشْهَدُ أَنْ لَا إِلٰهَ إِلَّا اللهُ وَحْدَهُ لَا شَرِيكَ لَهُ، وَ أَشْهَدُ أَنَّ مُحَمَّدًا عَبْدُهُ وَ رَسُولُهُ، وَ أَنَّ عَلِيَّ بْنَ أَبِي طَالِبٍ أَمِيرَ الْمُؤْمِنِينَ عَبْدُ اللهِ وَ أَخُو رَسُولِهِ، وَ أَنَّ الْأَئِمَّةَ الطَّاهِرِينَ مِنْ وُلْدِهِ حُجَجُ اللهِ عَلَىٰ خَلْقِهِ.	I testify that there is no god except Allah. He is One and has no partner. I testify that Muḥammad is His servant and apostle, that ᶜAlī ibn Abī Ṭālib, the Commander of the Faithful, is a servant of Allah and brother of His Apostle, and that the immaculate Imams of his descent are Allah's testaments to His creatures.

1 *Al-Mazār al-Kabīr*, 203.

2 *Biḥār*, xcvii, 330, b 4, h 29.

3 *Tuḥfat al-Zā'r*, 141-142.

4 *Hadīyat al-Zā'irīn*, 247.

5 *Biḥār*, xcvii, 377, b 5, h 10, from Shaykh Mufīd, Ibn Ṭāwūs and Shahīd Awwal, *Mazār*, 99-114.

Then enter and stand near the tomb of the Imam, facing it and with the back towards the *qiblah*. Then, after saying *takbīr* a hundred times, say,

اَلسَّلَامُ عَلَيْكَ يَا وَارِثَ آدَمَ خَلِيفَةِ اللّٰهِ، اَلسَّلَامُ عَلَيْكَ يَا وَارِثَ نُوحٍ صَفْوَةِ اللّٰهِ، اَلسَّلَامُ عَلَيْكَ يَا وَارِثَ إِبْرَاهِيمَ خَلِيلِ اللّٰهِ، اَلسَّلَامُ عَلَيْكَ يَا وَارِثَ مُوسَىٰ كَلِيمِ اللّٰهِ؛ اَلسَّلَامُ عَلَيْكَ يَا وَارِثَ عِيسَىٰ رُوحِ اللّٰهِ،

Peace be to you, O heir of Adam, Allah's vicegerent. Peace be to you, O heir of Noah, chosen of Allah! Peace be to you, O heir of Abraham, Allah's dedicated friend! Peace be to you, O heir of Moses, Allah's interlocutor! Peace be to you, O heir of Jesus, Allah's spirit!

اَلسَّلَامُ عَلَيْكَ يَا وَارِثَ مُحَمَّدٍ سَيِّدِ رُسُلِ اللّٰهِ، اَلسَّلَامُ عَلَيْكَ يَا أَمِيرَ الْمُؤْمِنِينَ، اَلسَّلَامُ عَلَيْكَ يَا إِمَامَ الْمُتَّقِينَ، اَلسَّلَامُ عَلَيْكَ يَا سَيِّدَ الْوَصِيِّينَ، اَلسَّلَامُ عَلَيْكَ يَا وَصِيَّ رَسُولِ رَبِّ الْعَالَمِينَ،

Peace be to you, O heir of Muhammad, the chief of Allah's apostles! Peace be to you, O Commander of the Faithful! Peace be to you, O leader of the Godwary! Peace be to you, O chief of the Legatees! Peace be to you, O legatee of the Apostle of the Lord of all the worlds!

اَلسَّلَامُ عَلَيْكَ يَا وَارِثَ عِلْمِ الْأَوَّلِينَ وَ الْآخِرِينَ، اَلسَّلَامُ عَلَيْكَ أَيُّهَا النَّبَأُ الْعَظِيمُ، اَلسَّلَامُ عَلَيْكَ أَيُّهَا الصِّرَاطُ الْمُسْتَقِيمُ، اَلسَّلَامُ عَلَيْكَ أَيُّهَا الْمُهَذَّبُ الْكَرِيمُ،

Peace be to you, O heir to the knowledge of the seers of the former and latter generations! Peace be to you, O Great Tiding! Peace be to you, O straight path! Peace be to you, O refined and noble one!

اَلسَّلَامُ عَلَيْكَ أَيُّهَا الْوَصِيُّ التَّقِيُّ، اَلسَّلَامُ عَلَيْكَ أَيُّهَا الرَّضِيُّ الزَّكِيُّ، اَلسَّلَامُ عَلَيْكَ أَيُّهَا الْبَدْرُ الْمُضِيءُ، اَلسَّلَامُ عَلَيْكَ أَيُّهَا الصِّدِّيقُ الْأَكْبَرُ، اَلسَّلَامُ عَلَيْكَ أَيُّهَا الْفَارُوقُ الْأَعْظَمُ،

Peace be to you, O pious legatee! Peace be to you, O admirable and immaculate one! Peace be to you, O bright full moon! Peace be to you, O the greatest of the truthful! Peace be to you, O greatest of separators of truth from falsehood!

Peace be to you, O radiant lamp! Peace be to you, O Imam of guidance! Peace be to you, O standard of piety! Peace be to you, O Allah's greatest testament!

اَلسَّلَامُ عَلَيْكَ أَيُّهَا السِّرَاجُ الْمُنِيرُ، اَلسَّلَامُ عَلَيْكَ يَا إِمَامَ الْهُدَى، اَلسَّلَامُ عَلَيْكَ يَا عَلَمَ التُّقَى، اَلسَّلَامُ عَلَيْكَ يَا حُجَّةَ اللهِ الْكُبْرَى،

Peace be to you, O Allah's exclusive and dedicated servant, Allah's trustee and His elect, the gateway to Allah and His testament, the repository of Allah's laws and His secrets, the reservoir of Allah's knowledge and His treasurer, and Allah's envoy among His creatures!

اَلسَّلَامُ عَلَيْكَ يَا خَاصَّةَ اللهِ وَ خَالِصَتَهُ، وَ أَمِينَ اللهِ وَ صَفْوَتَهُ، وَ بَابَ اللهِ وَ حُجَّتَهُ، وَ مَعْدِنَ حُكْمِ اللهِ وَ سِرِّهِ، وَ عَيْبَةَ عِلْمِ اللهِ وَ خَازِنَهُ، وَ سَفِيرَ اللهِ فِي خَلْقِهِ،

I testify that you maintained the prayer, paid the *zakat*, bade what is right, forbade what is wrong, followed the Apostle, complied with the book of Allah with the compliance worthy of it, communicated Allah's messages, fulfilled Allah's covenants and with you were fulfilled the words of Allah. (I testify that) you struggled for the sake of Allah with a struggle worthy of Him, worked sincerely for the sake of Allah and His Apostle, may Allah bless him and his Family.

أَشْهَدُ أَنَّكَ أَقَمْتَ الصَّلَاةَ، وَ آتَيْتَ الزَّكَاةَ، وَ أَمَرْتَ بِالْمَعْرُوفِ، وَ نَهَيْتَ عَنِ الْمُنْكَرِ، وَ اتَّبَعْتَ الرَّسُولَ، وَ تَلَوْتَ الْكِتَابَ حَقَّ تِلَاوَتِهِ، وَ بَلَّغْتَ عَنِ اللهِ، وَ وَفَيْتَ بِعَهْدِ اللهِ، وَ تَمَّتْ بِكَ كَلِمَاتُ اللهِ، وَ جَاهَدْتَ فِي اللهِ حَقَّ جِهَادِهِ، وَ نَصَحْتَ لِلّٰهِ وَ لِرَسُولِهِ صَلَّى اللهُ عَلَيْهِ وَ آلِهِ،

You made generous sacrifices, patiently and seeking only Allah's good pleasure, defending the religion of Allah, shielding the Apostle of Allah, seeking what is with Allah, desiring the fulfilment of Allah's promise, and you

وَ جُدْتَ بِنَفْسِكَ صَابِرًا مُحْتَسِبًا، مُجَاهِدًا عَنْ دِينِ اللهِ، مُوَقِّيًا لِرَسُولِ اللهِ، طَالِبًا مَا عِنْدَ اللهِ، رَاغِبًا فِيمَا

وَعَدَ اللهُ، وَ مَضَيْتَ لِلَّذِى كُنْتَ عَلَيْهِ
شَهِيدًا وَ شَاهِدًا وَ مَشْهُودًا.

passed away for the sake of what you stood for as a martyr, a witness and witnessed one!

فَجَزَاكَ اللهُ عَنْ رَسُولِهِ وَ عَنِ الْإِسْلَامِ
وَ أَهْلِهِ مِنْ صِدّيقٍ أَفْضَلَ الْجَزَاءِ،

May Allah reward you with the best of rewards for your truthfulness on behalf of His Apostle and on behalf of Islam and its followers.

أَشْهَدُ أَنَّكَ كُنْتَ أَوَّلَ الْقَوْمِ إِسْلَامًا،
وَ أَخْلَصَهُمْ إِيمَانًا، وَ أَشَدَّهُمْ يَقِينًا،
وَ أَخْوَفَهُمْ لِلّٰهِ، وَ أَعْظَمَهُمْ عَنَاءً، وَ
أَحْوَطَهُمْ عَلٰى رَسُولِ اللهِ صَلَّى اللهُ
عَلَيْهِ وَآلِهِ، وَ أَفْضَلَهُمْ مَنَاقِبَ، وَ
أَكْثَرَهُمْ سَوَابِقَ، وَ أَرْفَعَهُمْ دَرَجَةً،
وَ أَشْرَفَهُمْ مَنْزِلَةً، وَ أَكْرَمَهُمْ عَلَيْهِ؛
فَقَوِيتَ حِينَ وَهَنُوا، وَ لَزِمْتَ مِنْهَاجَ
رَسُولِ اللهِ صَلَّى اللهُ عَلَيْهِ وَ آلِهِ،

I testify that you were the first of the people to embrace Islam, the most dedicated of them in faith, the strongest of them in conviction, the most fearful of them before God, that you suffered the greatest hardships and distress, were the most watchful of them with regard to the Apostle of Allah, may Allah bless him and his Family. You were the most superior of them in merits, you had a record of greatest number of contributions to your credit, were the highest of them in rank, the most dignified of them in the station, the most generous of all the people in supporting him. You remained firm and strong when they weekend and stuck to the way of the Apostle of Allah, may Allah bless him and his Family.

وَ أَشْهَدُ أَنَّكَ كُنْتَ خَلِيفَتَهُ حَقًّا،
لَمْ تُنَازَعْ بِرَغْمِ الْمُنَافِقِينَ، وَ غَيْظِ
الْكَافِرِينَ، وَ ضِغْنِ الْفَاسِقِينَ، وَ قُمْتَ
بِالْأَمْرِ حِينَ فَشِلُوا، وَ نَطَقْتَ حِينَ
تَتَعْتَعُوا، وَ مَضَيْتَ بِنُورِ اللهِ إِذْ وَقَفُوا،
فَمَنِ اتَّبَعَكَ فَقَدِ اهْتَدَى.

I testify that you were his rightful successor, uncontested despite the dissent of the hypocrites, the rage of the faithless and the spite of the perverse, and that you stood your ground while they lost heart, spoke up while they stammered, and walked with the light of Allah while they stopped dead. So whoever follows you is the rightly guided.

كُنْتَ أَوَّلَهُمْ كَلامًا، وَ أَشَدَّهُمْ خِصَامًا،
وَ أَصْوَبَهُمْ مَنْطِقًا، وَ أَسَدَّهُمْ رَأْيًا، وَ
أَشْجَعَهُمْ قَلْبًا، وَ أَكْثَرَهُمْ يَقِينًا، وَ
أَحْسَنَهُمْ عَمَلًا، وَ أَعْرَفَهُمْ بِالْأُمُورِ،

You were the foremost of them in eloquence, the most vigorous of them in battling the enemy, the most rightful of them in speech, the most balanced of them in opinion, the most courageous of them in heart, the strongest of them in conviction, the most virtuous of them in conduct, and the most well-informed of them in all matters.

كُنْتَ لِلْمُؤْمِنِينَ أَبًا رَحِيمًا، إِذْ صَارُوا
عَلَيْكَ عِيَالًا، فَحَمَلْتَ أَثْقَالَ مَا عَنْهُ
ضَعُفُوا، وَ حَفِظْتَ مَا أَضَاعُوا، وَ رَعَيْتَ
مَا أَهْمَلُوا، وَ شَمَّرْتَ إِذْ جَبُنُوا، وَ عَلَوْتَ
إِذْ هَلِعُوا، وَ صَبَرْتَ إِذْ جَزِعُوا، كُنْتَ عَلَى
الْكَافِرِينَ عَذَابًا صَبًّا، وَ غِلْظَةً وَ غَيْظًا،
وَ لِلْمُؤْمِنِينَ غَيْثًا وَ خِصْبًا وَ عِلْمًا،

You were a kind father to the faithful, and they were like members of your family. You took upon yourself the burdens they were too weak to carry, preserving what they were prone to lose, observing what they neglected, setting to work when they shrank away, rising up when they despaired, being patient when they were dismayed. You were a punishment, harshness and rage to the faithless, and a merciful rain and source of abundance and knowledge for the faithful.

لَمْ تُفْلَلْ حُجَّتُكَ، وَ لَمْ يَزِغْ قَلْبُكَ، وَ لَمْ
تَضْعُفْ بَصِيرَتُكَ، وَ لَمْ تَجْبُنْ نَفْسُكَ؛
كُنْتَ كَالْجَبَلِ لَا تُحَرِّكُهُ الْعَوَاصِفُ، وَ
لَا تُزِيلُهُ الْقَوَاصِفُ، كُنْتَ كَمَا قَالَ
رَسُولُ اللهِ صَلَّى اللهُ عَلَيْهِ وَ آلِهِ قَوِيًّا
فِي بَدَنِكَ، مُتَوَاضِعًا فِي نَفْسِكَ، عَظِيمًا
عِنْدَ اللهِ، كَبِيرًا فِي الْأَرْضِ، جَلِيلًا فِي
السَّمَاءِ؛

Your arguments were indefeasible; your heart never swerved; your insight never weakened; your soul was dauntless, and you were like a mountain that stood unmoved before strong winds and firm before thunderous storms. You were as the Apostle of Allah, may Allah bless him and his Family, said, strong in body, humble in soul, greatly honoured with Allah, great in the earth and glorious in the heaven.

لَمْ يَكُنْ لِأَحَدٍ فِيكَ مَهْمَزٌ، وَ لَا لِقَائِلٍ فِيكَ مَغْمَزٌ، وَ لَا لِخَلْقٍ فِيكَ مَطْمَعٌ، وَ لَا لِأَحَدٍ عِنْدَكَ هَوَادَةٌ،

No one could find any reason to taunt you, nor any speaker could find fault with you. The people could not expect any unjust favours from you, nor you showed any indulgence for anyone.

يُوجَدُ الضَّعِيفُ الذَّلِيلُ عِنْدَكَ قَوِيًّا عَزِيزًا حَتَّىٰ تَأْخُذَ لَهُ بِحَقِّهِ، وَ الْقَوِيُّ الْعَزِيزُ عِنْدَكَ ضَعِيفًا (ذَلِيلًا) حَتَّىٰ تَأْخُذَ مِنْهُ الْحَقَّ، اَلْقَرِيبُ وَ الْبَعِيدُ عِنْدَكَ فِي ذٰلِكَ سَوَاءٌ.

The weak and the lowly were strong and mighty with you until you had restored their rights to them, and the strong and mighty were weak before you until they were brought to justice. In this respect, the stranger and the friend were equal before you.

شَأْنُكَ الْحَقُّ وَ الصِّدْقُ وَ الرِّفْقُ، وَ قَوْلُكَ حُكْمٌ وَ حَتْمٌ، وَ أَمْرُكَ حِلْمٌ وَ عَزْمٌ، وَ رَأْيُكَ عِلْمٌ وَ حَزْمٌ، اِعْتَدَلَ بِكَ الدِّينُ، وَ سَهُلَ بِكَ الْعَسِيرُ، وَ أُطْفِئَتْ بِكَ النِّيرَانُ، وَ قَوِيَ بِكَ الْإِيمَانُ، وَ ثَبَتَ بِكَ الْإِسْلَامُ، وَ هَدَّتْ مُصِيبَتُكَ الْأَنَامَ، فَإِنَّا لِلّٰهِ وَ إِنَّا إِلَيْهِ رَاجِعُونَ .

Your conduct was one infused with justice, truth and gentleness, and your speech was definitive judgment. Your manner was one of forbearance and resoluteness. Your opinion was informed with knowledge and judiciousness. Through you and your efforts the religion was well established, hardships in its way were removed, the flames of discord were extinguished, the faith was strengthened, Islam became established, and the tragedy of your martyrdom wrecked the people! Indeed we belong to Allah, and we will return to Him!

لَعَنَ اللّٰهُ مَنْ قَتَلَكَ، وَ لَعَنَ اللّٰهُ مَنْ خَالَفَكَ، وَ لَعَنَ اللّٰهُ مَنِ افْتَرَىٰ عَلَيْكَ، وَ لَعَنَ اللّٰهُ مَنْ ظَلَمَكَ وَ غَصَبَكَ حَقَّكَ، وَ لَعَنَ اللّٰهُ مَنْ

May Allah's curse be on those who killed you, and may Allah's curse be on those who opposed you! May the curse of Allah be on those who slandered you, and may Allah's curse be on those who wronged you and usurped your right! May the curse of Allah be on those who came to know about it and received it with approval! Indeed we repudiate them before Allah.

May the curse of Allah be upon the group which opposed you, contested your authority, supported others against you, shed your blood, avoided you and forsook you!

All praise belongs to Allah who has made hellfire their destination, and evil is that abode for those who enter it. I bear witness, O *walī* of Allah and His Apostle, may Allah bless him and his Family, that you delivered and fulfilled all that you were charged with.

I bear witness that you are the beloved of Allah and His gateway, that you are the vicinage of Allah and His Face, whereby He is faced and approached, and that you are the path of Allah, and that you are a servant of Allah and the brother of His Apostle, may Allah bless him and his Family!

I have come to visit you on account of your great standing and station with Allah and with His Apostle, seeking nearness to Allah by the means of this pilgrimage, requesting your intercession. Through your intercession I seek my deliverance and protection from the Fire, to rescue myself from the sins that I have piled up like firewood on my back, taking refuge with you, putting my hopes in the mercy of my Lord.

بَلَغَهُ ذلِكَ فَرَضِيَ بِهِ، إِنَّـا إِلَى اللهِ مِنْهُمْ بُرَآءُ،

لَعَـنَ اللهُ أُمَّةً خَالَفَتْـكَ، وَ جَحَدَتْ وِلايَتَكَ، وَ تَظَاهَرَتْ عَلَيْكَ وَ قَتَلَتْكَ، وَ حَادَتْ عَنْكَ وَ خَذَلَتْكَ.

اَلْحَمْـدُ لِلهِ الَّذِي جَعَلَ النَّارَ مَثْوَاهُمْ، وَ بِئْسَ الْوِرْدُ الْمَوْرُودُ. أَشْـهَدُ لَكَ يَا وَلِيَّ اللهِ وَ وَلِيَّ رَسُـولِهِ صَلَّى اللهُ عَلَيْهِ وَ آلِهِ بِالْبَلاغِ وَ الْأَدَاءِ،

وَ أَشْهَدُ أَنَّكَ حَبِيبُ اللهِ وَ بَابُهُ، وَ أَنَّكَ جَنْبُ اللهِ وَ وَجْهُـهُ الَّذِي مِنْهُ يُؤْتَى، وَ أَنَّكَ سَبِيلُ اللهِ، وَ أَنَّكَ عَبْدُ اللهِ وَ أَخُو رَسُولِهِ صَلَّى اللهُ عَلَيْهِ وَ آلِهِ،

أَتَيْتُكَ زَائِـرًا لِعَظِيمِ حَالِكَ وَ مَنْزِلَتِكَ عِنْـدَ اللهِ وَ عِنْدَ رَسُـولِهِ، مُتَقَرِّبًا إِلَى اللهِ بِزِيَارَتِكَ، رَاغِبًا إِلَيْكَ فِي الشَّفَاعَةِ، أَبْتَغِي بِشَـفَاعَتِكَ خَـلاصَ نَفْسِي، مُتَعَـوِّذًا بِكَ مِنَ النَّارِ، هَارِبًا مِنْ ذُنُوبِي الَّتِي احْتَطَبْتُهَا عَلَى ظَهْرِي، فَزِعًا إِلَيْكَ رَجَاءَ رَحْمَةِ رَبِّي،

أَتَيْتُكَ أَسْتَشْفِعُ بِكَ يَا مَوْلَايَ إِلَى اللهِ، وَ أَتَقَرَّبُ بِكَ إِلَيْهِ لِيَقْضِيَ بِكَ حَوَائِجِي، فَاشْفَعْ لِي يَا أَمِيرَ الْمُؤْمِنِينَ إِلَى اللهِ، فَإِنِّي عَبْدُ اللهِ وَ مَوْلَاكَ وَ زَائِرُكَ، وَ لَكَ عِنْدَ اللهِ الْمَقَامُ الْمَعْلُومُ، وَ الْجَاهُ الْعَظِيمُ، وَ الشَّأْنُ الْكَبِيرُ، وَ الشَّفَاعَةُ الْمَقْبُولَةُ.

I have come to you, my master, to plead for your intercession with Allah, and I seek nearness to Him through you, so that He may fulfil my needs for your sake. So intercede for me with Allah, O Commander of the Faithful, for indeed I am Allah's servant and your friend and pilgrim, and you have a distinguished station with Allah, a great honour, a high standing, and an intercession favoured with acceptance!

اَللّٰهُمَّ صَلِّ عَلَىٰ مُحَمَّدٍ وَ آلِ مُحَمَّدٍ، وَ صَلِّ عَلَىٰ عَبْدِكَ وَ أَمِينِكَ الْأَوْفَىٰ، وَ عُرْوَتِكَ الْوُثْقَىٰ، وَ يَدِكَ الْعُلْيَا، وَ كَلِمَتِكَ الْحُسْنَىٰ، وَ حُجَّتِكَ عَلَى الْوَرَىٰ، وَ صِدِّيقِكَ الْأَكْبَرِ، سَيِّدِ الْأَوْصِيَاءِ، وَ رُكْنِ الْأَوْلِيَاءِ، وَ عِمَادِ الْأَصْفِيَاءِ، أَمِيرِ الْمُؤْمِنِينَ، وَ يَعْسُوبِ الْمُتَّقِينَ، وَ قُدْوَةِ الصِّدِّيقِينَ، وَ إِمَامِ الصَّالِحِينَ، اَلْمَعْصُومِ مِنَ الزَّلَلِ، وَ الْمَفْطُومِ مِنَ الْخَلَلِ، وَ الْمُهَذَّبِ مِنَ الْعَيْبِ، وَ الْمُطَهَّرِ مِنَ الرَّيْبِ، أَخِي نَبِيِّكَ، وَ وَصِيِّ رَسُولِكَ، وَ الْبَائِتِ عَلَىٰ فِرَاشِهِ، وَ الْمُوَاسِي لَهُ بِنَفْسِهِ، وَ كَاشِفِ الْكَرْبِ عَنْ وَجْهِهِ، اَلَّذِي جَعَلْتَهُ سَيْفًا لِنُبُوَّتِهِ، وَ مُعْجِزًا لِرِسَالَتِهِ، وَ

O Allah, bless Muḥammad and the Family of Muḥammad and bless Your most loyal servant and trustee, Your firmest handle, Your uppermost hand, Your best word, Your testament to Your creatures, the greatest of Your truthful servants, the chief of the Legatees, the pillar of the saints, the pole of Your elect, the Commander of the Faithful, the leader of the Godwary, the exemplar of the truthful, the Imam of the righteous, who is preserved from error, exempted from fault, untarnished by defects, unpolluted by doubts, brother of Your Prophet, legatee of Your Apostle, who slept on the Prophet's bed sacrificing his life for his sake, who dispelled signs of distress from his face, whom You made the sword of his prophethood, the miracle of his apostleship, the manifest proof of his testament, the

دِلَالَةً وَاضِحَةً لِحُجَّتِهِ، وَ حَامِلًا لِرَايَتِهِ،
وَ وِقَايَةً لِمُهْجَتِهِ، وَ هَادِيًا لِأُمَّتِهِ، وَ يَدًا
لِبَأْسِهِ، وَ تَاجًا لِرَأْسِهِ، وَ بَابًا لِنَصْرِهِ، وَ
مِفْتَاحًا لِظَفَرِهِ، حَتَّىٰ هَزَمَ جُنُودَ الشِّرْكِ
بِأَيْدِكَ، وَ أَبَادَ عَسَاكِرَ الْكُفْرِ بِأَمْرِكَ،
وَ بَذَلَ نَفْسَهُ فِي مَرْضَاتِكَ وَ مَرْضَاةِ
رَسُولِكَ، وَ جَعَلَهَا وَقْفًا عَلَىٰ طَاعَتِهِ،
وَ مِجَنًّا دُونَ نَكْبَتِهِ، حَتَّىٰ فَاضَتْ
نَفْسُهُ صَلَّى اللهُ عَلَيْهِ وَ آلِهِ فِي كَفِّهِ،
وَ اسْتَلَبَ بَرْدَهَا وَ مَسَحَهُ عَلَىٰ وَجْهِهِ،

bearer of his banner, the shield of his heart, the guide of his *ummah*, the force of his might, the crown of his head, the gateway of his support, and the key to his victories, so that he defeated the armies of the idolaters with Your help, decimated the troops of unfaith by Your command, gave himself generously for the sake of Your good pleasure and that of Your Apostle, dedicating himself totally to obeying the Prophet, shielding him from disasters and calamities, until he—may Allah bless him and his Family—gave up the ghost in his hands, and he captured its coolness and stroked his face.

وَ أَعَانَتْهُ مَلَائِكَتُكَ عَلَىٰ غُسْلِهِ وَ
تَجْهِيزِهِ، وَ صَلَّى عَلَيْهِ وَ وَارَىٰ شَخْصَهُ، وَ
قَضَىٰ دَيْنَهُ، وَ أَنْجَزَ وَعْدَهُ، وَ لَزِمَ عَهْدَهُ،
وَ احْتَذَىٰ مِثَالَهُ، وَ حَفِظَ وَصِيَّتَهُ، وَ حِينَ
وَجَدَ أَنْصَارًا نَهَضَ مُسْتَقِلًّا بِأَعْبَاءِ
الْخِلَافَةِ، مُضْطَلِعًا بِأَثْقَالِ الْإِمَامَةِ،
فَنَصَبَ رَايَةَ الْهُدَىٰ فِي عِبَادِكَ، وَ نَشَرَ
ثَوْبَ الْأَمْنِ فِي بِلَادِكَ، وَ بَسَطَ الْعَدْلَ فِي
بَرِيَّتِكَ، وَ حَكَمَ بِكِتَابِكَ فِي خَلِيقَتِكَ،
وَ أَقَامَ الْحُدُودَ، وَ قَمَعَ الْجُحُودَ، وَ قَوَّمَ

The angels assisted him while he washed the Prophet's body, and he performed his funeral rites, offered the funeral prayer for him, buried his body, paid his debts, met his promises, remained loyal to his covenant, followed his example, preserved his legacy, and when he found supporters, stood up assuming the burdens of the caliphate and the solemn duties of the Imamate, to plant the banner of guidance in the midst of Your servants, to spread peace and security in Your lands, to disseminate justice amongst Your creatures, giving judgement for Your creatures according to Your Scripture, implementing Your laws, suppressing dissension, straightening deviance, stilling turmoil, dispelling weakness, closing the gaps and fighting against the perfidious, the perverse and the renegades, and he never ceased following the path of the Apostle of Allah, may Allah bless and his Family, and his policies, his gentle character, his graceful manners, following his methods, devoted to his high-mindedness and zeal, pursuing his practice and keeping his precedents always in his view, prompting Your servants to adopt them and inviting them to follow them, until his white hair were dyed in the blood of his head!

الزَّيْغَ، وَ سَكَّنَ الْغَمْرَةَ، وَ أَبَادَ الْفَتْرَةَ، وَ
سَدَّ الْفُرْجَةَ، وَ قَتَلَ النَّاكِثَةَ وَ الْقَاسِطَةَ
وَ الْمَارِقَةَ، وَ لَمْ يَزَلْ عَلىٰ مِنْهَاجِ رَسُولِ
اللهِ صَلَّى اللهُ عَلَيْهِ وَ آلِهِ وَ وَتِيرَتِهِ،
وَ لُطْفِ شَاكِلَتِهِ، وَ جَمَالِ سِيرَتِهِ،
مُقْتَدِيًا بِسُنَّتِهِ، مُتَعَلِّقًا بِهِمَّتِهِ، مُبَاشِرًا
لِطَرِيقَتِهِ، وَ أَمْثِلَتُهُ نَصْبُ عَيْنَيْهِ،
يَحْمِلُ عِبَادَكَ عَلَيْهَا، وَ يَدْعُوهُمْ إِلَيْهَا،
إِلىٰ أَنْ خُضِبَتْ شَيْبَتُهُ مِنْ دَمِ رَأْسِهِ.

O Allah, even as he never let doubt get the better of his conviction in obeying You and did not associate anyone with Your divinity even for a moment, bless him with a blessing that is increasing and enhancing, whereby he may attain to the rank of prophethood in Your paradise, and convey to him our greetings and *salām*, and grant us Your grace, favour, forgiveness and approval in our love for him. Indeed You are dispenser of a mighty grace, by Your mercy, O Most Merciful of the merciful!

اَللّٰهُمَّ فَكَمَا لَمْ يُؤْثِرْ فِي طَاعَتِكَ شَكًّا
عَلىٰ يَقِينٍ، وَ لَمْ يُشْرِكْ بِكَ طَرْفَةَ عَيْنٍ،
صَلِّ عَلَيْهِ صَلَاةً زَاكِيَةً نَامِيَةً يَلْحَقُ
بِهَا دَرَجَةَ النُّبُوَّةِ فِي جَنَّتِكَ، وَ بَلِّغْهُ
مِنَّا تَحِيَّةً وَ سَلَامًا، وَ آتِنَا مِنْ لَدُنْكَ
فِي مُوَالاتِهِ فَضْلًا وَ إِحْسَانًا، وَ مَغْفِرَةً
وَ رِضْوَانًا، إِنَّكَ ذُو الْفَضْلِ الْجَسِيمِ،
بِرَحْمَتِكَ يَا أَرْحَمَ الرَّاحِمِينَ.

Then kiss the *ḍarīḥ* and place your right cheek on it and then the left. Then offer the prayer of *ziyārah* facing the *qiblah*. After the prayer, supplicate for any need that you may have. Then, after performing the *tasbīḥ* of Ḥaḍrat Fāṭimah (*ᶜa*), say,

O Allah, You gave me the good

اَللّٰهُمَّ إِنَّكَ بَشَّرْتَنِي عَلىٰ لِسَانِ نَبِيِّكَ

وَ رَسُولِكَ مُحَمَّدٍ صَلَوَاتُكَ عَلَيْهِ وَ آلِهِ، فَقُلْتَ: وَ بَشِّرِ الَّذِينَ آمَنُوا أَنَّ لَهُمْ قَدَمَ صِدْقٍ عِنْدَ رَبِّهِمْ.

news by the tongue of Your Prophet and Apostle, Muḥammad, may Your blessings be upon him and his Family, saying: 'Give good news to the faithful that they are in good standing with their Lord.'[10:2]

اَللّٰهُمَّ وَ إِنِّي مُؤْمِنٌ بِجَمِيعِ أَنْبِيَائِكَ وَ رُسُلِكَ صَلَوَاتُكَ عَلَيْهِمْ، فَلَا تَقِفْنِي بَعْدَ مَعْرِفَتِهِمْ مَوْقِفًا تَفْضَحُنِي فِيهِ عَلَىٰ رُؤُوسِ الْأَشْهَادِ، بَلْ قِفْنِي مَعَهُمْ وَ تَوَفَّنِي عَلَى التَّصْدِيقِ بِهِمْ.

O Allah I have faith in all Your prophets and apostles, may Your blessings be upon them. So, after my knowledge of them, do not humiliate me on the Day of Resurrection in front of all and sundry! Rather grant me to stand in their company and make me die affirming them.

اَللّٰهُمَّ وَ أَنْتَ خَصَصْتَهُمْ بِكَرَامَتِكَ، وَ أَمَرْتَنِي بِاتِّبَاعِهِمْ. اَللّٰهُمَّ وَ إِنِّي عَبْدُكَ وَ زَائِرُكَ، مُتَقَرِّبًا إِلَيْكَ بِزِيَارَةِ أَخِي رَسُولِكَ، وَ عَلَىٰ كُلِّ مَأْتِيٍّ وَ مَزُورٍ حَقٌّ لِمَنْ أَتَاهُ وَ زَارَهُ، وَ أَنْتَ خَيْرُ مَأْتِيٍّ وَ أَكْرَمُ مَزُورٍ؛

O Allah, You have singled them out for Your generosity and have commanded me to follow them. O Allah, I am Your servant and pilgrim, seeking nearness to You through my visit to the brother of Your Apostle. Every host and everyone who is paid a visit owes a debt to his visitor and You are the best of those who are visited and the most munificent of those who receive.

فَأَسْأَلُكَ يَا اللّٰهُ يَا رَحْمَانُ يَا رَحِيمُ، يَا جَوَادُ يَا مَاجِدُ، يَا أَحَدُ يَا صَمَدُ، يَا مَنْ لَمْ يَلِدْ وَ لَمْ يُولَدْ وَ لَمْ يَكُنْ لَهُ كُفُوًا أَحَدٌ، وَ لَمْ يَتَّخِذْ صَاحِبَةً وَ لَا وَلَدًا، أَنْ تُصَلِّيَ عَلَىٰ مُحَمَّدٍ وَ آلِ مُحَمَّدٍ، وَ أَنْ تَجْعَلَ تُحْفَتَكَ إِيَّايَ مِنْ زِيَارَتِي أَخَا رَسُولِكَ

So I beseech You, O Allah, O All-beneficent, O All-merciful, O Generous One, O Praiseworthy One, O One, O All-embracing! O You who neither begat, nor were begotten, nor have You any equal, who have not taken any spouse or offspring, to bless Muḥammad and the Family of Muḥammad, and let Your gift to me for my *ziyārah* of Your Apostle's brother

فَكَاكَ رَقَبَتِي مِنَ النَّارِ، وَ أَنْ تَجْعَلَنِي مِمَّنْ يُسَارِعُ فِي الْخَيْرَاتِ، وَ يَدْعُوكَ رَغَبًا وَ رَهَبًا، وَ تَجْعَلَنِي لَكَ مِنَ الْخَاشِعِينَ.

be the release my neck from the noose of hellfire and to make me one of those who are active in performing good works, who call on You with fear and hope, and to make me one of those who are humble before You!

اَللّٰهُمَّ إِنَّكَ مَنَنْتَ عَلَيَّ بِزِيَارَةِ مَوْلَایَ عَلِيِّ بْنِ أَبِي طَالِبٍ وَ وِلَايَتِهِ وَ مَعْرِفَتِهِ، فَاجْعَلْنِي مِمَّنْ يَنْصُرُهُ وَ يَنْتَصِرُ بِهِ، وَ مُنَّ عَلَيَّ بِنَصْرِكَ لِدِينِكَ.

O Allah, You have favoured me with the *ziyārah* of my master, ʿAlī ibn Abī Ṭīlib and with adherence to his *wilāyah* and with the knowledge of his Imamate. So make me one of his supporters and one of those who are victorious through him, and favour me by enabling me to give support to Your religion.

اَللّٰهُمَّ وَ اجْعَلْنِي مِنْ شِيعَتِهِ، وَ تَوَفَّنِي عَلَىٰ دِينِهِ. اَللّٰهُمَّ أَوْجِبْ لِي مِنَ الرَّحْمَةِ وَ الرِّضْوَانِ، وَ الْمَغْفِرَةِ وَ الْإِحْسَانِ، وَ الرِّزْقِ الْوَاسِعِ الْحَلَالِ الطَّيِّبِ مَا أَنْتَ أَهْلُهُ، يَا أَرْحَمَ الرَّاحِمِينَ، وَ الْحَمْدُ لِلّٰهِ رَبِّ الْعَالَمِينَ

O Allah, appoint me among his followers and make me die on his creed. O Allah, assign me a share of Your mercy, Your approval, Your forgiveness and favour, and an expansive lawful and good provision that is worthy of You, O Most Merciful of the merciful! All praise belongs to Allah, the Lord of all the worlds!

It is mentioned in a reliable report[1] that Ḥaḍrat Khiḍr (ʿ*a*) appeared on the day of martyrdom of the Commander of the Faithful (ʿ*a*). He wept as he pronounced the words of *istirjāʿ* (*Innā lillāhi wa innā ilayhi rājiʿūn*). He came up hurrying and stood at the entrance of the house of the Commander of the Faithful (ʿ*a*) and said,

رَحِمَكَ اللهُ يَا أَبَا الْحَسَنِ كُنْتَ أَوَّلَ الْقَوْمِ إِسْلَاماً وَ أَخْلَصَهُمْ إِيمَاناً وَ أَشَدَّهُمْ يَقِيناً وَ أَخْوَفَهُمْ لِلّٰهِ

O Abūl Ḥasan! May Allah have mercy on you! You were foremost of all in submitting to God, the most dedicated of them in faith, the firmest of them in conviction and the most Godfearing among

[1] *Kāfī*, i, 454, Kitāb al-Ḥujjah, h 4, whence *Biḥār*, xcvii, 354, b 5, h 1. Ṣadūq's *Amālī*, 247, h 11. *Kamāl al-Dīn*, ii, 387, h 3, whence *Biḥār*, xlii, 303, b 128, h 4.

them!

Then he described many of the Imam's virtues in words that closely resemble those of the above *ziyārah*. Hence this *ziyārah* may appropriately be recited on the day of the Imam's martyrdom as well.

The text of Khiḍr's eulogy, which may be considered a *ziyārah* for the day of the Imam's martyrdom, has also been cited in my book *Hadīyat al-Zā'irīn*, and those interested may refer to that book.[1]

Earlier in the present book while describing the observances pertaining to the night of the Prophet's *mabʿath*, we have cited an account relating to the Imam's shrine from Ibn Baṭūṭah's account of his travels (vol. 1, p. 405-6). It will be appropriate to refer to it in the present context.

[1] *Hadīyat al-Zā'irīn*, 254-256.

Chapter Five

The Ziyarah of Kūfah

Kūfah is one of the four towns chosen by God Almighty. The expression "Mount Sīnā" (*Ṭūri Sīnīn*) mentioned in Sūrat al-Tīn has been interpreted as referring to it.[1] It is mentioned in a report[2] that it is Allah's sanctuary (*ḥaram*) and that of the Apostle of Allah (ṣ) and the Commander of the Faithful (*ᶜa*). It also says that a penny given in charity here equals a hundred offered elsewhere, and that two *rakᶜahs* offered here equal a hundred offered elsewhere.[3]

The Virtues of the Great Mosque of Kufah

These are more than what can be mentioned here. Its claim to sanctity is sufficiently borne out by its being one of the world's four mosques visiting which has been recommended for obtaining the blessings associated with them.[4]

It is one of the spots where a Muslim traveller has the option to

[1] Khiṣāl, i, 225, h 58, whence *Biḥār*, xcvi, 77, b 8, h 2, xcvi, 383, b 3, h 3, xcvii, 392, b 6, h 20. *Maᶜānī*, 364, h 1, whence *Wasā'il*, xiv, 361, b 16, h 19389, and *Biḥār*, lvii, 204, b 36, h 2. *Rawḍat al-Wāᶜiẓīn*, ii, 405.

[2] *Kāmil al-Ziyārāt*, b 8, h 2, whence *Wasā'il*, v, 258, b 44, h 2486. *Biḥār*, xcvii, 392, b 6, h 42.

[3] According to other reports, cited more widely in the sources, a *dirham* given in charity here equals a thousand offered elsewhere, and that a prayer offered here equals a thousand offered elsewhere. See the reports cited in *Kāfī*, iv, 586, h 1. *Faqīh*, i, 228, h 690, whence *Wasā'il*, v, 256, b 44, h 6478. *Kāmil al-Ziyārāt*, 29, h 8, whence *Biḥār*, xcvi, 242, b 44, h 10, xcvii, 400, b 6, h 51. Mufīd's *Mazār*, 5, b 1, 2. *Tahdhīb*, vi, 31, b 10, h 2. *Rawḍat al-Wāᶜiẓīn*, ii, 410. (Tr.)

[4] A report cited in *Faqīh* (i, 231, h 694, whence *Wasā'il*, v, 257, b 44, h 6482) and Khiṣāl (i, 143, whence *Biḥār*, xcvi, 240, b 44, h 2, xcvi, 379, b 2, h 2, *Wasā'il*, v, 262, b 46, h 6496) from Imam ᶜAlī (*ᶜa*) mentions three mosques meant for pilgrimage: the Holy Mosque at Makkah, the Prophet's Mosque at Madīnah and the Mosque of Kūfah. Another report from Imam ᶜAlī (*ᶜa*) cited in Ṭūsī's *Amālī* (369, majlis 13, whence *Wasā'il*, v, 282, b 57, h 6556, *Biḥār*, xcvi, 240, b 44, h4, xcvi, 380, b 2, h 4, xcix, 270, b 3, h 1) describes these three and al-Aqṣā Mosque in al-Quds as the "four palaces of paradise" on earth.

offer his obligatory prayers with or without *qaṣr*.[1] It has been said[2] that the reward of a prayer offered in this mosque equals that of a *ḥajj* pilgrimage approved and accepted by Allah, or that of a thousand prayers offered elsewhere.[3]

It is mentioned in some reports that it has been a place of worship for many prophets,[4] and that it will as well be the venue of prayer for Imam Mahdī, may Allah bless him.[5] According to one report, one thousand prophets and one thousand legatees of prophets have prayed in it.[6] Some reports[7] suggest that the Mosque of Kūfah is greater in merit than Al-Aqṣā Mosque in Bayt al-Maqdis.

Ibn Qūlawayh cites a report[8] that Imam Muḥammad al-Bāqir (*ᶜa*) said that if people knew the virtues of the Mosque of Kūfah they would definitely arrange the means of journey to visit this mosque from distant towns. He also said that the reward of performing an obligatory prayer in it equals that of an accepted *ḥajj* pilgrimage, and a supererogatory prayer therein equals in reward that of an accepted *ᶜumrah*.

1 *Kāfī*, iv, 586, h 2-5. *Kāmil al-Ziyārāt*, 249-250. Mufīd's *Mazār*, 136-138, h 1-4. Ṭūsī's *Miṣbāḥ*, 731. *Tahdhīb*, v, 431-432, b 26, h 143-146. *Istibṣār*, ii, 335, b 229, h 4-6. *Wasā'il*, viii, 528, b 25, h, 11355-11356, viii, 530-532, h 11365, 11367-11368, 11371. *Mustadrak*, vi, 545, b 18, h 7476/5. *Biḥār*, lxxxvi, 76-78, b 2, h 1-3, xcviii, 83, b 11, h 12.

2 See the sources cited below for Ibn Qūlawayh's report from Imam Muḥammad al-Bāqir (*ᶜa*).

3 See note 3 above.

4 *Kāfī*, iii, 492, h 3, 393, h 9. *Faqīh*, i, 231, h 693, 696. *Tahdhīb*, iii, 251-252, b 25, h 9, 11; vi, 31-32, b 10, h 1, 5, 6.

5 Ṣadūq's *Amālī*, 227-228, h 8, whence *Biḥār*, xcvii, 389, b 6, h 14. *Faqīh*, i, 231, 696, whence *Wasā'il*, v, 257, b 44, h 6484. *Rawḍat al-Wāᶜiẓīn*, ii, 637.

6 *Kāfī*, iii, 492, h 3, whence *Wasā'il*, v, 252, b 44, h 6468. *Faqīh*, i, 231, h 683. *Tahdhīb*, vi, 32, b 10, h 5, whence *Wasā'il*, v, 257, b 44, h 6481. *Jāmiᶜ al-Akhbār*, 69, 70, whence *Biḥār*, lxxx, 376, b 8, h 45 and *Mustadrak*, iii, 406-407, b 35, h 3887/13, 3889/15. *Biḥār*, lxxx. 359, b 8, h 12, xcvii, 394, b 6, h 28, and *Mustadrak*, iii, 407, b 36, h 3890/1, from *al-Ghārāt*, ii, 285. *Thawāb*, 30, whence *Biḥār*, xcvii, 397, b 6, h 37. *Kāmil al-Ziyārāt*, 28, whence *Biḥār*, xcvii, 400, b 6, h 48. *Rawḍat al-Wāᶜiẓīn*, ii, 410. *Manāqib*, ii, 200. Mufīd's *Mazār*, 7, b 2, h 2.

7 *Kāfī*, iii, 491, h 2, whence *Wasā'il*, v, 261, b 45, h 6495. *Tahdhīb*, iii, 251, b 25, h 9. *Tafsīr al-ᶜAyyāshī*, ii, 279, whence *Biḥār*, xviii, 385, b 3, h 91, xcvii, 405, b 6, h 62. *Kāmil al-Ziyārāt*, 32, b 8, h 18, whence *Biḥār*, xcvii, 403, b 6, h 59. *Mustadrak*, iii, 407, b 36, h 3890/1, 3891/2 from *al-Ghārāt* and Ibn al-Mashhadī's *Mazār*.

8 *Kāmil al-Ziyārāt*, 28, h 3, whence *Wasā'il*, v, 256, b 44, h 6480, and *Biḥār*, xcvii, 399, b 6, h 45. Mufīd's *Mazār*, 7, b 2, h 1. *Tahdhīb*, vi, 32, b 10, h 4. *Jāmiᶜ al-Akhbār*, 69, whence *Biḥār*, lxxx, 376, b 8, h 45.

According to another report,[1] the merit of performing obligatory and supererogatory prayers in it is like that of a *ḥajj* and *ᶜumrah* performed in the company of the Apostle of Allah (ṣ).

Shaykh Kulaynī and other major compilers of *ḥadith* have cited a report[2] on the authority of Hārūn b. Khārijah wherein he says, "Imam Jaᶜfar al-Ṣādiq (ᶜa) said to me, 'O Hārūn, how far is the Mosque of Kūfah from your place? Is it at a mile's distance?' 'No,' I said. 'Do you offer all your prayers there?' he asked me. 'No,' I replied. He said, 'Had I lived near that mosque, I would not miss performing a single prayer in it. Do you have any idea about the merit of that place? There has not been any righteous servant of God, nor any prophet, who has not prayed in the Mosque of Kūfah. When the Apostle of Allah (ṣ) was being taken on his nocturnal journey to the heavens, Gabriel asked him, "O Apostle of Allah, do you know where we are now? We are right in front of the Mosque of Kūfah." The Prophet (ṣ) said, "Ask the Lord to permit me to come down in it and offer two *rakᶜahs* of prayer." Gabriel sought God Almighty's permission and He granted it, whereat the Prophet (ṣ) alighted in the mosque and offered two *rakᶜahs* of prayer. Indeed there is a garden from among the gardens of paradise on its right side, another in its middle and a third at its rear. The reward of a single obligatory prayer offered therein equals that of a thousand prayers performed elsewhere, and the reward of one supererogatory prayer there equals that of five hundred prayers. Even just sitting there without reciting the Qur'ān or performing any *dhikr* has the reward of worship. If the people knew the merits of this place they would visit it, even if one could move only by crawling on the ground like an infant.' "

An account of the virtues of this mosque was given earlier under the seventh *ziyārah* of the Commander of the Faithful (ᶜa) (p. 136). From some reports it appears that the right side of the mosque has a greater merit than its left side.[3]

1 *Tahdhīb*, vi, 32, b 10, h 5, whence *Wasā'il*, v, 257, b 44, h 6481. *Jāmiᶜ al-Akhbār*, 69, whence *Biḥār*, lxxx, 376, b 8, h 45 and *Mustadrak*, iii, 406-407, b 35, h 3887/13, 3889/15. *Kāmil al-Ziyārāt*, 28, whence *Biḥār*, xcvii, 400, b 6, h 48. *Rawḍat al-Wāᶜẓīn*, ii, 410. Mufīd's *Mazār*, 7, b 2, h 2.

2 *Maḥāsin*, i, 56, b 68, h 86, whence *Biḥār*, xcvii, 398, b 6, h 39. *Kāfī*, iii, 490, h 1, whence *Wasā'il*, v, 252, b 44, h 6469. Ṣadūq's *Amālī*, 385, whence *Biḥār*, xcvii, 391, b 6, h 16-18. *Tahdhīb*, iii, 250, b 25, h 8. Ṭūsī's *Amālī*, 428, majlis 15, h 957, 14. *Al-Ghārāt*, ii, 285, whence *Biḥār*, lxxx, 359, b 8, h 11 and *Mustadrak*, iii, 399, b 35, h 3875/1. *Kāmil al-Ziyārāt*, 28, b 8, h 6.

3 *Kāfī*, iii, 490, h 1; iii, 493, h 9, whence *Wasā'il*, v, 251, b 44, h 6467 & *Biḥār*, xcvii, 389, b 6, h 13. *Tahdhīb*, iii, 350, b 25, h 8; iii, 252, b 25, h 11; vi, 32, b 10,

The Observances of the Mosque of Kufah

As described in the *Miṣbāḥ al-Zā'ir* and other books,[1] while entering the town of Kūfah one should say,

بِسْمِ اللهِ وَ بِاللهِ، وَ فِي سَبِيلِ اللهِ، وَ عَلَىٰ مِلَّةِ رَسُـــولِ اللهِ صَلَّى اللهُ عَلَيْهِ وَ آلِهِ، اَللّٰهُمَّ أَنْزِلْنِي مُنْزَلًا مُبَارَكًا وَ أَنْتَ خَيْرُ الْمُنْزِلِينَ.

In the Name of Allah, by Allah, on the path of Allah and in keeping with the creed of the Apostle of Allah, may Allah bless him and his Family. O Allah, conduct me to a blessed destination and You are the best of those who bring the voyagers to their destinations.

While on the way to the Mosque of Kūfah and till reaching its gate, keep saying,

اَللهُ أَكْبَرُ وَ لَا إِلٰهَ إِلَّا اللهُ وَ الْحَمْدُ لِلّٰهِ وَ سُبْحَانَ اللهِ.

Allah is greater. There is no god besides Allah. All praise belongs to Allah, and may Allah be glorified!

At the Entrance of the Mosque

On reaching the mosque, stop at the gate, say the following[2] and enter, preferably through the gate at the rear of the mosque, commonly known as "Bāb al-Fīl."

اَلسَّلَامُ عَلَىٰ سَيِّدِنَا رَسُولِ اللهِ مُحَمَّدِ بْنِ عَبْدِ اللهِ وَ آلِهِ الطَّاهِرِينَ. اَلسَّلَامُ عَلَىٰ أَمِيرِ الْمُؤْمِنِينَ عَلِيِّ بْنِ أَبِي طَالِبٍ وَ رَحْمَةُ اللهِ وَ بَرَكَاتُهُ، وَ عَلَىٰ مَجَالِسِهِ وَ مَشَاهِدِهِ،

Peace be to our master, Muḥammad ibn ᶜAbdillah, the Apostle of Allah, and his immaculate Family. Peace be to ᶜAlī ibn Abī Ṭālib, the Commander of the Faithful, and may Allah's mercy and His blessings be upon him and upon the venues of his sessions and aud-

h 6, whence *Wasā'il*, v, 252, b 44, h 6469. Mufīd's *Mazār*, 8, b 2, h 3. *Rawḍat al-Wāᶜẓīn*, ii, 410. *Jāmiᶜ al-Akhbār*, 69, whence *Biḥār*, lxxx, 376, b 8, h 45.

1 *Biḥār*, xcvii, 409, b 6, h 66, from Shaykh Mufīd, *Mazār al-Kabīr*, Ibn Ṭāwūs and Shahīd Awwal.

2 *Biḥār*, xcvii, 409, b 6, h 67, from *al-Mazār al-Kabīr*, 161, b 11, and Shahīd's *Mazār*, 230.

وَ مَقَامِ حِكْمَتِهِ، وَ آثَارِ آبَائِهِ آدَمَ وَ نُوحٍ وَ
إِبْرَاهِيمَ وَ إِسْمَاعِيلَ، وَ تِبْيَانِ بَيِّنَاتِهِ.

iences, the seats of his judgement and the relics of his forebears, Adam, Noah, Abraham and Ishmael, and the memorabilia of his proofs.

اَلسَّلَامُ عَلَى الْإِمَامِ الْحَكِيمِ الْعَدْلِ،
الصِّدِّيقِ الْأَكْبَرِ، اَلْفَارُوقِ بِالْقِسْطِ، اَلَّذِى
فَرَّقَ اللهُ بِهِ بَيْنَ الْحَقِّ وَ الْبَاطِلِ، وَ الْكُفْرِ
وَ الْإِيمَانِ، وَ الشِّرْكِ وَ التَّوْحِيدِ، لِيَهْلِكَ مَنْ
هَلَكَ عَنْ بَيِّنَةٍ، وَ يَحْيَا مَنْ حَيَّ عَنْ بَيِّنَةٍ.

Peace be to the wise and just Imam, the most veracious one, who set apart (truth from falsehood) on the basis of justice, through whom Allah separated the truth from falsehood, faith from unfaith, and monotheism from polytheism, so that he who perishes might perish by a manifest proof, and he who lives may live on by a manifest proof.

أَشْهَدُ أَنَّكَ أَمِيرُ الْمُؤْمِنِينَ وَ خَاصَّةُ
نَفْسِ الْمُنْتَجَبِينَ، وَ زَيْنُ الصِّدِّيقِينَ، وَ
صَابِرُ الْمُمْتَحَنِينَ، وَ أَنَّكَ حَكَمُ اللهِ فِى
أَرْضِهِ، وَ قَاضِى أَمْرِهِ، وَ بَابُ حِكْمَتِهِ، وَ
عَاقِدُ عَهْدِهِ، وَ النَّاطِقُ بِوَعْدِهِ، وَ الْحَبْلُ
الْمَوْصُولُ بَيْنَهُ وَ بَيْنَ عِبَادِهِ، وَ كَهْفُ
النَّجَاةِ، وَ مِنْهَاجُ التُّقَى، وَ الدَّرَجَةُ الْعُلْيَا،
وَ مُهَيْمِنُ الْقَاضِى الْأَعْلَى، يَا أَمِيرَ الْمُؤْمِنِينَ
بِكَ أَتَقَرَّبُ إِلَى اللهِ زُلْفَى، أَنْتَ وَلِيِّى وَ
سَيِّدِى وَ وَسِيلَتِى فِى الدُّنْيَا وَ الْآخِرَةِ.

I bear witness that you are the Commander of the Faithful, the choicest of the elect, the ornament of the truthful, the most steadfast of the tested ones, and that you are God's arbiter on His earth, adjudicator by His command, the gateway of His wisdom, concluder of His covenant, the declarer of His promise, and the connecting cord between Him and His servants, the haven of deliverance, the path of God-fearing, the highest degree and custodian of the Supreme Judge. O Commander of the Faithful, through you do I seek nearness to Allah and you are my guardian, my master and my recourse in this world and the Hereafter!

On entering the mosque say,

اَللهُ أَكْبَرُ، اَللهُ أَكْبَرُ، اَللهُ أَكْبَرُ، هٰذَا

Allah is greater. Allah is great-

مَقَامُ الْعَائِذِ بِـــالله، وَ بِمُحَمَّدٍ حَبِيبِ
اللهِ صَلَّى اللهُ عَلَيْهِ وَ آلِهِ، وَ بِوِلَايَةِ أَمِيرِ
الْمُؤْمِنِينَ، وَ الْأَئِمَّةِ الْمَهْدِيِّينَ الصَّادِقِينَ
النَّاطِقِينَ الرَّاشِــدِينَ، الَّذِيــنَ أَذْهَبَ
اللهُ عَنْهُــمُ الرِّجْسَ وَ طَهَّرَهُمْ تَطْهِيرًا،

er. Allah is greater. I, who stand here, take refuge with Allah, with Muḥammad, Allah's beloved, may Allah bless him and his Family, and in the *wilāyah* of the Commander of the Faithful and the Imams, the veracious guides and the rightly-guided ones, from whom Allah has repelled all impurity and purified them with a thorough purification.

رَضِيتُ بِهِــمْ أَئِمَّةً وَ هُـــدَاةً وَ مَوَالِيَّ،
سَلَّمْتُ لِأَمْرِ اللهِ لَا أُشْرِكُ بِهِ شَيْئًا، وَ لَا
أَتَّخِذُ مَعَ اللهِ وَلِيًّا، كَذَبَ الْعَادِلُونَ بِاللهِ
وَ ضَلُّوا ضَلَالًا بَعِيدًا، حَسْــبِيَ اللهُ وَ
أَوْلِيَاءُ اللهِ، أَشْهَدُ أَنْ لَا إِلٰهَ إِلَّا اللهُ وَحْدَهُ
لَا شَرِيكَ لَهُ، وَ أَشْهَدُ أَنَّ مُحَمَّدًا عَبْدُهُ وَ
رَسُولُهُ صَلَّى اللهُ عَلَيْهِ وَ آلِهِ، وَ أَنَّ عَلِيًّا
وَ الْأَئِمَّةَ الْمَهْدِيِّــينَ مِنْ ذُرِّيَّتِهِ عَلَيْهِمُ
السَّلَامُ أَوْلِيَائِي وَ حُجَّةُ اللهِ عَلَى خَلْقِهِ.

I am well-pleased with them as my Imams, guides and masters. I comply with Allah's commands and I do not ascribe any partner to Him, nor do I take anyone as guardian besides Allah. Those who equate others with Allah have lied and strayed into far error. Sufficient are for me Allah and His *awliyā*. I testify that there is no god besides Allah, that He is One and has no partner. I testify that Muḥammad is His servant and apostle—may Allah bless him and his Family—and that ᶜAlī and the rightly-guided Imams of his descent, peace be to them, are my masters and Allah's testament to His creation.

The Observance of the Fourth Pillar (Maqām-o Ibrāhīm)

Then proceed to the fourth pillar, associated with the Prophet Abraham (ᶜ*a*), which is near the "Bāb al-Anmāṭ" and besides the fifth pillar. There, offer four *rak*ᶜ*ahs*, two *rak*ᶜ*ahs* with al-Fātiḥah and Sūrat al-Tawḥīd and the remaining two with al-Fātiḥah and Sūrat al-Qadr.[1] After prayers, say the *tasbīḥ* of Ḥaḍrat Fāṭimah (ᶜ*a*) and then say,[2]

1 *Biḥār*, xcvii, 410, b 6, h 68, from *al-Mazār al-Kabīr* and Shahīd Awwal.
2 *Biḥār*, xcvii, 410-411, b 6, h 68, from Ibn Ṭāwūs.

Peace be to Allah's righteous and rightly-guided servants, from whom He has repelled all impurity and purified them with a thorough purification. He has made them prophetic envoys and appointed them to be testament to all His creation. *Peace be to the apostles and all praise belongs to Allah, the Lord of all the world. That is the ordaining of the All-mighty, the All-knowing.*(36:38.)

اَلسَّلَامُ عَلىٰ عِبَادِ اللهِ الصَّالِحِينَ الرَّاشِدِينَ، اَلَّذِينَ أَذْهَبَ اللهُ عَنْهُمُ الرِّجْسَ وَ طَهَّرَهُمْ تَطْهِيرًا، وَ جَعَلَهُمْ أَنْبِيَاءَ مُرْسَلِينَ، وَ حُجَّةً عَلَى الْخَلْقِ أَجْمَعِينَ، وَ سَلَامٌ عَلَى الْمُرْسَلِينَ، وَ الْحَمْدُ لِلّٰهِ رَبِّ الْعَالَمِينَ، ذٰلِكَ تَقْدِيرُ الْعَزِيزِ الْعَلِيمِ.

Then say seven times, "*Salāmun ᶜalā Nūḥin fil ᶜālamīn*" (*'Peace be to Noah, throughout the nations!*)(37:79) Then say,

O friend of the faithful, we remain loyal to the exhortation you made to the apostles and the truthful ones of your descent, and we are your followers and followers of our Prophet, Muḥammad, may Allah bless him and his Family, and bless you and all the apostles, prophets, and the truthful ones. We stand fast by the creed of Abraham and the religion of Muḥammad, the untaught prophet, the rightly-guided Imams, and by the *wilāyah* of our master, ᶜAli, the Commander of the Faithful.

نَحْنُ عَلىٰ وَصِيَّتِكَ يَا وَلِيَّ الْمُؤْمِنِينَ، اَلَّتِي أَوْصَيْتَ بِهَا ذُرِّيَّتَكَ مِنَ الْمُرْسَلِينَ وَ الصِّدِّيقِينَ، وَ نَحْنُ مِنْ شِيعَتِكَ وَ شِيعَةِ نَبِيِّنَا مُحَمَّدٍ صَلَّى اللهُ عَلَيْهِ وَ آلِهِ وَ عَلَيْكَ وَ عَلىٰ جَمِيعِ الْمُرْسَلِينَ وَ الْأَنْبِيَاءِ وَ الصَّادِقِينَ، وَ نَحْنُ عَلىٰ مِلَّةِ إِبْرَاهِيمَ، وَ دِينِ مُحَمَّدٍ النَّبِيِّ الْأُمِّيِّ، وَ الْأَئِمَّةِ الْمَهْدِيِّينَ، وَ وِلَايَةِ مَوْلَانَا عَلِيٍّ أَمِيرِ الْمُؤْمِنِينَ.

Peace be to the bearer of good news and the warner—may Allah's blessings, His mercy, pleasure and bounties be upon him and upon his legatee and successor, who was after him Allah's witness to His creation: ᶜAlī, the Commander of the Faithful, the

اَلسَّلَامُ عَلَى الْبَشِيرِ النَّذِيرِ، صَلَوَاتُ اللهِ عَلَيْهِ وَ رَحْمَتُهُ وَ رِضْوَانُهُ وَ بَرَكَاتُهُ، وَ عَلىٰ وَصِيِّهِ وَ خَلِيفَتِهِ، اَلشَّاهِدِ لِلّٰهِ مِنْ بَعْدِهِ عَلىٰ خَلْقِهِ، عَلِيٍّ أَمِيرِ الْمُؤْمِنِينَ، اَلصِّدِّيقِ

الْأَكْبَرِ، وَ الْفَارُوقِ الْمُبِينِ، اَلَّذِى
أَخَذْتَ بَيْعَتَهُ عَلَى الْعَالَمِينَ،

greatest of the truthful, the manifest separator (between truth and falsehood), for whom was taken the oath of allegiance from all the people.

رَضِيتُ بِهِمْ أَوْلِيَاءَ وَ مَوَالِيَ وَ حُكَّامًا فِي
نَفْسِي وَ وُلْدِى [وَلَدِى] وَ أَهْلِي، وَ مَالِي
وَ قِسْمِي، وَ حِلِّي وَ إِحْرَامِي، وَ إِسْلَامِي وَ
دِينِي، وَ دُنْيَايَ وَ آخِرَتِي، وَ مَحْيَايَ وَ مَمَاتِي،

I accept them as my guardians, masters and arbiters in relation to my own self, my children, family, property and share, in all my circumstances without and within the state of pilgrim sanctity, in my compliance and faith, my world and Hereafter, and my life and death.

أَنْتُمُ الْأَئِمَّةُ فِي الْكِتَابِ، وَ فَصْلُ الْمَقَامِ، وَ
فَصْلُ الْخِطَابِ، وَ أَعْيُنُ الْحَيِّ الَّذِى لَا يَنَامُ،

You are the Imams in the Scripture, the conclusive and final word, the sentinels of the Living One who does not sleep.

وَ أَنْتُمْ حُكَمَاءُ اللهِ، وَ بِكُمْ حَكَمَ
اللهُ، وَ بِكُمْ عُرِفَ حَقُّ اللهِ، لَا إِلٰهَ إِلَّا
اللهُ، مُحَمَّدٌ رَسُولُ اللهِ، أَنْتُمْ نُورُ اللهِ
مِنْ بَيْنِ أَيْدِينَا وَ مِنْ خَلْفِنَا، أَنْتُمْ سُنَّةُ
اللهِ الَّتِي بِهَا سَبَقَ الْقَضَاءُ.

You are Allah's sages: through you He judges, and through you Allah's rights are known. There is no god besides Allah, Muḥammad is the Apostle of Allah, and you are the light of Allah, in our own time and the future. You are Allah's precedent in whose favour the divine decree has already gone forth.

يَا أَمِيرَ الْمُؤْمِنِينَ، أَنَا لَكُمْ مُسَلِّمٌ
تَسْلِيمًا، لَا أُشْرِكُ بِاللهِ شَيْئًا، وَ لَا أَتَّخِذُ
مِنْ دُونِهِ وَلِيًّا. اَلْحَمْدُ لِلّٰهِ الَّذِى هَدَانِي
بِكُمْ، وَ مَا كُنْتُ لِأَهْتَدِيَ لَوْ لَا أَنْ
هَدَانِيَ اللهُ، اَللهُ أَكْبَرُ، اَللهُ أَكْبَرُ،
اَللهُ أَكْبَرُ، اَلْحَمْدُ لِلّٰهِ عَلَى مَا هَدَانَا.

O Commander of the Faithful, I am totally compliant to you. I do not ascribe any partner to Allah, nor seek any guardian besides Him. All praise belongs to Allah who guided me to you, and I would not have been guided had Allah not guided me. Allah is greater. Allah is greater. Allah is greater. Thanks to Allah for guiding us!

The Observances of Dikkat al-Qaḍā' and Bayt al-Ṭa<u>sh</u>t

The Dikkat al-Qaḍā' ('the Bench of Judgement') is a location in the mosque where the Commander of the Faithful (ᶜ*a*) used to sit in judgement. There was a short pillar in that place on which was inscribed the Qur'ānic verse,

إِنَّ اللهَ يَأْمُرُ بِالْعَدْلِ وَ الْإِحْسَان

Indeed Allah enjoins justice and kindness. (16:90)

The Bayt al-Ṭa<u>sh</u>t is the spot where a wonderful episode occurred involving an unmarried girl.[1] She had gone into a pond where a leech-like parasite had entered her womb and gradually grown in bulk by sucking blood. Her bulging belly had led her brothers to conclude that she was pregnant. They wanted to kill her for bringing shame on the family.

The case was brought before the Commander of the Faithful (ᶜ*a*). He had a curtain set up at one side of the mosque and sat the girl down behind it. Then he had her examined by a midwife, who after examining her declared that she was indeed carrying a child in her belly. Then at the Imam's order they brought a basin full of slime and mud and the girl was told to sit in it. The parasite came out of the girl's body at the smell of the slime. According to some accounts, the Imam miraculously stretched out his hand and fetched a handful of snow from the mountains of Syria and placed it by the basin, whereupon the parasite came out of the girl's belly.

A point to be noted here is concerning the sequence of the observances of this mosque. According to the customary order, after the above observance pertaining to the Fourth Pillar, one proceeds to perform the observance relating to the spot at the middle of the mosque. The observances pertaining to the Dikkat al-Qaḍā' and Bayt al-Ṭa<u>sh</u>t are performed at the end, after finishing the observance relating to the station of Imam Jaᶜfar al-Ṣādiq (ᶜ*a*).

However, the sequence given here follows the one given by Sayyid Ibn Ṭāwūs in *Miṣbāḥ al-Zā'ir*, by ᶜAllāmah Majlisī in the *Biḥār* and <u>Sh</u>ay<u>kh</u> <u>Kh</u>iḍr in the *Mazār*.[2] Those who wish to follow the customary sequence may perform the observances of Dikkat al-Qaḍā and Bayt

1 *Faḍā'il*, 157, whence *Biḥār*, xl, 278, b 97, h 42. *<u>Kh</u>arā'ij*, i, 210, whence *Biḥār*, xl, 242, b 97, h 20.

2 *Biḥār*, xcvii, 410-412.

al-Ṭashṭ after the observance of the Station of Imam Jaᶜfar al-Ṣādiq (ᶜ*a*), instead of after the observance of the Fourth Pillar.

The observance of Dikkat al-Qaḍā consists of offering two *rakᶜahs* of prayer in that place, with Sūrat al-Fātiḥah and any sūrah.[1] After the prayer and *tasbīḥ* of Ḥaḍrat Fātimah (ᶜ*a*) say,

يا مَالِكِي وَ مُمَلِّكِي وَ مُتَغَمِّدِي بِالنِّعَمِ الْجِسَامِ مِنْ غَيْرِ اسْتِحْقَاقٍ، وَجْهِي خَاضِعٌ لِمَا تَعْلُوهُ الْأَقْدَامُ لِجَلَالِ وَجْهِكَ الْكَرِيمِ.

O my Owner and Bestower of my possessions, who have enveloped me with Your immense blessings without my having deserved them! I lower and humble my face to the ground, which is trodden under feet, for the sake of the majesty of Your noble Face!

لَا تَجْعَلْ هٰذِهِ الشِّدَّةَ وَ لَا هٰذِهِ الْمِحْنَةَ مُتَّصِلَةً بِاسْتِيصَالِ الشَّأْفَةِ، وَ امْنَحْنِي مِنْ فَضْلِكَ مَا لَمْ تَمْنَحْ بِهِ أَحَدًا مِنْ غَيْرِ مَسْأَلَةٍ، أَنْتَ الْقَدِيمُ الْأَوَّلُ الَّذِي لَمْ تَزَلْ وَ لَا تَزَالُ، صَلِّ عَلَىٰ مُحَمَّدٍ وَ آلِ مُحَمَّدٍ وَ اغْفِرْ لِي وَ ارْحَمْنِي،

Do not let this hardship and ordeal lead up to utter destruction. Grant me, out of Your grace, that which You do not grant to anybody without his asking. You are the First and the Pre-eternal One who have always existed and will continue to exist. Bless Muḥammad and the Family of Muḥammad, and forgive me and have mercy on me.

وَ زَكِّ عَمَلِي، وَ بَارِكْ لِي فِي أَجَلِي، وَ اجْعَلْنِي مِنْ عُتَقَائِكَ وَ طُلَقَائِكَ مِنَ النَّارِ، بِرَحْمَتِكَ يَا أَرْحَمَ الرَّاحِمِينَ.

Purify my conduct and bless the span of my life and make me one of those whom You have spared and delivered from the Fire, O Most Merciful of the merciful!

The Observance of the Bayt al-Ṭashṭ

At the Bayt al-Ṭashṭ, which is next to the Dikkat al-Qaḍā, offer two *rakᶜahs*, as Imam al-Ṣādiq (ᶜ*a*) is reported[2] to have offered two *rakᶜahs* at this place. Then, after *salām* and *tasbīḥ*, say,

اَللّٰهُمَّ إِنِّي ذَخَرْتُ تَوْحِيدِي إِيَّاكَ،

O Allah, I treasure my faith in

1 *Biḥār*, xcvii, 411-412, b 6, h 68, from Ibn Ṭāwūs.

2 *Biḥār*, xcvii, 412, b 6, h 68.

Your Oneness, my knowledge of You, my dedication to You, my admission of Your Lordship, and I treasure as well my allegiance to Muḥammad and his Family—Your creatures with whose fellowship You have blessed me—for the day that I seek refuge in You, in life and after death.

وَ مَعْرِفَتِي بِكَ، وَ إِخْلَاصِي لَكَ، وَ إِقْرَارِي
بِرُبُوبِيَّتِكَ، وَ ذَخَرْتُ وِلَايَةَ مَنْ أَنْعَمْتَ
عَلَيَّ بِمَعْرِفَتِهِمْ مِنْ بَرِيَّتِكَ، مُحَمَّدٍ وَ عِتْرَتِهِ
صَلَّى اللّٰهُ عَلَيْهِمْ، لِيَوْمِ فَزَعِي إِلَيْكَ عَاجِلًا
وَ آجِلًا،

O my Master, I seek refuge with You and them, today and in this place where I stand, and beseech You to expand Your blessing, to spare me from Your vengeance, which I fear, to bless what You provide me with, and to protect my heart from every worry, affliction and sin, with regard to my faith, my conduct in this life and my condition in the Hereafter, O Most Merciful of the merciful!

وَ قَدْ فَزِعْتُ إِلَيْكَ وَ إِلَيْهِمْ يَا مَوْلَايَ فِي
هٰذَا الْيَوْمِ وَ فِي مَوْقِفِي هٰذَا، وَ سَأَلْتُكَ
مَادَّتِي مِنْ نِعْمَتِكَ، وَ إِزَاحَةَ مَا أَخْشَاهُ مِنْ
نِقْمَتِكَ، وَ الْبَرَكَةَ فِيمَا رَزَقْتَنِيهِ، وَ تَحْصِينَ
صَدْرِي مِنْ كُلِّ هَمٍّ وَ جَائِحَةٍ وَ مَعْصِيَةٍ فِي
دِينِي وَ دُنْيَايَ وَ آخِرَتِي، يَا أَرْحَمَ الرَّاحِمِينَ.

The Observance at the Mosque's Centre

This spot is called Dikkat al-Miʿrāj, apparently because the Apostle of Allah (ṣ) came down here with the permission of God Almighty and offered two *rakʿahs* at this place. The tradition pertaining to this episode was mentioned at the beginning of this chapter.

Two *rakʿahs* are to be offered at the middle of the mosque, with al-Fātiḥah and Sūrat al-Tawḥīd in the first and al-Fātiḥah and Sūrat al-Kāfirūn in the second.[1] After *salām* and *tasbīḥ* of Fāṭimah Zahrā (*ʿa*), say,

O Allah, You are Peace, from You proceeds all peace, and to You returns all peace, and Your abode is the abode of peace. Our Lord, greet us with Your greeting of 'Peace.'

اَللّٰهُمَّ أَنْتَ السَّلَامُ، وَ مِنْكَ السَّلَامُ، وَ
إِلَيْكَ يَعُودُ السَّلَامُ، وَ دَارُكَ دَارُ السَّلَامِ،
حَيِّنَا رَبَّنَا مِنْكَ بِالسَّلَامِ.

[1] *Biḥār*, xcvii, 412, b 6, h 68, from Ibn Ṭāwūs.

O Allah, I have offered this prayer, seeking Your mercy, Your pleasure and Your pardon, and to honour Your mosque. O Allah, bless Muḥammad and the Family of Muḥammad and raise my prayer to the *ᶜIllīyūn* and accept it from me, O Most Merciful of the merciful!

اَللّٰهُمَّ إِنِّي صَلَّيْتُ هٰذِهِ الصَّلَاةَ ابْتِغَاءَ
رَحْمَتِكَ وَ رِضْوَانِكَ وَ مَغْفِرَتِكَ، وَ تَعْظِيمًا
لِمَسْجِدِكَ. اَللّٰهُمَّ فَصَلِّ عَلَىٰ مُحَمَّدٍ وَ آلِ
مُحَمَّدٍ، وَ ارْفَعْهَا فِي عِلِّيِّينَ، وَ تَقَبَّلْهَا مِنِّي
يَا أَرْحَمَ الرَّاحِمِينَ.

The Observance of the Seventh Pillar

The seventh pillar is the place where God Almighty inspired Adam (*ᶜa*) to pray for repentance.[1] Proceed towards this place and, standing near the pillar, say while facing the *qiblah*,[2]

In Allah's Name, by Allah and following the creed of Allah's Apostle, may Allah bless him and his Family. There is no god besides Allah and Muḥamamd is the Apostle of Allah.

بِسْمِ اللّٰهِ وَ بِاللّٰهِ، وَ عَلَىٰ مِلَّةِ رَسُولِ اللّٰهِ
صَلَّى اللّٰهُ عَلَيْهِ وَ آلِهِ، وَ لَا إِلٰهَ إِلَّا اللّٰهُ
مُحَمَّدٌ رَسُولُ اللّٰهِ.

Peace be to Adam, our father, and Eve, our mother. Peace be to Abel, who was slain wrongfully and unjustly, out of envy for Allah's gifts and His approval. Peace be to Shayth, Allah's elect and His chosen trustee, and peace be to the paragons of veracity from his pure progeny, from the first of them to the last.

اَلسَّلَامُ عَلَىٰ أَبِينَا آدَمَ، وَ أُمِّنَا حَوَّاءَ. اَلسَّلَامُ عَلَىٰ
هَابِيلَ الْمَقْتُولِ ظُلْمًا وَ عُدْوَانًا عَلَىٰ مَوَاهِبِ
اللّٰهِ وَ رِضْوَانِهِ. اَلسَّلَامُ عَلَىٰ شَيْثٍ صَفْوَةِ اللّٰهِ
الْمُخْتَارِ الْأَمِينِ، وَ عَلَى الصَّفْوَةِ الصَّادِقِينَ مِنْ
ذُرِّيَّتِهِ الطَّيِّبِينَ، أَوَّلِهِمْ وَ آخِرِهِمْ.

Peace be to Abraham, Ishmael, Isaac, and Jacob and to their chosen descendants! Peace be to Moses, Allah's interlocutor! Peace be to Jesus, Allah's spirit!

اَلسَّلَامُ عَلَىٰ إِبْرَاهِيمَ وَ إِسْمَاعِيلَ وَ إِسْحَاقَ
وَ يَعْقُوبَ، وَ عَلَىٰ ذُرِّيَّتِهِمُ الْمُخْتَارِينَ.
اَلسَّلَامُ عَلَىٰ مُوسَىٰ كَلِيمِ اللّٰهِ. اَلسَّلَامُ عَلَىٰ
عِيسَىٰ رُوحِ اللّٰهِ.

1 *Miftāḥ al-Jinān*, 749. Untraced in the sources.
2 *Biḥār*, xcvii, 412-414, b 6, h 68, from Ibn Ṭāwūs.

Peace be to Muḥammad ibn ᶜAbd Allāh, the Seal of the Prophets. Peace be to the Commander of the Faithful and his immaculate descendants, and may Allah's mercy and blessings be upon them! Peace be to you, among the former generations! Peace be to you, among the latter generations!

اَلسَّلَامُ عَلَىٰ مُحَمَّدِ بْنِ عَبْدِ اللهِ خَاتَمِ
النَّبِيِّينَ. اَلسَّلَامُ عَلَىٰ أَمِيرِ الْمُؤْمِنِينَ وَ
ذُرِّيَّتِهِ الطَّيِّبِينَ، وَ رَحْمَةُ اللهِ وَ بَرَكَاتُهُ.
اَلسَّلَامُ عَلَيْكُمْ فِي الْأَوَّلِينَ، اَلسَّلَامُ
عَلَيْكُمْ فِي الْآخِرِينَ.

Peace be to Fāṭimah Zahrā! Peace be to the Imams, the guides and Allah's witnesses to His creation! Peace be to him who is the sentinel and witness over the nations on behalf of Allah, the Lord of all the worlds!

اَلسَّلَامُ عَلَىٰ فَاطِمَةَ الزَّهْرَاءِ. اَلسَّلَامُ عَلَى
الْأَئِمَّةِ الْهَادِينَ، شُهَدَاءِ اللهِ عَلَىٰ خَلْقِهِ.
اَلسَّلَامُ عَلَى الرَّقِيبِ الشَّاهِدِ عَلَى الْأُمَمِ
لِلّٰهِ رَبِّ الْعَالَمِينَ.

Then offer four *rakᶜahs*, with al-Fātiḥah and Sūrat al-Qadr in the first and al-Fātiḥah and Sūrat al-Tawḥīd in the second *rakᶜah*. The third and fourth *rakᶜahs* are to be offered in a similar manner. After the *tasbīḥ* of Ḥaḍrat Fāṭimah (*ᶜa*), say,

O Allah, though I have disobeyed You, yet I have been obedient to You with regard to my faith in You—a favour You have done me, not a favour I may have done—and I have obeyed You with regard to something which is dearest of all things in Your eyes: I did not ascribe any child to You nor any partner. Although I have sinned against You with regard to many things, that was not due to insolence on my behalf, nor due to a denial of my servanthood, nor a negation of Your lordship. Rather, I followed my desire and Satan made me stumble, after Your

اَللّٰهُمَّ إِنْ كُنْتُ قَدْ عَصَيْتُكَ فَإِنِّي قَدْ
أَطَعْتُكَ فِي الْإِيمَانِ مِنِّي بِكَ، مَنًّا مِنْكَ
عَلَيَّ، لَا مَنًّا مِنِّي عَلَيْكَ، وَ أَطَعْتُكَ فِي
أَحَبِّ الْأَشْيَاءِ لَكَ، لَمْ أَتَّخِذْ لَكَ وَلَدًا،
وَ لَمْ أَدْعُ لَكَ شَرِيكًا، وَ قَدْ عَصَيْتُكَ
فِي أَشْيَاءَ كَثِيرَةٍ عَلَىٰ غَيْرِ وَجْهِ الْمُكَابَرَةِ
لَكَ، وَ لَا الْخُرُوجِ عَنْ عُبُودِيَّتِكَ، وَ لَا
الْجُحُودِ لِرُبُوبِيَّتِكَ، وَ لٰكِنِ اتَّبَعْتُ
هَوَايَ، وَ أَزَلَّنِي الشَّيْطَانُ بَعْدَ الْحُجَّةِ

teaching had left me no room for any excuse!

عَلَيَّ وَ الْبَيَانِ،

If You punish me it will be because of my sins, and that will not be unjust, and if You pardon me and have mercy on me, that would be on account of Your generosity and magnanimity, O Munificent One!

فَإِنْ تُعَذِّبْنِي فَبِذُنُوبِي غَيْرَ ظَالِمٍ لِي، وَ إِنْ تَعْفُ عَنِّي وَ تَرْحَمْنِي فَبِجُودِكَ وَ كَرَمِكَ يَا كَرِيمُ.

O Allah, my sins have left me with no option but to pin hopes on Your pardon, though I have already made myself deserve its denial. O Allah, I seek what I do not deserve and desire what I do not merit.

اَللّٰهُمَّ إِنَّ ذُنُوبِي لَمْ يَبْقَ لَهَا إِلَّا رَجَاءُ عَفْوِكَ، وَ قَدْ قَدَّمْتُ آلَةَ الْحِرْمَانِ، فَأَنَا أَسْأَلُكَ اللّٰهُمَّ مَا لَا أَسْتَوْجِبُهُ، وَ أَطْلُبُ مِنْكَ مَا لَا أَسْتَحِقُّهُ.

O Allah, if You punish me for my sins, that will not be unjust of You, and if You forgive me, You are indeed the best of the merciful, O my Master! O Allah, You are You, and I am I! You keep on turning to me with clemency and I keep on reverting into sin! You go on being gracious to me out of Your forbearance, and I keep on regressing out of my ignorance!

اَللّٰهُمَّ إِنْ تُعَذِّبْنِي فَبِذُنُوبِي، وَ لَمْ تَظْلِمْنِي شَيْئًا، وَ إِنْ تَغْفِرْ لِي فَخَيْرُ رَاحِمٍ أَنْتَ يَا سَيِّدِي . اَللّٰهُمَّ أَنْتَ أَنْتَ وَ أَنَا أَنَا، أَنْتَ الْعَوَّادُ بِالْمَغْفِرَةِ، وَ أَنَا الْعَوَّادُ بِالذُّنُوبِ، وَ أَنْتَ الْمُتَفَضِّلُ بِالْحِلْمِ، وَأَنَا الْعَوَّادُ بِالْجَهْلِ

O Allah, I beseech You, O treasure of the weak, O worthy of great hopes, O saviour of the drowning, O deliverer of the perishing, O bringer of death to the living and quickener of the dead! You are Allah, there is no god besides You! To You pay reverence the rays of the Sun, the roar of the waters, the rustling of the trees, the light of the moon, the darkness of the night, the radi-

اَللّٰهُمَّ فَإِنِّي أَسْأَلُكَ يَا كَنْزَ الضُّعَفَاءِ، يَا عَظِيمَ الرَّجَاءِ، يَا مُنْقِذَ الْغَرْقَى، يَا مُنْجِيَ الْهَلْكَى، يَا مُمِيتَ الْأَحْيَاءِ، يَا مُحْيِيَ الْمَوْتَى، أَنْتَ اللّٰهُ لَا إِلٰهَ إِلَّا أَنْتَ، أَنْتَ الَّذِي سَجَدَ لَكَ شُعَاعُ الشَّمْسِ، وَ دَوِيُّ الْمَاءِ، وَ حَفِيفُ الشَّجَرِ، وَ نُورُ الْقَمَرِ، وَ ظُلْمَةُ

اللَّيْلِ، وَ ضَوْءُ النَّهَارِ، وَ خَفَقَانُ الطَّيْرِ،

ance of the day and the fluttering of the birds.

فَأَسْأَلُكَ اللّٰهُمَّ يا عَظِيمُ بِحَقِّكَ عَلىٰ مُحَمَّدٍ وَ آلِهِ الصَّادِقِينَ، وَ بِحَقِّ مُحَمَّدٍ وَ آلِهِ الصَّادِقِينَ عَلَيْكَ، وَ بِحَقِّكَ عَلىٰ عَلِيٍّ، وَ بِحَقِّ عَلِيٍّ عَلَيْكَ، وَ بِحَقِّكَ عَلىٰ فَاطِمَةَ، وَ بِحَقِّ فَاطِمَةَ عَلَيْكَ، وَ بِحَقِّكَ عَلَى الْحَسَنِ، وَ بِحَقِّ الْحَسَنِ عَلَيْكَ، وَ بِحَقِّكَ عَلَى الْحُسَيْنِ، وَ بِحَقِّ الْحُسَيْنِ عَلَيْكَ، فَإِنَّ حُقُوقَهُمْ عَلَيْكَ مِنْ أَفْضَلِ إِنْعَامِكَ عَلَيْهِمْ، وَ بِالشَّأْنِ الَّذِى لَكَ عِنْدَهُمْ، وَ بِالشَّأْنِ الَّذِى لَهُمْ عِنْدَكَ، صَلِّ عَلَيْهِمْ يَا رَبِّ صَلَاةً دَائِمَةً مُنْتَهَى رِضَاكَ، وَ اغْفِرْ لِي بِهِمُ الذُّنُوبَ الَّتِي بَيْنِي وَ بَيْنَكَ، وَ أَرْضِ عَنِّي خَلْقَكَ، وَ أَتْمِمْ عَلَيَّ نِعْمَتَكَ كَمَا أَتْمَمْتَهَا عَلىٰ آبَائِى مِنْ قَبْلُ، وَ لَا تَجْعَلْ لِأَحَدٍ مِنَ الْمَخْلُوقِينَ عَلَيَّ فِيهَا امْتِنَانًا، وَ امْنُنْ عَلَيَّ كَمَا مَنَنْتَ عَلىٰ آبَائِى مِنْ قَبْلُ، يَا كٓهٰيٰعٓصٓ.

O Allah, I beseech You, O Supreme One, by Your right on Muḥammad and the truthful Imams of his Family, and by the right that Muḥammad and the truthful ones of his Family have on You, by Your right on ʿAlī and by ʿAlī's right on You, by Your right on Fāṭimah and Fāṭimah's right on You, by Your right on al-Ḥasan and by al-Ḥasan's right on You, by Your right on al-Ḥusayn and by al-Ḥusayn's right on You, for indeed their rights on You are the best of Your blessings You have granted them! And by the station You have with them, and by the station they have with You, I beseech You to bless them, O Lord, with an everlasting blessing to an extent that will please You. For their sake, forgive me the sins that intervene between me and You! Reconcile Your creatures with me and complete Your blessing upon me, inasmuch as You completed for my ancestors before, and do not allow these blessings to be marred by favours from any of the creatures. Favour me as You have favoured my ancestors before, O Kāf-Hā-Yā-ʿAyn-Ṣād!

اَللّٰهُمَّ كَمَا صَلَّيْتَ عَلىٰ مُحَمَّدٍ وَ آلِهِ، فَاسْتَجِبْ لِي دُعَائِى فِيمَا سَأَلْتُ يَا كَرِيمُ يَا كَرِيمُ يَا كَرِيمُ.

O Allah, inasmuch as You have blessed Muḥammad and his Family, answer my petition about what I have asked You, O Munificent One, O Munificent One, O Munificent One!

Then[1] make prostration, and say while prostrating,

يَا مَنْ يَقْدِرُ عَلَىٰ حَوَائِجِ السَّائِلِينَ، وَ يَعْلَمُ مَا فِي ضَمِيرِ الصَّامِتِينَ، يَا مَنْ لَا يَحْتَاجُ إِلَى التَّفْسِيرِ، يَا مَنْ يَعْلَمُ خَائِنَةَ الْأَعْيُنِ وَ مَا تُخْفِي الصُّدُورُ، يَا مَنْ أَنْزَلَ الْعَذَابَ عَلَىٰ قَوْمِ يُونُسَ، وَ هُوَ يُرِيدُ أَنْ يُعَذِّبَهُمْ فَدَعَوْهُ وَ تَضَرَّعُوا إِلَيْهِ فَكَشَفَ عَنْهُمُ الْعَذَابَ، وَ مَتَّعَهُمْ إِلَىٰ حِينٍ، قَدْ تَرَىٰ مَكَانِي، وَ تَسْمَعُ دُعَائِي، وَ تَعْلَمُ سِرِّي وَ عَلَانِيَتِي وَ حَالِي، صَلِّ عَلَىٰ مُحَمَّدٍ وَ آلِ مُحَمَّدٍ، وَ اكْفِنِي مَا أَهَمَّنِي مِنْ أَمْرِ دِينِي وَ دُنْيَايَ وَ آخِرَتِي يَا سَيِّدِي.

O You who are able to grant the requests of all petitioners and know what is in the hearts of those who are mute! O You, who need no explanation! O You who know treacherous glances of the eyes and secrets concealed in the breasts! O You who sent down punishment on the people of Jonah, desiring to punish them, whereat they called You and entreated You, whereupon You removed their punishment and provided them for a while! You see my place and hear my call, knowing my private and public matters and my state! Bless Muḥammad and the Family of Muḥammad and suffice me with regard to all that is of concern to me in relation to my faith, my life in the world and the Hereafter, O my Master!

Repeat the phrase "*Yā sayyidī*" seventy times. Then, rising from prostration, say,

يَا رَبِّ أَسْأَلُكَ بَرَكَةَ هٰذَا الْمَوْضِعِ، وَ بَرَكَةَ أَهْلِهِ، وَ أَسْأَلُكَ أَنْ تَرْزُقَنِي مِنْ رِزْقِكَ رِزْقًا حَلَالًا طَيِّبًا تَسُوقُهُ إِلَيَّ بِحَوْلِكَ وَ قُوَّتِكَ، وَ أَنَا خَائِضٌ فِي عَافِيَةٍ، يَا أَرْحَمَ الرَّاحِمِينَ.

O Lord! I beseech You to grant me the *barakah* of this place and the *barakah* of its worthies. I beseech You to provide me with Your lawful and pure provision that You cater to me with Your power and might, while I continue to dwell in well-being, O Most Merciful of the merciful!

[1] It may be useful here to see the note on the following page concerning a variant version of this observance. (Tr.)

A Note

The book called "*al-Maẓār al-Qadīm*" suggests that after the words "*Yā karīmu, yā karīm...*" and before making prostration one should recite the supplication of the *Ṣaḥifah Sajjādiyyah* which begins with the words, "*Allāhumma yā man tuḥallu bihī ᶜuqadul makārih...,*" and was cited earlier in Book I (vol. 1, p. 328). After this supplication and before saying the above-mentioned supplication "*Yā man yaqdiru ᶜalā ḥawā'ij...*" in the state of prostration, one should say the following supplication.

اَللّٰهُـــمَّ إِنَّكَ تَعْلَمُ وَ لا أَعْلَمُ، وَ تَقْدِرُ وَ
لا أَقْدِرُ، وَ أَنْتَ عَـــلّامُ الْغُيُوبِ، صَلِّ
اللّٰهُمَّ عَلٰى مُحَمَّدٍ وَ آلِ مُحَمَّدٍ، وَ اغْفِرْ لِي
وَ ارْحَمْنِي وَ تَجَاوَزْ عَنِّي وَ تَصَدَّقْ عَلَيَّ مَا
أَنْتَ أَهْلُهُ، يَا أَرْحَمَ الرَّاحِمِينَ.

O Allah, You know and I do not know. You ordain and I do not. You are the knower of all the Unseen. Bless Muḥammad and the Family of Muḥammad and forgive me, have mercy on me, and overlook my faults, and grant me that which is worthy of You, O Most Merciful of the merciful!

It is to be noted that there are many reports concerning the virtues of this pillar.[1] Shaykh Kulaynī reports with a reliable chain of authorities that the Commander of the Faithful (ᶜa) used to offer prayers facing this pillar, standing close to it.[2] It is mentioned in a reliable report that every night 60,000 angels descend from the heaven to offer prayers at the seventh pillar.[3] This happens every night and will go on till the day of judgement, without any of the angels ever returning.

According to another reliable tradition,[4] Imam Jaᶜfar al-Ṣādiq (ᶜa)

1 *Wasā'il*, v, 263-265, b 47, h 6497-6502. *Biḥār*, xcvii, 388, 390, 392, 395, 396, 401, 406, b 6, h 11, 12, 15, 23, 30, 31, 54-56, 64, 65. *Mustadrak*, iii, 409-411, h 37, h 3893/1- 3897/5.

2 *Kāfī*, iii, 493, h 4, 8. Mufīd's *Mazār*, 10, b 3, h 1. Ṭūsī's *Amālī*, 51, majlis 2, h 67/36. *Tahdhīb*, vi, 33, b 10, h 8, whence *Wasā'il*, v, 363, b 47, h 6497-6498, *Biḥār*, xxxix, 130, b 79, h 1, lxxx, 377, b 8, h 45, xcvii, 392, 401, 406, b 6, h 23, 54, 64. *Mustadrak*, iii, 411, b 37, h 3897/5.

3 *Kāfī*, iii, 493, b 5, whence *Wasā'il*, v, 363, b 47, 6499, & *Biḥār*, xcvii, 401, b 6, h 55.

4 *Kāfī*, iii, 493, h 7. Mufīd's *Mazār*, 10, b 3, h 2. *Tahdhīb*, vi, 33, b 10, h 9. *Wasā'il*, v, 264, b 47, h 6501 and *Biḥār*, lxxx, 377, b 8, h 45, xcvii, 406, b 6, h 65. *Jāmiᶜ al-Akhbār*, 70.

is reported to have held that the seventh pillar is the station of Abraham (ʿ*a*).

Shaykh Kulaynī in *Kāfī* has cited a report[1] with a *ṣaḥīḥ* chain of authorities from Abū Ismāʿīl al-Sarrāj, from Muʿāwiyah b. Wahb, from Abū Ḥamzah al-Thumālī, from Aṣbagh b. Nubātah that Aṣbagh took Abū Ḥamzah's hand and while pointing to the seventh pillar said, "This pillar is the station of the Commander of the Faithful (ʿ*a*), where he used to pray. Imam al-Ḥasan (ʿ*a*) used to pray by the fifth pillar. At times, when the Commander of the Faithful was not present, he would offer prayers in the latter's place, and it is near Bāb Kindah." There are many reports describing the virtues of this spot, but our object here is brevity.

The Observance of the Fifth Pillar

Among the distinguished spots in the Mosque of Kūfah is the fifth pillar, where the pilgrim should offer prayer and supplicate God Almighty to grant his petitions. It is mentioned in reliable reports[2] that this was the place where the Prophet Abraham, the Friend of the All-beneficent, used to pray, and this is not contrary to the other reports, for it is possible that he used to offer prayers in all these spots. In a reliable report[3] Imam Jaʿfar al-Ṣādiq (ʿ*a*) is quoted as having said that the fifth pillar is the station of Gabriel (ʿ*a*), while according to the above-mentioned report it is also the station of Imam al-Ḥasan (ʿ*a*). That which can be inferred from the reports is that the spots near the fifth and the seventh pillar are the more meritorious locations of this mosque.

According to Sayyid Ibn Ṭāwūs,[4] one should offer near the fifth pillar two *rakʿahs*, with al-Fātiḥah and any other *sūrah*, and after *salām* and *tasbīḥ* say,

اَللّٰهُمَّ إِنِّي أَسْأَلُكَ بِجَمِيعِ أَسْمَائِكَ كُلِّهَا،

O Allah, I beseech You by all Your Names—those that we know and

[1] *Kāfī*, iii, 493, h 8, whence *Wasāʾil*, v, 263, b 47, h 6497 and *Biḥār*, xcvii, 406, b 6, h 64. Mufīd's *Mazār*, 10, b 3, h 1. *Tahdhīb*, vi, 33, b 10, h 8.

[2] *Kāfī*, iii, 493, h 6. *Tahdhīb*, iii, 251, b 25, h 10. *Wasāʾil*, v, 263, b 47, h 6500. *Biḥār*, xcvii, 388, 396, 401, b 6, h 11, 31, 56. *Mustadrak*, iii, 410, b 37, h 3894/2, 3895/3.

[3] *Kāfī*, iii, 493, h7. *Tahdhīb*, vi, 33, b 10, h 9. *Wasāʾil*, v, 263, b 47, h 6501. *Biḥār*, lxxx, 377, b 8, h 45, xcvii, 395, 406, b 6, h 30, 65.

[4] *Biḥār*, xcvii, 415, b 6, h 69, from Ibn Ṭāwūs.

those we do not—and I beseech You by Your great and supreme Name, the greatest and the supreme most, when someone invokes You by it You answer him, when someone requests You by it You grant him, when someone seeks Your help by it You help him, when someone pleads for Your pardon by it You forgive him, when someone seeks Your aid by it You assist him, when someone appeals to You by it for Your provision You provide him, when someone implores You by it for succour You succour him, and when someone beseeches Your mercy by it You have mercy on him, when someone seeks refuge with You by it You shelter him, when someone relies upon You by it You suffice him, when someone seeks Your protection by it You protect him, when someone entreats You by it to be saved from the Fire You deliver him, when someone pleads for Your kindness by it You are gentle to him, when someone pins his hope on You by it You grant him—Your Name by virtue of which You made Adam Your chosen one, Noah Your confidant, Abraham Your dedicated friend, Moses Your interlocutor, Jesus Your spirit, and Muḥammad Your beloved, ᶜAlī his legatee, may Allah bless them all, to fulfil my needs, to forgive my past sins, to grant me that which is worthy of You and to do the same for all the faithful, men and women, in the

مَا عَلِمْنَا مِنْهَا وَ مَا لَا نَعْلَمُ، وَ أَسْأَلُكَ
بِاسْمِكَ الْعَظِيمِ الْأَعْظَمِ الْكَبِيرِ
الْأَكْبَرِ الَّذِي مَنْ دَعَاكَ بِهِ أَجَبْتَهُ، وَ
مَنْ سَأَلَكَ بِهِ أَعْطَيْتَهُ، وَ مَنِ اسْتَنْصَرَكَ
بِهِ نَصَرْتَهُ، وَ مَنِ اسْتَغْفَرَكَ بِهِ غَفَرْتَ
لَهُ، وَ مَنِ اسْتَعَانَكَ بِهِ أَعَنْتَهُ، وَ مَنِ
اسْتَرْزَقَكَ بِهِ رَزَقْتَهُ، وَ مَنِ اسْتَغَاثَكَ
بِهِ أَغَثْتَهُ، وَ مَنِ اسْتَرْحَمَكَ بِهِ رَحِمْتَهُ،
وَ مَنِ اسْتَجَارَكَ بِهِ أَجَرْتَهُ، وَ مَنْ تَوَكَّلَ
عَلَيْكَ بِهِ كَفَيْتَهُ، وَ مَنِ اسْتَعْصَمَكَ بِهِ
عَصَمْتَهُ، وَ مَنِ اسْتَنْقَذَكَ بِهِ مِنَ النَّارِ
أَنْقَذْتَهُ، وَ مَنِ اسْتَعْطَفَكَ بِهِ تَعَطَّفْتَ
لَهُ، وَ مَنْ أَمَّلَكَ بِهِ أَعْطَيْتَهُ، الَّذِي
اتَّخَذْتَ بِهِ آدَمَ صَفِيًّا، وَ نُوحًا نَجِيًّا،
وَ إِبْرَاهِيمَ خَلِيلًا، وَ مُوسَىٰ كَلِيمًا،
وَ عِيسَىٰ رُوحًا، وَ مُحَمَّدًا حَبِيبًا، وَ
عَلِيًّا وَصِيًّا، صَلَّى اللّٰهُ عَلَيْهِمْ أَجْمَعِينَ،
أَنْ تَقْضِيَ لِي حَوَائِجِي، وَ تَعْفُوَ عَمَّا
سَلَفَ مِنْ ذُنُوبِي، وَ تَتَفَضَّلَ عَلَيَّ
بِمَا أَنْتَ أَهْلُهُ، وَ لِجَمِيعِ الْمُؤْمِنِينَ وَ

الْمُؤْمِنَاتِ لِلدُّنْيَا وَ الْآخِرَةِ، يَا مُفَرِّجَ هَمِّ الْمَهْمُومِينَ، وَ يَا غِيَاثَ الْمَلْهُوفِينَ، لَا إِلٰهَ إِلَّا أَنْتَ، سُبْحَانَكَ يَا رَبَّ الْعَالَمِينَ.

life of the world and the Hereafter, O Reliever of the worries of the anguished, O Succourer of the aggrieved, there is no god besides You, glory be to You, O Lord of all the worlds!

Imam Ja^cfar al-Ṣādiq (*^ca*) is reported[1] to have told one of his companions to offer two *rak^cahs* near the fifth pillar, where Abraham (*^ca*) offered prayers, and to say, "*Assalāmu ^calā abīnā Ādama wa ummunā Ḥawwā...*" A supplication with a similar wording, to be read while facing the *qiblah*, was cited in the observances of the seventh pillar.

The Observance of the Third Pillar at the Station of Imam Zayn al-^cĀbidīn (*^ca*)

Then one should proceed towards the station of Imam Zayn al-^cĀbidīn (*^ca*), which is near the third pillar and by the Bāb Kindah.

This place is opposite the platform at the gate of the Commander of the Faithful (*^ca*) in the direction of the *qiblah*, and from the western side opposite the Bāb Kindah, which has been closed.

It is said that it is better to offer the prayer here at a distance of five cubits from the pillar, where the platform used to be. Two *rak^cahs* are to be offered here with al-Fātiḥah and some other sūrah, and after *salām* and *tasbīḥ* one should say,[2]

بِسْمِ اللهِ الرَّحْمٰنِ الرَّحِيمِ، اَللّٰهُمَّ إِنَّ ذُنُوبِي قَدْ كَثُرَتْ وَ لَمْ يَبْقَ لَهَا إِلَّا رَجَاءُ عَفْوِكَ، وَ قَدْ قَدَّمْتُ آلَةَ الْحِرْمَانِ إِلَيْكَ، فَأَنَا أَسْأَلُكَ اللّٰهُمَّ مَا لَا أَسْتَوْجِبُهُ، وَ أَطْلُبُ مِنْكَ مَا لَا أَسْتَحِقُّهُ،

In the Name of Allah, the All-beneficent, the all-Merciful. O Allah, my sins are indeed numerous and they have left me with no option except to pin hopes on Your pardon, though I have already made myself deserve its denial. O Allah, I ask of You what I deserve not and seek from You what I merit not.

اَللّٰهُمَّ إِنْ تُعَذِّبْنِي فَبِذُنُوبِي وَ لَمْ تَظْلِمْنِي

O Allah, if You punish me for my sins, it will not be unjust of

1 *Biḥār*, xcvii, 388, b 6, h 11.

2 *Al-Mazār al-Kabīr*, 165, b 11. *Biḥār*, xcvii, 415-416, b 6, h 69, from Ibn Ṭāwūs. Shahīd Awwal's *Mazār*, 236.

You, and if You forgive me, You are indeed the best of the merciful, O my Master!

شَـيْئًا، وَ إِنْ تَغْفِرْ لِى فَخَيْرُ رَاحِمٍ أَنْتَ يَا سَيِّدِى.

O Allah, You are You and I am I! You keep on turning to me with pardon, and I keep on reverting to sin! You go one being gracious out of Your forbearance and I keep on regressing out of my ignorance!

اَللّٰهُمَّ أَنْتَ أَنْتَ وَ أَنَـا أَنَا، أَنْتَ الْعَوَّادُ بِالْمَغْفِـرَةِ، وَ أَنَا الْعَوَّادُ بِالذُّنُوبِ، وَ أَنْتَ الْمُتَفَضِّلُ بِالْحِلْمِ، وَ أَنَا الْعَوَّادُ بِالْجَهْلِ.

O Allah, I beseech You, O treasure of the weak, O worthy of great hopes, O rescuer of the drowning, O deliverer of the doomed, O bringer of death to the living and quickener of the dead! You are Allah, there is no god besides You, to You pay reverence the rays of the sun, the roar of the waters, the rustling of the trees, the light of the moon, the darkness of the night, the radiance of the day and the fluttering of the birds.

اَللّٰهُمَّ فَإِنِّى أَسْـأَلُكَ يَا كَنْزَ الضُّعَفَاءِ، يَا عَظِيمَ الرَّجَاءِ، يَا مُنْقِذَ الْغَرْقَى، يَا مُنْجِيَ الْهَلْكَى، يَـا مُمِيتَ الْأَحْيَـاءِ، يَا مُحْيِيَ الْمَوْتَى، أَنْـتَ اللهُ الَّذِى لَا إِلٰهَ إِلَّا أَنْتَ، أَنْتَ الَّذِى سَجَدَ لَكَ شُعَاعُ الشَّمْسِ، وَ نُورُ الْقَمَرِ، وَ ظُلْمَةُ اللَّيْلِ، وَ ضَوْءُ النَّهَارِ، وَ خَفَقَانُ الطَّيْرِ،

O Allah, I beseech You, O Supreme One, O Munificent One, by Your right on Muḥammad and the truthful ones of his Family, and by the right of Muḥammad and the truthful ones of his Family on You, by Your right on ʿAlī and by the right of ʿAlī on You, by Your right on Fāṭimah and the right of Fāṭimah on You, by Your right on al-Ḥasan and by the right of al-Ḥasan on You, by Your right on al-Ḥusayn and by the right of al-Ḥusayn on You, for indeed their rights on You are the best of blessings You have granted them.

فَأَسْأَلُكَ اللّٰهُمَّ يَا عَظِيمُ بِحَقِّكَ يَا كَرِيمُ عَلَى مُحَمَّدٍ وَ آلِهِ الصَّادِقِينَ، وَ بِحَقِّ مُحَمَّدٍ وَ آلِهِ الصَّادِقِينَ عَلَيْـكَ، وَ بِحَقِّكَ عَلَى عَلِيٍّ، وَ بِحَقِّ عَلِيٍّ عَلَيْـكَ، وَ بِحَقِّكَ عَلَى فَاطِمَـةَ، وَ بِحَقِّ فَاطِمَةَ عَلَيْكَ، وَ بِحَقِّكَ عَلَى الْحَسَـنِ، وَ بِحَقِّ الْحَسَنِ عَلَيْكَ، وَ بِحَقِّكَ عَلَى الْحُسَـيْنِ، وَ بِحَقِّ الْحُسَـيْنِ عَلَيْكَ، فَإِنَّ حُقُوقَهُمْ مِنْ أَفْضَلِ إِنْعَامِكَ

عَلَيْهِمْ، وَ بِالشَّـــأْنِ الَّذِى لَكَ عِنْدَهُمْ، وَ بِالشَّـــأْنِ الَّذِى لَهُمْ عِنْدَكَ، صَلِّ يَا رَبِّ عَلَيْهِمْ صَلاٰةً دَائِمَـــةً مُنْتَهَى رِضَاكَ، وَ اغْفِرْ لِي بِهِمُ الذُّنُوبَ الَّتِي بَيْنِي وَ بَيْنَكَ، وَ أَتْمِمْ نِعْمَتَكَ عَلَيَّ كَمَا أَتْمَمْتَهَا عَلَىٰ آبَائِى مِنْ قَبْلُ، يَا كٓهٰيٰعٓصٓ.

And I beseech You by the station You have with them, and by the station they have with You, to bless them, O Lord, with an everlasting blessing, to the extent that will please You, and forgive, for their sake, my sins that intervene between me and You, and complete Your blessing on me, inasmuch as You completed for my ancestors before, O Kāf-Hā-Yā-ᶜAyn-Ṣād!

اَللّٰهُمَّ كَمَا صَلَّيْتَ عَلَىٰ مُحَمَّدٍ وَ آلِ مُحَمَّدٍ، فَاسْتَجِبْ لِي دُعَائِي فِيمَا سَأَلْتُكَ،

O Allah, inasmuch as You have blessed Muḥammad and his Family, answer my petition with regard to what I have asked You.

Then make prostration and, laying the right cheek on the ground, say,

يَا سَيِّدِى يَا سَيِّدِى يَا سَيِّدِى، صَلِّ عَلَىٰ مُحَمَّـــدٍ وَ آلِ مُحَمَّدٍ، وَ اغْفِرْ لِي وَ اغْفِرْ لِي وَ اغْفِرْ لِي.

O my Master! O my Master! O my Master! Bless Muḥammad and the Family of Muḥammad, and forgive me! Forgive me! Forgive me!

Repeat these words several times in a state of tearful humility. Then laying the left cheek on the ground, say these words again repeatedly and make any petition you want.

An Observance for the Mosque's Visitors

Some popular and unreliable compilations mention an observance to be performed here. However, that observance, taught by Imam Jaᶜfar al-Ṣādiq (*ᶜa*) to one of his companions, is not limited to this spot. The manner of its performance, as taught by the Imam to a companion, is mentioned in a report.[1] The Imam is reported to have asked him, "Don't you pass by the great mosque of Kūfah while going out for work in the mornings?" "I do," he replied. The Imam said, "Offer four *rakᶜahs* in that mosque and after the prayer say,

[1] *Kāfī*, iii, 475, h 5. *Biḥār*, xcvii, 414-415, b 6, h 69, from Ibn Ṭāwūs.

إِلَهِي إِنْ كُنْتُ قَدْ عَصَيْتُكَ فَإِنِّي قَدْ
أَطَعْتُكَ فِي أَحَبِّ الْأَشْيَاءِ إِلَيْكَ، لَمْ
أَتَّخِذْ لَكَ وَلَدًا، وَ لَمْ أَدْعُ لَكَ شَرِيكًا،
وَ قَدْ عَصَيْتُكَ فِي أَشْيَاءَ كَثِيرَةٍ عَلَىٰ
غَيْرِ وَجْهِ الْمُكَابَرَةِ لَكَ، وَ لَا الْإِسْتِكْبَارِ
عَنْ عِبَادَتِكَ، وَ لَا الْجُحُودِ لِرُبُوبِيَّتِكَ،
وَ لَا الْخُرُوجِ عَنِ الْعُبُودِيَّةِ لَكَ،

My God, even if I have disobeyed You, I have obeyed You with regard to something which is dearest of things in Your eyes: I did not ascribe any child to You nor any partner. Although I have sinned against You with regard to many things, that was not due to insolence on my behalf, nor caused by an arrogant attitude towards Your worship, nor meant as a denial of Your Lordship, nor due to renunciation of my servanthood.

وَ لٰكِنِ اتَّبَعْتُ هَوَايَ، وَ أَزَلَّنِيَ
الشَّيْطَانُ بَعْدَ الْحُجَّةِ وَ الْبَيَانِ، فَإِنْ
تُعَذِّبْنِي فَبِذُنُوبِي غَيْرَ ظَالِمٍ أَنْتَ لِي،
وَ إِنْ تَعْفُ عَنِّي وَ تَرْحَمْنِي فَبِجُودِكَ وَ
كَرَمِكَ يَا كَرِيمُ.

Rather, I followed my desire and Satan made me stumble, after Your teaching had left me no room for any excuse! Hence if You punish me for my sins, that will not be unjust, and if You pardon me and have mercy on me, that will be on account of Your generosity and magnanimity, O Munificent One!

Also say,

غَدَوْتُ بِحَوْلِ اللهِ وَ قُوَّتِهِ، غَدَوْتُ بِغَيْرِ
حَوْلٍ مِنِّي وَ لَا قُوَّةٍ وَ لٰكِنْ بِحَوْلِ اللهِ
وَ قُوَّتِهِ، يَا رَبِّ أَسْأَلُكَ بَرَكَةَ هٰذَا الْبَيْتِ
وَ بَرَكَةَ أَهْلِهِ، وَ أَسْأَلُكَ أَنْ تَرْزُقَنِي
رِزْقًا حَلَالًا طَيِّبًا تَسُوقُهُ إِلَيَّ بِحَوْلِكَ وَ
قُوَّتِكَ، وَ أَنَا خَائِضٌ فِي عَافِيَتِكَ.

I rise in the morning with Allah's power and His might. I rise in the morning, not by my own power and strength, but by the power and might of Allah. O Lord, I beseech You to grant me the *barakah* of this house and the *barakah* of its worthies. I beseech You to provide me with Your lawful and pure provision that You cater to me with Your power and might while I continue to dwell in Your gift of wellbeing!

Shahīd Awwal and Muḥammad ibn al-Mashhadī[1] mention this ob-

[1] *Biḥār*, xcvii, 415, b 6, h 69.

servance as one pertaining to the courtyard of the mosque, to be performed after the observance of the fourth pillar. They prescribe a four-*rakʿah* prayer, with al-Fātiḥah and Sūrat al-Tawḥīd in the first two, and al-Fātiḥah with Sūrat al-Qadr in the next two *rakʿahs*, followed by the *tasbīḥ* of Fāṭimah Zahrā (*ʿa*).

In a reliable report,[1] Abū Ḥamzah al-Thumālī says, "One day, as I sat in the Mosque of Kūfah, I saw a man enter through the Bāb Kindah. He was the handsomest of men and well-dressed. A most pleasant fragrance hung around him. He had a turban on his head and wore a shirt and a gown. There were Arab shoes in his feet, which he removed as he approached the seventh pillar. While standing, he raised his hands to the ears and said the *takbīr* in a manner which made my hair stand and filled me with a feeling of awe. Then he offered four *rakʿahs* of prayer, performing the kneelings and prostrations in the worthiest manner. Then he recited the supplication *Ilāhî in kuntu qad ʿaṣaytuk...* until he reached the words *Yā karīm*. Then he prostrated as he repeated the words *Yā karīm* as many times as he could in a single breath. Then, while still prostrating, he said the supplication *Yā man yaqdiru ḥawâ'ijis sâ'ilīn...* followed by *Yā sayyidī!* seventy times." These supplications were cited above in the observance of the seventh pillar.

Abū Ḥamzah says, "When he raised his head, I recognized him. It was ʿAlī ibn al-Ḥusayn. I kissed his hands and asked him, 'What has brought you here?' The Imam replied, 'I came for what you saw me doing.' " That is, for prayer in the Mosque of Kūfah. An account of this report was given under the seventh *ziyārah* of the Commander of the Faithful (*ʿa*), where the Imam is described as taking along Abū Ḥamzah while proceeding for the *ziyārah* of the Commander of the Faithful (*ʿa*) (p. 136).

The Observance of Bāb al-Faraj, or the Station of Noah

After finishing the observance of the third pillar, proceed towards the bench at Bāb Amīr al-Mu'minīn (*ʿa*), which is a platform next to the door of the mosque that used to open toward the house of the Commander of the Faithful (*ʿa*). Offer four *rakʿahs* there with al-Fātiḥah and any other sūrah, and after the *tasbīḥ* say,[2]

[1] Shahīd Awwal's *Mazār*, 239-241 & *al-Mazār al-Kabīr*, 168 , whence *Biḥār*, xcvii, 388, b 6, h 12.

[2] *Biḥār*, xcvii, 416, b 6, h 69, from Ibn Ṭāwūs.

O Allah, bless Muḥammad and the Family of Muḥammad, and fulfil my need! O Allah, You don't disappoint those who ask You, nor are Your gifts ever exhausted. O fulfiller of needs, O answerer of supplications, O Lord of the heavens and the earths, O remover of distress, O bounteous giver of gifts, O repeller of adversities, O changer of vices into virtues, turn to me with Your bounteousness, grace and beneficence, and grant my petition concerning things that I ask You and beseech You for, by the right of Your Prophet, Your vicegerent and Your righteous *awliyā!*

اَللّٰهُمَّ صَلِّ عَلٰى مُحَمَّدٍ وَ آلِ مُحَمَّدٍ، وَ اقْضِ حَاجَتِي يَا اللهُ، يَا مَنْ لَا يَخِيبُ سَائِلُهُ، وَ لَا يَنْفَدُ نَائِلُهُ، يَا قَاضِيَ الْحَاجَاتِ، يَا مُجِيبَ الدَّعَوَاتِ، يَا رَبَّ الْأَرَضِينَ وَ السَّمَاوَاتِ، يَا كَاشِفَ الْكُرُبَاتِ، يَا وَاسِعَ الْعَطِيَّاتِ، يَا دَافِعَ النَّقِمَاتِ، يَا مُبَدِّلَ السَّيِّئَاتِ حَسَنَاتٍ، عُدْ عَلَيَّ بِطَوْلِكَ وَ فَضْلِكَ وَ إِحْسَانِكَ، وَ اسْتَجِبْ دُعَائِي فِيمَا سَأَلْتُكَ وَ طَلَبْتُ مِنْكَ، بِحَقِّ نَبِيِّكَ وَ وَصِيِّكَ وَ أَوْلِيَائِكَ الصَّالِحِينَ.

Another Prayer at this Place

Another observance for this station is a two-*rakʿah* prayer.[1] After the prayer and *tasbīḥ*, say,

O Allah, I have alighted in Your courtyard because of my knowledge that You are One and All-embracing, and that no one except You has the ability to fulfil my need. I know, my Lord, that whenever I have watched Your blessings on me, my need for You has become more intense!

اَللّٰهُمَّ إِنِّي حَلَلْتُ بِسَاحَتِكَ لِعِلْمِي بِوَحْدَانِيَّتِكَ وَ صَمَدَانِيَّتِكَ، وَ أَنَّهُ لَا قَادِرَ عَلٰى قَضَاءِ حَاجَتِي غَيْرُكَ، وَ قَدْ عَلِمْتُ يَا رَبِّ أَنَّهُ كُلَّمَا شَاهَدْتُ نِعْمَتَكَ عَلَيَّ اشْتَدَّتْ فَاقَتِي إِلَيْكَ،

My Lord, a crucial matter has befallen me, as You know, for You know without anyone informing You!

وَ قَدْ طَرَقَنِي يَا رَبِّ مِنْ مُهِمِّ أَمْرِي مَا قَدْ عَرَفْتَهُ، لِأَنَّكَ عَالِمٌ غَيْرُ مُعَلَّمٍ،

[1] *Biḥār*, xcvii, 417, b 6, h 69, from Ibn Ṭāwūs.

I beseech You by Your Name which made the heavens split when set on them, and spread out the earths, dispersed the stars and stabilized the mountains when set on them.

وَ أَسْأَلُكَ بِالْإِسْمِ الَّذِى وَضَعْتَهُ عَلَى السَّمَاوَاتِ فَانْشَقَّتْ، وَ عَلَى الْأَرَضِينَ فَانْبَسَطَتْ، وَ عَلَى النُّجُومِ فَانْتَشَرَتْ، وَ عَلَى الْجِبَالِ فَاسْتَقَرَّتْ،

I beseech You by the Name which You committed to Muḥammad, to ʿAlī, to al-Ḥasan, al-Ḥusayn and all the Imams, may Your blessings be upon them all, to bless Muḥammad and the Family of Muḥammad and to fulfil, my Lord, my need, remove its difficulty, and suffice me in getting through its ponderous part. Open for me its lock, for if You do, You are worthy of gratitude and praise, and if You do not, You are still worthy of gratitude and praise, for You are neither unjust in Your judgements nor unfair in dispensing justice!

وَ أَسْأَلُكَ بِالْإِسْمِ الَّذِى جَعَلْتَهُ عِنْدَ مُحَمَّدٍ وَ عِنْدَ عَلِيٍّ وَ عِنْدَ الْحَسَنِ وَ عِنْدَ الْحُسَيْنِ وَ عِنْدَ الْأَئِمَّةِ كُلِّهِمْ صَلَوَاتُ اللهِ عَلَيْهِمْ أَجْمَعِينَ، أَنْ تُصَلِّيَ عَلَىٰ مُحَمَّدٍ وَ آلِ مُحَمَّدٍ، وَ أَنْ تَقْضِيَ لِي يَا رَبِّ حَاجَتِي، وَ تُيَسِّرَ عَسِيرَهَا، وَ تَكْفِيَنِي مُهِمَّهَا، وَ تَفْتَحَ لِي قُفْلَهَا، فَإِنْ فَعَلْتَ ذٰلِكَ فَلَكَ الْحَمْدُ، وَ إِنْ لَمْ تَفْعَلْ فَلَكَ الْحَمْدُ، غَيْرَ جَائِرٍ فِي حُكْمِكَ، وَ لَا حَائِفٍ فِي عَدْلِكَ.

Then laying the right side of your face on the ground say,

O Allah, Jonah son of Matthew, Your servant and prophet, supplicated You in the fish's belly, whereupon You answered him, and I supplicate You so answer me by the right of Muḥammad and the Family of Muḥammad!

اَللّٰهُمَّ إِنَّ يُونُسَ بْنَ مَتّٰى عَبْدَكَ وَ نَبِيَّكَ دَعَاكَ فِي بَطْنِ الْحُوتِ فَاسْتَجَبْتَ لَهُ، وَ أَنَا أَدْعُوكَ فَاسْتَجِبْ لِي بِحَقِّ مُحَمَّدٍ وَ آلِ مُحَمَّدٍ.

Then supplicate for whatever need you may have. Then laying the left side of the face on the ground say,

O Allah, You have command-

اَللّٰهُمَّ إِنَّكَ أَمَرْتَ بِالدُّعَاءِ، وَ تَكَفَّلْتَ

ed Your servants to supplicate and promised to answer them. I supplicate to You as You have commanded me, so bless Muḥammad and the Family of Muḥammd and answer me as You have promised, O Munificent One!

بِالْإِجَابَةِ، وَ أَنَا أَدْعُوكَ كَمَا أَمَرْتَنِي،
فَصَلِّ عَلَىٰ مُحَمَّدٍ وَ آلِ مُحَمَّدٍ، وَ
اسْتَجِبْ لِي كَمَا وَعَدْتَنِي يَا كَرِيمُ.

Then laying your forehead on the ground, say,

O giver of might and honour to the weak and the abased! O humbler of the mighty, You know my distress. So bless Muḥammad and his Family and grant me relief, O Munificent One!

يَا مُعِزَّ كُلِّ ذَلِيلٍ، وَ يَا مُذِلَّ كُلِّ
عَزِيزٍ، تَعْلَمُ كُرْبَتِي، فَصَلِّ عَلَىٰ
مُحَمَّدٍ وَ آلِهِ، وَ فَرِّجْ عَنِّي يَا كَرِيمُ.

A Prayer for Need at this Place

This prayer consists of four *rakʿahs*.[1] After the prayer and *tasbīḥ*, say,

O Allah, I beseech You! O You who are neither seen by the eyes, nor comprehended by the minds, whom describers cannot describe, whom events cannot change and ages cannot annihilate!

اَللّٰهُمَّ إِنِّي أَسْأَلُكَ يَا مَنْ لَا تَرَاهُ
الْعُيُونُ، وَ لَا تُحِيطُ بِهِ الظُّنُونُ، وَ
لَا يَصِفُهُ الْوَاصِفُونَ، وَ لَا تُغَيِّرُهُ
الْحَوَادِثُ، وَ لَا تُفْنِيهِ الدُّهُورُ،

You know the weights of the mountains, the measures of the seas, the leaves of the trees and the sands of the deserts, and all that over which the sun and the moon shine, all that the night covers in darkness and the day illuminates! One heaven does not conceal another heaven from You, nor one earth another, nor does the mountains hide what lies at their roots, nor the oceans what lies in

تَعْلَمُ مَثَاقِيلَ الْجِبَالِ، وَ مَكَايِيلَ
الْبِحَارِ، وَ وَرَقَ الْأَشْجَارِ، وَ رَمْلَ
الْقِفَارِ، وَ مَا أَضَاءَتْ بِهِ الشَّمْسُ وَ
الْقَمَرُ، وَ أَظْلَمَ عَلَيْهِ اللَّيْلُ، وَ وَضَحَ
عَلَيْهِ النَّهَارُ، وَ لَا تُوَارِي مِنْكَ
سَمَاءٌ سَمَاءً، وَ لَا أَرْضٌ أَرْضًا، وَ لَا

[1] *Al-Mazār al-Kabīr*, 171. Shahīd's *Mazār*, 244. *Biḥār*, xcvii, 417-418, b 6, h 69, from Ibn Ṭāwūs.

جَبَلٌ مَا فِي أَصْلِهِ، وَ لَا بَحْرٌ مَا فِي قَعْرِهِ،

their depths!

أَسْأَلُكَ أَنْ تُصَلِّيَ عَلَىٰ مُحَمَّدٍ وَ آلِ مُحَمَّدٍ، وَ أَنْ تَجْعَلَ خَيْرَ أَمْرِي آخِرَهُ، وَ خَيْرَ أَعْمَالِي خَوَاتِيمَهَا، وَ خَيْرَ أَيَّامِي يَوْمَ أَلْقَاكَ، إِنَّكَ عَلَىٰ كُلِّ شَيْءٍ قَدِيرٌ.

I beseech You to bless Muḥammad and the Family of Muḥammad and to make the final part of my life its best part, the best part of my conduct their motives, and the best of my days the day that I shall meet You! Indeed You have power over all things!

اَللّٰهُمَّ مَنْ أَرَادَنِي بِسُوءٍ فَأَرِدْهُ، وَ مَنْ كَادَنِي فَكِدْهُ، وَ مَنْ بَغَانِي بِهَلَكَةٍ فَأَهْلِكْهُ، وَ اكْفِنِي مَا أَهَمَّنِي مِمَّنْ دَخَلَ هَمُّهُ عَلَيَّ.

O Allah, deter those who have evil intentions against me. Devise against those who plot against me. Destroy those who unjustly seek to destroy me. Take care of my concerns which cause me worry!

اَللّٰهُمَّ أَدْخِلْنِي فِي دِرْعِكَ الْحَصِينَةِ، وَ اسْتُرْنِي بِسِتْرِكَ الْوَاقِي، يَا مَنْ يَكْفِي مِنْ كُلِّ شَيْءٍ وَ لَا يَكْفِي مِنْهُ شَيْءٌ، اِكْفِنِي مَا أَهَمَّنِي مِنْ أَمْرِ الدُّنْيَا وَ الْآخِرَةِ، وَ صَدِّقْ قَوْلِي وَ فِعْلِي، يَا شَفِيقُ يَا رَفِيقُ، فَرِّجْ عَنِّي الْمَضِيقَ، وَ لَا تُحَمِّلْنِي مَا لَا أُطِيقُ.

O Allah, shelter me with Your secure shield and cover me with Your protective cover! O You who suffice against all things and against whom nothing can suffice! Suffice me with regard to my concerns pertaining to this world and the Hereafter and endorse my speech and conduct! O affectionate one, O gentle one, relieve me of the straits I am in and burden me not with what I cannot bear!

اَللّٰهُمَّ احْرُسْنِي بِعَيْنِكَ الَّتِي لَا تَنَامُ، وَ ارْحَمْنِي بِقُدْرَتِكَ عَلَيَّ، يَا أَرْحَمَ الرَّاحِمِينَ، يَا عَلِيُّ يَا عَظِيمُ، أَنْتَ عَالِمٌ بِحَاجَتِي، وَ عَلَىٰ قَضَائِهَا قَدِيرٌ، وَ هِيَ لَدَيْكَ يَسِيرٌ، وَ أَنَا إِلَيْكَ فَقِيرٌ، فَمُنَّ بِهَا عَلَيَّ يَا كَرِيمُ، إِنَّكَ عَلَىٰ كُلِّ شَيْءٍ قَدِيرٌ.

O Allah, guard me with Your eye that does not sleep and have mercy on me with Your power over me, O Most Merciful of the merciful! O Exalted and Supreme One, You know my need and have the power to fulfil it, and it is simple for You, while I stand in need of You! So do me a favour by granting it, O Munificent One! Indeed You have power over all things!

Then make prostration and say,

My God, You know my needs, so bless Muḥammad and his Family and fulfil them! You know all my sins, so bless Muḥammad and his Family and forgive them, O Munificent One!

إِلٰهِي قَــدْ عَلِمْتَ حَوَائِــجِي، فَصَلِّ عَلىٰ
مُحَمَّــدٍ وَ آلِ مُحَمَّــدٍ وَ اقْضِهَــا، وَ قَدْ
أَحْصَيْــتَ ذُنُوبِي، فَصَلِّ عَلىٰ مُحَمَّدٍ وَ آلِهِ
وَ اغْفِرْهَا، يَا كَرِيمُ.

Then laying the right cheek on the ground say,

If I have been a bad servant, You have been an excellent Lord! Treat me as is worthy of You, not as I deserve, O Most Merciful of the merciful!

إِنْ كُنْتُ بِئْسَ الْعَبْدُ، فَأَنْتَ نِعْمَ الرَّبُّ،
اِفْعَلْ بِي مَا أَنْتَ أَهْلُهُ، وَ لَا تَفْعَلْ بِي مَا
أَنَا أَهْلُهُ، يَا أَرْحَمَ الرَّاحِمِينَ

Then laying the left cheek on the ground say,

O Allah, if the sins of this servant of Yours have been monstrous, Your forgiveness will indeed be gracious, O Munificent One!

اَللّٰهُــمَّ إِنْ عَظُــمَ الذَّنْبُ مِــنْ عَبْدِكَ،
فَلْيَحْسُنِ الْعَفْوُ مِنْ عِنْدِكَ يَا كَرِيمُ.

Then laying your forehead on the ground say,

Have mercy on me, who, having acted meanly and sinfully, entreats You and admits his sins!

اِرْحَمْ مَنْ أَسَــاءَ وَ اقْتَرَفَ، وَ اسْتَكَانَ وَ
اعْتَرَفَ.

This supplication, up to the words "*Waghfirhā, yā karīm,*" is the same as the one prescribed in *al-Mazār al-Qadīm* for the observance pertaining to the station of Imam Zayn al-ʿAbidīn (*ʿa*) in the courtyard of the Sahlah Mosque.

The Observance at the Niche of the Commander of the Faithful (*ʿa*)

This is the place where the Commander of the Faithful (*ʿa*) was struck by the assassin's sword. The pilgrim performs a two-*rakʿah* prayer here with al-Fātiḥah and any *sūrah*. After *salām* and *tasbīḥ* say,[1]

يا مَنْ أَظْهَرَ الْجَمِيلَ وَ سَـــتَرَ الْقَبِيحَ، يا مَنْ لَـــمْ يُؤَاخِذْ بِالْجَرِيـــرَةِ، وَ لَمْ يَهْتِكِ السِّـــتْرَ وَ السَّرِيرَةَ، يا عَظِيـــمَ الْعَفْوِ، يا حَسَـــنَ التَّجَاوُزِ، يا وَاسِـــعَ الْمَغْفِرَةِ، يا بَاسِطَ الْيَدَيْنِ بِالرَّحْمَةِ،

O You who bring out all that is beautiful and cover up all that is ugly! O You who never take anyone to task for lapses of etiquette and do not expose hidden faults and secrets. O You whose clemency is great! O You who graciously overlook faults! O You whose forgiveness is immense! O You who have mercifully opened wide Your arms!

يا صَاحِـــبَ كُلِّ نَجْوَىٰ، يـــا مُنْتَهَىٰ كُلِّ شَـــكْوَىٰ، يا كَرِيمَ الصَّفْـــحِ، يا عَظِيمَ الرَّجَاءِ، يا سَيِّدِي صَلِّ عَلَىٰ مُحَمَّدٍ وَ آلِ مُحَمَّدٍ، وَ افْعَلْ بِي مَا أَنْتَ أَهْلُهُ يا كَرِيمُ.

O You who are companion to every secret discourse! O ultimate recourse of all complaints! O You who nobly overlook faults! O You in whom great hopes are placed! O my Master, bless Muḥammad and the Family of Muḥammad, and treat me as is worthy of You, O Munificent One!

THE MUNAJAT OF THE COMMANDER OF THE FAITHFUL ('A)[2]

اَللّٰهُمَّ إِنِّي أَسْـــأَلُكَ الْأَمَانَ يَوْمَ لَا يَنْفَعُ مَالٌ وَ لَا بَنُـــونَ إِلَّا مَنْ أَتَى اللهَ بِقَلْبٍ سَلِيمٍ.

O Allah, I beseech You to spare me on *the day when neither wealth nor children will avail, except him who comes to Allah with a sound heart.*(26:88-89)

وَأَسْأَلُكَ الْأَمَانَ يَوْمَ يَعَضُّ الظَّالِمُ عَلَىٰ يَدَيْهِ يَقُولُ يا لَيْتَنِي اتَّخَذْتُ مَعَ الرَّسُولِ سَبِيلًا.

I beseech You to spare me on the *day when the wrongdoer will bite his hands, saying, 'I wish I had followed the Apostle's way!'*(25:27)

وَ أَسْأَلُكَ الْأَمَانَ يَوْمَ يُعْرَفُ الْمُجْرِمُونَ

I beseech You to spare me on *the*

1 *Biḥār*, xcvii, 418, b 6, h 69, from Ibn Ṭāwūs.

2 The author of *al-Mazār al-Kabīr* and Shahīd Awwal cite the following *munājāt* of the Commander of the Faithful (*ʿa*) to be recited in this place. (Tr.) *Biḥār*, xcvii, 419-420, b 6, h 70, from *al-Mazār al-Kabīr* and Shahīd Awwal.

day when the guilty will be recognized by their mark; so they will be seized by the forelocks and the feet.[55:41]

بِسِيمَاهُمْ فَيُؤْخَذُ بِالنَّوَاصِى وَ الْأَقْدَامِ.

I beseech You to spare me on *the day— the day when a father shall not atone for his child, nor the child shall atone for its father in any wise. Indeed Allah's promise is true.*[31:33]

وَ أَسْأَلُكَ الْأَمَانَ يَوْمَ لَا يَجْزِى وَالِدٌ عَنْ وَلَدِهِ، وَ لَا مَوْلُودٌ هُوَ جَازٍ عَنْ وَالِدِهِ شَيْئًا، إِنَّ وَعْدَ اللهِ حَقٌّ.

I beseech You to spare me on *the day when the excuses of the wrong-doers will not benefit them, and the curse will lie on them, and for them will be the ills of the [ultimate] abode.*[40:52]

وَ أَسْأَلُكَ الْأَمَانَ يَوْمَ لَا يَنْفَعُ الظَّالِمِينَ مَعْذِرَتُهُمْ، وَ لَهُمُ اللَّعْنَةُ وَ لَهُمْ سُوءُ الدَّارِ.

I beseech You to spare me on the *day when no soul will be of any avail to another soul and all command that day will belong to Allah.*

وَ أَسْأَلُكَ الْأَمَانَ يَوْمَ لَا تَمْلِكُ نَفْسٌ لِنَفْسٍ شَيْئًا، وَ الْأَمْرُ يَوْمَئِذٍ لِلّٰهِ.

I beseech You to spare me on the *day when a man will evade his brother, his mother and father, his spouse and children—that day each of them will have a task to keep him preoccupied.*[80:34-37]

وَ أَسْأَلُكَ الْأَمَانَ يَوْمَ يَفِرُّ الْمَرْءُ مِنْ أَخِيهِ، وَ أُمِّهِ وَ أَبِيهِ، وَ صَاحِبَتِهِ وَ بَنِيهِ، لِكُلِّ امْرِىءٍ مِنْهُمْ يَوْمَئِذٍ شَأْنٌ يُغْنِيهِ.

I beseech You to spare me *on the day the guilty one will wish he could ransom himself from the punishment of that day at the price of his children, his spouse and his brother, his kin which had sheltered him and all those who are upon the earth, if that might deliver him. Never! Indeed it is a blazing fire, which strips away the scalp.*[70:11-16]

وَ أَسْأَلُكَ الْأَمَانَ يَوْمَ يَوَدُّ الْمُجْرِمُ لَوْ يَفْتَدِى مِنْ عَذَابِ يَوْمِئِذٍ بِبَنِيهِ، وَ صَاحِبَتِهِ وَ أَخِيهِ، وَ فَصِيلَتِهِ الَّتِى تُؤْوِيهِ، وَ مَنْ فِى الْأَرْضِ جَمِيعًا ثُمَّ يُنْجِيهِ، كَلَّا إِنَّهَا لَظَىٰ نَزَّاعَةً لِلشَّوَىٰ.

My Master! O My Master! You are the Master and I am the servant. Will anyone but the Master have mercy on His servant?

مَوْلَاىَ يَا مَوْلَاىَ، أَنْتَ الْمَوْلَىٰ وَ أَنَا الْعَبْدُ، وَ هَلْ يَرْحَمُ الْعَبْدَ إِلَّا الْمَوْلَىٰ؟

My Master! O My Master! You

مَوْلَاىَ يَا مَوْلَاىَ، أَنْتَ الْمَالِكُ وَ أَنَا

are the Owner and I am Your slave. Will anyone have mercy on the slave except the Owner?

الْمَمْلُوكُ، وَهَلْ يَرْحَمُ الْمَمْلُوكَ إِلَّا الْمَالِكُ؟

My Master! O My Master! You are the All-mighty and I am weak. Will anyone have mercy on someone who is weak except the All-mighty?

مَوْلَایَ یا مَوْلَایَ، أَنْتَ الْعَزِيزُ وَ أَنَا الذَّلِيلُ، وَ هَلْ يَرْحَمُ الذَّلِيلَ إِلَّا الْعَزِيزُ؟

My Master! O My Master! You are the Creator and I am Your creature. Will anyone have mercy on the creature except the Creator?

مَوْلَایَ یا مَوْلَایَ، أَنْتَ الْخَالِقُ وَ أَنَا الْمَخْلُوقُ، وَهَلْ يَرْحَمُ الْمَخْلُوقَ إِلَّا الْخَالِقُ؟

My Master! O My Master! You are Supreme One and I am puny. Will anyone have mercy on the puny except the Supreme One?

مَوْلَایَ یا مَوْلَایَ، أَنْتَ الْعَظِيمُ وَ أَنَا الْحَقِيرُ، وَ هَلْ يَرْحَمُ الْحَقِيرَ إِلَّا ا لْعَظِيمُ؟

My Master! O My Master! You are the All-strong and I am frail. Will anyone have mercy on the frail except the All-strong?

مَوْلَایَ يَا مَوْلَایَ، أَنْتَ الْقَوِيُّ وَ أَنَا الضَّعِيفُ، وَهَلْ يَرْحَمُ الضَّعِيفَ إِلَّا الْقَوِيُّ؟

My Master! O My Master! You are the All-sufficient and I am needy. Will anyone have mercy on the needy except the All-sufficient?

مَوْلَایَ يَا مَوْلَایَ، أَنْتَ الْغَنِيُّ وَ أَنَا الْفَقِيرُ، وَ هَلْ يَرْحَمُ الْفَقِيرَ إِلَّا الْغَنِيّ؟

My Master! O My Master! You are the Giver and I am the beggar. Will anyone have mercy on the beggar except the Giver?

مَوْلَایَ یا مَوْلَایَ، أَنْتَ الْمُعْطِي وَ أَنَا السَّائِلُ، وَ هَلْ يَرْحَمُ السَّائِلَ إِلَّا الْمُعْطِي؟

My Master! O My Master! You are the Living One and I am [essentially] devoid of life. Will anyone have mercy on the lifeless except the Living One?

مَوْلَایَ یا مَوْلَایَ، أَنْتَ الْحَيُّ وَ أَنَا الْمَيِّتُ، وَ هَلْ يَرْحَمُ الْمَيِّتَ إِلَّا الْحَيُّ؟

My Master! O My Master! You are the Everlasting One and I am ephemeral. Will anyone have mercy on the ephemeral except the Everlasting One?

مَوْلَایَ يَا مَوْلَایَ، أَنْتَ الْبَاقِي وَ أَنَا الْفَانِي، وَ هَلْ يَرْحَمُ الْفَانِيَ إِلَّا الْبَاقِي؟

My Master! O My Master! You are the Eternal One and I am transito-

مَوْلَایَ یا مَوْلَایَ، أَنْتَ الدَّائِمُ وَ أَنَا

ry. Will anyone except the Eternal One have mercy on one who is transitory?

الزَّائِلُ، وَ هَلْ يَرْحَمُ الزَّائِلَ إِلَّا الدَّائِمُ؟

My Master! O My Master! You are the All-provider and I am one who is provided. Will anyone except the All-provider have mercy on one who needs to be provided?

مَوْلَاىَ يَا مَوْلَاىَ، أَنْتَ الرَّازِقُ وَ أَنَا الْمَرْزُوقُ، وَهَلْ يَرْحَمُ الْمَرْزُوقَ إِلَّا الرَّازِقُ؟

My Master! O My Master! You are the All-generous and I am the one who is stingy. Will anyone except the All-generous have mercy on one who is stingy?

مَوْلَاىَ يَا مَوْلَاىَ، أَنْتَ الْجَوَادُ وَ أَنَا الْبَخِيلُ، وَ هَلْ يَرْحَمُ الْبَخِيلَ إِلَّا الْجَوَادُ؟

My Master! O My Master! You are the All-healer and I am afflicted. Will anyone except the All-healer have mercy on one who is afflicted?

مَوْلَاىَ يَا مَوْلَاىَ، أَنْتَ الْمُعَافِي وَ أَنَا الْمُبْتَلَى، وَ هَلْ يَرْحَمُ الْمُبْتَلَى إِلَّا الْمُعَافِي؟

My Master! O My Master! You are the All-great and I am insignificant. Will anyone except the All-great have mercy on one who is small?

مَوْلَاىَ يَا مَوْلَاىَ، أَنْتَ الْكَبِيرُ وَ أَنَا الصَّغِيرُ، وَ هَلْ يَرْحَمُ الصَّغِيرَ إِلَّا الْكَبِيرُ؟

My Master! O My Master! You are the Guide and I am the one who is astray. Will anyone except the Guide have mercy on the astray?

مَوْلَاىَ يَا مَوْلَاىَ، أَنْتَ الْهَادِي وَ أَنَا الضَّالُّ، وَ هَلْ يَرْحَمُ الضَّالَّ إِلَّا الْهَادِي؟

My Master! O My Master! You are the All-beneficent and I am the one who stands in need of mercy. Will anyone except the All-beneficent have mercy on one who stands in need of mercy?

مَوْلَاىَ يَا مَوْلَاىَ، أَنْتَ الرَّحْمٰنُ وَ أَنَا الْمَرْحُومُ، وَ هَلْ يَرْحَمُ الْمَرْحُومَ إِلَّا الرَّحْمٰنُ؟

My Master! O My Master! You are the Sovereign and I am the one in tribulation. Will anyone except the Sovereign have mercy on someone in tribulation?

مَوْلَاىَ يَا مَوْلَاىَ، أَنْتَ السُّلْطَانُ وَ أَنَا الْمُمْتَحَنُ، وَ هَلْ يَرْحَمُ الْمُمْتَحَنَ إِلَّا السُّلْطَانُ؟

My Master! O My Master! You are the Guide and I am bewildered and lost. Will anyone except the Guide

مَوْلَاىَ يَا مَوْلَاىَ، أَنْتَ الدَّلِيلُ وَ أَنَا الْمُتَحَيِّرُ، وَ هَلْ يَرْحَمُ الْمُتَحَيِّرَ إِلَّا

have mercy on the bewildered?

الدَّلِيلُ؟

My Master! O My Master! You are All-forgiving and I am the sinner. Will anyone except the All-forgiver have mercy on the sinner?

مَوْلَايَ يَا مَوْلَايَ، أَنْتَ الْغَفُورُ وَ أَنَا الْمُذْنِبُ، وَ هَلْ يَرْحَمُ الْمُذْنِبَ إِلَّا الْغَفُورُ؟

My Master! O My Master! You are the All-prevailing and I am subdued. Will anyone except the All-prevailing have mercy on the subdued?

مَوْلَايَ يَا مَوْلَايَ، أَنْتَ الْغَالِبُ وَ أَنَا الْمَغْلُوبُ، وَهَلْ يَرْحَمُ الْمَغْلُوبَ إِلَّا الْغَالِبُ؟

My Master! O My Master! You are the Lord and I am the servant. Will anyone except the Lord have mercy on the servant?

مَوْلَايَ يَا مَوْلَايَ، أَنْتَ الرَّبُّ وَ أَنَا الْمَرْبُوبُ، وَ هَلْ يَرْحَمُ الْمَرْبُوبَ إِلَّا الرَّبُّ؟

My Master! O My Master! You are the All-magnanimous Lord and I am Your submissive slave. Will anyone except the All-magnanimous Lord have mercy on His submissive slave?

مَوْلَايَ يَا مَوْلَايَ، أَنْتَ الْمُتَكَبِّرُ وَ أَنَا الْخَاشِعُ، وَ هَلْ يَرْحَمُ الْخَاشِعَ إِلَّا الْمُتَكَبِّرُ؟

My Master! O My Master! Have mercy on me out of Your mercifulness, be pleased with me out of Your generosity, munificence and grace, O Munificent and Kind One, O All-bountiful dispenser of favours, by Your mercy, O Most Merciful of the merciful!

مَوْلَايَ يَا مَوْلَايَ، ارْحَمْنِي بِرَحْمَتِكَ، وَ ارْضَ عَنِّي بِجُودِكَ وَ كَرَمِكَ وَ فَضْلِكَ، يَا ذَا الْجُودِ وَ الْإِحْسَانِ، وَ الطَّوْلِ وَ الْإِمْتِنَانِ، بِرَحْمَتِكَ يَا أَرْحَمَ الرَّاحِمِينَ.

Sayyid Ibn Ṭāwūs has mentioned an elaborate supplication, known as Duʿā al-Amān, to be recited after this *munājāt*, not cited here for reasons of space.[1] One may also recite here the sublime supplication that will be mentioned, God willing, in the observance pertaining to the Mosque of Zayd (p. 241).

1 *Biḥār*, xcvii, 420-425, b 6, h 70, from Ibn Ṭāwūs.

It should be noted that, as pointed out by us in *Hadīyat al-Zā'irīn*, there is a difference of opinion as to whether the niche where the Commander of the Faithful (ᶜa) was struck by the assassin's sword is the same as the well-known niche, or the one which is not in use. Caution would suggest that one perform the observances of the niche at both the places, or in one of the two locations on alternate visits.

The Observance at the Station of Imām al-Ṣādiq (ᶜa)

The next observance to be performed is at the station of Imam al-Ṣādiq (ᶜa) near the tomb of Muslim b. ᶜAqīl, may God be pleased with him. One is to offer there two *rakᶜahs*. After *salām* and *tasbīḥ* say,[1]

O Maker of all things that are made, O Restorer of all broken beings to wholeness, O You who are present at every gathering, O Witness to all secret discourses, O Knower of all hidden things, O present one who is never absent, O Prevailer who is never subdued, O Near One who is never far, O intimate friend of all who are lonely, O Living One who was living when there was no living being, O Giver of life to the lifeless and bringer of death to the living, O Sustainer of every soul despite what it earns, there is no god except You, bless Muḥammad and the Family of Muḥammad!	يَا صَانِعَ كُلِّ مَصْنُـوعٍ، وَيَا جَابِرَ كُلِّ كَسِيرٍ، وَيَا حَاضِرَ كُلِّ مَلَإٍ، وَيَا شَاهِدَ كُلِّ نَجْوَىٰ، وَيَا عَالِـمَ كُلِّ خَفِيَّةٍ، وَيَا شَـاهِدًا غَيْرَ غَائِبٍ، وَيَـا غَالِبًا غَيْرَ مَغْلُوبٍ، وَيَا قَرِيبًا غَـيْرَ بَعِيدٍ، وَيَا مُونِسَ كُلِّ وَحِيدٍ، وَيَا حَيًّا حِينَ لَا حَيَّ غَيْرُهُ، يَا مُحْيِيَ الْمَوْتَىٰ وَمُمِيتَ الْأَحْيَاءِ، اَلْقَائِمَ عَلَىٰ كُلِّ نَفْسٍ بِمَا كَسَبَتْ، لَا إِلٰهَ إِلَّا أَنْـتَ، صَلِّ عَلَىٰ مُحَمَّدٍ وَآلِ مُحَمَّدٍ.

As mentioned before, according to popular custom and the sequence mentioned in "*al-Mazar al-Qadīm*," next in order are the observances of the Dikkat al-Qaḍā and the Bayt al-Ṭa<u>sh</u>t, which we mentioned after the observance of the fourth pillar in accordance with *Miṣbāḥ al-Zā'ir* and the *Biḥār*.[2] Those who wish to follow the popular sequence should proceed to those spots to perform their observances, God willing.

1 *Biḥār*, xcvii, 425, b 6, h 68, from *al-Mazār al-Kabīr* and <u>Sh</u>ahīd Awwal.
2 *Biḥār*, xcvii, 409-414, b 6, h 67-68, citing Ibn Ṭāwūs.

THE ZIYARAH OF MUSLIM IBN ʿAQIL (R)

On finishing the observances of the Mosque of Kūfah one should proceed towards the tomb of Muslim ibn ᶜAqīl—may Allah be pleased with him—and standing near the grave say,[1]

All praise belongs to Allah, the Sovereign and the Manifest Reality, in front of whose greatness the rebellious tyrants cringe, whose Lordship is acknowledged by all denizens of the heavens and the earths, and whose Oneness is admitted universally by the creatures.

الْحَمْدُ لِلَّهِ الْمَلِكِ الْحَقِّ الْمُبِينِ،
اَلْمُتَصَاغِرِ لِعَظَمَتِهِ جَبَابِرَةُ الطَّاغِينَ،
اَلْمُعْتَرِفِ بِرُبُوبِيَّتِهِ جَمِيعُ أَهْلِ السَّمَاوَاتِ
وَ الْأَرَضِينَ، اَلْمُقِرِّ بِتَوْحِيدِهِ سَائِرُ الْخَلْقِ
أَجْمَعِينَ،

May Allah bless the chief of the creatures and his honoured Family with a blessing that may give them delight, in defiance of their enemies from mankind and Jinn. May the greetings of 'Peace' from Allah, the All-exalted and the Supreme, and those of His archangels, His apostles and prophets, His chosen Imams, His righteous servants and all the martyrs and saints, such as are the choicest and best of blessings, be every morning and evening upon you O Muslim ibn ᶜAqīl ibn Abī Ṭālib, and may Allah's mercy and bounties be upon you!

وَ صَلَّى اللهُ عَلٰى سَيِّدِ الْأَنَامِ وَ أَهْلِ بَيْتِهِ
الْكِرَامِ، صَلَاةً تَقَرُّ بِهَا أَعْيُنُهُمْ، وَ يَرْغَمُ
بِهَا أَنْفُ شَانِئِهِمْ مِنَ الْجِنِّ وَ الْإِنْسِ
أَجْمَعِينَ. سَلَامُ اللهِ الْعَلِيِّ الْعَظِيمِ وَ سَلَامُ
مَلَائِكَتِهِ الْمُقَرَّبِينَ وَ أَنْبِيَائِهِ الْمُرْسَلِينَ وَ
أَئِمَّتِهِ الْمُنْتَجَبِينَ وَ عِبَادِهِ الصَّالِحِينَ وَ جَمِيعِ
الشُّهَدَاءِ وَ الصِّدِّيقِينَ، وَ الزَّاكِيَاتُ الطَّيِّبَاتُ
فِيمَا تَغْتَدِي وَ تَرُوحُ عَلَيْكَ يَا مُسْلِمَ بْنَ
عَقِيلِ بْنِ أَبِي طَالِبٍ، وَ رَحْمَةُ اللهِ وَ بَرَكَاتُهُ.

I testify that you maintained the prayer, paid *zakāt*, bade what is right and forbade what is wrong and waged *jihād* for the sake of Allah as is worthy

أَشْهَدُ أَنَّكَ أَقَمْتَ الصَّلَاةَ، وَ آتَيْتَ الزَّكَاةَ،
وَ أَمَرْتَ بِالْمَعْرُوفِ، وَ نَهَيْتَ عَنِ الْمُنْكَرِ،
وَ جَاهَدْتَ فِي اللهِ حَقَّ جِهَادِهِ، وَ قُتِلْتَ

[1] *Biḥār*, xcvii, 426, b 6, h 70, from *al-Mazār al-Kabīr* and Shahīd Awwal.

of Him, and that you were slain following the path of the warriors of His way, until you met Allah while He was pleased with you!

عَلَىٰ مِنْهَاجِ الْمُجَاهِدِينَ فِى سَبِيلِهِ، حَتَّى لَقِيتَ اللّٰهَ عَزَّ وَ جَلَّ وَ هُوَ عَنْكَ رَاضٍ،

I testify that you fulfilled Allah's covenant and sacrificed yourself for the cause of supporting the testament of Allah and son of His testament until your demise.

وَ أَشْهَدُ أَنَّكَ وَفَيْتَ بِعَهْدِ اللّٰهِ، وَ بَذَلْتَ نَفْسَكَ فِى نُصْرَةِ حُجَّةِ اللّٰهِ وَ ابْنِ حُجَّتِهِ حَتَّى أَتَاكَ الْيَقِينُ،

I bear testimony to your compliance, loyalty and devotion to the son of the Apostle, the chosen grandson of the Prophet, the prescient guide, the legatee of the Messenger, and victim of wrongdoing and oppression. Hence, may Allah reward you on behalf of His Apostle, and on behalf of the Commander of the Faithful, al-Ḥasan and al-Ḥusayn, with the best of rewards for your patience, resignation and support. *How excellent is the reward of the [ultimate] abode!*[13:24]

أَشْهَدُ لَكَ بِالتَّسْلِيمِ وَ الْوَفَاءِ وَ النَّصِيحَةِ لِخَلَفِ النَّبِىِّ الْمُرْسَلِ، وَ السِّبْطِ الْمُنْتَجَبِ، وَ الدَّلِيلِ الْعَالِمِ، وَ الْوَصِىِّ الْمُبَلِّغِ، وَ الْمَظْلُومِ الْمُهْتَضَمِ؛ فَجَزَاكَ اللّٰهُ عَنْ رَسُولِهِ وَ عَنْ أَمِيرِ الْمُؤْمِنِينَ وَ عَنِ الْحَسَنِ وَ الْحُسَيْنِ أَفْضَلَ الْجَزَاءِ بِمَا صَبَرْتَ وَ احْتَسَبْتَ وَ أَعَنْتَ، فَنِعْمَ عُقْبَى الدَّارِ.

May the curse of Allah be on those who slew you, disregarded your right and made light of your sanctity. May Allah's curse be on those who swore allegiance to you and then betrayed you and forsook you, and handed you over to the enemy—those who rallied troops against you and did not assist you!

لَعَنَ اللّٰهُ مَنْ قَتَلَكَ، وَ لَعَنَ اللّٰهُ مَنْ أَمَرَ بِقَتْلِكَ، وَ لَعَنَ اللّٰهُ مَنْ ظَلَمَكَ، وَ لَعَنَ اللّٰهُ مَنِ افْتَرَىٰ عَلَيْكَ، وَ لَعَنَ اللّٰهُ مَنْ جَهِلَ حَقَّكَ وَ اسْتَخَفَّ بِحُرْمَتِكَ، وَ لَعَنَ اللّٰهُ مَنْ بَايَعَكَ وَ غَشَّكَ وَ خَذَلَكَ وَ أَسْلَمَكَ، وَ مَنْ أَلَّبَ عَلَيْكَ وَ لَمْ يُعِنْكَ.

All praise belongs to Allah who

اَلْحَمْدُ لِلّٰهِ الَّذِى جَعَلَ النَّارَ مَثْوَاهُمْ، وَ

has made *the Fire their ultimate abode—an evil goal for the incoming!*[11:98]

بِئْسَ الْوِرْدُ الْمَوْرُودُ.

I testify that you were slain wrongfully and that Allah has fulfilled the promise that He gave you!

أَشْهَدُ أَنَّكَ قُتِلْتَ مَظْلُومًا، وَ أَنَّ اللهَ مُنْجِزٌ لَكُمْ مَا وَعَدَكُمْ.

I come to you as a pilgrim, aware of your right, complying with your bidding, following your precedent, having prepared myself for your support, until God issues His judgement and He is the best of judges. I am certainly with you, not with your enemies.

جِئْتُكَ زَائِرًا عَارِفًا بِحَقِّكُمْ، مُسَلِّمًا لَكُمْ، تَابِعًا لِسُنَّتِكُمْ، وَ نُصْرَتِي لَكُمْ مُعَدَّةٌ، حَتَّىٰ يَحْكُمَ اللهُ وَ هُوَ خَيْرُ الْحَاكِمِينَ، فَمَعَكُمْ مَعَكُمْ لَا مَعَ عَدُوِّكُمْ،

May Allah's blessings be upon you, your spirits, your bodies, your outward and hidden being, and peace be to you and may Allah's mercy and His bounties be upon you! May Allah curse the lot who slew you with their hands and their tongues!

صَلَوَاتُ اللهِ عَلَيْكُمْ وَ عَلَىٰ أَرْوَاحِكُمْ وَ أَجْسَادِكُمْ وَ شَاهِدِكُمْ وَ غَائِبِكُمْ، وَ السَّلَامُ عَلَيْكُمْ وَ رَحْمَةُ اللهِ وَ بَرَكَاتُهُ، قَتَلَ اللهُ أُمَّةً قَتَلَتْكُمْ بِالْأَيْدِي وَ الْأَلْسُنِ.

In *al-Mazār al-Kabīr* the above text is given as a request for admittance (*i<u>dh</u>n al-du<u>kh</u>ūl*),[1] for after reciting it one is asked to enter the shrine and to cling to the grave. In accordance with the former report,[2] while pointing towards the *ḍarīḥ* one should say,

Peace be to you, O Allah's righteous servant, who were obedient to Allah and his Apostle and the Commander of the Faithful, al-Ḥasan and al-Ḥusayn, may peace be to them.

اَلسَّلَامُ عَلَيْكَ أَيُّهَا الْعَبْدُ الصَّالِحُ الْمُطِيعُ لِلّٰهِ وَ لِرَسُولِهِ وَ لِأَمِيرِ الْمُؤْمِنِينَ وَ الْحَسَنِ وَ الْحُسَيْنِ عَلَيْهِمُ السَّلَامُ.

All praise belongs to Allah, and may peace be to His chosen servants, Muḥammad and his Family. Peace be to you, and may Allah's

اَلْحَمْدُ لِلّٰهِ وَ سَلَامٌ عَلَىٰ عِبَادِهِ الَّذِينَ اصْطَفَىٰ مُحَمَّدٍ وَ آلِهِ، وَ السَّلَامُ عَلَيْكُمْ

1 *Al-Mazār al-Kabīr*, 177.

2 *Biḥār*, xcvii, 427.

mercy, bounties and forgiveness be upon you and your spirit and body!

وَ رَحْمَةُ اللهِ وَ بَرَكَاتُهُ وَ مَغْفِرَتُهُ وَ عَلَىٰ
رُوحِكَ وَ بَدَنِكَ،

I testify that you departed from the world upholding what was upheld by the warriors of Badr and the warriors of the path of Allah who did their utmost in waging struggle against His enemies and in giving support to His *awliyā'*! May Allah reward you with the best, the most abundant and plentiful of rewards that He has granted to any of those who fulfilled their pledges to Him, responded to His summons and obeyed those who have been invested with His authority!

أَشْهَدُ أَنَّكَ مَضَيْتَ عَلَىٰ مَا مَضَىٰ عَلَيْهِ
الْبَدْرِيُّونَ الْمُجَاهِدُونَ فِي سَبِيلِ اللهِ،
الْمُبَالِغُونَ فِي جِهَادِ أَعْدَائِهِ وَ نُصْرَةِ
أَوْلِيَائِهِ، فَجَزَاكَ اللهُ أَفْضَلَ الْجَزَاءِ وَ
أَكْثَرَ الْجَزَاءِ وَ أَوْفَرَ جَزَاءِ أَحَدٍ مِمَّنْ
وَفَىٰ بِبَيْعَتِهِ، وَ اسْتَجَابَ لَهُ دَعْوَتَهُ، وَ
أَطَاعَ وُلَاةَ أَمْرِهِ.

I testify that you did your utmost in sincere devotion, and offered your utmost effort. So Allah raised you with the martyrs; He placed your spirit among the spirits of the felicitous, granted you the best of stations and abodes and exalted your name among the inhabitants of the *ʿIllīyūn* and resurrected you "*with the prophets, the truthful, the martyrs and the righteous—and excellent companions are they!*"(4:69)

أَشْهَدُ أَنَّكَ قَدْ بَالَغْتَ فِي النَّصِيحَةِ، وَ
أَعْطَيْتَ غَايَةَ الْمَجْهُودِ حَتَّىٰ بَعَثَكَ اللهُ
فِي الشُّهَدَاءِ، وَ جَعَلَ رُوحَكَ مَعَ أَرْوَاحِ
السُّعَدَاءِ، وَ أَعْطَاكَ مِنْ جِنَانِهِ أَفْسَحَهَا
مَنْزِلًا، وَ أَفْضَلَهَا غُرَفًا، وَ رَفَعَ ذِكْرَكَ
فِي الْعِلِّيِّينَ، وَ حَشَرَكَ مَعَ النَّبِيِّينَ وَ
الصِّدِّيقِينَ وَ الشُّهَدَاءِ وَ الصَّالِحِينَ، وَ
حَسُنَ أُولَٰئِكَ رَفِيقًا.

I testify that you never flagged or flinched and that you departed in full possession of insight regarding your mission, following in the steps of the righteous and

أَشْهَدُ أَنَّكَ لَمْ تَهِنْ وَ لَمْ تَنْكُلْ، وَ أَنَّكَ
قَدْ مَضَيْتَ عَلَىٰ بَصِيرَةٍ مِنْ أَمْرِكَ،
مُقْتَدِيًا بِالصَّالِحِينَ، وَ مُتَّبِعًا لِلنَّبِيِّينَ،

فَجَمَعَ اللّٰهُ بَيْنَنَا وَ بَيْنَكَ وَ بَيْنَ رَسُولِهِ وَ أَوْلِيَائِهِ فِي مَنَازِلِ الْمُخْبِتِينَ، فَإِنَّهُ أَرْحَمُ الرَّاحِمِينَ.

the prophets. May Allah gather us with you, along with His Apostle and *awliyā*, in the abodes of the humble. Indeed He is the most merciful of the merciful!

Then offer a two-*rakᶜah* prayer at the head of the tomb and make a gift of it to the spirit of that illustrious martyr. Then say,

اَللّٰهُمَّ صَلِّ عَلَىٰ مُحَمَّدٍ وَآلِ مُحَمَّدٍ، وَ لَا تَدَعْ لِي ذَنْباً إِلَّا غَفَرْتَهُ، وَ لَا هَمّاً إِلَّا فَرَّجْتَهُ، وَ لَا مَرَضاً إِلَّا شَفَيْتَهُ، وَ لَا عَيْباً إِلَّا سَتَرْتَهُ، وَ لَا شَمْلاً إِلَّا جَمَعْتَهُ، وَ لَا غَائِباً إِلَّا حَفِظْتَهُ وَ أَدْنَيْتَهُ، وَ لَا عُرْياً إِلَّا كَسَوْتَهُ، وَ لَا رِزْقاً إِلَّا بَسَطْتَهُ، وَ لَا خَوْفاً إِلَّا آمَنْتَهُ، وَ لَا حَاجَةً مِنْ حَوَائِجِ الدُّنْيَا وَ الْآخِرَةِ لَكَ فِيهَا رِضًى وَ لِيَ فِيهَا صَلَاحٌ إِلَّا قَضَيْتَهَا، يَا أَرْحَمَ الرَّاحِمِينَ.

O Allah, bless Muḥammad and the Family of Muḥammad, and let not any of my sins remain unforgiven, nor any worries undispelled, nor any ailments uncured, nor any faults unconcealed, nor any disunion and separation unreplaced by union, nor anything that I have left behind unguarded and unrestored, nor any bareness uncovered, nor any provision unexpanded, nor any fear unrelieved, nor any of my needs pertaining to the world and the Hereafter, such as You approve of and are to my benefit, unfulfilled, O Most Merciful of the merciful!

This is the same supplication as the one which is made in the shrine of Ḥaḍrat ᶜAbbās (*ᶜa*) and will be mentioned later on (p. 295). One may as well take leave of Ḥaḍrat Muslim with the farewell text cited in the section on the *ziyārah* of Ḥaḍrat ᶜAbbās (*ᶜa*) (p. 297).

THE ZIYARAH OF HANI IBN ‘URWAH (R)

Standing at his graveside, first salute the Apostle of Allah (ṣ) and then say,[1]

سَلَامُ اللّٰهِ الْعَظِيمِ وَ صَلَوَاتُهُ عَلَيْكَ يَا هَانِيَ بْنَ عُرْوَةَ، اَلسَّلَامُ عَلَيْكَ أَيُّهَا

Greeting of ‘Peace” from Allah, the Supreme, be to you, and may His blessings be upon you, O Hānī

1 *Biḥār*, xcvii, 429, b 6, h 70, from *al-Mazār al-Kabīr* and Shahīd Awwal.

الْعَبْدُ الصَّالِحُ النَّاصِحُ لِلَّهِ وَ لِرَسُولِهِ وَ لِأَمِيرِ الْمُؤْمِنِينَ وَ الْحَسَنِ وَ الْحُسَيْنِ عَلَيْهِمُ السَّلَامُ.

ibn ʿUrwah! Peace be to you, O righteous servant of Allah, who were obedient to Allah and His Apostle and the Commander of the Faithful, al-Ḥasan and al-Ḥusayn, may peace be to them.

أَشْهَدُ أَنَّكَ قُتِلْتَ مَظْلُومًا، فَلَعَنَ اللَّهُ مَنْ قَتَلَكَ وَ اسْتَحَلَّ دَمَكَ، وَ حَشَا قُبُورَهُمْ نَارًا،

I testify that you were slain wrongfully and unjustly. May Allah's curse be on those who slew you, deeming it lawful to shed your blood, and may He fill their graves with fire.

أَشْهَدُ أَنَّكَ لَقِيتَ اللَّهَ وَ هُوَ رَاضٍ عَنْكَ بِمَا فَعَلْتَ وَ نَصَحْتَ،

I testify that you met Allah while He was pleased with you and your conduct and commitment (to Islam).

وَ أَشْهَدُ أَنَّكَ قَدْ بَلَغْتَ دَرَجَةَ الشُّهَدَاءِ، وَ جُعِلَ رُوحُكَ مَعَ أَرْوَاحِ السُّعَدَاءِ، بِمَا نَصَحْتَ لِلَّهِ وَ لِرَسُولِهِ مُجْتَهِدًا، وَ بَذَلْتَ نَفْسَكَ فِي ذَاتِ اللَّهِ وَ مَرْضَاتِهِ، فَرَحِمَكَ اللَّهُ وَ رَضِيَ عَنْكَ وَ حَشَرَكَ مَعَ مُحَمَّدٍ وَ آلِهِ الطَّاهِرِينَ، وَ جَمَعَنَا وَ إِيَّاكُمْ مَعَهُمْ فِي دَارِ النَّعِيمِ، وَ سَلَامٌ عَلَيْكَ وَ رَحْمَةُ اللَّهِ وَ بَرَكَاتُهُ.

I testify that you attained to the rank of the martyrs, and that your spirit has been joined to those of the felicitous by virtue of your commitment to Allah and His Apostle, and for your effort for their sake, and for your sacrifices for the sake of Allah and His pleasure. May Allah have mercy on you, and may He be pleased with you, and gather you with Muḥammad and his immaculate Family. May he gather you and us along with them in the abode of His blessing. Peace be to you and may Allah's mercy and His bounties be upon you!

Then offer a two-*rakʿah* prayer as a gift to the spirit of Hānī. Then make any petition that you may like. Then bid him farewell with words similar to those with which you have bidden farewell to Muslim.

Chapter Six

Some Other Mosques of Kūfah

The Virtues of the Sahlah Mosque

After the Mosque of Kūfah there is no mosque in the region that equals the Sahlah Mosque in its merit. It is said to have been the home of the prophets Idrīs (*ʿa*) and Abraham (*ʿa*) and a place frequented by Khiḍr (*ʿa*).[1]

Imam Jaʿfar al-Ṣādiq (*ʿa*) is reported to have said to Abū Baṣīr, "O Abū Muḥammad, it is as if I already see the Master of the Era (i.e. the Twelfth Imam) taking up residence with his family in the Sahlah Mosque. God Almighty has not sent any apostle without his having prayed in that mosque. Someone who stays in that mosque is like one who has tarried in the tent of the Apostle of Allah (*ṣ*). There is no faithful person, man or woman, whose heart does not long to visit that mosque. There is a rock in that mosque bearing portraits of the prophets. No one makes prayer in that mosque and supplicates with a genuine motive without going back with his petition answered. No one who prays for safety in that mosque is denied safety from what he fears." Describing further virtues of that mosque, the Imam said, "It is one of the holy spots where God loves to be called by His creatures. Every day and night angels arrive to visit that mosque and perform worship in it. Had I been living near where you live, I would have offered all my prayers in that mosque." He added, "O Abū Muḥammad, what I have not described of that mosque's virtues are more than what I have." Abū Baṣīr asked him if the Twelfth Imam will stay in it permanently. "Yes," he replied.[2]

The Observances of the Sahlah Mosque

A two-*rakʿah* prayer is to be offered here between *maghrib* and *ʿishā*. Imam Jaʿfar al-Ṣādiq (*ʿa*) is reported[3] to have said that God Almighty shall relieve the distress of those who make this prayer here and

1 *Biḥār*, xcvii, 436, b 17, h 1-4.

2 *Biḥār*, xcvii, 436, b 17, h 7.

3 Rāwandī's *Qiṣaṣ*, 79, b 2, h 62, whence *Biḥār*, xlvi, 182, b 11, h 45, xcvii, 434, b 7, h 2 & *Mustadrak*, iii, 413, b 39, h 3900/2.

supplicate Him. Ibn Ṭāwūs says[1] that the best time for visiting the Sahlah Mosque is on Wednesday eve (i.e. Tuesday night) between the times of *maghrib* and *ʿishā*.

At the Entrance of the Sahlah Mosque

It is mentioned in some works[2] on *ziyārah* that when entering the mosque, one should first stand near the gate and say,

بِسْمِ اللهِ وَ بِاللهِ وَ مِنَ اللهِ وَ إِلَى اللهِ، وَ مَا شَاءَ اللهُ، وَ خَيْرُ الْأَسْمَاءِ لِلهِ، تَوَكَّلْتُ عَلَى اللهِ وَ لَا حَوْلَ وَ لَا قُوَّةَ إِلَّا بِاللهِ الْعَلِيِّ الْعَظِيمِ.

In the Name of Allah, by Allah, from Allah, toward Allah, as Allah wishes, and the best of names belongs to Allah. I put my trust in Allah and there is no power or force except what derives from Allah, the All-exalted the All-supreme.

اَللّٰهُمَّ اجْعَلْنِي مِنْ عُمَّارِ مَسَاجِدِكَ وَ بُيُوتِكَ. اَللّٰهُمَّ إِنِّي أَتَوَجَّهُ إِلَيْكَ بِمُحَمَّدٍ وَ آلِ مُحَمَّدٍ، وَ أُقَدِّمُهُمْ بَيْنَ يَدَيْ حَوَائِجِي، فَاجْعَلْنِي اللّٰهُمَّ بِهِمْ عِنْدَكَ وَجِيهًا فِي الدُّنْيَا وَ الْآخِرَةِ وَ مِنَ الْمُقَرَّبِينَ.

O Allah, make me one of those who keep up Your mosques and houses of worship. O Allah, I turn to You through the mediation of Muḥammad and the Family of Muḥammad, setting them ahead of my petitions. O Allah, make me eminent with You through them in the world and the Hereafter and of those who are near to You.

اَللّٰهُمَّ اجْعَلْ صَلَاتِي بِهِمْ مَقْبُولَةً، وَ ذَنْبِي بِهِمْ مَغْفُورًا، وَ رِزْقِي بِهِمْ مَبْسُوطاً، وَ دُعَائِي بِهِمْ مُسْتَجَابًا، وَ حَوَائِجِي بِهِمْ مَقْضِيَّةً، وَ انْظُرْ إِلَيَّ بِوَجْهِكَ الْكَرِيمِ نَظْرَةً رَحِيمَةً أَسْتَوْجِبُ بِهَا الْكَرَامَةَ عِنْدَكَ، ثُمَّ لَا تَصْرِفْهُ

O Allah, for their sake accept my prayer, forgive my sins, expand my provision, answer my supplications, satisfy my needs and look at me mercifully with Your munificent Face, a look that will make me worthy of honour with You and which You will never turn away from

1 *Biḥār*, xcvii, 445, citing Ibn Ṭāwūs.

2 Untraced in the usual works. Abridged from a longer version meant to be recited while entering a mosque in Ṭūsī's *Miṣbāḥ*, 131-132, whence *Biḥār*, lxxxiv, 234, b 12, h 46 & *Miftāḥ*, 766-8.

عَنِّي أَبَدًا، بِرَحْمَتِكَ يَا أَرْحَمَ الرَّاحِمِينَ.

me ever, with Your mercy, O Most Merciful of the merciful!

يَا مُقَلِّبَ الْقُلُوبِ وَ الْأَبْصَارِ، ثَبِّتْ قَلْبِي عَلَىٰ دِينِكَ وَ دِينِ نَبِيِّكَ وَ وَلِيِّكَ، وَ لَا تُزِغْ قَلْبِي بَعْدَ إِذْ هَدَيْتَنِي، وَ هَبْ لِي مِنْ لَدُنْكَ رَحْمَةً، إِنَّكَ أَنْتَ الْوَهَّابُ.

O Changer of the hearts and visions, keep me steady on Your religion, and do not let my heart swerve after that You have guided me, and grant me Your mercy; indeed You are the All-bestower.

اَللّٰهُمَّ إِلَيْكَ تَوَجَّهْتُ، وَ مَرْضَاتَكَ طَلَبْتُ، وَ ثَوَابَكَ ابْتَغَيْتُ، وَ بِكَ آمَنْتُ، وَ عَلَيْكَ تَوَكَّلْتُ. اَللّٰهُمَّ فَأَقْبِلْ بِوَجْهِكَ إِلَيَّ، وَ أَقْبِلْ بِوَجْهِي إِلَيْكَ.

O Allah, I have turned to you, seeking Your pleasure and Your reward, placing faith in You and putting my trust in You! O Allah, turn to me by turning Your Face toward me and my face toward You!

Then one should recite the Throne Verse (2:255), Sūrat al-Falaq and Sūrat al-Nās, and after that say each of the following seven times: *"Subḥānallāh, "Walḥamdu lillāh," "Wa lâ ilāha illallāh," "wallāhu akbar."* Then say,[1]

اَللّٰهُمَّ لَكَ الْحَمْدُ عَلَىٰ مَا هَدَيْتَنِي، وَ لَكَ الْحَمْدُ عَلَىٰ مَا فَضَّلْتَنِي، وَ لَكَ الْحَمْدُ عَلَىٰ مَا شَرَّفْتَنِي، وَ لَكَ الْحَمْدُ عَلَىٰ كُلِّ بَلَاءٍ حَسَنٍ ابْتَلَيْتَنِي. اَللّٰهُمَّ تَقَبَّلْ صَلَاتِي وَ دُعَائِي، وَ طَهِّرْ قَلْبِي، وَ اشْرَحْ لِي صَدْرِي، وَ تُبْ عَلَيَّ، إِنَّكَ أَنْتَ التَّوَّابُ الرَّحِيمُ.

O Allah, to You belongs all praise for guiding me! To You belongs all praise for the grace You have granted me! To You belongs all praise for the honour You have conferred on me! To You belongs all praise for every fair trial with which You have tested me! O Allah, accept my prayers and my supplications, purge my heart, open up my breast, and accept my penitence! Indeed you are the All-clement, the All-merciful!

After entering, one should offer the *maghrib* prayer and its *nāfilah.*

[1] *Makārim*, 297, whence *Biḥār*, lxxxi, 24, b 9, h 16 & *Mustadrak*, iii, 391, b 30, h 3861/6.

Then offer the prayer of *taḥiyyah* of the mosque, seeking nearness to Allah. After the prayer of *taḥiyyah*, raise the hands towards the sky and say,[1]

أَنْتَ اللّٰهُ لَا إِلٰهَ إِلَّا أَنْتَ مُبْدِئُ الْخَلْقِ
وَ مُعِيدُهُمْ، وَ أَنْتَ اللّٰهُ لَا إِلٰهَ إِلَّا أَنْتَ
خَالِقُ الْخَلْقِ وَ رَازِقُهُمْ،

You are Allah, there being no god besides You, the Originator of the creatures and their Restorer. You are Allah, there being no god besides You, the Creator of the creatures and their Provider.

وَ أَنْتَ اللّٰهُ لَا إِلٰهَ إِلَّا أَنْتَ الْقَابِضُ
الْبَاسِطُ، وَ أَنْتَ اللّٰهُ لَا إِلٰهَ إِلَّا أَنْتَ،
مُدَبِّرُ الْأُمُورِ، وَ بَاعِثُ مَنْ فِي الْقُبُورِ،
أَنْتَ وَارِثُ الْأَرْضِ وَ مَنْ عَلَيْهَا.

You are Allah, there being no god besides You, the tightener and expander of provision. You are Allah, there being no god besides You, the director of all affairs, the Resurrector of those who are in the graves, the Inheritor of the earth and those who live upon it!

أَسْأَلُكَ بِاسْمِكَ الْمَخْزُونِ الْمَكْنُونِ
الْحَيِّ الْقَيُّومِ، وَ أَنْتَ اللّٰهُ لَا إِلٰهَ إِلَّا أَنْتَ
عَالِمُ السِّرِّ وَ أَخْفَىٰ،

I beseech You by Your hidden and treasured Name, the Living One and the All-sustainer! You are Allah, there being no god besides You, the Knower of all that is secret and that which is still more hidden!

أَسْأَلُكَ بِاسْمِكَ الَّذِي إِذَا دُعِيتَ بِهِ
أَجَبْتَ، وَ إِذَا سُئِلْتَ بِهِ أَعْطَيْتَ،

I beseech You by Your Name, when called by which You answer, and when invoked by it You grant!

وَ أَسْأَلُكَ بِحَقِّكَ عَلَىٰ مُحَمَّدٍ وَ أَهْلِ بَيْتِهِ،
وَ بِحَقِّهِمُ الَّذِي أَوْجَبْتَهُ عَلَىٰ نَفْسِكَ، أَنْ
تُصَلِّيَ عَلَىٰ مُحَمَّدٍ وَ آلِ مُحَمَّدٍ، وَ أَنْ تَقْضِيَ
لِي حَاجَتِي، اَلسَّاعَةَ، اَلسَّاعَةَ، يَا سَامِعَ
الدُّعَاءِ، يَا سَيِّدَاهْ يَا مَوْلَاهْ يَا غِيَاثَاهْ،

I beseech You by Your right over Muḥammad and his Family, and by their right which You have made incumbent on Yourself, to bless Muḥammad and the Family of Muḥammad, and to grant my need this very hour, O hearer of supplications! O Master! O my Guardian and Rescuer!

[1] *Al-Mazār al-Kabīr*, 138, b 5. *Biḥār*, xcvii, 442, b 7, h 21, from Shahīd Awwal's *Mazār*, 255.

I beseech You by every Name wherewith You have named Yourself or held secret in Your knowledge of the Unseen, to bless Muḥammad and the Family of Muḥammad and to grant me immediate relief, this very hour, O Changer of hearts and visions! O Hearer of supplications!

أَسْأَلُكَ بِكُلِّ اسْمٍ سَمَّيْتَ بِهِ نَفْسَكَ،
أَوِ اسْتَأْثَرْتَ بِهِ فِي عِلْمِ الْغَيْبِ عِنْدَكَ،
أَنْ تُصَلِّيَ عَلَىٰ مُحَمَّدٍ وَآلِ مُحَمَّدٍ، وَأَنْ
تُعَجِّلَ فَرَجَنَا السَّاعَةَ، يَا مُقَلِّبَ الْقُلُوبِ
وَالْأَبْصَارِ، يَا سَمِيعَ الدُّعَاءِ!

Then make prostration and humbly implore God for whatever request you may have.

At the Station of Abraham (ʿ*a*)

Then proceed towards the north-western corner of the mosque, the location of the house of the Prophet Abraham (ʿ*a*) from where he is said to have gone forth to fight the Amalekites. Offer two *rakʿahs* there. After the prayer and *tasbīḥ* say,[1]

O Allah, for the sake of the right of this sacred shrine and the rights of those who have worshipped You in it, as You know my need, bless Muḥammad and the Family of Muḥammad and fulfil it! As You know my sins, bless Muḥammad and the Family of Muḥammad and forgive them. O Allah, keep me alive so long as life is good for me, and take me away when death is better for me and in a state of devotedness to Your *awliyā* and hostility toward Your enemies, and treat me as is worthy of You, O Most Merciful of the merciful!

اَللّٰهُمَّ بِحَقِّ هٰذِهِ الْبُقْعَةِ الشَّرِيفَةِ، وَ بِحَقِّ
مَنْ تَعَبَّدَ لَكَ فِيهَا، قَدْ عَلِمْتَ حَوَائِجِي،
فَصَلِّ عَلَىٰ مُحَمَّدٍ وَ آلِ مُحَمَّدٍ وَ اقْضِهَا،
وَ قَدْ أَحْصَيْتَ ذُنُوبِي، فَصَلِّ عَلَىٰ مُحَمَّدٍ
وَ آلِ مُحَمَّدٍ وَ اغْفِرْهَا. اَللّٰهُمَّ أَحْيِنِي مَا
كَانَتِ الْحَيَاةُ خَيْرًا لِي، وَ أَمِتْنِي إِذَا كَانَتِ
الْوَفَاةُ خَيْرًا لِي، عَلَىٰ مُوَالَاةِ أَوْلِيَائِكَ وَ
مُعَادَاةِ أَعْدَائِكَ، وَ افْعَلْ بِي مَا أَنْتَ
أَهْلُهُ، يَا أَرْحَمَ الرَّاحِمِينَ.

1 *Al-Mazār al-Kabīr*, 140, b 6. *Biḥār*, xcvii, 443, b 7, h 22, from Shahīd Awwal's *Mazār*, 259.

At the Station of Idrīs (ʿa)

Then proceed towards another corner of the mosque towards the south-west and offer two *rakʿahs*. After the prayer, with raised hands say,[1]

O Allah! I have offered this prayer seeking Your pleasure, desiring Your gift, expecting Your hospitality and awards! So bless Muḥammad and the Family of Muḥammad and accept it from me with a most gracious acceptance, and enable me with Your mercy to attain what I aspire for, and treat me as is worthy of You, O Most Merciful of the merciful.	اَللّٰهُـــمَّ إِنِّي صَلَّيْتُ هٰـــذِهِ الصَّلَاةَ ابْتِغَاءَ مَرْضَاتِـــكَ، وَ طَلَبَ نَائِلِـــكَ، وَ رَجَاءَ رِفْدِكَ وَ جَوَائِزِكَ، فَصَلِّ عَلٰى مُحَمَّدٍ وَ آلِ مُحَمَّدٍ، وَ تَقَبَّلْهَا مِنِّي بِأَحْسَـــنِ قَبُولٍ، وَ بَلِّغْنِي بِرَحْمَتِـــكَ الْمَأْمُولَ، وَ افْعَلْ بِي مَا أَنْتَ أَهْلُهُ، يَا أَرْحَمَ الرَّاحِمِينَ.

Then make prostration and lay each side of the face on the ground.

At the Station of Khiḍr (ʿa)

Then proceed towards the spot on the eastern side of the mosque and offer two *rakʿahs*. After the prayer, raising your hands, say,[2]

O Allah, if my sins and offences have impaired my visage with You, preventing my voice from rising up to You and my prayers from being heard by You, I beseech You—by You, O Allah, who have no peer—taking recourse in the mediation of Muḥammad and his Family! I beseech You to bless Muḥammad and the Family of Muḥammad, and to turn to me with Your munificent Face and	اَللّٰهُـــمَّ إِنْ كَانَتِ الذُّنُـــوبُ وَ الْخَطَايَا قَدْ أَخْلَقَتْ وَجْهِي عِنْدَكَ، فَلَمْ تَرْفَعْ لِي إِلَيْكَ صَوْتًا، وَ لَمْ تَسْتَجِبْ لِي دَعْوَةً، فَإِنِّي أَسْأَلُكَ بِكَ يَـــا اللّٰهُ، فَإِنَّهُ لَيْسَ مِثْلَـــكَ أَحَدٌ، وَ أَتَوَسَّـــلُ إِلَيْكَ بِمُحَمَّدٍ وَ آلِهِ، وَ أَسْأَلُكَ أَنْ تُصَلِّيَ عَلٰى مُحَمَّدٍ وَ آلِ مُحَمَّدٍ، وَ أَنْ تُقْبِلَ

1 *Al-Mazār al-Kabīr*, 141, b 6. *Biḥār*, xcvii, 444, b 7, h 22, from Shahīd Awwal's *Mazār*, 260.

2 *Al-Mazār al-Kabīr*, 141, b 6. *Biḥār*, xcvii, 444, b 7, h 22, from Shahīd Awwal's *Mazār*, 260.

to turn my face toward You. Do not disappoint me when I supplicate You, and do not deprive me when I pin my hopes on You, O Most Merciful of the merciful!

إِلَيَّ بِوَجْهِكَ الْكَرِيمِ، وَ تُقْبِلَ بِوَجْهِي إِلَيْكَ، وَ لَا تُخَيِّبَنِي حِينَ أَدْعُوكَ، وَ لَا تَحْرِمَنِي حِينَ أَرْجُوكَ، يَا أَرْحَمَ الرَّاحِمِينَ.

At the Station of the the Righteous and the Prophets

In accordance with some lesser-known works[1] on *ziyārah*, after this observance one is to offer two *rakʿahs* at another spot (known as "Maqām al-Ṣāliḥīn wal-Anbiyâ' wal-Mursalīn") on the eastern side of the mosque, and say, after the prayer,

O Allah, I beseech You by Your Name, O Allah, to bless Muḥammad and the Family of Muḥammad and to make the final part of my life its best part, the best part of my works my last deeds, and the best of my days the day that I shall meet You! Indeed You have power over all things!

اَللّٰهُمَّ إِنِّي أَسْأَلُكَ بِاسْمِكَ يَا اللّٰهُ أَنْ تُصَلِّيَ عَلَىٰ مُحَمَّدٍ وَ آلِ مُحَمَّدٍ، وَ أَنْ تَجْعَلَ خَيْرَ عُمْرِي آخِرَهُ، وَ خَيْرَ أَعْمَالِي خَوَاتِيمَهَا، وَ خَيْرَ أَيَّامِي يَوْمَ أَلْقَاكَ فِيهِ، إِنَّكَ عَلَىٰ كُلِّ شَيْءٍ قَدِيرٌ.

O Allah, accept my supplication and hear my confidential petitions, O Most High, O All-supreme, O All-able, O All-dominant, O Living One who do not die, bless Muḥammad and the Family of Muḥammad and forgive my sins which stand between You and me, and do not humiliate me on the Day of Resurrection in front of all and sundry! Guard me with Your eye which does not sleep and have mercy on me with Your power over me, O Most Merciful of the merciful! May Allah bless our master, Muḥammad, and his immaculate Family, O Lord of all the worlds!

اَللّٰهُمَّ تَقَبَّلْ دُعَائِي، وَ اسْمَعْ نَجْوَايَ، يَا عَلِيُّ يَا عَظِيمُ، يَا قَادِرُ يَا قَاهِرُ، يَا حَيًّا لَا يَمُوتُ، صَلِّ عَلَىٰ مُحَمَّدٍ وَ آلِ مُحَمَّدٍ، وَ اغْفِرْ لِيَ الذُّنُوبَ الَّتِي بَيْنِي وَ بَيْنَكَ، وَ لَا تَفْضَحْنِي عَلَىٰ رُءُوسِ الْأَشْهَادِ، وَ احْرُسْنِي بِعَيْنِكَ الَّتِي لَا تَنَامُ، وَ ارْحَمْنِي بِقُدْرَتِكَ عَلَيَّ، يَا أَرْحَمَ الرَّاحِمِينَ، وَ صَلَّى اللّٰهُ عَلَىٰ سَيِّدِنَا مُحَمَّدٍ وَ آلِهِ الطَّاهِرِينَ، يَا رَبَّ الْعَالَمِينَ.

1 *Miftāḥ al-Jinān*, 770-771. Not traced in the usual sources.

At the Station of Imam Zayn al-ᶜĀbidīn (ᶜ*a*)

Thereafter offer two *rakᶜahs* in the chamber built in the middle of the mosque, (nowadays known as the station of Imam Zayn al-ᶜAbidīn (ᶜ*a*)), and after the prayer say,[1]

O You who are nearer to me than my jugular vein! O You who accomplish whatever You desire! O You who intervene between a man and his heart! Bless Muḥammad and his Family and, with Your power and might, intervene between us and those who torment us! O You who suffice against all things and against whom nothing can suffice! Suffice us with regard to all our concerns pertaining to the world and the Hereafter, O Most Merciful of the merciful!

يَا مَنْ هُوَ أَقْرَبُ إِلَيَّ مِنْ حَبْلِ الْوَرِيدِ، يَا فَعَّالًا لِمَا يُرِيدُ، يَا مَنْ يَحُولُ بَيْنَ الْمَرْءِ وَ قَلْبِهِ، صَلِّ عَلَىٰ مُحَمَّدٍ وَ آلِهِ، وَ حُلْ بَيْنَنَا وَ بَيْنَ مَنْ يُؤْذِينَا بِحَوْلِكَ وَ قُوَّتِكَ، يَا كَافِيَ مِنْ كُلِّ شَيْءٍ وَ لَا يَكْفِي مِنْهُ شَيْءٌ، اِكْفِنَا الْمُهِمَّ مِنْ أَمْرِ الدُّنْيَا وَ الْآخِرَةِ، يَا أَرْحَمَ الرَّاحِمِينَ.

Then, prostrating, lay each side of your face on the ground.

According to *Mazār Qadīm*,[2] here is to be recited, after a two-*rakᶜah* prayer, the supplication "*Allā·humma innî as'aluka, yā man lā tarāhul ᶜuyūn...*," which was cited (p. 218) in the observances pertaining to the location of the Door of the Commander of the Faithful (ᶜ*a*) in the Mosque of Kūfah.

At the Station of Imam Mahdī (ᶜ*a*)

Near this location is a building known as the Station of the Imam Mahdī (ᶜ*a*), and it is appropriate to perform his *ziyārah* in this place, and some works on *ziyārah* recommend the text "*Salāmul·lāhil kāmilut tâmmush shāmil...*," to be recited here in the standing position. This text is the same as the *istighāthah* (appeal for help) cited earlier in the Seventh Chapter of Book I (p. 334) from *al-Kalim al-Ṭayyib*. Ac-

1 *Biḥār*, xcvii, 445-446, b 7, h 22, citing Ibn Ṭāwūs.

2 *Dharīᶜah*, xx, 322-323, has five works (3217-3221) by unknown authors styled "*Mazār Qadīm*," two of which (3219 & 3221) contain observances of the Mosques of Kūfah and Sahlah.

cording to Sayyid Ibn Ṭāwūs,[1] this is also one of the texts of *ziyārah* meant to be recited after a two-*rakʿah* prayer in the holy basement at Sāmarrā.

Prayer and Supplication at Zayd's Mosque

After the observances of the Sahlah Mosque, one should proceed towards Zayd's Mosque, which is in its vicinity, and offer there two *rakʿahs*. After the prayer, with raised hands, say,[2]

إِلٰهِي قَدْ مَدَّ إِلَيْكَ الْخَاطِئُ الْمُذْنِبُ يَدَيْهِ بِحُسْنِ ظَنِّهِ بِكَ، إِلٰهِي قَدْ جَلَسَ الْمُسِيءُ بَيْنَ يَدَيْكَ مُقِرًّا لَكَ بِسُوءِ عَمَلِهِ، وَ رَاجِيًا مِنْكَ الصَّفْحَ عَنْ زَلَلِهِ.

My God, this sinner and offender stretches towards You his hands on account of his favourable opinion of You, warranting hope. My God, Your guilty servant sits before You having confessed to his evil conduct and expecting You to pardon his failings.

إِلٰهِي قَدْ رَفَعَ إِلَيْكَ الظَّالِمُ كَفَّيْهِ رَاجِيًا لِمَا لَدَيْكَ، فَلَا تُخَيِّبْهُ بِرَحْمَتِكَ مِنْ فَضْلِكَ.

My God, this wrongdoer has raised his hands hoping to receive that which is with You. Mercifully, do not disappoint him by denying him Your grace!

إِلٰهِي قَدْ جَثَا الْعَائِدُ إِلَى الْمَعَاصِي بَيْنَ يَدَيْكَ، خَائِفًا مِنْ يَوْمٍ تَجْثُو فِيهِ الْخَلَائِقُ بَيْنَ يَدَيْكَ.

My God, this one who keeps on relapsing into sin kneels before You, fearing the day when all creatures will be fallen on their knees before You!

إِلٰهِي جَاءَكَ الْعَبْدُ الْخَاطِئُ فَزِعًا مُشْفِقًا، وَ رَفَعَ إِلَيْكَ طَرْفَهُ حَذِرًا رَاجِيًا، وَ فَاضَتْ عَبْرَتُهُ مُسْتَغْفِرًا نَادِمًا،

My God, Your errant servant comes to You, full of anxiety and panic, raising up to You his glance in fear and hope, his tears flowing, remorseful and imploring Your forgiveness!

وَ عِزَّتِكَ وَ جَلَالِكَ مَا أَرَدْتُ بِمَعْصِيَتِي مُخَالَفَتَكَ، وَمَا عَصَيْتُكَ إِذْ عَصَيْتُكَ وَأَنَا

By Your might and glory, I did not wish to oppose You by my sinning. I did not disobey You when

1 *Biḥār*, xcix, 97, citing Ibn Ṭāwūs.

2 *Al-Mazār al-Kabīr*, 142, b 6. *Biḥār*, xcvii, 444, b 7, h 22, from Shahīd Awwal's *Mazār*, 261.

I sinned being ignorant of You, neither was it in order to expose myself to Your retribution, nor on account of disregard for You while You watched me! But my carnal soul tempted me and my wretchedness prompted me to commit it! The curtain You had drawn over my vices deluded me! Now who will save me from Your punishment?

بِكَ جَاهِلٌ، وَ لَا لِعُقُوبَتِكَ مُتَعَرِّضٌ، وَ لَا لِنَظَرِكَ مُسْتَخِفٌّ، وَ لٰكِنْ سَوَّلَتْ لِي نَفْسِي، وَ أَعَانَتْنِي عَلىٰ ذٰلِكَ شِقْوَتِي، وَ غَرَّنِي سِتْرُكَ الْمُرْخىٰ عَلَيَّ، فَمِنَ الْآنَ مِنْ عَذَابِكَ مَنْ يَسْتَنْقِذُنِي؟

Whose good offices shall I seek if You withhold Your support from me? What a shame will it be when tomorrow I am brought to stand before You and when those not encumbered with sins are told to pass on and those laded with sins are told to fall (into hell)! Will I pass on with the light-footed or fall with the laden?

وَ بِحَبْلِ مَنْ أَعْتَصِمُ إِنْ قَطَعْتَ حَبْلَكَ عَنِّي؟ فَيَا سَوْأَتَاهْ غَدًا مِنَ الْوُقُوفِ بَيْنَ يَدَيْكَ إِذَا قِيلَ لِلْمُخِفِّينَ جُوزُوا، وَ لِلْمُثْقِلِينَ حُطُّوا، أَ فَمَعَ الْمُخِفِّينَ أَجُوزُ؟ أَمْ مَعَ الْمُثْقِلِينَ أَحُطُّ؟

Woe to me! With growing age my sins multiply! Woe to me! The longer I live the more numerous are my offences! How often shall I repent and how often shall I relapse? Has not time yet come when I should be ashamed before my Lord?!!

وَيْلِي كُلَّمَا كَبُرَ سِنِّي كَثُرَتْ ذُنُوبِي! وَيْلِي كُلَّمَا طَالَ عُمْرِي كَثُرَتْ مَعَاصِيَّ! فَكَمْ أَتُوبُ وَ كَمْ أَعُودُ؟ أَ مَا آنَ لِي أَنْ أَسْتَحْيِيَ مِنْ رَبِّي؟

O Allah, by the right of Muḥammad and the Family of Muḥammad, forgive me and have mercy on me, O Most Merciful of the merciful and the Best of forgivers!

اَللّٰهُمَّ فَبِحَقِّ مُحَمَّدٍ وَ آلِ مُحَمَّدٍ اغْفِرْ لِي وَ ارْحَمْنِي يَا أَرْحَمَ الرَّاحِمِينَ وَ خَيْرَ الْغَافِرِينَ.

Then, mournfully, put your face on the ground say,

Have mercy on someone who having been guilty of misconduct and sin, now surrenders and confesses his sins!

إِرْحَمْ مَنْ أَسَاءَ وَ اقْتَرَفَ، وَ اسْتَكَانَ وَ اعْتَرَفَ.

Then placing the right cheek on the ground, say,

If I have been a bad servant, You are indeed an excellent Lord!	إِنْ كُنْتُ بِئْسَ الْعَبْدُ، فَأَنْتَ نِعْمَ الرَّبُّ.

Then place the left cheek on the ground, and say,

Inasmuch as Your servant's sin is great, it will be gracious of You to pardon him! O Munificent One!	عَظُمَ الذَّنْبُ مِنْ عَبْدِكَ فَلْيَحْسُنِ الْعَفْوُ مِنْ عِنْدِكَ يَا كَرِيمُ.

Then returning to the position of prostration, say 100 times *"Al-ᶜafw, al-ᶜafw..."*

This is one of the celebrated mosques of Kūfah and is known after Zayd b. Ṣūḥān, one of the distinguished companions of the Commander of the Faithful (*ᶜa*). He was considered one of his eminent votaries (*abdāl*). He was martyred in the Battle of the Camel while fighting in the Imam's camp. The supplication cited above is ascribed to him, and he used to recite it in nightly prayers.[1]

The Mosque of Ṣaʿsaʿah

Near the Mosque of Zayd is another ascribed to his brother Ṣaᶜsaᶜah b. Ṣūḥān, who was also one of Imam ᶜAlī's companions. Ṣaᶜṣaᶜah was one of those who knew the Imam's station and was a leading figure among the faithful. A gifted and eloquent speaker, the Commander of the Faithful (*ᶜa*) highly regarded his talent in oratory as well as his austere piety and support for the cause of the truth.[2]

On the night of the Imam's martyrdom, when his body was carried from Kūfah to Najaf, Ṣaᶜṣaᶜah was also among those who attended the funeral. After the burial, standing at the graveside, Ṣaᶜṣaᶜah smeared his head with a handful of dust and spoke, saying, "You are dearer to me than my own parents, O Commander of the Faithful! Rejoice in the dignity that God has granted you! O Abul Ḥasan! Immaculate was your birth, formidable was your patience and great was your *jihād*. You attained what you had longed for, making a prof-

1 *Al-Mazār al-Kabīr*, 143, b 6. Shahīd Awwal's *Mazār*, 263, whence *Biḥār*, xcvii, 445.

2 *Rijāl al-Kashshī*, 67-69. *Rijāl al-Najāshī*, 203. *Muntaha al-Maqāl*, iv, 27. *Aᶜyān al-Shīᶜah*, i, 167, 349, 480, vii, 101, 103, 325, 387. *Muᶜjam Rijāl al-Ḥadīth*, x, 112, no. 5923.

itable deal with God, and departed to His vicinage ..."

He wept bitterly as he spoke, making all listeners weep as well. It was really a mourning ceremony that was held in the dark of that night at the Imam's graveside. Ṣaᶜṣaᶜah's was a sermon delivered in this mourning session, attended by Imam al-Ḥasan, Imam al-Ḥusayn, Muḥammad ibn Ḥanafiyyah, Abū al-Faḍl al-ᶜAbbās and other sons and relatives of the Imam (*ᶜa*). After his speech those present offered condolences to Imam al-Ḥasan, Imam al-Ḥusayn and other sons of the Imam (*ᶜa*). Then they returned to Kūfah.[1]

The Mosque of Ṣaᶜṣaᶜah is one of the celebrated mosques of Kūfah and the Imam of the Era—may Allah's blessings be upon him—was seen there by a group of people during the month of Rajab. The Imam offered two *rakᶜahs* and recited the supplication *"Allāhumma, yā dhal minanis sābighah, wal ālâ'il wāziᶜah...,"* which has already been cited earlier in the observances of the month of Rajab (vol. 1, p. 374).[2] Apparently, the Imam's act indicates that this supplication is meant specifically for this noble mosque and is a part of its observances, like the supplications associated with the Sahlah Mosque and the Mosque of Zayd.

However, as the episode occurred during the month of Rajab, when the Imam recited this supplication, it may as well be one of the supplications meant for the days of Rajab. Accordingly, this supplication has also been mentioned among observances of the month of Rajab by the scholars in their books.[3]

1 *Biḥār*, xlii, 295-296.

2 *Iqbāl*, 644, whence *Biḥār*, xcv, 391, b 23, h 12, xcvii, 447, b 7, h 24 & *Mustadrak*, iii, 441, b 54, h 3952/10.

3 Ṭūsī's *Miṣbāḥ*, 802. *Iqbāl*, 644, whence *Biḥār*, xcv, 391, b 23, h 1. *Balad*, 178.

Chapter Seven

The Ziyārah of Karbalā

This chapter deals with the virtues of the *ziyārah* of Imam Abū ᶜAbdillāh al-Ḥusayn—may Allah's blessings be upon him—the etiquette to be observed by pilgrims during their journey to his holy shrine and within the shrine itself, and the manner of performing the Imam's *ziyārah*. It consists of three sections.

Section One
The Virtues of the Imam's Ziyarah

The virtues of the *ziyārah* of Imam al-Ḥusayn (ᶜ*a*) are more than can be described here.[1] It is mentioned in many reports that its excellence equals that of *ḥajj*, ᶜ*umrah* and *jihād*, or rather exceeds all of these by several degrees.[2] Among its virtues is that it brings about forgiveness for one's sins, an easy reckoning on the Day of Retribution, the elevation of one's rank, the acceptance of one's supplications, and prolongation of one's life-span.[3] Among its rewards are safety of one's body and property, expansion of one's provision, fulfilment of one's needs and removal of the causes of one's worries and distress. Its disregard causes injury to one's faith and amounts to disregarding a major right of the Apostle of Allah (*ṣ*).[4] The least reward of a visitor to the shrine of that Imam is that his sins are forgiven by God Almighty, his life and property remain safe until he returns to his family, and on the Day of Resurrection he will find God to be a

1 *Kāmil al-Ziyārat*, 111-184, b 38-74. *Al-Mazār al-Kabīr*, 325-354, b 1-11. *Wasā'il*, xiv, 409-428, b 37, h 19476-19523. *Biḥār*, xcviii, 1-81, b 1-10.

2 For its excellence in relation to *ḥajj* and ᶜ*umrah*, see *Kāmil al-Ziyārāt*, 154-164, b 63, h 1-10, b 64, h 1-9, b 65, h 1-15, b 66, h 1- 10, *Wasā'il*, xiv, 445-455, b 45, h 19566-19588, & *Biḥār*, xcviii, 28-45, b 5, h 1-84 from many sources; and in relation to *jihād*, see: *Kāfī*, iv, 444581, h 5 whence *Wasā'il*, xiv, 455, b 46, h 19589 & *Biḥār*, lxxi, 332, b 20, h 108. *Kāmil al-Ziyārāt*, 164, b 67, h 1, whence *Biḥār*, xcviii, 43, b 5, h 81 & *Mustadrak*, x, 277, b 34, h 12011/2. *Thawāb*, 87. Mufīd's *Mazār*, 38, b 15, h 2. *Tahdhīb*, vi, 44, b 16, h 9. *Rawḍat al-Wā*ᶜ*iẓīn*, i, 194. *Jāmi*ᶜ *al-Akhbār*, 24, faṣl 11.

3 *Kāmil al-Ziyārāt*, 150-154, 165-181, b 61, h 1-5, b 62, h 1-8, b 68, h 1-5, b 69, h 1-9, b 70, h 1-12, b 71, h 1-8, b 72, h 1-7.

4 *Wasā'il*, xiv, 428-435, b 38, h 19524-19544.

better protector of his person than in the world.

It is mentioned in many reports that the *ziyārah* of the Imam removes grief,[1] brings relief from agony at the time of death, and saves one from the terrors of the grave.[2] The money one spends for the pilgrimage journey has a reward 10,000 times greater than that of a similar sum spent in charity.[3] When the pilgrim proceeds towards the Imam's shrine, he is welcomed by 4000 angels, who escort him during his return journey.[4] The prophets of the old, their legatees, the immaculate Imams and the angels—may Allah's blessings of peace be to them all—regularly visit the Imam's shrine and pray for his pilgrims and give them good news.[5] God Almighty views the visitors to the shrine of Imam al-Ḥusayn (ᶜ*a*) with more compassion than He does the pilgrims assembled at ᶜArafāt.[6] On the Day of Resurrection, those who see the dignity and glory of the pilgrims of Imam al-Ḥusayn (ᶜ*a*) will wish they had visited his shrine during their life in this world.[7]

There are countless reports on this subject, and later on we will have occasion to refer to some of the virtues of the Imam's *ziyārah* when citing particular *ziyārahs*. Here we shall confine ourselves to citing just one such report.

Ibn Qūlawayh, Kulaynī, Sayyid Ibn Ṭāwūs and others have cited it in their works through reliable chains of transmission on the authority of Muᶜāwiyah b. Wahb al-Bajalī al-Kūfī, an eminent and trusted traditionist.[8] He says,

1 *Kāmil al-Ziyārāt*, 167-168, b 69, h 1-9. *Biḥār*, xcviii, 18, b 3, h 1.

2 *Kāmil al-Ziyārāt*, 149, b 60, h 1, whence *Biḥār*, xcviii, 77, b 10, h 34 & *Mustadrak*, x, 253, b 26, h 11956/46.

3 *Kāmil al-Ziyārāt*, 127-129, b 46, h 1-5. *Biḥār*, xcviii, 50-51, b 8, h 1-3.

4 *Kāfī*, v, 481, h 6, 7. *Kāmil al-Ziyārāt*, 119, 167, 189, 191, 192, b 41, h 1, 5, b 69, h 2, b 77, h 1, 2, 8, 9. Ṣadūq's *Amālī*, 14, 142, majlis 4, 29. *Thawāb*, 87, 88. Nuᶜmānī's *Ghaybah*, 311. *Rawḍat al-Wāᶜiẓīn*, i, 194. *Manāqib*, iv, 128. From various sources in *Wasā'il*, xiv, 309, 310, 320, 327, b 37, h 19476, 19477, 19501, 19523, *Biḥār*, xlv, 226, b 4, h 21, lii, 328, b 27, h 48, xcviii, 55, 62, 63, b 9, h 16, 20, 40, 42, 44 & *Mustadrak*, x, 242, 245, 254, b 26, h 11933/23, 11939/29, 11940/30, 11959/49.

5 *Biḥār*, xcviii, 58-64, b 9, h 26-48 from various sources.

6 *Kāmil al-Ziyārāt*, 170-171, b 70, h 3, 4, 5, 7. *Biḥār*, xcviii, 36, b 5, h 50.

7 *Kāmil al-Ziyārāt*, 135, b 50, h 1 whence *Wasā'il*, xiv, 424, b 37, h 19512 & *Biḥār*, xcviii, 72, b 10, h 18.

8 *Kāfī*, iv, 582, h 11, whence *Wasā'il*, xiv, 411, b 37, h 19482. *Kāmil al-Ziyārāt*, 116, b 40, h 2, whence *Biḥār*, xcviii, 8, 51, b 1, h 30, b 9, h 1. *Thawāb*, 94, whence *Mustadrak*, x, 230, b 26, h 11914/4. *Al-Mazār al-Kabīr*, 334-336. *Miṣbāḥ al-Zā'ir*, 193.

"Once when calling on Imam Jaᶜfar al-Ṣādiq (ᶜa) I found him engaged in prayer. I sat down and waited for him to finish. As he prayed, I heard him making an earnest supplication to his Lord. He was saying, 'O Allah, who have singled us out for the gift of Your honour, promised us the privilege of intercession, endowed us with the sciences of apostleship, made us heirs of the prophets, appointed us to be the final link in the chain of past nations, preferred us for the legacy of the Prophet (ṣ), granted us the knowledge of what is past and what is to come, and made the hearts of a part of mankind fond of us![1] Forgive me and my brethren, and forgive the pilgrims to the grave of my forbear, al-Ḥusayn ibn ᶜAlī—may Allah's blessings be on them—who spend their means and set out with their bodies, out of their fond devotion for us, expecting the reward that lies with You and to maintain their intimate relationship with us, expecting thereby to bring joy to Your Prophet, Muḥammad. They do so to comply with Your bidding, seeking Your pleasure and approval and inciting thereby the displeasure and rage of our enemies!'

'Recompense them on our behalf with Your pleasure and approval! Protect them night and day! In the best possible manner, take care in their absence of their families and children whom they leave behind! Be their companion, and protect them from the evil of every unruly tyrant, from the harm of any of Your creatures, weak and strong, and from the evil of every satan from humans or jinn! Grant them the best of what they expect from You while leaving their homelands, preferring nearness to us to the company of their children, families and kinsmen!'

'O Allah, our enemies fault them for going forth for our *ziyārah*. But that does not stop them from making up their minds against their wishes and setting out toward us. So have mercy on their faces which get scorched by the sun! Have mercy on the cheeks that rub the ground at the grave of Abū ᶜAbd Allah (ᶜa)! Have mercy on the eyes that flow with tears out of compassion for us! Have mercy on the hearts that become listless and burn for our sake! Have mercy on the cries of lamentation that rise for our sake! O Allah, I commit their souls and bodies to Your care until the time when You will give them to drink from the Pool of *Kaw<u>th</u>ar* on the Day of Thirst!' "

1 A reference to the Qur'ān, 14:37.

Ibn Wahb says,

> "The Imam—may Allah bless him—continued to supplicate in this manner as he prayed in prostration. When he had finished, I said to him, 'May my life be sacrificed for you, from what I have heard of your supplication, I guess, if it were said for someone who did not know God at all, the fire of hell would not touch him. By God, I wish I had visited him and not gone for ḥajj!'
>
> "The Imam said to me, 'How near is his tomb to your place! What has kept you from making his *ziyārah*? Don't neglect it, Muᶜāwiyah.' I said, 'May my life be sacrificed for you, I did not know that this matter had all this much significance.' He said, 'O Muᶜāwiyah, those who pray for the pilgrims of al-Ḥusayn are more in the heavens than those who pray for them on this earth. Do not forsake his pilgrimage for fear of anyone. For those who forsake it on account of fear will be so regretful that they will wish they had been killed and buried by his shrine. Would you not like to be seen by God among those for whom prayers are made by the Apostle of Allah, ᶜAlī, Fāṭimah and the infallible Imams? Would you not like to be among those with whom the angels will shake hands tomorrow? Would you not like to be among those who arrive on the scene of judgement without any trace of sin? Would you not like tomorrow to be among those with whom the Apostle of Allah (ṣ) will shake hands?' "

Section two

The Etiquette of the Imam's Ziyarah

(1) The first point of etiquette, according to the instructions given by Imam Jaᶜfar al-Ṣādiq (*ᶜa*) to Ṣafwān (in the report mentioned under the seventh *ziyārah*, p. 278), is to fast for three days before setting out on the pilgrimage journey and to take a bath on the third day.[1] Shaykh Muḥammad b. al-Mashhadī mentions the same observances in the preliminaries to be performed for the Imam's *ziyārah* on the days of the two *ᶜīds*. Afterwards, one should gather the members of one's family and say,[2]

[1] The bath is to be performed on the fourth day, according to *Biḥār*, xcviii, 257, b 18, h 41, from *al-Mazār al-Kabīr*, 427.

[2] *Biḥār*, xcviii, 356, b 30, h 2, from *al-Mazār al-Kabīr*, 417, b 2. A longer version is cited in Ṭūsī's *Miṣbāḥ*, 717 and *Biḥār*, xcviii, 257, b 18, h 41, from *al-Mazār al-Kabīr*, 427.

O Allah, today I commend to Your care my self, my family, my property, my children and all those who belong to me in some way or other—those of them that are present and those who are absent.	اَللّٰهُمَّ إِنِّي أَسْـتَوْدِعُكَ الْيَـوْمَ نَفْسِي وَ أَهْـلِي وَ مَـالِي وَ وَلَدِي، وَ كُلَّ مَنْ كَانَ مِنِّي بِسَبِيلٍ، اَلشَّاهِدَ مِنْهُمْ وَ الْغَائِبَ.
O Allah, guard us in Your protection with the shield of faith, and protect our means. O Allah, place us in Your fortification and do not strip us of Your blessings, nor alter the blessings and welfare You have given us to enjoy, and grant us more of Your grace. Indeed we beseech You!	اَللّٰهُمَّ احْفَظْنَا بِحِفْظِكَ بِحِفْظِ الْإِيمَانِ وَ احْفَظْ عَلَيْنَا. اَللّٰهُمَّ اجْعَلْنَا فِي حِرْزِكَ، وَ لَا تَسْـلُبْنَا نِعْمَتَكَ، وَ لَا تُغَيِّرْ مَا بِنَا مِنْ نِعْمَةٍ وَ عَافِيَةٍ، وَ زِدْنَا مِنْ فَضْلِكَ، إِنَّا إِلَيْكَ رَاغِبُونَ.

Then depart from your home in a state of humility, walking gently and with dignity, and say a lot, *Lâ ilāha illallāh, wallāhu akbar, wal ḥamdu lillāh,* and keep on praising Allah and calling down blessings on the Prophet and his Family, may Allah bless them.

(2) Imam Jaᶜfar al-Ṣādiq (*ᶜa*) is reported[1] to have said concerning the etiquette of pilgrimage to the shrine of Imam al-Ḥusayn (*ᶜa*): "Visit the shrine of Abū ᶜAbdillāh in a state of sorrow and grief, with dishevelled hair covered with dust (of the way), and with hunger and thirst (of the journey), as such was his condition at the time of his martyrdom. Make any requests that you may have and leave; do not settle there.

(3) While on the pilgrimage journey, one should abstain from carrying along or consuming delicious foods, such as roasted meat, sweets and dainties. It is better to have simple food, such as bread with milk or yogurt. Imam Jaᶜfar al-Ṣādiq (*ᶜa*) is reported[2] to have said in this regard, "I have heard that some people carry along roasted lambs and sweets while going for the *ziyārah* of Imam al-Ḥusayn (*ᶜa*). They would not carry along such food items when visiting the

1 *Kāfī*, iv, 587, h 2, whence *Wasā'il*, xiv, 540, b 77, h 19778. *Kāmil al-Ziyārāt*, 131, b 48, h 3, whence *Wasā'il*, xiv, 528, b 71, h 19751. *Thawāb*, 88, whence *Biḥār*, xcviii, 140, b 17, h 2. Mufīd's *Mazār*, 96, b 48. *Tahdhīb*, vi, 76, b 22, h 2.

2 *Faqīh*, ii, 281, h 2453, whence *Wasā'il*, xi, 422, b 41, h 15158. *Thawāb*, 89, whence *Biḥār*, xcviii, 141, b 17, h 7. Mufīd's *Mazār*, 97, b 48. *Kāmil al-Ziyārāt*, 129, 130, h 1, 3, whence *Wasā'il*, xiv, 541, b 77, h 19780. *Amān*, 56.

graves of their own ancestors and relatives."

In another reliable report,[1] the Imam is said to have told Mufaḍḍal b. ᶜUmar, "It is, of course, better to visit the shrine of Imam al-Ḥusayn than not to visit it, but at times it is better not to visit his shrine than to visit it." When asked to explain what he meant, the Imam said, "By God, when you set out to visit the graves of your fathers, you go in a state of sorrow and grief. But when visiting his shrine you take along delicacies in your provisions. Rather you should arrive at his shrine with dusty and dishevelled hair."

Hence the appropriate thing for pilgrims from wealthy and merchant families is to pay attention to this point in their pilgrimage journeys. When en route to Karbalā, they are invited by their friends in towns and furnished with victuals consisting of roasted chicken, Kebab and other delicacies to be carried along, they should decline and tell them, "We are travelling to Karbalā and it is not proper for us to have such things for meals."

Shaykh Kulaynī reports[2] that after the martyrdom of Imam al-Ḥusayn (*ᶜa*) one of his wives from Banū Kalb held a mourning ceremony for the Imam. She mourned for the Imam along with other women and servants, and they wept so much that their eyes dried up and they had no more tears left. Someone arranged a dinner consisting of roasted fowls and had it sent for them as a refreshment in the course of their mourning. When that lady noticed it, she asked what it was. She was told that it was a gift sent by someone for the mourners to refresh their strength. She said, "We are not celebrating a wedding. What shall we do with it!" Then she had it sent away.

(4) Among things desirable for the pilgrim during journeys to the shrine of Imam al-Ḥusayn (*ᶜa*) is to walk with humility, like a humble servant. Hence those who travel using the modern means of transport should be careful not to look down on other pilgrims and servants of God who have a tough time making their journey with their simple and primitive means.

In the accounts of the Companions of the Cave given by scholars, it is mentioned that they were courtiers of Daqyūs (Decius) and were like his ministers. When God's mercy prompted them to embrace monotheism and to reform themselves, they thought that it would be best for them to seclude themselves from the rest of the community and to take refuge in a cave for the sake of God's worship.

1 *Kāmil al-Ziyārāt*, 130, 131, b 47, h 4, b 48, h 2, whence *Wasā'il*, xi, 422, 542, b 41, h 15159, b 77, h 19781 & *Biḥār*, xcviii, 141, b 17, h 10.

2 *Kāfī*, i, 466, h 9, whence *Biḥār*, xlv, 170, b 39, h 18.

They mounted their steeds and left the town. After they had gone for about three miles, Tamlīkhā, one of them, said to the others,

يَا إِخْوَتَاهْ، جَاءَتْ مَسْكَنَةُ الْآخِرَةِ، وَ ذَهَبَ مُلْكُ الدُّنْيَا، اِنْزِلُوا عَنْ خُيُولِكُمْ، وَ امْشُوا عَلَىٰ أَرْجُلِكُمْ، لَعَلَّ اللهَ أَنْ يَجْعَلَ لَكُمْ مِنْ أَمْرِكُمْ فَرَجاً وَ مَخْرَجاً.

> "Brothers, mundane glory has departed and the humility of the Hereafter is upon us. Get down from your horses and walk on your feet! Maybe God will bring some relief, or open a way out of your predicament!"[1]

He meant to say, "Brothers, this is the path of the Hereafter and henceforth we must walk humbly like the poor and forsake patrician ways and the customs of worldly glory. Now we must dismount from horseback and proceed on foot towards the court of the Almighty. Maybe our Lord will have mercy on us, and help us on to rectitude in our affair." Thereupon, they dismounted from their horses. On that day those noble souls walked for seven parasangs until their feet were hurt and blood dripped from them.

The pilgrim to this holy shrine should keep this matter in his mind. He should know that inasmuch as one adopts humility and humbleness for God's sake in His way, it will elevate his station. Hence Imam Jaᶜfar al-Ṣādiq (ᶜa) is reported to have said concerning the etiquette of *ziyārah* of Imam al-Ḥusayn (ᶜa) that, for those who make pilgrimage to the Imam's shrine on foot, God Almighty writes for every step a thousand good deeds and erases a thousand sins from their record, and raises their rank by a thousand degrees in paradise.

On reaching the Euphrates, the pilgrim should bathe in it, and, baring his feet and holding his shoes in his hands, continue his foot journey toward the shrine, walking like a humble servant.

(5) On the way, when one comes across pilgrims making the journey on foot, who are tired and need help, one should try one's best to help them reach their destination, being careful not to have a dismissive attitude towards them.

Shaykh Kulaynī cites a report[2] on the authority of Abū Hārūn, who says, "I was present when Imam Jaᶜfar al-Ṣādiq (ᶜa) once said to a group of his visitors, 'What is the matter with you that you look

[1] Rāwandī's *Qiṣaṣ*, 259, faṣl 8, h 300, whence *Biḥār*, xiv, 216, b 27, h 1. *Irshād al-Qulūb*, ii, 262. Jazā'irī's *Qiṣaṣ*, 444.

[2] *Kāfī*, viii, 102, h 73, whence *Wāfī*, v, 988, h 63446 & *Wasā'il*, xii, 272, b 148, h 16286.

down upon us?' One of them, a man from Khorāsān, got up and said, 'God forbid, how can we ever be disrespectful towards you or anyone related to you?'

The Imam said to him, 'You are yourself one of those who have treated me with contempt.' That man said, 'I take refuge with God from ever acting with contempt toward you!' The Imam said, 'Woe to you, did you not hear that man on the way, who called out to you when the caravan was near Juḥfah and requested you to give him a ride for a mile, and he said to you, "By God, I am tired!" But you did not so much as even turn your head to look at him and disregarded his request? Whoever treats a faithful person with contempt is guilty of contempt toward us and disregard for God!' "

While describing the etiquette of *ziyārah*, we have mentioned an instructive episode pertaining to ᶜAlī ibn Yaqṭīn under the ninth of the points of etiquette (p. 15) which is relevant here. This point of etiquette is not limited to pilgrims of Imam al-Ḥusayn's shrine. We mention it here because such situations occur more often during such journeys.

(6) Muḥammad b. Muslim, an eminent and trustworthy authority, reports[1] that he asked Imam Muḥammad al-Bāqir (*ᶜa*), "When we go to visit the shrine of your forefather al-Ḥusayn ibn ᶜAlī (*ᶜa*), is it not as if we were on a *ḥajj* journey?" "Of course," he said. "Is it obligatory for us, then, to observe what is obligatory for *ḥajj* pilgrims?" asked Muḥammad.

The Imam replied, "That which is necessary for you to observe is to be kindly in your conduct towards your companions, to be parsimonious in your speech except when you have to say something good, and to remember God often. Among things to be observed is to put on clean clothes, to take a bath before entering the shrine precincts, to be humble and kindly in your deportment, to pray a lot, to invoke much blessings on Muḥammad and the Family of Muḥammad, to abstain from anything which is improper for you, to guard your looks from anything forbidden to look at or suspected to be such, to help your brethren-in-faith, to assist those who have run out of their means and to share your money with them. It is obligatory on you to observe *taqiyyah*, which is meant to preserve your religion, to refrain from things God has forbidden, and to avoid disputing and swearing, or engaging in arguments and debates that may involve swearing. When you conduct yourself in such a manner, you will receive the

[1] *Kāmil al-Ziyārāt*, 130, b 48, h 1, whence *Biḥār*, xcviii, 142, b 17, h 11.

full reward of *ḥajj* and *ᶜumrah* you deserve to receive from God, to whom you look up for reward for having spent your wealth and putting up with separation from your family, and return home while partaking of God's mercy and approval and with your sins forgiven."

(7) In a report[1] of Abū Ḥamzah al-Thumāli from Imam Jaᶜfar al-Ṣādiq (*ᶜa*) concerning the *ziyārah* of Imam al-Ḥusayn (*ᶜa*), the Imam is reported to have stated that on reaching Naynawā and setting down one's baggage, one should refrain from applying oil to one's body, using kohl, or eating meat as long as one stays in that place.

(8) Many traditions recommend that the pilgrim take bath in the water of the Euphrates. One report[2] mentions Imam Jaᶜfar al-Ṣādiq (*ᶜa*) as having said that someone who visits the tomb of Imam al-Ḥusayn (*ᶜa*) after taking bath in the Euphrates becomes as free from sin as he was at the time of his birth, even though he should have been guilty of major sins.

Another report[3] recounts that some people said to the Imam that at times, due to winter or some other reason, it was hard for them to take bath before performing the *ziyārah* of Imam al-Ḥusayn's tomb. The Imam said to them, "Someone who bathes in the Euphrates and visits the shrine of Imam al-Ḥusayn (*ᶜa*) has a merit written for him which is beyond reckoning."

Bashīr al-Dahhān reports[4] that Imam Jaᶜfar al-Ṣādiq (*ᶜa*) said that for someone who visits the tomb of al-Ḥusayn ibn ᶜAlī (*ᶜa*) after performing *wuḍū* and taking bath in the Euphrates, God Almighty writes a reward equal to that of *ḥajj* and *ᶜumrah* for every step that he takes. According to some reports,[5] the bath is to be taken in the Euphrates at the place facing the Imam's tomb. It is desirable on reaching the river, as mentioned in some reports,[6] to say "*Allāhu akbar*" a hundred times, and "*Lâ ilāha illallāh*" a hundred times and to invoke blessings

1 *Kāmil al-Ziyārat*, 226, h 17 whence *Biḥār*, xcviii, 175, b 18, h 33 & *Mustadrak*, x, 348, b 60, h 12153/1.

2 *Kāmil al-Ziyārat*, 184, b 75, h 1 whence *Wasā'il*, xiv, 485, b 59, h 19659 & *Biḥār*, xcviii, 143, b 17, h 14.

3 *Kāmil al-Ziyārat*, 188, b 76, h 1 whence *Wasā'il*, xiv, 489, b 60, h 19670 & *Biḥār*, xcviii, 145, b 17, h 27.

4 *Kāmil al-Ziyārat*, 186, b 75, h 7 whence *Biḥār*, xcviii, 146, b 17, h 31, & *Mustadrak*, x, 297, b 43, h 12048/2. *Tahdhīb*, i, 52, b 17, h 7, whence *Wasā'il*, xiv, 484, b 59, h 19655.

5 *Kāfī*, iv, 572, h 1, whence *Wasā'il*, xiv, 483, b 59, h 19653. *Kāmil al-Ziyārat*, 186, b 75, h 8, 201, h 3, whence *Biḥār*, xcviii, 146, 157, b 17, h 33, b 18, h 5, & *Mustadrak*, x, 297, b 43, h 12049/3.

6 *Al-Mazār al-Kabīr*, 428, b 3, whence *Biḥār*, xcviii, 257, 357, b 18, h 41, b 30, h 3.

on the Prophet and his Family a hundred times.

(9) While entering the sacred shrine precincts, to enter from the gate on the eastern side, as told by Imam Ja[c]far al-Ṣādiq ([c]a) to Yūsūf al-Kunāsī.[1]

(10) In a report cited by Ibn Qūlwayh,[2] Imam Ja[c]far al-Ṣādiq ([c]a) is mentioned as having told Mufaḍḍal b. [c]Umar, "O Mufaḍḍal, when you approach the tomb of Imam al-Ḥusayn ([c]a) stand at the door of the shrine and recite these words, to partake of God's mercy for each word that you say."

اَلسَّــلَامُ عَلَيْكَ يَا وَارِثَ آدَمَ صَفْوَةِ اللهِ،
اَلسَّــلَامُ عَلَيْكَ يَا وَارِثَ نُوحٍ نَبِيِّ اللهِ،
اَلسَّلَامُ عَلَيْكَ يَا وَارِثَ إِبْرَاهِيمَ خَلِيلِ اللهِ،
اَلسَّلَامُ عَلَيْكَ يَا وَارِثَ مُوسَىٰ كَلِيمِ اللهِ،
اَلسَّلَامُ عَلَيْكَ يَا وَارِثَ عِيسَىٰ رُوحِ اللهِ،

Peace be to you, O heir of Adam, the chosen of Allah! Peace be to you, O heir of Noah, the prophet of Allah! Peace be to you, O heir of Abraham, Allah's dedicated friend! Peace be to you, O heir of Moses, Allah's interlocutor! Peace be to you, O heir of Jesus, spirit of Allah!

اَلسَّــلَامُ عَلَيْكَ يَــا وَارِثَ مُحَمَّدٍ حَبِيبِ
اللهِ، اَلسَّــلَامُ عَلَيْكَ يَا وَارِثَ عَلِيٍّ وَصِيِّ
رَسُــولِ اللهِ، اَلسَّــلَامُ عَلَيْكَ يَا وَارِثَ
الْحَسَــنِ الرَّضِيِّ، اَلسَّلَامُ عَلَيْكَ يَا وَارِثَ
فَاطِمَةَ بِنْتِ رَسُولِ اللهِ،

Peace be to you, O heir of Muḥammad, the beloved of Allah! Peace be to you, O heir of [c]Alī, legatee of the Apostle of Allah! Peace be to you, O heir of al-Ḥasan, the approved one! Peace be to you, O heir of Fāṭimah, daughter of the Apostle of Allah!

اَلسَّلَامُ عَلَيْكَ أَيُّهَا الشَّــهِيدُ الصِّدِّيقُ،
اَلسَّــلَامُ عَلَيْكَ أَيُّهَا الْوَصِيُّ الْبَارُّ التَّقِيُّ،
اَلسَّلَامُ عَلَى الْأَرْوَاحِ الَّتِي حَلَّتْ بِفِنَائِكَ
وَ أَنَاخَتْ بِرَحْلِكَ، اَلسَّلَامُ عَلَىٰ مَلَائِكَةِ

Peace be to you, O martyr and truthful one! Peace be to you, O pious and Godwary legatee! Peace be to the spirits that have alighted in your courtyard and terminated their journey in your shrine! Peace be to the an-

[1] *Kāmil al-Ziyārat*, 201, h 3, whence *Wasā'il*, xiv, 483, b 59, h 19653 & *Biḥār*, xcviii, 157, b 18, h 5.

[2] *Kāmil al-Ziyārat*, 205, b 79, h 5, whence *Biḥār*, xcviii, 163, b 18, h 8, & *Mustadrak*, x, 299, b 45, h 12354/2.

اللهِ الْمُحْدِقِينَ بِكَ.	gels of Allah who surround you!
أَشْــهَدُ أَنَّكَ قَدْ أَقَمْتَ الصَّلَاةَ، وَ آتَيْتَ الزَّكَاةَ، وَ أَمَرْتَ بِالْمَعْرُوفِ، وَ نَهَيْتَ عَنِ الْمُنْكَرِ، وَ عَبَدْتَ اللهَ مُخْلِصاً حَتَّى أَتَاكَ الْيَقِينُ. اَلسَّلَامُ عَلَيْكَ وَ رَحْمَةُ اللهِ وَ بَرَكَاتُهُ	I testify that you maintained the prayer, and paid the *zakāt*, bade what is right and forbade what is wrong, and worshipped Allah exclusively until the last breath. Peace be to you and may Allah's mercy and His bounties be upon you!

Then approach the tomb. The report says that every step that one takes has the reward of a martyr slain in God's way. On reaching the grave, stroke it with your hand and say,

اَلسَّــلَامُ عَلَيْكَ يَا حُجَّةَ اللهِ فِي أَرْضِهِ وَ سَمَائِهِ.	Peace be to you, O God's testament on His earth and in His heaven!

Then proceed to offer prayer, says the report, adding that for every *rakᶜah* one offers by the Imam's graveside, one will receive the reward of someone who has performed *ḥajj* and *ᶜumrah* a thousand times, freed a thousand slaves and participated in *jihād* alongside one of God's prophetic envoys.[1]

(11) Abū Saᶜīd al-Madā'inī reports[2] that he asked Imam Jaᶜfar al-Ṣādiq (*ᶜa*), "Shall I visit the tomb of al-Ḥusayn, may peace be upon him?" The Imam replied, "Sure, O Abū Saᶜīd, visit the tomb of Ḥusayn, son of the Apostle of Allah, may Allah bless him and his Family, the best of the good, the purest of the pure, and the most pious of the pious. When you visit his tomb, say the *tasbīḥ* of the Commander of the Faithful (*ᶜa*) a thousand times at the head of the grave, and the *tasbīḥ* of Fāṭimah (*ᶜa*) a thousand times at the feet. Then offer two *rakᶜahs*, reciting the sūrahs Yā Sīn and al-Raḥmān during the prayer. When you have done that, God will write its reward for you, God willing." Abū Saᶜīd then asked the Imam to teach him the *tasbīḥs* of ᶜAlī (*ᶜa*) and Fāṭimah (*ᶜa*). The following is the *tasbīḥ* of ᶜAlī (*ᶜa*) as taught by the Imam.[3]

1 *Al-Mazār al-Kabīr*, 355, b 12, h 2.

2 *Kāmil al-Ziyārāt*, 214, h 10, whence *Biḥār*, xcviii, 166, b 18, h 17. Both *tasbīḥs* cited with some difference of wording in Kafᶜamī's *Miṣbāḥ*, 410 & *Balad*, 149.

3 A variant of Imam ᶜAlī's *tasbīḥ* is cited in Ṭūsī's *Miṣbāḥ*, 293 and *Jamāl*, 248,

Glory be to Him whose treasures are never spent. Glory be to Him whose beacons never pass away. Glory to Him, that which is with whom never perishes. Glory be to Him who has no partner sharing in His judgement. Glory be to Him whose glory never fades. Glory be to Him whose term has no end. Glory be to Him besides whom there is no god!

سُبْحَانَ الَّذِى لَا تَنْفَدُ خَزَائِنُهُ، سُبْحَانَ
الَّذِى لَا تَبِيدُ مَعَالِمُهُ، سُبْحَانَ الَّذِى
لَا يَفْنَىٰ مَا عِنْدَهُ، سُبْحَانَ الَّذِى لَا
يُشْرِكُ أَحَداً فِى حُكْمِهِ، سُبْحَانَ الَّذِى
لَا اضْمِحْلَالَ لِفَخْرِهِ، سُبْحَانَ الَّذِى لَا
انْقِطَاعَ لِمُدَّتِهِ، سُبْحَانَ الَّذِى لَا إِلٰهَ غَيْرُهُ.

The *tasbīḥ* of Fāṭimah (*ʿa*) is as follows.

Glory be to the Lord of lofty and supreme glory! Glory be to the Lord of sublime and exalted honour! Glory be to the Lord of the magnificent and eternal kingdom, ! Glory be to the Lord of splendour and beauty! Glory be to Him who dons the robes of light and dignity! Glory be to Him who sees the ant's track on a rock and the bird's trail in the air!

سُبْحَانَ ذِى الْجَلَالِ الْبَاذِخِ الْعَظِيمِ،
سُبْحَانَ ذِى الْعِزِّ الشَّامِخِ الْمُنِيفِ،
سُبْحَانَ ذِى الْمُلْكِ الْفَاخِرِ الْقَدِيمِ،
سُبْحَانَ ذِى الْبَهْجَةِ وَ الْجَمَالِ، سُبْحَانَ
مَنْ تَرَدَّىٰ بِالنُّورِ وَالْوَقَارِ، سُبْحَانَ مَنْ يَرَىٰ
أَثَرَ النَّمْلِ فِى الصَّفَا وَ وَقْعَ الطَّيْرِ فِى الْهَوَاءِ.

(12) While in Karbalā one should try to offer all one's obligatory and supererogatory prayers in the shrine of Imam al-Ḥusayn (*ʿa*), as prayers offered at his graveside are blessed with acceptance. Sayyid Ibn Ṭāwūs says that one should take full care not to miss any obligatory and *nāfilah* prayers in the holy precincts of the Ḥā'ir, as it is mentioned in the reports[1] that obligatory prayers offered at his graveside merit the reward of *ḥajj* and supererogatory prayers that of *ʿumrah*.

We have mentioned the tradition reported by Mufaḍḍal concerning the great reward of prayer in that holy shrine. In another reliable

whence *Biḥār*, lxxxviii, 172, h 5.

1 *Kāmil al-Ziyārāt*, 251, b 83, h 1, whence *Biḥār*, xcviii, 82, b 11, h 7 & *Mustaadrak*, x, 327, b 52, h 12107/5. Mufīd's *Mazār*, 133, b 59, h 1. *Tahdhīb*, vi, 73, b 22, h 10, whence *Wasā'il*, xiv, 518, b 69, h 19728. *Al-Mazār al-Kabīr*, 355, b 12, h 1

report, Imam Jaᶜfar al-Ṣādiq (ᶜ*a*) is reported to have said that someone who visits the Imam's shrine and offers two or four *rakᶜahs* at his graveside is granted the reward of *ḥajj* and ᶜ*umrah.*[1]

That which can be gathered from the traditions is that it is proper to offer the prayer of *ziyārah* and other prayers behind the tomb or at its head. However, while praying at the head of the tomb one should stand somewhat behind so as not to stand in the same line as the grave. In the narration of Abū Ḥamzah al-Thumālī from Imam Jaᶜfar al-Ṣādiq (ᶜ*a*), it is mentioned that one is to offer near the head two *rakᶜahs*, reciting al-Fātiḥah and Yā Sīn in the first and al-Fātiḥah and al-Raḥmān in the second.

One may as well pray behind the tomb if one wishes, but it is better to pray at the head. After the prayer of *ziyārah*, one may pray as much as one wishes. However, the two *rakᶜahs* of *ziyārah* are essential while visiting any of the shrines.

Ibn Qūlawayh reports[2] Imam Muḥammad al-Bāqir (ᶜ*a*) as having told someone, "When you have any need, what keeps you from approaching the tomb of al-Ḥusayn, may Allah bless him, and after offering four *rakᶜahs* there, asking for fulfilment of your need? Indeed an obligatory prayer performed at his graveside equals *ḥajj* and a supererogatory prayer has the reward of an ᶜ*umrah.*"

(13) One should know that the main part of observances performed in the holy shrine of al-Imam Ḥusayn (ᶜ*a*) is supplication, for answering of supplications under its dome is one of the things granted by God Almighty to the Imam for his martyrdom. The pilgrim must take advantage of this matter and, taking care not to neglect the opportunity to repent from sins, entreat God for forgiveness and make petitions for fulfilment of his/her needs.

Many supplications have been recommended by the Imams in the *ziyārahs* prescribed for the visitors, and we would have cited here some of them if it were not for considerations of brevity. It is preferable to recite as much as one can of the supplications of *al-Ṣaḥīfat al-Kāmilah,* which are the finest of supplications. At the end of this

1 *Tahdhīb*, vi, 79, b 26, h 4, whence *Wasā'il,* xiv, 330, 520, b 2, h 19329, b 69, h 19734. *Kāmil al-Ziyārāt,* 160, 251, b 65, h 14, b 83, h 3, whence *Biḥār*, xcvii, 119-120, b 2, h 18, 19. *Al-Mazār al-Kabīr*, 134, 185, b 59, h 3, b 11, h 3, whence *Mustadrak*, x, 229, b 52, h 12113/11.

2 *Kāmil al-Ziyārāt*, 251, b 83, h 1, whence *Biḥār*, xcviii, 82, b 11, h 7 & *Mustaadrak*, x, 327, b 52, h 12107/5. Mufīd's *Mazār*, 133, b 59, h 1. *Tahdhīb*, vi, 73, b22, h 10, whence *Wasā'il*, xiv, 518, b 69, h 19728. *Al-Mazār al-Kabīr*, 355, b 12, h 1

Book, after the common *ziyārahs*, we have cited a supplication that can be recited in any of the holy shrines (p. 543, see also p. 593). However, in order to obviate the fault of total omission in this place, we cite the following brief supplication which has been cited under one of the *ziyārahs*.[1] The supplication is to be recited within the shrine with hands raised towards the heaven.

O Allah, You see my place and hear my speech, and You observe me as I stand here, entreating You, having taken refuge by the tomb of Your testament and the son of Your Prophet. My Master, You know my needs, and my condition is not concealed from You!

اَللّٰهُمَّ قَدْ تَرَىٰ مَكَانِي، وَ تَسْـمَعُ كَلَامِي،
وَ تَرَىٰ مَقَامِي وَ تَضَرُّعِي وَ مَلَاذِي بِقَبْرِ
حُجَّتِكَ وَ ابْـنِ نَبِيِّكَ، وَ قَدْ عَلِمْتَ يَا
سَيِّدِي حَوَائِجِي، وَ لَا يَخْفَىٰ عَلَيْكَ حَالِي،

I have turned to You through the good offices of the son of Your Apostle, Your testament and trustee. I come to You seeking nearness to You and Your Apostle. So make me noteworthy with You in the world and the Hereafter and one of those near to You.

وَ قَـدْ تَوَجَّهْتُ إِلَيْكَ بِابْنِ رَسُـولِكَ وَ
حُجَّتِكَ وَ أَمِينِكَ، وَ قَدْ أَتَيْتُكَ مُتَقَرِّبًا بِهِ
إِلَيْكَ وَ إِلَىٰ رَسُولِكَ، فَاجْعَلْنِي بِهِ عِنْدَكَ
وَجِيهًا فِي الدُّنْيَا وَ الْآخِرَةِ وَ مِنَ الْمُقَرَّبِينَ،

Fulfil my hope by virtue of my *ziyārah*, and grant my desire. Grant me eagerness and ardour, and satisfy my needs, and do not turn me away disappointed. Do not dash my expectations. Do not deny my supplication, and confide to me with Your positive response to all that I have asked You for in relation to my religion, and my life in this world and the Hereafter.

وَ أَعْطِـنِي بِزِيَـارَتِي أَمَـلِي، وَ هَبْ لِي
مُنَايَ، وَ تَفَضَّلْ عَلَيَّ بِشَهْوَتِي وَ رَغْبَتِي،
وَ اقْضِ لِي حَوَائِجِي، وَ لَا تَرُدَّنِي خَائِبًا،
وَ لَا تَقْطَعْ رَجَائِي، وَ لَا تُخَيِّبْ دُعَائِي،
وَ عَرِّفْـنِي الْإِجَابَةَ فِي جَمِيعِ مَا دَعَوْتُكَ
مِنْ أَمْرِ الدِّينِ وَ الدُّنْيَا وَ الْآخِرَةِ،

Let me be one of Your servants from whom You turn away all afflictions, ailments, tribulations and accidents, and one of those

وَ اجْعَلْـنِي مِنْ عِبَـادِكَ الَّذِينَ صَرَفْتَ
عَنْهُمُ الْبَلَايَا وَ الْأَمْـرَاضَ، وَ الْفِتَنَ وَ

[1] *Tahdhīb*, vi, 61, b 18. *Biḥār*, xcviii, 212, b 18, h 33, from Mufīd and *al-Mazār al-Kabīr*, 111-112.

whom You will have them live in well-being and die in well-being, and admit them into paradise in a state of well-being, and shelter them in well-being from the Fire. With Your favour, enable me to succeed in obtaining the goodness and probity I seek for myself, my family, my children, my brethren, my property and all that You have blessed me with, O Most Merciful of the merciful!

الْأَعْرَاضِ، مِنَ الَّذِينَ تُحْيِيهِمْ فِي عَافِيَةٍ،
وَ تُمِيتُهُمْ فِي عَافِيَةٍ، وَ تُدْخِلُهُمُ الْجَنَّةَ فِي
عَافِيَـــةٍ، وَ تُجِيرُهُمْ مِنَ النَّارِ فِي عَافِيَةٍ، وَ
وَفِّقْ لِي بِمَنٍّ مِنْـــكَ صَلَاحَ مَا أُؤَمِّلُ فِي
نَفْسِي وَ أَهْلِي وَ وُلْدِي وَ إِخْوَانِي وَ مَالِي وَ
جَمِيعِ مَا أَنْعَمْتَ بِهِ عَلَيَّ، يَا أَرْحَمَ الرَّاحِمِينَ.

(14) Among observances to be performed in the shrine of Imam al-Ḥusayn (ᶜa) is to invoke blessings for him. A report prescribes that one should stand behind the grave near the Imam's shoulder and pronounce *ṣalawāt* on the Prophet (ṣ) and Imam al-Ḥusayn, may Allah bless him.

In *Miṣbāḥ al-Zā'ir*, under one of the *ziyārahs*, Sayyid Ibn Ṭāwūs has cited the following text of *ṣalawāt* to be pronounced for the Imam (ᶜ*a*).[1]

O Allah, bless Muḥammad and the Family of Muḥammad, and bless al-Ḥusayn, who was aggrieved and martyred, the bewailed martyr and captive of many sufferings, with a blessing which is burgeoning, enhancing and bountiful, ascending at its beginning and endless at its end, the best of what you have granted to any of the offspring of Your prophets and envoys, O Lord of all the worlds!

اَللّٰهُـــمَّ صَلِّ عَلىٰ مُحَمَّـــدٍ وَ آلِ مُحَمَّدٍ، وَ
صَلِّ عَلَى الْحُسَيْنِ الْمَظْلُومِ الشَّهِيدِ قَتِيلِ
الْعَبَرَاتِ وَ أَسِيرِ الْكُرُبَاتِ، صَلَاةً نَامِيَةً
زَاكِيَةً مُبَارَكَةً يَصْعَـــدُ أَوَّلُهَا وَ لَا يَنْفَدُ
آخِرُهَـــا، أَفْضَلَ مَا صَلَّيْتَ عَلىٰ أَحَدٍ مِنْ
أَوْلَادِ الْأَنْبِيَاءِ وَ الْمُرْسَلِينَ، يَا رَبَّ الْعَالَمِينَ

O Allah, bless the martyred Imam, who was forsaken and slain wrongfully, the master and leader, the devout and ascetic legatee and successor, the truthful Imam,

اَللّٰهُمَّ صَلِّ عَلَى الْإِمَامِ الشَّهِيدِ الْمَقْتُولِ
الْمَظْلُومِ الْمَخْذُولِ، وَ السَّـــيِّدِ الْقَائِدِ،
وَ الْعَابِـــدِ الزَّاهِـــدِ، اَلْـــوَصِيِّ الْخَلِيفَةِ،

1 *Biḥār*, xcviii, 225-226, b 18, h 34, from *Miṣbāḥ al-Zā'ir*, 248.

اَلْإِمَامِ الصِّدِّيقِ، اَلطُّهْرِ الطَّاهِرِ، اَلطَّيِّبِ الْمُبَارَكِ، وَ الرَّضِيِّ الْمَرْضِيِّ، وَ التَّقِيِّ الْهَادِى الْمَهْدِيِّ، اَلزَّاهِدِ الذَّائِدِ، اَلْمُجَاهِدِ الْعَالِمِ، إِمَامِ الْهُدَىٰ، سِبْطِ الرَّسُولِ، وَ قُرَّةِ عَيْنِ الْبَتُولِ، صَلَّى اللهُ عَلَيْهِ وَ آلِهِ وَ سَلَّمَ.

pure, immaculate, blameless, and blessed, pleased with God, pleasing to Him, the pious, rightly-guided guide, self-denying defender (of Islam), combatant and all-knowing Imam of guidance, grandson of the Apostle and apple of eye of Batūl, may Allah bless him and his Family and give them peace!

اَللّٰهُمَّ صَلِّ عَلَىٰ سَيِّدِى وَ مَوْلَاىَ كَمَا عَمِلَ بِطَاعَتِكَ، وَ نَهَىٰ عَنْ مَعْصِيَتِكَ، وَ بَالَغَ فِى رِضْوَانِكَ، وَ أَقْبَلَ عَلَىٰ إِيمَانِكَ، غَيْرَ قَابِلٍ فِيكَ عُذْرًا سِرًّا وَ عَلَانِيَةً، يَدْعُو الْعِبَادَ إِلَيْكَ، وَ يَدُلُّهُمْ عَلَيْكَ، وَ قَامَ بَيْنَ يَدَيْكَ، يَهْدِمُ الْجَوْرَ بِالصَّوَابِ، وَ يُحْيِي السُّنَّةَ بِالْكِتَابِ، فَعَاشَ فِى رِضْوَانِكَ مَكْدُودًا، وَ مَضَىٰ عَلَىٰ طَاعَتِكَ وَ فِى أَوْلِيَائِكَ مَكْدُوحًا، وَ قَضَىٰ إِلَيْكَ مَفْقُودًا، لَمْ يَعْصِكَ فِى لَيْلٍ وَ لَا نَهَارٍ، بَلْ جَاهَدَ فِيكَ الْمُنَافِقِينَ وَ الْكُفَّارَ.

O Allah, bless my master and guardian, inasmuch as he acted in obedience to You, forbade disobedience to You, did his utmost to please You, and dedicated himself to faith in You, not accepting any excuse, privately and openly, for opposing You, inviting the people to You and guiding them to You. He rose in Your presence to raze injustice through uprightness and revive the *sunnah* by the Scripture. He lived working hard for the sake of Your good pleasure, and passed away striving in obedience to You, surrendering his soul to You while being bereave for the sake of Your friends. He did not disobey You for a single night or day. Rather, he fought for Your sake the hypocrites and the faithless.

اَللّٰهُمَّ فَاجْزِهِ خَيْرَ جَزَاءِ الصَّادِقِينَ الْأَبْرَارِ، وَ ضَاعِفْ عَلَيْهِمُ الْعَذَابَ، وَ لِقَاتِلِيهِ الْعِقَابَ، فَقَدْ قَاتَلَ كَرِيمًا، وَ قُتِلَ مَظْلُومًا، وَ مَضَىٰ مَرْحُومًا، يَقُولُ

O Allah, reward him with the best of rewards received by Your truthful and pious servants, and double their punishment and that of those who slew him. He fought nobly, was slain wrongfully, and passed away receiving Your mercy, while telling them,

"I am the son of Muḥammad, the Apostle of Allah, and son of him who gave charity and worshipped God." But they slew him deliberately and intentionally for the sake of his faith and obeyed Satan in slaying him, not fearing the All-beneficent to shed his blood.

أَنَا ابْنُ رَسُــولِ اللهِ مُحَمَّــدٍ، وَ ابْنُ مَنْ زَكَّىٰ وَ عَبَدَ، فَقَتَلُــوهُ بِالْعَمْدِ الْمُعْتَمَدِ، قَتَلُوهُ عَلَى الْإِيمَــانِ، وَ أَطَاعُوا فِي قَتْلِهِ الشَّيْطَانَ، وَ لَمْ يُرَاقِبُوا فِيهِ الرَّحْمٰنَ.

O Allah, bless my master and guardian with a blessing that would exalt his name, and whereby You make his cause prevail and hasten his victory. Grant him the best share of Your grace on the Day of Resurrection! Enhance his dignity in the loftiest reaches of *ʿIllīyūn* and grant him the highest dignity of those held in honour with You. With Your mercy, raise the dignity of his station among those near to You in the highest of stations, and grant him the privilege of mediation and the most splendid station, merit and excellence and abundant honour!

اَللّٰهُمَّ فَصَلِّ عَلىٰ سَيِّدِي وَ مَوْلَايَ صَلَاةً تَرْفَــعُ بِهَا ذِكْرَهُ، وَ تُظْهِــرُ بِهَا أَمْرَهُ، وَ تُعَجِّلُ بِهَا نَــصْرَهُ، وَ اخْصُصْهُ بِأَفْضَلِ قِسَمِ الْفَضَائِلِ يَوْمَ الْقِيَامَةِ، وَ زِدْهُ شَرَفًا فِي أَعْلىٰ عِلِّيِّــينَ، وَ بَلِّغْــهُ أَعْلىٰ شَرَفِ الْمُكَرَّمِينَ، وَ ارْفَعْهُ مِنْ شَرَفِ رَحْمَتِكَ فِي شَرَفِ الْمُقَرَّبِــينَ فِي الرَّفِيعِ الْأَعْلىٰ، وَ بَلِّغْهُ الْوَسِــيلَةَ، وَ الْمَنْزِلَةَ الْجَلِيلَةَ، وَ الْفَضْلَ وَ الْفَضِيلَةَ، وَ الْكَرَامَةَ الْجَزِيلَةَ.

O Allah, reward him on our behalf with the best of rewards You have granted to an leader on behalf of his followers, and bless my master and guardian whenever his name is mentioned and when not mentioned!

اَللّٰهُــمَّ فَاجْزِهِ عَنَّا أَفْضَــلَ مَا جَازَيْتَ إِمَامًا عَنْ رَعِيَّتِهِ، وَ صَلِّ عَلىٰ سَــيِّدِي وَ مَوْلَايَ كُلَّمَا ذُكِرَ وَ كُلَّمَا لَمْ يُذْكَرْ.

My master and guardian, admit me into your party and camp, and secure my pardon from your Lord and mine, for you have such an eminence, worth and exalted station with Allah that He will grant whatever You ask and your inter-

يَــا سَــيِّدِي وَ مَــوْلَايَ أَدْخِلْــنِي فِي حِزْبِــكَ وَ زُمْرَتِكَ، وَ اسْــتَوْهِبْنِي مِنْ رَبِّكَ وَ رَبِّي، فَإِنَّ لَــكَ عِنْدَ اللهِ جَاهًا وَ قَــدْرًا وَ مَنْزِلَةً رَفِيعَةً، إِنْ سَــأَلْتَ

أُعْطِيتَ، وَ إِنْ شَفَعْتَ شُفِّعْتَ .

cession will be accepted.

اَللهَ اَللهَ فِي عَبْدِكَ وَ مَوْلَاكَ، لَا تُخَلِّنِي
عِنْدَ الشَّدَائِدِ وَ الْأَهْوَالِ لِسُوءِ عَمَلِي
وَ قَبِيحِ فِعْلِي وَ عَظِيمِ جُرْمِى، فَإِنَّكَ
أَمَلِي وَ رَجَائِى، وَ ثِقَتِي وَ مُعْتَمَدِى، وَ
وَسِيلَتِي إِلَى اللهِ رَبِّي وَ رَبِّكَ، لَمْ يَتَوَسَّلِ
الْمُتَوَسِّلُونَ إِلَى اللهِ بِوَسِيلَةٍ هِيَ أَعْظَمُ
حَقًّا وَ لَا أَوْجَبُ حُرْمَةً وَ لَا أَجَلُّ قَدْرًا
عِنْدَهُ مِنْكُمْ أَهْلَ الْبَيْتِ،

For God's sake, remember this servant and friend of yours! Do not abandon me in the distress and fear I face on account of my evil conduct, ugly deeds and my great offences! For you are my hope, my expectation, my trust, reliance and my mediator with Allah, my Lord and yours! The seekers of mediation with God have never sought mediation with anyone with a greater right, a more compelling honour and a greater worth than yours, O Family of the Prophet, with Him!

لَا خَلَّفَنِيَ اللهُ عَنْكُمْ بِذُنُوبِي، وَ جَمَعَنِي
وَ إِيَّاكُمْ فِي جَنَّةِ عَدْنٍ الَّتِي أَعَدَّهَا
لَكُمْ وَ لِأَوْلِيَائِكُمْ، إِنَّهُ خَيْرُ الْغَافِرِينَ
وَ أَرْحَمُ الرَّاحِمِينَ .

May Allah not separate me from you on account of my sins, and may He gather me with you in the gardens of Eden that He has prepared for you and your friends! Indeed He is the Best of those who forgive, and the Most Merciful of the merciful!

اَللّٰهُمَّ أَبْلِغْ سَيِّدِى وَ مَوْلَاىَ تَحِيَّةً كَثِيرَةً
وَ سَلَامًا، وَ ارْدُدْ عَلَيْنَا مِنْهُ السَّلَامَ،
إِنَّكَ جَوَادٌ كَرِيمٌ، وَ صَلِّ عَلَيْهِ كُلَّمَا ذُكِرَ
السَّلَامُ وَ كُلَّمَا لَمْ يُذْكَرْ، يَا رَبَّ الْعَالَمِينَ.

O Allah, convey to my master and guardian profuse greetings of 'Peace' and convey their response to us. Indeed You are generous and munificent. Bless him whenever 'Peace' is mentioned, and when not mentioned, O Lord of all the worlds!

At the end of this Book, we have cited texts of *ṣalawāt* to be pronounced for each of the Infallible Ones (*ʿa*), including a brief *ṣalawāt* for Imam al-Ḥusayn (*ʿa*) (p. 550). Its recitation should not be neglected.

(15) Among observances special to this shrine is for victims of

wrongdoing to pray against their oppressors. That is, it is desirable for the distressed victims to supplicate in this shrine against the authors of injustice. That supplication has been cited by Shaykh Ṭūsī in *Miṣbāḥ al-Mutjhajjid*[1] among observances of Friday, with the remark that it is preferable to recite it at the graveside of Imam Abū ᶜAbdillāh al-Ḥusayn (*ᶜa*). The supplication is as follows.

اَللّٰهُمَّ إِنِّي أَعْتَزُّ بِدِينِكَ، وَ أَكْرُمُ بِهِدَايَتِكَ، وَ فُلَانٌ يُذِلُّنِي بِشَرِّهِ، وَ يُهِينُنِي بِأَذِيَّتِهِ، وَ يُعِيبُنِي بِوَلَاءِ أَوْلِيَائِكَ، وَ يَبْهَتُنِي بِدَعْوَاهُ، وَ قَدْ جِئْتُ إِلَى مَوْضِعِ الدُّعَاءِ وَ ضَمَانِكَ الْإِجَابَةَ، اَللّٰهُمَّ صَلِّ عَلَىٰ مُحَمَّدٍ وَ آلِ مُحَمَّدٍ، وَ أَعْدِنِي عَلَيْهِ، اَلسَّاعَةَ، اَلسَّاعَةَ.

O Allah, I have been honoured by Your religion and granted dignity with Your guidance, and so-and-so humiliates me with his evil and insults me with his torments. He finds fault with me for befriending Your friends and stuns me with his allegations. I have come to this hub of supplication where You have guaranteed to answer it. O Allah, bless Muḥammad and the Family of Muḥammad and grant me victory over him at this very hour!

Then throwing yourself on the grave, say

مَوْلَايَ إِمَامِي، مَظْلُومٌ اسْتَعْدَىٰ عَلَىٰ ظَالِمِهِ، اَلنَّصْرَ اَلنَّصْرَ.

My master and Imam! I have been wronged and seek your help against him who has wronged me. Help me! Help me!

Continue saying "*an-naṣr*" for a full breath.

(16) Among the observances pertaining to this shrine is a supplication of Imam Jaᶜfar al-Ṣādiq (*ᶜa*) cited by Ibn Fahd (*r*) in *ᶜUddat al-Dāᶜī*.[2] The Imam has advised those who want God to fulfil any of their needs to say the following supplication while standing at the head of Imam al-Ḥusayn's graveside. God willing, their petition will be granted.

يَا أَبَا عَبْدِ اللّٰهِ، أَشْهَدُ أَنَّكَ تَشْهَدُ مَقَامِي وَ تَسْمَعُ كَلَامِي، وَ أَنَّكَ حَيٌّ عِنْدَ رَبِّكَ

O Abū ᶜAbdillāh! I testify that you see me standing here and hear my speech, and that you are

1 Ṭūsī's *Miṣbāḥ*, 279, whence *Biḥār*, lxxxvi, 306, b 3, h 11; xcviii, 285, b 23.

2 *ᶜUddah*, 64, whence *Mustadrak*, x, 345, b 59, h 12149/1.

living near Your Lord, provided by Him. Ask your Lord and mine to fulfil my needs!	تُرْزَقُ، فَاسْأَلْ رَبَّكَ وَ رَبِّي فِي قَضَاءِ حَوَائِجِي.

(17) Among observances pertaining to this shrine is a two-*rak*ᶜ*ah* prayer at the head of the holy graveside with *sūrahs* al-Raḥmān and al-Mulk. Ibn Ṭāwūs reports[1] that for those who perform this prayer, God, the All-munificent, will write a reward equal to that of twenty-five *ḥajj* pilgrimages performed in the company of the Apostle of Allah (*ṣ*).

(18) A practice associated with this shrine is that of *istikhārah* (lit. seeking something which is good, expedient and advisable from God). ᶜAllāmah Majlisī has described the manner of its performance on the basis of a report cited in Ḥimyarī's *Qurb al-Isnād* with a *ṣaḥīḥ* chain of authorities from Imam Jaᶜfar al-Ṣādiq (ᶜ*a*).[2] Anyone seeking divine counsel concerning the best course of action in a matter should stand at the head of Imam al-Ḥusayn's graveside and say,

All praise belongs to Allah. There is no god other than Allah. May glory be to Allah!	و الْحَمْدُ لِلّٰهِ وَ لَا إِلٰهَ إِلَّا اللّٰهُ وَ سُبْحَانَ اللّٰهِ.

Then, after glorifying God and praising Him in a manner worthy of Him, he should beseech Him a hundred times to guide him to the best course of action so that Almighty God may show him what is advisable for him to do in the matter. According to other reports,[3] while seeking Divine guidance one should say a hundred times,

I ask Allah to guide me with His mercy to the best choice in keeping with welfare.	أَسْتَخِيرُ اللّٰهَ بِرَحْمَتِهِ خِيَرَةً فِي عَافِيَةٍ.

(19) The perfect shaykh Abul Qāsim Jaᶜfar ibn Qūlawayh (*r*) reports[4] that Imam Jaᶜfar al-Ṣādiq (ᶜ*a*) said, "When you visit the shrine

1 *Miṣbāḥ al-Zā'ir*, 531.

2 *Qurb al-Isnād*, 28, whence *Wasā'il*, viii, 83, b 9, h 10140, *Biḥār*, lxxxviii, 260, b 7, h 9; xcviii, 285, b 23, h 1.

3 *Kāfī*, iii, 470, h 3. *Faqīh*, i, 562, h 1552. *Muqni*ᶜ*ah*, 219, b 29. Ṭūsī's *Miṣbāḥ*, 534. *Tahdhīb*, iii, 181, b 16, h 6. *Makārim*, 322. *Fatḥ al-Abwāb*, 181, 184, 187, 286, 298. Kafᶜamī's *Miṣbāḥ*, 390. 392. *Balad*, 159, 160.

4 *Kāmil al-Ziyārāt*, 86, b 29, h 16, whence *Biḥār*, xlv, 224, b 41, h 17.

of Abū ᶜAbdillāh (ᶜa), keep silent unless it is for some good purpose. Indeed the guardian angels of day and night meet the resident angels of the shrine and greet them. But their severe grief and mourning keep them from answering them. So they wait until noontime or until the time of daybreak when they can talk with them and question them concerning things pertaining to the matters of the heaven. But between these times they do not speak and their mourning and supplication do not cease."

The Imam is also reported[1] to have said that God Almighty sends four-thousand angels to the shrine of Imam al-Ḥusayn (ᶜa), who arrive there dusty and dishevelled, like persons in deep mourning, and mourn for him from daybreak until noon. At noon, these four thousand ascend to heaven and another four thousand angels descend and mourn him until daybreak. There are many traditions which mention this. These reports show that weeping for the Imam in his holy shrine and mourning him and reciting elegies is a desirable thing to do, and may justifiably be considered one of the observances of that blessed shrine, which is the house of mourning for his followers.

A report[2] narrated by Ṣafwān from Imam Jaᶜfar al-Ṣādiq (ᶜa) shows that the supplications of the angels and their entreaties before God condemning those who killed the Commander of the Faithful (ᶜa) and those who slew Imam al-Ḥusayn (ᶜa), the weeping of the angels gathered around the Imam's grave, and the lamentations of the jinn for his sake and the severity of their grief are such that if someone were to hear them, he will be so profoundly upset that he will find it hard to eat and drink anything and will be unable to rest and sleep.

It is mentioned in a report narrated by ᶜAbd Allāh b. Ḥammād al-Baṣrī[3] that Imam Jaᶜfar al-Ṣādiq (ᶜa) said to him, "I have heard that some people from the region surrounding Kūfah and others come to his shrine and the women wail for him and that this happens during the middle of the month of Shaᶜbān. Some of them recite the Qur'ān, some recount the episodes of the martyrs, some mourn and bewail him, and some recite elegies." The reporter says, "I said to him, 'Yes, I have myself seen some of what you describe.' " The Imam said, "May

1 *Kāmil al-Ziyārāt*, 85, 191, b 27, h 11, b77, h 6, whence *Biḥār*, xlv, 223, b 41, h 15, xcviii, 56, b 9, h 22 & *Mustadrak*, x, 243, b 26, h 11935/25.

2 *Kāmil al-Ziyārāt*, 92, 297, b 28, h 18, b 98, h 17, whence *Biḥār*, xcviii, 14, b 2, h 14. *Durūᶜ*, 74, faṣl 20.

3 *Kāmil al-Ziyārāt*, 324, b 108, h 1, whence *Biḥār*, xcviii, 73, b 10, h 21 & *Mustadrak*, x, 251, b 26, h 11952/42.

Allah be praised, who has appointed from among the people those who visit us, pay tribute to us, recite elegies for us, and appointed others from among our kinsmen and others, who discredit them, shed their blood with impunity (or, according to another reading, 'ridicule them') and condemn them for what they do."

At the beginning of this tradition, the Imam remarks concerning Imam al-Ḥusayn (ʿ*a*), "He was martyred as a stranger in an alien land. Those who visit him bewail him. Those who have not visited his shrine grieve for him. Those who have not met him are pained for his sake, and those who see his son's grave at the foot of his tomb feel pity for him. He was martyred in the wilderness without any friend or kindred, and denied his rights. The apostates supported one another against him until they slew him, stripped him and left his body for the animals of the wild, after they had withheld from him the water of the Euphrates from which even dogs drink freely, disregarding the rights of the Apostle of Allah and his exhortations concerning him and his family."

Ibn Qūlawayh also cites a report of al-Ḥāri<u>th</u> al-Aʿwar[1] which describes the Commander of the Faithful (ʿ*a*) as having said, "May my father and mother be the ransom of al-Ḥusayn, who will be martyred in a land beyond Kūfah. By God, it is as if I see the animals of the wild stretching their necks on his grave, bewailing and lamenting him day and night. When that happens, beware lest you should be found lacking in your considerateness towards him." There are many traditions on this subject.

(20) Sayyid Ibn Ṭāwūs (*r*) says[2] that when one wishes to leave the shrine after finishing the Imam's *ziyārah*, it is desirable to embrace the *ḍarīḥ* and say,

Peace be to you, my master! Peace be to you, O Allah's testament! Peace be to you, O Allah's chosen friend. Peace be to you, O Allah's favourite servant! Peace be to you, who were slain thirsty!

اَلسَّلامُ عَلَيْكَ يا مَوْلايَ، اَلسَّلامُ عَلَيْكَ
يا حُجَّةَ اللهِ، اَلسَّلامُ عَلَيْكَ يا صَفْوَةَ
اللهِ، اَلسَّلامُ عَلَيْكَ يا خالِصَةَ اللهِ،
اَلسَّلامُ عَلَيْكَ يا قَتِيلَ الظَّماءِ،

1 *Kāmil al-Ziyārāt*, 79, b 26, h 3, 291, b 77, h 3, whence *Biḥār*, xcviii, 6, b 1, h 23 & *Mustadrak*, x, 358, b 27, h 11965/5.

2 Ṭusī's *Miṣbāḥ*, 723. *Iqbāl*, 714, whence *Biḥār*, xcviii, 230, b 18, h 36. Also cited in *Biḥār*, xcviii, 268, b 18, h 42, from "an old manuscript."

Peace be to you, the most forlorn of the estranged!	اَلسَّلامُ عَلَيْكَ يا غَرِيبَ الْغُرَباءِ،
Peace be to you from one who departs, though not from boredom or dissatisfaction. If I leave, it is not due to weariness, and if I stay on it will not be due to distrust in the promise that Allah has given to the patient.	اَلسَّلامُ عَلَيْكَ سَلامَ مُوَدِّعٍ لا سَئِمٍ وَ لا قالٍ، فَإِنْ أَمْضِ فَلا عَنْ مَلالَةٍ، وَ إِنْ أُقِمْ فَلا عَنْ سُوءِ ظَنٍّ بِما وَعَدَ اللهُ الصّابِرِينَ،
May Allah not make this my last opportunity of performing your *ziyārah*, and may He grant me to return into your presence, to stand in your courtyard and tarry in your shrine, and Him do I beseech to grant me felicity through you, and to grant me your company in the world and the Hereafter!	لا جَعَلَهُ اللهُ آخِرَ الْعَهْدِ مِنِّي لِزِيارَتِكَ، وَ رَزَقَنِيَ اللهُ الْعَوْدَ إِلىٰ مَشْهَدِكَ، وَ الْمَقامَ بِفِنائِكَ، وَ الْقِيامَ فِي حَرَمِكَ، وَ إِيّاهُ أَسْأَلُ أَنْ يُسْعِدَنِي بِكُمْ، وَ يَجْعَلَنِي مَعَكُمْ فِي الدُّنْيا وَ الْآخِرَةِ.

Section Three

Ziyarah of Imam al-Ḥusayn and Ḥadrat ᶜAbbas

The *ziyārahs* prescribed by tradition for Imam al-Ḥusayn (ᶜ*a*) are of two kinds: those which are general, not meant for any special occasion, and those which are for specific days. These are cited in the following three sub-sections.

General Ziyārahs of Imām al-Ḥusayn (ᶜ*a*)

There are many of them and here we shall cite some.

The First Ziyarah

Shaykh Kulayni cites with his *isnād* a report[1] of al-Ḥusayn b. Thuwayr, who says,

"I, Yūnus b. Ẓabyān, Mufaḍḍal b. ᶜUmar and Abū Salamah al-Sarrāj

[1] *Kāfī*, iv, 575. h 2, whence *Wasā'il*, xiv, 490, b 62, h 19672 & *Wāfī*, xiv, 1485, b 190, h 114575. *Kāmil al-Ziyārāt*, 80, b 26, h 3, 197, b 79, h 2, whence *Biḥār*, xcviii, 151, b 18, h 3. *Faqīh*, ii, 594-598, h 3199. *Tahdhīb*, vi, 55, b 18, h 1.

were seated in the presence of Abū ᶜAbdillāh (Jaᶜfar ibn Muḥammad) (ᶜa). Yūnus, who was the most senior among us, spoke. He said to the Imam, 'You are dearer to me than my own life. At times I attend the gatherings of those people (meaning the ᶜAbbāsids). What should I say?' The Imam said to him, 'When you are present in their gatherings and you remember us, say, "O Allah, show us times of ease and delight!" And indeed you will obtain what you desire.'

Then Yūnus said, 'I often remember al-Ḥusayn, peace be to him. What should I say at such times?' The Imam replied, 'Say, *Ṣallal·lāhu ᶜalayka yâ Abā ᶜAbdillāh* (May Allah bless you, O Abū ᶜAbdillāh!), and repeat it three times, for indeed your greeting reaches him from far and near.' Then he added, 'When Abū ᶜAbdillāh al-Ḥusayn passed away, he was mourned by the seven heavens and the seven earths and whatever is in them and between them, as well as by the creatures of our Lord who inhabit paradise and hell, and those of them which are visible and those who are invisible. All of them wept over Abū ᶜAbdillāh al-Ḥusayn (ᶜa) except three, which did not feel sorrow for him.' 'What were they?' asked Yūnus. 'Those who did not feel sorrow for him were (the people of) Baṣrah and Damascus and the partisans (*shīᶜah*) of ᶜUthmān, may Allah condemn them.'

Yūnus said to the Imam, 'I intend to visit his tomb. What should I do, and what should I say?' The Imam replied, 'When you arrive at the shrine of Abū ᶜAbdillāh, take bath on the bank of the Euphrates and put on your clean clothes. Then set out barefooted, for there you are within one of the sanctuaries of Allah and His Apostle. As you walk, say a lot *Allāhu akbar, Lâ ilāha illal·lāh, Subḥānallāh* and *Alḥamdu lillāh*, and glorify and magnify God and invoke His blessings on Muḥammad and his Family, till you reach the gate of the shrine. On reaching the gate, say,

اَلسَّلامُ عَلَيْكَ يا حُجَّةَ اللهِ وَ ابْنَ حُجَّتِهِ، اَلسَّلامُ عَلَيْكُمْ يا مَلائِكَةَ اللهِ وَ زُوّارَ قَبْرِ ابْنِ نَبِيِّ اللهِ

Peace be to you, O testament of Allah and son of His testament! Peace be to you O Angels of Allah and pilgrims to the grave of the son of Allah's Prophet!

Then take ten steps and stop, and say thirty times *Allāhu akbar!* Then approach the tomb, facing the grave and with the *qiblah* to your rear.

Then say,[1]

Peace be to you, O Allah's testament and son of His testament! Peace be to you, O Allah's martyr and son of His martyr! Peace be to you, O slain one whose avenger is Allah, son of him whose avenger is Allah! Peace be to you, O slain one whose slaying aggrieved Allah and retribution for whose blood is sought by the denizens of the heavens and the earth!

اَلسَّلامُ عَلَيْكَ يا حُجَّةَ اللهِ وَ ابْنَ حُجَّتِهِ، اَلسَّلامُ عَلَيْكَ يا قَتِيلَ اللهِ وَ ابْنَ قَتِيلِهِ، اَلسَّلامُ عَلَيْكَ يا ثارَ اللهِ وَ ابْنَ ثارِهِ، اَلسَّلامُ عَلَيْكَ يا وِتْرَ اللهِ الْمَوْتُورَ فِي السَّماواتِ وَ الْأَرْضِ،

I testify that your blood settled in paradise making the canopies of God's Throne tremble, and that all the creation wept on its account, the seven heavens and the seven earths and whatever is in them and all that is between them, and all creatures of our Lord that dwell in the heaven and hell the visible and the invisible!

أَشْهَدُ أَنَّ دَمَكَ سَكَنَ فِي الْخُلْدِ، وَ اقْشَعَرَّتْ لَهُ أَظِلَّةُ الْعَرْشِ، وَ بَكى لَهُ جَمِيعُ الْخَلائِقِ، وَ بَكَتْ لَهُ السَّماواتُ السَّبْعُ وَ الْأَرَضُونَ السَّبْعُ، وَ ما فِيهِنَّ وَ ما بَيْنَهُنَّ، وَ مَنْ يَتَقَلَّبُ فِي الْجَنَّةِ وَ النّارِ مِنْ خَلْقِ رَبِّنا، وَ ما يُرى وَ ما لا يُرى،

I testify that you are the testament of Allah, son of His testament, and affirm that you and your father were slain in the way of Allah. I testify that you are the slain one whose avenger is Allah, son of him whose avenger is Allah! I testify that your slaying has aggrieved Allah, and retribution for your unavenged blood is sought by the denizens of the heavens and the earth!

أَشْهَدُ أَنَّكَ حُجَّةُ اللهِ وَ ابْنُ حُجَّتِهِ، وَ أَشْهَدُ أَنَّكَ قَتِيلُ اللهِ وَ ابْنُ قَتِيلِهِ، وَ أَشْهَدُ أَنَّكَ ثارُ اللهِ وَ ابْنُ ثارِهِ، وَ أَشْهَدُ أَنَّكَ وِتْرُ اللهِ الْمَوْتُورُ فِي السَّماواتِ وَ الْأَرْضِ،

I testify that you delivered all that you were charged with, were committed to the good of the *um-*

وَ أَشْهَدُ أَنَّكَ قَدْ بَلَّغْتَ وَ نَصَحْتَ، وَ وَفَيْتَ وَ أَوْفَيْتَ، وَ جاهَدْتَ فِي

[1] See *Biḥār*, xcviii, 154-157 for ᶜAllāmah Majlisī's exposition of the difficult phrases of this *ziyārah*.

سَبِيلِ اللهِ، وَ مَضَيْتَ لِلَّذِى كُنْتَ عَلَيْهِ شَهِيدًا وَ مُسْتَشْهِدًا وَ شَاهِدًا وَ مَشْهُودًا،

mah, discharged your obligations, lived fully up to your covenant, waged *jihād* in the way of Allah, and departed while upholding what you affirmed in life, as a martyr and witness standing in full view of all witnesses!

أَنَا عَبْدُ اللهِ وَ مَوْلَاكَ وَ فِى طَاعَتِكَ وَ الْوَافِدُ إِلَيْكَ، أَلْتَمِسُ كَمَالَ الْمَنْزِلَةِ عِنْدَ اللهِ، وَ ثَبَاتَ الْقَدَمِ فِى الْهِجْرَةِ إِلَيْكَ، وَ السَّبِيلَ الَّذِى لَا يَخْتَلِجُ دُونَكَ مِنَ الدُّخُولِ فِى كِفَالَتِكَ الَّتِى أُمِرْتَ بِهَا،

I am a servant of Allah and your protégé, committed to obeying you. I have come to you, seeking a perfect standing with Allah, a steadfastness in my journey towards you and on the path that would not keep me away from you and from entering your tutelage, which you have been charged with.

مَنْ أَرَادَ اللهَ بَدَأَ بِكُمْ، بِكُمْ يُبَيِّنُ اللهُ الْكَذِبَ، وَ بِكُمْ يُبَاعِدُ اللهُ الزَّمَانَ الْكَلِبَ، وَبِكُمْ فَتَحَ اللهُ، وَبِكُمْ يَخْتِمُ اللهُ، وَ بِكُمْ يَمْحُو مَا يَشَاءُ وَ يُثْبِتُ،

Whoever seeks Allah, starts with you. It is by your means that Allah exposes falsehoods and He shields His servants from the harassments of the times. Allah began with you and with you shall Allah conclude, and by your means He effaces or confirms whatever He wishes.

وَ بِكُمْ يَفُكُّ الذُّلَّ مِنْ رِقَابِنَا، وَ بِكُمْ يُدْرِكُ اللهُ تِرَةَ كُلِّ مُؤْمِنٍ يُطْلَبُ بِهَا، وَ بِكُمْ تُنْبِتُ الْأَرْضُ أَشْجَارَهَا، وَ بِكُمْ تُخْرِجُ الْأَرْضُ ثِمَارَهَا، وَ بِكُمْ تُنْزِلُ السَّمَاءُ قَطْرَهَا وَ رِزْقَهَا،

It is by your means that He delivers us from weakness and humiliation and by your means Allah makes it possible to avenge the wrongs done to every faithful person. It is by your means that the earth grows its vegetation and produces its fruits. It is by your means that the sky sends down its rain and provision.

وَ بِكُمْ يَكْشِفُ اللهُ الْكَرْبَ، وَ بِكُمْ يُنَزِّلُ اللهُ الْغَيْثَ، وَ بِكُمْ

It is by your means that Allah removes all distress and it is by your means that Allah sends the rains. It is by your means that the earth, which bears your bodies, glorifies Allah, and the mountains remain fixed to their anchors.

تُسَبِّحُ الْأَرْضُ الَّتِي تَحْمِلُ أَبْدَانَكُمْ، وَ تَسْتَقِرُّ جِبَالُهَا عَنْ مَرَاسِيهَا،

The will of the Lord in ordaining His affairs descends to you and issues from your houses, issuing as elaborated rules for the servants. Accursed be the people who slew you, those who opposed you, those who contested your authority, those who backed one another against you, and those who were present but would not submit to martyrdom.

إِرَادَةُ الرَّبِّ فِي مَقَادِيرِ أُمُورِهِ تَهْبِطُ إِلَيْكُمْ، وَ تَصْدُرُ مِنْ بُيُوتِكُمْ، وَ الصَّادِرُ عَمَّا فُصِّلَ مِنْ أَحْكَامِ الْعِبَادِ، لُعِنَتْ أُمَّةٌ قَتَلَتْكُمْ، وَ أُمَّةٌ خَالَفَتْكُمْ، وَ أُمَّةٌ جَحَدَتْ وِلَايَتَكُمْ، وَ أُمَّةٌ ظَاهَرَتْ عَلَيْكُمْ، وَ أُمَّةٌ شَهِدَتْ وَ لَمْ تُسْتَشْهَدْ.

All praise belongs to Allah, who has made hellfire their abode, an evil goal for the incoming and an evil abode for those who enter. All praise belongs to Allah, the Lord of all the worlds!

اَلْحَمْدُ لِلهِ الَّذِي جَعَلَ النَّارَ مَأْوَاهُمْ، وَ بِئْسَ وِرْدُ الْوَارِدِينَ وَ بِئْسَ الْوِرْدُ الْمَوْرُودُ، وَ الْحَمْدُ لِلهِ رَبِّ الْعَالَمِينَ .

Then say thrice,

May Allah bless you, O Abū ᶜAbd Allāh!

وَ صَلَّى اللهُ عَلَيْكَ يَا أَبَا عَبْدِ اللهِ.

And say thrice,

I repudiate before Allah those who opposed you!

أَنَا إِلَى اللهِ مِمَّنْ خَالَفَكَ بَرِيءٌ.

Then approach the grave of his son, ᶜAlī ibn al-Ḥusayn (ᶜa), who is buried at his father's feet, and say three times,

Peace be to you, O son of the Apostle of Allah! Peace be to you, O son of the Commander of the Faithful! Peace be to you,

اَلسَّلَامُ عَلَيْكَ يَا ابْنَ رَسُولِ، اللهِ، اَلسَّلَامُ عَلَيْكَ يَا ابْنَ أَمِيرِ الْمُؤْمِنِينَ، اَلسَّلَامُ

O son of al-Ḥasan and al-Ḥusayn! Peace be to you, O son of Khadījah and Fāṭimah! May Allah bless you! May Allah bless you! May Allah bless you! May Allah curse those who slew you!

عَلَيْــكَ يَا ابْنَ الْحَسَــنِ وَ الْحُسَــيْنِ، اَلسَّلَامُ عَلَيْكَ يَا ابْنَ خَدِيجَةَ وَ فَاطِمَةَ، صَــلَّى اللهُ عَلَيْكَ، صَــلَّى اللهُ عَلَيْكَ، صَلَّى اللهُ عَلَيْكَ، لَعَنَ اللهُ مَنْ قَتَلَكَ.

Say the last sentence three times. Then say thrice,

I repudiate them before Allah!

أَنَا إِلَى اللهِ مِنْهُمْ بَرِيءٌ

Then get up and pointing with the hand towards the grave of the martyrs— may Allah be pleased with them—say,

Peace be to you! Peace be to you! Peace be to you! By Allah, you triumphed! By Allah, you were triumphant! By Allah, you were triumphant! I wish I had been with you and attained such a great triumph!

اَلسَّــلَامُ عَلَيْكُمْ، اَلسَّلَامُ عَلَيْكُمْ، اَلسَّلَامُ عَلَيْكُمْ، فُزْتُمْ وَ اللهِ، فُزْتُمْ وَ اللهِ، فُزْتُــمْ وَ اللهِ، فَلَيْتَ أَنِّي مَعَكُمْ فَأَفُوزَ فَوْزًا عَظِيمًا.

Then moving back to the rear of the tomb offer six *rakᶜahs* of prayer facing the tomb of Abū ᶜAbdillāh (*ᶜa*). Having done it, you will have got through with the *ziyārah*, after which one can return if one wishes to do so.

This *ziyārah* has also been cited by Shaykh Ṭūsī in the *Tahdhīb* and by Shaykh Ṣadūq in *Man lā yaḥḍuruh al-Faqīh*. Shaykh Ṣadūq remarks, "I have cited various *ziyārahs* in my book on the topic of *mazār* and *maqtal*, and have chosen this *ziyārah* for this book, because it is the most reliable of them from the viewpoint of transmission and is sufficient for our purpose."[1]

The Second Ziyarah

Shaykh Kulaynī cites a report[2] that describes Imam ᶜAlī al-Naqi (*ᶜa*) as having said, "When visiting the shrine of al-Ḥusayn (*ᶜa*), say,

1 *Faqīh*, ii, 598.

2 *Kāfī*, iv, 577, h 3. *Kāmil al-Ziyārāt*, 209, h 7, whence *Biḥār*, xcviii, 172, b 18, h 26. *Tahdhīb*, vi, 114, h 18. Kafᶜamī's *Miṣbāḥ*, 498. *Balad*, 287.

اَلسَّلَامُ عَلَيْكَ يَا أَبَا عَبْدِ اللهِ، اَلسَّلَامُ
عَلَيْكَ يَا حُجَّةَ اللهِ فِي أَرْضِهِ، وَ شَاهِدَهُ
عَلَى خَلْقِهِ، اَلسَّلَامُ عَلَيْكَ يَا ابْنَ رَسُولِ
اللهِ، اَلسَّلَامُ عَلَيْكَ يَا ابْنَ عَلِيٍّ الْمُرْتَضَى،
اَلسَّلَامُ عَلَيْكَ يَا ابْنَ فَاطِمَةَ الزَّهْرَاءِ.

Peace be to you, O Abū ʿAbdillāh! Peace be to you, O Allah's testament on His earth and His witness to His creation! Peace be to you, O son of the Apostle of Allah! Peace be to you, O son of ʿAlī al-Murtaḍā! Peace be to you, O son of Fāṭimah Zahrā!

أَشْهَدُ أَنَّكَ قَدْ أَقَمْتَ الصَّلَاةَ، وَ آتَيْتَ
الزَّكَاةَ، وَ أَمَرْتَ بِالْمَعْرُوفِ، وَ نَهَيْتَ عَنِ
الْمُنْكَرِ، وَ جَاهَدْتَ فِي سَبِيلِ اللهِ حَتَّى
أَتَاكَ الْيَقِينُ، فَصَلَّى اللهُ عَلَيْكَ حَيًّا وَ مَيِّتًا.

I testify that you maintained the prayer, paid the *zakāt*, bade what is right and forbade what is wrong, and that you waged *jihād* in the way of Allah until your demise! So may Allah bless you, in life and death!

Then placing the right cheek on the grave, say,

أَشْهَدُ أَنَّكَ عَلَى بَيِّنَةٍ مِنْ رَبِّكَ، جِئْتُ
مُقِرًّا بِالذُّنُوبِ لِتَشْفَعَ لِي عِنْدَ رَبِّكَ يَا
ابْنَ رَسُولِ اللهِ.

I bear witness that you stood on a clear proof from your Lord! I come to you confessing my sins, that you may intercede for me with Allah, your Lord, O son of the Apostle of Allah!

Then mention each of the Imams by their names, and say,

أَشْهَدُ أَنَّكُمْ حُجَجُ اللهِ.

I testify that you are the testaments of Allah!

Then say,

أُكْتُبْ لِي عِنْدَكَ مِيثَاقًا وَ عَهْدًا إِنِّي
أَتَيْتُكَ مُجَدِّدًا الْمِيثَاقَ، فَاشْهَدْ لِي عِنْدَ
رَبِّكَ إِنَّكَ أَنْتَ الشَّاهِدُ.

Record my covenant and pledge with you. I have come to you to renew my covenant. So be my witness with Allah, for you are indeed an arch witness!

The Third Ziyarah

This is a short *ziyārah* cited by Sayyid Ibn Ṭāwūs in his *Miṣbāḥ al-Zā'ir* on the authority of Jābir b. Yazīd al-Juᶜfī from Imam Jaᶜfar al-Ṣādiq (ᶜ*a*), and many virtues are ascribed to it in the tradition.[1] In this report, the Imam asks Jābir, "How far is the grave of al-Ḥusayn (ᶜ*a*) from your place?" Jabir replies, "A day's journey and odd." "Do you visit him?" asks the Imam. "Yes, I do," replies Jābir. "Shall I gladden you with a description of some of its rewards?" "Yes," says Jābir, "May I be your ransom"

"When one of you prepares to visit his shrine, the denizens of the heaven spread around its good news among themselves, and when he emerges from his home, mounted or on foot, God appoints four thousand of His angels who keep on blessing him until he reaches the tomb of al-Ḥusayn (ᶜ*a*)."

Then the Imam describes the manner of performing the *ziyārah* as follows. "When you arrive at the tomb of al-Ḥusayn ibn ᶜAlī (ᶜ*a*), stop at the door and say these words, for each of which you will receive a portion of Divine mercy":

اَلسَّــلَامُ عَلَيْكَ يَا وَارِثَ آدَمَ صَفْوَةِ اللهِ،
اَلسَّــلَامُ عَلَيْكَ يَا وَارِثَ نُوحٍ نَبِيِّ اللهِ،
اَلسَّلَامُ عَلَيْكَ يَا وَارِثَ إِبْرَاهِيمَ خَلِيلِ اللهِ،
اَلسَّلَامُ عَلَيْكَ يَا وَارِثَ مُوسَىٰ كَلِيمِ اللهِ،
اَلسَّلَامُ عَلَيْكَ يَا وَارِثَ عِيسَىٰ رُوحِ اللهِ،

Peace be to you, O heir of Adam, Allah's chosen! Peace be to you, O heir of Noah, Allah's prophet! Peace be to you, O heir of Abraham, Allah's dedicated friend! Peace be to you, O heir of Moses, Allah's interlocutor! Peace be to you, O heir of Jesus, spirit of Allah!

اَلسَّلَامُ عَلَيْكَ يَا وَارِثَ مُحَمَّدٍ سَيِّدِ رُسُلِ اللهِ،
اَلسَّلَامُ عَلَيْكَ يَا وَارِثَ عَلِيٍّ أَمِيرِ الْمُؤْمِنِينَ
وَ خَيْرِ الْوَصِيِّينَ، اَلسَّلَامُ عَلَيْكَ يَا وَارِثَ
الْحَسَــنِ الرَّضِيِّ الطَّاهِرِ الرَّاضِي الْمَرْضِيِّ.

Peace be to you, O heir of Muḥammad, chief of God's apostles! Peace be to you, O heir of ᶜAlī, the Commander of the Faithful and the best of the Legatees! Peace be to you, O heir of al-Ḥasan, (Allah's) approved one, the pure one, pleased with Allah and pleasing to Him!

اَلسَّــلَامُ عَلَيْكَ أَيُّهَا الصِّدِّيقُ الْأَكْبَرُ،

Peace be to you, O most truth-

[1] *Biḥār*, xcviii, 229, 18, h 36 from *Miṣbāḥ al-Zā'ir*, 252.

اَلسَّلَامُ عَلَيْكَ أَيُّهَا الْوَصِيُّ الْبَرُّ التَّقِيُّ، اَلسَّلَامُ عَلَيْكَ وَ عَلَى الْأَرْوَاحِ الَّتِي حَلَّتْ بِفِنَائِكَ، وَ أَنَاخَتْ بِرَحْلِكَ، اَلسَّلَامُ عَلَيْكَ وَ عَلَى الْمَلَائِكَةِ الْحَافِّينَ بِكَ،

ful one! Peace be to you, O pious and Godwary legatee! Peace be to you and to the spirits that alight in your courtyard and terminate their journey in your shrine! Peace be to you and the angels who surround you!

أَشْهَدُ أَنَّكَ قَدْ أَقَمْتَ الصَّلَاةَ، وَ آتَيْتَ الزَّكَاةَ، وَ أَمَرْتَ بِالْمَعْرُوفِ، وَ نَهَيْتَ عَنِ الْمُنْكَرِ، وَ جَاهَدْتَ الْمُلْحِدِينَ، وَ عَبَدْتَ اللهَ حَتَّى أَتَاكَ الْيَقِينُ، اَلسَّلَامُ عَلَيْكَ وَ رَحْمَةُ اللهِ وَ بَرَكَاتُهُ.

I testify that you maintained the prayer, paid the *zakāt*, bade what is right and forbade what is wrong, and worshipped Allah devotedly until the last breath. Peace be to you and may Allah's mercy and His bounties be upon you!

"Then walk towards the tomb; for each step that you take, you will receive a reward like that of someone martyred in the way of Allah. On reaching the grave, stroke it with your hand and say,

اَلسَّلَامُ عَلَيْكَ يَا حُجَّةَ اللهِ فِي أَرْضِهِ.

Peace be to you, O Allah's testament on His earth!

"Then proceed to offer the prayer, and for every *rakʿah* you perform therein, you will receive a reward like that of someone who has performed a thousand *ḥajj* and *ʿumrah* pilgrimages, freed a thousand slaves, and rallied around a prophetic envoy on a thousand occasions for the sake of Allah."

A version of this report narrated on the authority of Mufaḍḍal b. ʿUmar was cited earlier in the section on the etiquette of the Imam's *ziyārah*.

The Fourth Ziyarah

The following *ziyārah* is cited in *Kāmil al-Ziyārāt*[1] in a report of Muʿāwiyah b. ʿAmmār from Imam Jaʿfar al-Ṣādiq (*ʿa*), in answer to his query as to what one should say on visiting the shrine of Imam al-Ḥusayn (*ʿa*).

1 *Kāmil al-Ziyārāt*, 205, h 4, whence *Biḥār*, xcviii, 122, b 18, h 7 & *Mustadrak*, x, 299, b 45, h 12053/1.

Peace be to you, O Abū ᶜAbdillāh! May Allah bless you, O Abū ᶜAbdillāh! May Allah's mercy be on you, O Abū ᶜAbdillāh! May Allah curse those who slew you, and may He curse those who participated in shedding your blood and may Allah curse those who heard about it approvingly. I repudiate all that before Allah!

اَلسَّلَامُ عَلَيْكَ يَا أَبَا عَبْدِ اللهِ، صَلَّى اللهُ عَلَيْكَ يَا أَبَا عَبْدِ اللهِ، رَحِمَكَ اللهُ يَا أَبَا عَبْدِ اللهِ، لَعَنَ اللهُ مَنْ قَتَلَكَ، وَ لَعَنَ اللهُ مَنْ شَرِكَ فِي دَمِكَ، وَ لَعَنَ اللهُ مَنْ بَلَغَهُ ذٰلِكَ فَرَضِيَ بِهِ، أَنَا إِلَى اللهِ مِنْ ذٰلِكَ بَرِيءٌ.

The Fifth Ziyarah

The following *ziyārah* is mentioned in a report of Ibrāhīm b. Abī al-Bilād, cited in *Kāmil al-Ziyārāt*.[1] It describes Imam Mūsā al-Kāẓim (ᶜ*a*) as asking Ibrāhīm, "What do you say while visiting the tomb of Imam Ḥusayn (ᶜ*a*)?" The Imam approves the following text which is recited by Ibrāhīm.

Peace be to you, O Abū ᶜAbdillāh! Peace be to you O son of the Apostle of Allah! I testify that you maintained the prayer, paid the *zakāt*, bade what is right and forbade what is wrong, and that you summoned to the way of your Lord with wisdom and good advice. I testify that those who shed your blood and violated your sanctity are the ones cursed, damned and condemned by David and Jesus son of Mary. *That because of their disobedience and the aggression that they used to commit!*(5:78)

اَلسَّلَامُ عَلَيْكَ يَا أَبَا عَبْدِ اللهِ، اَلسَّلَامُ عَلَيْكَ يَا ابْنَ رَسُولِ اللهِ، أَشْهَدُ أَنَّكَ قَدْ أَقَمْتَ الصَّلَاةَ، وَ آتَيْتَ الزَّكَاةَ، وَ أَمَرْتَ بِالْمَعْرُوفِ، وَنَهَيْتَ عَنِ الْمُنْكَرِ، وَدَعَوْتَ إِلَى سَبِيلِ رَبِّكَ بِالْحِكْمَةِ وَ الْمَوْعِظَةِ الْحَسَنَةِ، وَ أَشْهَدُ أَنَّ الَّذِينَ سَفَكُوا دَمَكَ وَاسْتَحَلُّوا حُرْمَتَكَ مَلْعُونُونَ مُعَذَّبُونَ عَلَى لِسَانِ دَاوُدَ وَ عِيسَى بْنِ مَرْيَمَ، ذٰلِكَ بِمَا عَصَوْا وَ كَانُوا يَعْتَدُونَ.

1 *Kāmil al-Ziyārāt*, 208, h 6, whence *Biḥār*, xcviii, 165, b 18, h 12 & *Mustadrak*, x, 303, b 45, h 12056/4.

THE SIXTH ZIYARAH

Ibn Qūlawayh cites in *Kāmil al-Ziyārāt* the report of ᶜAmmār b. Mūsā al-Sābāṭī,[1] wherein Imam Jaᶜfar al-Ṣādiq (*ᶜa*) is reported to have taught him this *ziyārah* to be said at the tomb of Imam Ḥusayn (*ᶜa*):

Peace be to you, O son of the Apostle of Allah! Peace be to you, O son of the Commander of the Faithful! Peace be to you, O Abū ᶜAbdillāh! Peace be to you, O doyen of the youth of paradise, and may Allah's mercy and His bounties be upon you!

اَلسَّلَامُ عَلَيْكَ يَا ابْنَ رَسُولِ اللهِ، اَلسَّلَامُ عَلَيْكَ يَا ابْنَ أَمِيرِ الْمُؤْمِنِينَ، اَلسَّلَامُ عَلَيْكَ يَا أَبَا عَبْدِ اللهِ، اَلسَّلَامُ عَلَيْكَ يَا سَيِّدَ شَبَابِ أَهْلِ الْجَنَّةِ، وَ رَحْمَةُ اللهِ وَ بَرَكَاتُهُ.

Peace be to you, whose pleasure and approval proceed from the pleasure of Allah, and whose displeasure proceeds from the displeasure of the All-beneficent! Peace be to you, O trustee of Allah, testament of Allah, gateway to Allah, guide to Allah, and summoner to Allah!

اَلسَّلَامُ عَلَيْكَ يَا مَنْ رِضَاهُ مِنْ رِضَى الرَّحْمٰنِ، وَ سَخَطُهُ مِنْ سَخَطِ الرَّحْمٰنِ، اَلسَّلَامُ عَلَيْكَ يَا أَمِينَ اللهِ وَ حُجَّةَ اللهِ وَ بَابَ اللهِ وَ الدَّلِيلَ عَلَى اللهِ وَ الدَّاعِيَ إِلَى اللهِ.

I testify that you allowed what Allah has made lawful and forbade what Allah has made unlawful, and that you maintained the prayer, paid the *zakāt*, bade what is right, forbade what is wrong, and summoned to the path of Allah with wisdom and good advice.

أَشْهَدُ أَنَّكَ قَدْ حَلَّلْتَ حَلَالَ اللهِ، وَ حَرَّمْتَ حَرَامَ اللهِ، وَ أَقَمْتَ الصَّلَاةَ، وَ آتَيْتَ الزَّكَاةَ، وَ أَمَرْتَ بِالْمَعْرُوفِ، وَ نَهَيْتَ عَنِ الْمُنْكَرِ، وَ دَعَوْتَ إِلَى سَبِيلِ رَبِّكَ بِالْحِكْمَةِ وَ الْمَوْعِظَةِ الْحَسَنَةِ،

I testify that you and those who were slain with you are martyrs, living and provided for near your Lord. And I testify that those who killed you are in hellfire. I follow Allah's religion

وَ أَشْهَدُ أَنَّكَ وَ مَنْ قُتِلَ مَعَكَ شُهَدَاءُ أَحْيَاءٌ عِنْدَ رَبِّكُمْ تُرْزَقُونَ، وَ أَشْهَدُ أَنَّ قَاتِلَكَ فِي النَّارِ، أَدِينُ اللهَ بِالْبَرَاءَةِ مِمَّنْ قَتَلَكَ، وَ

[1] *Kāmil al-Ziyārāt*, 212, h 9 whence *Biḥār*, xcviii, 166, b 18, h 15 & *Mustadrak*, x, 304, b 45, h 12059/7. Kafᶜamī's *Miṣbāḥ*, 499. *Balad*, 281.

by repudiating those who killed you and those who fought against you, took sides against you, rallied against you, and those who heard your call and did not help you. I wish I had been with you, for then I would have attained a great triumph!

مِمَّنْ قَاتَلَكَ وَ شَايَعَ عَلَيْكَ، وَ مِمَّنْ جَمَعَ عَلَيْكَ، وَ مِمَّنْ سَمِعَ صَوْتَكَ وَ لَمْ يُعِنْكَ، يا لَيْتَنِي كُنْتُ مَعَكُمْ فَأَفُوزَ فَوْزًا عَظِيمًا .

The Seventh Ziyarah

(Ziyārat Wāri<u>th</u>)

This *ziyārah* is mentioned in a report of Ṣafwān al-Jammāl cited by <u>Sh</u>ay<u>kh</u> Ṭūsī in the *Miṣbāḥ*.[1] Ṣafwān reports that he visited Imam Jaᶜfar al-Ṣādiq (ᶜ*a*) to take his leave while departing for the *ziyārah* of Imam al-Ḥusayn (ᶜ*a*) and asked him concerning the manner of its performance. The Imam said to him, "Fast for three days before your departure and take a bath on the third day. Then gather your family and say, *Allā·humma innî astawdiᶜukal yawma nafsī . . .*" (p. 249) Then the Imam taught him a supplication to be said on reaching the Euphrates.

He said, "Then take bath in the water of the Euphrates, for indeed my father recounted for me from his ancestors from the Apostle of Allah (ṣ) that he said, 'This son of mine, al-Ḥusayn, will be slain on the banks of the Euphrates. Whoever visits his tomb and bathes in the Euphrates will be relieved from sins to become as on the day his mother had borne him.' While taking the bath say,

In the Name of Allah, and by Allah! O Allah, make it a source of light, purity, safety and healing from every malady, disease, blight and infirmity! O Allah, purify with it my heart, open with it my breast and make easy my task!

بِسْمِ اللهِ وَ بِاللهِ. اَللّٰهُمَّ اجْعَلْهُ نُورًا وَ طَهُورًا وَ حِرْزًا وَ شِفَاءً مِنْ كُلِّ دَاءٍ وَ سُقْمٍ وَ آفَةٍ وَ عَاهَةٍ. اَللّٰهُمَّ طَهِّرْ بِهِ قَلْبِي، وَ اشْرَحْ بِهِ صَدْرِي، وَ سَهِّلْ لِي بِهِ أَمْرِي.

"After the bath, put on two pieces of clean clothing and offer two *rakᶜahs* of prayer outside the bank. That is the place concerning which Allah, the Glorious and Exalted, has said,

[1] Ṭūsī's *Miṣbāḥ*, 717, whence *Biḥār*, xcviii, 197, b 17, h 32. *Biḥār*, xcvii, 128, b 3, h 9 & *Mustadrak*, x, 402, b 86, h 12258/1 from Kafᶜamī's *Miṣbāḥ*.

وَ فِي الْأَرْضِ قِطَعٌ مُتَجَاوِرَاتٌ وَ جَنَّاتٌ مِنْ أَعْنَابٍ وَ زَرْعٌ وَ نَخِيلٌ صِنْوَانٌ وَ غَيْرُ صِنْوَانٍ يُسْقَىٰ بِمَاءٍ وَاحِدٍ وَ نُفَضِّلُ بَعْضَهَا عَلَىٰ بَعْضٍ فِي الْأُكُلِ

In the earth are neighbouring terrains [of diverse kinds] and vineyards, farms, and date palms growing from the same root and from diverse roots, [all] irrigated by the same water, and We give some of them an advantage over others in flavour. (13:4)

"After the prayer, set out towards the tomb walking with calm dignity and shorten your steps, because for every step that you take, God, the Most High, will write for you the reward of a *ḥajj* and *ʿumrah*. Approach the shrine with a humble heart and tearful eyes while continually saying *Allāhu akbar* and *Lâ ilāha illallāh,* praising God and invoking blessings on the Prophet (ṣ) and on al-Ḥusayn in particular, and pronouncing anathema on his killers and condemning those who opened the door to the wrongs and injustices committed against the Prophet's Family. Then stop on reaching the doors of the shrine, and say,

اَللّٰهُ أَكْبَرُ كَبِيرًا، وَ الْحَمْدُ لِلّٰهِ كَثِيرًا، وَ سُبْحَانَ اللّٰهِ بُكْرَةً وَ أَصِيلًا، اَلْحَمْدُ لِلّٰهِ الَّذِي هَدَانَا لِهٰذَا وَ مَا كُنَّا لِنَهْتَدِيَ لَوْ لَا أَنْ هَدَانَا اللّٰهُ، لَقَدْ جَاءَتْ رُسُلُ رَبِّنَا بِالْحَقِّ.

May Allah be magnified greatly. May He be praised most often. May He be glorified every morning and evening! All praise belongs to Allah, who guided us to this. We would never have been guided had not Allah guided us. Our Lord's apostles have indeed brought the truth.

"Then say,

اَلسَّلَامُ عَلَيْكَ يَا رَسُولَ اللّٰهِ، اَلسَّلَامُ عَلَيْكَ يَا نَبِيَّ اللّٰهِ، اَلسَّلَامُ عَلَيْكَ يَا خَاتَمَ النَّبِيِّينَ، اَلسَّلَامُ عَلَيْكَ يَا سَيِّدَ الْمُرْسَلِينَ، اَلسَّلَامُ عَلَيْكَ يَا حَبِيبَ اللّٰهِ،

Peace be to you, O Apostle of Allah! Peace be to you, O Prophet of Allah! Peace be to you, O seal of the Prophets! Peace be to you, O chief of the Apostles! Peace be to you, O beloved of Allah!

Peace be to you, O Commander of the Faithful! Peace be to you, O chief of the Legatees! Peace be to you, O leader of the matchless!

اَلسَّلَامُ عَلَيْكَ يَا أَمِيرَ الْمُؤْمِنِينَ، اَلسَّلَامُ عَلَيْكَ يَا سَيِّدَ الْوَصِيِّينَ، اَلسَّلَامُ عَلَيْكَ يَا قَائِدَ الْغُرِّ الْمُحَجَّلِينَ،

Peace be to you, O son of Fāṭimah, mistress of the world's womankind! Peace be to you and to the Imams of your descent! Peace be to you, O legatee of the Commander of the Faithful! Peace be to you, O truthful martyr!

اَلسَّلَامُ عَلَيْكَ يَا ابْنَ فَاطِمَةَ سَيِّدَةِ نِسَاءِ الْعَالَمِينَ، اَلسَّلَامُ عَلَيْكَ وَ عَلَى الْأَئِمَّةِ مِنْ وُلْدِكَ، اَلسَّلَامُ عَلَيْكَ يَا وَصِيَّ أَمِيرِ الْمُؤْمِنِينَ، اَلسَّلَامُ عَلَيْكَ أَيُّهَا الصِّدِّيقُ الشَّهِيدُ،

Peace be to you, O angels of Allah residing in this venerable place! Peace be to you, O angels of my Lord who surround the grave of al-Ḥusayn, may peace be to him! Peace be to you on my behalf as long as I live and as long as day and night endure!

اَلسَّلَامُ عَلَيْكُمْ يَا مَلَائِكَةَ اللهِ الْمُقِيمِينَ فِي هٰذَا الْمَقَامِ الشَّرِيفِ، اَلسَّلَامُ عَلَيْكُمْ يَا مَلَائِكَةَ رَبِّي الْمُحْدِقِينَ بِقَبْرِ الْحُسَيْنِ عَلَيْهِ السَّلَامُ، اَلسَّلَامُ عَلَيْكُمْ مِنِّي أَبَدًا مَا بَقِيتُ وَ بَقِيَ اللَّيْلُ وَ النَّهَارُ.

"After this say,

Peace be to you, O Abū ʿAbdillāh! Peace be to you, O son of the Apostle of Allah! Peace be to you, O son of the Commander of the Faithful! I, your servant, son of your servant and handmaid, acknowledge my servanthood, having renounced any opposition to you. A friend of your friends and enemy of your enemies, I have set out to your shrine, seeking shelter in your sanctuary and nearness to you, by making you the sole goal of my journey!

اَلسَّلَامُ عَلَيْكَ يَا أَبَا عَبْدِ اللهِ، اَلسَّلَامُ عَلَيْكَ يَا ابْنَ رَسُولِ اللهِ، اَلسَّلَامُ عَلَيْكَ يَا ابْنَ أَمِيرِ الْمُؤْمِنِينَ، عَبْدُكَ وَ ابْنُ عَبْدِكَ وَ ابْنُ أَمَتِكَ، اَلْمُقِرُّ بِالرِّقِّ، وَ التَّارِكُ لِلْخِلَافِ عَلَيْكُمْ، وَ الْمُوَالِي لِوَلِيِّكُمْ، وَ الْمُعَادِي لِعَدُوِّكُمْ، قَصَدَ حَرَمَكَ، وَ اسْتَجَارَ بِمَشْهَدِكَ، وَ تَقَرَّبَ إِلَيْكَ بِقَصْدِكَ.

May I enter, O Apostle of Allah? May I enter, O Prophet of Allah? May I enter, O Commander of the Faithful? May I enter, O chief of the Legatees? May I enter, O Fāṭimah, mistress of the world's womankind? May I enter, O my master, O Abū ᶜAbd Allāh? May I enter, O my master, O son of the Apostle of Allah?

أَأَدْخُلُ يَا رَسُولَ اللهِ؟ أَأَدْخُلُ يَا نَبِيَّ اللهِ؟ أَأَدْخُلُ يَا أَمِيرَ الْمُؤْمِنِينَ؟ أَأَدْخُلُ يَا سَيِّدَ الْوَصِيِّينَ؟ أَأَدْخُلُ يَا فَاطِمَةُ سَيِّدَةَ نِسَاءِ الْعَالَمِينَ؟ أَأَدْخُلُ يَا مَوْلَاىَ يَا أَبَا عَبْدِ اللهِ؟ أَأَدْخُلُ يَا مَوْلَاىَ يَا ابْنَ رَسُولِ اللهِ؟

"Then if your heart is moved and tears come to your eyes, it is a sign that you have the leave to enter. Then enter the shrine precincts and say,

All praise belongs to Allah, the Single, One, Singular and the All-embracing One, who guided me to your *wilāyah* and singled me out for your *ziyārah* and enabled me to set out toward you!

اَلْحَمْدُ لِلهِ الْوَاحِدِ الْأَحَدِ الْفَرْدِ الصَّمَدِ، الَّذِى هَدَانِى لِوِلَايَتِكَ، وَ خَصَّنِى بِزِيَارَتِكَ، وَ سَهَّلَ لِى قَصْدَكَ.

"Then approach the door of the domed building housing the tomb, and standing at a place near the head of the tomb, say,

Peace be to you, O heir of Adam, the chosen one of Allah! Peace be to you, O heir of Noah, the prophet of Allah! Peace be to you, O heir of Abraham, the dedicated friend of Allah! Peace be to you, O heir of Moses, Allah's interlocutor! Peace be to you, O heir of Jesus, spirit of Allah!

اَلسَّلَامُ عَلَيْكَ يَا وَارِثَ آدَمَ صَفْوَةِ اللهِ، اَلسَّلَامُ عَلَيْكَ يَا وَارِثَ نُوحٍ نَبِيِّ اللهِ، اَلسَّلَامُ عَلَيْكَ يَا وَارِثَ إِبْرَاهِيمَ خَلِيلِ اللهِ، اَلسَّلَامُ عَلَيْكَ يَا وَارِثَ مُوسَىٰ كَلِيمِ اللهِ، اَلسَّلَامُ عَلَيْكَ يَا وَارِثَ عِيسَىٰ رُوحِ اللهِ،

Peace be to you, O heir of Muḥammad, the beloved of Allah. Peace be to you, O heir of ᶜAli, the Commander of the Faithful, peace be to him! Peace be to you,

اَلسَّلَامُ عَلَيْكَ يَا وَارِثَ مُحَمَّدٍ حَبِيبِ اللهِ، اَلسَّلَامُ عَلَيْكَ يَا وَارِثَ أَمِيرِ الْمُؤْمِنِينَ عَلَيْهِ السَّلَامُ،

اَلسَّلَامُ عَلَيْكَ يَا ابْنَ مُحَمَّدٍ الْمُصْطَفَى،
اَلسَّلَامُ عَلَيْكَ يَا ابْنَ عَلِيٍّ الْمُرْتَضَى،

O son of Muḥammad al-Mustafa! Peace be to you, O son of ‘Alī al-Murtaḍā!

اَلسَّلَامُ عَلَيْكَ يَا ابْنَ فَاطِمَةَ الزَّهْرَاءِ،
اَلسَّلَامُ عَلَيْكَ يَا ابْنَ خَدِيجَةَ الْكُبْرَى،

Peace be to you, O son of Fāṭimah Zahrā. Peace be to you, O son of Khadījat al-Kubra!

اَلسَّلَامُ عَلَيْكَ يَا ثَارَ اللهِ وَ ابْنَ ثَارِهِ، وَ
الْوِتْرَ الْمَوْتُورَ،

Peace be to you, O slain one whose avenger is Allah, son of him whose avenger is Allah, and retribution for whose unavenged blood is sought!

أَشْهَدُ أَنَّكَ قَدْ أَقَمْتَ الصَّلَاةَ، وَ آتَيْتَ الزَّكَاةَ،
وَ أَمَرْتَ بِالْمَعْرُوفِ، وَ نَهَيْتَ عَنِ الْمُنْكَرِ، وَ
أَطَعْتَ اللهَ وَ رَسُولَهُ حَتَّى أَتَاكَ الْيَقِينُ،

I testify that you maintained the prayer, paid the *zakāt*, bade what is right and forbade what is wrong, and obeyed Allah and His Apostle till the last breath.

فَلَعَنَ اللهُ أُمَّةً قَتَلَتْكَ، وَ لَعَنَ اللهُ أُمَّةً
ظَلَمَتْكَ، وَ لَعَنَ اللهُ أُمَّةً سَمِعَتْ بِذٰلِكَ
فَرَضِيَتْ بِهِ .

So may Allah curse the lot who slew you, and may Allah curse the lot who oppressed you, and may Allah curse the lot who heard of it approvingly.

يَا مَوْلَايَ يَا أَبَا عَبْدِ اللهِ، أَشْهَدُ أَنَّكَ كُنْتَ
نُورًا فِي الْأَصْلَابِ الشَّامِخَةِ، وَ الْأَرْحَامِ
الْمُطَهَّرَةِ، لَمْ تُنَجِّسْكَ الْجَاهِلِيَّةُ بِأَنْجَاسِهَا،
وَ لَمْ تُلْبِسْكَ مِنْ مُدْلَهِمَّاتِ ثِيَابِهَا،

O my master! O Abū ʿAbdillāh! I testify that you were a light borne within the backs and breastbones of illustrious fathers and wombs of chaste mothers. The filth of the Age of pagan ignorance did not touch you, nor its defilements affected you.

وَ أَشْهَدُ أَنَّكَ مِنْ دَعَائِمِ الدِّينِ وَ أَرْكَانِ
الْمُؤْمِنِينَ، وَ أَشْهَدُ أَنَّكَ الْإِمَامُ الْبَرُّ التَّقِيُّ
الرَّضِيُّ الزَّكِيُّ الْهَادِي الْمَهْدِيُّ، وَ أَشْهَدُ أَنَّ

I testify that you are one of the pillars of God's religion and the mainstays of the faithful. I testify that you are an Imam, pious, Godwary, resigned to the will of Allah, pure, rightly-guiding and rightly-guided. I testify that the Imams of your progeny are the paragons of Godfearing, the standards of guidance, the firm handle of Allah and His testaments to the people of the world.

الْأَئِمَّةَ مِنْ وُلْدِكَ كَلِمَةُ التَّقْوَىٰ، وَ أَعْلَامُ الْهُدَىٰ، وَ الْعُرْوَةُ الْوُثْقَىٰ، وَ الْحُجَّةُ عَلَىٰ أَهْلِ الدُّنْيَا،

I call on Allah, His angels, His prophets and apostles to be my witnesses that I have faith in you and am certain of your return, as attested by the religious precepts I follow and my last deeds. My heart is at peace with your heart and my conduct in compliance with your instructions.

وَ أُشْهِدُ اللّٰهَ وَ مَلَائِكَتَهُ وَ أَنْبِيَاءَهُ وَ رُسُلَهُ أَنِّي بِكُمْ مُؤْمِنٌ، وَ بِإِيَابِكُمْ مُوقِنٌ، بِشَرَايِعِ دِينِي، وَ خَوَاتِيمِ عَمَلِي، وَ قَلْبِي لِقَلْبِكُمْ سِلْمٌ، وَ أَمْرِي لِأَمْرِكُمْ مُتَّبِعٌ،

May Allah's blessings be upon you, on your souls, your remains and your bodies, on the visible realms of your being and on those that are unseen, on those which are manifest and those which are hidden.

صَلَوَاتُ اللّٰهِ عَلَيْكُمْ، وَ عَلَىٰ أَرْوَاحِكُمْ، وَ عَلَىٰ أَجْسَادِكُمْ، وَ عَلَىٰ أَجْسَامِكُمْ، وَ عَلَىٰ شَاهِدِكُمْ، وَ عَلَىٰ غَائِبِكُمْ، وَ عَلَىٰ ظَاهِرِكُمْ، وَ عَلَىٰ بَاطِنِكُمْ.

"Then leaning over the *ḍarīḥ* embrace it and say,

O son of Allah's Apostle, you are dearer to me than my parents! O Abū ᶜAbdillāh, you are dearer to me than my father and mother! Your martyrdom was a great loss and calamity that befell us and all the denizens of the heavens and the earth!

بِأَبِي أَنْتَ وَ أُمِّي يَا ابْنَ رَسُولِ اللّٰهِ، بِأَبِي أَنْتَ وَ أُمِّي يَا أَبَا عَبْدِ اللّٰهِ، لَقَدْ عَظُمَتِ الرَّزِيَّةُ، وَ جَلَّتِ الْمُصِيبَةُ بِكَ عَلَيْنَا وَ عَلَىٰ جَمِيعِ أَهْلِ السَّمَاوَاتِ وَ الْأَرْضِ،

May Allah curse those who saddled their horses, bridled their mounts and prepared to fight you!

فَلَعَنَ اللّٰهُ أُمَّةً أَسْرَجَتْ وَ أَلْجَمَتْ وَ تَهَيَّأَتْ لِقِتَالِكَ،

O my master, O Abū ᶜAbdillāh! I have set out to your shrine

يَا مَوْلَايَ يَا أَبَا عَبْدِ اللّٰهِ، قَصَدْتُ

and come to your sanctuary to beseech Allah by your station and standing with Him, to bless Muḥammad and the Family of Muḥammad, and to admit me into your fold in this world and in the Hereafter!

حَرَمَكَ، وَ أَتَيْتُ إِلَىٰ مَشْهَدِكَ، أَسْأَلُ اللهَ
بِالشَّأْنِ الَّذِى لَكَ عِنْدَهُ، وَ بِالْمَحَلِّ الَّذِى
لَكَ لَدَيْهِ، أَنْ يُصَلِّيَ عَلَىٰ مُحَمَّدٍ وَ آلِ مُحَمَّدٍ،
وَ أَنْ يَجْعَلَنِي مَعَكُمْ فِي الدُّنْيَا وَ الْآخِرَةِ.

"Then stand up and offer a two-*rakᶜah* prayer at the head of the tomb, reciting any *sūrah* you like in these two *rakᶜahs*. After the prayer, say,

O Allah, I have prayed, bowed, and prostrated to you—You are One and have no partner—for it is not permissible to pray, bow and prostrate before anyone except You, for indeed You are Allah, there is no god other than you!

اَللّٰهُمَّ إِنِّي صَلَّيْتُ وَ رَكَعْتُ وَ سَجَدْتُ
لَكَ، وَحْدَكَ لَا شَرِيكَ لَكَ، لِأَنَّ الصَّلَاةَ
وَ الرُّكُوعَ وَ السُّجُودَ لَا يَكُونُ إِلَّا لَكَ،
لِأَنَّكَ أَنْتَ اللهُ لَا إِلٰهَ إِلَّا أَنْتَ.

O Allah, bless Muḥammad and the Family of Muḥammad and convey to them the best of my greetings and *salāms* and return to me their *salām*.

اَللّٰهُمَّ صَلِّ عَلَىٰ مُحَمَّدٍ وَ آلِ مُحَمَّدٍ، وَ
أَبْلِغْهُمْ عَنِّي أَفْضَلَ السَّلَامِ وَ التَّحِيَّةِ،
وَ ارْدُدْ عَلَيَّ مِنْهُمُ السَّلَامَ.

O Allah, these two *rakᶜahs* are a gift from me to my master al-Ḥusayn ibn ᶜAlī, may peace be to them! O Allah, bless Muḥammad and bless him, and accept it from me and reward me for it according to the best of my hope and expectations from You and Your *walī*, O Guardian of the faithful!

اَللّٰهُمَّ وَ هَاتَانِ الرَّكْعَتَانِ هَدِيَّةٌ مِنِّي إِلَىٰ
مَوْلَايَ الْحُسَيْنِ بْنِ عَلِيٍّ عَلَيْهِمَا السَّلَامُ،
اَللّٰهُمَّ صَلِّ عَلَىٰ مُحَمَّدٍ وَ عَلَيْهِ، وَ تَقَبَّلْ
مِنِّي وَ أْجُرْنِي عَلَىٰ ذٰلِكَ بِأَفْضَلِ أَمَلِي وَ
رَجَائِي فِيكَ وَ فِي وَلِيِّكَ يَا وَلِيَّ الْمُؤْمِنِينَ.

"Then move to the feet of the tomb, and standing at the head of the grave of ᶜAlī ibn al-Ḥusayn (ᶜ*a*), say,

Peace be to you, O son of the Apostle of Allah! Peace be to

اَلسَّلَامُ عَلَيْكَ يَا ابْنَ رَسُولِ اللهِ،

اَلسَّلَامُ عَلَيْكَ يَا ابْنَ نَبِيِّ اللهِ، اَلسَّلَامُ
عَلَيْكَ يَا ابْنَ أَمِيرِ الْمُؤْمِنِينَ، اَلسَّلَامُ
عَلَيْكَ يَا ابْنَ الْحُسَيْنِ الشَّهِيدِ،

you, O son of the Prophet of Allah! Peace be to you, O son of the Commander of the Faithful! Peace be to you, O son of al-Ḥusayn, the martyr!

اَلسَّلَامُ عَلَيْكَ أَيُّهَا الشَّهِيدُ، اَلسَّلَامُ
عَلَيْكَ أَيُّهَا الْمَظْلُومُ وَابْنُ الْمَظْلُومِ، لَعَنَ
اللهُ أُمَّةً قَتَلَتْكَ، وَلَعَنَ اللهُ أُمَّةً ظَلَمَتْكَ،
وَلَعَنَ اللهُ أُمَّةً سَمِعَتْ بِذٰلِكَ فَرَضِيَتْ بِهِ.

Peace be to you, O martyr! Peace be to you, O aggrieved one, son of the aggrieved Imam! May Allah curse those who slew you! May Allah curse those who aggrieved you! May Allah curse those who heard about it approvingly!

Then leaning on the grave, embrace it and say,

اَلسَّلَامُ عَلَيْكَ يَا وَلِيَّ اللهِ وَابْنَ وَلِيِّهِ، لَقَدْ
عَظُمَتِ الْمُصِيبَةُ، وَجَلَّتِ الرَّزِيَّةُ بِكَ
عَلَيْنَا وَعَلىٰ جَمِيعِ الْمُسْلِمِينَ، فَلَعَنَ اللهُ
أُمَّةً قَتَلَتْكَ، وَأَبْرَأُ إِلَى اللهِ وَإِلَيْكَ مِنْهُمْ.

Peace be to you, O *walī* of Allah and son of His *walī*! It was a great loss and a tremendous calamity that befell us and all Muslims because of your martyrdom! May Allah curse those who slew you, and I repudiate them before Allah and before you!

"Then proceed towards the door of exit at the feet of the grave of ʿAlī ibn al Ḥusayn (ʿ*a*) and turning towards the tomb of the other martyrs say,

اَلسَّلَامُ عَلَيْكُمْ يَا أَوْلِيَاءَ اللهِ وَأَحِبَّاءَهُ،
اَلسَّلَامُ عَلَيْكُمْ يَا أَصْفِيَاءَ اللهِ وَأَوِدَّاءَهُ،
اَلسَّلَامُ عَلَيْكُمْ يَا أَنْصَارَ دِينِ اللهِ،

Peace be to you, O friends of Allah and His dear ones! Peace be to you, O chosen ones of Allah and His lovers! Peace be to you, O helpers of the religion of Allah!

اَلسَّلَامُ عَلَيْكُمْ يَا أَنْصَارَ رَسُولِ
اللهِ، اَلسَّلَامُ عَلَيْكُمْ يَا أَنْصَارَ أَمِيرِ
الْمُؤْمِنِينَ، اَلسَّلَامُ عَلَيْكُمْ يَا أَنْصَارَ

Peace be to you, O helpers of the Apostle of Allah! Peace be to you, O helpers of the Commander of the Faithful! Peace be to you, O helpers of Fāṭimah, mistress of the world's womankind! Peace be to you, O helpers of Abū Muḥammad al-Ḥasan ibn ʿAlī, the *walī* and well-wisher of the *ummah*! Peace be to you, O helpers of Abū ʿAbdillāh! You are dearer to me than my father and mother! Blessed are you and blessed is the land where you are buried. You attained a great triumph, and how much I wish I had been with you and triumphed along with you!

فَاطِمَةَ سَيِّدَةِ نِسَاءِ الْعَالَمِينَ، اَلسَّلَامُ عَلَيْكُمْ يَا أَنْصَارَ أَبِي مُحَمَّدٍ الْحَسَنِ بْنِ عَلِيٍّ الْوَلِيِّ النَّاصِحِ، اَلسَّلَامُ عَلَيْكُمْ يَا أَنْصَارَ أَبِي عَبْدِ اللهِ، بِأَبِي أَنْتُمْ وَ أُمِّي، طِبْتُمْ وَ طَابَتِ الْأَرْضُ الَّتِي فِيهَا دُفِنْتُمْ، وَ فُزْتُمْ فَوْزًا عَظِيمًا، فَيَا لَيْتَنِي كُنْتُ مَعَكُمْ فَأَفُوزَ مَعَكُمْ .

"Then come back to the head of al-Ḥusayn's grave and supplicate as much as you can, for yourself and your family, children and brethren, for no supplication or petition is refused in his shrine."

This *ziyārah* is known as "Ziyārat Wār<u>ith</u>" and its source is <u>Sh</u>ay<u>kh</u> Ṭūsī's book *Miṣbāḥ al-Muhajjid*, a work considered most reliable by the scholars. I have cited this *ziyārah* directly from that noble work and its last words are *Fa yā laytanī kuntu maʿakum fa afūza maʿakum.*

Hence the addition at the end of this *ziyārah*, i.e. *Fil jināni maʿan nabī·yīna waṣ ṣiddīqīna wa<u>sh</u>·<u>sh</u>uhadâ'i waṣ ṣāliḥīn, wa ḥasuna ūlâ'ika rafīqa. Assalāmu ʿalā man kāna fil Ḥâ'iri minkum wa ʿalā man lam yakun fil Ḥâ'iri maʿakum...*, is an interpolation in the text of the *ḥadīth*.

In this regard, my teacher, <u>Sh</u>ay<u>kh</u> Nūrī, writes in his book *Luʾluʾ wa Marjān*,[1]

Such interpolations, apart from being unauthorized additions to the words of the Imam (ʿa) and innovations in religion, are plain falsehoods. Yet they have received such currency that they are proclaimed loudly day and night in the shrine of Abū ʿAbdillāh al-Ḥusayn (ʿa) in the presence of archangels and in the midst of divine prophets and apostles (ʿa), without anyone objecting or stopping the people from uttering these lies and being guilty of sin. Gradually, these words have found way into compilations of supplications and *ziyārahs*, made under some title or another by incompetent laymen, which are then printed and published, passing on from one of such compilations to another.

[1] *Luʾlu' wa Marjān*, 163-164, 168-169.

> The matter has reached such alarming proportions that it has created confusion even among students of religious studies. One day I saw a student reciting those reprehensible falsehoods in connection with the martyrs. I put my hand on his shoulder and he turned his attention to me. I said to him, 'Is it not shameful for the learned to utter such falsehoods in such a holy place?' He said, 'Are they not part of the transmitted tradition?' 'No,' I said, amazed at his question. 'I have seen this in a book,' he said. 'Which book? I asked him. 'In the *Miftāḥ al-Jinān*, he replied. I did not say anything, as someone who is so ill-informed to consider the compilation of a commoner as a 'book' and reliable source is not worthy of speaking to.

Continuing his remarks on the topic, the shaykh (*r*) writes,

> Leaving the common people to do what they like in such lesser heresies as the bath of Uways Qaran, the pottage of Abū Dardā—a loyal follower of Muᶜāwiyah— and the fast of silence, wherein one refrains from speech during the day, and other such things without anyone opposing them, has led to such brazenness that, with every month and year that passes, there appears a new prophet and imam and the people forsake the religion of God in throngs.

Reflect upon the statements of this august scholar who was well-informed about the temperament of the *sharīᶜah*. See how this matter has caused him great consternation. He knows the evil consequence of such actions, as against those who, being ignorant of the sciences of the Imams of the Prophet's Family, not knowing anything beyond some terminology, consider these interpolations not only as unimportant but even try to justify them and act in accordance with them. Inevitably, the matter has reached such proportions that such works as *Miṣbāḥ al-Mutahajjid, Iqbāl, Muhaj al-Daᶜawāt, Jamāl, Miṣbāḥ al-Zā'ir, Balad al-Amīn, Junnat al-Wāqiyah, Miftāḥ al-Falāḥ, Miqbās, Rabīᶜ al-Asābīᶜ, Tuḥfah, Zād al-Maᶜād,* and others like them, are consigned to oblivion and these silly compilations have become popular.

In eighty places in Duᶜā' al-Mujīr—a text that has been transmitted through a reliable chain of authorities—they insert the expression *bi ᶜafwik*, and nobody objects. For each passage of Duᶜā' al-Jawshan al-Kabīr, which is comprised of a hundred passages, they fabricate a particular virtue.

Despite the fact that we have so many splendid *ziyārahs* transmitted from the Imams (ᶜ*a*) which are superbly eloquent in wording and sublime in their teaching and content, they have devised an inane supplication named "Duᶜā' Ḥubbī," which is claimed to have descended from the divine Throne and for reciting which they have contrived such merits that leave one aghast. Some of the claimed virtues of the supplication are as follows: Gabriel is said to have told the Apostle of Allah (ṣ) on Almighty God's behalf, "I will not punish any of My servants who carries this supplication with himself even though he may deserve to go to hell, having spent all his life in sin, and even if he should not have bowed to me a single time. I will grant him a reward of seventy thousand prophets, seventy thousand ascetics, seventy thousand martyrs, seventy thousand devotees given to prayer, and the reward of someone who clothes seventy thousand persons without clothing, feeds seventy thousand hungry persons, a reward equal to grains of sands in the deserts, the reward of seventy thousand holy spots on the earth, the reward of the seal of prophesy of the Apostle of Allah and the reward of Jesus, the spirit of Allah, Abraham, Allah's dedicated friend, Ishmael, who was sacrificed for Allah, Moses, Allah's interlocutor, Jacob, Allah's prophet, Adam, Allah's chosen one, and that of Gabriel, Michael, Isrāfīl, ᶜIzrā'īl and other angels. O Muḥammad, I will forgive whoever recites this holy supplication or carries him on his person, and I feel ashamed to punish him..."

Such matters are more regrettable than funny. The Shīᶜī works of supplication have been compiled with great meticulous care. Most of those who made copies were scholars who would compare their manuscripts with copies written by other scholars and correct them. If they found any difference of wording, they would make a note of it on the margins. For instance, in a manuscript of Duᶜā' Makārim, it is indicated on the margin that the wording is *wablugh bi īmānī* in the manuscript of Ibn Ashnās and *Allāhumma abligh bi īmānī* in the report of Ibn Shādhān, or, for instance, it is pointed out how a certain word appears in the manuscript of Ibn Sakkūn and its variant in the manuscript of Shahīd Awwal.

The way things have turned out, the *Miftāḥ*, whose description was just given, has become the sole source-book for supplications. This book is considered authoritative by the common people as well the educated elite, Arabs and non-Arabs alike. The reason behind this is nothing but indifference on behalf of scholars in the field of *ḥadīth* and reports handed down by tradition, failure to refer to works of the scholars and jurists of the school of the Prophet's immaculate Family, and failure to check this kind of innovations, interpolations and corruption by ignorant compilers and falsifiers. The failure to restrain the incompetent and to stop the fools from making interpolations has reached such a degree that supplications are composed according to one's personal taste and inclination and *ziyārahs* and invocations of blessings on the Prophet and his Family are invented. Many of such collections of interpolated supplications have been printed and many mini-*Miftāḥs* have been born and come into circulation, and the disease has gradually spread to other books and become pandemic.

To give an example, the *Muntaha al-Aᶜmāl*, a work of mine, has been recently reprinted. One calligrapher has made interpolations in it according to suit his fancy. In the account of Mālik b. Yasr, the text appears as follows: "By the prayer of Imam Ḥusayn (*ᶜa*) both his hands became paralysed—thank God. During summer they would become like dry wood—thank God, and in winter blood would drip from them—thank God; and such was his evil fate—thank God."

The copyist, of his own accord, has added the phrase "thank God" (*Al-ḥamdu lillāh*) in four places in just two lines of text. In other places he has added the honorific "*k͟hānam*" after the names of Ḥaḍrat Zaynab and Ḥaḍrat Umm Kult͟hūm, so as to show, in his own opinion, respect for the two ladies. As he hated Ḥamīd b. Qaḥṭabah because of his evil character, he has spelled his name as Ḥamīd b. Qaḥbah, and for caution's sake added "Qaḥṭabah" in parenthesis as if to indicate an alternative spelling. He thought it was more correct to write the name ᶜAbd Rabbih as ᶜAbd Allah, and changed Zaḥr b. Qays to Zajar b. Qays in every place. Considering the name "Umm Salamah" to be an error, he has 'corrected' it as "Umm al-Salamah" wherever he could.

My purpose in mentioning these matters is twofold. One thing is that someone who made these interpolations in accordance with his judgement did so because he thought he was improving on the original text, which seemed to him to be deficient. The truth is that what he imagined to be an improvement has spoiled the original text. On this basis, one should know that what we add to original texts out of ignorance, or make modifications in the supplications by our deficient judgement, supposing that it would make them better, are in view of competent scholars destructive changes that impair them and deprive them of their reliability. Therefore, the proper thing is to refrain from making any alterations and to act in the manner that has been prescribed for us, without ever departing from it.

My second purpose was to point out that when the works of a living author, who is present, are treated in this manner, what will they do with other works and what credibility could be attached to the rest of printed books, unless it is a well-known work by one of the famous scholars and has been examined and approved by some trustworthy scholar of that discipline.

There is a report[1] concerning a book on daily religious observances by Yūnus b. ᶜAbd al-Raḥmān, a trustworthy scholar and a pioneering jurist from among the disciples of the Imams (ᶜ*a*). Abū Hās͟him al-Jaᶜfarī presented that book to Imam al-Ḥasan al-ᶜAskarī to be examined by him. After reading the entire book, he made this remark concerning it:

هٰذَا دِينِي وَ دِينُ آبَائِي كُلُّهُ وَ هُوَ الْحَقُّ كُلُّهُ

> This entire work is (genuine and it is) in accordance with my religion and that of my ancestors.

Note that despite his knowledge of the great learning, eminence and integrity of Yūnus, Abū Hās͟him al-Jaᶜfarī did not consider that sufficient for acting according to his book unless its contents were seen and approved by the Imam.

Also, it has been reported[2] that Būraq al-Būs͟hanjānī al-Harawī, a man known for his veracity and piety, visited Imam al-Ḥasan al-ᶜAskarī (ᶜ*a*) in Sāmarrā and gave him the *Kitāb al-Yawm wa al-Laylah* of the eminent scholar Faḍl b. S͟hād͟hān Nays͟hābūrī, and requested the Imam to examine it thoroughly, page by page. After reading it, the Imam told him,

هٰذَا صَحِيحٌ يَنْبَغِي أَنْ تَعْمَلَ بِهِ

> The contents of this book are genuine and it is proper for you to act upon it.

There are other similar reports. Although I am aware of the tastes of the people of these times and their lack of concern for such matters as these, I have done my utmost not to leave any room for excuse. As far as possible, I have cited the supplications and *ziyārah*s quoted in this book from the manuscripts of original works, compared them with different copies, and corrected them to the extent of my ability,

1 *Rijāl al-Kas͟hs͟hī*, 484. *Wasā'il*, xxvii, 100, b 8, h 33320.

2 *Rijāl al-Kas͟hs͟hī*, 537. *Wasā'il*, xxvii, 100, b 8, h 33321. *Muntaha al-Maqāl*, v, 198, no. 2282.

so that, God willing, the readers may be able to act upon them with confidence, provided that the copyists do not make interpolations in it and the readers too set aside their fancies and inventions.

Shaykh Kulaynī reports[1] on the authority of ᶜAbd al-Raḥīm al-Qaṣīr that once he said to Imam Jaᶜfar al-Ṣādiq (ᶜ*a*), "May I be your ransom, I have invented a supplication." The Imam told him, "Spare me of your inventions!" The Imam did not allow him to recite his composition and himself prescribed a supplication for him.

Shaykh Ṣadūq, may Allah fill his grave with fragrance, reports[2] on the authority of ᶜAbd Allāh b. Sinān that Imam Jaᶜfar al-Ṣādiq (ᶜ*a*) said to him, "Soon there will come a time when you will face uncertainty and will be left without a guide and leader. No one will find deliverance from that uncertainty except those who recite the Supplication of the Drowning (Duᶜā al-Gharīq)." When ᶜAbd Allāh asked the Imam as to what that supplication was, he told him, "Say,

يَا اللهُ يَا رَحْمَانُ يَا رَحِيمُ يَا مُقَلِّبَ الْقُلُوبِ ثَبِّتْ قَلْبِي عَلَىٰ دِينِكَ

'O Allah, O All-beneficent, O All-merciful, O You who change the hearts, keep my heart steady on Your religion!' "

ᶜAbd Allāh says, "I said,

يَا مُقَلِّبَ الْقُلُوبِ وَ الْأَبْصَارِ ثَبِّتْ قَلْبِي عَلَىٰ دِينِكَ

'O changer of hearts and visions, keep my heart steady on Your religion!'

"The Imam said to me, 'It is true that God Almighty is the changer of hearts and visions, but say exactly as I have told you: *Yā muqallibul qulūb, thabbit qalbī ᶜalā dīnik.*' "

For those who add words to the supplications and make interpolations, it will be sufficient to reflect on these two noble traditions. God protect us.

1 *Kāfī*, iii, 476, h 1. *Faqīh*, i, 559, h 1548. *Tahdhīb*, i, 116, b 5, h 37. Whence *Wasā'il*, iii, 333, b 20, h 3799, viii, 130, b 28, h 10234 & *Biḥār*, xcix, 229, h 3.

2 *Kamāl al-Dīn*, ii, 351, b 33, h 50, whence *Biḥār*, xcii, 326, b 115, h 1. *Muhaj*, 332.

The Ziyarah of ʿAbbas ibn ʿAli (ʿa)

The august shaykh Jaʿfar b. Qūlawayh reports[1] with a reliable chain of authorities from Abū Ḥamzah al-Thumālī that Imam Jaʿfar al-Ṣādiq (ʿa) said to Abū Ḥamzah, "When you visit the tomb of ʿAbbās ibn ʿAlī (ʿa), which is on the bank of the Euphrates facing the Ḥā'ir (i.e. the shrine of Imam Ḥusayn), stand at the door of the shrine and say,

To you be Allah's greetings of peace and the greetings of His archangels, prophets, and envoys, His righteous servants and all the martyrs and the truthful, as well as pure and felicitous benisons be showered on you every morning and evening, O son of the Commander of the Faithful!

سَلَامُ اللهِ وَ سَلَامُ مَلَائِكَتِهِ الْمُقَرَّبِينَ
وَ أَنْبِيَائِهِ الْمُرْسَلِينَ وَ عِبَادِهِ الصَّالِحِينَ
وَ جَمِيعِ الشُّهَدَاءِ وَ الصِّدِّيقِينَ،
وَالزَّاكِيَاتُ الطَّيِّبَاتُ فِيمَا تَغْتَدِي وَ
تَرُوحُ عَلَيْكَ يَا ابْنَ أَمِيرِ الْمُؤْمِنِينَ،

I testify to your submission and support, loyalty and devotion to the descendent of the Prophet and Apostle, may Allah bless him and his Family, and his distinguished grandson, the learned guide and the Apostle's legatee, who was charged with communicating the divine teachings, and who was wronged and oppressed!

أَشْهَدُ لَكَ بِالتَّسْلِيمِ وَ التَّصْدِيقِ
وَ الْوَفَاءِ وَ النَّصِيحَةِ لِخَلَفِ النَّبِيِّ
صَلَّى اللهُ عَلَيْهِ وَ آلِهِ الْمُرْسَلِ، وَ
السِّبْطِ الْمُنْتَجَبِ، وَ الدَّلِيلِ الْعَالِمِ، وَ
الْوَصِيِّ الْمُبَلِّغِ، وَ الْمَظْلُومِ الْمُهْتَضَمِ،

May Allah reward you on behalf of His Apostle, the Commander of the Faithful, Fāṭimah, al-Ḥasan and al-Ḥusayn, may Allah's blessings be upon them, with the best of rewards for your patience and resignation to Allah's will, and for the hardships you bore! *So how excellent is the reward of the (ultimate) abode!*

فَجَزَاكَ اللهُ عَنْ رَسُولِهِ وَ عَنْ
أَمِيرِ الْمُؤْمِنِينَ وَ عَنِ الْحَسَنِ وَ
الْحُسَيْنِ، صَلَوَاتُ اللهِ عَلَيْهِمْ، أَفْضَلَ
الْجَزَاءِ بِمَا صَبَرْتَ وَ احْتَسَبْتَ
وَ أَعَنْتَ، فَنِعْمَ عُقْبَى الدَّارِ .

May Allah curse those who

لَعَنَ اللهُ مَنْ قَتَلَكَ، وَ لَعَنَ اللهُ مَنْ

[1] *Kāmil al-Ziyārāt*, 256, b 85, h 1, whence *Biḥār*, xcviii, 277, b 20, h 1. Mufīd's *Mazār*, 121, b 55. Ṭūsī's *Miṣbāḥ*, 724. *Tahdhīb*, vi, 65, b 18.

slew you! May Allah curse those who disregarded your rights and made light of your sanctity! May Allah curse those who blocked your access to the waters of the Euphrates!	جَهِلَ حَقَّكَ وَ اسْتَخَفَّ بِحُرْمَتِكَ، وَ لَعَنَ اللّٰهُ مَنْ حَالَ بَيْنَكَ وَ بَيْنَ مَاءِ الْفُرَاتِ.
I testify that you were slain wrongfully and that Allah will fulfil the promise He has given you! O son of the Commander of the Faithful, I have come to you as a pilgrim to your shrine with a heart that submits to you and is compliant to your authority. I am your follower and ready to offer you help and support, *until Allah gives His judgment and He is the best of judges.*(10:109)	أَشْهَدُ أَنَّكَ قُتِلْتَ مَظْلُومًا، وَ أَنَّ اللّٰهَ مُنْجِزٌ لَكُمْ مَا وَعَدَكُمْ. جِئْتُكَ يَا ابْنَ أَمِيرِ الْمُؤْمِنِينَ وَافِدًا إِلَيْكُمْ، وَ قَلْبِي مُسَلِّمٌ لَكُمْ وَ تَابِعٌ، وَ أَنَا لَكُمْ تَابِعٌ، وَ نُصْرَتِي لَكُمْ مُعَدَّةٌ، حَتَّى يَحْكُمَ اللّٰهُ وَ هُوَ خَيْرُ الْحَاكِمِينَ.
I am with you and on your side, not with your enemy. I affirm my faith in you and in your return, and repudiate the faithless lot who opposed you and slew you. May Allah slay the lot who slew you with their hands and tongues!	فَمَعَكُمْ مَعَكُمْ لَا مَعَ عَدُوِّكُمْ، إِنِّي بِكُمْ وَ بِإِيَابِكُمْ مِنَ الْمُؤْمِنِينَ، وَ بِمَنْ خَالَفَكُمْ وَ قَتَلَكُمْ مِنَ الْكَافِرِينَ. قَتَلَ اللّٰهُ أُمَّةً قَتَلَتْكُمْ بِالْأَيْدِي وَ الْأَلْسُنِ.

Then enter the shrine and, embracing the *ḏarīḥ*, say the following (It is better to stand behind the tomb facing the *qiblah* while reciting this *ziyārah*, as mentioned by Shaykh Ṭūsī in the *Tahdhīb* [*Thummad·khul fan·kabba ʻalal-qabri wa qul, wa anta mustaqbilul-qiblah, Assalāmu ʻalayka ayyuhal ʻabduṣ ṣāliḥ...*]).[1]

Peace be to you, O righteous servant of Allah, who are obedient to Allah and His Apostle and the Commander of the faithful, al-Ḥasan and al-Ḥusayn, may Allah bless them and grant them peace. Peace be to you and may Allah's mercy, bounties, forgiveness and	اَلسَّلَامُ عَلَيْكَ أَيُّهَا الْعَبْدُ الصَّالِحُ، اَلْمُطِيعُ لِلّٰهِ وَ لِرَسُولِهِ وَ لِأَمِيرِ الْمُؤْمِنِينَ وَ الْحَسَنِ وَ الْحُسَيْنِ صَلَّى اللّٰهُ عَلَيْهِمْ وَ سَلَّمَ، اَلسَّلَامُ عَلَيْكَ وَ رَحْمَةُ اللّٰهِ

1 *Tahdhīb*, vi, 66, b 18.

good pleasure be with you and with your spirit and your body!

وَ بَرَكَاتُـــهُ وَ مَغْفِرَتُـــهُ وَ رِضْوَانُهُ، وَ عَلَىٰ رُوحِكَ وَ بَدَنِكَ،

I testify, and hold Allah to witness, that you departed from the world upholding what was upheld by the warriors of Badr and the warriors of the way of Allah, who were devoted to Him in waging *jihād* against His enemies, who did their utmost in giving support to His *awliyā'*, and defended His beloved servants!

أَشْـــهَدُ وَ أُشْـــهِدُ اللهَ أَنَّكَ مَضَيْتَ عَلَىٰ مَا مَضَىٰ بِهِ الْبَدْرِيُّـــونَ، وَ الْمُجَاهِدُونَ فِي سَبِيلِ اللهِ، اَلْمُنَاصِحُونَ لَهُ فِي جِهَادِ أَعْدَائِـــهِ، اَلْمُبَالِغُونَ فِي نُـــصْرَةِ أَوْلِيَائِهِ، اَلذَّابُّونَ عَنْ أَحِبَّائِهِ،

May Allah reward you with the best, the most abundant, the most plentiful and the complete of rewards that He has granted those who have fulfilled their pledges to Him, responded to His summons, and obeyed those who have been invested with authority by Him!

فَجَـــزَاكَ اللهُ أَفْضَلَ الْجَـــزَاءِ وَ أَكْثَرَ الْجَزَاءِ وَ أَوْفَرَ الْجَزَاءِ وَ أَوْفَىٰ جَزَاءِ أَحَدٍ مِمَّنْ وَفَىٰ بِبَيْعَتِهِ، وَ اسْتَجَابَ لَهُ دَعْوَتَهُ، وَ أَطَاعَ وُلَاةَ أَمْرِهِ.

I testify that you did your best in devotion and offered your utmost efforts. May Allah resurrect you with the martyrs and may He put your spirit among the spirits of the felicitous and may He grant you the most expansive and the best of stations and abodes, and may He exalt your name in the *ʿIlliyūn* and may He resurrect you *with the prophets, the truthful, the martyrs and the righteous, and excellent companions are they!* (4:69)

أَشْـــهَدُ أَنَّكَ قَدْ بَالَغْتَ فِي النَّصِيحَةِ، وَ أَعْطَيْتَ غَايَةَ الْمَجْهُـــودِ، فَبَعَثَكَ اللهُ فِي الشُّهَدَاءِ، وَ جَعَلَ رُوحَكَ مَعَ أَرْوَاحِ السُّعَدَاءِ، وَ أَعْطَاكَ مِنْ جِنَانِهِ أَفْسَحَهَا مَنْزِلًا وَ أَفْضَلَهَا غُرَفًـــا، وَ رَفَعَ ذِكْرَكَ فِي عِلِّيِّـــينَ، وَ حَشَرَكَ مَـــعَ النَّبِيِّينَ وَ الصِّدِّيقِينَ وَ الشُّـــهَدَاءِ وَ الصَّالِحِينَ، وَ حَسُنَ أُولٰئِكَ رَفِيقًا.

I testify that you never flagged

أَشْـــهَدُ أَنَّكَ لَمْ تَهِنْ وَ لَمْ تَنْكُلْ، وَ أَنَّكَ

مَضَيْتَ عَلىٰ بَصِيرَةٍ مِنْ أَمْرِكَ، مُقْتَدِيًا
بِالصَّالِحِينَ، وَ مُتَّبِعًا لِلنَّبِيِّينَ، فَجَمَعَ اللهُ
بَيْنَنَا وَ بَيْنَكَ وَ بَيْنَ رَسُولِهِ وَ أَوْلِيَائِهِ فِي
مَنَازِلِ الْمُخْبِتِينَ، فَإِنَّهُ أَرْحَمُ الرَّاحِمِينَ.

or flinched and that you departed in full possession of insight of your mission, emulating the righteous and following in the steps of the prophets. May Allah gather us with you, his Apostle and His *awliyā’* in the abodes of the humble. Indeed, He is the Most Merciful of the merciful!

The *ziyārah* of Ḥaḍrat ʿAbbās mentioned above was according to the report (cited by Ibn Qūlawayh). However, according to reports cited by Sayyid ʿAlī b. Ṭāwūs, Shaykh Mufīd and others,[1] after reciting the above text one should proceed towards the head of the tomb and offer two *rakʿahs* of prayer. After this, one may pray as much as one wishes and make petitions to God. After the prayers say,

اَللّٰهُمَّ صَلِّ عَلىٰ مُحَمَّدٍ وَ آلِ مُحَمَّدٍ، وَ لَا
تَدَعْ لِي فِي هٰذَا الْمَكَانِ الْمُكَرَّمِ وَ الْمَشْهَدِ
الْمُعَظَّمِ ذَنْبًا إِلَّا غَفَرْتَهُ، وَ لَا هَمًّا إِلَّا
فَرَّجْتَهُ، وَ لَا مَرَضًا إِلَّا شَفَيْتَهُ، وَ لَا عَيْبًا
إِلَّا سَتَرْتَهُ، وَ لَا رِزْقًا إِلَّا بَسَطْتَهُ، وَ لَا
خَوْفًا إِلَّا آمَنْتَهُ، وَ لَا شَمْلًا إِلَّا جَمَعْتَهُ،
وَ لَا غَائِبًا إِلَّا حَفِظْتَهُ وَ أَدْنَيْتَهُ، وَ لَا
حَاجَةً مِنْ حَوَائِجِ الدُّنْيَا وَ الْآخِرَةِ لَكَ
فِيهَا رِضًى وَ لِيَ فِيهَا صَلَاحٌ إِلَّا قَضَيْتَهَا،
يَا أَرْحَمَ الرَّاحِمِينَ.

O Allah, bless Muḥammad and the Family of Muḥammad and do not let any of my sins remain unforgiven in this venerated place and august shrine, nor any of my worries undispelled, nor any of my maladies uncured, nor any defect unconcealed, nor any provision unexpanded, nor any fear unrelieved, nor any disunion and separation unreplaced by union, nor anything that I have left behind unprotected and unrestored back to me, nor any of my needs pertaining to the world and the Hereafter–such as You approve of and are in my interest–unfulfilled, O Most Merciful of the merciful!

Then approaching the dharīḥ, stand at the feet of the tomb and say,

1 Mufīd's *Mazār*, 123, b 5, whence *Biḥār*, xcviii, 218, b 18, h 33.

Peace be to you, O Abul Faḍlil ᶜAbbās, son of the Commander of the Faithful Peace be to you, O son of the chief of the Legatees! Peace be to you, O son of him who was foremost of all people in embracing Islam and foremost of them in faith, the most steadfast of them in upholding Allah's religion, and most diligent of them in defending Islam!

اَلسَّـلَامُ عَلَيْكَ يَا أَبَا الْفَضْلِ الْعَبَّاسَ بْنَ أَمِيرِ الْمُؤْمِنِينَ، اَلسَّـلَامُ عَلَيْكَ يَا ابْنَ سَـيِّدِ الْوَصِيِّينَ، اَلسَّـلَامُ عَلَيْكَ يَا ابْـنَ أَوَّلِ الْقَوْمِ إِسْـلَامًا، وَ أَقْدَمِهِمْ إِيمَانًا، وَ أَقْوَمِهِمْ بِدِينِ اللهِ، وَ أَحْوَطِهِمْ عَلَى الْإِسْلَامِ.

I testify that you were devoted to Allah and His Apostle, and to your brother. How excellent and self-abnegating a brother you were!

أَشْـهَدُ لَقَدْ نَصَحْتَ لِلّٰهِ وَ لِرَسُـولِهِ وَ لِأَخِيكَ، فَنِعْمَ الْأَخُ الْمُوَاسِي،

May Allah curse those who slew you! May Allah curse those who wronged you! May Allah curse those who breached your sanctity and rights and violated the sanctity of Islam!

فَلَعَـنَ اللهُ أُمَّةً قَتَلَتْكَ، وَ لَعَنَ اللهُ أُمَّةً ظَلَمَتْكَ، وَ لَعَنَ اللهُ أُمَّةً اسْتَحَلَّتْ مِنْكَ الْمَحَارِمَ، وَ انْتَهَكَتْ حُرْمَةَ الْإِسْلَامِ،

How patient and gallant a warrior you have been! How devoted a supporter and helper! And how excellent a defender of your brother! How amenable to your Lord! How ardent in seeking the bountiful divine reward and elegant compliments, which others regarded with indifference! May Allah admit you into the ranks of your ancestors in the gardens of bliss!

فَنِعْمَ الصَّابِرُ الْمُجَاهِدُ الْمُحَامِي النَّاصِرُ، وَ الْأَخُ الدَّافِـعُ عَنْ أَخِيهِ، اَلْمُجِيبُ إِلَى طَاعَةِ رَبِّهِ، اَلرَّاغِبُ فِيمَا زَهِدَ فِيهِ غَيْرُهُ مِنَ الثَّوَابِ الْجَزِيلِ وَ الثَّنَاءِ الْجَمِيلِ، وَ أَلْحَقَكَ اللهُ بِدَرَجَـةِ آبَائِكَ فِي جَنَّاتِ النَّعِيمِ.

O Allah, I have undertaken the *ziyārah* of Your *awliyā*, being desirous of Your reward, expecting Your forgiveness, and Your generous kindness.

اَللّٰهُـمَّ إِنِّي تَعَرَّضْتُ لِزِيَـارَةِ أَوْلِيَائِكَ، رَغْبَةً فِي ثَوَابِكَ، وَ رَجَـاءً لِمَغْفِرَتِكَ وَ جَزِيلِ إِحْسَانِكَ،

فَأَسْأَلُكَ أَنْ تُصَلِّيَ عَلَىٰ مُحَمَّدٍ وَآلِهِ الطَّاهِرِينَ، وَأَنْ تَجْعَلَ رِزْقِي بِهِمْ دَارًّا، وَ عَيْشِي بِهِمْ قَارًّا، وَ زِيَارَتِي بِهِمْ مَقْبُولَةً، وَ حَيَاتِي بِهِمْ طَيِّبَةً، وَ أَدْرِجْنِي إِدْرَاجَ الْمُكْرَمِينَ،

I beseech You to bless Muḥammad and his immaculate Family and, through them, to make my provision plentiful, my lifestyle steady, my *ziyārah* received with acceptance, and grant me to live, through them, a good life. Record my name among those who are held in honour with You.

وَاجْعَلْنِي مِمَّنْ يَنْقَلِبُ مِنْ زِيَارَةِ مَشَاهِدِ أَحِبَّائِكَ مُفْلِحًا مُنْجِحًا، قَدِ اسْتَوْجَبَ غُفْرَانَ الذُّنُوبِ، وَسَتْرَ الْعُيُوبِ، وَ كَشْفَ الْكُرُوبِ، إِنَّكَ أَهْلُ التَّقْوَىٰ وَأَهْلُ الْمَغْفِرَةِ

Make me one of those who return from their *ziyārah* to the shrines of Your beloved ones with felicity and success, their sins forgiven, their faults concealed, and their distress removed. Indeed, You are worthy of being wary of and worthy to forgive!

When intending to bid farewell to Ḥaḍrat ʿAbbās, approach his tomb and say the following, as mentioned in the report of Abū Ḥamzah al-Thumālī as well as the works of the other scholars,

أَسْتَوْدِعُكَ اللهَ وَ أَسْتَرْعِيكَ، وَ أَقْرَأُ عَلَيْكَ السَّلَامَ، آمَنَّا بِاللهِ وَ بِرَسُولِهِ وَ بِكِتَابِهِ وَ بِمَا جَاءَ بِهِ مِنْ عِنْدِ اللهِ، اَللّٰهُمَّ فَاكْتُبْنَا مَعَ الشَّاهِدِينَ،

I commend you to Allah's care, committing you to His protection, and give you my *salām!* We have faith in Allah and His Apostle and the Scripture and whatever he has brought from Allah. O Allah, so write us among the witnesses.

اَللّٰهُمَّ لَا تَجْعَلْهُ آخِرَ الْعَهْدِ مِنْ زِيَارَتِي قَبْرَ ابْنِ أَخِي رَسُولِكَ صَلَّى اللهُ عَلَيْهِ وَ آلِهِ، وَ ارْزُقْنِي زِيَارَتَهُ أَبَدًا مَا أَبْقَيْتَنِي، وَ احْشُرْنِي مَعَهُ وَ مَعَ آبَائِهِ فِي الْجِنَانِ، وَ عَرِّفْ بَيْنِي وَ بَيْنَهُ وَ بَيْنَ رَسُولِكَ وَ

O Allah, do not let this be my last opportunity of *ziyārah* of the grave of the nephew of Your Apostle, may Allah bless him and his Family, and bless me by enabling me to perform his *ziyārah* often as long as you keep me alive. Raise me at resurrection along with his ancestors in para-

dise and bring about familiarity between me and him and your Apostle and *awliyā'*.	أَوْلِيَائِكَ،
O Allah, bless Muḥammad and the Family of Muḥammad and let my death be in the state of faith in you, coupled with affirmation of your Apostle and the *wilāyah* of ᶜAlī ibn Abī Ṭālib and the Imams of his descent, may peace be to them, and disapproval of their enemies, for indeed I endorse this creed! May Allah bless Muḥammad and the Family of Muḥammad!	اَللّٰهُمَّ صَلِّ عَلىٰ مُحَمَّدٍ وَ آلِ مُحَمَّدٍ، وَ تَوَفَّنِي عَلَى الْإِيمَانِ بِكَ، وَ التَّصْدِيقِ بِرَسُولِكَ، وَ الْوِلَايَةِ لِعَلِيِّ بْـنِ أَبِي طَالِبٍ وَ الْأَئِمَّةِ مِنْ وُلْدِهِ عَلَيْهِمُ السَّـلَامُ، وَ الْبَرَاءَةِ مِنْ عَدُوِّهِمْ، فَإِنِّي قَدْ رَضِيتُ يَا رَبِّي بِذٰلِكَ، وَ صَلَّى اللّٰهُ عَلىٰ مُحَمَّدٍ وَ آلِ مُحَمَّدٍ.

Then supplicate for yourself, your parents and other faithful and for the generality of Muslims and recite any supplication of your liking.

It is mentioned in a report[1] from Imam ᶜAlī ibn al-Ḥusayn al-Sajjād (ᶜ*a*) that he said, "May Allah's mercy be on ᶜAbbās. He sacrificed himself for his brother and gave his life for his sake. They severed his arms while he was serving his brother, and God Almighty rewarded him by giving him two wings with which he flies in paradise, like Jaᶜfar b. Abī Ṭālib. ᶜAbbās has a station with Allah which will be envied by all the martyrs on the Day of Resurrection and they will aspire to it."

According to reports,[2] Ḥaḍrat ᶜAbbās was thirty-four years old at the time of his martyrdom. His mother, Umm al-Banīn, would go out of the town and into the Baqīᶜ cemetery to mourn him and his brothers, and her wailing would move every passer-by to tears. It is not strange if her lamentations moved friends, for even Marwān b. al-Ḥakam, one of the staunchest enemies of the Prophet's family, is said to have wept on hearing her lamentations.[3] She is reported[4] to recite the following verses bewailing the martyrdom of ᶜAbbas and her other sons:

1 Ṣadūq's *Amālī*, 462, majlis 70, h 10. Khiṣāl, i, 68, h 101, whence *Biḥār*, xxii, 274, b 5, h 21, xliv, 298, b 35, h 4..
2 *Iᶜlām al-Warā*, 203, b 5.
3 Abū Mikhnaf's *Maqtal al-Ḥusayn*, 181.
4 *Ibid.*

يَا مَنْ رَأَى الْعَبَّاسَ كَرَّ عَلَىٰ جَمَاهِيرِ النَّـقَدِ وَوَرَاهُ مِنْ أَبْنَاءِ حَيْدَرَ كُلُّ لَيْثٍ ذِي لَبَـدِ
أُنْبِئْتُ أَنَّ ابْنِي أُصِيبَ بِرَأْسِهِ مَقْطُوعَ يَدِ وَيْلِي عَلَىٰ شِبْلِي أَمَالَ بِرَأْسِهِ ضَرْبُ الْعَـمَدِ
لَوْ كَانَ سَيْفُكَ فِي يَدِيْكَ لَمَا دَنَا مِنْهُ أَحَدٌ

O you who have seen ᶜAbbas assail the enemy's ranks
Along with the other sons of Haydar at his rear,
Like lions set on a flock of sheep!
Yet, I've been told that my son's head was struck
With a club, and his arms were cut off!
Alas! ᶜAbbās! If you had a sword in your hand
No one would have dared to approach you!

The following verses are also from her.[1]

لا تَدْعُونِّي وَيْـكِ أُمَّ الْبَـنِـيـنَ تُـذَكِّـرِينِي بِلِيُوثِ الْعَرِيـنِ
كَانَتْ بَنُونَ لِـي أُدْعَى بِهِـمْ وَالْيَوْمَ أَصْبَحْتُ وَلا مِنْ بَنِيـنَ
أَرْبَعَةٌ مِثْلُ نُسُـورِ الـرُّبَـى قَدْ وَاصَلُوا الْمَوْتَ بِقَطْعِ الْوَتِيـنِ
تَـنَـازَعَ الْخِـرْصَانُ أَشْلاءَهُمْ فَكُلُّهُـمْ أَمْسَىٰ صَرِيعًا طَعِيـنَ
يَا لَيْتَ شِعْرِي أَكَمَا أَخْـبَـرُوا بِأَنَّ عَبَّاسًـا قَطِيعُ الْيَـمِـينِ

Call me not "Ummul Banīn," don't call me by that name anymore,
For it reminds me of my sons, who were brave as lions.
Yes, I did have sons, and I was so called after them,
But today I am bereaved, having lost my dear ones.
Four of them they were, like eagles of the hills.
They met their death and their jugular veins were cut,
The Javelins contended for their bodies,
And they lay fallen, pierced by sharp points of the spears.
I wish someone would tell me if it was indeed true,
That ᶜAbbas's right arm was struck off in battle!

1 Abū Mikhnaf's *Maqtal al-Ḥusayn*, 182. *Riyāḥīn al-Sharīʿah*, iii, 294.

Imām Ḥusayn's Ziyārahs for Special Days

There are several *ziyārahs* of the Imam meant for specific occasions.

1. ZIYARAH FOR THE 1ST & 15TH OF RAJAB AND 15TH SHAʿBAN

Imam Jaʿfar al-Ṣādiq (ʿa) is reported[1] to have said that God Almighty forgives those who perform *ziyārah* of Imam al-Ḥusayn (ʿa) on the first day of Rajab. Ibn Abī Naṣr reports[2] that he asked Imam ʿAlī al-Riḍā (ʿa) as to what time was best for the *ziyārah* of Imam al-Ḥusayn (ʿa). "The middle of Rajab and the middle of Shaʿbān," he replied.

Shaykh Mufīd and Sayyid ʿAlī b. Ṭāwūs[3] have mentioned the following *ziyārah* as one meant for the first day of Rajab and the eve of 15th Shaʿbān. To these occasions, Shahīd Awwal[4] has added the eve of the first of Rajab, the eve and day of the 15th of Rajab and the day of the 15th Shaʿbān as well. Hence according to what he says, this *ziyārah* can be recited on these six occasions.

Following is the manner of its performance. When one intends to perform *ziyārah* of Imam al-Ḥusayn (ʿa) on any of these occasions, one should take bath and put on one's cleanest clothes. Then, standing at the gates of the holy shrine and facing in the direction of the *qiblah*, one should greet the Apostle of Allah (ṣ), the Commander of the Faithful, Ḥaḍrat Fāṭimah, Imam al-Ḥasan, Imam al-Ḥusayn, and the rest of the Imams, may Allah bless them.

The text of this greeting is cited under the request for admittance mentioned in the *ziyārah* of Imam al-Ḥusayn (ʿa) prescribed for the day of ʿArafah (p. 325). Then enter and approach the *ḍarīḥ*, and standing near it say *"Allāhu akbar"* one hundred times. Then say,

---

[1] *Kāmil al-Ziyārāt*, 172, 182, b 70, h 11, b 73, h 2, whence *Wasāʾil*, xiv, 467, b 50, h 18614 & *Biḥār*, xcviii, 89, 97, b 12, h 22, b 13, h 31. Mufīd's *Mazār*, 39, b 16, h 2. *Masār*, 57. Ṭūsī's *Miṣbāḥ*, 801.*Tahdhīb*, vi, 48, b 16, h 22, whence *Wasāʾil*, xiv, 265, b 50, h 19612. *Iqbāl*, 149.

[2] *Kāmil al-Ziyārāt*, 182, 73, h 1, *Tahdhīb*, vi, 48, b 16, h 23, whence *Wasāʾil*, xiv, 456, b 50, h 19612. Mufīd's *Mazār*, 40, b 17, h 1, whence *Biḥār*, xcviii, 246, b 27, h 1. *Iqbāl*, 257.

[3] *Biḥār*, xcviii, 336, b 26, h 1, citing Shaykh Mufīd and Ibn Ṭāwūs, mentions it as being meant for the day *and eve* of the first of Rajab and for the eve of 15th Shaʿbān.

[4] *Mazār*, 142-145. However, Shahīd Awwal here mentions only that it is meant for the eve and day of the first of Rajab and the *eve* of 15th Shaʿbān. There is no mention of 15th Rajab.

اَلسَّلامُ عَلَيْكَ يَا ابْنَ رَسُولِ اللهِ، اَلسَّلامُ عَلَيْكَ يَا ابْنَ خَاتَمِ النَّبِيِّينَ، اَلسَّلامُ عَلَيْكَ يَا ابْنَ سَيِّدِ الْمُرْسَلِينَ، اَلسَّلامُ عَلَيْكَ يَا ابْنَ سَيِّدِ الْوَصِيِّينَ،

Peace be to you, O son of the Apostle of Allah! Peace be to you, O son of the Seal of the Prophets! Peace be to you, O son of the Chief of the envoys! Peace be to you, O son of the chief of the Legatees!

اَلسَّلامُ عَلَيْكَ يَا أَبَا عَبْدِ اللهِ، اَلسَّلامُ عَلَيْكَ يَا حُسَيْنَ بْنَ عَلِيٍّ، اَلسَّلامُ عَلَيْكَ يَا ابْنَ فَاطِمَةَ سَيِّدَةِ نِسَاءِ الْعَالَمِينَ،

Peace be to you, O Abū ʿAbdillāh! Peace be to you, O Ḥusayn ibn ʿAlī! Peace be to you, O son of Fāṭimah, the mistress of the world's womankind!

اَلسَّلامُ عَلَيْكَ يَا وَلِيَّ اللهِ وَ ابْنَ وَلِيِّهِ، اَلسَّلامُ عَلَيْكَ يَا صَفِيَّ اللهِ وَ ابْنَ صَفِيِّهِ، اَلسَّلامُ عَلَيْكَ يَا حُجَّةَ اللهِ وَ ابْنَ حُجَّتِهِ، اَلسَّلامُ عَلَيْكَ يَا حَبِيبَ اللهِ وَ ابْنَ حَبِيبِهِ، اَلسَّلامُ عَلَيْكَ يَا سَفِيرَ اللهِ وَ ابْنَ سَفِيرِهِ،

Peace be to you, O *walī* of Allah and son of His *walī!* Peace be to you, O chosen of Allah and son of His chosen one! Peace be to you, O testament of Allah and son of His testament! Peace be to you, O beloved of Allah and son of His beloved! Peace be to you, O emissary of Allah and son of His emissary!

اَلسَّلامُ عَلَيْكَ يَا خَازِنَ الْكِتَابِ الْمَسْطُورِ، اَلسَّلامُ عَلَيْكَ يَا وَارِثَ التَّوْرَاةِ وَ الْإِنْجِيلِ وَ الزَّبُورِ، اَلسَّلامُ عَلَيْكَ يَا أَمِينَ الرَّحْمٰنِ، اَلسَّلامُ عَلَيْكَ يَا شَرِيكَ الْقُرْآنِ، اَلسَّلامُ عَلَيْكَ يَا عَمُودَ الدِّينِ، اَلسَّلامُ عَلَيْكَ يَا بَابَ حِكْمَةِ رَبِّ الْعَالَمِينَ،

Peace be to you, O custodian of the inscribed Scripture! Peace be to you, O inheritor of the Torah, the Evangel and the Psalms! Peace be to you, O trustee of the All-beneficent! Peace be to you, O counterpart of the Qur'ān! Peace be to you, O pillar of the faith! Peace be to you, O gateway to the wisdom of the Lord of all the worlds!

اَلسَّلامُ عَلَيْكَ يَا بَابَ حِطَّةٍ الَّذِى مَنْ

Peace be to you, O door to remission of sins, whoever enters

دَخَلَهُ كَانَ مِنَ الْآمِنِينَ، اَلسَّلَامُ عَلَيْكَ يَا عَيْبَةَ عِلْمِ اللهِ، اَلسَّلَامُ عَلَيْكَ يَا مَوْضِعَ سِرِّ اللهِ، اَلسَّلَامُ عَلَيْكَ يَا ثَارَ اللهِ وَ ابْنَ ثَارِهِ وَ الْوِتْرَ الْمَوْتُورَ،

which is secure from punishment! Peace be to you, O storehouse of Allah's knowledge! Peace be to you, O repository of Allah's secrets! Peace be to you, O slain one whose avenger is Allah, son of him whose avenger is Allah, and retribution for whose unavenged blood is sought!

اَلسَّلَامُ عَلَيْكَ وَ عَلَى الْأَرْوَاحِ الَّتِي حَلَّتْ بِفِنَائِكَ، وَ أَنَاخَتْ بِرَحْلِكَ،

Peace be to you and to the spirits that alight in your courtyard and conclude their journey in your shrine!

بِأَبِي أَنْتَ وَ أُمِّي وَ نَفْسِي يَا أَبَا عَبْدِ اللهِ، لَقَدْ عَظُمَتِ الْمُصِيبَةُ، وَ جَلَّتِ الرَّزِيَّةُ بِكَ عَلَيْنَا وَ عَلَىٰ جَمِيعِ أَهْلِ الْإِسْلَامِ،

You are dearer to me than my father and mother and my own self, O Abū ʿAbdillāh! Your martyrdom was a painful calamity and cause of great distress for us and all followers of Islam!

فَلَعَنَ اللهُ أُمَّةً أَسَّسَتْ أَسَاسَ الظُّلْمِ وَ الْجَوْرِ عَلَيْكُمْ أَهْلَ الْبَيْتِ، وَ لَعَنَ اللهُ أُمَّةً دَفَعَتْكُمْ عَنْ مَقَامِكُمْ، وَ أَزَالَتْكُمْ عَنْ مَرَاتِبِكُمُ الَّتِي رَتَّبَكُمُ اللهُ فِيهَا،

May Allah's curse be on those who instituted a regime of wrongdoing and injustice against you, O Prophet's Family! May Allah's curse be on those who hindered you from your rightful station and held you back from assuming the status that Allah had assigned you!

بِأَبِي أَنْتَ وَ أُمِّي وَ نَفْسِي يَا أَبَا عَبْدِ اللهِ، أَشْهَدُ لَقَدِ اقْشَعَرَّتْ لِدِمَائِكُمْ أَظِلَّةُ الْعَرْشِ مَعَ أَظِلَّةِ الْخَلَائِقِ، وَ بَكَتْكُمُ السَّمَاءُ وَ الْأَرْضُ وَ سُكَّانُ الْجِنَانِ وَ الْبَرِّ وَ الْبَحْرِ، صَلَّى اللهُ عَلَيْكَ عَدَدَ مَا فِي عِلْمِ اللهِ،

You are dearer to me than my father and mother and my own self, O Abū ʿAbdillāh! I testify that the spirits about the divine Throne and the spirits of the creatures trembled at the shedding of your blood, and heaven and earth wept for you as well as the denizens of paradise and those of land and sea! May Allah bless you to the extent and number in His knowledge!

لَبَّيْكَ دَاعِيَ اللهِ، إِنْ كَانَ لَمْ يُجِبْكَ بَدَنِي عِنْدَ اسْتِغَاثَتِكَ وَلِسَانِي عِنْدَ اسْتِنْصَارِكَ، فَقَدْ أَجَابَكَ قَلْبِي وَ سَمْعِي وَ بَصَرِي، سُبْحَانَ رَبِّنَا إِنْ كَانَ وَعْدُ رَبِّنَا لَمَفْعُولًا.

I am at your service, O summoner of Allah! Even if my body could not answer to your call for help, and my tongue could not respond to your call for assistance, my heart, my hearing and my sight respond to you! Glory be to our Lord, our Lord's promise is sure to be fulfilled!

أَشْهَدُ أَنَّكَ طُهْرٌ طَاهِرٌ مُطَهَّرٌ مِنْ طُهْرٍ طَاهِرٍ مُطَهَّرٍ، طَهُرْتَ وَ طَهُرَتْ بِكَ الْبِلَادُ، وَ طَهُرَتْ أَرْضٌ أَنْتَ بِهَا، وَ طَهُرَ حَرَمُكَ،

I testify that you are pure, immaculate and purified, being of an ancestry pure, immaculate and purified! Pure are you, and through you all the lands have been purified. Pure is the land where you are buried and pure is your shrine!

أَشْهَدُ أَنَّكَ قَدْ أَمَرْتَ بِالْقِسْطِ وَ الْعَدْلِ وَ دَعَوْتَ إِلَيْهِمَا، وَ أَنَّكَ صَادِقٌ صِدِّيقٌ، صَدَقْتَ فِيمَا دَعَوْتَ إِلَيْهِ، وَ أَنَّكَ ثَارُ اللهِ فِي الْأَرْضِ،

I testify that you enjoined justice and fairness and you called the people to them and that you are veracious and truthful, true in your summons! I testify that you are the slain one of the earth whose avenger is Allah.

وَ أَشْهَدُ أَنَّكَ قَدْ بَلَّغْتَ عَنِ اللهِ، وَ عَنْ جَدِّكَ رَسُولِ اللهِ، وَ عَنْ أَبِيكَ أَمِيرِ الْمُؤْمِنِينَ، وَ عَنْ أَخِيكَ الْحَسَنِ، وَ نَصَحْتَ وَ جَاهَدْتَ فِي سَبِيلِ اللهِ، وَ عَبَدْتَهُ مُخْلِصًا حَتَّى أَتَاكَ الْيَقِينُ، فَجَزَاكَ اللهُ خَيْرَ جَزَاءِ السَّابِقِينَ، وَ صَلَّى اللهُ عَلَيْكَ وَ سَلَّمَ تَسْلِيمًا.

I testify that you delivered all that you were charged with by Allah and by the Apostle of Allah, your grandfather, the Commander of the Faithful, your father, and al-Ḥasan, your brother, and that you were sincere and waged *jihād* in the way of Allah and served Him devoutly until the last breath! May Allah reward you with the best of what He has granted to the foremost (of His servants) and may He bless you and greet you in the worthiest manner!

اَللّٰهُمَّ صَلِّ عَلَىٰ مُحَمَّدٍ وَ آلِ مُحَمَّدٍ، وَ

O Allah bless Muḥammad and the

Family of Muḥammad and bless al-Ḥusayn, the aggrieved one and the rightly-guided martyr, the slain one mourned by the tearful, the victim of many sufferings, with a blessing that is growing, enhancing and bounteous, ascending at its front and endless at its end, the best of what You have granted to any of the offspring of Your prophets and envoys, O God of all the worlds!

صَلِّ عَلَى الْحُسَيْنِ الْمَظْلُومِ الشَّهِيدِ الرَّشِيدِ، قَتِيلِ الْعَبَرَاتِ، وَ أَسِيرِ الْكُرُبَاتِ، صَلَاةً نَامِيَةً زَاكِيَةً مُبَارَكَةً، يَصْعَدُ أَوَّلُهَا وَ لَا يَنْفَدُ آخِرُهَا، أَفْضَلَ مَا صَلَّيْتَ عَلَى أَحَدٍ مِنْ أَوْلَادِ أَنْبِيَائِكَ الْمُرْسَلِينَ، يَا إِلٰهَ الْعَالَمِينَ!

Then embrace the tomb, laying the right cheek on it and then the left. Then go around it and kiss its four corners.

According to Shaykh Mufīd's report,[1] one should then proceed towards the grave of ᶜAlī ibn al-Ḥusayn (ᶜa), and, standing near it, say,

Peace be to you O truthful, pure and immaculate one, the intimate and beloved of Allah, and son of the apple of eye of the Apostle of Allah! Peace be to you O martyr, who were resigned to the will of Allah, and may Allah's mercy and His bounties be upon you! How noble is your station and how dignified your final goal!

اَلسَّلَامُ عَلَيْكَ أَيُّهَا الصِّدِّيقُ الطَّيِّبُ الزَّكِيُّ الْحَبِيبُ الْمُقَرَّبُ، وَ ابْنَ رَيْحَانَةِ رَسُولِ اللهِ، اَلسَّلَامُ عَلَيْكَ مِنْ شَهِيدٍ مُحْتَسِبٍ، وَ رَحْمَةُ اللهِ وَ بَرَكَاتُهُ، مَا أَكْرَمَ مَقَامَكَ وَ أَشْرَفَ مُنْقَلَبَكَ،

I testify that Allah has appreciated your endeavour, rewarded you abundantly, and admitted you to the highest peak of dignity and nobility, and to the exalted abodes, even as He had favoured you earlier and made you one of the members of the Family of the Prophet from *whom Allah has repelled all impurity and purified them*

أَشْهَدُ لَقَدْ شَكَرَ اللهُ سَعْيَكَ، وَ أَجْزَلَ ثَوَابَكَ، وَ أَلْحَقَكَ بِالذِّرْوَةِ الْعَالِيَةِ حَيْثُ الشَّرَفُ كُلُّ الشَّرَفِ، وَ فِي الْغُرَفِ السَّامِيَةِ، كَمَا مَنَّ عَلَيْكَ مِنْ قَبْلُ وَ جَعَلَكَ مِنْ أَهْلِ الْبَيْتِ الَّذِينَ

[1] *Biḥār*, xcviii, 337, b 26, h 1, from Shaykh Mufīd.

with a thorough purification! (33:33) May the blessings of Allah be upon you and so may His mercy, bounties and good pleasure!

أَذْهَبَ اللهُ عَنْهُمُ الرِّجْسَ وَ طَهَّرَهُمْ تَطْهِيرًا، صَلَوَاتُ اللهِ عَلَيْكَ وَ رَحْمَةُ اللهِ وَ بَرَكَاتُهُ وَ رِضْوَانُهُ،

O immaculate master, intercede for me with your Lord concerning removal of the burden of sins from my back and relief from their weight! Have mercy on my lowliness and humbleness in front of you and your revered father, may Allah bless both of you!

فَاشْفَعْ أَيُّهَا السَّيِّدُ الطَّاهِرُ إِلَىٰ رَبِّكَ فِي حَطِّ الْأَثْقَالِ عَنْ ظَهْرِي، وَ تَخْفِيفِهَا عَنِّي، وَ ارْحَمْ ذُلِّي وَ خُضُوعِي لَكَ وَ لِلسَّيِّدِ أَبِيكَ صَلَّى اللهُ عَلَيْكُمَا.

Then embracing the grave, say,

May Allah enhance your dignity in the Hereafter, inasmuch as He has honoured you in the world, and may He make you felicitous, inasmuch as He has made His servants felicitous through you! I testify that you are the landmarks of God's religion and guiding stars for the world's people! Peace be to you and may Allah's mercy and His bounties be upon you!

زَادَ اللهُ فِي شَرَفِكُمْ فِي الْآخِرَةِ كَمَا شَرَّفَكُمْ فِي الدُّنْيَا، وَ أَسْعَدَكُمْ كَمَا أَسْعَدَ بِكُمْ، وَ أَشْهَدُ أَنَّكُمْ أَعْلَامُ الدِّينِ وَ نُجُومُ الْعَالَمِينَ، وَ السَّلَامُ عَلَيْكُمْ وَ رَحْمَةُ اللهِ وَ بَرَكَاتُهُ.

Then turn towards the tomb of the martyrs and say,

Peace be to you O helpers of Allah and the helpers of His Apostle, the helpers of ʿAlī ibn Abī Ṭālib, the helpers of Fāṭimah, the helpers of al-Ḥasan and al-Ḥusayn, and the helpers of Islam!

اَلسَّلَامُ عَلَيْكُمْ يَا أَنْصَارَ اللهِ وَ أَنْصَارَ رَسُولِهِ وَ أَنْصَارَ عَلِيِّ بْنِ أَبِي طَالِبٍ وَ أَنْصَارَ فَاطِمَةَ وَ أَنْصَارَ الْحَسَنِ وَ الْحُسَيْنِ وَ أَنْصَارَ الْإِسْلَامِ،

I testify that you served Allah

أَشْهَدُ أَنَّكُمْ لَقَدْ نَصَحْتُمْ لِلّٰهِ، وَ

جَاهَدْتُمْ فِي سَبِيلِهِ، فَجَزَاكُمُ اللهُ عَنِ الْإِسْلَامِ وَ أَهْلِهِ أَفْضَلَ الْجَزَاءِ، فُزْتُمْ وَ اللهِ فَوْزًا عَظِيمًا، يَا لَيْتَنِي كُنْتُ مَعَكُمْ فَأَفُوزَ فَوْزًا عَظِيمًا.	sincerely and waged *jihād* in His way! So may Allah reward you on behalf of Islam and its people with the best of rewards! By Allah, you attained a great triumph, and how I wish I had been with you and attained such a great triumph!
أَشْهَدُ أَنَّكُمْ أَحْيَاءٌ عِنْدَ رَبِّكُمْ تُرْزَقُونَ، أَشْهَدُ أَنَّكُمُ الشُّهَدَاءُ وَ السُّعَدَاءُ، وَ أَنَّكُمُ الْفَائِزُونَ فِي دَرَجَاتِ الْعُلَى، وَ السَّلَامُ عَلَيْكُمْ وَ رَحْمَةُ اللهِ وَ بَرَكَاتُهُ.	I testify that you are living and provided for near your Lord! I testify that you attained martyrdom and felicity and that you succeeded in attaining to the highest of degrees! Peace be to you and may Allah's mercy and His bounties be upon you!

Then return to the head of the tomb of Imam al-Ḥusayn (ᶜ*a*) and perform the prayer of *ziyārah* and supplicate for yourself, your parents and brethren in faith.

Sayyid ᶜAlī b. Ṭāwūs has cited[1] a *ziyārah* of Ḥaḍrat ᶜAlī Akbar and other martyrs wherein are mentioned their names. As it is very well-known, we refrain from citing it here for reasons of space.

2. Ziyarah for the 15th of Rajab

This *ziyārah* has been cited by Shaykh Mufīd in his *Kitāb al-Mazār*[2] as one meant for the middle of Rajab. It is known as "Ziyārat al-Ghufaylah," as the middle of Rajab is known as *ghufaylah* (drived from *ghaflah*, which means inattention or negligence) on account of the people's negligence and lack of attention to the virtues of this day.

When intending to perform the Imam's *ziyārah* at this time, enter the shrine and say three times "*Allāhu akbar.*" Then, standing near the tomb, say,

اَلسَّلَامُ عَلَيْكُمْ يَا آلَ اللهِ، اَلسَّلَامُ	Peace be to you, O family of Allah! Peace be to you, O

[1] *Iqbāl*, 572, whence *Biḥār*, xlv, 64-73, b 37, h 3, xcviii, 269-274, b 19, h 1 & *Mustadrak*, x, 408, b 86, h 12266/9.

[2] *Biḥār*, xcviii, 345, b 27, h 1, from Shaykh Mufīd. Shahīd Awwal's *Mazār*, 161-164.

chosen ones of Allah! Peace be to you, O elect of Allah from His creation! Peace be to you, O chiefs of all the chiefs! Peace be to you, O lions of the woods! Peace be to you, O arks of salvation!

عَلَيْكُمْ يَا صِفْوَةَ اللهِ، اَلسَّلَامُ عَلَيْكُمْ
يَا خِيَرَةَ اللهِ مِنْ خَلْقِهِ، اَلسَّلَامُ عَلَيْكُمْ يَا
سَادَةَ السَّادَاتِ، اَلسَّلَامُ عَلَيْكُمْ يَا لُيُوثَ
الْغَابَاتِ، اَلسَّلَامُ عَلَيْكُمْ يَا سُفُنَ النَّجَاةِ،

Peace be to you, O Abū ʿAbdillāh al-Ḥusayn! Peace be to you, O heir to the knowledge of all the prophets and may Allah's mercy and His bounties be upon you!

اَلسَّلَامُ عَلَيْكَ يَا أَبَا عَبْدِ اللهِ الْحُسَيْنِ،
اَلسَّلَامُ عَلَيْكَ يَا وَارِثَ عِلْمِ الْأَنْبِيَاءِ وَ
رَحْمَةُ اللهِ وَ بَرَكَاتُهُ.

Peace be to you, O heir of Adam, the chosen of Allah! Peace be to you, O heir of Noah, the prophet of Allah! Peace be to you, O heir of Abraham, the dedicated friend of Allah! Peace be to you, O heir of Ishmael, who was sacrificed for the sake of Allah! Peace be to you, O heir of Moses, the interlocutor of Allah! Peace be to you, O heir of Jesus, spirit of Allah!

اَلسَّلَامُ عَلَيْكَ يَا وَارِثَ آدَمَ صِفْوَةِ اللهِ،
اَلسَّلَامُ عَلَيْكَ يَا وَارِثَ نُوحٍ نَبِيِّ اللهِ،
اَلسَّلَامُ عَلَيْكَ يَا وَارِثَ إِبْرَاهِيمَ خَلِيلِ اللهِ،
اَلسَّلَامُ عَلَيْكَ يَا وَارِثَ إِسْمَاعِيلَ ذَبِيحِ اللهِ،
اَلسَّلَامُ عَلَيْكَ يَا وَارِثَ مُوسَىٰ كَلِيمِ اللهِ،
اَلسَّلَامُ عَلَيْكَ يَا وَارِثَ عِيسَىٰ رُوحِ اللهِ،

Peace be to you, O heir of Muḥammad, the beloved of Allah! Peace be to you, O son of Muḥammad al-Muṣṭafa! Peace be to you, O son of ʿAlī al-Murtaḍā! Peace be to you, O son of Fāṭimah Zahrā! Peace be to you, O son of Khadījat al-Kubrā!

اَلسَّلَامُ عَلَيْكَ يَا وَارِثَ مُحَمَّدٍ حَبِيبِ اللهِ،
اَلسَّلَامُ عَلَيْكَ يَا ابْنَ مُحَمَّدٍ الْمُصْطَفَىٰ،
اَلسَّلَامُ عَلَيْكَ يَا ابْنَ عَلِيٍّ الْمُرْتَضَىٰ،
اَلسَّلَامُ عَلَيْكَ يَا ابْنَ فَاطِمَةَ الزَّهْرَاءِ،
اَلسَّلَامُ عَلَيْكَ يَا ابْنَ خَدِيجَةَ الْكُبْرَىٰ،

Peace be to you, O martyr, son of martyr! Peace be to you, who were slain for the sake of Allah, son of him who was slain for

اَلسَّلَامُ عَلَيْكَ يَا شَهِيدُ بْنَ الشَّهِيدِ،
اَلسَّلَامُ عَلَيْكَ يَا قَتِيلُ بْنَ الْقَتِيلِ، اَلسَّلَامُ

عَلَيْكَ يَا وَلِيَّ اللهِ وَ ابْنَ وَلِيِّهِ، اَلسَّلَامُ عَلَيْكَ يَا حُجَّةَ اللهِ وَ ابْنَ حُجَّتِهِ عَلَىٰ خَلْقِهِ،

Allah! Peace be to you, O *walī* of Allah and son of His *walī*! Peace be to you, O testament of Allah and son of His testament to His creation!

أَشْهَدُ أَنَّكَ قَدْ أَقَمْتَ الصَّلَاةَ، وَ آتَيْتَ الزَّكَاةَ، وَ أَمَرْتَ بِالْمَعْرُوفِ، وَ نَهَيْتَ عَنِ الْمُنْكَرِ، وَ رُزِئْتَ [وَ بَرَرْتَ] بِوَالِدَيْكَ، وَ جَاهَدْتَ عَدُوَّكَ،

I testify that you maintained the prayer, paid the *zakāt*, bade what is right and forbade what is wrong, suffered the loss of [were kind to] your parents, and waged *jihād* against your enemies.

وَ أَشْهَدُ أَنَّكَ تَسْمَعُ الْكَلَامَ، وَ تَرُدُّ الْجَوَابَ، وَ أَنَّكَ حَبِيبُ اللهِ وَ خَلِيلُهُ وَ نَجِيبُهُ وَ صَفِيُّهُ وَ ابْنُ صَفِيِّهِ. يَا مَوْلَاى وَ ابْنَ مَوْلَاى، زُرْتُكَ مُشْتَاقًا فَكُنْ لِي شَفِيعًا إِلَى اللهِ يَا سَيِّدِى، وَ أَسْتَشْفِعُ إِلَى اللهِ بِجَدِّكَ سَيِّدِ النَّبِيِّينَ، وَ بِأَبِيكَ سَيِّدِ الْوَصِيِّينَ، وَ بِأُمِّكَ فَاطِمَةَ سَيِّدَةِ نِسَاءِ الْعَالَمِينَ،

I testify that you hear my speech and answer me, and that you are the beloved of Allah, His dedicated, select, and chosen friend and son of His chosen one! My master, son of my master, I have come eagerly for your pilgrimage. So intercede for me with Allah, O my master! I seek intercession with Allah through your grandfather, the Chief of the prophets, through your father, the chief of the Legatees, through your mother, Fāṭimah, the mistress of the world's womankind.

أَلَا لَعَنَ اللهُ قَاتِلِيكَ، وَ لَعَنَ اللهُ ظَالِمِيكَ، وَ لَعَنَ اللهُ سَالِبِيكَ وَ مُبْغِضِيكَ مِنَ الْأَوَّلِينَ وَ الْآخِرِينَ، وَ صَلَّى اللهُ عَلَىٰ سَيِّدِنَا مُحَمَّدٍ وَ آلِهِ الطَّيِّبِينَ الطَّاهِرِينَ.

May Allah's curse be on those who slew you! May Allah's curse be on those who wronged you! May Allah's curse be on those who robbed you and usurped your rights, from those of the former generations and the latter! May Allah bless our master, Muḥammad, and his pure and immaculate Family!

Then embrace the holy grave and turning toward the graves of ⁽ᶜ⁾Alī ibn al-Ḥusayn (ᶜa), perform his *ziyārah* and say,

Peace be to you, O my master, son of my master! May Allah's curse be on those who slew you! May Allah's curse be on those who wronged you! I seek nearness to Allah through my *ziyārah* and my love for you, and I repudiate your enemies before Allah! Peace be to you, O my master, and may Allah's mercy and His bounties be upon you!

اَلسَّـلامُ عَلَيْـكَ يَـا مَـوْلاىَ وَ ابْنَ مَوْلاىَ، لَعَـنَ اللهُ قَاتِلِيكَ، وَ لَعَنَ اللهُ ظَالِمِيكَ، إِنِّي أَتَقَرَّبُ إِلَى اللهِ بِزِيَارَتِكُمْ وَ بِمَحَبَّتِكُـمْ، وَ أَبْـرَأُ إِلَى اللهِ مِـنْ أَعْدَائِكُمْ، وَ السَّلامُ عَلَيْكَ يَا مَوْلاىَ وَ رَحْمَةُ اللهِ وَ بَرَكَاتُهُ.

Then proceed towards the graves of the martyrs, may Allah be pleased with them, and standing there, say,

Peace be to the spirits who have made the tomb of Abū ⁽ᶜ⁾Abdillāh al-Ḥusayn, peace be to him, the destination of their journey! Peace be to you, O pure souls, free of all defilement! Peace be to you, O rightly guided ones! Peace be to you, O pious servants of Allah! Peace be to you and to all the angels that surround your graves!

اَلسَّـلامُ عَلَى الْأَرْوَاحِ الْمُنِيخَةِ بِقَبْرِ أَبِي عَبْدِ اللهِ الْحُسَيْنِ عَلَيْهِ السَّلامُ، اَلسَّلامُ عَلَيْكُمْ يَا طَاهِرِينَ مِنَ الدَّنَسِ، اَلسَّلامُ عَلَيْكُمْ يَا مَهْدِيُّونَ، اَلسَّلامُ عَلَيْكُمْ يَا أَبْرَارَ اللهِ، اَلسَّـلامُ عَلَيْكُمْ وَ عَلَى الْمَلائِكَةِ الْحَافِّينَ بِقُبُورِكُمْ أَجْمَعِينَ،

May Allah gather us and you in the abode of His mercy and under His throne. Indeed He is the Most Merciful of the merciful! Peace be to you and may Allah's mercy and His bounties be upon you!

جَمَعَنَا اللهُ وَ إِيَّاكُمْ فِي مُسْتَقَرِّ رَحْمَتِهِ، وَ تَحْتِ عَرْشِـهِ، إِنَّهُ أَرْحَـمُ الرَّاحِمِينَ، وَ السَّلامُ عَلَيْكُمْ وَ رَحْمَةُ اللهِ وَ بَرَكَاتُهُ.

After this, proceed towards the shrine of al-ᶜAbbās, son of the Commander of the Faithful (ᶜa), and on reaching the door of the shrine chamber say, "*Salāmullāhi wa salāmu malâ'ikatihil muqarrabīn...*" The text of this *ziyārah* has been cited above (p. 292).

3. Ziyarah for the 15th of Sha'ban

One should know that there are many reports that mention the virtues of the Imam's *ziyārah* on the 15th of the month of Shaʿbān. It will be sufficient to mention here one report transmitted with several reliable *isnād* from Imam Zayn al-ʿĀbidīn (*ʿa*) and Imam Jaʿfar al-Ṣādiq (*ʿa*).

The Imams have been reported[1] to have said that whoever desires to shake hands with 124,000 prophets should perform the *ziyārah* of Abū ʿAbdillāh al Ḥusayn (*ʿa*) on the 15th of Shaʿban, for on this day the angels and the spirits of the prophets take leave and come for the *ziyārah* of the Imam. Happy are those who shake hands with them, for they are accompanied by their five *ulu al-ʿazm* apostles of Allah, namely, Noah, Abraham, Moses, Jesus and Muḥammad, may Allah bless him and his Family and all the prophets. When asked by the narrator of the report as to why the five of them were called *ūlu al-ʿazm*, the Imam explained that it was because they had been sent to the denizens of the East and the West, humankind and the jinn.

There are two versions of the text of the *ziyārah*. One of them is the same as the one cited for the first day of Rajab (p. 300). The other has been cited by Shaykh Kafʿamī in his book *al-Balad al-Amin* from Imam Jaʿfar al-Ṣādiq (*ʿa*).[2] According to this version, one should stand near the tomb of the Imam and say,

All praise belongs to Allah, the All-exalted, the All-supreme. Peace be to you, O Allah's righteous and noble servant! I entrust you with my testimony concerning you that will bring me near to you on the day of your intercession (with Allah).	اَلْحَمْدُ لِلّٰهِ الْعَلِيِّ الْعَظِيمِ، وَ السَّلَامُ عَلَيْكَ أَيُّهَا الْعَبْدُ الصَّالِحُ الزَّكِيُّ، أُودِعُكَ شَهَادَةً مِنِّي لَكَ تُقَرِّبُنِي إِلَيْكَ فِي يَوْمِ شَفَاعَتِكَ،

1 *Kāmil al-Ziyārāt*, 179, b 72, h 2, whence *Biḥār*, xi, 32, b 1, h 25, xcviii, 93, b 13, h 2 & *Mustadrak*, x, 288, b 38, h 12031/2. Mufīd's *Mazār*, 42, b 18, h 1. Ṭūsī's *Miṣbāḥ*, 830. *Tahdhīb*, vi, 48, b 16, h 24, whence *Wasā'il*, xiv, 467, b 51, h 19615. *Iqbāl*, 710, whence *Wasā'il*, xiv, 470, b 51, h 19622 & *Biḥār*, xi, 58, b 1, h 61. Jazā'rī's *Qiṣaṣ*, 5.

2 Kafʿamī's *Miṣbāḥ*, 498. *Balad*, 284, whence *Biḥār*, xcviii, 342, b 26, h 2.

أَشْهَدُ أَنَّكَ قُتِلْتَ وَ لَمْ تَمُتْ، بَلْ بِرَجَاءِ حَيَاتِكَ حَيِيَتْ قُلُوبُ شِيعَتِكَ، وَ بِضِيَاءِ نُورِكَ اهْتَدَى الطَّالِبُونَ إِلَيْكَ،

I testify that you were slain and died not. Rather it is by the hope of your life that the hearts of your followers are kept alive, and it is with your light that your seekers are guided to you!

وَ أَشْهَدُ أَنَّكَ نُورُ اللهِ الَّذِي لَمْ يُطْفَأْ وَ لَا يُطْفَأُ أَبَدًا، وَ أَنَّكَ وَجْهُ اللهِ الَّذِي لَمْ يَهْلِكْ وَ لَا يُهْلَكُ أَبَدًا،

I testify that you are Allah's light which was not nor will ever be extinguished, and that you are the Face of Allah that did not nor will ever perish.

وَ أَشْهَدُ أَنَّ هٰذِهِ التُّرْبَةَ تُرْبَتُكَ، وَ هٰذَا الْحَرَمَ حَرَمُكَ، وَ هٰذَا الْمَصْرَعَ مَصْرَعُ بَدَنِكَ، لَا ذَلِيلَ وَاللهِ مُعِزُّكَ، وَ لَا مَغْلُوبَ وَاللهِ نَاصِرُكَ، هٰذِهِ شَهَادَةٌ لِي عِنْدَكَ إِلَى يَوْمِ قَبْضِ رُوحِي بِحَضْرَتِكَ، وَ السَّلَامُ عَلَيْكَ وَ رَحْمَةُ اللهِ وَ بَرَكَاتُهُ.

I testify that this soil is the soil of your grave and this shrine is your sanctuary. This is the place where your body fell on the battlefield. By Allah, those who support you will never be weak and those who help you are never defeated! Let this testimony of mine be with you until the day my spirit is taken out of my body in your presence! Peace be to you and may Allah's mercy and His bounties be upon you!

4. Ziyarah for the Night(s) of Qadr

There are many traditions[1] mentioning the virtues of Imam al-Ḥusayn's *ziyārah* during the blessed month of Ramaḍān on the night of the first, fifteenth and last day of the month and especially on the Night of Qadr.

Imam Muḥammad al-Taqī (*ᶜa*) is reported[2] to have said that those who perform the *ziyārah* of Imam al-Ḥusayn (*ᶜa*) on the eve of the twenty-third of Ramaḍān—a night which is hoped to be the Night of Qadr and during which every matter of consequence is ordained—will be greeted by the spirits of twenty-four thousand angels and prophets who visit the Imam's shrine on this night with the permis-

[1] *Wasā'il*, xiv, 472-475, b 53, h 19628-19633. *Biḥār*, xcviii, 349, b 29, h 1-3.

[2] *Iqbāl*, 212, whence *Wasā'il*, xiv, 474, b 53, h 19632 & *Biḥār*, xcv, 166, xcviii, 100, b 13, h 31.

sion of God Almighty.

It is mentioned in another reliable report[1] from Imam Jaᶜfar al-Ṣādiq (ᶜa) that when the Night of Qadr befalls, a caller cries out from the seventh heaven, "God, the Most High, has forgiven all those who have visited the shrine of al-Ḥusayn for *ziyārah*."

It is mentioned in a report[2] that whoever offers two *rakᶜahs* of prayer, or whatever is feasible for him, at the shrine of Imam al-Ḥusayn on the Night of Qadr, and asks God to rescue him from the fire of hell and admit him into paradise, God grants his request and delivers him from hellfire.

Ibn Qūlawayh reports[3] that Imam Jaᶜfar al-Ṣādiq (ᶜa) said that someone who visits the shrine of Imam al-Ḥusayn during the month of Ramaḍān and dies during the pilgrimage journey will not be subjected to the reckoning of his works on the Day of Resurrection and will be told, "Enter paradise without any qualms."

The text of Imam al-Ḥusayn's *ziyārah* for the Night of Qadr has been cited by Shaykh Mufīd, Muḥammad b. al-Mashhadī, Sayyid Ibn Ṭāwūs and Shahīd Awwal.[4] They prescribe this text for this night as well for the days of ᶜĪd al-Fiṭr and ᶜĪd al-Aḍḥā.

Muḥammad b. al-Mashhadī reports[5] it with a reliable chain of authorities from Imam Jaᶜfar al-Ṣādiq (ᶜa), who is reported to have said: "When you intend to perform the *ziyārah* of Abū ᶜAbdillāh al-Ḥusayn (ᶜa), go to his shrine after having taken bath and putting on your cleanest clothes. While standing near his grave, turn your face towards his tomb with the back towards the *qiblah* and say,

اَلسَّلَامُ عَلَيْكَ يَا ابْنَ رَسُولِ اللهِ، اَلسَّلَامُ
عَلَيْكَ يَا ابْنَ أَمِيرِ الْمُؤْمِنِينَ، اَلسَّـلَامُ
عَلَيْكَ يَا ابْنَ الصِّدِّيقَةِ الطَّاهِرَةِ فَاطِمَةَ
سَيِّدَةِ نِسَاءِ الْعَالَمِينَ، اَلسَّلَامُ عَلَيْكَ يَا

Peace be to you, O son of the Apostle of Allah! Peace be to you, O son of the Commander of the Faithful! Peace be to you, O son of the truthful and the immaculate Fāṭimah, mistress of the world's womankind! Peace be to you, O

1 *Kāmil al-Ziyārāt*, 184, b 74, h 5, whence *Biḥār*, xcviii, 96, b 13, h 18. Mufīd's *Mazār*, 54, b 24, h 1. *Tahdhīb*, vi, 49, b 16, h 26, whence *Wasā'il*, xiv, 472, b 53, h 19628. *Iqbāl*, 212, whence *Wasā'il*, xiv, 474, b 53, h 19633 & *Biḥār*, xcv, 166, xcviii, 100, b 13, h 32.

2 *Iqbāl*, 212, whence *Biḥār*, xcviii, 99, b 13, h 30.

3 *Kāmil al-Ziyārāt*, 330, b 108, h 7, whence *Biḥār*, xcviii, 97, b 13, h 20.

4 *Biḥār*, xcviii, 350, b 29, h 2, citing Mufīd and Shahīd Awwal.

5 *Al-Mzār al-Kabīr*, 414, whence *Biḥār*, xcviii, 351, b 29, h 3.

my master, O Abu ᶜAbdillāh, and may Allah's mercy and His bounties be upon you!

مَــوْلاَيَ يَا أَبَا عَبْـدِ اللهِ وَ رَحْمَةُ اللهِ وَ بَرَكَاتُهُ،

I testify that you maintained the prayer, paid the *zakāt*, bade what is right and forbade what is wrong, followed the Scripture as it is worthy of being followed, waged *jihād* in the way of Allah as is worthy of Him, bore patiently all the torments for His sake and in resignation to His will, until the last breath!

أَشْـهَدُ أَنَّكَ قَدْ أَقَمْتَ الصَّلاَةَ، وَ آتَيْتَ الزَّكَاةَ، وَ أَمَرْتَ بِالْمَعْرُوفِ، وَ نَهَيْتَ عَنِ الْمُنْكَرِ، وَ تَلَوْتَ الْكِتَابَ حَقَّ تِلاَوَتِهِ، وَ جَاهَدْتَ فِي اللهِ حَقَّ جِهَادِهِ، وَ صَبَرْتَ عَلَى الْأَذَىٰ فِي جَنْبِهِ مُحْتَسِبًا حَتَّىٰ أَتَاكَ الْيَقِينُ،

I testify that those who opposed you and fought against you, those who forsook you and those who slew you, were accursed ones, cursed by the tongue of the untutored Prophet, and *whoever fabricates lies certainly fails.*

أَشْـهَدُ أَنَّ الَّذِينَ خَالَفُوكَ وَ حَارَبُوكَ وَ الَّذِينَ خَذَلُوكَ وَ الَّذِينَ قَتَلُوكَ مَلْعُونُونَ عَلَىٰ لِسَـانِ النَّبِيِّ الْأُمِّيِّ، وَ قَدْ خَابَ مَنِ افْتَرَىٰ،

May Allah's curse be on those who wronged you, those of the former and the latter generations, and may He double their painful punishment!

لَعَنَ اللهُ الظَّالِمِينَ لَكُـمْ مِنَ الْأَوَّلِينَ وَ الْآخِرِيـنَ، وَ ضَاعَفَ عَلَيْهِمُ الْعَذَابَ الْأَلِيمَ،

I come to you, my master, O son of the Apostle of Allah, as a pilgrim, well knowing your right, befriending your friends and despising your enemies, enlightened concerning the rightness of what you stood for, knowing well that those who opposed you were an astray lot! So intercede for me with your Lord!

أَتَيْتُكَ يَا مَوْلاَيَ يَا ابْنَ رَسُولِ اللهِ زَائِرًا عَارِفًا بِحَقِّكَ، مُوَالِيًـا لِأَوْلِيَائِكَ، مُعَادِيًا لِأَعْدَائِـكَ، مُسْـتَبْصِرًا بِالْهُدَى الَّذِي أَنْتَ عَلَيْهِ، عَارِفًا بِضَلاَلَةِ مَنْ خَالَفَكَ، فَاشْفَعْ لِي عِنْدَ رَبِّكَ.

Then embrace the tomb and lay your cheek on it. Then, after moving on towards the head of the tomb, say,

Peace be to you, O testament of Allah on His earth and in His heaven! May Allah bless your immaculate spirit and your pure body! Peace be to you, my master, and may Allah's mercy and His bounties be upon you!

اَلسَّلامُ عَلَيْكَ يا حُجَّةَ اللهِ فِي أَرْضِهِ
وَ سَمائِهِ، صَلَّى اللهُ عَلى رُوحِكَ الطَّيِّبِ
وَ جَسَدِكَ الطّاهِرِ، وَ عَلَيْكَ السَّلامُ يا
مَوْلايَ وَ رَحْمَةُ اللهِ وَ بَرَكاتُهُ.

Then embrace the tomb and put your cheek on it. Then offer a two-*rakʿah* prayer of *ziyārah* at the head of the tomb, and after that pray as much as is feasible for you. Then moving on towards the foot of the tomb, perform the *ziyārah* of ʿAlī ibn al-Ḥusayn (*ʿa*) and say,

Peace be to you, O my master, my master's son, and may Allah's mercy and His bounties be upon you! May Allah's curse be on those who wronged you! May the curse of Allah be on those who slew you and may He double their painful punishment!

اَلسَّلامُ عَلَيْكَ يا مَوْلايَ وَ ابْنَ مَوْلايَ وَ
رَحْمَةُ اللهِ وَ بَرَكاتُهُ، لَعَنَ اللهُ مَنْ ظَلَمَكَ،
وَ لَعَنَ اللهُ مَنْ قَتَلَكَ، وَ ضاعَفَ عَلَيْهِمُ
الْعَذابَ الْأَلِيمَ.

Then supplicate and make any petitions you wish. Then perform the *ziyārah* of the martyrs while facing the *qiblah* from the feet of the tomb, and say,

Peace be to you, O truthful ones! Peace be to you, O martyrs and patient souls! I testify that you waged *jihād* in the way of Allah and bore torments patiently for His sake! You worked devotedly for the cause of Allah and His Apostle until your demise!

اَلسَّلامُ عَلَيْكُمْ أَيُّهَا الصِّدِّيقُونَ، اَلسَّلامُ
عَلَيْكُمْ أَيُّهَا الشُّهَداءُ الصّابِرُونَ، أَشْهَدُ
أَنَّكُمْ جاهَدْتُمْ فِي سَبِيلِ اللهِ، وَ صَبَرْتُمْ
عَلَى الْأَذى فِي جَنْبِ اللهِ، وَ نَصَحْتُمْ لِلّٰهِ
وَ لِرَسُولِهِ حَتّى أَتاكُمُ الْيَقِينُ،

I testify that you are living and provided for near Allah!

أَشْهَدُ أَنَّكُمْ أَحْياءٌ عِنْدَ رَبِّكُمْ تُرْزَقُونَ،

فَجَزَاكُمُ اللهُ عَنِ الْإِسْلَامِ وَ أَهْلِهِ أَفْضَلَ جَزَاءِ الْمُحْسِنِينَ، وَ جَمَعَ بَيْنَنَا وَ بَيْنَكُمْ فِي مَحَلِّ النَّعِيمِ.

May Allah grant you the best of rewards that He grants to the virtuous on behalf of Islam and its followers! May He gather you and us together in the Abode of bliss!

Then proceed to perform the *ziyārah* of ᶜAbbās son of the Commander of the Faithful (*ᶜa*). On reaching the tomb, stand near the grave and say,

اَلسَّلَامُ عَلَيْكَ يَا ابْنَ أَمِيرِ الْمُؤْمِنِينَ، اَلسَّلَامُ عَلَيْكَ أَيُّهَا الْعَبْدُ الصَّالِحُ الْمُطِيعُ لِلّٰهِ وَ لِرَسُولِهِ، أَشْهَدُ أَنَّكَ قَدْ جَاهَدْتَ وَ نَصَحْتَ وَ صَبَرْتَ حَتّٰى أَتَاكَ الْيَقِينُ، لَعَنَ اللهُ الظَّالِمِينَ لَكُمْ مِنَ الْأَوَّلِينَ وَ الْآخِرِينَ، وَ أَلْحَقَهُمْ بِدَرْكِ الْجَحِيمِ.

Peace be to you, O son of the Commander of the Faithful! Peace be to you, O righteous servant of Allah, who were obedient to Allah and His Apostle! I testify that you waged *jihād* and strived with devotion and patience until the last breath! May Allah's curse be on those who wronged you, from those of the former and the latter generations, and may He consign them to the lowest reaches of hell!

Then pray as much as you may wish in the mosque of his shrine before leaving.

5. Ziyarah for the Eves of ʻĪd al-Fitr & al-Adha[1]

According to a report with a reliable *isnād*,[2] Imam Jaᶜfar al-Ṣādiq (*ᶜa*) said that those who perform *ziyārah* of Imam al-Ḥusayn's shrine on one of these three nights are forgiven their past and future sins: the eve of ᶜĪd al-Fiṭr, the eve of ᶜĪd al-Aḍḥā, and the eve of 15th Shaᶜbān.

According to another report with a reliable *isnād*,[3] Imam Mūsā al-Kāẓim (*ᶜa*) said that there are three nights wherein those who per-

[1] *Biḥār*, xcviii, 352-355.

[2] *Kāmil al-Ziyārāt*, 180, b 72, h 6, whence *Biḥār*, xcviii, 89, b 12, h 23, xcviii, 94, b 13, h 10 & *Mustadrak*, x, 290, b 40, h 12035/1. Mufīd's *Mazār*, 45, b 19, h 1. *Tahdhīb*, vi, 49, b 16, h 27, whence *Wasā'il*, xiv, 475, b 54, h 19634.

[3] *Biḥār*, xcviii, 101, b 13, h 36, from *Miṣbāḥ al-Zā'ir*.

form *ziyārah* of Imam al-Ḥusayn (*ᶜa*) are forgiven their past and future sins. They are: the eve of 15th of Shaᶜbān, eve of 23rd of Ramaḍān, and the eve of ᶜĪd al-Fiṭr.

Imam Jaᶜfar al-Ṣādiq (*ᶜa*) is reported[1] to have said that for those who perform *ziyārah* of Imam al-Ḥusayn (*ᶜa*) on the eve of 15th Shaᶜbān, the eve of ᶜĪd al-Fiṭr and the eve of ᶜArafah within a single year, God Almighty writes the reward of a thousand *ḥajj* and a thousand *ᶜumrah* pilgrimages blessed with acceptance, and fulfils a thousand of their needs pertaining to life in this world and the Hereafter.

Imam Muḥammad al-Bāqir (*ᶜa*) is reported[2] to have said that those who are present in Karbalā on the eve of ᶜArafah and stay there to perform the Imam's *ziyārah* on the day of ᶜĪd before returning home, God Almighty saves them from the harms of that year.

The scholars have narrated two *ziyārahs* for these two blessed occasions of ᶜĪd.[3] One of them is the same as the one mentioned for the Nights of Qadr. Their statements indicate that the aforementioned *ziyārah* is meant for these two ᶜīd days and that the following *ziyārah* is for the nights that precede them.

The manner of its performance has been mentioned as follows. When intending to perform the Imam's *ziyārah* on any of these two nights, one should stand at the door of the shrine chamber and while looking at the tomb recite the following text by way of appeal for the leave of admittance:[4]

O my master, O Abū ᶜAbd Allāh! O son of the Apostle of Allah! I, your humble servant and son of your handmaid, stand in your presence. Humble and inconsiderable in front of the sublimity of your station, I acknowledge your	يَا مَوْلَايَ يَا أَبَا عَبْدِ اللّٰهِ، يَا ابْنَ رَسُولِ اللّٰهِ، عَبْدُكَ وَ ابْنُ أَمَتِكَ، اَلذَّلِيلُ بَيْنَ يَدَيْكَ، وَ الْمُصَغَّرُ فِي عُلُوِّ قَدْرِكَ، وَ الْمُعْتَرِفُ بِحَقِّكَ، جَاءَكَ مُسْتَجِيرًا بِكَ،

1 *Kāmil al-Ziyārāt*, 170, b 70, h 6, 174, b 71, h 6, 182, b 73, h 2, whence *Wasā'il*, xiv, 469, b 51, h 19619, & *Biḥār*, xcviii, 90, 93, 105, b 12, h 24, b 13, h 1, b 14, h 15. Mufīd's *Mazār*, 50, b 21, h 1. Ṭūsī's *Miṣbāḥ*, 715, whence *Wasā'il*, xiv, 463, b 49, h 19606. *Iqbāl*, 332.

2 *Kāmil al-Ziyārāt*, 269, b 88, h 9, whence *Biḥār*, xcviii, 90, b 12, h 25. Mufīd's *Mazār*, 48, b 20, h 3. Ṭūsī's *Miṣbāḥ*, 716, whence *Wasā'il*, xiv, 464, b 49, h 19609, *Biḥār*, xcviii, 91, b 12, h 34 & *Mustadrak*, x, 287, b 36, h 12027/12. *Iqbāl*, 330, 421.

3 *Biḥār*, xcviii, 352-359, b 30.

4 *Biḥār*, xcviii, 352-355, b 30. *Miṣbāḥ al-Zā'ir*, 172-175. Shahīd Awwal's *al-Mazār*, 154-161.

قَاصِدًا إِلَىٰ حَرَمِكَ، مُتَوَجِّهًا إِلَىٰ مَقَامِكَ، مُتَوَسِّلًا إِلَى اللهِ تَعَالَىٰ بِكَ،

rights. I have come to you seeking refuge with you, having set out to your shrine and made it my destination, I seek your mediation with Allah, the Most High!

أَ أَدْخُلُ يَا مَوْلَايَ؟ أَ أَدْخُلُ يَا وَلِيَّ اللهِ؟ أَ أَدْخُلُ يَا مَلَائِكَةَ اللهِ الْمُحْدِقِينَ بِهٰذَا الْحَرَمِ، الْمُقِيمِينَ فِي هٰذَا الْمَشْهَدِ؟

May I enter, O my master? May I enter, O *walī* of Allah? May I enter, O angels of Allah who surround this sanctuary and reside in this shrine?

Then, if you feel humbleness descend into your heart and tears well up in your eyes, enter, advancing with the right foot. Then say,

بِسْمِ اللهِ وَ بِاللهِ وَ فِي سَبِيلِ اللهِ وَ عَلَىٰ مِلَّةِ رَسُولِ اللهِ، اَللّٰهُمَّ أَنْزِلْنِي مُنْزَلًا مُبَارَكًا وَ أَنْتَ خَيْرُ الْمُنْزِلِينَ.

In the Name of Allah, by Allah, in the way of Allah, following the creed of the Apostle of Allah. O Allah, *land me with a blessed landing, for You are the best of those who bring ashore!*(23:29)

Then say,

اَللهُ أَكْبَرُ كَبِيرًا، وَ الْحَمْدُ لِلّٰهِ كَثِيرًا، وَ سُبْحَانَ اللهِ بُكْرَةً وَ أَصِيلًا، وَ الْحَمْدُ لِلّٰهِ الْفَرْدِ الصَّمَدِ الْمَاجِدِ الْأَحَدِ، اَلْمُتَفَضِّلِ الْمَنَّانِ الْمُتَطَوِّلِ الْحَنَّانِ، اَلَّذِي مِنْ تَطَوُّلِهِ سَهَّلَ لِي زِيَارَةَ مَوْلَايَ بِإِحْسَانِهِ، وَ لَمْ يَجْعَلْنِي عَنْ زِيَارَتِهِ مَمْنُوعًا وَ لَا عَنْ ذِمَّتِهِ مَدْفُوعًا بَلْ تَطَوَّلَ وَ مَنَحَ.

May Allah be magnified greatly, may He be praised most often, and may He be glorified every morning and evening! All praise belongs to Allah, the Singular, the All-embracing, the All-praiseworthy, the One, the Gracious, the Favourer, the Bounteous and the Compassionate, who out of His bounty and kindness facilitated for me the *ziyārah* of my master, and did not deprive me of his *ziyārah* and nor withheld from me His protection and care, but rather treated me with generosity and kindness!

Then enter. On reaching the tomb, stand facing it with humility, and in a tearful and entreating manner say,

Peace be to you, O heir of Adam, the chosen of Allah! Peace be to you, O heir of Noah, the trustee of Allah! Peace be to you, O heir of Abraham, the dedicated friend of Allah! Peace be to you, O heir of Moses, the interlocutor of Allah! Peace be to you, O heir of Jesus, spirit of Allah!

اَلسَّلامُ عَلَيْكَ يا وَارِثَ آدَمَ صِفْوَةِ اللهِ، اَلسَّلامُ عَلَيْكَ يا وَارِثَ نُوحٍ أَمِينِ اللهِ، اَلسَّلامُ عَلَيْكَ يا وَارِثَ إِبْرَاهِيمَ خَلِيلِ اللهِ، اَلسَّلامُ عَلَيْكَ يا وَارِثَ مُوسَىٰ كَلِيمِ اللهِ، اَلسَّلامُ عَلَيْكَ يا وَارِثَ عِيسَىٰ رُوحِ اللهِ،

Peace be to you, O heir of Muḥammad, the beloved of Allah, may Allah bless him and his Family! Peace be to you, O heir of ᶜAlī, the testament of Allah! Peace be to you, O pious and Godwary legatee! Peace be to you, who were slain and whose avenger is Allah, son of him whose avenger is Allah, and retribution for whose unavenged blood is sought!

اَلسَّلامُ عَلَيْكَ يا وَارِثَ مُحَمَّدٍ صَلَّى اللهُ عَلَيْهِ وَ آلِهِ حَبِيبِ اللهِ، اَلسَّلامُ عَلَيْكَ يا وَارِثَ عَلِيٍّ حُجَّةِ اللهِ، اَلسَّلامُ عَلَيْكَ أَيُّهَا الْوَصِيُّ الْبَرُّ التَّقِيُّ، اَلسَّلامُ عَلَيْكَ يا ثَارَ اللهِ وَ ابْنَ ثَارِهِ، وَ الْوِتْرَ الْمَوْتُورَ،

I testify that you indeed maintained the prayer, paid the *zakāt*, bade what is right and forbade what is wrong, and that you waged *jihād* in the way of Allah as is worthy of Him until your sanctity was violated and you were slain wrongfully!

أَشْهَدُ أَنَّكَ قَدْ أَقَمْتَ الصَّلاةَ، وَ آتَيْتَ الزَّكَاةَ، وَ أَمَرْتَ بِالْمَعْرُوفِ، وَ نَهَيْتَ عَنِ الْمُنْكَرِ، وَ جَاهَدْتَ فِي اللهِ حَقَّ جِهَادِهِ حَتَّى اسْتُبِيحَ حَرَمُكَ، وَ قُتِلْتَ مَظْلُومًا.

Then with a humble heart and tearful eyes stand at the head of the grave and say,

Peace be to you, O Abū ᶜAbdillāh! Peace be to you, O son of

اَلسَّلامُ عَلَيْكَ يا أَبَا عَبْدِ اللهِ، اَلسَّلامُ

the Apostle of Allah! Peace be to you, O son of the chief of the Legatees! Peace be to you, O son of Fāṭimah Zahrā, the mistress of the world's womankind!

عَلَيْكَ يَا ابْنَ رَسُولِ اللهِ، اَلسَّلَامُ عَلَيْكَ يَا ابْنَ سَيِّدِ الْوَصِيِّينَ، اَلسَّلَامُ عَلَيْكَ يَا ابْنَ فَاطِمَةَ الزَّهْرَاءِ سَيِّدَةِ نِسَاءِ الْعَالَمِينَ،

Peace be to you, O hero of all Muslims! O my master, I testify that (before your conception) you were a light in the loins of noble fathers and wombs of chaste mothers, untainted by the defilements of the (pre-Islamic) era of ignorance and untouched by its blights.

اَلسَّلَامُ عَلَيْكَ يَا بَطَلَ ا لْمُسْلِمِينَ، يَا مَوْلَايَ أَشْهَدُ أَنَّكَ كُنْتَ نُورًا فِي الْأَصْلَابِ الشَّامِخَةِ، وَ الْأَرْحَامِ الْمُطَهَّرَةِ، لَمْ تُنَجِّسْكَ الْجَاهِلِيَّةُ بِأَنْجَاسِهَا، وَ لَمْ تُلْبِسْكَ مِنْ مُدْلَهِمَّاتِ ثِيَابِهَا،

I testify that you are one of the pillars of the faith, a champion of Muslims and a bastion of the faithful. I testify that you are a pious, Godwary, approved, blameless and a rightly-guided Imam and guide.

وَ أَشْهَدُ أَنَّكَ مِنْ دَعَائِمِ الدِّينِ، وَ أَرْكَانِ الْمُسْلِمِينَ، وَ مَعْقِلِ الْمُؤْمِنِينَ، وَ أَشْهَدُ أَنَّكَ الْإِمَامُ الْبَرُّ التَّقِيُّ الرَّضِيُّ الزَّكِيُّ الْهَادِي الْمَهْدِيُّ،

I testify that the Imams of your descent are models of Godfearing, banners of guidance, the firmest handle and testaments for the world's denizens.

وَ أَشْهَدُ أَنَّ الْأَئِمَّةَ مِنْ وُلْدِكَ كَلِمَةُ التَّقْوَىٰ، وَ أَعْلَامُ الْهُدَىٰ، وَ الْعُرْوَةُ الْوُثْقَىٰ، وَ الْحُجَّةُ عَلَىٰ أَهْلِ الدُّنْيَا،

Then, clinging to the tomb, embrace it and say,

Indeed we belong to Allah, and to Him do we return. My master! I love those who hold you dear and despise your enemies. I affirm my faith in you and conviction in your return as attested by the religious precepts that I follow and my final deeds. My heart

إِنَّا لِلّٰهِ وَ إِنَّا إِلَيْهِ رَاجِعُونَ، يَا مَوْلَايَ أَنَا مُوَالٍ لِوَلِيِّكُمْ، وَ مُعَادٍ لِعَدُوِّكُمْ، وَ أَنَا بِكُمْ مُؤْمِنٌ، وَ بِإِيَابِكُمْ مُوقِنٌ، بِشَرَائِعِ دِينِي وَ خَوَاتِيمِ عَمَلِي، وَ قَلْبِي لِقَلْبِكُمْ

is at peace with your hearts and my conduct is in compliance with your instructions.

سِلْمٌ، وَ أَمْرِى لِأَمْرِكُمْ مُتَّبِعٌ،

My master, I come to you in a state of fear, so give me safety. I come to you seeking asylum, so give me refuge. I come to you in indigence, so enrich me! My master and guardian! You, my guardian, are Allah's testament to the totality of His creation. I have faith in the occult and open, esoteric and exoteric aspects of your persons, and in the first of you and the last one.

يَا مَوْلَایَ أَتَيْتُكَ خَائِفًا فَآمِنِّى، وَ أَتَيْتُكَ مُسْتَجِيرًا فَأَجِرْنِى، وَ أَتَيْتُكَ فَقِيرًا فَأَغْنِنِى، سَيِّدِى وَ مَوْلَایَ أَنْتَ مَوْلَایَ حُجَّةُ اللهِ عَلَى الْخَلْقِ أَجْمَعِينَ، آمَنْتُ بِسِرِّكُمْ وَ عَلَانِيَتِكُمْ، وَ بِظَاهِرِكُمْ وَ بَاطِنِكُمْ، وَ أَوَّلِكُمْ وَ آخِرِكُمْ،

I testify that you are inseparable from the Scripture of Allah and His trustee who summon to Him with wisdom and good advice. May Allah's curse be on those who wronged you. May His curse lie on those who slew you and on those who heard about it approvingly.

وَ أَشْهَدُ أَنَّكَ التَّالِى لِكِتَابِ اللهِ، وَ أَمِينُ اللهِ، اَلدَّاعِى إِلَى اللهِ بِالْحِكْمَةِ وَ الْمَوْعِظَةِ الْحَسَنَةِ، لَعَنَ اللهُ أُمَّةً ظَلَمَتْكَ، وَ أُمَّةً قَتَلَتْكَ، وَ لَعَنَ اللهُ أُمَّةً سَمِعَتْ بِذٰلِكَ فَرَضِيَتْ بِهِ.

Then offer a two-*rakʿah* prayer at the head of the Imam's tomb and, after the *salām*, say,

O Allah, I pray to You and to You do I bow and prostrate. You are One and You have no partner. It is not permissible to pray, bow and prostrate to anyone except You, for You are Allah, besides whom there is no god.

اَللّٰهُمَّ إِنِّى لَكَ صَلَّيْتُ، وَ لَكَ رَكَعْتُ، وَ لَكَ سَجَدْتُ، وَحْدَكَ لَا شَرِيكَ لَكَ، فَإِنَّهُ لَا تَجُوزُ الصَّلَاةُ وَ الرُّكُوعُ وَ السُّجُودُ إِلَّا لَكَ، لِأَنَّكَ أَنْتَ اللهُ الَّذِى لَا إِلٰهَ إِلَّا أَنْتَ،

O Allah, bless Muḥammad and the Family of Muḥammad and convey to them the best of my greetings and *salām* and bring

اَللّٰهُمَّ صَلِّ عَلَى مُحَمَّدٍ وَ آلِ مُحَمَّدٍ، وَ أَبْلِغْهُمْ عَنِّى أَفْضَلَ السَّلَامِ وَ التَّحِيَّةِ، وَ

ارْدُدْ عَلَيَّ مِنْهُمُ السَّلَامَ،

back to me their response.

اَللّٰهُمَّ وَ هَاتَانِ الرَّكْعَتَانِ هَدِيَّةٌ مِنِّي إِلىٰ
سَيِّدِي الْحُسَيْنِ بْنِ عَلِيٍّ عَلَيْهِمَا السَّلَامُ،

O Allah, these two *rakᶜahs* are a gift from me for my master, al-Ḥusayn ibn ᶜAlī, peace be to them!

اَللّٰهُمَّ صَلِّ عَلىٰ مُحَمَّدٍ وَ عَلَيْهِ وَ تَقَبَّلْهُمَا
مِنِّي، وَ اجْزِنِي عَلَيْهِمَا أَفْضَلَ أَمَلِي وَ
رَجَائِي فِيكَ وَ فِي وَلِيِّكَ يَا وَلِيَّ الْمُؤْمِنِينَ.

O Allah, bless Muḥammad and him, and accept them from me, and grant me for them a reward in accordance with the best of my hopes and expectations that I have from You and Your *walī*, O Guardian of the faithful!

Then, clinging to the tomb, embrace it again and say,

اَلسَّلَامُ عَلَى الْحُسَيْنِ بْنِ عَلِيٍّ الْمَظْلُومِ
الشَّهِيدِ، قَتِيلِ الْعَبَرَاتِ وَ أَسِيرِ الْكُرُبَاتِ

Peace be to al-Ḥusayn ibn ᶜAlī, the aggrieved and bewailed martyr and victim of many sufferings.

اَللّٰهُمَّ إِنِّي أَشْهَدُ أَنَّهُ وَلِيُّكَ وَ ابْنُ وَلِيِّكَ،
وَ صَفِيُّكَ الثَّائِرُ بِحَقِّكَ، أَكْرَمْتَهُ
بِكَرَامَتِكَ، وَ خَتَمْتَ لَهُ بِالشَّهَادَةِ، وَ
جَعَلْتَهُ سَيِّدًا مِنَ السَّادَةِ، وَ قَائِدًا مِنَ
الْقَادَةِ، وَ أَكْرَمْتَهُ بِطِيبِ الْوِلَادَةِ، وَ
أَعْطَيْتَهُ مَوَارِيثَ الْأَنْبِيَاءِ، وَ جَعَلْتَهُ
حُجَّةً عَلىٰ خَلْقِكَ مِنَ الْأَوْصِيَاءِ،
فَأَعْذَرَ فِي الدُّعَاءِ، وَ مَنَحَ النَّصِيحَةَ، وَ
بَذَلَ مُهْجَتَهُ فِيكَ، حَتَّى اسْتَنْقَذَ عِبَادَكَ
مِنَ الْجَهَالَةِ وَ حَيْرَةِ الضَّلَالَةِ،

O Allah, I testify that he is Your *walī*, son of Your *walī* and Your chosen one, who stood up to establish Your truth/right, whom You dignified with Your honour and ended his life in martyrdom. You made him a master among masters and a leader among leaders. You honoured him with an immaculate birth and gave him the heritage of the prophets, making him a testament to Your creation and one of the Prophet's legatees. He left nothing to be desired in summoning people to You, working for their good, and offering his lifeblood for Your sake, in order to deliver Your servants from ignorance and the perplexity of error.

Those who were deceived by the world helped each other against him, exchanging their portion of the Hereafter for a paltry gain, and perished in pursuit of their desires. They incurred Your wrath and that of Your Prophet, obeying the heretics and hypocrites among Your servants and those laden with grave sins and deserving hellfire.

وَ قَدْ تَوَازَرَ عَلَيْهِ مَنْ غَرَّتْهُ الدُّنْيَا، وَ
بَاعَ حَظَّهُ مِنَ الْآخِرَةِ بِالْأَدْنَىٰ، وَ تَرَدَّىٰ
فِي هَوَاهُ، وَ أَسْخَطَكَ وَ أَسْخَطَ نَبِيَّكَ، وَ
أَطَاعَ مِنْ عِبَادِكَ أُولِي الشِّقَاقِ وَ النِّفَاقِ
وَ حَمَلَةَ الْأَوْزَارِ الْمُسْتَوْجِبِينَ النَّارَ،

He waged *jihād* against them with patience and resignation, facing them and without turning his back, undeterred by the blame of any blamer, until his blood was spilled in the way of obedience to You and his sanctity was violated.

فَجَاهَدَهُمْ فِيكَ صَابِرًا مُحْتَسِبًا
مُقْبِلًا غَيْرَ مُدْبِرٍ، لَا تَأْخُذُهُ فِي
اللهِ لَوْمَةُ لَائِمٍ، حَتَّىٰ سُفِكَ فِي
طَاعَتِكَ دَمُهُ، وَ اسْتُبِيحَ حَرِيمُهُ،

O Allah, requite them with a dire curse and punish them with a painful punishment!

اَللّٰهُمَّ الْعَنْهُمْ لَعْنًا وَبِيلًا، وَ عَذِّبْهُمْ
عَذَابًا أَلِيمًا.

Then turn towards the grave of ʿAlī ibn al-Ḥusayn (ʿ*a*) at the foot of Imam al-Ḥusayn's tomb and say,

Peace be to you, O *walī* of Allah! Peace be to you, O son of the Apostle of Allah! Peace be to you, O son of the Seal of the Prophets! Peace be to you, O son of Fāṭimah, mistress of the world's womankind! Peace be to you, O son of the Commander of the Faithful!

اَلسَّلَامُ عَلَيْكَ يَا وَلِيَّ اللهِ، اَلسَّلَامُ
عَلَيْكَ يَا ابْنَ رَسُولِ اللهِ، اَلسَّلَامُ عَلَيْكَ
يَا ابْنَ خَاتَمِ النَّبِيِّينَ، اَلسَّلَامُ عَلَيْكَ
يَا ابْنَ فَاطِمَةَ سَيِّدَةِ نِسَاءِ الْعَالَمِينَ،
اَلسَّلَامُ عَلَيْكَ يَا ابْنَ أَمِيرِ الْمُؤْمِنِينَ،

Peace be to you, who were aggrieved and martyred! Dearer to me than my father and mother, you lived felicitously and were slain wrongfully and martyred!

اَلسَّلَامُ عَلَيْكَ أَيُّهَا الْمَظْلُومُ الشَّهِيدُ،
بِأَبِي أَنْتَ وَ أُمِّي عِشْتَ سَعِيدًا وَ قُتِلْتَ
مَظْلُومًا شَهِيدًا.

Then turn towards the tomb of the other martyrs (r) and say,

Peace be to you, O defenders of Allah's Unity! *Peace be to you for your patience. How excellent is the reward of the abode of the Hereafter.* (13:24) Dearer to me than my father and mother, you attained a great triumph!

اَلسَّـــلَامُ عَلَيْكُـمْ أَيُّهَـا الذَّابُّونَ عَنْ تَوْحِيـدِ اللهِ، اَلسَّـلَامُ عَلَيْكُـمْ بِمَا صَبَرْتُمْ، فَنِعْمَ عُقْبَى الدَّارِ، بِأَبِي أَنْتُمْ وَ أُمِّي فُزْتُمْ فَوْزًا عَظِيمًا.

Then approach the shrine of ᶜAbbās ibn ᶜAlī (ᶜa) and standing near his *ḏarīḥ* say,

Peace be to you, O Allah's righteous servant and true helper and comforter of your brother. I testify that you had faith in Allah, you assisted the son of the Apostle of Allah and summoned the people to Allah's way and were self-abnegating. May the best of Allah's greetings and peace be to you!

اَلسَّـــلَامُ عَلَيْكَ أَيُّهَا الْعَبْدُ الصَّالِحُ وَ الصِّدِّيقُ الْمُوَاسِى، أَشْـــهَدُ أَنَّكَ آمَنْتَ بِاللهِ، وَ نَــصَرْتَ ابْنَ رَسُــولِ اللهِ، وَ دَعَـوْتَ إِلَى سَـبِيلِ اللهِ، وَ وَاسَـيْتَ بِنَفْسِكَ، فَعَلَيْكَ مِنَ اللهِ أَفْضَلُ التَّحِيَّةِ وَ السَّلَام.

Then embracing the tomb say,

O helper of Allah's religion, you are dearer to me than my father and mother! Peace be to you, O helper of al-Ḥusayn the truthful one. Peace be to you, O helper of al-Ḥusayn the martyr. Peace be to you from me, so long as I live and so long as day and night endure!

بِأَبِي أَنْــتَ وَ أُمِّي يَا نَــاصِرَ دِينِ اللهِ، اَلسَّـــلَامُ عَلَيْـكَ يَا نَاصِرَ الْحُسَـيْنِ الصِّدِّيـقِ، اَلسَّـــلَامُ عَلَيْـكَ يَا نَاصِرَ الْحُسَيْنِ الشَّـهِيدِ، عَلَيْكَ مِنِّي السَّلَامُ مَا بَقِيتُ وَ بَقِيَ اللَّيْلُ وَ النَّهَارُ.

Then offer two *rakᶜahs* near the head of the tomb, and after the prayer recite the supplication *Allā·humma innī ṣallaytu...*, which was recited at the head of Imam al-Ḥusayn's tomb (p. 284).

Then return to the shrine of Imam al-Ḥusayn (ᶜa) and remain near him for as long as you wish, but it is not desirable to lie down there for sleep overnight.

When bidding farewell, stand near the head of the tomb, cry and say,

اَلسَّلاٰمُ عَلَيْكَ يَا مَوْلاٰىَ سَلاٰمَ مُوَدِّعٍ
لاٰ قَالٍ وَ لاٰ سَئِمٍ، فَإِنْ أَنْصَرِفْ فَلاٰ عَنْ
مَلاٰلَةٍ، وَ إِنْ أُقِمْ فَلاٰ عَنْ سُوءِ ظَنٍّ بِمَا
وَعَدَ اللّٰهُ الصَّابِرِينَ، يَا مَوْلاٰىَ لاٰ جَعَلَهُ
اللّٰهُ آخِرَ الْعَهْدِ مِنِّى لِزِيٰارَتِكَ، وَ رَزَقَنِى
الْعَوْدَ إِلَيْكَ وَ الْمُقَامَ فِى حَرَمِكَ، وَ
الْكَوْنَ فِى مَشْهَدِكَ، آمِينَ رَبَّ الْعَالَمِينَ.

Peace be to you my master from one who departs, though not out of boredom or dissatisfaction. If I leave it is not out of weariness, and if I stay on, it will not be due to lack of trust in the promise that Allah has given to the patient. My master, may Allah not make this my last opportunity of your *ziyārah*, and may He grant me to return to you, to stand in your shrine and to be in your presence. Amen, O Lord of all the worlds!

Then kiss the *ḍarīḥ* and rub your body against it, for that will give you safety and protection. Then withdraw, walking backwards while facing the tomb and without turning your back toward it, and say,

اَلسَّلاٰمُ عَلَيْكَ يَا بَابَ الْمَقَامِ، اَلسَّلاٰمُ
عَلَيْكَ يَا شَرِيكَ الْقُرْآنِ، اَلسَّلاٰمُ عَلَيْكَ
يَا حُجَّةَ الْخِصَامِ، اَلسَّلاٰمُ عَلَيْكَ يَا سَفِينَةَ
النَّجَاةِ، اَلسَّلاٰمُ عَلَيْكُمْ يَا مَلاٰئِكَةَ رَبِّى
الْمُقِيمِينَ فِى هٰذَا الْحَرَمِ، اَلسَّلاٰمُ عَلَيْكَ
أَبَدًا مَا بَقِيتُ وَ بَقِىَ اللَّيْلُ وَ النَّهَارُ،

Peace be to you, O door to the divine sanctum! Peace be to you, O counterpart of the Qur'ān! Peace be to you, O testament against the adversaries of Islam! Peace be to you, O ark of salvation! Peace be to you, O my Lord's angels residing in this shrine. Peace be to you forever, as long as I live and as long as day and night endure!

And say,

إِنَّا لِلّٰهِ وَ إِنَّا إِلَيْهِ رَاجِعُونَ، وَ لاٰ حَوْلَ وَ
لاٰ قُوَّةَ إِلاّٰ بِاللّٰهِ الْعَلِيِّ الْعَظِيمِ.

We belong to Allah and to Him do we return. There is no power or force except what derives from Allah, the All-exalted and All-supreme!

Then depart. Sayyid ᶜAlī b. Ṭāwūs and Muḥammad b. al-Ma<u>sh</u>hadī mention that one who performs this *ziyārah* is like someone who has met God on His Throne.

6. Ziyarah of Imam Ḥusayn for the Day of ʿArafah

The reports from the Imams of the Prophet's immaculate Family (*ᶜa*) concerning the virtues and rewards of Imam Ḥusayn's *ziyārah* on the day of ᶜArafah are too numerous to be mentioned here. We will mention here some of them for the sake of rousing interest in the would-be pilgrims.

There is the report[1] of Ba<u>sh</u>īr al-Dahhān which has been transmitted with reliable *isnād*.

> Bashīr says: "I told Imam Jaᶜfar al-Ṣādiq (*ᶜa*) that at times having failed to make the *ḥajj* pilgrimage I spend the day of ᶜArafah at the shrine of Imam al-Ḥusayn (*ᶜa*). He said to me, 'What you do is good, O Bashīr. Every faithful person who performs the *ziyārah* of Imam al-Ḥusayn on any day other than the day of *ᶜīd* with the knowledge of his rights has a reward written for him equal to that of twenty *ḥajj* and twenty *ᶜumrahs* blessed with acceptance, as well as the reward of twenty instances of *jihād* waged alongside an apostle or a just imam. Those who perform the *ziyārah* of the Imam on the day of *ᶜīd*, God Almighty writes for them a reward equal to that of a hundred *ḥajj* and a hundred *ᶜumrahs* blessed with acceptance, as well as the reward of a hundred instances of *jihād* waged alongside an apostle or a just imam. Those who perform the *ziyārah* of Imam Ḥusayn on the day of ᶜArafah with the knowledge of his rights have a reward written for them equal to that of a thousand *ḥajj* and a thousand *ᶜumrahs* blessed with acceptance, as well as the reward of a thousand instances of *jihād* waged alongside an apostle or a just imam.' "
>
> Ba<u>sh</u>īr says, "I said to him, 'But where else can I receive the reward of being present at ᶜArafāt?!' The Imam gave me a look like that of someone who is annoyed and said, 'Ba<u>sh</u>īr, when a person with faith goes forth to perform the *ziyārah* of Imam Ḥusayn's

1 *Kāmil al-Ziyārāt*, 169, b 70, h 1, whence *Biḥār*, xcviii, 85, b 12, h 3 & *Mustadrak*, x, 281, b 36, h 12016/1. *<u>Th</u>awāb*, 143, majlis 29, h 11 & Ṭūsī's *Amālī*, 201, majlis 7, h 342/44, whence *Biḥār*, xcviii, 85, b 12, h 1, 2. With some difference in *Kāmil al-Ziyārāt*, 172, b 70, h 11, whence *Biḥār*, xcviii, 89, b 12, h 20 & *Mustadrak*, x, 286, b 36, h 12025/10. *Faqīh*, ii, 580, h 3169. Mufīd's *Mazār*, 48, b 20, h 4.

shrine on the day of ᶜArafah and approaches his tomb after taking bath in the water of the Euphrates, God Almighty writes for him for every step that he takes the reward of a *ḥajj* performed with all its rites.' Or he said, 'an *ᶜumrah*' " (or *ghazwah*, according to another manuscript).

There are many reports[1] with reliable *isnād* which state that on the day of ᶜArafah God Almighty first casts His merciful glance on the visitors of Imam Ḥusayn's shrine before He looks at the pilgrims gathered at ᶜArafāt. Another report[2] with reliable *isnād* is as follows.

Rifāᶜah says, "Imam Jaᶜfar al-Ṣādiq (*ᶜa*) asked me, 'Did you perform *ḥajj* this year?' I said to him, 'I didn't have the means to go on ḥajj pilgrimage. But I spent the day of ᶜArafah at the shrine of Imam Ḥusayn (*ᶜa*).' The Imam said to me, 'Rifāᶜah, you have not fallen behind those who were present at Minā. Were it not that I hate to see people forsake *ḥajj*, I would have narrated for you a *ḥadīth* after hearing which you would never miss the *ziyārah* of his shrine.'

He remained silent for a while. Then he said, 'My father narrated for me that whoever sets out for the shrine of Imam Ḥusayn (*ᶜa*) with the knowledge of his rights and without pride, is escorted by a thousand angels at his right and a thousand angels to his left and a reward is written for him equal to a thousand *ḥajj* and a thousand *ᶜumrahs* performed in the company of a prophet or his legatee.' "

The manner of performing this *ziyārah*, as mentioned by leading Shīᶜī scholars, is as follows.[3] When intending to perform the Imam's *ziyārah* on this day, one should take a bath, if possible, in the water of the Euphrates, or with any water that is available. Then one should put on one's cleanest clothes and approach the Imam's shrine, walk-

1 *Kāmil al-Ziyārāt*, 170, b 70, h 3, *Faqīh*, ii, 580, h 3171. *Thawāb*, 90, whence *Biḥār*, xcviii, 85, b 12, h 4 & *Mustadrak*, x, 282, b 36, h 12017/2. *Maᶜānī*, 391, h 36. Ṭūsī's *Miṣbāḥ*, 715. *Tahdhīb*, vi, 50, b 16, h 31, whence *Wasā'il*, xiv, 462, b 49, h 19601.

2 Ṭūsī's *Miṣbāḥ*, 716, whence *Wasā'il*, xiv, 463, b 49, h 19607 & *Biḥār*, xcviii, 91, b 12, h 32.

3 *Al-Mazār al-Kabīr*, 138-141. *Miṣbāḥ al-Zā'ir*, 184-185. Shahīd Awwal's *Mazār*, 170-178. *Biḥār* xcviii, 359-365, b 31, from Shaykh Mufīd, Ibn Ṭāwūs, and Shahīd Awwal,

ing slowly and with composure and dignity. On reaching the gates of the shrine, say, "*Allāhu akbar!*" Then say,

اَللّٰهُ أَكْــبَرُ كَبِيرًا، وَ الْحَمْدُ لِلّٰهِ كَثِيرًا، وَ سُــبْحَانَ اللّٰهِ بُكْـرَةً وَ أَصِيلًا، وَ الْحَمْدُ لِلّٰهِ الَّذِى هَدَانَا لِهٰذَا وَ مَا كُنَّا لِنَهْتَدِيَ لَوْ لَا أَنْ هَدَانَا اللّٰهُ، لَقَدْ جَاءَتْ رُسُــلُ رَبِّنَا بِالْحَقِّ،

May Allah be magnified greatly; may He be praised most often; and may He be glorified every morning and evening! *All praise belongs to Allah, who guided us to this. We would have never been guided had not Allah guided us. Our Lord's apostles have certainly brought the truth.*(7:43)

اَلسَّــلَامُ عَلٰى رَسُولِ اللّٰهِ صَلَّى اللّٰهُ عَلَيْهِ وَ آلِهِ، اَلسَّــلَامُ عَلٰى أَمِيرِ الْمُؤْمِنِينَ، اَلسَّلَامُ عَلٰى فَاطِمَةَ الزَّهْرَاءِ سَيِّدَةِ نِسَاءِ الْعَالَمِينَ، اَلسَّلَامُ عَلَى الْحَسَــنِ وَ الْحُسَيْنِ، اَلسَّلَامُ عَلٰى عَلِيِّ بْنِ الْحُسَيْنِ، اَلسَّلَامُ عَلٰى مُحَمَّدِ بْنِ عَلِيٍّ، اَلسَّلَامُ عَلٰى جَعْفَرِ بْنِ مُحَمَّدٍ، اَلسَّلَامُ عَلٰى مُوسَى بْنِ جَعْفَرٍ، اَلسَّلَامُ عَلٰى عَلِيِّ بْنِ مُوسٰى، اَلسَّلَامُ عَلٰى مُحَمَّدِ بْنِ عَلِيٍّ، اَلسَّلَامُ عَلٰى عَلِيِّ بْنِ مُحَمَّدٍ، اَلسَّلَامُ عَلَى الْحَسَنِ بْنِ عَلِيٍّ، اَلسَّلَامُ عَلَى الْخَلَفِ الصَّالِحِ الْمُنْتَظَرِ،

Peace be to the Apostle of Allah, may Allah bless him and his Family. Peace be to the Commander of the Faithful! Peace be to Fāṭimah, mistress of the world's womankind! Peace be to al-Ḥasan and al-Ḥusayn! Peace be to ʿAli ibn al-Ḥusayn! Peace be to Muḥammad ibn ʿAlī! Peace be to Jaʿfar ibn Muḥammad! Peace be to Mūsā ibn Jaʿfar! Peace be to ʿAlī ibn Mūsā! Peace be to Muḥammad ibn ʿAlī! Peace be to ʿAlī ibn Muḥammad! Peace be to al-Ḥasan ibn ʿAlī! Peace be to their righteous successor, the awaited Imam!

اَلسَّــلَامُ عَلَيْكَ يَا أَبَا عَبْدِ اللّٰهِ، اَلسَّلَامُ عَلَيْكَ يَا ابْنَ رَسُــولِ اللّٰهِ، عَبْدُكَ وَ ابْنُ عَبْدِكَ وَ ابْــنُ أَمَتِكَ، اَلْمُــوَالِي لِوَلِيِّكَ، اَلْمُعَادِي لِعَدُوِّكَ، اِسْــتَجَارَ بِمَشْهَدِكَ، وَ

Peace be to you, O Abū ʿAbdillāh! Peace be to you, O son of the Apostle of Allah! Your servant and son of your servant and maidservant, who befriends your friends and despises your enemies, has taken refuge in your shrine and seeks nearness to Allah through his visit to you.

تَقَرَّبَ إِلَى اللهِ بِقَصْدِكَ،

All praise belongs to Allah who has guided me to your *wilāyah*, singled me out for your *ziyārah*, and facilitated my visit to you!

اَلْحَمْدُ لِلَّهِ الَّذِي هَدَانِي لِوَلَايَتِكَ، وَ خَصَّنِي بِزِيَارَتِكَ، وَ سَهَّلَ لِي قَصْدَكَ.

Then enter and, standing near the head of the tomb, say,

Peace be to you, O heir of Adam, the chosen of Allah! Peace be to you, O heir of Noah, the prophet of Allah! Peace be to you, O heir of Abraham, the dedicated friend of Allah! Peace be to you, O heir of Moses, who conversed with Allah! Peace be to you, O heir of Jesus, spirit of Allah!

اَلسَّلَامُ عَلَيْكَ يَا وَارِثَ آدَمَ صِفْوَةِ اللهِ،
اَلسَّلَامُ عَلَيْكَ يَا وَارِثَ نُوحٍ نَبِيِّ اللهِ،
اَلسَّلَامُ عَلَيْكَ يَا وَارِثَ إِبْرَاهِيمَ خَلِيلِ اللهِ،
اَلسَّلَامُ عَلَيْكَ يَا وَارِثَ مُوسَىٰ كَلِيمِ اللهِ،
اَلسَّلَامُ عَلَيْكَ يَا وَارِثَ عِيسَىٰ رُوحِ اللهِ،

Peace be to you, O heir of Muḥammad, the beloved of Allah! Peace be to you, O heir of ʿAlī, the Commander of the Faithful. Peace be to you, O heir of Fāṭimah Zahrā! Peace be to you, O son of Muḥammad al-Muṣṭafā! Peace be to you, O son of ʿAlī al-Murtaḍā! Peace be to you, O son of Fāṭimah Zahrā. Peace be to you, O son of <u>Kh</u>adījat al-Kubrā!

اَلسَّلَامُ عَلَيْكَ يَا وَارِثَ مُحَمَّدٍ حَبِيبِ اللهِ،
اَلسَّلَامُ عَلَيْكَ يَا وَارِثَ أَمِيرِ الْمُؤْمِنِينَ،
اَلسَّلَامُ عَلَيْكَ يَا وَارِثَ فَاطِمَةَ الزَّهْرَاءِ،
اَلسَّلَامُ عَلَيْكَ يَا ابْنَ مُحَمَّدٍ الْمُصْطَفَىٰ،
اَلسَّلَامُ عَلَيْكَ يَا ابْنَ عَلِيٍّ الْمُرْتَضَىٰ،
اَلسَّلَامُ عَلَيْكَ يَا ابْنَ فَاطِمَةَ الزَّهْرَاءِ،
اَلسَّلَامُ عَلَيْكَ يَا ابْنَ خَدِيجَةَ الْكُبْرَىٰ،

Peace be to you, O slain one whose avenger is Allah, son of him whose avenger is Allah, and retribution for whose blood is sought !

اَلسَّلَامُ عَلَيْكَ يَا ثَارَ اللهِ وَ ابْنَ ثَارِهِ، وَ الْوِتْرَ الْمَوْتُورَ،

I testify that you indeed maintained the prayer, paid the

أَشْهَدُ أَنَّكَ قَدْ أَقَمْتَ الصَّلَاةَ، وَ آتَيْتَ

الزَّكَاةَ، وَ أَمَرْتَ بِالْمَعْرُوفِ، وَ نَهَيْتَ عَنِ الْمُنْكَرِ، وَ أَطَعْتَ اللهَ حَتّىٰ أَتاكَ الْيَقِينُ،	*zakāt*, bade what is right and forbade what is wrong, and obeyed Allah until the last breath.
فَلَعَنَ اللهُ أُمَّةً قَتَلَتْكَ، وَ لَعَنَ اللهُ أُمَّةً ظَلَمَتْكَ، وَ لَعَنَ اللهُ أُمَّةً سَمِعَتْ بِذٰلِكَ فَرَضِيَتْ بِهِ،	So may Allah's curse be on the people who slew you. May His curse be on those who wronged you and may His curse be on those who heard of it approvingly.
يا مَوْلاىَ يا أَبا عَبْدِ اللهِ، أُشْهِدُ اللهَ وَ مَلائِكَتَهُ وَ أَنْبِياءَهُ وَ رُسُلَهُ، أَنّي بِكُمْ مُؤْمِنٌ، وَ بِإِيابِكُمْ مُوقِنٌ، بِشَرائِعِ ديني وَ خَواتِيمِ عَمَلي وَ مُنْقَلَبي إِلىٰ رَبّي، فَصَلَواتُ اللهِ عَلَيْكُمْ وَ عَلىٰ أَرْواحِكُمْ وَ عَلىٰ أَجْسادِكُمْ وَ عَلىٰ شاهِدِكُمْ وَ عَلىٰ غائِبِكُمْ وَ ظاهِرِكُمْ وَ باطِنِكُمْ.	O my master! O Abū ʿAbdillah! I call on Allah, His angels, prophets and apostles to be witnesses to my faith in you and my conviction in your return, as attested by the religious precepts I follow, my final deeds, and my return to my Lord. May Allah's blessings be on you, your spirits and your bodies, and on the manifest and hidden aspects of your persons as well as on the exoteric and esoteric ones.
اَلسَّلامُ عَلَيْكَ يَا ابْنَ خاتَمِ النَّبِيّينَ، وَ ابْنَ سَيِّدِ الْوَصِيّينَ، وَ ابْنَ إِمامِ الْمُتَّقينَ، وَ ابْنَ قائِدِ الْغُرِّ الْمُحَجَّلِينَ إِلىٰ جَنّاتِ النَّعِيمِ،	Peace be to you, O son of the Seal of the Prophets, son of the chief of the Legatees, son of the Imam of the pious, and son of the leader of the devout with bright faces and hands into the gardens of bliss!
وَ كَيْفَ لا تَكُونُ كَذٰلِكَ وَ أَنْتَ بابُ الْهُدىٰ، وَ إِمامُ التُّقىٰ، وَ الْعُرْوَةُ الْوُثْقىٰ، وَ الْحُجَّةُ عَلىٰ أَهْلِ الدُّنْيا، وَ خامِسُ أَصْحابِ الْكِساءِ، غَذَتْكَ يَدُ الرَّحْمَةِ، وَ رَضَعْتَ [رُضِعْتَ]	How could you be otherwise, for you are the gateway of guidance, the leader of piety, the firmest handle (of God), God's testament to the world's denizens, and one of the Five People of the Cloak! You were nourished by the hand of mercy, fed at the breast of faith, and brought up in the laps of Islam! My soul is unhappy for being

مِـنْ ثَدْيِ الْإِيمَـانِ، وَ رُبِّيتَ فِي حِجْرِ الْإِسْلَامِ، فَالنَّفْسُ غَيْرُ رَاضِيَةٍ بِفِرَاقِكَ، وَ لَا شَـاكَّةٍ فِي حَيَاتِـكَ، صَلَـوَاتُ اللهِ عَلَيْـكَ وَ عَلَىٰ آبَائِـكَ وَ أَبْنَائِكَ،

separate from you and I have no doubts that you are alive. May Allah's blessings be on you, your ancestors and descendants.

اَلسَّلَامُ عَلَيْكَ يَا صَرِيعَ الْعَبْرَةِ السَّاكِبَةِ، وَ قَرِينَ الْمُصِيبَةِ الرَّاتِبَةِ،

Peace be to you, O slain one for whom the tears flow and who went through successive tragedies!

لَعَنَ اللهُ أُمَّةً اسْتَحَلَّتْ مِنْكَ الْمَحَارِمَ، وَ انْتَهَكَتْ فِيكَ حُرْمَةَ الْإِسْـلَامِ، فَقُتِلْتَ صَلَّى اللهُ عَلَيْكَ مَقْهُورًا، وَ أَصْبَحَ رَسُولُ اللهِ صَـلَّى اللهُ عَلَيْهِ وَ آلِهِ بِكَ مَوْتُورًا، وَ أَصْبَحَ كِتَابُ اللهِ بِفَقْدِكَ مَهْجُورًا،

May Allah's curse be on those who violated your sanctity and violated thereby the sanctity of Islam. You—may Allah bless you—were slain tyrannically and the Apostle of Allah was bereaved and aggrieved at your martyrdom and the Book of Allah was consigned to oblivion at your loss.

اَلسَّـلَامُ عَلَيْكَ وَ عَلَىٰ جَدِّكَ وَ أَبِيكَ وَ أُمِّكَ وَ أَخِيكَ، وَ عَلَى الْأَئِمَّةِ مِنْ بَنِيكَ، وَ عَلَى الْمُسْتَشْـهَدِينَ مَعَـكَ، وَ عَلَى الْمَلَائِكَةِ الْحَافِّينَ بِقَبْرِكَ، وَ الشَّاهِدِينَ لِـزُوَّارِكَ، اَلْمُؤَمِّنِـينَ بِالْقَبُولِ عَلَىٰ دُعَاءِ شِيعَتِكَ، وَ السَّـلَامُ عَلَيْكَ وَ رَحْمَةُ اللهِ وَ بَرَكَاتُهُ.

Peace be to you, to your grandfather, your father, mother and brother and to the Imams from among your descendants and those who were martyred with you, and to the angels who surround your tomb, who watch the visitors to your shrine and say 'Amen!' to the supplications of your followers! Peace be to you and may Allah's mercy and His bounties be upon you.

بِأَبِي أَنْتَ وَ أُمِّي يَا ابْنَ رَسُـولِ اللهِ، بِأَبِي أَنْتَ وَ أُمِّي يَا أَبَا عَبْدِ اللهِ، لَقَدْ عَظُمَتِ

O son of Allah's Apostle, You are dearer to me than my father and mother! O Abū ᶜAbdillāh, you are dearer to me than my father and mother! Your martyrdom was a tremendous loss and calamity that befell us and all the denizens of the heavens and the earth! May Allah's curse be on those who saddled and bridled their mounts and prepared to fight you!

الرَّزِيَّةُ، وَ جَلَّتِ الْمُصِيبَةُ بِكَ عَلَيْنَا وَ
عَلَىٰ جَمِيعِ أَهْلِ السَّمَاوَاتِ وَ الْأَرْضِ،
فَلَعَنَ اللهُ أُمَّةً أَسْرَجَتْ وَ أَلْجَمَتْ وَ
تَهَيَّأَتْ لِقِتَالِكَ،

O my master, O Abū ʿAbd Allāh! I have set out to your shrine and come to your sanctuary to beseech Allah by your station and standing with Him to bless Muḥammad and the Family of Muḥammad and, with His favour, generosity and munificence, to take me into your fold in this world and the Hereafter!

يَا مَوْلَايَ يَا أَبَا عَبْدِ اللهِ، قَصَدْتُ
حَرَمَكَ، وَ أَتَيْتُ مَشْهَدَكَ، أَسْأَلُ اللهَ
بِالشَّأْنِ الَّذِي لَكَ عِنْدَهُ، وَ بِالْمَحَلِّ
الَّذِي لَكَ لَدَيْهِ، أَنْ يُصَلِّيَ عَلَىٰ مُحَمَّدٍ وَ آلِ
مُحَمَّدٍ، وَ أَنْ يَجْعَلَنِي مَعَكُمْ فِي الدُّنْيَا وَ
الْآخِرَةِ، بِمَنِّهِ وَ جُودِهِ وَ كَرَمِهِ.

Then embrace the *ḏarīḥ* and proceed to offer two *rakʿahs* of prayer at the head of the tomb with any sūrahs that you may like to recite. After the prayer, say,

O Allah, I have prayed, bowed and prostrated to you—You are One and have no partner—for it is not permissible to pray, bow and prostrate before anyone except You, for indeed you are Allah, there is no god other than you!

اَللّٰهُمَّ إِنِّي صَلَّيْتُ وَ رَكَعْتُ وَ سَجَدْتُ
لَكَ، وَحْدَكَ لَا شَرِيكَ لَكَ، لِأَنَّ الصَّلَاةَ
وَ الرُّكُوعَ وَ السُّجُودَ لَا تَكُونُ إِلَّا لَكَ،
لِأَنَّكَ أَنْتَ اللهُ لَا إِلٰهَ إِلَّا أَنْتَ،

O Allah, bless Muḥammad and Muḥammad's Family and convey my best greetings and *salāms* to them and bring me their greeting and *salām*.

اَللّٰهُمَّ صَلِّ عَلَىٰ مُحَمَّدٍ وَ آلِ مُحَمَّدٍ، وَ
أَبْلِغْهُمْ عَنِّي أَفْضَلَ التَّحِيَّةِ وَ السَّلَامِ، وَ
ارْدُدْ عَلَيَّ مِنْهُمُ التَّحِيَّةَ وَ السَّلَامَ،

O Allah, these two *rakʿahs* of prayer are a gift from me to my

اَللّٰهُمَّ وَ هَاتَانِ الرَّكْعَتَانِ هَدِيَّةٌ مِنِّي إِلَىٰ

مَوْلَايَ وَ سَيِّدِي وَ إِمَامِي الْحُسَيْنِ بْنِ عَلِيٍّ
عَلَيْهِمَا السَّلَامُ،

master al-Ḥusayn ibn ʿAlī, may peace be to them!

اَللّٰهُمَّ صَلِّ عَلىٰ مُحَمَّدٍ وَ آلِ مُحَمَّدٍ، وَ تَقَبَّلْ
ذٰلِكَ مِنِّي وَ اجْزِنِي عَلىٰ ذٰلِكَ أَفْضَلَ أَمَلِي وَ
رَجَائِي فِيكَ وَ فِي وَلِيِّكَ يَا أَرْحَمَ الرَّاحِمِينَ.

O Allah, bless Muḥammad and bless him, and accept this from me. Reward me for it by the best of my hopes and expectations from You and Your *walī*, O Most Merciful of the merciful!

Then rise and move towards the feet of the tomb and perform the *ziyārah* of ʿAlī ibn al-Ḥusayn (*ʿa*), who is buried at the foot of Imam Ḥusayn's grave, and say,

اَلسَّلَامُ عَلَيْكَ يَا ابْنَ رَسُولِ اللهِ، اَلسَّلَامُ
عَلَيْكَ يَا ابْنَ نَبِيِّ اللهِ، اَلسَّلَامُ عَلَيْكَ
يَا ابْنَ أَمِيرِ الْمُؤْمِنِينَ، اَلسَّلَامُ عَلَيْكَ يَا
ابْنَ الْحُسَيْنِ الشَّهِيدِ، اَلسَّلَامُ عَلَيْكَ أَيُّهَا
الشَّهِيدُ بْنَ الشَّهِيدِ، اَلسَّلَامُ عَلَيْكَ أَيُّهَا
الْمَظْلُومُ بْنَ الْمَظْلُومِ،

Peace be to you, O son of the Apostle of Allah! Peace be to you, O son of the Prophet of Allah! Peace be to you, O son of Commander of the Faithful. Peace be to you, O son of al-Ḥusayn, the martyr! Peace be to you, O martyr! Peace be to you, O aggrieved one, son of the aggrieved Imam!

لَعَنَ اللهُ أُمَّةً قَتَلَتْكَ، وَ لَعَنَ اللهُ أُمَّةً
ظَلَمَتْكَ، وَ لَعَنَ اللهُ أُمَّةً سَمِعَتْ بِذٰلِكَ
فَرَضِيَتْ بِهِ،

May Allah's curse be upon those who slew you! May Allah's curse be on those who wronged you! May Allah's curse be on those who heard about it approvingly!

اَلسَّلَامُ عَلَيْكَ يَا مَوْلَايَ، اَلسَّلَامُ عَلَيْكَ يَا
وَلِيَّ اللهِ وَ ابْنَ وَلِيِّهِ، لَقَدْ عَظُمَتِ الْمُصِيبَةُ
وَ جَلَّتِ الرَّزِيَّةُ بِكَ عَلَيْنَا وَ عَلىٰ جَمِيعِ
الْمُؤْمِنِينَ، فَلَعَنَ اللهُ أُمَّةً قَتَلَتْكَ، وَ أَبْرَأُ

Peace be to you, my master! Peace be to you, O *walī* of Allah and son of His *walī*! Your martyrdom was a tremendous loss and a calamity that befell us and all the faithful! May Allah's curse be on those who slew you. I re-

إِلَى اللهِ وَ إِلَيْكَ مِنْهُمْ فِي الدُّنْيَا وَ الْآخِرَةِ،

pudiate them before Allah and before you in the world and the Hereafter!

Then turn towards the grave of the martyrs and perform their *ziyārah*, saying,

اَلسَّلَامُ عَلَيْكُمْ يَا أَوْلِيَاءَ اللهِ وَ أَحِبَّاءَهُ،
اَلسَّلَامُ عَلَيْكُمْ يَا أَصْفِيَاءَ اللهِ وَ أَوِدَّاءَهُ،
اَلسَّلَامُ عَلَيْكُمْ يَا أَنْصَارَ دِينِ اللهِ
وَ أَنْصَارَ نَبِيِّهِ وَ أَنْصَارَ أَمِيرِ الْمُؤْمِنِينَ
وَ أَنْصَارَ فَاطِمَةَ سَيِّدَةِ نِسَاءِ الْعَالَمِينَ،
اَلسَّلَامُ عَلَيْكُمْ يَا أَنْصَارَ أَبِي مُحَمَّدٍ
الْحَسَنِ الْوَلِيِّ النَّاصِحِ، اَلسَّلَامُ عَلَيْكُمْ
يَا أَنْصَارَ أَبِي عَبْدِ اللهِ الْحُسَيْنِ الشَّهِيدِ
الْمَظْلُومِ، صَلَوَاتُ اللهِ عَلَيْهِمْ أَجْمَعِينَ.

Peace be to you, O friends of Allah and His dear ones! Peace be to you, O chosen ones of Allah and His lovers! Peace be to you, O helpers of the religion of Allah! Peace be to you, O helpers of the Apostle of Allah! Peace be to you, O helpers of the Commander of the Faithful. Peace be to you, O helpers of Fāṭimah, mistress of the world's womankind! Peace be to you, O helpers of Abū Muḥammad al-Ḥasan ibn ʿAlī, the sincere *walī* (devoted to the good of the *ummah*)! Peace be to you, O helpers of Abū ʿAbd Allāh, the aggrieved martyr! May Allah's blessings be upon you all!

بِأَبِي أَنْتُمْ وَ أُمِّي، طِبْتُمْ وَ طَابَتِ الْأَرْضُ
الَّتِي فِيهَا دُفِنْتُمْ، وَ فُزْتُمْ وَ اللهِ فَوْزًا
عَظِيمًا، يَا لَيْتَنِي كُنْتُ مَعَكُمْ فَأَفُوزَ
مَعَكُمْ فِي الْجِنَانِ مَعَ الشُّهَدَاءِ وَ
الصَّالِحِينَ وَ حَسُنَ أُولٰئِكَ رَفِيقًا، وَ
السَّلَامُ عَلَيْكُمْ وَ رَحْمَةُ اللهِ وَ بَرَكَاتُهُ.

You are dearer to me than my father and mother! Happy are you and happy the land where you are buried. You attained a great triumph, and how much I wish I had been with you and triumphed along with you, to enter paradise in the company of *the martyrs and the righteous, and excellent companions are they!* Peace be to you and may Allah's mercy and His bounties be upon you!

Then return towards the head of Imam al-Ḥusayn's tomb and supplicate a lot for yourself, your family and your brethren in faith.

Sayyid ᶜAlī b. Ṭāwūs and Shahīd Awwal mention that one should then proceed towards the tomb of Ḥaḍrat ᶜAbbās (ᶜa) and standing near it, say,

Peace be to you, O Abul-Faḍlil-ᶜAbbās, son of the Commander of the Faithful! Peace be to you, O son of the chief of the Legatees! Peace be to you, O son of him who was foremost of his people in embracing Islam and foremost of them in faith, who was most steadfast in upholding Allah's religion, and most diligent of them in defending Islam!

اَلسَّلَامُ عَلَيْكَ يَا أَبَا الْفَضْلِ الْعَبَّاسَ بْنَ أَمِيرِ الْمُؤْمِنِينَ، اَلسَّلَامُ عَلَيْكَ يَا ابْنَ سَيِّدِ الْوَصِيِّينَ، اَلسَّلَامُ عَلَيْكَ يَا ابْنَ أَوَّلِ الْقَوْمِ إِسْلَامًا، وَ أَقْدَمِهِمْ إِيمَانًا، وَ أَقْوَمِهِمْ بِدِينِ اللهِ، وَ أَحْوَطِهِمْ عَلَى الْإِسْلَامِ،

I testify that you were devoted to Allah, His Apostle, and to your brother, and an excellent and self-abnegating brother you were!

أَشْهَدُ لَقَدْ نَصَحْتَ لِلّٰهِ وَ لِرَسُولِهِ وَ لِأَخِيكَ، فَنِعْمَ الْأَخُ الْمُوَاسِي،

May Allah's curse be on those who slew you! May Allah's curse be on those who wronged you! May Allah's curse be on those who breached your sanctity and rights and violated the sanctity of Islam!

فَلَعَنَ اللهُ أُمَّةً قَتَلَتْكَ، وَ لَعَنَ اللهُ أُمَّةً ظَلَمَتْكَ، وَ لَعَنَ اللهُ أُمَّةً اسْتَحَلَّتْ مِنْكَ الْمَحَارِمَ، وَ انْتَهَكَتْ فِي قَتْلِكَ حُرْمَةَ الْإِسْلَامِ،

What an excellent brother, a patient and gallant warrior you were! How devoted a supporter, helper and defender of your brother! How responsive to obeying your Lord, how ardent in seeking His plenteous reward and compliments, which others regarded with indifference! May Allah admit you into the ranks of your ancestors in the gardens of bliss! Indeed He is all-laudable, all-glorious.

فَنِعْمَ الْأَخُ الصَّابِرُ الْمُجَاهِدُ الْمُحَامِي النَّاصِرُ، وَ الْأَخُ الدَّافِعُ عَنْ أَخِيهِ، اَلْمُجِيبُ إِلَى طَاعَةِ رَبِّهِ، اَلرَّاغِبُ فِيمَا زَهِدَ فِيهِ غَيْرُهُ مِنَ الثَّوَابِ الْجَزِيلِ، وَ الثَّنَاءِ الْجَمِيلِ، وَ أَلْحَقَكَ اللهُ بِدَرَجَةِ آبَائِكَ فِي دَارِ النَّعِيمِ، إِنَّهُ حَمِيدٌ مَجِيدٌ.

Then clasping the *ḏarīḥ*, say,

اَللّٰهُمَّ لَكَ تَعَرَّضْتُ، وَ لِزِيَارَةِ أَوْلِيَائِكَ قَصَدْتُ، رَغْبَةً فِي ثَوَابِكَ، وَ رَجَاءً لِمَغْفِرَتِكَ وَ جَزِيلِ إِحْسَانِكَ،

O Allah, I have placed myself before Your mercy and undertaken the *ziyārah* of Your *awliyā'* in my pursuit of Your reward, expecting Your forgiveness and Your generous kindness!

فَأَسْأَلُكَ أَنْ تُصَلِّيَ عَلَىٰ مُحَمَّدٍ وَ آلِ مُحَمَّدٍ، وَ أَنْ تَجْعَلَ رِزْقِي بِهِمْ دَارًّا، وَ عَيْشِي بِهِمْ قَارًّا، وَ زِيَارَتِي بِهِمْ مَقْبُولَةً، وَ ذَنْبِي بِهِمْ مَغْفُورًا، وَ اقْلِبْنِي بِهِمْ مُفْلِحًا مُنْجِحًا مُسْتَجَابًا دُعَائِي بِأَفْضَلِ مَا يَنْقَلِبُ بِهِ أَحَدٌ مِنْ زُوَّارِهِ وَ الْقَاصِدِينَ إِلَيْهِ، بِرَحْمَتِكَ يَا أَرْحَمَ الرَّاحِمِينَ.

I beseech You to bless Muḥammad and the Family of Muḥammad and to make, through them, my provision plentiful, my lifestyle steady, my *ziyārah* received with acceptance, my sins forgiven, and, through them, bless my return home with success and felicity, my supplications answered with the best of what has been granted to any of his pilgrims and visitors, with Your mercy, O Most Merciful of the merciful!

Then embrace his *ḍarīḥ* and offer the prayer of *ziyārah* at his shrine and pray as much as you wish. When bidding farewell to Ḥaḍrat ᶜAbbās, one may recite the text mentioned earlier under his *ziyārah* (p. 297).

7. IMAM ḤUSAYN'S ZIYARAH FOR THE DAY OF ᶜĀSHURA

There are several texts prescribed for the Imam's *ziyārah* on the day of ᶜĀshūrā. For reasons of space, we shall cite only two of them here. We have also mentioned a *ziyārah* in Book Two (vol. 1, p. 766), in observances pertaining to the day of ᶜĀshūrā, whose contents are appropriate for this occasion.

FIRST ZIYARAH FOR THE DAY OF ʿĀSHURA

This is the well-known *ziyārah* for the day of ᶜĀshūrā which can be recited from far and near. It is mentioned in a report cited by Shaykh

Ṭūsī in the *Miṣbāḥ*.[1] Muḥammad b. Ismāᶜīl b. Baziᶜ reports from Ṣāliḥ b. ᶜUqbah from his father, from Imam Muḥammad al-Bāqir (*ᶜa*) that he told the narrator: "Whoever visits Ḥusayn ibn ᶜAlī (*ᶜa*) on the tenth of Muḥarram and weeps over him at his shrine will meet God Almighty on the day of Resurrection having been blessed with the reward of two thousand *ḥajj* and two thousand *ᶜumrah* pilgrimages as well as that of participating in two thousand campaigns (*ghazwah*), the reward of each of these being like that of someone who has performed the *ḥajj* and *ᶜumrah* pilgrimages with the Apostle of Allah (*ṣ*) and the Imams (*ᶜa*) and waged *jihād* alongside them."

The narrator asked the Imam concerning the reward of those in far off places who are unable to make the journey to Karbalā on the day of ᶜĀshūrā. The Imam replied, "Someone like that should go out of the town or ascend to an elevated place in his house and greet the Imam while pointing toward his shrine and make diligent supplications against his killers and offer a two-*rakᶜah* prayer. That should be done in the first part of the day, before noon. Then he should mourn Husayn (*ᶜa*) and weep over him and enjoin the members of his family, those of them whom he does not have to beware of, to weep for him and hold deep mourning in his house, expressing distress over his martyrdom, condoling with one another for the calamity that has befallen them on account of Ḥusayn's martyrdom. For those who do so, I vouch for them all of that reward from God, the Most High."

When asked by the narrator how they are to condole with each other, the Imam replied, "They should say to each other,

أَعْظَمَ اللهُ أُجُورَنَا بِمُصَابِنَا بِالْحُسَيْنِ عَلَيْهِ السَّلَامُ، وَ جَعَلَنَا وَ إِيَّاكُمْ مِنَ الطَّالِبِينَ بِثَارِهِ مَعَ وَلِيِّهِ الْإِمَامِ الْمَهْدِيِّ مِنْ آلِ مُحَمَّدٍ عَلَيْهِمُ السَّلَامُ.

May Allah reward us greatly for the grievous loss we have suffered due to the martyrdom of Ḥusayn, may peace be to him, and may He appoint us and you to be among those who seek to avenge his blood with Imam Mahdī, his heir from the Family of Muḥammad, may peace be to them.

The Imam further said, "If possible, do not go out on this day for any of your needs, as it is an inauspicious day on which the needs

[1] *Kāmil al-Ziyārāt*, 174, b 71, h 8, whence *Mustadrak*, x, 293, b 41, h 12042/6. *Miṣbāḥ*, 772-782, whence *Biḥār*, xcviii, 293-296, b 24, h 2 & *Wasā'il*, xiv, 477, b 55, h 19640.

of the faithful are not fulfilled, and if fulfilled are not blessed and they will not see any good come out of it. Any of you should not procure anything for storage on this day, and provisions thus obtained will not be blessed for him and his family. When they have acted in this manner, God, the Most High, will write for them the reward of a thousand *ḥajj* and a thousand *ʿumrah* pilgrimages and of participating in a thousand campaigns, each of them performed with the Apostle of Allah (ṣ), and their reward with God shall be like the reward for the ordeals undergone by every prophet, apostle, legatee, saint and martyr who has died, or was slain, from the time since God has created the world until the Day of Resurrection."

Ṣāliḥ b. ʿUqbah and Sayf b. ʿAmīrah report[1] that ʿAlqamah b. Muḥammad al-Ḥaḍramī said, "I said to Imam Muḥammad al-Bāqir (ʿa), 'Teach me a supplication that I may recite on this day when visiting his shrine, or when I greet him while pointing toward his shrine from my home in a distant town.' " The Imam said to him, "O ʿAlqamah, when you have offered two *rakʿahs* of prayer after having greeted him while pointing toward his shrine, then, after saying *takbīr* and while pointing toward his shrine, recite the following text. Indeed, when you recite it you will have made the supplication said by the angels who visit his shrine and God will write for you the reward of a million degrees, and you will be like those who were martyred along with al-Ḥusayn (ʿa), share with them in their degrees, and will not be known except as someone belonging to the martyrs who were slain with him. There will be written for you the reward of *ziyārah* of every prophet and apostle and the *ziyārah* of every pilgrim who has visited al-Ḥusayn (ʿa) since the day he was slain, may peace be to him and his family."

Peace be to you, O Abū ʿAbdillāh! Peace be to you, O son of the Apostle of Allah! (Peace be to you, O chosen one of Allah and son of His chosen one!) Peace be to you, O son of the Commander of the Faithful and the chief of the Legatees! Peace be to you, O son of Fāṭimah, the mis-

اَلسَّلَامُ عَلَيْكَ يَا أَبَا عَبْدِ اللهِ، اَلسَّلَامُ عَلَيْكَ يَا ابْنَ رَسُولِ اللهِ، (اَلسَّلَامُ عَلَيْكَ يَا خِــيَرَةَ اللهِ وَ ابْنَ خِيَرَتِهِ)، اَلسَّــلَامُ عَلَيْكَ يَا ابْنَ أَمِيرِ الْمُؤْمِنِينَ وَ ابْنَ سَــيِّدِ الْوَصِيِّينَ، اَلسَّلَامُ عَلَيْكَ

[1] *Kāmil al-Ziyārāt*, 175, b 71, h 8, whence *Biḥār*, xcviii, 290, b 24, h 1. *Al-Mazār al-Kabīr*, 480-485, b 7. S̲h̲ahīd Awwal's *Mazār*, 178-184, b 27. Kafʿamī's *Miṣbāḥ*, 482-485. *Balad*, 269-271.

tress of the world's womankind.

يَا ابْنَ فَاطِمَةَ سَيِّدَةِ نِسَاءِ الْعَالَمِينَ،

Peace be to you, avenger of whose blood is Allah, son of him avenger of whose blood is Allah, and whose blood remains unavenged! Peace be to you and to the spirits that descend in your courtyard. Peace from Allah be to you all on my behalf as long as I live and day and night endure!

اَلسَّلَامُ عَلَيْكَ يَا ثَارَ اللهِ وَ ابْنَ ثَارِهِ، وَ الْوِتْرَ الْمَوْتُورَ، اَلسَّلَامُ عَلَيْكَ وَ عَلَى الْأَرْوَاحِ الَّتِي حَلَّتْ بِفِنَائِكَ، عَلَيْكُمْ مِنِّي جَمِيعًا سَلَامُ اللهِ أَبَدًا مَا بَقِيتُ وَ بَقِيَ اللَّيْلُ وَ النَّهَارُ،

O Abū ᶜAbdillāh, your martyrdom was a great calamity and the cause of great distress for us and all followers of Islam! It was a tremendous calamity that befell the heavens and which affected all the denizens of the heavens!

يَا أَبَا عَبْدِ اللهِ لَقَدْ عَظُمَتِ الرَّزِيَّةُ، وَ جَلَّتْ وَ عَظُمَتِ الْمُصِيبَةُ بِكَ عَلَيْنَا وَ عَلَى جَمِيعِ أَهْلِ الْإِسْلَامِ، وَ جَلَّتْ وَ عَظُمَتْ مُصِيبَتُكَ فِي السَّمَاوَاتِ عَلَى جَمِيعِ أَهْلِ السَّمَاوَاتِ،

May Allah's curse be on those who instituted a regime of wrongdoing and injustice against you, people of the Prophet's Family! May Allah's curse be on those who sidelined you from your rightful station and withheld from you the status that Allah had assigned you! May Allah's curse be on those who slew you, and may His curse be on those who paved the way for them making it possible to wage war against you!

فَلَعَنَ اللهُ أُمَّةً أَسَّسَتْ أَسَاسَ الظُّلْمِ وَ الْجَوْرِ عَلَيْكُمْ أَهْلَ الْبَيْتِ، وَ لَعَنَ اللهُ أُمَّةً دَفَعَتْكُمْ عَنْ مَقَامِكُمْ، وَ أَزَالَتْكُمْ عَنْ مَرَاتِبِكُمُ الَّتِي رَتَّبَكُمُ اللهُ فِيهَا، وَ لَعَنَ اللهُ أُمَّةً قَتَلَتْكُمْ، وَ لَعَنَ اللهُ الْمُمَهِّدِينَ لَهُمْ بِالتَّمْكِينِ مِنْ قِتَالِكُمْ،

Before God and you, I repudiate them, their supporters, their followers and those who befriend them! O Abū ᶜAbdillāh! I make

بَرِئْتُ إِلَى اللهِ وَ إِلَيْكُمْ مِنْهُمْ وَ (مِنْ) أَشْيَاعِهِمْ وَ أَتْبَاعِهِمْ وَ أَوْلِيَائِهِمْ، يَا

peace with those who are at peace with you and will make war against those who are at war with you, till the Day of Resurrection.

أَبَا عَبْدِ اللهِ إِنِّي سِلْمٌ لِمَنْ سَالَمَكُمْ، وَ حَرْبٌ لِمَنْ حَارَبَكُمْ إِلَى يَوْمِ الْقِيَامَةِ،

May Allah's curse be on the clan of Ziyād and the clan of Marwān! May Allah's curse be on the generality of the Umayyads! May Allah's curse be on the son of Marjānah! May Allah's curse be on ʿUmar ibn Saʿd! May Allah's curse be on Shimr! May Allah's curse be on the lot who saddled and harnessed their mounts and patrolled the land for the battle against you!

وَ لَعَنَ اللهُ آلَ زِيَادٍ وَ آلَ مَرْوَانَ، وَ لَعَنَ اللهُ بَنِي أُمَيَّةَ قَاطِبَةً، وَ لَعَنَ اللهُ ابْنَ مَرْجَانَةَ وَ لَعَنَ اللهُ عُمَرَ بْنَ سَعْدٍ وَ لَعَنَ اللهُ شِمْرًا، وَ لَعَنَ اللهُ أُمَّةً أَسْرَجَتْ وَ أَلْجَمَتْ وَ تَنَقَّبَتْ لِقِتَالِكَ،

Dearer than my father and mother, your martyrdom has caused me great sorrow! I beseech Allah, who has honoured you with your station and honoured me through you, to enable me to avenge your blood with the God-aided Imam from the Family of Muḥammad, may Allah bless him and his Family!

بِأَبِي أَنْتَ وَ أُمِّي، لَقَدْ عَظُمَ مُصَابِي بِكَ، فَأَسْأَلُ اللهَ الَّذِي أَكْرَمَ مَقَامَكَ وَ أَكْرَمَنِي (بِكَ) أَنْ يَرْزُقَنِي طَلَبَ ثَارِكَ مَعَ إِمَامٍ مَنْصُورٍ مِنْ أَهْلِ بَيْتِ مُحَمَّدٍ صَلَّى اللهُ عَلَيْهِ وَ آلِهِ.

O Allah, make me eminent with You in the world and the Hereafter through Ḥusayn, peace be to him!

اَللّٰهُمَّ اجْعَلْنِي عِنْدَكَ وَجِيهًا بِالْحُسَيْنِ عَلَيْهِ السَّلَامُ فِي الدُّنْيَا وَ الْآخِرَةِ.

O Abū ʿAbd Allāh! I seek nearness to Allah, His Apostle, the Commander of the Faithful, Fāṭimah, al-Ḥasan and you, through my love for you and through my repudiation of (those who fought against you and waged war against you, and my repudiation of those who in-

يَا أَبَا عَبْدِ اللهِ، إِنِّي أَتَقَرَّبُ إِلَى اللهِ وَ إِلَى رَسُولِهِ وَ إِلَى أَمِيرِ الْمُؤْمِنِينَ وَ إِلَى فَاطِمَةَ وَ إِلَى الْحَسَنِ وَ إِلَيْكَ بِمُوَالاتِكَ، وَ بِالْبَرَاءَةِ (مِمَّنْ قَاتَلَكَ وَ نَصَبَ لَكَ الْحَرْبَ وَ بِالْبَرَاءَةِ مِمَّنْ

أَسَّسَ أَسَاسَ الظُّلْمِ وَ الْجَوْرِ عَلَيْكُمْ ،

stituted the regime of injustice and oppression against you.

وَ أَبْرَأُ إِلَى اللهِ وَ إِلَىٰ رَسُولِهِ) مِمَّنْ أَسَّسَ أَسَاسَ ذٰلِكَ، وَ بَنَىٰ عَلَيْهِ بُنْيَانَهُ، وَ جَرَىٰ فِي ظُلْمِهِ وَ جَوْرِهِ عَلَيْكُمْ وَ عَلَىٰ أَشْيَاعِكُمْ، بَرِئْتُ إِلَى اللهِ وَ إِلَيْكُمْ مِنْهُمْ،

And I do repudiate, before Allah and His Apostle,) those who created the grounds for that, those who built upon it and made injustice and wrongdoing against you and your followers their policy. I repudiate them before Allah and before you.

وَ أَتَقَرَّبُ إِلَى اللهِ ثُمَّ إِلَيْكُمْ بِمُوَالاٰتِكُمْ وَ مُوَالاٰةِ وَلِيِّكُمْ، وَ بِالْبَرَاءَةِ مِنْ أَعْدَائِكُمْ وَ النَّاصِبِينَ لَكُمُ الْحَرْبَ، وَ بِالْبَرَاءَةِ مِنْ أَشْيَاعِهِمْ وَ أَتْبَاعِهِمْ،

I seek nearness to Allah and you with my love for you and my love for your friends, and through my repudiation of your enemies and those who waged war against you as well as my repudiation of their supporters and followers!

إِنِّي سِلْمٌ لِمَنْ سَالَمَكُمْ، وَ حَرْبٌ لِمَنْ حَارَبَكُمْ، وَ وَلِيٌّ لِمَنْ وَالاٰكُمْ، وَ عَدُوٌّ لِمَنْ عَادَاكُمْ،

I am at peace with those who are at peace with you and at war with those who are at war with you. I befriend those who befriend you and am hostile to those who are hostile towards you.

فَأَسْأَلُ اللهَ الَّذِى أَكْرَمَنِي بِمَعْرِفَتِكُمْ وَ مَعْرِفَةِ أَوْلِيَائِكُمْ، وَ رَزَقَنِي الْبَرَاءَةَ مِنْ أَعْدَائِكُمْ، أَنْ يَجْعَلَنِي مَعَكُمْ فِي الدُّنْيَا وَ الْآخِرَةِ، وَ أَنْ يُثَبِّتَ لِي عِنْدَكُمْ قَدَمَ صِدْقٍ فِي الدُّنْيَا وَ الْآخِرَةِ،

I beseech Allah, who has honoured me with my appreciation of you and your friends and has enabled me to repudiate your enemies, to include me in your fold in the the present life and the Hereafter, and to grant me a steady and worthy standing with you in this life and the Hereafter.

وَ أَسْأَلُهُ أَنْ يُبَلِّغَنِي الْمَقَامَ الْمَحْمُودَ لَكُمْ عِنْدَ اللهِ، وَ أَنْ يَرْزُقَنِي طَلَبَ ثَارِى [ثَارَكُمْ] مَعَ إِمَامِ هُدًى ظَاهِرٍ نَاطِقٍ

I beseech Him to enable me to reach the praiseworthy station you have with Allah and to enable me to avenge your blood alongside the Imam of guidance from your Family, who is mani-

بِالْحَقِّ مِنْكُمْ،

fest and speaks in accordance with the truth.

وَ أَسْأَلُ اللهَ بِحَقِّكُمْ وَ بِالشَّأْنِ الَّذِى لَكُمْ عِنْدَهُ أَنْ يُعْطِيَنِى بِمُصَابِى بِكُمْ أَفْضَلَ مَا يُعْطِى مُصَابًا بِمُصِيبَتِهِ، مُصِيبَةً مَا أَعْظَمَهَا وَ أَعْظَمَ رَزِيَّتَهَا فِى الْإِسْلَامِ وَ فِى جَمِيعِ السَّمَاوَاتِ وَ الْأَرْضِ،

I beseech Allah by your right and your standing with Him, to grant me, by virtue of my sorrow for your sake, the best reward granted to anyone who has suffered a tragedy, which has been a great calamity and a tremendous loss that befall the world of Islam and affected all (the denizens of) the heavens and the earth!

اَللّٰهُمَّ اجْعَلْنِى فِى مَقَامِى هٰذَا مِمَّنْ تَنَالُهُ مِنْكَ صَلَوَاتٌ وَ رَحْمَةٌ وَ مَغْفِرَةٌ.

O Allah, include me, while I stand here, among those who receive Your blessings, mercy and forgiveness!

اَللّٰهُمَّ اجْعَلْ مَحْيَاىَ مَحْيَا مُحَمَّدٍ وَ آلِ مُحَمَّدٍ، وَ مَمَاتِى مَمَاتَ مُحَمَّدٍ وَ آلِ مُحَمَّدٍ.

O Allah, grant me to live as Muḥammad and his Family lived, and grant me to die like Muḥammad and the Family of Muḥammad!

اَللّٰهُمَّ إِنَّ هٰذَا يَوْمٌ تَبَرَّكَتْ بِهِ بَنُو أُمَيَّةَ وَ ابْنُ آكِلَةِ الْأَكْبَادِ، اَللَّعِينُ ابْنُ اللَّعِينِ عَلٰى لِسَانِكَ وَ لِسَانِ نَبِيِّكَ صَلَّى اللهُ عَلَيْهِ وَ آلِهِ فِى كُلِّ مَوْطِنٍ وَ مَوْقِفٍ وَقَفَ فِيهِ نَبِيُّكَ صَلَّى اللهُ عَلَيْهِ وَ آلِهِ.

O Allah, this was celebrated as an auspicious day by the clan of Umayyads and the scion of her who ate the livers (of the martyrs), the accursed scion of the one cursed by You and Your Prophet, may Allah bless him and his Family, in every place and situation Your Prophet, may Allah bless him and his Family, was present.

اَللّٰهُمَّ الْعَنْ أَبَا سُفْيَانَ وَ مُعَاوِيَةَ، وَ يَزِيدَ بْنَ مُعَاوِيَةَ، عَلَيْهِمْ مِنْكَ اللَّعْنَةُ أَبَدَ الْآبِدِينَ،

O Allah, curse Abū Sufyān, Muʿāwiyah, and Yazīd son of Muʿāwiyah, may Your curse be on them forever and ever.

وَ هٰذَا يَوْمٌ فَرِحَتْ بِهِ آلُ زِيَادٍ وَ آلُ مَرْوَانَ بِقَتْلِهِمُ الْحُسَيْنَ صَلَوَاتُ اللهِ عَلَيْهِ، اَللّٰهُمَّ فَضَاعِفْ عَلَيْهِمُ اللَّعْنَ

On this day the clan of Ziyād and the Marwānids rejoiced for having slain Ḥusayn, may Allah bless him. O Allah, amplify Your curse on them and heighten their painful punishment.

مِنْكَ وَ الْعَذَابَ الْأَلِيمَ.

O Allah, I seek nearness to You on this day and in this place, and throughout the days of my life, by repudiating them and cursing them and by befriending Your Prophet and his Family, may peace be to them!

اَللّٰهُمَّ إِنِّي أَتَقَرَّبُ إِلَيْكَ فِي هٰذَا الْيَوْمِ وَ فِي مَوْقِفِي هٰذَا وَ أَيَّامِ حَيَاتِي بِالْبَرَاءَةِ مِنْهُمْ، وَ اللَّعْنَةِ عَلَيْهِمْ، وَ بِالْمُوَالاةِ لِنَبِيِّكَ وَ آلِ نَبِيِّكَ عَلَيْهِ وَ عَلَيْهِمُ السَّلَامُ.

Then say a hundred times,

O Allah, let Your curse be on the first tyrant who breached the rights of Muḥammad and the Family of Muḥammad and the last follower of that policy. O Allah, curse the league that fought al-Ḥusayn and made alliances and pacts and agreed to kill him. O Allah, curse all of them!

اَللّٰهُمَّ الْعَنْ أَوَّلَ ظَالِمٍ ظَلَمَ حَقَّ مُحَمَّدٍ وَ آلِ مُحَمَّدٍ، وَ آخِرَ تَابِعٍ لَهُ عَلَىٰ ذٰلِكَ، اَللّٰهُمَّ الْعَنِ الْعِصَابَةَ الَّتِي جَاهَدَتِ الْحُسَيْنَ، وَ شَايَعَتْ وَ بَايَعَتْ وَ تَابَعَتْ عَلَىٰ قَتْلِهِ، اَللّٰهُمَّ الْعَنْهُمْ جَمِيعًا.

Then say a hundred times,

Peace be to you, O Abū ᶜAbdillāh and to the spirits that have alighted in your courtyard! Peace be to you from me so long as I live and so long as day and night endure! May Allah not make this my last opportunity of your *ziyārah*. Peace be to al-Ḥusayn, to ᶜAlī ibn al-Ḥusayn, to the children of al-Ḥusayn and the companions of al-Ḥusayn!

اَلسَّلَامُ عَلَيْكَ يَا أَبَا عَبْدِ اللهِ وَ عَلَى الْأَرْوَاحِ الَّتِي حَلَّتْ بِفِنَائِكَ، عَلَيْكَ مِنِّي سَلَامُ اللهِ أَبَدًا مَا بَقِيتُ وَ بَقِيَ اللَّيْلُ وَ النَّهَارُ، وَ لَا جَعَلَهُ اللهُ آخِرَ الْعَهْدِ مِنِّي لِزِيَارَتِكُمْ [لِزِيَارَتِكَ]، اَلسَّلَامُ عَلَى الْحُسَيْنِ، وَ عَلَىٰ عَلِيِّ بْنِ الْحُسَيْنِ، وَ عَلَىٰ أَوْلَادِ الْحُسَيْنِ، وَ عَلَىٰ أَصْحَابِ الْحُسَيْنِ.

Then say,

O Allah, single out for Your curse,

اَللّٰهُمَّ خُصَّ أَنْتَ أَوَّلَ ظَالِمٍ بِاللَّعْنِ مِنِّي،

on my behalf, the first tyrant, starting with him, then the second one, then the third one and then the fourth. O Allah, lay Your curse on Yazīd, the fifth one and curse ᶜUbayullāh ibn Ziyād, son of Marjānah, and ᶜUmar ibn Saᶜd, Shimr, the clan of Abū Sufyān and the clans of Ziyād and Marwān till the Day of Resurrection!

وَ ابْدَأْ بِهِ أَوَّلًا ثُمَّ [الْعَنِ] الثَّانِيَ وَ الثَّالِثَ
وَ الرَّابِعَ، اَللّٰهُمَّ الْعَنْ يَزِيدَ خَامِسًا، وَ
الْعَنْ عُبَيْدَ اللهِ بْنَ زِيَادٍ وَ ابْنَ مَرْجَانَةَ،
وَ عُمَرَ بْنَ سَعْدٍ وَ شِمْرًا، وَ آلَ أَبِي سُفْيَانَ
وَ آلَ زِيَادٍ وَ آلَ مَرْوَانَ إِلَىٰ يَوْمِ الْقِيَامَةِ.

Then make prostration and say,

O Allah, to You belongs all praise and to You are due thanks of the grateful for their afflictions. All praise belongs to Allah for this great calamity that has befallen me. O Allah, grant me al-Ḥusayn's intercession on my entry at the scene of Retribution, and grant me a steady and worthy standing with You alongside al-Ḥusayn and his companions, who gave their lifeblood defending al-Ḥusayn, peace be to him!

اَللّٰهُمَّ لَكَ الْحَمْدُ حَمْدَ الشَّاكِرِينَ لَكَ عَلَىٰ
مُصَابِهِمْ، اَلْحَمْدُ لِلّٰهِ عَلَىٰ عَظِيمِ رَزِيَّتِي،
اَللّٰهُمَّ ارْزُقْنِي شَفَاعَةَ الْحُسَيْنِ يَوْمَ الْوُرُودِ،
وَ ثَبِّتْ لِي قَدَمَ صِدْقٍ عِنْدَكَ مَعَ الْحُسَيْنِ
وَ أَصْحَابِ الْحُسَيْنِ، اَلَّذِينَ بَذَلُوا مُهَجَهُمْ
دُونَ الْحُسَيْنِ عَلَيْهِ السَّلَامُ.

ᶜAlqamah says that Imam Muḥammad al-Bāqir (ᶜ*a*) told him to perform this *ziyārah* from his home every day if he could and that he would receive all the rewards mentioned for this observance, God willing.

Muḥammad b. Khālid al-Ṭayālisī reports[1] that Sayf b. ᶜAmīrah said, "I went to Najaf (Gharī) with Ṣafwān b. Mihrān and a group of our companions after the departure of Imam Jaᶜfar al-Ṣādiq (ᶜ*a*), and from Ḥīrah we set out for Madīnah. After we had performed the *ziyārah* of the Commander of the Faithful (ᶜ*a*), Ṣafwān turned in the direction of the shrine of Abū ᶜAbdillāh al-Ḥusayn (ᶜ*a*) and said to us, 'Now perform the *ziyārah* of al-Ḥusayn from this spot at the head

1 Ṭūsī's *Miṣbāḥ*, 777, whence *Biḥār*, xcviii, 296, b 24, h 3. *Al-Mazār al-Kabīr*, 214, b 5, whence *Biḥār*, xcvii, 310, b 4, h 24. *Farḥat al-Gharī*, 96, b 6, whence *Wasā'il*, xiv, 401, b 32, h 19458.

of the graveside of the Commander of the Faithful (ᶜa), as was done by Imam Jaᶜfar al-Ṣādiq (ᶜa). I was with him, when he greeted Imam al-Ḥusayn (ᶜa) from this place while pointing towards his shrine.' "

Sayf says: "Then Ṣafwān recited the same *ziyārah* for the day of ᶜĀshūrā that ᶜAlqamah had narrated from Imam Muḥammad al-Bāqir (ᶜa). Then he offered two *rakᶜahs* at the head of the Commander of the Faithful's graveside. After the prayer, he bade farewell to the Commander of the Faithful (ᶜa) and then turning his face towards the shrine of Imam al-Ḥusayn (ᶜa) and pointing with his hand toward it, bade him farewell. The supplication that he recited after the prayer of Imam al-Ḥusayn's *ziyārah* was as follows."

Duᶜā ᶜAlqamah

Supplication After the Ziyārah of ʿĀshura

O Allah, O Allah, O Allah! O Answerer of the calls of the distressed! O Reliever of the anxieties of the troubled! O Succour of those who appeal for help! O Rescuer of those who cry out in distress!

يَا اَللّٰهُ يَا اَللّٰهُ يَا اَللّٰهُ، يَا مُجِيبَ دَعْوَةِ
الْمُضْطَرِّينَ، يَا كَاشِفَ كُرَبِ الْمَكْرُوبِينَ،
يَا غِيَاثَ الْمُسْتَغِيثِينَ، يَا صَرِيخَ
الْمُسْتَصْرِخِينَ،

O You who are nearer to me than my jugular vein! O You who intervene between a person and his heart! O You who are on the highest viewpoint and on the manifest horizon!

وَ يَا مَنْ هُوَ أَقْرَبُ إِلَيَّ مِنْ حَبْلِ الْوَرِيدِ،
وَ يَا مَنْ يَحُولُ بَيْنَ الْمَرْءِ وَ قَلْبِهِ، وَ يَا مَنْ
هُوَ بِالْمَنْظَرِ الْأَعْلَىٰ وَ بِالْأُفُقِ الْمُبِينِ،

O You who are the All-beneficent and the All-merciful, settled on the Throne! O You *who know the treachery of the eyes and what the breasts hide!* O You from whom no hidden thing is concealed!

وَ يَا مَنْ هُوَ الرَّحْمٰنُ الرَّحِيمُ عَلَى الْعَرْشِ
اسْتَوَىٰ، وَ يَا مَنْ يَعْلَمُ خَائِنَةَ الْأَعْيُنِ وَ مَا
تُخْفِي الصُّدُورُ، وَيَا مَنْ لَا يَخْفَىٰ عَلَيْهِ خَافِيَةٌ،

O You who are not confused by the great number of petitions! O You who are not wearied by the entreaties of the importunate! O

يَا مَنْ لَا تَشْتَبِهُ عَلَيْهِ الْأَصْوَاتُ، وَ يَا مَنْ
لَا تُغَلِّطُهُ الْحَاجَاتُ، وَ يَا مَنْ لَا يُبْرِمُهُ

إِلْحَاحُ الْمُلِحِّينَ، يَا مُدْرِكَ كُلِّ فَوْتٍ، وَ يَا جَامِعَ كُلِّ شَمْلٍ، وَ يَا بَارِئَ النُّفُوسِ بَعْدَ الْمَوْتِ، يَا مَنْ هُوَ كُلَّ يَوْمٍ فِي شَأْنٍ،

Restorer of everything that is missing! O Bringer about of all unions! O Reviver of the souls after death! O You who are engaged in some work every day!

يَا قَاضِيَ الْحَاجَاتِ، يَا مُنَفِّسَ الْكُرُبَاتِ، يَا مُعْطِيَ السُّؤْلَاتِ، يَا وَلِيَّ الرَّغَبَاتِ، يَا كَافِيَ الْمُهِمَّاتِ، يَا مَنْ يَكْفِي مِنْ كُلِّ شَيْءٍ وَ لَا يَكْفِي مِنْهُ شَيْءٌ فِي السَّمَاوَاتِ وَ الْأَرْضِ،

O Fulfiller of all needs! O Dispeller of worries! O Granter of requests! O Patron of all petitions! O Sufficer in all concerns! O You who suffice against [protect from] all things, and against whom nothing in the heavens and the earth can suffice!

أَسْأَلُكَ بِحَقِّ مُحَمَّدٍ خَاتَمِ النَّبِيِّينَ، وَ عَلِيٍّ أَمِيرِ الْمُؤْمِنِينَ، وَ بِحَقِّ فَاطِمَةَ بِنْتِ نَبِيِّكَ، وَ بِحَقِّ الْحَسَنِ وَ الْحُسَيْنِ، فَإِنِّي بِهِمْ أَتَوَجَّهُ إِلَيْكَ فِي مَقَامِي هٰذَا، وَ بِهِمْ أَتَوَسَّلُ وَ بِهِمْ أَتَشَفَّعُ إِلَيْكَ،

I beseech You by the right of Muḥammad, the Seal of the Prophets, and ʿAlī, the Commander of the Faithful, and by the right of Fāṭimah, daughter of Your Prophet, and by the rights of al-Ḥasan and al-Ḥusayn, for I turn to You through their mediation in this place where I stand and take recourse in their mediation and their intercession.

وَ بِحَقِّهِمْ أَسْأَلُكَ وَ أُقْسِمُ وَ أَعْزِمُ عَلَيْكَ، وَ بِالشَّأْنِ الَّذِي لَهُمْ عِنْدَكَ، وَ بِالْقَدْرِ الَّذِي لَهُمْ عِنْدَكَ، وَ بِالَّذِي فَضَّلْتَهُمْ عَلَى الْعَالَمِينَ، وَ بِاسْمِكَ الَّذِي جَعَلْتَهُ عِنْدَهُمْ، وَ بِهِ خَصَصْتَهُمْ دُونَ الْعَالَمِينَ، وَ بِهِ أَبَنْتَهُمْ وَ أَبَنْتَ فَضْلَهُمْ مِنْ فَضْلِ الْعَالَمِينَ، حَتَّى فَاقَ فَضْلُهُمْ فَضْلَ الْعَالَمِينَ جَمِيعًا،

I beseech You by their right and adjure and implore You by the standing and worth they have with You and by the preference You have granted them over all the world's denizens, and by Your Name that You have conferred on them, to exclusion of other denizens of the world, thus distinguishing them and exalting their excellence over that of all the world's denizens, so that their merit surpasses the merits of all the world's denizens.

I beseech You to bless Muḥammad and the Family of Muḥammad and to remove my grief, worries and anguish, to take care of my concerns of consequence, to pay my debts, and shelter me from poverty and need, to spare me from asking the creatures, to protect me from: those I fear would cause me worry, those I fear would cause me hardship, those I fear would cause me grief, and from the evil of those whose evil I fear, the cunning of those whose cunning I fear, from the envy of those whose envy I fear, from the injustice of those whose injustice I fear, from the authority of those whose authority I fear, and from the guile of those whose guile I fear, and the power of those whose power I fear, and to repel from me the stratagems of cunning persons and the ruses of the guileful.

أَسْأَلُكَ أَنْ تُصَلِّيَ عَلَىٰ مُحَمَّدٍ وَ آلِ مُحَمَّدٍ،
وَ أَنْ تَكْشِفَ عَنِّي غَمِّي وَ هَمِّي وَ
كَرْبِي، وَ تَكْفِيَنِي الْمُهِمَّ مِنْ أُمُورِي، وَ
تَقْضِيَ عَنِّي دَيْنِي، وَ تُجِيرَنِي مِنَ الْفَقْرِ،
وَ تُجِيرَنِي مِنَ الْفَاقَةِ، وَ تُغْنِيَنِي عَنِ
الْمَسْأَلَةِ إِلَى الْمَخْلُوقِينَ، وَ تَكْفِيَنِي
هَمَّ مَنْ أَخَافُ هَمَّهُ، وَ عُسْرَ مَنْ أَخَافُ
عُسْرَهُ، وَ حُزُونَةَ مَنْ أَخَافُ حُزُونَتَهُ، وَ
شَرَّ مَنْ أَخَافُ شَرَّهُ، وَ مَكْرَ مَنْ أَخَافُ
مَكْرَهُ، وَ بَغْيَ مَنْ أَخَافُ بَغْيَهُ، وَ جَوْرَ
مَنْ أَخَافُ جَوْرَهُ، وَ سُلْطَانَ مَنْ أَخَافُ
سُلْطَانَهُ، وَ كَيْدَ مَنْ أَخَافُ كَيْدَهُ، وَ
مَقْدُرَةَ مَنْ أَخَافُ مَقْدُرَتَهُ عَلَيَّ، وَ تَرُدَّ
عَنِّي كَيْدَ الْكَيَدَةِ وَ مَكْرَ الْمَكَرَةِ.

O Allah, whoever aims to harm me, target him! Whoever plots against me, scheme against him, and turn away from me his guile and schemes, his violence and designs, and keep him off from me in whatever manner You wish!

اَللّٰهُمَّ مَنْ أَرَادَنِي فَأَرِدْهُ، وَ مَنْ كَادَنِي
فَكِدْهُ، وَ اصْرِفْ عَنِّي كَيْدَهُ وَ مَكْرَهُ
وَ بَأْسَهُ وَ أَمَانِيَّهُ، وَ امْنَعْهُ عَنِّي كَيْفَ
شِئْتَ وَ أَنَّىٰ شِئْتَ.

O Allah, distract him from troubling me with a poverty which You will not redress, with an affliction You will not shield him

اَللّٰهُمَّ اشْغَلْهُ عَنِّي بِفَقْرٍ لَا تَجْبُرُهُ، وَ
بِبَلَاءٍ لَا تَسْتُرُهُ، وَ بِفَاقَةٍ لَا تَسُدُّهَا،

from, a want You will not remove, a malady from which You will not cure him, a disgrace You will not turn to honour, and a privation You will not relieve!

وَ بِسُقْمٍ لَا تُعَافِيهِ، وَ ذُلٍّ لَا تُعِزُّهُ، وَ بِمَسْكَنَةٍ لَا تَجْبُرُهَا.

O Allah, make degradation his prospect, send poverty into his home and let disease and sickness into his body, thus distracting him from troubling me with a preoccupation from which he finds no release. Make him forget me as You have made him forget You, and turn aside from me his hearing, sight, tongue, hands, feet, heart and all his bodily members and afflict him in all these with an illness which You will not heal, so that You make it the cause of his preoccupation which will distract him from troubling me and remembering me.

اَللّٰهُمَّ اضْرِبْ بِالذُّلِّ نَصْبَ عَيْنَيْهِ، وَ أَدْخِلْ عَلَيْهِ الْفَقْرَ فِي مَنْزِلِهِ، وَ الْعِلَّةَ وَ السُّقْمَ فِي بَدَنِهِ، حَتَّىٰ تَشْغَلَهُ عَنِّي بِشُغْلٍ شَاغِلٍ لَا فَرَاغَ لَهُ، وَ أَنْسِهِ ذِكْرِي كَمَا أَنْسَيْتَهُ ذِكْرَكَ، وَ خُذْ عَنِّي بِسَمْعِهِ وَ بَصَرِهِ وَ لِسَانِهِ وَ يَدِهِ وَ رِجْلِهِ وَ قَلْبِهِ وَ جَمِيعِ جَوَارِحِهِ، وَ أَدْخِلْ عَلَيْهِ فِي جَمِيعِ ذٰلِكَ السُّقْمَ، وَ لَا تَشْفِهِ حَتَّىٰ تَجْعَلَ ذٰلِكَ لَهُ شُغْلًا شَاغِلًا بِهِ عَنِّي وَ عَنْ ذِكْرِي،

Suffice me, O Sufficer, besides whom nothing can suffice, for You are the All-sufficing and there is no sufficer besides You. You are the Reliever and there is no reliever besides You. You are the Rescuer and there is no rescuer besides You. You are the Granter of refuge and there is no refuge besides You! Disappointed are those who take refuge in anyone other than You, and look for succour, sanctuary, shelter, haven with anyone other than You, and seek safety with a creature and not You.

وَ اكْفِنِي يَا كَافِيَ مَا لَا يَكْفِي سِوَاكَ، فَإِنَّكَ الْكَافِي لَا كَافِيَ سِوَاكَ، وَ مُفَرِّجٌ لَا مُفَرِّجَ سِوَاكَ، وَ مُغِيثٌ لَا مُغِيثَ سِوَاكَ، وَ جَارٌ لَا جَارَ سِوَاكَ، خَابَ مَنْ كَانَ جَارُهُ سِوَاكَ، وَ مُغِيثُهُ سِوَاكَ، وَ مَفْزَعُهُ إِلَىٰ سِوَاكَ، وَ مَهْرَبُهُ إِلَىٰ سِوَاكَ، وَ مَلْجَأُهُ إِلَىٰ غَيْرِكَ، وَ مَنْجَاهُ مِنْ مَخْلُوقٍ غَيْرِكَ،

So You are my reliance, my hope, my sanctuary, my shelter, my ha-

فَأَنْتَ ثِقَتِي وَ رَجَائِي وَ مَفْزَعِي وَ مَهْرَبِي

وَ مَلْجَئِى وَ مَنْجَاىَ، فَبِكَ أَسْـتَفْتِحُ وَ بِكَ أَسْتَنْجِحُ، وَ بِمُحَمَّدٍ وَ آلِ مُحَمَّدٍ أَتَوَجَّهُ إِلَيْكَ وَ أَتَوَسَّلُ وَ أَتَشَفَّعُ،

ven and my safety. You do I implore for victory and success, and to You do I turn through the good offices of Muḥammad and the Family of Muḥammad and seek their mediation and intercession!

فَأَسْــأَلُكَ يَا اَللّٰهُ يَا اَللّٰهُ يَا اَللّٰهُ، فَلَكَ الْحَمْدُ وَ لَكَ الشُّــكْرُ وَ إِلَيْكَ الْمُشْــتَكَىٰ وَ أَنْتَ الْمُسْتَعَانُ،

I beseech You, O Allah, O Allah, O Allah! For to You belongs all praise and to You are due all thanks. To You are addressed all complaints and You are our resort!

فَأَسْــأَلُكَ يَا اَللّٰهُ يَا اَللّٰهُ يَا اَللّٰهُ، بِحَقِّ مُحَمَّدٍ وَ آلِ مُحَمَّــدٍ، أَنْ تُصَــلِّيَ عَلَىٰ مُحَمَّــدٍ وَ آلِ مُحَمَّدٍ، وَ أَنْ تَكْشِــفَ عَنِّي غَمِّي وَ هَمِّي وَ كَرْبِي فِي مَقَامِي هٰذَا كَمَا كَشَــفْتَ عَنْ نَبِيِّــكَ هَمَّهُ وَ غَمَّهُ وَ كَرْبَهُ، وَ كَفَيْتَهُ هَوْلَ عَدُوِّهِ، فَاكْشِفْ عَنِّي كَمَا كَشَفْتَ عَنْهُ، وَ فَرِّجْ عَنِّي كَمَا فَرَّجْتَ عَنْهُ، وَ اكْفِنِي كَمَا كَفَيْتَهُ، وَ اصْرِفْ عَنِّي هَوْلَ مَا أَخَافُ هَوْلَهُ، وَ مَؤُونَةَ مَا أَخَافُ مَؤُونَتَهُ، وَ هَمَّ مَا أَخَافُ هَمَّهُ بِلَا مَؤُونَةٍ عَلَىٰ نَفْسِي مِنْ ذٰلِكَ،

I beseech You, O Allah, O Allah, O Allah, by the right of Muḥammad and the Family of Muḥammad, to bless Muḥammad and the Family of Muḥammad, and to remove my grief, my worries and anguish in this place where I stand, even as You removed the grief, worries and anguish of Your Prophet and sufficed him against the fear of his enemies! Remove my afflictions as You removed his. Give me relief as You gave him relief. Suffice me as You sufficed him. Repel from me the dangers, burdens and worries that I fear, without my having to bear any trouble on that account.

وَ اصْرِفْــنِي بِقَضَاءِ حَوَائِــجِي، وَ كِفَايَةِ مَا أَهَمَّنِي هَمُّهُ مِنْ أَمْرِ آخِرَتِي وَ دُنْيَاىَ،

Send me back with my needs fulfilled, having taken care of all that is of concern to me of the affairs of my Hereafter and present life!

يَا أَمِيرَ الْمُؤْمِنِينَ وَ يَا أَبَا عَبْدِ اللهِ، عَلَيْكُمَا

O Commander of the Faithful! O Abū ʿAbdillāh! May Allah's

Peace be to you on my behalf, so long as I live and so long as day and night endure, and may Allah not make this my last opportunity to perform your *ziyārah* and may He never separate me from you!	مِنِّي سَلَامُ اللهِ أَبَدًا مَا بَقِيتُ وَ بَقِيَ اللَّيْلُ وَ النَّهَارُ، وَ لَا جَعَلَهُ اللهُ آخِرَ الْعَهْدِ مِنْ زِيَارَتِكُمَا، وَ لَا فَرَّقَ اللهُ بَيْنِي وَ بَيْنَكُمَا.
O Allah, grant me to live like Muḥammad and his progeny and to die like them. Grant me to die while following their creed; raise me at resurrection in their fold; and do not ever separate me from them in this world or in the Hereafter even for so much as the twinkling of the eye!	اَللّٰهُمَّ أَحْيِنِي حَيَاةَ مُحَمَّدٍ وَ ذُرِّيَّتِهِ، وَ أَمِتْنِي مَمَاتَهُمْ، وَ تَوَفَّنِي عَلَىٰ مِلَّتِهِمْ، وَ احْشُرْنِي فِي زُمْرَتِهِمْ، وَ لَا تُفَرِّقْ بَيْنِي وَ بَيْنَهُمْ طَرْفَةَ عَيْنٍ أَبَدًا فِي الدُّنْيَا وَ الْآخِرَةِ
O Commander of the Faithful! O Abū ʿAbdillāh! I have come to you as a pilgrim, seeking Your mediation with Allah, your Lord and mine; turning to Him with your mediation, seeking your intercession with Allah, the Most High, with regard to this need of mine. So intercede for me, for indeed you have an admirable station with Allah, a preeminent eminence, and an exalted station and mediation.	يَا أَمِيرَ الْمُؤْمِنِينَ وَ يَا أَبَا عَبْدِ اللهِ، أَتَيْتُكُمَا زَائِرًا وَ مُتَوَسِّلًا إِلَى اللهِ رَبِّي وَ رَبِّكُمَا، وَ مُتَوَجِّهًا إِلَيْهِ بِكُمَا وَ مُسْتَشْفِعًا بِكُمَا إِلَى اللهِ تَعَالَىٰ فِي حَاجَتِي هٰذِهِ، فَاشْفَعَا لِي فَإِنَّ لَكُمَا عِنْدَ اللهِ الْمَقَامَ الْمَحْمُودَ وَ الْجَاهَ الْوَجِيهَ وَ الْمَنْزِلَ الرَّفِيعَ وَ الْوَسِيلَةَ،
I am returning from my visit to you, awaiting the fulfilment of this need, its satisfaction and completion by Allah with your intercession with Him in my favour in this regard. So let me not be disappointed, nor let my return be one of failure and loss. Rather, let my return be rewarded with favour and let it be one of felicity and success, with all my petitions	إِنِّي أَنْقَلِبُ عَنْكُمَا مُنْتَظِرًا لِتَنَجُّزِ الْحَاجَةِ وَ قَضَائِهَا وَ نَجَاحِهَا مِنَ اللهِ بِشَفَاعَتِكُمَا لِي إِلَى اللهِ فِي ذٰلِكَ، فَلَا أَخِيبُ وَ لَا يَكُونُ مُنْقَلَبِي مُنْقَلَبًا خَائِبًا خَاسِرًا، بَلْ يَكُونُ مُنْقَلَبِي

مُنْقَلَبًا رَاجِحًا مُفْلِحًا مُنْجِحًا مُسْتَجَابًا
بِقَضَاءِ جَمِيعِ حَوَائِجِى،

answered!

وَ تَشَفَّعَا لِى إِلَى اللهِ، اِنْقَلَبْتُ عَلَىٰ مَا
شَاءَ اللهُ وَ لَا حَوْلَ وَ لَا قُوَّةَ إِلَّا بِاللهِ،
مُفَوِّضًا أَمْرِى إِلَى اللهِ، مُلْجِئًا ظَهْرِى
إِلَى اللهِ، مُتَوَكِّلًا عَلَى اللهِ، وَ أَقُولُ حَسْبِيَ
اللهُ وَ كَفَىٰ، سَمِعَ اللهُ لِمَنْ دَعَا، لَيْسَ لِى
وَرَاءَ اللهِ وَ وَرَاءَكُمْ يَا سَادَتِى مُنْتَهىٰ،
مَا شَاءَ رَبِّى كَانَ، وَ مَا لَمْ يَشَأْ لَمْ يَكُنْ،
وَ لَا حَوْلَ وَ لَا قُوَّةَ إِلَّا بِاللهِ،

Intercede in my favour with Allah, so that I return as Allah wishes—there being no power or force except what proceeds from Allah—entrusting my matters to Allah, falling back on Allah, putting trust in Allah, and believing that Allah is sufficient for me and that He hears those who call Him. I have no resort beyond Allah and beyond you, my masters! Whatever my Lord wishes occurs and what He does not wish does not come about, and there is no power or force except what derives from Allah.

أَسْتَوْدِعُكُمَا اللهَ، وَ لَا جَعَلَهُ اللهُ آخِرَ
الْعَهْدِ مِنِّى إِلَيْكُمَا، اِنْصَرَفْتُ يَا سَيِّدِى
يَا أَمِيرَ الْمُؤْمِنِينَ وَ مَوْلَاىَ، وَ أَنْتَ يَا أَبَا
عَبْدِ اللهِ يَا سَيِّدِى، وَ سَلَامِى عَلَيْكُمَا
مُتَّصِلٌ مَا اتَّصَلَ اللَّيْلُ وَ النَّهَارُ، وَاصِلٌ
ذٰلِكَ إِلَيْكُمَا غَيْرُ مَحْجُوبٍ عَنْكُمَا
سَلَامِى إِنْ شَاءَ اللهُ، وَ أَسْأَلُهُ بِحَقِّكُمَا
أَنْ يَشَاءَ ذٰلِكَ وَ يَفْعَلَ، فَإِنَّهُ حَمِيدٌ مَجِيدٌ.

I commend both of you to Allah and may He not make this my last opportunity to visit the two of you! I am departing, O my master and guardian, the Commander of the Faithful, and you, my master, Abū ʿAbd Allāh! Peace be to you on my behalf, forever, as long as day and night continue, and may my greeting reach you, not kept out from your presence, God willing. I beseech Him by your right that He may wish so and do so. Indeed He is the All-praiseworthy and the All-glorious.

اِنْقَلَبْتُ يَا سَيِّدَىَّ عَنْكُمَا تَائِبًا،
حَامِدًا لِلّٰهِ شَاكِرًا، رَاجِيًا لِلْإِجَابَةِ غَيْرَ

O my masters, I depart from you as someone who being penitent, praises and thanks Allah, expecting his prayers to be heard. I am neither despondent nor lacking in hope, but always keen to return and come back again and again to visit the two of you, never being indisposed toward you and your *ziyārah*, but keen to come back again and again, God willing, and there is no power or force except what derives from Allah.

آيِسٍ وَ لَا قَانِطٍ، آيِبًا عَائِدًا رَاجِعًا إِلَىٰ زِيَارَتِكُمَا، غَيْرَ رَاغِبٍ عَنْكُمَا وَ لَا مِنْ زِيَارَتِكُمَا، بَلْ رَاجِعٌ عَائِدٌ إِنْ شَاءَ اللهُ، وَ لَا حَوْلَ وَ لَا قُوَّةَ إِلَّا بِاللهِ.

My masters, I have been keen to visit the two of you and perform your *ziyārah*, while the world's people remain indifferent to you and your *ziyārah*, so may not Allah disappoint me with regard to my hopes and expectations from your *ziyārah*. Indeed He is nearmost and responsive!

يَا سَادَتِي رَغِبْتُ إِلَيْكُمَا وَ إِلَىٰ زِيَارَتِكُمَا بَعْدَ أَنْ زَهِدَ فِيكُمَا وَ فِي زِيَارَتِكُمَا أَهْلُ الدُّنْيَا، فَلَا خَيَّبَنِيَ اللهُ مَا رَجَوْتُ وَ مَا أَمَّلْتُ فِي زِيَارَتِكُمَا، إِنَّهُ قَرِيبٌ مُجِيبٌ.

Sayf says, "I said to Ṣafwān that ᶜAlqamah b. Muḥammad had not narrated this supplication from Imam Muḥammad al-Bāqir (ᶜ*a*) and that the *ziyārah* was the only thing that he had narrated.

"Ṣafwān replied, saying, 'I have visited this place with my master Jaᶜfar al-Ṣādiq (ᶜ*a*) and he performed the *ziyārah* as we have done and made this supplication after performing a prayer just like the one we have offered at the time of bidding farewell, and he, too, bade farewell in the manner we have done.' Then he said to me, 'Imam Jaᶜfar al-Ṣādiq (ᶜ*a*) said to me,

> "Commit yourself to performing this *ziyārah* and making this supplication. I vouch for those who perform this *ziyārah* and make this supplication, whether they do so from far or near, that God, the Most High, will accept their *ziyārah* and thank their efforts. Their greeting will reach the Imam and will not go unacknowledged. Their needs, irrespective of their extent, will be answered by God Almighty and they will not be disappointed.
>
> "O Ṣafwān, I have received this *ziyārah* with such a guarantee from my father, and my father received it from ᶜAlī ibn al-Ḥusayn with this guarantee from al-Ḥusayn (ᶜ*a*), and al-Ḥusayn received it with this guarantee from his brother al-Ḥasan (ᶜ*a*), and Ḥasan

received it with this guarantee from his father, the Commander of the Faithful (ᶜa), and the Commander of the Faithful (ᶜa) received it with this guarantee from the Apostle of Allah (ṣ), and the Apostle of Allah (ṣ) received it with this guarantee from Gabriel (ᶜa), and Gabriel received it from Allah, the Almighty and the All-glorious, with this guarantee.

"Certainly, Allah, the Almighty and All-glorious, has sworn by His Self that He will accept the *ziyārah* of those who perform this *ziyārah* of al-Ḥusayn from far and near and make this supplication, that He will answer their petitions however great they may be, and that He will grant their requests, so they will not go back disappointed but will return joyous and happy due to the fulfilment of their needs, having won entry into paradise and emancipation from hellfire, as well as the acceptance of their intercession for whoever they may intercede, excepting the enemies of the Prophet's Family.

"God, the Most High, has sworn this by His Self, and He has made us testify to the witness that His angels have borne concerning this. Then Gabriel said, 'O Apostle of Allah, Allah has sent me to you to bring you joy and good news, and to bring joy and good news to ᶜAlī ibn Abī Ṭālib, Fāṭimah, al-Ḥasan and al-Ḥusayn and to the Imams of your descent until the Day of Resurrection. O Muḥammad, may your joy and the joy of ᶜAlī, Fāṭimah, al-Ḥasan, al-Ḥusayn, and the Imams and that of your followers be perpetual till the Day of Resurrection!' "

"Then Ṣafwān said to me, 'Imam Jaᶜfar al-Ṣādiq (ᶜa) said to me, "O Ṣafwān, whenever a need arises for you, perform this *ziyārah* wherever you should be, and make this supplication as well, requesting your Lord to satisfy your need, and Allah will answer your petition, for Allah does not breach any promise He has given to His Apostle out of His favour. And all praise belongs to Allah." ' "

The compiler says: After the Ziyārah Jāmiᶜah Kabīrah, we shall, God willing, cite from *al-Najm al-Thāqib* the episode of Ḥājj Sayyid Aḥmad Rashtī's encounter during his ḥajj journey with the Imam of the Era (ᶜa), in the course of which the Imam is reported as having urged the sayyid to recite this *ziyārah*, saying, "ᶜĀshūrā! ᶜĀshūrā! Why don't you recite the Ziyārah of ᶜĀshūrā?!" (see p. 537)

The Episode of Ḥājj Muḥammad ᶜAlī Yazdī

Shaykh Nūrī, my teacher, makes the following remarks in his book *al-Najm al-Thāqib*,[1] concerning the Ziyārah of ᶜĀshūrā.

> With respect to its merit and station, the Ziyārah of ᶜĀshūrā is not like the other *ziyārahs*, which were apparently composed or dictated by the infallible Imams (*ᶜa*). This is true, while granting that whatever comes from their immaculate hearts derives from the higher realm. However, this particular *ziyārah* belongs to the category of *aḥadīth qudsī*, and its contents, including the *ziyārah*, the anathemas, the greetings and the petitions, have been received in the same order by the Seal of the Prophets (*ṣ*) from Gabriel, the trusted divine emissary, from God.
>
> Experience shows that its regular recitation for forty days or less is unmatched in respect of fulfilment of needs, achievement of goals, and deterrence of enemies. But the best of its benefits, which can be achieved by its regular performance, is one which I have mentioned in my book *Dār al-Salām*. Here I will describe it briefly.
>
> This episode was narrated by Ḥājj Mullā Ḥasan Yazdī, a trustworthy and pious man and a devout resident of Najaf Ashraf who perpetually engaged in worship and *ziyārah* of the holy shrines. He narrated it from Ḥājj Muḥammad ᶜAlī Yazdī, who resided in Yazd and was a trustworthy, pious and learned person, constantly preoccupied with amending his affairs pertaining to the Hereafter.
>
> It was his regular practice to spend the nights in a cemetery, known locally as Mazār, outside the town, where a number of pious persons were buried. He had a neighbour whom he had known since his childhood days and as young boys they had taken lessons with the same teacher. Later on, he had taken up the profession of a tax collector. On his death, he was buried in the same cemetery near the place where this pious man used to spend his nights.
>
> One night, within a month, he saw his neighbour in a dream, appearing to be in good shape. Approaching the man, he said to him, 'I know you from beginning to end, and know your inner state as well as your outward condition. You were not one of those one might expect to have a virtuous heart. Your occupa-

[1] *Najm al-Thāqib*, ii, 716-718.

tion, too, was such that you hardly deserved anything but punishment. What action has helped you reach such a condition?'

'What you say is entirely true. I was undergoing severe punishment right from the day of my death, until yesterday when the wife of Ustād Ashraf, the blacksmith, died and was buried in this place,' said the deceased man, pointing to a spot nearly a hundred cubits away. 'On the night of her burial, Imam Abū ᶜAbdillāh al-Ḥusayn (*ᶜa*) visited her three times. On the third occasion, he ordered punishments to be lifted from this cemetery. Since then our condition has been good. Ease and blessing have fallen to our lot.'

Yazdī woke up in a state of amazement. Not knowing the blacksmith, he went to inquire about him in the bazaar of the blacksmiths. On finding the man, he asked him if he had a wife. 'Yes,' he replied, 'She died yesterday." After having confirmed that she had been buried in the same graveyard, Muḥammad ᶜAlī asked the man if his wife had ever made pilgrimage to the shrine of Imam Ḥusayn (*ᶜa*). She had not. Asked if she used to narrate the accounts of the Imam's martyrdom, he replied, 'No.' Asked if she used to hold mourning ceremonies at her house, his reply was 'No.' He asked the stranger, 'What are you after?' When Muḥammad ᶜAlī recounted his dream for him, he said, 'Yes, it was her custom to recite the Ziyārah of ᶜĀshūrā.' "

A Second Ziyarah for the Day of 'Āshura

This is a lesser-known *ziyārah*, but is similar to the popular one with respect to its reward, without involving the effort of pronouncing a hundred anathemas and a hundred *salāms*, and this is an advantage for those who may have some urgent matters to attend.

The manner of its performance, as mentioned in *al-Mazār al-Qadīm*,[1] is that someone intending to perform the Imam's *ziyārah* from far or near should take a bath, and then go out of the town or ascend to the roof of his house. There, he should perform two *rakᶜahs*, reciting Sūrat al-Tawḥīd in each. After *salām*, facing in the direction of the Imam's shrine and pointing toward it, say with humility:

Peace be to you, O son of the Apostle of Allah! Peace be to you,	اَلسَّلَامُ عَلَيْكَ يَا ابْنَ رَسُولِ اللهِ، اَلسَّلَامُ

1 *Mustadrak*, x, 412-416, b 86, h 12273/16 from *al-Mazār al-Qadīm*.

عَلَيْكَ يَا ابْنَ الْبَشِيرِ النَّذِيرِ، وَ بْنَ سَيِّدِ
الْوَصِيِّينَ، اَلسَّلَامُ عَلَيْكَ يَا ابْنَ فَاطِمَةَ
سَيِّدَةِ نِسَاءِ الْعَالَمِينَ، اَلسَّلَامُ عَلَيْكَ يَا
خِيَرَةَ اللهِ وَ ابْنَ خِيَرَتِهِ، اَلسَّلَامُ عَلَيْكَ
يَا ثَارَ اللهِ وَ ابْنَ ثَارِهِ، اَلسَّلَامُ عَلَيْكَ
أَيُّهَا الْوِتْرُ الْمَوْتُورُ،

O son of the bringer of good news and warnings and son of the chief of the Legatees! Peace be to you, O son of Fāṭimah, mistress of the world's womankind! Peace be to you, O chosen of Allah and son of His chosen one! Peace be to you, avenger of whose blood is Allah, son of him avenger of whose blood is Allah! Peace be to you, who were wrongfully slain and whose blood remains unavenged!

اَلسَّلَامُ عَلَيْكَ أَيُّهَا الْإِمَامُ الْهَادِي الزَّكِيُّ،
وَ عَلَى أَرْوَاحٍ حَلَّتْ بِفِنَائِكَ، وَ أَقَامَتْ
فِي جِوَارِكَ، وَ وَفَدَتْ مَعَ زُوَّارِكَ، اَلسَّلَامُ
عَلَيْكَ مِنِّي مَا بَقِيتُ وَ بَقِيَ اللَّيْلُ وَ النَّهَارُ،

Peace be to you, O Imam and immaculate guide, and to the spirits who have alighted in your courtyard and reside in the neighbourhood of your shrine and arrive escorting your pilgrims! Peace be to you, forever, as long as I live and as long as day and night endure!

فَلَقَدْ عَظُمَتْ بِكَ الرَّزِيَّةُ، وَ جَلَّتْ
فِي الْمُؤْمِنِينَ وَ الْمُسْلِمِينَ وَ فِي أَهْلِ
السَّمَاوَاتِ وَ أَهْلِ الْأَرَضِينَ أَجْمَعِينَ،
فَإِنَّا لِلّٰهِ وَ إِنَّا إِلَيْهِ رَاجِعُونَ،

Your martyrdom was a great tragedy that weighed heavy on the hearts of the faithful and the Muslims and all the denizens of the heavens and the earths! *Indeed we belong to Allah, and to Him do we return!*

صَلَوَاتُ اللهِ وَ بَرَكَاتُهُ وَ تَحِيَّاتُهُ عَلَيْكَ
يَا أَبَا عَبْدِ اللهِ الْحُسَيْنَ، وَ عَلَى آبَائِكَ
الطَّيِّبِينَ الْمُنْتَجَبِينَ، وَ عَلَى ذُرِّيَّاتِكُمُ
الْهُدَاةِ الْمَهْدِيِّينَ،

May Allah's blessings, His benisons and greeting be on you, O Abū ʿAbdillāh al-Ḥusayn, and on your ancestors, the immaculate and the elect, and your descendents, the rightly-guided guides!

لَعَنَ اللهُ أُمَّةً خَذَلَتْكَ وَ تَرَكَتْ
نُصْرَتَكَ وَ مَعُونَتَكَ، وَ لَعَنَ اللهُ أُمَّةً

May Allah's curse be on those who forsook you and denied you their help and support! May Allah's curse be on those who instituted the regime of oppression against you, paved the way for injustice against you, made persecution and violence against you a policy and implemented it throughout your districts and among your followers.

أَسَّسَتْ أَسَاسَ الظُّلْمِ لَكُمْ، وَ مَهَّدَتِ
الْجَوْرَ عَلَيْكُمْ، وَ طَرَّقَتْ إِلَىٰ أَذِيَّتِكُمْ
وَ تَحَيُّفِكُمْ، وَ جَارَتْ ذٰلِكَ فِي دِيَارِكُمْ
وَ أَشْيَاعِكُمْ،

I repudiate them and their supporters and followers before Allah, the Almighty and Glorious, and you, my masters, guardians and Imams.

بَرِئْتُ إِلَى اللهِ عَزَّ وَ جَلَّ وَ إِلَيْكُمْ يَا
سَادَاتِي وَ مَوَالِيَّ وَ أَئِمَّتِي مِنْهُمْ وَ مِنْ
أَشْيَاعِهِمْ وَ أَتْبَاعِهِمْ،

I beseech Allah, who has exalted your station, my guardians, and elevated your position and status, to honour me through your *wilāyah* and love and adherence to you, and through disavowal of your enemies!

وَ أَسْأَلُ اللهَ الَّذِي أَكْرَمَ يَا مَوَالِيَّ
مَقَامَكُمْ وَ شَرَّفَ مَنْزِلَتَكُمْ وَ شَأْنَكُمْ،
أَنْ يُكْرِمَنِي بِوِلَايَتِكُمْ وَ مَحَبَّتِكُمْ وَ
الْإِيتِمَامِ بِكُمْ وَ بِالْبَرَاءَةِ مِنْ أَعْدَائِكُمْ،

I beseech Allah, the All-benign and the All-merciful, to bless me with your friendship and to enable me to seek vengeance for your blood with the awaited Imam and guide from the Family of Muḥammad, to include me in your fold in the world and the Hereafter, and to enable me to attain to the praiseworthy station you have with Allah!

وَ أَسْأَلُ اللهَ الْبَرَّ الرَّحِيمَ أَنْ يَرْزُقَنِي
مَوَدَّتَكُمْ، وَ أَنْ يُوَفِّقَنِي لِلطَّلَبِ بِثَارِكُمْ مَعَ
الْإِمَامِ الْمُنْتَظَرِ الْهَادِي مِنْ آلِ مُحَمَّدٍ، وَ أَنْ
يَجْعَلَنِي مَعَكُمْ فِي الدُّنْيَا وَ الْآخِرَةِ، وَ أَنْ
يُبَلِّغَنِي الْمَقَامَ الْمَحْمُودَ لَكُمْ عِنْدَ اللهِ،

I beseech Allah, the Almighty and Glorious, by your right and the standing that Allah has granted you, to grant me for my sorrow on your account the best of what He has granted to any sufferer for his affliction. We

وَ أَسْأَلُ اللهَ عَزَّ وَ جَلَّ بِحَقِّكُمْ وَ بِالشَّأْنِ
الَّذِي جَعَلَ اللهُ لَكُمْ أَنْ يُعْطِيَنِي
بِمُصَابِي بِكُمْ أَفْضَلَ مَا أَعْطَىٰ مُصَابًا
بِمُصِيبَةٍ، إِنَّا لِلّٰهِ وَ إِنَّا إِلَيْهِ رَاجِعُونَ، يَا

لَهَا مِنْ مُصِيبَةٍ مَـا أَفْجَعَهَا وَ أَنْكَاهَا
لِقُلُوبِ الْمُؤْمِنِينَ وَ الْمُسْلِمِينَ، فَإِنَّا لِلّٰهِ
وَ إِنَّا إِلَيْهِ رَاجِعُونَ.

belong to Allah and to Him do we return! How terrible a tragedy it has been that has aggrieved the hearts of the faithful and the Muslims! *Indeed, we belong to Allah and to Him do we return!*

اَللّٰهُمَّ صَلِّ عَلَىٰ مُحَمَّدٍ وَ آلِ مُحَمَّدٍ، وَ
اجْعَلْنِي فِي مَقَامِي مِمَّنْ تَنَالُهُ مِنْكَ
صَلَوَاتٌ وَ رَحْمَةٌ وَ مَغْفِرَةٌ، وَ اجْعَلْنِي
عِنْدَكَ وَجِيهًا فِي الدُّنْيَا وَ الْآخِرَةِ وَ مِنَ
الْمُقَرَّبِينَ، فَإِنِّي أَتَقَرَّبُ إِلَيْكَ بِمُحَمَّدٍ وَ آلِ
مُحَمَّدٍ صَلَوَاتُكَ عَلَيْهِ وَ عَلَيْهِمْ أَجْمَعِينَ.

O Allah, bless Muḥammad and the Family of Muḥammad, and appoint me, as I stand in this place, to be among those who partake of Your blessings, mercy and forgiveness. Make me eminent with You in the world and the Hereafter and admit me among those near to You. For indeed I seek nearness to You through Muḥammad and the Family of Muḥammad, may Your blessings be upon him and them all.

اَللّٰهُمَّ وَ إِنِّي أَتَوَسَّلُ وَ أَتَوَجَّهُ بِصَفْوَتِكَ
مِنْ خَلْقِكَ وَ خِيَرَتِكَ مِنْ خَلْقِكَ مُحَمَّدٍ
وَ عَلِيٍّ وَ الطَّيِّبِينَ مِنْ ذُرِّيَّتِهِمَا.

O Allah, I seek with You the advocacy of Your elect and Your chosen ones from amongst Your creation, Muḥammad, ʿAlī and the immaculate ones of their descent, and I turn to You through them.

اَللّٰهُمَّ فَصَلِّ عَلَىٰ مُحَمَّدٍ وَ آلِ مُحَمَّدٍ، وَ
اجْعَلْ مَحْيَايَ مَحْيَاهُمْ، وَ مَمَاتِي مَمَاتَهُمْ،
وَ لَا تُفَرِّقْ بَيْنِي وَ بَيْنَهُمْ فِي الدُّنْيَا وَ
الْآخِرَةِ، إِنَّكَ سَمِيعُ الدُّعَاءِ.

O Allah, bless Muḥammad and the Family of Muḥammad, and grant me to live like them and to die like them, and do not ever separate me from them in the world or in the Hereafter! Indeed You hear all supplications!

اَللّٰهُمَّ وَ هٰذَا يَوْمٌ تُجَدِّدُ فِيهِ النِّقْمَةَ، وَ تُنْزِلُ
فِيهِ اللَّعْنَةَ عَلَى اللَّعِينِ يَزِيدَ وَ عَلَىٰ آلِ يَزِيدَ
وَ عَلَىٰ آلِ زِيَادٍ وَ عُمَرَ بْنِ سَعْدٍ وَ الشِّمْرِ.

O Allah, this is a day on which You renew indignation towards and anathemas on the accursed Yazīd, his clan and the clan of Ziyād and on ʿUmar ibn Saʿd and Shimr.

اَللّٰهُمَّ الْعَنْهُمْ وَ الْعَنْ مَنْ رَضِيَ بِقَوْلِهِمْ وَ فِعْلِهِمْ مِنْ أَوَّلٍ وَ آخِرٍ لَعْنًا كَثِيرًا، وَ أَصْلِهِمْ حَرَّ نَارِكَ، وَ أَسْكِنْهُمْ جَهَنَّمَ وَ سَاءَتْ مَصِيرًا، وَ أَوْجِبْ عَلَيْهِمْ وَ عَلىٰ كُلِّ مَنْ شَايَعَهُمْ وَ بَايَعَهُمْ وَ تَابَعَهُمْ وَ سَاعَدَهُمْ، وَ رَضِيَ بِفِعْلِهِمْ، وَ افْتَحْ لَهُمْ وَ عَلَيْهِمْ وَ عَلىٰ كُلِّ مَنْ رَضِيَ بِذٰلِكَ لَعَنَاتِكَ الَّتِي لَعَنْتَ بِهَا كُلَّ ظَالِمٍ وَ كُلَّ غَاصِبٍ وَ كُلَّ جَاحِدٍ وَ كُلَّ كَافِرٍ وَ كُلَّ مُشْرِكٍ وَ كُلَّ شَيْطَانٍ رَجِيمٍ وَ كُلَّ جَبَّارٍ عَنِيدٍ،

O Allah, curse them and those who approve of their statements and deeds, from the first of them to the last one, with copious anathemas, and burn them in the heat of Your Fire and settle them in hell, and it is an evil destination. Inflict on them and all those who have supported them, or made compacts with them, followed them, aided them and approved of their actions, Your anathema with which You have cursed every oppressor, usurper, denier, infidel, polytheist and every outcast Satan and every wilful tyrant!

اَللّٰهُمَّ الْعَنْ يَزِيدَ وَ آلَ يَزِيدَ وَ بَنِي مَرْوَانَ جَمِيعًا. اَللّٰهُمَّ وَ ضَعِّفْ غَضَبَكَ وَ سَخَطَكَ وَ عَذَابَكَ وَ نَقِمَتَكَ عَلىٰ أَوَّلِ ظَالِمٍ ظَلَمَ أَهْلَ بَيْتِ نَبِيِّكَ،

O Allah, curse Yazīd, the clan of Yazīd and the Marwānids, all together! O Allah, redouble Your wrath, indignation, punishment and vengeance against the first oppressor who oppressed the Family of Your Prophet!

اَللّٰهُمَّ وَ الْعَنْ جَمِيعَ الظَّالِمِينَ لَهُمْ وَ انْتَقِمْ مِنْهُمْ، إِنَّكَ ذُو نِقْمَةٍ مِنَ الْمُجْرِمِينَ.

O Allah, curse all those who have wronged them and take vengeance on them. Indeed You take vengeance on the criminals.

اَللّٰهُمَّ وَ الْعَنْ أَوَّلَ ظَالِمٍ ظَلَمَ آلَ بَيْتِ مُحَمَّدٍ، وَ الْعَنْ أَرْوَاحَهُمْ وَ دِيَارَهُمْ وَ قُبُورَهُمْ،

O Allah, curse the first oppressor who oppressed the Family of Muḥammad and curse their spirits, their dwellings and their graves.

وَ الْعَنِ اللّٰهُمَّ الْعِصَابَةَ الَّتِي نَازَلَتِ الْحُسَيْنَ بْنَ بِنْتِ نَبِيِّكَ، وَ حَارَبَتْهُ وَ قَتَلَتْ

O Allah, curse the league that clashed with al-Ḥusayn, son of Your Prophet's daughter, and

أَصْحَابَهُ وَ أَنْصَارَهُ وَ أَعْوَانَهُ وَ أَوْلِيَاءَهُ وَ شِيعَتَهُ وَ مُحِبِّيهِ وَ أَهْلَ بَيْتِهِ وَ ذُرِّيَّتَهُ،

fought him and slew his companions and supporters, his helpers and friends, his followers and votaries, his relatives and descendants!

وَ الْعَنِ اللّٰهُمَّ الَّذِينَ نَهَبُوا مَالَهُ، وَ سَلَبُوا [وَ سَبَوْا] حَرِيمَهُ، وَ لَمْ يَسْمَعُوا كَلَامَهُ وَ لَا مَقَالَهُ.

O Allah, curse those who plundered his belongings, took his womenfolk captive, and did not listen to his speech and address.

اَللّٰهُمَّ وَ الْعَنْ كُلَّ مَنْ بَلَغَهُ ذٰلِكَ فَرَضِيَ بِهِ مِنَ الْأَوَّلِينَ وَ الْآخِرِينَ وَ الْخَلَائِقِ أَجْمَعِينَ إِلَىٰ يَوْمِ الدِّينِ.

O Allah, curse everyone who on coming to know about it heard it approvingly, from those of the former and the latter generations and from the entire creation until the Day of Retribution!

اَلسَّلَامُ عَلَيْكَ يَا أَبَا عَبْدِ اللهِ الْحُسَيْنَ، وَ عَلَىٰ مَنْ سَاعَدَكَ وَ عَاوَنَكَ وَ وَاسَاكَ بِنَفْسِهِ، وَ بَذَلَ مُهْجَتَهُ فِي الذَّبِّ عَنْكَ،

Peace be to you, O Abū ʿAbdillāh al-Ḥusayn and to those who assisted and supported you, those who made sacrifices for you and gave their lifeblood in your defence!

اَلسَّلَامُ عَلَيْكَ يَا مَوْلَايَ وَ عَلَيْهِمْ، وَ عَلَىٰ رُوحِكَ وَ عَلَىٰ أَرْوَاحِهِمْ، وَ عَلَىٰ تُرْبَتِكَ وَ عَلَىٰ تُرْبَتِهِمْ. اَللّٰهُمَّ لَقِّهِمْ رَحْمَةً وَ رِضْوَانًا وَ رَوْحًا وَ رَيْحَانًا.

Peace be to you, my master, and to them, to your spirit and their spirits, to the soil of your graveside and to the soil of their graveside! O Allah, grant them Your mercy and approval, beatitude and euphoria!

اَلسَّلَامُ عَلَيْكَ يَا مَوْلَايَ يَا أَبَا عَبْدِ اللهِ، يَا ابْنَ خَاتَمِ النَّبِيِّينَ، وَ يَا ابْنَ سَيِّدِ الْوَصِيِّينَ، وَ يَا ابْنَ سَيِّدَةِ نِسَاءِ الْعَالَمِينَ.

Peace be to you, O my master, O Abū ʿAbdillāh, O son of the Seal of the Prophets, O son of the chief of the Legatees, O son of the mistress of the world's womankind!

اَلسَّلَامُ عَلَيْكَ يَا شَهِيدُ يَا ابْنَ الشَّهِيدِ.

Peace be to you, O martyr and martyr's son!

اَللّٰهُمَّ بَلِّغْهُ عَنِّي فِي هٰذِهِ السَّاعَةِ وَ فِي هٰذَا

O Allah, convey my greetings

اَلْيَــوْمِ وَ فِي هٰذَا الْوَقْتِ وَ كُلِّ وَقْتٍ تَحِيَّةً وَ سَلَامًا.

and *salām* to him, at this hour and day, at this time and at all times!

اَلسَّلَامُ عَلَيْكَ يَا ابْنَ سَيِّدِ الْعَالَمِينَ، وَ عَلَى الْمُسْتَشْهَدِينَ مَعَكَ سَلَامًا مُتَّصِلًا مَا اتَّصَلَ اللَّيْلُ وَ النَّهَارُ،

Peace be to you, O son of the Master of the world's denizens, and to those who were martyred along with you—a peace that is perpetual, continuing so long as day and night follow one another!

اَلسَّلَامُ عَلَى الْحُسَــيْنِ بْنِ عَلِيٍّ الشَّهِيدِ، اَلسَّــلَامُ عَلٰى عَلِيِّ بْنِ الْحُسَيْنِ الشَّهِيدِ، اَلسَّــلَامُ عَلَى الْعَبَّاسِ بْنِ أَمِيرِ الْمُؤْمِنِينَ الشَّهِيدِ،

Peace be to the martyr, al-Ḥusayn son of ᶜAlī! Peace be to the martyr, ᶜAlī son of al-Ḥusayn! Peace be to the martyr, ᶜAbbās son of the Commander of the Faithful!

اَلسَّــلَامُ عَلَى الشُّــهَدَاءِ مِــنْ وُلْدِ أَمِيرِ الْمُؤْمِنِينَ،

Peace be to the martyrs from among the sons of the Commander of the Faithful!

اَلسَّلَامُ عَلَى الشُّــهَدَاءِ مِنْ وُلْدِ جَعْفَرٍ وَ عَقِيلٍ،

Peace be to the martyrs from among the sons of Jaᶜfar and ᶜAqīl!

اَلسَّلَامُ عَلٰى كُلِّ مُسْتَشْهَدٍ مِنَ الْمُؤْمِنِينَ،

Peace be to all martyrs from among the faithful!

اَللّٰهُمَّ صَــلِّ عَلٰى مُحَمَّــدٍ وَ آلِ مُحَمَّدٍ، وَ بَلِّغْهُمْ عَنِّي تَحِيَّةً وَ سَلَامًا.

O Allah, bless Muḥammad and the Family of Muḥammad and convey my greetings and *salām* to them!

اَلسَّــلَامُ عَلَيْكَ يَا رَسُولَ اللهِ وَ عَلَيْكَ السَّلَامُ وَ رَحْمَةُ اللهِ وَ بَرَكَاتُهُ، أَحْسَنَ اللهُ لَكَ الْعَزَاءَ فِي وَلَدِكَ الْحُسَيْنِ عَلَيْهِ السَّلَامُ

Peace be to you, O Apostle of Allah! May peace and Allah's mercy and bounties be upon you! May Allah give you the best solace in your grief for your son al-Ḥusayn, may peace be to him!

اَلسَّــلَامُ عَلَيْــكَ يَــا أَبَا الْحَسَــنِ يَا

Peace be to you, O Abul Ḥasan,

O Commander of the Faithful! May peace and Allah's mercy and bounties be upon you! May Allah give you the best solace in your grief for your son al-Ḥusayn!

أَمِيرَ الْمُؤْمِنِينَ وَ عَلَيْكَ السَّلَامُ وَ رَحْمَةُ اللّٰهِ وَ بَرَكَاتُهُ، أَحْسَنَ اللّٰهُ لَكَ الْعَزَاءَ فِي وَلَدِكَ الْحُسَيْنِ.

Peace be to you, O Fāṭimah, daughter of the Apostle of the Lord of all the worlds! May peace and Allah's mercy and bounties be upon you! May Allah give you the best solace in your grief for your son al-Ḥusayn!

اَلسَّلَامُ عَلَيْكِ يَا فَاطِمَةُ يَا بِنْتَ رَسُولِ رَبِّ الْعَالَمِينَ وَ عَلَيْكِ السَّلَامُ وَ رَحْمَةُ اللّٰهِ وَ بَرَكَاتُهُ، أَحْسَنَ اللّٰهُ لَكِ الْعَزَاءَ فِي وَلَدِكِ الْحُسَيْنِ.

Peace be to you, O Abū Muḥammad al-Ḥasan! May peace and Allah's mercy and bounties be upon you! May Allah give you the best solace in your grief for your brother al-Ḥusayn!

اَلسَّلَامُ عَلَيْكَ يَا أَبَا مُحَمَّدٍ الْحَسَنَ وَ عَلَيْكَ السَّلَامُ وَ رَحْمَةُ اللّٰهِ وَ بَرَكَاتُهُ، أَحْسَنَ اللّٰهُ لَكَ الْعَزَاءَ فِي أَخِيكَ الْحُسَيْنِ.

Peace be to the spirits of all the faithful, men and women, the living among them and the dead! May peace and Allah's mercy and bounties be upon them! May Allah give them the best solace in their grief for their master, al-Ḥusayn!

اَلسَّلَامُ عَلَىٰ أَرْوَاحِ الْمُؤْمِنِينَ وَ الْمُؤْمِنَاتِ، اَلْأَحْيَاءِ مِنْهُمْ وَ الْأَمْوَاتِ، وَ عَلَيْهِمُ السَّلَامُ وَ رَحْمَةُ اللّٰهِ وَ بَرَكَاتُهُ، أَحْسَنَ اللّٰهُ لَهُمُ الْعَزَاءَ فِي مَوْلَاهُمُ الْحُسَيْنِ.

O Allah, appoint us to be among those who will seek to avenge his blood with the just Imam, through whom You will exalt Islam and its people, O Lord of all the worlds!

اَللّٰهُمَّ اجْعَلْنَا مِنَ الطَّالِبِينَ بِثَارِهِ مَعَ إِمَامٍ عَدْلٍ تُعِزُّ بِهِ الْإِسْلَامَ وَ أَهْلَهُ يَا رَبَّ الْعَالَمِينَ.

Then make prostration and say,

O Allah, to You belongs all praise for all the tragedies that have befallen us, and to You

اَللّٰهُمَّ لَكَ الْحَمْدُ عَلَىٰ جَمِيعِ مَا نَابَ مِنْ خَطْبٍ، وَ لَكَ الْحَمْدُ عَلَىٰ كُلِّ أَمْرٍ، وَ إِلَيْكَ

belongs all praise for all matters. To You do we complain for the great ordeals that have befallen Your *awliyā'* and chosen ones, and that is on account of the dignity and the bountiful grace that You have granted them.

الْمُشْتَكىٰ فِي عَظِيمِ الْمُهِمَّاتِ بِخِيَرَتِكَ وَ أَوْلِيَائِكَ، وَ ذٰلِكَ لِمَا أَوْجَبْتَ لَهُمْ مِنَ الْكَرَامَةِ وَ الْفَضْلِ الْكَثِيرِ،

O Allah, bless Muḥammad and the Family of Muḥammad, and grant me the intercession of al-Ḥusayn, may peace be to him, on the day of my entry at Resurrection, in the witnessed station and at the Pool (of Kaw<u>th</u>ar).

اَللّٰهُمَّ فَصَلِّ عَلىٰ مُحَمَّدٍ وَآلِ مُحَمَّدٍ، وَارْزُقْنِي شَفَاعَةَ الْحُسَيْنِ عَلَيْهِ السَّلَامُ يَوْمَ الْوُرُودِ وَ الْمَقَامَ الْمَشْهُودَ وَ الْحَوْضَ الْمَوْرُودَ،

Grant me a worthy standing with You in the company of al-Ḥusayn, may peace be to him and his companions, who made sacrifices for him, giving their lifeblood in his defence and waged *jihād* with him against Your enemies, seeking Your pleasure, expecting Your reward and affirming Your promise, and fearing Your threats. Indeed You are meticulous in bringing about what You wish, O Most Merciful of the merciful!

وَ اجْعَلْ لِي قَدَمَ صِدْقٍ عِنْدَكَ مَعَ الْحُسَيْنِ وَ أَصْحَابِ الْحُسَيْنِ عَلَيْهِ السَّلَامُ، اَلَّذِينَ وَاسَوْهُ بِأَنْفُسِهِمْ، وَ بَذَلُوا دُونَهُ مُهَجَهُمْ، وَ جَاهَدُوا مَعَهُ أَعْدَاءَكَ ابْتِغَاءَ مَرْضَاتِكَ وَ رَجَائِكَ، وَ تَصْدِيقًا بِوَعْدِكَ، وَ خَوْفًا مِنْ وَعِيدِكَ، إِنَّكَ لَطِيفٌ لِمَا تَشَاءُ، يَا أَرْحَمَ الرَّاحِمِينَ.

8. Ziyarah for the Day of Arbaʿin

The day of Arbaʿīn occurs on 20th of the month of Ṣafar. <u>Sh</u>ay<u>kh</u> Ṭūsī, in *Miṣbāḥ* and *Tah<u>dh</u>īb*, cites a report[1] quoting Imam al-Ḥasan al-Askarī (*ʿa*) that there are five signs of the faithful: 1) offering 51 *rakʿahs* of prayer during every night and day (17 *rakʿahs* of the daily obligatory and 34 *rakʿahs* of *nāfilah*); 2) performing the *ziyārah* of Arbaʿīn; 3) wearing a ring in the right hand; 4) laying the forehead on soil or clay (*turbah*) during prostration; and 5) saying the *basmalah*

1 Mufīd's *Mazār*, 53, b 23. Ṭūsī's *Miṣbāḥ*, 787. *Tah<u>dh</u>īb*, vi, 52, b 16, h 37, whence *Wasā'il*, xiv, 478, b 56, h 19643 & *Biḥār*, xcviii, 106, b 14, h 17. *Rawḍat al-Wāʿiẓīn*, i, 195. *Iqbāl*, 589, whence *Biḥār*, xcv, 348, b 11, h 1, xcviii, 329, b 25, h 1. *ʿAwālī*, iv, 37, from Imam Jaʿfar al-Ṣādiq (*ʿa*).

aloud during prayers.

Two versions of Imam Ḥusayn's (ᶜa) *ziyārah* for this day have been cited in *ḥadīth* works. One is the *ziyārah* cited by Shaykh Ṭūsī in the *Miṣbāḥ* from Ṣafwān al-Jammāl,[1] wherein Ṣafwān says that Imam Jaᶜfar al-Ṣādiq (ᶜa) told him to perform the *ziyārah* of ᶜArbaᶜīn during forenoon and to recite the following text.

Peace be to the *walī* of Allah and His beloved! Peace be to Allah's dedicated and select friend. Peace be to Allah's chosen friend and son of His chosen friend. Peace be to al-Ḥusayn, the aggrieved martyr. Peace be to the captive of many sufferings and the bewailed martyr.

اَلسَّلَامُ عَلٰى وَلِيِّ اللّٰهِ وَ حَبِيبِهِ، اَلسَّلَامُ عَلٰى خَلِيلِ اللّٰهِ وَ نَجِيبِهِ، اَلسَّلَامُ عَلٰى صَفِيِّ اللّٰهِ وَ ابْنِ صَفِيِّهِ، اَلسَّلَامُ عَلَى الْحُسَيْنِ الْمَظْلُومِ الشَّهِيدِ، اَلسَّلَامُ عَلٰى أَسِيرِ الْكُرُبَاتِ وَ قَتِيلِ الْعَبَرَاتِ.

O God, I testify that he is Your *walī*, the son of Your *walī*, Your chosen one and son of Your chosen one, and he is held in honour with You. You honoured him with martyrdom, rewarded him with felicity, selected for him an immaculate birth, appointed him a chief among the chiefs, a leader among the leaders, and a defender among the defenders of Your faith. You gave him the heritage of the prophets, and appointed him a testament to Your creation among the legatees.

اَللّٰهُمَّ إِنِّي أَشْهَدُ أَنَّهُ وَلِيُّكَ وَ ابْنُ وَلِيِّكَ، وَ صَفِيُّكَ وَ ابْنُ صَفِيِّكَ، اَلْفَائِزُ بِكَرَامَتِكَ، أَكْرَمْتَهُ بِالشَّهَادَةِ، وَ حَبَوْتَهُ بِالسَّعَادَةِ، وَ اجْتَبَيْتَهُ بِطِيبِ الْوِلَادَةِ، وَ جَعَلْتَهُ سَيِّدًا مِنَ السَّادَةِ وَ قَائِدًا مِنَ الْقَادَةِ وَ ذَائِدًا مِنَ الذَّادَةِ، وَ أَعْطَيْتَهُ مَوَارِيثَ الْأَنْبِيَاءِ، وَ جَعَلْتَهُ حُجَّةً عَلٰى خَلْقِكَ مِنَ الْأَوْصِيَاءِ،

In his summons, He left no room for any excuse, accorded sincere counsel, and gave his lifeblood for Your sake, to deliver Your servants from ignorance and the confusion of error.

فَأَعْذَرَ فِي الدُّعَاءِ، وَ مَنَحَ النُّصْحَ، وَ بَذَلَ مُهْجَتَهُ فِيكَ لِيَسْتَنْقِذَ عِبَادَكَ مِنَ الْجَهَالَةِ وَ حَيْرَةِ الضَّلَالَةِ،

Those who were deceived by the

وَ قَدْ تَوَازَرَ عَلَيْهِ مَنْ غَرَّتْهُ الدُّنْيَا، وَ

[1] Ṭūsī's *Miṣbāḥ*, 788-790. *Al-Mazār al-Kabīr*, 514-516.

world helped each other against him, exchanging their portion of the Hereafter for a paltry gain, and arrogantly perished in pursuit of their desires. They incurred Your wrath and that of Your Prophet, obeying the heretics and hypocrites among Your servants and those laden with grave sins and deserving hellfire.

بَاعَ حَظَّهُ بِالْأَرْذَلِ الْأَدْنىٰ، وَ شَرىٰ آخِرَتَهُ بِالثَّمَنِ الْأَوْكَسِ، وَ تَغَطْرَسَ وَ تَرَدّىٰ فِي هَوَاهُ، وَ أَسْخَطَكَ وَ أَسْخَطَ نَبِيَّكَ، وَ أَطَاعَ مِنْ عِبَادِكَ أَهْلَ الشِّقَاقِ وَ النِّفَاقِ وَ حَمَلَةَ الْأَوْزَارِ الْمُسْتَوْجِبِينَ النَّارَ،

He waged *jihād* against them with patience and resignation, until his blood was spilled in the way of obedience to You and his sanctity was violated.

فَجَاهَدَهُمْ فِيكَ صَابِرًا مُحْتَسِبًا حَتّىٰ سُفِكَ فِي طَاعَتِكَ دَمُهُ، وَ اسْتُبِيحَ حَرِيمُهُ.

O Allah, condemn them with a dire curse and punish them with a painful punishment!

اَللّٰهُمَّ فَالْعَنْهُمْ لَعْنًا وَبِيلًا، وَ عَذِّبْهُمْ عَذَابًا أَلِيمًا.

Peace be to you, O son of the Apostle of Allah! Peace be to you, O son of the chief of the Legatees!

اَلسَّلَامُ عَلَيْكَ يَا ابْنَ رَسُولِ اللهِ، اَلسَّلَامُ عَلَيْكَ يَا ابْنَ سَيِّدِ الْأَوْصِيَاءِ،

I affirm that you are indeed Allah's trustee and son of His trustee. You lived felicitously and were slain wrongfully and martyred!

أَشْهَدُ أَنَّكَ أَمِينُ اللهِ وَ ابْنُ أَمِينِهِ، عِشْتَ سَعِيدًا وَ مَضَيْتَ حَمِيدًا وَ مُتَّ فَقِيدًا مَظْلُومًا شَهِيدًا،

I affirm that Allah will fulfil His promise to you, destroy those who forsook you and punish those who slew you.

وَ أَشْهَدُ أَنَّ اللهَ مُنْجِزٌ مَا وَعَدَكَ، وَ مُهْلِكٌ مَنْ خَذَلَكَ، وَ مُعَذِّبٌ مَنْ قَتَلَكَ،

I testify that you fulfilled Allah's covenant and struggled in His way until your demise.

وَ أَشْهَدُ أَنَّكَ وَفَيْتَ بِعَهْدِ اللهِ، وَ جَاهَدْتَ فِي سَبِيلِهِ حَتّىٰ أَتَاكَ الْيَقِينُ،

So may Allah's curse be on those who slew you, and may He curse those who wronged you,

فَلَعَنَ اللهُ مَنْ قَتَلَكَ، وَ لَعَنَ اللهُ مَنْ ظَلَمَكَ، وَ لَعَنَ اللهُ أُمَّةً سَمِعَتْ بِذٰلِكَ

and may His curse be on those who heard of it approvingly.

فَرَضِيَتْ بِهِ.

O Allah, I testify that I befriend those who befriend him and am hostile to those who are hostile towards him.

اَللّٰهُمَّ إِنِّي أُشْهِدُكَ أَنِّي وَلِيٌّ لِمَنْ وَالاٰهُ، وَ عَدُوٌّ لِمَنْ عَادَاهُ.

You are dearer to me than my parents, O son of the Apostle of Allah! I testify that you were a light borne within the backs and breastbones of illustrious fathers and wombs of chaste mothers. The filth of the Age of pagan ignorance did not touch you, nor its defilements affected you. I testify that you are one of the pillars of God's religion and mainstays of the Muslim community and the faithful.

بِأَبِي أَنْتَ وَ أُمِّي يَا ابْنَ رَسُولِ اللهِ، أَشْهَدُ أَنَّكَ كُنْتَ نُورًا فِي الْأَصْلَابِ الشَّامِخَةِ، وَ الْأَرْحَامِ الْمُطَهَّرَةِ، لَمْ تُنَجِّسْكَ الْجَاهِلِيَّةُ بِأَنْجَاسِهَا، وَ لَمْ تُلْبِسْكَ الْمُدْلَهِمَّاتُ مِنْ ثِيَابِهَا، وَ أَشْهَدُ أَنَّكَ مِنْ دَعَائِمِ الدِّينِ، وَ أَرْكَانِ الْمُسْلِمِينَ، وَ مَعْقِلِ الْمُؤْمِنِينَ،

I testify that you are the pious and Godwary Imam, resigned to Allah's will, pure, rightly-guiding and rightly-guided. I testify that the Imams of your progeny are paragons of Godfearing, standards of guidance, the firm handle of Allah and His testaments to the world's denizens..

وَ أَشْهَدُ أَنَّكَ الْإِمَامُ الْبَرُّ التَّقِيُّ الرَّضِيُّ الزَّكِيُّ الْهَادِي الْمَهْدِيُّ، وَ أَشْهَدُ أَنَّ الْأَئِمَّةَ مِنْ وُلْدِكَ كَلِمَةُ التَّقْوَىٰ، وَ أَعْلَامُ الْهُدَىٰ، وَ الْعُرْوَةُ الْوُثْقَىٰ، وَ الْحُجَّةُ عَلَىٰ أَهْلِ الدُّنْيَا،

I affirm my faith in you and conviction in your return, as attested by the religious precepts I follow and my last deeds. My heart is at peace with your heart and my conduct in compliance with your instructions, and my help and support for you is ready until Allah gives His leave. So I am with

وَ أَشْهَدُ أَنِّي بِكُمْ مُؤْمِنٌ، وَ بِإِيَابِكُمْ مُوقِنٌ، بِشَرَائِعِ دِينِي، وَ خَوَاتِيمِ عَمَلِي، وَ قَلْبِي لِقَلْبِكُمْ سِلْمٌ، وَ أَمْرِي لِأَمْرِكُمْ مُتَّبِعٌ، وَ نُصْرَتِي لَكُمْ مُعَدَّةٌ حَتَّىٰ يَأْذَنَ اللهُ لَكُمْ،

you, not with your enemy.	فَمَعَكُمْ مَعَكُمْ لَا مَعَ عَدُوِّكُمْ،
May Allah's blessings be upon you, on your spirits, your remains, on the visible realms of your being and on those that are Unseen, on those that are manifest and those that are hidden. Amen! O Lord of all the worlds!	صَلَوَاتُ اللهِ عَلَيْكُمْ، وَ عَلَىٰ أَرْوَاحِكُمْ، وَ أَجْسَادِكُمْ وَ شَاهِدِكُمْ وَ غَائِبِكُمْ، وَ ظَاهِرِكُمْ وَ بَاطِنِكُمْ، آمِينَ رَبَّ الْعَالَمِينَ.

Then offer a two-*rakᶜah* prayer, and make any supplication that you wish before returning.

A second *ziyārah* is the one reported on the authority of ᶜAṭā from Jābir.[1] ᶜAṭā says: "I was with Jābir b. ᶜAbd Allāh al-Anṣārī on the 22nd of Ṣafar. On reaching G͟hādiriyyah, Jābir took a bath in the river and put on a clean shirt that he had brought with him. He asked me if I had any perfume. I had some *Suᶜd* (Cyperus), which he took and applied to his head and body. Then he set out barefoot until he stopped at the head of al-Ḥusayn's graveside. Saying thrice "*Allāhu akbar!*" he fell down unconscious. When he recovered from his swoon, I heard him say, '*Assalāmu ᶜalaykum yâ Ālallāh! Assalāmu ᶜalaykum yâ...*' "

The text of this *ziyārah* is almost the same as that of the *ziyārah* of 15th Rajab which was cited above, there being a slight difference of wording which may be due to different manuscripts, as suggested by S͟hahīd Awwal (*r*). Those who wish to recite that text also should refer to the *ziyārah* cited above for the 15th of Rajab (p. 300).

Besides the occasions mentioned above, there is a great merit in performing the *ziyārah* of Imam al-Ḥusayn (*ᶜa*) on other holy days and nights, especially on occasions which are associated with the Imam, such as the day of *Mubāhalah*, the day of revelation of the Sūrat Hal Atā (al-Dahr, or al-Insān), the anniversary of his noble birthday, and Friday eves.[2] According to that which can be inferred from a certain report, every Friday eve God Almighty casts His gracious look on the Imam and sends all the apostles and their legatees to visit him.[3]

Ibn Qūlawayh cites a report[4] in which Imam Jaᶜfar al-Ṣādiq (*ᶜa*) is mentioned as having said that those who perform the *ziyārah* of

1 *Biḥār*, xcviii, 329-330 b 42, from *Miṣbāḥ al-Zā'ir*, 151-152.

2 *Biḥār*, xcviii, 101, b 30.

3 *Kāmil al-Ziyārāt*, 112, b 38, h 4, whence *Biḥār*, xcviii, 60, b 26, h 32.

4 *Kāmil al-Ziyārāt*, 183, b 74, h 3, whence *Wasā'il*, xiv, 479, b 57, h 19646 & *Biḥār*, xcviii, 96, b 13, h 17.

Imam al-Ḥusayn's shrine on the eve of every Friday are forgiven their sins. They will not depart from the world with regret and will dwell in paradise with Imam al-Ḥusayn (*ᶜa*).

Al-Aᶜmash reports that a neighbour of his saw in a dream leaflets falling from the heaven bearing the promise of amnesty and safety for those who perform the *ziyārah* of Imam al-Ḥusayn (*ᶜa*) on Friday eves.[1] Later on, while describing the observances pertaining to Kāẓimayn, we will recount the story of Ḥājjī ᶜAlī Baghdādī concerning performance of *ziyārah* at this and other times (p. 399).

Imam Jaᶜfar al-Ṣādiq (*ᶜa*) is reported[2] as having been asked if there was a preferred time for the *ziyārah* of Imam Ḥusayn (*ᶜa*). He is reported to have replied, "Perform his *ziyārah* at any time and occasion, because there is a definite benefit and virtue in his *ziyārah*. Those who perform it more often will receive a greater benefit and those who perform it fewer times will receive a smaller reward. Try to perform his *ziyārah* at times of devotional significance, as virtuous acts performed during them have a reward superior by several degrees. During such times the angels descend from the heaven for the sake of his *ziyārah*."

I did not find any particular text prescribed for *ziyārah* on such occasions. Yes, there is a supplication prescribed by the Imam of the Era (*ᶜa*) for the 3rd of Shaᶜbān, the day of Imam al-Ḥusayn's birth, and one must recite it on this day. We have cited it in the observances pertaining to the month of Shaᶜbān (vol.1, p. 442).

One should know that there is also a great merit in performing the *ziyārah* of the Imam from places and towns far away from Karbalā. Here we will confine ourselves to mentioning two reports cited in *Kāfī*, *Tahdhīb* and *Faqīh*.

The first report[3] is that of Ibn Abī ᶜUmayr, from Hishām, in which Imam Jaᶜfar al-Ṣādiq (*ᶜa*) is reported to have said: "Whenever any of you resides in a place far off from our tombs, let him ascend to the roof of his house, offer two *rakᶜahs* of prayer and pronounce *salām* while pointing toward our tombs. Your greeting will definitely reach us."

The second report[4] is that of Ḥannān b. Sadīr, from his father,

1 *Al-Mazār al-Kabīr*, 107, whence *Biḥār*, xcviii, 58, b 26, h 26.

2 *Iqbāl*, 10, whence *Wasā'il*, xiv, 473, b 53, h 19630 & *Biḥār*, xcviii, 98, b 13, h 29.

3 *Faqīh*, ii, 599, h 3202, whence in *Wasā'il*, xiv, 577, b 95, h 19852.

4 *Kāmil al-Ziyārāt*, 287, 288, b 96, h 2, 7 whence *Wasā'il*, xiv, 580, b 96, h 19858 & *Biḥār*, xcviii, 365, 367, b 32, h 2, 10 & *Mustadrak*, x, 306, b 46, h 12063/2. *Faqīh*, ii, 599, h 3203. *Tahdhīb*, vi, 116, h 21.

who reports that Imam Ja^cfar al-Ṣādiq (^c*a*) asked him, "Sadīr, do you perform the *ziyārah* of al-Ḥusayn's shrine every day?" When Sadīr replied in the negative, the Imam said to him, "How unkind that is of you! Do you perform it every Friday?" Sadīr's reply was again a "No." "Do you perform it once a month?" The reply was again "No." "Do you perform it once a year?" Sadīr says, "I told him that it was several years since I had performed his *ziyārah*." The Imam said to him, "O Sadīr, how unkind that is of you to Imam al-Ḥusayn! Don't you know that God Almighty has two million (one million, in *Tahdhīb* and *Faqīh*) angels who visit him with dishevelled hair, covered with dust, and weep for him and do not become weary of lamentation. What stops you, Sadīr, from performing the *ziyārah* of his shrine once a day and five times on Fridays?" Sadīr says, "I told him that the shrine was at a distance of many parasangs from where I was." The Imam said, "Go up to the roof of your house and look to your right and left. Then turning toward his shrine and lifting your face towards the sky, say,

اَلسَّلَامُ عَلَيْكَ يَا أَبَا عَبْدِ اللهِ، اَلسَّلَامُ عَلَيْكَ وَ رَحْمَةُ اللهِ وَ بَرَكَاتُهُ	Peace be to you, O Abū ^cAbdillāh! May peace and Allah's mercy be on you!

"A reward equal to that of a ḥajj and ^cumrah pilgrimage will be written for you for your *ziyārah*." Sadīr says, "I often do this more than twenty times in a month."

At the head of the report pertaining to the first general *ziyārah* (p. 267) an account was given which is pertinent to the topic of these reports.

The Virtues of Imam al-Ḥusayn's Turbah

It should be known that there are many reports which describe the *turbah* of Imam Ḥusayn (^c*a*) as being a cure for every pain and malady except death and that it offers security from afflictions and safety from every danger and peril. The reports mentioning this matter are *mutawātir*.[1]

The miracles ensuing from the sacred *turbah* are more numerous than can be mentioned here. In my book *Fawā'id al-Raḍawīyah*, which deals with biographical accounts of Imāmī scholars, I have mentioned one of these miracles in the biographical account of the

[1] *Kāmil al-Ziyārāt*, 278-286, b 93-95. *Biḥār*, xcviii, 118-140, b 16, h 1-83.

erudite *muḥaddith* Sayyid Niᶜmatullāh Jazā'irī (*r*). That august scholar used to take great pains in the pursuit of knowledge. During the early years of his studies, he used to read by the light of the moon, as he could not afford lamplight. His eyesight became weak due to prolonged study in moonlight as well as due to severe strain resulting from intensive reading and writing. In order to recover his eyesight, he used to apply as kohl the holy *turbah* of Imam al-Ḥusayn (ᶜ*a*) and *turbah* from the sacred tombs of the Imams buried in Iraq. With the blessing of those *turbahs* his eyesight would be restored.

I wrote that account lest it should be a matter for disbelief for some persons of our times whose opinions have been affected due to social contact with atheists and the faithless.

Dimyarī in his book *Ḥayāt al-Ḥayawān* mentions that when the asp becomes blind on aging, God Almighty inspires it to rub its eyes on fresh fennel. It leaves the desert to find the herb in distant orchards and places where it is found. On rubbing its eyes on the herb, its eyesight is restored. This has been mentioned also by Zamakhsharī and other writers.

If God Almighty has given such a property to a herb, which is sought by a blind serpent to heal its blindness, there is no wonder if the *turbah* of the son of the Apostle of Allah (*ṣ*) who was martyred with his family and relatives for the sake of God, should be a cure from all diseases and be blessed with other beneficial properties for the good of his followers and lovers.

Here it will be sufficient to cite some reports in this regard.

(1) It is mentioned in a report that when the houris of paradise see an angel about to descend to the earth for some task, they request him to bring the *turbah* of Imam al-Ḥusayn's tomb for a gift.[1]

(2) According to another report[2] transmitted through a reliable chain of authorities, a person received a gift sent for him by Imam ᶜAlī al-Riḍā (ᶜ*a*) from Khurāsān. On opening the package, he saw some dust in it. On asking the person who had brought the gift, he was told that it was *turbah* from the tomb of Imam al-Ḥusayn (ᶜ*a*) and that the Imam did not send a garment or some other gift to anyone without putting some of the *turbah* within it, with the remark that it was pro-

[1] *Makārim*, 281, whence. *Biḥār*, lxxxii, 333, b 37, h 16. *Al-Mazār al-Kabīr*, 368, b 13, h 16, whence *Biḥār*, xcviii, 134, b 16, h 67 & *Mustadrak*, x, 345, b 58, h 12147/4.

[2] *Kāmil al-Ziyārāt*, 280, b 93, h 5, whence *Biḥār*, xcviii, 124, b 16, h 23 & *Mustadrak*, viii, 218, b 33, h 9295/1, Mufīd's *Mazār*, 144, b 62, h 6. *Makārim*, 255, whence *Biḥār*, lxxiii, 252, b 48, h 47.

tection against accident and injury by God's will.

(3) ᶜAbd Allāh b. Abī Yaᶜfūr reports[1] that he remarked to Imam Jaᶜfar al-Ṣādiq (ᶜa) that some persons who take the *turbah* of Imam Ḥusayn (ᶜa) did benefit from it while others did not. The Imam said to him, "By God, everyone who takes it with the belief that it would benefit him, does benefit from it."

(4) Abū Ḥamzah al-Thumālī reports[2] that he questioned Imam Jaᶜfar al-Ṣādiq (ᶜa), saying, "I have seen our companions collect the soil from the grave of Imam al-Ḥusayn (ᶜa) for the purpose of remedy. Does it really have the healing property they claim?" The Imam said to him,

> "The soil taken from within a distance of four miles (4000 cubits) from the tomb can be used as remedy, and so too the soil taken from the grave of my grandfather, the Apostle of Allah (ṣ), and from the grave of al-Ḥasan, ᶜAlī ibn al-Ḥusayn and Muḥammad ibn ᶜAlī. Collect it, as it is a cure for all maladies and a shield against any kind of danger. None of the things that are sought for remedy equals it except prayer (*duᶜā*).
>
> "Its effectiveness is not impaired by anything except improper receptacles in which it is placed or by lack of faith on behalf of those who use it for cure. But it suffices as a cure, by the leave of God, those who have conviction, sparing them of the need to take resort in other remedies. It is corrupted by devils and the faithless from among the jinn who rub themselves against it, and it sniffs everything that passes by. The devils and the faithless jinn envy humans on account of it and they touch it, making it lose most of its aroma. No *turbah* is brought out of the Ḥā'ir without a countless number of devils and faithless jinn going after it, and they rub against it while it is held in the hand of its owner. They cannot enter the Ḥā'ir because of the guarding angels.
>
> "If the *turbah* remains unimpaired, it will immediately cure anyone who is treated with it. Therefore, when you collect it, conceal it and mention over it the Name of God, the Almighty and the Glorious.

[1] *Kāfī*, iv, 588, h 3, whence *Wasā'il*, xiv, 522, b 70, h 19737. *Kāmil al-Ziyārāt*, 274, b 91, h 1, whence *Biḥār*, xcviii, 122, b 16, h 12 & *Mustadrak*, x, 329, b 53, h 12114/1,

[2] *Kāmil al-Ziyārāt*, 280, b 93, h 5, whence *Wasā'il*, xiv, 531, b 73, h 19757, whence and from Shaykh Bahā'ī's *Kashkūl* in *Biḥār*, xcviii, 128, b 11, h 39, lvii, 155, b 33, h 22 & *Mustadrak*, x, 332, b 53, h 12122/9, xvi, 204, b 43, h 19595/2.

"I have been informed that some of those who collect it make light of its worth, and some of them even place it in the saddle-bags of their camels, mules and donkeys, or in food utensils or bags that come into contact with hands. How can those who hold it in such low esteem obtain cure from it? The hearts lacking conviction and those who make light of something in which their good lies, spoil the fruits of their efforts."

(5) It is mentioned in a report[1] that someone who wants to take a small pinch of the *turbah* with his fingertips, should kiss it, hold it to his eyes and draw his hand over his body and take it after saying,

اَللّٰهُمَّ بِحَقِّ هٰذِهِ التُّرْبَةِ، وَ بِحَقِّ مَنْ حَلَّ
بِهَا وَ ثَوَىٰ فِيهَا، وَ بِحَقِّ جَدِّهِ وَ أَبِيهِ، وَ
أُمِّهِ وَ أَخِيهِ، وَ الْأَئِمَّةِ مِنْ وُلْدِهِ، وَ بِحَقِّ
الْمَلَائِكَةِ الْحَافِّينَ بِهِ، إِلَّا جَعَلْتَهَا شِفَاءً
مِنْ كُلِّ دَاءٍ، وَ بُرْءًا مِنْ كُلِّ مَرَضٍ، وَ نَجَاةً
مِنْ كُلِّ آفَةٍ، وَ حِرْزًا مِمَّا أَخَافُ وَ أَحْذَرُ.

O Allah, by the rights of this *turbah* and the rights of him who is buried in it and resides therein, and by the rights of his grandfather, father, mother, brother, and the Imams of his descent, and by the rights of the angels who surround him, make it a remedy for every malady, the cure for every disease, deliverance from every affliction, and protection from all that I fear and seek to avoid!

It is mentioned in a report that the way to keep the *turbah* under seal is to recite Sūrat al-Qadr over it.[2]

According to another report[3], while taking the *turbah* oneself, or giving it to someone to eat, one should say,

بِسْمِ اللهِ وَ بِاللهِ، اَللّٰهُمَّ اجْعَلْهُ رِزْقًا
وَاسِعًا، وَ عِلْمًا نَافِعًا، وَ شِفَاءً مِنْ

In the Name of Allah and by Allah. O Allah, make it the cause of plentiful provision, beneficial knowledge and cure for every malady.

1 Ṭūsī's *Amālī*, 318, majlis 11, h 636/93, whence *Wasā'il*, xiv, 522, b 70, h 19740 & *Biḥār*, xcviii, 119, b 16, h 4. *Bis͟hārah*, 217. *Makārim*, 167.

2 *Kāfī*, iv, 588, h 7, whence *Wasā'il*, xiv, 522, b 70, h 19738. *Kāmil al-Ziyārāt*, 284, b 94, h 1, thence and *Kāfī* in *Biḥār*, xcviii, 127, b 16, h 36 & *Mustadrak*, x, 341, b 56, h 12138/5.

3 *Kāmil al-Ziyārāt*, 284, b 94, h 1, whence *Biḥār*, xcviii, 129, b 16, h 40 & *Mustadrak*, x, 341, b 56, h 12139/6. Mufīd's *Mazār*, 149, b 65, h 1. Ṭūsī's *Miṣbāḥ*, 733 whence *Biḥār*, xcviii, 134, b 16, h 70. *Makārim*, 166. *Daʿawāt*, 187. *Biḥār*, xcii, 32.

Indeed You have power all things. كُلِّ دَاءٍ، إِنَّكَ عَلىٰ كُلِّ شَىْءٍ قَدِيرٌ.

There are many uses of the noble *turbah* of the Imam (ᶜ*a*) and it is *mustaḥab* to place it along with the corpse in the grave[1] and to use it for writing on the shroud. Another of its uses is for prostration during prayers. It has been reported that seven veils are removed for those who perform *sajdah* on it.[2] It means that it is the cause of acceptance of prayers and their ascent to the heaven.

Another of the uses of the Imam's *turbah* is to make rosary from its clay for the purpose of *dhikr* and holding it in one's hand, which acts have a great virtue. When held in one's hand it does *tasbīḥ* without one's saying it.[3] Evidently, that is something other than the *tasbīḥ* which is characteristic of all things and is mentioned by God, the Most High, in this verse,

وَإِنْ مِنْ شَىْءٍ إِلَّا يُسَبِّحُ بِحَمْدِهِ وَلٰكِنْ لَا تَفْقَهُونَ تَسْبِيحَهُمْ

There is not a thing but celebrates His praise, but you do not understand their glorification. (17:44)

And is referred to in these verses of Rūmī,

گر ترا از غیب چشمی باز شد	با تو ذرات جهان همراز شد
نطق خاك و نطق آب و نطق گل	هست محسوس حواس اهل دل
جمله ذرات در عالم نهان	با تو می‌گویند روزان و شبان
ما سمیعیم و بصیر و باهشیم	با شما نامحرمان ما خامشیم
از جمادی سوی جانِ جان شوید	غلغل اجزای عالم بشنوید
فاش تسبیح جمادات آیدت	وسوسه تاویل ها بزدایدت

Should the Hidden Hand open your inner eye,

1 *Tahdhīb*, vi, 76, b 22, h 18, whence *Wasā'il*, iii, 29, b 12, h 2946 & *Biḥār*, xcviii, 133, b 16, h 63. *Iḥtijāj*, ii, 489, whence *Biḥār*, liii, 164, b 31, h 4, lxxviii, 313, b 9, h 8, lxxix, 34, b 12, h 23.

2 Ṭūsī's *Miṣbāḥ*, 733, whence *Wasā'il*, v, 366, b 16, h 6808, vi, 456, b 16, h 8430 & *Biḥār*, lxxxii, 153, b 28, h 14, xcviii, 135, b 16, h 74. *Daᶜawāt*, 188.

3 Mufīd's *Mazār*, 150, b 66, h 2. Ṭūsī's *Miṣbāḥ*, 735, whence *Wasā'il*, vi, 456, b 16, h 8432 & *Biḥār*, lxxxii, 334, b 37, h 18, xcviii, 136, b 16, h 77. *Al-Mazār al-Kabīr*, 367, b 13, h 12, whence *Mustadrak*, x, 344, b 58, h 12145/2.

Tahdhīb, vi, 75, b 22, h 17, whence *Wasā'il*, xiv, 536, b 75, h 19771 & *Biḥār*, xcviii, 132, b 16, h 62. *Iḥtijāj*, ii, 489, whence *Wasā'il*, vi, 456, b 16, h 8433 & *Biḥār*, liii, 164, b 31, h 4, lxxxii, 327, b 37, h 1.

Mufīd's *Mazār*, 151, b 66, h 4. *Makārim*, 281, whence *Wasā'il*, vi, 455, b 16, h 8428 & *Biḥār*, lxxxii, 333, b 37, h 116. *Al-Mazār al-Kabīr*, 367, b 13, h 14, whence *Biḥār*, xcviii, 133, b 16, h 66 & *Mustadrak*, iv, 13, b 9, h 4058/4, x, 344, b 58, h 12146/3.

You would share the secrets that lie in the heart of every particle
The People of the Heart do hear the voices of earth, water and clay
Every particle will tell with you, day and night, in intimate discourse:
"We do hear, see, and are aware: we are mute only with strangers."
From the corporeal world, move on to the Soul of souls
Listen to the chorus of the world's constituents
You will hear distinctly the bodies praising the Lord
And be freed from the temptation to explain away (the Qur'anic saying).

Hence the *tasbīḥ* mentioned in this report is one which is particular to the *turbah* of the Doyen of the Martyrs (*ᶜa*).

(6) Imam ᶜAlī al-Riḍā (*ᶜa*) is reported[1] to have said that when someone says the following *dhikr* while fingering a rosary whose beads are made of the *turbah* of Imam al-Ḥusayn (*ᶜa*), God, the Most High, writes for him, for every bead, 6000 good deeds, erases 6000 of his sins, raises his rank by 6000 degrees and confers on him 6000 intercessions.

Glory be to Allah. All praise belongs to Allah. There is no god besides Allah and Allah is greater!	سُبْحَانَ اللهِ وَ الْحَمْدُ لِلّٰهِ وَ لَا إِلٰهَ إِلَّا اللهُ وَ اللهُ أَكْبَرُ.

Imam Jaᶜfar al-Ṣādiq (*ᶜa*) is reported to have said that someone who holds one bead (made of baked clay) of the *turbah* of Imam al-Ḥusayn (*ᶜa*) and says *istighfār* a single time, God writes it as having said it seventy times, and should he hold the rosary in his hand without saying *tasbīḥ*, for every bead is written a reward for having said it seven times.[2]

(7) It is mentioned in a reliable report[3] that once when Imam Jaᶜfar al-Ṣādiq (*ᶜa*) was visiting Iraq, a group of people approached him and said to him, "We know that the *turbah* of Imam al-Ḥusayn (*ᶜa*) is a cure for every illness. But does it also provide security from every

1 *Al-Mazār al-Kabīr*, 151, b 66, h 3, whence *Biḥār*, xcviii, 133, b 16, h 65 & *Mustadrak*, iv, 13, b 9, h 40573, x, 344, b 58, h 12144/1.

2 Ṭūsī's *Miṣbāḥ*, 735, whence *Wasā'il*, vi, 456, b 16, h 8432 & *Biḥār*, lxxxii, 332, b 37, h 184. *Al-Mazār al-Kabīr*, 150, b 66, h 2, whence *Mustadrak*, x, 344, b 58, h 12145/2.

3 *Falāḥ al-Sā'il*, 224, whence *Biḥār*, lxxxiii, 276, b 45, h 41.

danger?" The Imam (ʿa) told them that it does, adding that when someone wishes to be secure from every danger, he should take a rosary made of the Imam's *turbah* in his hand and recite the following supplication three times.

O Allah, I have risen this morning seeking resort in Your protection and invulnerable shelter—which is inviolable and unassailable—from the evil of every oppressor and harmful thing, from those which You have created, the silent ones of Your creatures and those that speak, thus shielding myself from every danger with a full and immune covering, which is the love of the Family of Your Prophet, Muḥammad, peace be to him and his Family, taking shelter against everyone intending to hurt me, by the means of the impregnable wall, which is my sincere admission of their rights, and taking hold of their cord, with the conviction that the truth belongs to them, that it is with them, from them, in them and through them. I befriend those they befriend and am hostile to those whom they regard as enemy, avoiding those they avoid.	أَصْبَحْتُ اللّٰهُمَّ مُعْتَصِمًا بِذِمَامِكَ وَ جِوَارِكَ الْمَنِيعِ الَّذِى لَا يُطَاوَلُ وَ لَا يُحَاوَلُ، مِنْ شَرِّ كُلِّ غَاشِمٍ وَ طَارِقٍ مِنْ سَائِرِ مَنْ خَلَقْتَ وَ مَا خَلَقْتَ مِنْ خَلْقِكَ الصَّامِتِ وَ النَّاطِقِ، فِى جُنَّةٍ مِنْ كُلِّ مَخُوفٍ بِلِبَاسٍ سَابِغَةٍ حَصِينَةٍ، وَ هِىَ وِلَاءُ أَهْلِ بَيْتِ نَبِيِّكَ مُحَمَّدٍ صَلَّى اللّٰهُ عَلَيْهِ وَ آلِهِ، مُحْتَجِزًا مِنْ كُلِّ قَاصِدٍ لِى إِلَىٰ أَذِيَّةٍ بِجِدَارٍ حَصِينٍ، اَلْإِخْلَاصِ فِى الْاِعْتِرَافِ بِحَقِّهِمْ، وَ التَّمَسُّكِ بِحَبْلِهِمْ جَمِيعًا، مُوقِنًا أَنَّ الْحَقَّ لَهُمْ وَ مَعَهُمْ وَ مِنْهُمْ وَ فِيهِمْ وَ بِهِمْ، أُوَالِى مَنْ وَالَوْا، وَ أُعَادِى مَنْ عَادَوْا، وَ أُجَانِبُ مَنْ جَانَبُوا،
So bless Muḥammad and his Family and grant me protection, O Allah, through them from the evil of all that I am wary of. O Supreme One, I shield myself from the enemies through the Originator of the heavens and the earth: *Indeed We have put a barrier before them and a barrier behind them, then We have*	فَصَلِّ عَلَىٰ مُحَمَّدٍ وَ آلِهِ، وَ أَعِذْنِى اللّٰهُمَّ بِهِمْ مِنْ شَرِّ كُلِّ مَا أَتَّقِيهِ، يَا عَظِيمُ حَجَزْتُ الْأَعَادِىَ عَنِّى بِبَدِيعِ السَّمَاوَاتِ وَ الْأَرْضِ، إِنَّا جَعَلْنَا مِنْ بَيْنِ أَيْدِيهِمْ سَدًّا وَ مِنْ خَلْفِهِمْ سَدًّا

فَأَغْشَيْنَاهُمْ فَهُمْ لَا يُبْصِرُونَ.

blind-folded them, so they do not see. (36:9)

Then kiss the rosary and rub it on your eyes and say,

اللّٰهُمَّ إِنِّي أَسْأَلُكَ بِحَقِّ هٰذِهِ التُّرْبَةِ الْمُبَارَكَةِ، وَ بِحَقِّ صَاحِبِهَا وَ بِحَقِّ جَدِّهِ وَ بِحَقِّ أَبِيهِ وَ بِحَقِّ أُمِّهِ وَ بِحَقِّ أَخِيهِ وَ بِحَقِّ وُلْدِهِ الطَّاهِرِينَ، اِجْعَلْهَا شِفَاءً مِنْ كُلِّ دَاءٍ، وَ أَمَانًا مِنْ كُلِّ خَوْفٍ، وَ حِفْظًا مِنْ كُلِّ سُوءٍ.

O Allah, I beseech You by the right of this blessed *turbah* and by the right of him to whom it belongs and by the right of his grandfather, by the right of his father, by the right of his brother and by the right of his immaculate descendants to make it a cure from every malady and safety from every fear and protection from every ill.

Then put it on your forehead. When one does so in the morning he will remain in God's protection until night and when done at night he will remain in God's protection until the morning.

According to another report,[1] when someone feels threatened by a ruler or someone else, he should perform this *ḥirz* to the end while leaving his house so as to be secure from their harm.

The compiler says: The commonly-held opinion of the scholars is that it is absolutely impermissible to eat any soil and clay, with the exception of the noble *turbah* of Imam Ḥusayn (*ᶜa*) with the purpose of healing and without any intent of pleasure, to the extent of a grain of gram or, to be more cautious, half a grain. It is better to place the *turbah* in one's mouth and drink a little water after that and to say,

اللّٰهُمَّ اجْعَلْهُ رِزْقًا وَاسِعًا، وَ عِلْمًا نَافِعًا، وَ شِفَاءً مِنْ كُلِّ دَاءٍ وَ سُقْمٍ.

O Allah, let it be a means of ample provision, beneficial knowledge and cure from every pain and illness.

ᶜAllāmah Majlisī (*r*) says that to be on the safe side, the rosaries and tablets (*muhr*) made of the Imam's *turbah* should not be sold and bought but rather be given and received as gift (*hadiyah*). Perhaps it is not bad to agree on an amount in return without making it a

[1] Ṭūsī's *Amālī*, 276, majlis 10, h 529/67, whence *Biḥār*, xcii, i, b 53, h 1. *Bishārah*, 129. *Makārim*, 277.

precondition, as it is mentioned in a reliable report from Imam Jaᶜfar al-Ṣādiq (*ᶜa*) that buying and selling the clay from the tomb of Imam al-Ḥusayn (*ᶜa*) is like buying and selling his flesh.[1]

The Compiler says: Our teacher, the erudite *muḥaddi<u>th</u>*, <u>Th</u>iqat al-Islām Nūrī (*r*) relates the following story in *Dār al-Salām*:[2]

> One day, when one of my brothers was with my late mother, she noticed that he had placed the *turbah* of Imam Ḥusayn (*ᶜa*) in the lower pocket of his cloak. My mother admonished him, pointing out that it was irreverent to carry the holy *turbah* in that manner, as the tablet might get pressed under his thigh and break. My brother said to her, "You are right. Till now I have broken two of these tablets." He promised not to carry it in his lower pocket.
>
> Some days after this episode, my learned father, who had no knowledge of this event, saw in a dream that our master Imam Abū ᶜAbdillāh al-Ḥusayn (*ᶜa*) had come to visit him. The Imam sat in the library room and was very kind and affectionate. He told my father to call his sons in order that he may give them some gifts. My father had his sons called, and they were five of them. They stood near the door facing the Imam, who had brought as gifts garments and other things. He then called each of us one by one and gave him a gift. When it was my brother's turn, the Imam glanced at him as if he were somewhat annoyed and, turning to my late father, remarked, "This son of yours has broken two tablets of the *turbah* of my grave under his thigh." Then without asking him to come forward like the others, he tossed the gift towards him. I still remember that it was a comb case made of embroidered silk. On waking up, my father recounted the dream to my late mother. When she told him what she had observed about my brother, he was amazed by the truthfulness of the dream.

1 *Kāmil al-Ziyārāt*, 286, b 95, h 5, whence *Wasā'il*, xxiv, 228, b 59, h 30405 & *Biḥār*, xcviii, 130, b 16, h 49.

2 *Dār al-Salām*, ii, 231-232.

Chapter Eight

The Ziyārah of Kāẓimayn

This chapter pertains to the virtues of the *ziyārah* of the Imams Mūsā al-Kāẓim (*ʿa*) and Muḥammad al-Taqī (*ʿa*) at Kāẓimayn and the manner of performing it. It also contains a description of the Barāthā Mosque and the *ziyārah* of Ḥaḍrat Salmān and the four deputies of the Imam of the Era (*ʿa*), may Allah be pleased with them. It consists of four sections.

Section One

The Virtues of the Ziyārah of Kāẓimayn and Its Manner

Many virtues have been mentioned for the *ziyārah* of these two infallible Imams (*ʿa*) and there are many reports stating that the *ziyārah* of Imam Musā al-Kāẓim (*ʿa*) is like that of the Apostle of Allah (ṣ).[1] According to one of such reports, someone who performs his *ziyārah* is like one who has performed the *ziyārah* of the Apostle of Allah (ṣ) and the Commander of the Faithful (*ʿa*).[2] According to another, the reward of those who perform his *ziyārah* is paradise.[3]

The eminent scholar Muḥammad b. Shahr Āshūb in his book *al-Manāqib* quotes ʿAlī b. Khallāl's statement cited by Khaṭīb in his book *Ta'rīkh Baghdād*. ʿAlī b. Khallāl says that there has been no occasion when his difficulty was not removed by God when he went to the tomb of Imam Mūsā ibn Jaʿfar (*ʿa*) to seek his mediation.[4]

It is said that in Baghdad a woman was seen walking in great haste. When asked as to where she was going, she replied, "To the shrine

1 *Kāmil al-Ziyārāt*, 299-300, b 99, h 5, 6, 9. Mufīd's *Mazār*, 191, b 14, h 3. *Muqniʿah*, 477, b 24. *Tahdhīb*, vi, 82, b 30, h 4. Whence *Wasā'il*, xiv, 545, b 80, h 19789; *Biḥār*, xcix, 4, b 1, h 17-20 & *Mustadrak*, x, 352, b 62, h 12164/1. *Jāmiʿ al-Akhbār*, 28, faṣl 13.

2 *Kāmil al-Ziyārāt*, 299, b 99, h 6, whence *Biḥār*, xcix, 4, b 1, h 19 & *Mustadrak*, x, 352, b 62, h 12165/2. *Rawḍat al-Wāʿiẓīn*, i, 221.

3 Mufīd's *Mazār*, 191, b 14, h 2. *Al-Fuṣūl al-Mukhtārah*, 130. *ʿUyūn Akhbār al-Riḍā* (*ʿa*), ii, 257, b 66, h 12. *Tahdhīb*, vi, 82, b 32, h 3, whence in *Wasā'il*, xiv, 545, b 80, h 19788 & *Biḥār*, xcix, 1, b 1, h 5. *Manāqib*, iv, 329 whence *Biḥār*, xcix, 1, b 1, h 3. *Jāmiʿ al-Akhbār*, 28, faṣl 13.

4 *Manāqib*, iv, 305, whence *Biḥār*, xcix, 1, b 1, h 1.

of Mūsā ibn Jaᶜfar (ᶜ*a*) to pray for my son who has been imprisoned." A man belonging to the Ḥanbalī sect ridiculed her, saying, "Your son will die in the prison." She said, "O God, I beseech you by him who was martyred in the prison to show me Your power!" Her son was released immediately and the son of the Ḥanbalī who had ridiculed her was arrested for the same offence.[1]

Shaykh Ṣadūq reports that Ibrāhīm b. ᶜUqbah wrote a letter to Imam ᶜAlī al-Naqī (ᶜ*a*) questioning him concerning the *ziyārah* of Imam Ḥusayn (ᶜ*a*) and that of Imam Mūsā al-Kāẓim (ᶜ*a*) and Imam Muḥammad al-Taqī (ᶜ*a*) as to which was preferable. The Imam wrote to him that priority lay with Imam Ḥusayn's *ziyārah* but that the *ziyārah* of the two Imams was greater in reward and more inclusive.[2]

As for the manner of performing the *ziyārah* at Kāẓimayn, some of the *ziyārahs* are specifically addressed to each of the Imams and some are common for both of them.

Individual Ziyārahs of Each Imam

Two *ziyārahs* have been given here for Imam Mūsā al-Kāẓim (ᶜ*a*) and three for Imam Muḥammad al-Taqī (ᶜ*a*).

First Ziyarah of Imam Musa al-Kazim (ʿa)

The first *ziyārah,* as described by Sayyid ᶜAlī b. Ṭāwūs[3] in *Miṣbāḥ al-Zā'ir,* is to be performed as follows. When intending to perform the Imam's *ziyārah*, the proper thing to do is to first take a bath. When approaching the shrine, one should walk with calm dignity. On reaching the gate of the shrine, one should stop and say,

Allah is greater. Allah is greater. There is no god other than Allah, and Allah is greater! All praise belongs to Allah for guiding us to His religion and enabling us to follow His path to which He has summoned (all mankind).	اَللّٰهُ أَكْبَرُ اللّٰهُ أَكْبَرُ، لاَ إِلٰهَ إِلَّا اللّٰهُ وَ اللّٰهُ أَكْبَرُ، الْحَمْدُ لِلَّهِ عَلٰى هِدٰايَتِهِ لِدِينِهِ، وَ التَّوْفِيقِ لِمٰا دَعٰا إِلَيْهِ مِنْ سَبِيلِهِ.
O Allah, You are the noblest of those who are sought and most	اَللّٰهُمَّ إِنَّكَ أَكْرَمُ مَقْصُودٍ وَ أَكْرَمُ

1 *Manāqib*, iv, 305, whence *Biḥār*, xcix, 1, b 1, h 2.

2 ᶜ*Uyūn Akhbār al-Riḍā* (ᶜ*a*), ii, 261, whence *Biḥār*, xcix, 2, b 50, h 7.

3 *Miṣbāḥ al-Zā'ir*, 198-200, whence *Biḥār*, xcix, 14-16, b 51, h 9.

مَأْتِيٍّ، وَ قَدْ أَتَيْتُكَ مُتَقَرِّبًا إِلَيْكَ بِابْنِ بِنْتِ نَبِيِّكَ صَلَوٰاتُكَ عَلَيْهِ وَ عَلٰى آبٰائِهِ الطّٰاهِرِينَ وَ أَبْنٰائِهِ الطَّيِّبِينَ.

generous of those who are approached in times of need! I come to You seeking nearness to You through the son of Your Prophet's daughter, may Your blessings be upon him, his immaculate ancestors and pure descendants!

اَللّٰهُمَّ صَلِّ عَلٰى مُحَمَّدٍ وَ آلِ مُحَمَّدٍ، وَ لٰا تُخَيِّبْ سَعْيِي، وَ لٰا تَقْطَعْ رَجٰائِي، وَ اجْعَلْنِي عِنْدَكَ وَجِيهًا فِي الدُّنْيٰا وَ الْآخِرَةِ وَ مِنَ الْمُقَرَّبِينَ

O Allah, bless Muḥammad and the Family of Muḥammad and do not let my efforts be disappointed, do not cut off my hope, make me honoured with You in the world and the Hereafter and admit me among those near to You!

Then enter with the right foot and say,

بِسْمِ اللّٰهِ وَ بِاللّٰهِ وَ فِي سَبِيلِ اللّٰهِ وَ عَلٰى مِلَّةِ رَسُولِ اللّٰهِ صَلَّى اللّٰهُ عَلَيْهِ وَ آلِهِ،

In the Name of Allah, by Allah, in the way of Allah and holding to the creed of the Apostle of Allah, may Allah bless him and his Family!

اَللّٰهُمَّ اغْفِرْ لِي وَ لِوٰالِدَيَّ وَ لِجَمِيعِ الْمُؤْمِنِينَ وَ الْمُؤْمِنٰاتِ.

O Allah, forgive me and my parents and all the faithful, men and women!

Stop on reaching the tomb chamber and say, seeking leave of admittance,

أَ أَدْخُلُ يٰا رَسُولَ اللّٰهِ؟ أَ أَدْخُلُ يٰا نَبِيَّ اللّٰهِ؟ أَ أَدْخُلُ يٰا مُحَمَّدَ بْنَ عَبْدِ اللّٰهِ؟ أَ أَدْخُلُ يٰا أَمِيرَ الْمُؤْمِنِينَ؟ أَ أَدْخُلُ يٰا أَبٰا مُحَمَّدٍ الْحَسَنَ؟ أَ أَدْخُلُ يٰا أَبٰا عَبْدِ اللّٰهِ الْحُسَيْنَ؟ أَ أَدْخُلُ يٰا أَبٰا مُحَمَّدٍ عَلِيَّ بْنَ الْحُسَيْنِ؟ أَ أَدْخُلُ يٰا أَبٰا جَعْفَرٍ مُحَمَّدَ بْنَ

May I enter O Apostle of Allah? May I enter O Prophet of Allah? May I enter O Muḥammad ibn ᶜAbd Allāh? May I enter, O Commander of the Faithful? May I enter, O Abū Muḥammad al-Ḥasan? May I enter, O Abū ᶜAbdillāh al-Ḥusayn? May I enter O Abū Muḥammad ᶜAlī ibn al-Ḥusayn? May I enter, O Abū Jaᶜfar Muḥammad ibn ᶜAlī? May I enter, O Abū ᶜAbdillāh Jaᶜfar ibn Muḥammad? May I enter, O my master Abul-Ḥasan Mūsā ibn Jaᶜfar? May I enter, O my master Abū Jaᶜfar? May I enter, O my master Muḥammad ibn ᶜAlī?

عَلِيٍّ؟ أَأَدْخُلُ يَا أَبَا عَبْدِ اللهِ جَعْفَرَ بْنَ
مُحَمَّدٍ؟ أَأَدْخُلُ يَا مَوْلَايَ يَا أَبَا الْحَسَنِ
مُوسَى بْنَ جَعْفَرٍ؟ أَأَدْخُلُ يَا مَوْلَايَ يَا أَبَا
جَعْفَرٍ؟ أَأَدْخُلُ يَا مَوْلَايَ مُحَمَّدَ بْنَ عَلِيٍّ؟

Then enter, and say four times "*Allāhu akbar!*" Then, facing the tomb and with the back towards the *qiblah*, say,

Peace to you, O *walī* of Allah and son of His *walī!* Peace to you, O testament of Allah and son of His testament! Peace to you, O chosen one of Allah and son of His chosen one! Peace to you, O trustee of Allah and son of His trustee! Peace to you, O light of Allah in the darkness of the earth!

اَلسَّلَامُ عَلَيْكَ يَا وَلِيَّ اللهِ وَ ابْنَ وَلِيِّهِ،
اَلسَّلَامُ عَلَيْكَ يَا حُجَّةَ اللهِ وَ ابْنَ حُجَّتِهِ،
اَلسَّلَامُ عَلَيْكَ يَا صَفِيَّ اللهِ وَ ابْنَ صَفِيِّهِ،
اَلسَّلَامُ عَلَيْكَ يَا أَمِينَ اللهِ وَ ابْنَ أَمِينِهِ،
اَلسَّلَامُ عَلَيْكَ يَا نُورَ اللهِ فِي ظُلُمَاتِ الْأَرْضِ

Peace to you, O Imam of guidance! Peace to you, O standard of faith and Godfearing! Peace to you, O repository of the knowledge of the prophets! Peace to you, O repository of the knowledge of the apostles! Peace to you, O deputy of the preceding legatees!

اَلسَّلَامُ عَلَيْكَ يَا إِمَامَ الْهُدَى، اَلسَّلَامُ
عَلَيْكَ يَا عَلَمَ الدِّينِ وَ التُّقَى، اَلسَّلَامُ
عَلَيْكَ يَا خَازِنَ عِلْمِ النَّبِيِّينَ، اَلسَّلَامُ
عَلَيْكَ يَا خَازِنَ عِلْمِ الْمُرْسَلِينَ، اَلسَّلَامُ
عَلَيْكَ يَا نَائِبَ الْأَوْصِيَاءِ السَّابِقِينَ،

Peace to you, O mine of clear revelations! Peace to you, O bearer of certain knowledge! Peace to you, O possessor of the knowledge of the apostles!

اَلسَّلَامُ عَلَيْكَ يَا مَعْدِنَ الْوَحْيِ الْمُبِينِ،
اَلسَّلَامُ عَلَيْكَ يَا صَاحِبَ الْعِلْمِ الْيَقِينِ،
اَلسَّلَامُ عَلَيْكَ يَا عَيْبَةَ عِلْمِ الْمُرْسَلِينَ،

Peace to you, O righteous Imam! Peace to you, O abstemious Imam! Peace to you, O de-

اَلسَّلَامُ عَلَيْكَ أَيُّهَا الْإِمَامُ الصَّالِحُ، اَلسَّلَامُ
عَلَيْكَ أَيُّهَا الْإِمَامُ الزَّاهِدُ، اَلسَّلَامُ عَلَيْكَ

vout Imam! Peace to you, O Imam and upright master! Peace to you, O you who were slain and martyred!

أَيُّهَا الْإِمَامُ الْعَابِدُ، اَلسَّلَامُ عَلَيْكَ أَيُّهَا الْإِمَامُ اَلسَّيِّدُ الرَّشِيدُ، اَلسَّلَامُ عَلَيْكَ أَيُّهَا الْمَقْتُولُ الشَّهِيدُ،

Peace to you, O son of the Apostle of Allah and son of his legatee! Peace to you, O Mūsā ibn Ja'far, my master, and may Allah's mercy and His bounties be upon you!

اَلسَّلَامُ عَلَيْكَ يَا ابْنَ رَسُولِ اللهِ وَ ابْنَ وَصِيِّهِ، اَلسَّلَامُ عَلَيْكَ يَا مَوْلَايَ مُوسَى بْنَ جَعْفَرٍ وَ رَحْمَةُ اللهِ وَ بَرَكَاتُهُ،

I testify that you communicated from Allah what You had been charged with, and preserved what He had entrusted to you, and that you allowed what Allah has made lawful and forbade what Allah has made unlawful, and that you upheld Allah's laws, followed His scripture, and patiently bore the torments for Allah's sake and waged *jihād* for His sake in the manner worthy of Him until the last breath!

أَشْهَدُ أَنَّكَ قَدْ بَلَّغْتَ عَنِ اللهِ مَا حَمَّلَكَ، وَ حَفِظْتَ مَا اسْتَوْدَعَكَ، وَ حَلَّلْتَ حَلَالَ اللهِ، وَ حَرَّمْتَ حَرَامَ اللهِ، وَ أَقَمْتَ أَحْكَامَ اللهِ، وَ تَلَوْتَ كِتَابَ اللهِ، وَ صَبَرْتَ عَلَى الْأَذَى فِي جَنْبِ اللهِ، وَ جَاهَدْتَ فِي اللهِ حَقَّ جِهَادِهِ حَتَّى أَتَاكَ الْيَقِينُ،

I testify that you passed away upholding what your immaculate fathers, your pure ancestors, the guiding legatees and the rightly-guided Imams passed away upholding. You did not choose blindness over guidance and never swerved from truth towards falsehood.

وَ أَشْهَدُ أَنَّكَ مَضَيْتَ عَلَى مَا مَضَى عَلَيْهِ آبَاؤُكَ الطَّاهِرُونَ، وَ أَجْدَادُكَ الطَّيِّبُونَ، اَلْأَوْصِيَاءُ الْهَادُونَ، اَلْأَئِمَّةُ الْمَهْدِيُّونَ، لَمْ تُؤْثِرْ عَمًى عَلَى هُدًى، وَ لَمْ تَمِلْ مِنْ حَقٍّ إِلَى بَاطِلٍ،

I testify that you worked sincerely for Allah, His Apostle and the Commander of the Faithful, fulfilled your trusts and did not betray them, and that you maintained the prayer and paid the *zakāt*, bade

وَ أَشْهَدُ أَنَّكَ نَصَحْتَ لِلّٰهِ وَ لِرَسُولِهِ وَ لِأَمِيرِ الْمُؤْمِنِينَ، وَ أَنَّكَ أَدَّيْتَ الْأَمَانَةَ، وَ اجْتَنَبْتَ الْخِيَانَةَ، وَ أَقَمْتَ الصَّلَاةَ، وَ

آتَيْتَ الزَّكَاةَ، وَ أَمَرْتَ بِالْمَعْرُوفِ، وَ نَهَيْتَ عَنِ الْمُنْكَرِ، وَ عَبَدْتَ اللهَ مُخْلِصا مُجْتَهِدا مُحْتَسِبا حَتَّى أَتَاكَ الْيَقِينُ،

what is right and forbade what is wrong, and worshipped Allah with dedication, devotion and resignation until the last breath.

فَجَزَاكَ اللهُ عَنِ الْإِسْلاَمِ وَ أَهْلِهِ أَفْضَلَ الْجَزَاءِ وَ أَشْرَفَ الْجَزَاءِ،

May Allah grant you the best and noblest reward on behalf of Islam and its followers!

أَتَيْتُكَ يَا ابْنَ رَسُولِ اللهِ زَائِرا عَارِفًا بِحَقِّكَ، مُقِرًّا بِفَضْلِكَ، مُحْتَمِلًا لِعِلْمِكَ، مُحْتَجِبًا بِذِمَّتِكَ، عَائِذًا بِقَبْرِكَ، لاَئِذًا بِضَرِيحِكَ، مُسْتَشْفِعًا بِكَ إِلَى اللهِ، مُوَالِيًا لِأَوْلِيَائِكَ، مُعَادِيًا لِأَعْدَائِكَ، مُسْتَبْصِرًا بِشَأْنِكَ وَ بِالْهُدَى الَّذِى أَنْتَ عَلَيْهِ، عَالِمًا بِضَلاَلَةِ مَنْ خَالَفَكَ، وَ بِالْعَمَى الَّذِى هُمْ عَلَيْهِ،

O son of the Apostle of Allah, I come to you as a pilgrim, knowing your rights, admitting your merits, assenting to your knowledge, seeking shelter under your protection, taking refuge by your tomb, taking shelter by your sepulchre, seeking your intercession with Allah, befriending your friends, despising your enemies, having insight of your station and the guidance you have been invested with, and knowing that your opponents are astray and blind.

بِأَبِي أَنْتَ وَ أُمِّي وَ نَفْسِي وَ أَهْلِي وَ مَالِي وَ وُلْدِى يَا ابْنَ رَسُولِ اللهِ، أَتَيْتُكَ مُتَقَرِّبًا بِزِيَارَتِكَ إِلَى اللهِ تَعَالَى، وَ مُسْتَشْفِعًا بِكَ إِلَيْهِ، فَاشْفَعْ لِي عِنْدَ رَبِّكَ لِيَغْفِرَ لِي ذُنُوبِي، وَ يَعْفُوَ عَنْ جُرْمِي، وَ يَتَجَاوَزَ عَنْ سَيِّئَاتِي، وَ يَمْحُوَ عَنِّي خَطِيئَاتِي، وَ يُدْخِلَنِي الْجَنَّةَ، وَ يَتَفَضَّلَ

O son of the Apostle of Allah, you are dearer to me than my father and mother and my own self, my family, children and property! I come to you seeking nearness to Allah by the means of your *ziyārah*, and seek your intercession with Allah. So intercede for me with your Lord that He may forgive my sins, pardon my offences, overlook my misdeeds, efface my errors and admit me into paradise, and to grant me that which is worthy of Him, and that He may forgive me, my ancestors, my brothers and sisters, and all the faithful, men and women, in the world's east and its west, north and south, out of His grace, generosity and favour!

عَلَيَّ بِمَا هُوَ أَهْلُهُ، وَ يَغْفِرَ لِي وَ لِآبَائِي
وَ لِإِخْوَانِي وَ أَخَوَاتِي وَ لِجَمِيعِ الْمُؤْمِنِينَ
وَ الْمُؤْمِنَاتِ فِي مَشَارِقِ الْأَرْضِ وَ
مَغَارِبِهَا بِفَضْلِهِ وَ جُودِهِ وَ مَنِّهِ.

Then leaning against the *ḍarīḥ* embrace it, and laying your cheeks on it make any petition that you wish. Then, returning to the head of graveside, say,

Peace be to you, O my master, Mūsā ibn Jaʿfar, and may Allah's mercy and bounties be on you! I testify that you are the Imam and guide, God's *walī* and mankind's preceptor, that you are the repository of God's revelations and their authorized interpreter, who bear the knowledge of the Torah and the Evangel, that you are knowing and just, truthful in speech and sincere in deeds!

اَلسَّلَامُ عَلَيْكَ يَا مَوْلَايَ يَا مُوسَى
بْنَ جَعْفَرٍ وَ رَحْمَةُ اللهِ وَ بَرَكَاتُهُ، أَشْهَدُ
أَنَّكَ الْإِمَامُ الْهَادِي، وَ الْوَلِيُّ الْمُرْشِدُ،
وَ أَنَّكَ مَعْدِنُ التَّنْزِيلِ، وَ صَاحِبُ
التَّأْوِيلِ، وَ حَامِلُ التَّوْرَاةِ وَ الْإِنْجِيلِ، وَ
الْعَالِمُ الْعَادِلُ، وَ الصَّادِقُ الْعَامِلُ،

My master, I repudiate your enemies before God and seek nearness to Him through my affection for you. May Allah bless you, your fathers, ancestors and descendants, as well as your followers and lovers, and may Allah's mercy and His bounties be upon you and them!

يَا مَوْلَايَ أَنَا أَبْرَأُ إِلَى اللهِ مِنْ أَعْدَائِكَ،
وَ أَتَقَرَّبُ إِلَى اللهِ بِمُوَالَاتِكَ، فَصَلَّى اللهُ
عَلَيْكَ وَ عَلَى آبَائِكَ وَ أَجْدَادِكَ وَ أَبْنَائِكَ
وَ شِيعَتِكَ وَ مُحِبِّيكَ، وَ رَحْمَةُ اللهِ وَ بَرَكَاتُهُ.

Then offer two *rakʿahs* as the prayer of *ziyārah*, reciting the *sūrahs* Yā Sīn and al-Raḥmān in them, or any other Qur'ānic *sūrahs* you can conveniently recite. Thereafter, make any petition that you would like to make.

Second Ziyarah of Imam Musa al-Kazim (ʻa)

Shaykh Mufīd, Shahīd Awwal, and Muḥammad b. al-Mashhadī have mentioned its manner of performance as follows.[1] When intending to perform the Imam's *ziyārah* on arriving in Baghdad, one should perform a bath with the intent of visiting the holy shrine. On arriving at the gate of the shrine, one should stop and seek leave of admittance. Then, while entering, one should say,

بِسْـمِ اللهِ وَ بِاللهِ وَ فِي سَبِيلِ اللهِ وَ عَلىٰ
مِلَّةِ رَسُولِ اللهِ صَلَّى اللهُ عَلَيْهِ وَ آلِهِ، وَ
السَّلاٰمُ عَلىٰ أَوْلِيَاءِ اللهِ.

In the Name of Allah, by Allah, in the way of Allah, and following the creed of the Apostle of Allah, may Allah bless him and his Family! Peace to the *awliyā'* of Allah!

After entering the shrine and approaching the Imam's tomb, say while facing it,

اَلسَّـلاٰمُ عَلَيْكَ يَا نُورَ اللهِ فِي ظُلُمَاتِ
الْأَرْضِ، اَلسَّلاٰمُ عَلَيْكَ يَا وَلِيَّ اللهِ، اَلسَّلاٰمُ
عَلَيْكَ يَا حُجَّةَ اللهِ، اَلسَّـلاٰمُ عَلَيْكَ يَا
بَابَ اللهِ، أَشْـهَدُ أَنَّكَ أَقَمْتَ الصَّلاٰةَ،
وَ آتَيْتَ الـزَّكَاةَ، وَ أَمَرْتَ بِالْمَعْرُوفِ، وَ
نَهَيْتَ عَنِ الْمُنْكَرِ، وَ تَلَوْتَ الْكِتَابَ حَقَّ
تِلاٰوَتِهِ، وَ جَاهَدْتَ فِي اللهِ حَقَّ جِهَادِهِ،
وَ صَبَرْتَ عَلَى الْأَذَى فِي جَنْبِهِ مُحْتَسِـبًا،
وَ عَبَدْتَـهُ مُخْلِصًا حَتَّى أَتَـاكَ الْيَقِينُ،

Peace to you, O light of Allah in the darkness of the earth! Peace to you, O *walī* of Allah! Peace to you, O testament of Allah! Peace to you, O gateway to Allah! I testify that you maintained the prayer, paid the *zakāt*, bade what is right and forbade what is wrong, followed the Scripture as it is worthy of being followed, waged *jihād* for the sake of Allah as is worthy of Him, bore with patience and resignation all the torments for His sake, and worshipped Him with dedication until your last breath!

أَشْهَدُ أَنَّكَ أَوْلَى بِاللهِ وَ بِرَسُولِهِ، وَ أَنَّكَ
ابْنُ رَسُـولِ اللهِ حَقًّا، أَبْرَأُ إِلَى اللهِ مِنْ

I testify that you are the nearest of all creation to Allah and His Apostle, and that you are

[1] *Al-Mazār al-Kabīr*, 177 & Shahīd Awwal's *Mazār*, 58, whence and from Mufīd in *Biḥār*, xcix, 11-13, b 51, h 7.

a veritable son of the Apostle of Allah. I repudiate your enemies before God and seek nearness to Him through your friendship. My master, I come to you knowing your rights, while I befriend your friends and despise your enemies. So intercede in my favour with your Lord!

أَعْدَائِكَ، وَ أَتَقَرَّبُ إِلَى اللهِ بِمُوَالاَتِكَ،
أَتَيْتُكَ يَا مَوْلاَىَ عَارِفًا بِحَقِّكَ، مُوَالِيًا
لِأَوْلِيَائِكَ، مُعَادِيًا لِأَعْدَائِكَ، فَاشْفَعْ
لِى عِنْدَ رَبِّكَ.

Then clinging to the tomb, embrace it, laying your cheeks upon it. Then approach the head of the grave and standing there, say,

Peace to you, O son of the Apostle of Allah! I testify that you were truthful. You discharged your mission sincerely, spoke faithfully, and passed away as a martyr. You did not prefer blindness to guidance and never swerved from truth towards falsehood. May Allah bless you, your immaculate ancestors and descendants!

اَلسَّلاَمُ عَلَيْكَ يَا ابْنَ رَسُولِ اللهِ،
أَشْهَدُ أَنَّكَ صَادِقٌ، أَدَّيْتَ نَاصِحًا، وَ
قُلْتَ أَمِينًا، وَ مَضَيْتَ شَهِيدًا، لَمْ تُؤْثِرْ
عَمًى عَلَى الْهُدَىٰ، وَ لَمْ تَمِلْ مِنْ حَقٍّ إِلَى
بَاطِلٍ، صَلَّى اللهُ عَلَيْكَ وَ عَلَىٰ آبَائِكَ وَ
اَبْنَائِكَ الطَّاهِرِينَ.

Then kiss the holy tomb and offer two *rakʿahs* as the prayer of *ziyārah*. After this and any other prayers you may want to make, bow down in prostration and say,

O Allah, on You do I rely and You are my goal. Expecting Your grace, I have visited the tomb of my Imam, obedience to whom You have made mandatory for me, and I seek his mediation with You. By their right, which You have made obligatory on Yourself, forgive me, my parents and all the faithful, O Munificent One!

اَللّٰهُمَّ إِلَيْكَ اعْتَمَدْتُ، وَ إِلَيْكَ قَصَدْتُ،
وَ بِفَضْلِكَ رَجَوْتُ، وَ قَبْرَ إِمَامِىَ الَّذِى
أَوْجَبْتَ عَلَىَّ طَاعَتَهُ زُرْتُ، وَ بِهِ إِلَيْكَ
تَوَسَّلْتُ، فَبِحَقِّهِمُ الَّذِى أَوْجَبْتَ عَلَىٰ
نَفْسِكَ، اِغْفِرْ لِى وَ لِوَالِدَىَّ وَ لِلْمُؤْمِنِينَ
يَا كَرِيمُ!

Then laying your right cheek on the ground, say,

O Allah, You know my needs, so bless Muḥammad and the Family of Muḥammad and fulfil them!

اَللّٰهُــمَّ قَدْ عَلِمْــتَ حَوَائِـجِي، فَصَلِّ
عَلىٰ مُحَمَّـدٍ وَ آلِ مُحَمَّـدٍ وَ اقْضِهَـا!

Then laying your left cheek on the ground, say,

O Allah, You know all my sins. By the rights of Muḥammad and the Family of Muḥammad, bless Muḥammad and the Family of Muḥammad and forgive them, and grant me that which is worthy of You!

اَللّٰهُمَّ قَدْ أَحْصَيْتَ ذُنُوبِي، فَبِحَقِّ مُحَمَّدٍ
وَ آلِ مُحَمَّدٍ، صَلِّ عَلىٰ مُحَمَّدٍ وَ آلِ مُحَمَّدٍ،
وَ اغْفِرْهَا، وَ تَصَدَّقْ عَلَيَّ بِمَا أَنْتَ أَهْلُهُ.

Then returning to the state of prostration say a hundred times, "Shukran!" After this, raising the head from prostration, make any supplication that you may like to make.

Ṣalawat for Imam Musa al-Kazim (ʿa)

The august sayyid ᶜAlī b. Ṭāwūs (*r*) has cited in his book *Miṣbāḥ al-Zā'ir*[1] an invocation of blessings (*ṣalawāt*) within a *ziyārah* for Imam Mūsā ibn Jaᶜfar (*ᶜa*) which contains hints about his merits and excellences, his diligent devotions, and the sufferings he went through. It is hoped that the pilgrims will not miss the benefit of reciting it.

O Allah, bless Muḥammad and his Family and bless Mūsā ibn Jaᶜfar, heir of the pious and Imam of the elect, the embodiment of light and inheritor of the composure and dignity of the prophets and heir to their legacy and wisdom,

He, who used to keep nightly vigils, remaining awake till the crack of dawn, being continuously engaged in prayer for forgiveness, during prolonged prostrations, amid flowing tears, profuse supplications and continuous en-

اَللّٰهُمَّ صَلِّ عَلىٰ مُحَمَّدٍ وَ أَهْلِ بَيْتِهِ، وَ صَلِّ
عَلىٰ مُوسَى بْنِ جَعْفَـرٍ وَصِيِّ الْأَبْرَارِ، وَ
إِمَامِ الْأَخْيَارِ، وَ عَيْبَةِ الْأَنْوَارِ، وَ وَارِثِ
السَّكِينَةِ وَ الْوَقَارِ، وَ الْحِكَمِ وَ الْآثَارِ،
اَلَّذِي كَانَ يُحْيِي اللَّيْلَ بِالسَّهَرِ إِلَى السَّحَرِ
بِمُوَاصَلَةِ الِاسْتِغْفَارِ، حَلِيفِ السَّجْدَةِ
الطَّوِيلَةِ، وَ الدُّمُوعِ الْغَزِيرَةِ، وَ الْمُنَاجَاةِ

1 *Al-Mazār al-Kabīr*, 201-202 whence *Biḥār*, xcix, 17-18, b 51, h 10,

treaties. He was the seat of wisdom and justice, goodness and merit, magnanimity and generosity.

الْكَثِيرَةِ، وَ الضَّرَاعَاتِ الْمُتَّصِلَةِ، وَ مَقَرِّ
النُّهَىٰ وَالْعَدْلِ، وَ الْخَيْرِ وَ الْفَضْلِ، وَ
النَّدَىٰ وَ الْبَذْلِ،

He was on intimate terms with suffering and patience. Having been weighed down by oppression, he was buried in a tyrannical manner, after being tormented in the pits of prisons and dark dungeons, his ankles bruised by shackles, and a derogatory announcement was made over his coffin.

وَمَأْلَفِ الْبَلْوَىٰ وَالصَّبْرِ، وَ الْمُضْطَهَدِ
بِالظُّلْمِ، وَ الْمَقْبُورِ بِالْجَوْرِ، وَ الْمُعَذَّبِ فِي
قَعْرِ السُّجُونِ وَ ظُلَمِ الْمَطَامِيرِ، ذِي السَّاقِ
الْمَرْضُوضِ بِحَلَقِ الْقُيُودِ، وَالْجَنَازَةِ الْمُنَادَىٰ
عَلَيْهَا بِذُلِّ الْإِسْتِخْفَافِ،

He met al-Muṣṭafā, his grandfather, and al-Murtaḍā, his father, and his mother, the mistress of the womankind, in such a state that his heritage had been usurped and he, after being denied due loyalty and support, was made to drink poison by those who sought to murder him.

وَ الْوَارِدِ عَلَىٰ جَدِّهِ الْمُصْطَفَىٰ وَ أَبِيهِ
الْمُرْتَضَىٰ وَ أُمِّهِ سَيِّدَةِ النِّسَاءِ بِإِرْثٍ
مَغْصُوبٍ، وَ وِلَاءٍ مَسْلُوبٍ، وَ أَمْرٍ
مَغْلُوبٍ، وَ دَمٍ مَطْلُوبٍ، وَ سَمٍّ مَشْرُوبٍ،

O Allah, as he patiently bore the severe ordeals, swallowed bitter rage and anguish, submitting to Your will and pleasure, obeyed You with dedication and absolute humility and submission, and opposed heresy and its followers without being affected by the blame of any blamer in regard to things You have commanded or forbidden, bless him with a blessing that is growing, appreciating, and enhancing, by virtue of which You will grant him the privilege of interceding in favour of the

اَللّٰهُمَّ وَ كَمَا صَبَرَ عَلَىٰ غَلِيظِ الْمِحَنِ،
وَ تَجَرَّعَ غُصَصَ الْكُرَبِ، وَ اسْتَسْلَمَ
لِرِضَاكَ، وَ أَخْلَصَ الطَّاعَةَ لَكَ، وَ مَحَضَ
الْخُشُوعَ، وَ اسْتَشْعَرَ الْخُضُوعَ، وَ عَادَى
الْبِدْعَةَ وَ أَهْلَهَا، وَ لَمْ يَلْحَقْهُ فِي شَيْءٍ
مِنْ أَوَامِرِكَ وَ نَوَاهِيكَ لَوْمَةُ لَائِمٍ، صَلِّ
عَلَيْهِ صَلَاةً نَامِيَةً مُنِيفَةً زَاكِيَةً تُوجِبُ
لَهُ بِهَا شَفَاعَةَ أُمَمٍ مِنْ خَلْقِكَ، وَ قُرُونٍ

nations and generations of Your creatures!

Convey our greetings and *salām* to him. Grant us, for our friendship and love for him, Your grace and kindness, forgiveness and approval! Indeed You are dispenser of an all-embracing grace and a great clemency, by Your mercy, O Most Merciful of the merciful!

مِنْ بَرَايَاكَ،

وَ بَلِّغْهُ عَنَّا تَحِيَّةً وَ سَلَامًا، وَ آتِنَا مِنْ لَدُنْكَ فِي مُوَالاتِهِ فَضْلًا وَ إِحْسَانًا، وَ مَغْفِرَةً وَ رِضْوَانًا، إِنَّكَ ذُو الْفَضْلِ الْعَمِيمِ، وَ التَّجَاوُزِ الْعَظِيمِ، بِرَحْمَتِكَ يَا أَرْحَمَ الرَّاحِمِينَ!

First Ziyarah of Imam Muhammad al-Taqi (ʿa)

The manner of performing it has also been mentioned by Shaykh Mufīd, Shahīd Awwal and Muḥammad b. al-Mashhadī as follows.[1] Having performed the *ziyārah* of Imam Mūsā al-Kāẓim (*ʿa*), one should turn toward the tomb of Imam Muḥammad al-Taqī (*ʿa*), buried behind his grandfather. Standing near the tomb, say,

Peace be to you, O *walī* of Allah! Peace be to you, O testament of Allah! Peace be to you, O light of Allah in the darkness of the earth!

اَلسَّلَامُ عَلَيْكَ يَا وَلِيَّ اللهِ، اَلسَّلَامُ عَلَيْكَ يَا حُجَّةَ اللهِ، اَلسَّلَامُ عَلَيْكَ يَا نُورَ اللهِ فِي ظُلُمَاتِ الْأَرْضِ،

Peace be to you, O son of the Apostle of Allah! Peace be to you and your ancestors! Peace be to you and your descendants! Peace be to you and your friends!

اَلسَّلَامُ عَلَيْكَ يَا ابْنَ رَسُولِ اللهِ، اَلسَّلَامُ عَلَيْكَ وَ عَلَىٰ آبَائِكَ، اَلسَّلَامُ عَلَيْكَ وَ عَلَىٰ أَبْنَائِكَ، اَلسَّلَامُ عَلَيْكَ وَ عَلَىٰ أَوْلِيَائِكَ،

I testify that you maintained the prayer and paid the *zakāt*, bade what is right and forbade what is wrong, followed the Book of Allah as it is worthy of being followed, waged *jihād* for the sake of Allah as is worthy of Him, and that you patiently bore the torments for

أَشْهَدُ أَنَّكَ قَدْ أَقَمْتَ الصَّلَاةَ، وَ آتَيْتَ الزَّكَاةَ، وَ أَمَرْتَ بِالْمَعْرُوفِ، وَ نَهَيْتَ عَنِ الْمُنْكَرِ، وَ تَلَوْتَ الْكِتَابَ حَقَّ تِلَاوَتِهِ، وَ جَاهَدْتَ فِي اللهِ حَقَّ جِهَادِهِ، وَ صَبَرْتَ

[1] *Al-Mazār al-Kabīr*, 177 & Shahīd Awwal's *Mazār*, 58, whence and from Shaykh Mufīd in *Biḥār*, xcix, 12-13, b 51, h 7.

Allah's sake until the last breath! عَلَى الْأَذَى فِي جَنْبِهِ حَتَّى أَتَاكَ الْيَقِينُ،

I have come to you as a pilgrim, knowing your rights, befriending your friends and despising your enemies. So intercede for me with your Lord! أَتَيْتُكَ زَائِرًا عَارِفًا بِحَقِّكَ، مُوَالِيًا لِأَوْلِيَائِكَ، مُعَادِيًا لِأَعْدَائِكَ، فَاشْفَعْ لِي عِنْدَ رَبِّكَ.

Then embrace the tomb and lay your cheek on the *ḍarīḥ*. Then offer two *rakʿahs* of the prayer of *ziyārah* and offer any other prayers that you wish. Then make prostration and say,

Have mercy on me, who having been guilty of misconduct and sin, now surrender and confess my sins! إِرْحَمْ مَنْ أَسَاءَ وَ اقْتَرَفَ، وَ اسْتَكَانَ وَ اعْتَرَفَ.

Then laying the right cheek on the ground, say,

If I have been a bad servant, You are indeed an excellent Lord! إِنْ كُنْتُ بِئْسَ الْعَبْدُ، فَأَنْتَ نِعْمَ الرَّبُّ.

Then place the left cheek on the ground and say,

Inasmuch as Your servant's sin is great, it will be gracious of You to pardon him! O Munificent One! عَظُمَ الذَّنْبُ مِنْ عَبْدِكَ، فَلْيَحْسُنِ الْعَفْوُ مِنْ عِنْدِكَ يَا كَرِيمُ!

Then returning to the position of prostration, say a hundred times "*Shukran!*"

Second Ziyarah of Imam Muhammad al-Taqi (ʿa)

Sayyid ʿAlī b. Ṭāwūs[1] writes in his book *Miṣbāḥ al-Zā'ir* that having performed the *ziyārah* of Imam Mūsā al-Kāẓim (ʿ*a*) one should approach the tomb of Imam Muḥammad al-Taqī (ʿ*a*) and, after embracing it, say,

Peace be to you, O Abū Jaʿfar Muḥammad ibn ʿAlī, O pious and Godwary Imam who have fulfilled اَلسَّلَامُ عَلَيْكَ يَا أَبَا جَعْفَرٍ مُحَمَّدَ بْنَ عَلِيٍّ، اَلْبَرَّ التَّقِيَّ، الْإِمَامَ الْوَفِيَّ، اَلسَّلَامُ

[1] *Miṣbāḥ al-Zā'ir*, 395, whence *Biḥār*, xcix, 20-22, b 51, h 7.

عَلَيْكَ أَيُّهَا الرَّضِيُّ الزَّكِيُّ، اَلسَّلَامُ عَلَيْكَ
يَا وَلِيَّ اللهِ، اَلسَّلَامُ عَلَيْكَ يَا نَجِيَّ اللهِ،
اَلسَّلَامُ عَلَيْكَ يَا سَفِيرَ اللهِ، اَلسَّلَامُ عَلَيْكَ
يَا سِرَّ اللهِ، اَلسَّلَامُ عَلَيْكَ يَا ضِيَاءَ اللهِ،
اَلسَّلَامُ عَلَيْكَ يَا سَنَاءَ اللهِ، اَلسَّلَامُ عَلَيْكَ
يَا كَلِمَةَ اللهِ، اَلسَّلَامُ عَلَيْكَ يَا رَحْمَةَ اللهِ،
اَلسَّلَامُ عَلَيْكَ أَيُّهَا النُّورُ السَّاطِعُ، اَلسَّلَامُ
عَلَيْكَ أَيُّهَا الْبَدْرُ الطَّالِعُ، اَلسَّلَامُ عَلَيْكَ
أَيُّهَا الطَّيِّبُ مِنَ الطَّيِّبِينَ، اَلسَّلَامُ عَلَيْكَ أَيُّهَا
الطَّاهِرُ مِنَ الْمُطَهَّرِينَ، اَلسَّلَامُ عَلَيْكَ أَيُّهَا الْآيَةُ
الْعُظْمَىٰ، اَلسَّلَامُ عَلَيْكَ أَيُّهَا الْحُجَّةُ الْكُبْرَىٰ،
اَلسَّلَامُ عَلَيْكَ أَيُّهَا الْمُطَهَّرُ مِنَ الزَّلَّاتِ،
اَلسَّلَامُ عَلَيْكَ أَيُّهَا الْمُنَزَّهُ عَنِ الْمُعْضِلَاتِ
[الْمُعْظِلَاتِ]، اَلسَّلَامُ عَلَيْكَ أَيُّهَا الْعَلِيُّ عَنْ
نَقْصِ الْأَوْصَافِ، اَلسَّلَامُ عَلَيْكَ أَيُّهَا الرَّضِيُّ
عِنْدَ الْأَشْرَافِ،

your mission. Peace be to you, O immaculate one, pleasing to Allah. Peace be to you, O *walī* of Allah! Peace be to you, O intimate friend of Allah! Peace be to you, O envoy of Allah! Peace be to you, O secret of Allah! Peace be to you, O radiance of Allah! Peace be to you, O brilliance of Allah! Peace be to you, O word of Allah! Peace be to you, O mercy of Allah!

Peace be to you, O brilliant light! Peace be to you, O ascendant full moon! Peace be to you, O good descendent of the good! Peace be to you, O pure descendent of the pure! Peace be to you, O greatest sign (of Allah)! Peace be to you, O greatest testament (of Allah)!

Peace be to you, O immaculate one who were untainted by lapses! Peace be to you, O pure one untouched by perplexities! Peace be to you, who were far exalted above having any defect of character! Peace be to you, who were admirable with the noble ones!

اَلسَّلَامُ عَلَيْكَ يَا عَمُودَ الدِّينِ، أَشْهَدُ أَنَّكَ
وَلِيُّ اللهِ وَ حُجَّتُهُ فِي أَرْضِهِ، وَ أَنَّكَ جَنْبُ
اللهِ وَ خِيَرَةُ اللهِ، وَ مُسْتَوْدَعُ عِلْمِ اللهِ وَ
عِلْمِ الْأَنْبِيَاءِ، وَ رُكْنُ الْإِيمَانِ وَ تَرْجُمَانُ

Peace be to you, O pillar of the faith! I testify that you are Allah's *walī* and His testament on His earth and that you are nearest to Allah and His chosen one, the repository of Allah's knowledge and that of the prophets, the mainstay of

الْقُرْآنِ،
وَ أَشْهَدُ أَنَّ مَنِ اتَّبَعَكَ عَلَى الْحَقِّ وَ
الْهُدَىٰ، وَ أَنَّ مَنْ أَنْكَرَكَ وَ نَصَبَ لَكَ
الْعَدَاوَةَ عَلَى الضَّلَالَةِ وَ الرَّدَىٰ، أَبْرَأُ إِلَى
اللهِ وَ إِلَيْكَ مِنْهُمْ فِي الدُّنْيَا وَ الْآخِرَةِ، وَ
السَّلَامُ عَلَيْكَ

faith and the interpreter of the Qur'ān.

I testify that those who follow you are on the right path and rightly guided, and that those who deny you and are hostile to you are on the path of error and destruction. I repudiate them before Allah and you in the world and the Hereafter. Peace be to you, so long as I survive and as long as day and night endure!

While invoking blessings on the Imam, say,

مَا بَقِيتُ وَ بَقِيَ اللَّيْلُ وَ النَّهَارِ.
اَللّٰهُمَّ صَلِّ عَلَىٰ مُحَمَّدٍ وَ أَهْلِ بَيْتِهِ، وَ صَلِّ
عَلَىٰ مُحَمَّدِ بْنِ عَلِيٍّ الزَّكِيِّ التَّقِيِّ، وَ الْبَرِّ
الْوَفِيِّ، وَ الْمُهَذَّبِ النَّقِيِّ، هَادِي الْأُمَّةِ،
وَ وَارِثِ الْأَئِمَّةِ، وَ خَازِنِ الرَّحْمَةِ، وَ
يَنْبُوعِ الْحِكْمَةِ، وَ قَائِدِ الْبَرَكَةِ، وَ عَدِيلِ
الْقُرْآنِ فِي الطَّاعَةِ، وَ وَاحِدِ الْأَوْصِيَاءِ فِي
الْإِخْلَاصِ وَ الْعِبَادَةِ، وَ حُجَّتِكَ الْعُلْيَا، وَ
مَثَلِكَ الْأَعْلَىٰ، وَ كَلِمَتِكَ الْحُسْنَىٰ، اَلدَّاعِي
إِلَيْكَ، وَ الدَّالِّ عَلَيْكَ، اَلَّذِي نَصَبْتَهُ عَلَمًا
لِعِبَادِكَ، وَ مُتَرْجِمًا لِكِتَابِكَ، وَ صَادِعًا
بِأَمْرِكَ، وَ نَاصِرًا لِدِينِكَ، وَ حُجَّةً عَلَىٰ
خَلْقِكَ، وَ نُورًا تَخْرُقُ بِهِ الظُّلَمَ، وَ قُدْوَةً

O Allah bless Muḥammad and his Family and bless Muḥammad ibn ʿAlī, pure and Godwary, pious and steadfast, refined and blameless guide of the *ummah*, the heir of the Imams, the storehouse of God's mercy, the fountainhead of wisdom, the dispenser of God's bounty, the counterpart of the Qur'ān with respect to the duty of obedience, one of the Prophet's successors with respect to dedication and worship, Your highest testament, Your exalted likeness, Your fairest word, who summoned and guided to You and whom You had appointed as a guidepost for Your servants, interpreter of Your scripture, executor of Your ordinances, defender of Your faith, testament to Your creatures, a light with which You dispel darkness, an exemplar through whom You dispense guidance and an intercessor through whom one may reach paradise!

تُدْرَكُ بِهَا الْهِدَايَةُ، وَ شَفِيعًا تُنَالُ بِهِ الْجَنَّةُ.

O Allah, by virtue of his due humbleness before You and his total awe for You, bless him well beyond the blessing You have granted to any of Your favourite servants You are pleased with whose obedience and accepted their service, and convey to him greetings and *salām* on our behalf, and grant us Your grace, kindness, forgiveness and approval by virtue of our friendship and love for him. Indeed You are the dispenser of eternal favours and a gracious pardon!

اَللّٰهُمَّ وَ كَمَا أَخَذَ فِي خُشُوعِهِ لَكَ حَظَّهُ، وَ اسْتَوْفَى مِنْ خَشْيَتِكَ نَصِيبَهُ، فَصَلِّ عَلَيْهِ أَضْعَافَ مَا صَلَّيْتَ عَلَىٰ وَلِيٍّ ارْتَضَيْتَ طَاعَتَهُ، وَ قَبِلْتَ خِدْمَتَهُ، وَ بَلِّغْهُ مِنَّا تَحِيَّةً وَ سَلَامًا، وَ آتِنَا فِي مُوَالَاتِهِ مِنْ لَدُنْكَ فَضْلًا وَ إِحْسَانًا، وَ مَغْفِرَةً وَ رِضْوَانًا، إِنَّكَ ذُو الْمَنِّ الْقَدِيمِ وَ الصَّفْحِ الْجَمِيلِ.

Then offer the prayer of *ziyārah*. After *salām* make this supplication:

O Allah, You are the Lord and I am Your servant. You are the Creator and I am Your creature. You are the Master and I am the slave. You are the Bestower, and I am the beseecher. You are the Provider and I am the provided one.

اَللّٰهُمَّ أَنْتَ الرَّبُّ وَ أَنَا الْمَرْبُوبُ، وَأَنْتَ الْخَالِقُ وَ أَنَا الْمَخْلُوقُ، وَ أَنْتَ الْمَالِكُ وَ أَنَا الْمَمْلُوكُ، وَ أَنْتَ الْمُعْطِي وَ أَنَا السَّائِلُ، وَ أَنْتَ الرَّازِقُ وَ أَنَا الْمَرْزُوقُ،

You are the All-able and I lack ability. You are the All-strong and I am weak. You are the Rescurer and I am the one who beseeches Your help. You are the Eternal One and I am ephemeral.

وَ أَنْتَ الْقَادِرُ وَ أَنَا الْعَاجِزُ، وَ أَنْتَ الْقَوِيُّ وَ أَنَا الضَّعِيفُ، وَ أَنْتَ الْمُغِيثُ وَ أَنَا الْمُسْتَغِيثُ، وَ أَنْتَ الدَّائِمُ وَ أَنَا الزَّائِلُ،

You are the All-great and I am a lowly being. You are the All-supreme and I am the puny one. You are the Master and I am Your servant. You are the Almighty and I am frail. You are the Most

وَ أَنْتَ الْكَبِيرُ وَ أَنَا الْحَقِيرُ، وَ أَنْتَ الْعَظِيمُ وَ أَنَا الصَّغِيرُ، وَ أَنْتَ الْمَوْلَىٰ وَ أَنَا الْعَبْدُ، وَ أَنْتَ الْعَزِيزُ وَ أَنَا الذَّلِيلُ، وَ أَنْتَ

الرَّفِيعُ وَ أَنَا الْوَضِيعُ،

High and I am lowly.

وَ أَنْتَ الْمُدَبِّرُ وَ أَنَا الْمُدَبَّرُ، وَ أَنْتَ الْبَاقِي
وَ أَنَا الْفَانِي، وَ أَنْتَ الدَّيَّانُ وَ أَنَا الْمُدَانُ،
وَ أَنْتَ الْبَاعِثُ وَ أَنَا الْمَبْعُوثُ، وَ أَنْتَ
الْغَنِيُّ وَ أَنَا الْفَقِيرُ، وَ أَنْتَ الْحَيُّ وَ أَنَا
الْمَيِّتُ.

You are Providence and I am subject to Your providence. You are the Judge and I am subject to Your judgements. You are the Resurrector, and I am the one to be raised from the dead. You are the Self-sufficient and I am all-needy. You are the Living One and I am (essentially) devoid of life.

تَجِدُ مَنْ تُعَذِّبُ يَا رَبِّ غَيْرِى، وَ لَا أَجِدُ
مَنْ يَرْحَمُنِي غَيْرَكَ،

My Lord, You will find others besides me to punish, but I will not find anyone besides You to have mercy on me!

اَللّٰهُمَّ صَلِّ عَلٰى مُحَمَّدٍ وَ آلِ مُحَمَّدٍ، وَ قَرِّبْ
فَرَجَهُمْ، وَ ارْحَمْ ذُلِّي بَيْنَ يَدَيْكَ، وَ تَضَرُّعِى
إِلَيْكَ، وَ وَحْشَتِي مِنَ النَّاسِ وَ أُنْسِى بِكَ،

O Allah, bless Muḥammad and the Family of Muḥammad and hasten their relief. Have mercy on my abjectness before You and my entreaties to You, my estrangement from the people and my intimacy with You!

يَا كَرِيمُ ثُمَّ تَصَدَّقْ عَلَيَّ فِي هَذِهِ السَّاعَةِ
بِرَحْمَةٍ مِنْ عِنْدِكَ، تَهْدِى بِهَا قَلْبِي، وَ
تَجْمَعُ بِهَا أَمْرِى، وَ تَلُمُّ بِهَا شَعَثِي، وَ تُبَيِّضُ
بِهَا وَجْهِى، وَ تُكْرِمُ بِهَا مَقَامِى، وَ تَحُطُّ
بِهَا عَنِّي وِزْرِى، وَ تَغْفِرُ بِهَا مَا مَضَى مِنْ
ذُنُوبِي، وَ تَعْصِمُنِي فِيمَا بَقِيَ مِنْ عُمُرِى،
وَ تَسْتَعْمِلُنِي فِي ذَلِكَ كُلِّهِ بِطَاعَتِكَ وَ مَا
يُرْضِيكَ عَنِّي، وَ تَخْتِمُ عَمَلِي بِأَحْسَنِهِ، وَ
تَجْعَلُ لِي ثَوَابَهُ الْجَنَّةَ،

O Munificent One, grant me, this very hour, Your mercy, whereby You will guide my heart, compose my dissipated affairs, help me to get back on my feet, brighten my face, elevate my station, relieve me of my burden, forgive my past sins and protect me from sinning in what remains of my life. Employ me throughout all that in acts of obedience to You and in pursuits that You approve of. Let my last actions be the best of them, and appoint paradise to be my reward.

Set me on the path of the righteous. Help me to make the best use of Your gifts, even as You help the righteous to make the best use of the gifts You grant them. Do not ever take away any good You bestow upon me, nor ever let me relapse into an evil You have rescued me from. Never let my enemies and those who are envious gloat over my misfortunes. Never abandon me to my own devices even for the twinkling of an eye nor for a time shorter or longer, O Lord of all the worlds!

وَ تَسْلُكُ بِي سَبِيلَ الصَّالِحِينَ، وَ تُعِينُنِي عَلَىٰ صَالِحِ مَا أَعْطَيْتَنِي، كَمَا أَعَنْتَ الصَّالِحِينَ عَلَىٰ صَالِحِ مَا أَعْطَيْتَهُمْ، وَ لَا تَنْزِعْ مِنِّي صَالِحاً أَعْطَيْتَنِيهِ أَبَداً، وَ لَا تَرُدَّنِي فِي سُوءٍ اسْتَنْقَذْتَنِي مِنْهُ أَبَداً، وَ لَا تُشْمِتْ بِي عَدُوّاً وَ لَا حَاسِداً أَبَداً، وَ لَا تَكِلْنِي إِلَىٰ نَفْسِي طَرْفَةَ عَيْنٍ أَبَداً، وَ لَا أَقَلَّ مِنْ ذٰلِكَ وَ لَا أَكْثَرَ يَا رَبَّ الْعَالَمِينَ!

O Allah, bless Muḥammad and the Family of Muḥammad and enable me to see what is true as true, so that I may pursue it, and to see what is false as false, so that I may avoid it, and do not let it appear to me as ambiguous, so that I may follow my desires without guidance from You. Let it be my desire to obey You, take from me what will make me approved with You, and, by Your leave, guide me where the truth is subject to controversy. Indeed You guide whomever You wish to a straight path!

اَللّٰهُمَّ صَلِّ عَلَىٰ مُحَمَّدٍ وَ آلِ مُحَمَّدٍ، وَ أَرِنِي الْحَقَّ حَقّاً فَأَتَّبِعَهُ، وَ الْبَاطِلَ بَاطِلًا فَأَجْتَنِبَهُ، وَ لَا تَجْعَلْهُ عَلَيَّ مُتَشَابِهاً فَأَتَّبِعَ هَوَايَ بِغَيْرِ هُدًى مِنْكَ، وَ اجْعَلْ هَوَايَ تَبَعاً لِطَاعَتِكَ، وَ خُذْ رِضَا نَفْسِكَ مِنْ نَفْسِي، وَ اهْدِنِي لِمَا اخْتُلِفَ فِيهِ مِنَ الْحَقِّ بِإِذْنِكَ، إِنَّكَ تَهْدِي مَنْ تَشَاءُ إِلَىٰ صِرَاطٍ مُسْتَقِيمٍ

Then plead with God to grant your request, which will be granted, God willing.[1]

Third Ziyarah of Imam Muhammad al-Taqi (ʿa)

Shaykh Ṣadūq (*r*) has cited this *ziyārah* in the *Faqīh*.[2] He writes: "When

[1] *Biḥār*, xcix, 21-22, b 2, h 11 from Sayyid Ibn Ṭāwūs..

[2] *Kāmil al-Ziyārāt*, 301, b 100, h 1, whence *Biḥār*, xcix, 7, b 1, h 1. *Faqīh*, ii, 600-602, h 3209.

intending to perform the Imam's *ziyārah*, one should first take a bath and put on clean clothes. Then recite this *ziyārah* when greeting the Imam,

اَللّٰهُمَّ صَلِّ عَلٰى مُحَمَّدِ بْنِ عَلِيٍّ، اَلْإِمَامِ
التَّقِيِّ، اَلنَّقِيِّ الرَّضِيِّ، الْمَرْضِيِّ، وَ حُجَّتِكَ
عَلٰى مَنْ فَوْقَ الْأَرْضِ وَ مَنْ تَحْتَ الثَّرٰى،
صَلَاةً كَثِيرَةً نَامِيَةً زَاكِيَةً مُبَارَكَةً
مُتَوَاصِلَةً مُتَرَادِفَةً مُتَوَاتِرَةً كَأَفْضَلِ
مَا صَلَّيْتَ عَلٰى أَحَدٍ مِنْ أَوْلِيَائِكَ،

O Allah, bless Muḥammad ibn ʿAlī, the Godwary and immaculate Imam, who is pleasing to You and well-pleased with You, Your testament to those who live on the earth and those who are under the ground, with a blessing that is abundant, growing, enhancing, plenteous, continuous, uninterrupted, and perpetual, and with the best of what You have blessed any of Your *awliyā'*.

وَ السَّلَامُ عَلَيْكَ يَا وَلِيَّ اللّٰهِ، اَلسَّلَامُ عَلَيْكَ
يَا نُورَ اللّٰهِ، اَلسَّلَامُ عَلَيْكَ يَا حُجَّةَ اللّٰهِ،
اَلسَّلَامُ عَلَيْكَ يَا إِمَامَ الْمُؤْمِنِينَ، وَ وَارِثَ
عِلْمِ النَّبِيِّينَ، وَ سُلَالَةَ الْوَصِيِّينَ. اَلسَّلَامُ
عَلَيْكَ يَا نُورَ اللّٰهِ فِي ظُلُمَاتِ الْأَرْضِ،
أَتَيْتُكَ زَائِرًا عَارِفًا بِحَقِّكَ، مُعَادِيًا لِأَعْدَائِكَ،
مُوَالِيًا لِأَوْلِيَائِكَ، فَاشْفَعْ لِي عِنْدَ رَبِّكَ

Peace be to You, O *walī* of Allah! Peace be to you, O light of Allah! Peace be to you, O testament of Allah! Peace to you, O Imam of the faithful and heir to the knowledge of the prophets and descendent of the legatees! Peace be to you, O light of Allah in the darkness of the earth! I come to you as a pilgrim with the knowledge of your rights, hating your enemies and befriending your friends! So intercede for me with your Lord!

"Then ask Allah for the fulfilment of your needs. After this offer, in the chamber wherein is situated the grave of Imam Muḥammad al-Taqī (ʿ*a*), four *rakʿahs*, two as prayer of *ziyārah* for Imam Mūsā al-Kāẓim (ʿ*a*) and two as that for Imam Muḥammad al-Taqī (ʿ*a*). Do not pray at the head of the tomb of Imam Musā al-Kāẓim (ʿ*a*) which faces graves belonging to the Quraysh and it is not permissible to pray facing them."

The compiler says: It appears from Shaykh Ṣadūq's words that during his time the tombs of the two Imams were situated in different chambers with separate doors.

Common Ziyarahs of the Two Imams

These are of two kinds. The first kind of common *ziyārahs* are those which must be recited separately for each Imam.

(1) The illustrious scholar Jaᶜfar b. Qūlawayh al-Qummī, in *Kāmil al-Ziyārāt*,[1] cites a *ziyārah* from Imam ᶜAlī al-Naqī (*ᶜa*) that is to be recited separately for each of the two Imams (*ᶜa*).

Peace be to you, O *walī* of Allah. Peace be to you, O testament of Allah! Peace be to you, O light of Allah in the darkness of the earth! Peace to you, concerning whom Allah's decision superseded His edict! I come to you as a pilgrim, knowing your rights, hating your enemies and befriending your friends. My master, intercede in my favour with your Lord!	اَلسَّلَامُ عَلَيْكَ يَا وَلِيَّ اللهِ، اَلسَّلَامُ عَلَيْكَ يَا حُجَّةَ اللهِ، اَلسَّلَامُ عَلَيْكَ يَا نُورَ اللهِ فِي ظُلُمَاتِ الْأَرْضِ، اَلسَّلَامُ عَلَيْكَ يَا مَنْ بَدَا لِلّٰهِ فِي شَأْنِهِ، أَتَيْتُكَ زَائِرًا عَارِفًا بِحَقِّكَ، مُعَادِيًا لِأَعْدَائِكَ، مُوَالِيًا لِأَوْلِيَائِكَ، فَاشْفَعْ لِي عِنْدَ رَبِّكَ يَا مَوْلَايَ!

This *ziyārah* is one of the most reliable ones and it has been cited by Shaykh Ṣadūq, Kulaynī and Ṭūsī with a slight difference of wording.

The second kind of common *ziyārahs* are those which jointly address the two Imams (*ᶜa*).

(2) Shaykh Mufīd, Shahīd Awwal and Muḥammad b. al-Mashhadī[2] have cited the following text of *ziyārah* to be recited at the tomb of the two Imams (*ᶜa*).

Peace be to you, O *walīs* of Allah! Peace be to you, O testaments of Allah! Peace be to you, O lights of Allah in the darkness of the earth!	اَلسَّلَامُ عَلَيْكُمَا يَا وَلِيَّيِ اللهِ، اَلسَّلَامُ عَلَيْكُمَا يَا حُجَّتَيِ اللهِ، اَلسَّلَامُ عَلَيْكُمَا يَا نُورَيِ اللهِ فِي ظُلُمَاتِ الْأَرْضِ،

[1] *Kāfī*, iv, 578, h 1. *Kāmil al-Ziyārāt*, 301-302, b 100, h 1 whence *Biḥār*, xcix, 7, b 2, h 1 & *Mustadrak*, x, 353, b 63, h 12168/1. *Tahdhīb*, iv, 82, 96, b 31, h 1, b 39, h 1. *Al-Mazār al-Kabīr*, 541, b 2.

[2] Shahīd Awwal's *Mazār*, 194, faṣl 6, h 31, whence and also from Mufīd and *al-Mazār al-Kabīr*, *Biḥār*, xcix, 13, b 2, h 7.

I testify that you communicated what you were charged with by Allah to deliver and you preserved what you were entrusted with, that you allowed what Allah has made lawful and forbade what He has made unlawful, that you upheld God's laws and followed the Book of Allah, that you bore all the torments for Allah's sake with patience and resignation until the last breath.

أَشْهَدُ أَنَّكُمَا قَدْ بَلَّغْتُمَا عَنِ اللهِ مَا حَمَّلَكُمَا، وَ حَفِظْتُمَا مَا اسْتُودِعْتُمَا، وَ حَلَّلْتُمَا حَلَالَ اللهِ، وَ حَرَّمْتُمَا حَرَامَ اللهِ، وَ أَقَمْتُمَا حُدُودَ اللهِ، وَ تَلَوْتُمَا كِتَابَ اللهِ، وَ صَبَرْتُمَا عَلَى الْأَذَى فِي جَنْبِ اللهِ مُحْتَسِبَيْنِ حَتَّى أَتَاكُمَا الْيَقِينُ،

I repudiate your enemies before Allah and seek nearness to Him through your *wilāyah*. I come to you as a pilgrim, knowing your rights, befriending your friends and despising your enemies, and possessing insight concerning the guidance vested in you and the error of those who opposed you! So intercede for me with your Lord, for indeed you are blessed with a great eminence and praiseworthy station with Allah!

أَبْرَأُ إِلَى اللهِ مِنْ أَعْدَائِكُمَا، وَ أَتَقَرَّبُ إِلَى اللهِ بِوِلَايَتِكُمَا، أَتَيْتُكُمَا زَائِرًا عَارِفًا بِحَقِّكُمَا، مُوَالِيًا لِأَوْلِيَائِكُمَا، مُعَادِيًا لِأَعْدَائِكُمَا، مُسْتَبْصِرًا بِالْهُدَى الَّذِي أَنْتُمَا عَلَيْهِ، عَارِفًا بِضَلَالَةِ مَنْ خَالَفَكُمَا، فَاشْفَعَا لِي عِنْدَ رَبِّكُمَا، فَإِنَّ لَكُمَا عِنْدَ اللهِ جَاهًا عَظِيمًا وَ مَقَامًا مَحْمُودًا.

Then kiss the noble ground of the shrine and place your right cheek on it. Then approach the head of the tomb and say,

Peace be to you, O testaments of Allah in His heaven and earth! Your servant and friend is a pilgrim at your tomb, seeking nearness to Allah through his visit to your shrines.

اَلسَّلَامُ عَلَيْكُمَا يَا حُجَّتَيِ اللهِ فِي أَرْضِهِ وَ سَمَائِهِ، عَبْدُكُمَا وَ وَلِيُّكُمَا زَائِرُكُمَا مُتَقَرِّبًا إِلَى اللهِ بِزِيَارَتِكُمَا،

O Allah, confer on me a worthy mention among your *awliyā'* and chosen ones, make me fond of their shrines, and admit me into their fold in the world and the

اَللّٰهُمَّ اجْعَلْ لِي لِسَانَ صِدْقٍ فِي أَوْلِيَائِكَ الْمُصْطَفَيْنَ، وَ حَبِّبْ إِلَيَّ مَشَاهِدَهُمْ، وَ اجْعَلْنِي مَعَهُمْ فِي الدُّنْيَا وَ الْآخِرَةِ يَا

Hereafter, O Most Merciful of the merciful!

أَرْحَمَ الرَّاحِمِينَ!

After this, offer the prayer of *ziyārah*, two *rakʿahs* for each of the Imams, and make any petitions to God that you wish to make.

The compiler says: As the Shīʿah had to observe intense *taqiyyah* in those days due to the dangers involved, the *ziyārahs* prescribed for these two Imams (*ʿa*) were brief for the sake of their safety from the harm of the tyrannical regimes of those days. However, if the pilgrim wishes to recite an elaborate text, the "*jāmiʿah*" *ziyārahs* are the best ones, especially the one which is related to Imam Mūsā al-Kāẓim (*ʿa*), as is evident from its report, and will be cited at the beginning of the section pertaining to *ziyārāt jāmiʿah* (p. 520).

When the pilgrim intends to leave the shrine city, he should bid the two Imams farewell by reciting one of the supplications that are recited at such times, such as the one cited by Shaykh Ṭūsī (*r*) in *Tahdhīb*.[1] He writes: "When intending to bid farewell to Imam Mūsā (*ʿa*), stand by his graveside and say,

Peace be to you, O my master, Abul-Ḥasan, and may Allah's mercy and His bounties be upon you! I entrust you to Allah and give you my *salām*. We have faith in Allah and the Apostle and whatever you have brought and guided us to. O Allah, write us among the witnesses!

اَلسَّلَامُ عَلَيْكَ يَا مَوْلَايَ يَا أَبَا الْحَسَنِ وَ رَحْمَةُ اللهِ وَ بَرَكَاتُهُ، أَسْتَوْدِعُكَ اللهَ وَ أَقْرَأُ عَلَيْكَ اَلسَّلَامَ، آمَنَّا بِاللهِ وَ بِالرَّسُولِ وَ بِمَا جِئْتَ بِهِ وَ دَلَلْتَ عَلَيْهِ، اَللّٰهُمَّ اكْتُبْنَا مَعَ الشَّاهِدِينَ.

Similarly, while bidding farewell to Imam Muḥammad al-Taqī (*ʿa*), he writes that one should say,[2]

Peace be to you, O my master, O son of the Apostle of Allah, may Allah's mercy and His bounties be upon you! I entrust you to Allah and give you my *salām*. We have faith in Allah and the Apostle and whatever you have

اَلسَّلَامُ عَلَيْكَ يَا مَوْلَايَ يَا ابْنَ رَسُولِ اللهِ وَ رَحْمَةُ اللهِ وَ بَرَكَاتُهُ، أَسْتَوْدِعُكَ اللهَ وَ أَقْرَأُ عَلَيْكَ اَلسَّلَامَ، آمَنَّا بِاللهِ وَ بِرَسُولِهِ وَ بِمَا جِئْتَ بِهِ وَ دَلَلْتَ

1 *Muqniʿah*, 478, b 26. *Tahdhīb*, vi, 83, b 32, whence *Biḥār*, xcix, 9, b 2, h 4..

2 *Muqniʿah*, 484, b 34. *Tahdhīb*, vi, 81, b 40, whence *Biḥār*, xcix, 9, b 2, h 4.

brought and guided us to. O Allah, write us among the witnesses! عَلَيْـــهِ، اَللّٰهُمَّ اكْتُبْنَا مَعَ الشَّـــاهِدِينَ.

Then beseech Allah not to make it your last occasion of *ziyārah* and to enable you to return. Then embrace the tomb and lay down each of your cheeks on it.

The Episode of Ḥajji Ali Baghdadi

The compiler says: It will be appropriate to cite here the episode of Ḥājjī ʿAlī Baghdādī, an upright and pious person, related by our teacher in his books, *Jannat al-Māwā* and *Najm al-Thāqib*. He remarks in *Najm al-Thāqib* that if there were nothing in that noble book except the authentic account of that episode, which contains many noteworthy points and is of recent occurrence, it would have been sufficient for its value and worth. After the introductory account, he quotes the said Ḥājjī as having said,

> A sum of eighty Tumans had accrued towards my obligation pertaining to the Imam's Share.[1] I went to Najaf Ashraf and paid 20 Tumans to His Eminence Shaykh Murtaḍā—the banner of guidance and piety, may Allah elevate his station—20 Tumans to His Eminence Shaykh Muḥammad Ḥusayn Mujtahid Kāẓimaynī, and 20 to His Eminence Shaykh Muḥammad Ḥasan Sharūqī. There remained 20 Tumans that I still owed, which I intended to pay on returning to Baghdad to His Eminence Shaykh Muḥammad Ḥasan Kāẓimaynī Āl-i Yā Sīn.
>
> On returning to Baghdad, as I wished to pay the debt as soon as possible, one Thursday I had the honour to visit the shrine of the Imams at Kāẓimayn (ʿ*a*). After the *ziyārah* I visited the Shaykh, may God protect him, and paid him part of the remaining 20 Tumans, promising him to pay the rest after selling off some of the merchandise when it was sent to me gradually. I decided to return to Baghdad in the afternoon that day. The Shaykh asked me to stay, but I excused myself for I had to pay the wages of workers at my wool-weaving factory. It was my custom to pay the weekly wages every Thursday afternoon.
>
> While returning, after I had covered a third part of the distance,

[1] I.e., the part of *Khums* known as *Sahm-e Imam*. The other part is *Sahm-e Sādāt*, the share of the sayyids..

I saw a dignified sayyid coming from Baghdad. On approaching, he greeted me and extended his hands for a handshake. "*Ahlan wa sahlan*," he said as we hugged and embraced each other. He wore a bright green turban and there was a large black mole on his blessed cheek.

"Ḥājj ᶜAlī, where are you bound?" he asked me, having halted. I told him that I had visited the Imams at Kāẓimayn and was returning to Baghdad. "Tonight is Friday eve! Go back!" He insisted. "*Sayyidī*," I said, "I can't do so." "Of course, you can," he replied, "Turn back, so that I may testify in your favour that you are one of the friends and followers (*mawālī*) of the Commander of the Faithful (*ᶜa*) and one of our friends, and so that the Shaykh, too, may give his testimony. God Almighty has commanded that one should take two witnesses."

What he had said was something that was already on my mind. I had wanted to request the Shaykh to write for me a testimony that I was one of the *mawālī* of the Prophet's Family (*ᶜa*), which I wished to be placed in my shroud at death.

I said to him, "What do you know about me, and what kind of testimony will you give?" He said, "How doesn't someone who receives the debt owed to him not know him who pays his debts?" "What debt?" I asked him. "What you have paid to my deputy," he replied. "Who is your deputy?" I inquired. "Shaykh Muḥammad Ḥasan," he answered. "He is your deputy?" I asked him "Yes, he is my deputy," he replied.

I wondered how this venerable sayyid had called me by name, though I did not know him. Then I thought that maybe he knew me and I had forgotten him. Then it occurred to me that perhaps the sayyid wanted to be given something from the Share of the sayyids and I was willing to give him something from the Share of the Imam. I said to him, "Sayyid, there was some money with me remaining from the Share of you folks and I have consulted His Eminence Shaykh Muḥammad Ḥasan concerning this matter to pay the Share of the sayyid with his permission." He smiled at me and said, "Yes, you have delivered part of our share to our deputies in Najaf Ashraf." I asked him if what I had paid had been accepted. "Yes," he replied.

Then it struck me that the sayyid spoke of our eminent scholars as "our deputies," and it appeared rather immoderate to me. But then I thought that the scholars were deputies authorised to receive the funds pertaining to the Share of the sayyids. These thoughts distracted me from realizing the identity of my companion.

Then he said to me, "Turn back and perform the *ziyārah* of my ancestor." I turned back. As we went along, his right hand was in my left. I noticed that a stream of clear water flowed to our right and there were trees of lemon, orange, and pomegranate as well as vines. We walked in their shade and there were fruits upon them, all at the same time, though it was not their season. "What is this stream, and what are these trees?" I asked him. He said, "They accompany everyone of our friends who visits our ancestor and visits us."

I said to him, "I want to ask a question. The late Shaykh ᶜAbd al-Razzāq was a teacher. One day when I was visiting him he told me that if someone were to spend all his lifetime keeping fast during days and performing worship at nights, and were he to perform forty *ḥajj* and forty *ᶜumrah* pilgrimages and then die between Ṣafā and Marwah, he would receive no reward for his works if he were not one of the *mawālī* of the Commander of the Faithful (*ᶜa*). Is that true?" "That is true," he replied, "By God, there is no reward for him."

Then I asked him concerning one of my relatives if he was one of the *mawālī* of the Commander of the Fatihful (*ᶜa*). "Yes, he is, and so is everyone that is related to you," he replied. Then I asked him another question: "The speakers at ceremonies held to mourn Imam Ḥusayn (*ᶜa*) narrate that Sulaymān Aᶜmash had questioned his neighbour concerning the *ziyārah* of the Doyen of the Martyrs (*ᶜa*) and was told that it was an innovation in religion (*bidᶜah*). Thereafter the neighbour saw in a dream a howdah being carried between the heaven and the earth. When asked as to who was in it, he was told that Fāṭimah Zahrah (*ᶜa*) and Khadījat al-Kubrā (*ᶜa*) were in it and as it was Friday eve they were going for the *ziyārah* of Imam Ḥusayn's shrine (*ᶜa*). Then he saw leaflets falling from the howdah on which was written, 'There is immunity from hellfire for the pilgrims of Ḥusayn who visit him on Friday eve. There is immunity for them on the Day of Resurrection.' Is this report authentic?" He answered, "Yes, it is true and genuine."

I asked him if it was true that those who perform the *ziyārah* of Imam Ḥusayn (*ᶜa*) on Friday eves are granted immunity. "Yes, by

God!" he said as his blessed eyes filled with tears.

"*Sayyidunā*," I said, "I have another question." "Do ask," he said. "In the year 1269 I had performed the *ziyārah* of Imam Riḍā (ᶜ*a*). At Dorood I met one of the Shurūqī Beduins who dwell in the east of Najaf Ashraf. I invited him to have dinner with me. Asked about the *wilāyah* of Imam Riḍā (ᶜ*a*), he said, 'It is paradise,' adding, 'Today is fifteenth day that I have eaten from provisions furnished by my master Imam Riḍā (ᶜ*a*). What business have the angels Munkir and Nakīr to approach me in the grave? My flesh and blood have grown with the food of the Imam at his guest house.' Is it true that Imam ᶜAlī ibn Mūsā al-Riḍā (ᶜ*a*) comes and rescues the dead from the hands of Munkir and Nakīr?" He replied, "Yes, by God, my grandfather has guaranteed safety."

Then I said, "*Sayyidunā*, I have a small question. Has my *ziyārah* of Imam Riḍā (ᶜ*a*) been accepted?" "It has been accepted, God willing," he replied. Then I asked him concerning Hājjī Muḥammad Ḥusayn, the garment merchant, the late Hājjī Aḥmad's son, whether his *ziyārah* was accepted. He was my companion in the journey to the shrine of Imam Riḍā (ᶜ*a*) and we had shared the expenses. "A righteous servant—his *ziyārah* is accepted," he answered. Then I asked him concerning a certain man from Baghdad who had accompanied us on this journey, if his *ziyārah* were also accepted. He remained silent. I asked him if he had heard my question. He did not reply. (Hājjī ᶜAlī recounted that they were several wealthy persons from Baghdad who throughout that journey were continually engaged in amusements and diversions, and that particular man had killed his mother.)

On the way, we reached the place in the environs of the blessed town of Kāẓimayn where there are orchards on both sides of the wide road. The strip of the road adjacent to the orchards on the right hand of someone coming from Baghdad had belonged to some sayyid orphans and the government had forcibly made it part of the road. Pious and cautious travellers from these two towns always avoided using that strip of land in that part of the road. However, I noticed him walking in that strip. I said to him, "Master, this place belongs to some sayyid orphans. It is not legitimate to use it." He said, "This place belongs to the Commander of the Faithful, our ancestor, his descendants and our children. It is permissible for our *mawālī* to use it."

Nearby on the right there was an orchard belonging to a man

known as Hājjī Mirza Hādī, a well-known wealthy Iranian who resided in Baghdad. I asked him, "*Sayyidunā*, is it true what they say, that the land of Hājjī Mirza Hādī's orchard belongs to Imam Mūsā ibn Jaᶜfar?" "What have you to do with this matter?" he said, avoiding a reply.

Then we reached the point where the canal that brings water from the Tigris to the orchards and farms in that area crosses the road. There the road divides in the direction of the town. One way is known as the King's Way. The other is called the Way of the Sayyids. When he turned towards the Way of the Sayyids, I said to him, "Let us take the other road," meaning the King's Way. But he said, "We will go by our own way."

As we went along, we had not gone more than a few steps that we found ourselves in the shrine courtyard, near the place where the shoes are left, without having seen the bazaar or the alleys that fall on the way. We entered the shrine portico from Bāb al-Murād on the eastern side towards the feet of the tomb. He did not stop at the door of the entrance hall, nor recited the appeal for admittance. After entering, he stopped at the threshold of the shrine chamber and said to me, "Recite the *ziyārah*." I replied that I was not adept at reciting. "Shall I recite for you," he asked me. Then he said,

أَ أَدْخُلُ يا اللهُ؟ السَّلامُ عَلَيْكَ يا رَسُولَ اللهِ، السَّلامُ عَلَيْكَ يا أَمِيرَ الْمُؤْمِنِين

(Shall I enter, O Allah? Peace be to you O Apostle of Allah! Peace be to you O Commander of the Faithful!)

Then he mentioned each of the Imams (ᶜ*a*), until he saluted Imam al-Ḥasan al-ᶜAskarī (ᶜ*a*) with these words,

السَّلامُ عَلَيْكَ يا أَبا مُحَمَّدٍ الْحَسَنَ الْعَسْكَرِيّ

(Peace be to you, O Abū Muḥammad al-Ḥasan al-ᶜAskarī!)

Then he asked me, "Do you know the Imam of your Era?" "How should I not know him!" I replied. "Salute your Imam," he told me. I said,

السَّلامُ عَلَيْكَ يا حُجَّةَ اللهِ يا صاحِبَ الزَّمانِ يا ابْنَ الْحَسَنِ

(Peace be to you O Testament of Allah, O Master of the Era, O Ibn al-Ḥasan!)

He smiled and said,

عَلَيْكَ السَّلامُ وَ رَحْمَةُ اللهِ وَ بَرَكَاتُهُ

(Peace be to you as well as Allah's mercy and His bounties!)

Then we entered the shrine and clinging to the holy tomb embraced it. Thereupon he told me to recite the *ziyārah* and I replied again that I was no reciter. "Shall I recite for you," he asked me, adding, "Which *ziyārah* do you want to be recited?" I replied that I would like him to recite the one which was superior. He remarked that the Ziyārah Amīn Allāh was superior, and began to recite it in this manner,

السَّلامُ عَلَيْكُما يا أَمِينَي اللهِ فِي أَرْضِهِ، و حُجَّتَيْهِ عَلَىٰ عِبادِهِ ...

(Peace be to the two of you, O God's trustees on His earth and His testaments to His servants...)

At that time they lit up the lamps within the shrine. I saw the candles burning, but within the shrine it was bright as if it were filled with sunlight. The candles appeared faint, like lamps lit in sunshine during day. However, I was so distracted that I did not pay attention to these clues.

After finishing the *ziyārah* we moved on from the foot of the tomb to its back on the eastern side. Halting there, he asked me, "Will you perform the *ziyārah* of Ḥusayn, my grandfather?" I replied that I will, seeing that it was Friday eve. Thereat he recited the Ziyārat Wāri<u>th</u>.

The call for the sunset prayer had just ended, and he said to me, "Offer your prayers and join the congregation."

Then he moved on to the mosque at the back of the blessed tomb where the congregational prayers were about to be held. He stood alone by himself on the right side of the imam who was leading the prayer, while I found a place for myself in the first row. When the prayers were over, I did not see him.

I came out from the mosque and looked around for him within the shrine chamber but could not find him. I wanted to give him some money and ask him to be my guest for the night. Then it struck me, who could that Sayyid be?

I realized the remarkable and inexplicable things that had

happened, including my consenting to his behest to turn back, despite having to attend to important business in Baghdad; his calling me by name though I had never seen him; his mention of the phrase 'our *mawālī*; his remark concerning the testimony; the orchards that appeared on our way with trees laden with out-of-season fruits, and other things. These convinced me that he was the Imam Mahdī (*ᶜa*). Also striking were his words while seeking admittance to the shrine, his questioning me after saluting Imam Ḥasan al-ᶜAskarī whether I knew my Imam of the Era, the smile he gave me and his reply on my saluting the Imam of the Era (*ᶜa*).

I approached the attendant who keeps the shoes and inquired about the sayyid. He had seen him leave and asked me if he were my companion. "Yes," I told him. Then I went to my host's place to stay for the night. In the morning I went to see His Eminence Shaykh Muḥammad Ḥasan and recounted for him what I had seen. He put his finger to his mouth and forbade me from divulging this secret, with the remark, "May God grant you success."

Accordingly, I kept it a secret and did not speak about the matter to anyone. A month after this episode, one day when I was in the blessed shrine a dignified sayyid approached me and asked what I had seen, referring to that day's incident. I denied having seen anything. He repeated his question and I was emphatic in my denial. After that he disappeared and I did not see him again.[1]

Section Two

Visit to the Baratha Mosque

The Barāthā Mosque is one of the well-known and highly-regarded mosques. It is situated midway between Baghdad and Kāẓimayn on the route commonly taken by the pilgrims. Yet most of them fail to partake of its blessing due to their indifference, despite many of its reported virtues. Yāqūt al-Ḥamawī, a historian of the 7th/13th century (d. 626/1228), writes in his book *Muᶜjam al-Buldān*,[2]

> Barāthā used to be a locality of Baghdad, to the south of Karkh and Bāb Muḥawwal. It had a central mosque (*jāmiᶜ*) where the Shīᶜah used to offer prayer. Later it fell into ruins and there also remained no trace of the locality. The *jāmiᶜ* was completed in

1 *Najm al-Thāqib*, ii, 573-582.

2 *Muᶜjam al-Buldān*, i, 362-363.

329/[940-41] and sermons were established in it. Earlier it used to be a mosque where some Shīcītes used to gather and condemn the Companions. Al-Rāḍī Billāh raided the mosque and those who were there were caught and imprisoned, and the mosque was razed to the ground. The Shīcah reported the matter to Bajkam al-Mākānī, the chief of the nobles of Baghdad, who ordered it to be rebuilt, and had it extended and fortified. He had al-Rāḍī's name inscribed over its entrance. Prayers used to be held in it until after 450/[1058], since when it has fallen into oblivion until the present.

Barāthā was a village before the founding of Baghdad and it is claimed that cAlī (c*a*) passed through it while setting out for the Battle of Nahrawān against the Khawārij and that he offered prayers at the spot where the aforesaid mosque stands. It is also said that he entered a public bath that existed in the village.

To this Barāthā belongs Abū Shucayb al-Barāthī, the ascetic, famed for his worship and devoutness. He was the first to take up residence at Barāthā, in a hut where he used to worship. A maiden, daughter of an eminent secretary and a great man of the world, who had been brought up in palaces, passed by his hut. On seeing Abū Shucayb and his condition, she was fascinated and captivated by his piety. She came to Abū Shucayb and told him that she would like to be his servant. He said to her, 'If you desire to do so, you will have to cast away all your worldly belongings and divest yourself of what you are in order to be suitable for what you wish to be.' Giving up all her worldly possessions, she came to him in an ascetic's garb. He married her. On entering the hut, she saw a piece of mat of palm leaves where Abū Shucayb used to sit in order to protect himself from the damp ground. She said to him, 'I will not stay with you until you remove it, for I have heard from you that the earth says: "O Son of Man, place whatever barrier you wish between me and yourself, but know that tomorrow you will rest in my belly." ' Thereat Abū Shucayb threw it away. She remained with him for several years and the two of them worshipped God devotedly until death."

In my book *Hadīyat al-Zā'irīn* I have cited some of the reports concerning the virtues of this mosque.[1] There, we have remarked that the traditions disclose several virtues of this mosque, which are such that if any one of them were true of any mosque it would behoove

1 *Hadīyat al-Zā'irīn*, 61-65.

one to travel long distances in order to partake of the blessing of offering prayers therein and making supplications.

The first of these virtues is that God Almighty has decreed that no leader commanding an army will alight in that place except a prophet or his legatee.

Second, the place had been a home for Mary (ᶜ*a*).

Third, that place is associated with Jesus (ᶜ*a*).

Fourth, a spring exists there which had gushed forth for Mary (ᶜ*a*).

Fifth, the spring was miraculously disclosed by the Commander of the Faithful (ᶜ*a*).

Sixth, there exists a white stone in the place on which Mary had laid the child Jesus (ᶜ*a*).

Seventh, the white stone was miraculously retrieved by the Commander of the Faithful (ᶜ*a*), who relocated it at the *qiblah* of the mosque.

Eighth, the Commander of the Faithful (ᶜ*a*) and his two sons, Imam Ḥasan (ᶜ*a*) and Imam Ḥusayn (ᶜ*a*), had prayed in this mosque.

Ninth, the Imam stayed in that place for four days for the sake of the holiness of the spot.

Tenth, prophets, especially Abraham (ᶜ*a*), the dedicated friend of the All-beneficent (ᶜ*a*), have offered prayers in that place.

Eleventh, there exists a prophet's tomb, probably that of Joshua (ᶜ*a*), as according to the S̲h̲ayk̲h̲ his grave is at the Barāt̲h̲ā Mosque outside Kāẓimayn.

Twelfth, there occurred the miraculous return of the sun for the Commander of the Faithful (ᶜ*a*).

Despite all these merits, divine signs and the miracles of the Commander of the Faithful (ᶜ*a*), it is amazing that not one out of a thousand pilgrims who pass by repeatedly stops at this mosque to partake of its blessings, though it stands on their route.

If occasionally some of them do stop there and find the door of the mosque closed, they are unwilling to pay a small sum of money to have it opened for them and choose to forego its enormous blessings. Yet they are willing to spend huge amounts of money for sightseeing in Baghdad and visiting edifices built by tyrants, not to speak of the enormous sums they spend to buy the sinister and unclean wares of its Jews, as if for most of them their pilgrimage would remain incomplete without it. God help us!

Section Three

Ziyarah of the Deputies of the Imam of the Era (ᶜa)

Their names are:

Abū ᶜAmr ᶜUthmān b. Saᶜīd (al-ᶜAmrawī) al-Asadī,

Abū Jaᶜfar Muḥammad b. ᶜUthmān,

Abū al-Qāsim Ḥusayn b. Rūḥ Nawbakhtī, and

Abū al-Ḥasan ᶜAlī b. Muḥammad al-Samurī, may Allah be pleased with them.

One of the duties of the pilgrims during their stay at Kāẓimayn is to visit Baghdad in order to perform the *ziyārah* of the four special deputies of the Imam of the Era (*ᶜa*). Had each of them been buried in separate distant towns, it would have been appropriate for one to travel long distances and put up with the toils of journey to obtain the blessing of visiting their shrines. That is because none among the close companions of the Imams (*ᶜa*) enjoys the high station possessed by them. For nearly seventy years they held that office, representing the Imam (*ᶜa*) and mediating between him and his followers, and many unusual and miraculous events took place at their hands. It is said that some scholars even believed that they were preserved from error (*ᶜiṣmah*).

Obviously, in the same way as those venerable personages were intermediaries in their lives between the Master of the Era (*ᶜa*) and his followers and it was among their duties to convey the messages and petitions of the people to him, so also even now they hold the same noble office and the people's petitions, which are written in difficult and testing circumstances, reach him through them, as has been established in its appropriate place. Their merits and virtues are more than can be mentioned here, and what has been said is sufficient to urge the pilgrims to pay them a visit.

As for the manner of their *ziyārah*, it has been described by Shaykh Ṭūsī (*r*) in *Tahdhīb* and Sayyid ibn Ṭāwūs (*r*) in *Miṣbāḥ al-Zā'ir* and attributed to Janāb Abū al-Qāsim Ḥusayn ibn Rūḥ (*r*), who has mentioned it as follows.[1]

First one should salute the Apostle of Allah and after him the Commander of the Faithful, Khadījat al-Kubrā, Fāṭimah Zahrā', Imam al-Ḥasan, Imam al-Ḥusayn and each of the Imams up to the Imam of

1 *Tahdhīb*, vi, 118, whence *Wāfī*, xiv, 1590, b 3, h 314664. *Biḥār*, xcix, 292, b 5, from Ibn Ṭāwūs.

the Era, may peace be upon them. After this, while mentioning the name of the personage whose tomb is visited and that of his father in the following text, say,

اَلسَّلاَمُ عَلَيْكَ يَا فُلاَنَ بْنَ فُلاَنٍ، أَشْهَدُ أَنَّكَ بَابُ الْمَوْلٰى، أَدَّيْتَ عَنْهُ وَ أَدَّيْتَ إِلَيْهِ، مَا خَالَفْتَهُ وَ لاَ خَالَفْتَ عَلَيْهِ، قُمْتَ خَاصًّا وَ انْصَرَفْتَ سَابِقًا، جِئْتُكَ عَارِفًا بِالْحَقِّ الَّذِى أَنْتَ عَلَيْهِ، وَ أَنَّكَ مَا خُنْتَ فِى التَّأْدِيَةِ وَ السِّفَارَةِ،

Peace be to you, O ... son of ...! I testify that you were the intermediary of the Master and that you carried out the tasks you were entrusted by him and fulfilled your duties to him. You did not oppose him, nor did you dispute concerning him. You acted as the Imam's special deputy and departed from the world as his foremost follower. I come to you convinced of the truth you had faith in and that you did not breach the trust placed in you in carrying out your duties as an emissary.

اَلسَّلاَمُ عَلَيْكَ مِنْ بَابٍ مَا أَوْسَعَهُ [أَوْسَعَكَ]، وَ مِنْ سَفِيرٍ مَا آمَنَكَ، وَ مِنْ ثِقَةٍ مَا أَمْكَنَكَ، أَشْهَدُ أَنَّ اللّٰهَ اخْتَصَّكَ بِنُورِهِ حَتّٰى عَايَنْتَ الشَّخْصَ، فَأَدَّيْتَ عَنْهُ وَ أَدَّيْتَ إِلَيْهِ.

Peace be to you, as you were an accessible intermediary, a trustworthy emissary, and a steadfast source of reliance. I testify that Allah singled you out for His light, so that you saw his person, and carried out your duties on his behalf and toward him!

After this again salute the Apostle of Allah and all the aforementioned members of his Family until the Master of the Era (ʿ*a*) and say,

جِئْتُكَ مُخْلِصًا بِتَوْحِيدِ اللّٰهِ وَ مُوَالاَةِ أَوْلِيَائِهِ، وَ الْبَرَاءَةِ مِنْ أَعْدَائِهِمْ [أَعْدَائِهِ]، وَ مِنَ الَّذِينَ خَالَفُوكَ يَا حُجَّةَ الْمَوْلٰى، وَ بِكَ إِلَيْهِمْ [اللّٰهُمَّ] تَوَجُّهِى، وَ بِهِمْ إِلَى اللّٰهِ [إِلَيْكَ] تَوَسُّلِى.

I come to you, with exclusive faith in Allah's Oneness, while I befriend His *awliyā* and repudiate their enemies and those who are opposed you. O testament of my Master, I turn to them through you, and seek mediation with Allah through them!

Then supplicate and make petitions to God Almighty for fulfilment of your needs, which will be granted, God willing.

It is also desirable to visit the tomb of the great and esteemed scholar Thiqat al-Islām Muḥammad b. Yaᶜqūb al-Kulaynī (*r*) who was a leading authority of the Shīᶜah in his times and the most reliable and trusted of Shīᶜah scholars of *ḥadīth*. The noble *Kāfī*, which is the most precious heritage of the Shīᶜah, was compiled by him in a period of twenty years, thus doing a great service to Shīᶜī scholarship. It was due to his outstanding station that Ibn Athīr, after having named the Eighth Imam (*ᶜa*) as reviver of the Imāmiyyah faith at the head of the 3rd century, has considered him its reviver (*mujaddid*) at the outset of the 4th century. In our book *Hadīyat al-Zā'irīn* we have mentioned most of the scholars who are buried in the precincts of the holy shrines. Those who are interested should refer to that book.

Section Four

Ziyarah of Ḥadrat Salman (r)

One of the duties of the pilgrims arriving at Kāẓimayn is to visit Madā'in to perform the *ziyārah* of Salmān Muḥammadī, God's righteous servant, may Allah be pleased with him. He was one of the four foremost followers of Imam ᶜAlī (*ᶜa*) known as *al-Arkān al-Arbaᶜah* (the four pillars), and was honoured by the Prophet's remark,[1]

سَلْمَانُ مِنَّا أَهْلَ الْبَيْتِ

(Salmān is one of the members our Family.)

The Apostle of Allah (*ṣ*) has said about him,

سَلْمَانُ بَحْرٌ لا يُنْزَفُ وَ كَنْزٌ لا يَنْفَدُ. سَلْمَانُ مِنَّا أَهْلَ الْبَيْتِ يَمْنَحُ الْحِكْمَةَ وَ يُؤْتِي الْبُرْهَانَ

(Salmān is an inexhaustible ocean and an endless treasure. Salmān is one of our Family, who bestows wisdom and confers proofs.)[2]

The Commander of the Faithful (*ᶜa*) likened him to Luqmān the

[1] *Tafsīr Furāt*, 171, h 218. *ᶜUyūn Akhbār al-Riḍā*, ii, 64, b 31, h 282. *Majmaᶜ al-Bayān*, ii, 269, v, 285, viii, 126. *Tafsīr al-Ṣāfī*, i, 36. Ṭabarī's *Tafsīr*, xxi, 162. Ṭabarānī's *Muᶜjam al-Kabīr*, vi, 213. Ḥākim's *Mustadrak*, iii, 598. Haythami's *Majmaᶜ al-Zawā'id*, vi, 130. *Kanz al-ᶜUmmāl*, xi, 690, h 33320.

[2] *Al-Ghārāt*, ii, 823. *Ikhtiṣāṣ*, 341, whence *Biḥār*, xxii, 348, b 10, h 64.

Sage,[1] and Imam Jaᶜfar al-Ṣādiq (ᶜ*a*) considered him even superior to Luqmān,[2] while Imam Muḥammad al-Bāqir (ᶜ*a*) has counted him as one of the "percipient" (*al-mutawasimīn*) mentioned in the Qur'ān (15.75).[3]

Among things which can be inferred from the traditions is that he knew the Greatest Divine Name,[4] and was one of those to whom angels spoke (*muḥaddath*).[5] There are ten degrees of faith and he enjoyed the tenth degree.[6] He had knowledge of unseen things and foreknowledge of deaths. He had partaken of the gifts of paradise in this world itself.[7] It was said of him that paradise eagerly awaited[8] his arrival, and that he was loved by God and His Apostle (ṣ). The Prophet was enjoined by God Almighty to be affectionate towards four persons, Salmān being one of them.[9] Several verses of the Qur'ān were revealed commending him and his peers[10] and every time that Gabriel came to the Apostle of Allah (ṣ), he would ask the Prophet (ṣ) to give greetings to Salmān on God's behalf.[11] The Prophet (ṣ) was told to impart to Salmān the knowledge of future events, tribulations

1 *Al-Ghārāt*, i, 101. *Iḥtijāj*, i, 259, whence *Biḥār*, x, 121, b 8, h 2, xxii, 329, b 10, xxxiv, 317, b 34.

2 *Baṣā'ir al-Darajāt*, 17, b 9, h 13, whence *Biḥār*, xxii, 331, b 10, h 42, xxv, 12, b 1, h 22.

3 *Rijāl al-Kashshī*, 12, h 28, whence *Biḥār*, xxii, 349, b 10, h 69.

4 *Rijāl al-Kashshī*, 13, h 29. *Ikhtiṣāṣ*, 11, whence *Biḥār*, xxii, 346, b 10, h 59.

5 *Baṣā'ir al-Darajāt*, 322, b 6, h 4. ᶜ*Ilal*, i, 183, b 146, h 2. *Rijāl al-Kashshī*, 12, 15, 19, h 27, 34, 36, 44. Ṭūsī's *Amālī*, 407, majlis 14, h 914/62. Whence in *Wasā'il*, xxvii, 146, b 11, h 33443. & *Biḥār*, xxii, 326, 331, 350, b 10, h 31, 41, 68, 70, 72, 74, xxvi, 27, b 2, h 4.

6 *Khiṣāl*, ii, 447, 448, h 48, 49; *Rawḍat al-Wā*ᶜ*iẓīn*, ii, 280; whence *Biḥār*, xxii, 342, 350, b 10, h 52, 75, lxvi, 168, b 32, h 9, xcix, 291, b 5, h 2.

7 *Rijāl al-Kashshī*, 9, h 19. *Muhaj*, 5. *Dalā'il al-Imāmah*, 28. Whence *Biḥār*, xxii, 352, b 10, h 81, xliii, 66, b 3, h 59, xci, 226, b 39, h 2, xcii, 32, b 56, h 22.

8 *Al-Yaqīn*, 147, b 15, whence *Biḥār*, xxii, 331, b 10, h 43. *Kashf al-Ghummah*, i, 344.

9 *Kitāb Sulaym*, 941, h 78. *Ṣaḥīfat al-Riḍā*, 62, h 99. *Tafsīr Furāt*, 67, b 53, h 67/38. *Qurb al-Isnād*, 27. *Khiṣāl*, i, 253, 254, h 126, 127. ᶜ*Uyūn Akhbār al-Riḍā*, ii, 32, b 31, h 63 whence *Biḥār*, xxii, 326, b 10, h 27. *Rijāl al-Kashshī*, 10, h 21. *Ikhtiṣāṣ*, 9. Mufīd's *Amālī*, 124, majlis 15, h 2. *Rawḍat al-Wā*ᶜ*iẓīn*, ii, 283. Whence and other sources in *Biḥār*, xxii, 322, 323, 324, 326, 345, 353, b 10, h 10, 18, 19, 20, 27, 58, 82, xxvi, 63, b 1, h 146, xxxi, 185, xxxix, 11, b 71.

10 *Tafsīr al-Imām*, 120, h 63. *Tafsīr al-Qummī*, i, 255, ii, 34, 46, 301. *Shawāhid al-Tanzīl*, i, 413, 519. *Manāqib*, ii, 11. Whence in *Biḥār*, iv, 151, b 6, h 2, viii, 123, b 23, h 18, xxii, 44, b 37, xxii, 322, 323, 349, b 10, h 13, 14, 17 & *Mustadrak*, xvi, 53, b 14, h 19124/1.

11 *Ikhtiṣāṣ*, 221, whence *Biḥār*, xxi, 347, b 10, h 62.

as well as lineages.[1] He used to have exclusive nightly sessions with the Prophet (ṣ)[2] and he and the Commander of the Faithful (ᶜa) had taught him secrets of Divine knowledge which none else had the capacity and strength to bear. He had attained such a station that Imam Jaᶜfar al-Ṣādiq (ᶜa) said about him that,

أَدْرَكَ سَلْمَانُ الْعِلْمَ الْأَوَّلَ وَ الْعِلْمَ الْآخِرَ وَ هُوَ بَحْرٌ لا يُنْزَحُ وَ هُوَ مِنَّا أَهْلَ الْبَيْتِ

(Salmān has attained the knowledge of the first and the knowledge of the last. He is an inexhaustible ocean and one of us, the Prophet's Household.)[3]

For the purpose of motivating the pilgrims and urging them to perform his *ziyārah*, it is sufficient to reflect over his distinguished station among all the Prophet's Companions and the entire *ummah*. At his death, the Commander of the Faithful (ᶜa) made a nightly journey to Madā'in from Madīnah to wash and shroud his body with his own blessed hands and offered the funeral prayer for him along with many rows of the angels and returned to Madīnah the same night.[4] How ennobling is the love of the Prophet's Family, which raises a human being to such a station of greatness and glory!

As for the manner of performing his *ziyārah*, Sayyid ibn Ṭāwūs has cited four texts for the *ziyārah* of that personage. Here we will confine ourselves to citing only the first of them.[5] In *Hadīyat al-Zā'irīn* we have cited the fourth *ziyārah*, also cited by Shaykh Ṭūsī in *Tahdhīb*.

When intending to perform his *ziyārah*, stand at his graveside facing the *qiblah* and say,

Peace be to the Apostle of Allah, Muḥammad ibn ᶜAbdillāh, the Seal of the Prophets! Peace be to the Commander of the Faithful and the chief of the legatees! Peace be to the infallible	اَلسَّلامُ عَلَىٰ رَسُولِ اللهِ مُحَمَّدِ بْنِ عَبْدِ اللهِ خَاتَمِ النَّبِيِّينَ، اَلسَّلامُ عَلَىٰ أَمِيرِ الْمُؤْمِنِينَ سَيِّدِ الْوَصِيِّينَ، اَلسَّلامُ عَلَى

1 *Ibidem.*

2 *Sharḥ Nahj al-Balāghah*, xviii, 36, whence *Biḥār*, xxii, 391, b 11.

3 *Al-Ghārāt*, i, 101. Ṣadūq's *Amālī*, 252, majlis 43, h 8. *Ikhtiṣāṣ*, 11. *Rijāl al-Kashshī*, 12, 16, h 25, 37. *Bishārat al-Muṣṭafā*, 209. *Rawḍat al-Wāᶜiẓīn*, ii, 281. *Ṭarā'if*, i, 118, h 183. Whence and other sources in *Biḥār*, xxii, 318, 350, b 10, h 4, 73, b 11, h 11, xxiii, 111, b 7, h 19, xxxiv, 314, b 34, xcii, 176, b 105, h 23.

4 Shādhān's *Faḍā'il*, 86, whence *Biḥār*, xxii, 380, b 11, h 13; xxii, 284, b 11, h 21 from *Mashāriq al-Anwār*.

5 *Biḥār*, xcix, 287, b 5, h 1, from Ibn Ṭāwūs.

and rightly-guided Imams! Peace be to the archangels!

الْأَئِمَّةِ الْمَعْصُومِينَ الرَّاشِدِينَ، اَلسَّلَامُ عَلَى الْمَلَائِكَةِ الْمُقَرَّبِينَ .

Peace be to you, O companion of the Trusted Apostle of Allah. Peace be to you O friend of the Commander of the Faithful! Peace be to you, O repository of the secrets of the Blessed Masters! Peace be to you, O God's remainder from among the pious of the old! Peace be to you, O Abū ᶜAbdillāh and may Allah's mercy and His bounties be upon you!

اَلسَّلَامُ عَلَيْكَ يَا صَاحِبَ رَسُولِ اللّٰهِ الْأَمِينِ [الْأَمِينَ]، اَلسَّلَامُ عَلَيْكَ يَا وَلِيَّ أَمِيرِ الْمُؤْمِنِينَ، اَلسَّلَامُ عَلَيْكَ يَا مُودَعَ أَسْرَارِ السَّادَةِ الْمَيَامِينِ، اَلسَّلَامُ عَلَيْكَ يَا بَقِيَّةَ اللّٰهِ مِنَ الْبَرَرَةِ الْمَاضِينَ، اَلسَّلَامُ عَلَيْكَ يَا أَبَا عَبْدِ اللّٰهِ وَ رَحْمَةُ اللّٰهِ وَ بَرَكَاتُهُ،

I testify that you obeyed Allah as He had commanded You, and followed the Apostle as He had ordered you, that you befriended his successor as He had required of you, and that you summoned the people to honour his descendents as you had been taught, and that you knew the truth with conviction and confirmed it as He had commanded you!

أَشْهَدُ أَنَّكَ أَطَعْتَ اللّٰهَ كَمَا أَمَرَكَ، وَ اتَّبَعْتَ الرَّسُولَ كَمَا نَدَبَكَ، وَ تَوَلَّيْتَ خَلِيفَتَهُ كَمَا أَلْزَمَكَ، وَ دَعَوْتَ إِلَى الْإِهْتِمَامِ بِذُرِّيَّتِهِ كَمَا وَقَفَكَ [وَفَّقَكَ]، وَ عَلِمْتَ الْحَقَّ يَقِينًا وَ اعْتَمَدْتَهُ كَمَا أَمَرَكَ،

I testify that you are the door to al-Muṣṭafā's legatee and the way of approach to al-Murtaḍā, the testament of Allah, and Allah's trustee with respect to the Sciences of the Elect that you were entrusted with. I testify that you were one of the Prophet's Family and the noble ones chosen to assist the Prophet's legatee.

[وَ] أَشْهَدُ أَنَّكَ بَابُ وَصِيِّ الْمُصْطَفَىٰ، وَ طَرِيقُ حُجَّةِ اللّٰهِ الْمُرْتَضَىٰ، وَ أَمِينُ اللّٰهِ فِيمَا اسْتُودِعْتَ مِنْ عُلُومِ الْأَصْفِيَاءِ، أَشْهَدُ أَنَّكَ مِنْ أَهْلِ بَيْتِ النَّبِيِّ النُّجَبَاءِ الْمُخْتَارِينَ لِنُصْرَةِ الْوَصِيِّ،

I testify that you possessed the tenth degree of faith and overwhelming proofs and argu-

أَشْهَدُ أَنَّكَ صَاحِبُ الْعَاشِرَةِ وَ الْبَرَاهِينِ وَ الدَّلَائِلِ الْقَاهِرَةِ، وَ أَقَمْتَ الصَّلَاةَ، وَ

ments, and that you maintained the prayer, paid the *zakāt*, bade what is right and forbade what is wrong, discharged your trusts, worked sincerely for the sake of Allah and His Apostle, and bore patiently the torments for His sake until your last breath.	آتَيْتَ الزَّكَاةَ، وَ أَمَرْتَ بِالْمَعْرُوفِ، وَ نَهَيْتَ عَنِ الْمُنْكَرِ، وَ أَدَّيْتَ الْأَمَانَةَ، وَ نَصَحْتَ لِلَّهِ وَ لِرَسُولِهِ، وَ صَبَرْتَ عَلَى الْأَذَى فِي جَنْبِهِ حَتَّى أَتَاكَ الْيَقِينُ،
May Allah's curse be on those who denied your rights and downgraded your worth. May Allah's curse be on those who tormented you due to your attachment to your masters and harassed you due to your relations with the Prophet's Family. May Allah's curse be on those who blamed you for the sake of your allegiance to your masters. May Allah's curse be on the enemies of Muḥammad's Family, from humans and jinn, those belonging to the former generation and the latter ones, and may He mete out to them an amplified painful punishment.	لَعَنَ اللَّهُ مَنْ جَحَدَكَ حَقَّكَ، وَ حَطَّ مِنْ قَدْرِكَ، لَعَنَ اللَّهُ مَنْ آذَاكَ فِي مَوَالِيكَ، لَعَنَ اللَّهُ مَنْ أَعْنَتَكَ فِي أَهْلِ بَيْتِكَ، لَعَنَ اللَّهُ مَنْ لَامَكَ فِي سَادَاتِكَ، لَعَنَ اللَّهُ عَدُوَّ آلِ مُحَمَّدٍ مِنَ الْجِنِّ وَ الْإِنْسِ مِنَ الْأَوَّلِينَ وَ الْآخِرِينَ، وَ ضَاعَفَ عَلَيْهِمُ الْعَذَابَ الْأَلِيمَ،
May Allah's blessings be on you, O Abū ᶜAbdillāh! May Allah bless you, O companion of the Apostle of Allah, may Allah bless him and his Family and you. O friend of the Commander of the Faithful, may Allah bless your immaculate spirit and your pure body and may He, with His favour and compassion, unite us, at our death, with you in the station of our blessed masters, and may He gather us with them in their neighbourhood in the gardens of bliss!	صَلَّى اللَّهُ عَلَيْكَ يَا أَبَا عَبْدِ اللَّهِ، صَلَّى اللَّهُ عَلَيْكَ يَا صَاحِبَ رَسُولِ اللَّهِ صَلَّى اللَّهُ عَلَيْهِ وَ آلِهِ وَ عَلَيْكَ يَا مَوْلَى أَمِيرِ الْمُؤْمِنِينَ، وَ صَلَّى اللَّهُ عَلَى رُوحِكَ الطَّيِّبَةِ، وَ جَسَدِكَ الطَّاهِرِ، وَ أَلْحَقَنَا بِمَنِّهِ وَ رَأْفَتِهِ إِذَا تَوَفَّانَا بِكَ وَ بِمَحَلِّ السَّادَةِ الْمَيَامِينِ، وَ جَمَعَنَا مَعَهُمْ بِجِوَارِهِمْ فِي جَنَّاتِ النَّعِيمِ،

[صَلَّى اللهُ عَلَيْكَ] يَا أَبَا عَبْدِ اللهِ، وَ
صَلَّى اللهُ عَلىٰ إِخْوَانِكَ الشِّيعَةِ الْبَرَرَةِ
مِنَ السَّلَفِ الْمَيَامِينِ، وَ أَدْخَلَ الرَّوْحَ
وَ الرِّضْوَانَ عَلَى الْخَلَفِ مِنَ الْمُؤْمِنِينَ،
وَ أَلْحَقَنَا وَ إِيَّاهُمْ بِمَنْ تَوَلَّاهُ مِنَ الْعِتْرَةِ
الطَّاهِرِينَ، وَ عَلَيْكَ وَ عَلَيْهِمُ السَّلَامُ
وَ رَحْمَةُ اللهِ وَ بَرَكَاتُهُ.

May Allah bless you, O Abū ᶜAbdillāh! May Allah bless your brethren, the pious Shīᶜīs among our blessed predecessors and may He grant the later generations of the faithful delight and bless them with His approval. May He unite us and them with the immaculate progeny of the Prophet whom we hold dear. May peace be to you and them and may Allah's mercy and His bounties be upon you and them!

Then recite Sūrat al-Qadr seven times and make any supererogatory prayers that you wish.

When intending to leave, stand near the tomb and recite the following text in bidding farewell. This text has been cited by Sayyid ᶜAlī b. Ṭāwūs at the end of the fourth *ziyārah*.[1]

اَلسَّلَامُ عَلَيْكَ يَا أَبَا عَبْدِ اللهِ، أَنْتَ
بَابُ اللهِ الْمُؤْتَى مِنْهُ وَ الْمَأْخُوذُ عَنْهُ،
أَشْهَدُ أَنَّكَ قُلْتَ حَقًّا، وَ نَطَقْتَ
صِدْقًا، وَ دَعَوْتَ إِلَى مَوْلَايَ وَ مَوْلَاكَ
عَلَانِيَةً وَ سِرًّا، أَتَيْتُكَ زَائِرًا، وَ حَاجَاتِي
لَكَ مُسْتَوْدِعًا، وَ هَا أَنَا ذَا مُوَدِّعُكَ،
أَسْتَوْدِعُكَ دِينِي وَ أَمَانَتِي وَ خَوَاتِيمَ
عَمَلِي وَ جَوَامِعَ أَمَلِي إِلَى مُنْتَهَى أَجَلِي،
وَ السَّلَامُ عَلَيْكَ وَ رَحْمَةُ اللهِ وَ بَرَكَاتُهُ،
وَ صَلَّى اللهُ عَلىٰ مُحَمَّدٍ وَ آلِهِ الْأَخْيَارِ.

Peace be to you, O Abū ᶜAbdillāh! You are Allah's gateway by which He is approached and from which His knowledge is obtained. I testify that you declared the truth and spoke truthfully, summoning the people to your master and mine, publicly and privately. I have come to you as a pilgrim and I entrust you with my needs, and as I bid you farewell I commit to your care my faith, my trusts, the motives of my works and all my hopes till the end of my life. Peace be to you and may Allah's mercy and His bounties be on You! May Allah's blessings be upon Muḥammad and his Family, the chosen ones!

1 *Biḥār*, xcix, 291, b 5, h 2, from Ibn Ṭāwūs.

Then supplicate God ardently and leave.

The pilgrim visiting the tomb of Salmān has two more tasks to accomplish after his *ziyārah*. The first of them is to offer two *rakʿahs* of prayer or more at Ṭāq-e Kisrā, a place where the Commander of the Faithful (ʿ*a*) offered prayer. According to a report of ʿAmmār al-Sābāṭī, the Commander of the Faithful (ʿ*a*) came to Madā'in and visited the Ṭāq-e Kisrā accompanied by Dulaf b. Baḥīr.[1]

He prayed in that place and rising up said to Dulaf, "Come with me!" Accompanied by a group of the people of Sābāṭ, who were also present, the Imam made a tour of the palace of Kisrā making remarks to Dulaf about how things used to be during the times of the Khusros, and Dulaf would confirm what he said, with the remark, "By God, it was exactly as you say!" Dulaf said to the Imam, "Master, you know these places as if you had yourself put these things in their place."

It is reported[2] that when the Imam was going around Madā'in inspecting the ruins and relics of the Khusros, one of those present recited the following verse:

جَرَتِ الرِّيَاحُ عَلَى رُسُومِ دِيَارِهِمْ   فَكَأَنَّهُــــمْ كَانُوا عَلَى مِيعَــادِ

The wind blows on the ruins of their dwellings,
As if they had to keep a promise to leave everything behind!

The Imam said to him, "Why don't you recite these verses of the Qur'an,

كَمْ تَرَكُوا مِنْ جَنَّاتٍ وَ عُيُونٍ وَ زُرُوعٍ وَ مَقَامٍ كَرِيمٍ وَ نَعْمَةٍ كَانُوا فِيهَا فَاكِهِينَ كَذَلِكَ وَ

أَوْرَثْنَاهَا قَوْماً آخَرِينَ فَمَا بَكَتْ عَلَيْهِمُ السَّمَاءُ وَ الْأَرْضُ وَ مَا كَانُوا مُنْظَرِينَ

(How many gardens and springs did they leave behind! Fields and splendid places, and the bounties wherein they rejoiced! So it was; and We bequeathed them to another people. So neither the sky wept for them, nor the earth; nor were they granted any respite.)(44:25-29)

Then he said to them,

1 Shādhān's *Faḍā'il*, 70, whence *Biḥār*, xli, 213, b 111, h 27 & *Mustadrak*, iii, 448, b 54, h 3964/22, and in xviii, 168, b 5, h 22410/1 from ʿ*Uyūn al-Muʿjizāt*.

2 *Kanz al-Fawā'id*, i, 315, whence *Biḥār*, lxxv, 84, b 16, h 91. Warrām's *Majmūʿah*, ii, 280.

إِنَّ هَؤُلاءِ كَانُوا وَارِثِينَ فَأَصْبَحُوا مَوْرُوثِينَ لَمْ يَشْكُرُوا النِّعْمَةَ فَسُلِبُوا دُنْيَاهُمْ بِالْمَعْصِيَةِ

إِيَّاكُمْ وَ كُفْرَ النِّعَمِ لا تَحُلَّ [تَحِلَّ] بِكُمُ النِّقَمُ)

(Indeed, they were themselves heirs who left behind their legacy to be inherited by others. They were not grateful for God's blessings and so their worldly possessions were taken away because of their disobedience. Beware of being ungrateful for the blessings you enjoy, lest the Divine punishments befall you.)

Another thing is to visit the tomb of Ḥudhayfah b. Yamān, one of the eminent Companions of the Apostle of Allah (ṣ) and an intimate friend of the Commander of the Faithful (ᶜa). He had a special position among the Companions in that he knew the hypocrites (*munāfiqūn*) and their names. When he refrained from attending anyone's funeral prayers, the second caliph would not pray for him. During his rule Ḥudhayfah was the governor of Madā'in for years, after which he was replaced by Salmān.

Ḥudhayfah was restored to the office after Salmān's death and he retained it until the caliphate of Imam ᶜAlī (ᶜa). The Imam sent an epistle from Madīnah to the people of Madā'in, informing them about his assumption of the caliphate and confirming Ḥudhayfah in his position. Hudhayfah died at Madā'in and was buried there after the Imam (ᶜa) had left Madīnah for Baṣrah—where he confronted the rebels in the Battle of the Camel—and before his arrival in Kūfah.

Abū Ḥamzah al-Thumālī reports[1] that at the time of his death Ḥudhayfah called his son to his bedside and counselled him, exhorting him to put his advice into practice. "Cut off all hopes in relation to what is in the hands of the people, for therein lie richness and freedom from want. Do not look up to the people to meet your needs, for that is unremitting poverty. Live in such a manner that your today is better than yesterday. When praying, pray as if it were the last prayer of your life. Never do anything for which you will have to apologize."

The central mosque (*jāmi*ᶜ) of Madā'in is situated beside Salmān's shrine and it is named after Imam al-Ḥasan al-ᶜAskarī (ᶜa). It is not clear whether the mosque was built by the Imam or he had offered prayers there. The pilgrim should not miss the benefit of offering two *rak*ᶜ*ahs* as prayer of *taḥiyyah* in the mosque.

1 Ṣadūq's *Amālī*, 323, majlis 52, h 11, whence *Biḥār*, lxxv, 447, b 33, h 8.

Chapter Nine

The Ziyārah of Imam Riḍā at Mashhad

This chapter contains a description of the virtues of the *ziyārah* of our master and chief of the creatures, Abū al-Ḥasan ᶜAlī ibn Mūsā al-Riḍā, the Imam of humankind and jinn—may Allah bless him and his ancestors and descendents, the Imams of guidance—and the manner of its performance.

The virtues of the Imam's Ziyarah

These are more than can be recounted here. Here we will mention a few reports, most of which are cited from *Tuḥfat al-Zā'ir*.

(1) The Apostle of Allah (*ṣ*) is reported[1] to have said: "A piece of my heart will be buried in the land of Khorāsān. No believer will visit him without being destined by God Almighty to be admitted into paradise and his body rescued from hellfire."

According to another report,[2] he said, "A piece of my heart will be buried in the land of Khorāsān. God Almighty will relieve the distress of those who visit him and forgive the sins of the sinners who perform his *ziyārah*."

(2) According to a reliable report,[3] Imam Mūsā al-Kāẓim (*ᶜa*) said, "Those who perform the *ziyārah* of my son ᶜAlī will be granted by God, the Most High, a reward equal to that of seventy accepted *ḥajj* pilgrimages." "Seventy *ḥajj* pilgrimages!" said Sulaymān b. Ḥafṣ al-Marwazī, the narrator, who was amazed at the Imam's statement. Thereat the Imam said to him, "Yes, rather the reward of seventy thousand *ḥajj* pilgrimages." Then he added, "How often it happens that *ḥajj* pilgrimages performed are not accepted. One who visits his tomb and spends a night at his graveside is like someone who has visited God, the Most High, on His Throne." The reporter expressed greater astonishment at the Imam's words, whereat he told him,

1 *ᶜUyūn Akhbār al-Riḍā* (*ᶜa*), ii, 255, b 66, h 4,

2 *ᶜUyūn Akhbār al-Riḍā* (*ᶜa*), ii, 257-8, b 66, h 14, whence *Wasā'il*, xiv, 557, b 82, h 19814.

3 *ᶜUyūn Akhbār al-Riḍā* (*ᶜa*), ii, 259-260, b 66, h 20, whence *Biḥār*, xcix, 35, b 4, h 17. *Rawḍat al-Wāᶜiẓīn*, i, 234. *Jāmiᶜ al-Akhbār*, 30, b 14.

"Yes, on the Day of Resurrection there will be on the Throne of God, the Most High, four from the former and four from the latter generations. As for those from the former ones, they will be Noah, Abraham, Moses and Jesus, and the four from the latter generations will be Muḥammad, ᶜAlī, al-Ḥasan and al-Ḥusayn, may God's blessings and peace be on them. Then the lines will be drawn and there will be seated along with us the pilgrims of the graves of the Imams. Indeed the highest of them in rank and closest of them in reward will be pilgrims of the grave of my son, ᶜAlī."

(3) Imam ᶜAlī al-Riḍā (*ᶜa*) is reported[1] to have said, "There is a spot in Khurāsān which will one day be a place frequented by angels. Throngs of angels will continually descend there from the heaven and throngs will continue to ascend and this will go on until the time when the Trumpet is blown." He was asked, "O son of the Apostle of Allah, what spot is that?" The Imam replied, "It is in the land of Ṭūs. By God, it is one of the gardens of paradise. One who visits me in that place is like someone who has visited the Apostle of Allah (*ṣ*) and God, the Most High, will write for him a reward equal to that of a thousand *ḥajj* and a thousand *ᶜumrah* pilgrimages, and I and my forefathers will intercede for him on the Day of Resurrection."

(4) There is a report[2] received through several *ṣaḥīḥ* chains of narrators from Ibn Abī Naṣr al-Bazanṭī that he said, "I read in a letter of Abū al-Ḥasan al-Riḍā (*ᶜa*), 'Inform our followers that the *ziyārah* of my tomb equals a thousand *ḥajj* pilgrimages with God.' Later I asked Imam Muḥammad al-Taqī (*ᶜa*) concerning it. He replied, "Yes, by God, there is a reward of a million *ḥajj* pilgrimages for someone who visits him with the knowledge of his right."

(5) According to a report[3] with several reliable *isnād*, Imam ᶜAlī al-Riḍā (*ᶜa*) said, "On the Day of Resurrection I will come and rescue on three occasions from the terrors of that day those who visit my tomb despite its far distance: at the time when the records of deeds are given into the right hands and the left hands of their owners, at the

[1] Ṣadūq's *Amālī*, 63, majlis 15, h 7. *Faqīh*, ii, 585, h 3193, whence *Wasā'il*, xiv, 567, b 87, h 19836. *ᶜUyūn Akhbār al-Riḍā* (*ᶜa*), ii, 255-6, b 66, h 5. *Tahdhīb*, vi, 108, b 52, h 6. *Rawḍat al-Wāᶜiẓīn*, i, 233. *Jāmiᶜ al-Akhbār*, 31, b 14.

[2] Ṣadūq's *Amālī*, 119, majlis 25, h 3. *Faqīh*, ii, 582, h 3182. *Thawāb*, 98 & *ᶜUyūn Akhbār al-Riḍā* (*ᶜa*), ii, 257, b 66, h 10, whence *Biḥār*, xcix, 33, b 4, h 5. *Rawḍat al-Wāᶜiẓīn*, i, 233. *Bishārat al-Muṣṭafā*, 22. *Jāmiᶜ al-Akhbār*, 29, 32, b 14.

[3] *Kāmil al-Ziyārāt*, 304, b 101, h 4. *ᶜUyūn Akhbār al-Riḍā* (*ᶜa*), ii, 255, b 66, h 2. *Khiṣāl*, i, 167, h 220. *Jāmiᶜ al-Akhbār*, 31, b 14.

bridge over hell (*ṣirāṭ*), and at the Scales [for weighing the deeds]."

(6) According to another report,[1] he said, "I will be killed wrongfully through poisoning and will be buried by the side of Hārūn. God will make my tomb the place of pilgrimage of my followers and lovers. Regarding whoever visits me in that alien land, it will be my duty to visit him on the Day of Resurrection. By Him who honoured Muḥammad (ṣ) with prophethood and chose him over His entire creation, none of you will offer two *rakᶜahs* of prayer at my graveside without deserving forgiveness from God, Almighty and Glorious, on the day that he will encounter Him. By Him who honoured us with the Imamate after Muḥammad (ṣ) and singled us out to be his successors and legatees, the visitor to my grave will the most honoured of guests with God on the Day of Resurrection. God, the Most High, will rescue from hellfire the body of any faithful person whose face is wet by so much as a single drop of rain while visiting my tomb."

(7) According to a report[2] with reliable *isnād*, Muḥammad b. Sulaymān asked Imam Muḥammad al-Taqī (*ᶜa*) concerning someone who completes the duty of *ḥajj*, having performed *ᶜumrah* followed by *ḥajj tamattuᶜ*. After *ḥajj* this person arrives in Madīnah and performs the *ziyārah* of the Apostle of Allah (ṣ). Then he proceeds to the shrine of the Commander of the Faithful (*ᶜa*) and performs his *ziyārah* with the knowledge of his rights and being aware that he is God's testament of to His creation and the gateway through which God is to be approached. Then he comes to the shrine of Abū ᶜAbdillāh al-Ḥusayn (*ᶜa*) and performs his *ziyārah*. Then he travels to Baghdad and performs the *ziyārah* of Abū al-Ḥasan Mūsā (*ᶜa*) and after that returns to his town. If God provides him with the means to perform *ḥajj* again, is it preferable for him to go for *ḥajj* or to depart for Khorāsān and to perform the *ziyārah* of ᶜAlī ibn Mūsā al-Riḍā (*ᶜa*), his father? The Imam replied, "It is preferable for him to go to Khorāsān and perform the *ziyārah* of my father. But that is in the month of Rajab, and it is not appropriate to do that during these days, as it will expose you and us to defamation by the rulers."

(8) In his book *Man Lā Yaḥḍuruh al-Faqīh*, Shaykh Ṣadūq cites a re-

1 *ᶜUyūn Akhbār al-Riḍā* (*ᶜa*), ii, 226-227, b 52, h 1,whence *Wasā'il*, xiv, 559, b 82, h 19820 & *Biḥār*, xcix, 36, b 4, h 24.

2 *Kāfī*, iv, 584, h 2, whence *Wasā'il*, xiv, 565, b 87, h 19834. *Kāmil al-Ziyārāt*, 305, b 101, h 7, whence *Mustadrak*, x, 359, b 67, h 12182/3. *ᶜUyūn Akhbār al-Riḍā* (*ᶜa*), ii, 258, b 66, h 15, whence *Biḥār*, xcix, 37, b 4, h 30. Ṭūsī's *Miṣbāḥ*, 820. *Tahdhīb*, vi, 84, b 34, h 2.

port[1] wherein Imam Muḥammad al-Taqī (ᶜa) is mentioned as having said, "Between the two hills of Ṭūs is a piece of land taken from paradise. Whoever enters it will be secure from hellfire on the Day of Resurrection."

(9) According to another report[2] the Imam said, "I guarantee on behalf of God, the Most High, that paradise will be the reward of those who visit my father's tomb at Ṭūs with the knowledge of his rights."

(10) In his book *ᶜUyūn Akhbār al-Riḍā*, Shaykh Ṣadūq reports[3] that a pious person saw the Apostle of Allah (ṣ) in a dream and asked him, "O Apostle of Allah, which one of your children should I visit for *ziyārah*?" The Prophet (ṣ) told him, "Some of my descendants have come to me after they were poisoned and some came after they were slain." "O Apostle of Allah, which of them should I visit, seeing that their shrines are scattered in different places," asked the man. "Visit the one who is nearest to you, who was buried in an alien land," said the Prophet (ṣ). The man said, "O Apostle of Allah, do you mean al-Riḍā?" "Say, 'May Allah bless him!' " (*Ṣallallāhu ᶜalayh*) said the Prophet, repeating these words thrice.

In *Wasā'il* and *Mustadrak* there are chapters dealing with the desirability (*istiḥbāb*) of obtaining blessings by visiting the shrine of Imam ᶜAlī al-Riḍā (ᶜa) and the shrines of the other Imams, as well as with the desirability of preferring the *ziyārah* of Imam ᶜAlī al-Riḍā (ᶜa) to that of Imam al-Ḥusayn (ᶜa) and other Imams (ᶜa) and to supererogatory *ḥajj* and *ᶜumrah*.[4] We confined ourselves to mentioning the above ten reports, as further details are beyond the scope of this book.

THE MANNER OF PERFORMING THE IMAM'S ZIYĀRAH

Among the several *ziyārahs* that have been narrated, the popular text is the one which is mentioned in reliable books and reported on the authority of the august scholar Muḥammad b. al-Ḥasan b. al-Walīd,

1 *Faqīh*, ii, 583, h 3185. *ᶜUyūn Akhbār al-Riḍā* (ᶜa), ii, 256, b 66, h 6, whence *Wasā'il*, xiv, 556, b 82, h 19810 & *Biḥār*, xcix, 37, b 4, h 25. *Tahdhīb*, vi, 109, b 52, h 8, b 34, h 2.

2 *Faqīh*, ii, 583, h 3186 & *ᶜUyūn Akhbār al-Riḍā* (ᶜa), ii, 256, b 66, h 7. Whence *Wasā'il*, xiv, 553, 556, b 82, h 19804, 19811 & *Biḥār*, xcix, 37, b 4, h 26.

3 *ᶜUyūn Akhbār al-Riḍā* (ᶜa), ii, 281, b 69, h 5, whence *Biḥār*, xlix, 329, b 23, h 5.

4 *Wasā'il*, xiv, 550-560, b 82, h 19798-19825; xiv, 562-568, b 84-87, h 19828-19838. *Mustadrak*, x, 355-357, b 64, h 12171/1-12177/7; x, 357-361, b 66-67, h 12178/1-12184/5

one of the teachers of S͟haykh Ṣadūq.[1] From Ibn Qūlawayh's work on *mazār* it appears that this text has been narrated from the Imams (ᶜ*a*).

First Ziyarah of Imam al-Rida (ʿa)

The manner of its performance, as described in *Man Lā Yaḥduruh al-Faqīh*, is that when intending to set out on the journey for the *ziyārah* of Imam ᶜAlī al-Riḍā (ᶜ*a*), one should take a bath before leaving one's house, and while taking the bath one should say,

O Allah, purify my heart, open my breast and make my tongue extol You and celebrate Your praise. Indeed there is no power except what derives from You. O Allah, make it a means of purification and cure for me!

اَللّٰهُمَّ طَهِّرْنِي وَ طَهِّرْ لِي قَلْبِي، وَ اشْرَحْ لِي صَدْرِي، وَ أَجْرِ عَلىٰ لِسَانِي مِدْحَتَكَ وَ الثَّنَاءَ عَلَيْكَ، فَإِنَّهُ لَا قُوَّةَ إِلا بِكَ، اَللّٰهُمَّ اجْعَلْهُ لِي طَهُورًا وَ شِفَاءً.

While leaving one's house, one should say,

In the Name of Allah, by Allah and towards Allah and toward the son of the Apostle of Allah. Allah is sufficient for me. I put my trust in Allah. O Allah, I turn to You, make You my goal and seek that which is with You!

بِسْمِ اللهِ وَ بِاللهِ وَ إِلَى اللهِ وَ إِلَى ابْنِ رَسُولِ اللهِ، حَسْبِيَ اللهُ، تَوَكَّلْتُ عَلَى اللهِ، اَللّٰهُمَّ إِلَيْكَ تَوَجَّهْتُ، وَ إِلَيْكَ قَصَدْتُ، وَ مَا عِنْدَكَ أَرَدْتُ.

On emerging from one's house, one should stand at the door and say,

O Allah, I turn my face toward you, and with You do I leave my family, property and whatever You have given into my possession. I put my reliance on You, so do not disappoint me, O You-who do not disappoint those who desire You and do not let perish those whom You protect.

اَللّٰهُمَّ إِلَيْكَ وَجَّهْتُ وَجْهِي، وَ عَلَيْكَ خَلَّفْتُ أَهْلِي وَ مَالِي وَ مَا خَوَّلْتَنِي، وَ بِكَ وَثِقْتُ، فَلَا تُخَيِّبْنِي، يَا مَنْ لَا يُخَيِّبُ مَنْ أَرَادَهُ، وَ لَا يُضَيِّعُ مَنْ حَفِظَهُ، صَلِّ عَلىٰ مُحَمَّدٍ وَ آلِ مُحَمَّدٍ، وَ احْفَظْنِي بِحِفْظِكَ،

[1] *Kāmil al-Ziyārāt*, 309, b 102, h 2. *Faqīh*, ii, 602, h 3210. ᶜ*Uyūn Akhbār, al-Riḍā*, whence *Biḥār*, xcix, 44, b 5, h 1. *Tahdhīb*, vi, 86, b 35. *Al-Mazār al-Kabīr*, 647, b 1.

فَإِنَّهُ لَا يَضِيعُ مَنْ حَفِظْتَ.

Bless Muḥammad and the Family of Muḥammad and guard me with Your protection; for those whom You protect do not perish!

On arriving in the holy city of Mashhad, when intending to proceed to the shrine, one should take a bath and while doing so say,

اَللّٰهُمَّ طَهِّرْنِي وَ طَهِّرْ لِي قَلْبِي، وَ اشْرَحْ
لِي صَدْرِي، وَ أَجْرِ عَلىٰ لِسَانِي مِدْحَتَكَ
وَ مَحَبَّتَكَ وَ الثَّنَاءَ عَلَيْكَ، فَإِنَّهُ لَا قُوَّةَ
إِلا بِكَ، وَ قَدْ عَلِمْتُ أَنَّ قِوَامَ دِينِي
التَّسْلِيمُ لِأَمْرِكَ، وَ الاتِّبَاعُ لِسُنَّةِ
نَبِيِّكَ، وَ الشَّهَادَةُ عَلىٰ جَمِيعِ خَلْقِكَ.

O Allah, purify me and purify my heart for me. Open for me my breast and make my tongue extol You and celebrate Your love and praise. Indeed there is no power except what derives from You. I know that the basis of my religion is compliance with Your commands, following the *sunnah* of Your Prophet, and bearing witness to all Your creation.

اَللّٰهُمَّ اجْعَلْهُ لِي شِفَاءً وَ نُورًا، إِنَّكَ عَلىٰ
كُلِّ شَيْءٍ قَدِيرٌ.

O Allah, make it healing and light for me. Indeed You have power over all things!

Then put on your cleanest clothes and, walking bare-footed and taking short steps, proceed with calmness and dignity, remembering God in your heart and saying "*Allāhu akbar; Lâ ilāha illallāh; Subḥānallāh; Wal ḥamdu lillāh.*" While entering the holy shrine, say,

بِسْمِ اللهِ وَ بِاللهِ وَ عَلىٰ مِلَّةِ رَسُولِ اللهِ
صَلَّى اللهُ عَلَيْهِ وَ آلِهِ، أَشْهَدُ أَنْ لَا إِلٰهَ إِلا
اللهُ وَحْدَهُ لَا شَرِيكَ لَهُ، وَأَشْهَدُ أَنَّ مُحَمَّدًا
عَبْدُهُ وَ رَسُولُهُ، وَ أَنَّ عَلِيًّا وَلِيُّ اللهِ.

In the Name of Allah, by Allah, and following the creed of the Apostle of Allah, may Allah bless him and his Family. I testify that there is no god other than Allah, He is One and has no partner. I testify that Muḥammad is His servant and Apostle and that ᶜAlī is Allah's *walī*.

Then approach the *ḍarīḥ* and facing it with the *qiblah* towards one's back, say,

أَشْهَدُ أَنْ لَا إِلَهَ إِلَّا اللهُ وَحْدَهُ لَا شَرِيكَ لَهُ، وَ أَشْهَدُ أَنَّ مُحَمَّدًا عَبْدُهُ وَ رَسُولُهُ، وَ أَنَّهُ سَيِّدُ الْأَوَّلِينَ وَ الْآخِرِينَ، وَ أَنَّهُ سَيِّدُ الْأَنْبِيَاءِ وَ الْمُرْسَلِينَ،

I testify that there is no god other than Allah, He is One and has no partner, and I testify that Muḥammad is His servant and Apostle, and that he is the master of the former and the latter generations and that he is the chief of the prophets and the apostles.

اَللَّهُمَّ صَلِّ عَلَى مُحَمَّدٍ عَبْدِكَ وَ رَسُولِكَ وَ نَبِيِّكَ وَ سَيِّدِ خَلْقِكَ أَجْمَعِينَ، صَلَاةً لَا يَقْوَى عَلَى إِحْصَائِهَا غَيْرُكَ،

O Allah, bless Muḥammad, Your servant, apostle and prophet, and the master of all Your creation, with a blessing whose extent none can reckon except You!

اَللَّهُمَّ صَلِّ عَلَى أَمِيرِ الْمُؤْمِنِينَ عَلِيِّ بْنِ أَبِي طَالِبٍ، عَبْدِكَ وَ أَخِي رَسُولِكَ، اَلَّذِي انْتَجَبْتَهُ بِعِلْمِكَ، وَ جَعَلْتَهُ هَادِيًا لِمَنْ شِئْتَ مِنْ خَلْقِكَ، وَ الدَّلِيلَ عَلَى مَنْ بَعَثْتَهُ بِرِسَالَاتِكَ، وَ دَيَّانَ الدِّينِ بِعَدْلِكَ، وَ فَصْلَ قَضَائِكَ بَيْنَ خَلْقِكَ، وَ الْمُهَيْمِنَ عَلَى ذَلِكَ كُلِّهِ، وَ السَّلَامُ عَلَيْهِ وَ رَحْمَةُ اللهِ وَ بَرَكَاتُهُ.

O Allah, bless the Commander of the Faithful, ʿAlī ibn Abī Ṭālib, Your servant and brother of Your Apostle, whom You chose with Your knowledge and appointed as guide for whoever of Your creatures that You wished, as a guide pointing to him whom You have sent with Your messages, a judge who judged by Your justice and decided by Your decrees between Your creatures, and was a custodian of all that, and may peace and Allah's mercy and bounties be upon him!

اَللَّهُمَّ صَلِّ عَلَى فَاطِمَةَ بِنْتِ نَبِيِّكَ، وَ زَوْجَةِ وَلِيِّكَ، وَ أُمِّ السِّبْطَيْنِ الْحَسَنِ وَ الْحُسَيْنِ سَيِّدَيْ شَبَابِ أَهْلِ الْجَنَّةِ، اَلطُّهْرَةِ الطَّاهِرَةِ الْمُطَهَّرَةِ التَّقِيَّةِ النَّقِيَّةِ الرَّضِيَّةِ الزَّكِيَّةِ، سَيِّدَةِ نِسَاءِ أَهْلِ الْجَنَّةِ أَجْمَعِينَ، صَلَاةً لَا يَقْوَى عَلَى إِحْصَائِهَا غَيْرُكَ.

O Allah, bless Fāṭimah, daughter of Your Prophet and spouse of Your *walī*, mother of the grandsons, al-Ḥasan and al-Ḥusayn, the doyens of the youth of paradise, the immaculate, pure and purified lady, the Godwary, blameless, admirable, and chaste mistress of all the women of paradise, with a blessing whose extent none can reckon except You!

O Allah, bless al-Ḥasan and al-Ḥusayn, the grandsons of Your Prophet and doyens of the youth of paradise, the upholders of Your faith amongst Your creatures and guides pointing to him whom You have sent with Your messages, judges who judged by Your justice, and decided by Your decrees between Your creatures.

اَللّٰهُمَّ صَلِّ عَلَى الْحَسَنِ وَ الْحُسَيْنِ سِبْطَيْ نَبِيِّكَ، وَ سَيِّدَيْ شَبَابِ أَهْلِ الْجَنَّةِ، اَلْقَائِمَيْنِ فِي خَلْقِكَ، وَ الدَّلِيلَيْنِ عَلٰى مَنْ بَعَثْتَ بِرِسَالاٰتِكَ، وَ دَيَّانَيِ الدِّينِ بِعَدْلِكَ، وَ فَصْلَيْ قَضَائِكَ بَيْنَ خَلْقِكَ.

O Allah, bless ʿAlī ibn al-Ḥusayn, Your servant, the upholder of Your religion amongst Your creatures, the guide to him whom You have sent with Your messages, the judge who judged by Your justice and decided by Your decrees amongst Your creatures, and the chief of the devout!

اَللّٰهُمَّ صَلِّ عَلٰى عَلِيِّ بْنِ الْحُسَيْنِ عَبْدِكَ الْقَائِمِ فِي خَلْقِكَ، وَالدَّلِيلِ عَلٰى مَنْ بَعَثْتَ بِرِسَالاٰتِكَ، وَدَيَّانِ الدِّينِ بِعَدْلِكَ، وَفَصْلِ قَضَائِكَ بَيْنَ خَلْقِكَ، سَيِّدِ الْعَابِدِينَ.

O Allah, bless Muḥammad ibn ʿAlī, Your servant and vicegerent on Your earth, the exponent of the knowledge of the prophets!

اَللّٰهُمَّ صَلِّ عَلٰى مُحَمَّدِ بْنِ عَلِيٍّ عَبْدِكَ وَ خَلِيفَتِكَ فِي أَرْضِكَ، بَاقِرِ عِلْمِ النَّبِيِّينَ.

O Allah, bless Jaʿfar ibn Muḥammad, the veracious Imam, Your servant, guardian of Your religion and Your testament to Your entire creation, the truthful and pious Imam!

اَللّٰهُمَّ صَلِّ عَلٰى جَعْفَرِ بْنِ مُحَمَّدٍ الصَّادِقِ عَبْدِكَ وَ وَلِيِّ دِينِكَ، وَ حُجَّتِكَ عَلٰى خَلْقِكَ أَجْمَعِينَ، اَلصَّادِقِ الْبَارِّ.

O Allah, bless Mūsā ibn Jaʿfar, Your righteous servant, Your spokesman for Your creatures, the proclaimer of Your judgements and Your testament to Your creatures!

اَللّٰهُمَّ صَلِّ عَلٰى مُوسَى بْنِ جَعْفَرٍ عَبْدِكَ الصَّالِحِ، وَ لِسَانِكَ فِي خَلْقِكَ، اَلنَّاطِقِ بِحُكْمِكَ، وَ الْحُجَّةِ عَلٰى بَرِيَّتِكَ.

O Allah, bless ʿAlī ibn Mūṣā al-Riḍā al-Murtaḍā, Your servant, the guardian of Your religion, the upholder of Your justice, the summoner to Your religion and

اَللّٰهُمَّ صَلِّ عَلٰى عَلِيِّ بْنِ مُوسَى الرِّضَا الْمُرْتَضٰى عَبْدِكَ وَ وَلِيِّ دِينِكَ، اَلْقَائِمِ بِعَدْلِكَ، وَ الدَّاعِي إِلَى دِينِكَ وَ دِينِ

آبَائِــهِ الصَّادِقِينَ، صَلاةً لَا يَقْوَىٰ عَلَىٰ إِحْصَائِهَا غَيْرُكَ.

the religion of his ancestors, the truthful guides, with a blessing whose extent none can reckon except You!

اَللّٰهُمَّ صَلِّ عَلَىٰ مُحَمَّدِ بْنِ عَلِيٍّ عَبْدِكَ وَ وَلِيِّكَ، اَلْقَائِمِ بِأَمْرِكَ، وَالدَّاعِي إِلَىٰ سَبِيلِكَ.

O Allah, bless Muḥammad ibn ᶜAlī, Your servant and *walī*, the upholder of Your ordinances and summoner to Your way!

اَللّٰهُمَّ صَلِّ عَلَىٰ عَلِيِّ بْنِ مُحَمَّدٍ عَبْدِكَ وَ وَلِيِّ دِينِكَ، اَللّٰهُمَّ صَلِّ عَلَى الْحَسَــنِ بْنِ عَلِيٍّ الْعَامِلِ بِأَمْرِكَ، الْقَائِمِ فِي خَلْقِكَ، وَ حُجَّتِكَ الْمُؤَدِّي عَنْ نَبِيِّكَ، وَ شَاهِدِكَ عَلَىٰ خَلْقِكَ، اَلْمَخْصُوصِ بِكَرَامَتِكَ، الدَّاعِي إِلَى طَاعَتِكَ وَ طَاعَةِ رَسُــولِكَ، صَلَوَاتُكَ عَلَيْهِمْ أَجْمَعِينَ.

O Allah, bless ᶜAlī ibn Muḥammad, Your servant and guardian of Your religion! O Allah, bless al-Ḥasan ibn ᶜAlī, the executor of Your ordinances, the upholder of Your religion among Your creation and Your testament who fulfilled his mission on behalf of Your Prophet and was a witness to Your creatures, whom You had singled out for Your favours, who summoned the people to obey You and Your Apostle, may Your blessings be upon them all!

اَللّٰهُمَّ صَلِّ عَلَىٰ حُجَّتِكَ وَ وَلِيِّكَ الْقَائِمِ فِي خَلْقِكَ، صَلاةً تَامَّــةً نَامِيَةً بَاقِيَةً تُعَجِّلُ بِهَــا فَرَجَهُ، وَ تَنْــصُرُهُ بِهَا، وَ تَجْعَلُنَا مَعَهُ فِي الدُّنْيَا وَ الْآخِرَةِ.

O Allah, bless Your testament and *walī*, the upholder of Your religion amongst Your creatures, with a blessing that is complete, enhancing and perpetual, whereby You hasten his relief and assist him, and put us by his side in the world and the Hereafter!

اَللّٰهُمَّ إِنِّي أَتَقَرَّبُ إِلَيْكَ بِحُبِّهِمْ، وَ أُوَالِي وَلِيَّهُمْ، وَ أُعَادِي عَدُوَّهُمْ، فَارْزُقْنِي بِهِمْ خَيْرَ الدُّنْيَا وَ الْآخِــرَةِ، وَ اصْرِفْ عَنِّي بِهِمْ شَرَّ الدُّنْيَــا وَ الْآخِرَةِ، وَ أَهْوَالَ يَوْمِ الْقِيَامَةِ.

O Allah, I seek nearness to You through their love and befriend their friends and despise their enemies. So grant me through them the good of the world and the Hereafter. Save me, through them, from the ills of the world and the Hereafter and from the terrors of the Day of Resurrection!

Then sit down near the head of the tomb and say,

اَلسَّلَامُ عَلَيْكَ يَا وَلِيَّ اللهِ، اَلسَّلَامُ عَلَيْكَ
يَا حُجَّةَ اللهِ، اَلسَّلَامُ عَلَيْكَ يَا نُورَ اللهِ فِي
ظُلُمَاتِ الْأَرْضِ، اَلسَّلَامُ عَلَيْكَ يَا عَمُودَ
الدِّينِ،

Peace be to you O *walī* of Allah! Peace be to you, O testament of Allah! Peace be to you, O light of Allah in the darkness of the earth! Peace be to you, O pillar of the faith!

اَلسَّلَامُ عَلَيْكَ يَا وَارِثَ آدَمَ صِفْوَةِ اللهِ،
اَلسَّلَامُ عَلَيْكَ يَا وَارِثَ نُوحٍ نَبِيِّ اللهِ،
اَلسَّلَامُ عَلَيْكَ يَا وَارِثَ إِبْرَاهِيمَ خَلِيلِ اللهِ،
اَلسَّلَامُ عَلَيْكَ يَا وَارِثَ إِسْمَاعِيلَ ذَبِيحِ اللهِ،
اَلسَّلَامُ عَلَيْكَ يَا وَارِثَ مُوسَى كَلِيمِ اللهِ،
اَلسَّلَامُ عَلَيْكَ يَا وَارِثَ عِيسَى رُوحِ اللهِ،

Peace be to you, O heir of Adam, the chosen of Allah! Peace be to you, O heir of Noah, the prophet of Allah! Peace be to you, O heir of Abraham, Allah's dedicated friend! Peace be to you, O heir of Ishmael, who was offered as sacrifice to Allah! Peace be to you, O heir of Moses, Allah's interlocutor! Peace be to you, O heir of Jesus, the spirit of Allah!

اَلسَّلَامُ عَلَيْكَ يَا وَارِثَ مُحَمَّدٍ رَسُولِ اللهِ،
اَلسَّلَامُ عَلَيْكَ يَا وَارِثَ أَمِيرِ الْمُؤْمِنِينَ
عَلِيٍّ وَلِيِّ اللهِ وَ وَصِيِّ رَسُولِ رَبِّ الْعَالَمِينَ،
اَلسَّلَامُ عَلَيْكَ يَا وَارِثَ فَاطِمَةَ الزَّهْرَاءِ،

Peace be to you, O heir of Muḥammad, the Apostle of Allah! Peace be to you, O heir of ᶜAlī, the Commander of the Faithful, the *walī* of Allah and legatee of the Apostle of the Lord of all the worlds! Peace be to you, O heir of Fāṭimah Zahrā!

اَلسَّلَامُ عَلَيْكَ يَا وَارِثَ الْحَسَنِ وَ الْحُسَيْنِ
سَيِّدَيْ شَبَابِ أَهْلِ الْجَنَّةِ، اَلسَّلَامُ عَلَيْكَ
يَا وَارِثَ عَلِيِّ بْنِ الْحُسَيْنِ زَيْنِ الْعَابِدِينَ،
اَلسَّلَامُ عَلَيْكَ يَا وَارِثَ مُحَمَّدِ بْنِ عَلِيٍّ بَاقِرِ
عِلْمِ الْأَوَّلِينَ وَ الْآخِرِينَ، اَلسَّلَامُ عَلَيْكَ

Peace be to you, O heir of al-Ḥasan and al-Ḥusayn, the doyens of the youth of paradise! Peace be to you, O heir of ᶜAlī ibn al-Ḥusayn, the ornament of the devout! Peace be to you, O heir of Muḥammad ibn ᶜAlī, exponent of the knowledge of the first and the last (of the prophets)! Peace be to you, O heir of

يَا وَارِثَ جَعْفَرِ بْنِ مُحَمَّدٍ الصَّادِقِ الْبَارِّ، اَلسَّلاَمُ عَلَيْكَ يَا وَارِثَ مُوسَى بْنِ جَعْفَرٍ، اَلسَّلاَمُ عَلَيْكَ أَيُّهَا الصِّدِّيقُ الشَّهِيدُ، اَلسَّلاَمُ عَلَيْكَ أَيُّهَا الْوَصِيُّ الْبَارُّ التَّقِيُّ،

Ja^c^far ibn Muḥammad, the veracious and the pious Imam! Peace be to you, O heir of Mūsā ibn Ja^c^far! Peace be to you, O truthful martyr! Peace be to you, O pious and Godwary legatee of the Prophet!

أَشْهَدُ أَنَّكَ قَدْ أَقَمْتَ الصَّلاَةَ، وَ آتَيْتَ الزَّكَاةَ، وَ أَمَرْتَ بِالْمَعْرُوفِ، وَ نَهَيْتَ عَنِ الْمُنْكَرِ، وَ عَبَدْتَ اللّٰهَ [مُخْلِصًا] حَتَّى أَتَاكَ الْيَقِينُ، اَلسَّلاَمُ عَلَيْكَ يَا أَبَا الْحَسَنِ وَ رَحْمَةُ اللهِ وَ بَرَكَاتُهُ .

I testify that you maintained the prayer, paid the *zakāt*, bade what is right and forbade what is wrong and worshipped Allah until the last breath! Peace be to you, O Abul Ḥasan and may Allah's mercy and His bounties be upon you!

Then clinging to the *ḍarīḥ*, say,

اَللّٰهُمَّ إِلَيْكَ صَمَدْتُ مِنْ أَرْضِي، وَ قَطَعْتُ الْبِلاَدَ رَجَاءَ رَحْمَتِكَ، فَلاَ تُخَيِّبْنِي وَ لاَ تَرُدَّنِي بِغَيْرِ قَضَاءِ حَاجَتِي، وَ ارْحَمْ تَقَلُّبِي عَلَى قَبْرِ ابْنِ أَخِي رَسُولِكَ صَلَوَاتُكَ عَلَيْهِ وَ آلِهِ،

O Allah, I have betaken myself to You from my homeland and journeyed across many a town expecting Your mercy! So disappoint me not, and turn me not away without fulfilling my need. Accept mercifully my visit to the grave of the son of Your Apostle's brother, may Your blessings be upon him and his Family.

بِأَبِي أَنْتَ وَ أُمِّي يَا مَوْلاَيَ، أَتَيْتُكَ زَائِرًا وَافِدًا عَائِذًا مِمَّا جَنَيْتُ عَلَى نَفْسِي، وَ احْتَطَبْتُ عَلَى ظَهْرِي، فَكُنْ لِي شَافِعًا إِلَى اللهِ يَوْمَ فَقْرِي وَ فَاقَتِي، فَلَكَ عِنْدَ اللهِ مَقَامٌ مَحْمُودٌ، وَ أَنْتَ عِنْدَهُ وَجِيهٌ.

O my master, dearer you are to me than my parents! I come to you as a pilgrim and visitor, seeking refuge from the offences I have committed against myself and the burden of sins that I have piled up on my back. So intercede for me with Allah on the day of my need and destitution. For you have a praiseworthy station with Allah and are eminent with Him!

Then, with the left hand extended over the tomb, raise your right hand and say,

O Allah, I seek nearness to You through my friendship and love for them. I love and follow the last of them like I love and follow the first of them, and forswear every favourite other than them.	اَللّٰهُمَّ إِنِّي أَتَقَرَّبُ إِلَيْكَ بِحُبِّهِمْ وَ بِوِلَايَتِهِمْ، أَتَوَلّٰى آخِرَهُمْ بِمَا تَوَلَّيْتُ بِهِ أَوَّلَهُمْ، وَ أَبْرَأُ مِنْ كُلِّ وَلِيجَةٍ دُونَهُمْ،
O Allah, lay Your curse on *those who changed Your blessing* (into unfaith and ingratitude), accused Your Prophet, contested Your signs, mocked Your appointed Imam and prompted those people to impose themselves on the Family of Muḥammad.	اَللّٰهُمَّ الْعَنِ الَّذِينَ بَدَّلُوا نِعْمَتَكَ، وَ اتَّهَمُوا نَبِيَّكَ، وَ جَحَدُوا بِآيَاتِكَ، وَ سَخِرُوا بِإِمَامِكَ، وَ حَمَلُوا النَّاسَ عَلٰى أَكْتَافِ آلِ مُحَمَّدٍ،
O Allah, I seek nearness to You by pronouncing anathema upon them and repudiating them in the world and the Hereafter, O All-beneficent!	اَللّٰهُمَّ إِنِّي أَتَقَرَّبُ إِلَيْكَ بِاللَّعْنَةِ عَلَيْهِمْ وَ الْبَرَاءَةِ مِنْهُمْ فِي الدُّنْيَا وَ الْآخِرَةِ، يَا رَحْمَانُ!

Then return towards the feet of the grave and say,

O Abul Ḥasan, may Allah bless you. May His blessings be on your spirit and body! You were patient, truthful and confirmedly veracious. May Allah slay those who slew you with their hands and tongues!	صَلَّى اللّٰهُ عَلَيْكَ يَا أَبَا الْحَسَنِ، صَلَّى اللّٰهُ عَلٰى رُوحِكَ وَ بَدَنِكَ، صَبَرْتَ وَ أَنْتَ الصَّادِقُ الْمُصَدَّقُ، قَتَلَ اللّٰهُ مَنْ قَتَلَكَ بِالْأَيْدِي وَ الْأَلْسُنِ.

Then supplicate fervently pronouncing anathema on the assassins of the Commander of the Faithful (*ᶜa*), al-Ḥasan (*ᶜa*), al-Ḥusayn (*ᶜa*) and those shed the blood of the Family of the Apostle of Allah (*ṣ*). Then passing from behind the tomb, proceed towards its head and offer there a two-*rakᶜah* prayer, reciting Sūrat Yā Sīn in the first and Sūrat al-Raḥmān in the second *rakᶜah*. Then supplicate fervently for yourself, your parents and all your brethren in faith. Stay as much as you like at the head of the graveside and offer your prayers near the Imam's tomb.

This is the best of the texts prescribed for *ziyārah* of the Imam. The phrase *sakhirū bi imāmika* (they mocked Your Imam) in the closing passage of this text, as cited in *Faqīh*, *ᶜUyūn* and the works of ᶜAllāmah Majlisī, appears as *sakhirū bi ayyāmika* (they mocked Your days) in *Miṣbāḥ al-Zā'ir*. The latter wording is also correct, or may be more appropriate considering that by the "days" are meant the Imams, as can be gathered from the report of Ṣaqr b. Abī Dulaf, which was cited in Chapter 5 of Book One (p. 170).

It is proper to pronounce the anathema in any language on those who were responsible for killing the Imams (ᶜ*a*). However, it is perhaps preferable to recite the following text excerpted from one of the supplications.[1]

O Allah, curse the assassins of the Commander of the Faithful, the killers of al-Ḥasan and al-Ḥusayn, may peace be to them, and the killers of the Family of Your Prophet! O Allah, curse the enemies of Muḥammad's Family and their killers and add to their punishment, abasement, disgrace and ignominy. O Allah, shove them forcibly towards the Fire, push them back into painful punishment, and gather them and those who followed them in throngs bound for hell!

اَللّٰهُمَّ الْعَنْ قَتَلَةَ أَمِيرِ الْمُؤْمِنِينَ، وَ قَتَلَةَ
الْحَسَنِ وَ الْحُسَيْنِ عَلَيْهِمُ السَّلَامُ، وَ
قَتَلَةَ أَهْلِ بَيْتِ نَبِيِّكَ، اَللّٰهُمَّ الْعَنْ أَعْدَاءَ
آلِ مُحَمَّدٍ وَ قَتَلَتَهُمْ، وَ زِدْهُمْ عَذَابًا فَوْقَ
الْعَذَابِ، وَ هَوَانًا فَوْقَ هَوَانٍ، وَ ذُلًّا فَوْقَ
ذُلٍّ، وَ خِزْيًا فَوْقَ خِزْيٍ. اَللّٰهُمَّ دُعَّهُمْ إِلَى
النَّارِ دَعًّا وَ أَرْكِسْهُمْ فِي أَلِيمِ عَذَابِكَ رَكْسًا
وَ احْشُرْهُمْ وَ أَتْبَاعَهُمْ إِلَى جَهَنَّمَ زُمَرًا.

According to *Tuḥfat al-Zā'ir*, Shaykh Mufīd has cited the following supplication as being *mustaḥab* for reciting after the prayer of *ziyārah* of Imam al-Riḍā (ᶜ*a*).[2]

O Allah, I beseech You! O Allah, Your sovereignty is eternal. Your might is enduring. Your author-

اَللّٰهُمَّ إِنِّي أَسْأَلُكَ يَا اللّٰهُ، اَلدَّائِمُ فِي
مُلْكِهِ، اَلْقَائِمُ فِي عِزِّهِ، اَلْمُطَاعُ فِي

1 Excerpted, apparently, with some difference of wording, from a longer text cited in *Muhaj*, 257, whence in *Biḥār*, lxxxii, 224, b 44, h 44 & *Mustadrak*, v, 140, b 5, h 5516/13.

2 *Biḥār*, xcix, 55-57, b 5, h 11.

سُلْطَانِهِ، اَلْمُتَفَرِّدُ فِى كِبْرِيَائِهِ، اَلْمُتَوَحِّدُ فِى دَيْمُومِيَّةِ بَقَائِهِ، اَلْعَادِلُ فِى بَرِيَّتِهِ، اَلْعَالِمُ فِى قَضِيَّتِهِ، اَلْكَرِيمُ فِى تَأْخِيرِ عُقُوبَتِهِ.

ity is obeyed. Your supremacy is unique. The eternity of Your Being is singular. You are just to Your creation. Your decrees are based on Your knowledge. You are magnanimous in putting off Your punishments.

إِلَهِى حَاجَاتِى مَصْرُوفَةٌ إِلَيْكَ، وَ آمَالِى مَوْقُوفَةٌ لَدَيْكَ، وَ كُلَّمَا وَفَّقْتَنِى مِنْ خَيْرٍ [بِخَيْرٍ] فَأَنْتَ دَلِيلِى عَلَيْهِ، وَ طَرِيقِى إِلَيْهِ، يَا قَدِيرًا لَا تَئُودُهُ الْمَطَالِبُ، يَا مَلِيًّا يَلْجَأُ إِلَيْهِ كُلُّ رَاغِبٍ، مَا زِلْتُ مَصْحُوبًا مِنْكَ بِالنِّعَمِ، جَارِيًا عَلَى عَادَاتِ الْإِحْسَانِ وَ الْكَرَمِ،

My God, my needs are addressed to You. My hopes wait on You. Whenever You have enabled me to obtain any good, You were my guide to it and my path toward it. O Omnipotent One who is not wearied by petitions! O Rich One who is the refuge of every seeker! I have always been endowed with Your blessings, proceeding in accordance with Your habitual kindness and munificence!

أَسْأَلُكَ بِالْقُدْرَةِ النَّافِذَةِ فِى جَمِيعِ الْأَشْيَاءِ، وَ قَضَائِكَ الْمُبْرَمِ الَّذِى تَحْجُبُهُ بِأَيْسَرِ الدُّعَاءِ، وَ بِالنَّظْرَةِ الَّتِى نَظَرْتَ بِهَا إِلَى الْجِبَالِ فَتَشَامَخَتْ، وَ إِلَى الْأَرَضِينَ فَتَسَطَّحَتْ، وَ إِلَى السَّمَاوَاتِ فَارْتَفَعَتْ، وَ إِلَى الْبِحَارِ فَتَفَجَّرَتْ،

I beseech You by Your power which permeates all things, by Your confirmed ordainments which You cause to be intercepted by the smallest of prayers, by Your glance that You cast on the mountains causing them to rise high, on the earths causing them to become levelled, on the heavens causing them to elevate, and on the oceans causing them to burst forth!

يَا مَنْ جَلَّ عَنْ أَدَوَاتِ لَحَظَاتِ الْبَشَرِ، وَ لَطُفَ عَنْ دَقَائِقِ خَطَرَاتِ الْفِكَرِ، لَا تُحْمَدُ يَا سَيِّدِى إِلَّا بِتَوْفِيقٍ مِنْكَ يَقْتَضِى حَمْدًا، وَ لَا تُشْكَرُ عَلَى أَصْغَرِ مِنَّةٍ إِلَّا

O You who are exalted and beyond the human faculties of perception and too subtle to be apprehended by the subtleties of thought! My Master, You are not praised without Your enabling and assistance, which require further praise! You are not thanked for the least of Your favours without that requiring further thanks. So when can anyone count all Your blessings, my God, and thank for Your gifts, my Master, or repay Your kindness?

اسْتَوْجَبْتَ بِهَا شُكْرًا، فَمَتَى تُحْصَى نَعْمَاؤُكَ يَا إِلَهِى؟ وَ تُجَازَى آلاؤُكَ يَا مَوْلَاىَ؟ وَ تُكَافَأُ صَنَائِعُكَ يَا سَيِّدِى؟

It is by Your blessing that the praisers praise You and the grateful give You thanks. You are relied upon to pardon sins, and You spread upon the erring the wings of Your clement veiling. You heal the injuries with Your hands.

وَ مِنْ نِعَمِكَ يَحْمَدُ الْحَامِدُونَ، وَ مِنْ شُكْرِكَ يَشْكُرُ الشَّاكِرُونَ، وَ أَنْتَ الْمُعْتَمَدُ لِلذُّنُوبِ فِي عَفْوِكَ، وَ النَّاشِرُ عَلَى الْخَاطِئِينَ جَنَاحَ سِتْرِكَ، وَ أَنْتَ الْكَاشِفُ لِلضُّرِّ بِيَدِكَ،

How many a vice You have kept hidden with Your forbearance until it has vanished, and how many a virtue Your grace has enlarged until Your reward for it became great! You are too exalted and great to be feared for anything except Your justice, and anything to be expected from You except Your kindness and grace! Favour me as demanded by Your grace, and forsake me not as demanded by Your justice!

فَكَمْ مِنْ سَيِّئَةٍ أَخْفَاهَا حِلْمُكَ حَتَّى دَخِلَتْ، وَ حَسَنَةٍ ضَاعَفَهَا فَضْلُكَ حَتَّى عَظُمَتْ عَلَيْهَا مُجَازَاتُكَ، جَلَلْتَ أَنْ يُخَافَ مِنْكَ إِلَّا الْعَدْلُ، وَ أَنْ يُرْجَى مِنْكَ إِلَّا الْإِحْسَانُ وَ الْفَضْلُ، فَامْنُنْ عَلَيَّ بِمَا أَوْجَبَهُ فَضْلُكَ، وَ لَا تَخْذُلْنِي بِمَا يَحْكُمُ بِهِ عَدْلُكَ،

My Master, were the earth to know about my sins it would make me sink into it, or the mountains would crash upon me, or the heavens would pluck me and tear me to pieces, or the seas would drown me!

سَيِّدِى لَوْ عَلِمَتِ الْأَرْضُ بِذُنُوبِي لَسَاخَتْ بِي، أَوِ الْجِبَالُ لَهَدَّتْنِي، أَوِ السَّمَاوَاتُ لَاخْتَطَفَتْنِي، أَوِ الْبِحَارُ لَأَغْرَقَتْنِي،

My Master, my Master, my Master! My Guardian, my Guardian,

سَيِّدِى سَيِّدِى سَيِّدِى، مَوْلَاىَ مَوْلَاىَ

my Guardian! Often have I stood as a guest in Your presence; so do not deprive me of what You have promised those who beseech You!

مَوْلاٰیَ، قَدْ تَكَرَّرَ وُقُوفِي لِضِيٰافَتِكَ، فَلاٰ تَحْرِمْنِي مَا وَعَدْتَ الْمُتَعَرِّضِينَ لِمَسْأَلَتِكَ،

O You who are known to the gnostics, are worshipped by the devout, and are thanked by the grateful! O Companion of those who remember You, You are praised by those who praise You, You are found by those who seek You, You are described by those who declare You to be the One, You are the beloved of those who love You, You are the succour of those who desire You, You are the goal of those who turn penitently to You!

يٰا مَعْرُوفَ الْعَارِفِينَ، يٰا مَعْبُودَ الْعَابِدِينَ، يٰا مَشْكُورَ الشَّاكِرِينَ، يٰا جَلِيسَ الذَّاكِرِينَ، يٰا مَحْمُودَ مَنْ حَمِدَهُ، يٰا مَوْجُودَ مَنْ طَلَبَهُ، يٰا مَوْصُوفَ مَنْ وَحَّدَهُ، يٰا مَحْبُوبَ مَنْ أَحَبَّهُ، يٰا غَوْثَ مَنْ أَرَادَهُ، يٰا مَقْصُودَ مَنْ أَنَابَ إِلَيْهِ،

The Unseen is known to none except You! There is none except You who can remove ills and evils! There is none except You who directs the world's affairs. There is none except You who forgives sins! There is none except You who creates the creation. There is none except You who sends down the rains! Bless Muḥammad and the Family of Muḥammad and forgive me, O Best of those who forgive!

يٰا مَنْ لاٰ يَعْلَمُ الْغَيْبَ إِلاّٰ هُوَ، يٰا مَنْ لاٰ يَصْرِفُ السُّوءَ إِلاّٰ هُوَ، يٰا مَنْ لاٰ يُدَبِّرُ الْأَمْرَ إِلاّٰ هُوَ، يٰا مَنْ لاٰ يَغْفِرُ الذَّنْبَ إِلاّٰ هُوَ، يٰا مَنْ لاٰ يَخْلُقُ الْخَلْقَ إِلاّٰ هُوَ، يٰا مَنْ لاٰ يُنَزِّلُ الْغَيْثَ إِلاّٰ هُوَ، صَلِّ عَلىٰ مُحَمَّدٍ وَآلِ مُحَمَّدٍ، وَاغْفِرْ لِي يٰا خَيْرَ الْغَافِرِينَ!

Lord, I seek Your forgiveness as one who is shamed! I seek Your forgiveness in hope! I seek Your forgiveness as one who is penitent! I seek Your forgiveness in eagerness! I seek Your forgiveness in fear and awe! I seek Your

رَبِّ إِنِّي أَسْتَغْفِرُكَ اسْتِغْفَارَ حَيٰاءٍ، وَأَسْتَغْفِرُكَ اسْتِغْفَارَ رَجَاءٍ، وَأَسْتَغْفِرُكَ اسْتِغْفَارَ إِنَابَةٍ، وَأَسْتَغْفِرُكَ اسْتِغْفَارَ رَغْبَةٍ، وَأَسْتَغْفِرُكَ اسْتِغْفَارَ رَهْبَةٍ، وَ

أَسْتَغْفِرُكَ اسْتِغْفَارَ طَاعَةٍ، وَ أَسْتَغْفِرُكَ اسْـتِغْفَارَ إِيمَانٍ، وَ أَسْتَغْفِرُكَ اسْتِغْفَارَ إِقْرَارٍ، وَ أَسْتَغْفِرُكَ اسْتِغْفَارَ إِخْلَاصٍ، وَ أَسْتَغْفِرُكَ اسْتِغْفَارَ تَقْوَىٰ، وَ أَسْتَغْفِرُكَ اسْتِغْفَارَ تَوَكُّلٍ، وَ أَسْـتَغْفِرُكَ اسْتِغْفَارَ ذِلَّةٍ، وَ أَسْتَغْفِرُكَ اسْـتِغْفَارَ عَامِلٍ لَكَ هَارِبٍ مِنْكَ إِلَيْكَ،

forgiveness as one who obeys You! I seek Your forgiveness as one who has faith in You! I seek Your forgiveness as one who admits his faults! I seek Your forgiveness sincerely! I seek Your forgiveness with an entreaty imbued with Godfearing! I seek Your forgiveness as one who trusts You! I seek Your forgiveness in lowliness! I seek Your forgiveness as one who works for You and who flees to You from You!

فَصَلِّ عَلَىٰ مُحَمَّدٍ وَ آلِ مُحَمَّدٍ، وَ تُبْ عَلَيَّ وَ عَلَىٰ وَالِدَيَّ بِمَا تُبْتَ وَ تَتُوبُ عَلَىٰ جَمِيعِ خَلْقِكَ، يَا أَرْحَمَ الرَّاحِمِينَ!

Bless Muḥammad and the Family of Muḥammad, and turn clemently to me and my parents inasmuch as You have turned before and continue to turn to all Your creatures, O Most Merciful of the merciful!

يَا مَنْ تَسَمَّىٰ (يُسَمَّىٰ) بِالْغَفُورِ الرَّحِيمِ، يَا مَنْ تَسَمَّىٰ بِالْغَفُورِ الرَّحِيمِ، يَا مَنْ تَسَمَّىٰ بِالْغَفُورِ الرَّحِيمِ، صَلِّ عَلَىٰ مُحَمَّدٍ وَ آلِ مُحَمَّدٍ، وَ اقْبَلْ تَوْبَتِي، وَ زَكِّ عَمَلِي، وَ اشْكُرْ سَعْيِي، وَ ارْحَمْ ضَرَاعَتِي، وَ لَا تَحْجُبْ صَوْتِي، وَ لَا تُخَيِّبْ مَسْأَلَتِي، يَا غَوْثَ الْمُسْتَغِيثِينَ!

O You who are called the All-forgiving and the All-merciful! O You who are called the All-forgiving and the All-merciful! O You who are called the All-forgiving and the All-merciful! Bless Muḥammad and the Family of Muḥammad and accept my repentance, purify my conduct, reward my efforts, have mercy on my entreaties, do not shut out my voice, and do not disappoint my petition, O Succour of all those who call for help!

وَ أَبْلِغْ أَئِمَّتِي سَلَامِي وَ دُعَائِي، وَ شَفِّعْهُمْ فِي جَمِيعِ مَا سَأَلْتُكَ، وَ أَوْصِلْ هَدِيَّتِي إِلَيْهِمْ كَمَا يَنْبَغِي لَهُمْ، وَ زِدْهُمْ

Convey my *salām* and prayers to my Imams and make them my intercessors concerning all that I have asked of You! Convey my gift to them in a manner that is

worthy of them and enhance it for them, as is worthy of You, so many times that none except You can count! There is no power or force except what derives from Allah, the All-exalted and the All-great! May Allah bless Muḥammad, the best of the Envoys, and his immaculate Family!	مِنْ ذَلِكَ مَا يَنْبَغِي لَكَ بِأَضْعَافٍ لَا يُحْصِيهَا غَيْرُكَ، وَ لَا حَوْلَ وَ لَا قُوَّةَ إِلَّا بِاللهِ الْعَلِيِّ الْعَظِيمِ، وَ صَلَّى اللهُ عَلَى أَطْيَبِ الْمُرْسَلِينَ مُحَمَّدٍ وَ آلِهِ الطَّاهِرِينَ .

ᶜAllamāh Majlisī, in *Biḥār*, has cited from an early Shīᶜī work a *ziyārah* of Imam ᶜAlī al-Riḍā (ᶜ*a*), known as *Jawādīyah.* At its end, one is told to offer the prayer of *ziyārah* and to perform the *tasbīḥ* as a gift to the Imam. Thereafter one is to recite the above-mentioned supplication which begins with the words *Allāhumma innî as'aluka, yâ Allāh, ad·dâ'imu...* Hence, whenever one performs that *ziyārah* in this holy shrine, one should not forget to recite this supplication as well.

SECOND ZIYARAH OF IMAM AL-RIDA (ʿA)

Ibn Qūlawayh reports[1] this *ziyārah* from one of the Imams (ᶜ*a*). According to it, on approaching the tomb of Imam ᶜAlī al-Riḍā (ᶜ*a*) one should say,

O Allah, bless ᶜAlī ibn Mūsā al-Riḍā al-Murtaḍā, the Godwary and immaculate Imam, Your testament to those who live on the earth's surface and those who lie buried under the ground, the veracious guide and martyr, with a blessing that is abundant, complete, growing, continuous, constant and uninterrupted, the best of what You have granted to any of Your *awliyā.*	اَللّٰهُمَّ صَلِّ عَلَى عَلِيِّ بْنِ مُوسَى الرِّضَا الْمُرْتَضَى، اَلْإِمَامِ التَّقِيِّ النَّقِيِّ، وَ حُجَّتِكَ عَلَى مَنْ فَوْقَ الْأَرْضِ وَ مَنْ تَحْتَ الثَّرَى، اَلصِّدِّيقِ الشَّهِيدِ صَلَاةً كَثِيرَةً تَامَّةً زَاكِيَةً مُتَوَاصِلَةً مُتَوَاتِرَةً مُتَرَادِفَةً، كَأَفْضَلِ مَا صَلَّيْتَ عَلَى أَحَدٍ مِنْ أَوْلِيَائِكَ .

[1] *Kāmil al-Ziyārāt*, 309, b 102, h 1, whence *Biḥār*, xcix, 50, b 5, h 7 & *Mustadrak*, x, 410, b 86, h 12270/13.. Kafᶜamī's *Miṣbāḥ*, 493.

Third Ziyarah of Imam al-Rida (ʿa)

This *ziyārah* is cited by Shaykh Mufīd in his book *al-Muqniʿah*.[1] Having taken bath and put on one's cleanest clothes, one should stand by the tomb and say,

Peace be to you O *walī* of Allah and son of His *walī*! Peace be to you, O testament of Allah and son of His testament! Peace be to you, O Imam of guidance and *the firmest handle*,(2:256) and may Allah's mercy and His bounties be upon you!

اَلسَّلَامُ عَلَيْكَ يَا وَلِيَّ اللهِ وَ ابْنَ وَلِيِّهِ، اَلسَّلَامُ عَلَيْكَ يَا حُجَّةَ اللهِ وَ ابْنَ حُجَّتِهِ، اَلسَّلَامُ عَلَيْكَ يَا إِمَامَ الْهُدَىٰ، وَ الْعُرْوَةَ الْوُثْقَىٰ، وَ رَحْمَةُ اللهِ وَ بَرَكَاتُهُ .

I testify that you passed away upholding that which was upheld by your immaculate ancestors, may Allah's blessings be upon them. You did not prefer blindness to guidance and did not incline from truth toward falsehood. I testify that you worked sincerely for the cause of Allah and His Apostle and you fulfilled your trusts. May Allah grant you the best reward on behalf of Islam and its followers!

أَشْهَدُ أَنَّكَ مَضَيْتَ عَلَىٰ مَا مَضَىٰ عَلَيْهِ آبَاؤُكَ الطَّاهِرُونَ صَلَوَاتُ اللهِ عَلَيْهِمْ، لَمْ تُؤْثِرْ عَمًى عَلَىٰ هُدًى، وَ لَمْ تَمِلْ مِنْ حَقٍّ إِلَىٰ بَاطِلٍ، وَ أَنَّكَ نَصَحْتَ لِلّٰهِ وَ لِرَسُولِهِ، وَ أَدَّيْتَ الْأَمَانَةَ، فَجَزَاكَ اللهُ عَنِ الْإِسْلَامِ وَ أَهْلِهِ خَيْرَ الْجَزَاءِ !

You are dearer to me than my father and mother! I come to you as a pilgrim, knowing your rights, befriending your friends and despising your enemies. So intercede for me with your Lord!

أَتَيْتُكَ بِأَبِي وَ أُمِّي زَائِرًا عَارِفًا بِحَقِّكَ، مُوَالِيًا لِأَوْلِيَائِكَ، مُعَادِيًا لِأَعْدَائِكَ، فَاشْفَعْ لِي عِنْدَ رَبِّكَ!

Then clinging to the grave, one should embrace it placing on it alternately one's right and left cheek. Then moving on towards the head of the tomb, say,

Peace be to you, my master, O son of the Apostle of Allah, and may

اَلسَّلَامُ عَلَيْكَ يَا مَوْلَايَ يَا ابْنَ رَسُولِ

[1] *Muqniʿah*, 480, b 29. *Al-Mazār al-Kabīr*, 551, b 2, whence *Biḥār*, xcix, 51-52, b 5, h 10.

اللهِ وَ رَحْمَةُ اللهِ وَ بَرَكَاتُهُ، أَشْهَدُ أَنَّكَ الْإِمَامُ الْهَادِي، وَ الْوَلِيُّ الْمُرْشِدُ، أَبْرَأُ إِلَى اللهِ مِنْ أَعْدَائِكَ، وَ أَتَقَرَّبُ إِلَى اللهِ بِوِلَايَتِكَ، صَلَّى اللهُ عَلَيْكَ وَ رَحْمَةُ اللهِ وَ بَرَكَاتُهُ	Allah's mercy and His bounties be upon you! I testify that you are the rightly-guiding Imam, *walī*. and spiritual guide. I repudiate before Allah your enemies and seek nearness to Allah through your *wilāyah*, may Allah bless you and may His mercy and bounties be upon you!

Then offer two *rakʿahs* of the prayer of *ziyārah* and any other prayers that you may like. Then move towards the feet of the tomb to make any supplications that you wish.

There is a great merit in performing the Imam's *ziyārah* on days of special significance, especially during the month of Rajab and on the 23rd and 25th of Dhū al-Qaʿdah, and on the 6th of the month of Ramaḍān, as mentioned in the observances pertaining to different months, as well as on other days that have a special relation to the Imam (*ʿa*).

When intending to bid farewell to the Imam (*ʿa*), one may recite the same text as was cited for bidding farewell to the Apostle of Allah (ṣ), i.e. *Lā jaʿlahullāhu āk͟hira taslīmī ʿalayk...*(p. 74) Or one may recite the following text.[1]

اَلسَّلَامُ عَلَيْكَ يَا وَلِيَّ اللهِ وَ رَحْمَةُ اللهِ وَ بَرَكَاتُهُ، اَللّٰهُمَّ لَا تَجْعَلْهُ آخِرَ الْعَهْدِ مِنْ زِيَارَتِي ابْنَ نَبِيِّكَ وَ حُجَّتَكَ عَلَى خَلْقِكَ، وَ اجْمَعْنِي وَ إِيَّاهُ فِي جَنَّتِكَ، وَ احْشُرْنِي مَعَهُ وَ فِي حِزْبِهِ مَعَ الشُّهَدَاءِ وَ الصَّالِحِينَ، وَ حَسُنَ أُولَئِكَ رَفِيقًا .	Peace be to you, O *walī* of Allah and may Allah's mercy and His bounties be upon you! O Allah, do not make this my last opportunity of *ziyārah* of Your Prophet's son and Your testament to Your creation. Join me with him in Your paradise and gather me, at Resurrection, with him and among his party along with *the martyrs and the righteous, and an excellent company are they!*
وَ أَسْتَوْدِعُكَ اللهَ وَ أَسْتَرْعِيكَ وَ أَقْرَأُ عَلَيْكَ السَّلَامَ، آمَنَّا بِاللهِ وَ بِالرَّسُولِ وَ	I commend you to Allah's care, committing you to His protection, and give you my *salām!* We have

1 Kafʿamī's *Miṣbāḥ*, 494. *Balad*, 283, whence *Biḥār*, xcix, 50, b 5, h 8.

faith in Allah and the Apostle and in your teaching and guidance. So write us among the witnesses.	بِمَا جِئْتَ بِهِ وَ دَلَلْتَ عَلَيْهِ، فَاكْتُبْنَا مَعَ الشَّاهِدِينَ !

Certain points are worthy of mention here.

(1) There is a report[1] with reliable *isnād* that Imam ᶜAlī al-Naqī (ᶜ*a*) said, "Someone who has a need to be fulfilled by God should visit the shrine of my grandfather Imam ᶜAlī al-Riḍa (ᶜ*a*) in the town of Ṭūs and, after having taken a bath, offer two *rak*ᶜ*ahs* of prayer at the head of his tomb and mention his petition during *qunūt*. His petition will indeed be granted unless it relates to something which is sinful or harmful for his relatives. The place of his tomb is one of the spots of paradise and no one possessing faith makes pilgrimage to his shrine without being granted release from hellfire and admission into paradise by God Almighty."

(2) ᶜAllāmah Majlisī, quoting from a text in the hand of the eminent scholar al-Ḥusayn b. ᶜAbd al-Ṣamad, father of Shaykh Bahā'ī, cites a report[2] narrated on the authority of Abū al-Ṭayyib Ḥusayn b. Aḥmad Faqīh al-Rāzī that for someone who performs the *ziyārah* of Imam ᶜAlī al-Riḍā (ᶜ*a*) or other Imams and offers the Prayer of Jaᶜfar at his shrine, there is written for every *rak*ᶜ*ah* a reward equal to that of someone who has performed a thousand ᶜ*umrah* and *ḥajj* pilgrimages, freed a thousand slaves for the sake of God, and participated a thousand times in *jihād* alongside a prophetic envoy. For every step that he takes he is granted a reward of performing a thousand ᶜ*umrah* and *ḥajj* pilgrimages and freeing a hundred slaves for the sake of Allah and there are written for him a hundred virtues, and a hundred of his vices are erased from the record of his deeds. The manner of performing the Prayer of Jaᶜfar was mentioned in the observances of Friday (Book One, p. 144)

(3) Mukhawwal (Miḥwal) al-Sijistanī[3] reports, "When al-Ma'mūn summoned Imam ᶜAlī al-Riḍā (ᶜ*a*) from Madīnah to Khurāsān, he entered the Prophet's Mosque to bid the Apostle of Allah (ṣ) farewell. Several times he bade him farewell came out and again returned to the Prophet's grave and each time his voice would rise as he wept. I approached him and greeted him. He returned my *salām*. When I

1 Ṣadūq's *Amālī*, 588, majlis 86, h 12, whence *Wasā'il*, xiv, 569, b 88, h 19840. ᶜ*Uyūn Akhbār al-Riḍā*, ii, 262, b 66, h 32, whence *Biḥār*, xcix, 59, b 5, h 4.

2 *Biḥār*, xcvii, 137, b 3, h 25, whence *Mustadrak*, vi, 233, b 8, h 6791/2, x, 402, b 86, h 12259/2.

3 ᶜ*Uyūn Akhbār al-Riḍā*, ii, 217, whence *Biḥār*, xlix, 117, b 10, h 2.

congratulated him, he said to me, 'Visit me (after my death), for I am departing from my grandfather's vicinage and will die far away from my native place and will be buried by the side of Hārūn.' "

Shaykh Yūsuf b Ḥātam al-Shāmī states in *al-Durr al-Naẓīm*[1] that it has been reported from a number of companions of Imam ᶜAlī al-Riḍā (ᶜ*a*) that the Imam said, "When I was about to leave Madīnah for Khorāsān, I gathered the members of my family and asked them to mourn for me until I heard their cries. Then I distributed twelve thousand dinars amongst them, telling them that I will not return again to my family. Then I took Abū Jaᶜfar al-Jawād to the Prophet's Mosque and placing his hands on the side of the grave pressed him against the blessed tomb and entrusted his safety to the Apostle of Allah (ṣ). I ordered all my deputies and servants to listen to him and obey his commands and not to oppose him. I let them understand that he is my successor."

Sayyid ᶜAbd al-Karīm ibn Ṭāwūs reports,[2] "When al-Ma'mūn summoned Imam ᶜAlī al-Riḍā (ᶜ*a*) from Madīnah to Khurāsān, he set out from Madīnah towards Baṣrah, and set out from there to Baghdad by the road to Kūfah without entering it. From there he set out towards Qum, and there he was met by its people who contested with one another as to which of them shall host him. The Imam (ᶜ*a*) told them that his camel was charged to take him to where he would stay. The camel went on until it kneeled down at a house whose owner had dreamt the night before that Imam Riḍā (ᶜ*a*) would be his guest the next day. After some time that location became a place of distinction and it is a thriving school in our own times."

Shaykh Ṣadūq reports[3] with his *isnād* from Isḥāq b Rāhawayh, When Imam Abū al-Ḥasan ᶜAlī al-Riḍā (ᶜ*a*) visited Nayshābūr on his journey to meet al-Ma'mūn, at the time of his departure when he was leaving the town, the scholars of *ḥadīth* gathered around him and said, "O son of the Apostle of Allah (ṣ), you are leaving us. Will you not narrate for us a *ḥadīth* which may be of benefit to us?" The Imam sat in a camel-borne litter. Thereupon, he popped his head out and said, "I heard my father Mūsā ibn Jaᶜfar say, I heard my father Jaᶜfar ibn Muḥammad say, I heard my father Muḥammad ibn ᶜAlī say,

1 *Al-Durr al-Naẓīm*, 678. *ᶜUyūn Akhbār al-Riḍā*, ii, 219. *Dalā'il al-Imāmah*, 176. *Madīnat al-Maᶜājiz*, vii, 179.

2 *Farḥat al-Gharī*, 105.

3 Ṣadūq's *Amālī*, 235, majlis 41, h 8; *Thawāb*, 6; *Maᶜānī*, 370, h 1; *Tawḥīd*, 25, b 1, h 23; *ᶜUyūn Akhbār al-Riḍā*, ii, 135, b 37, h 4, whence *Biḥār*, iii, 7, b 1, h 16, xlix, 123, b 11, h 4. *Bishārah*, 269.

I heard my father ᶜAlī ibn al-Ḥusayn say, I heard my father al-Ḥusayn ibn ᶜAlī say, I heard my father Amīr al-Mu'minīn ᶜAlī ibn Abī Ṭālib (ᶜ*a*) say, I heard the Apostle of Allah (*ṣ*) say, I heard Gabriel say, I heard Allah, the Most Majestic, say,

لاَ إِلَهَ إِلاَّ اللهُ حِصْنِي، فَمَنْ دَخَلَ حِصْنِي أَمِنَ مِنْ عَذَابِي

("There is no god except Allah" is My fort, and those who enter My fort shall be safe from My punishment.)

When the camel set out, he cried out,

بِشُرُوطِهَا وَ أَنَا مِنْ شُرُوطِهَا

(Along with its conditions! And I am one of its conditions!)

Abū al-Ṣalṭ reports[1] that when Imam ᶜAlī al-Riḍā (ᶜ*a*) reached Deh Surkh in his journey from Nayshābūr, he was told, "It is noontime. Will you pray?" He asked for water and they replied that they had no water with them. Thereupon he dug the ground with his blessed hand and water gushed forth from it. He and those who were with him performed their ablutions with it. That spring remains to this day and is called Riḍā's Spring. Then he entered Sanābād, where he reclined with his back resting on a rock on the mountainside from which they used to carve out cooking pots. He prayed, saying, "O God, make it beneficial and bless whatever is made and carved out of it. Then he ordered that cooking pots be carved out of that mountain for him, telling them that his food will not be cooked except in pots carved from it. He ate little and his food was light. From that day the people carved out their cooking pots from it and the blessings of his prayer concerning it became manifest.

(4) The author of *Maṭlaᶜ al-Shams*, relates that Shah ᶜAbbās I came to the holy city of Mashhad on the 25th of Dhū al-Ḥijjah in the year 1006 H. He recounts that the holy shrine had been plundered by the Uzbek ᶜAbd al-Mu'min Khān, after which there was nothing left there except the gold-plated enclosure (*maḥjar-e ṭalā*). On the 28th of Dhūl Ḥijjah he left Mashhad for Herat and recaptured it. After restoring order there he returned to Mashhad and stayed there for a month. He had the courtyard of the holy shrine repaired and treated kindly the keepers of the holy shrine, after which he returned to

[1] *Manāqib*, iv, 343.

Iraq. At the end of the year 1008 H. Shah ᶜAbbās went again to the holy Mashhad and spent the winter there, personally carrying out a servant's duties in the sacred shrine. One night when he was pruning the burnt candle ends with a clipper, Shaykh Bahā'ī composed this quartet extempore,

پیوسته بود ملایک عِلّیین   پروانه شمع روضه خلد آیین

مقراض به احتیاط زن ای خادم   ترسم ببُری شهپر جبریل امین

Angels of the lofty heavens constantly encircle this Edenic shrine,
Like moths encircling the candle's flame.
Be careful O servant lest your clippers,
Should clip a wing of Gabriel, the Trusted Archangel.

In the year 1009 H. Shah ᶜAbbās made a foot journey to Mashhad to fulfil an oath and covered the long distance in 28 days. The author of *Ta'rīkh-e ᶜĀlam Āra* has written these lines in this regard,

غلام شاه مردان شاه عباس   شه والا گهر خاقان امجد

به طوف مرقد شاه خراسان   پیاده رفت با اخلاص بی حد

Slave of the sovereign of men, Shah ᶜAbbās,
A worthy king and glorious monarch,
Came to pay homage to the shrine of the lord of Khorāsān
On foot with boundless dedication.

Towards the end of these verses he says,

پیاده رفت شد تاریخ رفتن   ز اصفاهان پیاده تا به مشهد

This is the chronogram of his foot journey:
'He went on foot to Mashhad from Isfahan.'

On reaching the holy city of Mashhad, he had the shrine courtyard extended. The Hall of ᶜAlī Shīr, which adjoined the blessed tomb and was on one side of the courtyard and appeared unseemly, was brought into the centre and a hall was constructed opposite it on the other side. A road was drawn extending from the city's western gate to the eastern, reaching the shrine courtyard from both sides. Wells were dug and water canals were constructed and brought to the city. A canal was drawn through the middle of the street and a large cistern was built in the middle of the courtyard. The water passed through the cistern and flowed toward the eastern street. Inscriptions written in the hand of Mīrzā Muḥammad Riḍā, the chief calligrapher, ᶜAlī Riḍā ᶜAbbāsī and Muḥammad Riḍā Imāmī were mounted on these structures. Also Shah ᶜAbbās had the shrine dome plated with gold, as is stated in the inscription on the shrine dome. The text of this inscription reads:

بسم الله الرحمن الرحيم من عظائم توفيقات الله سبحانه أن وفق السلطان الأعظم مولى ملوك العرب و العجم صاحب النسب الطاهر النبوي و الحسب الباهر العلوي تراب أقدام خدام هذه العتبة المطهرة اللاهوتية غبار نعال زوار هذه الروضة المنورة الملكوتية مروج آثار أجداده المعصومين السلطان بن السلطان أبو المظفر شاه عباس الحسيني الموسوي الصفوي بهادر خان فاستسعد بالمجيء ماشيا على قدميه من دار السلطنة أصفهان إلى زيارة هذا الحرم الأشرف و قد تشرف بزينة هذه القبة من خلص ماله في سنة ألف و عشر و تم في سنة ألف و ست و عشر

> In the Name of Allah, the All-beneficent, the All-merciful. Among the greatest of successes granted by Allah, the Glorious, was the success He granted to the great king, the lord of the princes of the Arabs and the non-Arabs, of the pure lineage of the Prophet and the distinguished ᶜAlawid ancestry, the dust of the feet of the servants of this immaculate and celestial shrine, the dust of the feet of the pilgrims of this luminous heavenly tomb, the propagator of the heritage of his infallible ancestors, the Sultan son of Sultan, Abū al-Muẓaffar Shah ᶜAbbās al-Ḥusaynī al-Mūsawī al-Ṣafawī Bahādur Khān. He obtained the felicity of having come on foot from the capital of Isfahan for the *ziyārah* of this most noble shrine, and had the honour of adorning this dome with his personal wealth in the year 1010 H., completed thereafter in the year 1016 H.

(5) Shaykh Ṭabrisī (d. 548/1153), after describing some of the miracles performed by Imam ᶜAlī al-Riḍā (*ᶜa*) in *Iᶜlām al-Warā*,[1] says,

> As for the miracles that have been manifested for the people since the martyrdom of the Imam until our times with the blessings of his holy shrine and the wonders and signs that have been observed by many people and are confirmed by the generality of

[1] *Iᶜlām al-Warā*, 326.

> laymen and scholars and admitted by friends and foes alike, they are many, or rather innumerable. The blind-born and the leprous were cured in that holy shrine, petitions were granted, needs were fulfilled and relief obtained from adversities and afflictions. We have ourselves observed many of these and have a certain knowledge of their occurrence, which is beyond doubt.

The august shaykh al-Ḥurr al-ᶜĀmilī, after quoting the above statement of Shaykh Ṭabrisī in his work *Ithbāt al-Hudāt*,[1] says,

> The author of this book, Muḥammad b. al-Ḥasan al-Ḥurr, says, 'I have seen and observed many of such miracles as were observed by Shaykh Ṭabrisī, and in the course of my 26 years of residence in the vicinage of the Imam's shrine in the Holy Mashhad, it has become a matter of certainty for me, as it did for him, and I have heard things about this matter that are beyond *tawātur*. I do not remember ever having prayed for any need in this shrine without my request being granted, and I thank God. There is no room for elaboration in this place and so I have confined myself to these brief remarks.'

The compiler of this book, ᶜAbbās Qummī, says: So many wonders and miracles have been manifested at this holy shrine in every era that there is no need to recount past occurrences. In Chapter 1 of Book Two (p. 410) in the observances of the 27th night of Rajab, we have cited something which is pertinent to this topic, and here there is no scope for further details. It will be better to conclude this chapter at this point with verses said in eulogy of that Imam (ᶜ*a*).

سَلامٌ عَلَى آلِ طٰهٰ وَ يٰس   سَلامٌ عَلَى آلِ خَيْرِ النَّبِيِّينَ

سَلامٌ عَلَى رَوْضَةٍ حَلَّ فِيهَا   إِمَامٌ يُبَاهِي بِهِ الْمُلْكُ وَالدِّينُ

Peace to the Progeny of Ṭā Hā and Yā Sīn,
Peace to the Progeny of the Best of Prophets.
Peace to the shrine where has alighted the Imam
Who receives the homage of terrestrial power and celestial faith.

امام بحق شاه مطلق که آمد   حریم درش قبله‌گاه سلاطین

شه کاخ عرفان گل شاخ احسان   دُرِ دُرج امکان مهِ بُرج تمکین

[1] *Ithbāt al-Hudāt*, iv, 359.

علی بن موسی الرضا کز خدایش	رضا شد لقب چون رضا بودش آیین
ز فضل و شرف بینی او را جهانی	اگر نبودت تیره چشـــم جهان بین
پی عطـــر رُوبند حـــوران جنّت	غبار درش را به گیسوی مشکین
اگر خواهی آری به کف دامن او	برو دامن از هر چه جز اوست برچین

The true Imam and absolute king, his sacred door is *qiblah* of kings.
Lord of the edifice of gnosis and flower of virtue's tree
Pearl of the realm of contingency and moon of the abode of glory,
ᶜAlī ibn Mūsā al-Riḍā, who received that appellation from his Lord
The Pleasing One was his title, as he was wont to be pleased with his Lord.
A world of merit and dignity you will see
If your sight is not blind to what is beyond the mundane world.
With tresses fragrant with musk, the Houris of paradise gather perfume
Sweeping the dust of his threshold.
Should you wish to hold on to the skirts of his cloak
Rid yourself of every attachment besides Him.

Chapter Ten

Ziyārah at Sāmarrā

This chapter pertains to the *ziyārah* of the two Imams buried at the shrine at Sāmarrā (*Surra Man Ra'ā*) and the observances relating to the Sacred Basement. It consists of two sections.

Section One
Joint Ziyarah of the Two Imams
ᶜAlī al-Naqī & al-Ḥasan al-ᶜAskarī (ᶜa)

On entering Sāmarrā, when intending to proceed for the *ziyārah* of the two Imams (ᶜ*a*) one should first take a bath, and, while being attentive to the points of etiquette pertaining to entry into the holy shrines (pp. 13-21), set out walking with 5dignity and measured steps. On reaching the gates of the holy shrine, one should recite the usual appeal for admittance, mentioned at the beginning of this Book (pp. 22-26). On entering the shrine to perform the *ziyārah* of the two Imams (ᶜ*a*), one may recite the following, one of the most authentic *ziyārah*-texts.[1]

Peace be to you, O *walīs* of Allah! Peace be to you, O testaments of Allah! Peace be to you, O lights of Allah in the darkness of the earth! Peace be to you, on behalf of whom there occurred *badā* for Allah.

اَلسَّـلَامُ عَلَيْكُمَا يَا وَلِيَّيِ اللهِ، اَلسَّلَامُ
عَلَيْكُمَا يَا حُجَّتَيِ اللهِ، اَلسَّلَامُ عَلَيْكُمَا
يَا نُورَيِ اللهِ فِي ظُلُمَاتِ الْأَرْضِ، اَلسَّلَامُ
عَلَيْكُمَا يَا مَنْ بَدَا لِلّٰهِ فِي شَأْنِكُمَا

I come to you as a pilgrim, knowing your rights, despising your enemies and befriending your friends, believing in what you believed and denying what you denied, endorsing what you endorsed, and repudiating what

أَتَيْتُكُمَا زَائِرًا عَارِفًا بِحَقِّكُمَا، مُعَادِيًا
لِأَعْدَائِكُمَا، مُوَالِيًا لِأَوْلِيَائِكُمَا، مُؤْمِنًا
بِمَا آمَنْتُمَا بِهِ، كَافِرًا بِمَا كَفَرْتُمَا بِهِ،
مُحَقِّقًا لِمَا حَقَّقْتُمَا، مُبْطِلًا لِمَا أَبْطَلْتُمَا،

[1] *Kāmil al-Ziyārāt*, 313, b 103, h 1, whence *Biḥār*, xcix, 61, b 6, h 5. *Tahdhīb*, vi, 94, b 44, h 1. Mufīd's *Mazār*, 209, b 19. *Al-Mazār al-Kabīr*, 552, b 7, h 1.

you repudiated. I beseech Allah, my Lord and yours, to make my reward of your *ziyārah* His blessing of Muḥammad and his Family and to grant me your company in paradise with your righteous ancestors.

أَسْأَلُ اللهَ رَبِّي وَ رَبَّكُمَا أَنْ يَجْعَلَ حَظِّي
مِنْ زِيَارَتِكُمَا الصَّلَاةَ عَلَىٰ مُحَمَّدٍ وَ آلِهِ
وَ أَنْ يَرْزُقَنِي مُرَافَقَتَكُمَا فِي الْجِنَانِ مَعَ
آبَائِكُمَا الصَّالِحِينَ،

I beseech Him to rescue me from hellfire, to grant me your intercession and companionship, to make us and you familiar with one another, not to divest me of your love and that of your righteous ancestors, not to make this my last opportunity of performing your *ziyārah*, and to join me at Resurrection with you in paradise, with His mercy!

وَ أَسْأَلُهُ أَنْ يُعْتِقَ رَقَبَتِي مِنَ النَّارِ، وَ
يَرْزُقَنِي شَفَاعَتَكُمَا وَ مُصَاحَبَتَكُمَا،
وَ يُعَرِّفَ بَيْنِي وَ بَيْنَكُمَا، وَ لَا يَسْلُبَنِي
حُبَّكُمَا وَ حُبَّ آبَائِكُمَا الصَّالِحِينَ، وَ أَنْ
لَا يَجْعَلَهُ آخِرَ الْعَهْدِ مِنْ زِيَارَتِكُمَا، وَ
يَحْشُرَنِي مَعَكُمَا فِي الْجَنَّةِ بِرَحْمَتِهِ.

O Allah, grant me the gift of their love and make me die while following their creed!

اَللّٰهُمَّ ارْزُقْنِي حُبَّهُمَا وَ تَوَفَّنِي عَلَىٰ مِلَّتِهِمَا ،

O Allah, curse those who usurped the rights of Muḥammad's Family and take vengeance on them. O Allah, curse those of them belonging to the former generations and the latter ones and double their punishment, and send them, their adherents, friends and followers to the lowest reaches of hell. Indeed You have power over all things!

اَللّٰهُمَّ الْعَنْ ظَالِمِي آلِ مُحَمَّدٍ حَقَّهُمْ، وَ
انْتَقِمْ مِنْهُمْ، اَللّٰهُمَّ الْعَنِ الْأَوَّلِينَ مِنْهُمْ
وَ الْآخِرِينَ، وَ ضَاعِفْ عَلَيْهِمُ الْعَذَابَ،
وَ ابْلُغْ بِهِمْ وَ بِأَشْيَاعِهِمْ وَ مُحِبِّيهِمْ وَ
مُتَّبِعِيهِمْ أَسْفَلَ دَرْكٍ مِنَ الْجَحِيمِ، إِنَّكَ
عَلَىٰ كُلِّ شَيْءٍ قَدِيرٌ .

O Allah, hasten the relief of Your *walī*, son of Your *walī*, and grant us relief along with theirs, O Most Merciful of the merciful!

اَللّٰهُمَّ عَجِّلْ فَرَجَ وَلِيِّكَ وَ ابْنِ وَلِيِّكَ، وَ
اجْعَلْ فَرَجَنَا مَعَ فَرَجِهِمْ، يَا أَرْحَمَ الرَّاحِمِينَ !

Then supplicate earnestly for yourself and your parents and make any petition that you wish. If possible, offer two *rakᶜahs* of prayer near the tombs. Otherwise enter the adjacent mosque and offer two *rakᶜahs* there and make any supplication that you wish to make, for it will be granted. This mosque was situated next to the house where the Imams were staying and the Imams ᶜAlī al-Naqī and al-Ḥasan al-ᶜAskarī used to pray there.

The above-mentioned text of *ziyārah* is in accordance with the version given in *Kāmil al-Ziyārāt* and by Shaykh Mufīd and Shaykh Muḥammad b. al-Mashhadī. Shahīd Awwal has also cited this *ziyārah* in his *Mazār* with a slight difference.[1] According to his version, after the words *fil jannati bi raḥmatih*, one should cast oneself on each of the two graves, laying alternately one's right and left cheek on it. Then raising one's head one is to resume recitation of the text from the words *Allāhummarzuqnī ḥubbahum wa tawaffanī ᶜalā millatihim...* until the end. After this, one should offer four *rakᶜahs* of prayer near the head of the tomb. After the prayer of *ziyārah* one may continue with prayers for as long as one wishes.

It is to be remembered that the two Imams were buried in their house, which had a door which was sometimes opened and the Shīᶜī visitors would enter and perform the *ziyārah* by the graves. At times, the door was closed and they performed the *ziyārah* in front of the grille in the wall facing the holy tomb. At the beginning of the very report relating to this *ziyārah*,[2] it is mentioned that after taking bath one is to approach the tomb, if possible, otherwise to perform the *ziyārah* while pointing towards it from in front of the grille facing the tomb. The pilgrim is then told to offer the prayer of *ziyārah* in the mosque. Later this house was dismantled and the domed shrine with its halls and chambers was built in the place and the mosque became part of the shrine. Nowadays it is well known that the rectangular hall behind the tomb of the two Imams (*ᶜa*) is a continuation of the same mosque. In any case, the pilgrims have been relieved of the former impediments.

There are also separate *ziyārahs* for each of the two Imams which are cited in books pertaining to *ziyārah*. Their copies are available in plenty, should one wish to perform them. If the pilgrim has the inclination and time, it would be appropriate for him to recite the Ziyārah Jāmiᶜah Kabīrah, which will be be cited later on, God willing (p. 522). Its eloquent words, which come from Imam ᶜAlī al-Naqī (*ᶜa*), embody in an inclusive manner the pilgrim's expression of his

1 Shahīd Awwal's *Mazār*, 201, faṣl, 8.

2 *Kāmil al-Ziyārāt*, 313, b 103, h 1, whence *Biḥār*, xcix, 61, b 6, h 5.

humility and awe and his admission of the greatness and majesty of the Imams (ᶜ*a*).

Ziyarah of Imam ʿAli al-Naqi (ʿa)

Sayyid ᶜAlī b. Ṭāwūs, in *Miṣbāḥ al-Zā'ir*, has cited an elaborate *ziyārah* for each of the two Imams along with a *ṣalawāt* and supplication to be made after the prayer of *ziyārah*.[1] It will be appropriate to cite it here despite its length on account of its many merits. On reaching Sāmarrā, he says, one should take bath and set out towards the shrine having put on one's cleanest clothes. Walking with calm dignity on the way, one should recite the following appeal for admittance on reaching the gates of the shrine.

May I enter, O Prophet of Allah? May I enter, O Commander of the Faithful? May I enter, O Fāṭimah Zahrā, the mistress of the world's womankind? May I enter, O my master, al-Ḥasan ibn ᶜAlī? May I enter, O my master, al-Ḥusayn ibn ᶜAlī?

أَأَدْخُلُ يا نَبِيَّ اللهِ؟ أَأَدْخُلُ يا أَمِيرَ الْمُؤْمِنِينَ؟ أَأَدْخُلُ يا فاطِمَةُ الزَّهْراءُ سَيِّدَةَ نِساءِ الْعالَمِينَ؟ أَأَدْخُلُ يا مَوْلاىَ الْحَسَنَ بْنَ عَلِيٍّ؟ أَأَدْخُلُ يا مَوْلاىَ الْحُسَيْنَ بْنَ عَلِيٍّ؟

May I enter, O my master, ᶜAlī ibn al-Ḥusayn? May I enter, O my master, Muḥammad ibn ᶜAlī? May I enter, O my master, Jaᶜfar ibn Muḥammad?

أَأَدْخُلُ يا مَوْلاىَ عَلِيَّ بْنَ الْحُسَيْنِ؟ أَأَدْخُلُ يا مَوْلاىَ مُحَمَّدَ بْنَ عَلِيٍّ؟ أَأَدْخُلُ يا مَوْلاىَ جَعْفَرَ بْنَ مُحَمَّدٍ؟

May I enter, O my master Mūsā ibn Jaᶜfar? May I enter, O my master, ᶜAlī ibn Mūsā? May I enter, O my master, Muḥammad ibn ᶜAlī? May I enter, O my master, Abul-Ḥasan ᶜAlī ibn Muḥammad? May I enter, O my master, Abū Muḥammad al-Ḥasan ibn ᶜAlī? May I enter, O Allah's angels who have been put in charge of this noble

أَأَدْخُلُ يا مَوْلاىَ مُوسَى بْنَ جَعْفَرٍ؟ أَأَدْخُلُ يا مَوْلاىَ عَلِيَّ بْنَ مُوسَى؟ أَأَدْخُلُ يا مَوْلاىَ مُحَمَّدَ بْنَ عَلِيٍّ؟ أَأَدْخُلُ يا مَوْلاىَ يا أَبَا الْحَسَنِ عَلِيَّ بْنَ مُحَمَّدٍ؟ أَأَدْخُلُ يا مَوْلاىَ يا أَبا مُحَمَّدٍ الْحَسَنَ بْنَ عَلِيٍّ؟ أَأَدْخُلُ يا مَلائِكَةَ اللهِ الْمُوَكَّلِينَ

[1] *Biḥār*, xcix, 63, b 6, h 8 from Ibn Ṭāwūs.

shrine?

بِهَذَا الْحَرَمِ الشَّرِيفِ؟

Then enter with the right foot. Standing by the *ḍarīḥ* of Imam ᶜAlī al-Naqī (ᶜ*a*), face the tomb with the back towards the *qiblah*, and say a hundred times *Allāhu akbar*. Then say,

اَلسَّلاٰمُ عَلَيْكَ يَا أَبَا الْحَسَنِ عَلِيَّ بْنَ مُحَمَّدٍ الزَّكِيَّ الرَّاشِدَ النُّورَ الثَّاقِبَ وَ رَحْمَةُ اللهِ وَ بَرَكَاتُهُ .

Peace be to you, O Abul Ḥasan ᶜAlī ibn Muḥammad, the blameless guide and the piercing light, and may Allah's mercy and His bounties be upon you!

اَلسَّلاٰمُ عَلَيْكَ يَا صَفِيَّ اللهِ، اَلسَّلاٰمُ عَلَيْكَ يَا سِرَّ اللهِ، اَلسَّلاٰمُ عَلَيْكَ يَا حَبْلَ اللهِ، اَلسَّلاٰمُ عَلَيْكَ يَا آلَ اللهِ، اَلسَّلاٰمُ عَلَيْكَ يَا خِيَرَةَ اللهِ، اَلسَّلاٰمُ عَلَيْكَ يَا صَفْوَةَ اللهِ، اَلسَّلاٰمُ عَلَيْكَ يَا أَمِينَ اللهِ،

Peace be to you, O chosen of Allah! Peace be to you, O Allah's secret! Peace be to you, O Allah's cord! Peace be to you, O (one of) Allah's clan! Peace be to you, O elect of Allah! Peace be to you, O Allah's favourite! Peace be to you, O Allah's trustee!

اَلسَّلاٰمُ عَلَيْكَ يَا حَقَّ اللهِ، اَلسَّلاٰمُ عَلَيْكَ يَا حَبِيبَ اللهِ، اَلسَّلاٰمُ عَلَيْكَ يَا نُورَ الْأَنْوَارِ، اَلسَّلاٰمُ عَلَيْكَ يَا زَيْنَ الْأَبْرَارِ، اَلسَّلاٰمُ عَلَيْكَ يَا سَلِيلَ الْأَخْيَارِ، اَلسَّلاٰمُ عَلَيْكَ يَا عُنْصُرَ الْأَطْهَارِ،

Peace be to you, O right of Allah! Peace be to you, O beloved of Allah! Peace be to you, O light of lights! Peace be to you, O ornament of the pious! Peace be to you, O scion of the elect! Peace be to you, who belong to the breed of the immaculate ones!

اَلسَّلاٰمُ عَلَيْكَ يَا حُجَّةَ الرَّحْمٰنِ، اَلسَّلاٰمُ عَلَيْكَ يَا رُكْنَ الْإِيمَانِ، اَلسَّلاٰمُ عَلَيْكَ يَا مَوْلَى الْمُؤْمِنِينَ، اَلسَّلاٰمُ عَلَيْكَ يَا وَلِيَّ الصَّالِحِينَ، اَلسَّلاٰمُ عَلَيْكَ يَا عَلَمَ الْهُدَىٰ،

Peace be to you, O testament of the All-beneficent! Peace be to you, O pillar of faith! Peace be to you, O guardian of the faithful! Peace be to you, O friend of the righteous! Peace be to you, O banner of guidance! Peace be to you, O ally of Godfearing!

Peace be to you, O mainstay of religion!

اَلسَّلَامُ عَلَيْكَ يَا حَلِيفَ التُّقَى، اَلسَّلَامُ عَلَيْكَ يَا عَمُودَ الدِّينِ،

Peace be to you, O son of the Seal of the Prophets! Peace be to you, O son of the chief of the Legatees! Peace be to you, O son of Fāṭimah Zahrā, mistress of the world's womankind!

اَلسَّلَامُ عَلَيْكَ يَا ابْنَ خَاتَمِ النَّبِيِّينَ، اَلسَّلَامُ عَلَيْكَ يَا ابْنَ سَيِّدِ الْوَصِيِّينَ، اَلسَّلَامُ عَلَيْكَ يَا ابْنَ فَاطِمَةَ الزَّهْرَاءِ سَيِّدَةِ نِسَاءِ الْعَالَمِينَ،

Peace be to you, O loyal and trustworthy Imam! Peace be to you, O approved personage! Peace be to you, O Godwary one free from worldly attachments! Peace be to you, O testament to all the creation!

اَلسَّلَامُ عَلَيْكَ أَيُّهَا الْأَمِينُ الْوَفِيُّ، اَلسَّلَامُ عَلَيْكَ أَيُّهَا الْعَلَمُ الرَّضِيُّ، اَلسَّلَامُ عَلَيْكَ أَيُّهَا الزَّاهِدُ التَّقِيُّ، اَلسَّلَامُ عَلَيْكَ أَيُّهَا الْحُجَّةُ عَلَى الْخَلْقِ أَجْمَعِينَ،

Peace be to you, O follower of the Qur'ān! Peace be to you, O exponent of the lawful as differentiated from the unlawful! Peace be to you, O devoted and sincere guardian! Peace be to you, O clear path! Peace be to you, O bright star!

اَلسَّلَامُ عَلَيْكَ أَيُّهَا التَّالِي لِلْقُرْآنِ، اَلسَّلَامُ عَلَيْكَ أَيُّهَا الْمُبَيِّنُ لِلْحَلَالِ مِنَ الْحَرَامِ، اَلسَّلَامُ عَلَيْكَ أَيُّهَا الْوَلِيُّ النَّاصِحُ، اَلسَّلَامُ عَلَيْكَ أَيُّهَا الطَّرِيقُ الْوَاضِحُ، اَلسَّلَامُ عَلَيْكَ أَيُّهَا النَّجْمُ اللَّائِحُ،

My master, O Abul Ḥasan, I testify that you are Allah's testament to His creation and His vicegerent among His creatures, His trustee in His towns and His witness to His servants!

أَشْهَدُ يَا مَوْلَايَ يَا أَبَا الْحَسَنِ أَنَّكَ حُجَّةُ اللهِ عَلَىٰ خَلْقِهِ، وَ خَلِيفَتُهُ فِي بَرِيَّتِهِ، وَ أَمِينُهُ فِي بِلَادِهِ، وَ شَاهِدُهُ عَلَىٰ عِبَادِهِ،

I testify that you are the word of Godfearing, the gateway of guidance, the firmest handle and the testament to those who are on the earth and those who are under the ground.

وَ أَشْهَدُ أَنَّكَ كَلِمَةُ التَّقْوَىٰ، وَ بَابُ الْهُدَىٰ، وَ الْعُرْوَةُ الْوُثْقَىٰ، وَ الْحُجَّةُ عَلَىٰ مَنْ فَوْقَ الْأَرْضِ وَ مَنْ تَحْتَ الثَّرَىٰ،

وَ أَشْهَدُ أَنَّكَ الْمُطَهَّرُ مِنَ الذُّنُوبِ، الْمُبَرَّأُ
مِنَ الْعُيُوبِ، وَ الْمُخْتَصُّ بِكَرَامَةِ اللهِ،
وَ الْمَحْبُوُّ بِحُجَّةِ اللهِ، وَ الْمَوْهُوبُ لَهُ كَلِمَةُ
اللهِ، وَ الرُّكْنُ الَّذِى يَلْجَأُ إِلَيْهِ الْعِبَادُ، وَ
تُحْيَا بِهِ الْبِلَادُ،

I testify that you are free from sin and defects, endowed by Allah with dignity and divine proofs, and blessed with His word, that you are the support with which God's servants take shelter, and through you communities and towns receive real life!

وَ أَشْهَدُ يَا مَوْلَاىَ أَنِّي بِكَ وَ بِآبَائِكَ وَ
أَبْنَائِكَ مُوقِنٌ مُقِرٌّ، وَ لَكُمْ تَابِعٌ فِي ذَاتِ
نَفْسِي وَ شَرَائِعِ دِينِي، وَ خَاتِمَةِ عَمَلِي،
وَ مُنْقَلَبِي وَ مَثْوَاىَ، وَ أَنِّي وَلِيٌّ لِمَنْ
وَالَاكُمْ، وَ عَدُوٌّ لِمَنْ عَادَاكُمْ، مُؤْمِنٌ
بِسِرِّكُمْ وَ عَلَانِيَتِكُمْ، وَ أَوَّلِكُمْ
وَ آخِرِكُمْ، بِأَبِي أَنْتَ وَ أُمِّي، وَ السَّلَامُ
عَلَيْكَ وَ رَحْمَةُ اللهِ وَ بَرَكَاتُهُ .

My master, I testify that I have conviction and professed belief in you, your ancestors and descendants, following you with regard to my self, the precepts of my religion, my final works, my life's itinerary and final goal. I befriend those who befriend you and despise those who are hostile to you, having faith in your esoteric and exoteric affairs, and in the first of you and the last one. You are dearer to me than my father and mother! Peace be to you and may Allah's mercy and His bounties be upon you!

Then embrace the *ḍarīḥ* laying your right and left cheek on it, and say,

اَللّٰهُمَّ صَلِّ عَلىٰ مُحَمَّدٍ وَآلِ مُحَمَّدٍ، وَ صَلِّ
عَلىٰ حُجَّتِكَ الْوَفِيِّ، وَ وَلِيِّكَ الزَّكِيِّ، وَ أَمِينِكَ
الْمُرْتَضىٰ، وَ صَفِيِّكَ الْهَادِى، وَ صِرَاطِكَ
الْمُسْتَقِيمِ، وَ الْجَادَّةِ الْعُظْمىٰ، وَ الطَّرِيقَةِ
الْوُسْطىٰ، نُورِ قُلُوبِ الْمُؤْمِنِينَ، وَ وَلِيِّ

O Allah, bless Muḥammad and the Family of Muḥammad, and bless Your loyal testament, Your blameless *walī*, Your approved trustee, Your chosen guide, Your straight path, Your greatest highway and middle path, the light of the hearts of the faithful, the guardian of the Godwary, and the companion of those who

الْمُتَّقِينَ، وَ صَاحِبِ الْمُخْلَصِينَ.

are totally dedicated to You!

اَللّٰهُمَّ صَلِّ عَلٰى سَيِّدِنَا مُحَمَّدٍ وَ أَهْلِ بَيْتِهِ، وَ صَلِّ عَلٰى عَلِيِّ بْنِ مُحَمَّدٍ الرَّاشِدِ، اَلْمَعْصُومِ مِنَ الزَّلَلِ، وَ الطَّاهِرِ مِنَ الْخَلَلِ، وَ الْمُنْقَطِعِ إِلَيْكَ بِالْأَمَلِ، اَلْمَبْلُوِّ بِالْفِتَنِ، وَ الْمُخْتَبَرِ بِالْمِحَنِ، وَ الْمُمْتَحَنِ بِحُسْنِ الْبَلْوٰى وَ صَبْرِ الشَّكْوٰى، مُرْشِدِ عِبَادِكَ، وَ بَرَكَةِ بِلَادِكَ، وَ مَحَلِّ رَحْمَتِكَ، وَ مُسْتَوْدَعِ حِكْمَتِكَ، وَ الْقَائِدِ إِلَى جَنَّتِكَ، الْعَالِمِ فِى بَرِيَّتِكَ، وَ الْهَادِى فِى خَلِيقَتِكَ، اَلَّذِى ارْتَضَيْتَهُ وَ انْتَجَبْتَهُ وَ اخْتَرْتَهُ لِمَقَامِ رَسُولِكَ فِى أُمَّتِهِ، وَ أَلْزَمْتَهُ حِفْظَ شَرِيعَتِهِ، فَاسْتَقَلَّ بِأَعْبَاءِ الْوَصِيَّةِ، نَاهِضًا بِهَا وَ مُضْطَلِعًا بِحَمْلِهَا، لَمْ يَعْثُرْ فِى مُشْكِلٍ، وَ لَا هَفَا فِى مُعْضِلٍ، بَلْ كَشَفَ الْغُمَّةَ، وَ سَدَّ الْفُرْجَةَ، وَ أَدَّى الْمُفْتَرَضَ.

O Allah, bless Muḥammad, our master, and his Family, and bless ʿAlī ibn Muḥammad, the infallible guide preserved by You from lapses and free from defects, who placed his hope exclusively in You, who was tried with ordeals, tested with tribulations, put to test through Your gracefully inflicted afflictions and his uncomplaining patience, the guide of Your servants, the blessing for Your towns, the abode of Your mercy, the repository of Your wisdom, the leader on the way to Your paradise, the sage amidst Your creatures, the guide amongst Your creation, whom You approved, chose and elected for the position of Your Apostle in his community and whom You charged with the preservation of his *sharīʿah*, whereupon he undauntedly shouldered the responsibilities of the Prophet's successorship, rising up to discharge them, and fulfilled them skilfully, without ever stumbling in any difficulty or making mistake in any problem. Rather, he overcame distressing conditions, filled the gaps and fulfilled his duties.

اَللّٰهُمَّ فَكَمَا أَقْرَرْتَ نَاظِرَ نَبِيِّكَ بِهِ، فَرَقِّهِ [فَارْفَعْ] دَرَجَتَهُ، وَ أَجْزِلْ لَدَيْكَ مَثُوبَتَهُ، وَ صَلِّ عَلَيْهِ، وَ بَلِّغْهُ مِنَّا تَحِيَّةً وَ سَلَامًا، وَ آتِنَا مِنْ لَدُنْكَ فِى مُوَالَاتِهِ

O Allah, as You have brought comfort to Your Prophet through him, raise his rank, make abundant His reward with You and bless him. Convey our greetings and *salām* to him, and grant us Your grace, beneficence, forgiveness and ap-

فَضْلًا وَ إِحْسَانًا، وَ مَغْفِرَةً وَ رِضْوَانًا،
إِنَّكَ ذُو الْفَضْلِ الْعَظِيمِ.

proval by virtue of our friendship and love for him. Indeed You are dispenser of a mighty grace.

Then perform the prayer of *ziyārah*, and after the *salām*, say,

يَا ذَا الْقُدْرَةِ الْجَامِعَةِ، وَ الرَّحْمَةِ الْوَاسِعَةِ،
وَ الْمِنَنِ الْمُتَتَابِعَةِ، وَ الْآلَاءِ الْمُتَوَاتِرَةِ، وَ
الْأَيَادِي الْجَلِيلَةِ، وَ الْمَوَاهِبِ الْجَزِيلَةِ،
صَلِّ عَلَى مُحَمَّدٍ وَ آلِ مُحَمَّدٍ الصَّادِقِينَ،
وَ أَعْطِنِي سُؤْلِي، وَ اجْمَعْ شَمْلِي، وَ لُمَّ
شَعْثِي، وَ زَكِّ عَمَلِي، وَ لَا تُزِغْ قَلْبِي
بَعْدَ إِذْ هَدَيْتَنِي، وَ لَا تُزِلَّ قَدَمِي،

O Possessor of all-encompassing power and inclusive mercy, O Bestower of continuous favours and uninterrupted bounties, O Granter of splendid blessings and generous gifts! Bless Muḥammad and the Family of Muḥammad, the truthful ones, and grant my petition, help me get back on my feet, compose my dissipated affairs, and purify my conduct. Do not let my heart swerve after that You have guided me and do not let my feet stumble.

وَ لَا تَكِلْنِي إِلَى نَفْسِي طَرْفَةَ عَيْنٍ أَبَدًا،
وَ لَا تُخَيِّبْ طَمَعِي، وَ لَا تُبْدِ عَوْرَتِي، وَ
لَا تَهْتِكْ سِتْرِي، وَ لَا تُوحِشْنِي وَ لَا
تُؤْيِسْنِي، وَ كُنْ بِي رَءُوفًا رَحِيمًا، وَ
اهْدِنِي وَ زَكِّنِي وَ طَهِّرْنِي، وَ صَفِّنِي وَ
اصْطَفِنِي، وَ خَلِّصْنِي وَ اسْتَخْلِصْنِي،
وَ اصْنَعْنِي وَ اصْطَنِعْنِي، وَ قَرِّبْنِي إِلَيْكَ
وَ لَا تُبَاعِدْنِي مِنْكَ، وَ الْطُفْ بِي وَ لَا
تَجْفُنِي، وَ أَكْرِمْنِي وَ لَا تُهِنِّي، وَ مَا
أَسْأَلُكَ فَلَا تَحْرِمْنِي، وَ مَا لَا أَسْأَلُكَ

Never consign me to my own devices, even for an instant; do not disappoint my hope; do not lay bare my defects; do not rend my cover; and do not leave me in desolation and despair. Be kind and merciful to me, guide me, purify me and purge me; rectify me conduct and help me get back on my feet: free me from all taints and make me totally dedicated to You; foster me and take me up into Your favour; draw me close to Yourself and do not turn me away; be gentle to me and do not be unkindly. Grant me honour and do not abase me. Do not deprive me of what I request You and put together for me that which I do not ask You, O Most

Merciful of the merciful.

فَاجْمَعْهُ لِي، بِرَحْمَتِكَ يا أَرْحَمَ الرَّاحِمِينَ!

I beseech You by the sanctity of Your munificent Face, by the sanctity of Muḥammad, may Your blessings be upon him and his Family, and by the sanctity of the members of Your Apostle's Family, ʿAlī, the Commander of the Faithful, al-Ḥasan, al-Ḥusayn, ʿAlī, Muḥammad, Jaʿfar, Mūsā, ʿAlī, Muḥammad, ʿAlī, al-Ḥasan and their surviving heir, may Your blessings and bounties be upon them, to bless them all and to hasten the relief of their Qā'im by Your command, and defend him and through him defend Your religion, and appoint me among those who attain deliverance through him and work with dedication in obedience to him.

وَ أَسْأَلُكَ بِحُرْمَةِ وَجْهِكَ الْكَرِيمِ، وَ بِحُرْمَةِ نَبِيِّكَ مُحَمَّدٍ صَلَوَاتُكَ عَلَيْهِ وَ آلِهِ، وَ بِحُرْمَةِ أَهْلِ بَيْتِ رَسُولِكَ أَمِيرِ الْمُؤْمِنِينَ عَلِيٍّ، وَ الْحَسَنِ وَ الْحُسَيْنِ، وَ عَلِيٍّ وَ مُحَمَّدٍ وَ جَعْفَرٍ وَ مُوسَى وَ عَلِيٍّ وَ مُحَمَّدٍ وَ عَلِيٍّ وَ الْحَسَنِ وَ الْخَلَفِ الْبَاقِي، صَلَوَاتُكَ وَ بَرَكَاتُكَ عَلَيْهِمْ، أَنْ تُصَلِّيَ عَلَيْهِمْ أَجْمَعِينَ، وَ تُعَجِّلَ فَرَجَ قَائِمِهِمْ بِأَمْرِكَ، وَ تَنْصُرَهُ وَ تَنْتَصِرَ بِهِ لِدِينِكَ، وَ تَجْعَلَنِي فِي جُمْلَةِ النَّاجِينَ بِهِ، وَ الْمُخْلِصِينَ فِي طَاعَتِهِ،

I beseech You by their right, to answer my prayer, fulfil my need, grant my petition, and suffice me with regard to all that is of concern to me of my affairs pertaining to the world and the Hereafter, O Most Merciful of the merciful! O Light, O Proof, O Giver of light and clarity, O my Lord! Protect me from the harm of all evils and the blights of the times, and I beseech You to deliver me on the Day the Trumpet is blown!

وَ أَسْأَلُكَ بِحَقِّهِمْ لَمَّا اسْتَجَبْتَ لِي دَعْوَتِي، وَ قَضَيْتَ لِي حَاجَتِي، وَ أَعْطَيْتَنِي سُؤْلِي، وَ كَفَيْتَنِي مَا أَهَمَّنِي مِنْ أَمْرِ دُنْيَايَ وَ آخِرَتِي، يَا أَرْحَمَ الرَّاحِمِينَ، يَا نُورُ يَا بُرْهَانُ، يَا مُنِيرُ يَا مُبِينُ، يَا رَبِّ اكْفِنِي شَرَّ الشُّرُورِ وَ آفَاتِ الدُّهُورِ، وَ أَسْأَلُكَ النَّجَاةَ يَوْمَ يُنْفَخُ فِي الصُّورِ.

Then supplicate and make any petitions that you wish, and say a lot,

O my Provision for the Day when provisions are counted on, O my Hope and reliance, my Refuge and shelter! O You who are Single and One! O (revealer of) *Say 'He is Allah, the One!'* O Allah, I beseech You by the right of those You have created from among Your creatures and did not create anyone like them among Your creatures, to bless them all and to fulfil my need!	يَا عُدَّتِي عِنْدَ الْعَدَدِ [الْعُدَدِ]، وَ يَا رَجَائِي وَ الْمُعْتَمَدَ، وَ يَا كَهْفِي وَ السَّنَدَ، يَا وَاحِدُ يَا أَحَدُ، وَ يَا قُلْ هُوَ اللهُ أَحَدٌ، أَسْأَلُكَ اللّٰهُمَّ بِحَقِّ مَنْ خَلَقْتَ مِنْ خَلْقِكَ، وَ لَمْ تَجْعَلْ فِي خَلْقِكَ مِثْلَهُمْ أَحَدًا، صَلِّ عَلَىٰ جَمَاعَتِهِمْ، وَ افْعَلْ بِي كَذَا وَ كَذَا .

Then mention your need. It is reported that the Imam said: "I have asked God, the Almighy and Glorious, not to disappoint anyone who makes this supplication by my grave."

ZIYARAH OF IMAM AL-ḤASAN AL-'ASKARI ('A)

Shaykh Ṭūsī reports[1] with a reliable *isnād* from Imam al-Ḥasan al-ᶜAskarī (ᶜ*a*) that he said, "My tomb at Surra Man Ra'ā will be a source of protection for the people on both sides." Majlisī I has interpreted this as meaning the Shiᶜah and the Ahl al-Sunnah.[2] He remarks that the blessings of the Imam's presence envelop friend and foe alike, like the shrine of the two Imams at Kaẓimiyyah, which is a source of safety for the people of Baghdad (from Divine punishment).

According to Sayyid Ibn Ṭāwūs,[3] when one intends to perform the *ziyārah* of Imam al-Ḥasan al-ᶜAskarī (ᶜ*a*) one should perform all the steps that were mentioned under the *ziyārah* of his father, Imam ᶜAlī al-Ḥādī (ᶜ*a*). Then standing near the Imam's tomb, say,

Peace be to you, O my master, Abū Muḥammad al-Ḥasan ibn ᶜAlī al-Haḍī, the rightly-guided Imam, and may Allah's mercy and His bounties be upon you!	اَلسَّلَامُ عَلَيْكَ يَا مَوْلَايَ يَا أَبَا مُحَمَّدٍ الْحَسَنَ بْنَ عَلِيٍّ الْهَادِيَ الْمُهْتَدِيَ وَ رَحْمَةُ اللهِ وَ بَرَكَاتُهُ،

1 *Tahdhīb*, vi, 93, b 43, h 3, whence *Wasā'il*, xiv, 572, b 90, h 19843. Mufīd's *Mazār*, 202, b 18, h 5. *Al-Mazār al-Kabīr*, 41, h 24..

2 *Rawḍat al-Muttaqīn*, v, 402.

3 *Biḥār*, xcix, 67, b 6, h 8 from Ibn Ṭāwūs.

اَلسَّلَامُ عَلَيْكَ يَا وَلِيَّ اللهِ وَ ابْنَ أَوْلِيَائِهِ، اَلسَّلَامُ عَلَيْكَ يَا حُجَّةَ اللهِ وَ ابْنَ حُجَجِهِ، اَلسَّلَامُ عَلَيْكَ يَا صَفِيَّ اللهِ وَ ابْنَ أَصْفِيَائِهِ، اَلسَّلَامُ عَلَيْكَ يَا خَلِيفَةَ اللهِ وَ ابْنَ خُلَفَائِهِ وَ أَبَا خَلِيفَتِهِ،

Peace be to you, O *walī* of Allah and son of His *awliyā'*! Peace be to you, O testament of Allah, son of His testaments! Peace be to you, O chosen of Allah and son of His chosen ones! Peace be to you O vicegerent of Allah, son of His vicegerents and father of His vicegerent!

اَلسَّلَامُ عَلَيْكَ يَا ابْنَ خَاتَمِ النَّبِيِّينَ، اَلسَّلَامُ عَلَيْكَ يَا ابْنَ سَيِّدِ الْوَصِيِّينَ، اَلسَّلَامُ عَلَيْكَ يَا ابْنَ أَمِيرِ الْمُؤْمِنِينَ، اَلسَّلَامُ عَلَيْكَ يَا ابْنَ سَيِّدَةِ نِسَاءِ الْعَالَمِينَ،

Peace be to you, O son of the Seal of the Prophets! Peace be to you O son of the Chief of the Legatees! Peace be to you, O son of the Commander of the Faithful! Peace be to you, O son of the mistress of the world's womankind

اَلسَّلَامُ عَلَيْكَ يَا ابْنَ الْأَئِمَّةِ الْهَادِينَ، اَلسَّلَامُ عَلَيْكَ يَا ابْنَ الْأَوْصِيَاءِ الرَّاشِدِينَ، اَلسَّلَامُ عَلَيْكَ يَا عِصْمَةَ الْمُتَّقِينَ، اَلسَّلَامُ عَلَيْكَ يَا إِمَامَ الْفَائِزِينَ، اَلسَّلَامُ عَلَيْكَ يَا رُكْنَ الْمُؤْمِنِينَ، اَلسَّلَامُ عَلَيْكَ يَا فَرَجَ الْمَلْهُوفِينَ،

Peace be to you, O son of the Imams and Guides! Peace be to you, O son of the rightly-guided legatees! Peace be to you, O protector of the pious! Peace be to you, O Imam of the triumphant! Peace be to you, O support of the faithful! Peace be to you, O relief of the grief-stricken!

اَلسَّلَامُ عَلَيْكَ يَا وَارِثَ الْأَنْبِيَاءِ الْمُنْتَجَبِينَ، اَلسَّلَامُ عَلَيْكَ يَا خَازِنَ عِلْمِ وَصِيِّ رَسُولِ اللهِ، اَلسَّلَامُ عَلَيْكَ أَيُّهَا الدَّاعِي بِحُكْمِ اللهِ، اَلسَّلَامُ عَلَيْكَ أَيُّهَا النَّاطِقُ بِكِتَابِ اللهِ،

Peace be to you, O heir of the chosen prophets! Peace be to you, O repository of the knowledge of the legatee of Allah's Apostle! Peace be to you, who summon by Allah's judgement! Peace be to you, who speak by the scripture of Allah!

اَلسَّلَامُ عَلَيْكَ يَا حُجَّةَ الْحُجَجِ، اَلسَّلَامُ

Peace be to you, O testament of the testaments! Peace be

to you, O guide of the nations! Peace be to you, O dispenser of the blessings! Peace be to you, O storehouse of knowledge! Peace be to you, O ship of forbearance!

عَلَيْكَ يَا هَادِىَ الْأُمَمِ، اَلسَّلَامُ عَلَيْكَ
يَا وَلِيَّ النِّعَمِ، اَلسَّلَامُ عَلَيْكَ يَا عَيْبَةَ
الْعِلْمِ، اَلسَّلَامُ عَلَيْكَ يَا سَفِينَةَ الْحِلْمِ،

Peace be to you, O father of the awaited Imam, whose evidence is manifest for the intelligent, whose knowledge is grounded in certitude, who is veiled from the eyes of the wrongdoers, hidden from the regime of the evil-doers, through whom our Lord will restore Islam anew after its obliteration, and refresh the Qur'ān after its effacement!

اَلسَّلَامُ عَلَيْكَ يَا أَبَا الْإِمَامِ الْمُنْتَظَرِ،
اَلظَّاهِرَةِ لِلْعَاقِلِ حُجَّتُهُ، وَ الثَّابِتَةِ فِي الْيَقِينِ
مَعْرِفَتُهُ، اَلْمُحْتَجَبِ عَنْ أَعْيُنِ الظَّالِمِينَ،
وَ الْمُغَيَّبِ عَنْ دَوْلَةِ الْفَاسِقِينَ، وَ الْمُعِيدِ
رَبُّنَا بِهِ الْإِسْلَامَ جَدِيدًا بَعْدَ الْإِنْطِمَاسِ،
وَ الْقُرْآنَ غَضًّا بَعْدَ الْإِنْدِرَاسِ،

O my master, I testify that you maintained the prayer, paid the *zakāt*, bade what is right and forbade what is wrong, summoned to the way of Your Lord with wisdom and good advice, and worshipped Allah with dedication until the last breath.

أَشْهَدُ يَا مَوْلَاىَ أَنَّكَ أَقَمْتَ الصَّلَاةَ،
وَ آتَيْتَ الزَّكَاةَ، وَ أَمَرْتَ بِالْمَعْرُوفِ، وَ
نَهَيْتَ عَنِ الْمُنْكَرِ، وَ دَعَوْتَ إِلَى سَبِيلِ
رَبِّكَ بِالْحِكْمَةِ وَ الْمَوْعِظَةِ الْحَسَنَةِ، وَ
عَبَدْتَ اللهَ مُخْلِصًا حَتَّى أَتَاكَ الْيَقِينُ،

I beseech Allah, by the station you have with Him, to accept my *ziyārah* of your shrine, to receive well my effort to reach out to you, to answer my supplication for your sake, and to make me one of the supporters of the truth, and its followers, partisans, sponsors and lovers. Peace be to you, and may Allah's mercy and His bounties be upon you!

أَسْأَلُ اللهَ بِالشَّأْنِ الَّذِى لَكُمْ عِنْدَهُ،
أَنْ يَتَقَبَّلَ زِيَارَتِي لَكُمْ، وَ يَشْكُرَ سَعْيِي
إِلَيْكُمْ، وَ يَسْتَجِيبَ دُعَائِى بِكُمْ، وَ
يَجْعَلَنِي مِنْ أَنْصَارِ الْحَقِّ وَ أَتْبَاعِهِ وَ
أَشْيَاعِهِ وَ مَوَالِيهِ وَ مُحِبِّيهِ، وَ السَّلَامُ
عَلَيْكَ وَ رَحْمَةُ اللهِ وَ بَرَكَاتُهُ .

Then mbrace the *ḍarīḥ*, placing your right cheek on it and then the left, and say,

O Allah, bless Muḥammad, our master, and his Family, and bless al-Ḥasan ibn ʿAlī, the guide to Your religion, the summoner to Your path, the banner of guidance and the minaret of piety, the mine of wisdom, the refuge of the intellect, the rain of mercy for mankind, the cloud of wisdom, the ocean of advice, the heir of the Imams, the witness to the *ummah*, who was preserved from sin, refined, meritorious, close to You, pure from all impurity, whom You made heir to the knowledge of the Scripture, inspired him with decisive speech, hoisted him as standard for those who follow Your *qiblah*, made obedience to him coequal to obeying You, and enjoined all Your creatures to love him!

اَللّٰهُمَّ صَلِّ عَلىٰ سَيِّدِنَا مُحَمَّدٍ وَ أَهْلِ بَيْتِهِ،
وَ صَلِّ عَلَى الْحَسَنِ بْنِ عَلِيٍّ الْهَادِى إِلَى
دِينِكَ، وَ الدَّاعِى إِلَى سَبِيلِكَ، عَلَمِ
الْهُدَىٰ، وَ مَنَارِ التُّقَىٰ، وَ مَعْدِنِ الْحِجَىٰ، وَ
مَأْوَى النُّهَىٰ، وَ غَيْثِ الْوَرَىٰ، وَ سَحَابِ
الْحِكْمَةِ، وَ بَحْرِ الْمَوْعِظَةِ، وَ وَارِثِ
الْأَئِمَّةِ، وَ الشَّهِيدِ عَلَى الْأُمَّةِ، اَلْمَعْصُومِ
الْمُهَذَّبِ، وَ الْفَاضِلِ الْمُقَرَّبِ، وَ الْمُطَهَّرِ
مِنَ الرِّجْسِ، اَلَّذِى وَرَّثْتَهُ عِلْمَ الْكِتَابِ،
وَ أَلْهَمْتَهُ فَصْلَ الْخِطَابِ، وَ نَصَبْتَهُ عَلَمًا
لِأَهْلِ قِبْلَتِكَ، وَ قَرَنْتَ طَاعَتَهُ بِطَاعَتِكَ،
وَ فَرَضْتَ مَوَدَّتَهُ عَلىٰ جَمِيعِ خَلِيقَتِكَ،

O Allah, as he turned to You with utmost dedication to Your Unity, demolished those who likened You to Your creatures, and defended those who had faith in You, bless him, Lord, with a blessing that will bring him to the station of the humble and raise him in paradise to the rank of his grandfather, the Seal of the Prophets.

اَللّٰهُمَّ فَكَمَا أَنَابَ بِحُسْنِ الْإِخْلَاصِ
فِى تَوْحِيدِكَ، وَ أَرْدَى مَنْ خَاضَ فِى
تَشْبِيهِكَ، وَ حَامَى عَنْ أَهْلِ الْإِيمَانِ بِكَ،
فَصَلِّ يَا رَبِّ عَلَيْهِ صَلَاةً يَلْحَقُ بِهَا مَحَلَّ
الْخَاشِعِينَ، وَ يَعْلُو فِى الْجَنَّةِ بِدَرَجَةِ جَدِّهِ
خَاتَمِ النَّبِيِّينَ،

Convey to him our greetings

وَ بَلِّغْهُ مِنَّا تَحِيَّةً وَ سَلَامًا، وَ آتِنَا مِنْ

لَدُنْكَ فِي مُوَالاتِهِ فَضْلًا وَ إِحْسَانًا، وَ مَغْفِرَةً وَ رِضْوَانًا، إِنَّكَ ذُو فَضْلٍ عَظِيمٍ وَ مَنٍّ جَسِيمٍ.

and *salām*, and grant us for our love for him Your grace and kindness, forgiveness and approval! Indeed You are dispenser of a mighty grace and great favour!

Then offer the prayer of *ziyārah*, and say when you have finished,

يَا دَائِمُ يَا دَيْمُومُ [يَا دَيُّومُ]، يَا حَيُّ يَا قَيُّومُ، يَا كَاشِفَ الْكَرْبِ وَ الْهَمِّ، [وَ] يَا فَارِجَ الْغَمِّ، وَ يَا بَاعِثَ الرُّسُلِ، [وَ] يَا صَادِقَ الْوَعْدِ، [وَ] يَا حَيُّ لَا إِلٰهَ إِلَّا أَنْتَ،

O Eternal and everlasting One! O Living One and All-sustainer! O Reliever of worries and distress! O Dispeller of sorrows! O Sender of the apostles! O You who are true to Your promises! O Living One, there is no god besides You,

أَتَوَسَّلُ إِلَيْكَ بِحَبِيبِكَ مُحَمَّدٍ، وَ وَصِيِّهِ عَلِيٍّ ابْنِ عَمِّهِ وَ صِهْرِهِ عَلَى ابْنَتِهِ، اَلَّذِي [اَللَّذَيْنِ] خَتَمْتَ بِهِمَا الشَّرَائِعَ، وَ فَتَحْتَ [بِهِمَا] التَّأْوِيلَ وَ الطَّلَائِعَ، فَصَلِّ عَلَيْهِمَا صَلَاةً يَشْهَدُ بِهَا الْأَوَّلُونَ وَ الْآخِرُونَ، وَ يَنْجُو بِهَا الْأَوْلِيَاءُ وَ الصَّالِحُونَ،

I turn to You through the mediation of Muḥammad, Your beloved, and ᶜAlī, his legatee, cousin and daughter's husband, the two with whom You brought to conclusion the prophetic *sharīᶜahs* and through whom You inaugurated interpretation and new beginnings. So bless both of them with a blessing that is witnessed by the former and latter generations and whereby are delivered Your friends and righteous servants!

وَ أَتَوَسَّلُ إِلَيْكَ بِفَاطِمَةَ الزَّهْرَاءِ وَالِدَةِ الْأَئِمَّةِ الْمَهْدِيِّينَ، وَ سَيِّدَةِ نِسَاءِ الْعَالَمِينَ، اَلْمُشَفَّعَةِ فِي شِيعَةِ أَوْلَادِهَا الطَّيِّبِينَ، فَصَلِّ عَلَيْهَا صَلَاةً دَائِمَةً أَبَدَ الْآبِدِينَ، وَ دَهْرَ الدَّاهِرِينَ،

And I turn to You through the mediation of Fāṭimah Zahrā, the mother of the Imams and guides and mistress of the world's womankind, who intercedes on behalf of the followers of her infallible descendants. So bless her with a blessing that is perpetual, eternal and everlasting!

وَ أَتَوَسَّلُ إِلَيْكَ بِالْحَسَنِ الرَّضِيِّ الطَّاهِرِ

And I turn to You through the

الزَّكِيِّ، وَ الْحُسَيْنِ الْمَظْلُومِ الْمَرْضِيِّ الْبَرِّ التَّقِيِّ، سَيِّدَيْ شَبَابِ أَهْلِ الْجَنَّةِ، الْإِمَامَيْنِ الْخَيِّرَيْنِ الطَّيِّبَيْنِ التَّقِيَّيْنِ النَّقِيَّيْنِ الطَّاهِرَيْنِ الشَّهِيدَيْنِ الْمَظْلُومَيْنِ الْمَقْتُولَيْنِ، فَصَلِّ عَلَيْهِمَا مَا طَلَعَتْ شَمْسٌ وَ مَا غَرَبَتْ، صَلَاةً مُتَوَالِيَةً مُتَتَالِيَةً،

mediation of al-Ḥasan, the admirable, immaculate and pure Imam, and al-Ḥusayn, the admirable, benign and pious Imam, who was slain wrongfully, both of them doyens of the youth of paradise, the benevolent, pure, pious, faultless, immaculate Imams and martyrs who were slain wrongfully. So bless the two of them, as long as the sun rises and sets, with a blessing that is continuous and uninterrupted!

وَ أَتَوَسَّلُ إِلَيْكَ بِعَلِيِّ بْنِ الْحُسَيْنِ سَيِّدِ الْعَابِدِينَ، الْمَحْجُوبِ مِنْ خَوْفِ الظَّالِمِينَ، وَ بِمُحَمَّدِ بْنِ عَلِيٍّ الْبَاقِرِ الطَّاهِرِ النُّورِ الزَّاهِرِ، الْإِمَامَيْنِ السَّيِّدَيْنِ، مِفْتَاحَيِ الْبَرَكَاتِ، وَ مِصْبَاحَيِ الظُّلُمَاتِ، فَصَلِّ عَلَيْهِمَا مَا سَرَى لَيْلٌ وَ مَا أَضَاءَ نَهَارٌ، صَلَاةً تَغْدُو وَ تَرُوحُ،

And I turn to You through the mediation of ʿAlī ibn al-Ḥusayn, the doyen of the devout, who dwelt in seclusion for the fear of tyrants, and through the mediation of Muḥammad ibn ʿAlī, the immaculate exponent, the shining light, the two Imams and leaders who were keys of Divine blessings and lamps in the darkness. So bless them, as long as the night falls and the day shines, with a blessing sustained morning and evening!

وَ أَتَوَسَّلُ إِلَيْكَ بِجَعْفَرِ بْنِ مُحَمَّدٍ الصَّادِقِ عَنِ اللهِ، وَ النَّاطِقِ فِي عِلْمِ اللهِ، وَ بِمُوسَى بْنِ جَعْفَرٍ الْعَبْدِ الصَّالِحِ فِي نَفْسِهِ، وَ الْوَصِيِّ النَّاصِحِ، الْإِمَامَيْنِ الْهَادِيَيْنِ الْمَهْدِيَّيْنِ الْوَافِيَيْنِ الْكَافِيَيْنِ،

And I turn to You through the mediation of Jaʿfar ibn Muḥammad, who spoke truly on Allah's behalf and articulated Allah's knowledge, and Mūsā ibn Jaʿfar, the righteous servant of Allah, legatee of the Apostle and well-wisher of the *ummah*, both of whom were Imams and rightly-guided guides who fulfilled their mission and sufficed the *ummah*'s need for guidance.

So bless them, as long as the angels extol You and the firmament is in movement, with a blessing that grows and increases, not perishing or passing away!

فَصَلِّ عَلَيْهِمَا مَا سَبَّحَ لَكَ مَلَكٌ، وَ تَحَرَّكَ لَكَ فَلَكٌ، صَلَاةً تُنْمَىٰ وَ تَزِيدُ، وَ لَا تَفْنَىٰ وَ لَا تَبِيدُ،

And I turn to You through the mediation of ᶜAlī ibn Mūsā al-Riḍā and Muḥammad ibn ᶜAlī al-Murtaḍā, the two immaculate Imams and chosen of Allah. So bless them, as long as the morning shines and lasts, with a blessing whereby You elevate them to the station of Your pleasure in the *Illīyūn* in Your paradise!

وَ أَتَوَسَّلُ إِلَيْكَ بِعَلِيِّ بْنِ مُوسَى الرِّضَا، وَ بِمُحَمَّدِ بْنِ عَلِيٍّ الْمُرْتَضَىٰ، الْإِمَامَيْنِ الْمُطَهَّرَيْنِ الْمُنْتَجَبَيْنِ، فَصَلِّ عَلَيْهِمَا مَا أَضَاءَ صُبْحٌ وَ دَامَ، صَلَاةً تُرَقِّيهِمَا إِلَىٰ رِضْوَانِكَ فِي الْعِلِّيِّينَ مِنْ جِنَانِكَ،

And I turn to You through the mediation of ᶜAlī ibn Muḥammad, the rightly-guided, and al-Ḥasan ibn ᶜAlī, the guide, who were the upholders of Your command, Your servants who were tested with terrible ordeals and who bore patiently with provocative hatred. So bless them, as the recompense of the patient and the reward of the felicitous, with a blessing that will provide for their exaltation!

وَ أَتَوَسَّلُ إِلَيْكَ بِعَلِيِّ بْنِ مُحَمَّدٍ الرَّاشِدِ، وَ الْحَسَنِ بْنِ عَلِيٍّ الْهَادِي، اَلْقَائِمَيْنِ بِأَمْرِ عِبَادِكَ، اَلْمُخْتَبَرَيْنِ بِالْمِحَنِ الْهَائِلَةِ، وَ الصَّابِرَيْنِ فِي الْإِحَنِ الْمَائِلَةِ، فَصَلِّ عَلَيْهِمَا كِفَاءَ أَجْرِ الصَّابِرِينَ، وَ إِزَاءَ ثَوَابِ الْفَائِزِينَ، صَلَاةً تُمَهِّدُ لَهُمَا الرِّفْعَةَ،

And I turn to You, my Lord, through the mediation of our Imam, the authority of our age, 'the Promised Day,' the witness and the witnessed, the brilliant light, the resplendent radiance, assisted by Allah through his awe-inspiring presence, and granted victory with felicity. So bless him with a blessing as numerous as leaves and fruits of the trees, particles in clay and as nu-

وَ أَتَوَسَّلُ إِلَيْكَ يَا رَبِّ بِإِمَامِنَا وَ مُحَقِّقِ زَمَانِنَا، الْيَوْمِ الْمَوْعُودِ، وَ الشَّاهِدِ الْمَشْهُودِ، وَ النُّورِ الْأَزْهَرِ، وَ الضِّيَاءِ الْأَنْوَرِ، اَلْمَنْصُورِ بِالرُّعْبِ، وَ الْمُظَفَّرِ بِالسَّعَادَةِ، فَصَلِّ عَلَيْهِ عَدَدَ الثَّمَرِ، وَ أَوْرَاقِ الشَّجَرِ، وَ أَجْزَاءِ الْمَدَرِ، وَ عَدَدَ

merous as hair and fur and as great as a number that Your knowledge can count and Your Book can encompass, a blessing that would be envied by all creatures from the first to the last.

الشَّعْرِ وَ الْوَبَرِ، وَ عَدَدَ مَا أَحَاطَ بِهِ
عِلْمُكَ، وَ أَحْصَاهُ كِتَابُكَ، صَلَاةً يَغْبِطُهُ
بِهَا الْأَوَّلُونَ وَ الْآخِرُونَ،

O Allah, gather us in his group, sustain us in obedience to him, guard us with his governance, bless us with his *wilāyah*, help us against our enemies with his might and make us, our Lord, among those who turn to You penitently, O Most Merciful of the merciful!

اَللّٰهُمَّ وَ احْشُرْنَا فِي زُمْرَتِهِ، وَ احْفَظْنَا عَلَىٰ
طَاعَتِهِ،وَاحْرُسْنَابِدَوْلَتِهِ،وَأَتْحِفْنَابِوِلَايَتِهِ،
وَ انْصُرْنَا عَلَىٰ أَعْدَائِنَا بِعِزَّتِهِ، وَ اجْعَلْنَا
يَا رَبِّ مِنَ التَّوَّابِينَ، يَا أَرْحَمَ الرَّاحِمِينَ!

O Allah, the rebellious and accursed Iblīs asked You for a reprieve to pervert Your creatures and You granted him. He asked for time to lead astray Your servants, and You granted him time with Your prior knowledge about him. He has established himself, his troops have multiplied in number and his armies have proliferated. His preachers have spread in the earth's quarters and they have misled Your servants, corrupted Your religion, distorted the meanings of words, and divided Your servants into splintered groups and mutinous parties.

اَللّٰهُمَّ وَ إِنَّ إِبْلِيسَ الْمُتَمَرِّدَ اللَّعِينَ قَدِ
اسْتَنْظَرَكَ لِإِغْوَاءِ خَلْقِكَ فَأَنْظَرْتَهُ، وَ
اسْتَمْهَلَكَ لِإِضْلَالِ عَبِيدِكَ فَأَمْهَلْتَهُ
بِسَابِقِ عِلْمِكَ فِيهِ، وَ قَدْ عَشَّشَ وَ
كَثُرَتْ جُنُودُهُ، وَ ازْدَحَمَتْ جُيُوشُهُ، وَ
انْتَشَرَتْ دُعَاتُهُ فِي أَقْطَارِ الْأَرْضِ، فَأَضَلُّوا
عِبَادَكَ، وَ أَفْسَدُوا دِينَكَ، وَ حَرَّفُوا
الْكَلِمَ عَنْ مَوَاضِعِهِ، وَ جَعَلُوا عِبَادَكَ
شِيَعًا مُتَفَرِّقِينَ، وَ أَحْزَابًا مُتَمَرِّدِينَ،

Certainly, You have promised to dismantle his edifice and tear his work to pieces. So destroy his offspring and armies, purge Your lands of his fabrications and schisms, relieve Your servants of his creeds and fallacies. Bring

وَ قَدْ وَعَدْتَ نَقْضَ بُنْيَانِهِ، وَ تَمْزِيقَ
شَأْنِهِ، فَأَهْلِكْ أَوْلَادَهُ وَ جُيُوشَهُ، وَ طَهِّرْ
بِلَادَكَ مِنِ اخْتِرَاعَاتِهِ وَ اخْتِلَافَاتِهِ، وَ
أَرِحْ عِبَادَكَ مِنْ مَذَاهِبِهِ وَ قِيَاسَاتِهِ،

وَ اجْعَلْ دَائِرَةَ السَّوْءِ عَلَيْهِمْ، وَ ابْسُطْ
عَدْلَكَ، وَ أَظْهِرْ دِينَكَ، وَ قَوِّ أَوْلِيَاءَكَ،
وَ أَوْهِنْ أَعْدَاءَكَ، وَ أَوْرِثْ دِيَارَ إِبْلِيسَ
وَ دِيَارَ أَوْلِيَائِهِ أَوْلِيَاءَكَ، وَ خَلِّدْهُمْ فِي
الْجَحِيمِ، وَ أَذِقْهُمْ مِنَ الْعَذَابِ الْأَلِيمِ،
وَ اجْعَلْ لَعَائِنَكَ الْمُسْتَوْدَعَةَ فِي مَنَاحِسِ
[مَنَاحِيسِ] الْخِلْقَةِ، وَ مَشَاوِيهِ الْفِطْرَةِ
دَائِرَةً عَلَيْهِمْ، وَ مُوَكَّلَةً بِهِمْ، وَ جَارِيَةً فِيهِمْ
كُلَّ صَبَاحٍ وَ مَسَاءٍ، وَ غُدُوٍّ وَ رَوَاحٍ، رَبَّنَا
آتِنَا فِي الدُّنْيَا حَسَنَةً، وَ فِي الْآخِرَةِ حَسَنَةً، وَ
قِنَا بِرَحْمَتِكَ عَذَابَ النَّارِ، يَا أَرْحَمَ الرَّاحِمِينَ!

about their downfall, spread Your justice, make Your religion prevail, strengthen Your friends, and weaken Your enemies. Deliver the lands of Iblīs and those of his henchmen into the hands of Your friends. Put them forever into hell and make them taste its painful punishment.

Lay Your anathema on their inauspicious characters and ugly natures, to pursue, overtake and afflict them every morning and evening, day and night! Our Lord, give us good in this world and good in the Hereafter, and save us with Your mercy from the punishment of the Fire, O Most Merciful of the merciful!

Then supplicate and make any petitions you wish for yourself and your brethren.

ZIYARAH OF THE TWELFTH IMAM'S MOTHER (ᶜA)

Thereafter, perform the following *ziyārah* of the world's first lady, mother of the Imam of the Era (ᶜ*a*), whose grave is behind Imam al-Ḥasan al-ᶜAskarī's tomb.[1]

اَلسَّلَامُ عَلَىٰ رَسُولِ اللّٰهِ صَلَّى اللّٰهُ عَلَيْهِ وَ
آلِهِ، اَلصَّادِقِ الْأَمِينِ، اَلسَّلَامُ عَلَىٰ مَوْلَانَا
أَمِيرِ الْمُؤْمِنِينَ، اَلسَّلَامُ عَلَى الْأَئِمَّةِ
الطَّاهِرِينَ الْحُجَجِ الْمَيَامِينِ،

Peace be to the Apostle of Allah, the truthful and trustworthy prophet, may Allah bless him and his Family. Peace be to our master, the Commander of the Faithful. Peace be to the Immaculate Imams, the blessed testaments of God!

1 *Al-Mazār, al-Kabīr*, 660, b 3. *Biḥār*, xcix, 70, b 6, from Ibn Ṭāwūs. Shahīd Awwal's *Mazār*, 211.

Peace be to the mother of the Imam, the repository of the secrets of the All-knowing Sovereign and the mother who bore the noblest of creatures! Peace be to you, O truthful and approved lady!

اَلسَّلَامُ عَلٰى وَالِدَةِ الْإِمَامِ، وَ الْمُودَعَةِ أَسْرَارَ الْمَلِكِ الْعَلَّامِ، وَ الْحَامِلَةِ لِأَشْرَفِ الْأَنَامِ، اَلسَّلَامُ عَلَيْكِ أَيَّتُهَا الصِّدِّيقَةُ الْمَرْضِيَّةُ،

Peace be to you, O counterpart of the mother of Moses and daughter of the disciple of Jesus! Peace be to you, O pious and pure lady! Peace be to you, who were pleased with Allah and pleasing to Him!

اَلسَّلَامُ عَلَيْكِ يَا شَبِيهَةَ أُمِّ مُوسَىٰ وَ ابْنَةَ حَوَارِيِّ عِيسَىٰ، اَلسَّلَامُ عَلَيْكِ أَيَّتُهَا التَّقِيَّةُ النَّقِيَّةُ، اَلسَّلَامُ عَلَيْكِ أَيَّتُهَا الرَّضِيَّةُ الْمَرْضِيَّةُ،

Peace be to you, whose description appears in the Gospel, whose hand was sought from God's Trustworthy Spirit, whose marital tie was sought by Muḥammad, the chief of the Apostles, and who were entrusted with the secrets of the Lord of all the worlds!

اَلسَّلَامُ عَلَيْكِ أَيَّتُهَا الْمَنْعُوتَةُ فِي الْإِنْجِيلِ، اَلْمَخْطُوبَةُ مِنْ رُوحِ اللّٰهِ الْأَمِينِ، وَ مَنْ رَغِبَ فِي وُصْلَتِهَا مُحَمَّدٌ سَيِّدُ الْمُرْسَلِينَ، وَ الْمُسْتَوْدَعَةُ أَسْرَارَ رَبِّ الْعَالَمِينَ،

Peace be to you and to your ancestors, the disciples of Jesus! Peace be to you, and to your husband and child! Peace be to you and to your spirit and pure body!

اَلسَّلَامُ عَلَيْكِ وَ عَلٰى آبَائِكِ الْحَوَارِيِّينَ، اَلسَّلَامُ عَلَيْكِ وَ عَلٰى بَعْلِكِ وَ وَلَدِكِ، اَلسَّلَامُ عَلَيْكِ وَ عَلٰى رُوحِكِ وَ بَدَنِكِ الطَّاهِرِ،

I testify that you did your best in fostering your child; fulfilled your trust; strived diligently for the sake of Allah's pleasure; bore with the ordeals for the sake of Allah; guarded Allah's secret; bore the *walī* of Allah; took utmost care in guarding the testa-

أَشْهَدُ أَنَّكِ أَحْسَنْتِ الْكَفَالَةَ، وَ أَدَّيْتِ الْأَمَانَةَ، وَ اجْتَهَدْتِ فِي مَرْضَاةِ اللّٰهِ، وَ صَبَرْتِ فِي ذَاتِ اللّٰهِ، وَ حَفِظْتِ سِرَّ اللّٰهِ، وَ حَمَلْتِ وَلِيَّ اللّٰهِ، وَ بَالَغْتِ فِي

ment of Allah; ardently cherished the tie with the descendants of the Apostle of Allah, knowing well their rights, had faith in their truthfulness, acknowledged their station, possessed insight concerning their affair, had compassion for them and set their wishes above your own.

حِفْظِ حُجَّـةِ اللهِ، وَ رَغِبْتِ فِي وُصْلَةِ
أَبْنَاءِ رَسُولِ اللهِ، عَارِفَةً بِحَقِّهِمْ، مُؤْمِنَةً
بِصِدْقِهِمْ، مُعْتَرِفَةً بِمَنْزِلَتِهِمْ، مُسْتَبْصِرَةً
بِأَمْرِهِمْ، مُشْفِقَةً عَلَيْهِمْ، مُؤْثِرَةً هَوَاهُمْ،

I testify that you passed away possessing full insight of your faith, following in the footsteps of the righteous, while you were pleased with God and He was pleased with you, and you were Godwary, pure and blameless. May Allah be pleased with you and may He make you pleased, and may He make paradise your abode and destination, for indeed He gave you all the benisons that He did and granted you an honour that suffices you, may He gladden you and make you relish the dignity He has granted you.

وَ أَشْهَدُ أَنَّكِ مَضَيْتِ عَلَىٰ بَصِيرَةٍ مِنْ
أَمْرِكِ، مُقْتَدِيَـةً بِالصَّالِحِينَ، رَاضِيَةً
مَرْضِيَّـةً تَقِيَّـةً نَقِيَّةً زَكِيَّـةً، فَرَضِيَ
اللهُ عَنْكِ وَ أَرْضَـاكِ، وَ جَعَلَ الْجَنَّةَ
مَنْزِلَكِ وَ مَـأْوَاكِ، فَلَقَدْ أَوْلَاكِ مِنَ
الْخَـيْرَاتِ مَـا أَوْلَاكِ، وَ أَعْطَاكِ مِنَ
الشَّرَفِ مَا بِهِ أَغْنَاكِ، فَهَنَّاكِ اللهُ بِمَا
مَنَحَكِ مِنَ الْكَرَامَةِ وَ أَمْرَأَكِ .

Then raise your head and say,

O Allah, I put my reliance in You, seek Your good pleasure, and turn to You through the mediation of Your *awliyā*. I put my trust in Your forgiveness and forbearance, seeking protection with You, and I cling to the grave of Your *walī*'s mother.

اَللّٰهُمَّ إِيَّاكَ اعْتَمَدْتُ، وَ لِرِضَاكَ طَلَبْتُ،
وَ بِأَوْلِيَائِـكَ إِلَيْـكَ تَوَسَّـلْتُ، وَ عَلَىٰ
غُفْرَانِكَ وَ حِلْمِـكَ اتَّكَلْتُ، وَ بِكَ
اعْتَصَمْتُ، وَ بِقَبْرِ أُمِّ وَلِيِّكَ لُذْتُ،

So bless Muḥammad and the Family of Muḥammad and grant me the benefit of her *ziyārah*, keep me steady in my love for

فَصَلِّ عَلَىٰ مُحَمَّدٍ وَ آلِ مُحَمَّدٍ، وَ انْفَعْنِي
بِزِيَارَتِهَـا، وَ ثَبِّتْـنِي عَلَىٰ مَحَبَّتِهَا، وَ لَا

her, do not deprive me of her intercession and that of her son, bless me with her company, gather me at Resurrection with her and her son, even as You have enabled me to perform her *ziyārah* and that of her son!

تَحْرِمْنِي شَفَاعَتَهَا وَ شَفَاعَةَ وَلَدِهَا، وَ ارْزُقْنِي مُرَافَقَتَهَا، وَ احْشُرْنِي مَعَهَا وَ مَعَ وَلَدِهَا كَمَا وَفَّقْتَنِي لِزِيَارَةِ وَلَدِهَا وَ زِيَارَتِهَا،

O Allah, I turn to You through the mediation of the Immaculate Imams and have recourse to You through the blessed testaments from the Family of Ṭā-Hā and Yā-Sīn and beseech You to bless Muḥammad and the Family of Muḥammad, the immaculate ones. Appoint me among those who are content, joyous, triumphant, and rejoicing, *for whom there will be no fear nor who will ever grieve,* and make me one of those whose efforts are accepted by You, whose matters are facilitated, whose distress is removed and whose fears are allayed by You!

اَللّٰهُمَّ إِنِّي أَتَوَجَّهُ إِلَيْكَ بِالْأَئِمَّةِ الطَّاهِرِينَ، وَ أَتَوَسَّلُ إِلَيْكَ بِالْحُجَجِ الْمَيَامِينِ، مِنْ آلِ طٰهٰ وَ يٰس، أَنْ تُصَلِّيَ عَلىٰ مُحَمَّدٍ وَ آلِ مُحَمَّدٍ الطَّيِّبِينَ، وَ أَنْ تَجْعَلَنِي مِنَ الْمُطْمَئِنِّينَ الْفَائِزِينَ الْفَرِحِينَ الْمُسْتَبْشِرِينَ، اَلَّذِينَ لَا خَوْفٌ عَلَيْهِمْ وَ لَا هُمْ يَحْزَنُونَ، وَ اجْعَلْنِي مِمَّنْ قَبِلْتَ سَعْيَهُ، وَ يَسَّرْتَ أَمْرَهُ، وَ كَشَفْتَ ضُرَّهُ، وَ آمَنْتَ خَوْفَهُ،

O Allah, by the right of Muḥammad and the Family of Muḥammad, bless Muḥammad and the Family of Muḥammad and do not make this my last opportunity to perform her *ziyārah*. Grant me to keep on returning to her as long as You keep me alive; and when You make me die, to gather me in her fold, to admit me into intercession made by her and her son.

اَللّٰهُمَّ بِحَقِّ مُحَمَّدٍ وَ آلِ مُحَمَّدٍ صَلِّ عَلىٰ مُحَمَّدٍ وَ آلِ مُحَمَّدٍ، وَ لَا تَجْعَلْهُ آخِرَ الْعَهْدِ مِنْ زِيَارَتِي إِيَّاهَا، وَ ارْزُقْنِي الْعَوْدَ إِلَيْهَا أَبَدًا مَا أَبْقَيْتَنِي، وَ إِذَا تَوَفَّيْتَنِي فَاحْشُرْنِي فِي زُمْرَتِهَا، وَ أَدْخِلْنِي فِي شَفَاعَةِ وَلَدِهَا وَ شَفَاعَتِهَا،

Forgive me, my parents and all

وَ اغْفِرْ لِي وَ لِوَالِدَيَّ وَ لِلْمُؤْمِنِينَ وَ

the faithful, men and women, and give us good in this world and good in the Hereafter, and save us with Your mercy from the punishment of the Fire. May peace be to you, my masters, and may Allah's mercy and His bounties be upon you!	الْمُؤْمِنَاتِ، وَ آتِنَا فِي الدُّنْيَا حَسَـنَةً، وَ فِي الْآخِرَةِ حَسَـنَةً، وَ قِنَـا بِرَحْمَتِكَ عَذَابَ النَّارِ، وَ السَّلَامُ عَلَيْكُمْ يَا سَادَاتِي وَ رَحْمَةُ اللهِ وَ بَرَكَاتُهُ .

It has been reported[1] that Zayd al-Shaḥḥām asked Imam Jaᶜfar al-Ṣādiq (ᶜa) concerning the reward for performing the *ziyārah* of any of the Imams. The Imam replied that it was like the reward of someone who performs the *ziyārah* of the Apostle of Allah (ṣ). Earlier we have cited the report from Imam Jaᶜfar al-Ṣādiq (ᶜa) that a reward of a *ḥajj* and *ᶜumrah* pilgrimage is written for someone who performs the *ziyārah* of an Imam obeying whom is obligatory, and offers four *rakᶜahs* of prayer by his tomb.

ZIYARAH OF HADRAT HAKIMAH (R)

In our book *Hadīyat al-Zā'irīn*[2] we have mentioned the merits of Ḥaḍrat Ḥakīmah, the daughter of Imam Muḥammad al-Taqī (ᶜa), whose grave is at the feet of the tomb of the two Imams. Despite her high station no specific text has been mentioned in the sources for her *ziyārah*. Hence it is fitting that one perform her *ziyārah* by reciting the text that has been narrated for *ziyārah* of the decedents of the Imams (ᶜa), or to recite the following text which has been narrated for *ziyārah* of Ḥaḍrat Maᶜṣūmah bint Mūsā (ᶜa), her illustrious aunt.[3] The following text is to be recited while facing in the direction of the *qiblah*.

Peace be to Adam, the chosen of Allah. Peace be to Noah, the	اَلسَّلَامُ عَلَىٰ آدَمَ صِفْوَةِ اللهِ، اَلسَّلَامُ عَلَىٰ

[1] *Kāfī*, iv, 579, h 1, 585, h 5. *Kāmil al-Ziyārāt*, 147, 150, b 59, h 1, b 60, h 3, 4. *Faqīh*, ii, 578, h 3163. *ᶜIlal*, ii, 460, b 221, h 6. *ᶜUyūn Akhbār al-Riḍā*, ii, 262, b 66, h 31. Mufīd's *Mazār*, 183, b 11, h 1. *Tahdhīb*, vi, 79, 93, b 26, h 5, b 43, h 1. From these sources in *Wasā'il*, xiv, 327, 543, 571, b 2, h 19324, b b 79, h 19783, b 90, h 19842; *Biḥār*, xcvii, 117, 119, b 2, h 5, 15, xcviii, 76, b 10, h 29; & *Mustadrak*, x, 185, b 2, h 11806/11.

[2] *Hadīyat al-Zā'irīn*, 83-84.

[3] *Biḥār*, xlviii, 316, xcix, 265, b 1, h 3 & *Mustadrak*, x, 368, b 74, h 12198/3.

prophet of Allah. Peace be to Abraham, the dedicated friend of Allah. Peace be to Moses, Allah's interlocutor. Peace be to Jesus, the spirit of Allah.

نُوحٍ نَبِيِّ اللهِ، اَلسَّلاٰمُ عَلىٰ إِبْرَاهِيمَ خَلِيلِ اللهِ، اَلسَّلاٰمُ عَلىٰ مُوسَى كَلِيمِ اللهِ، اَلسَّلاٰمُ عَلىٰ عِيسَى رُوحِ اللهِ،

Peace be to you, O Apostle of Allah! Peace be to you, O best of Allah's creation! Peace be to you, O favourite of Allah! Peace be to you, O Muḥammad ibn ᶜAbd Allah, the Seal of the Prophets! Peace be to you, O ᶜAlī ibn Abī Ṭālib, the Commander of the Faithful and legatee of the Apostle of Allah! Peace be to you, O Fāṭimah, mistress of the world's womankind!

اَلسَّــلاٰمُ عَلَيْكَ يَا رَسُــولَ اللهِ، اَلسَّلاٰمُ عَلَيْكَ يَا خَيْرَ خَلْقِ اللهِ، اَلسَّلاٰمُ عَلَيْكَ يَا صَفِيَّ اللهِ، اَلسَّلاٰمُ عَلَيْكَ يَا مُحَمَّدَ بْنَ عَبْدِ اللهِ خَاتَمَ النَّبِيِّينَ، اَلسَّلاٰمُ عَلَيْكَ يَا أَمِيرَ الْمُؤْمِنِينَ عَلِيَّ بْــنَ أَبِي طَالِبٍ وَصِيَّ رَسُولِ اللهِ، اَلسَّلاٰمُ عَلَيْكِ يَا فَاطِمَةُ سَيِّدَةَ نِسَاءِ الْعَالَمِينَ،

Peace be to you, O grandsons of the Prophet of Mercy and doyens of the youth of paradise. Peace be to you, O ᶜAli ibn al-Ḥusayn, foremost of the devout and delight of the onlookers! Peace be to you, O Muḥammad ibn ᶜAlī, exponent of Divine knowledge after the Prophet! Peace be to you, O Jaᶜfar ibn Muḥammad, the truthful, pious and trustworthy Imam!

Peace be to you, O Mūsā ibn Jaᶜfar, the pure and immaculate Imam! Peace be to you, O ᶜAlī ibn Mūsā, the approved and favoured Imam! Peace be to you, O Muḥammad ibn ᶜAlī, the Godwary Imam. Peace be to you , O ᶜAlī ibn Muḥammad, the

اَلسَّــلاٰمُ عَلَيْكُمَا يَا سِــبْطَيِ الرَّحْمَةِ، وَ سَيِّدَيْ شَبَابِ أَهْلِ الْجَنَّةِ، اَلسَّلاٰمُ عَلَيْكَ يَا عَلِيَّ بْنَ الْحُسَــيْنِ سَيِّدَ الْعَابِدِينَ، وَ قُرَّةَ عَيْنِ النَّاظِرِينَ، اَلسَّلاٰمُ عَلَيْكَ يَا مُحَمَّدَ بْنَ عَلِيٍّ بَاقِرَ الْعِلْمِ بَعْدَ النَّبِيِّ، اَلسَّلاٰمُ عَلَيْكَ يَا جَعْفَرَ بْنَ مُحَمَّدٍ الصَّادِقَ الْبَارَّ الْأَمِينَ،

اَلسَّلاٰمُ عَلَيْكَ يَا مُوسَى بْنَ جَعْفَرٍ الطَّاهِرَ الطُّهْرَ، اَلسَّلاٰمُ عَلَيْكَ يَا عَلِيَّ بْنَ مُوسَى الرِّضَا الْمُرْتَضَىٰ، اَلسَّلاٰمُ عَلَيْكَ يَا مُحَمَّدَ بْنَ عَلِيٍّ التَّقِيَّ، اَلسَّلاٰمُ عَلَيْكَ يَا عَلِيَّ بْنَ مُحَمَّدٍ النَّقِيَّ

النَّاصِحَ الْأَمِينَ، اَلسَّلَامُ عَلَيْكَ يَا حَسَنَ
بْنَ عَلِيٍّ، اَلسَّلَامُ عَلَى الْوَصِيِّ مِنْ بَعْدِهِ.
اَللّٰهُمَّ صَلِّ عَلىٰ نُورِكَ وَ سِرَاجِكَ، وَ وَلِيِّ
وَلِيِّكَ وَ وَصِيِّ وَصِيِّكَ، وَ حُجَّتِكَ عَلىٰ
خَلْقِكَ،

blameless and trustworthy advisor! Peace be to you, O Ḥasan ibn ᶜAlī! Peace be to the legatee after him!

O Allah, bless Your light and lamp, the *walī* of Your *walī*, the legatee of Your legatee and Your testament to Your creation!

اَلسَّلَامُ عَلَيْكِ يَا بِنْتَ رَسُولِ اللهِ، اَلسَّلَامُ
عَلَيْكِ يَا بِنْتَ فَاطِمَةَ وَ خَدِيجَةَ، اَلسَّلَامُ
عَلَيْكِ يَا بِنْتَ أَمِيرِ الْمُؤْمِنِينَ، اَلسَّلَامُ
عَلَيْكِ يَا بِنْتَ الْحَسَنِ وَ الْحُسَيْنِ، اَلسَّلَامُ
عَلَيْكِ يَا بِنْتَ وَلِيِّ اللهِ، اَلسَّلَامُ عَلَيْكِ يَا
أُخْتَ وَلِيِّ اللهِ، اَلسَّلَامُ عَلَيْكِ يَا عَمَّةَ
وَلِيِّ اللهِ، اَلسَّلَامُ عَلَيْكِ يَا بِنْتَ مُحَمَّدِ بْنِ
عَلِيٍّ التَّقِيِّ، وَ رَحْمَةُ اللهِ وَ بَرَكَاتُهُ ،

Peace be to you, O daughter of the Apostle of Allah! Peace be to you, O daughter of Fāṭimah and Khadījah! Peace be to you, O daughter of the Commander of the Faithful! Peace be to you, O daughter of al-Ḥasan and al-Ḥusayn! Peace be to you, O daughter of Allah's *walī!* Peace be to you, O sister of Allah's *walī!* Peace be to you, O aunt of Allah's *walī!* Peace be to you, O daughter of Muḥammad ibn ᶜAlī al-Taqī, and may Allah's mercy and His bounties be upon you!

اَلسَّلَامُ عَلَيْكِ عَرَّفَ اللهُ بَيْنَنَا وَ بَيْنَكُمْ
فِي الْجَنَّةِ، وَ حَشَرَنَا فِي زُمْرَتِكُمْ، وَ
أَوْرَدَنَا حَوْضَ نَبِيِّكُمْ، وَ سَقَانَا بِكَأْسِ
جَدِّكُمْ، مِنْ يَدِ عَلِيِّ بْنِ أَبِي طَالِبٍ،
صَلَوَاتُ اللهِ عَلَيْكُمْ،

Peace be to you, may Allah acquaint us and you with one another in paradise and gather us in your fold and admit us at the Pool of the Prophet and give us to drink from the cup of your ancestor, by the hand of ᶜAlī ibn Abī Ṭālib! May Allah's blessings be upon you.

أَسْأَلُ اللهَ أَنْ يُرِيَنَا فِيكُمُ السُّرُورَ وَ
الْفَرَجَ، وَ أَنْ يَجْمَعَنَا وَ إِيَّاكُمْ فِي زُمْرَةِ

I beseech Allah to show us delight and relief in you and to gather us and you in the fold of your ancestor, Muḥammad,

جَدِّكُمْ مُحَمَّدٍ صَلَّى اللهُ عَلَيْهِ وَ آلِهِ، وَ
أَنْ لَا يَسْلُبَنَا مَعْرِفَتَكُمْ، إِنَّهُ وَلِيٌّ قَدِيرٌ،

may Allah bless him and his Family, and not to divest us of your knowledge. Indeed He is the all-powerful guardian.

أَتَقَرَّبُ إِلَى اللهِ بِحُبِّكُمْ، وَ الْبَرَاءَةِ
مِنْ أَعْدَائِكُمْ، وَ التَّسْلِيمِ إِلَى اللهِ،
رَاضِيًا بِهِ غَيْرَ مُنْكِرٍ وَ لَا مُسْتَكْبِرٍ، وَ
عَلَى يَقِينِ مَا أَتَى بِهِ مُحَمَّدٌ وَ بِهِ رَاضٍ،
نَطْلُبُ بِذَلِكَ وَجْهَكَ يَا سَيِّدِي، اَللّٰهُمَّ
وَ رِضَاكَ وَ الدَّارَ الْآخِرَةَ، يَا حَكِيمَةُ
اشْفَعِي لِي فِي الْجَنَّةِ، فَإِنَّ لَكِ عِنْدَ اللهِ
شَأْنًا مِنَ الشَّأْنِ .

I seek nearness to Allah through my love for you and my repudiation of your enemies, through my submission to Allah out of compliance to Him, without denial and defiance, and through my conviction in the teachings brought by Muḥammad, while I am satisfied and pleased with them, and with that I seek Your pleasure, O my Master., O Allah, our fate in the abode of the Hereafter depends on Your approval! O Ḥakīmah, intercede for me in paradise, for you have indeed an eminent station with Allah!

اَللّٰهُمَّ إِنِّي أَسْأَلُكَ أَنْ تَخْتِمَ لِي بِالسَّعَادَةِ،
فَلَا تَسْلُبْ مِنِّي مَا أَنَا فِيهِ، وَ لَا حَوْلَ وَ
لَا قُوَّةَ إِلَّا بِاللهِ الْعَلِيِّ الْعَظِيمِ،

O Allah, I beseech You to conclude my life with felicity, and do not take away from me what (faith) I presently possess. There is no power or force except what derives from Allah, the All-exalted and the All-great!

اَللّٰهُمَّ اسْتَجِبْ لَنَا، وَ تَقَبَّلْهُ بِكَرَمِكَ وَ
عِزَّتِكَ، وَ بِرَحْمَتِكَ وَ عَافِيَتِكَ، وَ صَلَّى
اللهُ عَلَى مُحَمَّدٍ وَ آلِهِ أَجْمَعِينَ، وَ سَلَّمَ
تَسْلِيمًا يَا أَرْحَمَ الرَّاحِمِينَ.

O Allah, answer our petitions and accept our devotions with Your generosity, Your might, Your mercy, and Your gift of well-being. May Allah bless Muḥammad and all his Family and greet them with the worthiest greetings! O Most Merciful of the merciful!

It is well known that a number of illustrious descendents of the Prophet (ṣ) are buried near the tombs of the two Imams at Sāmarrā. Among them is al-Ḥusayn, son of Imam ʿAlī al-Naqī (*ʿa*). I could not find the details of his life, but he appears to have been an illustrious *sayyid* and an exalted character. According to some reports, Imam al-Ḥasan al-ᶜAskarī and his brother al-Ḥusayn ibn ᶜAlī were called "*sibṭayn*" and they were likened to their forbears, Imam Ḥasan (ᶜ*a*) and Imam Ḥusayn (ᶜ*a*), the two grandsons of the Prophet of Mercy (*ṣ*).

In a report of Abū al-Ṭayyib it is stated that Ḥusayn had a voice resembling that of Ḥaḍrat Ḥujjat, the Imam of the Era, may Allah bless him. According to *Shajarat al-Awliyā* of Sayyid Aḥmad Ardakāni Yazdī, a jurist, *muḥaddith* and philosopher, it is stated in the account of Imam ᶜAlī al-Naqī's children that Ḥusayn, his son, was known for his piety and saintliness, and that he acknowledged the Imamate of his brother. Perhaps an adept researcher will be able to uncover further details concerning that venerable personage.

Ziyarah of Sayyid Muhammad (r), Son of Imam ᶜAlī al-Naqī (ᶜa)

Near the city of Sāmarrā is the well-known shrine of Sayyid Muḥammad, son of Imam ᶜAlī al-Naqī (ᶜ*a*), famous for its holy and miraculous character. The generality of people visit the shrine, where they make petitions and offer lots of gifts and endowments. All the Arabs living in the area regard it with awe and veneration. Many miracles of his have been reported which we refrain from mentioning for reasons of space. It is a sufficient token of his eminence that he had the ability to assume the office of Imamate as the eldest son of Imam ᶜAlī al-Naqī (ᶜ*a*).

Our teacher Thiqat al-Islām Nūrī, may Allah brighten his grave, held his *ziyārah* in great esteem and made efforts for the repairs of his blessed shrine. He wrote the following inscription which appears on the *ḍarīḥ*.

> This is the resting place of the august sayyid Abū Jaᶜfar Muḥammad, son of Imam Abū al-Ḥasan ᶜAlī al-Ḥadī, may peace be upon him, a great and highly regarded figure. The Shīᶜah used to think that he would succeed his father, may peace be upon him, as the Imam. When he died, his father designated Abū Muḥammad al-Zakī (ᶜ*a*), his brother, as successor, and said to him, "Thank God, for he has brought this about for you." His father had left him at Madīnah as a child and he joined him at maturity in Sāmarrā. Having set out to return to the Ḥijāz, he fell ill and died after reaching a town, nine parasangs on the way, and there stands his

shrine. Grieved at his death, Abū Muḥammad tore his shirt at the neck and said to those who found fault with his action, "Moses tore his shirt at the death of his brother Aaron, when he died after having lived for about 252 years."

Leave of Departure at the Shrine at Sāmarrā

When bidding farewell to the two Imams (ʿ*a*), stand beside the tomb and say,[1]

اَلسَّلَامُ عَلَيْكُمَا يَا وَلِيَّيِ اللهِ، أَسْتَوْدِعُكُمَا اللهَ وَ أَقْرَأُ عَلَيْكُمَا اَلسَّلَامَ، آمَنَّا بِاللهِ وَ بِالرَّسُولِ وَ بِمَا جِئْتُمَا بِهِ وَ دَلَلْتُمَا عَلَيْهِ، اَللّٰهُمَّ اكْتُبْنَا مَعَ الشَّاهِدِينَ،

Peace be to you, O *walīs* of Allah! I entrust you both to the care of Allah and give you my *salām!* We have faith in Allah and the Apostle and the teachings that you have brought and the guidance you have given. O Allah, write us among the witnesses!

اَللّٰهُمَّ لَا تَجْعَلْهُ آخِرَ الْعَهْدِ مِنْ زِيَارَتِي إِيَّاهُمَا، وَارْزُقْنِي الْعَوْدَ إِلَيْهِمَا، وَاحْشُرْنِي مَعَهُمَا وَ مَعَ آبَائِهِمَا الطَّاهِرِينَ، وَ الْقَائِمِ الْحُجَّةِ مِنْ ذُرِّيَّتِهِمَا، يَا أَرْحَمَ الرَّاحِمِينَ!

O Allah, do not make this my last opportunity of their *ziyārah* and grant me to return to them again. Gather me at Resurrection with the two of them, their immaculate ancestors, and the Restorer and Testament belonging to their descent, O Most Merciful of the merciful!

Section Two
The Observances of the Holy Basement

This section deals with the observances of the Holy Basement and the manner of *ziyārah* of Imam al-Mahdī, the Master of the Era, Allah's Testament to His servants, and His Remnant in the towns, may Allah bless him and his ancestors.

Before describing the related observances, I would like to call attention to a point mentioned in the *Hadiyyah*, from another book, the

[1] First of the two passages of this text is cited in: Mufīd's *Mazār*, 204, b 19; *Muqniʿah*, 488, b 39; *Tahdhīb*, vi, 95, b 45, whence *Wāfī*, xiv, 1564, h 14652/3 & *Biḥār*, xcix, 63, b 6.

Taḥiyyah, that the basement used to be part of the house of the two Imams. Formerly, before the new structure and courtyard were built, its entrance was located behind the tombs near the grave of Narjis Khātūn, from where they used to go downstairs, passing through a dark hallway before reaching the door of the basement, whose walls have now been covered with mirror-work, with a skylight, towards the *qiblah*, opening into the shrine courtyard. The former door was located at the middle of the basement, and has been replaced now by a niche covered with ceramic tiles.

All the observances pertaining to the three Imams, may peace be to them, were performed within a single building. Hence the Shahīd Awwal has mentioned the *ziyārah* of the basement after that of the two Imams (*ʿa*), followed by the *ziyārah* of Narjis Khātūn.

More than a hundred years ago, Aḥmad Khān Dunbalī, spending a large sum, built the present courtyard for the shrine of the two Imams (*ʿa*), as well as the shrine chamber and the high dome, an in addition a separate courtyard for the sacred basement, with an independent entrance, stairs and door with a special passage for women, as is the case at the present. The former passage, stairs and entrance of the basement have been completely closed and there remains no trace of them, nor any occasion for some of the earlier observances. However, there is no change in regard to the *ziyārah* of the basement itself.

First Ziyarah of the Twelfth Imam (ʻa)

Requesting permission to enter and reciting the appeal of admittance is a common feature of the *ziyārahs* and a custom to be observed at every shrine in accordance with the advice of the scholars. It is a practice to be observed here as well and one should not enter this revered shrine without seeking permission.

The request for admittance especially meant for the Holy Basement is the same as the *ziyārah* cited below (p. 480) which begins with the words "*Assalāmu ʿalayka yā khalīfatallāh...*" In it, the request for permission of entry is mentioned at the end of the *ziyārah*, and it should be recited at the door of the Basement before going down the stairs.

Sayyid Ibn Ṭāwūs has cited another text[1] for the appeal for admittance which is very similar to the First Appeal for Admittance cited

[1] *Biḥār*, xcix, 83, b 7, h 2 from Ibn Ṭāwūs.

at the outset of Chapter 2 of Book Three (p. 22).

ᶜAllāmah Majlisī has cited another text for the leave of entry, which he quotes from an old manuscript of a work compiled by a Shīᶜah scholar.[1] It begins with the words *"Allā·humma, inna hāḏhihī buqᶜatun ṭahhartahā, wa ᶜaqwatun sharraftahā...,"* and it has been cited earlier as a general appeal for admittance (p. 24).

Having sought the permission to enter, one should enter the Basement and perform the *ziyārah* of the Imam in the manner taught by him. The august shaykh Aḥmad b. Abū Ṭālib al-Ṭabrisī (*r*) reports in his noble work *al-Iḥtijāj* that the Imam of the Era (ᶜ*a*) wrote the following in a letter addressed to Muḥammad al-Ḥimyarī, after replying to certain questions that the latter had asked the Imam.[2]

بِسْمِ اللهِ الرَّحْمَنِ الرَّحِيمِ، لا لِأَمْرِهِ تَعْقِلُونَ وَ لا مِـــنْ أَوْلِيَائِهِ تَقْبَلُونَ، حِكْمَةٌ بَالِغَةٌ، فَمَا تُغْنِي النُّذُرُ [عَنْ قَوْمٍ لا يُؤْمِنُونَ]. السَّلامُ عَلَيْنَا وَ عَلَى عِبَادِ اللهِ الصَّالِحِين.

"In the Name of Allah, the All-beneficent, the All-merciful. Neither do you give thought to His ordinances, nor do you accept from His *awliyā'*. [They represent] *far-reaching wisdom; but warnings are of no avail* (to a people who have no faith)! Peace be to us and His righteous servants.

"Whenever you wish to pay attention to Allah, the Blessed and Exalted, through our means, say, as Allah, the Most High, has said,

سَلَامٌ عَلَىٰ آلِ يٰسٓ، اَلسَّـــلَامُ عَلَيْكَ يَا دَاعِيَ اللهِ وَ رَبَّانِيَّ آيَاتِهِ، اَلسَّلَامُ عَلَيْكَ يَا بَابَ اللهِ وَ دَيَّانَ دِينِهِ، اَلسَّلَامُ عَلَيْكَ يَا خَلِيفَةَ اللهِ وَ نَاصِرَ حَقِّهِ، اَلسَّلَامُ عَلَيْكَ يَا حُجَّــةَ اللهِ وَ دَلِيلَ إِرَادَتِهِ، اَلسَّـــلَامُ عَلَيْـــكَ يَا تَالِيَ كِتَـــابِ اللهِ وَ تَرْجُمَانَهُ،

"Peace be to the progeny of Yā Sīn! Peace be to you, O Allah's summoner and preceptor of His signs! Peace be to you, O Allah's doorway and the governor of His religion! Peace be to you, O vicegerent of Allah and defender of His Truth/right! Peace be to you, O testament of Allah and index of His will and purpose! Peace be to you, O follower of Allah's Book and its interpreter!

اَلسَّلَامُ عَلَيْكَ فِي آنَاءِ لَيْلِكَ وَ أَطْرَافِ

Peace be to you, throughout

1 *Biḥār*, xcix, 115, b 7.

2 *Al-Iḥtijāj*, ii, 317-318, whence *Biḥār*, xcix, 81-83, 92-94, b 7, h 1.

نَهَارِكَ، اَلسَّلَامُ عَلَيْكَ يَا بَقِيَّةَ اللهِ فِى أَرْضِهِ، اَلسَّلَامُ عَلَيْكَ يَا مِيثَاقَ اللهِ الَّذِى أَخَذَهُ وَ وَكَّدَهُ، اَلسَّلَامُ عَلَيْكَ يَا وَعْدَ اللهِ الَّذِى ضَمِنَهُ، اَلسَّلَامُ عَلَيْكَ أَيُّهَا الْعَلَمُ الْمَنْصُوبُ، وَ الْعِلْمُ الْمَصْبُوبُ، وَ الْغَوْثُ وَ الرَّحْمَةُ الْوَاسِعَةُ، وَعْدًا غَيْرَ مَكْذُوبٍ.

your nights and at the ends of your days! Peace be to you, O Allah's remnant and relic on His earth! Peace be to you, O Allah's covenant that He made and confirmed (with His creatures)! Peace be to you, O Allah's promise which He has guaranteed! Peace be to you, O raised banner, O downpour of divine knowledge, O succourer, O expansive mercy and undeniable promise!

اَلسَّلَامُ عَلَيْكَ حِينَ تَقُومُ، اَلسَّلَامُ عَلَيْكَ حِينَ تَقْعُدُ، اَلسَّلَامُ عَلَيْكَ حِينَ تَقْرَأُ وَ تُبَيِّنُ، اَلسَّلَامُ عَلَيْكَ حِينَ تُصَلِّى وَ تَقْنُتُ، اَلسَّلَامُ عَلَيْكَ حِينَ تَرْكَعُ وَ تَسْجُدُ، اَلسَّلَامُ عَلَيْكَ حِينَ تُهَلِّلُ وَ تُكَبِّرُ، اَلسَّلَامُ عَلَيْكَ حِينَ تَحْمَدُ وَ تَسْتَغْفِرُ،

Peace be to you when you rise up! Peace be to you when you remain seated! Peace be to you when you read and expound! Peace be to you when you pray and supplicate! Peace be to you when you kneel and prostrate! Peace be to you when you celebrate Allah's Oneness and greatness! Peace be to you when you celebrate His praise and seek His forgiveness!

اَلسَّلَامُ عَلَيْكَ حِينَ تُصْبِحُ وَ تُمْسِى، اَلسَّلَامُ عَلَيْكَ فِى اللَّيْلِ إِذَا يَغْشَى، وَ النَّهَارِ إِذَا تَجَلَّى، اَلسَّلَامُ عَلَيْكَ أَيُّهَا الْإِمَامُ الْمَأْمُونُ، اَلسَّلَامُ عَلَيْكَ أَيُّهَا الْمُقَدَّمُ الْمَأْمُولُ، اَلسَّلَامُ عَلَيْكَ بِجَوَامِعِ السَّلَامِ .

Peace be to you at every morning and evening. Peace be to you at *night when it envelopes* and by *day when it brightens!* Peace be to you, O trusted Imam! Peace be to you, O foremost one who is the focus of all hopes! Peace be to you, with the omneity of peace!

أُشْهِدُكَ يَا مَوْلَايَ أَنِّى أَشْهَدُ أَنْ لَا إِلَهَ إِلَّا اللهُ وَحْدَهُ لَا شَرِيكَ لَهُ، وَ أَنَّ مُحَمَّدًا عَبْدُهُ

Be witness, O my master, to my testimony that there is no god besides Allah, He is One and has no partner, and that Muḥammad

وَ رَسُولُهُ، لَا حَبِيبَ إِلَّا هُوَ وَ أَهْلُهُ،

is His servant and Apostle and that I befriend none but him and his Family!

وَ أُشْهِدُكَ يَا مَوْلَاىَ أَنَّ عَلِيًّا أَمِيرَ الْمُؤْمِنِينَ حُجَّتُهُ، وَ الْحَسَنَ حُجَّتُهُ، وَ الْحُسَيْنَ حُجَّتُهُ، وَ عَلِيَّ بْنَ الْحُسَيْنِ حُجَّتُهُ، وَ مُحَمَّدَ بْنَ عَلِيٍّ حُجَّتُهُ، وَ جَعْفَرَ بْنَ مُحَمَّدٍ حُجَّتُهُ، وَ مُوسَى بْنَ جَعْفَرٍ حُجَّتُهُ، وَ عَلِيَّ بْنَ مُوسَى حُجَّتُهُ، وَ مُحَمَّدَ بْنَ عَلِيٍّ حُجَّتُهُ، وَ عَلِيَّ بْنَ مُحَمَّدٍ حُجَّتُهُ، وَ الْحَسَنَ بْنَ عَلِيٍّ حُجَّتُهُ، وَ أَشْهَدُ أَنَّكَ حُجَّةُ اللهِ.

Be witness, O my master, to my testimony that ᶜAlī, the Commander of the Faithful, is His testament, and that al-Ḥasan is His testament, that al-Ḥusayn is His testament, that ᶜAlī ibn al-Ḥusayn is His testament, that Muḥammad ibn ᶜAlī is His testament, that Jaᶜfar ibn Muḥammad is His testament, that Mūsā ibn Jaᶜfar is His testament, that ᶜAlī ibn Mūsā is His testament, that Muḥammad ibn ᶜAlī is His testament, that ᶜAlī ibn Muḥammad is His testament, and that al-Ḥasan ibn ᶜAlī is His testament, and I testify that You are the testament of Allah.

أَنْتُمُ الْأَوَّلُ وَ الْآخِرُ، وَ أَنَّ رَجْعَتَكُمْ حَقٌّ لَا رَيْبَ فِيهَا يَوْمَ لَا يَنْفَعُ نَفْسًا إِيمَانُهَا لَمْ تَكُنْ آمَنَتْ مِنْ قَبْلُ أَوْ كَسَبَتْ فِي إِيمَانِهَا خَيْرًا، وَ أَنَّ الْمَوْتَ حَقٌّ، وَ أَنَّ نَاكِرًا وَ نَكِيرًا حَقٌّ،

I testify that you are the first and the last and that your return is a verity, wherein there is no doubt–on the day *when faith shall not benefit any soul that had not believed beforehand and had not earned some goodness in its faith.*(6:158) I testify that death is a fact and that the angels Nākir and Nakīr are real.

وَ أَشْهَدُ أَنَّ النَّشْرَ حَقٌّ، وَ الْبَعْثَ حَقٌّ، وَ أَنَّ الصِّرَاطَ حَقٌّ، وَ الْمِرْصَادَ حَقٌّ، وَ الْمِيزَانَ حَقٌّ، وَ الْحَشْرَ حَقٌّ، وَ الْحِسَابَ حَقٌّ، وَ الْجَنَّةَ وَ النَّارَ حَقٌّ، وَ الْوَعْدَ وَ الْوَعِيدَ بِهِمَا حَقٌّ. يَا مَوْلَاىَ شَقِيَ مَنْ

I testify that the Resurrection and raising of the dead is true, that the *ṣirāṭ* is true, the observation is a truth, the Balance is true, the mustering (of the creatures at judgement) is a truth, the reckoning of deeds is true, paradise and hell are realities and the promise and threat pertaining to them are

خَالَفَكُمْ، وَ سَعِدَ مَنْ أَطَاعَكُمْ.

true! O my master, the wretched are those who oppose you and the felicitous are those who obey you!

فَاشْهَدْ عَلَىٰ مَا أَشْهَدْتُكَ عَلَيْهِ، وَ أَنَا وَلِيٌّ لَكَ بَرِيءٌ مِنْ عَدُوِّكَ، فَالْحَقُّ مَا رَضِيتُمُوهُ، وَ الْبَاطِلُ مَا أَسْخَطْتُمُوهُ، وَ الْمَعْرُوفُ مَا أَمَرْتُمْ بِهِ، وَ الْمُنْكَرُ مَا نَهَيْتُمْ عَنْهُ،

So testify in my favour to that which I have held you to be my witness. I befriend you and repudiate your enemies. The truth is that which you approve and the falsehood is what you disapprove of. The right thing is what you command and the wrong thing is what you forbid.

فَنَفْسِي مُؤْمِنَةٌ بِاللّٰهِ وَحْدَهُ لَا شَرِيكَ لَهُ، وَ بِرَسُولِهِ وَ بِأَمِيرِ الْمُؤْمِنِينَ وَ بِكُمْ يَا مَوْلَايَ أَوَّلِكُمْ وَ آخِرِكُمْ، وَ نُصْرَتِي مُعَدَّةٌ لَكُمْ، وَ مَوَدَّتِي خَالِصَةٌ لَكُمْ، آمِينَ آمِينَ.

My soul has convinced faith in Allah, who is One and has no partner, and in His Apostle, in the Commander of the Faithful and you, O my master, in the first one of you and the last one. My assistance and help is ready for you and my friendship and love are exclusively for you! Amen! Amen!

"Then recite the following supplication:

اَللّٰهُمَّ إِنِّي أَسْأَلُكَ أَنْ تُصَلِّيَ عَلَىٰ مُحَمَّدٍ نَبِيِّ رَحْمَتِكَ، وَ كَلِمَةِ نُورِكَ، وَ أَنْ تَمْلَأَ قَلْبِي نُورَ الْيَقِينِ، وَ صَدْرِي نُورَ الْإِيمَانِ، وَ فِكْرِي نُورَ النِّيَّاتِ، وَ عَزْمِي نُورَ الْعِلْمِ، وَ قُوَّتِي نُورَ الْعَمَلِ، وَ لِسَانِي نُورَ الصِّدْقِ، وَ دِينِي نُورَ الْبَصَائِرِ مِنْ عِنْدِكَ، وَ بَصَرِي نُورَ الضِّيَاءِ، وَ سَمْعِي نُورَ الْحِكْمَةِ،

"O Allah, I beseech You to bless Muḥammad and the Family of Muḥammad, the Prophet of Your mercy and Your word of light, and to fill my heart with the light of conviction, my breast with the light of faith, my mind with the light of good intentions, my will with the light of knowledge, my strength with the light of action, my tongue with the light of truthfulness, my religion with the light of insights from You, my vision with the light of radiance, my hearing with the light of wisdom, my affections with the light of love for Muḥammad and his Family, may peace be to them, until I encounter You in a state wherein I shall have fulfilled my pledge and covenant with You whereat You will enfold me in Your mercy, O Guardian and Praiseworthy One!

وَ مَوَدَّتِي نُـــورَ الْمُوَالاةِ لِمُحَمَّدٍ وَ آلِهِ عَلَيْهِمُ السَّـــلامُ، حَتَّى أَلْقَاكَ وَ قَدْ وَفَيْتُ بِعَهْدِكَ وَ مِيثَاقِكَ، فَتُغَشِّيَنِي رَحْمَتَكَ يا وَلِيُّ يا حَمِيدُ.

O Allah, bless Muḥammad, Your testament on Your earth and Your vicegerent in Your towns, the summoner to Your path, the maintainer of Your justice, who stands to uphold Your ordinances, being a guardian to the faithful and bane for the faithless, who dispels darkness with light, making the truth shine forth, and speaks with wisdom and truthfulness. He is Your complete Word on Your earth, fearful and vigilant. He is the sincere guardian, the ship of deliverance, the banner of guidance, the light of the people's eyes, the best one to have donned a shirt and robe, and the giver of light to the blind, who will fill the earth with justice and fairness inasmuch as it is filled with wrongdoing and injustice. Indeed You have power over all things.

اَللّٰهُمَّ صَلِّ عَلىٰ مُحَمَّدٍ حُجَّتِكَ فِي أَرْضِكَ، وَ خَلِيفَتِكَ فِي بِلادِكَ، وَ الدَّاعِي إِلَى سَبِيلِكَ، وَ الْقَائِمِ بِقِسْطِكَ، وَ الثَّائِرِ بِأَمْرِكَ، وَلِيِّ الْمُؤْمِنِينَ، وَ بَوَارِ الْكَافِرِينَ، وَ مُجَلِّي الظُّلْمَةِ، وَ مُنِيرِ الْحَقِّ، وَ النَّاطِقِ بِالْحِكْمَةِ وَ الصِّـــدْقِ، وَ كَلِمَتِكَ التَّامَّةِ فِي أَرْضِـــكَ، الْمُرْتَقِبِ الْخَائِفِ، وَ الْوَلِيِّ النَّاصِحِ، سَفِينَةِ النَّجَاةِ، وَ عَلَمِ الْهُدَىٰ، وَ نُورِ أَبْصَارِ الْوَرَىٰ، وَ خَيْرِ مَنْ تَقَمَّصَ وَ ارْتَدَىٰ، وَ مُجَلِّي الْعَـــمَىٰ، الَّذِي يَمْلَأُ الْأَرْضَ عَدْلًا وَ قِسْطًا كَمَا مُلِئَتْ ظُلْمًا وَ جَوْرًا، إِنَّكَ عَلَىٰ كُلِّ شَيْءٍ قَدِيرٌ.

O Allah, bless Your *walī* and son of Your *awliyā'*, obedience to whom has been made mandatory by You, making it obligatory (for all) to observe their rights, having *repelled from them all impurity and purifying them with a thorough purification.*(33:33)

اَللّٰهُمَّ صَلِّ عَلىٰ وَلِيِّكَ وَ ابْنِ أَوْلِيَائِكَ، الَّذِينَ فَرَضْتَ طَاعَتَهُـــمْ، وَ أَوْجَبْتَ حَقَّهُمْ، وَ أَذْهَبْـــتَ عَنْهُمُ الرِّجْسَ وَ طَهَّرْتَهُمْ تَطْهِيرًا.

اَللّٰهُمَّ انْصُرْهُ وَ انْتَصِرْ بِهِ لِدِينِكَ، وَ انْصُرْ بِهِ أَوْلِيَاءَكَ وَ أَوْلِيَاءَهُ وَ شِيعَتَهُ وَ أَنْصَارَهُ، وَ اجْعَلْنَا مِنْهُمْ.

O Allah, help him and defend Your religion by his means and assist by his means Your friends and his friends, followers and supporters, and appoint us to be among them.

اَللّٰهُمَّ أَعِذْهُ مِنْ شَرِّ كُلِّ بَاغٍ وَ طَاغٍ، وَ مِنْ شَرِّ جَمِيعِ خَلْقِكَ، وَ احْفَظْهُ مِنْ بَيْنِ يَدَيْهِ وَ مِنْ خَلْفِهِ، وَ عَنْ يَمِينِهِ وَ عَنْ شِمَالِهِ، وَ احْرُسْهُ وَ امْنَعْهُ مِنْ أَنْ يُوصَلَ إِلَيْهِ بِسُوءٍ، وَ احْفَظْ فِيهِ رَسُولَكَ وَ آلَ رَسُولِكَ، وَ أَظْهِرْ بِهِ الْعَدْلَ، وَ أَيِّدْهُ بِالنَّصْرِ، وَ انْصُرْ نَاصِرِيهِ، وَ اخْذُلْ خَاذِلِيهِ، وَ اقْصِمْ قَاصِمِيهِ، وَ اقْصِمْ بِهِ جَبَابِرَةَ الْكُفْرِ، وَ اقْتُلْ بِهِ الْكُفَّارَ وَ الْمُنَافِقِينَ، وَ جَمِيعَ الْمُلْحِدِينَ، حَيْثُ كَانُوا مِنْ مَشَارِقِ الْأَرْضِ وَ مَغَارِبِهَا، بَرِّهَا وَ بَحْرِهَا، وَ امْلَأْ بِهِ الْأَرْضَ عَدْلًا، وَ أَظْهِرْ بِهِ دِينَ نَبِيِّكَ صَلَّى اللّٰهُ عَلَيْهِ وَ آلِهِ،

O Allah, protect him from the evil of every rebel and tyrant and the evil of all Your creatures. Guard him from his front and rear, from his right and left. Protect him and guard him from any harm that may reach him. By protecting him, safeguard Your Apostle and his progeny, and make justice prevail through him. Strengthen him by Your help and help his helpers. Forsake those who forsake him and shatter his mortal enemies. Through him shatter the tyrants who represent unfaith, and slay through him the infidels, the hypocrites, and all the heathen, wherever they should be, in the earth's east and its west, on land and sea, and through him fill the earth with justice and make the religion of Your Prophet, may Allah bless him and his Family, prevail!

وَ اجْعَلْنِي اللّٰهُمَّ مِنْ أَنْصَارِهِ وَ أَعْوَانِهِ، وَ أَتْبَاعِهِ وَ شِيعَتِهِ، وَ أَرِنِي فِي آلِ مُحَمَّدٍ عَلَيْهِمُ السَّلَامُ مَا يَأْمُلُونَ، وَ فِي عَدُوِّهِمْ مَا يَحْذَرُونَ، إِلٰهَ الْحَقِّ آمِينَ، يَا

O Allah, make me one of his helpers, supporters, followers and votaries, and show me in the Family of Muḥammad what they hope for, and in their enemies what they fear, O God of Truth! Amen, O Majestic and Munificent One, O Most Merciful of the merciful!"

ذَا الْجَلَالِ وَ الْإِكْرَامِ، يَا أَرْحَمَ الرَّاحِمِينَ!

Second Ziyarah of the Twelfth Imam (ʿA)

Another *ziyārah* has been cited in reliable works of Shīʿī scholars.[1] According to it, while standing at the entrance of the Imam's shrine, one should say:

Peace be to you, O vicegerent of Allah and vicegerent of your ancestors, the (God-appointed) guides! Peace be to you, O successor of the preceding legatees! Peace be to you, O preserver of the secrets of the Lord of all the worlds! Peace be to you, O remnant of Allah from among His elect and chosen servants!

اَلسَّلَامُ عَلَيْكَ يَا خَلِيفَةَ اللهِ وَ خَلِيفَةَ
آبَائِهِ الْمَهْدِيِّينَ، اَلسَّلَامُ عَلَيْكَ يَا وَصِيَّ
الْأَوْصِيَاءِ الْمَاضِينَ، اَلسَّلَامُ عَلَيْكَ يَا
حَافِظَ أَسْرَارِ رَبِّ الْعَالَمِينَ، اَلسَّلَامُ عَلَيْكَ
يَا بَقِيَّةَ اللهِ مِنَ الصَّفْوَةِ الْمُنْتَجَبِينَ،

Peace be to you, O descendent of the radiant lights! Peace be to you, O descendent of the brilliant luminaries! Peace be to you, O scion of the immaculate Family! Peace be to you, O mine of prophetic knowledge! Peace be to you, O sole Gateway for approach to Allah! Peace be to you, O Path of Allah, paths other than which lead those who pursue them to perish!

اَلسَّلَامُ عَلَيْكَ يَا ابْنَ الْأَنْوَارِ الزَّاهِرَةِ،
اَلسَّلَامُ عَلَيْكَ يَا ابْنَ الْأَعْلَامِ الْبَاهِرَةِ،
اَلسَّلَامُ عَلَيْكَ يَا ابْنَ الْعِتْرَةِ الطَّاهِرَةِ،
اَلسَّلَامُ عَلَيْكَ يَا مَعْدِنَ الْعُلُومِ النَّبَوِيَّةِ،
اَلسَّلَامُ عَلَيْكَ يَا بَابَ اللهِ الَّذِي لَا يُؤْتَى
إِلَّا مِنْهُ، اَلسَّلَامُ عَلَيْكَ يَا سَبِيلَ اللهِ الَّذِي
مَنْ سَلَكَ غَيْرَهُ هَلَكَ،

Peace be to you, O spectator of the Tree of Ṭūbā and the Lotus of the Boundary. Peace be to you, O inextinguishable light of Allah! Peace be to you, O uncon-

اَلسَّلَامُ عَلَيْكَ يَا نَاظِرَ شَجَرَةِ طُوبَى وَ
سِدْرَةِ الْمُنْتَهَى، اَلسَّلَامُ عَلَيْكَ يَا نُورَ اللهِ
الَّذِي لَا يُطْفَى، اَلسَّلَامُ عَلَيْكَ يَا حُجَّةَ

[1] *Biḥār*, xcix, 113-117 (from al-Shaykh al-Mufīd, al-Mashhadī, *al-Mazār al-Kabīr*, 194-196, al-Shahīd al-Awwal, *Mazār*, 62-64); xcix, 103-104 (from *Miṣbāḥ al-Zā'ir*, 229-230 and *al-Mazār al-Kabīr*, 216-217).

اللهِ الَّتِي لَا تَخْفَىٰ، اَلسَّلَامُ عَلَيْكَ
يَا حُجَّةَ اللهِ عَلَىٰ مَنْ فِي الْأَرْضِ وَ
السَّمَاءِ، اَلسَّلَامُ عَلَيْكَ سَلَامَ مَنْ
عَرَفَكَ بِمَا عَرَّفَكَ بِهِ اللهُ، وَ نَعَتَكَ
بِبَعْضِ نُعُوتِكَ الَّتِي أَنْتَ أَهْلُهَا وَ فَوْقَهَا.

cealed testament of Allah! Peace be to you, O Allah's testament to the denizens of the earth and the heaven! Peace be to you, from someone who knows you as you have been introduced by Allah, who has described some of your qualities, which you are worthy of and even surpass them.

أَشْهَدُ أَنَّكَ الْحُجَّةُ عَلَىٰ مَنْ مَضَىٰ وَ
مَنْ بَقِيَ، وَ أَنَّ حِزْبَكَ هُمُ الْغَالِبُونَ، وَ
أَوْلِيَاءَكَ هُمُ الْفَائِزُونَ، وَ أَعْدَاءَكَ هُمُ
الْخَاسِرُونَ، وَ أَنَّكَ خَازِنُ كُلِّ عِلْمٍ،
وَ فَاتِقُ كُلِّ رَتْقٍ، وَ مُحَقِّقُ كُلِّ حَقٍّ، وَ
مُبْطِلُ كُلِّ بَاطِلٍ،

I testify that you are God's testament to those who have passed away and those who remain and that your party is the one which is victorious, your friends are triumphant and your enemies are the losers. I testify that you are the storehouse of all knowledge, the solver of every problem, the affirmer of every truth and falsifier of every falsehood.

رَضِيتُكَ يَا مَوْلَايَ إِمَامًا وَ هَادِيًا وَ وَلِيًّا
وَ مُرْشِدًا، لَا أَبْتَغِي بِكَ بَدَلًا، وَ لَا أَتَّخِذُ
مِنْ دُونِكَ وَلِيًّا.

My master, I am pleased with you as my Imam, guide, guardian and preceptor. I do not seek any substitute for you, nor do I consider anyone as my guardian besides you.

أَشْهَدُ أَنَّكَ الْحَقُّ الثَّابِتُ الَّذِي لَا عَيْبَ
فِيهِ، وَ أَنَّ وَعْدَ اللهِ فِيكَ حَقٌّ، لَا أَرْتَابُ
لِطُولِ الْغَيْبَةِ وَ بُعْدِ الْأَمَدِ، وَ لَا أَتَحَيَّرُ مَعَ
مَنْ جَهِلَكَ وَ جَهِلَ بِكَ، مُنْتَظِرٌ مُتَوَقِّعٌ
لِأَيَّامِكَ ،

I testify that you are the enduring truth, free from any kind of defect, and that Allah's promise concerning you is true. I doubt it not because of the long duration of your occultation and I am not bewildered along with those who are ignorant about you and know you not. I await and look forward to the days of your appearance.

وَ أَنْتَ الشَّافِعُ الَّذِي لَا يُنَازَعُ [تُنَازَعُ]،

You are the incontestable intercessor and the irresistible master.

وَ الْوَلِيُّ الَّذِى لَا يُدَافَعُ [تُدَافَعُ]، ذَخَرَكَ اللّٰهُ لِنُصْرَةِ الدِّينِ، وَ إِعْزَازِ الْمُؤْمِنِينَ، وَ الْإِنْتِقَامِ مِنَ الْجَاحِدِينَ الْمَارِقِينَ،

Allah has treasured you for the support of the faith, for the empowerment of the faithful, and for taking vengeance on the infidels and the apostates.

أَشْهَدُ أَنَّ بِوِلَايَتِكَ تُقْبَلُ الْأَعْمَالُ، وَ تُزَكَّى الْأَفْعَالُ، وَ تُضَاعَفُ الْحَسَنَاتُ، وَ تُمْحَى السَّيِّئَاتُ، فَمَنْ جَاءَ بِوِلَايَتِكَ وَ اعْتَرَفَ بِإِمَامَتِكَ قُبِلَتْ أَعْمَالُهُ، وَ صُدِّقَتْ أَقْوَالُهُ، وَ تَضَاعَفَتْ حَسَنَاتُهُ، وَ مُحِيَتْ سَيِّئَاتُهُ، وَ مَنْ عَدَلَ عَنْ وِلَايَتِكَ، وَ جَهِلَ مَعْرِفَتَكَ، وَ اسْتَبْدَلَ بِكَ غَيْرَكَ، كَبَّهُ اللّٰهُ عَلَىٰ مَنْخَرِهِ فِي النَّارِ، وَ لَمْ يَقْبَلِ اللّٰهُ لَهُ عَمَلًا، وَ لَمْ يُقِمْ لَهُ يَوْمَ الْقِيَامَةِ وَزْنًا.

I testify that it is by virtue of your *wilāyah* that the people's works are accepted by Allah, their conduct is purified, their virtues are redoubled, and their vices are expunged. So the works of those who embrace your *wilāyah* and acknowledge your Imamate are accepted, their beliefs are confirmed, their virtues are redoubled and their vices are erased. But as for those who turn away from your *wilāyah*, remain ignorant of your station, and who give your place to others, Allah will cast them headlong into hellfire, never accepting their works and not attaching them any weight on the Day of Resurrection.

أُشْهِدُ اللّٰهَ وَ أُشْهِدُ مَلَائِكَتَهُ وَ أُشْهِدُكَ يَا مَوْلَايَ بِهٰذَا، ظَاهِرُهُ كَبَاطِنِهِ، وَ سِرُّهُ كَعَلَانِيَتِهِ، وَ أَنْتَ الشَّاهِدُ عَلَىٰ ذٰلِكَ، وَ هُوَ عَهْدِي إِلَيْكَ، وَ مِيثَاقِي لَدَيْكَ، إِذْ أَنْتَ نِظَامُ الدِّينِ، وَ يَعْسُوبُ الْمُتَّقِينَ، وَ عِزُّ الْمُوَحِّدِينَ، وَ بِذٰلِكَ أَمَرَنِي رَبُّ الْعَالَمِينَ، فَلَوْ تَطَاوَلَتِ الدُّهُورُ، وَ تَمَادَتِ الْأَعْمَارُ [الْأَعْصَارُ]، لَمْ أَزْدَدْ فِيكَ إِلَّا يَقِينًا، وَ لَكَ

I make Allah my witness, as well as His angels and you, my master, to this declaration, whose inner and subjective truth conforms to its ostensible and objective form and you are witness to that. It is my pledge and covenant with you, as you represent the order and system of religion, being the leader of the Godwary and the might and dignity of the monotheists, and this has been enjoined upon me by the Lord of all the worlds. Hence, should ages pass by and lifetimes go by,

إِلَّا حُبًّا، وَ عَلَيْكَ إِلَّا مُتَّكِلًا وَ مُعْتَمِدًا،
وَ لِظُهُورِكَ إِلَّا مُتَوَقِّعًا وَ مُنْتَظِرًا [تَوَقُّعًا
وَ انْتِظَارًا]، وَ لِجِهَادِي بَيْنَ يَدَيْكَ مُتَرَقِّبًا
[إِلَّا تَرَقُّبًا]، فَأَبْذُلُ نَفْسِي وَ مَالِي وَ وَلَدِي
وَ أَهْلِي وَ جَمِيعَ مَا خَوَّلَنِي رَبِّي بَيْنَ يَدَيْكَ،
وَ التَّصَرُّفَ بَيْنَ أَمْرِكَ وَ نَهْيِكَ،

that will not increase me in anything but conviction and my love for you and my trust and reliance upon you, my expectations of your appearance and my anticipation of participating in *jihād* in your presence, when I will sacrifice my life, property, wealth, my children and family and whatever my Lord has granted me for you and at your beck and call!

مَوْلَايَ فَإِنْ أَدْرَكْتُ أَيَّامَكَ الزَّاهِرَةَ،
وَ أَعْلَامَكَ الْبَاهِرَةَ، فَهَا أَنَا ذَا عَبْدُكَ
الْمُتَصَرِّفُ بَيْنَ أَمْرِكَ وَ نَهْيِكَ، أَرْجُو
بِهِ الشَّهَادَةَ بَيْنَ يَدَيْكَ، وَ الْفَوْزَ لَدَيْكَ،
مَوْلَايَ فَإِنْ أَدْرَكَنِي الْمَوْتُ قَبْلَ ظُهُورِكَ،
فَإِنِّي أَتَوَسَّلُ بِكَ وَ بِآبَائِكَ الطَّاهِرِينَ إِلَى
اللهِ تَعَالَى وَ أَسْأَلُهُ أَنْ يُصَلِّيَ عَلَىٰ مُحَمَّدٍ وَ
آلِ مُحَمَّدٍ، وَ أَنْ يَجْعَلَ لِي كَرَّةً فِي ظُهُورِكَ،
وَ رَجْعَةً فِي أَيَّامِكَ، لِأَبْلُغَ مِنْ طَاعَتِكَ
مُرَادِي، وَ أَشْفِيَ مِنْ أَعْدَائِكَ فُؤَادِي.

My master, should I live to see the shining days of your rule and your brilliant banners, I will be your servant at your beck and call, expecting martyrdom and victory in your service! But if, my master, should death overtake me before your appearance, I implore your mediation and that of your immaculate ancestors with Allah, the Most High, and beseech Him to bless Muḥammad and the Family of Muḥammad and to grant me another turn during the period of your appearance and allow me to return during the days of your rule, so that I may attain my goal in obedience to you and heal my heart by taking vengeance upon your enemies.

مَوْلَايَ وَقَفْتُ فِي زِيَارَتِكَ مَوْقِفَ الْخَاطِئِينَ
النَّادِمِينَ الْخَائِفِينَ مِنْ عِقَابِ رَبِّ
الْعَالَمِينَ، وَ قَدِ اتَّكَلْتُ عَلَىٰ شَفَاعَتِكَ، وَ
رَجَوْتُ بِمُوَالاتِكَ وَ شَفَاعَتِكَ مَحْوَ ذُنُوبِي،

My master, I stand, in this visit, as one who, having erred, is regretful and fearful of the retribution of the Lord of all the worlds, and I do rely on your intercession and pin my hopes on your love and intercession for effacement

وَ سَتْرَ عُيُوبِي، وَ مَغْفِرَةَ زَلَلِي، فَكُنْ لِوَلِيِّكَ يَا مَوْلاَيَ عِنْدَ تَحْقِيقِ أَمَلِهِ،

of my sins, concealment of my defects and pardon of my lapses. So, my master, enable this friend of yours to realize his hope!

وَ اسْأَلِ اللهَ غُفْرَانَ زَلَلِهِ، فَقَدْ تَعَلَّقَ بِحَبْلِكَ، وَ تَمَسَّكَ بِوِلاَيَتِكَ، وَ تَبَرَّأَ مِنْ أَعْدَائِكَ.

Ask Allah to forgive my lapses as someone who clings to your cord, holds on to your *wilāyah* and repudiates your enemies.

اَللّٰهُمَّ صَلِّ عَلىٰ مُحَمَّدٍ وَ آلِهِ، وَ أَنْجِزْ لِوَلِيِّكَ مَا وَعَدْتَهُ، اَللّٰهُمَّ أَظْهِرْ كَلِمَتَهُ، وَ أَعْلِ دَعْوَتَهُ، وَ انْصُرْهُ عَلىٰ عَدُوِّهِ وَ عَدُوِّكَ، يَا رَبَّ الْعَالَمِينَ!

O Allah, bless Muḥammad and his Family and fulfil what You have promised Your *walī*! O Allah, do make his word prevail, exalt his summons and help him against his enemy and Yours, O Lord of all the worlds!

اَللّٰهُمَّ صَلِّ عَلىٰ مُحَمَّدٍ وَ آلِ مُحَمَّدٍ، وَ أَظْهِرْ كَلِمَتَكَ التَّامَّةَ، وَ مُغَيَّبَكَ فِي أَرْضِكَ، اَلْخَائِفَ الْمُتَرَقِّبَ.

O Allah, bless Muḥammad and the Family of Muḥammad, manifest Your consummate Word who dwells in occultation on Your earth in a state of fear and vigilance.

اَللّٰهُمَّ انْصُرْهُ نَصْرًا عَزِيزًا وَ افْتَحْ لَهُ فَتْحًا يَسِيرًا، اَللّٰهُمَّ وَ أَعِزَّ بِهِ الدِّينَ بَعْدَ الْخُمُولِ، وَ أَطْلِعْ بِهِ الْحَقَّ بَعْدَ الْأُفُولِ، وَ أَجْلِ بِهِ الظُّلْمَةَ، وَ اكْشِفْ بِهِ الْغُمَّةَ.

O Allah, grant him a mighty help and inaugurate for him an easy victory! O Allah, through him, strengthen the faith after its weakness, make the truth rise after its setting, and through him dispel the darkness and remove the distress!

اَللّٰهُمَّ وَ آمِنْ بِهِ الْبِلاَدَ، وَ اهْدِ بِهِ الْعِبَادَ، اَللّٰهُمَّ امْلَأْ بِهِ الْأَرْضَ عَدْلًا وَ قِسْطًا كَمَا مُلِئَتْ ظُلْمًا وَ جَوْرًا، إِنَّكَ سَمِيعٌ مُجِيبٌ.

O Allah, through him, bring safety to the towns and guide Your servants! O Allah, through him, fill the earth with justice and fairness as much as it is filled with injustice and oppression! Indeed You are all-hearing and responsive!

اَلسَّلَامُ عَلَيْكَ يَا وَلِيَّ اللهِ، اِئْذَنْ لِوَلِيِّكَ فِي الدُّخُولِ إِلَى حَرَمِكَ، صَلَوَاتُ اللهِ عَلَيْكَ وَ عَلَى آبَائِكَ الطَّاهِرِينَ وَ رَحْمَةُ اللهِ وَ بَرَكَاتُه.

Peace be to you, O *walī* of Allah! Permit your friend to enter your shrine, may Allah's blessings be upon you and your immaculate ancestors, and may Allah's mercy and bounties be upon you!

Then proceed towards the basement of the Imam's occultation and standing in the doorway and while holding the doors, say "ahem" or clear your throat like someone seeking permission to enter. Then say *Bismillā hir·raḥmā·nir·raḥīm* and go down in an unhurried and reverential manner. Offer two *rakʿahs* of prayer in the basement chamber and then say:

اَللهُ أَكْبَرُ، اَللهُ أَكْبَرُ، اَللهُ أَكْبَرُ، لَا إِلَهَ إِلَّا اللهُ وَ اللهُ أَكْبَرُ، وَ لِلّهِ الْحَمْدُ، اَلْحَمْدُ لِلّهِ الَّذِي هَدَانَا لِهَذَا، وَ عَرَّفَنَا أَوْلِيَاءَهُ وَ أَعْدَاءَهُ، وَ وَفَّقَنَا لِزِيَارَةِ أَئِمَّتِنَا، وَ لَمْ يَجْعَلْنَا مِنَ الْمُعَانِدِينَ النَّاصِبِينَ، وَ لَا مِنَ الْغُلَاةِ الْمُفَوِّضِينَ، وَ لَا مِنَ الْمُرْتَابِينَ الْمُقَصِّرِينَ.

Allah is greater! Allah is greater! Allah is greater! There is no god except Allah and Allah is greater. To Him belongs all praise! All praise belongs to Allah, who guided us to this and made His friends and enemies known to us, and enabled us to perform the *ziyārah* of our Imams, not making us like those who are opposed and hostile to them, nor like the *ghulāt* who believe in *tafwīḍ*, nor of those who entertain doubts concerning their station and detract from it.

اَلسَّلَامُ عَلَى وَلِيِّ اللهِ وَ ابْنِ أَوْلِيَائِهِ، اَلسَّلَامُ عَلَى الْمُدَّخَرِ لِكَرَامَةِ أَوْلِيَاءِ اللهِ وَ بَوَارِ أَعْدَائِهِ، اَلسَّلَامُ عَلَى النُّورِ الَّذِي أَرَادَ أَهْلُ الْكُفْرِ إِطْفَاءَهُ، فَأَبَى اللهُ إِلَّا أَنْ يُتِمَّ نُورَهُ بِكُرْهِهِمْ، وَ أَيَّدَهُ بِالْحَيَاةِ حَتَّى يُظْهِرَ عَلَى يَدِهِ الْحَقَّ بِرَغْمِهِمْ،

Peace be to the *walī* of Allah and descendent of His *awliyā*. Peace be to him who has been saved up for the sake of honouring Allah's *awliyā*. and destroying His enemies! Peace be to the light which the faithless desired to extinguish, and Allah was intent on perfecting His light despite their aversion and confirmed him with a long life in order to make the truth prevail at his hands against their will.

أَشْهَدُ أَنَّ اللهَ اصْطَفَاكَ صَغِيرًا، وَ أَكْمَلَ لَكَ عُلُومَهُ كَبِيرًا، وَ أَنَّكَ حَيٌّ لَا تَمُوتُ حَتَّى تُبْطِلَ الْجِبْتَ وَ الطَّاغُوتَ.

I testify that Allah chose you in your childhood and perfected your divine knowledge in your mature years and that you are alive and will not die without confuting the Idol and the Rebel!

اَللّٰهُمَّ صَلِّ عَلَيْهِ وَ عَلٰى خُدَّامِهِ وَ أَعْوَانِهِ عَلٰى غَيْبَتِهِ وَ نَأْيِهِ، وَ اسْتُرْهُ سَتْرًا عَزِيزًا، وَ اجْعَلْ لَهُ مَعْقِلًا حَرِيزًا، وَ اشْدُدِ اللّٰهُمَّ وَطْأَتَكَ عَلٰى مُعَانِدِيهِ، وَ احْرُسْ مَوَالِيَهُ وَ زَائِرِيهِ.

O Allah, bless him and those who serve him and assist him during his occultation and inaccessibility, and conceal him with a mighty cover and appoint for him a safe sanctuary. O Allah, deliver a harsh blow to his enemies and safeguard his friends and visitors.

اَللّٰهُمَّ كَمَا جَعَلْتَ قَلْبِي بِذِكْرِهِ مَعْمُورًا، فَاجْعَلْ سِلَاحِي بِنُصْرَتِهِ مَشْهُورًا، وَ إِنْ حَالَ بَيْنِي وَ بَيْنَ لِقَائِهِ الْمَوْتُ الَّذِى جَعَلْتَهُ عَلٰى عِبَادِكَ حَتْمًا، وَ أَقْدَرْتَ بِهِ عَلٰى خَلِيقَتِكَ رَغْمًا، فَابْعَثْنِي عِنْدَ خُرُوجِهِ ظَاهِرًا مِنْ حُفْرَتِي، مُؤْتَزِرًا كَفَنِي، حَتَّى أُجَاهِدَ بَيْنَ يَدَيْهِ فِي الصَّفِّ الَّذِى أَثْنَيْتَ عَلٰى أَهْلِهِ فِي كِتَابِكَ فَقُلْتَ كَأَنَّهُمْ بُنْيَانٌ مَرْصُوصٌ.

O Allah, as You have animated my heart with his remembrance, so also make my weapon ready for helping him, and should death—which You have made certain for Your servants and ordained it inevitably for Your creatures—intervene between me and my meeting with him, raise me, at the time of his appearance, from my grave, donning my shroud, that I may fight at his side in the ranks of those whom You have commended in Your Book, saying, "*[Indeed Allah loves those who fight in His way in ranks,] as if they were a compact structure.*"(61:4)

اَللّٰهُمَّ طَالَ الْإِنْتِظَارُ، وَ شَمِتَ مِنَّا الْفُجَّارُ، وَ صَعُبَ عَلَيْنَا الْإِنْتِصَارُ. اَللّٰهُمَّ أَرِنَا وَجْهَ وَلِيِّكَ الْمَيْمُونَ فِي حَيَاتِنَا وَ بَعْدَ

O Allah, the waiting has been long and the wicked have gloated over us, and it has been hard for us to defend ourselves. O Allah, show us the blessed face of Your *walī* in our lives and after

الْمَنُونِ.

death as well.

اَللّٰهُمَّ إِنِّي أَدِينُ لَكَ بِالرَّجْعَةِ بَيْنَ يَدَيْ صَاحِبِ هَذِهِ الْبُقْعَةِ، اَلْغَوْثَ الْغَوْثَ الْغَوْثَ يَا صَاحِبَ الزَّمَانِ! قَطَعْتُ فِي وُصْلَتِكَ الْخُلَّانَ، وَ هَجَرْتُ لِزِيَارَتِكَ الْأَوْطَانَ، وَ أَخْفَيْتُ أَمْرِي عَنْ أَهْلِ الْبُلْدَانِ، لِتَكُونَ شَفِيعًا عِنْدَ رَبِّكَ وَ رَبِّي وَ إِلَى آبَائِكَ وَ مَوَالِيَّ فِي حُسْنِ التَّوْفِيقِ لِي، وَ إِسْبَاغِ النِّعْمَةِ عَلَيَّ، وَ سَوْقِ الْإِحْسَانِ إِلَيَّ.

O Allah, in the presence of the master of this shrine, I profess faith in You through belief in the Return! I appeal for help! Help me! Help me! O Master of the Era, I have parted from my dear ones to join you! I have left behind my hometown to visit your shrine! I have kept my affair hidden from the people of the towns, so that you may be my intercessor with your Lord and mine, and with your ancestors and my masters, that He may grant me utmost success and fullness of blessing and bestow upon me His kindness and benevolence!

اَللّٰهُمَّ صَلِّ عَلَى مُحَمَّدٍ وَ آلِ مُحَمَّدٍ، أَصْحَابِ الْحَقِّ، وَ قَادَةِ الْخَلْقِ، وَ اسْتَجِبْ مِنِّي مَا دَعَوْتُكَ، وَ أَعْطِنِي مَا لَمْ أَنْطِقْ بِهِ فِي دُعَائِي مِنْ صَلَاحِ دِينِي وَ دُنْيَايَ، إِنَّكَ حَمِيدٌ مَجِيدٌ، وَ صَلَّى اللّٰهُ عَلَى مُحَمَّدٍ وَ آلِهِ الطَّاهِرِينَ.

O Allah, bless Muḥammad and the Family of Muḥammad, the patrons of the Truth and the leaders of the creatures, and answer my petitions and grant me also what I have not mentioned in my supplication concerning what is good for my religion and my life in the world. Indeed You are the All-laudable, the All-glorious! May Allah bless Muḥammad and his immaculate Family!

Then enter the hallway and after offering two *rakʿah* of prayer say:

اَللّٰهُمَّ عَبْدُكَ الزَّائِرُ فِي فِنَاءِ وَلِيِّكَ الْمَزُورِ، اَلَّذِي فَرَضْتَ طَاعَتَهُ عَلَى الْعَبِيدِ وَ الْأَحْرَارِ، وَ أَنْقَذْتَ بِهِ

O Allah, this servant of Yours stands as a pilgrim in the courtyard of Your *walī*, obedience to whom You have made obligatory for all and sundry, freeman and slave, and through whom You have delivered Your friends from punishment of the Fire.

أَوْلِيَاءَكَ مِنْ عَذَابِ النَّارِ.

O Allah, accept this *ziyārah* and answer my petitions, as they come from someone who affirms without doubt the truthfulness of Your *walī*.

اَللّٰهُمَّ اجْعَلْهَا زِيَارَةً مَقْبُولَةً ذَاتَ دُعَاءٍ مُسْتَجَابٍ، مِنْ مُصَدِّقٍ بِوَلِيِّكَ غَيْرِ مُرْتَابٍ.

O Allah, do not make this my last *ziyārah* and visit to his shrine. Do not cut off my relation with his shrine and with the *ziyārah* of his father and grandfather!

اَللّٰهُمَّ لَا تَجْعَلْهُ آخِرَ الْعَهْدِ بِهِ وَ لَا بِزِيَارَتِهِ، وَ لَا تَقْطَعْ أَثَرِي مِنْ مَشْهَدِهِ وَ زِيَارَةِ أَبِيهِ وَ جَدِّهِ.

O Allah, recompense me for the expenses of my journey, and grant me and my brethren, parents and family the benefit of all that You have provided us in the world and the Hereafter!

اَللّٰهُمَّ أَخْلِفْ عَلَيَّ نَفَقَتِي، وَ انْفَعْنِي بِمَا رَزَقْتَنِي فِي دُنْيَايَ وَ آخِرَتِي لِي وَ لِإِخْوَانِي وَ أَبَوَيَّ وَ جَمِيعِ عِتْرَتِي.

O Imam, through whom the faithful shall triumph and at whose hands the faithless deniers will perish, I entrust you to Allah.

أَسْتَوْدِعُكَ اللهَ أَيُّهَا الْإِمَامُ الَّذِي يَفُوزُ بِهِ الْمُؤْمِنُونَ، وَ يَهْلِكُ عَلَىٰ يَدَيْهِ الْكَافِرُونَ الْمُكَذِّبُونَ!

O Son of Ḥasan ibn ʿAlī, O my master! I have come to visit you, Your father and grandfather, sure of obtaining victory through you and keeping faith in your Imamate!

يَا مَوْلَايَ يَا ابْنَ الْحَسَنِ بْنِ عَلِيٍّ، جِئْتُكَ زَائِرًا لَكَ وَ لِأَبِيكَ وَ جَدِّكَ، مُتَيَقِّنًا الْفَوْزَ بِكُمْ مُعْتَقِدًا إِمَامَتَكُمْ!

O Allah, record for me this testimony and *ziyārah* with You in the *ʿIllīyūn*. Enable me to reach the station of the righteous; and enable me to profit from their love, O Lord of all the worlds!

اَللّٰهُمَّ اكْتُبْ هَذِهِ الشَّهَادَةَ وَ الزِّيَارَةَ لِي عِنْدَكَ فِي عِلِّيِّينَ، وَ بَلِّغْنِي بَلَاغَ الصَّالِحِينَ، وَ انْفَعْنِي بِحُبِّهِمْ يَا رَبَّ الْعَالَمِينَ!

THIRD ZIYARAH OF THE TWELFTH IMAM ('A)

According to another *ziyārah* cited by Sayyid ibn Ṭāwūs,[1] one should say,

اَلسَّلَامُ عَلَى الْحَقِّ الْجَدِيدِ، وَ الْعَالِمِ الَّذِي عِلْمُهُ لَا يَبِيدُ، اَلسَّلَامُ عَلَى مُحْيِي الْمُؤْمِنِينَ وَ مُبِيرِ الْكَافِرِينَ.

Peace be to the fresh and evergreen Truth and the Sage whose knowledge is imperishable. Peace be to him who gives life to the faithful and destroys the faithless.

اَلسَّلَامُ عَلَى مَهْدِيِّ الْأُمَمِ، وَ جَامِعِ الْكَلِمِ، اَلسَّلَامُ عَلَى خَلَفِ السَّلَفِ وَ صَاحِبِ الشَّرَفِ، اَلسَّلَامُ عَلَى حُجَّةِ الْمَعْبُودِ، وَ كَلِمَةِ الْمَحْمُودِ،

Peace be to the Guide of the nations and Embodiment of divine wisdom. Peace be to the heir of the past sages and paragon of dignity. Peace to the Testament of the Lord and Word of the All-praiseworthy Lord.

اَلسَّلَامُ عَلَى مُعِزِّ الْأَوْلِيَاءِ وَ مُذِلِّ الْأَعْدَاءِ، اَلسَّلَامُ عَلَى وَارِثِ الْأَنْبِيَاءِ وَ خَاتِمِ الْأَوْصِيَاءِ،

Peace be to him who will confer honour on the friends and humiliate the enemies. Peace be to the Heir of the prophets and the Seal of the Legatees.

اَلسَّلَامُ عَلَى الْقَائِمِ الْمُنْتَظَرِ وَ الْعَدْلِ الْمُشْتَهَرِ، اَلسَّلَامُ عَلَى السَّيْفِ الشَّاهِرِ وَ الْقَمَرِ الزَّاهِرِ [وَ النُّورِ الْبَاهِرِ]، اَلسَّلَامُ عَلَى شَمْسِ الظَّلَامِ وَ بَدْرِ التَّمَامِ، اَلسَّلَامُ عَلَى رَبِيعِ الْأَنَامِ وَ نَضْرَةِ الْأَيَّامِ، اَلسَّلَامُ عَلَى صَاحِبِ الصَّمْصَامِ وَ فَلَّاقِ الْهَامِ، اَلسَّلَامُ عَلَى الدِّينِ الْمَأْثُورِ وَ الْكِتَابِ الْمَسْطُورِ،

Peace be to the awaited Restorer and Establisher of universal justice. Peace be to the Unsheathed Sword, the shining Moon and the dazzling Light. Peace be to the Sun that expunges the world's darkness, and the Full Moon (which illuminates its nights). Peace be to the Springtime of the earth's denizens and the verdure of its days. Peace be to the wielder of the sword and the cleaver of the crowns (of tyrants). Peace be to the soul of traditional religion and the inscribed scripture.

[1] *Biḥār*, xcix, 101, b 7. Shahīd Awwal's *Mazār*, 208. Kafʿamī's *Miṣbāḥ*, 497.

اَلسَّلَامُ عَلَىٰ بَقِيَّةِ اللهِ فِي بِلَادِهِ، وَ حُجَّتِهِ عَلَىٰ عِبَادِهِ، اَلْمُنْتَهَىٰ إِلَيْهِ مَوَارِيثُ الْأَنْبِيَاءِ، وَ لَدَيْهِ مَوْجُودٌ آثَارُ الْأَصْفِيَاءِ، [اَلسَّلَامُ عَلَى] الْمُؤْتَمَنِ عَلَى السِّرِّ، وَ الْوَلِيِّ لِلْأَمْرِ،

Peace be to Allah's remnant in His lands and His testament to His servants, the ultimate heir to the legacy of the prophets, with whom is the heritage of God's elect and who is the trustee of His secrets and one invested with His authority.

اَلسَّلَامُ عَلَى الْمَهْدِيِّ الَّذِي وَعَدَ اللهُ عَزَّ وَ جَلَّ بِهِ الْأُمَمَ أَنْ يَجْمَعَ بِهِ الْكَلِمَ، وَ يَلُمَّ بِهِ الشَّعَثَ، وَ يَمْلَأَ بِهِ الْأَرْضَ قِسْطًا وَ عَدْلًا، وَ يُمَكِّنَ لَهُ وَ يُنْجِزَ بِهِ وَعْدَ الْمُؤْمِنِينَ.

Peace be to the Mahdī, promised by Allah, the Almighty and Glorious, to the nations, through whom He shall bring about their unity of belief, remove their divisions, fill the earth with justice, and establish his power and authority to fulfil through him His promise to the faithful.

أَشْهَدُ يَا مَوْلَايَ أَنَّكَ وَ الْأَئِمَّةَ مِنْ آبَائِكَ أَئِمَّتِي وَ مَوَالِيَّ فِي الْحَيَاةِ الدُّنْيَا وَ يَوْمَ يَقُومُ الْأَشْهَادُ،

O my master, I testify that you and the Imams from among your ancestors are my Imams and guardians in the life of this world and on the Day when the witnesses shall stand up to testify.

أَسْأَلُكَ يَا مَوْلَايَ أَنْ تَسْأَلَ اللهَ تَبَارَكَ وَ تَعَالَىٰ فِي صَلَاحِ شَأْنِي، وَ قَضَاءِ حَوَائِجِي، وَ غُفْرَانِ ذُنُوبِي، وَ الْأَخْذِ بِيَدِي فِي دِينِي وَ دُنْيَايَ وَ آخِرَتِي لِي وَ لِإِخْوَانِي وَ أَخَوَاتِي الْمُؤْمِنِينَ وَ الْمُؤْمِنَاتِ كَافَّةً، إِنَّهُ غَفُورٌ رَحِيمٌ.

I beseech you, my master, to ask Allah, the Blessed and Exalted, to set right my affairs, fulfil my needs, forgive my sins, and to assist me and all my faithful brothers and sisters with regard to our religion and life in the world and the Hereafter! He is indeed all-forgiving and all-merciful!

Then perform the prayer of *ziyārah* in the aforementioned manner. That is, offer twelve *rakʿahs* of prayer, performing the *tasbīḥ* of Fāṭimah Zahrā (ʿ*a*) after *salām* following every two *rakʿahs* and make a gift of them to the Imam (ʿ*a*). On finishing the prayer of *ziyārah*, say,[1]

O Allah, bless Your testament on Your earth and Your vicegerent in Your lands, the summoner to Your way, the restorer of Your justice, who shall triumph by Your command, the friend of the faithful and destroyer of the faithless, who shall dispel the darkness and make the truth shine forth, the promulgator of wisdom, good advice and truthfulness, Your Word, the repository of Your knowledge, Your witness on Your earth, vigilant and fearful, the benevolent *walī*, the ship of deliverance, the banner of guidance, the light of the eyes of God's creatures, the best of those who don garments, the avenger of the blood of the martyrs, the reliever of distress, the remover of sorrows and afflictions, may Allah bless him and his ancestors, the Imams, guides and blessed leaders, as long as the morning stars rise, the trees foliate, fruits ripen, day and night alternate, and the birds sing.

اَللّٰهُمَّ صَلِّ عَلىٰ حُجَّتِكَ فِي أَرْضِكَ، وَ خَلِيفَتِكَ فِي بِلَادِكَ، اَلدَّاعِي إِلَىٰ سَبِيلِكَ، وَ الْقَائِمِ بِقِسْطِكَ وَ الْفَائِزِ بِأَمْرِكَ، وَلِيِّ الْمُؤْمِنِينَ، وَ مُبِيرِ الْكَافِرِينَ، وَ مُجَلِّي الظُّلْمَةِ، وَ مُنِيرِ الْحَقِّ، وَ الصَّادِعِ بِالْحِكْمَةِ وَ الْمَوْعِظَةِ الْحَسَنَةِ وَ الصِّدْقِ، وَ كَلِمَتِكَ وَ عَيْبَتِكَ وَ عَيْنِكَ فِي أَرْضِكَ، اَلْمُتَرَقِّبِ الْخَائِفِ، اَلْوَلِيِّ النَّاصِحِ، سَفِينَةِ النَّجَاةِ، وَ عَلَمِ الْهُدَىٰ، وَ نُورِ أَبْصَارِ الْوَرَىٰ، وَ خَيْرِ مَنْ تَقَمَّصَ وَ ارْتَدَىٰ، وَ الْوِتْرِ الْمَوْتُورِ، وَ مُفَرِّجِ الْكَرْبِ، وَ مُزِيلِ الْهَمِّ، وَ كَاشِفِ الْبَلْوَىٰ، صَلَوَاتُ اللّٰهِ عَلَيْهِ وَ عَلىٰ آبَائِهِ الْأَئِمَّةِ الْهَادِينَ وَ الْقَادَةِ الْمَيَامِينِ، مَا طَلَعَتْ كَوَاكِبُ الْأَسْحَارِ، وَ أَوْرَقَتِ الْأَشْجَارُ، وَ أَيْنَعَتِ الْأَثْمَارُ، وَ اخْتَلَفَ اللَّيْلُ وَ النَّهَارُ، وَ غَرَّدَتِ الْأَطْيَارُ.

O Allah, grant us to benefit by our love for him and gather us in his fold and under his banner, O God of the Truth. Amen, Lord of all the worlds!

اَللّٰهُمَّ انْفَعْنَا بِحُبِّهِ، وَ احْشُرْنَا فِي زُمْرَتِهِ وَ تَحْتَ لِوَائِهِ، إِلٰهَ الْحَقِّ آمِينَ رَبَّ الْعَالَمِينَ!

1 *Biḥār*, xcix, 101-102, b 7.

Another Ṣalawat for the Twelfth Imam (ʿa)[1]

اَللّٰهُمَّ صَلِّ عَلٰى مُحَمَّدٍ وَ أَهْلِ بَيْتِهِ، وَ صَلِّ عَلٰى وَلِيِّ الْحَسَنِ وَ وَصِيِّهِ وَ وَارِثِهِ، اَلْقَائِمِ بِأَمْرِكَ، وَ الْغَائِبِ فِي خَلْقِكَ، وَ الْمُنْتَظِرِ لِإِذْنِكَ،

O Allah, bless Muḥammad and his Family and bless al-Ḥasan's vicegerent, legatee and heir, who will rise by Your command, who is hidden amongst Your creatures, and who awaits Your permission.

اَللّٰهُمَّ صَلِّ عَلَيْهِ، وَ قَرِّبْ بُعْدَهُ، وَ أَنْجِزْ وَعْدَهُ، وَ أَوْفِ عَهْدَهُ، وَ اكْشِفْ عَنْ بَأْسِهِ حِجَابَ الْغَيْبَةِ، وَ أَظْهِرْ بِظُهُورِهِ صَحَائِفَ الْمِحْنَةِ.

O Allah, bless him and change our separation from him into nearness, fulfil Your promise to him, carry out Your covenant with him, remove the veil of occultation from his power and divulge with his appearance the records of the days of ordeal.

وَ قَدِّمْ أَمَامَهُ الرُّعْبَ، وَ ثَبِّتْ بِهِ الْقَلْبَ، وَ أَقِمْ بِهِ الْحَرْبَ، وَ أَيِّدْهُ بِجُنْدٍ مِنَ الْمَلَائِكَةِ مُسَوِّمِينَ، وَ سَلِّطْهُ عَلٰى أَعْدَاءِ دِينِكَ أَجْمَعِينَ.

Let awe go forth at his front (to put terror into the enemies' hearts). Make the hearts (of the faithful) steady through him. Wage war through him (against the faithless). Strengthen him with an army of deployed angels. Make him prevail over all enemies of Your religion.

وَ أَلْهِمْهُ أَنْ لَا يَدَعَ مِنْهُمْ رُكْنًا إِلَّا هَدَّهُ، وَ لَا هَامًا إِلَّا قَدَّهُ، وَ لَا كَيْدًا إِلَّا رَدَّهُ، وَ لَا فَاسِقًا إِلَّا حَدَّهُ، وَ لَا فِرْعَوْنَ إِلَّا أَهْلَكَهُ، وَ لَا سِتْرًا إِلَّا هَتَكَهُ، وَ لَا عَلَمًا إِلَّا نَكَّسَهُ، وَ لَا سُلْطَانًا إِلَّا كَسَبَهُ، وَ لَا رُمْحًا إِلَّا قَصَفَهُ، وَ لَا مِطْرَدًا إِلَّا خَرَقَهُ، وَ لَا

Prompt him not to leave any of their pillars without demolishing, nor anything of importance to them without shattering it to pieces, nor any of their stratagems not turned back on themselves, nor any of their evildoers left unpunished, nor to let any of their tyrants escape destruction, nor any of their covers without being rent, nor any of their flags not hauled down, nor any of their authority not taken over by him, nor any of their spears, nor any of their javelins unbroken, nor to leave any troops that are not

[1] *Biḥār*, xcix, 103, b 7.

جُنْدًا إِلَّا فَرَّقَهُ، وَ لَا مِنْبَرًا إِلَّا أَحْرَقَهُ،
وَ لَا سَيْفًا إِلَّا كَسَرَهُ، وَ لَا صَنَمًا إِلَّا
رَضَّهُ، وَ لَا دَمًا إِلَّا أَرَاقَهُ، وَ لَا جَوْرًا إِلَّا
أَبَادَهُ، وَ لَا حِصْنًا إِلَّا هَدَمَهُ، وَ لَا بَابًا
إِلَّا رَدَمَهُ، وَ لَا قَصْراً إِلَّا خَرَّبَهُ، وَ لَا
مَسْكَنًا إِلا فَتَّشَهُ، وَ لَا سَهْلًا إِلَّا أَوْطَأَهُ،
وَ لَا جَبَلًا إِلَّا صَعِدَهُ، وَ لَا كَنْزًا إِلَّا
أَخْرَجَهُ، بِرَحْمَتِكَ يَا أَرْحَمَ الرَّاحِمِينَ!

disbanded, nor leave any of their pulpits that is not burnt down, nor any sword unbroken, nor any idol that is not smashed, nor any blood that has not been spilled, nor any injustice that has not been abolished, nor any fortress that has not been demolished, nor any passage that has not been blocked, nor any palace that has not been razed, nor any house that has not been ransacked, nor any plain that has not been trodden, nor any mountain that has not been scaled, nor any treasure that has not been dug out, with Your mercy, O Most Merciful of the merciful!

The compiler says: After citing the Second Ziyārah that begins with the words "*Allāhu akbar. Allāhu akbar. Lâ ilāha illallāhu wallāhu akbar*...," Shaykh Mufīd (and Shahīd Awwal) say that according to an alternate report, after entering the Holy Basement one should recite the *ziyārah* which begins with the words "*Assalāmu ʿalal ḥaqqil jadīd*...," until its end (i.e., until the words *innahū ghafūrur raḥīm*) and then perform twelve *rakʿahs* of prayer with every two *rakʿahs* followed by a *salām*. After the prayer recite the following supplication reported from the Twelfth Imam (*ʿa*).[1]

اَللّٰهُمَّ عَظُمَ الْبَلَاءُ، وَ بَرِحَ الْخَفَاءُ، وَ
انْكَشَفَ الْغِطَاءُ، وَ ضَاقَتِ الْأَرْضُ، وَ
مَنَعَتِ السَّمَاءُ، وَ إِلَيْكَ يَا رَبِّ الْمُشْتَكَى،
وَ عَلَيْكَ الْمُعَوَّلُ فِي الشِّدَّةِ وَ الرَّخَاءِ!

O Allah, our ordeal has become great; the secret is out and the veil has been lifted; the earth has become narrow and the heaven has withheld its boons, and to You, my Lord, I address my complaint, and on You is my reliance in times of ease and distress.

اَللّٰهُمَّ صَلِّ عَلَىٰ مُحَمَّدٍ وَ آلِهِ، اَلَّذِينَ
فَرَضْتَ عَلَيْنَا طَاعَتَهُمْ، فَعَرَّفْتَنَا بِذَٰلِكَ

O Allah, bless Muḥammad and his Family, whom You have enjoined us to obey, thereby acquainting us with their station,

[1] The compiler is actually quoting ʿAllāmah Majlisī in *Biḥār*, xcix, 119, b 7.

and grant us relief for the sake of their right, a relief that is as prompt as the twinkling of the eye or faster.	مَنْزِلَتَهُمْ، فَرِّجْ عَنَّا بِحَقِّهِمْ فَرَجًا عَاجِلًا كَلَمْحِ الْبَصَرِ، أَوْ هُوَ أَقْرَبُ مِنْ ذَلِكَ.
O Muḥammad! O ᶜAlī! O ᶜAlī, O Muḥammad! Help me, for you are indeed my helpers! And suffice me, for you are indeed sufficient for me. O my Master, O Master of the Era! Help me! Help me! Help me! Come to my rescue! Come to my rescue! Come to my rescue!	يَا مُحَمَّدُ يَا عَلِيُّ، يَا عَلِيُّ يَا مُحَمَّدُ، أُنْصُرَانِي فَإِنَّكُمَا نَاصِرَايَ، وَ اكْفِيَانِي فَإِنَّكُمَا كَافِيَايَ، يَا مَوْلَايَ يَا صَاحِبَ الزَّمَانِ، اَلْغَوْثَ الْغَوْثَ الْغَوْثَ، أَدْرِكْنِي أَدْرِكْنِي أَدْرِكْنِي !

This is a sublime supplication which is worthy of being recited often in other places as well. We have cited its text with a slight difference in Book One (pp. 143, 330).

Fourth Ziyārah of the Twelfth Imam (ᶜa)

There is another method of *ziyārah* cited by Sayyid Ibn Ṭāwūs,[1] according to which, after offering two *rakᶜahs,* one should recite the text of the *ziyārah* "*Salāmullāhil kāmilut tāmmush shāmil...*" which has already been cited in Chapter 7 of Book One (p. 334) as an *istighāthah,* from Sayyid ᶜAlī Khan's *al-Kalim al-Ṭayyib.*

Four Related Observances

In his book *Miṣbāḥ al-Zā'ir*, Sayyid Ibn Ṭāwūs has devoted a chapter to observances pertaining to the Holy Basement. There he cites six *ziyārahs*, and remarks that there are four other observances relating to this chapter: (1) Duᶜā al-Nudbah; (2) the *ziyārah* with which the Imam of the Age (*ᶜa*) is addressed every day after the morning prayer (and this may be considered a seventh *ziyārah*); (3) Duᶜā al-ᶜAhd, whose recitation has been prescribed for the period of the Imam's occultation; (4) the supplication which is to be recited while returning from his noble shrine. Following in the steps of that saintly scholar we will also mention these four observances in this blessed book.

1 *Biḥār*, xcix, 97-98, b 7 from Ibn Ṭāwūs.

1. THE NUDBAH SUPPLICATION

The first of them is Duʿā al-Nudbah. It is *mustaḥab* to recite this supplication on the occasions of the four *ʿīds*, namely, ʿĪd al-Fiṭr, ʿĪd al-Aḍḥā, ʿĪd al-Ghadīr, and Fridays. Its text is as follows.[1]

الْحَمْدُ لِلَّهِ رَبِّ الْعَالَمِينَ، وَ صَلَّى اللَّهُ عَلَى سَيِّدِنَا مُحَمَّدٍ نَبِيِّهِ وَ آلِهِ وَ سَلَّمَ تَسْلِيمًا.

All praise belongs to Allah, the Lord of all the worlds. May Allah bless our master and His Prophet, Muḥammad, and his Family, and may peace be to them.

اَللَّهُمَّ لَكَ الْحَمْدُ عَلَى مَا جَرَى بِهِ قَضَاؤُكَ فِي أَوْلِيَائِكَ، الَّذِينَ اسْتَخْلَصْتَهُمْ لِنَفْسِكَ وَ دِينِكَ، إِذِ اخْتَرْتَ لَهُمْ جَزِيلَ مَا عِنْدَكَ مِنَ النَّعِيمِ الْمُقِيمِ الَّذِى لَا زَوَالَ لَهُ وَ لَا اضْمِحْلَالَ، بَعْدَ أَنْ شَرَطْتَ عَلَيْهِمُ الزُّهْدَ فِي دَرَجَاتِ هَذِهِ الدُّنْيَا الدَّنِيَّةِ، وَ زُخْرُفِهَا وَ زِبْرِجِهَا، فَشَرَطُوا لَكَ ذَلِكَ وَ عَلِمْتَ مِنْهُمُ الْوَفَاءَ بِهِ،

O Allah, to You belongs all praise for what You have ordained concerning Your *awliyā'*, whom You chose for Yourself and Your religion, preferring for them Your endless blessings that will never disappear or dwindle, after that You had taken their pledge to remain detached from the ranks and reaches of this lowly world and its glitter and lustre. They pledged to that, and You knew that they would remain loyal to it.

فَقَبِلْتَهُمْ وَ قَرَّبْتَهُمْ، وَ قَدَّمْتَ لَهُمُ الذِّكْرَ الْعَلِيَّ، وَ الثَّنَاءَ الْجَلِيَّ، وَ أَهْبَطْتَ عَلَيْهِمْ مَلَائِكَتَكَ، وَ كَرَّمْتَهُمْ بِوَحْيِكَ، وَ رَفَدْتَهُمْ بِعِلْمِكَ، وَ جَعَلْتَهُمُ الذَّرِيعَةَ إِلَيْكَ، وَ الْوَسِيلَةَ إِلَى رِضْوَانِكَ،

Thereat You received them, drew them close to Yourself and conferred upon them an exalted repute and clear compliments, sending down to them Your angels, honouring them with Your revelations, and assisting them with Your knowledge, and made them the means of approach to You and of attaining Your pleasure and approval.

فَبَعْضٌ أَسْكَنْتَهُ جَنَّتَكَ إِلَى أَنْ أَخْرَجْتَهُ

You settled one of them in Your

[1] *Al-Mazār al-Kabīr*, 573-584. *Biḥār*, xcix, 104, b 7 from *Miṣbāḥ al-Zā'ir*, 230-234. *Iqbāl*, 295.

مِنْهَا، وَ بَعْضٌ حَمَلْتَهُ فِي فُلْكِكَ، وَ نَجَّيْتَهُ وَ مَنْ آمَنَ مَعَهُ مِنَ الْهَلَكَةِ بِرَحْمَتِكَ،

paradise, until You expelled him from it. You carried one of them in Your ark and rescued him from perishing and those who had believed with him with Your mercy.

وَ بَعْضٌ اتَّخَذْتَهُ لِنَفْسِكَ خَلِيلًا، وَ سَأَلَكَ لِسَانَ صِدْقٍ فِي الْآخِرِينَ، فَأَجَبْتَهُ وَ جَعَلْتَ ذٰلِكَ عَلِيًّا، وَ بَعْضٌ كَلَّمْتَهُ مِنْ شَجَرَةٍ تَكْلِيمًا، وَ جَعَلْتَ لَهُ مِنْ أَخِيهِ رِدْءًا وَ وَزِيرًا، وَ بَعْضٌ أَوْلَدْتَهُ مِنْ غَيْرِ أَبٍ، وَ آتَيْتَهُ الْبَيِّنَاتِ، وَ أَيَّدْتَهُ بِرُوحِ الْقُدُسِ،

You took one of them for a dedicated friend and he asked You to grant him a good name in the posterity, whereat You answered his prayer and exalted it. You spoke to one of them from a tree, and made his brother his helper and minister. You caused one of them to be born without a father and gave him manifest signs, and strengthened him with the Holy Spirit.

وَ كُلٌّ شَرَعْتَ لَهُ شَرِيعَةً، وَ نَهَجْتَ لَهُ مِنْهَاجًا، وَ تَخَيَّرْتَ لَهُ أَوْصِيَاءَ مُسْتَحْفِظًا بَعْدَ مُسْتَحْفِظٍ، مِنْ مُدَّةٍ إِلَى مُدَّةٍ، إِقَامَةً لِدِينِكَ، وَ حُجَّةً عَلَى عِبَادِكَ، وَ لِئَلَّا يَزُولَ الْحَقُّ عَنْ مَقَرِّهِ، وَ يَغْلِبَ الْبَاطِلُ عَلَى أَهْلِهِ، وَ لَا يَقُولَ أَحَدٌ لَوْ لَا أَرْسَلْتَ إِلَيْنَا رَسُولًا مُنْذِرًا، وَ أَقَمْتَ لَنَا عَلَمًا هَادِيًا، فَنَتَّبِعَ آيَاتِكَ مِنْ قَبْلِ أَنْ نَذِلَّ وَ نَخْزَى،

For each of them You laid down a code of law and appointed for him a way, choosing for him successors so that they may—one after another and from one period to another—safeguard and uphold Your religion, as Your testaments to Your servants, to ensure that the truth is not supplanted and ousted from its place and falsehood does not take hold of the minds of the followers of the truth. (You did all this) so that none should be able to say, "Why did You not send an envoy to warn us and appoint a beacon to guide us so that we might follow Your signs instead of falling into degradation and disrepute."

إِلَى أَنِ انْتَهَيْتَ بِالْأَمْرِ إِلَى حَبِيبِكَ وَ

This process went on until You finally conferred Your authority on

Your beloved and Your chosen one, Muḥammad, may Allah bless him and his Family. Being Your chosen one, he was the chief of Your creatures, the select of Your chosen ones, the best of those You had selected, and the noblest of those who enjoyed Your confidence.

نَجِيبِكَ مُحَمَّدٍ صَلَّى اللّٰهُ عَلَيْهِ وَ آلِهِ، فَكَانَ كَمَا انْتَجَبْتَهُ سَيِّدَ مَنْ خَلَقْتَهُ، وَ صَفْوَةَ مَنِ اصْطَفَيْتَهُ، وَ أَفْضَلَ مَنِ اجْتَبَيْتَهُ، وَ أَكْرَمَ مَنِ اعْتَمَدْتَهُ،

You made him the foremost of Your prophets and sent him to both races of humans and jinn from among Your servants. You set the earth's east and west under his feet, and, putting the *Burāq* at his disposal, made his spirit [him] ascend to Your heaven.

قَدَّمْتَهُ عَلَىٰ أَنْبِيَائِكَ، وَ بَعَثْتَهُ إِلَى الثَّقَلَيْنِ مِنْ عِبَادِكَ، وَ أَوْطَأْتَهُ مَشَارِقَكَ وَ مَغَارِبَكَ، وَ سَخَّرْتَ لَهُ الْبُرَاقَ، وَ عَرَجْتَ بِرُوحِهِ [بِهِ] إِلَى سَمَائِكَ،

You entrusted him with the knowledge of what has been and what will be until the end of Your creation. Further, You assisted him through awe (that You cast into the hearts of his enemies) and encircled him with Gabriel and Michael and those who were dispatched from among Your angels. You promised to make his religion *prevail over all other religions though the polytheists should be averse.*

وَ أَوْدَعْتَهُ عِلْمَ مَا كَانَ وَ مَا يَكُونُ إِلَى انْقِضَاءِ خَلْقِكَ، ثُمَّ نَصَرْتَهُ بِالرُّعْبِ، وَ حَفَفْتَهُ بِجَبْرَئِيلَ وَ مِيكَائِيلَ، وَ الْمُسَوِّمِينَ مِنْ مَلَائِكَتِكَ، وَ وَعَدْتَهُ أَنْ تُظْهِرَ دِينَهُ عَلَى الدِّينِ كُلِّهِ وَ لَوْ كَرِهَ الْمُشْرِكُونَ.

That was after You had settled him in a worthy station amongst his kindred and appointed for him and them *the first house to be set up for mankind, which is the one at Bakkah, blessed and a guidance for all nations. In it are manifest signs [and] Abraham's Station, and whoever enters it shall be secure.*(3:96-97) And You said, *Indeed Allah desires to keep off all impurity from you, O People of the Family, and purify you with a thor-*

وَ ذٰلِكَ بَعْدَ أَنْ بَوَّأْتَهُ مُبَوَّأَ صِدْقٍ مِنْ أَهْلِهِ، وَ جَعَلْتَ لَهُ وَ لَهُمْ أَوَّلَ بَيْتٍ وُضِعَ لِلنَّاسِ، لَلَّذِي بِبَكَّةَ مُبَارَكًا وَ هُدًى لِلْعَالَمِينَ، فِيهِ آيَاتٌ بَيِّنَاتٌ، مَقَامُ إِبْرَاهِيمَ، وَ مَنْ دَخَلَهُ كَانَ آمِنًا، وَ قُلْتَ إِنَّمَا يُرِيدُ اللّٰهُ لِيُذْهِبَ عَنْكُمُ الرِّجْسَ

ough purification. (33:33)

أَهْلَ الْبَيْتِ، وَ يُطَهِّرَكُمْ تَطْهِيرًا.

Then You decreed in Your Scripture that the recompense for Muḥammad, may Your blessings be upon him and his Family, shall be the love of his Family, and You said, *Say, 'I do not ask you any reward for it except love of [my] relatives.'*(43:23) And You said, *Say, 'Whatever reward I may have asked you is for your own good.*(34:47) And You said, *Say, 'I do not ask you any reward for it, except that anyone who wishes should take the way to his Lord.'*(25:57) So they are the way to You and the path that leads to Your pleasure.

ثُمَّ جَعَلْتَ أَجْرَ مُحَمَّدٍ صَلَوَاتُكَ عَلَيْهِ وَ آلِهِ مَوَدَّتَهُمْ فِي كِتَابِكَ، فَقُلْتَ قُلْ لَا أَسْئَلُكُمْ عَلَيْهِ أَجْرًا إِلَّا الْمَوَدَّةَ فِي الْقُرْبَى، وَ قُلْتَ: مَا سَأَلْتُكُمْ مِنْ أَجْرٍ فَهُوَ لَكُمْ، وَ قُلْتَ: مَا أَسْئَلُكُمْ عَلَيْهِ مِنْ أَجْرٍ إِلَّا مَنْ شَاءَ أَنْ يَتَّخِذَ إِلَى رَبِّهِ سَبِيلًا، فَكَانُوا هُمُ السَّبِيلَ إِلَيْكَ، وَ الْمَسْلَكَ إِلَى رِضْوَانِكَ.

When the days of his life were near their end, he installed ᶜAlī ibn Abī Ṭālib—may Your blessings be on both of them and their Family—as the guide, as he was *the warner and there is a guide for every nation.* So he addressed the audience before him declaring, "This ᶜAlī is the master of all those who have me for their master. O Allah, befriend those who befriend him and be the enemy of his enemies. Assist those who help him and forsake those who forsake him."

فَلَمَّا انْقَضَتْ أَيَّامُهُ أَقَامَ وَلِيَّهُ عَلِيَّ بْنَ أَبِي طَالِبٍ، صَلَوَاتُكَ عَلَيْهِمَا وَ آلِهِمَا هَادِيًا، إِذْ كَانَ هُوَ الْمُنْذِرَ وَ لِكُلِّ قَوْمٍ هَادٍ، فَقَالَ وَ الْمَلَأُ أَمَامَهُ، مَنْ كُنْتُ مَوْلَاهُ فَعَلِيٌّ مَوْلَاهُ، اَللّٰهُمَّ وَالِ مَنْ وَالَاهُ، وَ عَادِ مَنْ عَادَاهُ، وَ انْصُرْ مَنْ نَصَرَهُ، وَ اخْذُلْ مَنْ خَذَلَهُ،

He also said, "ᶜAlī is the commander of those who regards me as his prophet." And he also said, "I and ᶜAlī are from the same tree, and the rest of the people are from various trees."

وَ قَالَ مَنْ كُنْتُ أَنَا نَبِيَّهُ فَعَلِيٌّ أَمِيرُهُ،

وَ قَالَ أَنَا وَ عَلِيٌّ مِنْ شَجَرَةٍ وَاحِدَةٍ، وَ سَائِرُ النَّاسِ مِنْ شَجَرٍ شَتَّى،

He assigned ᶜAlī a position that Aaron possessed in relation to Mo-

وَ أَحَلَّهُ مَحَلَّ هَارُونَ مِنْ مُوسَى،

فَقالَ لَهُ أَنْتَ مِنِّي بِمَنْزِلَةِ هَارُونَ
مِنْ مُوسَى، إِلَّا أَنَّهُ لا نَبِيَّ بَعْدِي،

ses, when he said to him, "You are to me as Aaron was in relation to Moses, except that there will be no prophet after me."

وَ زَوَّجَهُ ابْنَتَهُ سَيِّدَةَ نِسَاءِ الْعَالَمِينَ، وَ
أَحَلَّ لَهُ مِنْ مَسْجِدِهِ مَا حَلَّ لَهُ، وَ سَدَّ
الْأَبْوَابَ إِلَّا بَابَهُ، ثُمَّ أَوْدَعَهُ عِلْمَهُ وَ
حِكْمَتَهُ، فَقَالَ أَنَا مَدِينَةُ الْعِلْمِ وَ عَلِيٌّ
بَابُهَا، فَمَنْ أَرَادَ الْمَدِينَةَ وَ الْحِكْمَةَ
فَلْيَأْتِهَا مِنْ بَابِهَا،

He wedded ᶜAlī to his daughter, the Mistress of the world's womankind. He allowed ᶜAlī a privilege in relation to his mosque which was permitted only to himself, and he closed all the doors that opened into the mosque except that of ᶜAlī. He entrusted ᶜAlī with his knowledge and wisdom and declared, "I am the city of knowledge and ᶜAlī is its gate. Whoever desires to enter the city and acquire wisdom should enter through its gate."

ثُمَّ قَالَ أَنْتَ أَخِي وَ وَصِيِّي وَ وَارِثِي،
لَحْمُكَ مِنْ لَحْمِي، وَ دَمُكَ مِنْ دَمِي،
وَ سِلْمُكَ سِلْمِي، وَ حَرْبُكَ حَرْبِي، وَ
الْإِيمَانُ مُخَالِطٌ لَحْمَكَ وَ دَمَكَ كَمَا
خَالَطَ لَحْمِي وَ دَمِي، وَ أَنْتَ غَدًا عَلَى
الْحَوْضِ خَلِيفَتِي، وَ أَنْتَ تَقْضِي دَيْنِي،
وَ تُنْجِزُ عِدَاتِي، وَ شِيعَتُكَ عَلَى مَنَابِرَ
مِنْ نُورٍ مُبْيَضَّةً وُجُوهُهُمْ حَوْلِي فِي
الْجَنَّةِ، وَ هُمْ جِيرَانِي، وَ لَوْ لَا أَنْتَ يَا
عَلِيُّ لَمْ يُعْرَفِ الْمُؤْمِنُونَ بَعْدِي،

He further said, "You are my brother, my legatee and my heir. Your flesh is my flesh and your blood is my blood. Your peace treaties are my peace treaties and the wars waged by you are my wars. Faith permeates your blood and flesh in the same way as it does my flesh and blood. Tomorrow you will be my vicegerent at the Pool. You are the one who will pay off my debts and fulfil my promises. Your followers will stand around me in paradise on pulpits of light with their faces shining, and they will be my neighbours. O cAlī, were it not for you, the faithful would not be distinguishable (from the faithless) after me."

وَ كَانَ بَعْدَهُ هُدًى مِنَ الضَّلَالِ، وَ
نُورًا مِنَ الْعَمَى، وَ حَبْلَ اللهِ الْمَتِينَ، وَ

After the Prophet, ᶜAlī represented guidance as against error and as light and vision as opposed to blindness. He was the firm lifeline of Allah and His straight path, unsurpassed by anyone with regard to nearness to the Prophet in kinship or with regard to his precedence in faith, unmatched by anyone in any of his virtues. He followed in the footsteps of the Apostle, may Allah bless them and their Family, and fought to reinstate the genuine meanings of the Scripture, undeterred by the blame of any blamer.

صِرَاطَهُ الْمُسْتَقِيمَ، لَا يُسْبَقُ بِقَرَابَةٍ فِي رَحِمٍ، وَ لَا بِسَابِقَةٍ فِي دِينٍ، وَ لَا يُلْحَقُ فِي مَنْقَبَةٍ مِنْ مَنَاقِبِهِ، يَحْذُو حَذْوَ الرَّسُولِ صَلَّى اللهُ عَلَيْهِمَا وَ آلِهِمَا، وَ يُقَاتِلُ عَلَى التَّأْوِيلِ، وَ لَا تَأْخُذُهُ فِي اللهِ لَوْمَةُ لَائِمٍ،

In the course of this he offended the leaders of the Arabs, slew their heroes and engaged their wolves in combat, and, as a consequence, made their hearts full of bitterness and resentment because of Badr, Khaybar, Ḥunayn and other battles. As a result, they harboured his enmity and launched wars against him, in the course of which he killed the rebels, the perverse and the renegades.

قَدْ وَتَرَ فِيهِ صَنَادِيدَ الْعَرَبِ، وَ قَتَلَ أَبْطَالَهُمْ وَ نَاوَشَ ذُؤْبَانَهُمْ، فَأَوْدَعَ قُلُوبَهُمْ أَحْقَادا بَدْرِيَّةً وَ خَيْبَرِيَّةً وَ حُنَيْنِيَّةً وَ غَيْرَهُنَّ، فَأَضَبَّتْ عَلَى عَدَاوَتِهِ، وَأَكَبَّتْ عَلَى مُنَابَذَتِهِ، حَتَّى قَتَلَ النَّاكِثِينَ وَالْقَاسِطِينَ وَالْمَارِقِينَ،

Even after he had fulfilled his pledge and was assassinated by the biggest wretch of the latter generations, who followed in the footsteps of the most wretched of the former generations, they never abided by the commands of the Apostle of Allah, may Allah bless him and his Family, concerning the guides, one after another, and the *ummah* was bent on hostility towards him and—excepting a few who loyally observed their due rights—it rallied to violate the rights of his Family and to banish his progeny.

وَ لَمَّا قَضَى نَحْبَهُ وَ قَتَلَهُ أَشْقَى الْآخِرِينَ، يَتْبَعُ أَشْقَى الْأَوَّلِينَ، لَمْ يُمْتَثَلْ أَمْرُ رَسُولِ اللهِ صَلَّى اللهُ عَلَيْهِ وَ آلِهِ فِي الْهَادِينَ بَعْدَ الْهَادِينَ، وَ الْأُمَّةُ مُصِرَّةٌ عَلَى مَقْتِهِ، مُجْتَمِعَةٌ عَلَى قَطِيعَةِ رَحِمِهِ، وَ إِقْصَاءِ وَلَدِهِ، إِلَّا الْقَلِيلَ مِمَّنْ وَفَى لِرِعَايَةِ الْحَقِّ فِيهِمْ.

Thus some of them were slain,

فَقُتِلَ مَنْ قُتِلَ، وَ سُبِيَ مَنْ سُبِيَ،

وَ أُقْصِيَ مَنْ أُقْصِيَ، وَ جَرَى الْقَضَاءُ لَهُمْ بِمَا يُرْجَى لَهُ حُسْنُ الْمَثُوبَةِ، إِذْ كَانَتِ الْأَرْضُ لِلّٰهِ يُورِثُهَا مَنْ يَشَاءُ مِنْ عِبَادِهِ، وَ الْعَاقِبَةُ لِلْمُتَّقِينَ، وَ سُبْحَانَ رَبِّنَا إِنْ كَانَ وَعْدُ رَبِّنَا لَمَفْعُولًا، وَ لَنْ يُخْلِفَ اللّٰهُ وَعْدَهُ وَ هُوَ الْعَزِيزُ الْحَكِيمُ.

some were made captives, some were banished, and the fate that had been ordained for them came to pass, with the hope of a splendid reward, as *the earth belongs to Allah and and He gives its inheritance to whomever He wishes of His servants, and the outcome will be in favour of the Godwary.*[7:128] *And immaculate is our Lord! Indeed Our Lord's promise is bound to be fulfilled* [17:108] and *Allah shall never break His promise* [22:47] and *He is the Almighty and the All-wise.*

فَعَلَى الْأَطَائِبِ مِنْ أَهْلِ بَيْتِ مُحَمَّدٍ وَ عَلِيٍّ صَلَّى اللّٰهُ عَلَيْهِمَا وَ آلِهِمَا فَلْيَبْكِ الْبَاكُونَ، وَ إِيَّاهُمْ فَلْيَنْدُبِ النَّادِبُونَ، وَ لِمِثْلِهِمْ فَلْتُذْرَفِ الدُّمُوعُ، وَ لْيَصْرُخِ الصَّارِخُونَ، وَ يَضِجَّ الضَّاجُّونَ، وَ يَعِجَّ الْعَاجُّونَ،

So let the weepers weep and the mourners mourn over the immaculate souls of the Family of Muḥammad and ᶜAlī, may Allah bless them and their Family, and for them and their likes let tears be shed and for them let the keeners keen and the wailers wail and let the lamenters lament them!!

أَيْنَ الْحَسَنُ أَيْنَ الْحُسَيْنُ؟ أَيْنَ أَبْنَاءُ الْحُسَيْنِ؟ صَالِحٌ بَعْدَ صَالِحٍ، وَ صَادِقٌ بَعْدَ صَادِقٍ، أَيْنَ السَّبِيلُ بَعْدَ السَّبِيلِ؟ أَيْنَ الْخِيَرَةُ بَعْدَ الْخِيَرَةِ؟

Where is Ḥasan!? Where is Ḥusayn!? Where are the descendants of Ḥusayn, one righteous soul after another, one truthful spirit after another, one guide after another, one elect of the creation after another!?

أَيْنَ الشُّمُوسُ الطَّالِعَةُ؟ أَيْنَ الْأَقْمَارُ الْمُنِيرَةُ؟ أَيْنَ الْأَنْجُمُ الزَّاهِرَةُ؟ أَيْنَ أَعْلَامُ الدِّينِ وَ قَوَاعِدُ الْعِلْمِ؟ أَيْنَ بَقِيَّةُ

Where are those brilliant suns? Where are those shining moons? Where are those bright stars? Where are those beacons of the faith and the pillars of knowledge? Where is the remnant of God,

اللهِ الَّتِي لَا تَخْلُو مِنَ الْعِتْرَةِ الْهَادِيَةِ؟
أَيْنَ الْمُعَدُّ لِقَطْعِ دَابِرِ الظَّلَمَةِ؟ أَيْنَ
الْمُنْتَظَرُ لِإِقَامَةِ الْأَمْتِ وَ الْعِوَجِ؟ أَيْنَ
الْمُرْتَجَى لِإِزَالَةِ الْجَوْرِ وَ الْعُدْوَانِ؟ أَيْنَ
الْمُدَّخَرُ لِتَجْدِيدِ الْفَرَائِضِ وَ السُّنَنِ؟
أَيْنَ الْمُتَخَيَّرُ لِإِعَادَةِ الْمِلَّةِ وَ الشَّرِيعَةِ؟
أَيْنَ الْمُؤَمَّلُ لِإِحْيَاءِ الْكِتَابِ وَ
حُدُودِهِ؟ أَيْنَ مُحْيِي مَعَالِمِ الدِّينِ وَ
أَهْلِهِ؟

who is always present among the (Prophet's) guiding progeny?

Where is he who has been prepared to cut off the roots of the world's oppressors? Where is the awaited one, expected to straighten out crookedness and deviance? Where is the expected one, who is hoped to remove injustice and aggression? Where is he who has been held in store for the revival of divine duties and norms? Where is he who is chosen to restore the genuine creed and laws? Where is he who is looked forward to for the revival of the Scripture and its precepts? Where is the reviver of the principles of Islam and its worthies?

أَيْنَ قَاصِمُ شَوْكَةِ الْمُعْتَدِينَ؟ أَيْنَ هَادِمُ
أَبْنِيَةِ الشِّرْكِ وَ النِّفَاقِ؟ أَيْنَ مُبِيدُ أَهْلِ
الْفُسُوقِ وَ الْعِصْيَانِ وَ الطُّغْيَانِ؟ أَيْنَ
حَاصِدُ فُرُوعِ الْغَيِّ وَ الشِّقَاقِ؟ أَيْنَ
طَامِسُ آثَارِ الزَّيْغِ وَ الْأَهْوَاءِ؟

Where is the shatterer of the might of the aggressors? Where is the demolisher of the mansions of polytheism and hypocrisy? Where is the destroyer of the agents of depravity, sin and rebellion against God? Where is he who will cut off the offshoots of perversity and schism [hypocrisy]? Where is the annihilator of deviation and heresy?

أَيْنَ قَاطِعُ حَبَائِلِ الْكِذْبِ وَ الْإِفْتِرَاءِ؟
أَيْنَ مُبِيدُ الْعُتَاةِ وَ الْمَرَدَةِ؟ أَيْنَ
مُسْتَأْصِلُ أَهْلِ الْعِنَادِ وَ التَّضْلِيلِ وَ
الْإِلْحَادِ؟ أَيْنَ مُعِزُّ الْأَوْلِيَاءِ وَ مُذِلُّ
الْأَعْدَاءِ؟ أَيْنَ جَامِعُ الْكَلِمَةِ عَلَى
التَّقْوَىٰ؟

Where is he who will clear the snares of falsehood and fabrication? Where is the destroyer of the defiant and the arrogant? Where is he who will extirpate the agents of misguidance, apostasy and resistance to truth? Where is he who will bring power and honour to the friends and reduce God's enemies? Where is he who will bring about unity and accord on the basis of Godfearing?

Where is God's gateway, through whom He can be approached? Where is the Visage of God, towards which His friends turn? Where is the lifeline linking the earth to the heaven? Where is the master of the day of victory who will unfurl the banner of guidance? Where is he who will bring about a harmonious and righteous order and general satisfaction? Where is the avenger of the prophets and their progeny? Where is the avenger of the blood of the one slain at Karbalā?

أَيْنَ بَابُ اللهِ الَّذِى مِنْهُ يُؤْتَىٰ؟ أَيْنَ
وَجْهُ اللهِ الَّذِى إِلَيْهِ يَتَوَجَّهُ الْأَوْلِيَاءُ؟
أَيْنَ السَّبَبُ الْمُتَّصِلُ بَيْنَ الْأَرْضِ
وَ السَّمَاءِ؟ أَيْنَ صَاحِبُ يَوْمِ الْفَتْحِ
وَ نَاشِرُ رَايَةِ الْهُدَىٰ؟ أَيْنَ مُؤَلِّفُ
شَمْلِ الصَّلَاحِ وَ الرِّضَا؟ أَيْنَ الطَّالِبُ
بِذُحُولِ الْأَنْبِيَاءِ وَ أَبْنَاءِ الْأَنْبِيَاءِ؟
أَيْنَ الطَّالِبُ بِدَمِ الْمَقْتُولِ بِكَرْبَلَاءَ؟

Where is he who will be helped by God against those who transgress against him and slander him? Where is *'the distressed one'* who is answered when he calls? Where is the chief of the creatures, who is pious and Godfearing? Where is the son of the Chosen Prophet (al-Muṣṭafā), the son of ᶜAlī, with whom God is pleased (al-Murtaḍā), the son of the noble Khadījah, and the son of the great Fāṭimah?

أَيْنَ الْمَنْصُورُ عَلَىٰ مَنِ اعْتَدَىٰ عَلَيْهِ
وَ افْتَرَىٰ؟ أَيْنَ الْمُضْطَرُّ الَّذِى يُجَابُ
إِذَا دَعَا؟ أَيْنَ صَدْرُ الْخَلَائِقِ ذُو الْبِرِّ
وَ التَّقْوَىٰ؟ أَيْنَ ابْنُ النَّبِيِّ الْمُصْطَفَىٰ؟
وَ ابْنُ عَلِيٍّ الْمُرْتَضَىٰ؟ وَ ابْنُ خَدِيجَةَ
الْغَرَّاءِ؟ وَ ابْنُ فَاطِمَةَ الْكُبْرَىٰ؟

You are dearer to me than my father and mother, and dearer than my own life! I am willing to shield and support you with my life! O son of masters close to God! O son of the most distinguished and noble ancestors! O son of the rightly-guided guides! O son of God's elect and refined souls! O son of the great and noblest ancestors! O son of the best of immaculate

بِأَبِى أَنْتَ وَ أُمِّى وَ نَفْسِى لَكَ الْوِقَاءُ
وَ الْحِمَىٰ، يَا ابْنَ السَّادَةِ الْمُقَرَّبِينَ، يَا
ابْنَ النُّجَبَاءِ الْأَكْرَمِينَ، يَا ابْنَ الْهُدَاةِ
الْمَهْدِيِّينَ، يَا ابْنَ الْخِيَرَةِ الْمُهَذَّبِينَ،
يَا ابْنَ الْغَطَارِفَةِ الْأَنْجَبِينَ، يَا ابْنَ
الْأَطَائِبِ الْمُطَهَّرِينَ، يَا ابْنَ الْخَضَارِمَةِ

الْمُنْتَجَبِينَ، يَا ابْنَ الْقَمَاقِمَةِ الْأَكْرَمِينَ،

souls! O son of the select of the munificent! O son of the most generous of the magnanimous!

يَا ابْنَ الْبُدُورِ الْمُنِيرَةِ، يَا ابْنَ السُّرُجِ الْمُضِيئَةِ، يَا ابْنَ الشُّهُبِ الثَّاقِبَةِ، يَا ابْنَ الْأَنْجُمِ الزَّاهِرَةِ، يَا ابْنَ السُّبُلِ الْوَاضِحَةِ، يَا ابْنَ الْأَعْلَامِ اللَّائِحَةِ، يَا ابْنَ الْعُلُومِ الْكَامِلَةِ، يَا ابْنَ السُّنَنِ الْمَشْهُورَةِ، يَا ابْنَ الْمَعَالِمِ الْمَأْثُورَةِ،

O scion of the bright full moons! O son of the radiant lamps! O scion of the piercing stars! O scion of the brilliant stars! O scion of the manifest paths (leading to God)! O scion of the shining luminaries! O scion of the embodiments of perfect knowledge! O scion of the (the founders of) illustrious traditions! O son of (the sources of) traditional teachings!

يَا ابْنَ الْمُعْجِزَاتِ الْمَوْجُودَةِ، يَا ابْنَ الدَّلَائِلِ الْمَشْهُودَةِ، يَا ابْنَ الصِّرَاطِ الْمُسْتَقِيمِ، يَا ابْنَ النَّبَإِ الْعَظِيمِ، يَا ابْنَ مَنْ هُوَ فِي أُمِّ الْكِتَابِ لَدَى اللهِ عَلِيٌّ حَكِيمٌ،

O heir to the enduring miracles! O inheritor of the celebrated proofs! O scion of the Straight Path! O son of the Great Tiding! O son of him who is described in the Mother Book as being sublime and wise with Allah!

يَا ابْنَ الْآيَاتِ وَ الْبَيِّنَاتِ، يَا ابْنَ الدَّلَائِلِ الظَّاهِرَاتِ، يَا ابْنَ الْبَرَاهِينِ الْوَاضِحَاتِ الْبَاهِرَاتِ، يَا ابْنَ الْحُجَجِ الْبَالِغَاتِ، يَا ابْنَ النِّعَمِ السَّابِغَاتِ، يَا ابْنَ طٰهٰ وَ الْمُحْكَمَاتِ، يَا ابْنَ يٰس وَ الذَّارِيَاتِ، يَا ابْنَ الطُّورِ وَ الْعَادِيَاتِ، يَا ابْنَ مَنْ دَنَا فَتَدَلَّى فَكَانَ قَابَ قَوْسَيْنِ أَوْ أَدْنَى، دُنُوًّا وَ اقْتِرَابًا مِنَ الْعَلِيِّ الْأَعْلَى،

O heir to the signs and the manifest proofs! O inheritor of manifest guidelines! O heir to the clear and brilliant proofs! O son of (God's) conclusive testaments! O son of the bountiful blessings! O son of Ṭā Ḥā and heir to the definitive Signs! O scion of Yā Sīn and al-*Dhāriyāt!* O guardian of *al-Ṭūr* and *al-ᶜĀdiyāt!* O son of him who *drew near and nearer until he was within two bows' length or even nearer* to the Most High and the Most Exalted.

لَيْتَ شِعْرِي أَيْنَ اسْتَقَرَّتْ بِكَ النَّوَى، بَلْ

I wish I knew your final desti-

أَىُّ أَرْضٍ تُقِلُّكَ أَوْ ثَرَىٰ، أَ بِرَضْوَىٰ أَوْ غَيْرِهَا أَمْ ذِى طُوَىٰ، عَزِيزٌ عَلَيَّ أَنْ أَرَى الْخَلْقَ وَ لَا تُرَىٰ، وَ لَا أَسْمَعَ لَكَ حَسِيسًا وَ لَا نَجْوَىٰ، عَزِيزٌ عَلَيَّ أَنْ تُحِيطَ بِكَ دُونِيَ الْبَلْوَىٰ، وَ لَا يَنَالَكَ مِنِّي ضَجِيجٌ وَ لَا شَكْوَىٰ،

nation and the land where you are sojourning, whether it is Raḍwā, or Dhū Ṭuwā, or some other place! It is hard for me to see all and sundry and yet be unable to see you, or hear from you so much as a whisper or murmur! It pains me that afflictions should besiege you instead of me, without any of my cries and complaints reaching you!

بِنَفْسِي أَنْتَ مِنْ مُغَيَّبٍ لَمْ يَخْلُ مِنَّا، بِنَفْسِي أَنْتَ مِنْ نَازِحٍ مَا نَزَحَ عَنَّا، بِنَفْسِي أَنْتَ أُمْنِيَّةُ شَائِقٍ يَتَمَنَّىٰ، مِنْ مُؤْمِنٍ وَ مُؤْمِنَةٍ ذَكَرَا فَحَنَّا، بِنَفْسِي أَنْتَ مِنْ عَقِيدِ عِزٍّ لَا يُسَامَىٰ، بِنَفْسِي أَنْتَ مِنْ أَثِيلِ مَجْدٍ لَا يُجَارَىٰ، بِنَفْسِي أَنْتَ مِنْ تِلَادِ نِعَمٍ لَا تُضَاهَىٰ، بِنَفْسِي أَنْتَ مِنْ نَصِيفِ شَرَفٍ لَا يُسَاوَىٰ،

By my life, you are hidden from us without being distant! By my life, you are far without being cut off from us! By my life, you are the earnest longing of every faithful man and woman who remembers you with tenderness and affection! By my life, you belong to a lineage unsurpassed in its long-standing dignity! By my life, you are heir to a legacy unmatched in its blessings! By my life, your share of honour and dignity is unequalled!

إِلَىٰ مَتَىٰ أَحَارُ فِيكَ يَا مَوْلَايَ؟ وَ إِلَىٰ مَتَىٰ وَ أَيَّ خِطَابٍ أَصِفُ فِيكَ وَ أَيَّ نَجْوَىٰ؟ عَزِيزٌ عَلَيَّ أَنْ أُجَابَ دُونَكَ وَ أُنَاغَىٰ، عَزِيزٌ عَلَيَّ أَنْ أَبْكِيَكَ وَ يَخْذُلَكَ الْوَرَىٰ، عَزِيزٌ عَلَيَّ أَنْ يَجْرِيَ عَلَيْكَ دُونَهُمْ مَا جَرَىٰ،

My master, how long shall I remain distraught about you? Till when and with what words or muted petitions shall I implore (God) concerning you? It pains me to be able to receive responses and kindly messages but not from you! Hard it is upon me that I bewail you while the people have forsaken you! Hard it is upon me that of all you should endure what have endured!

هَــلْ مِنْ مُعِينٍ فَأُطِيلَ مَعَــهُ الْعَوِيلَ وَ الْبُكَاءَ؟ هَلْ مِنْ جَزُوعٍ فَأُسَاعِدَ جَزَعَهُ إِذَا خَلا؟ هَلْ قَذِيَتْ عَيْنٌ فَسَــاعَدَتْهَا عَيْــنِي عَلَى الْقَذَىٰ؟ هَــلْ إِلَيْكَ يَا ابْنَ أَحْمَدَ سَــبِيلٌ فَتُلْقَىٰ؟ هَلْ يَتَّصِلُ يَوْمُنَا مِنْكَ بِعِدَةٍ فَنَحْظَىٰ؟

Is there any helper with whom I can prolong my laments and groans? Is there any restless lonely soul whom I may assist in its restlessness? Is there an anguished heart that I may assist in its anguish? Is there any means of meeting you, O son of Aḥmad? Will our days ever reach a tryst when we will enjoy your company?

مَتَىٰ نَــرِدُ مَنَاهِلَكَ الرَّوِيَّــةَ فَنَرْوَىٰ؟ مَتَىٰ نَنْتَقِعُ مِنْ عَذْبِ مَائِكَ فَقَدْ طَالَ الصَّدَىٰ؟ مَتَىٰ نُغَادِيكَ وَ نُرَاوِحُكَ فَنُقِرَّ عَيْنًا؟ مَتَىٰ تَرَانَا وَ نَــرَاكَ وَ قَدْ نَشَرْتَ لِوَاءَ النَّصْرِ تُــرَىٰ؟ أَ تَرَانَا نَحُفُّ بِكَ وَ أَنْــتَ تَؤُمُّ الْمَلَأَ وَ قَــدْ مَلَأْتَ الْأَرْضَ عَــدْلًا، وَ أَذَقْــتَ أَعْــدَاءَكَ هَوَانًا وَ عِقَابًا، وَ أَبَــرْتَ الْعُتَاةَ وَ جَحَدَةَ الْحَقِّ، وَ قَطَعْتَ دَابِرَ الْمُتَكَبِّرِينَ، وَ اجْتَثَثْتَ أُصُولَ الظَّالِمِــينَ، وَ نَحْنُ نَقُولُ الْحَمْدُ لِلَّهِ رَبِّ الْعَالَمِينَ!

When shall we arrive at your fountain to quench our thirst? When shall we be satiated with your agreeable water, for we have thirsted for so long? When shall our mornings and evenings be spent by your side that we may be delighted? When will it be when we look at you and you look at us and you are seen unfolding the banner of victory? Will you ever see us surrounding you when you lead the hosts, having filled the earth with justice, after making your enemies taste disgrace and punishment, annihilating the tyrants and opponents of the truth, rooting out the arrogant and eradicating the roots of the wrongdoers, when we will say '*All praise belongs to Allah, the Lord of all the worlds*'?

اَللَّهُمَّ أَنْتَ كَشَّافُ الْكُرَبِ وَ الْبَلْوَىٰ، وَ إِلَيْكَ أَسْتَعْدِي فَعِنْدَكَ الْعَدْوَىٰ، وَ أَنْتَ رَبُّ الْآخِرَةِ وَ الدُّنْيَا،

O Allah, You are the Remover of afflictions and distress and to You do I appeal for deliverance, for all help is with You and You are the Lord of the world and the Hereafter!

So help me, Your insignificant and afflicted servant, O Succour of those who appeal for help! Show me my master, O Possessor of great powers, and through him relieve my ardent love and pain and satiate my thirst, O You who preside over the Throne and toward whom is the ultimate return and destination!

فَأَغِثْ يَا غِيَاثَ الْمُسْتَغِيثِينَ عُبَيْدَكَ الْمُبْتَلَى، وَ أَرِهِ سَيِّدَهُ يَا شَدِيدَ الْقُوَى، وَ أَزِلْ عَنْهُ بِهِ الْأَسَى وَ الْجَوَى، وَ بَرِّدْ غَلِيلَهُ يَا مَنْ عَلَى الْعَرْشِ اسْتَوَى، وَ مَنْ إِلَيْهِ الرُّجْعَى وَ الْمُنْتَهَى،

O Allah, we are Your servants eager to see Your *walī* who reminds us about You and Your Prophet! You created him as our protector and shelter, as the means of our sustenance and refuge, made him the Imam of the faithful amongst us! So convey to him our *salām* and greetings and thereby increase us, O Lord, in Your favour and kindness. Make his staying place our abode and residence, and complete Your blessing upon us by making him appear in front of us, until You admit us into Your paradise, into the company of the martyrs from among Your elect!

اَللّٰهُمَّ وَ نَحْنُ عَبِيدُكَ التَّائِقُونَ إِلَى وَلِيِّكَ الْمُذَكِّرِ بِكَ وَ بِنَبِيِّكَ، خَلَقْتَهُ لَنَا عِصْمَةً وَ مَلَاذًا، وَ أَقَمْتَهُ لَنَا قِوَامًا وَ مَعَاذًا، وَ جَعَلْتَهُ لِلْمُؤْمِنِينَ مِنَّا إِمَامًا، فَبَلِّغْهُ مِنَّا تَحِيَّةً وَ سَلَامًا، وَ زِدْنَا بِذَلِكَ يَا رَبِّ إِكْرَامًا، وَ اجْعَلْ مُسْتَقَرَّهُ لَنَا مُسْتَقَرًّا وَ مُقَامًا، وَ أَتْمِمْ نِعْمَتَكَ بِتَقْدِيمِكَ إِيَّاهُ أَمَامَنَا حَتَّى تُورِدَنَا جِنَانَكَ، وَ مُرَافَقَةَ الشُّهَدَاءِ مِنْ خُلَصَائِكَ.

O Allah, bless Muḥammad and the Family of Muḥammad and bless Muḥammad, his ancestor and Your Apostle, the greatest master, and bless ʿAlī, his forefather, the lesser master, and his foremother, Fāṭimah, daughter of Muḥammad and the most veracious lady, and the chosen ones of his pious forefathers, and him with the best, most perfect, complete, enduring, numerous

اَللّٰهُمَّ صَلِّ عَلَى مُحَمَّدٍ وَ آلِ مُحَمَّدٍ، وَ صَلِّ عَلَى مُحَمَّدٍ جَدِّهِ وَ رَسُولِكَ، اَلسَّيِّدِ الْأَكْبَرِ، وَ عَلَى أَبِيهِ، اَلسَّيِّدِ الْأَصْغَرِ، وَ جَدَّتِهِ الصِّدِّيقَةِ الْكُبْرَى فَاطِمَةَ بِنْتِ مُحَمَّدٍ، وَ عَلَى مَنِ اصْطَفَيْتَ مِنْ آبَائِهِ الْبَرَرَةِ، وَ عَلَيْهِ أَفْضَلَ وَ أَكْمَلَ، وَ

<table>
<tr>
<td>and abundant of blessings with which You have blessed any of Your elect and chosen servants from among Your creatures, and bless him with a blessing that is limited neither by number, nor bound by extent, and whose duration never ends.</td>
<td dir="rtl">أَتَمَّ وَ أَدْوَمَ، وَ أَكْثَرَ وَ أَوْفَرَ مَا صَلَّيْتَ
عَلَىٰ أَحَدٍ مِنْ أَصْفِيَائِكَ، وَ خِيَرَتِكَ مِنْ
خَلْقِكَ، وَ صَلِّ عَلَيْهِ صَلَاةً لَا غَايَةَ
لِعَدَدِهَا، وَ لَا نِهَايَةَ لِمَدَدِهَا، وَ لَا نَفَادَ
لِأَمَدِهَا.</td>
</tr>
<tr>
<td>O Allah, establish the truth through him and refute the falsehood. Through him guide Your friends and humiliate Your enemies.</td>
<td dir="rtl">اَللّٰهُمَّ وَ أَقِمْ بِهِ الْحَقَّ، وَ أَدْحِضْ بِهِ الْبَاطِلَ،
وَ أَدِلْ بِهِ أَوْلِيَاءَكَ، وَ أَذْلِلْ بِهِ أَعْدَاءَكَ،</td>
</tr>
<tr>
<td>O Allah, join us to him with a link that will lead us to the company of his forefathers and make us of those who take hold of their handhold and abide in their shade. Help us to observe his rights, to strive in obeying him and to refrain from disobeying him. Favour us by making him pleased with us and grant us his compassion, mercy, prayers and goodness whereby we may attain to Your bountiful mercy and triumph with You!</td>
<td dir="rtl">وَ صِلِ اللّٰهُمَّ بَيْنَنَا وَ بَيْنَهُ وُصْلَةً تُؤَدِّي
إِلَىٰ مُرَافَقَةِ سَلَفِهِ، وَ اجْعَلْنَا مِمَّنْ يَأْخُذُ
بِحُجْزَتِهِمْ، وَ يَمْكُثُ فِي ظِلِّهِمْ، وَ أَعِنَّا
عَلَىٰ تَأْدِيَةِ حُقُوقِهِ إِلَيْهِ، وَ الْإِجْتِهَادِ فِي
طَاعَتِهِ، وَ اجْتِنَابِ مَعْصِيَتِهِ، وَ امْنُنْ
عَلَيْنَا بِرِضَاهُ، وَ هَبْ لَنَا رَأْفَتَهُ وَ رَحْمَتَهُ،
وَ دُعَاءَهُ وَ خَيْرَهُ، مَا نَنَالُ بِهِ سَعَةً مِنْ
رَحْمَتِكَ، وَ فَوْزًا عِنْدَكَ،</td>
</tr>
<tr>
<td>Through him, accept our prayers, and for his sake forgive our sins, answer our supplications, expand our provisions, remove our worries, fulfil our needs and turn to us with Your munificent Face!</td>
<td dir="rtl">وَ اجْعَلْ صَلَاتَنَا بِهِ مَقْبُولَةً، وَ ذُنُوبَنَا
بِهِ مَغْفُورَةً، وَ دُعَاءَنَا بِهِ مُسْتَجَابًا، وَ
اجْعَلْ أَرْزَاقَنَا بِهِ مَبْسُوطَةً، وَ هُمُومَنَا بِهِ
مَكْفِيَّةً، وَ حَوَائِجَنَا بِهِ مَقْضِيَّةً، وَ أَقْبِلْ
إِلَيْنَا بِوَجْهِكَ الْكَرِيمِ،</td>
</tr>
</table>

Welcome our efforts to draw near to You and look at us with the look of mercy whereby we may attain complete honour and favour with You! Thereafter, through Your generosity, do not turn it away from us and give us to drink from the Pool of his ancestor, may Allah bless him and his Family, from his cup and with his hand, a drink that is satiating, agreeable and pleasant after which there will be no thirst, O Most Merciful of the merciful!

وَ اقْبَلْ تَقَرُّبَنَا إِلَيْكَ، وَ انْظُرْ إِلَيْنَا نَظْرَةً رَحِيمَةً نَسْتَكْمِلُ بِهَا الْكَرَامَةَ عِنْدَكَ، ثُمَّ لَا تَصْرِفْهَا عَنَّا بِجُودِكَ، وَ اسْقِنَا مِنْ حَوْضِ جَدِّهِ صَلَّى اللّٰهُ عَلَيْهِ وَ آلِهِ بِكَأْسِهِ وَ بِيَدِهِ رَيًّا رَوِيًّا هَنِيئًا سَائِغًا لَا ظَمَأَ بَعْدَهُ، يَا أَرْحَمَ الرَّاحِمِينَ!

Then offer the prayer of *ziyārah* in the above-mentioned manner, and make any petitions that you may wish, which will be granted, God willing.

2. A Ziyarah of the Imam of the Era (ʿa)

This is a *ziyārah* with which our master, the Imam of the Age (*ʿa*), is addressed every day after the morning prayer.[1] Its text is as follows.

O Allah, convey to my master, the Master of the Era—may Allah's blessings be upon him—on behalf of all the faithful, men and women, all over the earth's east and west, on land and sea, in its plains and mountains, the living among them and those who have passed away, and on behalf of my parents and children and me, blessings and greetings as weighty as Your Throne, as abundant as the ink needed to write Your words, and to the utmost degree of Your satisfaction, and as numerous as all

اللّٰهُمَّ بَلِّغْ مَوْلَايَ صَاحِبَ الزَّمَانِ، صَلَوَاتُ اللّٰهِ عَلَيْهِ، عَنْ جَمِيعِ الْمُؤْمِنِينَ وَ الْمُؤْمِنَاتِ، فِي مَشَارِقِ الْأَرْضِ وَ مَغَارِبِهَا، وَ بَرِّهَا وَ بَحْرِهَا، وَ سَهْلِهَا وَ جَبَلِهَا، حَيِّهِمْ وَ مَيِّتِهِمْ، وَ عَنْ وَالِدَيَّ وَ وُلْدِي وَ عَنِّي، مِنَ الصَّلَوَاتِ وَ التَّحِيَّاتِ، زِنَةَ عَرْشِ اللّٰهِ، وَ مِدَادَ كَلِمَاتِهِ، وَ مُنْتَهَى رِضَاهُ، وَ عَدَدَ مَا

[1] *Al-Mazār, al-Kabīr*, 662, b 4. *Biḥār*, xcix, 100, b 7, from Ibn Ṭāwūs..

أَحْصَاهُ كِتَابُهُ وَ أَحَاطَ بِهِ عِلْمُهُ.

that is encompassed by Your Book and embraced by Your knowledge.

اللّٰهُمَّ إِنِّي أُجَدِّدُ لَهُ فِي هٰذَا الْيَوْمِ، وَ فِي كُلِّ يَوْمٍ، عَهْدًا وَ عَقْدًا وَ بَيْعَةً فِي رَقَبَتِي.

O Allah, on this day and every day, I renew my covenant and compact with him and my oath of allegiance to him.

اللّٰهُمَّ كَمَا شَرَّفْتَنِي بِهٰذَا التَّشْرِيفِ، وَ فَضَّلْتَنِي بِهٰذِهِ الْفَضِيلَةِ، وَ خَصَصْتَنِي بِهٰذِهِ النِّعْمَةِ، فَصَلِّ عَلىٰ مَوْلَايَ وَ سَيِّدِي صَاحِبِ الزَّمَانِ، وَ اجْعَلْنِي مِنْ أَنْصَارِهِ وَ أَشْيَاعِهِ وَ الذَّابِّينَ عَنْهُ، وَ اجْعَلْنِي مِنَ الْمُسْتَشْهَدِينَ بَيْنَ يَدَيْهِ، طَائِعًا غَيْرَ مُكْرَهٍ، فِي الصَّفِّ الَّذِي نَعَتَّ أَهْلَهُ فِي كِتَابِكَ، فَقُلْتَ صَفًّا كَأَنَّهُمْ بُنْيَانٌ مَرْصُوصٌ، عَلىٰ طَاعَتِكَ وَ طَاعَةِ رَسُولِكَ وَ آلِهِ عَلَيْهِمُ السَّلَامُ. اللّٰهُمَّ هٰذِهِ بَيْعَةٌ لَهُ فِي عُنُقِي إِلىٰ يَوْمِ الْقِيَامَةِ.

O Allah, in the same way as You have granted me this honour and favour and singled me out for this blessing, bless my master and guardian, the Master of the Era, and appoint me among his supporters, followers and defenders, and make me one of those who obtain martyrdom in his service, willingly and without reserve, amid the ranks of those whom You have extolled in Your Book, saying, *"as if they were a compact structure,"* (61:4) and in obedience to You, Your Apostle and his Family, may peace be to them. O Allah, this is my pledge of allegiance to him until the Day of Resurrection!

The compiler says: After citing this *ziyārah* and prayer in the *Biḥār al-Anwār*, ᶜAllāmah Majlisī (*r*) remarks that certain olden works he had seen suggest that on reciting this supplication one should place one's right hand on one's left as a sign of one's pledge of allegiance.

We have cited above four *ziyārah*s while describing the observances pertaining to the Holy Basement. Hence this is the fifth *ziyārah* of our book. Moreover, we have cited still another *ziyārah* of the Imam of the Age (ᶜ*a*) for Fridays in Book One, while describing the *ziyārah*s of the Infallibles in the chapter on observances pertaining to the days of the week (p. 183).

3. Du‘a al-‘Ahd

Imam Jacfar al-Ṣādiq (*ᶜa*) is reported[1] to have said that those who recite this *ᶜahd* (i.e., ‘pledge’ or ‘covenant’) every morning for forty days will be among the helpers of the Qā’im (*ᶜa*), and should any of them die before his appearance, God Almighty will bring him forth from his grave to be in the service of the Imam, and for its every word God Almighty will reward him with a thousand good deeds and efface a thousand of his sins. Its text is as follows.

O Allah, Lord of the great light, the Exalted Throne and the surging sea, revealer of the Torah, the Evangel and Psalms, Lord of the shade and the nightly torrid wind, revealer of the Great Qur’ān, Lord of the archangels, the prophets and the apostles.

اَللّٰهُمَّ رَبَّ النُّورِ الْعَظِيمِ، وَ رَبَّ الْكُرْسِيِّ
الرَّفِيعِ، وَ رَبَّ الْبَحْرِ الْمَسْجُورِ، وَ مُنْزِلَ
التَّوْرَاةِ وَ الْإِنْجِيلِ وَ الزَّبُورِ، وَ رَبَّ الظِّلِّ
وَ الْحَرُورِ، وَ مُنْزِلَ الْقُرْآنِ الْعَظِيمِ، وَ رَبَّ
الْمَلَائِكَةِ الْمُقَرَّبِينَ، وَالْأَنْبِيَاءِ وَالْمُرْسَلِينَ،

O Allah I beseech You by Your munificent Face, by the light of Your brilliant Visage and Your eternal kingdom! O Living One, O All-sustainer! I beseech You by Your Name which illuminates the heavens and the earths, by Your Name by which the former and the latter generations have thrived and prospered, O Living One prior to every living thing, O Living One posterior to every living thing! O Living One when there was no living thing! O You who revive the dead and bring death to the living! O Living One, besides You there is no god!

اَللّٰهُمَّ إِنِّي أَسْأَلُكَ بِوَجْهِكَ الْكَرِيمِ، وَ بِنُورِ
وَجْهِكَ الْمُنِيرِ، وَ مُلْكِكَ الْقَدِيمِ، يَا حَيُّ
يَا قَيُّومُ، أَسْأَلُكَ بِاسْمِكَ الَّذِى أَشْرَقَتْ بِهِ
السَّمَاوَاتُ وَ الْأَرَضُونَ، وَ بِاسْمِكَ الَّذِى
يَصْلَحُ بِهِ الْأَوَّلُونَ وَ الْآخِرُونَ، يَا حَيًّا
قَبْلَ كُلِّ حَيٍّ، وَ يَا حَيًّا بَعْدَ كُلِّ حَيٍّ، وَ
يَا حَيًّا حِينَ لَا حَيَّ، يَا مُحْيِيَ الْمَوْتَى، وَ
مُمِيتَ الْأَحْيَاءِ، يَا حَيُّ لَا إِلَهَ إِلَّا أَنْتَ.

O Allah, convey blessings to our Master, the Imam, the right-

اَللّٰهُمَّ بَلِّغْ مَوْلَانَا الْإِمَامَ الْهَادِيَ الْمَهْدِيَّ

[1] *Al-Mazār al-Kabīr*, 663. *Biḥār*, lxxxiii, 284, b 45, h 47; xci, 41, b 28, h 25 & xcix, 110, b 7 from Ibn Ṭāwūs and other sources. Kafᶜamī’s *Miṣbāḥ*, 550. *Balad*, 82.

ly-guided guide and maintainer of Your Law, may Allah's blessings be upon him and his immaculate ancestors, on behalf of all the faithful, men and women, in the earth's east and west, in its plains and mountains, on land and sea, and from me and my parents–blessings as weighty as the Throne of Allah, as much as the ink needed to write Your words and as numerous as can be encompassed only by Your knowledge and contained in Your Book!

الْقَائِمَ بِأَمْرِكَ، صَلَوَاتُ اللهِ عَلَيْهِ وَ عَلىٰ آبَائِهِ الطَّاهِرِينَ، عَنْ جَمِيعِ الْمُؤْمِنِينَ وَ الْمُؤْمِنَاتِ، فِي مَشَارِقِ الْأَرْضِ وَ مَغَارِبِهَا، سَهْلِهَا وَ جَبَلِهَا، وَ بَرِّهَا وَ بَحْرِهَا، وَ عَنِّي وَ عَنْ وَالِدَيَّ، مِنَ الصَّلَوَاتِ زِنَةَ عَرْشِ اللهِ، وَ مِدَادَ كَلِمَاتِهِ، وَ مَا أَحْصَاهُ عِلْمُهُ وَ أَحَاطَ بِهِ كِتَابُهُ.

O Allah, I renew this morning, today and every day for the remainder of my life, my pledge, covenant and allegiance to him, binding on me, which I shall never retract or forsake.

اَللّٰهُمَّ إِنِّي أُجَدِّدُ لَهُ فِي صَبِيحَةِ يَوْمِي هَذَا وَ مَا عِشْتُ مِنْ أَيَّامِي، عَهْدًا وَ عَقْدًا وَ بَيْعَةً لَهُ فِي عُنُقِي، لَا أَحُولُ عَنْهَا وَ لَا أَزُولُ أَبَدًا.

O Allah, include me amongst his helpers and defenders, among those who are prompt in carrying out his demands, who follow his commands, support him, take the lead in carrying out his goals, and are martyred in his service.

اَللّٰهُمَّ اجْعَلْنِي مِنْ أَنْصَارِهِ وَ أَعْوَانِهِ وَ الذَّابِّينَ عَنْهُ، وَ الْمُسَارِعِينَ إِلَيْهِ، فِي قَضَاءِ حَوَائِجِهِ، وَ الْمُمْتَثِلِينَ لِأَوَامِرِهِ، وَ الْمُحَامِينَ عَنْهُ، وَ السَّابِقِينَ إِلَى إِرَادَتِهِ، وَ الْمُسْتَشْهَدِينَ بَيْنَ يَدَيْهِ.

O Allah, should death— which You have made certain for Your servants—intervene between me and him, bring me forth from my grave, donning my shroud, unsheathing my sword, drawing my spear, responding to the call of the caller amongst towspeople

اَللّٰهُمَّ إِنْ حَالَ بَيْنِي وَ بَيْنَهُ الْمَوْتُ الَّذِي جَعَلْتَهُ عَلىٰ عِبَادِكَ حَتْمًا مَقْضِيًّا، فَأَخْرِجْنِي مِنْ قَبْرِي مُؤْتَزِرًا كَفَنِي، شَاهِرًا سَيْفِي، مُجَرِّدًا قَنَاتِي، مُلَبِّيًا دَعْوَةَ

and the countryfolk.

الدَّاعِي فِي الْحَاضِرِ وَ الْبَادِي.

O Allah, grace me with the sight of that discerning glance and that bright and admirable visage, and brighten my eyes with his sight! Hasten his relief, facilitate his appearance, widen his way, lead me on to his path, enforce his authority and fortify his strength.

اَللّٰهُمَّ أَرِنِي الطَّلْعَةَ الرَّشِيدَةَ، وَ الْغُرَّةَ الْحَمِيدَةَ، وَ اكْحُلْ نَاظِرِي بِنَظْرَةٍ مِنِّي إِلَيْهِ، وَ عَجِّلْ فَرَجَهُ، وَ سَهِّلْ مَخْرَجَهُ، وَ أَوْسِعْ مَنْهَجَهُ، وَ اسْلُكْ بِي مَحَجَّتَهُ، وَ أَنْفِذْ أَمْرَهُ، وَ اشْدُدْ أَزْرَهُ،

O Allah, through him make Your cities flourish and give new life to Your servants, for Indeed You have said, and Your words are true, that "*Corruption has appeared in land and sea because of the doings of the people's hands.*" (30:41)

وَ اعْمُرِ اللّٰهُمَّ بِهِ بِلَادَكَ، وَ أَحْيِ بِهِ عِبَادَكَ، فَإِنَّكَ قُلْتَ، وَ قَوْلُكَ الْحَقُّ، ظَهَرَ الْفَسَادُ فِي الْبَرِّ وَ الْبَحْرِ بِمَا كَسَبَتْ أَيْدِي النَّاسِ،

O Allah, send forth for us Your *walī* and son of Your Prophet's daughter, the namesake of Your Apostle, so that he may tear to pieces every falsehood that he encounters and establish every truth!

فَأَظْهِرِ اللّٰهُمَّ لَنَا وَلِيَّكَ وَ ابْنَ بِنْتِ نَبِيِّكَ، اَلْمُسَمَّى بِاسْمِ رَسُولِكَ، حَتَّى لَا يَظْفَرَ بِشَيْءٍ مِنَ الْبَاطِلِ إِلَّا مَزَّقَهُ، وَ يُحِقَّ الْحَقَّ وَ يُحَقِّقَهُ،

O Allah make him the refuge for Your oppressed servants and helper for those who have no helper besides You; make him the reviver of the forsaken ordinances of Your Book, the restorer of the landmarks of Your religion and the traditions of Your Prophet, may Allah bless him and his family.

وَ اجْعَلْهُ اللّٰهُمَّ مَفْزَعًا لِمَظْلُومِ عِبَادِكَ، وَ نَاصِرًا لِمَنْ لَا يَجِدُ لَهُ نَاصِرًا غَيْرَكَ، وَ مُجَدِّدًا لِمَا عُطِّلَ مِنْ أَحْكَامِ كِتَابِكَ، وَ مُشَيِّدًا لِمَا وَرَدَ مِنْ أَعْلَامِ دِينِكَ وَ سُنَنِ نَبِيِّكَ صَلَّى اللهُ عَلَيْهِ وَ آلِهِ،

O Allah guard him like those whom You protect from the vi-

وَ اجْعَلْهُ اللّٰهُمَّ مِمَّنْ حَصَّنْتَهُ مِنْ بَأْسِ

olence of aggressors. O Allah, gladden Your Prophet Muhammad, may Allah bless him and his Family, with his appearance and those who follow his summons and have mercy on our state of abasement after his occultation.

الْمُعْتَدِينَ، اَللّٰهُمَّ وَ سُرَّ نَبِيَّكَ مُحَمَّدًا صَلَّى
اللهُ عَلَيْهِ وَ آلِهِ بِرُؤْيَتِهِ، وَ مَنْ تَبِعَهُ عَلَىٰ
دَعْوَتِهِ، وَ ارْحَمِ اسْتِكَانَتَنَا بَعْدَهُ.

O Allah, through his presence remove this affliction and sorrow from this *ummah* and hasten for us his appearance, *for indeed they see it to be far off, and We see it to be near,* (70:6-7) by Your mercy, O Most Merciful of the merciful!.

اَللّٰهُمَّ اكْشِفْ هَذِهِ الْغُمَّةَ عَنْ هَذِهِ
الْأُمَّةِ بِحُضُورِهِ، وَ عَجِّلْ لَنَا ظُهُورَهُ،
إِنَّهُمْ يَرَوْنَهُ بَعِيدًا وَ نَرَاهُ قَرِيبًا،
بِرَحْمَتِكَ يَا أَرْحَمَ الرَّاحِمِينَ!

On completing the *duᶜā*, strike your right thigh with the right hand three times, saying each time "*al-ᶜajal, al-ᶜajal, yā mawlāya, ya Ṣāḥibaz Zamān!*" (Hasten, hasten, my master, O Master of the Era!)

4. The Supplication at Departure

According to Sayyid Ibn Ṭāwūs,[1] when intending to depart from the shrine, one should return to the Holy Basement and engage in prayer for as long as one wishes. Then, one should recite the following supplication while standing facing the *qiblah*. Before leaving, one should plead with God as much as one can.

We cite the text of this supplication from Shaykh Ṭūsī's *Miṣbāḥ*, where it is reported from Imam ᶜAlī al-Riḍā (ᶜ*a*). The Shaykh writes that the Imam had told Yūnus b. ᶜAbd al-Raḥmān that this supplication be made for Imam Mahdī (ᶜ*a*).

O Allah, repel from Your *walī*, Your vicegerent and Your testament to Your creatures, Your spokesman, preacher of Your wisdom, Your watchful eye by Your sanction, Your witness to Your servants, the chief of the warriors, who takes shelter in

اَللّٰهُمَّ ادْفَعْ عَنْ وَلِيِّكَ وَ خَلِيفَتِكَ، وَ
حُجَّتِكَ عَلَىٰ خَلْقِكَ، وَ لِسَانِكَ الْمُعَبِّرِ
عَنْكَ، اَلنَّاطِقِ بِحِكْمَتِكَ، وَ عَيْنِكَ
النَّاظِرَةِ بِإِذْنِكَ، وَ شَاهِدِكَ عَلَىٰ عِبَادِكَ،

1 Ṭūsī's *Miṣbāḥ*, 409, *Jamāl*, 506, whence *Biḥār*, xcii, 330, b 115, h 4 & xcix, 112, b 7. Kafᶜamī's *Miṣbāḥ*, 548. *Balad*, 81.

You and worships You, from the evil of all that You have created, authored, produced and fashioned. Protect him from his front and rear, from his right and left, and from above and below with Your protection, which does not put at risk anyone You protect with. By safeguarding him, protect Your Apostle and the Imams, his ancestors and the pillars of Your religion!

الْجَحْجَاحِ الْمُجَاهِدِ، الْعَائِذِ بِكَ، الْعَابِدِ عِنْدَكَ، وَ أَعِذْهُ مِنْ شَرِّ جَمِيعِ مَا خَلَقْتَ وَ بَرَأْتَ، وَ أَنْشَأْتَ وَ صَوَّرْتَ، وَ احْفَظْهُ مِنْ بَيْنِ يَدَيْهِ وَ مِنْ خَلْفِهِ، وَ عَنْ يَمِينِهِ وَ عَنْ شِمَالِهِ، وَ مِنْ فَوْقِهِ وَ مِنْ تَحْتِهِ، بِحِفْظِكَ الَّذِى لَا يَضِيعُ مَنْ حَفِظْتَهُ بِهِ، وَ احْفَظْ فِيهِ رَسُولَكَ وَ آبَاءَهُ أَئِمَّتَكَ وَ دَعَائِمَ دِينِكَ،

Guard him in Your imperishable custody, in Your inviolable sanctuary, and under Your invulnerable cover and might! Keep him safe in Your reliable security, which does not forsake those whom You protect therewith. Take him into Your invincible sanctuary; help him with Your mighty help; strengthen him with Your indomitable hosts; empower him with Your strength; and have him escorted by Your angels. Love those who love him, and hate those who hate him. Shield him with Your impregnable shield and surround him with encircling angels!

وَ اجْعَلْهُ فِى وَدِيعَتِكَ الَّتِى لَا تَضِيعُ، وَ فِى جِوَارِكَ الَّذِى لَا يُخْفَرُ، وَ فِى مَنْعِكَ وَ عِزِّكَ الَّذِى لَا يُقْهَرُ، وَ آمِنْهُ بِأَمَانِكَ الْوَثِيقِ، الَّذِى لَا يُخْذَلُ مَنْ آمَنْتَهُ بِهِ، وَ اجْعَلْهُ فِى كَنَفِكَ الَّذِى لَا يُرَامُ مَنْ كَانَ فِيهِ، وَ انْصُرْهُ بِنَصْرِكَ الْعَزِيزِ، وَ أَيِّدْهُ بِجُنْدِكَ الْغَالِبِ، وَ قَوِّهِ بِقُوَّتِكَ، وَ أَرْدِفْهُ بِمَلَائِكَتِكَ، وَ وَالِ مَنْ وَالَاهُ، وَ عَادِ مَنْ عَادَاهُ، وَ أَلْبِسْهُ دِرْعَكَ الْحَصِينَةَ، وَ حُفَّهُ بِالْمَلَائِكَةِ حَفًّا.

O Allah, through him turn our disunity into unity, remove our divisions, put an end to oppression, make justice prevail, and beautify the earth by prolonging his life-span!

اَللَّهُمَّ اشْعَبْ بِهِ الصَّدْعَ، وَ ارْتُقْ بِهِ الْفَتْقَ، وَ أَمِتْ بِهِ الْجَوْرَ، وَ أَظْهِرْ بِهِ الْعَدْلَ، وَ زَيِّنْ بِطُولِ بَقَائِهِ الْأَرْضَ،

Strengthen him with Your

وَ أَيِّدْهُ بِالنَّصْرِ، وَ انْصُرْهُ بِالرُّعْبِ، وَ قَوِّ

help, help him by inspiring awe in his enemies, fortify his helpers and forsake those who forsake him! Demolish those who are hostile to him and annihilate those who are disloyal to him.

نَاصِرِيهِ، وَ اخْذُلْ خَاذِلِيهِ، وَ دَمْدِمْ مَنْ
نَصَبَ لَهُ، وَ دَمِّرْ مَنْ غَشَّهُ،

Through him, slay the tyrants and the leaders and supporters of unfaith! Through him, crush the leaders of error, the disseminators of heresy, the obliterators of the *Sunnah* and the promoters of falsehood! Through him, humble the tyrants and expunge the faithless and all the apostates in the world's east and west, in land and sea, in its plains and mountains, until You do not leave any inhabitant from among them and there remains no trace of them!

وَ اقْتُلْ بِهِ جَبَابِرَةَ الْكُفْرِ، وَ عَمَدَهُ
[عُمُدَهُ] وَ دَعَائِمَهُ، وَ اقْصِمْ بِهِ رُؤُوسَ
الضَّلَالَةِ، وَ شَارِعَةَ الْبِدَعِ، وَ مُمِيتَةَ
السُّنَّةِ، وَ مُقَوِّيَةَ الْبَاطِلِ، وَ ذَلِّلْ بِهِ
الْجَبَّارِينَ، وَ أَبِرْ بِهِ الْكَافِرِينَ، وَ جَمِيعَ
الْمُلْحِدِينَ فِي مَشَارِقِ الْأَرْضِ وَ
مَغَارِبِهَا، وَ بَرِّهَا وَ بَحْرِهَا، وَ سَهْلِهَا وَ
جَبَلِهَا، حَتَّى لَا تَدَعَ مِنْهُمْ دَيَّارًا، وَ لَا
تُبْقِيَ لَهُمْ آثَارًا.

O Allah, purge Your towns of them and thereby heal the hearts of Your servants! Through him give might and honour to the faithful, and revive the traditions of Your apostles and the forsaken precepts of the prophets!

اَللّٰهُمَّ طَهِّرْ مِنْهُمْ بِلَادَكَ، وَ اشْفِ مِنْهُمْ
عِبَادَكَ، وَ أَعِزَّ بِهِ الْمُؤْمِنِينَ، وَ أَحْيِ بِهِ
سُنَنَ الْمُرْسَلِينَ، وَ دَارِسَ حُكْمِ النَّبِيِّينَ،

Through him reestablish the teachings of Your religion which have fallen into oblivion and Your laws which have been altered, until through him and at his hands, Your religion is renewed and refreshed, and restored to its pristine purity and health, free of all crookedness

وَ جَدِّدْ بِهِ مَا امْتَحَى مِنْ دِينِكَ، وَ بُدِّلَ
مِنْ حُكْمِكَ، حَتَّى تُعِيدَ دِينَكَ بِهِ وَ عَلَى
يَدَيْهِ جَدِيدًا غَضًّا مَحْضًا صَحِيحًا، لَا
عِوَجَ فِيهِ وَ لَا بِدْعَةَ مَعَهُ، وَ حَتَّى تُنِيرَ
بِعَدْلِهِ ظُلَمَ الْجَوْرِ، وَ تُطْفِئَ بِهِ نِيرَانَ

and heresy, and until through the means of his justice You remove the darkness of injustice, extinguish the fires of unfaith, clarify the complexities of the truth and the obscurities of justice!

الْكُفْرِ، وَ تُوضِحَ بِهِ مَعَاقِدَ الْحَقِّ وَ مَجْهُولَ الْعَدْلِ.

For indeed he is Your servant, whom You have made Your favourite, choosing him for Your knowledge of the Unseen, preserved him from all sin, kept him free from all defects, pure from all defilements and secure from every impurity!

فَإِنَّهُ عَبْدُكَ الَّذِى اسْتَخْلَصْتَهُ لِنَفْسِكَ، وَ اصْطَفَيْتَهُ عَلَىٰ غَيْبِكَ، وَ عَصَمْتَهُ مِنَ الذُّنُوبِ، وَ بَرَّأْتَهُ مِنَ الْعُيُوبِ، وَ طَهَّرْتَهُ مِنَ الرِّجْسِ، وَ سَلَّمْتَهُ مِنَ الدَّنَسِ.

O Allah, on the Day of Resurrection, the day the Catastrophe shall befall, we will bear witness that he never committed any sin, was never guilty of any slip, never committed any disobedience, never neglected obedience to You, never violated any of Your sanctities, never altered any of Your prescribed duties, that he never changed any of Your laws, and that he is the true guide, rightly-guided, pure, blameless, Godfearing, admirable and chaste!

اَللّٰهُمَّ فَإِنَّا نَشْهَدُ لَهُ يَوْمَ الْقِيَامَةِ، وَ يَوْمَ حُلُولِ الطَّامَّةِ، أَنَّهُ لَمْ يُذْنِبْ ذَنْبًا، وَ لَا أَتَى حُوبًا، وَلَمْ يَرْتَكِبْ مَعْصِيَةً، وَ لَمْ يُضَيِّعْ لَكَ طَاعَةً، وَ لَمْ يَهْتِكْ لَكَ حُرْمَةً، وَ لَمْ يُبَدِّلْ لَكَ فَرِيضَةً، وَ لَمْ يُغَيِّرْ لَكَ شَرِيعَةً، وَ أَنَّهُ الْهَادِى الْمُهْتَدِى الطَّاهِرُ التَّقِيُّ النَّقِيُّ الرَّضِيُّ الزَّكِيُّ.

O Allah, grant him in relation to himself, his family, his children, his progeny, his people and all his subjects, that which will make him delighted and pleased. Bring under his control all the dominions, near and distant, the strong and the weak, so that his rule holds sway over every rule and his truth prevails over every falsehood!

اَللّٰهُمَّ أَعْطِهِ فِى نَفْسِهِ وَ أَهْلِهِ، وَ وَلَدِهِ وَ ذُرِّيَّتِهِ، وَ أُمَّتِهِ وَ جَمِيعِ رَعِيَّتِهِ، مَا تُقِرُّ بِهِ عَيْنَهُ، وَ تَسُرُّ بِهِ نَفْسَهُ، وَ تَجْمَعُ لَهُ مُلْكَ الْمَمْلَكَاتِ كُلِّهَا، قَرِيبِهَا وَ بَعِيدِهَا، وَ عَزِيزِهَا وَ ذَلِيلِهَا، حَتَّى تَجْرِىَ حُكْمُهُ عَلَىٰ كُلِّ حُكْمٍ، وَ تَغْلِبَ بِحَقِّهِ كُلَّ بَاطِلٍ.

O Allah, lead us through him on the path of guidance, on the supreme way and the middle path to which every extremist must return and with every laggard must catch up! Grant us the strength to obey him, make us steadfast in accompanying him, and favour us by enabling us to follow him.

اَللّٰهُمَّ اسْلُكْ بِنَا عَلٰى يَدَيْهِ مِنْهَاجَ الْهُدَىٰ، وَ الْمَحَجَّةَ الْعُظْمَىٰ، وَ الطَّرِيقَةَ الْوُسْطَى الَّتِي يَرْجِعُ إِلَيْهَا الْغَالِي، وَيَلْحَقُ بِهَا التَّالِي، وَ قَوِّنَا عَلٰى طَاعَتِهِ، وَ ثَبِّتْنَا عَلٰى مُشَايَعَتِهِ، وَ امْنُنْ عَلَيْنَا بِمُتَابَعَتِهِ.

Place us in his party, which carries out his commands, remains patiently by his side, and seeks Your pleasure by being his well-wisher, until You gather us on the Day of Resurrection among his helpers, supporters and promoters of his authority!

وَ اجْعَلْنَا فِي حِزْبِهِ الْقَوَّامِينَ بِأَمْرِهِ، اَلصَّابِرِينَ مَعَهُ، اَلطَّالِبِينَ رِضَاكَ بِمُنَاصَحَتِهِ، حَتَّى تَحْشُرَنَا يَوْمَ الْقِيَامَةِ فِي أَنْصَارِهِ وَ أَعْوَانِهِ، وَ مُقَوِّيَةِ سُلْطَانِهِ.

O Allah, make all that free from every kind of doubt, ambiguity, dissemblance and hypocrisy, so that our sole goal therein is You and we seek therewith only Your approval, until You admit us into his company, and place us into paradise with him!

اَللّٰهُمَّ وَ اجْعَلْ ذٰلِكَ لَنَا خَالِصًا مِنْ كُلِّ شَكٍّ وَ شُبْهَةٍ، وَ رِيَاءٍ وَ سُمْعَةٍ، حَتَّى لَا نَعْتَمِدَ بِهِ غَيْرَكَ، وَ لَا نَطْلُبَ بِهِ إِلَّا وَجْهَكَ، وَ حَتَّى تُحِلَّنَا مَحَلَّهُ، وَ تَجْعَلَنَا فِي الْجَنَّةِ مَعَهُ،

Protect us from weariness, lethargy and slackness, and appoint us to be among those through whom You help Your religion and reinforce the aid of Your *walī*, and do not substitute others in our place, for it is a simple matter for You to replace us with others and it will be a tremendous loss for us!

وَ أَعِذْنَا مِنَ السَّأْمَةِ، وَ الْكَسَلِ وَ الْفَتْرَةِ، وَ اجْعَلْنَا مِمَّنْ تَنْتَصِرُ بِهِ لِدِينِكَ، وَ تُعِزُّ بِهِ نَصْرَ وَلِيِّكَ، وَ لَا تَسْتَبْدِلْ بِنَا غَيْرَنَا، فَإِنَّ اسْتِبْدَالَكَ بِنَا غَيْرَنَا عَلَيْكَ يَسِيرٌ، وَ هُوَ عَلَيْنَا كَثِيرٌ.

O Allah, bless his successors and the Imams who come after him and enable them to attain their goals and enhance the

اَللّٰهُمَّ صَلِّ عَلٰى وُلَاةِ عَهْدِهِ وَ الْأَئِمَّةِ مِنْ بَعْدِهِ، وَ بَلِّغْهُمْ آمَالَهُمْ، وَ زِدْ فِي آجَالِهِمْ،

span of their lives! Grant them a mighty help, bring to completion the missions You have entrusted to them, consolidate their supports and appoint us to be their helpers and supporters of Your religion!

وَ أَعِزَّ نَصْرَهُمْ، وَ تَمِّمْ لَهُمْ مَا أَسْنَدْتَ
إِلَيْهِمْ مِنْ أَمْرِكَ لَهُمْ، وَ ثَبِّتْ دَعَائِمَهُمْ، وَ
اجْعَلْنَا لَهُمْ أَعْوَانًا، وَ عَلَىٰ دِينِكَ أَنْصَارًا،

For they are the repository of Your words, the custodians of Your knowledge, the pillars of Your Unity, the supports of Your religion, the dispensers of Your authority, Your favourites from among Your servants, the elect of Your creatures, Your *awliyā'* and descendants of Your *awliyā'*, the elect of the progeny of Your Prophet, may peace be to him and them, and may Allah's mercy and His bounties be upon them!

فَإِنَّهُمْ مَعَادِنُ كَلِمَاتِكَ، وَ خُزَّانُ
عِلْمِكَ، وَ أَرْكَانُ تَوْحِيدِكَ، وَ دَعَائِمُ
دِينِكَ، وَ وُلَاةُ أَمْرِكَ، وَ خَالِصَتُكَ
مِنْ عِبَادِكَ، وَ صَفْوَتُكَ مِنْ خَلْقِكَ،
وَ أَوْلِيَاؤُكَ وَ سَلَائِلُ أَوْلِيَائِكَ، وَ
صَفْوَةُ أَوْلَادِ نَبِيِّكَ، وَ السَّلَامُ عَلَيْهِ
وَ عَلَيْهِمْ وَ رَحْمَةُ اللهِ وَ بَرَكَاتُه.

Chapter Eleven

The Ziyārāt Jāmiᶜah & Ṣalawāt

This chapter contains the common (*jāmiᶜah*) *ziyārahs*, the after-*ziyārah* supplication, and the *ṣalawāt* invoked for each of the Infallibles (*ᶜa*). It consists of three sections.

Section One

Ziyārāt Jāmiᶜah

The *jāmiᶜah* or 'common' *ziyārahs* are texts which can be recited while performing the *ziyārah* of any of the Imams (*ᶜa*). There are many of them, and here we will confine ourselves to citing a few.

1. First Ziyarah Jami'ah

The text of this *ziyārah* has been cited in *Man lā Yaḥḍuruh al-Faqīh* by Shaykh Ṣādūq,[1] who narrates that when Imam ᶜAlī al-Riḍā (*ᶜa*) was asked concerning the manner of approaching the tomb of Imam Mūsā al-Kāẓim (*ᶜa*), he replied that the visitor should first offer prayer in any of the mosques in the neighbourhood of the tomb, and that the text prescribed by him suffices for all places (implying, apparently, either that it is sufficient for the *ziyārah* of any of the Imams, or that it is good for *ziyārah* when visiting any of the holy shrines in general, including those of the prophets and other Imams).

Peace be to the *awliyā* of Allah and His chosen ones! Peace be to the trustees of Allah and His friends! Peace be to the helpers of Allah and His vicegerents! Peace be to the repositories of the gnosis of Allah! Peace be to the abodes of Allah's remembrance! Peace

اَلسَّلاٰمُ عَلىٰ أَوْلِيٰاءِ اللّٰهِ وَ أَصْفِيٰائِهِ، اَلسَّلاٰمُ
عَلىٰ أُمَنٰاءِ اللّٰهِ وَ أَحِبّٰائِهِ، اَلسَّلاٰمُ عَلىٰ
أَنْصٰارِ اللّٰهِ وَ خُلَفٰائِهِ، اَلسَّلاٰمُ عَلىٰ مَحٰالِّ
مَعْرِفَةِ اللّٰهِ، اَلسَّلاٰمُ عَلىٰ مَسٰاكِنِ ذِكْرِ

1 *Kāmil al-Ziyārāt*, 315, b 104, h 1, whence *Mustadrak*, x, 354, b 63, h 12170/3. *Faqīh*, ii, 608, h 3212. *ᶜUyūn Akhbār al-Riḍā*, ii, 271, h 1, whence *Biḥār*, xcix, 126, b 8, h 1. *Tahdhīb*, vi, 102, h 2.

اللهِ، اَلسَّلَامُ عَلَىٰ مُظْهِرِي أَمْرِ اللهِ وَ نَهْيِهِ،

be to the promulgators of Allah's ordinances and His prohibitions!

اَلسَّلَامُ عَلَى الدُّعَاةِ إِلَى اللهِ، اَلسَّلَامُ عَلَى الْمُسْتَقِرِّينَ فِي مَرْضَاةِ اللهِ، اَلسَّلَامُ عَلَى الْمُخْلِصِينَ فِي طَاعَةِ اللهِ، اَلسَّلَامُ عَلَى الْأَدِلَّاءِ عَلَى اللهِ،

Peace be to the summoners to Allah! Peace be to them who are entrenched in the paths of Allah's pleasure! Peace be to them who are dedicated to obeying Allah! Peace be to them who are guides to Allah!

اَلسَّلَامُ عَلَى الَّذِينَ مَنْ وَالَاهُمْ فَقَدْ وَالَى اللهَ، وَ مَنْ عَادَاهُمْ فَقَدْ عَادَى اللهَ، وَ مَنْ عَرَفَهُمْ فَقَدْ عَرَفَ اللهَ، وَ مَنْ جَهِلَهُمْ فَقَدْ جَهِلَ اللهَ، وَ مَنِ اعْتَصَمَ بِهِمْ فَقَدِ اعْتَصَمَ بِاللهِ، وَ مَنْ تَخَلَّى مِنْهُمْ فَقَدْ تَخَلَّى مِنَ اللهِ عَزَّ وَ جَلَّ،

Peace be to them whose friends are Allah's friends and whose enemies are Allah's enemies, those who know them know Allah and those who are ignorant of them are ignorant about Allah, those who hold fast to them hold fast to Allah and those who forsake them are those who have forsaken Allah, the Almighty and Glorious!

وَ أُشْهِدُ اللهَ أَنِّي سِلْمٌ لِمَنْ سَالَمْتُمْ، وَ حَرْبٌ لِمَنْ حَارَبْتُمْ، مُؤْمِنٌ بِسِرِّكُمْ وَ عَلَانِيَتِكُمْ، مُفَوِّضٌ فِي ذَلِكَ كُلِّهِ إِلَيْكُمْ. لَعَنَ اللهُ عَدُوَّ آلِ مُحَمَّدٍ مِنَ الْجِنِّ وَ الْإِنْسِ، وَ أَبْرَأُ إِلَى اللهِ مِنْهُمْ، وَ صَلَّى اللهُ عَلَى مُحَمَّدٍ وَ آلِهِ

Allah be my witness that I am at peace with those who are at peace with you, and at war with those who are at war with you, having faith in your esoteric and exoteric affairs, and consigning all matters in these respects to you! May Allah banish from His mercy the enemies of the Family of Muḥammad, from jinn and humans, and I repudiate them before Allah. May Allah bless Muḥammad and his Family!

This *ziyārah* is also cited in *Kāfi*, *Kāmil al-Ziyārāṭ* and *Tahdhīb*. In all these books, the above-mentioned text of *ziyārah* is followed by a passage wherein one is enjoined to invoke profuse benedictions on Muḥammad (ṣ) and his Family (ᶜa), mentioning each of them by name, and to make disavowals of their enemies, and, thereafter, to make any petitions that one wishes for oneself and the faithful, men and women.[1] Apparently, this passage is part of the *ḥadīth*.

In any case, leading scholars of *ḥadīth* have considered this text to suffice for the purpose of *ziyārah* in all the shrines, and they have cited it in chapters pertaining to the common *ziyārahs*. This is also confirmed by the beginning of the tradition as well as by the wording of the *ziyārah* itself, which is not specific. Accordingly, one is assured of its being a general-purpose *ziyārah*, which may be recited in all the shrines including those of the prophets and their legatees, and therefore some scholars have mentioned it in observances pertaining to the shrine of the Prophet Jonah (ᶜa).

As for the injunction in the passage at the end of the *ziyārah* concerning invoking *ṣalawāt* for each of the Infallibles, the *ṣalawāt* reported by Abu al-Ḥasan al-Ḍarrāb al-Iṣfahānī, which was cited at the end of Friday observances (p. 164), is quite suitable for this purpose.

2. Second Ziyarah Jami'ah
(Ziyārah Jāmiᶜah Kabīrah)

In *Faqīh* and *ᶜUyūn*, Shaykh Ṣadūq[2] reports on the authority of Mūsā b. ᶜAbdillāh al-Nakhaᶜī that he asked Imam ᶜAlī al-Naqī (ᶜa) to teach him a comprehensive and inclusive text with which he may perform the *ziyārah* of any one of the Imams. Thereat the Imam told him that when the pilgrim arrives at the gate of the shrine, having taken a bath, he should stop and say the *shahādatayn*,

I testify that there is no god besides Allah—He is One and has no partner—and I testify that Muḥammad, may Allah bless him and his Family, is His servant and apostle.	أَشْـهَدُ أَنْ لَا إِلَهَ إِلَّا اللهُ وَحْـدَهُ لَا شَرِيكَ لَهُ، وَ أَشْهَدُ أَنَّ مُحَمَّدًا صَلَّى اللهُ عَلَيْهِ وَ آلِهِ عَبْدُهُ وَ رَسُولُهُ.

Then on entering when he sights the tomb he should halt and say 30 times *Allāhu akbar*. Then coming somewhat nearer, taking short steps and walking in a peaceful and dignified manner, he should stop

1 *Kāfī*, iv, 578-9, h 2. *Kāmil a-Ziyārāṭ*, 301-2, b 100, h 1. *Tahdhīb*, vi, 102, b 46, h 2.

2 *Faqīh*, ii, 609, h 3213. *ᶜUyūn Akhbār al-Riḍā*, ii, 272, h 1, whence *Biḥār*, xcix, 127, b 8, h 4. *Tahdhīb*, vi, 95, b 46, h 1, whence *Wāfī*, xiv, 1566, b 2, h 14654. *Al-Mazār, al-Kabīr*, 521, b 1.

again and say *Allāhu akbar* another 30 times. Then on approaching the tomb he should say *Allāhu akbar* 40 times, thus saying it hundred times in all. Then he should recite the *ziyārah* whose text is as follows.

(Perhaps, as remarked by (Muḥammad Taqī) Majlisī I, the reason for the instruction concerning the *takbīrāt* is to obviate the tendency of most of the people to fall into *ghulū* on account of the expressions found in this *ziyārah*, or to prevent them from becoming oblivious of the greatness of God, the Glorious and Exalted.)

Peace be to you, O members of the house of prophethood, the locus of apostleship, the frequent resort of the angels, the landing place of divine revelations, the source of Divine mercy, the repositories of Divine knowledge, the foremost ones in gentleness, the sources of high-mindedness, the guides of the nations, the arbiters of Allah's blessings, the elements of piety, the citadels of the elect, the shepherds of God's servants, the mainstays of the lands, the portals of the faith, the trustees of the All-beneficent, the progeny of the prophets, the quintessence of the apostles and the kindred of the favourite of the Lord of all the worlds, and may Allah's mercy and bounties be upon you!

اَلسَّلَامُ عَلَيْكُمْ يَا أَهْلَ بَيْتِ النُّبُوَّةِ، وَ
مَوْضِعَ الرِّسَالَةِ، وَ مُخْتَلَفَ الْمَلَائِكَةِ،
وَ مَهْبِطَ الْوَحْيِ، وَ مَعْدِنَ الرَّحْمَةِ، وَ
خُزَّانَ الْعِلْمِ، وَ مُنْتَهَى الْحِلْمِ، وَ أُصُولَ
الْكَرَمِ، وَ قَادَةَ الْأُمَمِ، وَ أَوْلِيَاءَ النِّعَمِ،
وَ عَنَاصِرَ الْأَبْرَارِ، وَ دَعَائِمَ الْأَخْيَارِ،
وَ سَاسَةَ الْعِبَادِ، وَ أَرْكَانَ الْبِلَادِ، وَ
أَبْوَابَ الْإِيمَانِ، وَ أُمَنَاءَ الرَّحْمٰنِ، وَ
سُلَالَةَ النَّبِيِّينَ، وَ صَفْوَةَ الْمُرْسَلِينَ، وَ
عِتْرَةَ خِيَرَةِ رَبِّ الْعَالَمِينَ، وَ رَحْمَةُ اللهِ
وَ بَرَكَاتُهُ.

Peace be to the Imams of Divine guidance, the beacons in the darkness, the standards of Godfearing, the paragons of wisdom, possessors of the intellect, refuge for the creatures, heirs to the prophets, the loftiest exemplars, the best of summoners, the testaments of Al-

اَلسَّلَامُ عَلَىٰ أَئِمَّةِ الْهُدَىٰ، وَ مَصَابِيحِ
الدُّجَىٰ، وَ أَعْلَامِ التُّقَىٰ، وَ ذَوِي النُّهَىٰ،
وَ أُولِي الْحِجَىٰ، وَ كَهْفِ الْوَرَىٰ، وَ وَرَثَةِ
الْأَنْبِيَاءِ، وَ الْمَثَلِ الْأَعْلَىٰ، وَ الدَّعْوَةِ

الْحُسْنَىٰ، وَ حُجَجِ اللهِ عَلَىٰ أَهْلِ الدُّنْيَا وَ الْآخِرَةِ وَ الْأُولَىٰ، وَ رَحْمَةُ اللهِ وَ بَرَكَاتُهُ.

lah to the people of this world and the Hereafter, and may Allah's mercy and His bounties be upon you!

اَلسَّلَامُ عَلَىٰ مَحَالِّ مَعْرِفَةِ اللهِ، وَ مَسَاكِنِ بَرَكَةِ اللهِ، وَ مَعَادِنِ حِكْمَةِ اللهِ، وَ حَفَظَةِ سِرِّ اللهِ، وَ حَمَلَةِ كِتَابِ اللهِ، وَ أَوْصِيَاءِ نَبِيِّ اللهِ، وَ ذُرِّيَّةِ رَسُولِ اللهِ، صَلَّى اللهُ عَلَيْهِ وَ آلِهِ، وَ رَحْمَةُ اللهِ وَ بَرَكَاتُهُ.

Peace be to the bearers of the gnosis of Allah, the abodes of His bounties, the mines of His wisdom, the custodians of His secrets, the bearers of His scripture, the legatees of the Prophet of Allah, and the seed of the Apostle of Allah, may Allah bless him and his Family, and may Allah's mercy and His bounties be upon you!

اَلسَّلَامُ عَلَى الدُّعَاةِ إِلَى اللهِ، وَ الْأَدِلَّاءِ عَلَىٰ مَرْضَاةِ اللهِ، وَ الْمُسْتَقِرِّينَ فِي أَمْرِ اللهِ، وَ التَّامِّينَ فِي مَحَبَّةِ اللهِ، وَ الْمُخْلِصِينَ فِي تَوْحِيدِ اللهِ، وَ الْمُظْهِرِينَ لِأَمْرِ اللهِ وَ نَهْيِهِ، وَ عِبَادِهِ الْمُكْرَمِينَ الَّذِينَ لَا يَسْبِقُونَهُ بِالْقَوْلِ وَ هُمْ بِأَمْرِهِ يَعْمَلُونَ، وَ رَحْمَةُ اللهِ وَ بَرَكَاتُهُ.

Peace be to the summoners to Allah, the exponents of the purposes of Allah, the ones entrenched in upholding the ordinances of Allah, the ones perfect in the love of Allah, who are dedicated in their exclusive faith in the Oneness of Allah, the promulgators of Allah's commandments and His prohibitions, His honoured servants who do not preempt Him in speech and who act only according to His commands, and may Allah's mercy and His bounties be upon you!

اَلسَّلَامُ عَلَى الْأَئِمَّةِ الدُّعَاةِ، وَ الْقَادَةِ الْهُدَاةِ، وَ السَّادَةِ الْوُلَاةِ، وَ الذَّادَةِ الْحُمَاةِ، وَ أَهْلِ الذِّكْرِ، وَ أُولِي الْأَمْرِ، وَ بَقِيَّةِ اللهِ، وَ خِيَرَتِهِ وَ حِزْبِهِ وَ عَيْبَةِ عِلْمِهِ وَ حُجَّتِهِ وَ صِرَاطِهِ وَ نُورِهِ وَ بُرْهَانِهِ، وَ

Peace be to the Imams and the summoners, the leaders and guides, the masters and guardians, the defenders and supporters, the keepers of divine remembrance, those invested with God's authority, the remainder of Allah on the earth, His chosen ones, His partisans, the repositories of His knowledge, His testaments, His

رَحْمَةُ اللهِ وَ بَرَكَاتُهُ.

path, His light, and His proof, and may Allah's mercy and His bounties be upon you!

أَشْهَدُ أَنْ لَا إِلَهَ إِلَّا اللهُ وَحْدَهُ لَا شَرِيكَ لَهُ، كَمَا شَهِدَ اللهُ لِنَفْسِهِ، وَ شَهِدَتْ لَهُ مَلَائِكَتُهُ وَ أُولُوا الْعِلْمِ مِنْ خَلْقِهِ، لَا إِلَهَ إِلَّا هُوَ الْعَزِيزُ الْحَكِيمُ،

I testify that there is no god besides Allah. He is One and has no partner, as He has testified concerning Himself, and so have the angels and those vested with knowledge from amongst His creation, that there is no god besides Him, the Almighty and the All-wise.

وَ أَشْهَدُ أَنَّ مُحَمَّدًا عَبْدُهُ الْمُنْتَجَبُ، وَ رَسُولُهُ الْمُرْتَضَى، أَرْسَلَهُ بِالْهُدَى وَ دِينِ الْحَقِّ، لِيُظْهِرَهُ عَلَى الدِّينِ كُلِّهِ وَ لَوْ كَرِهَ الْمُشْرِكُونَ.

And I testify that Muḥammad is His chosen servant and His approved apostle, whom He sent with guidance and true religion that He may cause it to prevail over all religions, however much the polytheists may be averse.

وَ أَشْهَدُ أَنَّكُمُ الْأَئِمَّةُ الرَّاشِدُونَ الْمَهْدِيُّونَ الْمَعْصُومُونَ الْمُكَرَّمُونَ الْمُقَرَّبُونَ الْمُتَّقُونَ الصَّادِقُونَ الْمُصْطَفَوْنَ الْمُطِيعُونَ لِلَّهِ، اَلْقَوَّامُونَ بِأَمْرِهِ، اَلْعَامِلُونَ بِإِرَادَتِهِ، اَلْفَائِزُونَ بِكَرَامَتِهِ،

And I testify that you are the rightly-guided Imams, guides to the right path, preserved from sin, honoured by and near to God, Godfearing, truthful, and chosen by Allah, obedient to Him, upholders of His commandments, acting in accordance with His will, and triumphant by His munificence and grace.

اِصْطَفَاكُمْ بِعِلْمِهِ، وَ ارْتَضَاكُمْ لِغَيْبِهِ، وَ اخْتَارَكُمْ لِسِرِّهِ، وَ اجْتَبَاكُمْ بِقُدْرَتِهِ، وَ أَعَزَّكُمْ بِهُدَاهُ، وَ خَصَّكُمْ بِبُرْهَانِهِ، وَ انْتَجَبَكُمْ لِنُورِهِ، وَ أَيَّدَكُمْ بِرُوحِهِ، وَ رَضِيَكُمْ خُلَفَاءَ فِي أَرْضِهِ،

He selected you with His knowledge, approved you for His knowledge of the Unseen, preferred you to confide in you His secrets, elected you with His power, empowered you with His guidance, distinguished you with His proofs, chose you for His light, strengthened you with His Spirit, approved you as His vicegerents on His earth, as His testaments to His creation, as defenders of His religion, as guardians of His secrets, as treasurers of His knowledge, as repositories of His wisdom, as interpreters of His revelations, as pillars of faith in His Unity, as witnesses to His creation, as beacons for His servants, as minarets for His towns, and as guides to His path.

وَ حُجَجًا عَلَىٰ بَرِيَّتِهِ، وَ أَنْصَارًا لِدِينِهِ، وَ حَفَظَةً لِسِرِّهِ، وَ خَزَنَةً لِعِلْمِهِ، وَ مُسْتَوْدَعًا لِحِكْمَتِهِ، وَ تَرَاجِمَةً لِوَحْيِهِ، وَ أَرْكَانًا لِتَوْحِيدِهِ، وَ شُهَدَاءَ عَلَىٰ خَلْقِهِ، وَ أَعْلَامًا لِعِبَادِهِ، وَ مَنَارًا فِي بِلَادِهِ، وَ أَدِلَّاءَ عَلَىٰ صِرَاطِهِ،

Allah has preserved you from slips, secured you from seductions, kept you clean of pollution, *repelled all impurity from you and purified you with a thorough purification.*(33:33)

عَصَمَكُمُ اللّٰهُ مِنَ الزَّلَلِ، وَ آمَنَكُمْ مِنَ الْفِتَنِ، وَ طَهَّرَكُمْ مِنَ الدَّنَسِ، وَ أَذْهَبَ عَنْكُمُ الرِّجْسَ، وَ طَهَّرَكُمْ تَطْهِيرًا.

You, too, extolled His majesty, magnified His station, praised His munificence, perpetuated His remembrance, confirmed His covenant, strengthened the bond of obedience to Him, were sincerely devoted to Him in secret and open, called people to His way with wisdom and good advice, sacrificed yourselves for the sake of His pleasure, and endured patiently whatever befell you in the way of His cause!

فَعَظَّمْتُمْ جَلَالَهُ، وَ أَكْبَرْتُمْ شَأْنَهُ، وَ مَجَّدْتُمْ كَرَمَهُ، وَ أَدَمْتُمْ ذِكْرَهُ وَ وَكَّدْتُمْ مِيثَاقَهُ، وَ أَحْكَمْتُمْ عَقْدَ طَاعَتِهِ، وَ نَصَحْتُمْ لَهُ فِي السِّرِّ وَ الْعَلَانِيَةِ، وَ دَعَوْتُمْ إِلَىٰ سَبِيلِهِ بِالْحِكْمَةِ وَ الْمَوْعِظَةِ الْحَسَنَةِ، وَ بَذَلْتُمْ أَنْفُسَكُمْ فِي مَرْضَاتِهِ، وَ صَبَرْتُمْ عَلَىٰ مَا أَصَابَكُمْ فِي جَنْبِهِ،

You maintained the prayer, paid the *zakāt*, enjoined what is right and forbade what is wrong, strove for Allah with an endeavour which is worthy of Him, until you proclaimed His summons, expounded His prescribed duties, implement-

وَ أَقَمْتُمُ الصَّلَاةَ، وَ آتَيْتُمُ الزَّكَاةَ، وَ أَمَرْتُمْ بِالْمَعْرُوفِ، وَ نَهَيْتُمْ عَنِ الْمُنْكَرِ، وَ جَاهَدْتُمْ فِي اللّٰهِ حَقَّ جِهَادِهِ، حَتَّىٰ أَعْلَنْتُمْ دَعْوَتَهُ، وَ بَيَّنْتُمْ فَرَائِضَهُ، وَ

أَقَمْتُمْ حُدُودَهُ، وَ نَشَرْتُمْ شَرَائِعَ أَحْكَامِهِ، وَ سَنَنْتُمْ سُنَّتَهُ، وَ صِرْتُمْ فِي ذَلِكَ مِنْهُ إِلَى الرِّضَا، وَ سَلَّمْتُمْ لَهُ الْقَضَاءَ، وَ صَدَّقْتُمْ مِنْ رُسُلِهِ مَنْ مَضَى،

ed the legal limits set by Him, promulgated the edicts of His law, established His conventions, persevering therein for His pleasure, surrendering yourselves to His ordainments, and confirming the veracity of earlier apostles.

فَالرَّاغِبُ عَنْكُمْ مَارِقٌ، وَ اللاَّزِمُ لَكُمْ لاَحِقٌ، وَ الْمُقَصِّرُ فِي حَقِّكُمْ زَاهِقٌ، وَ الْحَقُّ مَعَكُمْ وَ فِيكُمْ وَ مِنْكُمْ وَ إِلَيْكُمْ، وَ أَنْتُمْ أَهْلُهُ وَ مَعْدِنُهُ، وَ مِيرَاثُ النُّبُوَّةِ عِنْدَكُمْ، وَ إِيَابُ الْخَلْقِ إِلَيْكُمْ، وَ حِسَابُهُمْ عَلَيْكُمْ، وَ فَصْلُ الْخِطَابِ عِنْدَكُمْ، وَ آيَاتُ اللهِ لَدَيْكُمْ، وَ عَزَائِمُهُ فِيكُمْ، وَ نُورُهُ وَ بُرْهَانُهُ عِنْدَكُمْ، وَ أَمْرُهُ إِلَيْكُمْ،

Hence one who is averse to you is a renegade, and one who adheres to you is united with you, and anyone who belittles your rights is ruined. The truth is with you and in you, it proceeds from you and returns to you: you are its votaries and repository. The heritage of the Prophesy is with you, to you will be the return of the creatures, and with you will lie their reckoning. In you is vested conclusive speech, with you are the signs of Allah, in you are vested His purposes, with you are His light and proofs, and His command is entrusted to you.

مَنْ وَالاَكُمْ فَقَدْ وَالَى اللهَ، وَ مَنْ عَادَاكُمْ فَقَدْ عَادَى اللهَ، وَ مَنْ أَحَبَّكُمْ فَقَدْ أَحَبَّ اللهَ، وَ مَنْ أَبْغَضَكُمْ فَقَدْ أَبْغَضَ اللهَ، وَ مَنِ اعْتَصَمَ بِكُمْ فَقَدِ اعْتَصَمَ بِاللهِ،

He who befriends you, befriends Allah; he who is hostile to you is hostile to Allah; he who loves you, loves Allah; he who hates you, hates Allah; and he who holds fast to you, holds fast to Allah.

أَنْتُمُ الصِّرَاطُ الْأَقْوَمُ [السَّبِيلُ الْأَعْظَمُ]، وَ شُهَدَاءُ دَارِ الْفَنَاءِ، وَ شُفَعَاءُ دَارِ الْبَقَاءِ،

You are the firmest path, the witnesses of the transient abode, and intercessors of the permanent abode, the perpet-

وَ الرَّحْمَةُ الْمَوْصُولَةُ، وَ الْآيَةُ الْمَخْزُونَةُ، وَ الْأَمَانَةُ الْمَحْفُوظَةُ، وَ الْبَابُ الْمُبْتَلَى بِهِ النَّاسُ، مَنْ أَتَاكُمْ نَجَا، وَ مَنْ لَمْ يَأْتِكُمْ هَلَكَ،

ual mercy, the treasured sign, the guarded trust, and the gate of tribulation for mankind. He who comes to you is delivered, and he who does not come to you perishes.

إِلَى اللهِ تَدْعُونَ، وَ عَلَيْهِ تَدُلُّونَ، وَ بِهِ تُؤْمِنُونَ، وَ لَهُ تُسَلِّمُونَ، وَ بِأَمْرِهِ تَعْمَلُونَ، وَ إِلَى سَبِيلِهِ تُرْشِدُونَ، وَ بِقَوْلِهِ تَحْكُمُونَ،

You summon towards Allah, you guide towards Him, you have faith in Him, you surrender to Him, you act according to His commandments, you direct the people toward His path, and judge according to His Word.

سَعِدَ مَنْ وَالَاكُمْ، وَ هَلَكَ مَنْ عَادَاكُمْ، وَ خَابَ مَنْ جَحَدَكُمْ، وَ ضَلَّ مَنْ فَارَقَكُمْ، وَ فَازَ مَنْ تَمَسَّكَ بِكُمْ، وَ أَمِنَ مَنْ لَجَأَ إِلَيْكُمْ، وَ سَلِمَ مَنْ صَدَّقَكُمْ، وَ هُدِيَ مَنِ اعْتَصَمَ بِكُمْ،

Felicitous are they who befriend you; ruined are they who are hostile to you. Those who impugn you fail, and those who part from you go astray. Those who hold fast to you triumph; those who seek refuge in you remain secure; those who confirm you are safe; and those who cling with you are rightly guided.

مَنِ اتَّبَعَكُمْ فَالْجَنَّةُ مَأْوَاهُ، وَ مَنْ خَالَفَكُمْ فَالنَّارُ مَثْوَاهُ، وَ مَنْ جَحَدَكُمْ كَافِرٌ، وَ مَنْ حَارَبَكُمْ مُشْرِكٌ، وَ مَنْ رَدَّ عَلَيْكُمْ فِي أَسْفَلِ دَرْكٍ مِنَ الْجَحِيمِ.

Paradise is the destination of those who follow you, and hell is the abode of those who oppose you. Those who impugn you are faithless, those who fight against you are polytheists, and those who reject you will be in the lowest reach of hell.

أَشْهَدُ أَنَّ هٰذَا سَابِقٌ لَكُمْ فِيمَا مَضَى، وَ جَارٍ لَكُمْ فِيمَا بَقِيَ، وَ أَنَّ أَرْوَاحَكُمْ وَ نُورَكُمْ وَ طِينَتَكُمْ وَاحِدَةٌ، طَابَتْ وَ طَهُرَتْ بَعْضُهَا مِنْ بَعْضٍ.

I testify that this has been the mode concerning you in the past and so shall it remain for you in the future, and that your spirits, your light and your nature are one, free from all taints and pure, identical with one another.

Allah created you as lights, and set you encircling His Throne, until He favoured us with you, and placed you *in houses that Allah has allowed to be raised and wherein His Name is celebrated.*(24:36) He has made our invocations of blessings on you, and your *wilāyah* with which He has distinguished us, as the cause of soundness of our inborn character and the purity of our souls, and a means of purgation for us, as well as the expiation of our sins. As a result, with Him, we are those who acknowledge your superior position and are well-known for our affirmation of your station.

خَلَقَكُمُ اللهُ أَنْوَارًا فَجَعَلَكُمْ بِعَرْشِهِ مُحْدِقِينَ، حَتَّى مَنَّ عَلَيْنَا بِكُمْ، فَجَعَلَكُمْ فِي بُيُوتٍ أَذِنَ اللهُ أَنْ تُرْفَعَ وَ يُذْكَرَ فِيهَا اسْمُهُ، وَ جَعَلَ صَلَاتَنَا [صَلَوَاتِنَا] عَلَيْكُمْ وَ مَا خَصَّنَا بِهِ مِنْ وِلَايَتِكُمْ طِيبا لِخَلْقِنَا [لِخُلُقِنَا]، وَ طَهَارَةً لِأَنْفُسِنَا، وَ تَزْكِيَةً لَنَا، وَ كَفَّارَةً لِذُنُوبِنَا، فَكُنَّا عِنْدَهُ مُسَلِّمِينَ بِفَضْلِكُمْ، وَ مَعْرُوفِينَ بِتَصْدِيقِنَا إِيَّاكُمْ،

For Allah has elevated you to the noblest of the stations of those honoured with Him, to the most elevated degrees of those nearest to Him, and to the most exalted ranks of the apostles, where no achiever can reach, which no topper can exceed, no forerunner can overtake, and no aspirant can attain—inasmuch as there does not remain any archangel, or any prophetic envoy, or any saint or martyr, nor anyone learned or ignorant, nor any of the lowly or the distinguished, nor any righteous believer nor any depraved profligate, nor any obdurate tyrant nor any rebellious devil, nor any creature in-between these extremes without being informed of the

فَبَلَغَ اللهُ بِكُمْ أَشْرَفَ مَحَلِّ الْمُكَرَّمِينَ، وَ أَعْلَى مَنَازِلِ الْمُقَرَّبِينَ، وَ أَرْفَعَ دَرَجَاتِ الْمُرْسَلِينَ، حَيْثُ لَا يَلْحَقُهُ لَاحِقٌ، وَ لَا يَفُوقُهُ فَائِقٌ، وَ لَا يَسْبِقُهُ سَابِقٌ، وَ لَا يَطْمَعُ فِي إِدْرَاكِهِ طَامِعٌ، حَتَّى لَا يَبْقَى مَلَكٌ مُقَرَّبٌ، وَ لَا نَبِيٌّ مُرْسَلٌ، وَ لَا صِدِّيقٌ، وَ لَا شَهِيدٌ، وَ لَا عَالِمٌ وَ لَا جَاهِلٌ، وَ لَا دَنِيٌّ وَ لَا فَاضِلٌ، وَ لَا مُؤْمِنٌ صَالِحٌ، وَ لَا فَاجِرٌ طَالِحٌ، وَ لَا جَبَّارٌ عَنِيدٌ، وَ لَا شَيْطَانٌ

مَرِيدٌ، وَ لَا خَلْقٌ فِيمَا بَيْنَ ذَٰلِكَ شَهِيدٌ،
إِلَّا عَرَّفَهُمْ جَلَالَةَ أَمْرِكُمْ، وَ عِظَمَ
خَطَرِكُمْ، وَ كِبَرَ شَأْنِكُمْ، وَ تَمَامَ نُورِكُمْ،
وَ صِدْقَ مَقَاعِدِكُمْ، وَ ثَبَاتَ مَقَامِكُمْ،
وَ شَرَفَ مَحَلِّكُمْ وَ مَنْزِلَتِكُمْ عِنْدَهُ، وَ
كَرَامَتَكُمْ عَلَيْهِ، وَ خَاصَّتَكُمْ لَدَيْهِ، وَ
قُرْبَ مَنْزِلَتِكُمْ مِنْهُ،

majesty of your office, the greatness of your position, the supremacy of your standing, the perfection of your light, the worthiness of your situation, the perpetuity of your position, the dignity of your place and station with Him, your prestige and especial status with Him, and the proximity of your station to Him!

بِأَبِي أَنْتُمْ وَ أُمِّي وَ أَهْلِي وَ مَالِي وَ أُسْرَتِي،
أُشْهِدُ اللهَ وَ أُشْهِدُكُمْ أَنِّي مُؤْمِنٌ
بِكُمْ وَ بِمَا آمَنْتُمْ بِهِ، كَافِرٌ بِعَدُوِّكُمْ
وَ بِمَا كَفَرْتُمْ بِهِ، مُسْتَبْصِرٌ بِشَأْنِكُمْ
وَ بِضَلَالَةِ مَنْ خَالَفَكُمْ، مُوَالٍ لَكُمْ وَ
لِأَوْلِيَائِكُمْ، مُبْغِضٌ لِأَعْدَائِكُمْ وَ مُعَادٍ
لَهُمْ، سِلْمٌ لِمَنْ سَالَمَكُمْ، وَ حَرْبٌ لِمَنْ
حَارَبَكُمْ،

May my father and mother, my family, kin and wealth be sacrificed for your sake! Allah be my witness and you be my witnesses, that I have faith in you and believe in what you believe! That I disown your enemies and reject whatever you have rejected. That I have insight concerning your station as well as the error of your opponents. That I pledge my loyalty to you and to those who are loyal to you. That I bear hatred and hostility towards your enemies. That I am at peace with those who are at peace with you and at war with those who are at war with you.

مُحَقِّقٌ لِمَا حَقَّقْتُمْ، مُبْطِلٌ لِمَا أَبْطَلْتُمْ،
مُطِيعٌ لَكُمْ، عَارِفٌ بِحَقِّكُمْ، مُقِرٌّ
بِفَضْلِكُمْ، مُحْتَمِلٌ لِعِلْمِكُمْ، مُحْتَجِبٌ
بِذِمَّتِكُمْ، مُعْتَرِفٌ بِكُمْ، مُؤْمِنٌ
بِإِيَابِكُمْ، مُصَدِّقٌ بِرَجْعَتِكُمْ، مُنْتَظِرٌ

That I confirm whatever you confirm, and refute whatever you refute. That I declare my obedience to you, being aware of your due rights, acknowledging your excellence, accepting your knowledge, seeking security only under the care of your guardianship, accepting your Imamate,

لِأَمْرِكُمْ، مُرْتَقِبٌ لِدَوْلَتِكُمْ، آخِذٌ بِقَوْلِكُمْ، عَامِلٌ بِأَمْرِكُمْ، مُسْتَجِيرٌ بِكُمْ، زَائِرٌ لَكُمْ، لَائِذٌ عَائِذٌ بِقُبُورِكُمْ،

believing in your return, affirming your coming back, awaiting your orders, looking forward to the establishment of your regime, accepting your word, acting according to your order, seeking refuge with you, visiting you, taking shelter and seeking refuge by your graves,

مُسْتَشْفِعٌ إِلَى اللهِ عَزَّ وَ جَلَّ بِكُمْ، وَ مُتَقَرِّبٌ بِكُمْ إِلَيْهِ، وَ مُقَدِّمُكُمْ أَمَامَ طَلِبَتِي وَ حَوَائِجِي وَ إِرَادَتِي فِي كُلِّ أَحْوَالِي وَ أُمُورِي، مُؤْمِنٌ بِسِرِّكُمْ وَ عَلَانِيَتِكُمْ، وَ شَاهِدِكُمْ وَ غَائِبِكُمْ، وَ أَوَّلِكُمْ وَ آخِرِكُمْ، وَ مُفَوِّضٌ فِي ذٰلِكَ كُلِّهِ إِلَيْكُمْ، وَ مُسَلِّمٌ فِيهِ مَعَكُمْ، وَ قَلْبِي لَكُمْ مُسَلِّمٌ، وَ رَأْيِي لَكُمْ تَبَعٌ، وَ نُصْرَتِي لَكُمْ مُعَدَّةٌ، حَتَّى يُحْيِيَ اللهُ تَعَالَى دِينَهُ بِكُمْ، وَ يَرُدَّكُمْ فِي أَيَّامِهِ، وَ يُظْهِرَكُمْ لِعَدْلِهِ، وَ يُمَكِّنَكُمْ فِي أَرْضِهِ،

Seeking your intercession with Allah, the Almighty and Glorious, and seeking nearness to Him through you, setting you ahead of my petitions, my needs and my desires, in all circumstances and in all my affairs, having faith in your esoteric and exoteric affairs, your perceptible and imperceptible persons, and the first of you and the last one, and entrusting all my affairs in these respects to you and surrendering all that to you, with a heart that submits to you, and a mind that acquiesces in your judgement, and having readied my assistance for you, until Allah the Most High revives His religion through you, restores you in His days, makes you prevail for the sake of His justice and empowers you on His earth!

فَمَعَكُمْ مَعَكُمْ لَا مَعَ غَيْرِكُمْ، آمَنْتُ بِكُمْ، وَ تَوَلَّيْتُ آخِرَكُمْ بِمَا تَوَلَّيْتُ بِهِ أَوَّلَكُمْ، وَ بَرِئْتُ إِلَى اللهِ عَزَّ وَ جَلَّ مِنْ أَعْدَائِكُمْ، وَ مِنَ الْجِبْتِ وَ الطَّاغُوتِ وَ

Hence I am with you and only you, not with anyone besides you! I have faith in you, pledging my friendship and loyalty to the last of you as I have pledged my loyalty to the first of you. I forswear before Allah, the Almighty and

Glorious, your enemies, and repudiate the idol, the rebel, the satans and their confederates who wronged you, contested your rights, reneged on your authority, usurped your inheritance, being sceptical about you and who turned away from you. I forswear any friend and confidant other than you, forswear obedience to anyone except you, and forswear the leaders who invite towards hellfire!

So may Allah keep me steadfast, as long as I live, in being loyal to you, holding you dear and following your religion! May He help me to obey you, favour me with your intercession, and include me among the best of your followers who follow your summons.

May He place me among those who follow in your footsteps, walk on your path, follow your directions, gather in your throng, return at your restoration, are granted authority and power in your regime, are honoured in the era of your welfare, are empowered during your days, and whose eyes will be gladdened tomorrow by your sight!

May my father and mother, my family, kin and wealth be sacrificed for your sake! Whoever desires Allah must begin with

الشَّيَاطِينِ، وَ حِزْبِهِمُ الظَّالِمِينَ لَكُمْ،

[وَ] الْجَاحِدِينَ لِحَقِّكُمْ، وَ الْمَارِقِينَ

مِنْ وِلَايَتِكُمْ، وَ الْغَاصِبِينَ لِإِرْثِكُمْ،

[وَ] الشَّاكِّينَ فِيكُمْ، [وَ] الْمُنْحَرِفِينَ

عَنْكُمْ، وَ مِنْ كُلِّ وَلِيجَةٍ دُونَكُمْ، وَ

كُلِّ مُطَاعٍ سِوَاكُمْ، وَ مِنَ الْأَئِمَّةِ الَّذِينَ

يَدْعُونَ إِلَى النَّارِ،

فَثَبَّتَنِي اللّٰهُ أَبَدًا مَا حَيِيتُ عَلَى مُوَالَاتِكُمْ

وَ مَحَبَّتِكُمْ وَ دِينِكُمْ، وَ وَفَّقَنِي

لِطَاعَتِكُمْ، وَ رَزَقَنِي شَفَاعَتَكُمْ، وَ

جَعَلَنِي مِنْ خِيَارِ مَوَالِيكُمُ التَّابِعِينَ لِمَا

دَعَوْتُمْ إِلَيْهِ،

وَ جَعَلَنِي مِمَّنْ يَقْتَصُّ آثَارَكُمْ، وَ يَسْلُكُ

سَبِيلَكُمْ، وَ يَهْتَدِى بِهُدَاكُمْ، وَ يُحْشَرُ

فِي زُمْرَتِكُمْ، وَ يَكِرُّ فِي رَجْعَتِكُمْ،

وَ يُمَلَّكُ فِي دَوْلَتِكُمْ، وَ يُشَرَّفُ فِي

عَافِيَتِكُمْ، وَ يُمَكَّنُ فِي أَيَّامِكُمْ، وَ

تَقَرُّ عَيْنُهُ غَدًا بِرُؤْيَتِكُمْ،

بِأَبِي أَنْتُمْ وَ أُمِّي وَ نَفْسِي وَ أَهْلِي وَ

مَالِي، مَنْ أَرَادَ اللّٰهَ بَدَأَ بِكُمْ، وَ مَنْ

وَحَّدَهُ قَبِلَ عَنْكُمْ، وَ مَنْ قَصَدَهُ تَوَجَّهَ
بِكُمْ، مَوَالِيَّ لَا أُحْصِي ثَنَاءَكُمْ، وَ
لَا أَبْلُغُ مِنَ الْمَدْحِ كُنْهَكُمْ، وَ مِنَ
الْوَصْفِ قَدْرَكُمْ،

you. Whoever asserts His Unity, accepts your teaching. Whoever sets out for Him, must turn to you! My guardians! I cannot recount your admirable qualities, nor can I fathom with my praise the depths of your reality, nor describe your excellence as is worthy of it!

وَ أَنْتُمْ نُورُ الْأَخْيَارِ، وَ هُدَاةُ الْأَبْرَارِ، وَ
حُجَجُ الْجَبَّارِ، بِكُمْ فَتَحَ اللهُ وَ بِكُمْ
يَخْتِمُ، وَ بِكُمْ يُنَزِّلُ الْغَيْثَ، وَ بِكُمْ
يُمْسِكُ السَّمَاءَ أَنْ تَقَعَ عَلَى الْأَرْضِ
إِلَّا بِإِذْنِهِ، وَ بِكُمْ يُنَفِّسُ الْهَمَّ، وَ
يَكْشِفُ الضُّرَّ، وَ عِنْدَكُمْ مَا نَزَلَتْ
بِهِ رُسُلُهُ، وَ هَبَطَتْ بِهِ مَلَائِكَتُهُ،
وَ إِلَى جَدِّكُمْ (وَ إِلَى أَخِيكَ) بُعِثَ
الرُّوحُ الْأَمِينُ،

You are light of the elect, guides of the pious, and testaments of the All-compeller! By you has Allah initiated (the realm of contingent being) and by you will He seal it. Through you He brings the rains, and through you He holds the heavens from falling to the earth, except by His will. Through you He removes worries and relieves distress! With you are the messages brought by His messengers and with which His angels descended, and it was to your grandfather (/to your brother) that the Trustworthy Spirit was sent!

(While performing the *ziyārah* of the Commander of the Faithful (*ʿa*) say *wa ilā akhīka* (to your brother) instead of *wa ilā jaddikum*.)

آتَاكُمُ اللهُ مَا لَمْ يُؤْتِ أَحَدًا مِنَ
الْعَالَمِينَ، طَأْطَأَ كُلُّ شَرِيفٍ لِشَرَفِكُمْ،
وَ بَخَعَ كُلُّ مُتَكَبِّرٍ لِطَاعَتِكُمْ، وَ خَضَعَ
كُلُّ جَبَّارٍ لِفَضْلِكُمْ، وَ ذَلَّ كُلُّ شَيْءٍ
لَكُمْ، وَ أَشْرَقَتِ الْأَرْضُ بِنُورِكُمْ، وَ فَازَ

Allah has given you what He has not given to any of the world's beings! All the eminent bow their heads before your eminence. All the arrogant humble themselves before you. All the tyrants are submissive before you. Everything is lowly before you. The earth shines with your light. The triumphant attain

الْفَائِزُونَ بِوِلَايَتِكُمْ، بِكُمْ يُسْلَكُ إِلَى الرِّضْوَانِ، وَ عَلَى مَنْ جَحَدَ وِلَايَتَكُمْ غَضَبُ الرَّحْمَنِ.

success by virtue of your *wilāyah*. The pleasure of Allah is pursued through allegiance to you and the wrath of the All-beneficent befalls those who contest your *wilāyah!*

بِأَبِي أَنْتُمْ وَ أُمِّي وَ نَفْسِي وَ أَهْلِي وَ مَالِي، ذِكْرُكُمْ فِي الذَّاكِرِينَ، وَ أَسْمَاؤُكُمْ فِي الْأَسْمَاءِ، وَ أَجْسَادُكُمْ فِي الْأَجْسَادِ، وَ أَرْوَاحُكُمْ فِي الْأَرْوَاحِ، وَ أَنْفُسُكُمْ فِي النُّفُوسِ، وَ آثَارُكُمْ فِي الْآثَارِ، وَ قُبُورُكُمْ فِي الْقُبُورِ، فَمَا أَحْلَى أَسْمَاءَكُمْ، وَ أَكْرَمَ أَنْفُسَكُمْ، وَ أَعْظَمَ شَأْنَكُمْ، وَ أَجَلَّ خَطَرَكُمْ، وَ أَوْفَى عَهْدَكُمْ [وَ أَصْدَقَ وَعْدَكُمْ]،

May my father and mother, my life, my family, kin and wealth be sacrificed for your sake! Your account pervades all accounts; your names permeate all names; your bodies permeate all bodies; your spirits are present throughout all spirits; your souls prevail through all souls; your effects pervade all effects; your corporeal nature is present in all corporeal natures. So how sweet are your names! How dignified are your souls! How great is your station! How majestic is your position! How faithful is your covenant! How true is your promise!

كَلَامُكُمْ نُورٌ، وَ أَمْرُكُمْ رُشْدٌ، وَ وَصِيَّتُكُمُ التَّقْوَى، وَ فِعْلُكُمُ الْخَيْرُ، وَ عَادَتُكُمُ الْإِحْسَانُ، وَ سَجِيَّتُكُمُ الْكَرَمُ، وَ شَأْنُكُمُ الْحَقُّ وَ الصِّدْقُ وَ الرِّفْقُ، وَ قَوْلُكُمْ حُكْمٌ وَ حَتْمٌ، وَ رَأْيُكُمْ عِلْمٌ وَ حِلْمٌ وَ حَزْمٌ.

Your speech is light! Your commands are uprightness itself! (And similarly) your advice is piety! Your works are goodness! Your habit is benevolence! Your disposition is generosity! Your conduct is truth, honesty and kindness! Your word is judgement and certainty! Your opinion is knowledge, gentleness, and judiciousness!

إِنْ ذُكِرَ الْخَيْرُ كُنْتُمْ أَوَّلَهُ وَ أَصْلَهُ، وَ فَرْعَهُ وَ مَعْدِنَهُ، وَ مَأْوَاهُ وَ مُنْتَهَاهُ،

Whenever good is mentioned, you are its origin, its root, its branch, its source, its abode and its ultimate limit.

May my father and my mother and my life be sacrificed for you! How shall I extol your praise and recount your gracious gifts?

بِأَبِي أَنْتُمْ وَ أُمِّي وَ نَفْسِي، كَيْفَ
أَصِفُ حُسْنَ ثَنَائِكُمْ، وَ أُحْصِي
جَمِيلَ بَلَائِكُمْ،

Through you, Allah has rescued us from abasement and weakness, relieved us from the agonies of distress, and delivered us from the brink of perdition and from hell-fire!

وَ بِكُمْ أَخْرَجَنَا اللهُ مِنَ الذُّلِّ، وَ فَرَّجَ
عَنَّا غَمَرَاتِ الْكُرُوبِ، وَ أَنْقَذَنَا مِنْ
شَفَا جُرُفِ الْهَلَكَاتِ وَ مِنَ النَّارِ،

May my father my mother and my life be sacrificed for you! Through loyalty and love for you Allah has taught us the guiding principles of our religion and removed the perversions and pitfalls of our temporal affairs!

بِأَبِي أَنْتُمْ وَ أُمِّي وَ نَفْسِي، بِمُوَالاتِكُمْ
عَلَّمَنَا اللهُ مَعَالِمَ دِينِنَا، وَ أَصْلَحَ مَا
كَانَ فَسَدَ مِنْ دُنْيَانَا،

Through love and loyalty for you the Word was fulfilled, the blessings superabounded, and the gaps and separations were bridged! Through love and loyalty for you our obligatory acts of obedience are accepted, and to you belong the mandatory love, the elevated ranks, the praiseworthy station and the distinguished position with Allah, the Almighty and Glorious, along with tremendous dignity, great standing, and approved intercession!

وَ بِمُوَالاتِكُمْ تَمَّتِ الْكَلِمَةُ، وَ
عَظُمَتِ النِّعْمَةُ، وَ ائْتَلَفَتِ الْفُرْقَةُ، وَ
بِمُوَالاتِكُمْ تُقْبَلُ الطَّاعَةُ الْمُفْتَرَضَةُ،
وَ لَكُمُ الْمَوَدَّةُ الْوَاجِبَةُ، وَ الدَّرَجَاتُ
الرَّفِيعَةُ، وَ الْمَقَامُ الْمَحْمُودُ، وَ الْمَكَانُ
[وَ الْمَقَامُ] الْمَعْلُومُ عِنْدَ اللهِ عَزَّ وَ
جَلَّ، وَ الْجَاهُ الْعَظِيمُ، وَ الشَّأْنُ الْكَبِيرُ،
وَ الشَّفَاعَةُ الْمَقْبُولَةُ،

Our Lord, we believe in what You have sent down, and we follow the Apostle, so write us among the witnesses. (3:53) *Our Lord! Do not make our hearts swerve after You have guided us, and*

رَبَّنَا آمَنَّا بِمَا أَنْزَلْتَ وَ اتَّبَعْنَا الرَّسُولَ
فَاكْتُبْنَا مَعَ الشَّاهِدِينَ، رَبَّنَا لَا تُزِغْ
قُلُوبَنَا بَعْدَ إِذْ هَدَيْتَنَا وَ هَبْ لَنَا مِنْ

لَدُنْكَ رَحْمَةً، إِنَّكَ أَنْتَ الْوَهَّابُ، سُبْحَانَ رَبِّنَا إِنْ كَانَ وَعْدُ رَبِّنَا لَمَفْعُولًا.

bestow Your mercy on us. Indeed You are the All-munificent.[3:8] *Immaculate is our Lord! Indeed Our Lord's promise is bound to be fulfilled.*[17:108]

يَا وَلِيَّ اللهِ إِنَّ بَيْنِي وَ بَيْنَ اللهِ عَزَّ وَ جَلَّ ذُنُوبًا لَا يَأْتِي عَلَيْهَا إِلَّا رِضَاكُمْ، فَبِحَقِّ مَنِ ائْتَمَنَكُمْ عَلَىٰ سِرِّهِ، وَ اسْتَرْعَاكُمْ أَمْرَ خَلْقِهِ، وَ قَرَنَ طَاعَتَكُمْ بِطَاعَتِهِ، لَمَّا اسْتَوْهَبْتُمْ ذُنُوبِي وَ كُنْتُمْ شُفَعَائِي، فَإِنِّي لَكُمْ مُطِيعٌ، مَنْ أَطَاعَكُمْ فَقَدْ أَطَاعَ اللهَ، وَ مَنْ عَصَاكُمْ فَقَدْ عَصَى اللهَ، وَ مَنْ أَحَبَّكُمْ فَقَدْ أَحَبَّ اللهَ، وَ مَنْ أَبْغَضَكُمْ فَقَدْ أَبْغَضَ اللهَ،

O *walī* of Allah! There are sins (which form a barrier) between me and Allah, the Almighty and Glorious, which cannot be removed except by your consent. Therefore, for the sake of Him who entrusted you with His secrets and made you guardians of the affairs of His creatures, equating obedience to you with obedience to Him, ask Allah to pardon my sins, as you are my intercessor. For indeed I am obedient to you, and whoever obeys you obeys Allah, and whoever disobeys you disobeys Allah; whoever loves you loves Allah, and whoever bears enmity towards you bears enmity towards Allah!

اَللّٰهُمَّ إِنِّي لَوْ وَجَدْتُ شُفَعَاءَ أَقْرَبَ إِلَيْكَ مِنْ مُحَمَّدٍ وَ أَهْلِ بَيْتِهِ الْأَخْيَارِ الْأَئِمَّةِ الْأَبْرَارِ، لَجَعَلْتُهُمْ شُفَعَائِي،

O Allah, had I found any intercessors who were nearer to You than Muhammad and his Family, the chosen ones and the pious Imams, I would have certainly advanced them as my intercessors.

فَبِحَقِّهِمُ الَّذِي أَوْجَبْتَ لَهُمْ عَلَيْكَ، أَسْأَلُكَ أَنْ تُدْخِلَنِي فِي جُمْلَةِ الْعَارِفِينَ بِهِمْ وَ بِحَقِّهِمْ، وَ فِي زُمْرَةِ الْمَرْحُومِينَ بِشَفَاعَتِهِمْ، إِنَّكَ أَرْحَمُ الرَّاحِمِينَ!

Hence, for the sake of their right whose observance You have made incumbent upon Yourself, I beseech You to admit me among those who recognize them and their rights, and in the fold of those who receive Your mercy through their intercession. Indeed You are the Most Merciful of the merciful!

وَ صَلَّى اللهُ عَلَىٰ مُحَمَّدٍ وَ آلِهِ الطَّاهِرِينَ، وَ سَلَّمَ [تَسْلِيمًا] كَثِيرًا، وَ حَسْبُنَا اللهُ

May Allah bless Muḥammad and his immaculate Family, along with His abundant greetings of peace.

Allah is sufficient for us, and He is an excellent trustee.(3:173) وَ نِعْمَ الْوَكِيلُ.

This *ziyārah* has also been cited in *Tahdhīb* by Shaykh Ṭūsī, who also cites a farewell supplication after it. We have not cited it here for reasons of space. As remarked by ᶜAllāmah Majlisī, this is the best of all common *ziyārahs* with respect to its composite content, its eloquent prose and the chain of its transmission. His revered father, in his commentary on *Faqīh*, says that it is the best and most complete of all *ziyārahs* and that throughout the period of his sojourn in the shrine cities of Iraq he never used any other text for the *ziyārah* of the Imams (*ᶜa*).[1]

The Episode of Ḥajj Sayyid Ahmad Rashti

My teacher Shaykh Ḥusayn Nūrī has cited a narrative in his book *Najm al-Thāqib*,[2] which underscores the significance of reciting this *ziyārah* frequently and not neglecting it. The story is as follows.

> About seventeen years ago a pious person named Sayyid Aḥmad, son of Sayyid Hāshim b. Sayyid Ḥasan Mūsawī—may Allah grant him help and strength—a merchant and resident of the city of Rasht, had the honour of visiting Najaf Ashraf. One day he came to visit this non-descript along with the scholar and divine Shaykh ᶜAlī Rashtī (about whom we will have more to say, God willing, in the next narrative). At the time of leaving, the Shaykh, while commending his companion for his upright character, remarked that he once had a wonderful experience. However, the occasion was not fit for him to elaborate.
>
> When I met the Shaykh some days later, I was told that the Sayyid had left. When the Shaykh recounted for me the story of his experience along with an account of his life, I regretted greatly for not having heard it directly from him, although I do not have the smallest doubt about the Shaykh's veracity. Since that year the matter was on my mind until some months ago during the month of Jumādā al-Thāniyah of this year, on returning from Najaf Ashraf, I met that pious sayyid again in Sāmarrā as he was preparing to leave for Iran. I asked him about his past life includ-

1 *Rawḍat al-Muttaqīn*, v, 452.

2 *Najm al-Thāqib*, ii, 712-715, ḥikāyat 70.

ing the episode I had heard about. His account was exactly as I had been told before.

His narrative ran as follows. "In the year 1280 H. (1863-64) I left Rasht for the purpose of pilgrimage to the God's Holy House at Makkah and arrived in Tabriz, where I stayed at the house of Hājī Ṣafar ᶜAlī, a well-known merchant of the city. As there was no caravan for Makkah, I was puzzled. When Ḥājī Jabbār Jelodār Sedehī Iṣfahānī set out with the escort for Trabzon, I too hired some travelling equipment from him and went along.

"On reaching the first halt, three other persons were persuaded by Hājī Ṣafar ᶜAlī to join us. One of them was Ḥājī Mullā Bāqir Tabrīzī, well-known to the clerics as a professional *hajj* proxy, Ḥājī Sayyid Ḥusayn, a merchant of Tabrīz, and one Ḥājj ᶜAlī, a servant. We set out together until we reached Erzurum. From there we set out for Trabzon. In the course of our journey between these two cities, Ḥājī Jabbār Jelodār approached us and said that as the way that lay ahead of us was dangerous, we better make haste in setting out to accompany the caravan. This was because earlier we had been following the caravan at a distance most of the time. Accordingly, we got ready and set out with the caravan nearly two-and-a-half or three hours before daybreak.

"We must have gone about a half or three-fourth parasang when it grew dark and the snow began to fall. My companions covered their heads and moved on at a faster pace. However I tried to keep pace with them I failed to do so. As a result they moved ahead and I found myself alone. I got down from my horse and sat down by wayside. I became very worried as I had with me nearly six hundred Tumans, my expense for the journey. After some thought, I decided to wait where I was until the dawn, and to go back to the place from where we had set out. From there I planned to pursue the caravan while taking along a number of guards with me.

"In that state, my eyes fell on an orchard in which a gardener was striking the trees with his spade in order to relieve the branches of the snow. He approached me and coming near stopped at a distance. 'Who are you?' he asked me. I told him that my companions had gone ahead and I had lost my way. 'Perform a *nāfilah* prayer to find the way!' he said in Persian. I began to pray, and when I had finished the *tashahhud* he came again and said, 'Haven't you gone?' 'By God, I don't know the way,' I replied.

'Recite the *Jāmiᶜah*!' he suggested.

"I did not remember the *Jāmiᶜah* by heart, nor do I now, though I have visited the shrines of the Imams many times. Yet I got up and recited the entire *ziyārah jāmiᶜah* from memory. He appeared again and asked me, 'Are you still here?' I could not hold my tears and replied, 'Yes, I am here! I don't know the way.' 'Recite the *ziyārah* of ᶜĀshurā!' he advised. I did not remember the *ziyārah* of ᶜĀshūrā, and even now I don't remember it by heart. Yet I got up and began to recite it from memory and recited all the anathemas and the greetings along with the Supplication of ᶜAlqamah. I saw him approach again, and he said, 'Are you still there?!' I replied that I will wait until the morning. Thereupon he told me that he will take me to join the caravan.

"He went and returned riding an ass with his spade resting on his shoulder. 'Get on behind me,' he said. I mounted the ass behind him while holding the reins of my horse. I pulled at the reins but it refused to budge. 'Give me the reins,' he said to me. I gave him the reins which he caught in his right hand, holding the spade on his left shoulder.

"We set out and the horse followed obediently. Then placing his hand on my knee he said, 'Why don't you perform the *nāfilah* prayers? *Nāfilah, nāfilah, nāfilah!*' Then, after a while he said, 'Why don't you recite the *ziyārah* of ᶜĀshūrā? ᶜĀshūrā, ᶜĀshūrā, ᶜĀshūrā!' Then he said, 'Why don't you recite the *ziyārah jāmiᶜah*?! *Jāmiᶜah, jāmiᶜah, jāmiᶜah!*' During the journey he went on a curved path. Suddenly he turned to me and said, 'There are your companions!' They had come down by the side of a stream and were making ablutions for the morning prayer.

"I alighted from the ass, and when I tried to mount my horse I could not. He alighted and driving his spade into the snow, helped me get on the horse's back and turned its head in the direction of my companions. At that time my curiosity was roused about this man. He spoke Persian in a place where only Turkish was common and where most inhabitants were Christians. How could he have brought me to my companions in such a short time? I looked back but I did not see anyone and there was no trace of him. Then I joined my companions."

3. Third Ziyarah Jami'ah

ᶜAllāmah Majlisī has cited this *ziyārah* in *Tuḥfat al-Zā'ir* as the eighth of the common *ziyārahs* given in his book. He says that Sayyid Ibn Ṭāwūs has narrated it from Imam Jaᶜfar al-Ṣādiq (ᶜ*a*) among supplications relating to the day of ᶜArafah, with the remark that it may be recited in any place and on any occasion, especially on the day of ᶜArafah. Its text is as follows.[1]

اَلسَّلَامُ عَلَيْكَ يَا رَسُولَ اللهِ، اَلسَّلَامُ
عَلَيْكَ يَا نَبِيَّ اللهِ، اَلسَّلَامُ عَلَيْكَ
يَا خِيَرَةَ اللهِ مِنْ خَلْقِهِ، وَ أَمِينَهُ عَلَىٰ
وَحْيِهِ، اَلسَّلَامُ عَلَيْكَ يَا مَوْلَايَ يَا أَمِيرَ
الْمُؤْمِنِينَ، اَلسَّلَامُ عَلَيْكَ يَا مَوْلَايَ
أَنْتَ حُجَّةُ اللهِ عَلَىٰ خَلْقِهِ، وَ بَابُ
عِلْمِهِ، وَ وَصِيُّ نَبِيِّهِ، وَ الْخَلِيفَةُ مِنْ
بَعْدِهِ فِي أُمَّتِهِ، لَعَنَ اللهُ أُمَّةً غَصَبَتْكَ
حَقَّكَ، وَ قَعَدَتْ مَقْعَدَكَ، أَنَا بَرِيءٌ
مِنْهُمْ وَ مِنْ شِيعَتِهِمْ إِلَيْكَ.

Peace be to you, O Apostle of Allah! Peace be to you, O Prophet of Allah! Peace be to you, O chosen one of Allah's creatures and the trustee of His revelations! Peace be to you, O my master, O Commander of the Faithful! Peace be to you, O my master, you are Allah's testament to His creatures, the gateway to His knowledge, the legatee of His Prophet and His vicegerent within his *ummah* after him! May Allah's curse be on the lot who usurped your rights and sat in your seat. I repudiate them and their followers before you!

اَلسَّلَامُ عَلَيْكِ يَا فَاطِمَةُ الْبَتُولُ، اَلسَّلَامُ
عَلَيْكِ يَا زَيْنَ نِسَاءِ الْعَالَمِينَ، اَلسَّلَامُ
عَلَيْكِ يَا بِنْتَ رَسُولِ رَبِّ الْعَالَمِينَ،
صَلَّى اللهُ عَلَيْكِ وَ عَلَيْهِ، اَلسَّلَامُ
عَلَيْكِ يَا أُمَّ الْحَسَنِ وَ الْحُسَيْنِ، لَعَنَ

Peace be to you, O Fāṭimah, the Batūl! Peace be to you, O ornament of the world's womankind! Peace be to you, O daughter of the Apostle of the Lord of the worlds! May Allah bless you and him! Peace be to you, O mother of al-Ḥasan and al-Ḥusyan! May Allah's curse be on the lot who usurped your rights and denied you what

[1] *Iqbāl*, 382, whence *Biḥār*, xcv, 252, xcviii, 374, b 32, h 16. & *Mustadrak*, x, 369, b 75, h 12200/2.

اللهُ أُمَّــةً غَصَبَتْكِ حَقَّكِ، وَ مَنَعَتْكِ مَا جَعَلَهُ اللهُ لَــكِ حَلاَلاً، أَنَا بَرِیءٌ إِلَيْكِ مِنْهُمْ وَ مِنْ شِيعَتِهِمْ.

Allah had made lawfully yours! I repudiate them and their followers before you!

اَلسَّــلاَمُ عَلَيْكَ يَا مَوْلاَیَ يَا أَبَا مُحَمَّدٍ الْحَسَنَ الزَّكِيَّ. اَلسَّلاَمُ عَلَيْكَ يَا مَوْلاَیَ، لَعَنَ اللهُ أُمَّةً قَتَلَتْكَ، وَ بَايَعَتْ فِي أَمْرِكَ وَ شَــايَعَتْ، أَنَا بَرِیءٌ إِلَيْكَ مِنْهُمْ وَ مِنْ شِيعَتِهِمْ.

Peace be to you, O Abū Muḥammad al-Ḥasan, O blameless one! Peace be to you, O my master! May Allah's curse be on those who killed you and colluded and cooperated against you! I repudiate them and their followers before you!

اَلسَّلاَمُ عَلَيْكَ يَا مَوْلاَیَ يَا أَبَا عَبْدِ اللهِ الْحُسَيْنَ بْنَ عَلِيٍّ، صَلَوَاتُ اللهِ عَلَيْكَ وَ عَلَى أَبِيكَ وَ جَدِّكَ مُحَمَّدٍ صَلَّى اللهُ عَلَيْهِ وَ آلِهِ، لَعَــنَ اللهُ أُمَّةً اسْــتَحَلَّتْ دَمَكَ، وَ لَعَــنَ اللهُ أُمَّةً قَتَلَتْكَ وَ اسْــتَبَاحَتْ حَرِيمَــكَ، وَ لَعَــنَ اللهُ أَشْــيَاعَهُمْ وَ أَتْبَاعَهُــمْ، وَ لَعَــنَ اللهُ الْمُمَهِّدِينَ لَهُمْ بِالتَّمْكِينِ مِنْ قِتَالِكُــمْ، أَنَا بَرِیءٌ إِلَى اللهِ وَ إِلَيْكَ مِنْهُمْ.

Peace be to you, O my master Abū ʿAbd Allah al-Ḥusayn ibn ʿAlī, may Allah's blessings be upon you, your father and your grandfather, Muḥammad, may Allah bless him and his Family! May Allah's curse be on the people who sanctioned the shedding of your blood! May Allah's curse be upon those who slew you and violated your sanctity! May Allah's curse be upon their allies and followers! May Allah's curse be upon those who prepared the ground for them to wage war against you! I repudiate them before Allah and before you!

اَلسَّلاَمُ عَلَيْكَ يَا مَوْلاَیَ يَا أَبَا مُحَمَّدٍ عَلِيَّ بْنَ الْحُسَيْنِ، اَلسَّلاَمُ عَلَيْكَ يَا مَوْلاَیَ يَا أَبَا جَعْفَرٍ مُحَمَّدَ بْنَ عَلِيٍّ، اَلسَّلاَمُ عَلَيْكَ

Peace be to you, O my master, O Abū Muḥammad ʿAlī ibn al-Ḥusayn! Peace be to you, O my master Abū Jaʿfar Muḥammad ibn ʿAlī! Peace be to you, O my master Abū ᶜAbdillāh Jaᶜfar ibn Muḥammad! Peace be to you, O my master, Abū al-Ḥasan Mūsā ibn Jaᶜfar! Peace be to you, O my master Abū al-Ḥasan ᶜAlī ibn Mūsā! Peace be to you, O my master, Abū Jaᶜfar Muḥammad ibn ᶜAlī! Peace be to you, O my master, Abū al-Ḥasan ᶜAlī ibn Muḥammad! Peace be to you, O my master, Abū Muḥammad al-Ḥasan ibn ᶜAlī!

يَا مَوْلَايَ يَا أَبَا عَبْدِ اللهِ جَعْفَرَ بْنَ مُحَمَّدٍ، اَلسَّلَامُ عَلَيْكَ يَا مَوْلَايَ يَا أَبَا الْحَسَنِ مُوسَى بْنَ جَعْفَرٍ، اَلسَّلَامُ عَلَيْكَ يَا مَوْلَايَ يَا أَبَا الْحَسَنِ عَلِيَّ بْنَ مُوسَى، اَلسَّلَامُ عَلَيْكَ يَا مَوْلَايَ يَا أَبَا جَعْفَرٍ مُحَمَّدَ بْنَ عَلِيٍّ، اَلسَّلَامُ عَلَيْكَ يَا مَوْلَايَ يَا أَبَا الْحَسَنِ عَلِيَّ بْنَ مُحَمَّدٍ، اَلسَّلَامُ عَلَيْكَ يَا مَوْلَايَ يَا أَبَا مُحَمَّدٍ الْحَسَنَ بْنَ عَلِيٍّ،

Peace be to you, O my master Abū al-Qāsim Muḥammad ibn al-Ḥasan, Master of the Era! May Allah bless you and your pure and immaculate progeny!

اَلسَّلَامُ عَلَيْكَ يَا مَوْلَايَ يَا أَبَا الْقَاسِمِ مُحَمَّدَ بْنَ الْحَسَنِ صَاحِبَ الزَّمَانِ، صَلَّى اللهُ عَلَيْكَ وَ عَلَىٰ عِتْرَتِكَ الطَّاهِرَةِ الطَّيِّبَةِ.

O my masters, be my intercessors in ridding me of the burden of my sins and offenses! I have faith in Allah and that which has been revealed to you! I give my love and loyalty to the last of you as to the first of you, and I forswear the idol and the rebel, the Lāt and the ᶜUzzā! O my masters, I make peace with those who are at peace with you and at war with those who are at war with you, being enemy of your enemies and friend of your friends till the Day of Resurrection!

يَا مَوَالِيَّ كُونُوا شُفَعَائِي فِي حَطِّ وِزْرِي وَ خَطَايَايَ، آمَنْتُ بِاللهِ وَ بِمَا أُنْزِلَ إِلَيْكُمْ، وَ أَتَوَالَى آخِرَكُمْ بِمَا أَتَوَالَى أَوَّلَكُمْ، وَ بَرِئْتُ مِنَ الْجِبْتِ وَ الطَّاغُوتِ وَ اللَّاتِ وَ الْعُزَّى، يَا مَوَالِيَّ أَنَا سِلْمٌ لِمَنْ سَالَمَكُمْ، وَ حَرْبٌ لِمَنْ حَارَبَكُمْ، وَ عَدُوٌّ لِمَنْ عَادَاكُمْ، وَ وَلِيٌّ لِمَنْ وَالَاكُمْ إِلَى يَوْمِ الْقِيَامَةِ،

May Allah's curse be upon those who wronged you and

وَ لَعَنَ اللهُ ظَالِمِيكُمْ وَ غَاصِبِيكُمْ، وَ

لَعَنَ اللهُ أَشْيَاعَهُمْ وَ أَتْبَاعَهُمْ وَ أَهْلَ مَذْهَبِهِمْ، وَ أَبْرَأُ إِلَى اللهِ وَ إِلَيْكُمْ مِنْهُمْ.

usurped your rights! May Allah's curse be on their allies and followers and those who follow their way! I repudiate them before Allah and before you!

4. FOURTH ZIYARAH JAMIʿAH

One of the common *ziyārahs* is the well-known text known as "Ziyārah Amīn Allāh," which begins with the words *Assalāmu ᶜalayka yâ amīnallāhi fī arḍih, wa ḥujjatahū ᶜalā ᶜibādih. As͟hhadu annaka jāhadta filllāh...* It was cited as the second *ziyārah* (p. 106) in the section on the *ziyārah* of the Commander of the Faithful (*ᶜa*).

5. FIFTH ZIYĀRAH JĀMIᶜAH

This *ziyārah* begins with the words *Alḥamdu lillāhil lad͟hî as͟hhadanā mas͟hhada awliyâ'ihī fī Rajab*, which was cited in the section on observances relating to the month of Rajab (see vol. 1, p. 380). Thus far we have cited five general *ziyārah*s in this blessed anthology, which will be sufficient, God willing.

SECTION TWO
THE COMMON AFTER-ZIYARAH SUPPLICATION

This supplication may be recited after the *ziyārah* of any of the Imams (*ᶜa*). Sayyid Ibn Ṭāwūs (*r*) states that it is *mustaḥab* to recite it after *ziyārah* of the Imams (*ᶜa*).[1]

اَللّٰهُمَّ إِنْ كَانَتْ ذُنُوبِي قَدْ أَخْلَقَتْ وَجْهِي عِنْدَكَ، وَ حَجَبَتْ دُعَائِي عَنْكَ، وَ حَالَتْ بَيْنِي وَ بَيْنَكَ، فَأَسْأَلُكَ أَنْ تُقْبِلَ عَلَيَّ بِوَجْهِكَ الْكَرِيمِ، وَ تَنْشُرَ عَلَيَّ رَحْمَتَكَ، وَ تُنَزِّلَ عَلَيَّ بَرَكَاتِكَ،

O Allah, if my sins have impaired my visage with You, keeping my supplications from being heard by You, and they have become an obstacle between me and You, I beseech You to turn Your munificent Face towards me, to spread Your mercy over me, and to send down Your bounties on me!

وَ إِنْ كَانَتْ قَدْ مَنَعَتْ أَنْ تَرْفَعَ لِي إِلَيْكَ

And if they stop my voice from

1 *Biḥār*, xcix, 172, b 8 from Ibn Ṭāwūs.

صَوْتًا، أَوْ تَغْفِرَ لِي ذَنْبًا، أَوْ تَتَجَاوَزَ عَنْ
خَطِيئَةٍ مُهْلِكَةٍ، فَهَا أَنَا ذَا مُسْتَجِيرٌ
بِكَرَمِ وَجْهِكَ وَ عِزِّ جَلالِكَ، مُتَوَسِّلٌ
إِلَيْكَ، مُتَقَرِّبٌ إِلَيْكَ، بِأَحَبِّ خَلْقِكَ
إِلَيْكَ، وَ أَكْرَمِهِمْ عَلَيْكَ، وَ أَوْلاهُمْ
بِكَ، وَ أَطْوَعِهِمْ لَكَ، وَ أَعْظَمِهِمْ مَنْزِلَةً وَ
مَكَانًا عِنْدَكَ، مُحَمَّدٍ وَ بِعِتْرَتِهِ الطَّاهِرِينَ
الْأَئِمَّةِ الْهُدَاةِ الْمَهْدِيِّينَ، الَّذِينَ فَرَضْتَ
عَلَى خَلْقِكَ طَاعَتَهُمْ، وَ أَمَرْتَ بِمَوَدَّتِهِمْ،
وَ جَعَلْتَهُمْ وُلاةَ الْأَمْرِ مِنْ بَعْدِ رَسُولِكَ
صَلَّى اللهُ عَلَيْهِ وَ آلِهِ،

rising up to You or keep You from pardoning my sin, or from disregarding my fatal offenses, now I take refuge with Your munificent Face and Your might and majesty, taking resort in You, seeking nearness to You through the dearest of Your creatures, the most honoured of them with You, the nearest of them to You, the most obedient of them to You, who possesses the greatest station and standing with You, that is, Muḥammad and his immaculate Family, the Imams, the rightly-guided guides, obedience to whom You have made obligatory on Your creatures, whom You have commanded to be loved, investing them with authority after Your Apostle, may Allah bless him and his Family!

يَا مُذِلَّ كُلِّ جَبَّارٍ عَنِيدٍ، وَ يَا مُعِزَّ
الْمُؤْمِنِينَ، بَلَغَ مَجْهُودِي فَهَبْ لِي نَفْسِيَ
السَّاعَةَ، وَ رَحْمَةً مِنْكَ تَمُنُّ بِهَا عَلَيَّ، يَا
أَرْحَمَ الرَّاحِمِينَ!

O humiliator of every obdurate tyrant and empowerer of the faithful, my endurance is at its end, so grant me prompt amnesty and Your mercy, thus showing me Your favour, O Most Merciful of the merciful!

Then embrace the grave and, rubbing each side of the face on it, say,

اللَّهُمَّ إِنَّ هَذَا مَشْهَدٌ لا يَرْجُو مَنْ
فَاتَتْهُ فِيهِ رَحْمَتُكَ أَنْ يَنَالَهَا فِي غَيْرِهِ،
وَ لا أَحَدٌ أَشْقَى مِنِ امْرِئٍ قَصَدَهُ مُؤَمِّلًا
فَآبَ عَنْهُ خَائِبًا،

O Allah, this is a shrine where those who fail to receive Your mercy cannot hope to obtain it elsewhere! There is no one more wretched than the person who comes to it hopefully and returns disappointed!

O Allah, I take refuge in You from an evil return, from despair at death and from a rigorous reckoning (of my deeds at Resurrection and) Judgement!

اَللّٰهُـمَّ إِنِّى أَعُوذُ بِكَ مِنْ شَرِّ الْإِيَابِ، وَ خَيْبَةِ الْمُنْقَلَبِ، وَ الْمُنَاقَشَـةِ عِنْدَ الْحِسَابِ،

Far it is from You, my Lord, that You should equate obedience to Your *walī* with obedience to Yourself and love for him with the love of You, and disobedience to him with disobedience to You and then disappoint the pilgrim to his shrine who comes to his tomb after bearing the hardships of journey from distant towns!

وَ حَاشَـاكَ يَا رَبِّ أَنْ تَقْـرِنَ طَاعَةَ وَلِيِّكَ بِطَاعَتِكَ، وَ مُوَالَاتَهُ بِمُوَالَاتِكَ، وَ مَعْصِيَتَـهُ بِمَعْصِيَتِـكَ، ثُمَّ تُؤْيِسَ زَائِـرَهُ وَ الْمُتَحَمِّلَ مِنْ بُعْدِ الْبِلَادِ إِلَى قَبْرِهِ،

O my Lord, by Your honour, my heart is not persuaded to such treatment from You when all hearts testify to Your graciousness!

وَ عِزَّتِكَ يَـا رَبِّ لَا يَنْعَقِدُ عَلَى ذَلِكَ ضَمِـيرِى، إِذْ كَانَتِ الْقُلُـوبُ إِلَيْكَ بِالْجَمِيلِ تُشِيرُ.

Then offer the prayer of *ziyārah*. Shaykh Mufīd has also cited this supplication; but he adds that after reciting it one should recite the following.[1]

O *walī* of Allah, between me and Allah, Almighty and Glorious, there are sins that nothing can take away except your consent. So, by the right of Him who has entrusted you with His secrets and made you guardian of the affairs of His creatures, equating obedience to you with obedience to Himself, and loyalty and love towards you with loyalty and love for Him, to assume the setting right of my case with Allah, Almighty and Glorious!

As the benefit of my visit to you,

يَـا وَلِيَّ اللهِ إِنَّ بَيْنِـى وَ بَيْنَ اللهِ عَزَّ وَ جَـلَّ ذُنُوبًـا لَا يَـأْتِى عَلَيْهَا إِلَّا رِضَاكَ، فَبِحَقِّ مَنِ ائْتَمَنَكَ عَلَى سِرِّهِ، وَاسْتَرْعَاكَ أَمْرَ خَلْقِهِ، وَ قَرَنَ طَاعَتَكَ بِطَاعَتِهِ، وَ مُوَالَاتَـكَ بِمُوَالَاتِهِ، تَوَلَّ صَلَاحَ حَالِى مَعَ اللهِ عَزَّ وَ جَلَّ، وَاجْعَلْ حَظِّـى مِنْ زِيَارَتِكَ تَخْلِيطِى

[1] *Biḥār*, xcix, 173, b 8 citing Shaykh Mufīd's *Mazār*.

admit me into your sincere pilgrims concerning whom you beseech Allah to free them from hellfire and to grant them a good reward.	بِخَالِصِي زُوَّارِكَ، اَلَّذِينَ تَسْأَلُ اللهَ عَزَّ وَ جَلَّ فِي عِتْقِ رِقَابِهِمْ، وَ تَرْغَبُ إِلَيْهِ فِي حُسْنِ ثَوَابِهِمْ،
Here I am today, having taken refuge by your tomb and recourse in your good offices! So, my master, respond to me and come to my rescue, and request Allah, Almighty and Glorious, concerning me, for you have an honoured position and a great eminence with Allah. May Allah bless You and His worthy greetings be to you!	وَ هَا أَنَا الْيَوْمَ بِقَبْرِكَ لَائِذٌ، وَ بِحُسْنِ دِفَاعِكَ عَنِّي عَائِذٌ، فَتَلَافَنِي يَا مَوْلَايَ وَ أَدْرِكْنِي، وَ اسْأَلِ اللهَ عَزَّ وَ جَلَّ فِي أَمْرِي، فَإِنَّ لَكَ عِنْدَ اللهِ مَقَامًا كَرِيمًا وَ جَاهًا عَظِيمًا، صَلَّى اللهُ عَلَيْكَ وَ سَلَّمَ تَسْلِيمًا.

When intending to depart and bid farewell, say,[1]

Peace be to you, O Family of prophethood and the repository of apostleship, from one who says farewell, though not from weariness or dissatisfaction, and may Allah's mercy and bounties be upon you!	اَلسَّلَامُ عَلَيْكُمْ يَا أَهْلَ بَيْتِ النُّبُوَّةِ وَ مَعْدِنَ الرِّسَالَةِ، سَلَامَ مُوَدِّعٍ لَا سَئِمٍ وَ لَا قَالٍ، وَ رَحْمَةُ اللهِ وَ بَرَكَاتُهُ.

It is better for the pilgrim, when making any petition in the holy shrine, or, for that matter, at any place and time, to supplicate for the safety of the sacred person of the Imam of the Era (ʿa). This practice has significant benefits which cannot be elaborated here. They have been explained by our teacher, Shaykh Ḥusayn Nūrī, in the tenth chapter of *Najm al-Thāqib,* where he has cited some supplications that are suitable for this purpose. Those interested should refer to that book. The shortest of such supplications is the one which we have cited earlier in the observances of the 23rd night of the month of Ramaḍān, among supplications relating to the last ten days of that

1 This passage appears in the original *Mafatīḥ*, following the *Biḥār*, before the supplication cited from Shaykh Mufīd, an order which does not suit the pilgrim's convenience and benefit. (Tr.)

month (p. 606). Also, in the section on the etiquette to be observed while visiting the shrine of Imam al-Ḥusayn (ᶜa) (Vol. 2, p. 258) we have cited another supplication which may be recited in all the holy shrines.

SECTION THREE
ṢALAWAT FOR THE INFALLIBLES (ᶜA)

While describing the observances for Friday, Shaykh Ṭūsī cites in the *Miṣbāḥ* a report from his teachers, from Abū al-Faḍl al-Shaybānī from Abū Muḥammad ᶜAbd Allāh b. Muḥammad al-ᶜĀbid, narrated by him at a place called Dāliyah. ᶜAbd Allāh says that in the year 255 H. he asked Imam al-Ḥasan al-ᶜAskarī (ᶜa) at his residence in Sāmarrā to dictate to him the manner of invoking *ṣalawāt* on the Apostle of Allah (ṣ) and his successors. ᶜAbd Allāh had brought with him a large piece of paper and a pen for this purpose. The Imam (ᶜa) dictated to him verbatim the following texts without looking into any book.[1]

1. ṢALAWAT FOR THE APOSTLE OF ALLAH (Ṣ)

O Allah, bless Muḥammad, as he bore (the burden of) Your revelations and delivered Your messages! Bless Muḥammmad, as he sanctioned what You have made lawful, prohibited what You have made unlawful, and taught Your Scripture! Bless Muḥammad, as he established the prayer, paid the *zakāt* and summoned the people to Your religion.	اَللّٰهُمَّ صَلِّ عَلىٰ مُحَمَّدٍ كَمَا حَمَلَ وَحْيَكَ، وَ بَلَّغَ رِسَالاٰتِكَ، وَ صَلِّ عَلىٰ مُحَمَّدٍ كَمَا أَحَلَّ حَلاٰلَكَ، وَ حَرَّمَ حَرَامَكَ، وَ عَلَّمَ كِتَابَــكَ، وَ صَلِّ عَلىٰ مُحَمَّــدٍ كَمَا أَقَامَ الصَّلاٰةَ، وَ آتَى الزَّكَاةَ، وَ دَعَا إِلَى دِينِكَ،
Bless Muḥammad, as he confirmed Your promise and warned concerning Your threats! Bless Muḥammad, inasmuch as You forgive our sins for his sake, and conceal our defects through him and remove our sorrows through him!	وَ صَلِّ عَلىٰ مُحَمَّــدٍ كَمَا صَدَّقَ بِوَعْدِكَ، وَ أَشْفَقَ مِنْ وَعِيدِكَ، وَ صَلِّ عَلىٰ مُحَمَّدٍ كَمَــا غَفَرْتَ بِهِ الذُّنُوبَ، وَ سَــتَرْتَ بِهِ الْعُيُوبَ، وَ فَرَّجْتَ بِهِ الْكُرُوبَ،

[1] Ṭūsī's *Miṣbāḥ*, 399-406 . *Jamāl*, 483-494, whence *Biḥār*, xci, 73, b 30, h 1. *Zād al-Maᶜād*, 471-2.

Bless Muḥammad, as You have removed through him our wretchedness, relieved our sorrows, answered our supplications, and delivered us from afflictions through him!

وَ صَلِّ عَلىٰ مُحَمَّدٍ كَمَا دَفَعْتَ بِهِ الشَّقَاءَ، وَ كَشَفْتَ بِهِ الْغَمَّاءَ، وَ أَجَبْتَ بِهِ الدُّعَاءَ، وَ نَجَّيْتَ بِهِ مِنَ الْبَلَاءِ،

Bless Muḥammad, inasmuch as You have mercy on Your servants through him, revive Your towns through him, crush the tyrants through him and destroy despots through him!

وَ صَلِّ عَلىٰ مُحَمَّدٍ كَمَا رَحِمْتَ بِهِ الْعِبَادَ، وَ أَحْيَيْتَ بِهِ الْبِلَادَ، وَ قَصَمْتَ بِهِ الْجَبَابِرَةَ، وَ أَهْلَكْتَ بِهِ الْفَرَاعِنَةَ،

Bless Muḥammad, inasmuch as You have enhanced through him our wealth several fold, protected us through him from terrible things, broken the idols through him and shown mercy to Your creatures through him!

وَ صَلِّ عَلىٰ مُحَمَّدٍ كَمَا أَضْعَفْتَ بِهِ الْأَمْوَالَ، وَ أَحْرَزْتَ بِهِ مِنَ الْأَهْوَالِ، وَ كَسَرْتَ بِهِ الْأَصْنَامَ، وَ رَحِمْتَ بِهِ الْأَنَامَ،

Bless Muḥammad, inasmuch as You have sent him with the best of all religions, given through him strength and honour to faith, destroyed thorough him the idols and granted greatness and splendour to Your Sacred House! Bless Muḥammad and his Family, the immaculate and the elect, and greet them with the worthiest greetings!

وَ صَلِّ عَلىٰ مُحَمَّدٍ كَمَا بَعَثْتَهُ بِخَيْرِ الْأَدْيَانِ، وَ أَعْزَزْتَ بِهِ الْإِيمَانَ، وَ تَبَّرْتَ بِهِ الْأَوْثَانَ، وَ عَظَّمْتَ بِهِ الْبَيْتَ الْحَرَامَ، وَ صَلِّ عَلىٰ مُحَمَّدٍ وَ أَهْلِ بَيْتِهِ الطَّاهِرِينَ الْأَخْيَارِ وَ سَلِّمْ تَسْلِيمًا .

2. Ṣalawat for the Commander of the Faithful (ʻa)

O Allah, bless ʿAlī ibn Abī Ṭālib, the Commander of the Faithful, brother of Your Prophet and his heir, his chosen one [his legatee] and minister, the repository of his knowledge, the keeper of his secrets, the gateway of

اَللّٰهُمَّ صَلِّ عَلىٰ أَمِيرِ الْمُؤْمِنِينَ عَلِيِّ بْنِ أَبِي طَالِبٍ، أَخِي نَبِيِّكَ وَ وَلِيِّهِ، وَ صَفِيِّهِ [وَ وَصِيِّهِ] وَ وَزِيرِهِ، وَ مُسْتَوْدَعِ عِلْمِهِ، وَ مَوْضِعِ سِرِّهِ، وَ بَابِ حِكْمَتِهِ،

his wisdom, the proclaimer of his proofs, the summoner to his Law, his successor in his *ummah*, the reliever of his worries, the subduer of the infidels, and the humbler of the wicked, whom You placed in relation to Your Prophet in the position of Aaron in relation to Moses!

وَ النَّاطِقِ بِحُجَّتِهِ، وَ الدَّاعِى إِلَى شَرِيعَتِهِ،
وَ خَلِيفَتِهِ فِى أُمَّتِهِ، وَ مُفَرِّجِ الْكُرَبِ
[الْكَرْبِ] عَنْ وَجْهِهِ، قَاصِمِ الْكَفَرَةِ،
وَ مُرْغِمِ الْفَجَرَةِ، اَلَّذِى جَعَلْتَهُ مِنْ
نَبِيِّكَ بِمَنْزِلَةِ هَارُونَ مِنْ مُوسَى.

O Allah, befriend those who befriend him and be hostile to those who are hostile towards him! Help those who help him and forsake those who forsake him! Curse his enemies from the former and the latter generations and bless him with the best of blessings You have granted to any of the legatees of Your prophets, O Lord of all the worlds!

اَللّٰهُمَّ وَالِ مَنْ وَالاٰهُ، وَ عَادِ مَنْ عَادَاهُ،
وَ انْصُرْ مَنْ نَصَرَهُ، وَ اخْذُلْ مَنْ خَذَلَهُ،
وَ الْعَنْ مَنْ نَصَبَ لَهُ مِنَ الْأَوَّلِينَ وَ
الْآخِرِينَ، وَ صَلِّ عَلَيْهِ أَفْضَلَ مَا صَلَّيْتَ
عَلىٰ أَحَدٍ مِنْ أَوْصِيَاءِ أَنْبِيَائِكَ، يَا رَبَّ
الْعَالَمِينَ!

3. ṢALAWAT FOR FATIMAH ZAHRA ('A)

O Allah, bless Fāṭimah, the truthful and immaculate one, the beloved of Your beloved Prophet, mother of Your beloved and chosen ones, whom You have chosen, preferred and elected over all the world's womankind!

اَللّٰهُمَّ صَلِّ عَلَى الصِّدِّيقَةِ فَاطِمَةَ الزَّكِيَّةِ،
حَبِيبَةِ حَبِيبِكَ وَ نَبِيِّكَ، وَ أُمِّ أَحِبَّائِكَ وَ
أَصْفِيَائِكَ، اَلَّتِي انْتَجَبْتَهَا وَ فَضَّلْتَهَا وَ
اخْتَرْتَهَا عَلىٰ نِسَاءِ الْعَالَمِينَ،

O Allah, avenge her against those who wronged her and made light of her rights, and avenge, O Allah, the blood of her progeny!

O Allah, inasmuch as You made her the mother of the Imams of guidance, the spouse of the bearer of the banner of Your praise,

اَللّٰهُمَّ كُنِ الطَّالِبَ لَهَا مِمَّنْ
ظَلَمَهَا، وَ اسْتَخَفَّ بِحَقِّهَا، وَ
كُنِ الثَّائِرَ اللّٰهُمَّ بِدَمِ أَوْلَادِهَا،
اَللّٰهُمَّ وَ كَمَا جَعَلْتَهَا أُمَّ الْأَئِمَّةِ الْهُدَى،

وَ حَلِيلَةَ صَاحِبِ اللِّوَاءِ، وَ الْكَرِيمَةَ عِنْدَ الْمَلَإِ الْأَعْلَى، فَصَلِّ عَلَيْهَا وَ عَلَى أُمِّهَا صَلَاةً تُكْرِمُ بِهَا وَجْهَ مُحَمَّدٍ [أَبِيهَا] صَلَّى اللهُ عَلَيْهِ وَ آلِهِ، وَ تُقِرُّ بِهَا أَعْيُنَ ذُرِّيَّتِهَا، وَ أَبْلِغْهُمْ عَنِّي فِي هَذِهِ السَّاعَةِ أَفْضَلَ التَّحِيَّةِ وَ السَّلَامِ.

she who is honoured and eminent with the Supernal Elite, bless her and her mother with such blessings as would honour Muḥammad, may Allah bless him and his Family, and gladden her descendants, and convey to them on my behalf at this very hour the best of greetings and *salāms!*

4. Ṣalawat for the Imams al-Ḥasan and al-Ḥusayn ('a)

اَللَّهُمَّ صَلِّ عَلَى الْحَسَنِ وَ الْحُسَيْنِ، عَبْدَيْكَ وَ وَلِيَّيْكَ، وَ ابْنَيْ رَسُولِكَ، وَ سِبْطَيِ الرَّحْمَةِ، وَ سَيِّدَيْ شَبَابِ أَهْلِ الْجَنَّةِ، أَفْضَلَ مَا صَلَّيْتَ عَلَى أَحَدٍ مِنْ أَوْلَادِ النَّبِيِّينَ وَ الْمُرْسَلِينَ. اَللَّهُمَّ صَلِّ عَلَى الْحَسَنِ بْنِ سَيِّدِ النَّبِيِّينَ، وَ وَصِيِّ أَمِيرِ الْمُؤْمِنِينَ.

O Allah, bless al-Ḥasan and al-Ḥusayn, Your servants and vicegerents, sons of Your Apostle and grandsons of (the Prophet of)Mercy, and the doyens of the youth of paradise, with the best of blessings You have granted to any of the progeny of Your prophets and apostles! O Allah, bless al-Ḥasan, son of the Chief of the Prophets, and legatee of the Commander of the Faithful!

اَلسَّلَامُ عَلَيْكَ يَا ابْنَ رَسُولِ اللهِ، اَلسَّلَامُ عَلَيْكَ يَا ابْنَ سَيِّدِ الْوَصِيِّينَ.

Peace be to you, O son of the Apostle of Allah! Peace be to you, O son of the Chief of the Legatees!

أَشْهَدُ أَنَّكَ يَا ابْنَ أَمِيرِ الْمُؤْمِنِينَ أَمِينُ اللهِ وَ ابْنُ أَمِينِهِ، عِشْتَ مَظْلُومًا وَ مَضَيْتَ شَهِيدًا، وَ أَشْهَدُ أَنَّكَ الْإِمَامُ الزَّكِيُّ الْهَادِي الْمَهْدِيُّ.

I testify that you are son of the Commander of the Faithful, the trustee of Allah and son of His trustee! You were treated wrongfully in life and passed away as a martyr! I testify that you are an Imam, a blameless and rightly-guided guide.

O Allah, bless him and convey the best of greetings and *salāms* on my behalf to his spirit and body!

اَللّٰهُمَّ صَلِّ عَلَيْهِ وَ بَلِّغْ رُوحَهُ وَ جَسَدَهُ عَنِّي
فِي هٰذِهِ السَّاعَةِ أَفْضَلَ التَّحِيَّةِ وَ السَّلَامِ.

O Allah, bless al-Ḥusayn ibn ʿAlī, who was wronged and martyred, slain by the faithless and repudiated by the wicked.

اَللّٰهُمَّ صَلِّ عَلَى الْحُسَيْنِ بْنِ عَلِيٍّ الْمَظْلُومِ
الشَّهِيدِ، قَتِيلِ الْكَفَرَةِ وَ طَرِيحِ الْفَجَرَةِ.

Peace be to you, O Abū ʿAbdillāh! Peace be to you, O son of the Apostle of Allah! Peace be to you, O son of the Commander of the Faithful!

اَلسَّلَامُ عَلَيْكَ يَا أَبَا عَبْدِ اللّٰهِ، اَلسَّلَامُ
عَلَيْكَ يَا ابْنَ رَسُولِ اللّٰهِ، اَلسَّلَامُ
عَلَيْكَ يَا ابْنَ أَمِيرِ الْمُؤْمِنِينَ،

I testify with conviction that you are Allah's trustee, son of His trustee! You were slain wrongfully and passed away as a martyr. I testify that Allah, the Exalted, will avenge your blood and fulfil His promise of help and support in destroying your enemies and promulgating your summons!

أَشْهَدُ مُوقِنًا أَنَّكَ أَمِينُ اللّٰهِ وَ ابْنُ أَمِينِهِ،
قُتِلْتَ مَظْلُومًا وَ مَضَيْتَ شَهِيدًا، وَ
أَشْهَدُ أَنَّ اللّٰهَ تَعَالَى الطَّالِبُ بِثَارِكَ، وَ
مُنْجِزٌ مَا وَعَدَكَ مِنَ النَّصْرِ وَ التَّأْيِيدِ،
فِي هَلَاكِ عَدُوِّكَ وَ إِظْهَارِ دَعْوَتِكَ،

I testify that you fulfilled Allah's covenant, struggled in His way, and worshipped Him with total dedication until your last breath!

وَ أَشْهَدُ أَنَّكَ وَفَيْتَ بِعَهْدِ اللّٰهِ، وَ
جَاهَدْتَ فِي سَبِيلِ اللّٰهِ، وَ عَبَدْتَ اللّٰهَ
مُخْلِصًا حَتَّى أَتَاكَ الْيَقِينُ،

May Allah's curse be on those who killed you, and may His curse be on those who forsook you. May His curse be on those who rallied against you! I repudiate before Allah, the Most High, those who denied you, made light of your right, and consented to shed your blood!

لَعَنَ اللّٰهُ أُمَّةً قَتَلَتْكَ، وَ لَعَنَ اللّٰهُ أُمَّةً
خَذَلَتْكَ، وَ لَعَنَ اللّٰهُ أُمَّةً أَلَّبَتْ عَلَيْكَ،
وَ أَبْرَأُ إِلَى اللّٰهِ تَعَالَى مِمَّنْ أَكْذَبَكَ، وَ
اسْتَخَفَّ بِحَقِّكَ، وَ اسْتَحَلَّ دَمَكَ.

O Abū ʿAbdillāh, you are dearer to me than my father and mother!

بِأَبِي أَنْتَ وَ أُمِّي يَا أَبَا عَبْدِ اللّٰهِ، لَعَنَ

May Allah's curse be on those who slew you. May Allah's curse be on those who forsook you. May Allah's curse be on those who heard your call, but neither responded nor helped you.

اللهُ قَاتِلَكَ، وَ لَعَنَ اللهُ خَاذِلَكَ، وَ لَعَنَ اللهُ مَنْ سَمِعَ وَاعِيَتَكَ فَلَمْ يُجِبْكَ وَ لَمْ يَنْصُرْكَ،

May Allah's curse be on those who made your womenfolk captives! I forswear them before Allah as well as those who befriended them, sided with them and assisted them in doing that!

وَ لَعَنَ اللهُ مَنْ سَبَى نِسَاءَكَ، أَنَا إِلَى اللهِ مِنْهُمْ بَرِيءٌ وَ مِمَّنْ وَالاهُمْ وَ مَالَأَهُمْ وَ أَعَانَهُمْ عَلَيْهِ،

I testify that you and the Imams of your descent are the paragons of piety, the gateways of guidance, *the firmest handle* and God's testament to the world's denizens.

وَ أَشْهَدُ أَنَّكَ وَ الْأَئِمَّةَ مِنْ وُلْدِكَ كَلِمَةُ التَّقْوَىٰ، وَ بَابُ الْهُدَىٰ، وَ الْعُرْوَةُ الْوُثْقَىٰ، وَ الْحُجَّةُ عَلَىٰ أَهْلِ الدُّنْيَا،

I testify that I have faith in you and am convinced of your station. I follow you with my entire being, and with regard to the precepts of my religion, my final deeds and goals, in this life and in the Hereafter!

وَ أَشْهَدُ أَنِّي بِكُمْ مُؤْمِنٌ، وَ بِمَنْزِلَتِكُمْ مُوقِنٌ، وَ لَكُمْ تَابِعٌ بِذَاتِ نَفْسِي وَ شَرَائِعِ دِينِي وَ خَوَاتِيمِ عَمَلِي وَ مُنْقَلَبِي فِي دُنْيَايَ وَ آخِرَتِي.

5. Ṣalawat for ʻAli ibn al-Ḥusayn (ʻa)

O Allah, bless ᶜAlī ibn al-Ḥusayn, the doyen of the devout, whom You have chosen to be Your favourite and have appointed from his descendants *the Imams of guidance, who guide by the truth and do justice thereby.*[7:159] You have chosen him for Yourself, purged him of all impurity, elected him and made him a rightly-guided guide.

اَللّٰهُمَّ صَلِّ عَلَىٰ عَلِيِّ بْنِ الْحُسَيْنِ سَيِّدِ الْعَابِدِينَ، اَلَّذِي اسْتَخْلَصْتَهُ لِنَفْسِكَ، وَ جَعَلْتَ مِنْهُ أَئِمَّةَ الْهُدَىٰ، الَّذِينَ يَهْدُونَ بِالْحَقِّ وَ بِهِ يَعْدِلُونَ، اِخْتَرْتَهُ لِنَفْسِكَ، وَ طَهَّرْتَهُ مِنَ الرِّجْسِ، وَ اصْطَفَيْتَهُ وَ جَعَلْتَهُ هَادِيًا مَهْدِيًّا.

O Allah, bless him with the best of blessings You have granted to any of the progeny of Your prophets, to the extent that You would make him glad in this world and the Hereafter! Indeed, You are almighty and all-wise!

اَللّٰهُمَّ فَصَلِّ عَلَيْهِ أَفْضَلَ مَا صَلَّيْتَ عَلىٰ أَحَدٍ مِنْ ذُرِّيَّةِ أَنْبِيَائِكَ، حَتّىٰ يَبْلُغَ بِهِ مَا تَقَرُّ بِهِ عَيْنُهُ فِي الدُّنْيَا وَ الْآخِرَةِ، إِنَّكَ عَزِيزٌ حَكِيمٌ.

6. ṢALAWAT FOR MUHAMMAD IBN ʻALI (ʻA)

O Allah, bless Muḥammad ibn ʿAlī, the exponent of knowledge, the Imam of guidance, the leader of the Godwary and the chosen of Your servants!

اَللّٰهُمَّ صَلِّ عَلىٰ مُحَمَّدِ بْنِ عَلِيٍّ بَاقِرِ الْعِلْمِ، وَ إِمَامِ الْهُدىٰ، وَ قَائِدِ أَهْلِ التَّقْوىٰ، وَ الْمُنْتَجَبِ مِنْ عِبَادِكَ.

O Allah, inasmuch as You made him the hallmark for Your servants, the minaret for Your towns, the repository of Your wisdom, and the interpreter of Your revelations, commanding all people to obey him, warning them from disobeying him, bless him, O Lord, with the best blessings You have granted to any of the progeny of Your prophets, Your elect, Your apostles and trustees, O Lord of all the worlds!

اَللّٰهُمَّ وَ كَمَا جَعَلْتَهُ عَلَمًا لِعِبَادِكَ، وَ مَنَارًا لِبِلَادِكَ، وَ مُسْتَوْدَعًا لِحِكْمَتِكَ، وَ مُتَرْجِمًا لِوَحْيِكَ، وَ أَمَرْتَ بِطَاعَتِهِ، وَ حَذَّرْتَ مِنْ مَعْصِيَتِهِ، فَصَلِّ عَلَيْهِ يَا رَبِّ أَفْضَلَ مَا صَلَّيْتَ عَلىٰ أَحَدٍ مِنْ ذُرِّيَّةِ أَنْبِيَائِكَ وَ أَصْفِيَائِكَ وَ رُسُلِكَ وَ أُمَنَائِكَ يَا رَبَّ الْعَالَمِينَ!

7. ṢALAWAT FOR JAʻFAR IBN MUHAMMAD (ʻA)

O Allah, bless Jaʿfar ibn Muḥammad, the truthful one, the custodian of Your knowledge, the summoner to You by the truth, and the manifest light!

اَللّٰهُمَّ صَلِّ عَلىٰ جَعْفَرِ بْنِ مُحَمَّدٍ الصَّادِقِ، خَازِنِ الْعِلْمِ، اَلدَّاعِي إِلَيْكَ بِالْحَقِّ، اَلنُّورِ الْمُبِينِ.

O Allah, inasmuch as You made him the repository of Your Word

اَللّٰهُمَّ وَ كَمَا جَعَلْتَهُ مَعْدِنَ كَلَامِكَ

وَ وَحْيِكَ، وَ خَازِنَ عِلْمِكَ، وَ لِسَانَ
تَوْحِيدِكَ، وَ وَلِيَّ أَمْرِكَ، وَ مُسْتَحْفَظَ
دِينِكَ، فَصَلِّ عَلَيْهِ أَفْضَلَ مَا صَلَّيْتَ
عَلَىٰ أَحَدٍ مِنْ أَصْفِيَائِكَ وَ حُجَجِكَ،
إِنَّكَ حَمِيدٌ مَجِيدٌ.

and revelations, the custodian of Your knowledge, the proclaimer of Your Oneness, the one invested with Your authority, and the sanctuary of Your religion, bless him with the best of blessings You have granted to any of Your elect and Your testaments. Indeed You are praiseworthy and glorious!

8. ṢALAWAT FOR MUSA IBN JA'FAR ('A)

اَللّٰهُمَّ صَلِّ عَلَى الْأَمِينِ الْمُؤْتَمَنِ
مُوسَى بْنِ جَعْفَرٍ، اَلْبَرِّ الْوَفِيِّ، الطَّاهِرِ
الزَّكِيِّ، اَلنُّورِ الْمُبِينِ [الْمُنِيرِ]، الْمُجْتَهِدِ
الْمُحْتَسِبِ، اَلصَّابِرِ عَلَى الْأَذَى فِيكَ،

O Allah, bless Your trustworthy trustee Mūsā ibn Jaʿfar, the pious, loyal, pure and blameless Imam, who was a manifest [radiant] light, who strived diligently in Your way, patiently and resignedly bearing all the torments for Your sake!

اَللّٰهُمَّ وَ كَمَا بَلَّغَ عَنْ آبَائِهِ مَا اسْتُودِعَ
مِنْ أَمْرِكَ وَ نَهْيِكَ، وَ حَمَلَ عَلَى الْمَحَجَّةِ،
وَ كَابَدَ أَهْلَ الْعِزَّةِ وَ الشِّدَّةِ، فِيمَا كَانَ
يَلْقَىٰ مِنْ جُهَّالِ قَوْمِهِ، رَبِّ فَصَلِّ عَلَيْهِ
أَفْضَلَ وَ أَكْمَلَ مَا صَلَّيْتَ عَلَىٰ أَحَدٍ
مِمَّنْ أَطَاعَكَ وَ نَصَحَ لِعِبَادِكَ، إِنَّكَ
غَفُورٌ رَحِيمٌ.

O Allah, inasmuch as he communicated Your commands and prohibitions, which were entrusted to him by his ancestors, and led the people on the straight path, underwent ordeals at the hands of the powerful because of what he had to face from the ignorant of his people, bless him, Lord, with the best and most complete of blessings You have granted to those who are obedient to You and are well-wishers of Your servants. Indeed You are all-forgiving and all-merciful!

9. ṢALAWAT FOR 'ALI IBN MUSA ('A)

اَللّٰهُمَّ صَلِّ عَلَىٰ عَلِيِّ بْنِ مُوسَى الَّذِي

O Allah, bless ʿAlī ibn Mūsā, with whom You were pleased and through whom You have pleased whomsoever of Your creatures that You wished.

ارْتَضَيْتَهُ، وَ رَضَّيْتَ بِهِ مَنْ شِئْتَ مِنْ خَلْقِكَ،

O Allah, inasmuch as You have made him Your testament to Your creatures, the maintainer of Your ordinances, the defender of Your religion and the witness to Your servants, and inasmuch as he was sincerely concerned with their well-being, in secret and open, called the people to Your path with wisdom and good advice, bless him with the best of blessings You have granted to any of Your friends and chosen ones from Your creatures. Indeed You are generous and munificent!

اَللّٰهُمَّ وَ كَمَا جَعَلْتَهُ حُجَّةً عَلٰى خَلْقِكَ، وَ قَائِمًا بِأَمْرِكَ، وَ نَاصِرًا لِدِينِكَ، وَ شَاهِدًا عَلٰى عِبَادِكَ، وَ كَمَا نَصَحَ لَهُمْ فِي السِّرِّ وَ الْعَلَانِيَةِ، وَ دَعَا إِلَى سَبِيلِكَ بِالْحِكْمَةِ وَ الْمَوْعِظَةِ الْحَسَنَةِ، فَصَلِّ عَلَيْهِ أَفْضَلَ مَا صَلَّيْتَ عَلٰى أَحَدٍ مِنْ أَوْلِيَائِكَ وَ خِيَرَتِكَ مِنْ خَلْقِكَ، إِنَّكَ جَوَادٌ كَرِيمٌ.

10. Ṣalawat for Muhammad ibn ʿAli ibn Musa (ʿa)

O Allah, bless Muḥammad ibn ʿAlī ibn Mūsā, the paragon of God-fearing, the light of guidance, the model of loyalty, the heir of the immaculate ones, the successor of the preceding legatees and Your trustee over Your revelations!

اَللّٰهُمَّ صَلِّ عَلٰى مُحَمَّدِ بْنِ عَلِيِّ بْنِ مُوسَى عَلَمِ التُّقٰى، وَ نُورِ الْهُدٰى، وَ مَعْدِنِ الْوَفَاءِ، وَ فَرْعِ الْأَزْكِيَاءِ، وَ خَلِيفَةِ الْأَوْصِيَاءِ، وَ أَمِينِكَ عَلٰى وَحْيِكَ،

O Allah, inasmuch as You have guided people through him out of error, rescued them from perplexity, shown the right path to those who were guided aright, and cleansed those who were purified, bless him with the best of blessings that You have granted to any of Your friends and heirs of Your vicegerents! Indeed You are al-

اَللّٰهُمَّ فَكَمَا هَدَيْتَ بِهِ مِنَ الضَّلَالَةِ، وَ اسْتَنْقَذْتَ بِهِ مِنَ الْحَيْرَةِ، وَ أَرْشَدْتَ بِهِ مَنِ اهْتَدٰى، وَ زَكَّيْتَ بِهِ مَنْ تَزَكّٰى، فَصَلِّ عَلَيْهِ أَفْضَلَ مَا صَلَّيْتَ عَلٰى أَحَدٍ مِنْ أَوْلِيَائِكَ وَ

بَقِيَّـةِ أَوْصِيٰائِكَ، إِنَّـكَ عَزِيزٌ حَكِيمٌ.

mighty and all-wise!

11. Ṣalawat for 'Ali ibn Muhammad ('a)

اَللّٰهُمَّ صَلِّ عَلىٰ عَلِيِّ بْنِ مُحَمَّدٍ وَصِيِّ الْأَوْصِيٰاءِ، وَإِمَامِ الْأَتْقِيٰاءِ، وَ خَلَفِ أَئِمَّةِ الدِّينِ، وَ الْحُجَّةِ عَلَى الْخَلَائِقِ أَجْمَعِينَ.

O Allah, bless ᶜAlī ibn Muḥammad, the legatee of the Legatees, the Imam of the Godwary, scion of the leaders of the faith and (God's) testament to all the creatures.

اَللّٰهُمَّ كَمَا جَعَلْتَهُ نُورًا يَسْتَضِيءُ بِهِ الْمُؤْمِنُونَ، فَبَشَّرَ بِالْجَزِيلِ مِنْ ثَوَابِكَ، وَ أَنْذَرَ بِالْأَلِيمِ مِنْ عِقَابِكَ، وَ حَذَّرَ بَأْسَكَ، وَ ذَكَّرَ بِآيَاتِكَ، وَ أَحَلَّ حَلَالَكَ، وَ حَرَّمَ حَرَامَكَ، وَ بَيَّنَ شَرَائِعَكَ وَ فَرَائِضَكَ، وَ حَضَّ عَلىٰ عِبَادَتِكَ، وَ أَمَرَ بِطَاعَتِكَ، وَ نَهَى عَنْ مَعْصِيَتِكَ، فَصَلِّ عَلَيْهِ أَفْضَلَ مَا صَلَّيْتَ عَلىٰ أَحَدٍ مِنْ أَوْلِيٰائِكَ وَ ذُرِّيَّةِ أَنْبِيٰائِكَ، يا إِلٰهَ الْعَالَمِينَ!

O Allah, inasmuch as You made him a source of light for the faithful, and he gave them the good news of Your plentiful reward and warned them of Your retribution and punishment for sins, reminded them of Your signs, allowed what You have permitted and forbade what You have prohibited, expounded Your laws and obligations, urged them on to Your worship, enjoined them to obey You and forbade them from disobeying You, bless him with the best of blessings You have granted to any of Your friends and the progeny of Your prophets! O God of all the worlds!

The narrator of this report, Abū Muḥammad ᶜAbd Allāh al-Yamanī, says, on reaching the *ṣalawāt* to be said for his own self, the Imam fell silent. When I asked him about it, he said, "Were it not a matter of religion, which God has commanded us to communicate and deliver to its seekers, I would have preferred to remain silent. However, it is a matter of the faith, so write..."

12. Ṣalawat for Ḥasan ibn 'Ali ibn Muhammad ('a)

اَللّٰهُمَّ صَلِّ عَلَى الْحَسَنِ بْنِ عَلِيِّ بْنِ مُحَمَّدٍ

O Allah, bless al-Ḥasan ibn ᶜAlī ibn Muḥammad, the pious, God-

wary and veracious Imam, true to his word, the radiant light, the custodian of Your knowledge, the preacher of Your Unity, invested with Your authority, the scion of the leaders of the faith, the rightly-guided guides, and Your testament to the world's denizens.	الْبَرِّ التَّقِيِّ، اَلصَّادِقِ الْوَفِيِّ، اَلنُّورِ الْمُضِيءِ، خَازِنِ عِلْمِكَ، وَ الْمُذَكِّرِ بِتَوْحِيدِكَ، وَ وَلِيِّ أَمْرِكَ، وَ خَلَفِ أَئِمَّةِ الدِّينِ الْهُدَاةِ الرَّاشِدِينَ، وَ الْحُجَّةِ عَلَىٰ أَهْلِ الدُّنْيَا،
Bless him, O Lord, with the best of blessings You have granted to any of Your chosen servants, testaments and descendants of Your apostles, O God of all the worlds!	فَصَلِّ عَلَيْهِ يَا رَبِّ أَفْضَلَ مَا صَلَّيْتَ عَلَىٰ أَحَدٍ مِنْ أَصْفِيَائِكَ. وَ حُجَجِكَ وَ أَوْلَادِ رُسُلِكَ، يَا إِلَٰهَ الْعَالَمِينَ!

13. ṢALAWAT FOR THE AWAITED IMAM OF THE ERA (‘A)

O Allah, bless Your *walī*, son of Your *awliyā*, obedience to whom You have made obligatory along with observance of their rights. *You have repelled all impurity from them and purified them with a through purification.*	اَللّٰهُمَّ صَلِّ عَلَىٰ وَلِيِّكَ وَ ابْنِ أَوْلِيَائِكَ، اَلَّذِينَ فَرَضْتَ طَاعَتَهُمْ، وَ أَوْجَبْتَ حَقَّهُمْ، وَ أَذْهَبْتَ عَنْهُمُ الرِّجْسَ وَ طَهَّرْتَهُمْ تَطْهِيرًا.
O Allah, help him and make Your religion triumph through him, assist through him Your *awliyā* and his friends, followers and helpers, and appoint us to be among them.	اَللّٰهُمَّ انْصُرْهُ وَ انْتَصِرْ بِهِ لِدِينِكَ، وَ انْصُرْ بِهِ أَوْلِيَاءَكَ وَ أَوْلِيَاءَهُ، وَ شِيعَتَهُ وَ أَنْصَارَهُ، وَ اجْعَلْنَا مِنْهُمْ.
O Allah, protect him from the evil of every rebel and tyrant and from the evil of all Your creatures. Protect him from his front and rear, right and left, and guard him and shield him lest any ill should reach him. Preserve through his safety Your Apostle and the progeny of Your Apostle.	اَللّٰهُمَّ أَعِذْهُ مِنْ شَرِّ كُلِّ بَاغٍ وَ طَاغٍ، وَ مِنْ شَرِّ جَمِيعِ خَلْقِكَ، وَ احْفَظْهُ مِنْ بَيْنِ يَدَيْهِ وَ مِنْ خَلْفِهِ، وَ عَنْ يَمِينِهِ وَ عَنْ شِمَالِهِ، وَ احْرُسْهُ وَ امْنَعْهُ أَنْ يُوصَلَ إِلَيْهِ بِسُوءٍ، وَ احْفَظْ فِيهِ رَسُولَكَ وَ آلَ رَسُولِكَ،

وَ أَظْهِرْ بِهِ الْعَدْلَ، وَ أَيِّدْهُ بِالنَّصْرِ، وَ
انْصُرْ نَاصِرِيهِ، وَ اخْذُلْ خَاذِلِيهِ، وَ اقْصِمْ
بِهِ جَبَابِرَةَ الْكُفْرِ، وَ اقْتُلْ بِهِ الْكُفَّارَ وَ
الْمُنَافِقِينَ، وَ جَمِيعَ الْمُلْحِدِينَ، حَيْثُ
كَانُوا مِنْ مَشَارِقِ الْأَرْضِ وَ مَغَارِبِهَا،
وَ بَرِّهَا وَ بَحْرِهَا، وَ امْلَأْ بِهِ الْأَرْضَ
عَدْلًا، وَ أَظْهِرْ بِهِ دِينَ نَبِيِّكَ عَلَيْهِ وَ
آلِهِ السَّلَامُ،

Make justice prevail through him and confirm him with victory. Help his helpers and forsake those who abandon him. Through him, shatter the pagan tyrants and slay the faithless and the hypocrites and all the pagans, wheresoever they may be in the earth's east and west, land and sea. Through him, fill the earth with justice, and through him make the religion of Your Prophet prevail, peace be to him and his Family.

وَ اجْعَلْنِي اللّٰهُمَّ مِنْ أَنْصَارِهِ وَ أَعْوَانِهِ،
وَ أَتْبَاعِهِ وَ شِيعَتِهِ، وَ أَرِنِي فِي آلِ مُحَمَّدٍ
مَا يَأْمُلُونَ، وَ فِي عَدُوِّهِمْ مَا يَحْذَرُونَ،
إِلَهَ الْحَقِّ آمِينَ!

Appoint me, O Allah, to be among his helpers and supporters, his adherents and followers. Let me see in the Family of Muḥammad what they hope for, and in their enemies what they are scared of, O God of the truth! Amen!

Conclusion

This chapter pertains to the *ziyārah* of the great prophets, may peace be to them, and that of the *Imāmzādahs* (descendants of the Imams of the Prophet's Family) as well as the *ziyārah* of the graves of the faithful, may Allah settle them in the Abode of Peace. It consists of three sections.

Section One
Ziyarah of the Great Prophets (ʿa)

It should be known that it is an obligation affirmed by human reason as well the Divine *sharīʿah* to revere the prophets, may peace be to them, and to hold them in high regard, without making any distinction between them:

لا نُفَرِّقُ بَيْنَ أَحَدٍ مِنْ رُسُلِهِ

> [The faithful declare,] 'We make no distinction between any of His apostles.'(2:285)

It is a commendable practice to perform their *ziyārah*, as expressly stated by the scholars. Although the number of those personage is very large, their known places of burial are few. The locations of their tombs, as can be pointed out offhand are as follows:

Prophet Adam (ʿ*a*) and Prophet Noah (ʿ*a*) are buried in the luminous shrine of the Commander of the Faithful (ʿ*a*); Prophet Abraham (ʿ*a*) is buried at the holy al-Khalīl, near Bayt al-Maqdis (Jerusalem); his wife Sarah and the prophets Isaac (ʿ*a*), Jacob (ʿ*a*) and Joseph (ʿ*a*) are also buried in his vicinity. Prophet Ishmael (ʿ*a*) and his mother Hagar (ʿ*a*) are buried in the Ḥijr (by the Holy Kaʿbah) in the Masjid al-Ḥarām, wherein are also graves of many prophets.

According to a report from Imam Muḥammad al-Bāqir (ʿ*a*), the area between the Rukn and the Maqām is filled with the graves of the prophets (ʿ*a*), and Imam Jaʿfar al-Ṣādiq (ʿ*a*) is reported to have said that seventy prophets are buried in the space between al-Rukn al-Yamānī and the Black Stone.

A number of prophets are buried at Bayt al-Maqdis, such as David (ᶜa), Soloman (ᶜa) and others, may peace be to all of them, and their tombs are well known among its residents. The tomb of Prophet Zechariah (ᶜa) is well known at Aleppo and there is a well-known shrine pertaining to Prophet Jonah (ᶜa) by the canal in Kūfah. The shrine of the prophets Hūd (ᶜa) and Ṣāliḥ (ᶜa) at Najaf Ashraf is famous. The tomb of the Prophet Dhu al-Kifl (ᶜa) by the Euphrates, at a distance of a few parasang from Kūfah is well known. The tomb of the Prophet Jirjīs (ᶜa) is in the city of Mosul and that of Shīth Hibat Allah is outside the town. At Shūsh is the tomb of the Prophet Daniel (ᶜa) and by the Mosque of Burāthah are the tombs of Joshua (ᶜa) and other prophets, may peace be to them all.

However, as for the manner of performing their *ziyārah*, we have not come across any particular relevant report excepting the *ziyārah* of Adam and Noah (ᶜa), which was mentioned in the chapter pertaining to the *ziyārah* of the Commander of the Faithful (ᶜa).

From the report related to the first Ziyārah Jāmiᶜah, cited in the related chapter (p. 520), it appears that one may also perform the *ziyārah* of the prophets (ᶜa) with the same text. That which supports such a conclusion is that the august shaykh Muḥammad b. al-Mashhadī in his *Mazār*, and the most august sayyid Ibn Ṭāwūs in *Miṣbāḥ al-Zā'ir* and other scholars, may Allah be pleased with them, have cited the same *ziyārah* for the shrine of the Prophet Jonah (ᶜa)[1] and it may be presumed that their citation is based on the general inference that can apparently be drawn from the said report.

In any case, it will be appropriate to recite that text for *ziyārah* of the holy shrines of the prophets (ᶜa). As it has already been mentioned before, there is no need to cite it again. Those who wish may refer to the first *ziyārah* of the chapter on Ziyārāt Jāmiᶜah (p. 520) and benefit from its great reward.

Section Two
Ziyarah of Imamzadahs (ʿa)

This section deals with the *ziyārah* of the illustrious descendents of the Imams (ᶜa) and those lofty personages whose shrines are founts of blessing and *barakah* for being foci of Divine mercy and attention. Leading scholars have expressly affirmed the *istiḥbāb* of the *ziyārah* of their tombs. Thanks to God, the Most High, their tombs exist in most of the Shīᶜīte towns and even in villages and around hills and valleys, where they serve as refuge for the helpless and the weary,

1 *Al-Mazār al-Kabīr*, 155, b 10.

and as solace for withering hearts and shelter for the oppressed, and so will they continue to be until the Day of Resurrection. Wonders and miraculous occurrences are known to occur in many of these shrines.

However, in order that one may be confident of obtaining a shrine's blessing or relief from one's affliction at an Imāmzadah's tomb, one should first confirm two things before deciding to make a journey and setting out for it. First, one should ascertain from sources dealing with *ḥadīth* and genealogy concerning the spiritual station and eminence of the personage buried at the shrine, as well as his/her illustrious lineage; second, ascertain the authenticity of attribution of the tomb to the personage in question. Cases where these two things can be ascertained are very few. We have mentioned some of them in our book *Hadīyat al-Zā'irīn* and made remarks about Muḥsin ibn al-Ḥusayn (ᶜa) in *Nafthat al- Maṣdūr* and *Muntaha al-Āmāl*. As this book does not have the scope for an elaborate treatment, we shall confine ourselves to a brief mention of two of those personages.

1. FATIMAH BINT MUSA IBN JA'FAR ('A)

The shrine of this august *sayyidah*, Fāṭimah bint Mūsā ibn Jaᶜfar (ᶜa), known as Maᶜṣūmah, may peace be to her, is situated in the holy city of Qum and is well known. The shrine has a sublime dome and *ḍarīḥ* and several courtyards and is served by a retinue of staff. Many endowments are associated with it. It is the apple of the eye of the people of Qum and a refuge for the generality of pilgrims.

Every year large numbers of people arrive here after making painstaking journeys from distant towns for the sake of obtaining the blessings of the *ziyārah* of that august lady, whose merit and high station is manifest from many reports.

Shaykh Ṣadūq cites a report[1] of Saᶜd b. Saᶜd with a '*ḥasan*' *iṣnād*, on a par with *ṣaḥīḥ*, from Imam ᶜAlī al-Riḍā (ᶜa) that when asked about Fāṭimah b. Mūsā b. Jaᶜfar (ᶜa) he replied that whoever visits her shrine will be admitted into paradise.

According to another report[2] with reliable *isnād*, Imam Muḥammad al-Taqī (ᶜa) said, "Whoever that performs the *ziyārah* of my aunt at Qum will be admitted into paradise."

[1] *Kāmil al-Ziyārāt*, 324, b 106, h 1; *Thawāb*, 98; *ᶜUyūn Akhbār al-Riḍā*, ii, 267, b 7, h 1; whence *Wasā'il*, xiv, 576, b 94, h 19850 & *Biḥār*, xcv, 265, b 1, h 1; lvii, 228, b 38, h 60; xlviii, 316.

[2] *Kāmil al-Ziyārāt*, 324, b 106, h 2; whence *Biḥār*, xcix, 265, b 1, h 3, xlviii, 316.

ᶜAllāmah Majlisī (*r*) cites a report[1] from some works on *ziyārah* from ᶜAlī b. Ibrāhīm from his father, from Saᶜd al-Aṣhᶜarī al-Qummī from Imam ᶜAlī al-Riḍā (*ᶜa*) that he told Saᶜd, "There is a tomb in your vicinage belonging to our family." When asked if he meant the grave of Fāṭimah daughter of Mūsā ibn Jaᶜfar, the Imam (*ᶜa*) replied, "Yes. Whoever visits her shrine with the knowledge of her right will be admitted into paradise. When you reach her tomb, stand at the head of the graveside facing the *qiblah* and say, *Allāhu akbar* 34 times, *Subḥānallāh* 33 times, and *Alḥamdu lillāh* 33 times. Then say,

اَلسَّــلَامُ عَلٰى آدَمَ صِفْوَةِ اللهِ، اَلسَّــلَامُ عَلٰى نُوحٍ نَبِيِّ اللهِ، اَلسَّلَامُ عَلٰى إِبْرَاهِيمَ خَلِيلِ اللهِ، اَلسَّــلَامُ عَلٰى مُوسَىٰ كَلِيمِ اللهِ، اَلسَّلَامُ عَلٰى عِيسَىٰ رُوحِ اللهِ،

Peace be to Adam, the chosen of Allah. Peace be to Noah, the prophet of Allah. Peace be to Abraham, the dedicated friend of Allah. Peace be to Moses, Allah's interlocutor. Peace be to Jesus, the spirit of Allah.

اَلسَّــلَامُ عَلَيْكَ يَا رَسُولَ اللهِ، اَلسَّلَامُ عَلَيْــكَ يَا خَــيْرَ خَلْقِ اللهِ، اَلسَّــلَامُ عَلَيْكَ يَا صَفِيَّ اللهِ، اَلسَّلَامُ عَلَيْكَ يَا مُحَمَّدَ بْنَ عَبْدِ اللهِ خَاتَمَ النَّبِيِّينَ،

Peace be to you, O Apostle of Allah! Peace be to you, O best of Allah's creation! Peace be to you, O chosen of Allah! Peace be to you, O Muḥammad ibn ᶜAbdillāh, the Seal of the Prophets!

اَلسَّــلَامُ عَلَيْكَ يَا أَمِيرَ الْمُؤْمِنِينَ عَلِيَّ بْنَ أَبِي طَالِبٍ وَصِيَّ رَسُولِ اللهِ، اَلسَّلَامُ عَلَيْكِ يَا فَاطِمَةُ سَيِّدَةَ نِسَاءِ الْعَالَمِينَ، اَلسَّلَامُ عَلَيْكُمَا يَا سِبْطَيْ نَبِيِّ الرَّحْمَةِ وَ سَيِّدَيْ شَبَابِ أَهْلِ الْجَنَّةِ،

Peace be to you, O ᶜAlī ibn Abī Ṭālib, the Commander of the Faithful and legatee of the Apostle of Allah! Peace be to you, O Fāṭimah, mistress of the world's womankind! Peace be to you, O grandsons of the Prophet of Mercy and doyens of the youth of paradise!

اَلسَّلَامُ عَلَيْكَ يَا عَلِيَّ بْنَ الْحُسَيْنِ سَيِّدَ الْعَابِدِينَ وَ قُرَّةَ عَيْنِ النَّاظِرِينَ، اَلسَّلَامُ

Peace be to you, O ᶜAli ibn al-Ḥusayn, the foremost of the devout and the delight of the

[1] *Biḥār*, xlviii, 316, xcix, 265, b 1, h 3 & *Mustadrak*, x, 368, b 74, h 12198/3.

عَلَيْكَ يا مُحَمَّدَ بْنَ عَلِيٍّ بَاقِرَ الْعِلْمِ بَعْدَ النَّبِيِّ، اَلسَّلامُ عَلَيْكَ يا جَعْفَرَ بْنَ مُحَمَّدٍ الصَّادِقَ الْبَارَّ الْأَمِينَ،

onlookers! Peace be to you, O Muḥammad ibn ʿAlī, the exponent of knowledge after the Prophet! Peace be to you, O Jaʿfar ibn Muḥammad, the truthful, pious and trustworthy Imam!

اَلسَّلامُ عَلَيْكَ يا مُوسَى بْنَ جَعْفَرٍ الطَّاهِرَ الطُّهْرَ، اَلسَّلامُ عَلَيْكَ يا عَلِيَّ بْنَ مُوسَى الرِّضَا الْمُرْتَضَى، اَلسَّلامُ عَلَيْكَ يا مُحَمَّدَ بْنَ عَلِيٍّ التَّقِيَّ،

Peace be to you, O Mūsā ibn Jaʿfar, the pure and immaculate one! Peace be to you, O ʿAlī ibn Mūsā al-Riḍā, the approved one! Peace be to you, O Muḥammad ibn ʿAlī, the Godwary!

اَلسَّلامُ عَلَيْكَ يا عَلِيَّ بْنَ مُحَمَّدٍ النَّقِيَّ النَّاصِحَ الْأَمِينَ، اَلسَّلامُ عَلَيْكَ يا حَسَنَ بْنَ عَلِيٍّ،

Peace be to you, O ʿAlī ibn Muḥammad, the pure one and the trustworthy advisor! Peace be to you, O Ḥasan ibn ʿAlī!

اَلسَّلامُ عَلَى الْوَصِيِّ مِنْ بَعْدِهِ. اَللّٰهُمَّ صَلِّ عَلىٰ نُورِكَ وَ سِرَاجِكَ، وَ وَلِيِّ وَلِيِّكَ وَ وَصِيِّ وَصِيِّكَ، وَ حُجَّتِكَ عَلىٰ خَلْقِكَ.

Peace be to the legatee after him! O Allah, bless Your light and lamp, the *walī* of Your *walī*, the legatee of Your legatee and Your testament to Your creation!

اَلسَّلامُ عَلَيْكِ يا بِنْتَ رَسُولِ اللهِ، اَلسَّلامُ عَلَيْكِ يا بِنْتَ فَاطِمَةَ وَ خَدِيجَةَ، اَلسَّلامُ عَلَيْكِ يا بِنْتَ أَمِيرِ الْمُؤْمِنِينَ، اَلسَّلامُ عَلَيْكِ يا بِنْتَ الْحَسَنِ وَ الْحُسَيْنِ، اَلسَّلامُ عَلَيْكِ يا بِنْتَ وَلِيِّ اللهِ، اَلسَّلامُ عَلَيْكِ يا أُخْتَ وَلِيِّ اللهِ، اَلسَّلامُ عَلَيْكِ يا عَمَّةَ وَلِيِّ اللهِ، اَلسَّلامُ عَلَيْكِ يا بِنْتَ

Peace be to you, O daughter of the Apostle of Allah! Peace be to you, O daughter of Fāṭimah and Khadījah! Peace be to you, O daughter of the Commander of the Faithful! Peace be to you, O daughter of al-Ḥasan and al-Ḥusayn! Peace be to you, O daughter of Allah's *walī*! Peace be to you, O sister of Allah's *walī*! Peace be to you, O aunt of Allah's *walī*! Peace be to you, O daughter of Mūsā ibn Jaʿfar, and may Allah's mercy and His bounties be

مُوسَى بْـنِ جَعْفَرٍ وَ رَحْمَةُ اللهِ وَ بَرَكَاتُهُ،

upon you!

اَلسَّلَامُ عَلَيْكِ عَرَّفَ اللهُ بَيْنَنَا وَ بَيْنَكُمْ فِي الْجَنَّةِ، وَ حَشَرَنَا فِي زُمْرَتِكُمْ، وَ أَوْرَدَنَا حَوْضَ نَبِيِّكُمْ، وَ سَقَانَا بِكَأْسِ جَدِّكُمْ مِنْ يَدِ عَلِيِّ بْنِ أَبِي طَالِبٍ، صَلَوَاتُ اللهِ عَلَيْكُمْ.

Peace be to you, may Allah acquaint us with you in paradise and gather us in your fold and admit us at the Pool of your Prophet and give us to drink from the cup of your ancestor, by the hand of ʿAlī ibn Abī Ṭālib! May Allah's blessings be upon you.

أَسْأَلُ اللهَ أَنْ يُرِيَنَا فِيكُمُ السُّرُورَ وَ الْفَرَجَ، وَ أَنْ يَجْمَعَنَا وَ إِيَّاكُمْ فِي زُمْرَةِ جَدِّكُمْ مُحَمَّدٍ صَلَّى اللهُ عَلَيْهِ وَ آلِهِ، وَ أَنْ لَا يَسْلُبَنَا مَعْرِفَتَكُمْ، إِنَّهُ وَلِيٌّ قَدِيرٌ.

I beseech Allah to enable us to find delight and relief in you and to gather us and you in the fold of your ancestor, Muḥammad, may Allah bless him and his Family, and not to divest us of your knowledge. Indeed, He is the all-powerful guardian.

أَتَقَرَّبُ إِلَى اللهِ بِحُبِّكُمْ، وَ الْبَرَاءَةِ مِنْ أَعْدَائِكُمْ، وَ التَّسْلِيمِ إِلَى اللهِ رَاضِيًا بِهِ، غَيْرَ مُنْكِرٍ وَ لَا مُسْتَكْبِرٍ، وَ عَلَى يَقِينِ مَا أَتَى بِهِ مُحَمَّدٌ وَ بِهِ رَاضٍ، نَطْلُبُ بِذَلِكَ وَجْهَكَ يَا سَيِّدِي، اَللّٰهُمَّ وَ رِضَاكَ وَ الدَّارَ الْآخِرَةَ، يَا فَاطِمَةُ اشْفَعِي لِي فِي الْجَنَّةِ، فَإِنَّ لَكِ عِنْدَ اللهِ شَأْنًا مِنَ الشَّأْنِ.

I seek nearness to Allah through my love for you and my repudiation of your enemies, through my submission to Allah out of compliance to Him, without denial and defiance, and through my conviction in the teachings brought by Muḥammad, being satisfied and pleased with them, and with that I seek, my Master, Your pleasure, O Allah, Your approval and the abode of the Hereafter! O Fāṭimah, intercede for my admittance into paradise, for you have an eminent station with Allah!

اَللّٰهُمَّ إِنِّي أَسْأَلُكَ أَنْ تَخْتِمَ لِي بِالسَّعَادَةِ، فَلَا تَسْلُبْ مِنِّي مَا أَنَا فِيهِ، وَ لَا حَوْلَ

O Allah, I beseech You to conclude my life with felicity, so do not take away from me what (faith) I presently possess. There

وَ لا قُوَّةَ إِلَّا بِاللهِ الْعَلِيِّ الْعَظِيمِ.

is no power or force except what derives from Allah, the All-exalted and the All-supreme!

اَللّٰهُمَّ اسْتَجِبْ لَنَا، وَ تَقَبَّلْهُ بِكَرَمِكَ وَ عِزَّتِكَ، وَ بِرَحْمَتِكَ وَ عَافِيَتِكَ، وَ صَلَّى اللهُ عَلىٰ مُحَمَّدٍ وَ آلِهِ أَجْمَعِينَ، وَ سَلَّمَ تَسْلِيمًا يَا أَرْحَمَ الرَّاحِمِينَ!

O Allah, answer our petitions and accept our devotions, by Your generosity, might, mercy, and Your grace of well-being. O Allah bless Muḥammad and all his Family and greet them with the worthiest of greetings! O Most Merciful of the merciful!

2. Sayyid ʻAbd al-ʻAzim al-Ḥasani (ʻa)

The noble lineage of the venerable Imāmzadah ᶜAbd al-ᶜAẓīm reaches, through a chain of four ancestors, Imam al-Ḥasan al-Mujtabā (*ᶜa*), the great grandson of the Best of the Creatures, the Apostle of Allah (*ṣ*). He is ᶜAbd al-ᶜAẓīm, son of ᶜAbd Allāh, son of ᶜAlī, son of al-Ḥasan, son of Zayd, son of al-Ḥasan ibn ᶜAlī ibn Abī Ṭālib, may peace be upon him. His noble tomb at Ray is well-known, being the refuge of the generality of people.

His high station and eminence is quite manifest, as besides being a descendent of the Seal of the Prophets (*ᶜa*), he was one of the leading scholars of *ḥadīth*, eminent among the learned and distinguished for his piety, worship and saintliness. He was one of the companions of the Imams Muḥammad al-Jawād (*ᶜa*) and ᶜAlī al-Hādī (*ᶜa*) and was extremely devoted to them.

He has narrated many traditions from them and is the author of a compilation of the sermons of the Commander of the Faithful (*ᶜa*), *Khuṭab Amīr al-Mu'minīn*, and a *Kitāb Yawm wa Laylah*. He was the one who presented his creed before Imam ᶜAlī al-Hādī (*ᶜa*), the Imam of his era, and the Imam, while confirming it, said to him,

يَا أَبَا الْقَاسِمِ هٰذَا وَ اللهِ دِينُ اللهِ الَّذِي ارْتَضَاهُ لِعِبَادِهِ، فَاثْبُتْ عَلَيْهِ، ثَبَّتَكَ اللهُ بِالْقَوْلِ الثَّابِتِ فِي الدُّنْيَا وَ الْآخِرَةِ.

> O Abū al-Qāsim, by God, this is the religion of God which He has approved for His servants. Hold on to it firmly, may God strengthen you with an immutable belief in this world and Hereafter.

Ṣāḥib b. ᶜAbbād has written a short biographical treatise about him, from which our teacher, the late Thiqat al-Islām Nūrī, has cited at the end of the *Mustadrak*.[1] It is mentioned there, as also in Najāshī's *Rijāl*, that Ḥaḍrat ᶜAbd al-ᶜAẓīm fled due to the fear of the ruler of his time, moving on from one town to another in the guise of a messenger, until he reached Ray where he hid, according to Najāshī's account, in the basement of a house belonging to a Shīᶜah man in Sikkat al-Mawālī. There he used to worship God, fasting during days and praying at nights. He used to visit a tomb, which now lies opposite his own grave on the other side of the road that lies between them, and he would say that it belonged to one of the descendants of Imam Mūsā ibn Jaᶜfar (*ᶜa*). He continued to take refuge in that basement until, one after another, most of the Shīᶜīs came to know about him.

One of the Shīᶜīs saw the Apostle of Allah in a dream. "A man from among my descendants will be carried from Sikkat al-Mawālī and buried near the apple tree in the orchard belonging to ᶜAbd al-Jabbār b. ᶜAbd al-Wahhāb," the Prophet (ṣ) told him, and pointed to the spot where the grave was to be dug. When the man went to buy the plot of land from its owner, he asked him, "Why do you want to buy that tree and the land where it stands?" He related the dream for him. The owner of the land had also seen a similar dream, whereat he made an endowment of the land where the tree stood as well as the entire orchard for that sayyid and as a graveyard for the Shīᶜah.

Then ᶜAbd al-ᶜAẓīm fell ill and died. When his clothes were taken off for the body to be washed, they found in his pocket a note on which he had written his genealogy. It read, "I am Abū al-Qāsim ᶜAbd al-ᶜAẓīm, son of ᶜAbd Allāh, son of ᶜAlī, son of al-Ḥasan, son of Zayd, son of al-Ḥasan ibn ᶜAlī ibn Abī Ṭālib, may peace be upon them."[2]

Concerning his learning, Ṣāḥib b. ᶜAbbād cites a report of Abū Turāb al-Rūyānī from Abū Ḥammād al-Rāzī that he said, I met Imam ᶜAlī ibn Muḥammad al-Naqī (*ᶜa*) at Sāmarrā and asked him certain questions concerning the lawful and the unlawful. He answered my questions and when I bade him farewell he said to me, 'O Abū Ḥammād, when you have any problem in your region concerning any matter of your religion, ask ᶜAbd al-ᶜAẓīm concerning it and convey to him *salām* on my behalf'"[3]

Muḥaqqiq Mīr Dāmād writes in the *Rawāshiḥ* that there are many reports concerning the virtues of the *ziyārah* of ᶜAbd al-ᶜAẓīm and it is narrated that paradise is obligatory for those who perform the

1 *Mustadrak*, xvii, 321, b 11, h 21470/32, from Ṣāḥib's *Risālah*.

2 Najāshī's *Rijāl*, no. 653, p. 348, whence *Biḥār*, xcix, 368, b 2, h 3.

3 *Mustadrak*, xvii, 321, b 11, h 21470/32, from Ṣāḥib's *Risālah*.

ziyārah of his shrine. Shahīd Thānī has cited the same report in his gloss on the *Khulāṣah* from some scholars of genealogy (*ansāb*). Ibn Bābawayh and Ibn Qūlawayh report with a reliable *isnād* that when a man from Ray met Imam ʿAlī al-Naqī (ʿ*a*), the Imam asked him where he had been. He replied that he had gone for the *ziyārah* of Imam Ḥusayn (ʿ*a*). The Imam told him that had he visited the tomb of ʿAbd al-ʿAẓīm, which was in the vicinity of his home, it would have been like performing the *ziyārah* of Imam Ḥusayn (ʿ*a*).[1]

The scholars have not reported any text for the *ziyārah* of this personage, except that Fakhr al-Muḥaqqiqīn Āqā Jamāl al-Dīn has written in his work on *mazār* that it is appropriate to say the following while performing his *ziyārah*.

Peace be to Adam, the chosen of Allah. Peace be to Noah, the prophet of Allah. Peace be to Abraham, the dedicated friend of Allah. Peace be to Moses, Allah's interlocutor. Peace be to Jesus, the spirit of Allah.	اَلسَّلَامُ عَلَىٰ آدَمَ صِفْوَةِ اللهِ، اَلسَّلَامُ عَلَىٰ نُوحٍ نَبِيِّ اللهِ، اَلسَّلَامُ عَلَىٰ إِبْرَاهِيمَ خَلِيلِ اللهِ، اَلسَّلَامُ عَلَىٰ مُوسَىٰ كَلِيمِ اللهِ، اَلسَّلَامُ عَلَىٰ عِيسَىٰ رُوحِ اللهِ،
Peace be to you, O Apostle of Allah! Peace be to you, O best of Allah's creation! Peace be to you, O chosen of Allah! Peace be to you, O Muḥammad ibn ʿAbd Allāh, the Seal of the Prophets!	اَلسَّلَامُ عَلَيْكَ يَا رَسُولَ اللهِ، اَلسَّلَامُ عَلَيْكَ يَا خَيْرَ خَلْقِ اللهِ، اَلسَّلَامُ عَلَيْكَ يَا صَفِيَّ اللهِ، اَلسَّلَامُ عَلَيْكَ يَا مُحَمَّدَ بْنَ عَبْدِ اللهِ خَاتَمَ النَّبِيِّينَ،
Peace be to you, O ʿAlī ibn Abī Ṭālib, the Commander of the Faithful and legatee of the Apostle of Allah! Peace be to you, O Fāṭimah, mistress of the world's womankind! Peace be to you, O grand-sons of the Prophet of Mercy and doyens of the youth of paradise	اَلسَّلَامُ عَلَيْكَ يَا أَمِيرَ الْمُؤْمِنِينَ عَلِيَّ بْنَ أَبِي طَالِبٍ وَصِيَّ رَسُولِ اللهِ، اَلسَّلَامُ عَلَيْكِ يَا فَاطِمَةُ سَيِّدَةَ نِسَاءِ الْعَالَمِينَ، اَلسَّلَامُ عَلَيْكُمَا يَا سِبْطَيِ الرَّحْمَةِ، وَ سَيِّدَيْ شَبَابِ أَهْلِ الْجَنَّةِ،

[1] *Kāmil al-Ziyārāt*, 324, b 107, h 1 & *Thawāb*, 99, whence *Wasāʾil*, xiv, 575, b 93, h 19849 & *Biḥār*, xcix, 368, b 2, h 1, 2.

Peace be to you, O ᶜAli ibn al-Ḥusayn, the foremost of the devout and delight of the onlookers! Peace be to you, O Muḥammad ibn ᶜAlī, the exponent of knowledge after the Prophet! Peace be to you, O Jaᶜfar ibn Muḥammad, the truthful, pious and trustworthy one!

اَلسَّـــلامُ عَلَيْكَ يا عَلِيَّ بْنَ الْحُسَيْنِ
سَيِّدَ الْعَابِدِينَ وَ قُرَّةَ عَيْنِ النَّاظِرِينَ،
اَلسَّلامُ عَلَيْكَ يا مُحَمَّدَ بْنَ عَلِيٍّ بَاقِرَ
الْعِلْمِ بَعْدَ النَّبِيِّ، اَلسَّـــلامُ عَلَيْكَ يا
جَعْفَرَ بْنَ مُحَمَّدٍ الصَّادِقَ الْبَارَّ الْأَمِينَ

Peace be to you, O Mūsā ibn Jaᶜfar, the pure and immaculate one! Peace be to you, O ᶜAlī ibn Mūsā, al-Riḍā, the approved one! Peace be to you, O Muḥammad ibn ᶜAlī, the Godwary!

اَلسَّـــلامُ عَلَيْكَ يا مُوسَى بْنَ جَعْفَرٍ
الطَّاهِرَ الطُّهْرَ، اَلسَّلامُ عَلَيْكَ يا عَلِيَّ
بْنَ مُوسَى الرِّضَا الْمُرْتَضَى، اَلسَّـــلامُ
عَلَيْكَ يا مُحَمَّدَ بْنَ عَلِيٍّ التَّقِيِّ،

Peace be to you, O ᶜAlī ibn Muḥammad, the pure one and the trustworthy advisor! Peace be to you, O Ḥasan ibn ᶜAlī!

اَلسَّلامُ عَلَيْكَ يا عَلِيَّ بْنَ مُحَمَّدٍ النَّقِيَّ
النَّاصِحَ الْأَمِينَ، اَلسَّـــلامُ عَلَيْكَ يا
حَسَنَ بْنَ عَلِيٍّ،

Peace be to the legatee after him! O Allah, bless Your light and lamp, the *walī* of Your *walī*, the legatee of Your legatee and Your testament to Your creation!

اَلسَّـــلامُ عَلَى الْوَصِيِّ مِنْ بَعْدِهِ، اَللّٰهُمَّ
صَـــلِّ عَلٰى نُـــورِكَ وَ سِرَاجِكَ، وَ وَلِيِّ
وَلِيِّكَ وَ وَصِيِّ وَصِيِّـــكَ، وَ حُجَّتِكَ
عَلٰى خَلْقِكَ،

Peace be to you, O blameless sayyid and the immaculate and chosen one! Peace be to you, O son of the immaculate chiefs! Peace be to you, O son of the chosen ones and the elect!

اَلسَّـــلامُ عَلَيْكَ أَيُّهَا السَّيِّدُ الزَّكِيُّ وَ
الطَّاهِـــرُ الصَّفِيُّ، اَلسَّـــلامُ عَلَيْكَ يا
ابْنَ السَّادَةِ الْأَطْهَارِ، اَلسَّلامُ عَلَيْكَ
يا ابْنَ الْمُصْطَفَيْنَ الْأَخْيَارِ،

اَلسَّلَامُ عَلَىٰ رَسُولِ اللهِ وَ عَلَىٰ ذُرِّيَّةِ رَسُولِ اللهِ وَ رَحْمَةُ اللهِ وَ بَرَكَاتُهُ،

Peace be to the Apostle of Allah and the descendants of the Apostle of Allah, and may Allah's mercy and His bounties be upon them!

اَلسَّلَامُ عَلَى الْعَبْدِ الصَّالِحِ، اَلْمُطِيعِ لِلَّهِ رَبِّ الْعَالَمِينَ، وَ لِرَسُولِهِ وَ لِأَمِيرِ الْمُؤْمِنِينَ، اَلسَّلَامُ عَلَيْكَ يَا أَبَا الْقَاسِمِ، ابْنَ السِّبْطِ الْمُنْتَجَبِ الْمُجْتَبَىٰ، اَلسَّلَامُ عَلَيْكَ يَا مَنْ بِزِيَارَتِهِ ثَوَابُ زِيَارَةِ سَيِّدِ الشُّهَدَاءِ يُرْتَجَىٰ،

Peace be to you, God's righteous servant, who were obedient to Allah, the Lord of the worlds, and to His Apostle and the Commander of the Faithful. O Abul Qāsim, son of al-Mujtabā, the Prophet's grandson, the chosen one. Peace be to you, whose *ziyārah* is expected to bring the reward of the *ziyārah* of the Doyen of the Martyrs!

السَّلَامُ عَلَيْكَ عَرَّفَ اللهُ بَيْنَنَا وَ بَيْنَكُمْ فِي الْجَنَّةِ، وَ حَشَرَنَا فِي زُمْرَتِكُمْ، وَ أَوْرَدَنَا حَوْضَ نَبِيِّكُمْ، وَ سَقَانَا بِكَأْسِ جَدِّكُمْ مِنْ يَدِ عَلِيِّ بْنِ أَبِي طَالِبٍ، صَلَوَاتُ اللهِ عَلَيْكُمْ،

Peace be to you, may Allah acquaint us with you in paradise and gather us in your fold and admit us at the Pool of your Prophet and give us to drink from the cup of your ancestor, by the hand of ʿAlī ibn Abī Ṭālib! May Allah's blessings be upon you.

أَسْأَلُ اللهَ أَنْ يُرِيَنَا فِيكُمُ السُّرُورَ وَ الْفَرَجَ، وَ أَنْ يَجْمَعَنَا وَ إِيَّاكُمْ فِي زُمْرَةِ جَدِّكُمْ مُحَمَّدٍ صَلَّى اللهُ عَلَيْهِ وَ آلِهِ، وَ أَنْ لَا يَسْلُبَنَا مَعْرِفَتَكُمْ، إِنَّهُ وَلِيٌّ قَدِيرٌ.

I beseech Allah to enable us to find delight and relief in you and to gather us and you in the fold of your ancestor, Muḥammad, may Allah bless him and his Family, and not to divest us of your knowledge. Indeed He is the all-powerful guardian.

أَتَقَرَّبُ إِلَى اللهِ بِحُبِّكُمْ، وَ الْبَرَاءَةِ مِنْ أَعْدَائِكُمْ، وَ التَّسْلِيمِ إِلَى اللهِ رَاضِيًا بِهِ، غَيْرَ مُنْكِرٍ وَ لَا مُسْتَكْبِرٍ، وَ عَلَىٰ

I seek nearness to Allah through my love for you and my repudiation of your enemies, through my submission to Allah out of compliance to Him, without denial and defiance, and through my con-

يَقِينِ مَا أَتَى بِهِ مُحَمَّدٌ، نَطْلُبُ بِذَلِكَ وَجْهَكَ يَا سَيِّدِى. اَللّٰهُمَّ وَ رِضَاكَ وَ الدَّارَ الْآخِرَةَ، يَا سَيِّدِى وَ ابْنَ سَيِّدِى، اِشْفَعْ لِى فِى الْجَنَّةِ، فَإِنَّ لَكَ عِنْدَ اللّٰهِ شَأْنًا مِنَ الشَّأْنِ.

viction in the teachings brought by Muḥammad, being satisfied and pleased with them, and with that I seek Your pleasure, my Master, O Allah, I seek Your approval and the abode of the Hereafter. O master, son of my master, intercede for my admittance into paradise, for you have an eminent station with Allah!

اَللّٰهُمَّ إِنِّى أَسْأَلُكَ أَنْ تَخْتِمَ لِى بِالسَّعَادَةِ، فَلا تَسْلُبْ مِنِّى مَا أَنَا فِيهِ، وَ لَا حَوْلَ وَ لَا قُوَّةَ إِلا بِاللّٰهِ الْعَلِيِّ الْعَظِيمِ.

O Allah, I beseech You to conclude my life with felicity. So do not take away from me what (faith) I presently possess. There is no power or force except what derives from Allah, the All-exalted and the All-great!

اَللّٰهُمَّ اسْتَجِبْ لَنَا، وَ تَقَبَّلْهُ بِكَرَمِكَ وَ عِزَّتِكَ، وَ بِرَحْمَتِكَ وَ عَافِيَتِكَ، وَ صَلَّى اللّٰهُ عَلَىٰ مُحَمَّدٍ وَ آلِهِ أَجْمَعِينَ، وَ سَلَّمَ تَسْلِيمًا يَا أَرْحَمَ الرَّاحِمِينَ!

O Allah, answer our petitions and accept our devotions, by Your generosity and Your might, Your mercy, and Your grace of well-being. O Allah, bless Muḥammad and his Family and greet them with the worthiest of greetings! O Most Merciful of the merciful!

The aforementioned writer adds that according to some reports during the period the Imāmzādah ᶜAbd al-ᶜAẓīm dwelt in hiding in Ray, he would often emerge to visit the tomb that now stands facing his own on the other side of the road. He used to say that it is the grave of a man from among the descendants of Imam Mūsā ibn Jaᶜfar (*ᶜa*). Presently, there is a tomb there which is attributed to the Imāmzādah Ḥamzah, a son of Imam Mūsā al-Kāẓim (*ᶜa*). Apparently, it is the same tomb which was visited by Imāmzādah ᶜAbd al-ᶜAẓīm. One should also visit his shrine and recite there the same *ziyārah*, omitting the words *Assalāmu ᶜalayka yâ Abal Qāsimibnas sibṭil muntajabil Mujtabā.*

There is a grave in the courtyard of the Imāmzādah Ḥamzah's shrine belonging to the august shaykh Jamāl al-Dīn Abū al-Futūḥ Ḥusayn b. ᶜAlī al-Khuzāᶜī (*r*) author of the famous exegesis of the

Qur'ān and a leading figure among Qur'ān commentators. His tomb should also be visited, and one should not forget to visit the tomb of Shaykh Ṣadūq, known as Ibn Bābawayh, the chief of the *muḥaddith-ūn*, which is in the vicinity of the shrine of Shāh ᶜAbd al-ᶜAẓīm.

Section Three

Ziyarah of the Graves of the Faithful

The trustworthy traditionist and venerable Shaykh Jaᶜfar b. Qūl-awayh reports on the authority of ᶜAmr b. ᶜUthmān that he heard Imam Abū al-Ḥasan Mūsā ibn Jaᶜfar (*ᶜa*) say, "Those who do not have the ability to visit us, let them visit the righteous from among our friends (*mawālī*) so that the reward (*thawāb*) of having visited us is written for them, and let those who do not have access to us show kindness and benevolence towards the righteous among our friends so that a reward of having been kind to us is written for them."[1]

He also cites a report[2] with *ṣaḥīḥ isnād* from Muḥammad b. Aḥmad b. Yaḥyā al-Ashᶜarī that he said, "I was with ᶜAlī b. Bilāl at Fayd—a place on the way to Makkah—and as we were walking together towards the grave of Muḥammad b. Ismāᶜīl b. Bazīᶜ, ᶜAlī b. Bilāl said to me, 'The person who is buried here related to me from Imam ᶜAlī al-Riḍā (*ᶜa*) that he said, "When someone approaches the grave of his faithful brother and, with his hand placed on the grave, recites the Sūrat al-Qadr seven times, he will be safe on the Day of greatest terror," implying safety from the terrors of the Day of Resurrection.

Another report[3] has a similar text except that it adds that one should be facing the *qiblah*. The 'safety' mentioned in the above-mentioned report may refer either to someone who recites the *sūrah* at the grave—as is apparent from its literal meaning—or it may pertain to the dead person who is visited, as indicated by the report cited below from Sayyid Ibn Ṭāwūs.

Another report[4] is cited in *Kāmil al-Ziyārāt* on the authority of ᶜAbd

[1] *Kāmil al-Ziyārāt*, 319, b 105, h 1, whence *Biḥār*, xcix, 295, b 6, h 1.

[2] *Kāfī*, iii, 229, h 9, whence *Wasā'il*, iii, 226, b 57, h 3475. *Kāmil al-Ziyārāt*, 319, b 105, h 3, whence *Biḥār*, xcix, 295, b 6, h 3 & *Mustadrak*, ii, 371, b 48, h 2218/2. Mufīd's *Mazār*, 217, b 27, h 2. *Tahdhīb*, i, 104, b 49, h1.

[3] *Kāmil al-Ziyārāt*, 320, b 105, h 4.

[4] *Kāfī*, iii, 200, h 3, whence *Wasā'il*, iii, 198, b 33, h 3398. *Kāmil al-Ziyārāt*, 320, b 105, h 5, whence *Biḥār*, xcix, 295, b 6, h 5 & *Mustadrak*, ii, 370, b 48, h 2217/1. *Tahdhīb*, i, 462, b 23, h153, vi, 105, b 50, h 2. Mufīd's *Mazār*, 219, b 28, h 2. *Da ᶜawāt*, 271, h 774.

al-Raḥmān b. Abī ᶜAbd Allāh from Imam Jaᶜfar al-Ṣādiq (ᶜ*a*) wherein he asks the Imam concerning the manner one should place one's hand on a Muslim's grave. The Imam pointed at the ground and laid his hand on it, as he faced the *qiblah*.

According to a report[1] with *ṣaḥīḥ isnād*, Imam Jaᶜfar al-Ṣādiq (ᶜ*a*) when asked about the manner one should greet the dead, told ᶜAbd Allāh b Sinān to say,

Peace be to the people of this abode from among the faithful and Muslims. You have gone ahead of us and we too, God willing, shall join you!	السَّلامُ عَلىٰ أَهْلِ الدِّيَارِ مِنَ الْمُؤْمِنِينَ وَ الْمُسْلِمِينَ، أَنْتُمْ لَنَا فَرَطٌ وَ نَحْنُ إِنْ شَاءَ اللهُ بِكُمْ لاٰحِقُونَ!

According to another report,[2] Imam Ḥusayn (ᶜ*a*) said that when someone says the following on entering a graveyard, God Almighty writes for him good deeds equal in number to the creatures that have and will live since Adam until the Day of Resurrection.

O Allah, Lord of these ephemeral spirits, decayed bodies and worm-eaten bones, which departed from the world with faith in You! Grant them repose and refreshment from Yourself and give them *salām* on my behalf!	اللّٰهُمَّ رَبَّ هَذِهِ الْأَرْوَاحِ الْفَانِيَةِ، وَ الْأَجْسَادِ الْبَالِيَةِ، وَ الْعِظَامِ النَّخِرَةِ الَّتِي خَرَجَتْ مِنَ الدُّنْيَا وَ هِيَ بِكَ مُؤْمِنَةٌ، أَدْخِلْ عَلَيْهِمْ رَوْحًا مِنْكَ وَ سَلامًا مِنِّي.

The Commander of the Faithful (ᶜ*a*) is reported[3] to have said that for those who recite the following supplication on entering a graveyard, God Almighty writes a reward of fifty years of worship and wipes away fifty years' of their sins, as well as those of their parents.

In the Name of Allah, the All-beneficent, the All-merciful. Peace be to the votaries of 'There is no god except Allah,' on behalf of the	بِسْمِ اللهِ الرَّحْمَٰنِ الرَّحِيمِ، السَّلامُ عَلىٰ أَهْلِ لاٰ إِلَٰهَ إِلَّا اللهُ، مِنْ أَهْلِ لاٰ إِلَٰهَ إِلَّا

1 *Kāfī*, iii, 229, h 5, whence *Wasā'il*, iii, 225, b 56, h 3470. *Kāmil al-Ziyārāt*, 321, b 105, h 9, whence *Biḥār*, xcix, 297, b 6, h 12 & *Mustadrak*, ii, 365, b 47, h 2205/1.

2 *Sharḥ Nahj al-Balāghah*, vi, 192. *Biḥār*, xcix, 300, b 6, h 31 whence *Mustadrak*, ii, 373, b 49, h 2223/3.

3 *Biḥār*, xcix, 301, b 6, h 31, whence *Mustadrak*, ii, 369, b 47, h 2215/11.

اللّٰهُ،

votaries of 'There is no god except Allah'!

يَا أَهْلَ لَا إِلٰهَ إِلَّا اللّٰهُ، بِحَقِّ لَا إِلٰهَ إِلَّا اللّٰهُ، كَيْفَ وَجَدْتُمْ قَوْلَ لَا إِلٰهَ إِلَّا اللّٰهُ مِنْ لَا إِلٰهَ إِلَّا اللّٰهُ؟

O votaries of 'There is no god except Allah,' how did you find the belief 'There is no god except Allah' with Allah, besides whom there is no god?

يَا لَا إِلٰهَ إِلَّا اللّٰهُ، بِحَقِّ لَا إِلٰهَ إِلَّا اللّٰهُ، اِغْفِرْ لِمَنْ قَالَ لَا إِلٰهَ إِلَّا اللّٰهُ، وَ احْشُرْنَا فِي زُمْرَةِ مَنْ قَالَ لَا إِلٰهَ إِلَّا اللّٰهُ، مُحَمَّدٌ رَسُولُ اللّٰهِ، عَلِيٌّ وَلِيُّ اللّٰهِ!

O Allah, except whom there is no god, for the sake of 'There is no god except Allah,' forgive those who say 'There is no god except Allah,' and resurrect us in the fold of those who say, 'There is no god except Allah, Muḥammad is the Apostle of Allah and ᶜAlī is the *walī* of Allah'!

According to another report,[1] an appropriate thing to say while passing through a graveyard is to stand and say,

اللّٰهُمَّ وَلِّهِمْ مَا تَوَلَّوْا، وَ احْشُرْهُمْ مَعَ مَنْ أَحَبُّوا.

O Allah, take them on the path that they went and gather them (at Resurrection) with those whom they loved!

Sayyid Ibn Ṭāwūs writes[2] in *Miṣbāḥ al-Zā'ir* that when one intends to visit the graves of the faithful, it is preferable to do so on Thursday, although one may do it whenever one wishes. The manner of their *ziyārah* is to place one's hand on the grave while facing in the direction of the *qiblah* and to say,

اللّٰهُمَّ ارْحَمْ غُرْبَتَهُ، وَ صِلْ وَحْدَتَهُ، وَ آنِسْ وَحْشَتَهُ، وَ آمِنْ رَوْعَتَهُ، وَ أَسْكِنْ إِلَيْهِ مِنْ رَحْمَتِكَ رَحْمَةً يَسْتَغْنِي بِهَا عَنْ رَحْمَةِ

O Allah, have mercy on his isolation, remove his solitariness, be his solace in his loneliness, appease his fear and comfort him with Your mercy, a mercy whereby he will

1 *Biḥār*, xcix, 301, b 6, h 32, whence *Mustadrak*, ii, 373, b 49, h 2224/24.

2 *Kāfī*, iii, 229, h 6. *Kāmil al-Ziyārāt*, 321, b 105, h 10, whence *Biḥār*, xcix, 295, b 6, h 1. Mufīd's *Mazār*, 218, b 28. *Tahdhīb*, vi, 105, b 50, h 1, whence *Wasā'il*, xiv, 591, b 101, h 19882. *Daᶜawāt*, 271, h 773. *Jamāl*, 180. *Biḥār*, xcix, 299, b 6, h 25, from *Miṣbāḥ al-Zā'ir*.

مَنْ سِوَاكَ، وَ أَلْحِقْهُ بِمَنْ كَانَ يَتَوَلَّاهُ.

not need anyone else's mercy, and join him with those whom he used to befriend and follow!

Then recite Sūrat al-Qadr seven times.

There is another report[1] concerning the virtues of performing the *ziyārah* of the faithful and the reward of it, narrated by Fuḍayl, wherein it is said that when someone recites Sūrat al-Qadr seven times by the graveside of a faithful person God Almighty sends an angel to his grave to worship God by his graveside and He writes the reward of that worship for the deceased person. On rising from his grave at Resurrection he will not encounter any of the horrors of the Day of Resurrection without God Almighty turning away that horror from him on account of that angel until he is admitted by God into paradise.

However, along with reciting Sūrat al-Qadr seven times, one should also recite the sūrahs al-Fātiḥah, al-Falaq, al-Nās and al-Tawḥīd, as well as the Throne Verse (2:255), three times each.

The virtues of the *ziyārah* of the faithful are also mentioned in a report of Muḥammad b. Muslim from Imam Jaʿfar al-Ṣādiq (ʿ*a*).[2] Muḥammad b. Muslim says, "I asked the Imam if we should visit the dead. 'Of course,' he replied. I asked him if they knew when we visited them. 'By God, they certainly know and are gladdened by your visit. They become acquainted with you and get on familiar terms with you.' I asked him as to what we should say when we visit them. He said, 'Say,

اللّٰهُمَّ جَافِ الْأَرْضَ عَنْ جُنُوبِهِمْ، وَ صَاعِدْ إِلَيْكَ أَرْوَاحَهُمْ، وَ لَقِّهِمْ مِنْكَ رِضْوَانًا، وَ أَسْكِنْ إِلَيْهِمْ مِنْ رَحْمَتِكَ مَا تَصِلُ بِهِ وَحْدَتَهُمْ، وَ تُونِسُ بِهِ وَحْشَتَهُمْ، إِنَّكَ عَلَىٰ كُلِّ شَيْءٍ قَدِيرٌ.

O Allah, make the earth recede from their sides, raise their spirits up to You, let them encounter Your good pleasure, and reassure them of Your mercy, whereby You will dispel their solitariness, and cheer them up in their loneliness. Indeed You have power over all things.' "

1 *Kāmil al-Ziyārāt*, 322, b 105, h 12, whence *Biḥār*, xcix, 298, b 6, h 17 & *Mustadrak*, ii, 371, b 48, h 2219/3. *Jamāl*, 180, faṣl 9.

2 *Falāḥ al-Sā'il*, 85, whence *Mustadrak*, ii, 372, b 49, h 2222/2. From *Miṣbāḥ al-Zā'ir* in *Biḥār*, xcix, 300, b 6, h 26 whence *Mustadrak*, x, 384, b 80, h 12232/1.

Sayyid Ibn Ṭāwūs adds[1] that when present in a graveyard of the faithful, one should recite Sūrat al-Tawḥīd eleven times and make a gift of it to them, and it is reported that God Almighty rewards one who does so by the number of the dead buried therein.

According to a report[2] cited in *Kāmil al-Ziyārāt* Imam Jaᶜfar al-Ṣādiq (*ᶜa*) said, "When one visits the dead before sunrise, they hear and answer you, and if visited after sunrise, they hear but do not respond."

In Rāwandī's *Daᶜawāt* is cited a report from the Apostle of Allah (ṣ) concerning the undesirability (*karāhah*) of visiting graves at night, as the Prophet (ṣ) is quoted as having advised Abū Dharr, saying,

يَا أَبَا ذَرٍّ أُوصِيكَ فَاحْفَظْ لَعَلَّ اللهَ يَنْفَعُكَ بِهِ جَاوِرِ الْقُبُورَ تَذَكَّرْ بِهَا الْآخِرَةَ وَ زُرْهَا أَحْيَاناً بِالنَّهَارِ وَ لَا تَزُرْهَا بِاللَّيْلِ.

(O Abū Dharr, take my advice and remember it so that God may benefit you by it. Be a neighbour of the graves so that they remind you of the Hereafter. Visit them occasionally by day and do not visit them at night.)

In Shahīd Awwal's *Majmūᶜah* it is reported that the Apostle of Allah (ṣ) said[3] that no one says the following by the graveside of a dead person without God Almighty saving him from punishment on the Day of Resurrection.

O Allah, I beseech You by the right of Muḥammad and the Family of Muḥammad not to punish this dead person.	اللّٰهُمَّ إِنِّي أَسْأَلُكَ بِحَقِّ مُحَمَّدٍ وَ آلِ مُحَمَّدٍ أَنْ لَا تُعَذِّبَ هٰذَا الْمَيِّتَ.

It is reported[4] in *Jāmiᶜ al-Akhbār* from one of the Prophet's Companions that the Prophet (ṣ) said, "Send gifts for your dead." When asked what kind of gifts those might be, the Prophet replied, "Chari-

1 *Biḥār*, xcix, 300, b 6, h 26 whence *Mustadrak*, x, 384, b 80, h 12232/1, from *Miṣbāḥ al-Zā'ir.*

2 From ᶜAlī b. Asbāṭ's *Nawādir* in *Biḥār*, xcix, 297, b 6, h 11, whence *Mustadrak*, ii, 487, b 79, h 2526/25. Not found in *Kāmil al-Ziyārāt*.

3 *Daᶜawāt*, 270, whence *Biḥār*, lxxix, 54, b 12 & *Mustadrak*, ii, 372, b 49, h 2221/1. From Shahīd Awwal's *Majmūᶜah* in *Mustadrak*, ii, 373, b 49, h 2226/6.

4 *Jāmiᶜ al-Akhbār*, 169, faṣl 134, whence *Mustadrak*, ii, 484, b 79, h 2524/23.

ty (*ṣadaqah*) and supplication (*du*ᶜ*ā*)."

The Prophet (ṣ) also said,[1]

> "Indeed the spirits of the dead arrive every Friday at the lowest heaven and stop opposite their homes and dwellings. Each of them cries out with a sad and doleful voice as they weep, 'O my relatives, O my children, O my father, O my mother, O my kinsmen! Give us, may God have mercy on you, out of that which was once in our own hands and for which we will be answerable at Judgement and on account of which we face affliction and distress here, while others benefit from it.' Everyone of them cries out to his relatives, 'Give us a penny, a loaf of bread, or a piece of clothing, may Allah clothe you with the garments of paradise!'"

Thereat the Prophet (ṣ) wept and his Companions wept along with him. He wept so intensely that he could not speak for a while. Then he said,

> "They were your brethren in faith who became decayed bones and dust after having experienced the joys and bliss of life, and now they are crying out, cursing themselves, saying, 'Woe to us! Had we spent what we once possessed in our hands in obeying God and for the sake of His pleasure, we would not have stood in need of you!' Then they return with regret and remorse, and cry out, 'Make haste in sending charities for the dead!' "

The Prophet (ṣ) is also reported to have said, "Whatever charity is given for the dead, is taken by an angel in a brilliant tray of light whose radiance reaches the seven heavens. Then standing at the edge of the pit he says, 'Peace be to you O inhabitants of the graves! Your relatives have sent these gifts for you!' So the dead person takes his gift and reenters his grave with it, whereby his resting place becomes roomier." Then he added, "Behold! Whoever does kindness to a dead person through an act of charity will receive from God a reward like the mountain of Uḥud, and on the Day of Resurrection he will be in the shade of the Divine Throne, when there will no other shade. That is how the living and the dead obtain deliverance through such a charity."[2]

1 *Jāmi*ᶜ *al-Akhbār*, 169, faṣl 134, whence *Mustadrak*, ii, 484, b 79, h 2525/24.

2 *Jāmi*ᶜ *al-Akhbār*, 169, faṣl 134, whence *Mustadrak*, ii, 114, b 20, h 1577/11.

It is related that they saw the emir of Khurāsān in a dream and he was pleading, "Send for me what you throw for your dogs, for I am in need of it."

It should be known that the *ziyārah* of the graves of the faithful has a great reward and there are many additional benefits in it such as prompting one to take lesson from the dead, becoming more aware of one's situation in life, cultivating an attitude of detachment towards the world and and its attractions and inclining towards the Hereafter. One should visit the graveyards at times of great grief and great joy. Wise are those who take lesson from the dead, so that the charms of worldly life are driven out from their heart. The honey of mundane pleasures turns bitter in their mouths, prompting them to reflect on the transient nature of the world and its changing conditions and to remember that soon he too shall be like them, unable to perform any works, and become a lesson for others.

Well has Shaykh Niẓāmī said,

زنده دلی در صف افسردگان   رفت به همسایگی مردگان
حرف فنا خواند ز هر لوح پاك   روح بقا جست ز هر روح پاك
کارشناسی پی تفتیش حال   کرد از او بر سر راهی سؤال
کین همه از زنده رمیدن چراست   رخت سوی مرده کشیدن چراست
گفت پلیدان به مغاك اندرند   پاك نهادان ته خاك اندرند
مرده دلانند به روی زمین   بهر چه با مرده شوم همنشین
همدمی مرده دهد مردگی   صحبت افسرده دل افسردگی
زیر گل آنانکه پراکنده‌اند   گرچه به تن مرده به دل زنده‌اند
مرده دلی بود مرا پیش از این   بسته هر چون و چرا پیش از این
زنده شدم از نظر پاکشان   آب حیات است مرا خاکشان

A lively soul abandoned the company of the sombre,
 for the neighbourhood of the dead
Reading the message of impermanence on every grave,
Seeking the spirit of immortality from every pious soul.
A curious veteran asked him, as he passed by,
'Why run from the living to take lodgings with the dead?'

He said, 'The vicious abound in the town,
While the pure-minded lie buried beneath the ground.
People dead at heart abound in this land,
What's the use of keeping company of the dead?
The company of the dead is deadening,
And the society of the sombre is sad,
The dead scattered under the ground,
Though dead in body are live in soul,
Dead in heart I was, bound by worldly chores,
Their chaste looks have revived me; their dust is the elixir of life.

There is a report (narrated by Abū Baṣīr from Imam Jaᶜfar al-Ṣādiq (ᶜ*a*)) that

أَوْحَى اللهُ إِلَىٰ عِيسَى بْنِ مَرْيَمَ يَا عِيسَى (ع) : هَبْ لِي مِنْ عَيْنَيْكَ الدُّمُوعَ، وَ مِنْ قَلْبِكَ الْخُشُوعَ، وَ اكْحَلْ عَيْنَيْكَ بِمِيلِ الْحُزْنِ إِذَا ضَحِكَ الْبَطَّالُونَ، وَ قُمْ عَلَىٰ قُبُورِ الْأَمْوَاتِ فَنَادِهِمْ بِالصَّوْتِ الرَّفِيعِ، لَعَلَّكَ تَأْخُذُ مَوْعِظَتَكَ مِنْهُمْ، وَ قُلْ إِنِّي لَاحِقٌ بِهِمْ فِي اللَّاحِقِينَ .

God revealed to Jesus, Mary's son, saying, "Jesus, let your tears be the offering of your eyes and let humility be the offering of your heart. Let sorrow be the kohl of your eyes when the vain laugh. Stand over the graves and call the dead to take admonition from them, and say, "I will be joining them together with other arrivals."[1]

That which was ordained to be recorded in this noble book was completed on the eve of Sunday, 10th of D͟hū al-Qaᶜdah of the year 1344 H. (May 23, 1926), the night of the auspicious birth anniversary of our master the Eighth Imam, Abū al-Ḥasan al-Riḍā, may Allah bless him. As I received on this day a letter bearing the news of my mother's death, I request my faithful brethren who will benefit from this book to make supplication and *ziyārah* for her—may God forgive her and have mercy on her—as well as for my father and myself, in life and after death. وَ الْحَمْدُ لِلّٰهِ أَوَّلًا وَ آخِرًا وَ صَلَّى اللهُ عَلَىٰ مُحَمَّدٍ وَ آلِهِ الطَّاهِرِينَ

[1] Mufīd's *Amālī*, 236, majlis 27, h 7, whence *Biḥār*, lxix, 71, b 97, h 2. Ṭūsī's *Amālī*, 12, majlis 1, 15/15, whence *Biḥār*, xiv, 320, b 21, h 23. *Irs͟hād al-Qulūb*, i, 95, b 23. Rāwandī's *Qiṣaṣ*, 272, faṣl 5, h 320. *Mustadrak*, xi, 243, b 15, h 12874/28.

Appendices

Appendix One

(Continued from volume 1, p 793)

3. A Ziyarah Jamiʿah of the Imams

This is a general *ziyārah* text with which one can perform the *ziyārah* of any of the Imams at any time, that is, on any day of the week and during any month. This *ziyārah* has been narrated by Sayyid Ibn Ṭāwūs in *Miṣbāḥ al-Zāʾir* from the Imams (*ʿa*).[1] After mentioning certainly preliminaries consisting of supplication and prayer at the time of setting out on the journey of *ziyārah*, he says while taking the bath one should say,

In the Name of Allah, by Allah, in the way of Allah and following the creed of the Apostle of Allah. O Allah, wash away from me the defilement of sin and the dirt of defects, purify me with the water of repentance, clothe me with the armour that protects from sin, and strengthen me with Your gentleness, enabling me to perform righteous deeds. Indeed You are dispenser of a great grace!

بِسْـــمِ اللّٰهِ وَ بِاللّٰهِ وَ فِي سَبِيلِ اللّٰهِ وَ عَلٰى
مِلَّةِ رَسُولِ اللّٰهِ، اَللّٰهُمَّ اغْسِلْ عَنِّي دَرَنَ
الذُّنُوبِ وَ وَسَخَ الْعُيُوبِ، وَ طَهِّرْنِي بِمَاءِ
التَّوْبَةِ، وَ أَلْبِسْنِي رِدَاءَ الْعِصْمَةِ، وَ أَيِّدْنِي
بِلُطْفٍ مِنْـــكَ يُوَفِّقُنِي لِصَالِحِ الْأَعْمَالِ،
إِنَّكَ ذُو الْفَضْلِ الْعَظِيمِ.

While approaching the gates of the holy shrine, say,

All praise belongs to Allah who has enabled me to call on His *walī* and to visit His testament, and He has admitted me into his sanctuary and did not diminish my share of pilgrimage to his tomb and entry into the precincts of this shrine and the site of his grave.

الْحَمْـــدُ لِلّٰهِ الَّذِى وَفَّقَـــنِي لِقَصْدِ وَلِيِّهِ
وَ زِيٰـــارَةِ حُجَّتِـــهِ، وَ أَوْرَدَنِي حَرَمَهُ، وَ
لَمْ يَبْخَسْـــنِي حَظِّي مِنْ زِيٰارَةِ قَبْرِهِ، وَ
النُّزُولِ بِعَقْوَةِ مُغَيَّبِهِ، وَ سَاحَةِ تُرْبَتِهِ.

1 *Al-Mazār al-Kabīr*, 292, thence and from Ibn Ṭāwūs in *Biḥār*, xcix, 163, b 8.

اَلْحَمْدُ لِلّٰهِ الَّذِی لَمْ يَسِمْنِي بِحِرْمَانِ مَا
أَمَّلْتُهُ، وَ لَا صَرَفَ عَنِّي مَا رَجَوْتُهُ،
وَ لَا قَطَعَ رَجَائِي فِيمَا تَوَقَّعْتُهُ، بَلْ
أَلْبَسَنِي عَافِيَتَهُ، وَ أَفَادَنِي نِعْمَتَهُ، وَ
آتَانِي كَرَامَتَهُ.

All praise belongs to Allah who did not mark me out for denial of my hope, did not refuse me what I expected, and did not cut off my hope from what I looked forward to. Rather, He clothed me with well-being, bestowed on me His blessings, and granted me His grace.

On entering the shrine, stand facing the holy tomb, and say,

اَلسَّلَامُ عَلَيْكُمْ أَئِمَّةَ الْمُؤْمِنِينَ، وَ
سَادَةَ الْمُتَّقِينَ، وَ كُبَرَاءَ الصِّدِّيقِينَ، وَ
أُمَرَاءَ الصَّالِحِينَ، وَ قَادَةَ الْمُحْسِنِينَ،
وَ أَعْلَامَ الْمُهْتَدِينَ، وَ أَنْوَارَ الْعَارِفِينَ،
وَ وَرَثَةَ الْأَنْبِيَاءِ، وَ صَفْوَةَ الْأَوْصِيَاءِ،
وَ شُمُوسَ الْأَتْقِيَاءِ، وَ بُدُورَ الْخُلَفَاءِ، وَ
عِبَادَ الرَّحْمٰنِ، وَ شُرَكَاءَ الْقُرْآنِ، وَ مَنْهَجَ
الْإِيمَانِ، وَ مَعَادِنَ الْحَقَائِقِ، وَ شُفَعَاءَ
الْخَلَائِقِ، وَ رَحْمَةُ اللهِ وَ بَرَكَاتُهُ،

Peace be to you, Imams of the faithful, leaders of the Godwary, chiefs of the truthful, commanders of the righteous, leaders of the virtuous and beacons for the seekers of guidance, the lights of the gnostics, the heir of the prophets, the elect of the legatees, the suns of the pious, the full moons amongst the vicegerents, the servants of the All-beneficent, the partners of the Qur'ān, the highways of the faith, the repositories of the truths, and the intercessors of the creatures (with God), and may Allah's mercy and His bounties be upon you!

أَشْهَدُ أَنَّكُمْ أَبْوَابُ اللهِ، وَ مَفَاتِيحُ
رَحْمَتِهِ، وَ مَقَالِيدُ مَغْفِرَتِهِ، وَ سَحَائِبُ
رِضْوَانِهِ، وَ مَصَابِيحُ جِنَانِهِ، وَ حَمَلَةُ
فُرْقَانِهِ، وَ خَزَنَةُ عِلْمِهِ، وَ حَفَظَةُ سِرِّهِ، وَ
مَهْبِطُ وَحْيِهِ، وَ عِنْدَكُمْ أَمَانَاتُ النُّبُوَّةِ،

I testify that you are the gateways to God, the keys of His mercy and His forgiveness, the rain clouds of His good pleasure, the lamps of His paradise, the exponents of His Criterion, the custodians of His knowledge, the guards of His secrets, the receivers of His revelations, and with you are the trusts of prophecy

and the deposits of apostleship.	وَ وَدَائِعُ الرِّسَالَةِ.
You are the trustees of Allah, His lovers, His servants, His elect, the defenders of His Unity and the pillars of His magnification, the summoners to His Scriptures, the guards of His creatures, and the protectors of His trusts.	أَنْتُمْ أُمَنَاءُ اللهِ وَ أَحِبَّاؤُهُ، وَ عِبَادُهُ، وَ أَصْفِيَاؤُهُ، وَ أَنْصَارُ تَوْحِيدِهِ، وَ أَرْكَانُ تَمْجِيدِهِ، وَ دُعَاتُهُ إِلَىٰ كُتُبِهِ، وَ حَرَسَةُ خَلَائِقِهِ، وَ حَفَظَةُ وَدَائِعِهِ،
The eulogies of the angels do not surpass you with respect to sincerity and humility, nor are you contested by any supplicant and possessor of submissiveness.	لَا يَسْبِقُكُمْ ثَنَاءُ الْمَلَائِكَةِ فِي الْإِخْلَاصِ وَ الْخُشُوعِ، وَ لَا يُضَادُّكُمْ ذُو ابْتِهَالٍ وَ خُضُوعٍ،
How could that be, when you have hearts disciplined with fear and hope under Allah's tutelage and He made them repositories of thanksgiving and praise, making them secure from the dangers of negligence and purging them of the vices of languor and slackness.	أَنَّىٰ وَ لَكُمُ الْقُلُوبُ الَّتِي تَوَلَّى اللهُ رِيَاضَتَهَا بِالْخَوْفِ وَ الرَّجَاءِ، وَ جَعَلَهَا أَوْعِيَةً لِلشُّكْرِ وَ الثَّنَاءِ، وَ آمَنَهَا مِنْ عَوَارِضِ الْغَفْلَةِ، وَ صَفَّاهَا مِنْ سُوءِ الْفَتْرَةِ،
Rather, the denizens of the heavens seek nearness to God through your love and through refutation of your enemies, by mourning continuously over your sorrows and by pleading for forgiveness for your followers and friends.	بَلْ يَتَقَرَّبُ أَهْلُ السَّمَاءِ بِحُبِّكُمْ وَ بِالْبَرَاءَةِ مِنْ أَعْدَائِكُمْ، وَ تَوَاتُرِ الْبُكَاءِ عَلَىٰ مُصَابِكُمْ، وَ الْإِسْتِغْفَارِ لِشِيعَتِكُمْ وَ مُحِبِّيكُمْ،
Allah, my creator, is my witness and so are His angels and prophets, and you too, my masters, be my witnesses that I have faith in your *wilāyah*, believe in your Imamate, acknowledge	فَأَنَا أُشْهِدُ اللهَ خَالِقِي وَ أُشْهِدُ مَلَائِكَتَهُ وَ أَنْبِيَاءَهُ، وَ أُشْهِدُكُمْ يَا مَوَالِيَّ، أَنِّي مُؤْمِنٌ بِوِلَايَتِكُمْ، مُعْتَقِدٌ

لِإِمَامَتِكُمْ، مُقِرٌّ بِخِلَافَتِكُمْ، عَارِفٌ بِمَنْزِلَتِكُمْ، مُوقِنٌ بِعِصْمَتِكُمْ، خَاضِعٌ لِوَلَايَتِكُمْ، مُتَقَرِّبٌ إِلَى اللهِ بِحُبِّكُمْ وَ بِالْبَرَاءَةِ مِنْ أَعْدَائِكُمْ، عَالِمٌ بِأَنَّ اللهَ قَدْ طَهَّرَكُمْ مِنَ الْفَوَاحِشِ مَا ظَهَرَ مِنْهَا وَ مَا بَطَنَ، وَ مِنْ كُلِّ رِيبَةٍ وَ نَجَاسَةٍ، وَ دَنِيَّةٍ وَ رَجَاسَةٍ، وَ مَنَحَكُمْ رَايَةَ الْحَقِّ الَّتِي مَنْ تَقَدَّمَهَا ضَلَّ، وَ مَنْ تَأَخَّرَ عَنْهَا زَلَّ، وَ فَرَضَ طَاعَتَكُمْ عَلَى كُلِّ أَسْوَدَ وَ أَبْيَضَ،

your vicegerency, recognize your station, am convinced of your infallibility, and submit to your *wilāyah*, seeking nearness to Allah through your love and by refuting your enemies, knowing that Allah has purified you from indecencies, outward and inward, and from every kind of doubt, impurity, baseness and defilement, and He has conferred on you the banner of the truth—those who overtake it are lost and those who lag behind it stumble and fall. He has made obedience to you obligatory on all and sundry.

وَ أَشْهَدُ أَنَّكُمْ قَدْ وَفَيْتُمْ بِعَهْدِ اللهِ وَ ذِمَّتِهِ، وَ بِكُلِّ مَا اشْتَرَطَ عَلَيْكُمْ فِي كِتَابِهِ، وَ دَعَوْتُمْ إِلَى سَبِيلِهِ، وَ أَنْفَذْتُمْ طَاقَتَكُمْ فِي مَرْضَاتِهِ، وَ حَمَلْتُمُ الْخَلَائِقَ عَلَى مِنْهَاجِ النُّبُوَّةِ، وَ مَسَالِكِ الرِّسَالَةِ، وَ سِرْتُمْ فِيهِ بِسِيرَةِ الْأَنْبِيَاءِ وَ مَذَاهِبِ الْأَوْصِيَاءِ، فَلَمْ يُطَعْ لَكُمْ أَمْرٌ، وَ لَمْ تُصْغَ إِلَيْكُمْ أُذُنٌ، فَصَلَوَاتُ اللهِ عَلَى أَرْوَاحِكُمْ وَ أَجْسَادِكُمْ.

I testify that you fulfilled the covenant of Allah and His pledge and everything He had stipulated for you in His Scripture, and that you have summoned the people to His path and spent all your strength for the sake of His pleasure. You directed the creatures to the path of prophethood and the ways of apostleship and in all this you acted in accordance with the precedents of the prophets and the ways of the legatees. Yet your commands were not obeyed and your advices went unheard. May Allah's blessings be upon your spirits and bodies!

Then clinging to the holy tomb, say,

بِأَبِي أَنْتَ وَ أُمِّي يَا حُجَّةَ اللهِ، لَقَدْ

May my father and mother be

أُرْضِعْـــتَ بِثَدْيِ الْإِيمَـــانِ، وَ فُطِمْتَ
بِنُورِ الْإِسْلَامِ، وَ غُذِّيتَ بِبَرْدِ الْيَقِينِ،
وَ أُلْبِسْتَ حُلَلَ الْعِصْمَةِ، وَ اصْطُفِيتَ
وَ وُرِّثْتَ عِلْمَ الْكِتَابِ، وَ لُقِّنْتَ فَصْلَ
الْخِطَابِ، وَ أُوضِـــحَ بِمَكَانِكَ مَعَارِفُ
التَّنْزِيلِ وَ غَوَامِضُ التَّأْوِيلِ، وَ سُلِّمَتْ
إِلَيْـــكَ رَايَةُ الْحَـــقِّ، وَ كُلِّفْـــتَ هِدَايَةَ
الْخَلْقِ، وَ نُبِذَ إِلَيْـــكَ عَهْدُ الْإِمَامَةِ، وَ
أُلْزِمْتَ حِفْظَ الشَّرِيعَةِ،

your ransom! O Testament of Allah! Indeed you were nursed at the breast of faith and weaned with the light of Islam. You were nourished with the coolness of certitude and clothed in the robes of infallibility. You were chosen and given the heritage of the knowledge of the Book and inspired with decisive speech. The teachings of the revealed text and the mysteries of its interpretation were clarified by your station. You were handed over the banner of the truth and charged with the guidance of the creatures. The covenant of the Imamate was passed to you, and you were made responsible for the preservation of the *shari'ah*.

وَ أَشْهَدُ يَا مَوْلَايَ أَنَّكَ وَفَيْتَ بِشَرَائِطِ
الْوَصِيَّـــةِ، وَ قَضَيْتَ مَا لَزِمَكَ مِنْ حَدِّ
الطَّاعَةِ، وَ نَهَضْـــتَ بِأَعْبَاءِ الْإِمَامَةِ،
وَ احْتَذَيْتَ مِثَالَ النُّبُـــوَّةِ، فِي الصَّبْرِ وَ
الْإِجْتِهَادِ، وَ النَّصِيحَةِ لِلْعِبَادِ، وَ كَظْمِ
الْغَيْـــظِ وَ الْعَفْوِ عَنِ النَّاسِ، وَ عَزَمْتَ
عَلَى الْعَـــدْلِ فِي الْبَرِيَّـــةِ، وَ النَّصَفَةِ فِي
الْقَضِيَّةِ، وَ وَكَّـــدْتَ الْحُجَجَ عَلَى الْأُمَّةِ
بِالدَّلَائِلِ الصَّادِقَةِ، وَ الشَّرِيعَةِ النَّاطِقَةِ،

I testify, my master, that you fulfilled the provisions of the legacy, and discharged what had been incumbent upon you with utmost obedience. You carried all the burdens of the office of the Imamate and acted in accordance with the example of the prophets in patience, endeavour, earnest concern for the good of God servants, suppressing your rage and overlooking the faults of the people. You were resolute in establishing justice and fair judgment among the people, reinforcing the proofs for the *ummah* with genuine arguments and explicit laws.

وَ دَعَـــوْتَ إِلَى اللهِ بِالْحِكْمَةِ الْبَالِغَةِ، وَ
الْمَوْعِظَةِ الْحَسَنَةِ، فَمَنَعْتَ مِنْ تَقْوِيمِ

You summoned to Allah with far-reaching wisdom and good advice. Yet you were hindered from straightening what was crooked, from closing the gaps, rectifying the flaws, overcoming stubborn resistance, reviving the *sunnah* and laying heresies to rest, until you departed from the world as a martyr and joined the Apostle of Allah, may Allah bless him and his Family, with a praiseworthy record, may the blessings of Allah, perpetual and enhancing, be upon you!

الزَّيْغِ، وَ سَدِّ الثُّلَمِ، وَ إِصْلَاحِ الْفَاسِدِ، وَ
كَسْرِ الْمُعَانِدِ، وَ إِحْيَاءِ السُّنَنِ، وَ إِمَاتَةِ
الْبِدَعِ، حَتَّى فَارَقْتَ الدُّنْيَا وَ أَنْتَ شَهِيدٌ،
وَ لَقِيتَ رَسُولَ اللهِ صَلَّى اللهُ عَلَيْهِ وَ
آلِهِ وَ أَنْتَ حَمِيدٌ، صَلَوَاتُ اللهِ عَلَيْكَ
تَتَرَادَفُ وَ تَزِيدُ.

Then moving towards the foot of the blessed tomb, say,

O my masters, O Family of the Apostle of Allah, I seek nearness to Allah, the Glorious and Exalted, by opposing those who betrayed you, broke their pledge of allegiance to you, denied your *wilāyah*, refused to acknowledge your station, renounced obedience to you, forsook the means of your friendship, sought nearness to their tyrants by repudiating you and turning away from you. They prevented you from implementing divine ordinances, from rooting out unbelief, from removing disunity, from promoting unity, overcoming social flaws, straightening out crookedness, implementing the divine laws and from cultivation of Islam, and prevention of sin.

يَا سَادَتِي يَا آلَ رَسُولِ اللهِ، إِنِّي بِكُمْ
أَتَقَرَّبُ إِلَى اللهِ جَلَّ وَ عَلَا بِالْخِلَافِ
عَلَى الَّذِينَ غَدَرُوا بِكُمْ، وَ نَكَثُوا
بَيْعَتَكُمْ، وَ جَحَدُوا وِلَايَتَكُمْ، وَ
أَنْكَرُوا مَنْزِلَتَكُمْ، وَ خَلَعُوا رِبْقَةَ
طَاعَتِكُمْ، وَ هَجَرُوا أَسْبَابَ مَوَدَّتِكُمْ،
وَ تَقَرَّبُوا إِلَى فَرَاعِنَتِهِمْ بِالْبَرَاءَةِ مِنْكُمْ وَ
الْإِعْرَاضِ عَنْكُمْ، وَ مَنَعُوكُمْ مِنْ إِقَامَةِ
الْحُدُودِ، وَ اسْتِيصَالِ الْجُحُودِ، وَ شَعْبِ
الصَّدْعِ، وَ لَمِّ الشَّعَثِ، وَ سَدِّ الْخَلَلِ،
وَ تَثْقِيفِ الْأَوَدِ، وَ إِمْضَاءِ الْأَحْكَامِ، وَ
تَهْذِيبِ الْإِسْلَامِ، وَ قَمْعِ الْآثَامِ،

They raised up against you the dust storms of war and subver-

وَ أَرْهَجُوا عَلَيْكُمْ نَقْعَ الْحُرُوبِ وَ

الْفِتَنِ، وَ أَنْحَوْا عَلَيْكُمْ سُيُوفَ الْأَحْقَادِ، وَ هَتَكُوا مِنْكُمُ السُّتُورَ، وَ ابْتَاعُوا بِخُمْسِكُمُ الْخُمُورَ، وَ صَرَفُوا صَدَقَاتِ الْمَسَاكِينِ إِلَى الْمُضْحِكِينَ وَ السَّاخِرِينَ،

sion, drew upon you the swords of enmity, violated your dignity, bought intoxicants and wines with the one-fifth due to you, and spent the charities meant for the poor on clowns and jesters.

وَ ذَلِكَ بِمَا طَرَّقَتْ لَهُمُ الْفَسَقَةُ الْغُوَاةُ، وَ الْحَسَدَةُ الْبُغَاةُ، أَهْلُ النَّكْثِ وَ الْغَدْرِ، وَ الْخِلَافِ وَ الْمَكْرِ، وَ الْقُلُوبِ الْمُنْتِنَةِ مِنْ قَذَرِ الشِّرْكِ، وَ الْأَجْسَادِ الْمُشْحَنَةِ مِنْ دَرَنِ الْكُفْرِ، الَّذِينَ أَضَبُّوا عَلَى النِّفَاقِ، وَ أَكَبُّوا عَلَى عَلَائِقِ الشِّقَاقِ،

That was made conducive for them by the perverse evildoers, the envious oppressors, the perfidious traitors, the cunning antagonists, with their putrid hearts rotting with the filth of idolatry, and bodies burdened with the dirt of unfaith—those who rallied to hypocrisy and pursued eagerly factional ties.

فَلَمَّا مَضَى الْمُصْطَفَى صَلَّى اللهُ عَلَيْهِ وَ آلِهِ، اِخْتَطَفُوا الْغِرَّةَ، وَ انْتَهَزُوا الْفُرْصَةَ، وَ انْتَهَكُوا الْحُرْمَةَ، وَ غَادَرُوهُ عَلَى فِرَاشِ الْوَفَاةِ، وَ أَسْرَعُوا لِنَقْضِ الْبَيْعَةِ، وَ مُخَالَفَةِ الْمَوَاثِيقِ الْمُؤَكَّدَةِ، وَ خِيَانَةِ الْأَمَانَةِ الْمَعْرُوضَةِ عَلَى الْجِبَالِ الرَّاسِيَةِ، وَ أَبَتْ أَنْ تَحْمِلَهَا وَ حَمَلَهَا الْإِنْسَانُ الظَّلُومُ الْجَهُولُ، ذُو الشِّقَاقِ وَ الْعِزَّةِ بِالْآثَامِ الْمُولِمَةِ، وَ الْأَنَفَةِ عَنِ الْإِنْقِيَادِ لِحَمِيدِ الْعَاقِبَةِ،

So when al-Muṣṭafā, may Allah bless him and his Family, passed away, they seized on the people's neglect, grabbed the opportunity, and violated his sanctity, betrayed him as he lay on his deathbed and hastened to break the allegiance (they had sworn) and counter pledges solemnly made and betrayed the trust that had been presented to the firmly set mountains and which they had refused to bear and which was borne by the most ignorant and unfair man,[33:72] given to schism, to a hubris fed by harrowing sins, and defiant before (the call to) compliance for the sake of a commendable destiny.

فَحُشِرَ سِفْلَةُ الْأَعْرَابِ، وَ بَقَايَا الْأَحْزَابِ

Thus it was that the dregs of the

Arabs and remnants of the idolatrous hordes of the confederates were gathered at the house of prophecy and apostleship, the venue of the descent of revelations and angels, the seat of authority of *wilāyah* and the repository of Prophet's legacy, vicegerency and Imamate, until they broke the covenant taken by al-Muṣṭafā touching his brother, the banner of guidance and beacon of the path of deliverance as distinct from the paths of perdition.

إِلَى دَارِ النُّبُوَّةِ وَ الرِّسَالَةِ، وَ مَهْبِطِ الْوَحْيِ وَ الْمَلَائِكَةِ، وَ مُسْتَقَرِّ سُلْطَانِ الْوِلَايَةِ، وَ مَعْدِنِ الْوَصِيَّةِ وَ الْخِلَافَةِ وَ الْإِمَامَةِ، حَتَّىٰ نَقَضُوا عَهْدَ الْمُصْطَفَىٰ فِي أَخِيهِ عَلَمِ الْهُدَىٰ، وَ الْمُبَيِّنِ طَرِيقَ النَّجَاةِ مِنْ طُرُقِ الرَّدَىٰ،

And they wounded the heart of the Best of Creation by aggrieving his daughter and oppressing his darling, the flesh of his flesh and blood of his blood.

وَ جَرَحُوا كَبِدَ خَيْرِ الْوَرَىٰ فِي ظُلْمِ ابْنَتِهِ، وَ اضْطِهَادِ حَبِيبَتِهِ، وَ اهْتِضَامِ عَزِيزَتِهِ، بَضْعَةِ لَحْمِهِ وَ فِلْذَةِ كَبِدِهِ،

They forsook her husband, making light of his worth, infringing his sanctity, disregarding his blood relationship with the Prophet, denying his brotherhood with the Apostle, forsaking his friendship, and disobeying him and contesting his *wilāyah*, thus prompting even the slaves to covet the caliphate. They dragged him to give allegiance to them with drawn out swords and pointed spears. His heart full of bitterness and himself aflame with anger, he kept his extreme patience and suppressed his rage.

وَ خَذَلُوا بَعْلَهَا، وَ صَغَّرُوا قَدْرَهُ، وَ اسْتَحَلُّوا مَحَارِمَهُ، وَ قَطَعُوا رَحِمَهُ، وَ أَنْكَرُوا أُخُوَّتَهُ، وَ هَجَرُوا مَوَدَّتَهُ، وَ نَقَضُوا طَاعَتَهُ، وَ جَحَدُوا وِلَايَتَهُ، وَ أَطْمَعُوا الْعَبِيدَ فِي خِلَافَتِهِ، وَ قَادُوهُ إِلَىٰ بَيْعَتِهِمْ مُصْلِتَةً سُيُوفَهَا، مُقْذِعَةً أَسِنَّتَهَا، وَ هُوَ سَاخِطُ الْقَلْبِ، هَائِجُ الْغَضَبِ شَدِيدُ الصَّبْرِ، كَاظِمُ الْغَيْظِ،

They summoned him to give allegiance to them, an allegiance whose sinister character has cast a long shadow on Islam and sowed

يَدْعُونَهُ إِلَىٰ بَيْعَتِهِمُ الَّتِي عَمَّ شُومُهَا الْإِسْلَامَ، وَ زَرَعَتْ فِي قُلُوبِ أَهْلِهَا

the seeds of sinfulness into the hearts of its followers, alienated the likes of Salmān, drove away the likes of Miqdād, banished the likes of Abū Dhar, ripped open the bellies of the likes of Ammār, corrupted the meanings of the Qur'ān, altered the laws, changed the Station (of Abraham's location), permitted their one-fifth to be consumed by those who had been set free by the Prophet, imposed the rule of offspring of those cursed by the Prophet on the honour and blood of the people, mixed up the lawful with the unlawful, degraded faith and Islam, pulled down the Kaʿbah, pillaged the city of the Prophet's migration during the episode of Ḥarrah, brought out the daughters of the Immigrants and the Helpers for molestation and torture, put on them the clothes of shame and disgrace, giving a free licence to men of doubtful birth to kill the Family of the chosen of Allah and to annihilate his posterity, efface his traces, make his womenfolk captive, kill his supporters, smash his pulpit, overthrow the objects of his pride, extinguish his faith, and to obliterate his name!

الْآثَامَ، وَ عَقَّتْ سَلْمَانَهَا، وَ طَرَدَتْ مِقْدَادَهَا، وَ نَفَتْ جُنْدُبَهَا، وَ فَتَقَتْ بَطْنَ عَمَّارِهَا، وَ حَرَّفَتِ الْقُرْآنَ، وَ بَدَّلَتِ الْأَحْكَامَ، وَ غَيَّرَتِ الْمَقَامَ، وَ أَبَاحَتِ الْخُمُسَ لِلطُّلَقَاءِ، وَ سَلَّطَتْ أَوْلَادَ اللُّعَنَاءِ عَلَى الْفُرُوجِ وَ الدِّمَاءِ، وَ خَلَطَتِ الْحَلَالَ بِالْحَرَامِ، وَ اسْتَخَفَّتْ بِالْإِيمَانِ وَ الْإِسْلَامِ، وَ هَدَمَتِ الْكَعْبَةَ، وَ أَغَارَتْ عَلَى دَارِ الْهِجْرَةِ يَوْمَ الْحَرَّةِ، وَ أَبْرَزَتْ بَنَاتِ الْمُهَاجِرِينَ وَ الْأَنْصَارِ لِلنَّكَالِ وَ السَّوْرَةِ، وَ أَلْبَسَتْهُنَّ ثَوْبَ الْعَارِ وَ الْفَضِيحَةِ، وَ رَخَّصَتْ لِأَهْلِ الشُّبْهَةِ فِي قَتْلِ أَهْلِ بَيْتِ الصَّفْوَةِ، وَ إِبَادَةِ نَسْلِهِ، وَ اسْتِيصَالِ شَأْفَتِهِ، وَ سَبْيِ حَرَمِهِ، وَ قَتْلِ أَنْصَارِهِ، وَ كَسْرِ مِنْبَرِهِ، وَ قَلْبِ مَفْخَرِهِ، وَ إِخْفَاءِ دِينِهِ، وَ قَطْعِ ذِكْرِهِ.

My masters, had al-Muṣṭafā watched you and seen the arrows of the *ummah* sunk into your hearts, their spears piercing your throats, their swords drenched in your blood, the sons of har-

يَا مَوَالِيَّ فَلَوْ عَايَنَكُمُ الْمُصْطَفَى وَ سِهَامُ الْأُمَّةِ مُغْرَقَةٌ فِي أَكْبَادِكُمْ، وَ رِمَاحُهُمْ مُشْرَعَةٌ فِي نُحُورِكُمْ، وَ سُيُوفُهَا مُولَغَةٌ فِي

دِمَائِكُمْ، يَشْفِي أَبْنَاءُ الْعَوَاهِرِ غَلِيلَ الْفِسْقِ مِنْ وَرَعِكُمْ، وَ غَيْظَ الْكُفْرِ مِنْ إِيمَانِكُمْ، وَ أَنْتُمْ بَيْنَ صَرِيعٍ فِي الْمِحْرَابِ قَدْ فَلَقَ السَّيْفُ هَامَتَهُ، وَ شَهِيدٍ فَوْقَ الْجَنَازَةِ قَدْ شُكَّتْ أَكْفَانُهُ بِالسِّهَامِ، وَ قَتِيلٍ بِالْعَرَاءِ قَدْ رُفِعَ فَوْقَ الْقَنَاةِ رَأْسُهُ، وَ مُكَبَّلٍ فِي السِّجْنِ قَدْ رُضَّتْ بِالْحَدِيدِ أَعْضَاؤُهُ، وَ مَسْمُومٍ قَدْ قُطِّعَتْ بِجُرَعِ السَّمِّ أَمْعَاؤُهُ، وَ شَمْلُكُمْ عَبَادِيدُ تُفْنِيهِمُ الْعَبِيدُ وَ أَبْنَاءُ الْعَبِيدِ.

lots appeasing their lust for transgression with your piety and their rage of perfidy with your faith, while one of you lay prostrate in the prayer niche the crown of his head cleft with the sword, while another martyr had his shroud pierced with arrows rained on his funeral, while another lay slain on open ground as his head was raised on spearheads, and another languished in the prison in shackles, his limbs bruised by the irons, and another victim of poisoning, his bowels cut to pieces with vials of deadly poison! Your assemblage broken up and dispersed, decimated by slaves and sons of slaves!

فَهَلِ الْمِحَنُ يَا سَادَتِي إِلَّا الَّتِي لَزِمَتْكُمْ؟ وَ الْمَصَائِبُ إِلَّا الَّتِي عَمَّتْكُمْ؟ وَ الْفَجَائِعُ إِلَّا الَّتِي خَصَّتْكُمْ؟ وَ الْقَوَارِعُ إِلَّا الَّتِي طَرَقَتْكُمْ؟ صَلَوَاتُ اللهِ عَلَيْكُمْ وَ عَلَىٰ أَرْوَاحِكُمْ وَ أَجْسَادِكُمْ وَ رَحْمَةُ اللهِ وَ بَرَكَاتُهُ.

My masters, is tribulation anything other than what has attended you? Is disaster anything except what has overtaken you? Is calamity anything except what has fallen to your share? Is catastrophe anything except what struck you? May Allah's blessings be upon you, your spirits and your bodies, and may Allah's mercy and bounties be upon you!

Then embrace the blessed tomb and say,

بِأَبِي أَنْتُمْ وَ أُمِّي يَا آلَ الْمُصْطَفَىٰ، إِنَّا لَا نَمْلِكُ إِلَّا أَنْ نَطُوفَ حَوْلَ مَشَاهِدِكُمْ، وَ نُعَزِّيَ فِيهَا أَرْوَاحَكُمْ عَلَىٰ هَٰذِهِ الْمَصَائِبِ الْعَظِيمَةِ الْحَالَّةِ بِفِنَائِكُمْ،

O Family of al-Muṣṭafā, may my father and mother be your ransom. All that we can do is to circle your shrines and offer consolation to your spirits for these great calamities that befell you and the grievous tragedies that alighted at

وَ الرَّزَايَا الْجَلِيلَةِ النَّازِلَةِ بِسَاحَتِكُمْ، اَلَّتِي أَثْبَتَتْ فِي قُلُوبِ شِيعَتِكُمُ الْقُرُوحَ، وَ أَوْرَثَتْ أَكْبَادَهُمُ الْجُرُوحَ، وَ زَرَعَتْ فِي صُدُورِهِمُ الْغُصَصَ،

your threshold, which have made a lasting gash in the hearts of your followers and left a wound in their hearts, and sown rage in their breasts!

فَنَحْنُ نُشْهِدُ اللهَ أَنَّا قَدْ شَارَكْنَا أَوْلِيَاءَكُمْ وَ أَنْصَارَكُمُ الْمُتَقَدِّمِينَ، فِي إِرَاقَةِ دِمَاءِ النَّاكِثِينَ وَ الْقَاسِطِينَ وَ الْمَارِقِينَ، وَ قَتَلَةِ أَبِي عَبْدِ اللهِ سَيِّدِ شَبَابِ أَهْلِ الْجَنَّةِ عَلَيْهِ السَّلَامُ يَوْمَ كَرْبَلَاءَ، بِالنِّيَّاتِ وَ الْقُلُوبِ وَ التَّأَسُّفِ عَلَى فَوْتِ تِلْكَ الْمَوَاقِفِ الَّتِي حَضَرُوا لِنُصْرَتِكُمْ، وَ عَلَيْكُمْ مِنَّا السَّلَامُ وَ رَحْمَةُ اللهِ وَ بَرَكَاتُهُ.

Allah is our witness that we stand by your friends and supporters of the former generations in shedding the blood of those who broke their allegiance to you, the perverts, the renegades and the murderers of Abū ʿAbdillah, the doyen of the youth of paradise, may peace be to him, during the episode of Karbalā, and we stand by them with our intentions, sentiments and sorrow for our absence at those scenes at which they were present to offer you help. May peace be to you from us, and may Allah's mercy and His bounties be upon you!

Then standing behind the grave and facing in the direction of *Kaʿbah*, say,

اَللّٰهُمَّ يَا ذَا الْقُدْرَةِ الَّتِي صَدَرَ عَنْهَا الْعَالَمُ مُكَوَّنًا مَبْرُوءًا عَلَيْهَا مَفْطُورًا تَحْتَ ظِلِّ الْعَظَمَةِ، فَنَطَقَتْ شَوَاهِدُ صُنْعِكَ فِيهِ بِأَنَّكَ أَنْتَ اللهُ لَا إِلٰهَ إِلَّا أَنْتَ مُكَوِّنُهُ وَ بَارِئُهُ وَ فَاطِرُهُ، اَبْتَدَعْتَهُ لَا مِنْ شَيْءٍ، وَ لَا عَلَى شَيْءٍ،

O Allah, O Possessor of the power from which the world emerged and was brought into being, created and originated under the shade of Your supremacy. The evidence of Your handiwork therein declare that You are indeed Allah, there is no god except You, who brought it into existence, and that You are its creator, maker and originator, who initiated it, not from something, nor over something nor in something, nor on account of any loneliness that may have affected You, when there was no one except You, nor because of any need that may have arisen, prompting You to bring it into being, nor because You sought help from the creation thereafter. Rather You produced it that it may serve as an evidence pointing to You, indicating that You are separate from Your handiwork. Hence no one with a fair mind will deny You, nor anyone with a sound understanding will dispute You.

وَ لَا فِي شَيْءٍ، وَ لَا لِوَحْشَةٍ دَخَلَتْ
عَلَيْكَ إِذْ لَا غَيْرُكَ، وَ لَا حَاجَةٍ بَدَتْ
لَكَ فِي تَكْوِينِهِ، وَ لَا لِإِسْتِعَانَةٍ مِنْكَ
عَلَى الْخَلْقِ بَعْدَهُ، بَلْ أَنْشَأْتَهُ لِيَكُونَ
دَلِيلًا عَلَيْكَ بِأَنَّكَ بَائِنٌ مِنَ الصُّنْعِ،
فَلَا يُطِيقُ الْمُنْصِفُ لِعَقْلِهِ إِنْكَارَكَ، وَ
الْمَوْسُومُ بِصِحَّةِ الْمَعْرِفَةِ جُحُودَكَ،

I beseech You by the dignity of the pristine conception of Your Unity and the sanctity of attachment to Your Scripture and by the Family of Your Prophet, to bless Adam, the wonder of Your creation and Your first testament, the voice of Your power and Your vicegerent on Your vast earth, and to bless Muḥammad, the choicest of Your elect, the seeker of Your knowledge, the trusted explorer of Your hidden secrets by virtue of Your blessing and help, and to bless all the prophets, the honoured elect, the legatees and the truthful who have passed during the interval between the two of them, and to forgive me for the sake of this Imam!

أَسْأَلُكَ بِشَرَفِ الْإِخْلَاصِ فِي تَوْحِيدِكَ،
وَ حُرْمَةِ التَّعَلُّقِ بِكِتَابِكَ وَ أَهْلِ بَيْتِ
نَبِيِّكَ، أَنْ تُصَلِّيَ عَلَىٰ آدَمَ بَدِيعِ فِطْرَتِكَ،
وَ بِكْرِ حُجَّتِكَ، وَ لِسَانِ قُدْرَتِكَ،
وَ الْخَلِيفَةِ فِي بَسِيطَتِكَ، وَ عَلَىٰ مُحَمَّدٍ
الْخَالِصِ مِنْ صَفْوَتِكَ، وَ الْفَاحِصِ
عَنْ مَعْرِفَتِكَ، وَ الْغَائِصِ الْمَأْمُونِ
عَلَىٰ مَكْنُونِ سَرِيرَتِكَ، بِمَا أَوْلَيْتَهُ مِنْ
نِعْمَتِكَ بِمَعُونَتِكَ، وَ عَلَىٰ مَنْ بَيْنَهُمَا
مِنَ النَّبِيِّينَ وَ الْمُكَرَّمِينَ، وَ الْأَوْصِيَاءِ
وَ الصِّدِّيقِينَ، وَ أَنْ تَهَبَنِي لِإِمَامِي هٰذَا.

Then place your hand on the blessed tomb and say,

O Allah, for the sake of the station of this master, by virtue of his obedience to You, and his standing with You, do not make me die a sudden death and deprive me not of repentance.

اَللّٰهُمَّ بِمَحَلِّ هٰذَا السَّيِّدِ مِنْ طَاعَتِكَ، وَ بِمَنْزِلَتِهِ عِنْدَكَ، لَا تُمِتْنِي فُجَاءَةً، وَ لَا تَحْرِمْنِي تَوْبَةً،

Grant me piety and restraint from what You have forbidden me in relation to religion and worldly life. Engage me in the matters of the Hereafter, not with seeking worldly success. Grant me success in achieving that which You love and approve of, and prevent me from pursuing desires and being deluded by falsehoods and vain hopes.

وَ ارْزُقْنِي الْوَرَعَ عَنْ مَحَارِمِكَ دِينًا وَ دُنْيَا، وَ اشْغَلْنِي بِالْآخِرَةِ عَنْ طَلَبِ الْأُولَىٰ، وَ وَفِّقْنِي لِمَا تُحِبُّ وَ تَرْضَىٰ، وَ جَنِّبْنِي اتِّبَاعَ الْهَوَىٰ، وَ الْإِغْتِرَارَ بِالْأَبَاطِيلِ وَ الْمُنَىٰ.

O Allah, confer rectitude upon my speech, give righteousness to my actions, let my pledges and promises be imbued with honesty and loyalty, give me commitment and vigilance in discharging my agreements and covenants, and put piety and kindness into my work and character. Grant me an inclusive welfare and an all-embracing well-being. Turn toward me Your graciousness and help, grant me in plenty Your gifts of success and facility. Lord, make me live felicitously and enable me to die as a martyr, and purify me to be prepared and ready for death and whatever lies beyond it!

اَللّٰهُمَّ اجْعَلِ السَّدَادَ فِي قَوْلِي، وَ الصَّوَابَ فِي فِعْلِي، وَ الصِّدْقَ وَ الْوَفَاءَ فِي ضَمَانِي وَ وَعْدِي، وَ الْحِفْظَ وَ الْإِينَاسَ مَقْرُونَيْنِ بِعَهْدِي وَ وَعْدِي، وَ الْبِرَّ وَ الْإِحْسَانَ مِنْ شَأْنِي وَ خُلُقِي، وَ اجْعَلِ السَّلَامَةَ لِي شَامِلَةً، وَ الْعَافِيَةَ بِي مُحِيطَةً مُلْتَفَّةً، وَ لَطِيفَ صُنْعِكَ وَ عَوْنِكَ مَصْرُوفًا إِلَيَّ، وَ حُسْنَ تَوْفِيقِكَ وَ يُسْرِكَ مَوْفُورًا عَلَيَّ، وَ أَحْيِنِي يَا رَبِّ سَعِيدًا، وَ تَوَفَّنِي شَهِيدًا، وَ طَهِّرْنِي لِلْمَوْتِ وَ مَا بَعْدَهُ.

O Allah, put health and light into my hearing and sight, sufficiency and wealth in the paths of

اَللّٰهُمَّ وَ اجْعَلِ الصِّحَّةَ وَ النُّورَ فِي سَمْعِي وَ بَصَرِي، وَ الْجِدَةَ وَ الْخَيْرَ فِي طُرُقِي، وَ

الْهُدَىٰ وَ الْبَصِيرَةَ فِي دِينِي وَ مَذْهَبِي، وَ الْمِيزَانَ أَبَدًا نَصْبَ عَيْنِي، وَ الذِّكْرَ وَ الْمَوْعِظَةَ شِعَارِي وَ دِثَارِي، وَ الْفِكْرَةَ وَ الْعِبْرَةَ أُنْسِي وَ عِمَادِي، وَ مَكِّنِ الْيَقِينَ فِي قَلْبِي، وَ اجْعَلْهُ أَوْثَقَ الْأَشْيَاءِ فِي نَفْسِي، وَ اغْلِبْهُ عَلَىٰ رَأْيِي وَ عَزْمِي، وَ اجْعَلِ الْإِرْشَادَ فِي عَمَلِي، وَ التَّسْلِيمَ لِأَمْرِكَ مِهَادِي وَ سَنَدِي،

my life, and guidance and insight in my faith and religion. Let the Scales of Justice (to be set up at Judgement) be always before my eyes. Let admonition and advise be my motto and emblem, and let reflection and taking lesson be my refuge and mainstay. Establish certainty in my heart and make it the strongest thing in my soul. Make it predominant over my opinions and decisions. Let my conduct be imbued with rectitude and let submission to Your commands be my rest and reliance.

وَ الرِّضَا بِقَضَائِكَ وَ قَدَرِكَ أَقْصَىٰ عَزْمِي وَ نِهَايَتِي، وَ أَبْعَدَ هَمِّي وَ غَايَتِي، حَتَّىٰ لَا أَتَّقِيَ أَحَدًا مِنْ خَلْقِكَ بِدِينِي، وَ لَا أَطْلُبَ بِهِ غَيْرَ آخِرَتِي، وَ لَا أَسْتَدْعِيَ مِنْهُ إِطْرَائِي وَ مَدْحِي، وَ اجْعَلْ خَيْرَ الْعَوَاقِبِ عَاقِبَتِي، وَ خَيْرَ الْمَصَايِرِ مَصِيرِي، وَ أَنْعَمَ الْعَيْشِ عَيْشِي، وَ أَفْضَلَ الْهُدَىٰ هُدَايَ، وَ أَوْفَرَ الْحُظُوظِ حَظِّي، وَ أَجْزَلَ الْأَقْسَامِ قِسْمِي وَ نَصِيبِي،

Let resignation to Your decrees and ordainments be my ultimate aim and goal and my highest intention and end, so that I will not be afraid of any of Your creatures with regard to my religion and will not seek anything therewith except my Hereafter, nor seek from it my own praise and fame. Let my end be the best of ends, my destination the best of destinations, my life the most blessed of lives, my guidance the best of guidances, my portion the most abundant of portions, my share the most plentiful of shares!

وَ كُنْ لِي يَا رَبِّ مِنْ كُلِّ سُوءٍ وَلِيًّا، وَ إِلَىٰ كُلِّ خَيْرٍ دَلِيلًا وَ قَائِدًا، وَ مِنْ كُلِّ بَاغٍ وَ حَسُودٍ ظَهِيرًا وَ مَانِعًا.

O Lord, be my protector from every evil and harm, be my guide to every good, and be my supporter and defender against every aggressor and envier!

اَللّٰهُمَّ بِكَ اعْتِدَادِي وَ عِصْمَتِي وَ ثِقَتِي وَ

O Allah, in You is my reliance, my protection, my trust, my

success, my power and strength and for Your sake is my life and death. In Your control are my movements and pauses and I hold fast to Your firmest handle. My reliance and trust is in You in all matters. With You is my deliverance and rescue from the punishment of hell and the touch of the Inferno. With You is my home and destination in the abode of Your security and munificence. And at the hands of my masters and guardians, the progeny of Muḥammad al-Muṣṭafā, lies my triumph and relief.

تَوْفِيقِي وَ حَـوْلِي وَ قُوَّتِي، وَ لَكَ مَحْيَايَ وَ
مَمَاتِي، وَ فِي قَبْضَتِكَ سُكُونِي وَ حَرَكَتِي، وَ
إِنَّ بِعُرْوَتِكَ الْوُثْقَى اسْتِمْسَاكِي وَ وُصْلَتِي،
وَ عَلَيْكَ فِي الْأُمُورِ كُلِّهَا اعْتِمَادِي وَ تَوَكُّلِي،
وَ مِنْ عَذَابِ جَهَنَّمَ وَ مَسِّ سَـقَرَ نَجَاتِي
وَ خَـلَاصِي، وَ فِي دَارِ أَمْنِكَ وَ كَرَامَتِكَ
مَثْـوَايَ وَ مُنْقَلَبِي، وَ عَلَىٰ أَيْدِي سَـادَتِي
وَ مَـوَالِيَّ آلِ الْمُصْطَفَىٰ فَـوْزِي وَ فَرَجِي.

O Allah, bless Muḥammad and the Family of Muḥammad and forgive the faithful, men and women, and the Muslims, men and women, and forgive me, my parents, their offspring, my family and neighbours and those faithful men and women who have done me any favour! Indeed You are dispenser of a great grace!

اَللّٰهُمَّ صَلِّ عَلَىٰ مُحَمَّدٍ وَ آلِ مُحَمَّدٍ، وَ اغْفِرْ
لِلْمُؤْمِنِينَ وَ الْمُؤْمِنَاتِ وَ الْمُسْـلِمِينَ وَ
الْمُسْـلِمَاتِ، وَ اغْفِرْ لِي وَ لِوَالِدَيَّ وَ مَا
وَلَدَا، وَ أَهْـلِ بَيْتِي وَ جِيرَانِي، وَ لِكُلِّ مَنْ
قَلَّدَنِي يَدًا مِنَ الْمُؤْمِنِـينَ وَ الْمُؤْمِنَاتِ،
إِنَّكَ ذُو فَضْلٍ عَظِيمٍ.

4. AN AFTER-ZIYARAH SUPPLICATION

This is a supplication containing sublime themes which is recited after the *ziyārah* of any of the Imams (*ʿa*). Sayyid Ib Ṭāwūs, has cited it in the *Miṣbāḥ al-Zā'ir* after the aforementioned comprehensive *ziyārah*.[1] The text of this noble supplication is as follows.

O Allah, I visit this Imam, acknowledging his Imamate, believing in the duty to obey him. I have set out for his shrine de-

اَللّٰهُمَّ إِنِّي زُرْتُ هٰذَا الْإِمَامَ مُقِرًّا بِإِمَامَتِهِ،
مُعْتَقِـدًا لِفَـرْضِ طَاعَتِـهِ، فَقَصَدْتُ

1 From Ibn Ṭāw3s in . *Biḥār*, xcix, 169, b 8.

spite my sins and shortcomings, my mortal sins, my many misdeeds and vices, and whatever You know concerning me, seeking asylum in Your pardon, taking shelter in Your forbearance, putting hope in Your mercy, taking refuge in Your support, seeking protection in Your compassion, beseeching the intercession of Your *walī* and descendant of Your *awliyā*, Your elect one and scion of Your elect, Your trustee and scion of Your trustees, Your vicegerent and scion of Your vicegerents, whom You have made the means of Your mercy and approval, the media of Your compassion and forgiveness.

مَشْهَدَهُ بِذُنُوبِي وَ عُيُوبِي وَ مُوبِقَاتِ
آثَامِي وَ كَثْرَةِ سَيِّئَاتِي وَ خَطَايَايَ وَ مَا
تَعْرِفُهُ مِنِّي، مُسْتَجِيرًا بِعَفْوِكَ، مُسْتَعِيذًا
بِحِلْمِكَ، رَاجِيًا رَحْمَتَكَ، لَاجِئًا إِلَىٰ
رُكْنِكَ، عَائِذًا بِرَأْفَتِكَ، مُسْتَشْفِعًا
بِوَلِيِّكَ وَ ابْنِ أَوْلِيَائِكَ، وَ صَفِيِّكَ وَ ابْنِ
أَصْفِيَائِكَ، وَ أَمِينِكَ وَ ابْنِ أُمَنَائِكَ،
وَ خَلِيفَتِكَ وَ ابْنِ خُلَفَائِكَ، اَلَّذِينَ
جَعَلْتَهُمُ الْوَسِيلَةَ إِلَىٰ رَحْمَتِكَ وَ رِضْوَانِكَ،
وَ الذَّرِيعَةَ إِلَىٰ رَأْفَتِكَ وَ غُفْرَانِكَ،

O Allah, my first need from You is that You forgive me my past sins despite their great number and protect me from sin in what remains of my life. Purify my religion from that which pollutes, disfigures and detracts it, and protect it from doubt, uncertainty, corruption and polytheism. Make me steadfast in obeying You, Your Apostle and his descendants, the felicitous and chosen ones, may Your blessings, mercy, greetings and Your bounties be upon them.

اَللّٰهُمَّ وَ أَوَّلُ حَاجَتِي إِلَيْكَ أَنْ تَغْفِرَ لِي
مَا سَلَفَ مِنْ ذُنُوبِي عَلَىٰ كَثْرَتِهَا، وَ أَنْ
تَعْصِمَنِي فِيمَا بَقِيَ مِنْ عُمْرِي، وَ تُطَهِّرَ
دِينِي مِمَّا يُدَنِّسُهُ وَ يَشِينُهُ وَ يُزْرِي بِهِ، وَ
تَحْمِيَهُ مِنَ الرَّيْبِ وَ الشَّكِّ، وَ الْفَسَادِ وَ
الشِّرْكِ، وَ تُثَبِّتَنِي عَلَىٰ طَاعَتِكَ وَ طَاعَةِ
رَسُولِكَ وَ ذُرِّيَّتِهِ النُّجَبَاءِ السُّعَدَاءِ،
صَلَوَاتُكَ عَلَيْهِمْ وَ رَحْمَتُكَ وَ سَلَامُكَ
وَ بَرَكَاتُكَ،

Let my life, so long as You keep me alive, be in obedience to

وَ تُحْيِيَنِي مَا أَحْيَيْتَنِي عَلَىٰ طَاعَتِهِمْ، وَ

them, and let my death, when You make me die, be in obedience to them. Do not efface their love and affection from my heart, nor the hatred of their enemies, nor fellowship of their friends and kindness towards them.

تُمِيتَنِي إِذَا أَمَتَّنِي عَلَىٰ طَاعَتِهِمْ، وَ أَنْ
لَا تَمْحُوَ مِنْ قَلْبِي مَوَدَّتَهُمْ وَ مَحَبَّتَهُمْ،
وَ بُغْضَ أَعْدَائِهِمْ، وَ مُرَافَقَةَ أَوْلِيَائِهِمْ
وَ بِرَّهُمْ،

O Lord, I beseech You to accept all that from me. Make me fond of Your worship, careful in observing it, and lively in performing it. Make me abhor acts of disobedience to You and dislike committing what You have made unlawful, and withhold me from performing them. Dissuade me from being negligent of my prayers, from taking them lightly, and from delaying them. Enable me to offer them as You have prescribed and commanded, with humility and awe, in accordance with the *sunnah* of Your Apostle, may Your blessings, mercy and bounties be upon him and his Family.

وَ أَسْأَلُكَ يَا رَبِّ أَنْ تَقْبَلَ ذَٰلِكَ مِنِّي، وَ
تُحَبِّبَ إِلَيَّ عِبَادَتَكَ وَ الْمُوَاظَبَةَ عَلَيْهَا،
وَ تُنَشِّطَنِي لَهَا، وَ تُبَغِّضَ إِلَيَّ مَعَاصِيَكَ
وَ مَحَارِمَكَ وَ تَدْفَعَنِي عَنْهَا، وَ تُجَنِّبَنِي
التَّقْصِيرَ فِي صَلَوَاتِي وَ الْإِسْتِهَانَةَ بِهَا وَ
التَّرَاخِيَ عَنْهَا، وَ تُوَفِّقَنِي لِتَأْدِيَتِهَا كَمَا
فَرَضْتَ وَ أَمَرْتَ بِهِ عَلَىٰ سُنَّةِ رَسُولِكَ
صَلَوَاتُكَ عَلَيْهِ وَ آلِهِ وَ رَحْمَتُكَ وَ
بَرَكَاتُكَ خُضُوعًا وَ خُشُوعًا،

Open up my heart for the payment of *zakāt*, giving of charities and doing acts of kindness, assistance and empathy toward the followers of the Family of Muḥammad, may peace be upon them.

وَ تَشْرَحَ صَدْرِي لِإِيتَاءِ الزَّكَاةِ، وَ
إِعْطَاءِ الصَّدَقَاتِ، وَ بَذْلِ الْمَعْرُوفِ
وَ الْإِحْسَانِ إِلَىٰ شِيعَةِ آلِ مُحَمَّدٍ عَلَيْهِمُ
السَّلَامُ وَ مُوَاسَاتِهِمْ،

Let not die except after You have enabled me to perform the pilgrimage to Your Holy House and the *ziyārah* of the grave of Your Prophet and the graves of the Imams, may peace be upon them.

وَ لَا تَتَوَفَّانِي إِلَّا بَعْدَ أَنْ تَرْزُقَنِي حَجَّ
بَيْتِكَ الْحَرَامِ، وَ زِيَارَةَ قَبْرِ نَبِيِّكَ وَ قُبُورِ
الْأَئِمَّةِ عَلَيْهِمُ السَّلَامُ،

O Lord, I beseech You to grant me success in performing sincere repentance, one that You approve of, in harbouring intentions that You regard as commendable, and in performing righteous deeds that will be acceptable to You. Forgive me and have mercy upon me when You make me die. Make the throes of death easy for me, and resurrect me in the fold of Muḥammad and his Family, may Allah's blessings be upon him and them, and admit me with Your mercy into paradise.

وَ أَسْأَلُكَ يَا رَبِّ تَوْبَةً نَصُوحًا تَرْضَاهَا، وَ نِيَّةً تَحْمَدُهَا، وَ عَمَلًا صَالِحاً تَقْبَلُهُ، وَ أَنْ تَغْفِرَ لِي وَ تَرْحَمَنِي إِذَا تَوَفَّيْتَنِي، وَ تُهَوِّنَ عَلَيَّ سَكَرَاتِ الْمَوْتِ، وَ تَحْشُرَنِي فِي زُمْرَةِ مُحَمَّدٍ وَ آلِهِ صَلَوَاتُ اللهِ عَلَيْهِ وَ عَلَيْهِمْ، وَ تُدْخِلَنِي الْجَنَّةَ بِرَحْمَتِكَ،

Make my tears flow profuse in obedience to You and let them flow for that which brings me near to You. Make my heart compassionate towards Your *awliyā* and preserve me in this world from handicaps, blights, severe diseases and chronic illnesses and all kinds of afflictions and accidents.

وَ تَجْعَلَ دَمْعِي غَزِيرًا فِي طَاعَتِكَ، وَ عَبْرَتِي جَارِيَةً فِيمَا يُقَرِّبُنِي مِنْكَ، وَ قَلْبِي عَطُوفًا عَلَىٰ أَوْلِيَائِكَ، وَ تَصُونَنِي فِي هٰذِهِ الدُّنْيَا مِنَ الْعَاهَاتِ وَ الْآفَاتِ، وَ الْأَمْرَاضِ الشَّدِيدَةِ، وَ الْأَسْقَامِ الْمُزْمِنَةِ، وَ جَمِيعِ أَنْوَاعِ الْبَلَاءِ وَ الْحَوَادِثِ،

Restrain my heart from that which is unlawful and make acts of disobedience to You hateful to me. Make me fond of what is lawful, open for me its doors and steady my intentions and conduct with regard to that.

وَ تَصْرِفَ قَلْبِي عَنِ الْحَرَامِ، وَ تُبَغِّضَ إِلَيَّ مَعَاصِيَكَ، وَ تُحَبِّبَ إِلَيَّ الْحَلَالَ وَ تَفْتَحَ لِي أَبْوَابَهُ، وَ تُثَبِّتَ نِيَّتِي وَ فِعْلِي عَلَيْهِ،

Extend the span of my life and spare me of ordeals. Do not strip me of what You have favoured me with, and do not withdraw any kindness that You have granted me and do not strip me of the

وَ تَمُدَّ فِي عُمْرِي، وَ تُغْلِقَ أَبْوَابَ الْمِحَنِ عَنِّي، وَ لَا تَسْلُبَنِي مَا مَنَنْتَ بِهِ عَلَيَّ، وَ لَا تَسْتَرِدَّ شَيْئًا مِمَّا أَحْسَنْتَ بِهِ إِلَيَّ، وَ

blessings that You have bestowed upon me! Enhance what You have bestowed on me and increase it manifold times and provide me with a wealth which is plenty, vast, wholesome, agreeable, ever-increasing and sufficient, with an honour that is lasting and appropriate, with a prestige that is broad and secure, and with a blessing that is plentiful and inclusive, sparing me thereby from fruitless pursuits and toilsome means of livelihood.

لَا تَنْزِعَ مِنِّي النِّعَمَ الَّتِي أَنْعَمْتَ بِهَا عَلَيَّ، وَ تَزِيدَ فِيمَا خَوَّلْتَنِي وَ تُضَاعِفَهُ أَضْعَافًا مُضَاعَفَةً، وَ تَرْزُقَنِي مَالًا كَثِيرًا وَاسِعًا سَائِغًا هَنِيئًا نَامِيًا وَافِيًا، وَ عِزًّا بَاقِيًا كَافِيًا، وَ جَاهًا عَرِيضًا مَنِيعًا، وَ نِعْمَةً سَابِغَةً عَامَّةً، وَ تُغْنِيَنِي بِذَلِكَ عَنِ الْمَطَالِبِ الْمُنَكَّدَةِ، وَ الْمَوَارِدِ الصَّعْبَةِ،

Spare me from these while giving me to enjoy well-being in my faith, in my self, my children and all that You have given me and bestowed upon me. Preserve for me my wealth and all that You have given into my possession. Keep off from me the hands of oppressors. Return me to my homeland. Enable me to attain my ultimate hopes in the world and the Hereafter. Let my ultimate end be one that is praiseworthy, good and wholesome.

وَ تُخَلِّصَنِي مِنْهَا مُعَافًى فِي دِينِي وَ نَفْسِي وَ وَلَدِي وَ مَا أَعْطَيْتَنِي وَ مَنَحْتَنِي، وَ تَحْفَظَ عَلَيَّ مَالِي وَ جَمِيعَ مَا خَوَّلْتَنِي، وَ تَقْبِضَ عَنِّي أَيْدِيَ الْجَبَابِرَةِ، وَ تَرُدَّنِي إِلَى وَطَنِي، وَ تُبَلِّغَنِي نِهَايَةَ أَمَلِي فِي دُنْيَايَ وَ آخِرَتِي، وَ تَجْعَلَ عَاقِبَةَ أَمْرِي مَحْمُودَةً حَسَنَةً سَلِيمَةً،

Make me broad-minded, prosperous, good-natured, disinclined to stinginess, to withholding help from others, and to hypocrisy, falsehood, slander, and false speech, and make the love of Muḥammad and the Family of Muḥammad and their followers fixed in my heart.

وَ تَجْعَلَنِي رَحِيبَ الصَّدْرِ، وَاسِعَ الْحَالِ، حَسَنَ الْخُلُقِ، بَعِيدًا مِنَ الْبُخْلِ وَ الْمَنْعِ وَ النِّفَاقِ وَ الْكِذْبِ وَ الْبَهْتِ وَ قَوْلِ الزُّورِ، وَ تُرْسِخَ فِي قَلْبِي مَحَبَّةَ مُحَمَّدٍ وَ آلِ مُحَمَّدٍ وَ شِيعَتِهِمْ،

O Lord, protect me with regard to my self, my family, my proper-

وَ تَحْرُسَنِي يَا رَبِّ فِي نَفْسِي وَ أَهْلِي وَ

مَالِي وَ وَلَدِي وَ أَهْلِ حُزَانَتِي وَ إِخْوَانِي وَ
أَهْلِ مَوَدَّتِي وَ ذُرِّيَّتِي، بِرَحْمَتِكَ وَ جُودِكَ.

ty, my children, my dependants, my brethren, friends and descendants, with Your mercy and generosity.

اَللّٰهُمَّ هٰذِهِ حَاجَاتِي عِنْدَكَ، وَ قَدِ
اسْتَكْثَرْتُهَا لِلُؤْمِي وَ شُحِّي، وَ هِيَ عِنْدَكَ
صَغِيرَةٌ حَقِيرَةٌ، وَ عَلَيْكَ سَهْلَةٌ يَسِيرَةٌ،

O Allah, these are my requests to You, which I regard as exorbitant on account of my meanness and miserliness, though there are petty and insignificant in Your sight and simple and easy for You.

فَأَسْأَلُكَ بِجَاهِ مُحَمَّدٍ وَ آلِ مُحَمَّدٍ عَلَيْهِ وَ
عَلَيْهِمُ السَّلَامُ عِنْدَكَ، وَ بِحَقِّهِمْ عَلَيْكَ،
وَ بِمَا أَوْجَبْتَ لَهُمْ، وَ بِسَائِرِ أَنْبِيَائِكَ
وَ رُسُلِكَ وَ أَصْفِيَائِكَ وَ أَوْلِيَائِكَ
الْمُخْلَصِينَ مِنْ عِبَادِكَ، وَ بِاسْمِكَ
الْأَعْظَمِ الْأَعْظَمِ، لَمَّا قَضَيْتَهَا كُلَّهَا وَ
أَسْعَفْتَنِي بِهَا، وَ لَمْ تُخَيِّبْ أَمَلِي وَ رَجَائِي.

So I beseech You by the high standing that Muḥammad and the Family of Muḥammad, may peace be to him and them, have with You, and by their right on You and that to which You have entitled them and the rest of Your prophets, apostles, elect and *awliyā,* the dedicated of Your servants, and by Your supreme Name, the supreme most, to fulfil all of them and to grant these wishes of mine, and do not disappoint my hope and expectations!

اَللّٰهُمَّ وَ شَفِّعْ صَاحِبَ هٰذَا الْقَبْرِ فِيَّ. يَا
سَيِّدِي يَا وَلِيَّ اللهِ يَا أَمِينَ اللهِ، أَسْأَلُكَ
أَنْ تَشْفَعَ لِي إِلَى اللهِ عَزَّ وَ جَلَّ فِي هٰذِهِ
الْحَاجَاتِ كُلِّهَا، بِحَقِّ آبَائِكَ الطَّاهِرِينَ،
وَ بِحَقِّ أَوْلَادِكَ الْمُنْتَجَبِينَ، فَإِنَّ لَكَ عِنْدَ
اللهِ تَقَدَّسَتْ أَسْمَاؤُهُ الْمَنْزِلَةَ الشَّرِيفَةَ،
وَ الْمَرْتَبَةَ الْجَلِيلَةَ، وَ الْجَاهَ الْعَرِيضَ.

O Allah, make the owner of this grave my intercessor. O my master, O *walī* of Allah, O trustee of Allah! I beseech you to intercede with Allah, the Almighty and Glorious, on my behalf concerning all these requests of mine by the right of your immaculate ancestors and by the right of Your elect descendants! For You have with Allah, hallowed be His Names, a noble standing, an august rank and a consummate eminence.

اَللّٰهُمَّ لَوْ عَرَفْتُ مَنْ هُوَ أَوْجَهُ عِنْدَكَ

O Allah, had I known someone who had a greater eminence

with You than this Imam and his immaculate ancestors and descendants, may peace and blessings be upon them, I would have made them my intercessors and advanced them before these requests of mine. So hear me and answer my pleas, and treat me as is worthy of You, O Most Merciful of the merciful!

مِنْ هٰـذَا الْإِمَامِ وَ مِنْ آبَائِـهِ وَ أَبْنَائِهِ الطَّاهِرِيـنَ عَلَيْهِمُ السَّـلَامُ وَ الصَّلَاةُ لَجَعَلْتُهُـمْ شُـفَعَائِي، وَ قَدَّمْتُهُمْ أَمَامَ حَاجَتِي وَ طَلِبَاتِي هٰذِهِ، فَاسْـمَعْ مِنِّي وَ اسْتَجِبْ لِي، وَ افْعَلْ بِي مَا أَنْتَ أَهْلُهُ يَا أَرْحَمَ الرَّاحِمِينَ.

O Allah, whatever I have failed to mention in my petitions, or been unable to express, or even failed to comprehend, of things good for my religion, my worldly life and Hereafter, favour me with them.

Protect and safeguard me, pardon my faults and forgive me. Keep off from me the hands of those who wish to cause me harm or nuisance, including rebellious demons, wilful rulers, antagonists in religion, contenders in worldly matters, the envious who envy my blessings, wrongdoers and aggressors. Turn away from me their malice. Make them preoccupied with their own selves. Suffice me in relation to their evil and that of their followers and henchmen. Shelter me from all that which may cause me harm and injury. Grant me all that is good, including what I know and what I do not know.

اَللّٰهُمَّ وَمَا قَصُرَتْ عَنْهُ مَسْأَلَتِي، وَعَجَزَتْ عَنْهُ قُوَّتِي، وَ لَمْ تَبْلُغْهُ فِطْنَتِي مِنْ صَالِحِ دِينِي وَ دُنْيَايَ وَ آخِرَتِي، فَامْنُنْ بِهِ عَلَيَّ، وَ احْفَظْنِي وَ احْرُسْنِي، وَ هَبْ لِي وَ اغْفِرْ لِي، وَ مَنْ أَرَادَنِي بِسُوءٍ أَوْ مَكْرُوهٍ مِنْ شَيْطَانٍ مَرِيدٍ، أَوْ سُلْطَانٍ عَنِيدٍ، أَوْ مُخَالِفٍ فِي دِينٍ، أَوْ مُنَازِعٍ فِي دُنْيَا، أَوْ حَاسِدٍ عَلَيَّ نِعْمَةً، أَوْ ظَالِمٍ أَوْ بَاغٍ، فَاقْبِضْ عَنِّي يَدَهُ، وَ اصْرِفْ عَنِّي كَيْدَهُ، وَ اشْغَلْهُ عَنِّي بِنَفْسِهِ، وَ اكْفِنِي شَرَّهُ وَ شَرَّ أَتْبَاعِهِ وَ شَيَاطِينِهِ، وَ أَجِرْنِي مِنْ كُلِّ مَا يَضُرُّنِي وَ يُجْحِفُ بِي، وَ أَعْطِنِي جَمِيعَ الْخَيْرِ كُلِّهِ مِمَّا أَعْلَمُ وَ مِمَّا لَا أَعْلَمُ.

O Allah, bless Muḥammad and the Family of Muḥammad, and

اَللّٰهُمَّ صَلِّ عَلَىٰ مُحَمَّدٍ وَ آلِ مُحَمَّدٍ، وَ

اغْفِرْ لِي وَ لِوَالِدَيَّ، وَ لِإِخْوَانِي وَ أَخَوَاتِي،
وَ أَعْمَامِي وَ عَمَّاتِي، وَ أَخْوَالِي وَ خَالَاتِي،
وَ أَجْدَادِي وَ جَدَّاتِي، وَ أَوْلَادِهِمْ وَ
ذَرَارِيهِمْ، وَ أَزْوَاجِي وَ ذُرِّيَّاتِي، وَ أَقْرِبَائِي
وَ أَصْدِقَائِي، وَ جِيرَانِي وَ إِخْوَانِي فِيكَ
مِنْ أَهْلِ الشَّرْقِ وَ الْغَرْبِ، وَ لِجَمِيعِ
أَهْلِ مَوَدَّتِي مِنَ الْمُؤْمِنِينَ وَ الْمُؤْمِنَاتِ،
اَلْأَحْيَاءِ مِنْهُمْ وَ الْأَمْوَاتِ، وَ لِجَمِيعِ مَنْ
عَلَّمَنِي خَيْرًا أَوْ تَعَلَّمَ مِنِّي عِلْمًا.

forgive me, my parents, my brothers, my sisters, my paternal uncles and aunts, my maternal uncles and aunts, my grandfathers, my grandmothers, their offspring and descendants, my spouse(s), my descendants, my relatives, my friends, my neighbours and my brothers in Your religion from among the people who live in the east and the west and all those who are dear to me of the faithful, men and women, the living among them and the dead, and all those who have taught me anything good and those who have received instruction and knowledge from me!

اَللّٰهُمَّ أَشْرِكْهُمْ فِي صَالِحِ دُعَائِي وَ زِيَارَتِي
لِمَشْهَدِ حُجَّتِكَ وَ وَلِيِّكَ، وَ أَشْرِكْنِي
فِي صَالِحِ أَدْعِيَتِهِمْ بِرَحْمَتِكَ يَا أَرْحَمَ
الرَّاحِمِينَ، وَ بَلِّغْ وَلِيَّكَ مِنْهُمُ السَّلَامَ،

O Allah, appoint them a share in my good supplications and my *ziyārah* of the shrine of Your testament and *walī*, and grant me a share in their good supplications, with Your mercy, O Most Merciful of the merciful! Convey Your *walī* *salām* from them!

وَ السَّلَامُ عَلَيْكَ وَ رَحْمَةُ اللهِ وَ بَرَكَاتُهُ، يَا
سَيِّدِي يَا مَوْلَايَ (يَا فُلَانَ بْنَ فُلَانٍ)

O my master and guardian, (so-and-so son of so-and-so), peace be to You and may Allah's mercy and His bounties be upon you!

(Mention here the name of the Imam and that of his father.)

صَلَّى اللهُ عَلَيْكَ وَ عَلَىٰ رُوحِكَ وَ بَدَنِكَ،
أَنْتَ وَسِيلَتِي إِلَى اللهِ، وَ ذَرِيعَتِي إِلَيْهِ،
وَ لِي حَقُّ مُوَالَاتِي وَ تَأْمِيلِي، فَكُنْ
شَفِيعِي إِلَى اللهِ عَزَّ وَ جَلَّ فِي الْوُقُوفِ

May the blessings of Allah be upon you, your spirit and your body! You are my means of recourse to Allah and my intermediary with Him. I have a right arising from my love for you and my hope. So be my intercessor

عَلٰى قِصَّـــتِي هٰذِهِ، وَ صَرْفِي عَنْ مَوْقِفِي هٰذَا بِالنُّجْحِ بِمَا سَـــأَلْتُهُ كُلِّهِ بِرَحْمَتِهِ وَ قُدْرَتِهِ.

with Allah, Almighty and Glorious, in giving attention to this tale of mine and enabling me to return from this place with success in achieving all that I have asked for, by His mercy and power.

اَللّٰهُمَّ ارْزُقْنِي عَقْلًا كَامِلًا، وَ لُبًّا رَاجِحًا، وَ عِزًّا بَاقِيًا، وَ قَلْبًا زَكِيًّا، وَ عَمَلًا كَثِيرًا، وَ أَدَبًا بَارِعًا، وَ اجْعَلْ ذٰلِكَ كُلَّهُ لِي وَ لَا تَجْعَلْهُ عَلَيَّ، بِرَحْمَتِكَ يَا أَرْحَمَ الرَّاحِمِينَ!

O Allah, grant me a perfect intellect, a superior mind, an enduring honour, a pure heart and plenty of good works and excellent morals, and make all that beneficial for me and not detrimental to me, with Your mercy O Most Merciful of the merciful!

5. A Farewell Ziyarah

This is a *ziyārah* of farewell with which one can take leave of any of the Imams (a). It should be known that at the time of departure from the town, the pilgrims taking leave of someone who is he is visiting is part of the etiquette of *ziyārah* and bidding him farewell in the way as has been taught by them, a feature which is found in most of the *ziyārah*'s. in the Mafatih in the book of *ziyārah* we have cited the texts to be recited at farewell while taking leave of any of the Imams, may Allah's blessings be upon them. For the farewell of Imams Hussain, the doyen of the martyr, we confine ourselves to mentioning the same *ziyārah* of farewell that was cited in the 20th etiquette pertaining to the *ziyārah* of that Imams.

Here we cite the following *ziyārah* of farewell narrated by Muḥammad ibn al-Ma<u>sh</u>hadī in the chapter on farewell of his book his book *Al-Mazār al-Kabīr.* Sayyid Ibn *Ṭāwūs* has cited it after the aforementioned common *ziyārah*.[1] The texts of *ziyārah* given here is in accordance with *Miṣbāḥ al-Zā'ir*. When the pilgrim wants to return from any of the shrine cities, he should say,

اَلسَّــلَامُ عَلَيْكُمْ يَا أَهْلَ بَيْتِ النُّبُوَّةِ، وَ مَعْدِنَ الرِّسَــالَةِ، سَــلَامَ مُوَدِّعٍ لَا

Peace to you O Family of prophecy and repository of apostleship, a greeting from one who bids you farewell, without boredom or dis-

1 *Faqīh*, ii, 617. *ʿUyūn A<u>kh</u>bār al-Riḍā*, ii, 277, b 68, whence *Biḥār*, xcix, 134, b 8. *Al-Mazār al-Kabīr*, 535. *Tah<u>dh</u>īb*, vi, 101. *Balad*, 309. Wāfī, xiv, 1575.

inclination, and may the mercy of Allah and His bounties be upon you, Family of the Prophet, indeed He is all-praiseworthy and glorious.

سَئِمٍ وَ لَا قَالٍ، وَ رَحْمَةُ اللهِ وَ بَرَكَاتُهُ
عَلَيْكُمْ أَهْلَ الْبَيْتِ، إِنَّهُ حَمِيدٌ مَجِيدٌ،

This greeting is from a friend who departs, not out of any feelings of distaste or an intent to turn away from you, or to find a substitute for you, or for preferring someone over you, or because he sets little store by nearness to you. May Allah not make this my last opportunity of visiting your graves and coming to your shrines.

سَلَامَ وَلِيٍّ غَيْرِ رَاغِبٍ عَنْكُمْ، وَ لَا
مُنْحَرِفٍ عَنْكُمْ، وَ لَا مُسْتَبْدِلٍ بِكُمْ،
وَ لَا مُؤْثِرٍ عَلَيْكُمْ، وَ لَا زَاهِدٍ فِي
قُرْبِكُمْ؛ لَا جَعَلَهُ اللهُ آخِرَ الْعَهْدِ مِنْ
زِيَارَةِ قُبُورِكُمْ، وَ إِتْيَانِ مَشَاهِدِكُمْ،

Peace be to you! May Allah gather me in your fold, admit me at your Pool, make you pleased with me, enable me in your reign, resurrect me at the time of your return, empower me during your era, attach weight to my efforts for your sake, forgive my sins through your intercession, overlook my slips for the sake of my affection for you, raise my rank on account of my love for you, grant me dignity for obeying you, honour me with your guidance, and make me of those who return home blessed with felicity, success, safety, profit, welfare, sufficiency and achievement of God's approval, grace and protection, with the best of what any of your pilgrims, friends, lovers and followers has returned to his

وَ السَّلَامُ عَلَيْكُمْ، وَ حَشَرَنِيَ اللهُ
فِي زُمْرَتِكُمْ، وَ أَوْرَدَنِي حَوْضَكُمْ،
وَ أَرْضَاكُمْ عَنِّي، وَ مَكَّنَنِي فِي
دَوْلَتِكُمْ، وَ أَحْيَانِي فِي رَجْعَتِكُمْ، وَ
مَلَّكَنِي فِي أَيَّامِكُمْ، وَ شَكَرَ سَعْيِي
لَكُمْ، وَ غَفَرَ ذُنُوبِي بِشَفَاعَتِكُمْ،
وَ أَقَالَ عَثْرَتِي بِحُبِّكُمْ، وَ أَعْلَى كَعْبِي
بِمُوَالَاتِكُمْ، وَ شَرَّفَنِي بِطَاعَتِكُمْ، وَ
أَعَزَّنِي بِهُدَاكُمْ، وَ جَعَلَنِي مِمَّنْ يَنْقَلِبُ
مُفْلِحًا مُنْجِحًا سَالِمًا غَانِمًا مُعَافًا غَنِيًّا
فَائِزًا بِرِضْوَانِ اللهِ وَ فَضْلِهِ وَ كِفَايَتِهِ،
بِأَفْضَلِ مَا يَنْقَلِبُ بِهِ أَحَدٌ مِنْ زُوَّارِكُمْ

home!

وَ مَوَالِيكُمْ وَ مُحِبِّيكُمْ وَ شِـيعَتِكُمْ،

May Allah grant me to return again and again and again, so long as my Lord keeps me alive, with sincere intentions, faith, Godfearing, surrender and a provision that is plenty, lawful and good!

وَ رَزَقَنِيَ اللهُ الْعَوْدَ ثُمَّ الْعَوْدَ ثُمَّ الْعَوْدَ مَا أَبْقَانِي رَبِّي، بِنِيَّةٍ صَادِقَةٍ وَ إِيمَانٍ وَ تَقْوىٰ وَ إِخْبَاتٍ، وَ رِزْقٍ وَاسِعٍ حَلَالٍ طَيِّبٍ .

O Allah, do not make this my last opportunity to perform their ziyārah, to celebrate their memory and invoke blessings upon them, and appoint for me forgiveness, mercy, goodness, beneficence, light, faith, and a gracious response to my petitions such as You have granted to Your friends who know their rights, consider obedience to them obligatory, are eager to make their ziyārah and seek nearness to You and them!

اَللّٰهُـــمَّ لَا تَجْعَلْهُ آخِرَ الْعَهْدِ مِنْ زِيَارَتِهِمْ وَ ذِكْرِهِمْ وَ الصَّـلَاةِ عَلَيْهِمْ، وَ أَوْجِبْ لِيَ الْمَغْفِرَةَ وَ الرَّحْمَـةَ، وَ الْخَيْرَ وَ الْبَرَكَةَ، وَ النُّـورَ وَ الْإِيمَانَ وَ حُسْـنَ الْإِجَابَةِ، كَمَا أَوْجَبْتَ لِأَوْلِيائِكَ الْعَارِفِينَ بِحَقِّهِمْ، اَلْمُوجِبِـينَ طَاعَتَهُـمْ، وَ الرَّاغِبِـينَ فِي زِيَارَتِهِمْ، اَلْمُتَقَرِّبِينَ إِلَيْكَ وَ إِلَيْهِمْ.

May my father and mother be your ransom, and may my soul, wealth and family be sacrificed for you! Make me part of your concern, receive me into your party, admit me into your intercession, and remember me with your Lord!

بِأَبِي أَنْتُمْ وَ أُمِّي وَ نَفْسِي وَ مَالِي وَ أَهْلِي، اِجْعَلُـونِي مِنْ هَمِّكُـمْ، وَ صَيِّرُونِي فِي حِزْبِكُمْ، وَ أَدْخِلُونِي فِي شَفَاعَتِكُمْ، وَ اذْكُرُونِي عِنْدَ رَبِّكُمْ.

O Allah, bless Muḥammad and the Family of Muḥammad, and convey to their spirits and bodies my many salāms and greetings!

اَللّٰهُمَّ صَلِّ عَلىٰ مُحَمَّدٍ وَ آلِ مُحَمَّدٍ، وَ أَبْلِغْ أَرْوَاحَهُمْ وَ أَجْسَـادَهُمْ عَنِّي تَحِيَّةً كَثِيرَةً وَ سَلَامًا،

May peace be to you and may Allah's mercy and blessings be upon you!

وَ السَّلَامُ عَلَيْكُمْ وَ رَحْمَةُ اللهِ وَ بَرَكَاتُهُ.

8. ZIYARAH BY A PROXY

It should be known that it is possible to make a gift of the reward of the *ziyārah* of the Apostle of Allah (ṣ) and any of the Imams to the holy spirit of one of them and similarly to the spirit of one of the faithful, and one can perform *ziyārah* as a proxy on their behalf.

Hence it is reported with a reliable *isnād* that Dāwūd al-Ṣarmī said to Imam ᶜAli Naqī (ᶜ*a*), "I perform the *ziyārah* of your father and offer it as a gift to you." The Imam said to him, "You will have a great reward with God and thanks and appreciation from us."[1]

It is mentioned in another report that Imam ᶜAli Naqī (ᶜ*a*) sent a person to the shrine of Imam Ḥusayn (ca) to perform the *ziyārah* on his behalf and to pray for him.[2]

In a report with a reliable *isnād*, Imam Mūsā ibn Jaᶜfar (ᶜ*a*) is reported to have said, "When you visit the shrine of the Apostle of Allah (ṣ), after finishing the observances pertaining to the *ziyārah*, offer a two-*rak*ᶜ*ah* prayer near the head of the tomb of the Apostle of Allah (ṣ) and say,

Peace be to you O Prophet of Allah on behalf of my father and mother, my spouse and my children and dependants, and all the people of my town, the freemen and the slaves, the black and the white.	اَلسَّلَامُ عَلَيْكَ يَا نَبِيَّ اللهِ مِنْ أَبِي وَ أُمِّي وَ زَوْجَتِي وَ وَلَدِي وَ حَامَّتِي وَ مِنْ جَمِيعِ أَهْلِ بَلَدِي حُرِّهِمْ وَ عَبْدِهِمْ وَ أَبْيَضِهِمْ وَ أَسْوَدِهِمْ.

Then if you tell any of your townsman that you have conveyed his greetings to the Apostle (ṣ), you would be telling the truth."[3]

It is mentioned in some reports[4] that some of the Imams, may Allah's blessings by upon all of them, were asked concerning a person who offers a two-rakᶜah prayer, or keeps fast a day, or performs the ḥajj or ᶜumrah pilgrimages or perform is the *ziyārah* of the apostle of

1 *Tahdhīb*, vi, 110, b 52, h 15, whence *Wasā'il*, xiv, 593, b 103, h 19884 & *Biḥār*, xcix, 256, b 11, h 3.

2 *Al-Mazār al-Kabīr*, 595, b 1, h 2, whence *Biḥār*, xcix, 257, b 11, h 5. Mufīd's *Mazār*, 209, b 22, h 2.

3 *Kāfī*, iv, 316, h 8, whence *Wasā'il*, xi, 205, b 30, h 14633, xiv, 357, b 14, h 19382. *Biḥār*, xcix, 255, b 11, h 1, from *Tahdhīb*, vi, 109, b 52, h 9 and *Kāfī*.

4 *Al-Mazār al-Kabīr*, 599, b 2, h 2, whence *Biḥār*, xcix, 259, b 11, h 6 & Mustadrak, x, 385, b 82, h 12234/1..

Allah (ṣ) and all one of the infallible Imams (ᶜa) and makes a gift of its reward to his parents or one of his brethren in faith, whether there is any reward for him. They said that the reward of that action will reach the person to whom it has been gifted without anything being diminished from his own reward.

Shaykh Ṭūsī in his *Tahdhib* says,[1] 'Someone who goes on a journey to perform *ziyārah* as a proxy on behalf of his brother in faith for a fee, should say, after performing the back of *ziyārah* -- or the *ziyārah* itself, in accordance with some manuscripts:

O Allah, whatever hardship, exertion, dishevelment, and exhaustion that have affected me, give its reward to (so-and-so, child of so-and-so) and reward me for carrying out this observance on his behalf.	اَللّٰهُمَّ مَا أَصَابَنِي مِنْ تَعَبٍ أَوْ نَصَبٍ أَوْ شَعَثٍ أَوْ لُغُوبٍ فَأْجُرْ فُلَانَ بْنَ فُلَانٍ فِيهِ، وَ أْجُرْنِي فِي قَضَائِي عَنْهُ.

Then, when performing *ziyārah*, he should say that the close:

Peace be to you, my master, on behalf of so-and-so child of so-and-so, on whose behalf I have come on pilgrimage. So intercede for him/her with your Lord.	السَّلَامُ عَلَيْكَ يَا مَوْلَايَ عَنْ فُلَانِ بْنِ فُلَانٍ، أَتَيْتُكَ زَائِرًا عَنْهُ فَاشْفَعْ لَهُ عِنْدَ رَبِّكَ.

Then he can make any petition for him. Shaykh Ṭūsī also says[2] that someone desiring to make *ziyārah* as a proxy on behalf of someone else should say,

O Allah, (so-and so, child of so-and-so) has sent me forth to his master and mine in order that I pay you a visit on his behalf, expecting a generous reward and avoiding default at Judgement.	اَللّٰهُمَّ إِنَّ فُلَانَ بْنَ فُلَانٍ أَوْفَدَنِي إِلَى مَوَالِيهِ وَ مَوَالِيَّ لِأَزُورَ عَنْهُ، رَجَاءً لِجَزِيلِ الثَّوَابِ، وَ فِرَارًا مِنْ سُوءِ الْحِسَابِ،
O Allah, he addresses to You his appeal through the mediation of Your *awliyā*, who guide to You,	اَللّٰهُمَّ إِنَّهُ يَتَوَجَّهُ إِلَيْكَ بِأَوْلِيَائِهِ الدَّالِّينَ عَلَيْكَ، فِي غُفْرَانِكَ ذُنُوبَهُ، وَ حَطِّ

1 *Muqniᶜah*, 443, b 29, 493, b 48. Mufī's Mazār, 210, b 22. *Tahdhīb*, vi, 105, b 51, whence *Biḥār*, xcix, 255, b 11, h 2.

2 *Tahdhīb*, vi, 116, b 53, h 9, thence and *Kāfī* in *Biḥār*, xcix, 256, b 11, h 4.

for Your forgiveness of his sins and release from the burden of his misdeeds, and he takes recourse to You through their mediation at the shrine of his Imam, may Allah's blessings by upon them!

سَيِّئَاتِهِ، وَ يَتَوَسَّلُ إِلَيْكَ بِهِمْ عِنْدَ مَشْهَدِ إِمَامِهِ صَلَوَاتُ اللهِ عَلَيْهِمْ.

O Allah, accept that from him and accept the intercession of his masters in his favour, may Allah's blessings by upon them.

اَللّٰهُمَّ فَتَقَبَّلْ مِنْهُ، وَ اقْبَلْ شَفَاعَةَ أَوْلِيَائِهِ صَلَوَاتُ اللهِ عَلَيْهِمْ فِيهِ،

O Allah, reward him for the sake of his good intentions, right beliefs and his genuine love and devotion, by the best of what You have rewarded any of Your faithful servants. Make perpetual the gifts that You grant him, and enable him to use rightly what You have given him and do not make me the last person to be sent forth by him.

اَللّٰهُمَّ جَازِهِ عَلىٰ حُسْنِ نِيَّتِهِ، وَ صَحِيحِ عَقِيدَتِهِ، وَ صِحَّةِ مُوَالاتِهِ أَحْسَنَ مَا جَازَيْتَ أَحَدًا مِنْ عَبِيدِكَ الْمُؤْمِنِينَ، وَ أَدِمْ لَهُ مَا خَوَّلْتَهُ وَ اسْتَعْمِلْهُ صَالِحًا فِيمَا آتَيْتَهُ، وَ لَا تَجْعَلْنِي آخِرَ وَافِدٍ لَهُ يُوفِدُهُ.

O Allah, release his neck from hellfire, expand for him Your good and lawful provision, and make him one of the companions of Muḥammad and the Family of Muḥammad. Bless him in his children, wealth, family and slaves.

اَللّٰهُمَّ أَعْتِقْ رَقَبَتَهُ مِنَ النَّارِ، وَ أَوْسِعْ عَلَيْهِ مِنْ رِزْقِكَ الْحَلَالِ الطَّيِّبِ، وَ اجْعَلْهُ مِنْ رُفَقَاءِ مُحَمَّدٍ وَ آلِ مُحَمَّدٍ، وَ بَارِكْ لَهُ فِي وُلْدِهِ وَ مَالِهِ وَ أَهْلِهِ وَ مَا مَلَكَتْ يَمِينُهُ.

O Allah, bless Muḥammad and the Family of Muḥammad and set a barrier between him and disobedience to You so that he will not disobey You. Assist him to obey You and Your *awliyā* so that You will not miss him where You had required him to be present, nor see him in

اَللّٰهُمَّ صَلِّ عَلىٰ مُحَمَّدٍ وَ آلِ مُحَمَّدٍ، وَ حُلْ بَيْنَهُ وَ بَيْنَ مَعَاصِيكَ حَتّىٰ لَا يَعْصِيَكَ، وَ أَعِنْهُ عَلىٰ طَاعَتِكَ وَ طَاعَةِ أَوْلِيَائِكَ، حَتّىٰ لَا تَفْقِدَهُ حَيْثُ

a place where You had forbidden him to be.

أَمَرْتَهُ، وَ لَا تَرَاهُ حَيْثُ نَهَيْتَهُ.

O Allah, bless Muḥammad and the Family of Muḥammad and forgive him, have mercy upon him, and pardon him and all the faithful, men and women.

اَللّٰهُمَّ صَلِّ عَلٰى مُحَمَّدٍ وَ آلِ مُحَمَّدٍ، وَ اغْفِرْ لَهُ وَ ارْحَمْهُ وَ اعْفُ عَنْهُ وَ عَنْ جَمِيعِ الْمُؤْمِنِينَ وَ الْمُؤْمِنَاتِ.

O Allah, bless Muḥammad and the Family of Muḥammad and protect him from terror at the approach of death, from the horrors of the Day of Resurrection, from ending up at an evil destination, and from the darkness and solitude of the grave, and from mortifying situations and settings in the world and the Hereafter.

اَللّٰهُمَّ صَلِّ عَلٰى مُحَمَّدٍ وَ آلِ مُحَمَّدٍ، وَ أَعِذْهُ مِنْ هَوْلِ الْمُطَّلَعِ، وَ مِنْ فَزَعِ يَوْمِ الْقِيَامَةِ، وَ سُوءِ الْمُنْقَلَبِ، وَ مِنْ ظُلْمَةِ الْقَبْرِ وَ وَحْشَتِهِ، وَ مِنْ مَوَاقِفِ الْخِزْيِ فِي الدُّنْيَا وَ الْآخِرَةِ.

O Allah, bless Muḥammad and the Family of Muḥammad and let his reward at this stage be Your forgiveness. At this point where I stand by the side of my Imams, may Allah bless him, let Your gift to him be to overlook his slips, to accept his excuses, and to disregard his misdeeds, and to make God-fearing his provision, to give him the good which is with You at the time of his return, to resurrect him in the fold of Muḥammad and the Family of Muḥammad, may Allah bless him and his Family, and to forgive him and his parents. Indeed You are the best of those who are beseeched and the noblest of those who are asked that Your servants rely upon.

اَللّٰهُمَّ صَلِّ عَلٰى مُحَمَّدٍ وَ آلِ مُحَمَّدٍ، وَ اجْعَلْ جَائِزَتَهُ فِي مَوْقِفِي هٰذَا غُفْرَانَكَ، وَ تُحْفَتَهُ فِي مَقَامِي هٰذَا عِنْدَ إِمَامِي صَلَّى اللّٰهُ عَلَيْهِ أَنْ تُقِيلَ عَثْرَتَهُ، وَ تَقْبَلَ مَعْذِرَتَهُ، وَ تَتَجَاوَزَ عَنْ خَطِيئَتِهِ، وَ تَجْعَلَ التَّقْوَى زَادَهُ، وَ مَا عِنْدَكَ خَيْرًا لَهُ فِي مَعَادِهِ، وَ تَحْشُرَهُ فِي زُمْرَةِ مُحَمَّدٍ وَ آلِ مُحَمَّدٍ صَلَّى اللّٰهُ عَلَيْهِ وَ آلِهِ، وَ تَغْفِرَ لَهُ وَ لِوَالِدَيْهِ، فَإِنَّكَ خَيْرُ مَرْغُوبٍ إِلَيْهِ، وَ أَكْرَمُ مَسْئُولٍ اعْتَمَدَ الْعِبَادُ عَلَيْهِ.

O Allah, there is a gift for every guest and an honour for every vis-

اَللّٰهُمَّ وَ لِكُلِّ مُوفِدٍ جَائِزَةٌ، وَ لِكُلِّ زَائِرٍ

كَرَامَــةٌ، فَاجْعَلْ جَائِزَتَــهُ فِي مَوْقِفِي هٰــذَا غُفْرَانَكَ، وَ الْجَنَّــةَ لَهُ وَ لِجَمِيعِ الْمُؤْمِنِينَ وَ الْمُؤْمِنَاتِ.

itor. Let his reward, while I stand in this place, be Your forgiveness and paradise for him and for all the faithful, men and women!

اَللّٰهُمَّ وَ أَنَا عَبْــدُكَ الْخَاطِئُ الْمُذْنِبُ الْمُقِرُّ بِذُنُوبِهِ، فَأَسْــأَلُكَ يَا اللهُ بِحَقِّ مُحَمَّــدٍ وَ آلِ مُحَمَّدٍ أَنْ لَا تَحْرِمَنِي بَعْدَ ذَلِــكَ الْأَجْــرَ وَ الثَّوَابَ، مِــنْ فَضْلِ عَطَائِكَ، وَ كَرَمِ تَفَضُّلِكَ.

O Allah I am Your servant, sinful and full of faults, who confesses to his sins. I beseech You, O Allah, for the sake of the right of Muḥammad and the Family of Muḥammad, not to deprive me, after that reward and recompense, of Your gracious gifts and munificent favours!

Then approaching the ḍarīḥ and lifting one's hands towards the sky and facing in the direction of the *Qiblah*, one should say,

يَا مَــوْلَايَ يَا إِمَامِي، عَبْدُكَ فُلَانُ بْنُ فُلَانٍ، أَوْفَدَنِي زَائِرًا لِمَشْهَدِكَ، يَتَقَرَّبُ إِلَى اللهِ عَزَّ وَ جَلَّ بِذٰلِكَ وَ إِلَى رَسُولِهِ وَ إِلَيْكَ، يَرْجُو بِذٰلِكَ فَكَاكَ رَقَبَتِهِ مِنَ النَّارِ مِنَ الْعُقُوبَةِ، فَاغْفِرْ لَهُ وَ لِجَمِيعِ الْمُؤْمِنِينَ وَ الْمُؤْمِنَاتِ،

O my master and my Imam, Your servant [so-and-so child of so-and-so] has sent me on pilgrimage to your shrine, seeking thereby nearness to Allah, Almighty and Glorious, and to His Apostle and to you, expecting thereby to be rescued from hellfire and its punishment. So forgive him and all the faithful, men and women.

يَا اَللهُ يَا اَللهُ يَا اَللهُ يَا اَللهُ يَا اَللهُ يَا اَللهُ يَا اَللهُ، لَا إِلٰهَ إِلَّا اللهُ الْحَلِيمُ الْكَرِيمُ، لَا إِلٰهَ إِلَّا اللهُ الْعَلِيُّ الْعَظِيمُ، أَسْــأَلُكَ أَنْ تُصَــلِّيَ عَلَى مُحَمَّــدٍ وَ آلِ مُحَمَّدٍ، وَ تَسْــتَجِيبَ لِي فِيهِ وَ فِي جَمِيعِ إِخْوَانِي

O Allah, O Allah, O Allah, O Allah, O Allah, O Allah, O Allah! There is no god except Allah, the All-forbearing and the All-munificent. There is no god except Allah, the All-exalted and the All-great! I beseech You to bless Muḥammad and the Family of Muḥammad and to answer my prayers concerning all my brothers and sisters, my children and my family, with Your generosity and munificence, O Most Merciful of the merciful!

وَ أَخَوَاتِي وَ وَلَدِي وَ أَهْلِي، بِجُودِكَ وَ
كَرَمِكَ يَا أَرْحَمَ الرَّاحِمِينَ!

APPENDIX TWO

(Continued fom Volume 1, p 793)

The author of the *Mafatih al-Jinan* mentions several supplications in his book without citing their complete text on account of their length. Those supplications are given in this appendix so that the readers do not need to refer to other books. Moreover, as there was no *ziyārah* for the Imāmzādahs in the *Mafātīḥ*, a *ziyārah* for them has also been included here with the hope that the pious readers will appreciate the efforts of the compiler, the calligrapher, and the sponsor of this print. God is the One who grants success.

1. Complete text of the Supplication of the Prayer of Imam al-Ḥusayn (ᶜ*a*). (see vol. 1, p. 132)

2. The Supplication recited after the *ziyārah* of Imam Muḥammad al-Taqī al-Jawād (ᶜ*a*). (see p. 392 above)

3. Another *ziyārah* of Imam Muḥammad al-Jawād (al-Taqī) (ᶜ*a*). (see below)

4 & 5 Two *ziyārahs* of the Imāmzādahs. (see next page)

6. The remaining part of the *tasbīḥ* pertaining to observances of the Day of ᶜArafah, which begins with the words *Subḥānallāhi qabla kulli aḥad*. (see vol. 1, p. 690)

3. ANOTHER ZIYARAH OF IMAM MUHAMMAD AL-JAWAD (ʿA)

Another text for the Imam's *ziyārah* that has been reported is as follows.[1]

Peace be to the most accessible of doors (to God), the truest of paths, the confirmed possessor of knowledge, the mainspring of wisdom, the lamp of darkness, the chief of the Arabs and non-Arabs, the guide to the path of rectitude,

السَّلَامُ عَلَى الْبَابِ الْأَقْصَدِ، وَ الطَّرِيقِ
الْأَرْشَدِ، وَ الْعَالِمِ الْمُؤَيَّدِ، يَنْبُوعِ
الْحِكَمِ وَ مِصْبَاحِ الظُّلَمِ، سَيِّدِ الْعَرَبِ
وَ الْعَجَمِ، اَلْهَادِي إِلَى الرَّشَادِ، اَلْمُوَفَّقِ

[1] *Biḥār*, xcix, 22-23, b 2, h 12 from Sayyid Ibn Ṭāwūs.

the one blessed with divine endorsement and approval, my master, Abū Jaᶜfar Muḥammad ibn ᶜAlī al-Jawād!

I testify, O *walī* of Allah, that you maintained the prayer, paid the *zakāt*, bade what is right and forbade what is wrong, and struggled in the way of Allah with a struggle that is worthy of Him, and worshipped Allah with dedication until your demise! You lived a felicitous life and passed away as a martyr! *I wish I were with you so that I had achieved a great success!'* May Allah's mercy and His blessings be upon you!

بِالتَّأْيِيدِ وَ السَّــــدَادِ، مَوْلَايَ أَبِي جَعْفَرٍ
مُحَمَّدِ بْنِ عَلِيٍّ الْجَوَادِ.
أَشْــــهَدُ يَا وَلِيَّ اللهِ أَنَّكَ أَقَمْتَ الصَّلَاةَ،
وَ آتَيْتَ الــزَّكَاةَ، وَ أَمَرْتَ بِالْمَعْرُوفِ، وَ
نَهَيْتَ عَنِ الْمُنْكَرِ، وَ جَاهَدْتَ فِي سَبِيلِ
اللهِ حَقَّ جِهَادِهِ، وَ عَبَدْتَ اللهَ مُخْلِصًا
حَتَّى أَتَاكَ الْيَقِينُ، فَعِشْــتَ سَعِيدًا، وَ
مَضَيْتَ شَهِيدًا، يَا لَيْتَنِي كُنْتُ مَعَكُمْ
فَأَفُوزَ فَوْزًا عَظِيمًا، وَ رَحْمَةُ اللهِ وَ بَرَكَاتُهُ.

Then kiss the blessed tomb and place your right cheek on it. Then offer a two-*rakᶜah* prayer of *ziyārah* and make any petition that you may have.

4 & 5. TWO ZIYARAHS OF THE IMAMZADAHS (R)

The august sayyid, ᶜAlī ibn Ṭāwūs has mentioned two *ziyārahs* in his book *Miṣbāḥ al-Zā'ir* for the Imāmzādahs, and it would be appropriate to cite them here.[1] He writes that when intending to perform the *ziyārah* of any of them, such as Qāsim son of Imam Mūsā al-Kāẓim (*ᶜa*), or that of al-ᶜAbbās son of the Commander of the Faithful (*ᶜa*), or ᶜAlī Akbar son of Imam Ḥusayn (*ᶜa*), who was slain at Karbalā, or someone like them, one should stand at the head their graveside and say,

4. FIRST ZIYĀRAH

Peace be to you, O pure master, immaculate *walī,* and compassionate summoner! I testify that you spoke the truth, declared what is veritable and true, sum-

السَّلَامُ عَلَيْكَ أَيُّهَا السَّيِّدُ الزَّكِيُّ الطَّاهِرُ
الْوَلِيُّ، وَ الدَّاعِي الْحَفِيُّ، أَشْهَدُ أَنَّكَ قُلْتَ
حَقًّا، وَ نَطَقْتَ حَقًّا وَ صِدْقًا، وَ دَعَوْتَ

[1] *Biḥār*, xcix, 272-273, b 4, h 1 from Sayyid Ibn Ṭāwūs..

moned (the people) openly and secretly to my master and yours. Those who follow you are successful and those who affirm you are saved. Those who impugned you and stayed away from you failed and were losers.

إِلَى مَوْلَايَ وَ مَوْلَاكَ عَلَانِيَةً وَ سِرّاً،
فَازَ مُتَّبِعُكَ، وَ نَجَا مُصَدِّقُكَ، وَ خَابَ
وَ خَسِرَ مُكَذِّبُكَ، وَ الْمُتَخَلِّفُ عَنْكَ،

Be witness to this testimony of mine so that I may be among the successful by virtue of my knowledge of your station, my compliance to you, my affirmation of your veracity and my following you.

اِشْهَدْ لِي بِهٰذِهِ الشَّهَادَةِ، لِأَكُونَ مِنَ
الْفَائِزِينَ بِمَعْرِفَتِكَ وَ طَاعَتِكَ، وَ
تَصْدِيقِكَ وَ اتِّبَاعِكَ،

Peace be to you, O my master, descendant of my master! You are the door of Allah by which people may approach Him and receive from Him! I come to you as a pilgrim and I leave my petitions in your care and invoke your custodianship in regard to my faith, my trusts, the final phase of my works, and the totality of my hopes till the end of my lifetime! Peace be to you and may Allah's mercy and His blessings be upon you!

وَ السَّلَامُ عَلَيْكَ يَا سَيِّدِي وَ ابْنَ
سَيِّدِي، أَنْتَ بَابُ اللهِ الْمُؤْتَى مِنْهُ وَ
الْمَأْخُوذُ عَنْهُ، أَتَيْتُكَ زَائِرًا وَ حَاجَاتِي
لَكَ مُسْتَوْدِعًا، وَ هَا أَنَا ذَا أَسْتَوْدِعُكَ
دِينِي وَ أَمَانَتِي وَ خَوَاتِيمَ عَمَلِي وَ
جَوَامِعَ أَمَلِي إِلَى مُنْتَهَى أَجَلِي، وَ السَّلَامُ
عَلَيْكَ وَ رَحْمَةُ اللهِ وَ بَرَكَاتُهُ.

5. Second Ziyārah

Another *ziyārah* for the descendants of the Imams (ᶜ*a*) is as follows:

Peace be to (Muḥammad) al-Muṣṭafā, your ancestor! Peace be to (ᶜAlī) al-Murtaḍā al-Rida! Peace be to the two masters, al-Ḥasan and al-Ḥusayn! Peace be to Khadījah, mother of the Mistress of the world's womankind! Peace be to Fāṭimah, mother of the Immacu-

اَلسَّلَامُ عَلَى جَدِّكَ الْمُصْطَفَى، اَلسَّلَامُ
عَلَى أَبِيكَ الْمُرْتَضَى الرِّضَا، اَلسَّلَامُ عَلَى
السَّيِّدَيْنِ الْحَسَنِ وَ الْحُسَيْنِ، اَلسَّلَامُ
عَلَى خَدِيجَةَ أُمِّ سَيِّدَةِ نِسَاءِ الْعَالَمِينَ،

اَلسَّلَامُ عَلىٰ فَاطِمَةَ أُمِّ الْأَئِمَّةِ الطَّاهِرِينَ،

late Imams!

اَلسَّـــلَامُ عَلَى النُّفُوسِ الْفَاخِـــرَةِ، بُحُورِ الْعُلُومِ الزَّاخِرَةِ، شُـــفَعَائِي فِي الْآخِرَةِ، وَ أَوْلِيَائِي عِنْدَ عَوْدِ الـــرُّوحِ إِلَى الْعِظَامِ النَّاخِرَةِ، أَئِمَّةِ الْخَلْقِ وَ وُلَاةِ الْحَقِّ،

Peace be to these splendid souls, the abounding oceans of knowledge, my intercessors in the Hereafter, my patrons at the time of the spirit's return to my decayed bones, the Imams of the creation and the guardians of the truth!

اَلسَّلَامُ عَلَيْكَ أَيُّهَا الشَّخْصُ الشَّرِيفُ الطَّاهِرُ الْكَرِيمُ،

May peace be to you, O noble, blameless and magnanimous personage!

أَشْـــهَدُ أَنْ لَا إِلٰـــهَ إِلَّا اللهُ وَ أَنَّ مُحَمَّدًا عَبْدُهُ وَ مُصْطَفَـــاهُ، وَ أَنَّ عَلِيّاً وَلِيُّهُ وَ مُجْتَبَاهُ، وَ أَنَّ الْإِمَامَـــةَ فِي وُلْدِهِ إِلَى يَوْمِ الدِّيـــنِ، نَعْلَـــمُ ذٰلِكَ عِلْـــمَ الْيَقِينِ، وَ نَحْـــنُ لِذٰلِكَ مُعْتَقِـــدُونَ، وَ فِي نَصْرِهِمْ مُجْتَهِدُونَ.

I testify that there is no god except Allah and that Muḥammad is His servant and His chosen one; that ᶜAlī is His *walī* and His elect, and that the Imamate will remain in his descendants until the Day of Retribution. We know that with certain knowledge and that is our confirmed belief and we are doing our best to assist them!

APPENDIX THREE

1. Duᶜā Makārim al-Akhlāq. (see vol. 1, p. 301)
2. Sūrat al-ᶜAnkabūt. vol. 1, p. 33)
3. Sūrat al-Rūm. (vol. 1, p. 42)
4. Sūrat al-Dukhān. (vol. 1, p. 50)
5. Ḥadīth al-Kisā. (see vol. 1, p. 794)

Bibliography

ᶜAbd b. Ḥumayd (d. 249), *al-Muntak͟hab min Musnad ᶜAbd b. Ḥumayd*, ed. S. Ṣ. B. al-Sāmarā'ī and M. M. K͟h. Al-Ṣaᶜīdī, Cairo: Maktabat al-Nahḍat al-ᶜArabiyyah, 1408/1988.

ᶜAbd al-Karīm b. Ṭāwūs al-Ḥillī (d. 692), *Farḥat al-G͟harī*, Najaf, 1368.

Abū Dāwūd = Sulaymān b. As͟hᶜat͟h al-Sijistānī (d. 275), *Sunan*, Beirut: Dār al-Maᶜrifah, n.d.

Abū Mikhnaf, Maqtal al-Ḥusayn,

Aḥkām al-Qur'ān, by Aḥmad b. ᶜAlī al-Jaṣṣāṣ (d. 370), Beirut: Dār Iḥyā' al-Turāt͟h al-ᶜArabī, 1405.

Aḥmad b. Muḥammad b. Ḥanbal (d. 241), *Faḍā'il Amīr al-Mu'minīn ᶜAlī b. Abī Ṭālib ᶜAlayh al-Salām*, ed. Sayyid ᶜAbd al-ᶜAzīz al-Ṭabāṭabā'ī, Qum: Dār al-Tafsīr, 1433/1390 Sh.

Aᶜlām al-Dīn, see Daylamī

Āl Ṭawq = Aḥmad b. Ṣāliḥ al-Qaṭīfī (fl. 1245), *Rasā'il Āl Ṭawq*, Beirut: Dār al-Muṣṭafā li Iḥyā' al-Turāt͟h, 1422.

ᶜAlī b. Jaᶜfar al-ᶜUrayḍī (early 3rd ᶜentury), *Masā'il*, Qum: Āl al-Bayt, 1409.

ᶜAllāmah Ḥillī = al-Ḥasan b. Yūsuf b. al-Muṭahhar al-Asadī (d. 726), *Kashf al-Yaqīn*, Tehran: Ministry of Islamic Guidance, 1411.

—*Tad͟hkirat al-Fuqahā'*, Qum: Mu'assasat Āl al-Bayt, n.d.

—*Qawāᶜid al-Aḥkām fā Maᶜrifat al-Ḥalāl wal-Ḥarām*, Qum: Jāmiᶜ al-Mudarrisīn, 1413.

—*Taḥrīr al-Aḥkām al-S͟harᶜīiyyah ᶜalā Mad͟hhab al-Imāmiyyah*, Qum: Nas͟hr-e Ṭūs, n.d.

ᶜAllāmah Majlisī II= Muḥammad Bāqir b. Muḥammad Taqī (d. 1110), *Biḥār al-Anwār*, Beirut: Mu'assasat al-Wafā', 1404.

—*Mir'āt al-ᶜUqūl fī S͟harḥ Ak͟hbār Āl-i al-Rasūl*, ed. S. Hās͟him Rasūlī, Tehran: Dār al-Kutub al-Islāmiyyah, 1404.

—*Tuḥfat al-Zā'ir*, ed. Mu'assaseh Imām Hādī, Qum: Payām-e Imām Hādī, 1386 H. Sh.

—*Zād al-Maᶜād (be hamrahe Miftāḥ al-Jinān.)*, ed. Yūsuf Asad-Zādeh, Qum: Payām-e Muqaddas, 1389 H.Sh. (A similar combined Arabic version has been publisehd in Beirut by Mu'assasat al-Aᶜlamī lil Maṭbūᶜāt, 1423/2003. Its page numbers appear in paranthesis in the references)

Ansāb al-Ashrāf, by Aḥmad b. Muḥammad b. Yaḥyā b. Jābir al-Balādhurī (d. 279), ed. M. F. al-ᶜAẓm, Damascus, 1996; Beirut: Dār al-Fikr, n.d.

Asbāb Nuzūl al-Āyāt, by al-Wāḥidī = Abū al-Ḥasan ᶜAlī b. Aḥmad b. Mattawayh al-Nayshābūrī (d. 468), Cairo: Mu'assasat al-Ḥalabī, 1388/1968.

Ashᶜarī = Aḥmad b. Muḥammad b. ᶜĪsā al-Ashᶜarī (d. *circa* 203), *al-Nawādir*, Qum: Madrasah Imam Mahdī, 1408.

ᶜ*Awālī* = ᶜ*Awālī al-Li'ālī*, by Abū Jaᶜfar Muḥammad b. ᶜAlī b. Ibrāhīm, Ibn Abī Jumhūr (alive in 901), Qum: Intishārāt Sayyid al-Shuhadā', 1405.

ᶜ*Awālim*= ᶜ*Awālim al-*ᶜ*Ulūm wal-Ma*ᶜ*ārif wal-Aḥwāl min al-Āyāt wal-Akhbār wal-Aqwāl (Mustadrak Sayyidat al-Nisā' ilal-Imām al-Jawād)* by ᶜAbd Allāh b. Nūr Allāh al-Baḥrāni al-Iṣfahānī (fl. 12th/18th cent.), ed. Muḥammad Bāqir Muwaḥḥid Abṭaḥī Iṣfahānī, Qum: Mu'assasat al-Imām al-Mahdī, 1413.

*A*ᶜ*yān al-Shī*ᶜ*ah*, Sayyid Muḥsin b. ᶜAbd al-Karīm al-Amīn al-Ḥusaynī al-ᶜĀmilī (d. 1371), Beirut: Dār al-Taᶜāruf lil Maṭbūᶜāt, 1406.

Bahā'ī = Bahā' al-Dīn Muḥammad b. al-Ḥusayn al-ᶜĀmilī (d. 1031), *al-Ḥabl al-Matīn fī Aḥkām al-Dīn*, ed. M. Aḥmadiyān, Qum: Maktabah Baṣīratī, 1390.

Al-Baḥr al-Muḥīṭ = Abū Ḥayyān Muḥammad b. Yūsuf al-Andalūsī (d.), ed. Ṣ. M. Jamīl, Beirut Dār al-Fikr, 1420.

Al-Baḥrānī = Sayyid Hāshim b. Sulaymān al-Baḥrānī al-Katkānī (d. 1107), *al-Burhān fī Tafsīr al-Qur'ān*, Tehran: Bunyād-e Biᶜthat, 1416.

—*Madīnah Ma*ᶜ*ājiz al-A'immah al-Ithnā* ᶜ*Ashar wa Dalā'il al-Ḥujaj* ᶜ*alā al-Bashar*, Tehran, 1300/1882; Qum: Mu'assasat al-Maᶜārif al-Islāmiyyah, 1413.

Baṣā'r al-Darajāt, by al-Ṣaffār = Abū Jaᶜfar Muḥammad b. al-Ḥasan b. Farrukh al-Qummī (d. 290), Qum: Āyatullah Marᶜashī Library, 1404.

Al-Bayhaqī = Abū Bakr Aḥmad b. al-Ḥusayn al-Nayshābūrī (d. 458), *al-Sunan al-Kubrā*, Hyderabad, 1344; Beirut: Dār al-Fikr, n.d.

Al-Bidāyah wa al-Nihāyah, by Ibn Kathīr = Abū al-Faḍl Ismāᶜīl b. ᶜUmar al-Qurashī al-Dimashqī (d. 774), Beirut: Dār al-Fikr, n.d., ed. ᶜA, Shīrī, Beirut: Dār Iḥyā' al-Turāth al-ᶜArabī, 1408/1988.

*Bishārat al-Muṣtabā li Shī*ᶜ*at al-Murtaḍā*, Abū Jaᶜfar ᶜImād al-Dīn Muḥammad b. Abī al-Qāsim ᶜAlī b. Muḥammad b. ᶜAlī al-Ṭabarī, (alive in 553), Najaf: Ḥaydarīyah, 1383/1963.

*Da*ᶜ*ā'im* = *Da*ᶜ*ā'im al-Islam*, by Abū Ḥanīfah Nuᶜmān b. Muḥammad al-

Tamīmī al-Maghribī (d. 363), Cairo: Dār al-Maᶜārif, 1385.
Daᶜawāt, see Rāwandī
Dalā'il = *Kitāb Dalā'il al-Imāmah*, by Muḥammad b. Jarīr b. Rustam al-Ṭabarī, Qum: Dār al-Dhakhā'r li al-Maṭbūᶜāt, n.d.
Daylamī = Ḥasan b. Abī al-Ḥasan Muḥammad (8th ᶜentury), *Aᶜlām al-Dīn*, Qum: Āl al-Bayt, 1408.
—*Irshād al-Qulūb*, Qum: Intishārāt Sharīf Raḍī, 1412.
Dīwān Imām ᶜAlī, Imam ᶜAlī b. Abī Ṭālib, Qum: Intishārāt-e Payām-e Islām, 1369 Sh.
Al-Durar fī Ikhtiṣār al-Maghāzī wa al-Siyar, by Ibn ᶜAbd al-Brrr, Abū ᶜUmar Yūsuf b. ᶜAbd Allāh al-Qurṭubī (d. 463), Cairo: Ministry of Awqāf, n.d.
Al-Durr al-Manthūr = *al-Durr al-Manthūr fī Tafsīr al-Ma'thūr*, by Jalāl al-Dīn al-Suyūṭī (d. 911), Qum: Ayatullah Marᶜashī Library, 1404.
Faḍā'il Shahr Rajab, see al-Ḥākim al-Ḥaskānī
Falāḥ al-Sā'il, see Ibn Ṭāwūs.
Faqīh, see Ṣadūq.
Fayḍ=Muḥammad Muḥsin b. Murtaḍā al-Kāshānī (d. 1091), *Khulāṣat al-Adhkār*, ms. 5747, 139 folios, Kitābkhāneh Āstān-e Quds-e Raḍawī, Mashhad. Black & white images of the manuscript in *Majmūᶜeh Āthār-e ᶜAllamāh Fayḍ Kāshānī*, a software made by C.R.C.I.S., Qum.
—*al-Tafsīr al-Ṣāfī*, Qum: Mu'assasat al-Hādī, 1416/1375 Sh.
—*Al-Wāfī*, ed. Ḍ. Ḥ, al-Iṣfahānī, Iṣfahān: Maktabat al-Imam Amīr al-Mu'minīn ᶜAlī (*ᶜa*), 1406.
Fiqh al-Riḍā, (attributed) Imam ᶜAlī b. Mūsā al-Riḍā (*ᶜa*) (d. 202), Mashhad: Kungreh Jahānī-ye Imam Riḍā, 1406.
Al-Fuṣūl al-Muhimmah fī Maᶜrifat al-A'immah, by Ibn al-Ṣabbāgh = ᶜAlī b. Muḥammad b. Aḥmad al-Makkī al-Mālikī (d. 855), Qum: Dār al-Ḥadīth, 1422.
Al-Ghadīr fī al-Kitāb wa al-Sunnah wa al-Adab, by ᶜAbd al-Ḥusayn b. Aḥmad al-Tabrīzī al-Najafī al-Amīnī (d. 1390), Beirut, 1397/1977; Tehran, 1408.
Ghanā'im al-Ayyām fī mā Yataᶜallaqu bil Ḥalāl wal Ḥarām, by Mīrzā Abū al-Qāsim b, Muḥammad Ḥasan al-Jīlānī al-Qummī (d. *circa* 1232), n. d.
Ghārāt = *Kitāb al-Ghārāt*, by Ibrāhīm b. Muḥammad al-Thaqafī al-Kūfī (d. 283), ed. S. J. M. Urmawi, Tehran, 1395; Qum, 1410.
Ḥabl al-Matīn, see Bahā'ī
Ḥadā'iq = *al-Ḥadā'iq al-Nāḍirah fī Aḥkām al-ᶜIṭrat al-ṭāhirah*, by Yūsuf b.

Aḥmad b. Ibrāhīm al-Baḥrānī (d. 1186). ed. M. T. Īrwānī and S. ᶜA. R. Muqram, Qum: Jāmiᶜ al-Mudarrisīn, 1405.
Ḥākim=Abū ᶜAbdillāh Muḥammad b. ᶜAbd Allāh al-Nayshābūrī (d. 405), al-*Mustadrak ᶜala al-Ṣaḥīḥayn*, ed. Yūsuf ᶜAbd al-Raḥmān al-Marᶜashlī, n.d.
al-Ḥākim al-Ḥaskānī, Abū ᶜAbdillāh al-Ḥaskānī (d. after 470), *Faḍā'il Shahr Rajab*, Tehran: Ministry of Islamic Guidance, 1411.
—*Shawāhid al-Tanzīl*, ed. M. B. Maḥmūdī, Tehran: Ministry of Islamic Guidance, 1400/1990.
Taḥrīr al-Aḥkām, see ᶜAllāmah Ḥillī.
Ḥurr al-ᶜĀmilī = Muḥammad b. al-Ḥasan al-Mashgharī (d. 1104), *Ithbāt al-Hudāt*, Beirut: Mu'assasat al-Aᶜlamī lil Maṭbūᶜāt, 1425/2004.
—*Wasā'il al-Shīᶜah*, Qum: Āl al-Bayt, 1408.
Ḥusayn b. Saᶜīd al-Ahwāzī (first half of 3rd ᶜentury), *Kitāb al-Mu'min*, Qum, 1401.
—*Kitāb al-Zuhd*, ed. Gh. ᶜIrfāniyān, Qum, 1402.
1409.
Ibn Abī Shaybah = Abū Bakú ᶜAbd Allāh b. Muḥammad b. Abī Shaybah al-ᶜAbsī (d. 235), *Muṣannaf*, ed. Saᶜīd al-Laḥḥām, Beirut: Dār al-Fikr, 1409/1989.
Ibn Bābawayh, see Ṣadūq
Ibn Hishām = Abū Muḥammad ᶜAbd al-Malik b. Hishām al-Ḥimyarī (d. 217), *al-Sīrah al-Nabawiyyah*, ed. M. al-Saqqā et al., Cairo, 1936; Beirut: Dār al-Maᶜrifah.
Ibn Rāhwayh = Isḥāq b. Ibrāhīm b. Makhlad al-Ḥanzalī al-Marwazī (d. 238), *Musnad Ibn Rāhwayh*, ed. ᶜA. ᶜA. Ḥ. B. al-Balūsī, Madīnah: Maktabat al-Īmān, 1412.
Ibn Shādhān, Abū al-Ḥasan Muḥammad b. Aḥmad b. ᶜAlī al-Qummī (d.), *Mi'at Manqibah*, Qum: Madrasah al-Imam al-Mahdī, 1407.
Ibn Ṭāwūs = Raḍī al-Dīn ᶜAlī b. Mūsā b. Ṭāwūs al-Ḥasanī al-Ḥillī (d. 664), *al-Amān*, Qum: Mu'assasat Āl al-Bayt, 1409.
—*Al-Durū al-Wāqiyah*, Beirut: Mu'assasat Āl al-Bayt, 1415/1995.
— *Falāḥ al-Sā'il*, ed. Gh. Al-Majīdī, Qum, 1419.
—*Fatḥ al-Abwāb*, ed. Ḥ. al-Khaffāf, Qum: Āl al-Bayt, 1409.
—*Jamāl al-Usbūᶜ*, Qum: Intishārāt Sharīf Raḍī, n.d.
—*Al-Mujjtanā min dᶜā al-Mujtabā*, Qum: Dār al-Dhakhā'ir, 1411.
—Miṣbāḥ al-Zā'ir,
—*Al-Taḥṣīn*, Qum: Mu'assasah Dār al-Kitāb, 1413.
—*Al-Ṭarā'if*, Qum: Intishārāt-e Khayyām, 1400.
—*Al-Yaqīn*, Qum: Mu'assasah Dār al-Kitāb, 1413.

Al-Iḥtijāj, by Abū Manṣūr Aḥmad b. ᶜAlī al-Ṭabrisī (6th century), Ma<u>sh</u>had: Na<u>sh</u>r-e Murtaḍā, 1403.

Ikhtiṣāṣ, see Mufīd.

ᶜIlal, see Ṣadūq

Iᶜlām al-Warā, by Abū ᶜAlī Faḍl b. al-Ḥasan al-Ṭabarisī, Amīn al-Islām (d. 548), *Iᶜlām al-Warā*, Tehran: Dār al-Kutub al-Islamiyyah, 1379

—*Majmaᶜ al-Bayān*, Beirut: Mu'assasat al-Aᶜlamī, 1415/1995.

Imtāᶜ al-Asmāᶜ, by Aḥmad b. ᶜAlī al-Maqrīzī, (d. 845), ed. M. ᶜAbd al-Ḥamī al-Numaysī, Beirut: Dār al-Kutub al-ᶜIlmiyyah, 1420/1999.

Ithbāt al-Hudāt, see Ḥurr al-ᶜĀmilī.

Al-Jaᶜfarīyāt (al-A<u>sh</u>ᶜa<u>th</u>īyāt), by Abū ᶜAlī Muḥammad b. Muḥammad b. al-A<u>sh</u>ᶜa<u>th</u> al-Kūfī (alive in 313), Tehran: Maktabah Naynawā, n.d.

Jamāl, see Ibn Ṭāwūs

Jāmiᶜ al-A<u>kh</u>bār, by Tāj al-Dīn <u>Sh</u>aᶜīrī [sic.] , Qum: Inti<u>sh</u>ārāt-e <u>Sh</u>arīf Raḍī, 1363 Sh. (The author's name is Muḥammad b. Muḥammad al-Sabzawārī [alive in 679], and the book's original title is *Maᶜārij al-Yaqīn fī Uṣūl al-Dīn*, ed. ᶜAlā' Āl Jaᶜfar, Qum: Āl al-Bayt, 1410/1993)

Jawāhir = *Jawāhir al-Kalām fī <u>Sh</u>arḥ <u>Sh</u>arā'iᶜ al-Islām*, by Muḥammad Ḥasan b. Bāqir b. ᶜAbd al-Raḥīm al-Najafī (d. 1266), ed. ᶜA. Al-Qūchānī, Beirut: Dār Iḥyā' al-Turā<u>th</u> al-ᶜArabī.

Jazā'irī = Sayyid Niᶜmat Allāh al-Mūsawī (d.), *Qiṣaṣ al-Anbiyā'*, Qum: Ayatullah Marᶜashī Library, 1404.

Kafᶜamī = Taqī al-Dīn Ibrāhīm b. ᶜAlī (d. 905), *al-Balad al-Amīn*, lithograph.

—*Al-Miṣbāḥ* (*Junnat al-Amān al-Wāqiyah wa Jannat al-Īmān al-Bāqiyah*) Qum: Inti<u>sh</u>ārāt <u>Sh</u>arīf al-Raḍī, 1405; Beirut: Mu'assasat al-Aᶜlamī lil Maṭbūᶜāt, 1414/1994).

Al-Kāfī, by Abū Jaᶜfar Muḥammad b. Yaᶜqūb al-Kulaynī (d. 329), Tehran: Dār al-Kutub al-Islāmiyyah, 1365 <u>Sh</u>.

Kalimah Ṭayyibah, see Nūrī.

Al-Kalim al-Ṭayyib, by Ibn Maᶜṣūm = ᶜAlī Ṣadr al-Dīn b. Aḥmad Niẓām al-Dīn b. Muḥammad Maᶜṣūm al-Ḥusaynī al-Madanī, Sayyid ᶜAlī Khān Shīrāzī (d. 1120), ed. Qāsim Ḥusayn 'Iwaḍ, 1st edition, Kuwait, 1435/2014.

Kāmil al-Ziyārāt, by Ibn Qūlawayh = Abū al-Qāsim Jaᶜfar b. Muḥammad b. Qūlawayh al-Qummī (d. 369), Najaf: 1365.

Al-Kāmil fi al-Ta'rīkh, by Ibn al-Athīr al-Jazarī (d. 630/1232), Beirut: Dā Ṣādir, 1385.

Kanz al-Fawā'id, by Abū al-Fatḥ Muḥammad b. ᶜU<u>th</u>mān al-Karājikī (d. 449), Qum: Dār al-<u>Dh</u>a<u>kh</u>ā'ir, 1410.

Kanz al-ᶜUmmāl, by ᶜAlī al-Muttaqī al-Hindī = ᶜAlā' al-Dīn ᶜAlī b. Ḥusām al-Dīn al-Burhānpūrī (d. 975), ed. B. Ḥayyānī and Ṣ. al-Saqqā, Beirut: Mu'assasat al-Risālah, 1409/1989.

Kashf al-Ghummah fī Maᶜrifat al-A'immah, by Bahā' al-Dīn Abū al-Ḥasan ᶜAlī b. ᶜĪsā al-Irbilī (d. 692), Tabriz: Maktabah Banī Hāshimī, 1381.

Kashf al-Ghiṭā' = *Kashf al-Ghiṭā' ᶜan Mubhamāt al-Sharīᶜat al-Gharrā'*, by Kāshif al-Ghiṭā' = Jaᶜfar b. K͟hiḍr al-Mālikī al-Najafī (d. 1228), Qum: Maktab al-Alām al-Islāmī, n.d.

Kas͟hf al-Yaqīn, see ᶜAllāmah Ḥillī

Al-Kas͟hf wal Bayān ᶜan Tafsīr al-Qur'ān, by Abū Isḥāq Aḥmad b. Ibrāhīm al-al-T͟haᶜlabī al-Nays͟hābūrī (5th ᶜentury), Beirut: Dār Iḥyā' al-Turāt͟h al-ᶜArabī, 1422.

Kas͟hs͟hāf = al-Kashshāf *ᶜan Ḥaqā'iq G͟hawāmiḍ al-Tanzīl*, by Abū al-Qāsim Muḥammad b. ᶜUmar al-Zamak͟hs͟harī, Jār Allāh (d. 538), Beirut: Dār al-Kutub al-ᶜArabī, 1407.

K͟harā'ij, see Rāwandī

K͟haṣāṣ al-A'immah by Muḥammad b. al-Ḥusayn al-S͟harīf al-Raḍī (d. , Mas͟hhad: Āstā-e Quds Raḍawī, 1406.

Al-K͟hilāf, see Ṭūsī

K͟hiṣāl, see Ṣadūq

Al-K͟hunsārī, Sayyid Jamāl al-Dīn Muḥammad (d. 1058) , *al-Mazār*, 109

Kifāyat al-At͟har, by Abū al-Qāsim ᶜAlī b. Muḥammad b. ᶜAlī al-K͟hazzāz al-Qummī al-Rāzī (d. late 4th ᶜentury), Qum: Intis͟hārāt Bīdār, 1401.

Kitāb Sulaym b. Qays al-Ḥilālī, Qum: Intis͟hārāt al-Hādī, 1415.

Al-Mabsūṭ, see Ṭūsī

Maᶜālim al-Tanzīl fī Tafsīr al-Qur'ān, by al-Ḥusayn b. Masᶜūd al-Bag͟hawī al-Farrā' (d. 510), ed. ᶜA. Al-Mahdī, Beirut: Dār Iḥyā' al-Turāt͟h al-ᶜArabī, 1420.

Maᶜdan al-Jawāhir, by Abū al-Futūḥ Muḥammad b. ᶜUthmān al-Karājikī (d. 499), Tehran: Murtaḍawīyah, 1394.

Madīnat Maᶜājiz see Baḥrānī.

Madārik al-ᶜUrwah, by Yūsuf Ārām al-Ḥā'irī al-Biyārjomandī al-Khurāsānī (d. 1394), Najaf: Maṭbaᶜat al-Nuᶜmān, n.d.

Al-Maghāzī, by Muḥammad b. ᶜUmar al-Wāqidī (d. 207/822), Beirut: Aᶜlamī, 1409.

Al-Maḥāsin, by Abū Jaᶜfar Aḥmad b. Muḥammad b. K͟hālid al-Barqī al-Qummī (d. 274-280), ed. J. M. Urmawī, Tehran, 1370.

Mafātīḥ al-G͟hayb, by Fak͟hr al-Dīn Abū ᶜAbdillāh Muḥammad b. ᶜUmar al-Rāzī (d. 606), Beirut: Dār Iḥyā' al-Turāt͟h al-ᶜArabī, 1420.

Majlisī II, see ᶜAllāmah Majlisī

Majma^c al-Bayān, see Ṭabrisī.
Majma^c al-Zawā'id, Nūr al-Dīn ^cAlī b. Abī Bakr al-Haythamī, (d. 807), Beirut: Dār al-Kutub al-^cIlmiyyah, 1408/1988.
Majmū^cat Warrām, = *Tanbīh al-Khawāṭir*, by Abū al-Ḥusayn Warrām b. Abī al-Firās al-Fātiḥahānī al-Ḥillī (d. 606), Qum: Maktabat al-Faqīh, n.d.
Al-Maghāzī, by Abū ^cAbdillāh Muḥammad b. ^cUmar al-Wāqidī (d. 207), ed. M. Jones., London, 1966; Beirut: A^clamī, n.d.
Makārim = *Makārim al-Akhlāq*, by Raḍī al-Dīn Abū Naṣr Ḥasan b. al-Faḍl al-Ṭabrisī (mid 6th ^century), Qum: Intishārāt Sharīf al-Raḍī, 1412.
Manāqib = *Manāqib Āl Abī Ṭālib*, by Abū Ja^cfar Muḥammad b. Ja^cfar b. Shahrāshūb (d. 588), Qum: Intishārāt ^cAllāmah, 1379.
Maqtal al-Ḥusayn (*^ca*), by Abū Mikhnaf (d. 157), ed. Ḥ. al-Ghaffārī, Qum: Maṭba^cat al-^cIlmiyyah, n.d.
Maṣābīḥ al-Ẓalām, by al-Waḥīd al-Behbahānī = Muḥammad Bāqir b. Muḥammad Akmal (d. 1205 or 1206), Qum: Mu'assasat al-^cAllāmah al-Waḥīd al-Behbahānī, 1424.
Mawāhib al-Raḥmān fī Tafsīr al-Qur'ān, by Sayyid ^cAbd al-A^clā al-Mūsawī al-Sabzawārī (d. 1414), Beirut: Mu'assasat Ahl al-Bayt, 1409.
Mawsū^cat al-^cAqā'id al-Islāmiyyah, by Muḥammad Rayshahrī, Qum: Dār al-Ḥadīth, 1425.
Mawsū'at Ṭabaqāt al-Fuqahaā', by Ja^cfar Subḥānī, Qum: Mu'assaseh Imam Ṣādiq.
Al-Mazār al-Kabīr, by Muḥammad b. al-Mashhadī (d. 610), J. al-Qayyūmī al-iṣfahānī, Qum: Jāmi^c al-Mudarrisīn, 1419.
Miftāḥ=*Miftāḥ al-Jinān*, by an anonymous compiler, though attributed to Asad Allāh Tehrānī Ḥā'irī (d. 1333). A recent reprint appears along with ^cAllāmah Maljilisī's *Zād al-Ma^cād (be hamrahe Miftāḥ al-Jinān.*), ed. Yūsuf Asad-Zādeh, Qum: Payām-e Muqaddas, 1389 Sh.
Miftāḥ al-Falāḥ, by Bahā' al-Dīn al-^cĀmilī (d. 1030), Beirut: Dār al-Aḍwā', 1405.
Miṣbāḥ al-Hudā fā Sharḥ al-^cUrwat al-Wuthqā, by Mīrzā Muḥammad Taqī al-Āmulī (d. 1391), Tehran, 1380.
Mishkāt al-Anwār, by Abū al-Ḥasan ^cAlī b. Ḥasan al-Ṭabrisī (7th century), Najaf: Ḥaydarīyah, 1385.
Mir'āt al-^cUqūl, see ^cAllāmah Majlisī
Al-Mīzān fī Tafsīr al-Qur'ān, by Sayyid Muḥammad Ḥusayn al-Ṭabāṭabā'ī (d. 1402), Qum: Jāmi^c al-Mudarrisīn, 1417.
Mufīd= Abū ^cAbdillāh Muḥammad b. Muḥammad b. al-Nu^cmān al-^cUkbarī al-Baghdādī, Ibn Mu^callim (d. 413), *al-Amālī*, Qum: Kun-

greh Jahānī-ye S͟haykh Mufīd, 1413.

—*Al-Fuṣūl al-Muk͟htārah*, Qum: Kungreh Jahānī-ye S͟haykh Mufīd, 1413.

—*Kitāb al-Ik͟htiṣāṣ* (attributed), ed. ᶜA. A. al-G͟hafārī and S. M. al-Zarandī, Beirut: Dār al-Mufīd, 1414/1993.

—*Al-Irshād*, Qum, 1413.

—*Masār al-S͟hīᶜah*, Qum: Kungreh Jahānī-ye S͟haykh Mufīd, 1413.

—*Al-Muqniᶜah*, Qum: Kungreh Jahānī-ye S͟haykh Mufīd, 1413.

Muᶜjam al-Buldān, by Abū ᶜAbdillāh Yāqūt b. ᶜAbd Allāh al-Ḥamawī (d. 626), Berut, 1957; Beirut: Dār Ṣādir, n.d.

Muᶜjam Rijāl al-Ḥadīth, by Sayyid Abū al-Qāsim b. ᶜAlī Akbar al-Mūsawī al-K͟hū'ī (d. 1413), Beirut, 1983.

Al-Muḥarrar al-Wajīz = ᶜAbd al-Ḥaqq b. G͟hālib, Ibn ᶜAṭiyyah al-Andalūsī (d. 542), ed. ᶜA. ᶜA. Muḥammad, Beirut: Dār al-Kutub al-ᶜIlmiyyah, 1422.

Muntaha al-Maqāl fī Aḥwāl al-Rijāl, by Abū ᶜAlī Muḥammad b. Ismāᶜīl al-Ḥā'irī (d. 1216), Qum: Āl al-Bayt, 1416.

Muntak͟hab al-Anwār al-Muḍī'ah, by ᶜAlī b. ᶜAbd al-Karīm al-Nīlī al-Najafī (d.), Qum: K͟hayyām, 1401.

Murūj al-D͟hahab wa Maᶜādin al-Jawhar, by al-Masᶜūdī = Abū al-Ḥasan ᶜAlī b. al-Ḥusayn b. ᶜAlī al-Hud͟halī al-Bag͟hdādī (d. 346), ed. Asᶜad Dāg͟hir, Qum: Dār al-Hijrat, 1409.

Musnad Aḥmad = *Musnad*, by Abū ᶜAbdillāh Aḥmad b. Muḥammad b. Ḥanbal al-S͟haybānī al-Marwazī (d. 241), Beirut: Dār Ṣādir, n.d.

Mustadrak, see Nūrī.

Mustadrak Safīnat al-Biḥār, by ᶜAlī Namāzī Shāhrūdī (d. 1405), ed. Ḥasan b. ᶜAlī Namāzī, Qum: Jāmiᶜ al-Mudarrisīn, 1418.

Muslim = Abū al-Ḥusayn Muslim b. al-Ḥajjāj al-Qusayrī al-Nays͟hābūrī (d. 261), *Ṣaḥīḥ*, Beirut: Dār al-Fikr, n.d.

Musnad Abī Dāwūd =*Musnad* by Abū Dawūd Sulaymān b. Dāwūd b. al-Jārūd al-Ṭayālisī (d. 204), ed. M. ᶜA. al-Turkī, Cairo, 1999; Beirut: Dār al-Maᶜrifah, n.d.

Nahj al-Balāghah, by Muḥammad b. al-Ḥusayn al-S͟harīf al-Raḍī, ed. Ṣ. al-Ṣāliḥ, Qum: Dār al-Hijrah, n.d. *Nihāyah*, see Ṭūsī

Nuᶜmānī = Abū ᶜAbdillāh Muḥammad b. Ibrāhīm al-Kātib, Ibn Abī Zaynab (mid. 4th ᶜentury), *Kitāb al-G͟haybah*, Tehran: Maktabat al-Ṣadūq, 1397.

Nūr al-T͟haqalayn = ᶜAbd ᶜAlī b. Jumuᶜah al-ᶜArūsī al-Ḥuwayzī al-S͟hīrāzī (d. alive in 1073), ed. S. H. R. Maḥallātī, Qum: Ismāᶜīliyān, 1415.

Nūrī = Ḥusayn b. Muḥammad Taqī al-Nūrī, Muḥaddit͟h (d. 1320), *Dār al-Salām*, Beirut: Mu'assasat al-Ta'rīkh al-ᶜArabī, 1429/2008.

— *Jannat al-Māwā fī D͟hikr man Fāzā bi Liqā'i al-Ḥujjah ʻalayh al-salām*,

Najaf: Markaz al-Dirāsāt al-Takhaṣṣuṣiyah fī al-Imām al-Mahdī.
—*Kalimah Ṭayyibah*, has several printed editions, one available at: http://alhassanain.org/persian/?com=book&id=302
— *Lu'lu' wa Marjān, Taḥrīfīt-e ᶜĀshūrā*, ed. Muṣṭfā Darāyetī, Qum: Intishārāt-e Aḥmad Muṭahharī, 1420/1379 Sh.
—*Mustadrik al-Wasā'il*, Beirut: Āl al-Bayt, 1408.
—*Al-Najm al-Thāqib fī Aḥwāl al-Imām al-Ghā'ib*, Qum: Masjid-e Jamkarān, 1384 Sh.
— *Ṣaḥifah ᶜAlawiyyah Thāniyyah*, see *Ṣaḥifah ᶜAlawiyyah.*
Nuzhah = *Nuzhat al-Nāẓir*, by Yaḥyā b. Saᶜīd al-Hudhalī al-Ḥillī (d. 689), Qum: Intishārāt Sharīf Raḍī, 1394.
Qawāᶜid, see ᶜAllāmah Ḥillī
Al-Qawāᶜid wa l-Fawā'id, see Shahīd Awwal
Qummī = Shaykh ᶜAbbās b. Muḥammad Riḍā al-Qummī (d. 1359 H.), *Hadīyyat al-Zā'irīn wa Bahjat al-Nāẓirīn*, Qum: Mu'assaseh Jahānī-ye Sibṭayn, 1383 H. Sh./2004.
—*Manāzil al-Ākhirah wa Maṭālib al-Fākhirah*, Isfahan: Markaz-e Fahangī-ye Shahī Mudarris, 1387 H. Sh.
Qurb al-Isnād, by ᶜAbd Allāh b. Jaᶜfar al-Ḥimyarī al-Qummī (late 3rd ᶜentury), Qum: Mu'assah Āl al-Bayt, 1413.
Rāwandī = Quṭb al-Dīn Saᶜīd b. Hibat Allāh al-Rāwandī (d. 573), *al-Da ᶜawāt*, Qum: Mu'assaseh Imam Mahdī, 1409.
—*Fiqh al-Qur'ān*, Qum: Ayatullah Marᶜashī Library, 1405.
—*Al-Kharā'ij wa al-Jarā'iḥ*, Qum: Mu'assaseh Imam Mahdī, 1409.
—*Qiṣaṣ al-Anbiyā'*, Mashhad: Āstān-e Quds Raḍawī, 1409.
Rāwandī = Sayyid Ḍiyā' al-Dīn Faḍl Allāh al-Rāwandī al-Kāshānī (d. circa 550), *al-Nawādir*, Qum: Mu'assasah Dār al-Kitāb, n.d.
Rawḍ al-Jinān = *Rawḍ al-Jinān wa Rawḥ al-Janān fī Tafsīr al-Qur'ān*, by Abū al-Futūḥ Ḥusayn b. ᶜAlī (6th century), Mashhad: Āstān-e Quds-e Raḍawī, 1408.
Al-Rawḍ al-Unuf fī Sharḥ al-Sīrah al-Nabawiyyah, by ᶜAbd al-Raḥmān al-Suhaylī (d. 581), Beirut: Dār Iḥyā' al-Turāth al-ᶜArabī, n.d.
Rawḍat al-Muttaqīn fī Sharḥ Man lā Yaḥḍuruh al-Faqīh, by Majlisī I, Muḥammad Taqī b. Maqṣūd ᶜAlī al-Iṣfahānī (d. 1070), ed. S. Ḥ. Mūsawī Kirmānī, et al., Qum: Kūshanpūr, 1406.
Rawḍat al-Wāᶜiẓīn, by Muḥamad b. Aḥmad b. ᶜAlī al-Fārisī, al-Fattāl al-Nayshābūrī (d. 508), Qum: Intishārāt Sharīf Raḍī, n.d.
Riḥlah Ibn Baṭṭūṭah, Muḥammad Ibn Baṭṭūṭah (d. 1368), ed. Muḥammad ᶜAbd al-Munᶜim al-ᶜAryān and Muṣṭafā al-Qaṣṣāṣ, Beirut: Dār Iḥyā al-ᶜUlūm, 1407/1987..

Rijāl al-Kashshī, by Abū ᶜAmr Muḥammad b. ᶜUmar b. ᶜAbd al-ᶜAzīz (early 4th ᶜentury), ed. Ḥ. Al-Muṣṭafawī, Mashhad: Mashhad University, 1348 Sh./1970.

Rijāl al-Najāshī = *Fihrist Asmā' Muṣannifī al-Shīᶜah*, by Abū al-ᶜAbbās Aḥmad b. ᶜAlī al-Asadī al-Kūfī (d. 450), ed. Sh. Zanjānī, Qum: Jāmiᶜ al-Mudarrisīn, 1407.

Risālat al-Fakhriyyah = *al-Risālat al-Fakhriyyah fī Maᶜrifat al-Niyyah*, Fakhr al-Muḥaqqiqīn, Muḥammad b. al-Ḥasan b. Yūsuf al-Asadī al-Ḥillī (d. 771), ed. Ṣ. al-Baṣrī, Mashhad: Majmaᶜ al-Buḥūth al-Islāmiyyah, 1411.

Rūḥ al-Maᶜānī fī Tafsīr al-Qur'ān al-ᶜAẓīm, by Sayyid Maḥmūd Ālūsī (d. 1270), Beirut: Dār al-Kutub al-ᶜIlmiyyah, 1415.

Sabīl al-Najāt = *Sabīl al-Najāt fī Tatimmat al-Murājaᶜāt*, by Ḥusayn al-Rāḍī, published along with *al-Murājiᶜāt*, Beirut: 1402/1982.

Sadād al-ᶜIbād = *Sadād al-ᶜIbād wa Rashād al-ᶜIbād*, by al-Ḥusayn b. Muḥammad al-Baḥrānī, Āl ᶜUṣfūr (d. 1216), ed. Muḥsin Āl ᶜUṣfūr, Qum: Maḥallātī, 1412.

Ṣadūq = Abū Jaᶜfar Muḥammad b. ᶜAlī b. Bābawayh al-Qummī (d. 381), *al-Amālī*, Tehran: Kitābkhāneh Islāmiyyah, 1362 H. Sh.

—*Faḍā'il al-Ashhur al-Thalāthah*, Qum: Dāwarī, n.d.

—*ᶜIlal al-Sharā'iᶜ*, Qum: Maktabeh Dāwarī, n.d.

—*Kamāl al-Dīn*, ed. ᶜA. A. Ghaffārī, Qum: Dār al-Kutub al-Islāmiyyah, 1395.

—*Kitāb al-Tawḥīd*, Qum: Jāmiᶜ al-Mudarrisīn, 1398.

—*Maᶜānī al-Akhbār*, Qum: Jāmiᶜ al-Mudarrisīn, 1361 Sh.

—*Thawāb al-Aᶜmāl*, Qum: Intishārāt Sharīf Raḍī, 1364 Sh.

— *ᶜUyūn Akhbār al-Riḍā*, Qum: Intishārāt Jahān, 1378.

al-Ṣaḥīfah al-ᶜAlawiyyah, by ᶜAbd Allāh b. Ṣāliḥ al-Samāhījī, published along with *al-Ṣaḥīfah al-ᶜAlawiyyah al-Thāniyyah*, by Mīrzā Ḥusayn Nūrī, with Persian translation of both compilations as *Tarjumeh Ṣaḥīfeh ᶜAlawiyyeh*, trans. & ed. S. Hāshim Rasūlī Maḥallātī, Qum: Bostān-e Kitāb, 1391 Sh.

Al-Ṣaḥīfat al-Kāmilah=The Psalms of Islam, Al-Ṣaḥīfar al-Kāmilat al-Sajjādiyya, Imam Zayn al-ᶜĀbidīn ᶜAlī ibn al-Ḥusayn, Trans. William C. Chttick, London: The Muhammdi Trust, 1987.

Ṣaḥīḥ Ibn Ḥibbān bi Tartīb Ibn Balbān, by Abū Ḥātim Muḥammad b. Ḥibbān al-Bustī (d. 354), ed. Sh. al-Arna'ūṭ, Beirut: Mu'assasat al-Risālah, 1414/1993.

Al-Ṣaḥīḥ min Sīrat al-Nabī al-Aᶜẓam, by Sayyid Jaᶜfar Murtaḍā al-ᶜĀmilī, Beirut.

Sarā'ir = *Mustaṭrifāt*, Muḥammad b. Idrīs al-ᶜIjlī al-Ḥillī (d. 598), Qum: Jāmiᶜ al-Mudarrisīn, 1411.

Al-Ṣawārim al-Muhraqah, by Nūr Allāh al-Tustarī (d. 1019), Tehran: Nahḍat, 1367.

S̲h̲ād̲h̲ān b. Jibrāīl al-Qummī (alive in 651), *al-Faḍā'il*, Qum: Intis̲h̲ārāt S̲h̲arīf Raḍī, 1363 Sh.

S̲h̲ahīd Awwal = S̲h̲ams al-Dīn Muḥammad b. Makkī al-ᶜAmilī (d. 786), *D̲h̲ikrā al-S̲h̲īᶜah fī Aḥkām al-S̲h̲arīᶜah*, Qum, 1419.

—*Al-Durūs al-S̲h̲arᶜiyyah fī Fiqh al-Imāmiyyah*, Qum: Jāmiᶜ al-Mudar-risīn, 1417.

—*al-Mazār fī Kayfiyyat Ziyārāt al-Nabī wa al-A'immat al-Aṭhār (ᶜa)*, Qum: Madrasat al-Imam Mahdī (ᶜa), 1410.

—*Al-Qawāᶜid wal Fawā'id*, ed. S. ᶜA. al-Ḥakīm, Qum: Maktabat al-Mufīd, 1400.

S̲h̲ahīd T̲h̲ānī = Zayd al-Dīn b. ᶜAlī b. Aḥmad al-Jubaᶜī al-Āmilī (d. 966), *Musakkin al-Fu'ād*, Qum: Āl al-Bayt, 1407.

—"Risālah Ṣalāt al-Jumuᶜah," in *Rasā'il al-S̲h̲ahīd al-Thānī*, Qum: Intis̲h̲ārāt Daftar-e Tablīghāt-e Islāmī, 1421 H., i, 171-249.

Al-S̲h̲āmī, S̲h̲ayk̲h̲ Yūsuf b Ḥātim (fl. 7th cent., *Al-Durr al-Naẓīm fī Manāqib al-A'immat al-Lahāmīm*, Qum: Jāmiᶜeh Mudarrisīn, 1420.

Sharḥ Nahj al-Balāg̲h̲ah, by Ibn Abī al-Ḥadīd, ᶜIzz al-Dīn ᶜAbd al-Ḥamīd b. Hibat Allāh al-Madā'inī (d. 655), ed. M. A. Ibrāhīm, Cairo, 1380/1960.

S̲h̲awāhid al-Tanzīl, see al-Ḥākim al-Ḥaskānī

Shifā' al-Ṣudūr fī S̲h̲arḥ Ziyārat al-ᶜĀs̲h̲ūr, Mīrzā Abū al-Faḍl Kalāntarī Ṭehrānī (d. c. 1317), ed. S. Ḥasan-zādeh, Qum: Intis̲h̲ārāt Āl-e ᶜAlī, 1390 Sh.

Ṣiffīn = *Waqᶜat Ṣiffīn*, by Naṣr b. Muzāḥim b. Sayyār al-Minqarī (d. 212), ed. ᶜA. M. Hārūn, Qum: Ayatullah Marᶜas̲h̲ī Library, 1403.

Sunan al-Nasā'ī = *Sunan*, by Abū ᶜAbd al-Raḥmān Aḥmad b. ᶜAlī b. Shu-ᶜayb (d. 303), Beirut: Dār al-Fikr, 1348/1930.

Ṭabarānī = Abū al-Qāsim Sulaymān b. Aḥmad b. Ayyūb (d. 360), *al-Muᶜjam al-Kabīr*, ed. Ḥ. ᶜA. al-Ṣalafī, Beirut: Dār Iḥyā al-Turāt̲h̲ al-ᶜArabī, 1405/1985.

Al-Ṭabaqāt al-Kubrā, by Muḥammad b. Saᶜd Kātib al-Wāqidī (d. 230), Beirut, Dār al-Kutub al-ᶜIlmiyyah, 1418/1997.

Ṭabarī, Abū Jaᶜfar Muḥammad b. Jarīr (d. 310), Tafsīr = *Jāmiᶜ al-Bayān*, ed. K̲h̲alīl Almis, Beirut: Dār al-Fikr, 1415/1995.

—*Ta'rīk̲h̲ al-Umam wa al-Mulūk*, ed. M. A. Ibrāhīm, Cairo, 1960; Beirut: Dār al-Turāt̲h̲, n.d.

Ta<u>dh</u>kirah, see ᶜAllāmah Ḥillī

Tafsīr Abū Ḥamzah Thumālī, by Abū Ḥamzah <u>Th</u>ābit b. Dīnār al-<u>Th</u>umālī (2nd century), ᶜA. M. Ḥ. Ḥirz al-Dīn and M. H. Maᶜrifat, Beirut: Dār al-Mufīd, 1420.

Tafsīr al-ᶜAyyāshī = Kitāb al-Tafsīr, by Abū al-Naḍr Muḥammad b. Masᶜūd al-Sulamī al-Samarqandī (early 4th ᶜentury), Tehran: ᶜIlmiyyah, 1390.

Tafsīr al-Burhān, see al-Baḥrānī.

Tafsīr Ibn Abī Ḥātim, by ᶜAbd al-Raḥmān b. ᶜUmar al-Ḥanẓalī al-Rāzī, Ibn Abī Ḥātim (d. 327), ed. A. M. al-Ṭayyib, Ṣaydā: al-Maktabat al-ᶜAṣriyyah, n.d.

Tafsīr al-Imām = Tafsīr al-Imām al-ᶜAskarī (attributed), al-Imam Abū Muḥammad al-Ḥasan b. ᶜAlī al-ᶜAskarī (d. 260), ed. S. M. B. M. al-Abṭaḥī, Qum: Madrasat al-Imam al-Mahdī, 1409.

Tafsīr al-Qummī, by Abū al-Ḥasan ᶜAlī b. Ibrāhīm al-Qummī (alive in 307), Qum: Mu'assasah Dār al-Kitāb, 1404.

Tafsīr Muqātil = Tafsār Muqātil b. Sulaymān, <u>by</u> Muqātil b. Sulaymān b. Ba<u>sh</u>īr al-Azdī (d. 150), ᶜA. M. <u>Sh</u>aḥḥātah, Beirut: Dār Iḥyā' al-Turā<u>th</u> al-ᶜArabī, 1423.

Tah<u>dh</u>īb, see Ṭūsī

Taḥrīr al-Aḥkām, see ᶜAllāmah Ḥillī

Taḥṣīn, see Ibn Ṭāwūs.

Tanzīh al-Anbiyā', by Abū al-Qāsim ᶜAlī b. al-Ḥusayn al-Mūsawī, ᶜAlam al-Hudā, al-<u>Sh</u>arīf al-Murtaḍā (d. 436), Qum: Inti<u>sh</u>ārāt <u>Sh</u>arīf Raḍī, n.d.

Ta'rī<u>kh</u> al-<u>Kh</u>amīs fī Aḥwāl Anfus al-Nafīs, by Ḥusayn b. Muḥammad al-Diyārbakrī (d. 966), Beirut: Dār Ṣādir, n.d.

Tawḥīd, see Ṣadūq

Ta'wīl al-Āyāt al-Ẓāhirah, Sayyid <u>Sh</u>araf al-Dīn ᶜAlī al-Ḥusynī al-Astarābādī (d. 940), Qum: Jāmiᶜ al-Mudarrisīn, 1409.

<u>Th</u>awāb, see Ṣadūq

Ṭibb al-A'immah, by ᶜAbd Allāh and Ḥusayn, sons of Bisṭām b. Sābūr al-Zayyāt (early 4th ᶜentury), Qum: Inti<u>sh</u>ārāt <u>Sh</u>arīf Raḍī, 1411.

Ṭibb al-Nabī, by Abū al-Abbās al-Mustag<u>h</u>firī, Qum: Inti<u>sh</u>ārāt <u>Sh</u>arīf Raḍī, 1362 Sh.

Ṭibb al-Riḍā, Imam ᶜAlī b. Mūsā al-Riḍā (ᶜ*a*), Qum: Inteshārāt <u>Kh</u>ayyām, 1402.

Sunan Tirmi<u>dh</u>ī = al-Jāmiᶜ al-Ṣaḥīḥ, by Abū ᶜĪsā Muḥammad b. ᶜĪsā al-Sulamī al-Tirmi<u>dh</u>ī (d. 279), ed. ᶜA. M. ᶜUthmān, Beirut: Dār al-Fikr, 1403/1983.

Tuḥaf al-ᶜUqūl, by Abū Muḥammad al-Ḥasan b. ᶜAlī b. Shubah al-Ḥarrānī (mid-4th ᶜentury), ᶜA. A. al-Ghaffārī, Qum: Jāmiᶜ al-Mudarrisīn, 1404.

Ṭūsī = Abū Jaᶜfar Umḥammad b. al-Ḥasan, Shaykh al-Ṭā'ifah (d. 460), *al-Amālī*, Qum: Intishārāt Dār al-Thaqāfah, 1414.

—*Al-Istibṣār*, Tehran: Dār al-Kutub al-Islaāmiyyah, 1390 Sh.

—*Al-Khilāf*, ed. ᶜA. al-Khurāsānī et. al, Qum: Jāmiᶜ al-Mudarrisīn, 1407.

—*Kitāb al-Ghaybah*, Qum: Mu'assaseh Maᶜārif-e Islāmī, 1411.

—*Al-Mabsūṭ fī Fiqh al-Imāmiyyah*, Tehran: Al-Maktabat al-Murtaḍawiyyah li Iḥyā' al-Āthār al-Jaᶜfariyyah, ed. S. M. T. al-Kashfī, 1387.

—*Miṣbāḥ al-Mutahajjid*, Beirut: Mu'assasat al-Fiqh al-Shīᶜah, 1411.

—*Al-Nihāyah fī Mujarrid al-Fiqh wa al-Fatāwā,* Beirut: Dār al-Kitāb al-ᶜArabī, 1400.

—*Al-Tibyān fī Tafsīr al-Qur'ān*, ed. A. Sh. Al-Amīn and A. Ḥ. Q. al-ᶜĀmilī, Beirut: Dār Iḥyā' al-Turāth al-ᶜArabī, 1376-83.

—*Al-Tahdhīb*, Tehran: Dār al-Kutub al-Islāmiyyah, 1365 Sh.

ᶜUdad = *ᶜUdad al-Qawiyyah*, by Raḍī al-Dīn ᶜAlī b. Yūsuf al-Ḥillī (d.), Qum: Ayatullah Marᶜashī Library, 1407.

ᶜUddah = *ᶜUddat al-Dāᶜī*, by Aḥmad b. Muḥammad b. Fahd al-Asadī al-Ḥillī (d. 841), Tehran: Dār al-Kitāb al-Islāmī, 1407.

ᶜUmdah = *ᶜUmdat ᶜUyūn Ṣiḥāḥ al-Akhbār*, by Ibn Biṭrīq = Yaḥyā b. al-Ḥasan al-Asadī al-Ḥillī (d. 600), Qum: Jāmiᶜ al-Mudarrisīn, 1407.

ᶜUyūn Akhbār al-Riḍā, see Ṣadūq

Al-Wāfī, see Fayḍ.

Wasā'il, see Ḥurr al-ᶜĀmilī

Al-Wasīlah, by Ibn Ḥamzah al-Ṭūsī (d. *circa* 560), Qum: Ayatullah Marᶜashī Library, 1408.

Yaqīn, see ᶜAllāmah Ḥillī.

Yaᶜqūbī = Aḥmad b. Muḥammad b. Isḥāq b. Jaᶜfar b. Wahb al-Baghdādī, Ibn Wāḍiḥ (d. 284), *Ta'rīkh*, Qum: Ahl Bayt; Beirut, 1960.

Index

www.ingramcontent.com/pod-product-compliance
Lightning Source LLC
Chambersburg PA
CBHW021656120626
46545CB00004B/1258
9781955725354